PHILIP'S

ROAD ATLA

Britain

About Philip's maps

This atlas contains maps at different scales to get you to your destination as easily and as quickly as possible.

Route planning maps show the whole country at a glance, so you can choose the most direct route, whether on motorways or A-roads: Road numbers, junction numbers, motorway services and dual carriageways are all clearly marked.

Road maps at 3 miles to 1 inch (Scottish Highlands and Islands at 4 miles to 1 inch) show the road network in detail and mark hundreds of places of interest. The roads are colour coded according to importance. Scenic routes are highlighted and in country areas lanes over 4 metres wide are coloured yellow.

Approach maps at 1 mile to 1 inch guide you through the suburbs of major cities, and give road names as well as numbers.

Town plans show the streets in the central area and mark one ways, car parks, stations and important buildings.

Philip's road maps were voted the clearest and most detailed in an independent consumer survey with 442 respondents.

First published in 2006 by
Philip's a division of
Octopus Publishing Group Ltd
2–4 Heron Quays, London E14 4JP
www.philips-maps.co.uk
First edition 2006
First impression 2006
Cartography by Philip's
Copyright © 2006 Philip's

 Ordnance Survey®

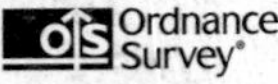

Data for the speed cameras provided by PocketGPSWorld.com Ltd.

Information for Tourist Attractions in England supplied by the British Tourist Authority / English Tourist Board.

Information for National Parks, Areas of Outstanding Natural Beauty, National Trails and Country Parks in Wales supplied by the Countryside Council for Wales.

Information for National Parks, Areas of Outstanding Natural Beauty, National Trails and Country Parks in England supplied by the Countryside Agency.

Data for Regional Parks, Long Distance Footpaths and Country Parks in Scotland provided by Scottish Natural Heritage.

Gaelic name forms used in the Western Isles provided by Comhairle nan Eilean.

Data for the National Nature Reserves in England provided by English Nature.

Data for the National Nature Reserves in Wales provided by Countryside Council for Wales. Darparwyd data'n ymwneud â Gwarchodfeydd Natur Cenedlaethol Cymru gan Gyngor Cefn Gwlad Cymru.

Information on the location of National Nature Reserves in Scotland was provided by Scottish Natural Heritage.

Data for National Scenic Areas in Scotland provided by the Scottish Executive Office. Crown copyright material is reproduced with the permission of the Controller of HMSO and the Queen's Printer for Scotland. Licence number C02W0003960.

The town plans of Calais and Boulogne are based on data supplied by Hachette Livre. The road mapping of Northern France was supplied by Blay-Foldex SA Copyright © Blay-Foldex SA

Printed in Italy by Rotolito

Cover photograph: Buttermere, Lake District National Park, Cumbria 98 C3

Photographic acknowledgements:
Cover: nagelestock.com / Alamy • Page II top Mark Sykes / Alamy • Page II bottom South West Images Scotland / Alamy • Page III, clockwise from top right: Jack Sullivan / Alamy; Adrian Sherratt / Alamy; Tony Charnock / Alamy; Iain Cooper / Alamy; Simon Holdcroft / Alamy; Mike Harrington / Alamy

Contents

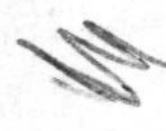

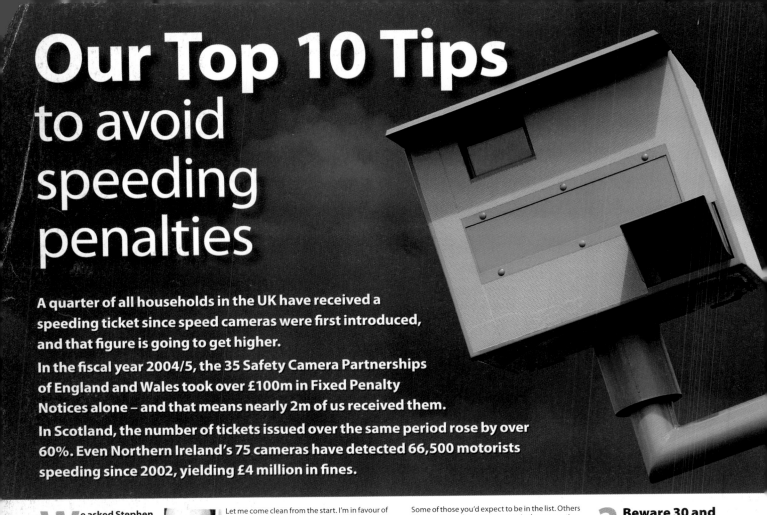

Our Top 10 Tips
to avoid speeding penalties

A quarter of all households in the UK have received a speeding ticket since speed cameras were first introduced, and that figure is going to get higher.

In the fiscal year 2004/5, the 35 Safety Camera Partnerships of England and Wales took over £100m in Fixed Penalty Notices alone – and that means nearly 2m of us received them.

In Scotland, the number of tickets issued over the same period rose by over 60%. Even Northern Ireland's 75 cameras have detected 66,500 motorists speeding since 2002, yielding £4 million in fines.

We asked Stephen Mesquita, speed camera expert, who last year spearheaded a national television campaign to publicise camera locations, to give his Top 10 Tips about what you can and can't do to avoid the cost of speeding fines, and keep the penalty points off your licence.

First, some facts: There are now over 3,300 fixed camera sites in the UK and about 3,400 'located' mobile sites listed on the official web sites. So the total's climbing towards 7,000 (far more than the 4,500 some websites quote).

If you are caught speeding, you can agree to pay a fixed £60 fine and get 3 points on your licence. The points normally stay on your licence for 4 years (11 if the conviction was drink- or drug-related or you failed to provide a specimen for analysis). In some cases, breaking a temporary speed limit where there are roadworks will only trigger the fine, not the endorsement. If you get 12 points on your licence within a three year period – or just 6 in your first two years as a driver – you will be banned from driving.

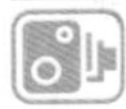

 …what's left is a legacy of inconsistency…

If you go over the speed limit by too much, you'll get an automatic summons – then, at the discretion of the court, the fines will be higher and the points could go up to 6 or even a ban.

You can challenge the penalty in court. But if you lose, it's likely to prove expensive.

Let me come clean from the start. I'm in favour of speed cameras where they do genuinely stop accidents (most people are). And I'm in favour of safe driving. But what the UK has ended up with is a mess.

Originally police forces were allowed to make their own decisions, place cameras where they liked, and raise as much money as possible. Then, when the government saw how unpopular speed cameras were becoming, they backtracked. First, cameras had to be placed only at accident black spots. Then the fines had to be siphoned back into road safety via the Treasury. Now the government has decreed that new cameras are only to be used if it can be proved that they are the best way to reduce accidents. That's fine – but what's left is a legacy of inconsistency that, unless it is sorted out, will continue to baffle and upset the law-abiding motorist.

So read on – because, if this hasn't affected you yet, it may well do in the future.

1 Beware camera-infested counties

Yes, I know. It's not a very practical suggestion but there is a serious point behind it. The Safety Camera Partnerships set up in each county stress that there are strict criteria for the siting of cameras – but there seems to be a concentration of cameras in some counties which aren't necessarily the busiest or the most dangerous to drive in. Which either means that the rules aren't being consistently applied or we are still living with cameras located before the rules came into being.

England and Wales

So, if the number of fixed cameras is anything to go by, here are the Top 10 counties to avoid in England and Wales (in order of fixed camera numbers)

1	London	6	Mid and South Wales
2	Staffordshire	7	West Yorkshire
3	Lancashire	8	Derbyshire
4	West Midlands	9	Hertfordshire
5	Thames Valley	10	Devon and Cornwall

Some of those you'd expect to be in the list. Others are a surprise. There are some quite busy counties, like Hampshire and Surrey, that have less than a third of the fixed cameras of any of those in our list. That's because their Safety Camera Partnerships didn't inherit a speed-camera jungle so were able to apply the accident black spot rules from scratch.

But more to the point, which counties raised the most revenue – and were they the ones with the most fixed cameras? Here are the top 10 income generators from Fixed Penalty Notices in 2004-5 Financial Year in England and Wales:

1	London	6	Northumbria
2	Mid and South Wales	7	West Yorks
3	Thames Valley	8	Kent
4	Avon and Somerset	9	Nottinghamshire
5	Essex	10	Lancashire

You'd expect London to be top. But productivity in Northumbria, whose web site lists only around 120 fixed and mobile sites, is remarkable. Similarly, Nottinghamshire, at number 9, lists under 100 fixed cameras and no mobile sites.

 …productivity in Northumbria is remarkable

We haven't produced a similar table for 'located' mobile sites, because it is impossible to find a consistent measure. Some counties only publicise the sites they are likely to monitor that week. Others give no mobile site information at all. Some define a mobile site with pinpoint accuracy, while others, like Fife in Scotland, simply highlight a stretch of road that could be 10 miles long. And how on earth did the inhabitants of Carmarthenshire earn a quarter of all the mobile locations in Wales? Confused by all this? So are we.

Scotland

Don't think you can escape in Scotland. There are fewer fixed cameras in the whole of Scotland than in any of the Top 5 English counties, but not surprisingly, Strathclyde and Lothian and Borders are the most camera-infested regions, with few or no fixed cameras in Highland, Fife or Dumfries and Galloway. Mobile camera sites are more evenly spread through the regions.

Ireland

In the North, there are only 4 fixed cameras and 71 mobile sites. In the Republic, there are just 3 cameras working in 20 boxes at any one time. But beware: a government report has recommended privatising speed cameras and allowing 600 of them to be operated by private operators – and not just at accident black spots. Not surprisingly, this has caused an outcry among the motoring organizations ('like shooting fish in a barrel' said one) – so watch this space.

2 Beware 30 and 40 mph limits

What are the speed limits for the majority of camera locations?

If your vision of the most common speeding ticket is the event we all see by the side of the motorway (a car stopped by the police car doing well over 70 then you're in for a surprise. The majority of speeding cameras – over 70% of both fixed and 'located' mobile cameras – are in zones where the limit is 30 to 40 mph.

Of course, mobile cameras can be anywhere. But tip No 2 is – be especially careful of 30 and 40 mile hour limits. Other than in London, the least guarded speed limit is 50 mph.

3 Stick to the B-Roads and Motorways

Fact: over 60% of the fixed camera sites and over 50% of the 'located' mobile sites are on A-Roads. Most of the rest are on unclassified roads – general in towns and villages. B-Roads and Motorways are relatively unsurveyed – although the M-ways may have a lot of 'unlocated' sites.

4 Drive like a woman (it's safer)

More than 80% of all speeding penalties are given to men.

There are two types of speeder – the deliberate speeder and the accidental speeder.

If you are interested in the camera locations in this atlas so that you can break the speed limit between them, you're a deliberate speeder, and almost certainly a man. Read on. Our Top 10 Tips might make you more conscious of the chances – and consequences – of being caught.

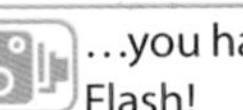

 …you haven't seen the sign. Flash!

Who are the accidental speeders? Almost everyone at some time. We've all done it. You're in an area that you're not familiar with. It's dark. You're quite alert but you're caught up in the rush hour and the traffic is moving fast. You've gone from a 40 zone to a 30 but you haven't seen the sign. Flash!

The truth is – most of us speed both deliberately and accidentally at some stage in our driving careers. The message is – cameras are widespread and they're not very forgiving.

Speed limits (mph)	Built-up area	Single carriageway	Dual carriageway	Motorway
Cars and motorcycles	30	60	70	70
Cars towing caravans and trailers	30	50	60	60
Buses and Coaches	30	50	60	60
Goods vehicles under 7.5 tonnes	30	50	60	70 (60 if articulated or towing)
Goods vehicles over 7.5 tonnes	30	40	50	60

So if you don't want the fine or the endorsement, you need to concentrate as much on your speed as you concentrate on not having an accident.

If you are a conscientious driver who feels the need to develop your skills of concentration in particular and defensive driving in general, then I'd recommend The Institute of Advanced Motorists (IAM) tel: 020 8996 9600.

5 Know your speed limit rules

Street lights = 30mph, unless it says otherwise. It's a horrible rule. Lots of people who should know about it don't. Lots of people who do know about it would like to see it changed.

Add to that the apparently arbitrary definition of 30mph and 40mph limits, and the frequency with which they change, and you have a recipe for confusion. Again, lots of inconsistencies to baffle the motorist.

...done for speeding at 31mph in a 30 mph zone

The round white sign with a black diagonal flash through it means 60 mph max, except on dual carriageways and M-ways.

How much leeway do you have? Is it zero tolerance? Is it the ACPO guidelines of +10%+2mph (that's the Association of Chief Police Officers, by the way)? Or is it somewhere in between? Well, the law is this – you can be done for speeding at 31mph in a 30 mph zone. As to the complicated equation, the police stress that guidelines are just that and they do not alter the law. But they probably would admit that they would be inundated if they stopped every motorist who is driving a couple of mph over the limit.

You are probably getting a bit of help from your speedometer. It's the clever idea of the car makers to set our speedometers 2–3mph faster than we are actually going. Now that so many of us have GPS in the car, this is getting more widely known. Now you know, it might be wiser to use the extra mph as air between you and a ticket.

6 Learn to tell your Gatso from your Digital Specs

Here's a concise guide to cameras. There are loads of different species, so we're only going to describe the main families.

Gatso – the most common ones. Generally in yellow boxes, they flash you from the back and store your number plate on film. As the film only has 400 exposures, don't assume, if you see the flash in your rear-view mirror, that you've been done. In fact it's reckoned that you have a three in four chance that the one you've just passed is not working.

Truvelo – pink-eyes. The pink eye gives you an infrared flash from the front, after sensors in the road have registered your speed. Unlike the GATSO, which can't identify the driver (worth remembering if you want to argue) the TRUVELO gets a mug-shot.

Digital Specs – pairs of video cameras set some distance apart to create a no-speeding zone between them. If your average speed over the distance exceeds the limit, you are snapped with an infrared flash. So they are much more testing for the driver. It's one thing slowing down when you see a camera, it's another thing maintaining an average speed over a distance of several miles. Still relatively rare.

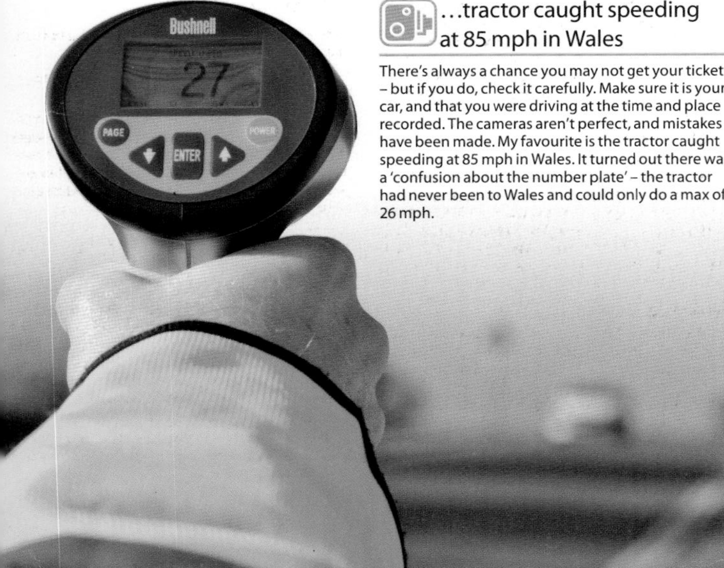

DS2s – strips in the road detect your speed and pass the information to an innocent-looking post at the side of the road. Look out for the detector van nearby, because that's what does the business.

Red light cameras – the UK total is creeping up towards 1,000. If you drive through a traffic light when it's at red, sensors in the road tell the camera to flash you.

All of the above can be detected using GPS devices for fixed cameras but not these -

Lasers – most mobile cameras are Lasers. You normally see a tripod in a van with the backdoors open and facing you; or on a motorway bridge or hand-held by the side of the road. They work – although rumour has it not in very bad weather – and they can't be detected by any of the GPS devices. If you happen to see a local villager touting a laser gun, you may get a letter asking you to drive more carefully but not a fine or penalty points.

7 Know where the cameras are

If you are serious about not getting caught speeding, there are some obvious precautions you can take before setting out.

- Check in this atlas whether there are fixed cameras on the route you are planning to take (they are marked on the map as small yellow squares)
- Check in the listings whether there are 'located' mobile sites on your route.
- Use a camera detector, such as those marketed by Road Angel, Road Pilot or Cyclops. These are perfectly legal, if expensive; they just tell you where the cameras are. Devices that detect and jam police laser detectors are about to be banned.
- Use the web sites for up-to-date information, including guidelines (but only guidelines) about where the police are locating their mobile vans each week. Each Safety Camera Partnership has a website (search for the county name followed by Safety Camera Partnership). Don't use the Department for Transport listings, which were 18 months out of date at the time we went to press.

8 If you do get a ticket, check it carefully

Even if there is film in the camera, you may not get a ticket.

A close study of the accounts of each of the Safety Camera Partnerships of England and Wales reveals a varying success in actually sending out the tickets and collecting the money. Some areas are collecting 100% of their fines. Others, particularly in the major urban areas, collect only just over 50%. The official reason is that tickets are not issued to owners of unregistered cars, foreign-registered cars and emergency vehicles being caught on camera(!). As an example, one coastal county with a lot of ferry traffic collected at 77% in 2004/5.

...tractor caught speeding at 85 mph in Wales

There's always a chance you may not get your ticket – but if you do, check it carefully. Make sure it is your car, and that you were driving at the time and place recorded. The cameras aren't perfect, and mistakes have been made. My favourite is the tractor caught speeding at 85 mph in Wales. It turned out there was a 'confusion about the number plate' – the tractor had never been to Wales and could only do a max of 26 mph.

9 Don't challenge a penalty without good reason

If you are caught speeding, you've got two choices. Pay the £60 and accept the 3 points. It's humiliating and irritating but then that's the idea. Or contest it.

From the 2004/05 Partnership accounts, about 10% of people challenge and don't pay the fixed penalty fines. Rumour is that the percentage is rising. You may get off, but if you contest a penalty and lose, you could pay a stiffer penalty.

If you do decide to fight, do as much research and get as much information about the circumstances as you can; and get as much case-study information as you can about the camera involved. The more witnesses and information you have, the more a good lawyer can build a case on your behalf.

Again, www.speed-trap.co.uk has some interesting case studies.

But don't expect success with any of these fabrications:

- Falsely nominate a fictitious person, or a real one from a foreign country, as the driver
- Nominate a person at an address that doesn't exist or at a derelict house
- Nominate a fictitious person at a real address
- Say the car was 'on a test drive' or that you don't have the name of the person who was driving it'
- Say you weren't in the area at the time – it must have been a cloned car'
- Give another registration number or change yours
- Register the car with incorrect details e.g. a wrong house number
- Say you don't know who was driving the car – 'it could have been one of several people'
- Ask your partner to pay the fixed penalty because you've already got points on your licence

These ten ingenious lies come to you courtesy of DriveSafe, who are the Greater Manchester Casualty Reduction Partnership, with the message that they know the scams to look out for, both the ones listed here and many more.

Lies can turn a simple speeding fine into something much more serious. In fact, you can be prosecuted for trying to pervert the course of justice. A criminal record can cost you much more than the £60 fixed penalty.

10 Avoid the points by going back to school

In a few counties, the police are giving drivers who are caught speeding another option. They can go on a Speed Awareness Scheme. These normally last half a day, you have to pay for them (probably more than £60) but you don't get the penalty points. So, if you like the sound of this as an option, it's worth considering.

Your alternative is to ask for your case to go forward for prosecution (see Top Tip No. 9)

And finally...

If you've got this far, you're obviously a bit of an aficionado on the subject of speeding, so I'm going to allow myself just one bit of preaching.

The 'Speed Kills' slogan has become much-used. But here are three pieces of information that certainly make me think twice about letting the needle stray over the prescribed limit:

1 Every year we kill over 3,000 of our fellow-citizens on our roads and we seriously injure 35,000. If you happen to live in a reasonable-sized town, just work that out as a percentage of the population of where you live. Road deaths have not fallen substantially since the proliferation of speed cameras – but the evidence seems to be reasonably conclusive that speed cameras reduce the number of deaths and serious injuries at the sites themselves.

2 The argument rages about whether speed is the cause of accidents or not. But that's all rather academic (isn't it?). A car that's not moving is not likely to injure someone. If the accident happens when the car is in motion, speed is at least part of the cause.

But here's the point. This is the 'if I hit a pedestrian, will I kill them?' chart ➤

So if you hit a pedestrian in a 30mph area and you're doing just 35mph (just on the 10% plus 2mph leeway) you're more than twice as likely to kill them. Not a nice thought. Maybe I should have called that the 'if I am hit by a car while on foot, will I be killed by it?' chart.

3 Every death costs us, as taxpayers, £1.5m and every serious injury £100,000. And that's doesn't take into account the human cost.

So, at the end of all this, my 11th Top 10 Tip is

11 Don't press the pedal to the metal

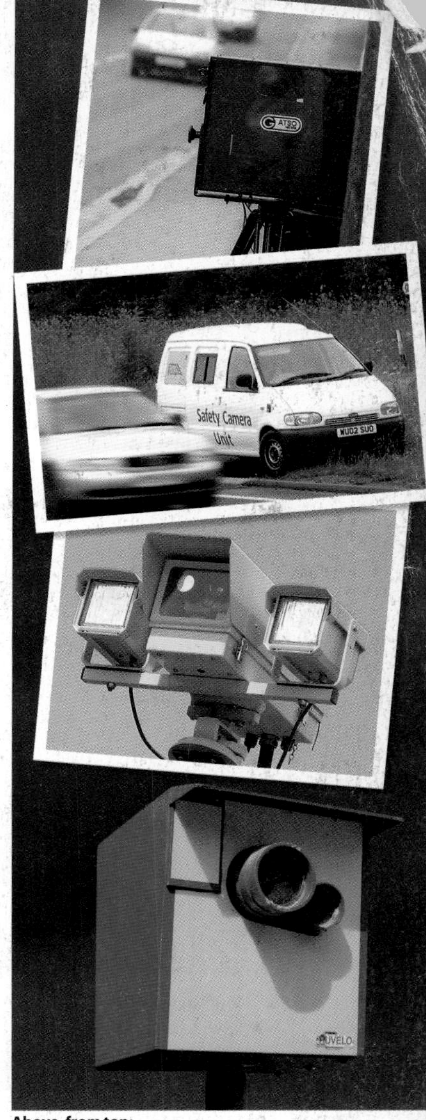

Above, from top: • Portable Gatso camera • Mobile safety camera unit • SPECS camera in Nottingham • Truvelo camera

Websites for further information

Official

Safety Camera Partnerships (use Google and put in Safety Camera Partnership plus the area you want)

- www.safetycamera.org.uk • www.dvla.gov.uk
- www.thinksafety.org.uk • www.dft.gov.uk
- www.road-safe.org

Safety pressure groups

- www.rospa.com • www.transport2000.org.uk
- www.roadpeace.org • www.brake.org.uk

Anti-camera pressure groups and web sites

- www.speed-trap.co.uk • ukgatsos.com
- www.ukspeedcameras.co.uk • www.abd.org.uk
- www.ukspeedtraps.co.uk • www.speedcam.co.uk
- www.speedcamerasuk.com

Case studies and news reports

- www.bbc.co.uk

Below The probability that a pedestrian will be killed when struck by a vehicle travelling between 20mph and 40mph

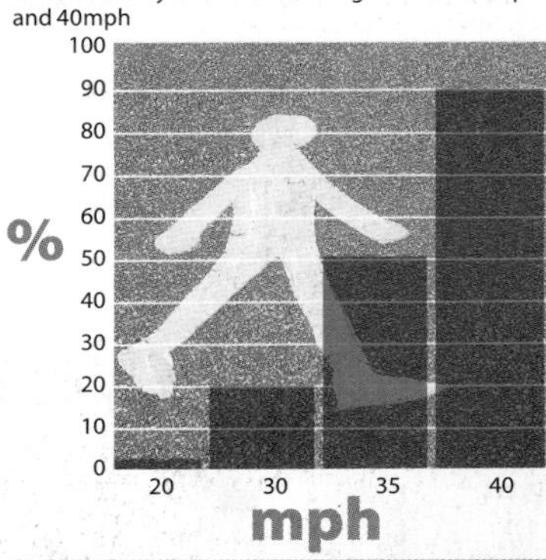

Mobile speed camera sites

The vast majority of speed cameras used on Britain's roads are operated by safety camera partnerships. This table lists the sites where each safety camera partnership may enforce speed limits through the use of mobile cameras or detectors. These are usually set up on the roadside or a bridge spanning the road and operated by a police or civilian enforcement officer. The speed limit at each site (if available) is shown in red type, followed by the approximate location in black type.

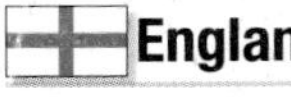

England

Avon and Somerset

Bath and North East Somerset, Bristol, North Somerset, Somerset, South Gloucestershire

M32
- 60 Bristol Stadium

A4
- 30 Bath, Newbridge Rd
- 30 Bristol, Anchor Rd
- 30 Bristol, Totterdown Bridge
- 50 Nr Keynsham, Keynsham Bypass jct A4175 Durley Hill
- 50 Portway
- 30 Portway, nr A4176 Bridge Valley Rd

A4/B4054
- 30 Bristol, Avonmouth Rd

A30
- 50 Cricket St Thomas
- 30 East Chinnock
- 40 Roundham
- 40 Yeovil, Hospital Rdbt
- 30 Yeovil, Sherborne Rd

A37
- 30 Bristol, Wells Rd (nr jct Airport Rd)
- 30 Bristol, Wells Rd (nr St Johns La)
- 60 Chilthorne Domer (east)
- 50 Emborough
- 30 Gurney Slade (north)
- 60 Lydford to Bristol
- 40 Lydford to Yeovil
- 60 Nr Podimore, Fosse Way, north of Podimore Rdbt
- 30 Shepton Mallet

A38
- 40 Aztec West, nr Bradley Stoke Way
- 30 Bathpool
- 40 Bedminster Down, Bridgwater Rd
- 40 Bristol, Bedminster Down Rd nr Bishopsworth Rd
- 30 Bristol, Bedminster Down Rd/West St
- 30 Bristol, Cheltenham Rd/Gloucester Rd, nr Cranbrook Rd
- 30 Bristol, Gloucester Rd nr B4052 Ashley Down Rd
- 30 Bristol, Stokes Croft nr Bond St
- 40 Churchill – Langford
- 40 Cross
- 30 East Reach/Toneway
- 40 Filton, Gloucester Rd (north) nr B4057 Gypsy Patch Lane
- 50 Heatherton Grange
- 40,30 North Petherton
- 40 Patchway, Gloucester Rd nr Highwood Rd
- 50 Pawlett (south)
- 50 Redhill
- 30 Rooks Bridge (east)
- 30 Taunton – Bridgwater
- 30 Taunton, Wellington Rd (inbound)
- 30 Taunton, Wellington Rd (outbound)
- 30 West Huntspill (north)

A39
- 30 Ashcott
- 30 Bilbrook
- 30 Bridgwater, Bath Rd
- 30 Bridgwater, North Broadway nr A38 Taunton Rd
- 30 Bridgwater, North Broadway/Broadway/Monmouth St
- 30 Chewton Mendip
- 40 Coxley nr Wells
- 50 Green Ore (south)
- 40 Horsey, Bath Rd
- 30 Quantock Rd
- 30 Walton

A46
- 60 Bath to Wickwar Rd
- 40 Dunkirk

A303
- 30 Buckland St Mary
- 50 Downhead nr Ilchester

A303/A3088
- 70 Cartgate Rdbt

A357
- 30 Templecombe

A303/A358
- 60 Southfields Rdbt

A358
- 60 Ashill
- 30 Donyatt
- 30 Henlade, nr M5 jct 25
- 40 Hornsbury Mill
- 40 Pen Elm (south)
- 30 Staplegrove Rd
- 30 Taunton Deane, Priorswood Rd
- 30 Taunton, Greenway Rd

A359
- 30 Mudford (north)

A361
- 30 Doulting
- 40 Durston
- 60 Frome Bypass
- 30 Othery
- 30 Pilton
- 30 West Pennard

A362
- 40 Terry Hill

A367
- 30 Bath, Green Park Rd
- 30 Bath, Bear Flat
- 30 Radstock, Wells Rd

A369
- 40 Abbots Leigh
- 60 Easton-in-Gordano, Martcombe Rd nr M5 jct 19

A370
- 30 Cleeve Village
- 30 Congresbury, Station Rd, Bristol Rd
- 30 Flax Bourton nr B3130
- 40 Long Ashton Bypass, Bristol End
- 30 West Wick, Somerset Avenue, west of M5 jct 21
- 30 Weston-super-Mare, Beach Rd
- 50 Weston-super-Mare, Herluin Way nr Winterstoke Rd
- 50 Weston-super-Mare, Somerset Avenue (central reservation)
- 50 Weston-super-Mare, Somerset Avenue, jct Moor Lane
- 30 Weston-super-Mare, Winterstoke Rd

A371
- 30 Draycott
- 40 Priestleigh (south)
- 30 Winscombe, Sidcot Lane nr jct A38,

A372
- 30 Aller

A378
- 30 Curry Rivel
- 40 Wrantage

A403
- 40 Avonmouth Docks

A420
- 30 Bristol, Lawrence Hill
- 30 Kingswood, Two Mile Hill Rd, Regent St
- 30 Old Market, nr Temple Way/Bond St
- 30 Redfield, Church Rd
- 30 St George, Clouds Hill Rd/Bell Hill Rd
- 30 Warmley, High St London Rd nr A4175 Bath Rd
- 60 Wick, Tog Hill

A432
- 30 Bristol, Fishponds Rd nr B4048 Lodge Causeway
- 30 Bristol, Fishponds Rd nr B4469 Royate Hill
- 30 Bristol, Fishponds Rd with B4469 Muller Rd
- 30 Bristol, Stapleton Rd nr jct A4320 Easton Way
- 40 Hambrook, Badminton Rd nr A4174 Avon Ring Rd
- 40 Kendleshire
- 30 Yate, Station Rd/B4059 Stover Rd

A3027
- 30 North St/East St

A3029
- 40 Bristol, Avon Bridge

A3039
- 30 Devonshire Rd

A3088
- 30 Yeovil, Lysander Rd

A3259
- 30 Monkton Heathfield

A4018
- 30 Bristol, Black Boy Hill/Whiteladies Rd
- 30 Bristol, Cribbs Causeway jct 17 M5
- 30 Bristol, Westbury Rd nr B4054 North View
- 30 Bristol, Whiteladies Rd into Queens Rd
- 30 Westbury on Trym, Falcondale Rd

A4044
- 30 Bristol, Temple Way/Redcliffe Way

A4081
- 40 Catbrain

A4162
- 30 Bristol, Sylvan Way/Dingle Rd/Canford Lane

A4174
- 50 Avon Ring Rd nr jct 1 M32
- 30 Bristol, Hartcliffe Way
- 40 Bristol, Hengrove Way/Airport Rd nr Creswicke Rd
- 50 Bromley Heath
- 50 Filton, Filton Rd/Avon Ring Rd nr Coldharbour Lane
- 40 Filton, Station Rd, nr Great Stoke Way

A4320
- 30 Bristol, at A4 Bath Rd nr Sandy Park Rd

B3124
- 30 Clevedon, Walton Rd

B3130
- 30 Nailsea, Stockway (north)/Chapel Avenue
- 30,40 Wraxall

B3133
- 30 Clevedon, Central Way

B3139
- 30,40 Mark Causeway
- 30 Chilcompton

B3140
- 30 Berrow, Coast Rd

B3141
- 30 East Huntspill

B3151
- 30 Compton Dundon
- 30 Ilchester
- 30 St, Somerton Rd

B3153
- 30 Keinton Mandeville (east Somerton)

B3170
- 30 Shoreditch Rd

B3440
- 30 Weston-super-Mare, Locking Rd/Regent St/Alexandra Parade

B4051
- 30 Bristol, Park Row/Perry Rd

B4054
- 30 Sea Mills, Shirehampton Rd

B4056
- 30 Bristol, Northumbria Drive/Linden Rd/Westbury Park
- 30 Bristol, Southmead Rd nr Pen Park Rd
- 30 Bristol, Southmead Rd nr Wellington Hill

B4057
- 30 Bristol, Crow Lane nr A4018 Passage Rd
- 30 Gypsy Patch Lane nr Hatchet Rd
- 50 Winterbourne Rd nr B4427 Gloucester Rd

B4058
- 30 Bristol, Frenchay Park Rd
- 30 Winterbourne, Winterbourne Hill/High St

B4059
- 30 Yate, Goose Green Way

B4060
- 30 Yate, Station Rd/Bowling Hill/Rounceval St

B4061
- 30 Thornbury, Bristol Rd

B4465
- 30 Mangotsfield, Broad St

B4465
- 30 Staple Hill, Staple Hill Rd/High St nr Forest Rd

Unclassified
- 30 Bristol, Bishopsworth, Whitchurch/Hareclive Rd
- 30 Bristol, Bishport Avenue
- 30 Knowle Bristol, Broadwalk
- 30 Bristol, Hengrove, Hawkfield Rd nr A4174 Hartcliffe Way
- 30 Bristol, Kingsway
- 30 Bristol, Long Cross, Lawrence Weston
- 30 Bristol, Stoke Hill/Stoke Rd nr Saville Rd, Clifton
- 30 Bristol, Sturminster Rd
- 30 Bristol, Whitchurch Lane nr Dundry Rd
- 30 Little Stoke, Little Stoke Lane
- 30 Taunton, Cheddon Rd
- 30 Taunton, Chestnut Drive
- 30 Taunton, Lisieux Way
- 30 Taunton, Trull Rd
- 50 Watergore, Harp Rd
- 30 Yeovil, Combe St

Bedfordshire and Luton

A5
- 60 Battlesden
- 40 Hockcliffe
- 60 Kensworth

A6
- 60 Gravenhurst, Barton Rd
- 30 Kempston, Ampthill Rd
- 30 Luton, New Bedford Rd
- 60 Pulloxhill, Barton Rd
- 60 Silsoe, Barton Rd

A421
- 50 Brogborough
- 60 Link Rd

A428
- 30 Bedford, Bromham Rd
- 30 Bedford, Goldington Rd

A505
- 30 Dunstable, Luton Rd
- 60 Leighton to Linslade Bypass

A507
- 30 Ridgmont, High St East
- 30 Ridgmont, High St West
- 60 Shefford, nr New Rd

A603
- 30 Bedford, Cardington Rd
- 30 Bedford, Lovell Rd
- 40 Willington

A1081
- 60 Luton, Airport Way

A4146
- 40 Leighton Buzzard, Billington Rd

A5120
- 40 Houghton Regis, Bedford Rd
- 30 Toddington, Station Rd

A5134
- 30 Kempston, High St

B530
- 60 Houghton Conquest

B1040
- 30 Biggleswade, Potton Rd

Unclassified
- 30 Bedford, Roff Avenue
- 30 Bromham, Stagsden Rd
- 30 Clapham, Highbury Grange
- 30 Cranfield, High St
- 30 Eaton Bray, Bower Lane
- 30 Flitwick, Ampthill Rd
- 30 Flitwick, Dunstable Rd
- 30 Heath and Reach, Woburn Rd
- 30 Leighton Buzzard, Heath Rd
- 30 Luton, Crawley Green Rd
- 30 Luton, Grange Avenue
- 30 Luton, Leagrave High St
- 30 Luton, Marsh Rd
- 30 Luton, Park Viaduct
- 30 Luton, Waller Avenue
- 30 Luton, Whitehorse Vale
- 30 Slip End, Markyate Rd

Berkshire

see Thames Valley

Bucks

see Thames Valley

Cambridgeshire

A14(E)
- 70 2km west of A1 Brampton Hut
- 70 East/Westbound

A15
- 30 New Fletton, London Rd

A47
- 70 Thorney Toll

A141
- 60 Clews Corner
- 60 Warboys
- 60 Wimblington/Doddington Bypass

A142
- 60 Soham Bypass
- 60 Witchford Bypass

A605
- 60 Elton, Bullock Rd
- 40 Kings Dyke

A1073
- 60 Eye Green, Peterborough Rd

A1123
- 60 Bluntisham, Needingworth Bypass

A1123
- 40 St Ives, Houghton Hill
- 40 Wiburton Village

A1307
- 70 Bartlow crossroads
- 30 Hills Rd
- 60 Linton Bypass

B645
- 40 Tilbrook Bends

Cheshire

A50
- 30 Grappenhall, Knutsford Rd
- 30 Knutsford, Manchester/Toft Rd
- 30 Warrington, Long Lane

A54
- 60 Ashton, Kelsall Rd

A56
- 40 Lymm, Camsley Lane

A57
- 40 Paddington, New Manchester Rd

A523
- 30 Poynton, London Rd

A532
- 30 Crewe, West St

A533
- 40 Middlewich, Booth Lane

A537
- 50 Macclesfield, Buxton Rd nr Wildboarclough

A5019
- 30 Crewe, Mill St

A5032
- 30 Whitby, Chester Rd

A5034
- 60 Mere, Mereside Rd

A5104
- 30 Chester, Hough Green

B5071
- 30 Crewe, Gresty Rd

B5078
- 30 Alsager, Sandbach Rd North

B5082
- 30 Northwich, Middlewich Rd

B5132
- 30 Ellesmere Port, Overpool Rd

B5463
- 30 Little Sutton, Station Rd

B5470
- 30 Macclesfield, Rainow Rd

Unclassified
- 30 Burtonwood, Lumber Lane
- 30 Ellesmere Port, Overpool Rd
- 30 Fearnhead, Harpers Rd
- 30 Hough Green, Prescot Rd
- 30 Howley, Battersby Lane
- 40 Runcorn, Astmoor Rd
- 30 Runcorn, Boston Avenue
- 30 Runcorn, Clifton Rd
- 30 Runcorn, Halton Rd
- 30 Runcorn, Heath Rd
- 30 Runcorn, Northwich Rd
- 30 Runcorn, Warrington Rd
- 30 Vale Royal, Woodford Lane (St John's Drive)
- 30 Whitecross, Lovely Lane
- 30 Widnes, Birchfield Rd
- 30 Widnes, Hough Green Rd
- 30 Wilmslow, Hough Lane
- 40 Winsford, Bradford Rd

Cleveland

Darlington, Hartlepool, Middlesbrough, Redcar and Cleveland

A171
- 50 Redcar, Charltons

A172
- 40 Middlesbrough, Morton Rd from crossroads to St Lukes
- 30 Middlesbrough, Morton Rd from Longlands to St Lukes
- 40 Middlesbrough, Stokesley – from Guisborough Rd jct to Captain Cooks Crescent

A177
- 50,60 Stockton, Durham Rd

A178
- 30 Seaton Carew, The Front

A179
- 30 Hartlepool, Easington Rd/Powlett Rd

A689
- 50 to 40 Hartlepool, from Sappers Corner

B1380
- 40 Middlesbrough, from Marton Crossroads to Ormesby Rd
- 30 Redcar, Eston

Unclassified
- 30 Dormanstow, Broadway
- 30 Eaglescliffe, Yarm Rd
- 30 Hartlepool, Catcote Rd
- 40,30 Hartlepool, Coronation Drive
- 30 Hartlepool, Owton Manor Lane and Wynyard Rd
- 30 Hartlepool, Oxford Rd
- 30 Hartlepool, Raby Rd
- 30 Hartlepool, Throston Grange Lane
- 30 Hartlepool, Winterbottom Avenue
- 30 Middlesbrough, Acklam Rd
- 40 Middlesbrough, Acklam Rd from Blue Bell to the Crematorium
- 30 Middlesbrough, Mandale Rd
- 30 Middlesbrough, Ormesby Rd
- 30 Middlesbrough, Trimdon Avenue
- 30 Ormesby, Normanby Rd
- 30 Redcar, Bankfields Rd
- 30 Redcar, Carlin How
- 30 Redcar, Church Lane
- 30 Redcar, Flatts Lane
- 30 Redcar, Greenstones Rd
- 30,40 Redcar, Kirkleatham Lane
- 30 Redcar, Marske High St
- 30 Redcar, Normanby Rd
- 30 Redcar, Ormesby Bank
- 30 Redcar, Redcar Lane
- 30 Redcar, Redcar Rd
- 30 Redcar, Stanghow Rd
- 30 Redcar, West Dyke Rd
- 30 Seaton Carew, Seaton Lane
- 30 Seaton Carew, Station Lane
- 40 Stockton, Bishopton Avenue
- 30 Stockton, Bishopton Rd West
- 30 Stockton, Darlington Lane
- 30 Stockton, Harrogate Lane
- 30 Stockton, Junction Rd
- 30 Stockton, Thames Rd
- 30 Stockton, Thornaby Rd
- 30 Stockton, Whitehouse Rd
- 30 Thornaby, Acklam Rd
- 30 Thornaby, Cunningham Drive

Cumbria

M6
- 70 Brunthwaite
- 70 Capplerigg
- 70 Cowperthwaite
- 70 Tebay

A6
- 60 Garnett Bridge/Hollowgate
- 30 Kendal, Milnthorpe Rd
- 30 Kendal, Shap Rd
- 30 London Rd
- 30 Penrith, Scotland Rd
- 60 Thiefside

A7
- 60 Westlinton Crossroads

A65
- 30 Kendal, Burton Rd
- 40 Kirby Lonsdale, Devils Bridge
- 60 Kirkby Lonsdale, Hollin Hall to Hornsbarrow

A66
- 60 Brigham/Broughton to Chapel Brow
- 60 Crackenthorpe
- 60 Dubwath/Bass Lake
- 60 Sandford Rd Ends
- 60 Troutbeck/Mungrisdale
- 60 Warcop, Brough Hill

A69
- 60 Aglionby
- 60 Scarrow Hill

A74
- 70 Kendal, Floriston

A590
- 60 Bouth Rd Ends
- 60 Haverthwaite/Backbarrow
- 70 Heaves/Levens/Gilpin
- 60 Newlands

A592
- 30,40 Rayrigg Rd

A595
- 60 Broughton, Wreaks End
- 30 Carlisle, Wigton Rd
- 60 Red Dial, Greenhill Hotel
- 60 West Woodside/Curthwaite Jct
- 40 Whitehaven, Loop Rd

A596
- 60 Micklethwaite

A683
- 60 Middleton to Cautley

A685
- 30 Kendal, Appleby Rd

A686
- 60 Edenhall to Meathaw Hill

A5087
- 30 Ulverston

B5277
- 30 Grange, Lindale Rd

B5299
- 40 Carlisle, Dalston Rd

Unclassified
- 30 Carlisle, Durdar Rd/Blackwell Rd
- 30 Barrow in Furness, Abbey Rd
- 30 Barrow in Furness, Michelson Rd

Derbyshire

A6
- 30 Allestree
- 30 Alvaston to Raynesway
- 40 Ambergate, Matlock Rd nr Chase Rd
- 30 Bakewell
- 40 Bakewell, Buxton Rd nr Holme Lane
- 30 Belper
- 40 Darley Dale, Dale Rd North nr The Parkway
- 40 Darley Dale, Dale Rd North opp The Parkway
- 30 Derby, London Rd
- 30 Fairfield, Fairfield Rd nr North Rd
- 40 Matlock Bath to Matlock, Dale Rd nr St John's Rd
- 40 Matlock Bath to Matlock, Dale Rd opp No. 138
- 40 Rock Corner, Buxton Rd
- 50 Taddington to Buxton

A52
- 30 Derby, Ashbourne Rd
- 40 Mackworth

A53
- 30 Buxton, Station Rd o/s Railway Station
- 30 Buxton, Station Rd opp Railway Station

A57
- 30 Glossop, Dinting Vale nr Primary School
- 30 Glossop, Dinting Vale opp Dinting Lane
- 30 Glossop, High St West nr Glossop Brook Rd

A61
- 30 Chesterfield, Derby Rd nr Herriot Drive
- 30 Chesterfield, Derby Rd nr Langer Lane
- 50 Stretton, Main Rd nr B6014
- 50 Stretton, Main Rd nr Straw Lane

A444
- 30 Overseal, Acresford Rd nr Valley Rd
- 30 Overseal, Burton Rd nr Lullington Rd
- 30 Stanton, Woodland Rd nr Piddocks Rd
- 30 Stanton, Woodland Rd opp Park Rd

A511
- 40 Bretby, Ashby Rd East nr Greary Lane
- 30 Hatton, Station Rd
- 30 Swadlincote, Ashby Rd nr Field Lane
- 30 Swadlincote, Burton Rd nr Eureka Rd
- 30 Swadlincote, Burton Rd nr Lincoln Way
- 30 Swadlincote, Burton Rd nr Sandcliffe Rd
- 30 Swadlincote, Burton Rd nr Springfield Rd
- 30 Woodville, Burton Rd nr Sorrel Drive
- 30 Woodville, High St nr Butt Lane

A514
- 30 Derby, Osmaston Rd nr Keble Close
- 30 Derby, Osmaston Rd nr Shaftesbury St
- 30 Derby, Osmaston Rd opp Cotton Lane
- 30 Hartshorne
- 30 Shelton Lock, Chellaston Rd nr Shelton Drive
- 30 Swadlincote
- 40 Swadlincote to Hartshorne
- 30 Ticknall

A516
- 30 Uttoxeter, New Rd

A601
- 30 Derby, Abbey St

A608
- 30 Heanor, Church St nr Hands Rd
- 30 Heanor, Heanor Rd nr Peatburn Ave
- 30 Heanor, Mansfield Rd adj Watson Ave
- 30 Heanor, Mansfield Rd opp Watson Ave
- 30 Langley Mill, Station Rd adj Aldred's Lane
- 30 Smalley

A609
- 30 Ilkeston, Nottingham Rd opp Ashdale Rd
- 30 Ilkeston, Nottingham Rd opp Little Hallam Lane
- 30 Kilburn to Horsley Woodhouse

A610
- 40 Codnor Gate
- 40 Ripley, Nottingham Rd nr Brittain Dr

A615
- 60 Tansley to Wessington

A616
- 30 Clowne
- 30 Creswell

A617
- 40 Bramley Vale
- 40 Glapwell to Pleasley

A6175
- 30 Holmewood
- 30 North Wingfield

A618
- 30 Killamarsh, Rotherham Rd

A619
- 50 Barlborough, Worksop Rd nr Van Dyks Hotel
- 40 Brimington, Chesterfield Rd opp Lansdowne Rd
- 30 Brimington, Ringwood Rd nr Foljambe Rd
- 30 Chesterfield, Chatsworth Rd nr Chatsworth Ave
- 30 Chesterfield, Chatsworth Rd opp Church View
- 30 Chesterfield, Chatsworth Rd opp Haddon Close
- 30 Hollingwood, Chesterfield Rd opp Ringwood Hall
- 40 Mastin Moor, Worksop Rd nr Norbriggs Rd
- 40 Mastin Moor, Worksop Rd nr Renishaw Rd
- 30 Middlecroft, Chesterfield Rd nr Ringwood Ave
- 30 Staveley, Chesterfield Rd nr Middlecroft Rd
- 50 Whitwell Common, Worksop Rd opp Highwood Lane
- 50 Whitwell, Barlborough nr Southgate Bungalows
- 50 Whitwell, Clinthill Lane o/s Southgate Bungalows

A623
- 30 Stoney Middleton

A624
- 40 Hayfield, Chapel Rd nr Church
- 40 Hayfield, Chapel Rd nr New Mills Rd

A632
- 30 Bolsover
- 30 Bolsover, Langwith Rd
- 30 Calow, Top Rd o/s No.33
- 30 Calow, Top Rd o/s No.62
- 40 Duckmanton, Chesterfield Rd nr Staveley Rd
- 40 Duckmanton, Chesterfield Rd opp Arkwright Arms Pub
- 30 Langwith, Main Rd nr Langwith Drive
- 30 Langwith, Main Rd nr Whaley Rd
- 30 Matlock

A5111
- 40 Derby, Harvey Rd nr Cockayne St North
- 40 Derby, Harvey Rd nr Neilson St
- 40 Derby, Harvey Rd nr Wyndham St
- 40 Derby, Harvey Rd o/s Newsagents
- 40 Derby, Osmaston Park Rd nr Arkwright St

A5250
- 30 Derby, Burton Rd
- 30 Littleover, Burton Rd

A6005
- 30 Draycott to Breaston
- 30 Long Eaton, Derby Rd opp Russell St
- 30 Long Eaton, Nottingham Rd nr Charlton Ave
- 30 Long Eaton, Nottingham Rd opp Cleveland Ave
- 30 Spondon, Derby Rd nr Derwent Rd
- 30 Spondon, Derby Rd o/s Asda
- 30 Spondon, Nottingham Rd nr Angler's Lane

A6007
- 30 Codnor to Heanor
- 30 Ilkeston, Heanor Rd nr Westfield Ave
- 40 Ilkeston, Heanor Rd nr Broadway
- 40 Ilkeston, Heanor Rd nr Hospital
- 40 Ilkeston, Heanor Rd nr Woodside Crescent
- 40 Shipley, Hardy Barn o/s No.64
- 40 Shipley, Hassock Lane North nr Algrave Hall Farm
- 40 Shipley, Hassock Lane South nr Pitt Lane

A6096
- 30 Kirk Hallam, Ladywood Rd nr Godfrey Dr
- 30 Kirk Hallam, Ladywood Rd nr Goole Ave
- 30 Spondon, Dale Rd nr Dreyfus Close
- 30 Spondon, Dale Rd nr Wood Rd
- 30 Spondon, Dale Rd opp Sandringham Dr

B5010
- 30 Sandiacre, Derby Rd adj Brook St
- 30 Sandiacre, Derby Rd adj Friesland Drive
- 30 Sandiacre, Derby Rd adj Woodside Rd

B5036
- 30 Cromford, Cromford Rd

B5353
- 30 Newhall, Park Rd

B6002
- 30 Sandiacre, Longmoor Rd nr Springfield Ave
- 30 Sandiacre, Longmoor Rd o/s No.108
- 30 Sandiacre, Longmoor Rd nr Queen's Drive

B6019
- 30 Alfreton, Mansfield Rd nr Prospect St
- 30 South Normanton, Mansfield Rd nr Carter Lane West
- 30 South Normanton, Mansfield Rd nr Storth Lane
- 30 South Normanton, The Common nr Market St
- 30 South Normanton, The Common nr The Hamlet

B6051
- 30 Chesterfield, Newbold Rd
- 30 Newbold, Newbold Rd

B6052
- 30 Eckington, High St nr j/w School St
- 30 Eckington, West St nr j/w Fanshaw Rd
- 30 Whittington

B6056
- 30 Eckington, Dronfield Rd opp Ravenscar Rd
- 30 Marsh Lane, Main Rd nr School Lane
- 30 Marsh Lane, Main Rd o/s No.45

B6062
- 30 Chinley

B6179
- 30 Little Eaton
- 40 Lower Kilburn
- 50 Lower Kilburn to Little Eaton
- 30 Ripley to Marehay

B6407
- 30 Shirebrook, Portland Rd adj Ashbourne St
- 30 Shirebrook, Portland Rd opp Ashbourne St

B6540
- 30 Long Eaton, Tamworth Rd nr Charles St
- 30 Long Eaton, Tamworth Rd nr Wyvern Ave
- 30 Long Eaton, Tamworth Rd opp Draycott Rd
- 30 Long Eaton, Tamworth Rd opp No.559
- 30 Long Eaton, Tamworth Rd opp Shaftesbury Ave

Unclassified
- 30 Chaddesden, Nottingham Rd nr No.427 (Cemetery)
- 30 Chaddesden, Nottingham Rd nr Pentagon Island

30 Chaddesden, Nottingham Rd o/s No.590 (Cherry Tree)
30 Charlesworth, Long Lane
30 Chesterfield, Boythorpe Rd
30 Chesterfield, Linacre Rd
30 Chesterfield, Old Rd
30 Denby, St Lane
30 Derby, Blagraves Lane
30 Derby, Kedleston Rd
30 Derby, Stenson Rd
30 Langley Mill, Upper Dunstead Rd
30 Shardlow, London Rd
40 Stenson Fields, Stenson Rd
30 Swadlincote, Hearthcote Rd

Devon and Cornwall

A30
60 Chiverton Cross
70 Highgate (Eastbound)
70 Highgate Hill
40 Sowton
60 Temple
A38
70 Bittaford Straight, Wrangaton
70 Deep Lane
70 Lee Mill, Lee Mill On-slip
70 Lower Clicker Tor
70 Smithaleigh
70 Smithaleigh, Smithaleigh Overbridge
70 Wrangaton, Bittaford Straight
A39
60 Barras Moor
30 Camelford, Valley Truckle
40 Perranarworthal, nr Truro
A361
50 Ashford
30 Barnstaple, Eastern Avenue
40 Knowle
30 Knowle (Westerland)
30 Wrafton
A374
30 Ebford
40 Plymouth, Plymouth Rd (Inbound)
40 Plymouth, Plymouth Rd (Outbound)
30 Torpoint, Anthony Rd
A376
30 Exmouth, Exeter Rd
A377
30 Copplestone
30 Crediton, Western Rd
30 Exeter, Alphington Rd
A379
30 Brixton Village
30 Paignton, Dartmouth Rd
30 Starcross
30 Starcross, The Strand
30 Teignmouth, Teignmouth Rd
30 Torquay, Babbacombe Rd
30 Yealmpton
A380
40 Kingskerswell, Newton Rd
A381
30 Newton Abbott, East St
A385
30 Collaton St Mary, Totnes Rd
30 Totnes, Ashburton Rd
A386
60 Chubb Tor
30 Plymouth, Outland Rd
60 Plymouth, Roborough Down
40 Plymouth, Tavistock Rd
A388
30 Kelly Bray
A390
60 Penstraze
60 Sticker Bypass
A394
40 Kenneggy Downs
A396
30 Rewe
30 Stoke Canon, Exeter Rd
A3015
30 Exeter, Topsham Rd
A3047
30 Carbis Bay
30 Pool, Trevenson Rd
30 Tuckingmill
A3058
30 Trewoon
A3064
30 Plymouth, St Budeaux Bypass
A3075
60 Rosecliston
B3165
30 Raymonds Hill, Crewkerne Rd
B3174
30 Ottery St Mary, Barrack Rd
B3183
30 Exeter, Heavitree Rd
30 Exeter, New North Rd
B3212
30 Exeter, Dunsford Rd
30 Exeter, Pinhoe Rd
B3213
30 Wrangaton Village, nr South Brent
B3233
30 Barnstaple, Bickington Rd
B3250
30 Plymouth, North Hill
B3284
60 Liskey
30 Liskey, Perranporth
30 Chudleigh, Station Hill
B3396
30 Plymouth, Milehouse Rd
Unclassified
30 Avonwick Village
30 Buddle Lane, Exwick Rd
30 Elburton, Haye Rd
30 Exeter, Exwick Lane
30 Fraddon Village, nr Indian Queens
60 Goss Moor, Castle an Dinas
30 Honicknowle, Shakespeare Rd
30 Ivybridge, Exeter Rd
40 Monkton Village
30 Paignton, Colley End Rd
30 Paignton, Preston Down Rd
30 Plymouth, Beacon Park Rd
30 Plymouth, Church Hill
30 Plymouth, Devonport Rd
30 Plymouth, Eggbuckland Rd
30 Plymouth, Glen Rd
30 Plymouth, Honicknowle Lane
30 Plymouth, Honicknowle Lane (North)
30 Plymouth, Lipson Rd
30 Plymouth, Mannamead Rd
30 Plymouth, Molesworth Rd
30 Plymouth, North Prospect Rd
40 Plymouth, Novorrossiysk Rd
30 Plymouth, Pomphlett Rd
30 Plymouth, Southway Drive
30 Plymouth, St Levan Rd
30 Plymouth, Tamerton Foliot Rd
30 Plymouth, Union St
30 Plymouth, Weston Park Rd
30 Plymouth, Wolseley Rd (Both Directions)
30 Plympton, Glen Rd
30 Saltash, Callington Rd
30 St Judes, Grenville Rd

Dorset

A30
Babylon Hill
Shaftesbury, Long Cross
A35
Bakers Arms Rdbt, Lytchett Minster Rdbt j/w A350
Bere Regis nr Woodbury Cross
Bridport, Cross Dykes nr Whiteway Cross
Christchurch Bypass
Dorchester, Friary Press
Kingston Russell
Lyndhurst Rd
nr Morden Hill and Slepe
Organford
Poole, Upton Rd
Sea Rd South
Vinney Cross nr Bridport
A37
Holywell Cross
Long Ash Lane
Staggs Folly
A348
Bear Cross, Ringwood Rd
A338
Cooper Dean, Wessex Way
Bournemouth, Spur Rd
A350
Holes Bay Rd
Poole Rd
Poole, Upton Country Park to A35 j/w Creekmoor
Stourplane, Shashton Rd
A352
Wool, Dorchester Rd
A354
Dorchester Rd/Ridgeway Hill
Poole, Gravel Hill
Redlands, Dorchester Rd
Upwey, Dorchester Rd
Weymouth, Buxton Rd
B3065
Poole, Pinecliff Rd
Poole, The Avenue
B3073
West Parley, Christchurch Rd
Wimborne, Oakley Hill
B3074
Broadstone, Higher Blandford Rd
B3082
Blandford Rd nr Badbury Rings
B3092
Gillingham, Colesbrook
B3157
Limekiln Hill
Portesham
Weymouth, Chickerell Rd
Weymouth, Lanehouse Rocks Rd
B3369
Poole, Sandbanks Rd
Poole, Shore Rd
Unclassified
Blandford, Salisbury Rd
Bournemouth, Branksome Wood Rd
Bournemouth, Carbery Avenue
Bournemouth, Littledown Avenue
Bournemouth, Southbourne Overcliff Drive
Dorchester Rd (Manor Rdbt to Weymouth Hospital)
Poole, Herbert Avenue
Poole, Old Wareham Rd
Portland, Weston Rd
Staplehill, Wimbourne Rd
Upton, Poole Rd

Durham

A66
Bowes Moor/Galley Bank/ Greta Bridge
A67
Conniscliffe
A167
Chester-le-St, North Lodge
Darlington, North Rd
Durham, Whitesmocks and Tollhouse Rd
A690
Crook, Low Willington to West Rd
Durham, West Rainton
A1086
Crimdon to Horden
B6188
Dipton, New Kyo to Flint Hill
B6280
Darlington, Yarm Rd
B6282
Bishop Auckland, Etherley and B6284 Ediscum Garth
B6288
Spennymoor/A167 Croxdale
Unclassified
Darlington, McMullen Rd
Durham, Finchale Rd
Peterlee, Essington Way

Essex

A12
Braintree, Overbridge nr Kelvedon Interchange
A13
30 Castle Point, High St (Hadleigh twds London)
30 Leigh on Sea, London Rd
Southend, Bournes Green Chase
Southend, North Shoebury
Southend, Southchurch Boulevard
A113
30 Epping, High Rd
A120
Little Bentley, Pellens Corner
A121
30 Epping, High Rd
30 Loughton, Goldings Hill (j/w Monkchester Close)
Loughton, High Rd
Waltham Abbey, Farm Hill Rd
Waltham Abbey, Sewardstine Rd
A126
30 Grays, London Rd
30 Tilbury, Montreal Rd
A128
Chipping Ongar, High St
30 Ingrave/Herongate, Brentwood Rd
A129
30 Basildon, Crays Hill
Billericay, Southend Rd
Rayleigh, London Rd
30 Wickford, London Rd
Wickford, Southend Rd
A130
30 Canvey Island, Long Rd
South Benfleet, Canvey Way
A133
30 Elmstead Market, Clacton Rd
A133
Little Bentley, Colchester Rd
A134
40 Great Horkesley, Nayland Rd
A137
30 Lawford, Wignall St
A1016
30 Chelmsford, Waterhouse Lane
A1017
30 Sible Hedingham, Swan St
A1023
30 Brentwood, Chelmsford Rd
30 Brentwood, London Rd
30 Brentwood, Shenfield Rd
A1025
40 Harlow, Third Avenue
A1060
Little Hallingbury, Lower Rd
A1090
30 Purfleet, London Rd
30 Purfleet, Tank Hill Rd
A1124
30 Colchester, Lexden Rd
A1158
30 Westcliff on Sea, Southbourne Grove
A1168
30 Loughton, Rectors Lane
A1169
40 Harlow, Southern Way
A1205
40 Harlow, Second Avenue
B170
Loughton, Roding Lane
Chigwell, Chigwell Rise
B172
Theydon Bois, Coppice Row
B173
Chigwell, Lambourne Rd
B184
40 Great Easton, Snow Hill
B186
30 South Ockendon, South Rd
B1002
30 Ingatestone, High St
B1007
30 Billericay, Laindon Rd
40 Chelmsford, Stock Rd
B1007
30 Billericay, Stock Rd
B1008
30 Chelmsford, Broomfield Rd
B1013
30 Hawkwell, High Rd
30 Hawkwell, Main Rd
30 Hockley/Hawkwell, Southend Rd
Rayleigh, High Rd
30 Rayleigh, Hockley Rd
B1014
30 South Benfleet, Benfleet Rd
B1018
30 Latchingdon, The St
30 Maldon, The Causeway
B1019
30 Hatfield Peveral, Maldon Rd
B1021
Burnham on Crouch, Church Rd
B1022
30 Colchester, Maldon Rd
30 Heckfordbridge, Maldon Rd
30 Maldon, Colchester Rd
30 Tiptree Heath, Maldon Rd
B1027
30 Clacton-on-Sea, Valley Rd/Old Rd
30 St Osyth, Pump Hill
40 Wivenhoe, Brightlingsea Rd
B1028
30 Wivenhoe, Colchester Rd
30 Wivenhoe, The Avenue
B1033
30 Kirby Cross, Frinton Rd
B1335
40 South Ockendon, Stifford Rd
B1352
Harwich, Main Rd
B1383
30 Newport, London Rd
Stansted Mountfitchet, Cambridge Rd
B1389
30 Witham, Colchester Rd
30 Witham, Hatfield Rd
B1393
30 Epping, Palmers Hill
B1441
30 Clacton-on-Sea, London Rd
B1442
30 Clacton-on-Sea, Thorpe Rd
B1464
30 Bowers Gifford, London Rd
Unclassified
40 Alresford, St Osyth Rd
30 Aveley, Purfleet Rd
Aveley, Romford Rd
30 Barstable, Sandon Rd
30 Basildon, Ashlyns
40 Basildon, Cranes Farm Rd (j/w Honywood Rd)
Basildon, Crayhill Rd
30 Basildon, Felmores
Basildon, London Rd, Wickford
30 Basildon, Vange Hill Drive
30 Basildon, Whitmore Way
30 Basildon, Wickford Avenue
30 Billericay, Mountnessing Rd
30 Bowers Gifford, London Rd
30 Braintree, Coldnailhurst Avenue
30 Brentwood, Eagle Way (nr j/w Clive Rd twds Warley Rd)
30 Buckhurst Hill, Buckhurst Way/Albert Rd
30 Canvey Island, Dovervelt Rd
30 Canvey Island, Link Rd
30 Canvey Island, Thorney Bay Rd
Chadwell St Mary, Brentwood Rd
30 Chadwell St Mary, Linford Rd
30 Chadwell St Mary, Riverview
30 Chelmsford, Baddow Rd
30 Chelmsford, Chignall Rd
30 Chelmsford, Copperfield Rd
Chelmsford, Galleywood Rd
30 Chelmsford, Longstomps Avenue
30 Clacton-on-Sea, St Johns Rd
30 Clacton, Kings Parade
30 Clacton, Marine Parade East
30 Colchester, Abbots Rd
30 Colchester, Avon Way
30 Colchester, Bromley Rd
Colchester, Ipswich Rd
30 Colchester, Old Heath Rd
30 Colchester, Shrub End Rd
30 Corringham, Southend Rd
30 Corringham, Springhouse Rd
Danbury, Maldon Rd
30 Daws Heath, Daws Heath Rd
30 Eastwood, Green Lane j/w Kendal Way
30 Eastwood, Western Approaches j/w Rockall
30 Grays, Blackshots Lane
30 Grays, Lodge Lane
Grays, London Rd (nr Angel Rd)
Grays, London Rd (nr Bransons Way)
40 Harlow, Abercrombie Way, twds Southern Way
40 Harlow, Howard Way
30 Hullbridge, Coventry Hill
30 Laindon, Durham Rd
30 Laindon, Nightingales
30 Laindon, Wash Rd
Langdon Hills, High Rd
30 Leigh on Sea, Belton Way East
30 Leigh on Sea, Belton Way West
30 Leigh on Sea, Blenhelm Chase
30 Leigh on Sea, Grand Parade/ Cliff Parade
30 Leigh on Sea, Hadleigh Rd
30 Leigh on Sea, Highlands Boulevard
30 Leigh on Sea, Manchester Drive
30 Leigh on Sea, Mountdale Gardens
30 Leigh on Sea, Western Rd
30 Loughton, Alderton Hill
30 Loughton, Loughton Way
Loughton, Valley Hill
30 Maldon, Fambridge Rd
30 Maldon, Holloway Rd
30 Maldon, Mundon Rd
30 Pitsea, Rectory Rd
30 Prittlewell, Kenilworth Gardens
30 Prittlewell, Prittlewell Chase
30 Rayleigh, Bull Lane
Rayleigh, Downhall Rd
30 Rayleigh, Trinity Rd, nr Church Rd
30 Rochford, Ashingdon Rd
30 Rochford, Rectory Rd
Rush Green, St Osyth Rd
30 Shoeburyness, Ness Rd
30 South Woodham Ferrers, Hullbridge Rd
30 South Woodham Ferrers, Inchbonnie Rd
30 Southend on Sea, Lifstan Way
Southend, Bournemouth Park Rd
30 Southend, Hamstel Rd
Southend, Western Esplanade/Westcliff on Sea
30 Southend, Woodgrange Drive j/w Sandringham Rd
30 Springfield, New Bowers Way
30 Stanford le Hope, London Rd
30 Tendring, Burrs Rd, Clacton
Tendring, Harwich Rd, Wix Arch Cottages to Cansey Lane
Theydon Bois, Piercing Hill
30 Thorpe Bay, Barnstaple Rd
30 Thorpe Bay, Thorpe Hall Avenue
Waltham Abbey, Paternoster Hill
Weeley Heath, Clacton Rd
30 West Thurrock, London Rd
30 Westcliff on Sea, Chalkwell Avenue
30 Westcliff on Sea, Kings Rd
30 Wickford, Radwinter Avenue
30 Witham, Powers Hall End
30 Witham, Rickstones Rd

Gloucestershire

A38
40 Twigworth
A40
60 Andoversford
30 Churcham
60 Farmington
40 Gloucester Rd
60 Hampnett
60 Hazleton
60 Northleach
60 The Barringtons
60 Whittington Area
A46
30 Ashchurch
40 North of Nailsworth
A48
60 Stroat
A417
70 Burford Jct
40 Corse, Gloucester Rd
70 Dartley Bottom
40 Lechlade
30 Maisemore
40 North of Hartpury
A419
40 Oldends Lane to Stonehouse Court
A429
60 Nr Bourton-on-the-Water
40 Fossebridge
A430
40 Hempsted Bypass
A435
60 Colesbourne
A436
60 Jct with B4068
A4013
30 Gloucester, Princess Elizabeth Way
30 Gloucester, Princess Elizabeth Way (Arle)
A4019
50 Uckington
A4136
40 Brierley
40 Coleford, Lower Lane
40 Harrow Hill
40 Little London
A4151
40 Steam Mills
A4173
30 nr St Peters School
B4008
40 Hardwicke, Bristol Rd south of Tesco rdbt
30 Olympus Park Area, Bristol Rd
30 Stonehouse, Gloucester Rd
B4060
30 Katharine Lady Berkeley's School
B4215
50 South east of Rudford
50 South of Newent Bypass
B4221
30 Picklenash School
40 Kilcot Village
B4226
60 Speech House
B4228
30 Coleford, Old Station Way
40 Perrygrove
B4231
30 Bream, Coleford Rd
B4633
30 Cheltenham, Gloucester Rd
Unclassified
30 Gloucester, Abbeymead Avenue
30 Gloucester, Barrow Hill
30 Gloucester, Chesterton Lane
30 Gloucester, Parkend Fancy Rd
30 Gloucester, St Georges Rd
30 Gloucester, Swindon Lane
30 Gloucester, Wymans Lane
30 Lydney, Highfield Rd
40 Minchinhampton Common
30 Siddington
40 Tewkesbury, Gloucester Rd

Greater Manchester

A6
30 Devonshire, Stockport Rd
30 Heaton Chapel, Wellington Rd
30 Longsight, Stockport Rd
30 Stockport Rd (North)
30 Stockport Rd (South East)
A34
30 Birchfield Rd (North)
40 Didsbury, Kingsway (North)
40 Gatley
A49
30 Marus Bridge, Warrington Rd (South)
30 Standish, Wigan Rd (South)
A56
30 Bury, Manchester Rd (North)
30 Derby, Bury New Rd (North)
30 Shuttleworth, Whalley Rd (North)
30 White City, Chester Rd
A57
30 Godley, Mottram Rd (West)
30 Hyde Rd
30 Hyde, Manchester Rd (West)
30 West Gorton, Hyde Rd
A58
30 Ashton, Liverpool Rd (West)
30 Bamfurlong (South West), Lily Lane
30 Bury, Bolton Rd (North East)
30 Bury, Bolton Rd (South West)
40 Hunger Hill, Wigan Rd (Doyle Rd)
A62
30 Ancoats, Oldham Rd
30 Ancoats, Oldham Rd (North East)
30 Newton Heath, Oldham Rd
30 Newton Heath, Oldham Rd (North East)
A571
30 Wigan, Victoria St (South West)
A572
30 Astley, Chaddock Lane (West)
30 Lowton, Newton Rd (South)
A574
30 Leigh, Warrington Rd (South)
A576
30 Crumpsall, Middleton Rd
30 Crumpsall, Middleton Rd (South)
A579
50 Leigh, Atherleigh Way (South)
A580
70 Leigh, East Lancashire Rd
A635
40 Ardwick, Mancunian Way
Beswick, Ashton Old Rd
40 Mancunian Way (East)
30 Openshaw, Ashton Old Rd
30 Openshaw, Ashton Old Rd (East)
30 Stalybridge, Stamford St (West)
A662
30 Beswick, Ashton New Rd
30 Clayton, Ashton New Rd
A664
Blackley, Rochdale Rd
30 Collyhurst, Rochdale Rd
30 Harpurhey, Rochdale Rd
30 Rochdale Rd (Whitemoss) (North)
A665
30 Cheetham Hill Rd (Alms Hill) (North)
30 Cheetham Hill, Cheetham Hill Rd
30 Prestwich, Bury Old Rd
A667
30 Radcliffe, Ringley Rd (West)
A670
30 Hazelhurst, Mossley Rd (South West)
A5079
30 Kingsway/Slade Lane (South West)
A5103
30 Princess Rd (Greame St) (North)
40 Princess Rd (Whitchurch) (North)
40 Withington, Princess Rd
30 Edge Lane (West)
A5209
30 Almond Brook Rd (East)
30 Crow Orchard Rd
A6010
30 West Gorton, Pottery Lane
A6104
40 Higher Blackley, Victoria Avenue
A6144
30 Harboro Rd (West)
30 Warburton Lane (South West)
A6145
30 Hulton Lane (North)
B5165
30 Timperley, Park Rd
B5213
30 Flixton, Church Rd (East)
30 Flixton, Church Rd (West)
30 Urmston, Church Rd (West)
B5217
30 Seymour Grove (South)
B5218
30 Upper Chorlton Rd (South)
B5235
40 Westhoughton/Atherton Boundary
B5237
30 Bickershaw Lane (West)
B5375
30 Shevington, Miles Lane (South)
B6177
30 Mossley, Stamford Rd
B6226
30 Horwich, Chorley Old Rd
Unclassified
30 Bird Hall Lane (North) (facing south)
30 Bury, Radcliffe Rd (North East)
30 Councillor Lane (West)
30 Crumpsall, Hazelbottom Rd
30 Great Moor (Mile End), Buxton Rd (South)
30 Hazelbottom Rd (North)
30 Kings Rd (East)
30 Kings Rd (West)
30 Marple Rd Offerton (South East)
30 Queensway (South)

Hampshire and Isle of Wight

A3
70 Liphook
30 Petersfield
A27
40 Fareham (east and west bound)
30 Fareham, Portchester Rd (eastbound)
30 Fareham, Portchester Rd (westbound)
30 Fareham, The Avenue
A30
30 Blackwater
30 Hook, London Rd
A32
30 West Meon
A33
50 Basingstoke
50 Chandlers Green
50 Sherfield on Loddon
50 Southampton, Millbrook Rd (western end of Flyover to Regents Park Rd)
30 West Quay Rd
A35
50 Totton
A325
40 East Hampshire (south)
70 Farnborough, Farnborough Rd
40 Rushmoor (north)
A334/B2177
40 Wickham
A335
30 Eastleigh
A337
30 New Forest (east)
40 New Forest (west)
A338
40 New Forest (south and north bound)
A339
60 Lasham
A340
30 Basingstoke
30 Tadley
A343
30 Hurstbourne Tarrant
A3020
40 Blackwater Rd
A3024
40 Bursledon Rd
30 Northam Rd to southern river bank
A3054
30 Newport, Fairlee Rd
30 Wootton / Lushington Hill, High St
B3037/A335
30,40 Eastleigh
B3055
40 New Forest
B3395
30 Sandown, Culver Parade
Unclassified
30 Apse Heath
30 Binstead Hill
30 Brading, High St New Rd
30 East Cowes, Victoria Grove/ Adelaide Grove
30 East Cowes, York Avenue
40 Fareham, Western Way
30 Fleet, Reading Rd South
30 Newport, Staplers Rd/Long Lane
30 Portsmouth, Northern Rd (north and south bound)
40 Southampton, The Avenue (north and south bound)
30 Swanick, Swanick Lane
50 Totton / Redbridge, Redbridge Flyover

Herefordshire

see West Mercia

Hertfordshire

A41
40 Watford, North Western Avenue
A119
30 Hertford, North Rd
A411
30 Bushey, London Rd
30 Watford, Hempstead Rd
A414
40 Hemel Hempstead, St Albans Rd
40 Hertford, Hertingfordbury Rd
A505
30 Hitchin, Cambridge Rd
A600
30 Hitchin, Bedford Rd
A602
40 Hitchin, Stevenage Rd
40 Stevenage, Broadhall Way (north of j/w Valley Way)
40 Stevenage, Monkswood Way
A1000
40 Bishop's Stortford, Barnet Rd
A1057
40 Hemel Hempstead, St Albans Rd West
30 St Albans, Hatfield Rd
A1170
30 Wormley, High Rd nr Macers Lane Jct
30 Wormley, High Rd nr Slipe Lane Jct
A4125
40 South Oxhey, Sandy Lane
30 Watford, Eastbury Rd
30 Watford, Tolpits Lane by jct with Scammell Close
A4251
30 Bourne End, London Rd
A5183
30 St Albans, Frogmore Rd
A6141
30 Baldock, London Rd
60 Letchworth, Letchworth Gate
B156
30 Broxbourne, Goffs Lane
B176
30 Cheshunt, High St
B197
30 Stevenage, North Rd
B487
30 Hatching Green, Redbourn Lane
40 Hemel Hempstead, Queensway
B488
40 Tring, Icknield Way at j/w Little Tring Rd
B556
30 Potters Bar, Mutton Lane
B1004
30 Bishop's Stortford, Windhill
B1502
30 Hertford, Stansted Rd
B5378
30 Elstree, Allum Lane
40 Shenley, Shenleybury
Unclassified
30 Cheshunt, Hammond St Rd
30 Hoddesdon, Essex Rd
30 Letchworth, Pizmore Way
30 Royston, Old North Rd
30 South Oxhey, Hayling Rd
30 St Albans, Sandpit Lane

30 Stevenage, Clovelly Way 75m south of j/w Scarborough Avenue
30 Stevenage, Clovelly Way jct of Eastbourne Avenue
30 Stevenage, Grace Way (200m north of Vardon Rd)
30 Stevenage, Grace Way (200m south of Vardon Rd)
40 Stevenage, Gresley Way (nr Dene Lane Footbridge)
40 Stevenage, Gresley Way (nr Woodcock Rd Jct)
30 Watford, Radlett Rd
30 Watford, Whippendell Rd (o/s Wemco House)
30 Welwyn Garden City, Heronswood Rd
30 Welwyn Garden City, Howlands

Humberside

East Riding of Yorkshire, Hull, North East Lincolnshire, North Lincolnshire

M180
70 North Lincolnshire, West of River Trent
A18
60 North East Lincolnshire, Barton St Central
60 North East Lincolnshire, Barton St North
60 North East Lincolnshire, Barton St South
30 North Lincolnshire, Wrawby
A63
50 East Riding, Melton
40 Hull, Castle St
40 Hull, Daltry St Flyover
A161
30 Belton
A163
30 Holme on Spalding Moor
A164
30 Leconfield
A165
30 Beeford
40 East Riding, Coniston
30 Freetown Way
40 Holderness Rd
30 Skirlaugh
A180
70 Great Coates Jct
A614
40 Holme on Spalding Moor
30 Middleton on the Wolds
60 Shiptonthorpe, north of rdbt
60 Shiptonthorpe, south of the village
A1033
40 Thomas Clarkson Way
30 Thorngumbald, Main St
30 Withernsea
A1077
30 Barton
A1079
50 Barmby Moor
30 Bishop Burton
30 Hull, Beverley Rd (Desmond Ave to Riverdale Rd)
40 Hull, Beverley Rd (Sutton Rd to Mizzen Rd)
A1084
30 Brigg, Bigby High Rd
A1174
30 Dunswell
30 Woodmansey
B1206
30 Barrow, Wold Rd
B1230
40 Gilberdyke
40 Newport
B1398
40 Greetwell
Unclassified
30 Ashby, Grange Lane South
30 Ashby, Messingham Rd
30 Belton, Westgate Rd
30 Beverley, Hull Bridge Rd
30 Bilton, Main Rd
30 Bridlington, Kingsgate
30 Bridlington, Quay Rd/St John's St
30 Broughton, High St
30 Cleethorpes, Clee Rd
30 East Halton, College Rd
30 Goole, Airmyn Rd
30 Grimsby, Cromwell Rd
30 Grimsby, Great Coates Rd
30 Grimsby, Laceby Rd
30 Grimsby, Louth Rd
30 Grimsby, Waltham Rd
30 Grimsby, Weelsby Rd
30 Hessle, Beverley Rd
30 Hornsea, Rolston Rd
30 Howden, Thorpe Rd
30 Hull, Anlaby Rd
40 Hull, Boothferry Rd
30 Hull, Bricknell Avenue
30 Hull, Greenwood Avenue
30 Hull, Hall Rd
30 Hull, John Newton Way/Bude Rd
30 Hull, Leads Rd
30 Hull, Marfleet Lane
30 Hull, Marfleet Lane/Marfleet Avenue
30 Hull, Priory Rd
30 Hull, Saltshouse Rd
40 Hull, Spring Bank West
30 Hull, Wawne Rd
30 Humberston, Tetney Rd
30 Immingham, Pelham Rd
70 Laceby Bypass
30 Preston, Station Rd
30 Scunthorpe, Ashby Rd
30 Scunthorpe, Cambridge Avenue
30 Scunthorpe, Cottage Beck Rd
40 Scunthorpe, Doncaster Rd
30 Scunthorpe, Luneburg Way
40 Scunthorpe, Queensway
30 Scunthorpe, Rowland Rd
30 South Killingholme, Top Rd
30 Yaddlethorpe, Moorwell Rd

Kent and Medway

A2
70 Canterbury
60 Dover, Guston
70 Dover, Lydden
40 Medway, London Rd
A20
70,40 Dover, Dover Rd/Archcliffe
40,50 Tonbridge and Malling, London Rd
A21
70 Sevenoaks Bypass
60 Tonbridge and Malling, Castle Hill
60 Tunbridge Wells, Key's Green
A25
30 Sevenoaks, Seal Rd
A26
40 Tonbridge and Malling, Maidstone Rd
A28
40 Ashford, Ashford Rd
A224
30 Sevenoaks, Tubs Hill
A225
30 Sevenoaks, Sevenoaks Rd
A226
50 Gravesham, Rochester Rd/Gravesend Rd through Chalk
50 Gravesham, Rochester Rd/Gravesend Rd through Shorne
40 Gravesham, Rochester Rd/Gravesend Rd through Higham
A227
30 Gravesham, through Culverstone Green
40 Gravesham, through Istead Rise
30 Gravesham, through Meopham Green
A228
40 Medway, Ratcliffe Highway
A229
50 Maidstone, Bluebell Hill
40,30 Maidstone, Linton Rd/Loose Rd
30 Medway, City Way
40 Tunbridge Wells, Angley Rd (Hartley Rd)
A249
70 Maidstone, Chalky Rd/Rumstead Lane, South St
70 Swale, Chestnut St
A253
30 Thanet, Canterbury Rd West
A256
70 Dover
30 Dover, London Rd
40 Thanet, Haine Rd
A258
50 Dover, Dover Rd
A259
40 Shepway
60 Shepway, Guldeford Lane
30 Shepway, High St
A262
30 Ashford, High St
A268
30 Tunbridge Wells, Queen St
A289
50 Medway, Medway Tunnel
70 Medway, Wainscott Bypass
A290
30 Canterbury, Blean
A291
30 Canterbury, Canterbury Rd
A292
30 Ashford, Mace Lane
A2033
30 Shepway, Dover Rd
A2990
60 Canterbury, Old Thanet Way
B258
30 Dartford, Barn End Lane
B2015
40 Nettlestead Green, Maidstone Rd
B2017
30 Tunbridge Wells, Badsell Rd
B2067
60 Ashford, Ashford Rd
30 Ashford, Woodchurch Rd
B2071
30 Shepway, Littlestone Rd
B2097
30 Rochester, Maidstone Rd
B2205
30 Swale, Mill Way
Unclassified
30 Canterbury, Mickleburgh Hill
30 Canterbury, Rough Common Rd
30 Dartford, Ash Rd/Hartley Rd
30 Gravesham, Sole St
30 Medway, Beechings Way
30 Medway, Esplanade
30 Medway, Maidstone Rd
30 Medway, St End Rd
30 Medway, Walderslade Rd
30 Sevenoaks, Ash Rd/Hartley Rd
30 Swale, Lower Rd
30 Thanet, Shottendane Rd

Lancashire

A6
40 Broughton, Garstang Rd (north of M55)
30 Chorley, Bolton Rd
30 Fulwood, Garstang Rd (south of M55)
30 Fulwood, Garstang Rd, north of Blackpool Rd
30 Lancaster, Greaves Rd
50 Lancaster, Scotforth Rd nr Burrow Lane Bailrigg
30 Preston, North Rd
30 Preston, Ringway
A56
30 Colne, Albert Rd
30 Colne, Burnley Rd
30 Nelson, Leeds Rd
A59
60 Gisburn, Gisburn Rd
50 Hutton, Liverpool Rd
30 Preston, New Hall Lane
A65
40 Lancaster, Cowan Bridge
A570
40 Scarisbrick, Southport Rd, Brook House Farm
A581
40 Ulnes Walton, Southport Rd
A583+A5073
30 Blackpool, Whitegate Drive/Waterloo Rd
A583+B5266
30 Blackpool, Church St/Newton Drive
A584
30 Blackpool, Promenade
30 Lytham, West/Central Beach
30 Warton, Lytham Rd
A584+A587
30 Blackpool, Promenade/ Fleetwood Rd
A587
30 Blackpool, East/North Park Drive
30 Cleveleys, Rossall Rd/ Crescent East
A588
60 Pilling, Head Dyke Lane
60 Wyre, Lancaster Rd, Cockerham at Gulf Lane
A666
30 Darwen, Blackburn Rd
30 Darwen, Bolton Rd nr Cross St
30 Darwen, Duckworth St
A671
30 Read, Whalley Rd
A674
30 Cherry Tree, Preston Old Rd
A675
50 Belmont, Belmont Rd (south of village)
50 Darwen, Belmont Rd, north of Belmont Village
60 Withnell, Bolton Rd (Dole Lane to Calf Hey Bridge)
A680
40 Edenfield, Rochdalee Rd
A682
60 Barrowford, Gisburn Rd nr Moorcock Inn
30 Brierfield, Colne Rd
40 Crawshawbooth, Burnley Rd
60 Gisburn, Gisburn Rd
60 Gisburn, Long Preston Rd
A683
30 Lancaster, Morecambe Rd
A5073
30 Blackpool, Waterloo Rd
A5085
30 Lane Ends, Blackpool Rd
A5209
30 Newburgh, Course Lane/Ash Brow
A6068
50 Barrowford, Barrowford Rd
A6114
30 Burnley, Casterton Avenue
A6177
50 Haslingden, Grane Rd West of Holcombe Rd
50 Hyndburn, Haslingden Rd/Elton Rd
B5192
30 Kirkham, Preston St
B5251
30 Chorley, Pall Mall
B5254
30 Lostock Hall, Leyland Rd/Watkin Lane
30 South Ribble, Leyland Rd (north of Talbot Rd to A59 Golden Way Rbdt, Penwortham)
B5256
30 Leyland, Turpin Green Lane
B5269
40 Goosnargh, Whittingham Lane
B6231
30 Oswaldtwistle, Union Rd
Unclassified
60 Belmont, Egerton Rd
30 Blackburn, East Park Rd
30 Blackburn, Whalley Old Rd, west of Railway Bridge
30 Blackpool, Dickson Rd, Queens St to Pleasant St
30 Briercliffe, Burnley Rd
30 Darwen, Lower Eccleshill Rd
60 Galgate, Bay Horse Rd
30 Nelson, Netherfield Rd
30 Preston, Lytham Rd
30 Preston, St Georges Rd
30 St Anne's, Church Rd to Albany Rd, nr High School

Leicestershire and Rutland

A1
70 Empingham, Great North Rd
70 Stretton, Great North Rd
A5
60 Hinckley, Watling St (B578 to M69)
50 Hinckley, Watling St (M69 to A47)
70 Sharnford, Watling St (Highcross to B4114)
A6
40 Birstall, Loughborough Rd
40 Leicester, Abbey Lane
30 Leicester, London Rd (Knighton Drive)
30 Loughborough, Derby Rd
40 Oadby, Glen Rd/Harborough Rd
A47
60 Barrowden, Peterborough Rd
60 Bisbrooke, Uppingham Rd
30 Earl Shilton, Hinckley Rd
40 Houghton on the Hill, Uppingham Rd
30 Leicester, Hinckley Rd
30 Leicester, Humberstone Rd
50 Morcott, Glaston Rd
50 Skeffington, Uppingham Rd
50 Tugby, Uppingham Rd
A50
70 Hemmington to Lockington
40 Leicester/Glenfield, Groby Rd/Leicester Rd
30 Woodgate
A426
50 Dunton Bassett, Lutterworth Rd
40 Glen Parva, Leicester Rd
60 Lutterworth, Leicester Rd
60 Whetstone, Lutterworth Rd
A444
60 Fenny Drayton, Atherstone Rd
30 Twycross Village, Main St
60 Twycross, Norton Juxta
A447
60 Cadeby, Hinckley Rd
40 Ravenstone, Wash Lane
A512
30 Loughborough, Ashby Rd
40 Shepshed, Ashby Rd Central
A563
30 Leicester, Attlee Way
30 Leicester, Colchester Rd/Hungarton Boulevard
30 Leicester, Glenhills Way
40 Leicester, Krefield Way
30 Leicester, New Parks Way
A594
30 Leicester, St Georges Way
A606
60 Barnsdale, Stamford Rd
60 Leicester, Broughton/Old Dalby
60 Tinwell, Stamford Rd
A607
30 Leicester, Melton Rd
30 Melton, Norman Way
70 Thurmaston, Newark Rd
60 Waltham on the Wolds, Melton Rd
60 Waltham/Croxton Kerrial, Melton Rd
A4304
40 Market Harborough, Lubbenham Hill
A5199
30 Leicester, Welford Rd
30 Wigston, Bull Head St
30 Wigston, Leicester Rd
A5460
40 Leicester, Narborough Rd
A6004
30 Loughborough, Alan Moss Rd
A6030
30 Leicester, Wakerley Rd/Broad Avenue
A6121
30 Ketton, Stamford Rd
B568
30 Leicester, Victoria Park Rd
B581
30 Broughton Astley, Broughton Way
B582
30 Blaby, Little Glen Rd
B590
30 Hinckley, Rugby Rd
B591
60 Charley, Loughborough Rd
B676
60 Freeby, Saxby Rd
B4114
40 Enderby/Narborough, Leicester Rd/King Edward Avenue
30 Leicester, Sharnford
B4616
30 Leicester, East Park Rd
B4666
30 Hinckley, Coventry Rd
B5003
40 Norris Hill, Ashby Rd
B5366
30 Leicester, Saffron Lane
B5350
30 Loughborough, Foreset Rd
30 Loughborough, Nanpantan Rd
Unclassified
30 Barrow upon Soar, Sileby Rd
30 Blaby, Lutterworth Rd
30 Ibstock, Leicester Rd
30 Leicester, Fosse Rd South
30 Shepshed, Leicester Rd

Lincolnshire

A15
60 Ashby Lodge
60 Aswarby
A15-B1191
60 Dunsby Hollow
A16
60 Boston, Boston Tytton Lane
40 Burwell
60 Deeping Bypass
60 Grainsby to Holton-le-Clay
60 North Thoresby
A17
60 Fleet Hargate
60 Hoffleet Stow
60 Moulton Common
A52
60 Bridge End
60 Horbling and Swaton
60 Ropsley
A153
40 Billinghay
50 Tattershall
A158
50 Scremby to Candlesby
A631
60 Hemswell
60 West Rasen, Dale Bridge
B1188
30 Branston
60 Canwick, Highfield House
60 Potterhanworth

London

M11
Chadwell
M25
Egham
Elmbridge, Byfleet
Hillingdon
Hillingdon, Colnbrook
Runneymeade
Spelthorne
Wraysbury
A3
Kingston Bypass
Wandsworth, Kingston Rd
A4
Hounslow, Brentford, Great West Rd
Hounslow, Great West Rd
A5
Barnet, Hendon Broadway
Brent, Edgware Rd
A10
Enfield, Great Cambridge Rd
Hackney, Stamford Hill
A13
Barking and Dagenham, Alfreds Way
Barking and Dagenham, Ripple Rd
Dagenham, Ripple Rd
Newham, Alfreds Way
A20
Bexley, Sidcup Rd
Bromley, Sidcup Bypass
Greenwick, Sidcup Rd
A21
Lewisham, Bromley Rd
A22
Croydon, Godstone Rd
A40
City of Westminster, Westway
Ealing, Perivale
Ealing, Western Avenue
Hammersmith and Fulham, Westway
Hillingdon, Ruislip, Western Avenue
A110
Enfield, Enfield Rd
A124
Newham, Barking Rd
A205
Richmond upon Thames
Richmond upon Thames, Upper Richmond Rd West
A213
Bromley, Croydon Rd
A214
Wandsworth, Trinity Rd
A215
Croydon, Beulah Hill
A217
Croydon, Garratt Lane
A219
Hammersmith and Fulham, Scrubs Lane
A222
Bromley, Bromley Rd
A232
Sutton, Cheam Rd
A298
West Barnes, Bushey Rd
A312
Hillingdon
A315
Hounslow, High St
A406
Barking and Dagenham, Barking Relief Rd
Barnet, North Circular Rd
Redbridge, Southend Rd
A501
Camden, Euston Rd
A503
Haringey, Seven Sisters Rd
A3220
Wandsworth, Latchmere Rd
A4006
Brent, Kenton Rd
B178
Barking and Dagenham, Ballards Rd
B272
Sutton, Foresters Rd
B278
Sutton, Green Lane
B279
Sutton, Tudor Drive
Unclassified
Barnet, Oakleigh Rd South
Bexley, Abbey Rd
Bexley, Bellegrove Rd
Bexley, Erith Rd
Bexley, Farady Avenue
Bexley, King Harolds Way
Bexley, Lower Rd
Bexley, Penhill Rd
Bexley, Pickford Lane
Bexley, Well Hall Rd
Bexley, Woolwich Rd
Brent, Crest Rd
Brent, Hillside
Brent, Kingsbury Rd
Brent, Kingsbury, Fryent Way
Brent, Sudbury, Watford Rd
Brent, Wembley, Watford Rd
Brent, Woodcock Hill
Bromley, Beckenham Rd
Bromley, Burnt Ash Lane
Bromley, Crystal Palace Park Rd
Bromley, Elmers End Rd
Bromley, Main Rd
Bromley, Sevenoaks Way
Bromley, Wickham Way
City of Westminster, Great Western Rd
City of Westminster, Millbank
City of Westminster, Vauxhall Bridge Rd
Croydon, Addiscombe, Long Lane
Croydon, Brigstock Rd
Croydon, Coulsdon, Coulsdon Rd
Croydon, Coulsdon, Portnalls Rd
Croydon, Thornton Rd
Ealing, Greenford, Greenford Rd
Ealing, Horn Lane
Ealing, Lady Margaret Rd
Ealing, Ruislip Rd
Ealing, Southall, Greenford Rd
Ealing, Uxbridge Rd
Eastcote, Field End Rd
Enfield, Fore St
Forest Hill, Stanstead Rd
Forest Hill, Stanstead Rd
Greenwick, Beresford St
Greenwick, Court Rd
Greenwick, Creek Rd
Greenwick, Glenesk Rd
Greenwick, Rochester Way
Greenwick, Rochester Way
Greenwick, Woolwich Church St
Hackney, Clapton Common
Hackney, Seven Sisters Rd
Hackney, Upper Clapton Rd
Hammersmith and Fulham, Fulham Palace Rd
Hammersmith and Fulham, Uxbridge Rd
Hammersmith and Fulham, Westway
Haringey, Belmont Rd
Haringey, Bounds Green Rd
Haringey, Seven Sisters Rd
Haringey, White Hart Lane
Harrow, Alexandra Avenue
Harrow, Harrow View
Harrow, Harrow Weald, Uxbridge Rd
Harrow, Honeypot Lane
Harrow, Porlock Avenue
Harrow, Watford Rd
Havering, Chase Cross Rd
Havering, Eastern Avenue
Havering, Eastern Avenue East
Havering, Hall Lane
Havering, Hornchurch, Parkstone Avenue
Havering, Ockenden Rd
Havering, Romford, Brentwood Rd
Havering, Wingletye Lane
Hillingdon, Cowley, Cowley Rd
Hillingdon, Cowley, High Rd
Hillingdon, Harefield, Church Hill
Hillingdon, Hayes, Kingshill Avenue
Hillingdon, Hayes, Uxbridge Rd
Hillingdon, Northwood Hills, Joel St
Hillingdon, Park Rd
Hillingdon, Stockley Rd
Hillingdon, Uxbridge, Cowley Rd
Hounslow, Bedfont, Hatton Rd
Hounslow, Great West Rd
Hounslow, Hanworth, Castle Way
Hounslow, Harlington Rd West
Islington, Holloway Rd
Islington, Seven Sisters Rd
Islington, Upper St
Kensington and Chelsea, Barlby Rd
Kensington and Chelsea, Chelsea Embankment
Kensington and Chelsea, Chesterton Rd
Kensington and Chelsea, Holand Park Avenue
Kensington and Chelsea, Holland Villas Rd
Kensington and Chelsea, Kensington Park Rd
Kensington and Chelsea, Kensington Rd
Kensington and Chelsea, Ladbroke Grove
Kensington and Chelsea, Latimer Rd
Kensington and Chelsea, Royal Hospital Rd
Kensington and Chelsea, Sloane St
Kensington and Chelsea, St Helens Gardens
Kingston upon Thames, Kingston Rd
Kingston upon Thames, Manor Drive North
Kingston upon Thames, Richmond Rd
Lambeth, Atkins Rd
Lambeth, Brixton Hill
Lambeth, Brixton Rd
Lambeth, Clapham Rd
Lambeth, Herne Hill Rd
Lambeth, Kennington Park Rd
Lambeth, Kings Avenue
Lambeth, Streatham High Rd
Lewisham, Brockley Rd
Lewisham, Brownhill Rd
Lewisham, Burnt Ash Hill
Lewisham, Lee High Rd
Lewisham, Lewisham Way
Lewisham, Westwood Hill
Merton, Central Rd
Merton, Colliers Wood, High St
Merton, Hillcross Avenue
Merton, London Rd
Merton, Martin Way
Merton, Ridgway Place
Merton, West Barnes Lane
Newham, Barking Rd
Newham, Romford Rd
Newham, Royal Albert Dock, Spine Rd
Newham, Royal Docks Rd
North Dagenham, Rainham Rd
Redbridge, Hainault, Manford Way
Redbridge, Woodford Avenue
Redbridge, Woodford Rd
Richmond upon Thames, Kew Rd
Richmond upon Thames, Sixth Cross Rd
Richmond upon Thames, Uxbridge Rd
Southwark, Albany Rd
Southwark, Alleyn Park
Southwark, Brenchley Gardens
Southwark, Camberwell New Rd
Southwark, Denmark Hill
Southwark, Kennington Park Rd
Southwark, Linden Grove
Southwark, Old Kent Rd
Southwark, Peckham Rye
Southwark, Salter Rd
Southwark, Sunray Avenue
Streatham, Streatham High Rd
Sutton, Beddington Lane
Sutton, Cheam Common Rd
Sutton, Maiden Rd
Sutton, Middleton Rd
Tower Hamlets, Bow Rd
Tower Hamlets, Cambridge Heath Rd
Tower Hamlets, Homerton High Rd
Tower Hamlets, Manchester Rd
Tower Hamlets, Mile End Rd
Tower Hamlets, Upper Clapton Rd
Tower Hamlets, Westferry Rd
Waltham Forest, Chingford Rd
Waltham Forest, Hoe St
Waltham Forest, Larksall Rd
Wandsworth, Battersea Park Rd
Wandsworth, Garratt Lane
Wandsworth, Upper Richmond Rd
Woolwich, Woolwich Church St

Norfolk

A10
60 Stow Bardolph
60 Tottenhill/Watlington
A11
70 Attleborough Bypass
70 Ketteringham
70 Roundham
70 Snetterton
70 Wymondham/Bestthorpe
A12
70 Hopton
A17
60 Terrington St Clement
A47
60 East Winch
60 Emneth
60 Honington/Easton
50 Lingwood/Acle
60 Mautby/Halvergate
60 Narborough
70 Postwick
70 Pullover Rdbt
60 Scarning
60 Swaffham/Sporle
70 Terrington St John
70 Tuddenham
60 Wendling/Framsham
A140
60 Aylsham
60 Dickleburgh Moor
60 Erpingham
60 Long Stratton/Tivetshall St Mary
60 Newton Flotman
40 Newton Flotman/Saxlingham Thorpe
30 Norwich, Harford Bridge
40 Roughton village
70 Scole Bypass
60 St. Faiths
A143
60 Billingford/Brockdish
A146
60 Hales
A148
60 Bodham
60 Fakenham Bypass
40 King's Lynn, Grimston Rd
60 Pretty Corner
50 Thursford
A149
70 Caister Bypass
60 Catfield
40 Catfield/Potter Heigham
30 Hunstanton
60 Kings Lynn/Nth Runcton
60 Knights Hill
60 Little Snoring
60 Roughton (N and S Repps)
60 Sandringham
50 Wayford Bridge East
50 Wayford Bridge West/ Smallburgh
A1065
60 Hilbrough
60 South Acre
60 Weeting with Broomhill
A1066
70 Rushford
60 South Lopham
40 Thetford, Mundford Rd
A1067
50 Bawdeswell
60 Morton/Attlebridge
A1075
60 Wretham (heath)
A1082
30 Sheringham
A1122
60 Swaffham/Beachamwell
A1151
60 Rackheath/Wroxham
B111
30 East Harling
B1108
30 Norwich, Earlham Rd
B1135
50 Wymondham/Wreningham
B1149
60 Horsford Woods
B1150
50 Scottow
50 Westwick
B1152
60 Orby
B1332
50 Ditchingham
Unclassified
70 Caister, High St/Norwich Rd
30 Caister, Ormesby Rd
60 Drayton, Reepham Rd
30 Shipdham, High St
30 Walton

North Yorkshire

A1
70 Catterick
A59
60 Beamsley
A64
70 Malton
A65
60 Clapham
60 Settle
Unclassified
30 Tunstall, Main St

Key to 3-mile map pages

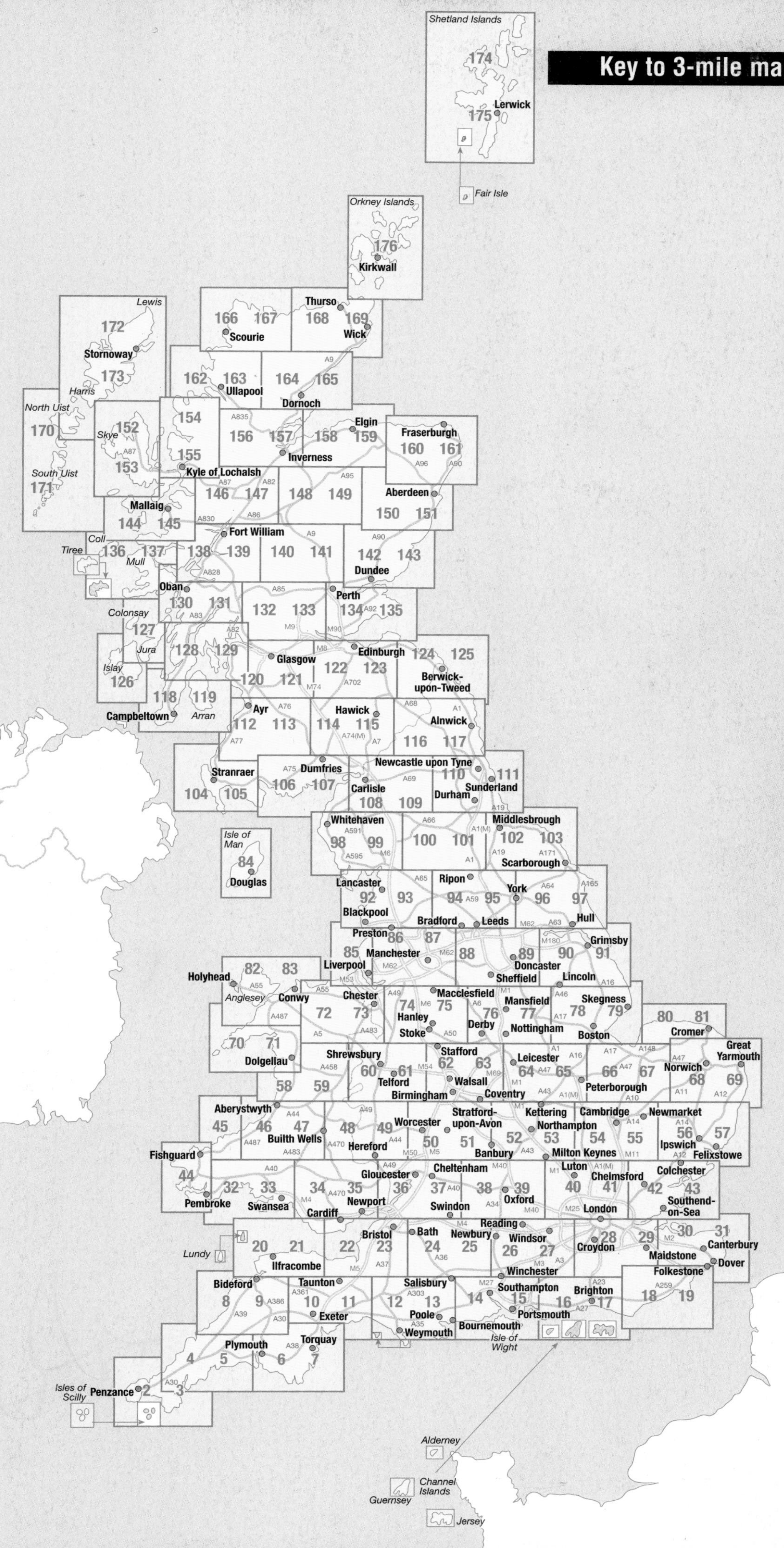
Shetland Islands
174
Lerwick
175
Fair Isle
Orkney Islands
176
Kirkwall
Lewis
172
Stornoway
173
Harris
North Uist
170
South Uist
171
Skye
152
153
166
167
Scourie
Thurso
168
169
Wick
162
163
Ullapool
164
165
Dornoch
154
155
156
157
158
159
Elgin
Inverness
Fraserburgh
160
161
Kyle of Lochalsh
146
147
148
149
Aberdeen
150
151
Mallaig
144
145
Fort William
138
139
140
141
142
143
Dundee
Coll
Tiree
136
137
Mull
Oban
130
131
132
133
Perth
134
135
Colonsay
127
Jura
128
129
Islay
126
Glasgow
120
121
Edinburgh
122
123
124
125
Berwick-upon-Tweed
118
119
Arran
Campbeltown
Ayr
112
113
Hawick
114
115
Alnwick
116
117
Stranraer
104
105
Dumfries
106
107
Carlisle
108
109
Newcastle upon Tyne
110
111
Sunderland
Durham
Whitehaven
98
99
100
101
Middlesbrough
102
103
Scarborough
Isle of Man
84
Douglas
Lancaster
92
93
Blackpool
Ripon
94
95
York
96
97
Bradford
Leeds
Hull
Preston
86
87
85
Manchester
88
89
Doncaster
90
91
Grimsby
Liverpool
Sheffield
Lincoln
Holyhead
82
83
Anglesey
Conwy
Chester
72
73
74
75
Macclesfield
Hanley
Stoke
76
Derby
Mansfield
77
Nottingham
Skegness
78
79
Boston
80
81
Cromer
70
71
Dolgellau
Shrewsbury
58
59
60
61
Telford
62
63
Stafford
Walsall
Birmingham
Coventry
Leicester
64
65
66
67
Peterborough
Norwich
68
69
Great Yarmouth
Aberystwyth
45
46
47
Builth Wells
48
49
Hereford
Worcester
50
51
Stratford-upon-Avon
Banbury
52
53
Kettering
Northampton
54
Cambridge
55
Newmarket
56
57
Ipswich
Felixstowe
Fishguard
44
Pembroke
32
33
Swansea
34
35
Cardiff
Newport
Gloucester
36
Cheltenham
37
38
39
Oxford
Swindon
Luton
40
Milton Keynes
41
Chelmsford
Colchester
42
43
Southend-on-Sea
London
Lundy
20
21
Ilfracombe
22
Bristol
23
Bath
24
Newbury
25
Reading
Windsor
26
27
28
Croydon
29
Maidstone
30
31
Canterbury
Dover
Folkestone
Winchester
Bideford
8
9
Taunton
10
11
Exeter
Salisbury
12
13
Poole
Weymouth
14
Southampton
15
Portsmouth
Bournemouth
16
Brighton
17
18
19
Isle of Wight
4
5
Plymouth
6
Torquay
7
Isles of Scilly
Penzance
2
3
Alderney
Channel Islands
Guernsey
Jersey

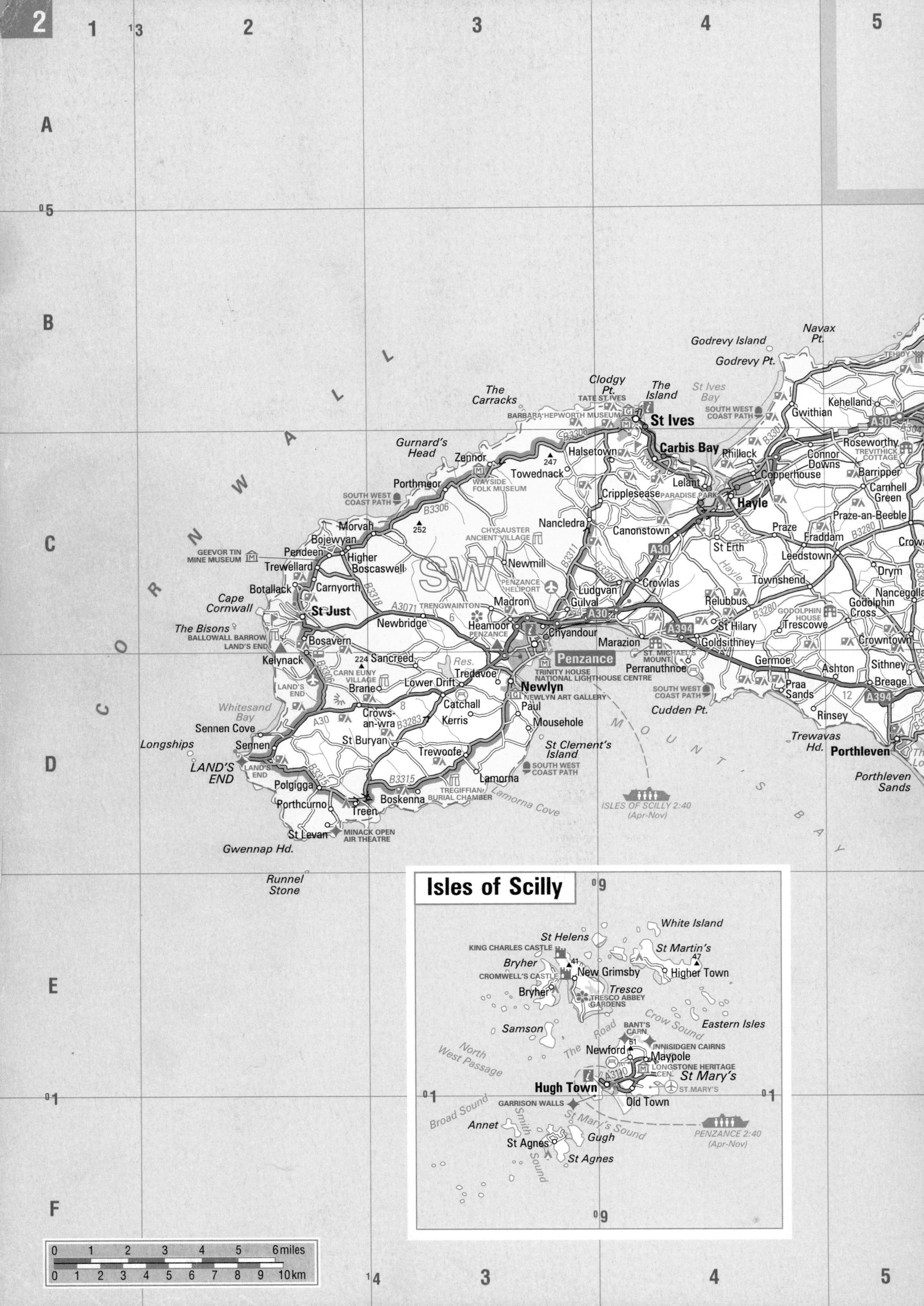
CORNWALL
SW
Godrevy Island
Navax Pt.
Godrevy Pt.
Clodgy Pt.
The Island
St Ives Bay
The Carracks
TATE ST IVES
BARBARA HEPWORTH MUSEUM
SOUTH WEST COAST PATH
St Ives
Carbis Bay
Gwithian
Kehelland
Gurnard's Head
Zennor
Halsetown
Phillack
Connor Downs
Roseworthy
TREVITHICK COTTAGE
Barripper
Porthmeor
WAYSIDE FOLK MUSEUM
Towednack
Lelant
Copperhouse
Carnhell Green
Cripplesease
PARADISE PARK
Hayle
Praze-an-Beeble
Morvah
Bojewyan
Nancledra
Canonstown
Praze
Fraddam
CHYSAUSTER ANCIENT VILLAGE
St Erth
Leedstown
GEEVOR TIN MINE MUSEUM
Pendeen
Higher Boscaswell
Trewellard
Newmill
Drym
Botallack
Carnyorth
PENZANCE HELIPORT
Ludgvan
Crowlas
Townshend
Nancegollan
Cape Cornwall
St Just
TRENGWAINTON
Madron
Gulval
Relubbus
GODOLPHIN HOUSE
Godolphin Cross
The Bisons
BALLOWALL BARROW
LAND'S END
Newbridge
Heamoor
PENZANCE
Chyandour
St Hilary
Trescowe
Bosavern
Marazion
Goldsithney
Crowntown
Kelynack
Sancreed
Res.
Penzance
ST. MICHAEL'S MOUNT
Germoe
Ashton
Sithney
CARN EUNY VILLAGE
Tredavoe
TRINITY HOUSE NATIONAL LIGHTHOUSE CENTRE
Perranuthnoe
Brane
Lower Drift
Newlyn
Praa Sands
Breage
Whitesand Bay
LAND'S END
Catchall
NEWLYN ART GALLERY
SOUTH WEST COAST PATH
Paul
Crows-an-wra
Kerris
Mousehole
Cudden Pt.
Rinsey
Sennen Cove
MOUNT'S BAY
Longships
Sennen
St Buryan
Trewoofe
St Clement's Island
Trewavas Hd.
Porthleven
LAND'S END
SOUTH WEST COAST PATH
Polgigga
Lamorna
Porthleven Sands
TREGIFFIAN BURIAL CHAMBER
Porthcurno
Boskenna
Lamorna Cove
ISLES OF SCILLY 2:40 (Apr-Nov)
Treen
St Levan
MINACK OPEN AIR THEATRE
Gwennap Hd.
Runnel Stone
A30
A3071
A394
B3306
B3311
B3309
B3318
B3283
B3315
B3302
B3280
B3301
247
252
224
Isles of Scilly
White Island
St Helens
St Martin's
KING CHARLES CASTLE
Bryher
New Grimsby
Higher Town
CROMWELL'S CASTLE
Tresco
TRESCO ABBEY GARDENS
Samson
Crow Sound
Eastern Isles
BANT'S CARN
North West Passage
The Road
Newford
INNISIDGEN CAIRNS
Maypole
LONGSTONE HERITAGE CEN.
St Mary's
Hugh Town
ST.MARY'S
Broad Sound
GARRISON WALLS
Old Town
Annet
Smith Sound
St Mary's Sound
Gugh
PENZANCE 2:40 (Apr-Nov)
St Agnes
0 1 2 3 4 5 6 miles
0 1 2 3 4 5 6 7 8 9 10 km

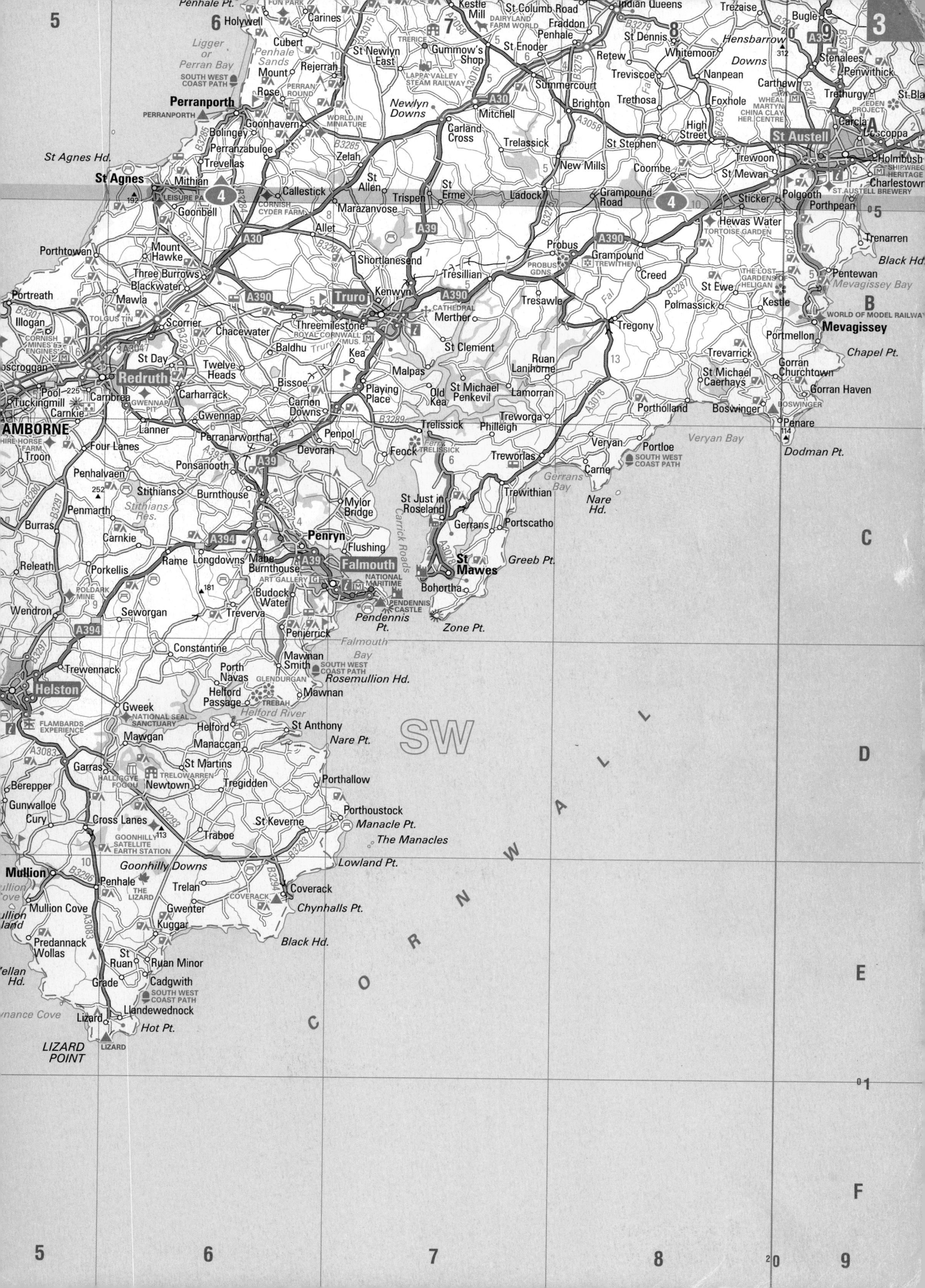
3
Perranporth
St Agnes
Truro
Redruth
Camborne
Falmouth
Penryn
St Mawes
Helston
St Austell
Mevagissey
Mullion
Lizard
LIZARD POINT
SW
CORNWALL
Newquay
Probus
Tregony
Mitchell
St Just in Roseland
Coverack
St Keverne
Perran Bay
Falmouth Bay
Veryan Bay
Mevagissey Bay
Carrick Roads
Helford River
Goonhilly Downs
Dodman Pt.
Zone Pt.
Nare Hd.
Black Hd.
Hot Pt.
SOUTH WEST COAST PATH
5
6
7
8
9
A
B
C
D
E
F

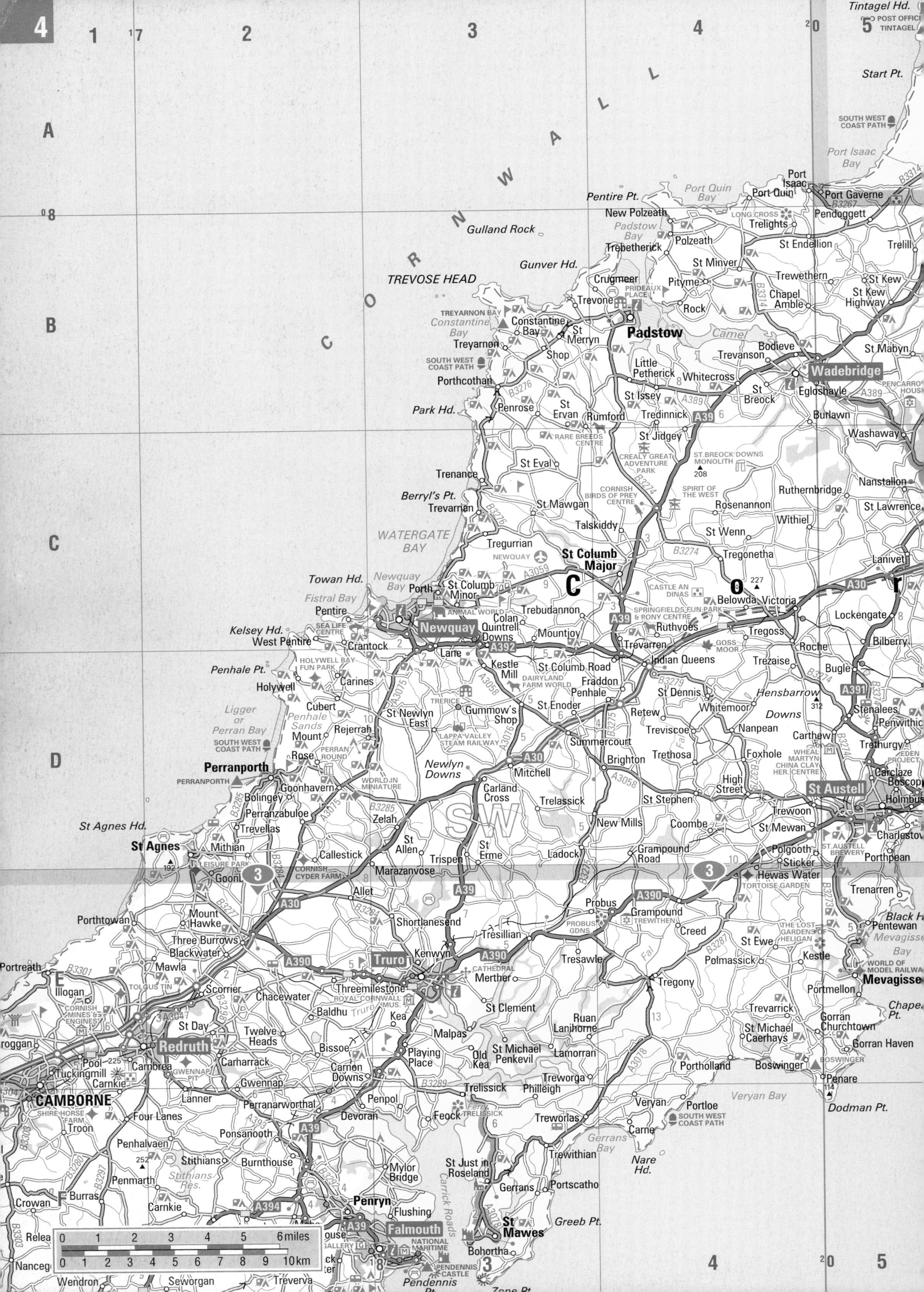

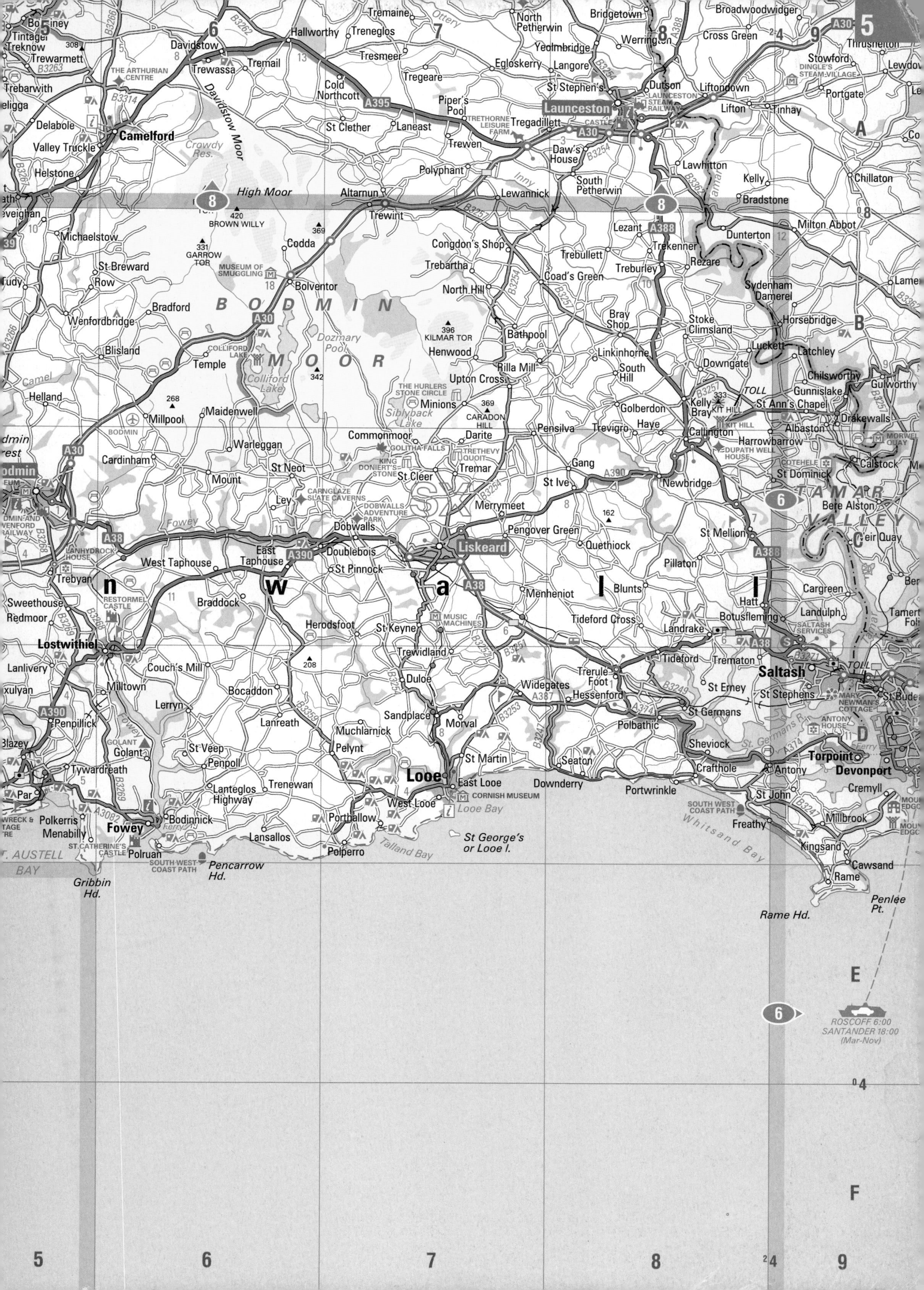
5
Tintagel
Treknow
Trewarmett
Trebarwith
Delabole
Camelford
Valley Truckle
Helstone
Michaelstow
St Breward
Row
Wenfordbridge
Bradford
Blisland
Helland
Millpool
Maidenwell
Cardinham
Bodmin
Lanhydrock House
Trebyan
Sweethouse
Redmoor
Lostwithiel
Restormel Castle
Lanlivery
Milltown
Penpillick
Par
Tywardreath
Polkerris
Menabilly
Fowey
Polruan
Bodinnick
Golant
Gribbin Hd.
Pencarrow Hd.
South West Coast Path
Davidstow
Trewassa
Tremail
The Arthurian Centre
Crowdy Res.
Davidstow Moor
High Moor
Brown Willy
Garrow Tor
Museum of Smuggling
Bolventor
Codda
BODMIN MOOR
Dozmary Pool
Colliford Lake
Temple
Warleggan
Mount
St Neot
Ley
Carnglaze Slate Caverns
Dobwalls Adventure Park
Dobwalls
Doublebois
East Taphouse
West Taphouse
Braddock
Couch's Mill
Bocaddon
Lerryn
Lanreath
St Veep
Penpoll
Lanteglos Highway
Trenewan
Lansallos
Polperro
Talland Bay
Hallworthy
Treneglos
Tremaine
Tresmeer
Cold Northcott
St Clether
Laneast
Tregeare
Altarnun
Trewint
Piper's Pool
Trethorne Leisure Farm
Tregadillett
Trewen
Polyphant
Lewannick
Congdon's Shop
Trebartha
North Hill
Kilmar Tor
Henwood
Upton Cross
Rilla Mill
The Hurlers Stone Circle
Minions
Siblyback Lake
Caradon Hill
Darite
Commonmoor
Golitha Falls
King Doniert's Stone
St Cleer
Trethevy Quoit
Tremar
Merrymeet
Liskeard
St Pinnock
Herodsfoot
St Keyne
Music Machines
Trewidland
Duloe
Sandplace
Morval
Muchlarnick
Pelynt
Looe
East Looe
West Looe
Cornish Museum
Looe Bay
St Martin
Porthallow
St George's or Looe I.
North Petherwin
Bridgetown
Werrington
Yeolmbridge
Egloskerry
Langore
St Stephen's
Dutson
Launceston
Launceston Steam Railway
Castle
Daw's House
South Petherwin
Lawhitton
Lezant
Trekenner
Trebullett
Treburley
Rezare
Coad's Green
Bray Shop
Bathpool
Linkinhorne
South Hill
Golberdon
Kelly Bray
Kit Hill
Callington
Haye
Trevigro
Pensilva
Gang
St Ive
Newbridge
Pengover Green
Quethiock
Pillaton
Blunts
Menheniot
Tideford Cross
Landrake
Tideford
Trerule Foot
Widegates
Hessenford
Polbathic
St Germans
Seaton
Downderry
Portwrinkle
Crafthole
Sheviock
Broadwoodwidger
Cross Green
Thrushelton
Stowford
Dingle's Steam Village
Lewdown
Liftondown
Lifton
Tinhay
Portgate
Kelly
Chillaton
Bradstone
Dunterton
Milton Abbot
Sydenham Damerel
Horsebridge
Luckett
Latchley
Downgate
Chilsworthy
Gunnislake
Gulworthy
St Ann's Chapel
Drakewalls
Albaston
Harrowbarrow
Dupath Well House
Cotehele
Morwellham Quay
Calstock
St Dominick
TAMAR VALLEY
Bere Alston
St Mellion
Cargreen
Landulph
Hatt
Botusfleming
Saltash Services
Saltash
Trematon
St Erney
St Stephens
Mary Newman's Cottage
Antony House
Torpoint
Devonport
Antony
St John
Cremyll
Millbrook
Freathy
Whitsand Bay
Kingsand
Cawsand
Rame
Rame Hd.
Penlee Pt.
ROSCOFF 6:00
SANTANDER 18:00
(Mar-Nov)
A30
A38
A39
A395
A388
A390
A374
A387
B3254
B3257
B3266
B3268
B3269
B3314
B3263
B3359
B3253
B3247
B3251
B3252
TOLL
A
B
C
D
E
F
5
6
7
8
9

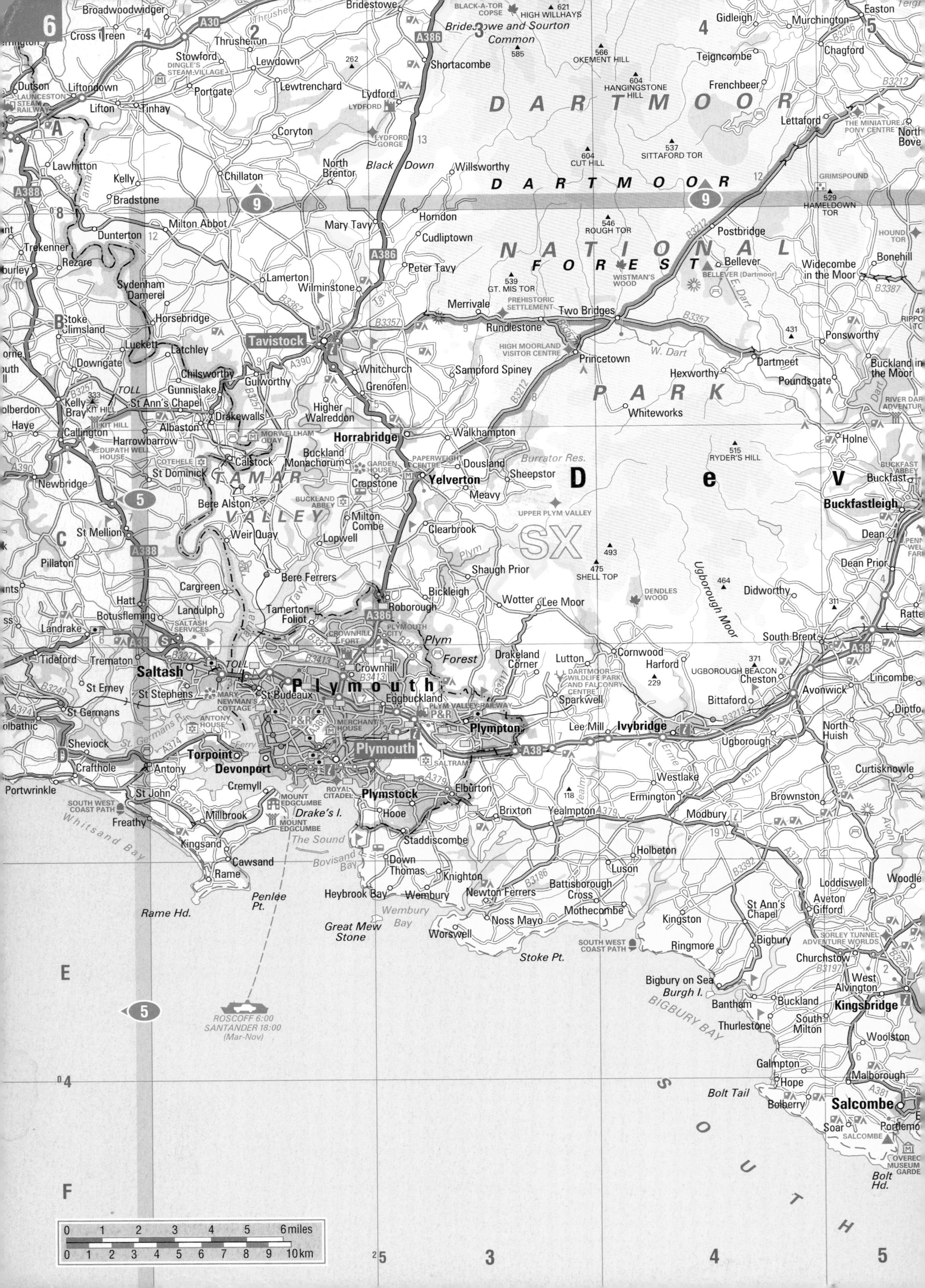
Broadwoodwidger
Cross Green
A30
Thrushelton
Bridestowe
BLACK-A-TOR COPSE
HIGH WILLHAYS
Bridestowe and Sourton Common
Gidleigh
Murchington
Easton
Stowford
DINGLE'S STEAM VILLAGE
Lewdown
Shortacombe
A386
OKEMENT HILL
Teigncombe
Chagford
Dutson
Liftondown
Lewtrenchard
Portgate
Lydford
HANGINGSTONE HILL
Frenchbeer
LAUNCESTON STEAM RAILWAY
Lifton
Tinhay
LYDFORD
DARTMOOR
Lettaford
THE MINIATURE PONY CENTRE
Coryton
LYDFORD GORGE
SITTAFORD TOR
CUT HILL
Lawhitton
Kelly
Chillaton
North Brentor
Black Down
Willsworthy
GRIMSPOUND
A388
Bradstone
Tamar
HAMELDOWN TOR
Horndon
Milton Abbot
Mary Tavy
Dunterton
ROUGH TOR
Postbridge
Trekenner
Cudliptown
NATIONAL
HOUND TOR
Rezare
A386
Peter Tavy
FOREST
Bellever
Widecombe in the Moor
Bonehill
Lamerton
GT. MIS TOR
WISTMAN'S WOOD
BELLEVER (Dartmoor)
Sydenham Damerel
Wilminstone
B3387
Merrivale
PREHISTORIC SETTLEMENT
Two Bridges
B3362
E. Dart
Horsebridge
Stoke Climsland
B3357
Rundlestone
Ponsworthy
Tavistock
Luckett
Latchley
HIGH MOORLAND VISITOR CENTRE
Princetown
W. Dart
Dartmeet
Buckland in the Moor
Downgate
A390
Whitchurch
Sampford Spiney
Hexworthy
Poundsgate
Chilsworthy
Gunnislake
Gulworthy
Grenofen
B3212
PARK
B3257
TOLL
Kelly Bray
KIT HILL
St Ann's Chapel
Higher Walreddon
Whiteworks
Callington
Drakewalls
Albaston
MORWELLHAM QUAY
Horrabridge
Walkhampton
Holne
Haye
Harrowbarrow
DUPATH WELL HOUSE
COTEHELE HOUSE
Calstock
Buckland Monachorum
GARDEN HOUSE
PAPERWEIGHT CENTRE
Dousland
Burrator Res.
RYDER'S HILL
St Dominick
TAMAR
Sheepstor
BUCKFAST ABBEY
Newbridge
Crapstone
Yelverton
D
e
V
Buckfast
Meavy
Buckfastleigh
Bere Alston
BUCKLAND ABBEY
VALLEY
UPPER PLYM VALLEY
St Mellion
Milton Combe
Clearbrook
Weir Quay
Lopwell
SX
Dean
A388
Plym
Pillaton
Shaugh Prior
SHELL TOP
Ugborough Moor
Dean Prior
Bere Ferrers
Cargreen
DENDLES WOOD
Bickleigh
Didworthy
Hatt
Wotter
Lee Moor
Landulph
Tamerton Foliot
Roborough
Botusfleming
SALTASH SERVICES
A386
Landrake
CROWNHILL FORT
PLYMOUTH CITY
Plym
South Brent
A38
Forest
Drakeland Corner
Lutton
Cornwood
Harford
Tideford
Trematon
B3271
TOLL
Crownhill
DARTMOOR WILDLIFE PARK AND FALCONRY CENTRE
UGBOROUGH BEACON
Cheston
Lincombe
Saltash
B3413
Plymouth
St Erney
St Stephens
St Budeaux
Eggbuckland
Sparkwell
Avonwick
MARY NEWMAN'S COTTAGE
PLYM VALLEY RAILWAY
Bittaford
St Germans
ANTONY HOUSE
P&R
MERCHANT'S HOUSE
Plympton
Lee Mill
Ivybridge
Diptford
St. Germans R.
Ferry
Plymouth
A38
Ugborough
North Huish
Sheviock
A374
Torpoint
Crafthole
Antony
Devonport
SALTRAM
Erme
Westlake
Curtisknowle
Portwrinkle
Cremyll
A379
Elburton
Ermington
Brownston
SOUTH WEST COAST PATH
St John
MOUNT EDGCUMBE
ROYAL CITADEL
Plymstock
Brixton
Yealmpton
Modbury
Freathy
Millbrook
Drake's I.
Hooe
Yealm
Whitsand Bay
Kingsand
MOUNT EDGCUMBE
The Sound
Staddiscombe
Holbeton
Cawsand
Bovisand Bay
Down Thomas
Luson
Rame
Knighton
B3392
Loddiswell
Woodle
Penlee Pt.
Heybrook Bay
Wembury
Newton Ferrers
Battisborough Cross
Aveton Gifford
Rame Hd.
Wembury Bay
Noss Mayo
Mothecombe
Kingston
St Ann's Chapel
Great Mew Stone
Worswell
SOUTH WEST COAST PATH
Ringmore
Bigbury
SORLEY TUNNEL ADVENTURE WORLDS
Stoke Pt.
Churchstow
E
Bigbury on Sea
Burgh I.
West Alvington
Bantham
Buckland
Kingsbridge
BIGBURY BAY
ROSCOFF 6:00
SANTANDER 18:00
(Mar-Nov)
Thurlestone
South Milton
Woolston
Galmpton
Hope
Malborough
Bolt Tail
Bolberry
Salcombe
Soar
Portlemo
SALCOMBE
OVEREC MUSEUM GARDE
SOUTH
Bolt Hd.
F
0 1 2 3 4 5 6 miles
0 1 2 3 4 5 6 7 8 9 10 km

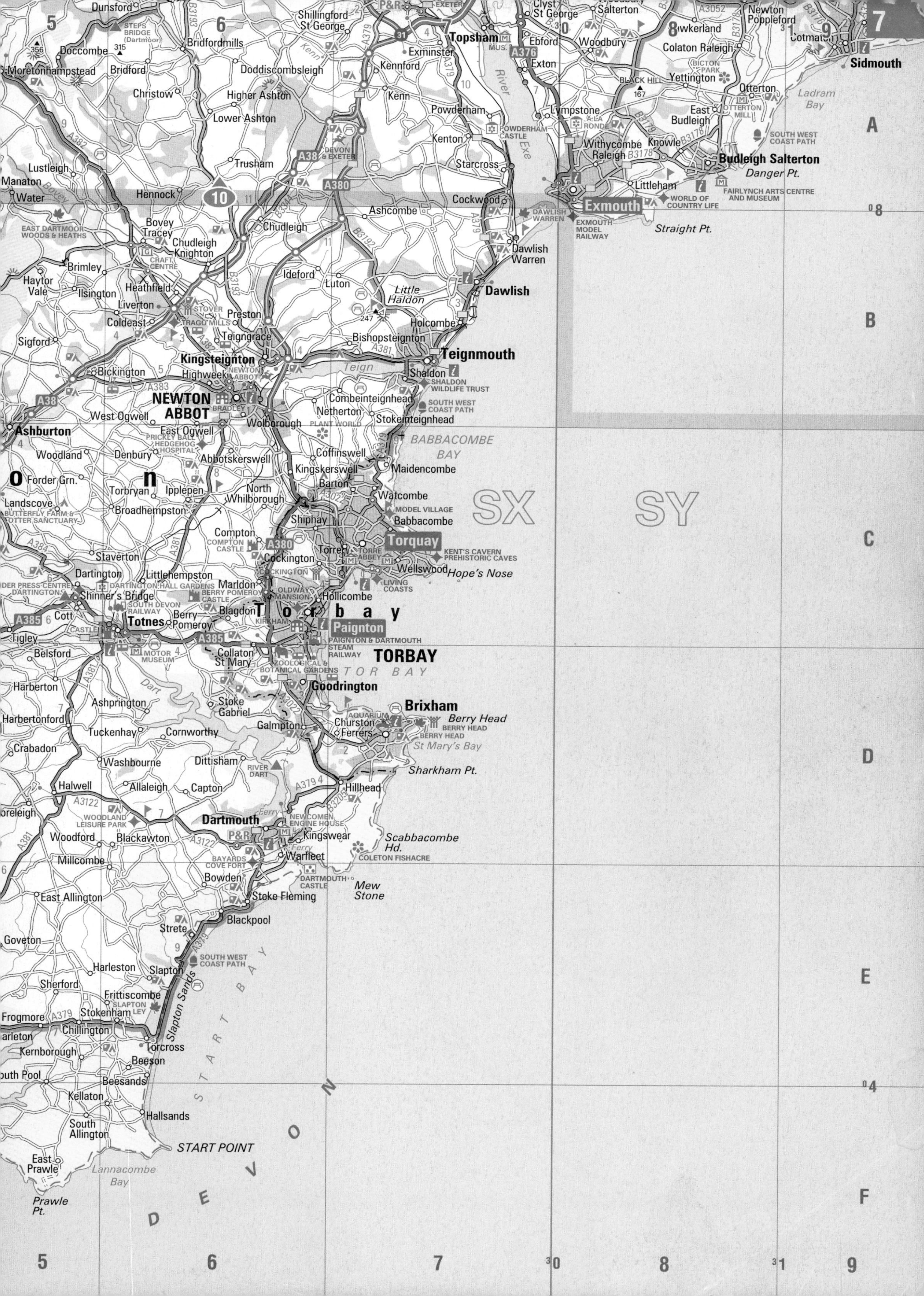
7
Dunsford
Steps Bridge (Dartmoor)
Bridfordmills
Shillingford St George
Exeter
Topsham
Clyst St George
Salterton
Newton Poppleford
Cotmaton
Sidmouth
Doccombe
Moretonhampstead
Bridford
Doddiscombsleigh
Kennford
Exminster
Ebford
Woodbury
Colaton Raleigh
Exton
Bicton Park
Black Hill
Yettington
Christow
Higher Ashton
Kenn
Otterton
Ladram Bay
Lower Ashton
Powderham
Powderham Castle
Lympstone
A La Ronde
East Budleigh
Otterton Mill
Kenton
Withycombe Raleigh
Knowle
South West Coast Path
Trusham
Starcross
Budleigh Salterton
Danger Pt.
Lustleigh
Manaton
Water
Hennock
Littleham
Fairlynch Arts Centre and Museum
Cockwood
Exmouth
World of Country Life
Ashcombe
Dawlish Warren
Exmouth Model Railway
Straight Pt.
Bovey Tracey
East Dartmoor Woods & Heaths
Chudleigh
Chudleigh Knighton
Craft Centre
Brimley
Haytor Vale
Ilsington
Heathfield
Ideford
Luton
Little Haldon
Dawlish
Liverton
Stover
Trago Mills
Preston
Coldeast
Holcombe
Teigngrace
Sigford
Bishopsteignton
Kingsteignton
Teignmouth
Teign
Bickington
Highweek
Shaldon
Shaldon Wildlife Trust
Newton Abbot
Bradley
Combeinteignhead
Netherton
South West Coast Path
West Ogwell
East Ogwell
Wolborough
Plant World
Stokeinteignhead
Ashburton
Prickly Ball Hedgehog Hospital
Babbacombe Bay
Woodland
Denbury
Abbotskerswell
Coffinswell
Kingskerswell
Maidencombe
Forder Grn.
Torbryan
Ipplepen
North Whilborough
Barton
Watcombe
Landscove
Butterfly Farm & Otter Sanctuary
Broadhempston
Model Village
SX
SY
Shiphay
Babbacombe
Compton
Compton Castle
Torquay
Staverton
Cockington
Torre
Torre Abbey
Kent's Cavern Prehistoric Caves
Wellswood
Hope's Nose
Dartington
Littlehempston
Dartington Hall Gardens
Marldon
Living Coasts
Shinner's Bridge
South Devon Railway
Berry Pomeroy Castle
Oldway Mansion
Hollicombe
Torbay
Cott
Totnes
Berry Pomeroy
Blagdon
Kirkham
Paignton
Tigley
Motor Museum
Paignton & Dartmouth Steam Railway
TORBAY
Belsford
Collaton St Mary
Zoological & Botanical Gardens
Tor Bay
Harberton
Goodrington
Dart
Brixham
Berry Head
Ashprington
Stoke Gabriel
Harbertonford
Aquarium
Churston Ferrers
Tuckenhay
Cornworthy
Galmpton
St Mary's Bay
Crabadon
Washbourne
Dittisham
River Dart
Sharkham Pt.
Halwell
Allaleigh
Capton
Hillhead
Woodland Leisure Park
Dartmouth
Newcomen Engine House
Woodford
Blackawton
Kingswear
Scabbacombe Hd.
Millcombe
Bayards Cove Fort
Warfleet
Coleton Fishacre
Bowden
Dartmouth Castle
Mew Stone
East Allington
Stoke Fleming
Blackpool
Strete
Goveton
South West Coast Path
Harleston
Slapton
Start Bay
Sherford
Frittiscombe
Slapton Ley
Slapton Sands
Frogmore
Stokenham
Chillington
Torcross
Kernborough
Beeson
Beesands
Kellaton
Hallsands
South Allington
Start Point
East Prawle
Lannacombe Bay
Prawle Pt.
DEVON
A
B
C
D
E
F
5
6
7
8
9

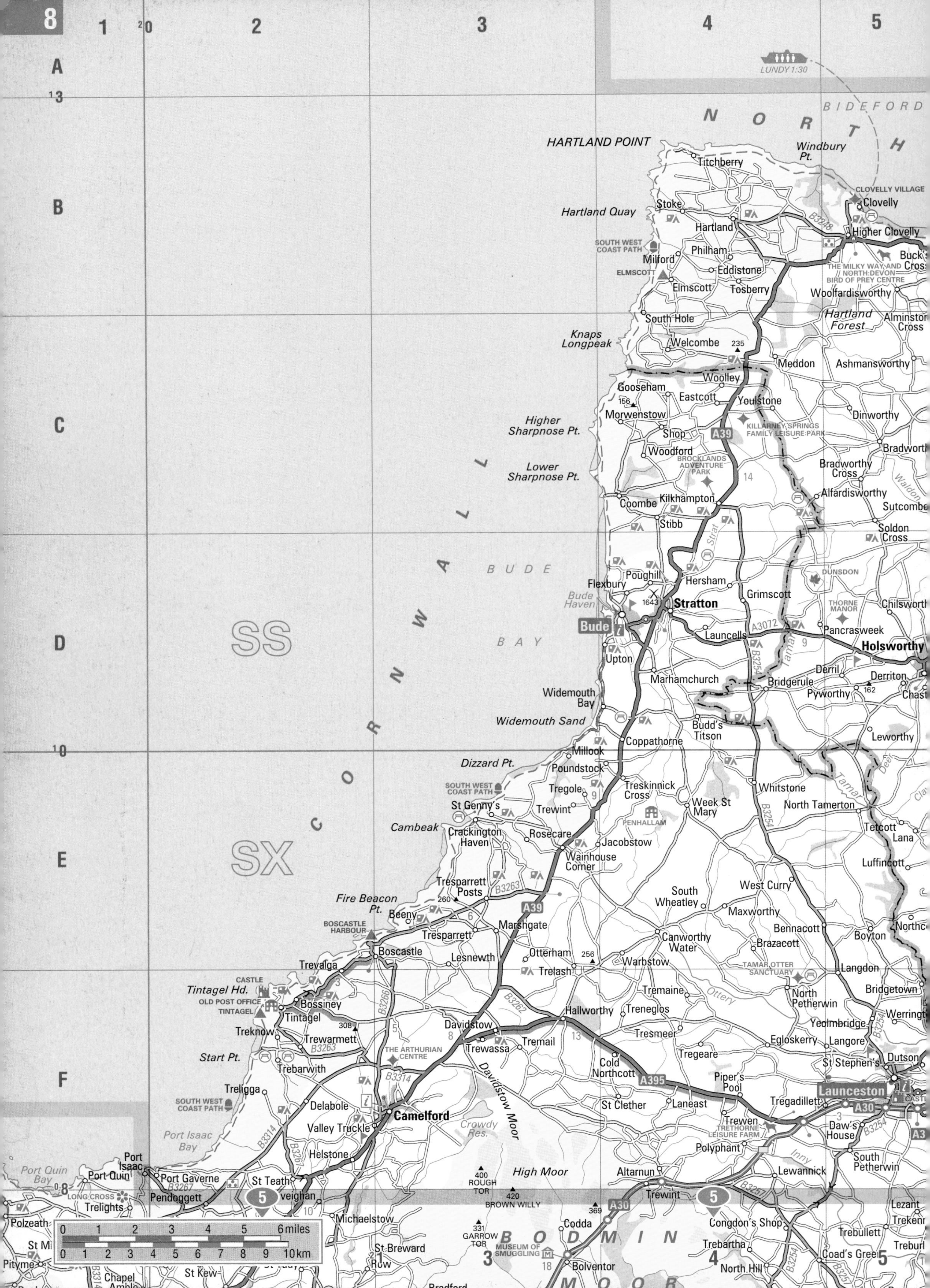

1   20   2   3   4   5

A
13
LUNDY 1:30

B I D E F O R D

N O R T H

HARTLAND POINT
Titchberry
Windbury Pt.
Stoke
Hartland Quay
Hartland
SOUTH WEST COAST PATH
Milford
Philham
ELMSCOTT
Elmscott
Eddistone
Tosberry
South Hole
Welcombe   235
Knaps
Longpeak
Gooseham   156
Morwenstow
Shop
Woodford
A39
Coombe
Kilkhampton
Stibb
Flexbury
Poughill
Bude Haven
Bude
Upton
Marhamchurch
Widemouth Bay
Widemouth Sand
Dizzard Pt.
Millook
Poundstock
Tregole
St Genny's
Trewint
Cambeak
Crackington Haven
Rosecare
Wainhouse Corner
Jacobstow
Tresparrett Posts
B3263
Fire Beacon Pt.
Beeny   260
BOSCASTLE HARBOUR
Marshgate
A39
Boscastle
Tresparrett
Lesnewth
Otterham
Trelash
Trevalga
CASTLE
Tintagel Hd.
OLD POST OFFICE TINTAGEL
Bossiney
Tintagel
Treknow
Trewarmett   308
Davidstow
Trewassa
Tremail
START Pt.
B3263
THE ARTHURIAN CENTRE
Trebarwith
Treligga
SOUTH WEST COAST PATH
Delabole
Camelford
Valley Truckle
Helstone
Port Quin Bay
Port Isaac
Port Gaverne
St Teath
LONG CROSS
Trelights
Pendoggett
eveighan
Polzeath
St Mi
Pityme
Michaelstow
St Breward
St Kew
Chapel Amble

HARTLAND FIELD
Woolfardisworthy
Clovelly
Higher Clovelly
THE MILKY WAY AND NORTH DEVON BIRD OF PREY CENTRE
Buck Cross
Hartland Forest
Alminstor Cross
Meddon
Ashmansworthy
Woolley
Eastcott
Youlstone
Dinworthy
KILLARNEY SPRINGS FAMILY LEISURE PARK
Bradwort
BROCKLANDS ADVENTURE PARK   14
Bradworthy Cross
Waldon
Alfardisworthy
Sutcombe
Hersham
Grimscott
DUNSDON
Soldon Cross
X 1643
Stratton
THORNE MANOR
Chilsworth
Launcells
A3072
Pancrasweek
Holsworthy
Derril
Bridgerule
Pyworthy   162
Derriton
Chast
Budd's Titson
Leworthy
Coppathorne
Whitstone
North Tamerton
Tetcott
Lana
Luffincott
Treskinnick Cross   9
PENHALLAM
Week St Mary
West Curry
Northc
South Wheatley
Maxworthy
Boyton
Canworthy Water
Bennacott
Brazacott
Langdon
Warbstow   256
TAMAR OTTER SANCTUARY
Bridgetown
Tremaine
North Petherwin
Werringt
Hallworthy
Treneglos
Yeolmbridge
Davidstow   8   13
Tresmeer
Egloskerry
Langore
Tregeare
St Stephen's
Cold Northcott
A395
Piper's Pool
Laneast
Tregadillett
Launceston
St Clether
Trewen TRETHORNE LEISURE FARM
Daw's House
A30
Polyphant
Lewannick
South Petherwin
High Moor
400 ROUGH TOR
Altarnun
Trewint   5
A30
B3257
Lezant
Trekenr
420 BROWN WILLY
Codda   369
Congdon's Shop
Trebullett
331 GARROW TOR   MUSEUM OF SMUGGLING   18
Bolventor
Trebartha
Coad's Gree
B O D M I N

M O O R

0   1   2   3   4   5   6 miles
0   1   2   3   4   5   6   7   8   9   10 km

SS

SX

C O R N W A L L

B U D E

B A Y

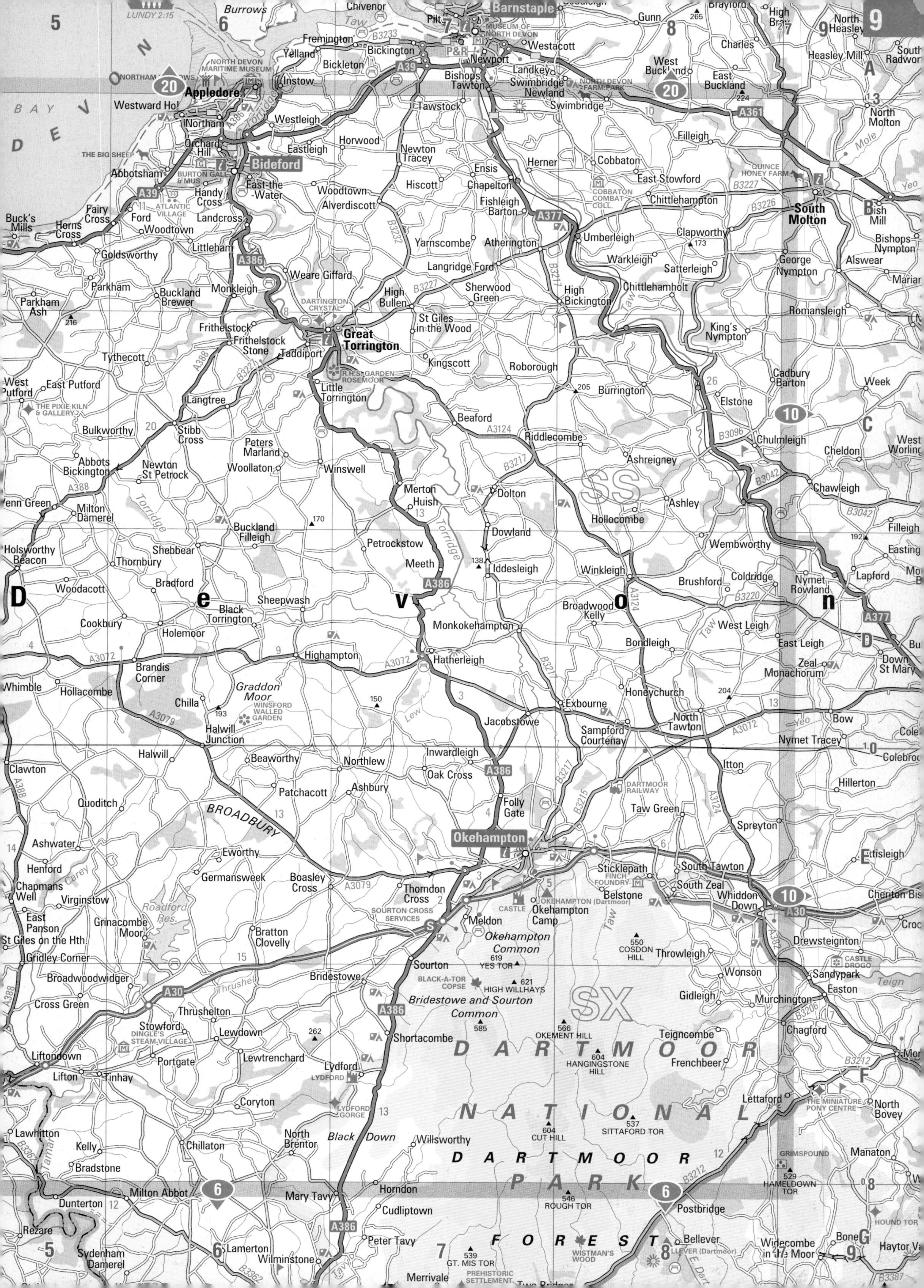
LUNDY 2:15
Burrows
Chivenor
Barnstaple
Brayford
High Bray
North Heasley
Pilton
MUSEUM OF NORTH DEVON
Gunn
265
Fremington
Yelland
Bickington
Bickleton
Westacott
Charles
Heasley Mill
South Radworthy
NORTH DEVON MARITIME MUSEUM
Instow
Newport
Landkey
Bishops Tawton
Swimbridge Newland
NORTH DEVON FARM PARK
West Buckland
East Buckland
224
NORTHAM BURROWS
Appledore
Westward Ho!
Northam
Tawstock
Swimbridge
North Molton
BAY
DEVON
Westleigh
Filleigh
A361
A39
Orchard Hill
THE BIG SHEEP
Eastleigh
Horwood
Newton Tracey
Herner
Cobbaton
Mole
QUINCE HONEY FARM
Abbotsham
BURTON GALL & MUS
Bideford
East-the-Water
Ensis
Hiscott
Chapelton
East Stowford
COBBATON COMBAT COLL.
B3227
Woodtown
Alverdiscott
Handy Cross
ATLANTIC VILLAGE
Fishleigh Barton
Chittlehampton
B3226
South Molton
Bish Mill
Yeo
Buck's Mills
Fairy Cross
Horns Cross
Ford
Landcross
Woodtown
A377
Umberleigh
Clapworthy
173
Bishops Nympton
Littleham
Goldsworthy
Yarnscombe
Atherington
Warkleigh
Satterleigh
George Nympton
Alswear
A386
Weare Giffard
Langridge Ford
B3232
Mariansleigh
Parkham
Buckland Brewer
Monkleigh
High Bullen
Sherwood Green
High Bickington
Chittlehamholt
Parkham Ash
216
DARTINGTON CRYSTAL
St Giles in the Wood
B3217
Romansleigh
Frithelstock
Great Torrington
King's Nympton
Tythecott
Frithelstock Stone
Taddiport
Kingscott
Roborough
West Putford
East Putford
R.H.S. GARDEN ROSEMOOR
Little Torrington
205
Burrington
Cadbury Barton
Week
THE PIXIE KILN & GALLERY
Langtree
A388
B3227
Elstone
Bulkworthy
Stibb Cross
Beaford
A3124
Riddlecombe
B3096
Chulmleigh
Cheldon
West Worlington
Peters Marland
Abbots Bickington
Newton St Petrock
Woollaton
Winswell
Ashreigney
Torridge
B3042
Chawleigh
Merton
Dolton
Fenn Green
Milton Damerel
Huish
SS
Ashley
Hollocombe
B3042
Buckland Filleigh
170
Dowland
Filleigh
Holsworthy Beacon
Shebbear
Petrockstow
Wembworthy
192
Eastington
Thornbury
Meeth
138
Iddesleigh
Winkleigh
Brushford
Coldridge
Nymet Rowland
Lapford
Woodacott
Bradford
Sheepwash
Broadwood Kelly
B3220
Cookbury
Black Torrington
Holemoor
Monkokehampton
Taw
West Leigh
A377
Bondleigh
East Leigh
A3072
Brandis Corner
Highampton
Hatherleigh
Zeal Monachorum
Down St Mary
Whimble
Hollacombe
Graddon Moor
Chilla
193
WINSFORD WALLED GARDEN
150
Lew
Exbourne
Honeychurch
204
Halwill Junction
A3079
Jacobstowe
Sampford Courtenay
North Tawton
Bow
Yeo
Nymet Tracey
Colebrooke
Halwill
Beaworthy
Northlew
Inwardleigh
Clawton
Oak Cross
Itton
DARTMOOR RAILWAY
Quoditch
Patchacott
Ashbury
BROADBURY
Folly Gate
B3215
Hillerton
Taw Green
Spreyton
Ashwater
Okehampton
Eworthy
Ettisleigh
Henford
Germansweek
Boasley Cross
Sticklepath
FINCH FOUNDRY
South Tawton
South Zeal
Chapmans Well
Carey
Virginstow
Roadford Res.
Thorndon Cross
A3079
Belstone
Whiddon Down
Cheriton Bishop
East Panson
Grinacombe Moor
SOURTON CROSS SERVICES
CASTLE
OKEHAMPTON (Dartmoor)
Okehampton Camp
A30
St Giles on the Hth.
Bratton Clovelly
Meldon
Okehampton Common
550 COSDON HILL
Throwleigh
Drewsteignton
Crockernwell
Gridley Corner
Sourton
619 YES TOR
CASTLE DROGO
Sandypark
Broadwoodwidger
Bridestowe
BLACK-A-TOR COPSE
621 HIGH WILLHAYS
Wonson
Teign
Easton
Thrushel
Bridestowe and Sourton Common
SX
Gidleigh
Murchington
Cross Green
Thrushelton
585
566 OKEMENT HILL
Chagford
B3206
Stowford
DINGLE'S STEAM VILLAGE
262
Shortacombe
Teigncombe
Lewdown
DARTMOOR
604 HANGINGSTONE HILL
Frenchbeer
Liftondown
Portgate
Lewtrenchard
Lydford
LYDFORD
B3212
Moretonhampstead
Lifton
Tinhay
Lettaford
THE MINIATURE PONY CENTRE
North Bovey
Coryton
LYDFORD GORGE
NATIONAL
Lawhitton
604 CUT HILL
537 SITTAFORD TOR
Kelly
North Brentor
Black Down
Willsworthy
Chillaton
DARTMOOR
Manaton
Tamar
Bradstone
GRIMSPOUND
529 HAMELDOWN TOR
B3362
PARK
Milton Abbot
Horndon
Mary Tavy
546 ROUGH TOR
Postbridge
Dunterton
B3212
HOUND TOR
Cudliptown
Rezare
Peter Tavy
FOREST
Bellever
Widecombe in the Moor
Bonehill
Haytor Vale
Sydenham Damerel
Lamerton
539 GT. MIS TOR
WISTMAN'S WOOD
LLEVER (Dartmoor)
Wilminstone
Tavy
E. Dart
B3357
B3387
Merrivale
PREHISTORIC SETTLEMENT
Two Bridges

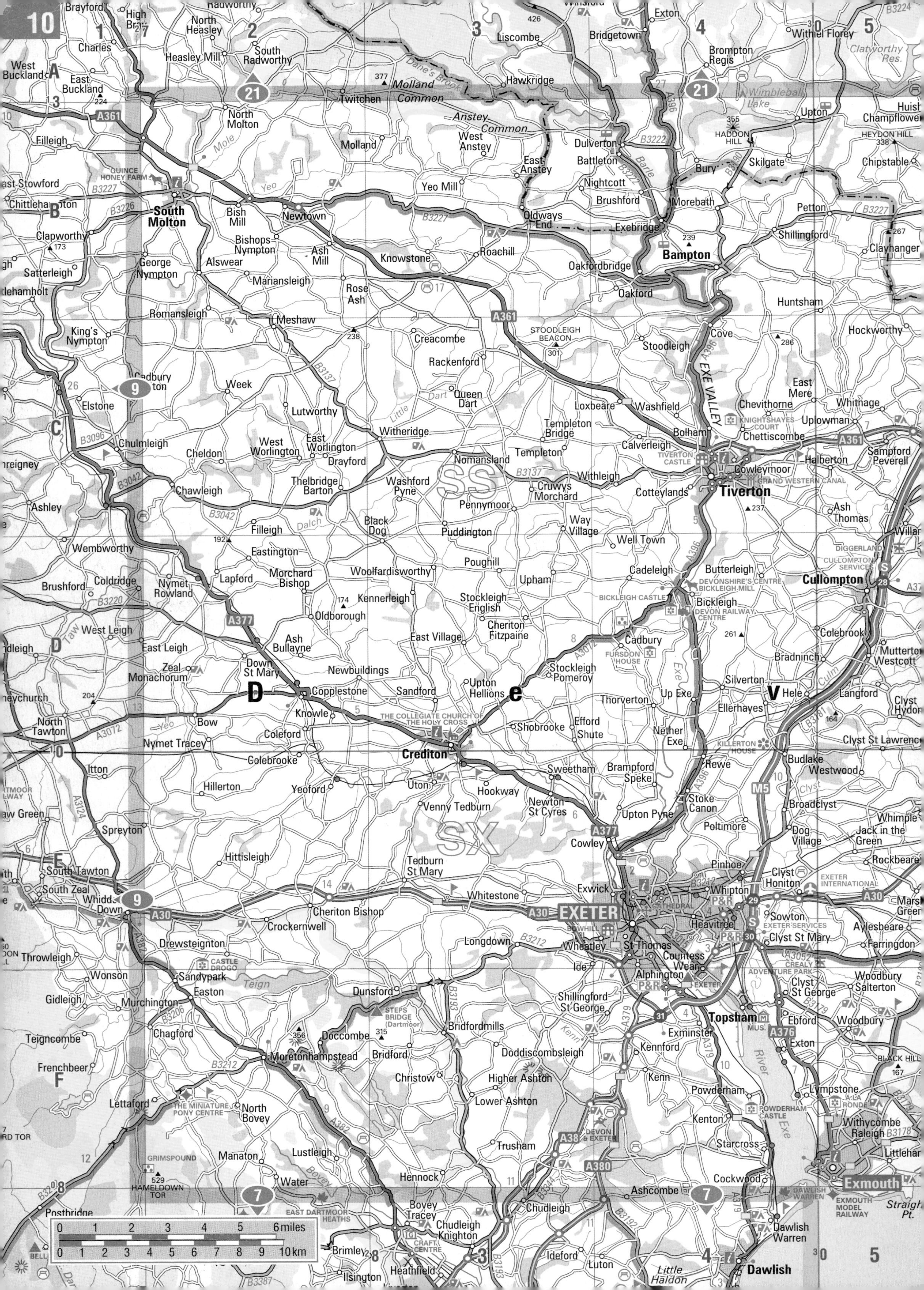
South Molton
Tiverton
Crediton
Exeter
Exmouth
Topsham
Cullompton
Bampton
Dulverton
Moretonhampstead
Chagford
Dawlish
Chudleigh
Bovey Tracey
Witheridge
Chulmleigh
Copplestone
Bickleigh
Silverton
Exe Valley
Molland Common
Anstey Common
Grand Western Canal
0 1 2 3 4 5 6 miles
0 1 2 3 4 5 6 7 8 9 10 km

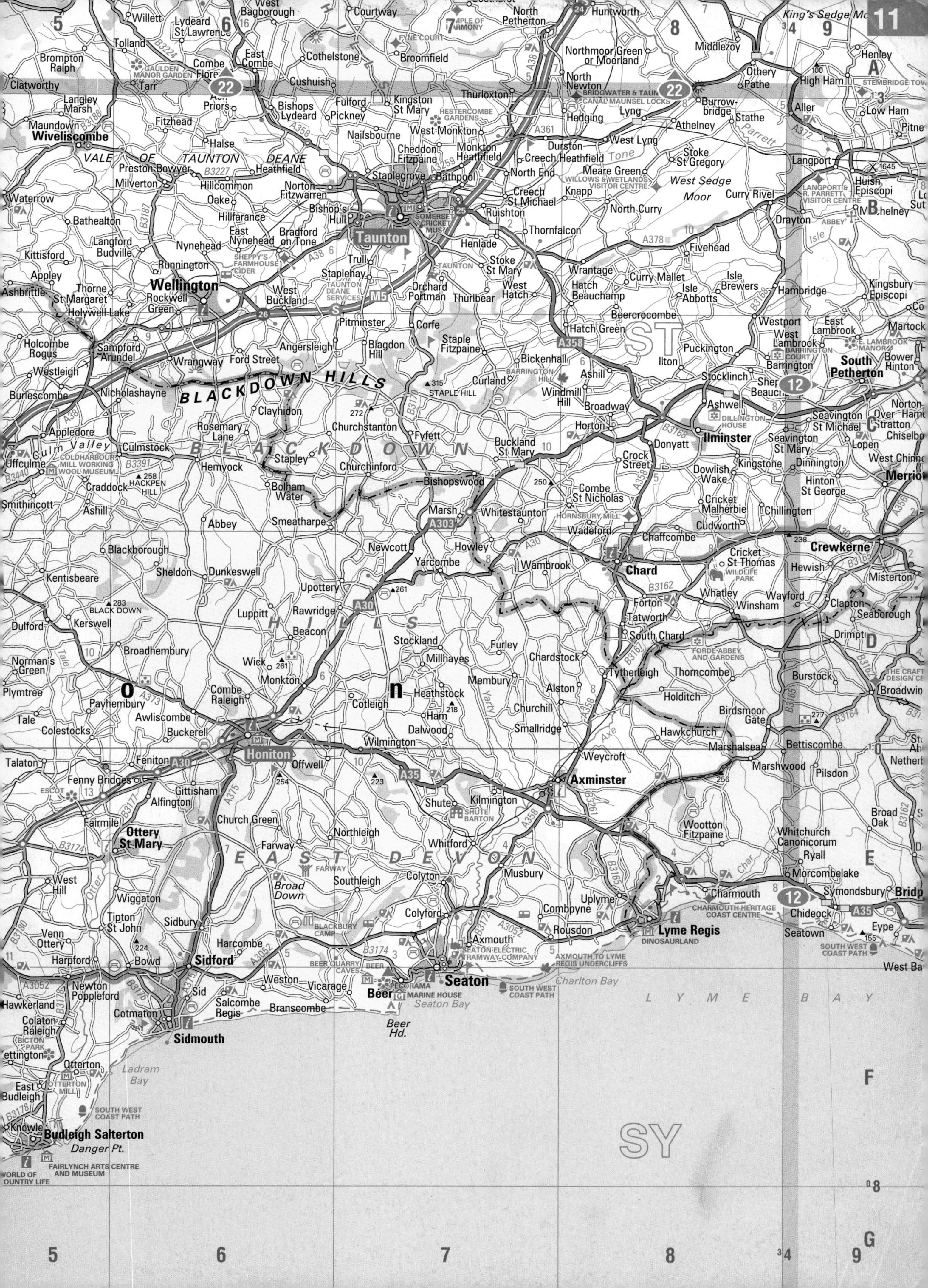

5
6
7
8
9
A
B
C
D
E
F
G
Willett
Lydeard St Lawrence
West Bagborough
Courtway
North Petherton
Huntworth
King's Sedge Moor
Middlezoy
Tolland
Cothelstone
Broomfield
Northmoor Green or Moorland
Henley
Brompton Ralph
Combe Florey
East Combe
Othery
Pathe
High Ham
GAULDEN MANOR GARDEN
Clatworthy
Tarr
Cushuish
North Newton
Thurloxton
BRIDGWATER & TAUNTON CANAL
MAUNSEL LOCKS
Burrow-bridge
Stathe
Aller
Low Ham
Langley Marsh
Ash Priors
Bishops Lydeard
Fulford
Pickney
Kingston St Mary
HESTERCOMBE GARDENS
Hedging
Lyng
Athelney
Maundown
Wiveliscombe
Fitzhead
Nailsbourne
West Monkton
Durston
West Lyng
Langport
Huish Episcopi
Halse
VALE OF TAUNTON DEANE
Cheddon Fitzpaine
Monkton Heathfield
Creech Heathfield
Tone
Stoke St Gregory
LANGPORT & R. PARRETT VISITOR CENTRE
Preston Bowyer
Heathfield
Staplegrove
Bathpool
North End
Meare Green
WILLOWS & WETLANDS VISITOR CENTRE
West Sedge Moor
Milverton
Hillcommon
Norton Fitzwarren
Creech St Michael
Knapp
Curry Rivel
Waterrow
Oake
Bishop's Hull
SOMERSET CRICKET MUS.
Ruishton
North Curry
Drayton
Muchelney
Bathealton
Hillfarance
Taunton
Thornfalcon
ABBEY
East Nynehead
Bradford on Tone
Langford Budville
Nynehead
Henlade
Fivehead
Isle
Kittisford
SHEPPY'S FARMHOUSE CIDER
Trull
TAUNTON
Stoke St Mary
Wrantage
Runnington
Appley
Thorne St Margaret
Wellington
Staplehay
TAUNTON DEANE SERVICES
Orchard Portman
Thurlbear
West Hatch
Hatch Beauchamp
Curry Mallet
Isle Abbotts
Isle Brewers
Hambridge
Kingsbury Episcopi
Ashbrittle
Rockwell Green
West Buckland
Holywell Lake
Pitminster
Corfe
Beercrocombe
Westport
East Lambrook
Martock
Holcombe Rogus
Sampford Arundel
Angersleigh
Blagdon Hill
Staple Fitzpaine
Hatch Green
West Lambrook
E. LAMBROOK MANOR
Wrangway
Ford Street
Bickenhall
Ilton
Puckington
BARRINGTON COURT
Barrington
South Petherton
Bower Hinton
Westleigh
BLACKDOWN HILLS
STAPLE HILL
Curland
BARRINGTON HILL
Ashill
Stocklinch
Shepton Beauchamp
Burlescombe
Nicholashayne
Windmill Hill
Broadway
Ashwell
DILLINGTON HOUSE
Seavington St Michael
Norton
Over Stratton
Clayhidon
Rosemary Lane
Churchstanton
Fyfett
Horton
Ilminster
Seavington St Mary
Chiselborough
Appledore
Culm Valley
Culmstock
BLACKDOWN
Buckland St Mary
Donyatt
Lopen
West Chinnock
Uffculme
COLDHARBOUR MILL WORKING WOOL MUSEUM
HACKPEN HILL
Hemyock
Stapley
Churchinford
Crock Street
Dowlish Wake
Kingstone
Dinnington
Merriott
Craddock
Bolham Water
Bishopswood
Combe St Nicholas
Hinton St George
Smithincott
Ashill
Marsh
Whitestaunton
HORNSBURY MILL
Cricket Malherbie
Chillington
Abbey
Smeatharpe
Wadeford
Cudworth
Chaffcombe
Blackborough
Newcott
Howley
Cricket St Thomas
WILDLIFE PARK
Crewkerne
Sheldon
Dunkeswell
Yarcombe
Wambrook
Chard
Hewish
Kentisbeare
Misterton
Upottery
B3162
Forton
Whatley
Wayford
Clapton
BLACK DOWN
Luppitt
Rawridge
Tatworth
Winsham
Seaborough
Dulford
Kerswell
HILLS
Beacon
South Chard
FORDE ABBEY AND GARDENS
Drimpton
Stockland
Furley
Broadhembury
Millhayes
Chardstock
Tytherleigh
Thorncombe
Burstock
THE CRAFT DESIGN CENTRE
Norman's Green
Wick
Monkton
Membury
Alston
Holditch
Broadwindsor
Plymtree
Payhembury
Combe Raleigh
Heathstock
Yarty
Churchill
Birdsmoor Gate
Awliscombe
Cotleigh
Ham
Smallridge
Tale
Colestocks
Buckerell
Dalwood
Axe
Hawkchurch
Wilmington
Marshalsea
Bettiscombe
Talaton
Feniton
Honiton
Offwell
Weycroft
Marshwood
Pilsdon
Netherbury
Fenny Bridges
ESCOT
Gittisham
Axminster
Alfington
Shute
Kilmington
SHUTE BARTON
Fairmile
Ottery St Mary
Church Green
Northleigh
Wootton Fitzpaine
Whitchurch Canonicorum
Broad Oak
Farway
EAST DEVON
Whitford
Ryall
Morcombelake
FARWAY
Musbury
West Hill
Broad Down
Southleigh
Colyton
Charmouth
Symondsbury
Bridport
Wiggaton
Uplyme
CHARMOUTH HERITAGE COAST CENTRE
Chideock
Tipton St John
Sidbury
Colyford
Combpyne
Rousdon
Lyme Regis
DINOSAURLAND
Seatown
Eype
Venn Ottery
BLACKBURY CAMP
Axmouth
SEATON ELECTRIC TRAMWAY COMPANY
Harcombe
SOUTH WEST COAST PATH
Harpford
Bowd
Sidford
AXMOUTH TO LYME REGIS UNDERCLIFFS
West Bay
BEER QUARRY CAVES
Weston
Vicarage
PECORAMA
Seaton
Charlton Bay
Newton Poppleford
Sid
Beer
MARINE HOUSE
Seaton Bay
LYME BAY
Hawkerland
Salcombe Regis
Branscombe
Cotmaton
Colaton Raleigh
Beer Hd.
Sidmouth
BICTON PARK
Otterton
Ladram Bay
OTTERTON MILL
East Budleigh
SOUTH WEST COAST PATH
Knowle
Budleigh Salterton
Danger Pt.
SY
ST
FAIRLYNCH ARTS CENTRE AND MUSEUM
WORLD OF COUNTRY LIFE

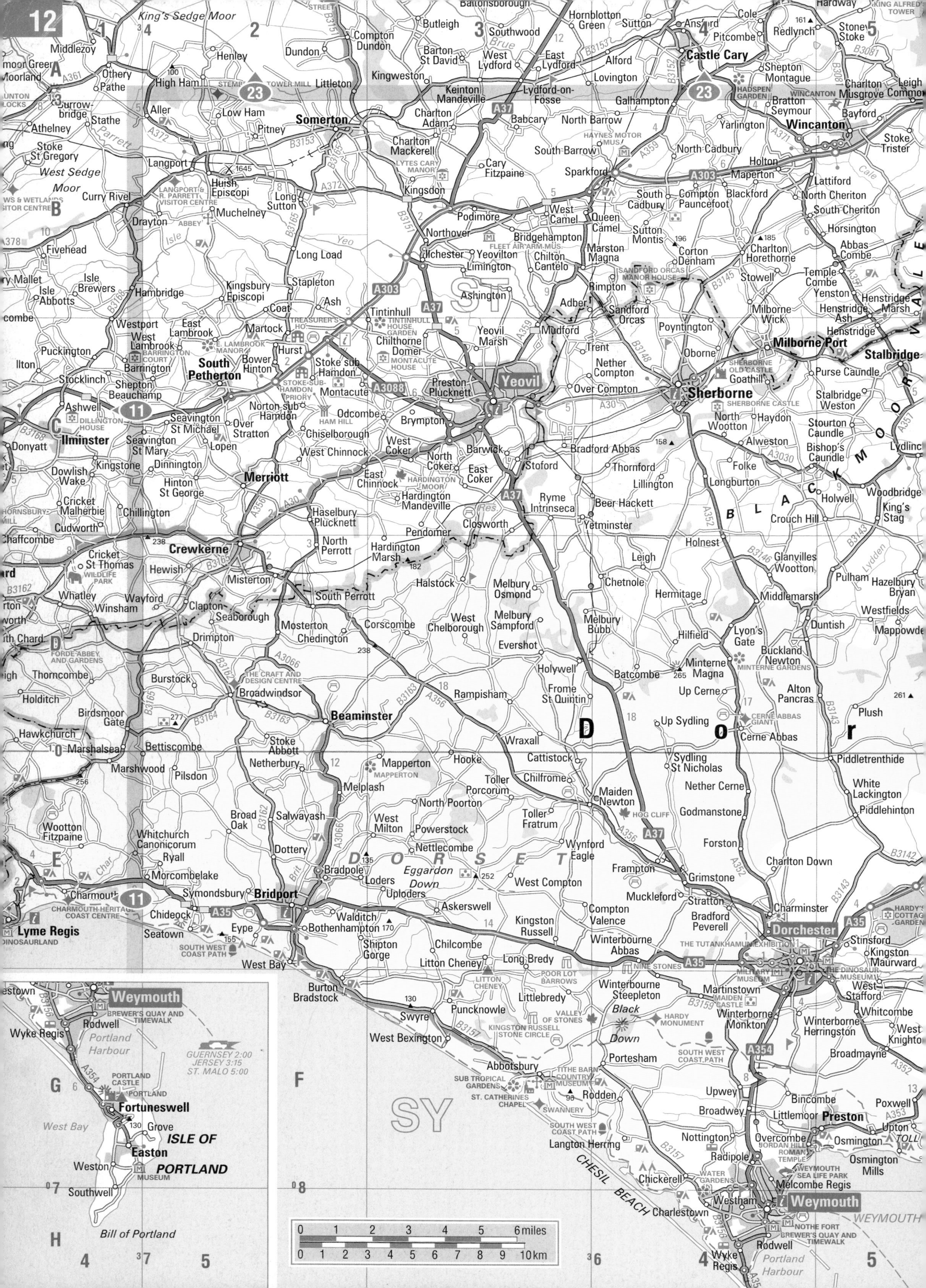
King's Sedge Moor
Middlezoy
Othery
Pathe
Henley
High Ham
Aller
Low Ham
Pitney
Dundon
Compton Dundon
Butleigh
Barton St David
Littleton
Kingweston
Somerton
Southwood
West Lydford
East Lydford
Baltonsborough
Hornblotton Green
Sutton
Ansford
Cole
Pitcombe
Redlynch
Stoney Stoke
Castle Cary
Alford
Lovington
Shepton Montague
Charlton Musgrove
Leigh Common
Keinton Mandeville
Lydford-on-Fosse
Galhampton
Bratton Seymour
Wincanton
Bayford
Charlton Adam
Charlton Mackerell
Babcary
North Barrow
Yarlington
Stoke Trister
Lytes Cary Manor
Cary Fitzpaine
South Barrow
Haynes Motor Mus
North Cadbury
Holton
Sparkford
Maperton
Burrow-bridge
Stathe
Athelney
Stoke St Gregory
West Sedge Moor
Langport
Huish Episcopi
Long Sutton
Kingsdon
Langport & R. Parrett Visitor Centre
Curry Rivel
Drayton
Muchelney
Podimore
West Camel
Queen Camel
South Cadbury
Compton Pauncefoot
Blackford
Lattiford
North Cheriton
South Cheriton
Horsington
Abbas Combe
Northover
Ilchester
Yeovilton
Limington
Fleet Air Arm Mus.
Bridgehampton
Chilton Cantelo
Marston Magna
Sutton Montis
Corton Denham
Charlton Horethorne
Long Load
Fivehead
Isle Brewers
Isle Abbotts
Hambridge
Kingsbury Episcopi
Stapleton
Ash
Coat
Martock
East Lambrook
West Lambrook
E. Lambrook Manor
Barrington Court
Barrington
Puckington
Westport
Tintinhull
Tintinhull House Garden
Treasurer's Ho
Chilthorne Domer
Montacute House
Ashington
Yeovil Marsh
Mudford
Adber
Rimpton
Sandford Orcas
Sandford Orcas Manor House
Poyntington
Milborne Wick
Stowell
Temple Combe
Yenston
Henstridge
Henstridge Marsh
Henstridge Ash
Milborne Port
Stalbridge
Ilton
Stocklinch
Shepton Beauchamp
South Petherton
Bower Hinton
Hurst
Stoke sub Hamdon
Stoke-sub-Hamdon Priory
Montacute
Preston Plucknett
Yeovil
Trent
Nether Compton
Over Compton
Oborne
Sherborne
Sherborne Old Castle
Goathill
Purse Caundle
Stalbridge Weston
Sherborne Castle
Ashwell
Dillington House
Ilminster
Seavington St Michael
Seavington St Mary
Over Stratton
Lopen
Norton sub Hamdon
Odcombe
Ham Hill
Chiselborough
Brympton
West Coker
West Chinnock
North Coker
East Coker
Barwick
Stoford
Bradford Abbas
North Wootton
Haydon
Stourton Caundle
Alweston
Bishop's Caundle
Lydlinch
Donyatt
Dowlish Wake
Kingstone
Dinnington
Hinton St George
Merriott
East Chinnock
Hardington Moor
Hardington Mandeville
Thornford
Lillington
Folke
Longburton
Holwell
Woodbridge
King's Stag
Cricket Malherbie
Chillington
Cudworth
Chaffcombe
Haselbury Plucknett
Ryme Intrinseca
Beer Hackett
Yetminster
Crouch Hill
Blackmoor Vale
Crewkerne
Cricket St Thomas
Wildlife Park
Hewish
Misterton
North Perrott
Pendomer
Closworth
Hardington Marsh
Holnest
Glanvilles Wootton
Leigh
Chetnole
Melbury Osmond
Halstock
Pulham
Hazelbury Bryan
Whatley
Winsham
Wayford
Clapton
Seaborough
South Perrott
Hermitage
Middlemarsh
Westfields
Mappowder
Chard
Forde Abbey and Gardens
Drimpton
Mosterton
Chedington
Corscombe
West Chelborough
Melbury Sampford
Melbury Bubb
Hilfield
Lyon's Gate
Buckland Newton
Dungton
Evershot
Thorncombe
Holditch
Burstock
The Craft and Design Centre
Broadwindsor
Holywell
Frome St Quintin
Batcombe
Minterne Magna
Minterne Gardens
Alton Pancras
Up Cerne
Rampisham
Beaminster
Birdsmoor Gate
Hawkchurch
Marshalsea
Bettiscombe
Stoke Abbott
Netherbury
Up Sydling
Cerne Abbas
Cerne Abbas Giant
Plush
Wraxall
Cattistock
Sydling St Nicholas
Piddletrenthide
Marshwood
Pilsdon
Mapperton
Hooke
Toller Porcorum
Chilfrome
Maiden Newton
Nether Cerne
White Lackington
Piddlehinton
Melplash
North Poorton
Hog Cliff
Godmanstone
Wootton Fitzpaine
Broad Oak
Salwayash
West Milton
Powerstock
Toller Fratrum
Whitchurch Canonicorum
Ryall
Dottery
Nettlecombe
Wynford Eagle
Forston
Morcombelake
Bradpole
Loders
Eggardon Down
Frampton
Grimstone
Charlton Down
Dorset
Charmouth
Charmouth Heritage Coast Centre
Symondsbury
Bridport
Uploders
West Compton
Muckleford
Stratton
Charminster
Lyme Regis
Dinosaurland
Chideock
Seatown
Eype
Walditch
Bothenhampton
Askerswell
Kingston Russell
Compton Valence
Bradford Peverell
Dorchester
Stinsford
Kingston Maurward
Hardy's Cottage Garden
South West Coast Path
West Bay
Shipton Gorge
Chilcombe
Litton Cheney
Long Bredy
Winterbourne Abbas
Nine Stones
The Tutankhamun Exhibition
Military Museum
The Dinosaur Museum
West Stafford
Burton Bradstock
Poor Lot Barrows
Littlebredy
Winterbourne Steepleton
Martinstown
Maiden Castle
Whitcombe
Swyre
Puncknowle
Valley of Stones
Black Down
Hardy Monument
Winterborne Monkton
Winterborne Herringston
West Knighton
West Bexington
Kingston Russell Stone Circle
Portesham
Broadmayne
Abbotsbury
Sub Tropical Gardens
Tithe Barn Country Museum
St. Catherine's Chapel
Swannery
Rodden
Upwey
Bincombe
Poxwell
Broadwey
Littlemoor
Preston
Upton
Langton Herring
Chesil Beach
Nottington
Overcombe
Jordan Hill Roman Temple
Osmington
Osmington Mills
Radipole
Chickerell
Water Gardens
Weymouth Sea Life Park
Melcombe Regis
Westham
Weymouth
Charlestown
Nothe Fort
Brewer's Quay and Timewalk
Rodwell
Wyke Regis
Portland Harbour
Guernsey 2:00
Jersey 3:15
St. Malo 5:00
Portland Castle
Fortuneswell
West Bay
Grove
Isle of Portland
Easton
Weston
Museum
Southwell
Bill of Portland
SY
ST
0 1 2 3 4 5 6 miles
0 1 2 3 4 5 6 7 8 9 10 km

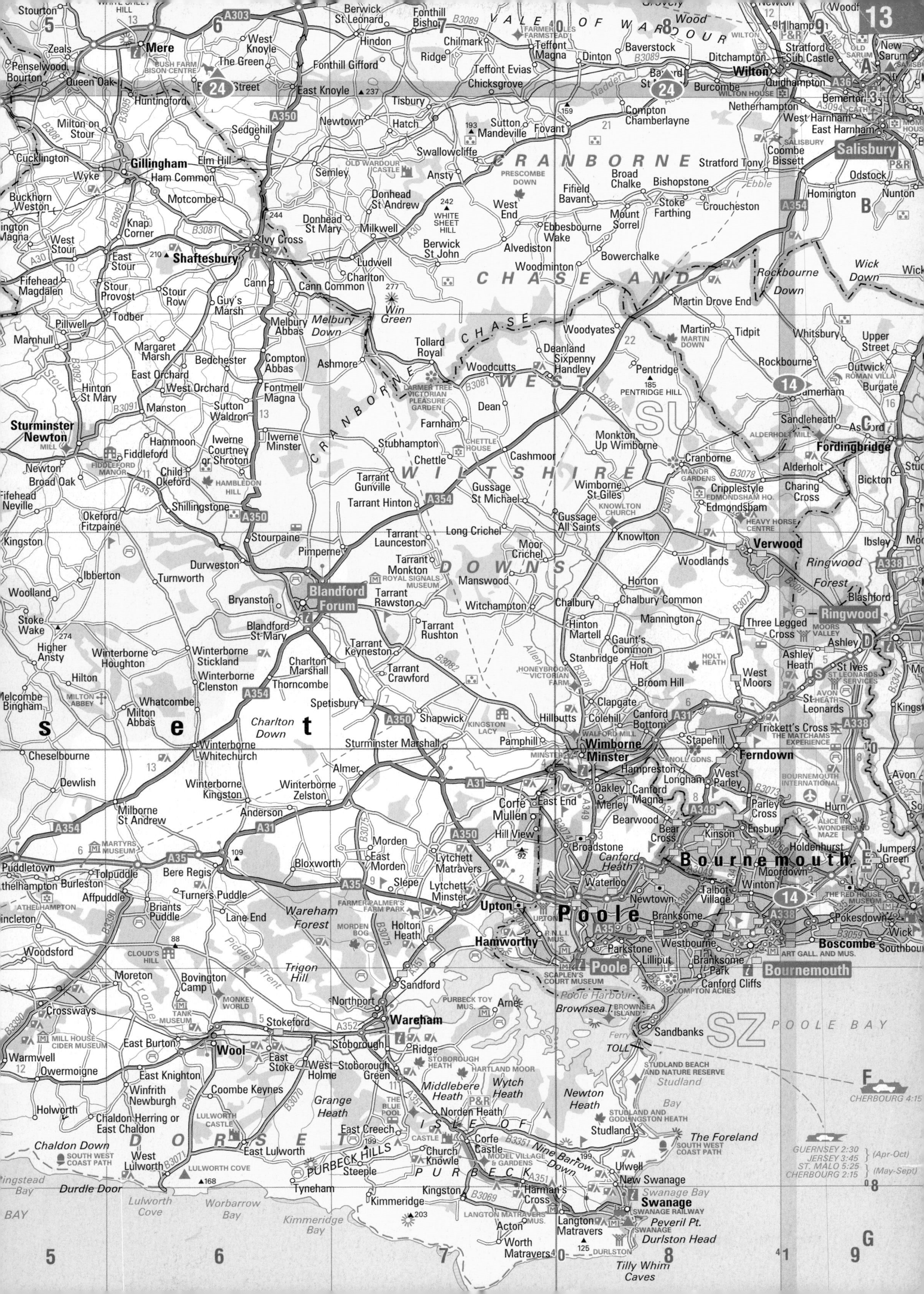
13
Stourton
Mere
West Knoyle
The Green
Bush Farm Bison Centre
Street
Berwick St Leonard
Hindon
Fonthill Gifford
Fonthill Bishop
Chilmark
Ridge
Farmer Giles Farmstead
Teffont Magna
Teffont Evias
Chicksgrove
Dinton
Baverstock
Vale of Wardour
Wood
Ditchampton
Wilton
Stratford sub Castle
Old Sarum
New Sarum
Quidhampton
Bemerton
Burcombe
Barford St Martin
Wilton House
Netherhampton
West Harnham
East Harnham
Salisbury
Zeals
Penselwood
Bourton
Queen Oak
Huntingford
East Knoyle
Tisbury
Newtown
Hatch
Sutton Mandeville
Fovant
Compton Chamberlayne
Milton on Stour
Sedgehill
Cucklington
Gillingham
Elm Hill
Ham Common
Wyke
Swallowcliffe
Old Wardour Castle
Semley
Ansty
Prescombe Down
Cranborne
Stratford Tony
Coombe Bissett
Broad Chalke
Bishopstone
Fifield Bavant
Stoke Farthing
Croucheston
Odstock
Homington
Nunton
Buckhorn Weston
Motcombe
Donhead St Andrew
Donhead St Mary
White Sheet Hill
West End
Mount Sorrel
Ebbesbourne Wake
Knap Corner
Milkwell
Berwick St John
Alvediston
Bowerchalke
West Stour
Ivy Cross
Shaftesbury
East Stour
Ludwell
Charlton
Woodminton
Chase and
Rockbourne Down
Wick Down
Fifehead Magdalen
Stour Provost
Stour Row
Cann
Cann Common
Guy's Marsh
Win Green
Martin Drove End
Todber
Pillwell
Melbury Abbas
Melbury Down
Woodyates
Martin
Martin Down
Tidpit
Whitsbury
Upper Street
Marnhull
Margaret Marsh
Bedchester
Compton Abbas
Ashmore
Tollard Royal
Cranborne Chase
Deanland
Sixpenny Handley
Pentridge
Pentridge Hill
Rockbourne
Outwick
Roman Villa
Burgate
Damerham
East Orchard
West Orchard
Hinton St Mary
Fontmell Magna
Woodcutts
West
Larmer Tree Victorian Pleasure Garden
Dean
Sandleheath
Ashford
Sturminster Newton
Manston
Sutton Waldron
Iwerne Minster
Farnham
SU
Monkton Up Wimborne
Alderholt Mill
Fordingbridge
Mill
Fiddleford Manor
Fiddleford
Hammoon
Iwerne Courtney or Shroton
Stubhampton
Chettle House
Chettle
Cashmoor
Cranborne
Manor Gardens
Alderholt
Bickton
Newton
Broad Oak
Child Okeford
Hambledon Hill
Tarrant Gunville
Wiltshire
Gussage St Michael
Wimborne St Giles
Cripplestyle
Edmondsham Ho.
Edmondsham
Charing Cross
Fifehead Neville
Shillingstone
Tarrant Hinton
Knowlton Church
Okeford Fitzpaine
Long Crichel
Gussage All Saints
Heavy Horse Centre
Kingston
Stourpaine
Tarrant Launceston
Moor Crichel
Knowlton
Verwood
Ibsley
Pimperne
Tarrant Monkton
Downs
Woodlands
Ringwood Forest
Ibberton
Durweston
Turnworth
Royal Signals Museum
Manswood
Horton
Blashford
Woolland
Blandford Forum
Tarrant Rawston
Chalbury
Chalbury Common
Ringwood
Bryanston
Witchampton
Mannington
Three Legged Cross
Moors Valley
Stoke Wake
Blandford St Mary
Tarrant Rushton
Hinton Martell
Higher Ansty
Winterborne Houghton
Winterborne Stickland
Tarrant Keyneston
Gaunt's Common
Ashley
Ashley Heath
Stanbridge
Holt
Holt Heath
Charlton Marshall
Tarrant Crawford
Honeybrook Victorian Farm
St Ives
St Leonards Services
Hilton
Winterborne Clenston
Thorncombe
Broom Hill
West Moors
Melcombe Bingham
Milton Abbey
Whatcombe
Spetisbury
Clapgate
Avon Heath
St Leonards
Milton Abbas
Charlton Down
Shapwick
Kingston Lacy
Hillbutts
Colehill
Canford Bottom
Trickett's Cross
The Matchams Experience
Winterborne Whitechurch
Sturminster Marshall
Pamphill
Walford Mill
Wimborne Minster
Stapehill
Cheselbourne
Ferndown
Dewlish
Almer
Hampreston
Knoll Gdns.
Longham
West Parley
Bournemouth International
Avon
Winterborne Kingston
Winterborne Zelston
Corfe Mullen
East End
Oakley
Merley
Canford Magna
Parley Cross
Hurn
Milborne St Andrew
Anderson
Bearwood
Bear Cross
Alice in Wonderland Maze
Kinson
Ensbury
Holdenhurst
Jumpers Green
Martyrs Museum
Morden
East Morden
Hill View
Broadstone
Canford Heath
Bournemouth
Puddletown
Tolpuddle
Bere Regis
Bloxworth
Lytchett Matravers
Moordown
Winton
Athelhampton
Burleston
Affpuddle
Turners Puddle
Slepe
Lytchett Minster
Waterloo
Newtown
Talbot Village
The Red House Museum
Briants Puddle
Lane End
Wareham Forest
Farmer Palmer's Farm Park
Upton
Poole
Branksome
Pokesdown
Morden Bog
Holton Heath
Hamworthy
Upton
R.N.L.I. Mus.
Westbourne
Boscombe
Art Gall. and Mus.
Southbourne
Woodsford
Cloud's Hill
Trigon Hill
Parkstone
Lilliput
Branksome Park
Scaplen's Court Museum
Poole
Bournemouth
Canford Cliffs
Compton Acres
Moreton
Bovington Camp
Sandford
Poole Harbour
Brownsea I.
Brownsea Island
Monkey World
Northport
Purbeck Toy Mus.
Arne
Crossways
Tank Museum
Stokeford
Wareham
SZ
Poole Bay
Mill House Cider Museum
East Burton
Wool
East Stoke
Stoborough
Ridge
Sandbanks
Ferry
Toll
Warmwell
Owermoigne
East Knighton
West Holme
Stoborough Green
Stoborough Heath
Hartland Moor
Studland Beach and Nature Reserve
Studland
Winfrith Newburgh
Coombe Keynes
Grange Heath
Middlebere Heath
Wytch Heath
Newton Heath
Bay
Cherbourg 4:15
Holworth
Chaldon Herring or East Chaldon
Lulworth Castle
The Blue Pool
Norden Heath
Studland and Godlingston Heath
Studland
Dorset
East Creech
Isle of
Corfe Castle
The Foreland
South West Coast Path
Chaldon Down
South West Coast Path
East Lulworth
Purbeck Hills
Church Knowle
Model Village & Gardens
Nine Barrow Down
Ulwell
Guernsey 2:30
Jersey 3:45
(Apr-Oct)
St. Malo 5:25
Cherbourg 2:15
(May-Sept)
West Lulworth
Lulworth Cove
Steeple
Purbeck
New Swanage
Ringstead Bay
Durdle Door
Tyneham
Kingston
Harman's Cross
Swanage Bay
Swanage
Swanage Railway
Bay
Lulworth Cove
Worbarrow Bay
Kimmeridge
Kimmeridge Bay
Langton Matravers
Langton Matravers Mus.
Acton
Peveril Pt.
Durlston Head
Worth Matravers
Durlston
Tilly Whim Caves

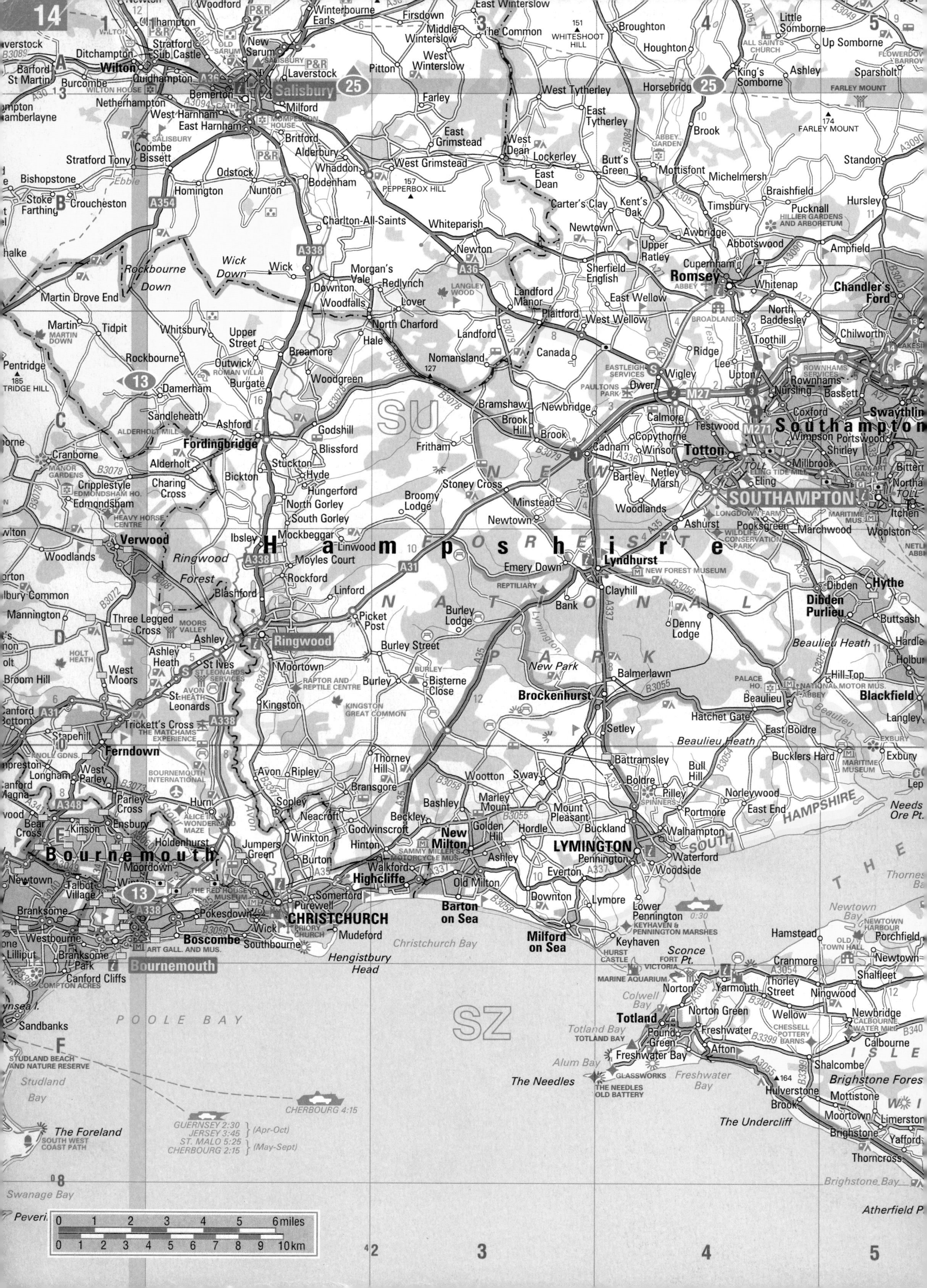
Woodford
Winterbourne Earls
Firsdown
East Winterslow
Middle Winterslow
The Common
151 WHITESHOOT HILL
Broughton
Little Somborne
Up Somborne
Houghton
ALL SAINTS CHURCH
Laverstock
Ditchampton
Wilton
Stratford sub Castle
Old Sarum
New Sarum
Salisbury
Barford St Martin
Burcombe
Quidhampton
WILTON HOUSE
Bemerton
Pitton
West Winterslow
King's Somborne
Ashley
Sparsholt
FLOWERDOWN BARROW
Horsebridge
FARLEY MOUNT
174 FARLEY MOUNT
West Tytherley
Netherhampton
Milford
Farley
East Tytherley
Brook
West Harnham
East Harnham
MOMPESSON HOUSE
Britford
Alderbury
East Grimstead
West Dean
Lockerley
Butt's Green
Mottisfont
Michelmersh
ABBEY GARDEN
Standon
Coombe Bissett
SALISBURY
Stratford Tony
Whaddon
West Grimstead
East Dean
Braishfield
Bishopstone
Odstock
Bodenham
157 PEPPERBOX HILL
Stoke Farthing
Croucheston
Homington
Nunton
Ebble
Carter's Clay
Kent's Oak
Timsbury
Pucknall
Hursley
HILLIER GARDENS AND ARBORETUM
Charlton-All-Saints
Whiteparish
Newtown
Awbridge
Abbotswood
Ampfield
Upper Ratley
Newton
Wick Down
Wick
Rockbourne Down
Morgan's Vale
Redlynch
Sherfield English
Cupernham
Romsey
ABBEY
Whitenap
Chandler's Ford
Martin Drove End
Downton
Woodfalls
LANGLEY WOOD
Lover
Landford Manor
Plaitford
East Wellow
West Wellow
North Baddesley
Martin
MARTIN DOWN
Tidpit
Whitsbury
Upper Street
North Charford
Hale
Landford
BROADLANDS
Test
Chilworth
Toothill
Pentridge
185 TRIDGE HILL
Rockbourne
Outwick
ROMAN VILLA
Breamore
Nomansland
127
Canada
Ridge
Lee
Upton
EASTLEIGH SERVICES
Wigley
ROWNHAMS SERVICES
Rownhams
Damerham
Burgate
Woodgreen
PAULTONS PARK
Ower
Nursling
Bassett
SU
Sandleheath
Ashford
Bramshaw
Newbridge
Calmore
Testwood
Coxford
Swaythling
Brook Hill
Brook
Southampton
Wimpson
Portswood
Cranborne
ALDERHOLT MILL
Fordingbridge
Godshill
Copythorne
Cadnam
Winsor
Totton
Shirley
MANOR GARDENS
Alderholt
Stuckton
Blissford
Fritham
Netley Marsh
Bartley
Millbrook
ELING TIDE MILL
CITY ART GALLERY
Bitterne
Cripplestyle
EDMONDSHAM HO.
Charing Cross
Bickton
Hyde
Hungerford
Eling
Northam
Edmondsham
North Gorley
Broomy Lodge
Stoney Cross
Minstead
SOUTHAMPTON
HEAVY HORSE CENTRE
South Gorley
Newtown
Woodlands
LONGDOWN FARM
Ashurst
Pooksgreen
Marchwood
MARITIME MUS.
Itchen
Woolston
Verwood
Ibsley
Mockbeggar
Linwood
WILDLIFE CONSERVATION PARK
Hampshire
Woodlands
Ringwood Forest
Moyles Court
Emery Down
Lyndhurst
NEW FOREST MUSEUM
Rockford
REPTILIARY
Clayhill
Dibden
Hythe
Dibden Purlieu
Blashford
Linford
NATIONAL PARK
Mannington
Three Legged Cross
MOORS VALLEY
Picket Post
Burley Lodge
Bank
Denny Lodge
Buttsash
Ashley
Ringwood
Ashley Heath
West Moors
Burley Street
Beaulieu Heath
Hardley
Holbury
HOLT HEATH
St Ives
ST LEONARDS SERVICES
Moortown
New Park
Lymington
Broom Hill
AVON HEATH
St. Leonards
RAPTOR AND REPTILE CENTRE
Burley
BURLEY
Bisterne Close
Balmerlawn
Brockenhurst
PALACE HO.
Beaulieu
NATIONAL MOTOR MUS.
ABBEY
Hill Top
Blackfield
Kingston
KINGSTON GREAT COMMON
Hatchet Gate
Langley
Trickett's Cross
THE MATCHAMS EXPERIENCE
Setley
East Boldre
Stapehill
Ferndown
Beaulieu Heath
Bucklers Hard
EXBURY
Exbury
MARITIME MUSEUM
Thorney Hill
Battramsley
Avon
Ripley
West Parley
BOURNEMOUTH INTERNATIONAL
Bransgore
Wootton
Sway
Bull Hill
Boldre
Pilley
SPINNERS
Norleywood
Longham
Parley Cross
Sopley
Bashley
Marley Mount
Mount Pleasant
East End
Portmore
HAMPSHIRE
Needs Ore Pt.
Lepe
Ensbury
Hurn
ALICE IN WONDERLAND MAZE
Neacroft
Godwinscroft
Beckley
Golden Hill
Hordle
Buckland
Walhampton
Bear Cross
Kinson
Holdenhurst
Jumpers Green
Winkton
Hinton
New Milton
SAMMY MILLER'S MOTORCYCLE MUS
Ashley
LYMINGTON
Pennington
Waterford
Woodside
SOUTH
THE
Bournemouth
Moordown
Burton
Walkford
Highcliffe
Old Milton
Everton
Newtown
Talbot Village
THE RED HOUSE MUSEUM
Somerford
Purewell
Barton on Sea
Downton
Lymore
Lower Pennington
0:30
Thorness Bay
Branksome
Pokesdown
CHRISTCHURCH
Milford on Sea
KEYHAVEN & PENNINGTON MARSHES
Newtown Bay
NEWTOWN HARBOUR
Porchfield
Westbourne
Boscombe
Wick
PRIORY CHURCH
Mudeford
Keyhaven
Hamstead
Lilliput
Branksome Park
ART GALL. AND MUS.
Southbourne
Christchurch Bay
Sconce Pt.
OLD TOWN HALL
Newtown
Bournemouth
Hengistbury Head
HURST CASTLE
FORT VICTORIA
Cranmore
Canford Cliffs
COMPTON ACRES
MARINE AQUARIUM
Yarmouth
Thorley Street
Shalfleet
Colwell Bay
Norton
Ningwood
POOLE BAY
SZ
Totland
Norton Green
Wellow
Newbridge
CALBOURNE WATER MILL
Sandbanks
Totland Bay
TOTLAND BAY
Pound Green
Freshwater
CHESSELL POTTERY BARNS
Calbourne
STUDLAND BEACH AND NATURE RESERVE
Afton
Alum Bay
Freshwater Bay
Shalcombe
ISLE
Studland Bay
The Needles
GLASSWORKS
THE NEEDLES OLD BATTERY
Freshwater Bay
164
Brighstone Forest
Hulverstone
Mottistone
Brook
CHERBOURG 4:15
Moortown
Limerstone
The Foreland
SOUTH WEST COAST PATH
GUERNSEY 2:30
JERSEY 3:45
ST. MALO 5:25
CHERBOURG 2:15
(Apr-Oct)
(May-Sept)
The Undercliff
Brighstone
Yafford
Thorncross
Swanage Bay
Brighstone Bay
Atherfield P
0 1 2 3 4 5 6 miles
0 1 2 3 4 5 6 7 8 9 10 km

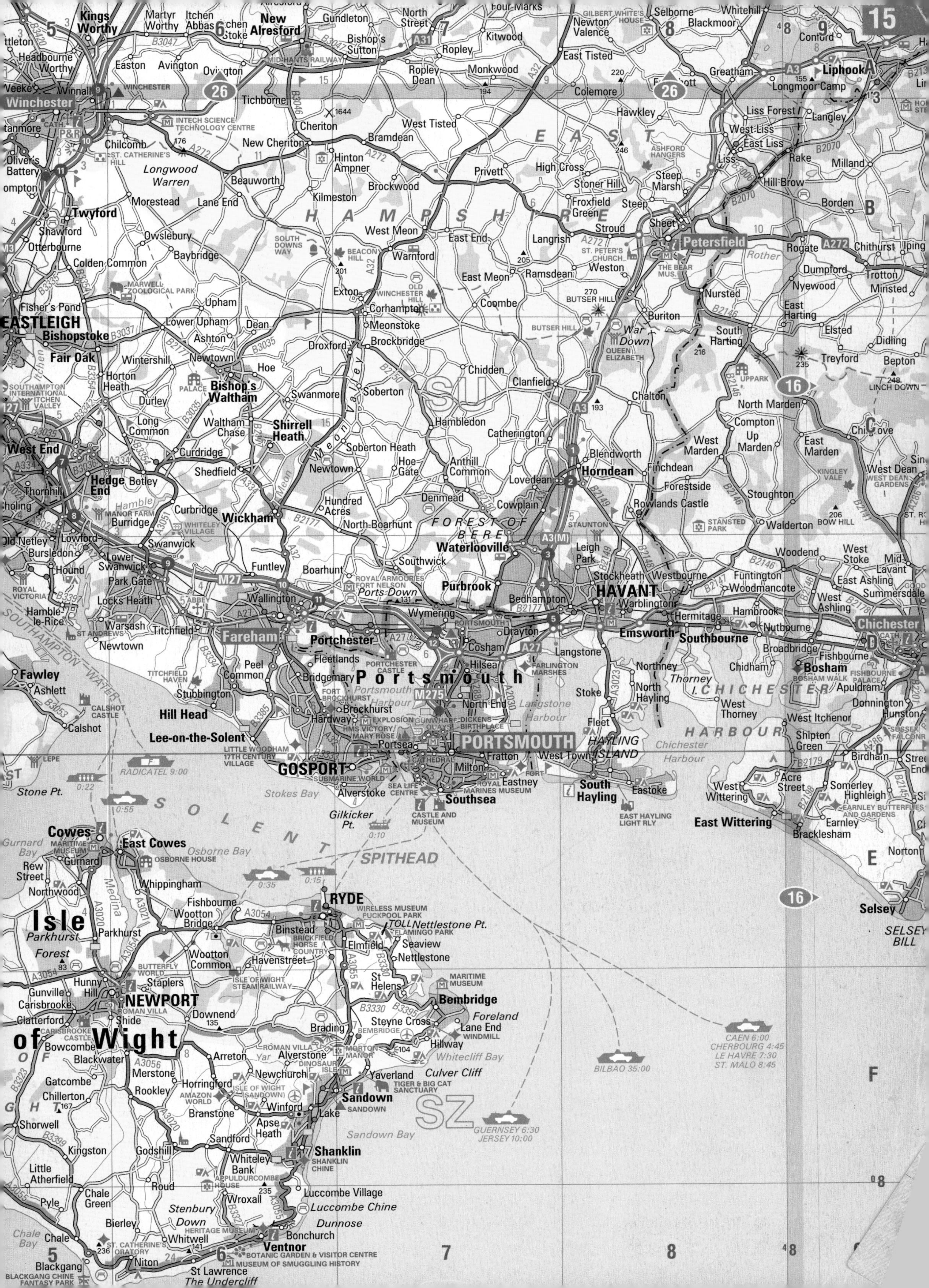
15
Kings Worthy
Martyr Worthy
Itchen Abbas
Itchen Stoke
New Alresford
Gundleton
North Street
Four Marks
Gilbert White's House
Selborne
Newton Valence
Whitehill
Blackmoor
Conford
Headbourne Worthy
Easton
Avington
Ovington
Bishop's Sutton
Mid-Hants Railway
Ropley
Kitwood
East Tisted
Greatham
Liphook
Weeke
Winnall
Winchester
Ropley Dean
Monkwood
Colemore
Longmoor Camp
Tichborne
Cheriton
Intech Science Technology Centre
West Tisted
Hawkley
Liss Forest
Langley
Chilcomb
New Cheriton
Bramdean
West Liss
East Liss
St. Catherine's Hill
Hinton Ampner
Ashford Hangers
Liss
Rake
Milland
Oliver's Battery
Longwood Warren
Beauworth
Privett
High Cross
Steep Marsh
Hill Brow
Brockwood
Stoner Hill
Kilmeston
Morestead
Lane End
Froxfield Green
Steep
Borden
Twyford
Hampshire
Sheet
Shawford
Owslebury
West Meon
East End
Langrish
Stroud
Petersfield
Rogate
Chithurst
Iping
Otterbourne
South Downs Way
Baybridge
Beacon Hill
Warnford
St. Peter's Church
The Bear Mus.
Rother
Dumpford
Trotton
Colden Common
East Meon
Ramsdean
Weston
Nyewood
Minsted
Marwell Zoological Park
Exton
Old Winchester Hill
Butser Hill
Nursted
Fisher's Pond
Upham
Corhampton
Coombe
Buriton
East Harting
Eastleigh
Lower Upham
Dean
Meonstoke
Butser Hill
War Down
South Harting
Elsted
Bishopstoke
Ashton
Droxford
Brockbridge
Queen Elizabeth
Didling
Fair Oak
Wintershill
Newtown
Hoe
Chidden
Treyford
Bepton
Southampton International
Itchen Valley
Horton Heath
Palace
Bishop's Waltham
Swanmore
Soberton
Clanfield
Uppark
Linch Down
Durley
Meon Valley
Chalton
North Marden
Long Common
Waltham Chase
Shirrell Heath
Hambledon
Compton
Up Marden
West Marden
Chilgrove
West End
Curdridge
Soberton Heath
Catherington
Blendworth
East Marden
Hedge End
Botley
Shedfield
Newtown
Hoe Gate
Anthill Common
Horndean
Finchdean
Kingley Vale
West Dean
West Dean Gardens
Thornhill
Hamble
Lovedean
Forestside
Stoughton
Manor Farm
Curbridge
Hundred Acres
Denmead
Cowplain
Rowlands Castle
Bow Hill
Burridge
Whiteley Village
Wickham
North Boarhunt
Forest of Bere
Staunton
Stansted Park
Walderton
Netley
Lowford
Bursledon
Swanwick
Waterlooville
Leigh Park
Woodend
West Stoke
Mid Lavant
Lower Swanwick
Funtley
Boarhunt
Southwick
Hound
Royal Victoria
Park Gate
Royal Armouries Fort Nelson
Ports Down
Purbrook
Stockheath
Westbourne
Funtington
Woodmancote
East Ashling
Locks Heath
Abbey
Wallington
Bedhampton
Havant
Warblington
West Ashling
Summersdale
Hamble-le-Rice
Warsash
Wymering
Hermitage
Hambrook
St Andrews
Titchfield
Fareham
Portsmouth
Drayton
Emsworth
Nutbourne
Chichester
Southampton Water
Newtown
Portchester
Cosham
Southbourne
Broadbridge
Langstone
Fleetlands
Portchester Castle
Hilsea
Farlington Marshes
Northney
Chidham
Fishbourne
Bosham
Fawley
Titchfield Haven
Peel Common
Bridgemary
Portsmouth
Bosham Walk
Fishbourne Palace
Ashlett
Stubbington
Fort Brockhurst
Portsmouth Harbour
North Hayling
Thorney I.
Chichester
Apuldram
Calshot Castle
Hill Head
Brockhurst
North End
Stoke
West Thorney
Donnington
Hunston
Calshot
Hardway
HMS Victory
Mary Rose
Explosion
Gunwharf Quays
Dickens Birthplace
Langstone Harbour
Fleet
Harbour
West Itchenor
Sussex Falconry
Lee-on-the-Solent
Portsea
Portsmouth
Hayling Island
Chichester Harbour
Shipton Green
Little Woodham 17th Century Village
Cathedral
Fratton
West Town
Birdham
Lepe
Radicatel 9:00
Gosport
Submarine World
Milton
Fort
Royal Marines Museum
Eastney
Acre Street
West Wittering
Somerley
Highleigh
Stone Pt.
Alverstoke
Sea Life Centre
Southsea
South Hayling
Eastoke
Earnley Butterflies and Gardens
Stokes Bay
Solent
Castle and Museum
East Hayling Light Rly
East Wittering
Earnley
Bracklesham
Gilkicker Pt.
Cowes
Gurnard Bay
Maritime Museum
Gurnard
East Cowes
Osborne Bay
Osborne House
Spithead
Norton
Rew Street
Whippingham
Northwood
Medina
Fishbourne
Ryde
Wireless Museum
Puckpool Park
Nettlestone Pt.
Toll
Flamingo Park
Selsey
Isle of Wight
Parkhurst
Parkhurst Forest
Wootton Bridge
Binstead
Brickfields Horse Country
Seaview
Elmfield
Selsey Bill
Wootton Common
Havenstreet
Nettlestone
Butterfly World
Hunny Hill
Staplers
Isle of Wight Steam Railway
St Helens
Maritime Museum
Gunville
Carisbrooke
Newport
Roman Villa
Bembridge
Clatterford
Carisbrooke Castle
Shide
Downend
Foreland
Brading
Steyne Cross
Lane End
Windmill
Bowcombe
Roman Villa
Morton Manor
Hillway
Caen 6:00
Cherbourg 4:45
Le Havre 7:30
St. Malo 8:45
Blackwater
Arreton
Yar
Alverstone
Dinosaur Isle
Whitecliff Bay
Bilbao 35:00
Merstone
Newchurch
Yaverland
Culver Cliff
Gatcombe
Horringford
Isle of Wight (Sandown)
Tiger & Big Cat Sanctuary
Rookley
Amazon World
Sandown
Chillerton
Winford
Lake
Shorwell
Branstone
Apse Heath
Guernsey 6:30
Jersey 10:00
Sandford
Sandown Bay
Kingston
Godshill
Whiteley Bank
Shanklin
Shanklin Chine
Little Atherfield
Appuldurcombe House
Roud
Luccombe Village
Pyle
Chale Green
Wroxall
Luccombe Chine
Stenbury Down
Dunnose
Bierley
Heritage Museum
Chale Bay
Chale
Whitwell
Bonchurch
St. Catherine's Oratory
Ventnor
Botanic Garden & Visitor Centre
Museum of Smuggling History
Blackgang
Blackgang Chine Fantasy Park
Niton
St Lawrence
The Undercliff
SU
SZ

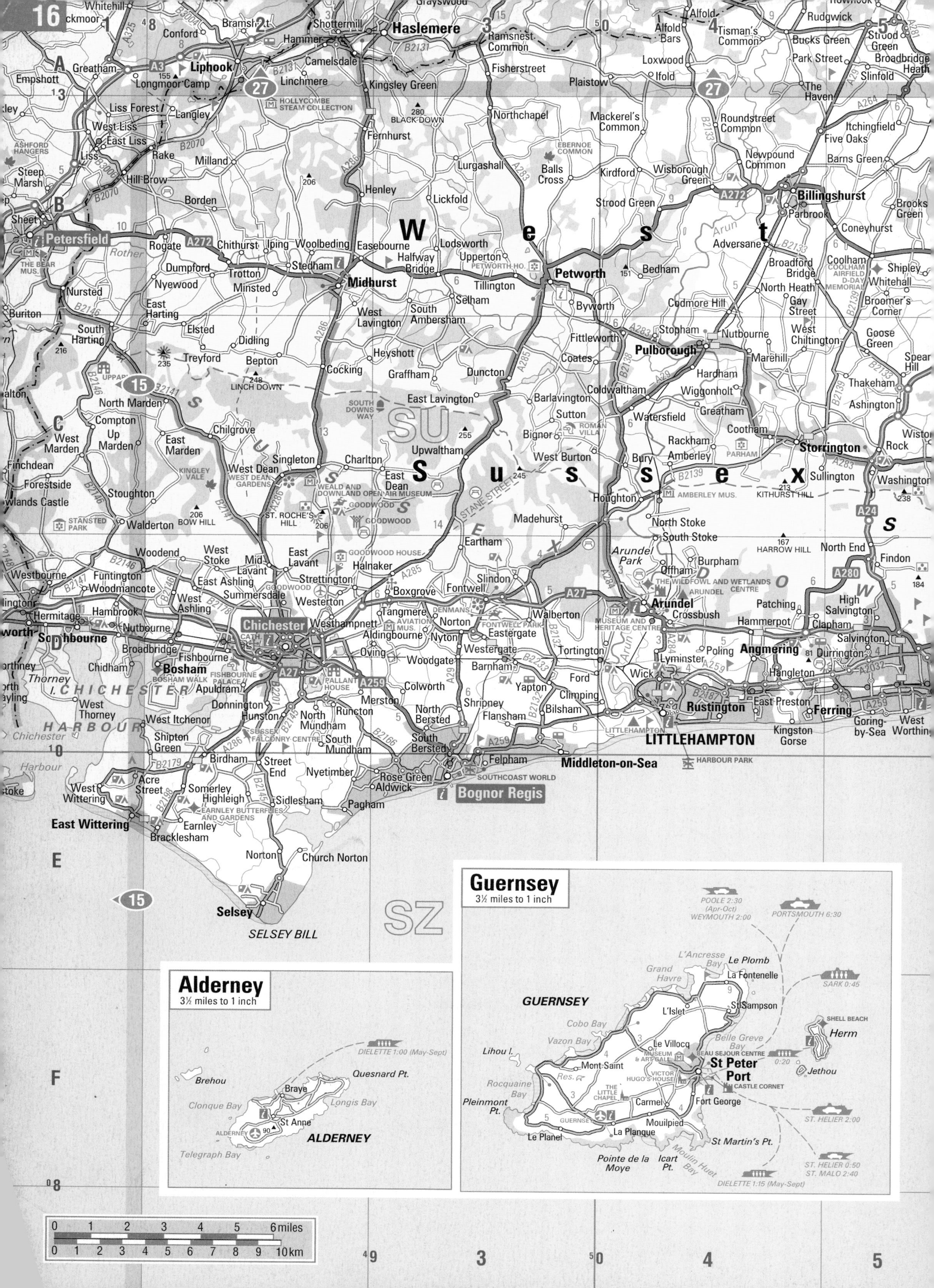
West Sussex
Haslemere
Liphook
Petersfield
Midhurst
Petworth
Billingshurst
Pulborough
Storrington
Arundel
Chichester
Bognor Regis
LITTLEHAMPTON
Middleton-on-Sea
Rustington
Angmering
Ferring
East Wittering
Selsey
SELSEY BILL
CHICHESTER HARBOUR
Bosham
SU
SZ
Guernsey
3½ miles to 1 inch
GUERNSEY
St Peter Port
St Sampson
Herm
Jethou
Alderney
3½ miles to 1 inch
ALDERNEY
St Anne
Braye
Brehou
Quesnard Pt.
Telegraph Bay
0 1 2 3 4 5 6 miles
0 1 2 3 4 5 6 7 8 9 10 km

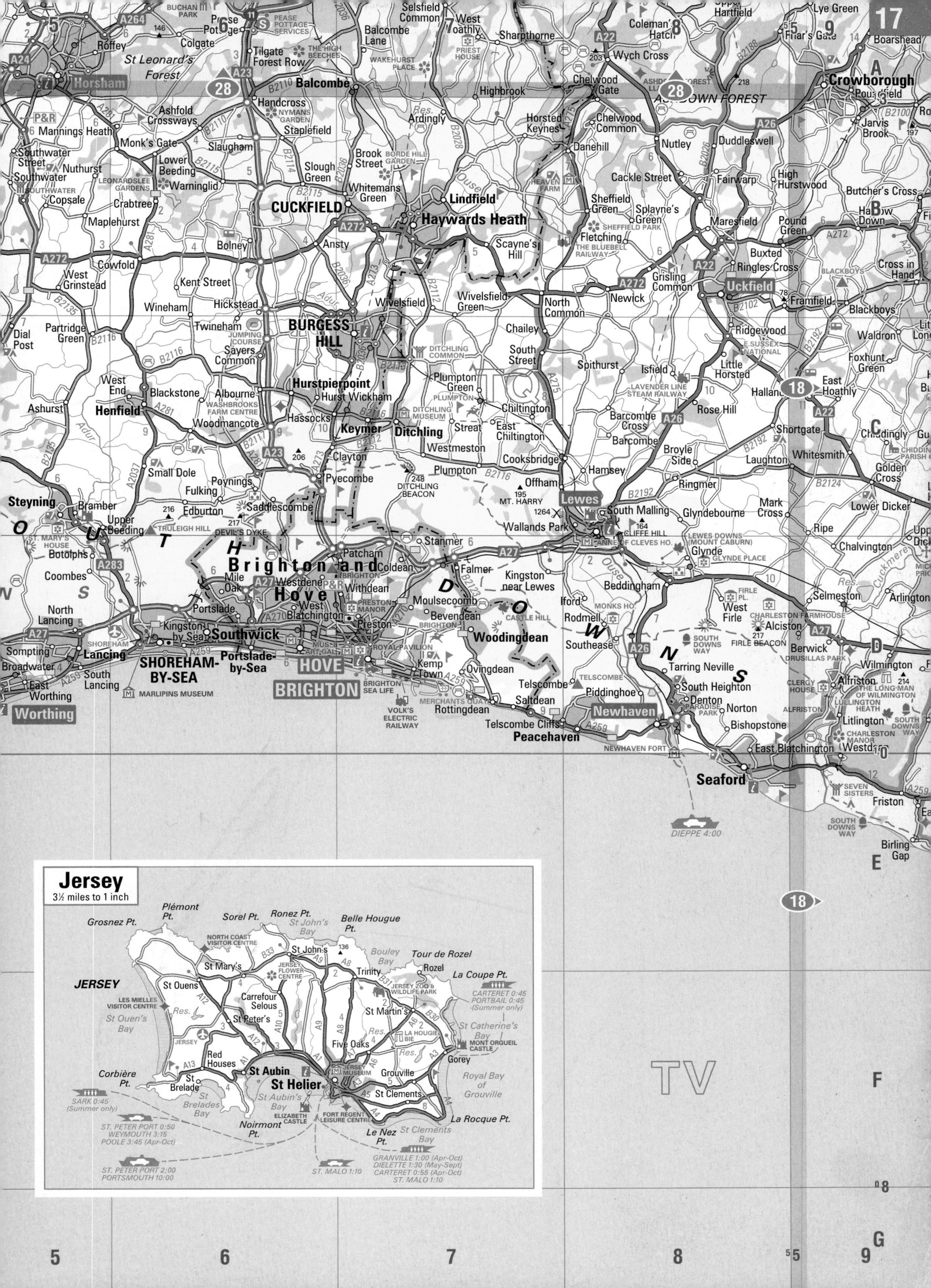
Horsham
Roffey
Colgate
St Leonard's Forest
Pease Pottage
PEASE POTTAGE SERVICES
Tilgate Forest Row
Balcombe Lane
Balcombe
Selsfield Common
West Hoathly
Sharpthorne
PRIEST HOUSE
WAKEHURST PLACE
Coleman's Hatch
Wych Cross
Lye Green
Boarshead
Crowborough
Poundfield
Jarvis Brook
Chelwood Gate
ASHDOWN FOREST
Highbrook
Ardingly
Horsted Keynes
Chelwood Common
Danehill
Nutley
Duddleswell
Handcross
NYMANS GARDEN
Ashfold Crossways
Mannings Heath
Monk's Gate
Slaugham
Staplefield
Southwater Street
Nuthurst
Southwater
Lower Beeding
LEONARDSLEE GARDENS
Warninglid
Slough Green
Brook Street
BORDE HILL GARDEN
Whitemans Green
CUCKFIELD
Lindfield
Haywards Heath
Copsale
Crabtree
Maplehurst
Bolney
Ansty
Scayne's Hill
HEAVEN FARM
Sheffield Green
SHEFFIELD PARK
Splayne's Green
Fletching
THE BLUEBELL RAILWAY
Cackle Street
Fairwarp
High Hurstwood
Butcher's Cross
Maresfield
Pound Green
Hadlow Down
Buxted
Ringles Cross
Cross in Hand
BLACKBOYS
Cowfold
West Grinstead
Kent Street
Wineham
Hickstead
Wivelsfield
Wivelsfield Green
North Common
Newick
Grisling Common
Uckfield
Framfield
Blackboys
Dial Post
Partridge Green
Twineham
JUMPING COURSE
Sayers Common
BURGESS HILL
DITCHLING COMMON
Chailey
South Street
Spithurst
Isfield
Ridgewood
E. SUSSEX NATIONAL
Little Horsted
Waldron
Foxhunt Green
East Hoathly
Halland
West End
Blackstone
Albourne
Henfield
Ashurst
WASHBROOKS FARM CENTRE
Hurstpierpoint
Hurst Wickham
Plumpton Green
PLUMPTON
LAVENDER LINE STEAM RAILWAY
Barcombe Cross
Barcombe
Rose Hill
Woodmancote
Hassocks
Keymer
Ditchling
DITCHLING MUSEUM
Streat
East Chiltington
Chiltington
Westmeston
Shortgate
Chiddingly
Broyle Side
Laughton
Whitesmith
Golden Cross
Small Dole
Clayton
Pyecombe
Plumpton
Cooksbridge
Hamsey
Offham
195 MT. HARRY
248 DITCHLING BEACON
Ringmer
Fulking
Poynings
Steyning
Bramber
Edburton
Saddlescombe
Upper Beeding
216 TRULEIGH HILL
217 DEVIL'S DYKE
ST. MARY'S HOUSE
Botolphs
Coombes
Lewes
South Malling
164 CLIFFE HILL
Wallands Park
ANNE OF CLEVES HO.
Glyndebourne
Mark Cross
Lower Dicker
Ripe
LEWES DOWNS (MOUNT CABURN)
Glynde
GLYNDE PLACE
Chalvington
SOUTH DOWNS
Stanmer
Patcham
Brighton and Hove
Coldean
Falmer
Kingston near Lewes
Mile Oak
Westdene
Withdean
PRESTON MANOR
Moulsecoomb
Bevendean
Beddingham
Iford
MONKS HO.
Rodmell
FIRLE PL.
West Firle
CHARLESTON FARMHOUSE
Selmeston
Arlington
North Lancing
Portslade
West Blatchington
Preston
Woodingdean
CASTLE HILL
Southease
217 FIRLE BEACON
Alciston
Berwick
DRUSILLAS PARK
Wilmington
Kingston by Sea
Southwick
Sompting
Lancing
SHOREHAM-BY-SEA
Portslade-by-Sea
HOVE
BRIGHTON
ROYAL PAVILION
MUS. & ART GALL.
Kemp Town
Ovingdean
Telscombe
TELSCOMBE
Piddinghoe
Tarring Neville
South Heighton
Denton
PARADISE PARK
Norton
Bishopstone
Alfriston
CLERGY HOUSE
214 THE LONG MAN OF WILMINGTON
LULLINGTON HEATH
Litlington
CHARLESTON MANOR
Broadwater
East Worthing
South Lancing
MARLIPINS MUSEUM
Worthing
BRIGHTON SEA LIFE
VOLK'S ELECTRIC RAILWAY
MERCHANTS QUAY
Rottingdean
Saltdean
Telscombe Cliffs
Peacehaven
Newhaven
NEWHAVEN FORT
East Blatchington
Westdean
Seaford
SEVEN SISTERS
Friston
DIEPPE 4:00
SOUTH DOWNS WAY
Birling Gap
TQ
TV
A24 A264 A23 A22 A26 A272 A281 A273 A2037 A283 A27 A270 A259 A275 B2110 B2114 B2115 B2116 B2135 B2036 B2112 B2028 B2026 B2102 B2192 B2124 B2123 B2117 B2100 B2188
Jersey
3½ miles to 1 inch
Plémont Pt.
Grosnez Pt.
Sorel Pt.
Ronez Pt.
St John's Bay
Belle Hougue Pt.
NORTH COAST VISITOR CENTRE
St John's
Bouley Bay
Tour de Rozel
Rozel
La Coupe Pt.
St Mary's
JERSEY FLOWER CENTRE
Trinity
JERSEY ZOO & WILDLIFE PARK
JERSEY
St Ouens
LES MIELLES VISITOR CENTRE
Carrefour Selous
CARTERET 0:45
PORTBAIL 0:45
(Summer only)
St Martin's
St Ouen's Bay
St Peter's
St Catherine's Bay
LA HOUGUE BIE
Five Oaks
MONT ORGUEIL CASTLE
Red Houses
Gorey
St Aubin
St Helier
JERSEY MUSEUM
Grouville
Royal Bay of Grouville
Corbière Pt.
St Brelade
St Brelades Bay
St Aubin's Bay
St Clements
ELIZABETH CASTLE
FORT REGENT LEISURE CENTRE
SARK 0:45 (Summer only)
La Rocque Pt.
Noirmont Pt.
Le Nez Pt.
St Clements Bay
ST. PETER PORT 0:50
WEYMOUTH 3:15
POOLE 3:45 (Apr-Oct)
ST. PETER PORT 2:00
PORTSMOUTH 10:00
ST. MALO 1:10
GRANVILLE 1:00 (Apr-Oct)
DIELETTE 1:30 (May-Sept)
CARTERET 0:55 (Apr-Oct)
ST. MALO 1:10
5
6
7
8
9
A
B
C
D
E
F
G

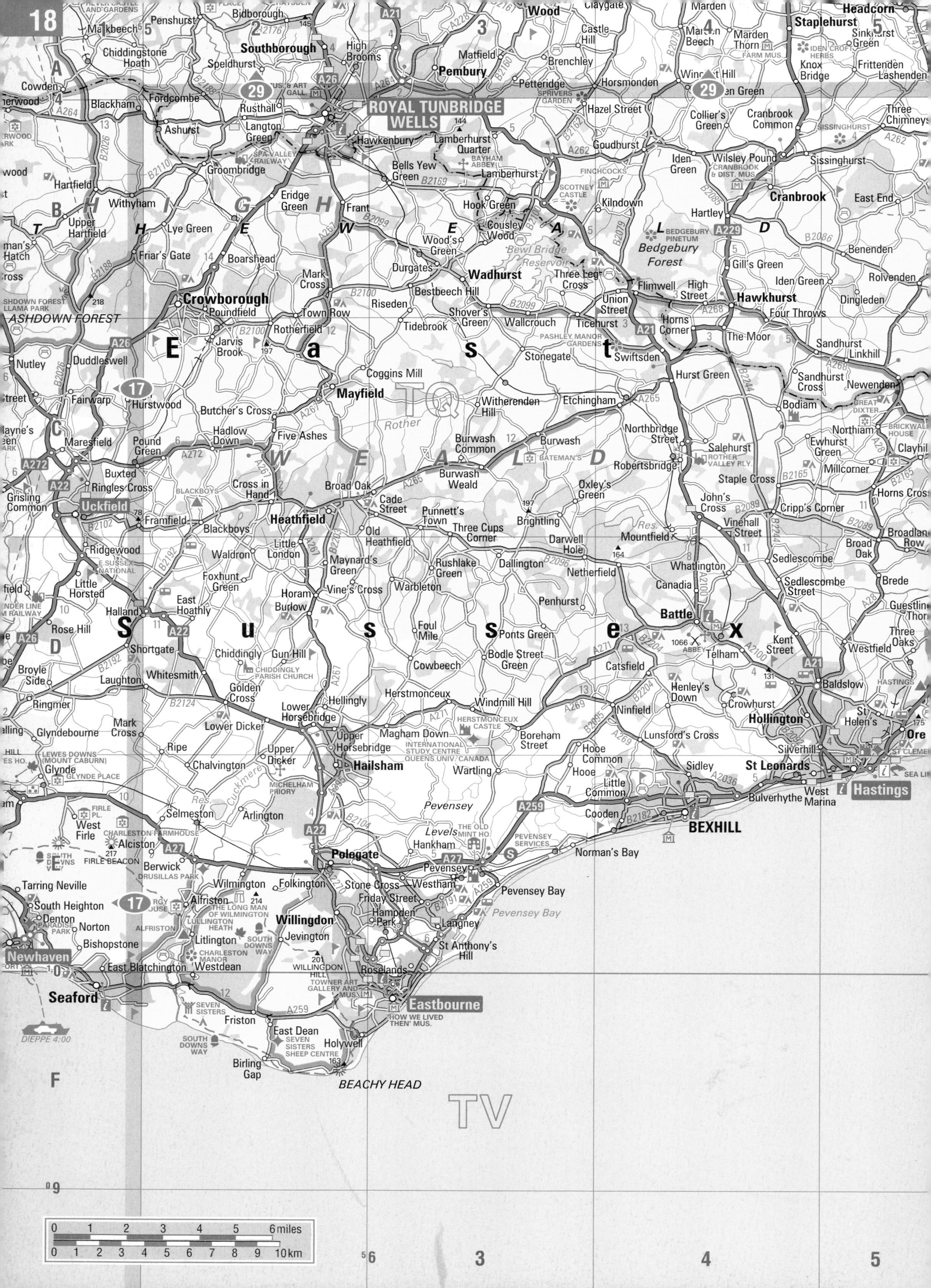

Markbeech
Penshurst
Bidborough
Southborough
High Brooms
Chiddingstone Hoath
Speldhurst
Cowden
Blackham
Fordcombe
Rusthall
ROYAL TUNBRIDGE WELLS
Ashurst
Langton Green
Hawkenbury
Groombridge
Spa Valley Railway
Hartfield
Withyham
Eridge Green
Frant
Upper Hartfield
Lye Green
Friar's Gate
Boarshead
Mark Cross
Crowborough
Poundfield
Ashdown Forest
Town Row
Rotherfield
Jarvis Brook
Nutley
Duddleswell
Fairwarp
Hurstwood
Maresfield
Pound Green
Buxted
Ringles Cross
Uckfield
Framfield
Blackboys
Heathfield
Cross in Hand
Five Ashes
Hadlow Down
Butcher's Cross
Mayfield
Coggins Mill
Ridgewood
Little Horsted
Halland
East Hoathly
Waldron
Foxhunt Green
Little London
Horam
Burlow
Rose Hill
Shortgate
Laughton
Whitesmith
Chiddingly
Gun Hill
Golden Cross
Broyle Side
Ringmer
Glyndebourne
Mark Cross
Lower Dicker
Upper Dicker
Ripe
Chalvington
Glynde
Selmeston
Arlington
West Firle
Alciston
Berwick
Wilmington
Folkington
Alfriston
Tarring Neville
South Heighton
Denton
Norton
Bishopstone
Litlington
Westdean
Newhaven
East Blatchington
Seaford
Friston
East Dean
Birling Gap
Beachy Head
Holywell
Eastbourne
Willingdon
Jevington
Polegate
Hailsham
Hellingly
Lower Horsebridge
Upper Horsebridge
Magham Down
Herstmonceux
Windmill Hill
Boreham Street
Wartling
Pevensey Levels
Hankham
Pevensey
Westham
Stone Cross
Friday Street
Hampden Park
Langney
St Anthony's Hill
Roselands
Pevensey Bay
Norman's Bay
Cooden
BEXHILL
Little Common
Hooe
Hooe Common
Ninfield
Lunsford's Cross
Sidley
Bulverhythe
St Leonards
West Marina
Hastings
Silverhill
Hollington
Crowhurst
Henley's Down
Catsfield
Battle
Telham
Baldslow
Ore
St Helen's
Westfield
Three Oaks
Kent Street
Canadia
Whatlington
Sedlescombe
Sedlescombe Street
Brede
Broad Oak
Vinehall Street
Cripp's Corner
Staple Cross
John's Cross
Mountfield
Netherfield
Darwell Hole
Penhurst
Ponts Green
Bodle Street Green
Cowbeech
Foul Mile
Warbleton
Rushlake Green
Dallington
Brightling
Punnett's Town
Three Cups Corner
Old Heathfield
Cade Street
Broad Oak
Maynard's Green
Vine's Cross
Burwash Weald
Burwash Common
Burwash
Etchingham
Witherenden Hill
Robertsbridge
Salehurst
Northbridge Street
Oxley's Green
Millcorner
Ewhurst Green
Northiam
Bodiam
Newenden
Sandhurst Cross
Sandhurst
Hurst Green
The Moor
Hawkhurst
Four Throws
Horns Corner
Swiftsden
Ticehurst
Stonegate
Wallcrouch
Shover's Green
Tidebrook
Riseden
Bestbeech Hill
Wadhurst
Durgates
Wood's Green
Cousley Wood
Hook Green
Three Leg Cross
Flimwell
Union Street
Kilndown
Bedgebury Forest
Hartley
Cranbrook
Benenden
Gill's Green
Iden Green
Rolvenden
Dingleden
Sissinghurst
Wilsley Pound
Iden Green
Colliers' Green
Cranbrook Common
Goudhurst
Hazel Street
Horsmonden
Brenchley
Pembury
Matfield
Petteridge
Lamberhurst
Lamberhurst Quarter
Bells Yew Green
Castle Hill
Marden
Marden Beech
Marden Thorn
Staplehurst
Headcorn
Sinkhurst Green
Frittenden
Knox Bridge
Three Chimneys
East End
Bewl Bridge Reservoir
E a s t
S u s s e x
W E A L D
H I G H
TQ
TV
DIEPPE 4:00
0 1 2 3 4 5 6 miles
0 1 2 3 4 5 6 7 8 9 10 km

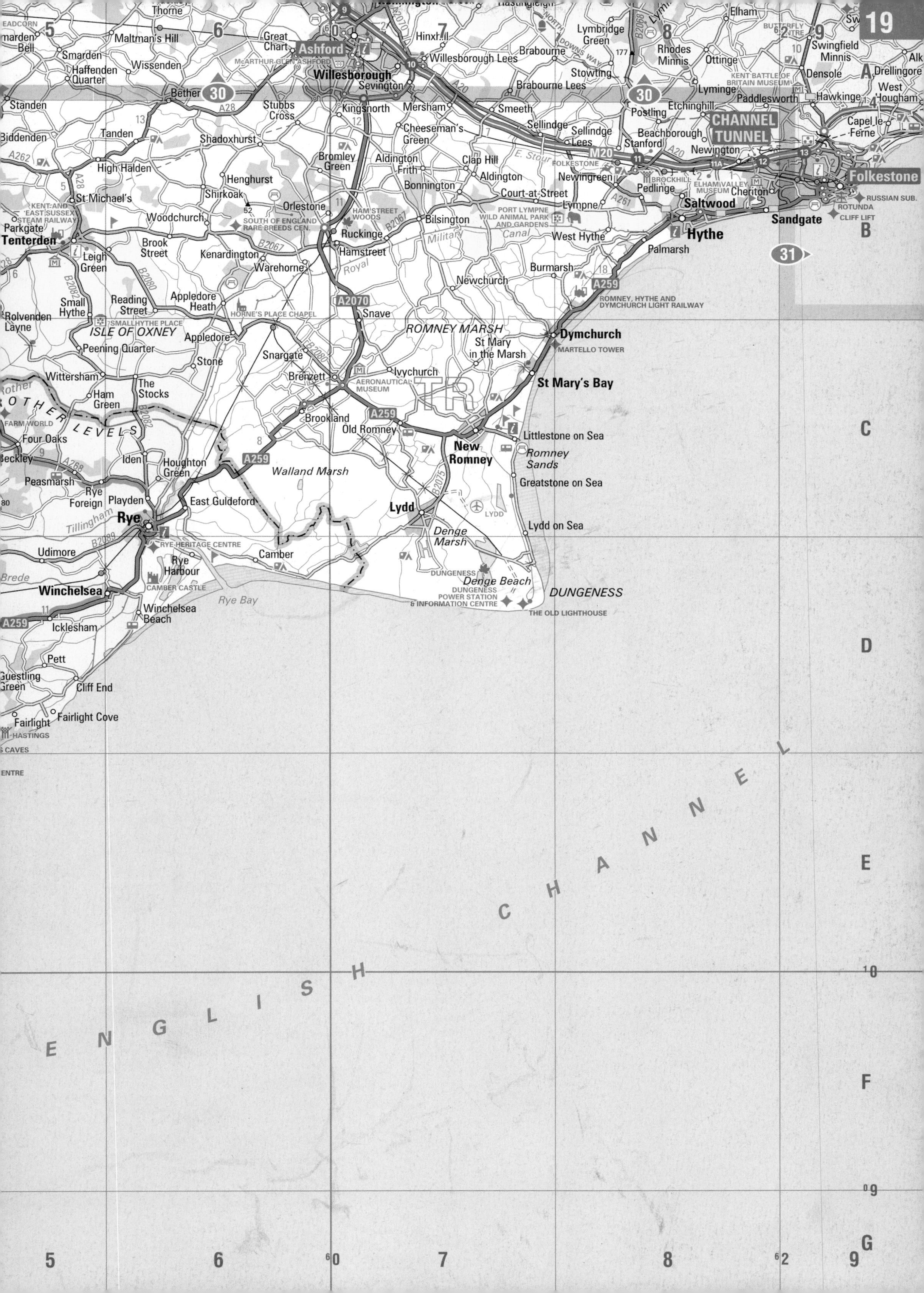
Ashford
Willesborough
Tenterden
Rye
Winchelsea
New Romney
Lydd
Hythe
Folkestone
Dymchurch
St Mary's Bay
Saltwood
Sandgate
CHANNEL TUNNEL
ROMNEY MARSH
ISLE OF OXNEY
Walland Marsh
Denge Marsh
DUNGENESS
Rye Bay
Littlestone on Sea
Greatstone on Sea
Lydd on Sea
Romney Sands
Camber
Appledore
Brenzett
Ivychurch
Brookland
Old Romney
Snargate
Snave
Newchurch
Burmarsh
Hamstreet
Ruckinge
Bilsington
Aldington
Smeeth
Sellindge
Mersham
Kingsnorth
Sevington
Shadoxhurst
High Halden
Woodchurch
Wittersham
Peasmarsh
Icklesham
Pett
Fairlight
Fairlight Cove
Cliff End
Udimore
Playden
Iden
Hinxhill
Brabourne
Stowting
Postling
Etchinghill
Lyminge
Elham
Densole
Hawkinge
Newington
Cheriton
Pedlinge
Lympne
Palmarsh
West Hythe
Stanford
ENGLISH CHANNEL
A259
A2070
M20
A20
A28
A268
A261
B2067
B2080
B2082
B2075
30
31
5
6
7
8
9
A
B
C
D
E
F
G
TR

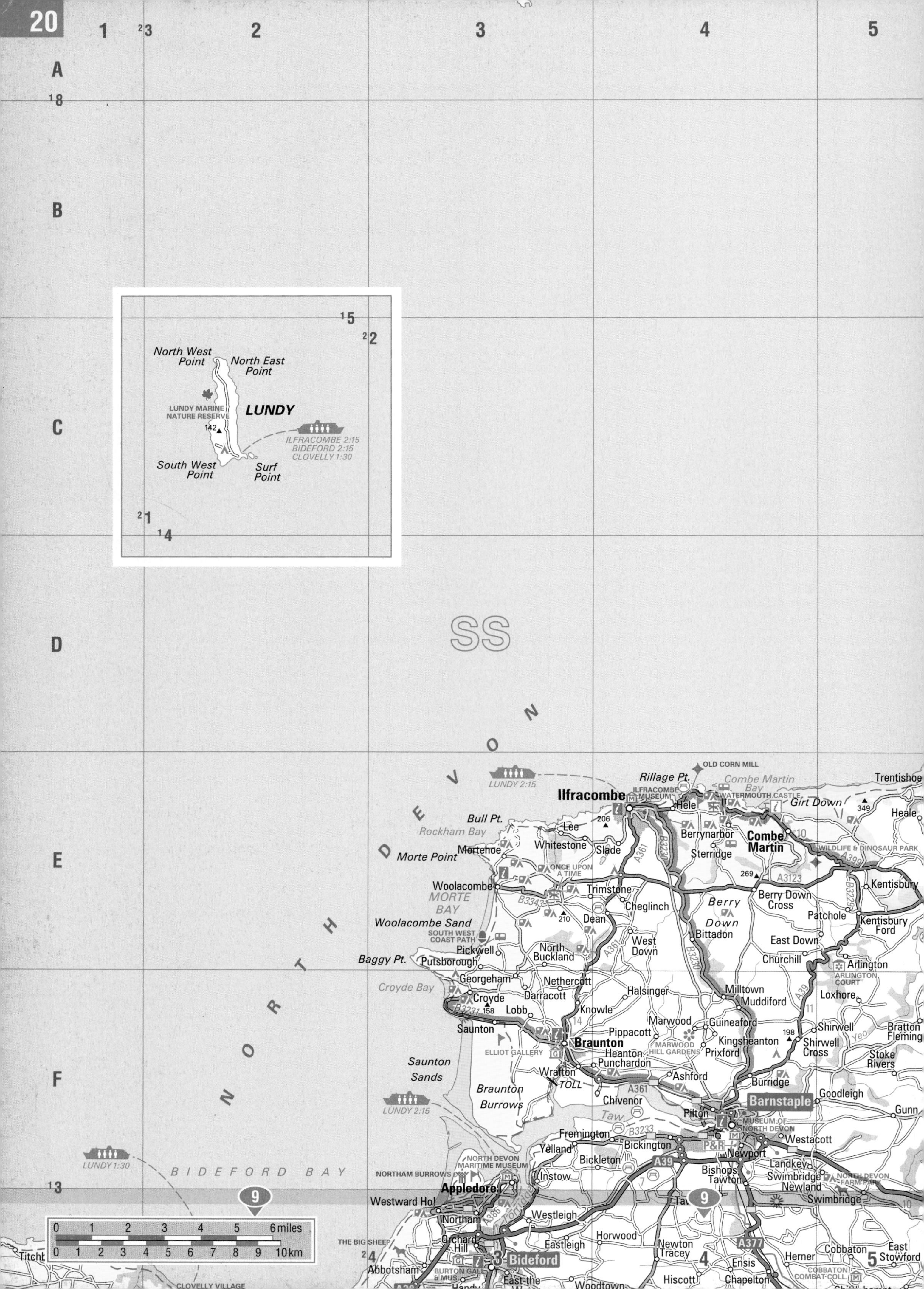

A

B

C

North West Point
North East Point

LUNDY MARINE NATURE RESERVE

LUNDY

142

South West Point

Surf Point

ILFRACOMBE 2:15
BIDEFORD 2:15
CLOVELLY 1:30

D

SS

**N
O
R
T
H

D
E
V
O
N**

LUNDY 2:15

Rillage Pt.
Combe Martin Bay
Trentishoe

OLD CORN MILL

Ilfracombe
ILFRACOMBE MUSEUM
WATERMOUTH CASTLE
Girt Down
Heale

Bull Pt.
Hele
349

Rockham Bay
Lee
Whitestone
206
Berrynarbor
Sterridge
Combe Martin
WILDLIFE & DINOSAUR PARK

E

Mortehoe
Slade

Morte Point
ONCE UPON A TIME
Trimstone
269
Berry Down Cross
Patchole
Kentisbury

Woolacombe
Cheglinch
Berry Down
Kentisbury Ford

MORTE BAY
210
Dean
West Down
Bittadon
East Down

Woolacombe Sand
SOUTH WEST COAST PATH
Pickwell
North Buckland
Churchill
Arlington

Baggy Pt.
Putsborough
Nethercott
Halsinger
Milltown
ARLINGTON COURT
Loxhore

Croyde Bay
Georgeham
Marwood
Muddiford
198

Croyde
158
Darracott
Knowle
Pippacott
Guineaford
Shirwell
Bratton Fleming

Lobb
MARWOOD HILL GARDENS
Prixford
Shirwell Cross
Stoke Rivers

Saunton
14
Pilton
Kingsheanton

ELLIOT GALLERY
Braunton
Heanton Punchardon
Ashford
Burridge
Goodleigh

F

Saunton Sands
Wrafton
TOLL
Chivenor
Barnstaple
Gunn

Braunton Burrows
MUSEUM OF NORTH DEVON
Westacott

LUNDY 2:15
Taw
Fremington
B3233
Newport
Landkey

LUNDY 1:30
Yelland
Bickington
P&R
Bishops Tawton
Swimbridge Newland
NORTH DEVON FARM PK

BIDEFORD BAY
NORTH DEVON MARITIME MUSEUM
Instow
Swimbridge

9

Appledore
Westward Ho!
Northam
Westleigh
Newton Tracey
A377
Cobbaton
East Stowford

NORTHAM BURROWS

THE BIG SHEEP
Orchard Hill
BURTON GALL & MUS
Bideford
Eastleigh
Horwood
Ensis
Herner
COBBATON COMBAT COLL
East

Titchb...
Abbotsham
Hiscott
Chapelton

CLOVELLY VILLAGE
Woodtown

0 1 2 3 4 5 6 miles
0 1 2 3 4 5 6 7 8 9 10km

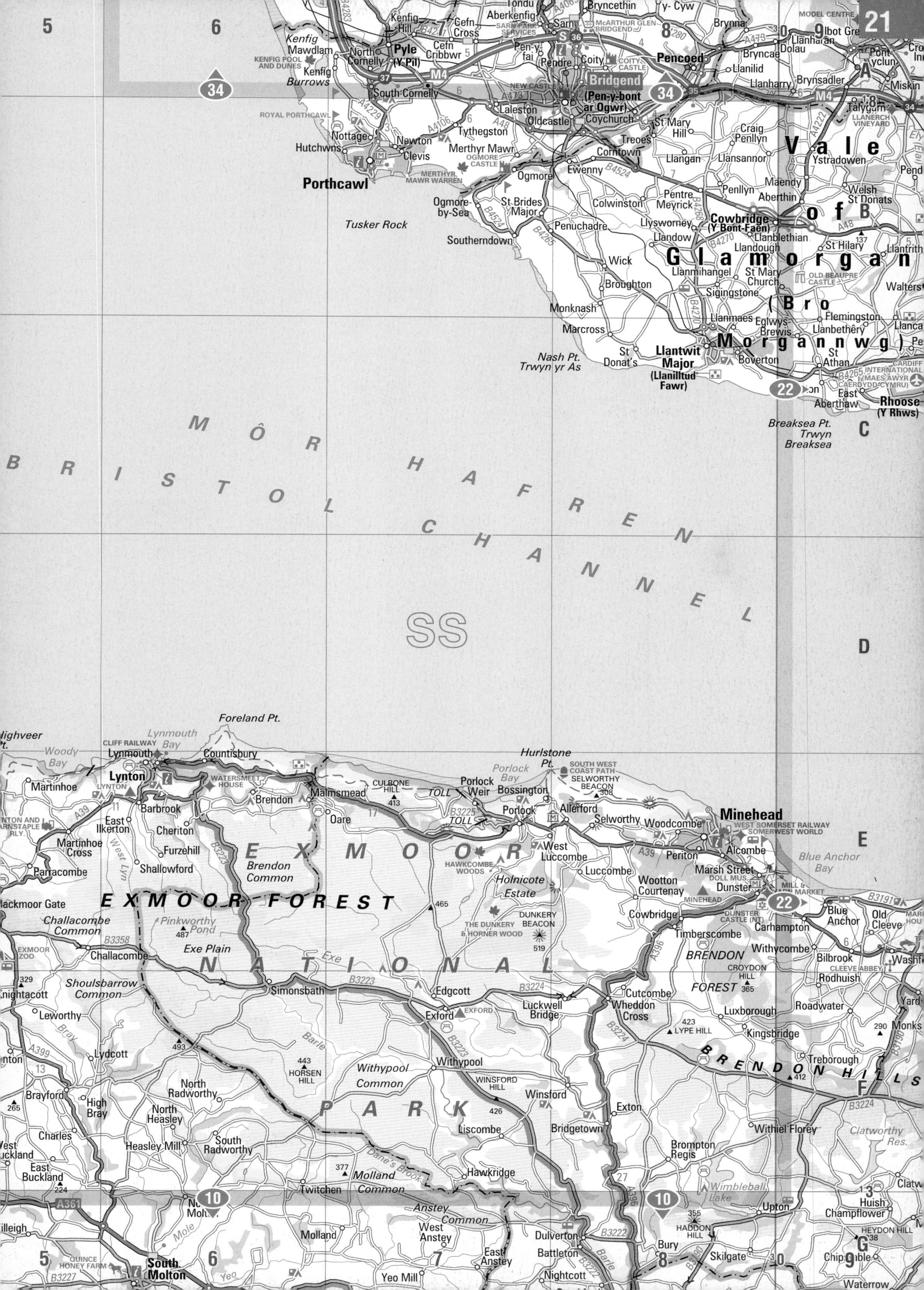

21
MODEL CENTRE
Kenfig Hill
Cefn Cross
Aberkenfig
SARN PARK SERVICES
Sarn
Bryncethin
McARTHUR GLEN BRIDGEND
Brynna
Llanharan
Dolau
Kenfig
Mawdlam
KENFIG POOL AND DUNES
Kenfig Burrows
North Cornelly
Pyle (Y Pil)
Cefn Cribbwr
Pen-y-fai
Pendre
Coity
COITY CASTLE
Pencoed
Bryncae
Llanilid
Llanharry
Brynsadler
Pont-y-clun
Miskin
M4
South Cornelly
NEW CASTLE
Bridgend (Pen-y-bont ar Ogwr)
Talygarn
LLANERCH VINEYARD
ROYAL PORTHCAWL
Laleston
Oldcastle
Coychurch
St Mary Hill
Craig Penllyn
Nottage
Newton
Tythegston
Treoes
Hutchwns
Clevis
Merthyr Mawr
OGMORE CASTLE
Corntown
Llangan
Llansannor
Ystradowen
MERTHYR MAWR WARREN
Ogmore
Ewenny
Porthcawl
Vale of Glamorgan (Bro Morgannwg)
Pentre Meyrick
Penllyn
Maendy
Aberthin
Welsh St Donats
Ogmore-by-Sea
St Brides Major
Colwinston
Llysworney
Cowbridge (Y Bont-Faen)
Llanblethian
Tusker Rock
Southerndown
Penuchadre
Llandow
Llandough
St Hilary
Llantrithyd
Wick
Llanmihangel
St Mary Church
OLD BEAUPRE CASTLE
Broughton
Sigingstone
Walterston
Monknash
Llanmaes
Eglwys-Brewis
Flemingston
Llanbethery
Llancarfan
Marcross
St Donat's
Llantwit Major (Llanilltud Fawr)
Boverton
St Athan
CARDIFF INTERNATIONAL (MAES AWYR CAERDYDD CYMRU)
Nash Pt. Trwyn yr As
East Aberthaw
Rhoose (Y Rhws)
Breaksea Pt. Trwyn Breaksea
MÔR HAFREN
BRISTOL CHANNEL
SS
Foreland Pt.
Highveer Pt.
Lynmouth Bay
Woody Bay
CLIFF RAILWAY
Lynmouth
Countisbury
Hurlstone Pt.
SOUTH WEST COAST PATH
SELWORTHY BEACON
Porlock Bay
Martinhoe
Lynton
WATERSMEET HOUSE
Malmsmead
CULBONE HILL
TOLL
Porlock Weir
Bossington
Brendon
Oare
Porlock
Allerford
Selworthy
Woodcombe
Minehead
WEST SOMERSET RAILWAY
SOMERWEST WORLD
Barbrook
East Ilkerton
Cheriton
West Luccombe
Periton
Alcombe
Martinhoe Cross
West Lyn
Furzehill
EXMOOR
Blue Anchor Bay
Parracombe
Shallowford
Brendon Common
HAWKCOMBE WOODS
Luccombe
Wootton Courtenay
Marsh Street
Dunster
DOLL MUS.
MILL & MARKET
Holnicote Estate
MINEHEAD
Blackmoor Gate
EXMOOR FOREST
DUNSTER CASTLE (NT)
Blue Anchor
Old Cleeve
Cowbridge
Challacombe Common
Pinkworthy Pond
THE DUNKERY & HORNER WOOD
DUNKERY BEACON
Timberscombe
Carhampton
EXMOOR ZOO
Challacombe
Exe Plain
NATIONAL
BRENDON
Withycombe
Bilbrook
CLEEVE ABBEY
Washford
CROYDON HILL
Rodhuish
Shoulsbarrow Common
Simonsbath
Edgcott
Cutcombe
FOREST
Knightacott
Exford
Luckwell Bridge
Wheddon Cross
Luxborough
Roadwater
Leworthy
LYPE HILL
Kingsbridge
Monksilver
Bray
Barle
Lydcott
HORSEN HILL
Withypool
Treborough
Withypool Common
BRENDON HILLS
Brayford
North Radworthy
WINSFORD HILL
Winsford
High Bray
PARK
Exton
North Heasley
Charles
Liscombe
Bridgetown
Withiel Florey
Clatworthy Res.
West Buckland
Heasley Mill
South Radworthy
Brompton Regis
East Buckland
Molland Common
Hawkridge
Dane's Brook
Twitchen
Wimbleball Lake
Huish Champflower
North Molton
Anstey Common
Upton
HADDON HILL
Filleigh
Mole
Molland
West Anstey
Dulverton
HEYDON HILL
Bury
QUINCE HONEY FARM
South Molton
East Anstey
Battleton
Skilgate
Chipstable
Yeo
Yeo Mill
Nightcott
Waterrow

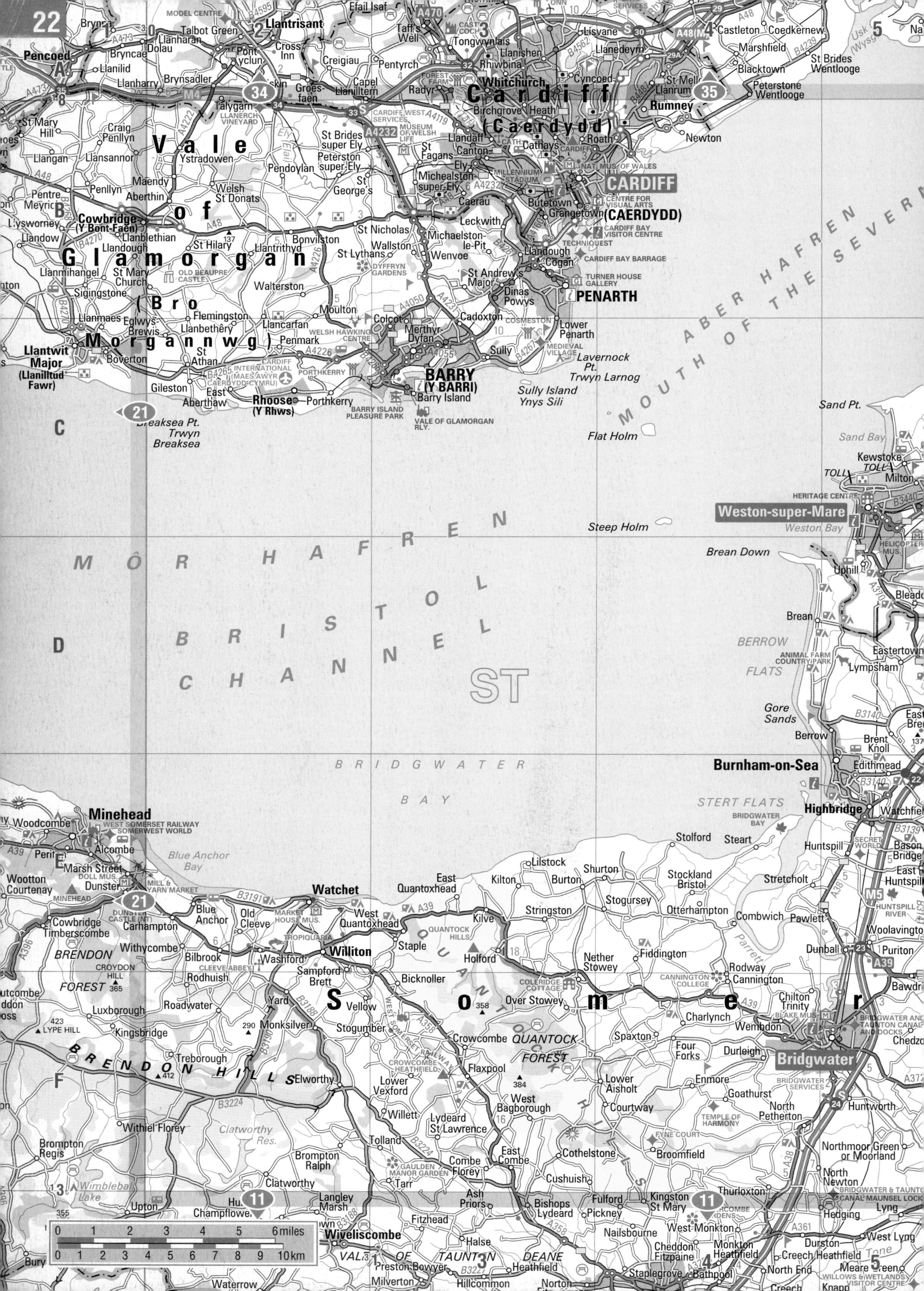

A
B
C
D
E
F
1
2
3
4
5
Pencoed
Llantrisant
Talbot Green
Llanharan
Dolau
Bryncae
Llanilid
Llanharry
Brynsadler
Pont-y-clun
Cross Inn
Efail Isaf
Taff's Well
Tongwynlais
Creigiau
Pentyrch
Capel Llanilltern
Groes-faen
Radyr
Llanishen
Rhiwbina
Whitchurch
Lisvane
Llanedeyrn
Cyncoed
Castleton
Coedkernew
Marshfield
Blacktown
St Brides Wentlooge
Peterstone Wentlooge
St Mellons
Llanrumney
Rumney
Cardiff
(Caerdydd)
Birchgrove
Heath
Cathays
Roath
Newton
St Mary Hill
Craig Penllyn
Talygarn
Llangan
Llansannor
Ystradowen
Vale
of
Glamorgan
(Bro
Morgannwg)
St Brides super Ely
Peterston super-Ely
Pendoylan
St Fagans
Llandaff
Canton
Ely
Michaelston-super-Ely
Caerau
St George's
Penllyn
Maendy
Welsh St Donats
Aberthin
Pentre Meyrick
Llysworney
Cowbridge
(Y Bont-Faen)
Llanblethian
St Hilary
Llandow
Llandough
Llantrithyd
Bonvilston
St Nicholas
Wallston
St Lythans
Dyffryn Gardens
Wenvoe
Michaelston-le-Pit
Leckwith
Butetown
Grangetown
CARDIFF
(CAERDYDD)
Centre for Visual Arts
Cardiff Bay Visitor Centre
Techniquest
Cardiff Bay Barrage
Turner House Gallery
Llandough
Cogan
PENARTH
Llanmihangel
St Mary Church
Old Beaupre Castle
Walterston
Sigingstone
St Andrew's Major
Dinas Powys
Llanmaes
Eglwys-Brewis
Flemingston
Llanbethery
Llancarfan
Moulton
Colcot
Merthyr-Dyfan
Cadoxton
Cosmeston
Lower Penarth
Sully
Medieval Village
Lavernock Pt.
Trwyn Larnog
Llantwit Major
(Llanilltud Fawr)
Boverton
St Athan
Penmark
Welsh Hawking Centre
Cardiff International
Porthkerry
BARRY
(Y BARRI)
Barry Island
Barry Island Pleasure Park
Vale of Glamorgan Rly.
Gileston
East Aberthaw
Rhoose
(Y Rhws)
Porthkerry
Sully Island
Ynys Sili
Breaksea Pt.
Trwyn Breaksea
Flat Holm
ABER HAFREN
MOUTH OF THE SEVERN
Sand Pt.
Sand Bay
Kewstoke
Milton
Heritage Centre
Weston-super-Mare
Weston Bay
Helicopter Mus.
Steep Holm
Brean Down
Uphill
Bleadon
Brean
MÔR HAFREN
BRISTOL CHANNEL
ST
BERROW FLATS
Animal Farm Country Park
Eastertown
Lympsham
Gore Sands
Berrow
Brent Knoll
Burnham-on-Sea
Edithmead
BRIDGWATER BAY
STERT FLATS
Bridgwater Bay
Highbridge
Watchfield
Minehead
Woodcombe
West Somerset Railway
Somerwest World
Alcombe
Periton
Blue Anchor Bay
Marsh Street
Dunster
Doll Mus.
Mill & Yarn Market
Wootton Courtenay
Watchet
Market House Mus.
East Quantoxhead
Kilton
Lilstock
Shurton
Burton
Stolford
Steart
Stockland Bristol
Huntspill
Bason Bridge
East Huntspill
Secret World
Stretcholt
Blue Anchor
Old Cleeve
West Quantoxhead
Kilve
Stringston
Stogursey
Otterhampton
Combwich
Pawlett
Huntspill River
Woolavington
Cowbridge
Timberscombe
Carhampton
Tropiquaria
Quantock Hills
Withycombe
Bilbrook
Washford
Williton
Staple
Holford
Nether Stowey
Fiddington
Dunball
Puriton
Brendon
Croydon Hill
Forest
Cleeve Abbey
Rodhuish
Sampford Brett
Bicknoller
Coleridge Cottage
Rodway
Cannington
Cannington College
Bawdrip
Roadwater
Yard
Vellow
Over Stowey
Chilton Trinity
Somer
Luxborough
Lype Hill
Kingsbridge
Monksilver
Stogumber
Charlynch
Wembdon
Blake Mus.
Bridgwater and Taunton Canal and Docks
Chedzoy
Crowcombe
Quantock
Forest
Spaxton
Four Forks
Durleigh
Bridgwater
Brendon Hills
Treborough
Elworthy
Crowcombe Heathfield
Flaxpool
Lower Aisholt
Enmore
Bridgwater Services
Goathurst
Lower Vexford
West Bagborough
Courtway
North Petherton
Huntworth
Withiel Florey
Clatworthy Res.
Willett
Lydeard St Lawrence
Temple of Harmony
Fyne Court
Brompton Regis
Tolland
Brompton Ralph
Gaulden Manor Garden
Combe Florey
East Combe
Cothelstone
Broomfield
Northmoor Green or Moorland
Wimbleball Lake
Clatworthy
Tarr
Cushuish
North Newton
Upton
Huish Champflower
Langley Marsh
Ash Priors
Bishops Lydeard
Fulford
Pickney
Kingston St Mary
Thurloxton
Bridgwater & Taunton Canal Maunsel Lock
Hedging
Lyng
Fitzhead
West Monkton
Hestercombe Gardens
Wiveliscombe
Halse
Nailsbourne
Cheddon Fitzpaine
Monkton Heathfield
Durston
West Lyng
Creech Heathfield
Bury
Vale of Taunton Deane
Preston Bowyer
Heathfield
Staplegrove
Bathpool
North End
Meare Green
Willows & Wetlands Visitor Centre
Milverton
Waterrow
Hillcommon
Norton
Creech
Knapp
0 1 2 3 4 5 6 miles
0 1 2 3 4 5 6 7 8 9 10 km
M4
M5
A48
A470
A4232
A4226
A4050
A39
A358
A38
A361
B3224
B3191
B3140

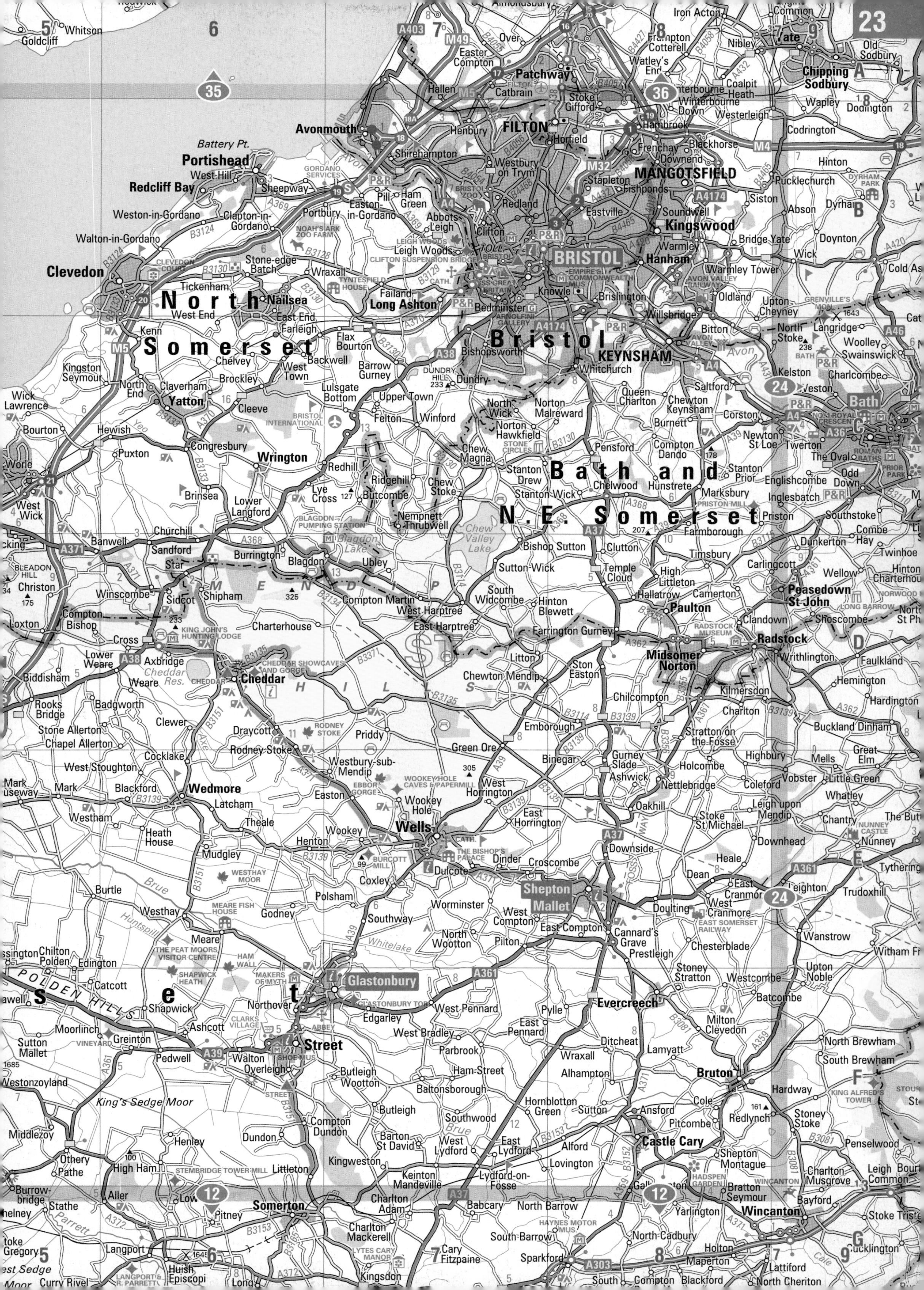
Goldcliff
Whitson
35
36
Avonmouth
Battery Pt.
Portishead
West Hill
Redcliff Bay
Sheepway
Portbury
Pill
Easton-in-Gordano
Ham Green
Weston-in-Gordano
Clapton-in-Gordano
Walton-in-Gordano
Clevedon
Tickenham
Nailsea
North Somerset
West End
East End
Farleigh
Kenn
Flax Bourton
Backwell
Chelvey
Brockley
West Town
Barrow Gurney
Kingston Seymour
North End
Claverham
Yatton
Cleeve
Wick Lawrence
Bourton
Hewish
Congresbury
Puxton
Wrington
Brinsea
Lower Langford
Churchill
Banwell
Sandford
Burrington
Blagdon
Ubley
Star
Winscombe
Sidcot
Shipham
Christon
Compton Bishop
Loxton
Cross
Axbridge
Cheddar
Cheddar Res.
Lower Weare
Weare
Biddisham
Rooks Bridge
Badgworth
Stone Allerton
Chapel Allerton
Clewer
Draycott
Rodney Stoke
Priddy
Cocklake
West Stoughton
Mark
Blackford
Wedmore
Latcham
Theale
Westham
Heath House
Mudgley
Burtle
Westhay
Meare
Godney
Chilton Polden
Edington
Catcott
POLDEN HILLS
Shapwick
Ashcott
Moorlinch
Greinton
Sutton Mallet
Pedwell
Walton
Overleigh
Street
Westonzoyland
King's Sedge Moor
Middlezoy
Othery
Pathe
Henley
High Ham
Burrowbridge
Stathe
Aller
Low Ham
Pitney
Langport
Huish Episcopi
Curry Rivel
Somerton
Long Sutton
Dundon
Compton Dundon
Littleton
Kingweston
Butleigh
Butleigh Wootton
Barton St David
Keinton Mandeville
Charlton Adam
Charlton Mackerell
Kingsdon
Glastonbury
Northover
Edgarley
West Pennard
West Bradley
East Pennard
Parbrook
Ham Street
Baltonsbury
Southwood
West Lydford
East Lydford
Lydford-on-Fosse
Babcary
North Barrow
South Barrow
Sparkford
Hornblotton Green
Alford
Lovington
Castle Cary
Ansford
Pitcombe
Shepton Montague
Bratton Seymour
Yarlington
North Cadbury
Holton
Maperton
Wincanton
Bayford
Charlton Musgrove
Penselwood
Stoney Stoke
Redlynch
Bruton
Hardway
North Brewham
South Brewham
Lamyatt
Ditcheat
Wraxall
Alhampton
Pylle
Evercreech
Milton Clevedon
Batcombe
Westcombe
Stoney Stratton
Prestleigh
Cannard's Grave
East Compton
Shepton Mallet
West Compton
Pilton
North Wootton
Worminster
Southway
Polsham
Coxley
Dulcote
Dinder
Croscombe
Wells
Wookey
Wookey Hole
Easton
Henton
Westbury-sub-Mendip
West Horrington
East Horrington
Green Ore
Binegar
Gurney Slade
Ashwick
Oakhill
Downside
Doulting
East Cranmore
West Cranmore
Chesterblade
Emborough
Chewton Mendip
Litton
Ston Easton
Chilcompton
Farrington Gurney
Midsomer Norton
Radstock
Paulton
Camerton
Hallatrow
High Littleton
Timsbury
Temple Cloud
Clutton
Bishop Sutton
Sutton Wick
South Widcombe
Hinton Blewett
West Harptree
East Harptree
Compton Martin
Charterhouse
Nempnett Thrubwell
Butcombe
Ridgehill
Lye Cross
Redhill
Chew Stoke
Chew Magna
Chew Valley Lake
Blagdon Lake
Stanton Drew
Stanton Wick
Pensford
Norton Hawkfield
North Wick
Norton Malreward
Winford
Felton
Upper Town
Lulsgate Bottom
Dundry
Bishopsworth
Whitchurch
Bristol
BRISTOL
Bedminster
Long Ashton
Failand
Wraxall
Leigh Woods
Abbots Leigh
Clifton
Redland
Westbury on Trym
Henbury
Shirehampton
Hallen
Catbrain
Patchway
Easter Compton
Over
Stoke Gifford
FILTON
Horfield
Frenchay
Hambrook
Winterbourne
Winterbourne Down
Frampton Cotterell
Watley's End
Iron Acton
Nibley
Yate
Chipping Sodbury
Old Sodbury
Wapley
Dodington
Codrington
Coalpit Heath
Westerleigh
Downend
MANGOTSFIELD
Stapleton
Fishponds
Eastville
Soundwell
Kingswood
Hanham
Warmley
Siston
Pucklechurch
Hinton
Dyrham
Abson
Bridge Yate
Doynton
Wick
Warmley Tower
Oldland
Upton Cheyney
Willsbridge
Bitton
North Stoke
Langridge
Woolley
Swainswick
Kelston
Weston
Charlcombe
Bath
KEYNSHAM
Brislington
Knowle
Saltford
Queen Charlton
Chewton Keynsham
Burnett
Corston
Newton St Loe
Twerton
The Oval
Odd Down
Englishcombe
Compton Dando
Chelwood
Hunstrete
Stanton Prior
Marksbury
Priston
Farmborough
Inglesbatch
Southstoke
Dunkerton
Combe Hay
Twinhoe
Carlingcott
Wellow
Peasedown St John
Shoscombe
Clandown
Writhlington
Kilmersdon
Charlton
Faulkland
Hemington
Hardington
Buckland Dinham
Stratton on the Fosse
Holcombe
Highbury
Mells
Great Elm
Vobster
Little Green
Coleford
Whatley
Nettlebridge
Stoke St Michael
Leigh upon Mendip
Chantry
Downhead
Nunney
Dean
Heale
Tytherington
Trudoxhill
Leighton
Wanstrow
Witham Friary
Upton Noble
Bath and N.E. Somerset
Somerset
24
12

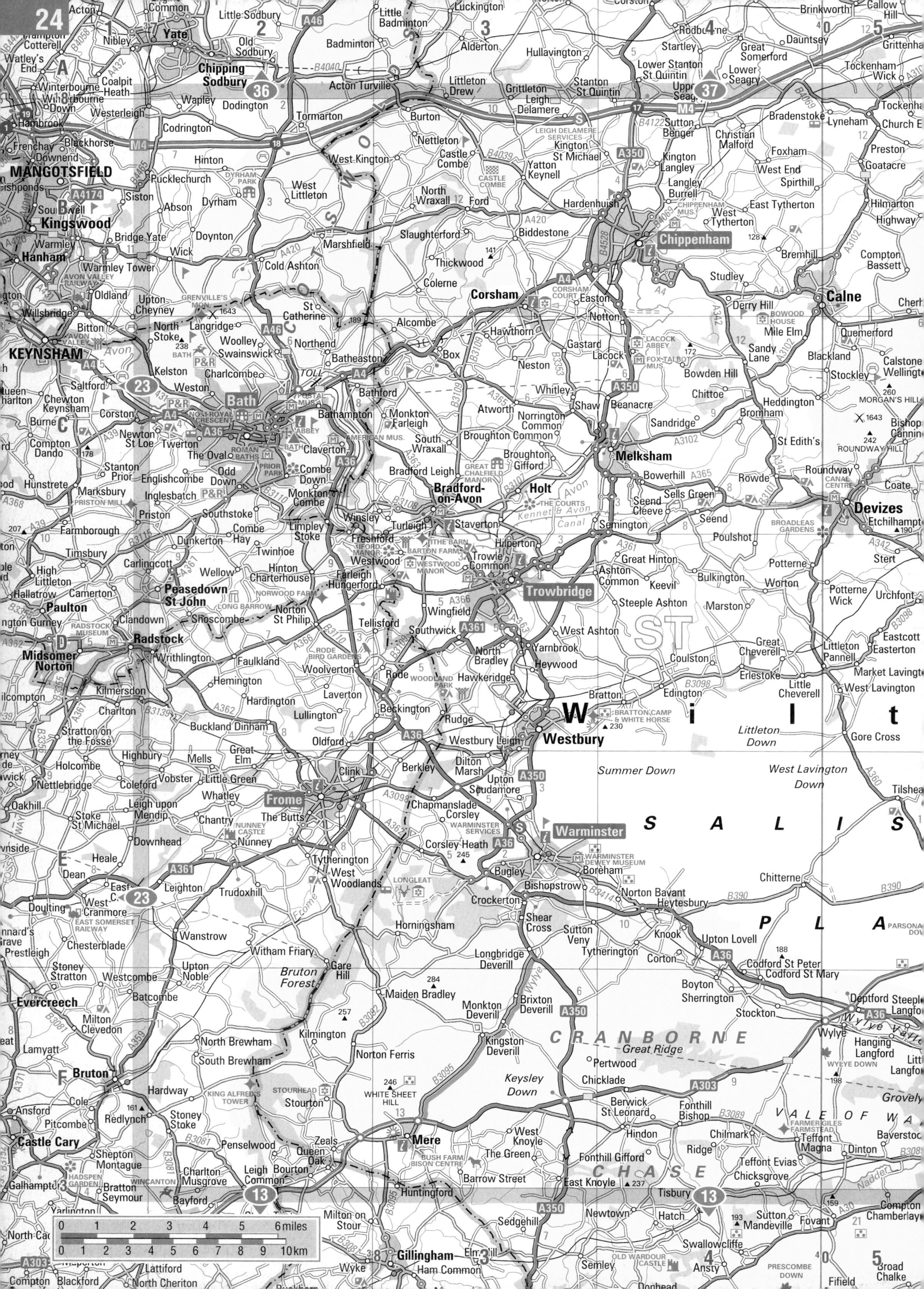
Acton
Nibley
Yate
Little Sodbury
Old Sodbury
Chipping Sodbury
Little Badminton
Badminton
Luckington
Alderton
Hullavington
Rodbourne
Startley
Great Somerford
Dauntsey
Brinkworth
Callow Hill
Grittenham
Tockenham Wick
Lower Seagry
Lower Stanton St Quintin
Stanton St Quintin
Winterbourne
Coalpit Heath
Frampton Cotterell
Watley's End
Westerleigh
Wapley
Dodington
Acton Turville
Littleton Drew
Grittleton
Leigh Delamere
Tormarton
Burton
Codrington
Hambrook
Frenchay
Downend
Blackhorse
MANGOTSFIELD
Pucklechurch
Hinton
Dyrham Park
Dyrham
West Littleton
Nettleton
West Kington
Castle Combe
Kington St Michael
Yatton Keynell
Leigh Delamere Services
Sutton Benger
Christian Malford
Bradenstoke
Lyneham
Kington Langley
Foxham
West End
Spirthill
Preston
Goatacre
Langley Burrell
Hardenhuish
Chippenham
East Tytherton
West Tytherton
Hilmarton
Highway
Bremhill
Compton Bassett
Siston
Abson
Soundwell
Kingswood
Bridge Yate
Doynton
Wick
North Wraxall
Ford
Biddestone
Slaughterford
Marshfield
Thickwood
Cold Ashton
Colerne
Warmley
Hanham
Warmley Tower
Avon Valley Railway
Oldland
Upton Cheyney
Willsbridge
Bitton
Grenville's Mon.
Langridge
North Stoke
Woolley
Swainswick
St Catherine
Alcombe
Corsham
Corsham Court
Easton
Notton
Hawthorn
Studley
Derry Hill
Bowood House
Calne
Mile Elm
Quemerford
KEYNSHAM
Kelston
Charlcombe
Northend
Batheaston
Box
Gastard
Neston
Lacock
Lacock Abbey
Fox Talbot Mus.
Sandy Lane
Bowden Hill
Blackland
Calstone Wellington
Stockley
Saltford
Weston
Bath
Bathford
Whitley
Shaw
Beanacre
Chittoe
Heddington
Morgan's Hill
Chewton Keynsham
Corston
Newton St Loe
Twerton
Royal Crescent
Abbey
Bathampton
Monkton Farleigh
Atworth
Norrington Common
Broughton Common
Sandridge
Bromham
Bishops Cannings
Burnett
Compton Dando
The Oval
Roman Baths
Claverton
American Mus.
South Wraxall
Melksham
St Edith's
Roundway Hill
Stanton Prior
Englishcombe
Odd Down
Prior Park
Combe Down
Bradford Leigh
Great Chalfield Manor
Broughton Gifford
Bowerhill
Rowde
Roundway
Coate
Hunstrete
Marksbury
Priston Mill
Inglesbatch
Monkton Combe
Bradford-on-Avon
Holt
The Courts
Seend Cleeve
Sells Green
Devizes
Canal Centre
Priston
Southstoke
Combe Hay
Winsley
Turleigh
Staverton
Seend
Etchilhampton
Farmborough
Dunkerton
Limpley Stoke
Freshford
Tithe Barn
Barton Farm
Semington
Kennet & Avon Canal
Poulshot
Broadleas Gardens
Timsbury
Twinhoe
Iford Manor
Westwood
Westwood Manor
Hilperton
Trowle Common
Great Hinton
Potterne
Stert
High Littleton
Carlingcott
Wellow
Hinton Charterhouse
Farleigh Hungerford
Trowbridge
Ashton Common
Keevil
Bulkington
Worton
Potterne Wick
Urchfont
Hallatrow
Camerton
Peasedown St John
Norwood Farm
Steeple Ashton
Marston
Paulton
Clandown
Shoscombe
Long Barrow
Norton St Philip
Wingfield
Tellisford
Southwick
West Ashton
Eastcott
Easterton
Radstock Museum
Radstock
Midsomer Norton
Writhlington
Faulkland
Rode Bird Gardens
North Bradley
Yarnbrook
Heywood
Great Cheverell
Coulston
Littleton Pannell
Market Lavington
Hemington
Woolverton
Rode
Woodland Park
Hawkeridge
Erlestoke
Edington
Little Cheverell
West Lavington
Kilmersdon
Hardington
Laverton
Bratton
Bratton Camp & White Horse
Charlton
Lullington
Beckington
Rudge
Westbury
Stratton on the Fosse
Buckland Dinham
Oldford
Westbury Leigh
Littleton Down
Gore Cross
Holcombe
Highbury
Mells
Great Elm
Clink
Berkley
Dilton Marsh
Summer Down
West Lavington Down
Nettlebridge
Coleford
Vobster
Little Green
Upton Scudamore
Tilshead
Oakhill
Whatley
Frome
Chapmanslade
Corsley
Stoke St Michael
Leigh upon Mendip
Chantry
Nunney Castle
The Butts
Warminster Services
Warminster
SALIS
Downhead
Nunney
Corsley Heath
Warminster Dewey Museum
Boreham
Heale
Tytherington
Bugley
Dean
West Woodlands
Longleat
Bishopstrow
Chitterne
Leighton
East Cranmore
West Cranmore
East Somerset Railway
Doulting
Trudoxhill
Crockerton
Norton Bavant
Heytesbury
Horningsham
Shear Cross
Sutton Veny
Knook
Upton Lovell
PLA
Wanstrow
Chesterblade
Witham Friary
Tytherington
Longbridge Deverill
Corton
Codford St Peter
Codford St Mary
Stoney Stratton
Westcombe
Upton Noble
Bruton Forest
Gare Hill
Boyton
Sherrington
Batcombe
Maiden Bradley
Monkton Deverill
Brixton Deverill
Evercreech
Milton Clevedon
Kilmington
Stockton
Deptford
Steeple Langford
Wylye
Wylye Valley
Lamyatt
North Brewham
Norton Ferris
Kingston Deverill
CRANBORNE
Great Ridge
Hanging Langford
Wylye Down
South Brewham
Pertwood
Bruton
Hardway
King Alfred's Tower
Stourhead
Stourton
White Sheet Hill
Keysley Down
Chicklade
Berwick St Leonard
Fonthill Bishop
Grovely
Cole
Redlynch
Stoney Stoke
VALE OF WA
Ansford
Pitcombe
Castle Cary
Penselwood
Zeals
Mere
West Knoyle
Hindon
Chilmark
Farmer Giles Farmstead
Teffont Magna
Dinton
Baverstock
Shepton Montague
Queen Oak
Bush Farm Bison Centre
The Green
Fonthill Gifford
Ridge
Teffont Evias
Hadspen Garden
Charlton Musgrove
Leigh Common
Bourton
Barrow Street
CHASE
Chicksgrove
Galhampton
Bratton Seymour
Wincanton
Bayford
Huntingford
East Knoyle
Tisbury
Compton Chamberlayne
Yarlington
Milton on Stour
Sedgehill
Newtown
Hatch
Sutton Mandeville
Fovant
North Cadbury
Gillingham
Swallowcliffe
Lattiford
Ham Common
Semley
Old Wardour Castle
Ansty
Prescombe Down
Broad Chalke
Fifield
Compton
Blackford
North Cheriton
Wyke
0 1 2 3 4 5 6 miles
0 1 2 3 4 5 6 7 8 9 10 km

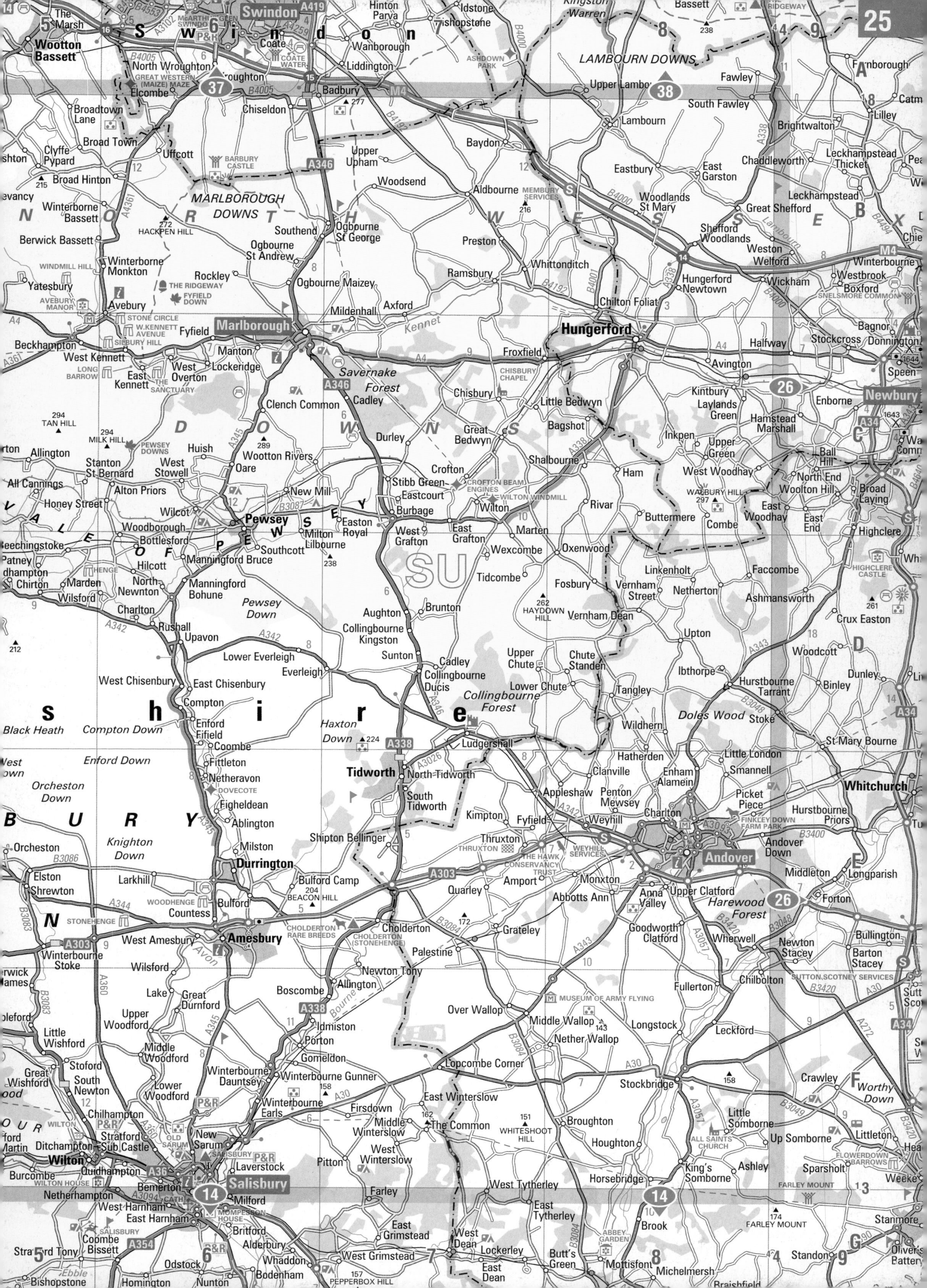
Swindon
Wootton Bassett
Marlborough
Hungerford
Newbury
Pewsey
Tidworth
Andover
Whitchurch
Durrington
Amesbury
Salisbury
Wilton
Stockbridge
LAMBOURN DOWNS
MARLBOROUGH DOWNS
Savernake Forest
Collingbourne Forest
Harewood Forest
Doles Wood
Pewsey Down
Lambourn
Aldbourne
Ramsbury
Avebury
Chiseldon
Ogbourne St George
Burbage
Ludgershall
Upavon
Enford
Netheravon
Bulford
Shrewton
Over Wallop
Middle Wallop
Nether Wallop
Kintbury
Inkpen
Hurstbourne Tarrant
St Mary Bourne
Longparish
Winterslow
King's Somborne
Mottisfont

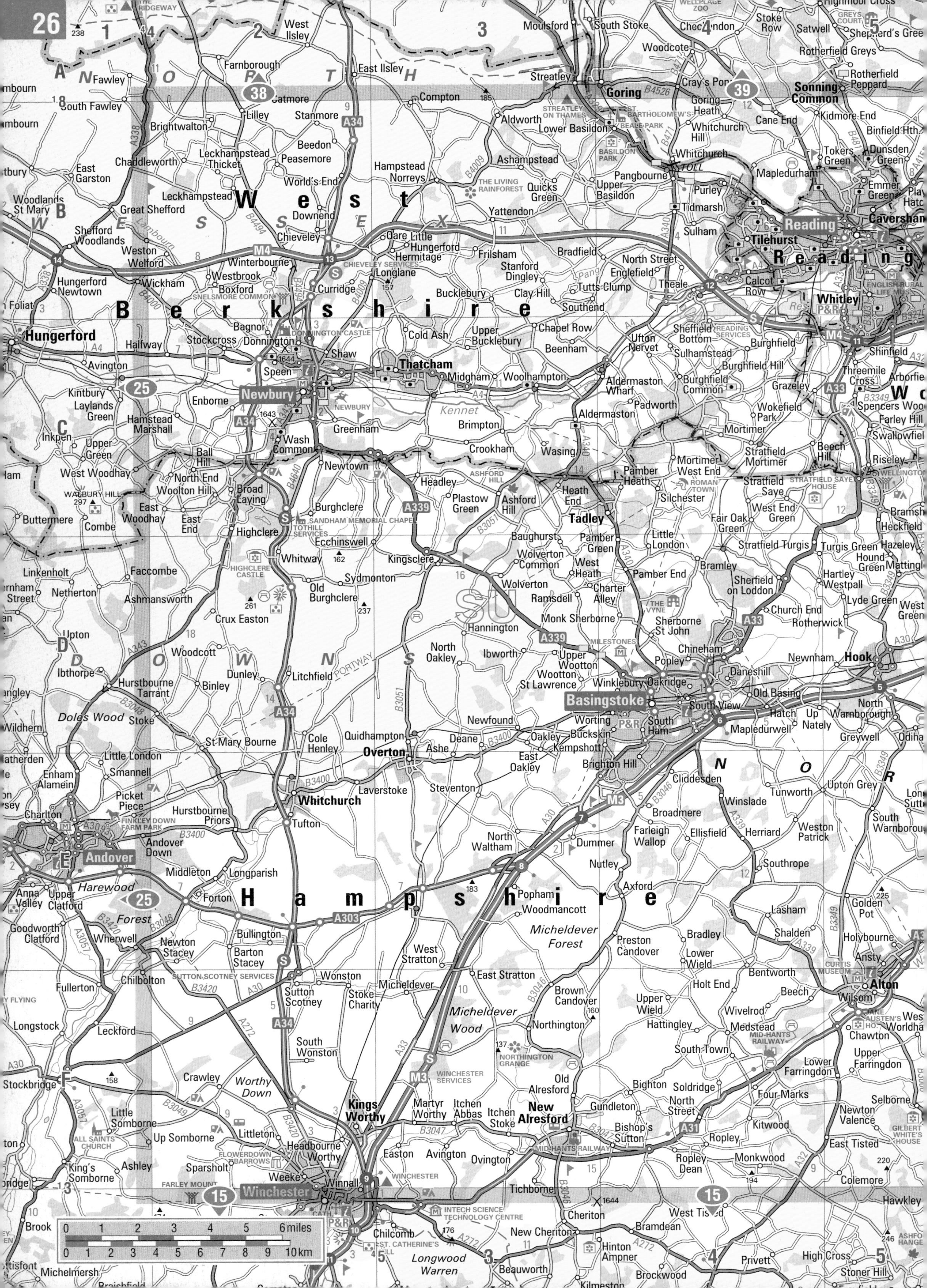
West Berkshire
Hampshire
Newbury
Reading
Basingstoke
Andover
Winchester
Hungerford
Thatcham
Tadley
Overton
Whitchurch
Goring
Alton
New Alresford
Kings Worthy
Whitley
Tilehurst
Caversham
Hook
Sonning Common
Streatley
Pangbourne
Theale
Kingsclere
Highclere
Burghclere
Stockbridge
0 1 2 3 4 5 6 miles
0 1 2 3 4 5 6 7 8 9 10 km

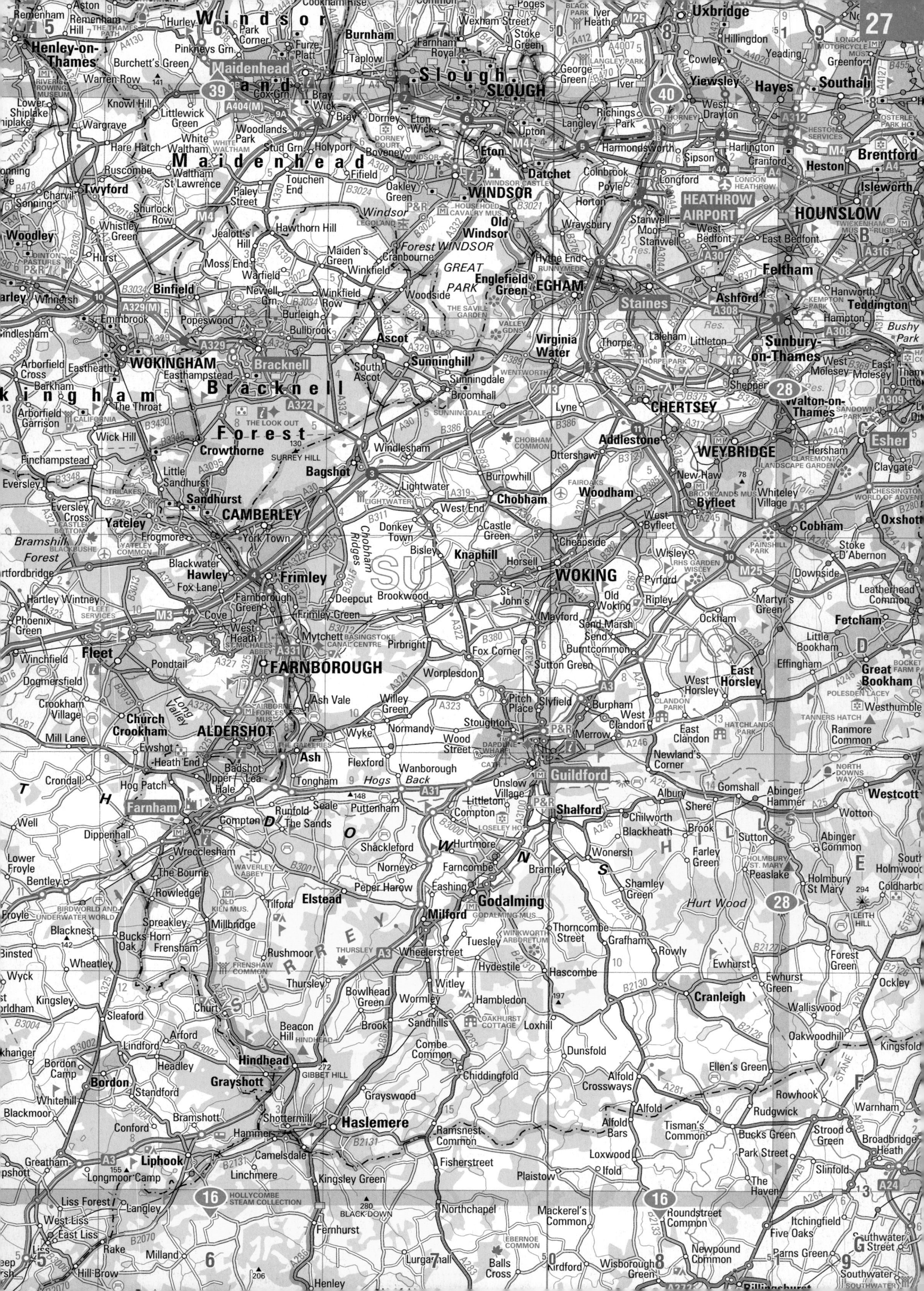
Windsor and Maidenhead
Henley-on-Thames
Burnham
Slough
SLOUGH
Uxbridge
Hillingdon
Yeading
Cowley
Yiewsley
Hayes
Southall
Maidenhead
39
40
Taplow
Farnham Royal
Stoke Green
George Green
Iver
West Drayton
Bray
Dorney
Eton Wick
Langley
Richings Park
Eton
Datchet
Harmondsworth
Sipson
Harlington
Cranford
Heston
Brentford
Twyford
Woodley
Sonning
Ruscombe
Waltham St Lawrence
White Waltham
Holyport
Fifield
Oakley Green
WINDSOR
Colnbrook
Poyle
Longford
HEATHROW AIRPORT
Isleworth
HOUNSLOW
Horton
Wraysbury
Stanwell Moor
Stanwell
West Bedfont
East Bedfont
Feltham
Old Windsor
Forest WINDSOR
GREAT PARK
Englefield Green
EGHAM
Staines
Ashford
Hanworth
Teddington
Binfield
Warfield
Winkfield
Ascot
Sunninghill
Sunningdale
Virginia Water
Thorpe
Laleham
Littleton
Sunbury-on-Thames
Shepperton
28
Walton-on-Thames
West Molesey
East Molesey
WOKINGHAM
Bracknell
Easthampstead
Wokingham
Bracknell Forest
Crowthorne
Bagshot
Windlesham
Lightwater
Chobham
Lyne
CHERTSEY
Addlestone
Ottershaw
WEYBRIDGE
Hersham
Esher
Claygate
Woodham
New Haw
Byfleet
Whiteley Village
Cobham
Oxshott
Sandhurst
CAMBERLEY
Yateley
Frimley
Hawley
Blackwater
Knaphill
Horsell
WOKING
Pyrford
Wisley
Ripley
Stoke D'Abernon
Downside
Leatherhead Common
Fetcham
Fleet
FARNBOROUGH
Mytchett
Pirbright
Worplesdon
Send
Burntcommon
Ockham
East Horsley
West Horsley
Effingham
Great Bookham
Church Crookham
ALDERSHOT
Ash
Ash Vale
Normandy
Stoughton
Guildford
Merrow
Burpham
West Clandon
East Clandon
Westcott
Farnham
Shalford
Chilworth
Gomshall
Shere
Abinger Hammer
Albury
Compton
Puttenham
The Sands
Milford
Godalming
Elstead
Tilford
Farncombe
Bramley
Wonersh
Shamley Green
Peaslake
Holmbury St Mary
Hurt Wood
Hindhead
Grayshott
Bordon
Haslemere
Liphook
Chiddingfold
Dunsfold
Cranleigh
Ewhurst
Alfold
Rudgwick
Loxwood
Plaistow
Northchapel
Fernhurst
Wisborough Green
Kirdford
Billingshurst
Rake
Liss
Milland
Henley
SURREY HILLS
16

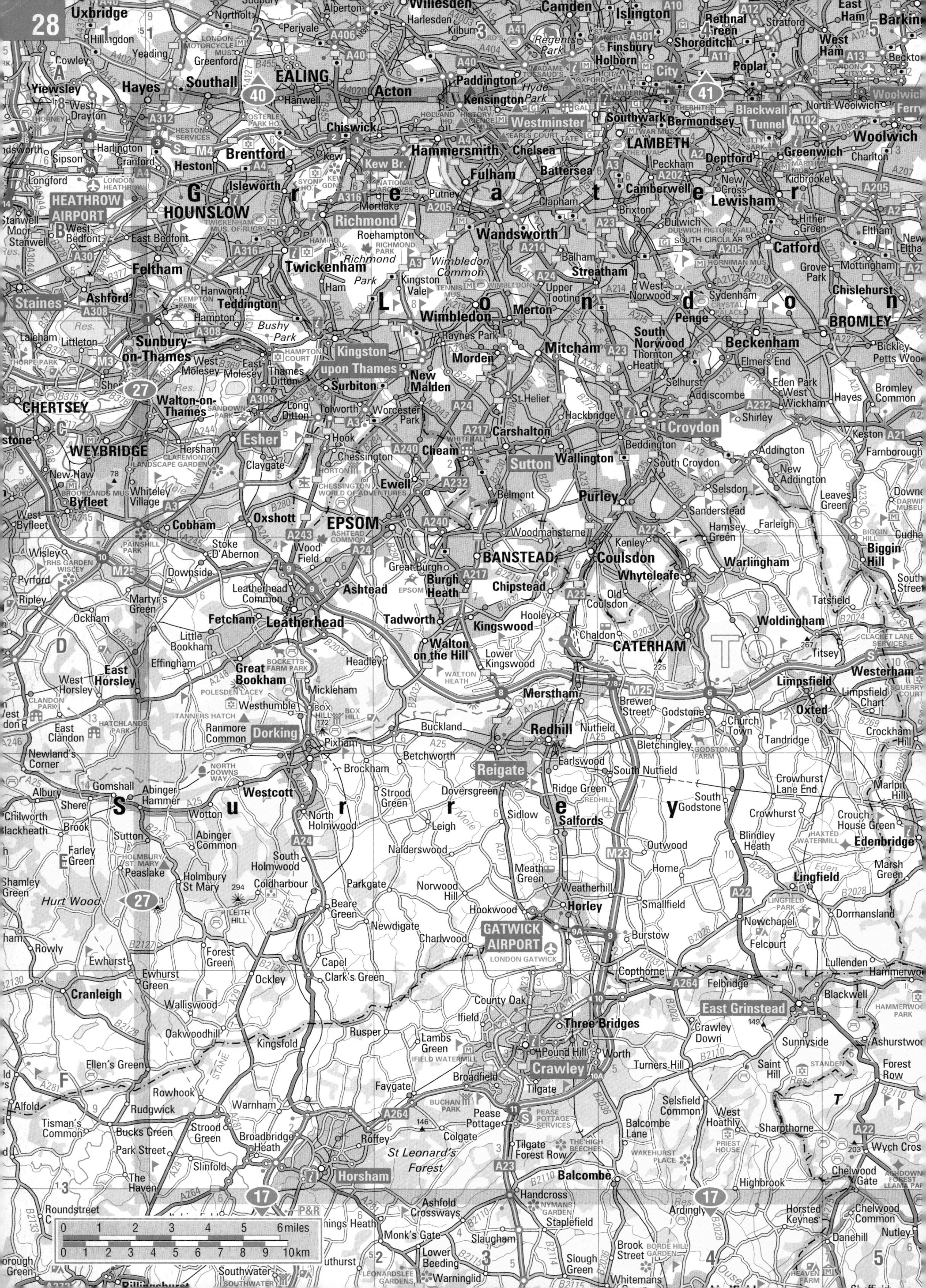

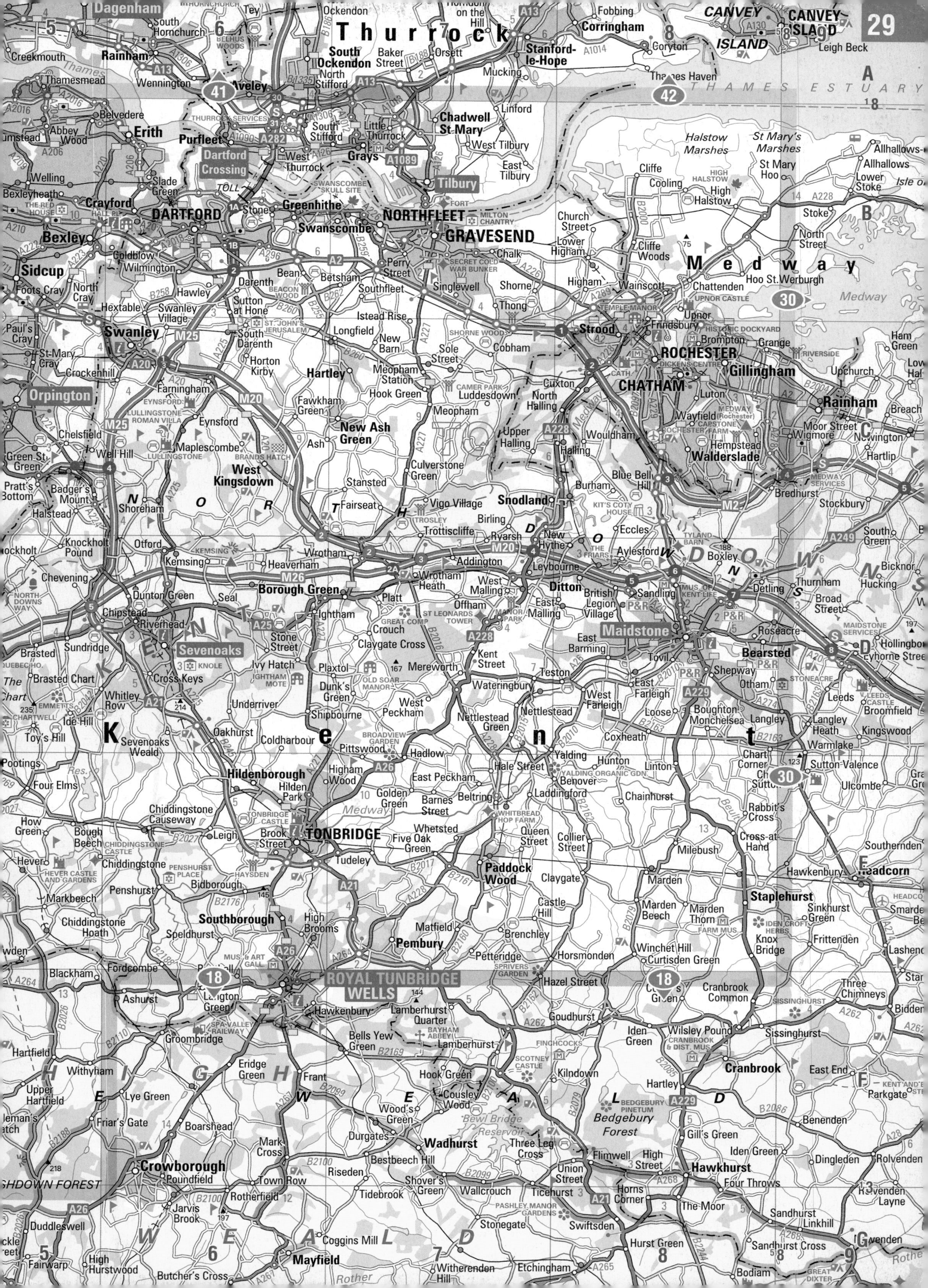

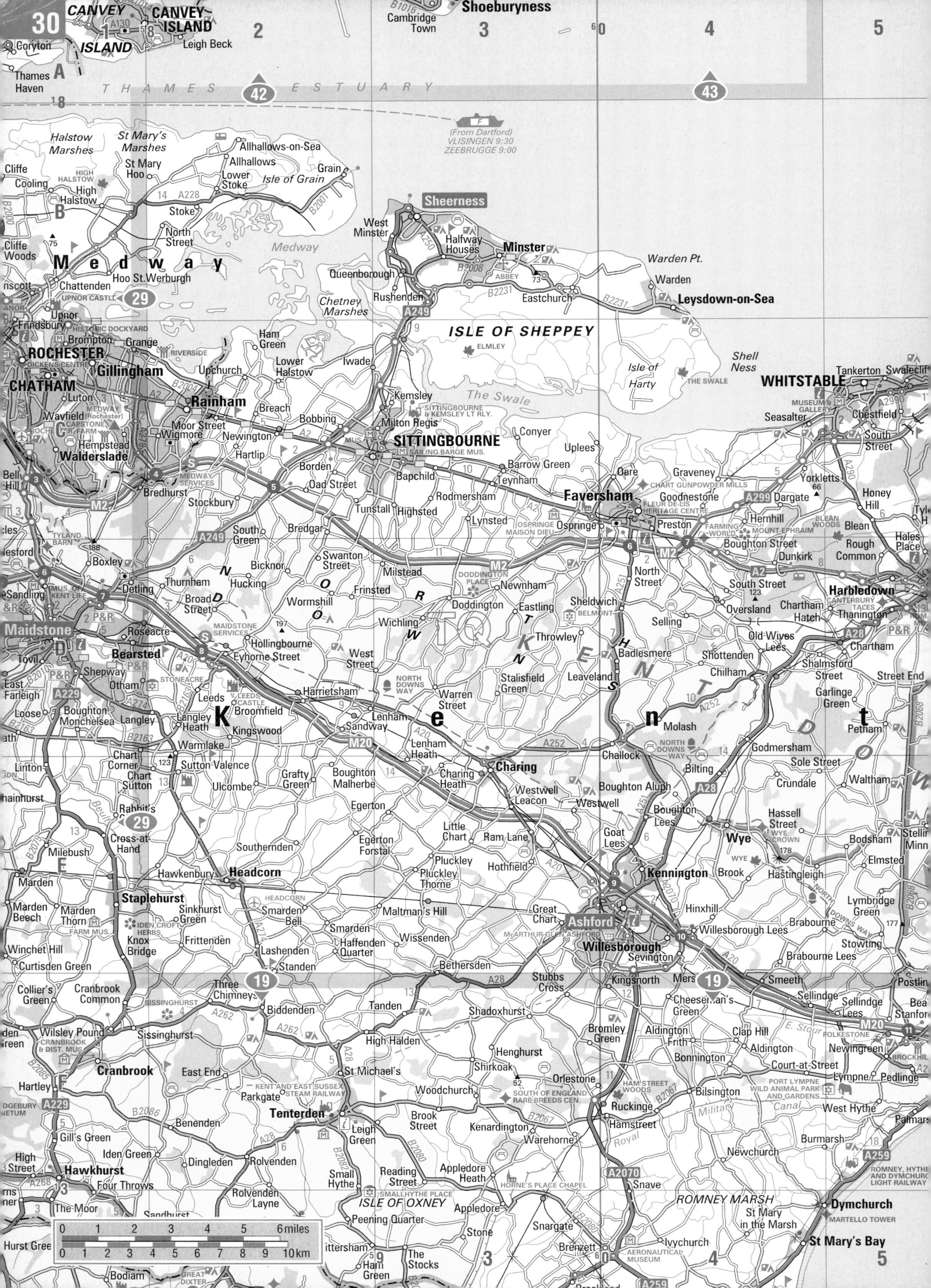
CANVEY ISLAND
CANVEY ISLAND
Coryton
Thames Haven
Leigh Beck
Shoeburyness
Cambridge Town
THAMES ESTUARY
42
43
(From Dartford)
VLISINGEN 9:30
ZEEBRUGGE 9:00
Halstow Marshes
St Mary's Marshes
Allhallows-on-Sea
Allhallows
St Mary Hoo
Grain
Lower Stoke
Isle of Grain
Cliffe
Cooling
HIGH HALSTOW
High Halstow
Stoke
North Street
Medway
Cliffe Woods
Medway
Chattenden
Hoo St.Werburgh
UPNOR CASTLE
29
Upnor
Frindsbury
HISTORIC DOCKYARD
Brompton
Grange
ROCHESTER
DICKENS CENTRE
Gillingham
RIVERSIDE
CHATHAM
Luton
Wayfield
CAPSTONE FARM
Hempstead
Walderslade
Upchurch
Rainham
Moor Street
Wigmore
Newington
Hartlip
Bredhurst
MEDWAY SERVICES
Stockbury
Sheerness
West Minster
Halfway Houses
Minster
ABBEY
Queenborough
Rushenden
Chetney Marshes
Eastchurch
Warden Pt.
Warden
Leysdown-on-Sea
ISLE OF SHEPPEY
ELMLEY
Ham Green
Lower Halstow
Iwade
Kemsley
The Swale
Isle of Harty
THE SWALE
Shell Ness
Breach
Bobbing
SITTINGBOURNE & KEMSLEY LT RLY.
Milton Regis
SITTINGBOURNE
SAILING BARGE MUS.
Conyer
Uplees
Borden
Oad Street
Bapchild
Barrow Green
Teynham
Oare
Faversham
CHART GUNPOWDER MILLS
FLEUR DE LIS HERITAGE CENTRE
Graveney
Goodnestone
Dargate
Tunstall
Highsted
Rodmersham
Lynsted
OSPRINGE MAISON DIEU
Ospringe
Preston
FARMING WORLD
MOUNT EPHRAIM
Hernhill
Tankerton
Swalecliffe
WHITSTABLE
MUSEUM & GALLERY
Seasalter
Chestfield
South Street
Yorkletts
Honey Hill
Blean
BLEAN WOODS
Rough Common
Hales Place
Boughton Street
Dunkirk
Harbledown
CANTERBURY TALES
TYLAND BARN
Boxley
South Green
Bredgar
Bicknor
Swanton Street
Milstead
DODDINGTON PLACE
Newnham
Doddington
North Street
Sheldwich
BELMONT
Eastling
South Street
Oversland
Selling
Chartham Hatch
Thanington
Thurnham
Detling
Hucking
Sandling
MUS. OF KENT LIFE
Broad Street
Wormshill
Frinsted
Wichling
Maidstone
Roseacre
MAIDSTONE SERVICES
Hollingbourne
Bearsted
Eyhorne Street
West Street
Throwley
Badlesmere
Shottenden
Old Wives Lees
Chartham
Tovil
Shepway
Otham
STONEACRE
East Farleigh
Loose
Leeds
LEEDS CASTLE
Broomfield
Harrietsham
NORTH DOWNS WAY
Warren Street
Stalisfield Green
Leaveland
Chilham
Shalmsford Street
Street End
Garlinge Green
Boughton Monchelsea
Langley
Langley Heath
Kingswood
Lenham
Sandway
Molash
Petham
Kent
NORTH DOWNS
Warmlake
Chart Corner
Chart Sutton
Sutton Valence
Lenham Heath
Charing
Challock
NORTH DOWNS WAY
Godmersham
Sole Street
Linton
Ulcombe
Grafty Green
Boughton Malherbe
Charing Heath
Westwell Leacon
Westwell
Boughton Aluph
Bilting
Crundale
Waltham
Rabbit's Cross
Egerton
Boughton Lees
Hassell Street
WYE CROWN
Milebush
Cross-at-Hand
Southernden
Egerton Forstal
Little Chart
Ram Lane
Goat Lees
Wye
Bodsham
Elmsted
Marden
Hawkenbury
Headcorn
Pluckley
Pluckley Thorne
Hothfield
Kennington
Brook
Hastingleigh
Staplehurst
Sinkhurst Green
HEADCORN
Smarden Bell
Maltman's Hill
Great Chart
Ashford
Hinxhill
Lymbridge Green
Marden Beech
Marden Thorn
FARM MUS.
IDEN CROFT HERBS
Smarden
Haffenden Quarter
Wissenden
McARTHUR GLEN ASHFORD
Willesborough
Willesborough Lees
Brabourne
Stowting
Knox Bridge
Frittenden
Lashenden
Sevington
Brabourne Lees
Winchet Hill
Curtisden Green
Standen
Bethersden
Stubbs Cross
Kingsnorth
Mersham
Smeeth
Postling
Collier's Green
Cranbrook Common
Three Chimneys
19
SISSINGHURST
Biddenden
Tanden
Shadoxhurst
Cheeseman's Green
Sellindge
Sellindge Lees
Stanford
Wilsley Pound
CRANBROOK & DIST. MUS.
Sissinghurst
High Halden
Bromley Green
Aldington Frith
Clap Hill
Aldington
FOLKESTONE
Newingreen
Henghurst
Bonnington
Court-at-Street
Cranbrook
East End
St Michael's
Shirkoak
Orlestone
Lympne
Pedlinge
Hartley
KENT AND EAST SUSSEX STEAM RAILWAY
Parkgate
Woodchurch
SOUTH OF ENGLAND RARE BREEDS CEN.
HAM STREET WOODS
Ruckinge
Bilsington
PORT LYMPNE WILD ANIMAL PARK AND GARDENS
West Hythe
Royal Military Canal
Tenterden
Benenden
Leigh Green
Brook Street
Kenardington
Warehorne
Hamstreet
Gill's Green
Iden Green
Dingleden
Rolvenden
Newchurch
Burmarsh
High Street
Hawkhurst
Four Throws
Small Hythe
Reading Street
Appledore Heath
HORNE'S PLACE CHAPEL
Snave
ROMNEY, HYTHE AND DYMCHURCH LIGHT RAILWAY
The Moor
Rolvenden Layne
SMALLHYTHE PLACE
ISLE OF OXNEY
Appledore
ROMNEY MARSH
Dymchurch
MARTELLO TOWER
Sandhurst
Peening Quarter
Snargate
St Mary in the Marsh
Hurst Green
Wittersham
Stone
Brenzett
AERONAUTICAL MUSEUM
Ivychurch
St Mary's Bay
Ham Green
The Stocks
Bodiam
GREAT DIXTER
0 1 2 3 4 5 6 miles
0 1 2 3 4 5 6 7 8 9 10 km

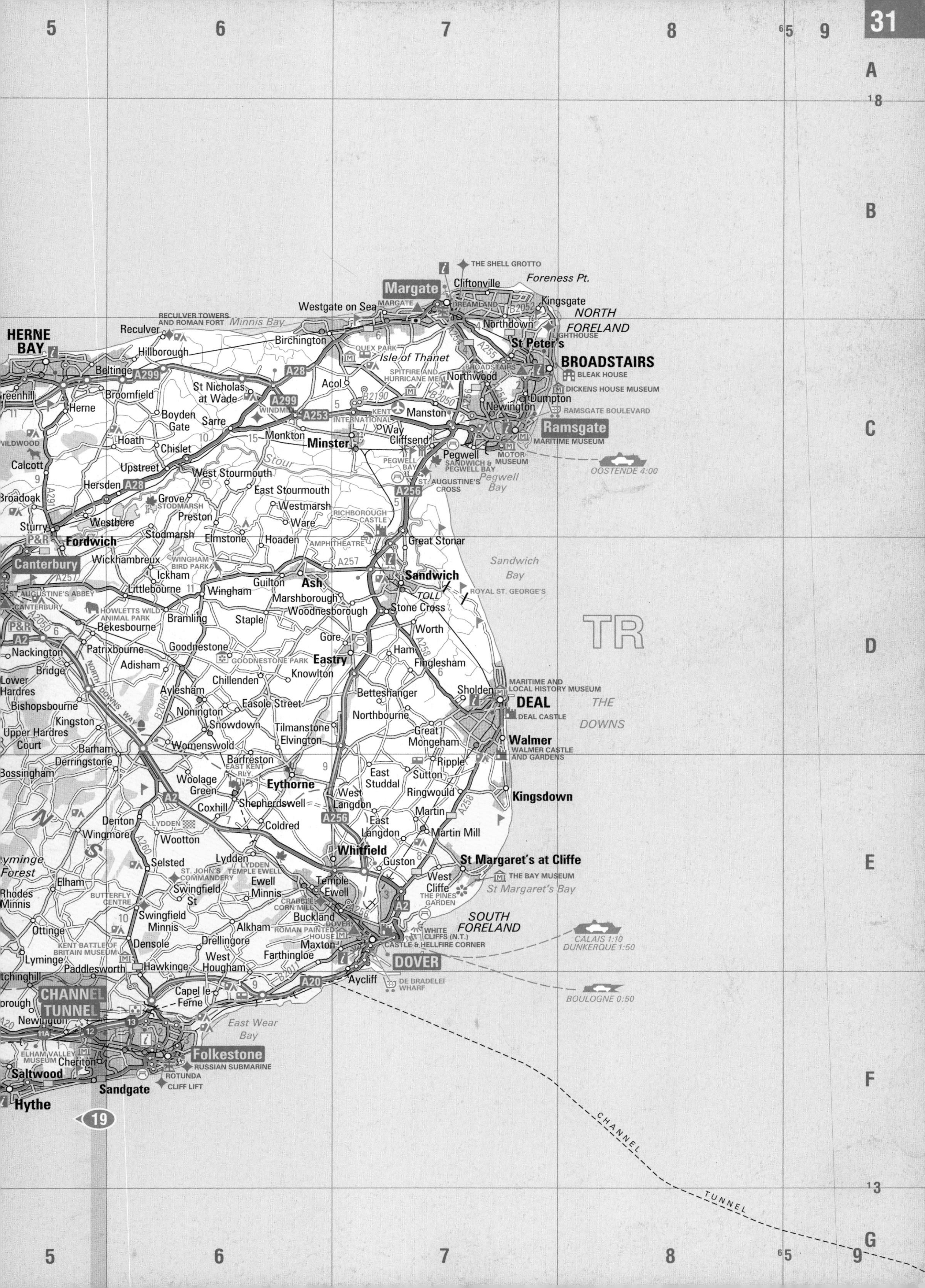
31
5
6
7
8
9
A
B
C
D
E
F
G
THE SHELL GROTTO
Foreness Pt.
Margate
Cliftonville
Kingsgate
NORTH
FORELAND
LIGHTHOUSE
Westgate on Sea
MARGATE
DREAMLAND
B2052
Northdown
RECULVER TOWERS
AND ROMAN FORT
Minnis Bay
Reculver
HERNE
BAY
Birchington
St Peter's
Hillborough
QUEX PARK
Isle of Thanet
BROADSTAIRS
Beltinge
A299
A28
SPITFIRE AND
HURRICANE MEM.
Northwood
BLEAK HOUSE
Greenhill
Broomfield
St Nicholas
at Wade
Acol
B2190
DICKENS HOUSE MUSEUM
Herne
Boyden
Gate
Sarre
A299
WINDMILL
A253
KENT
INTERNATIONAL
Manston
B2050
Newington
Dumpton
RAMSGATE BOULEVARD
WILDWOOD
Hoath
Chislet
Monkton
Minster
Way
Cliffsend
Ramsgate
MARITIME MUSEUM
Calcott
Upstreet
Stour
Pegwell
PEGWELL
BAY
MOTOR
MUSEUM
SANDWICH &
PEGWELL BAY
OOSTENDE 4:00
West Stourmouth
Hersden
A28
ST. AUGUSTINE'S
CROSS
Pegwell
Bay
East Stourmouth
A256
Broadoak
Grove
STODMARSH
Westmarsh
Preston
Ware
RICHBOROUGH
CASTLE
Sturry
Westbere
Fordwich
Stodmarsh
Elmstone
Hoaden
AMPHITHEATRE
Great Stonar
Canterbury
Wickhambreux
WINGHAM
BIRD PARK
A257
Sandwich
Bay
Ickham
Guilton
Ash
Sandwich
A257
Littlebourne
Wingham
TOLL
ROYAL ST. GEORGE'S
ST. AUGUSTINE'S ABBEY
CANTERBURY
Marshborough
Woodnesborough
Stone Cross
HOWLETTS WILD
ANIMAL PARK
Bramling
Staple
Worth
TR
Bekesbourne
A2050
A2
Gore
Nackington
Patrixbourne
Goodnestone
Ham
A258
GOODNESTONE PARK
Eastry
Finglesham
Adisham
Bridge
NORTH DOWNS WAY
Knowlton
Lower
Hardres
Chillenden
MARITIME AND
LOCAL HISTORY MUSEUM
Betteshanger
Sholden
THE
Bishopsbourne
Aylesham
B2046
Easole Street
DEAL
Nonington
Northbourne
DEAL CASTLE
DOWNS
Kingston
Snowdown
Tilmanstone
Upper Hardres
Court
Great
Mongeham
Walmer
Barham
Womenswold
Elvington
WALMER CASTLE
AND GARDENS
Derringstone
Barfreston
EAST KENT
RLY.
Ripple
Bossingham
Woolage
Green
Eythorne
East
Studdal
Sutton
Ringwould
Kingsdown
A2
Coxhill
Shepherdswell
West
Langdon
Martin
A256
A258
Denton
LYDDEN
Coldred
East
Langdon
Wingmore
Wootton
Martin Mill
A260
Whitfield
Lyminge
Forest
Selsted
Lydden
ST. JOHN'S
COMMANDERY
LYDDEN
TEMPLE EWELL
Guston
St Margaret's at Cliffe
Temple
Ewell
West
Cliffe
THE BAY MUSEUM
Elham
Swingfield
St
Ewell
Minnis
St Margaret's Bay
Rhodes
Minnis
BUTTERFLY
CENTRE
CRABBLE
CORN MILL
A2
THE PINES
GARDEN
Swingfield
Minnis
Buckland
DOVER
SOUTH
FORELAND
Ottinge
Alkham
ROMAN PAINTED
HOUSE
WHITE
CLIFFS (N.T.)
CALAIS 1:10
DUNKERQUE 1:50
KENT BATTLE OF
BRITAIN MUSEUM
Densole
Drellingore
Maxton
CASTLE & HELLFIRE CORNER
Lyminge
Paddlesworth
Hawkinge
West
Hougham
Farthingloe
DOVER
Etchinghill
B2011
A20
Aycliff
DE BRADELEI
WHARF
CHANNEL
TUNNEL
Capel le
Ferne
BOULOGNE 0:50
Newington
East Wear
Bay
ELHAM VALLEY
MUSEUM
Cheriton
Folkestone
RUSSIAN SUBMARINE
Saltwood
ROTUNDA
Sandgate
CLIFF LIFT
Hythe
19
CHANNEL
TUNNEL

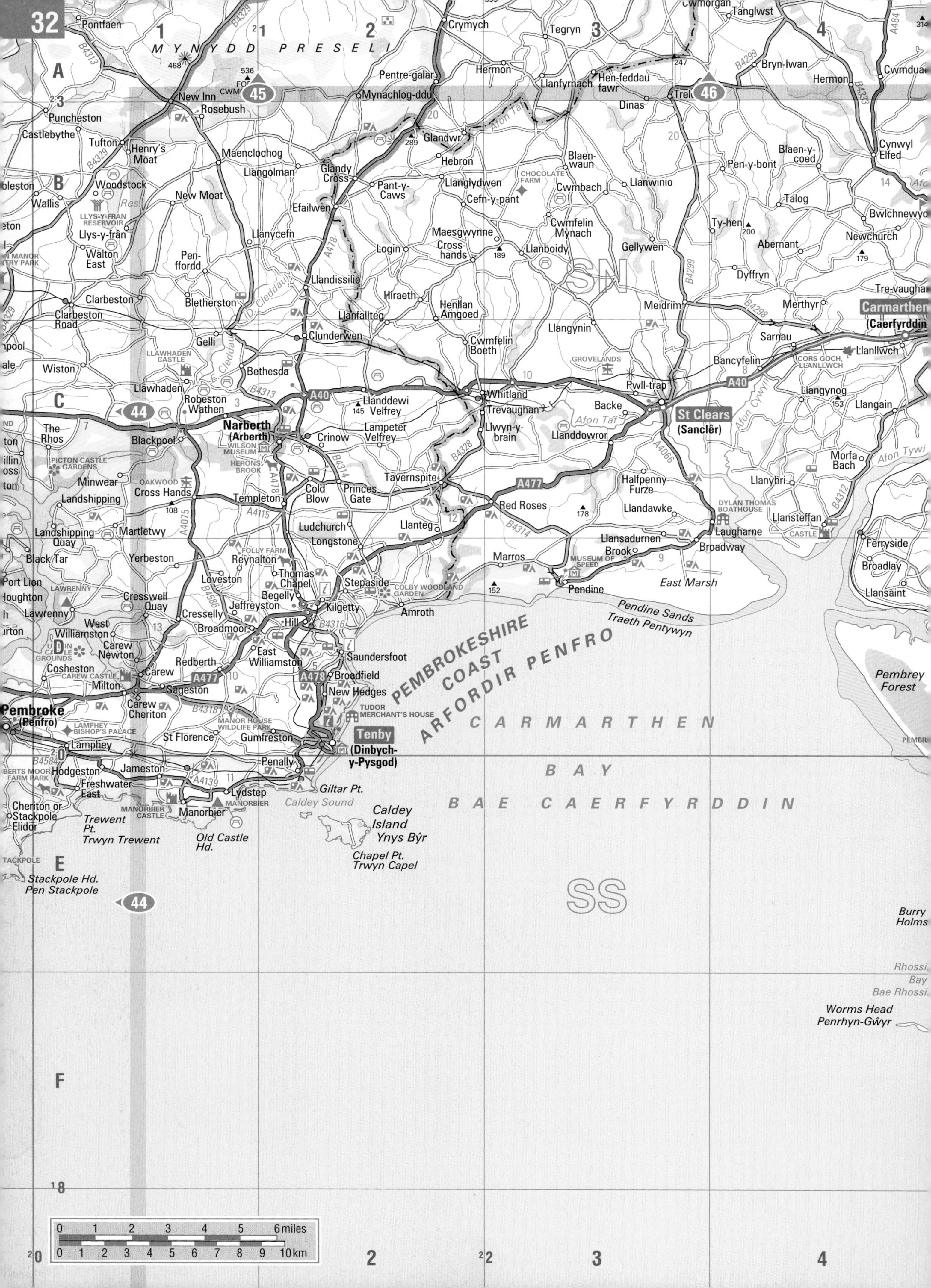
MYNYDD PRESELI
Crymych
Tegryn
Pontfaen
New Inn
Rosebush
Puncheston
Castlebythe
Tufton
Henry's Moat
Maenclochog
Llangolman
Glandy Cross
Mynachlog-ddu
Pentre-galar
Hermon
Llanfyrnach
Hen-feddau fawr
Dinas
Glandwr
Hebron
Llanglydwen
Cefn-y-pant
Cwmbach
Blaen-waun
Llanwinio
Pant-y-Caws
Efailwen
Woodstock
Wallis
New Moat
Llys-y-frân
Walton East
Llanycefn
Pen-ffordd
Bletherston
Clarbeston
Clarbeston Road
Llandissilio
Login
Maesgwynne
Cross-hands
Llanboidy
Cwmfelin Mynach
Gellywen
Hiraeth
Henllan Amgoed
Llanfallteg
Clunderwen
Gelli
Cwmfelin Boeth
Llangynin
Meidrim
Wiston
Bethesda
Llawhaden
Robeston Wathen
Narberth (Arberth)
Llanddewi Velfrey
Whitland
Trevaughan
Llwyn-y-brain
Lampeter Velfrey
Crinow
Blackpool
The Rhos
Minwear
Cross Hands
Landshipping
Templeton
Cold Blow
Princes Gate
Tavernspite
Red Roses
Landshipping Quay
Martletwy
Black Tar
Yerbeston
Reynalton
Loveston
Ludchurch
Longstone
Llanteg
Marros
Pendine
Thomas Chapel
Begelly
Jeffreyston
Stepaside
Kilgetty
Amroth
Cresswell Quay
Cresselly
Broadmoor
Hill
West Williamston
Carew Newton
Lawrenny
Port Lion
Cosheston
Redberth
East Williamston
Saundersfoot
Milton
Carew
Sageston
Broadfield
New Hedges
Pembroke (Penfro)
Carew Cheriton
Lamphey
St Florence
Gumfreston
Tenby (Dinbych-y-Pysgod)
Hodgeston
Jameston
Penally
Freshwater East
Lydstep
Manorbier
Cheriton or Stackpole Elidor
Trewent Pt. Trwyn Trewent
Old Castle Hd.
Gilltar Pt.
Caldey Sound
Caldey Island Ynys Bŷr
Chapel Pt. Trwyn Capel
Stackpole Hd. Pen Stackpole
PEMBROKESHIRE COAST ARFORDIR PENFRO
CARMARTHEN BAY
BAE CAERFYRDDIN
SN
SS
Tanglwst
Bryn-Iwan
Hermon
Cwmduad
Cynwyl Elfed
Blaen-y-coed
Pen-y-bont
Talog
Bwlchnewydd
Ty-hen
Abernant
Newchurch
Dyffryn
Tre-vaughan
Merthyr
Carmarthen (Caerfyrddin)
Sarnau
Llanllwch
Bancyfelin
Pwll-trap
St Clears (Sanclêr)
Backe
Llanddowror
Llangynog
Llangain
Morfa Bach
Llanybri
Halfpenny Furze
Llandawke
Llansteffan
Laugharne
Llansadurnen
Brook
Broadway
East Marsh
Pendine Sands Traeth Pentywyn
Ferryside
Broadlay
Llansaint
Pembrey Forest
Burry Holms
Rhossili Bay Bae Rhossili
Worms Head Penrhyn-Gŵyr
A40
A477
A478
A4066
B4313
B4329
B4314
B4328
B4299
B4298
B4333
B4312
B4316
B4318
B4586
B4585
A4075
A4115
A4139
A484
45
46
44
0 1 2 3 4 5 6 miles
0 1 2 3 4 5 6 7 8 9 10 km

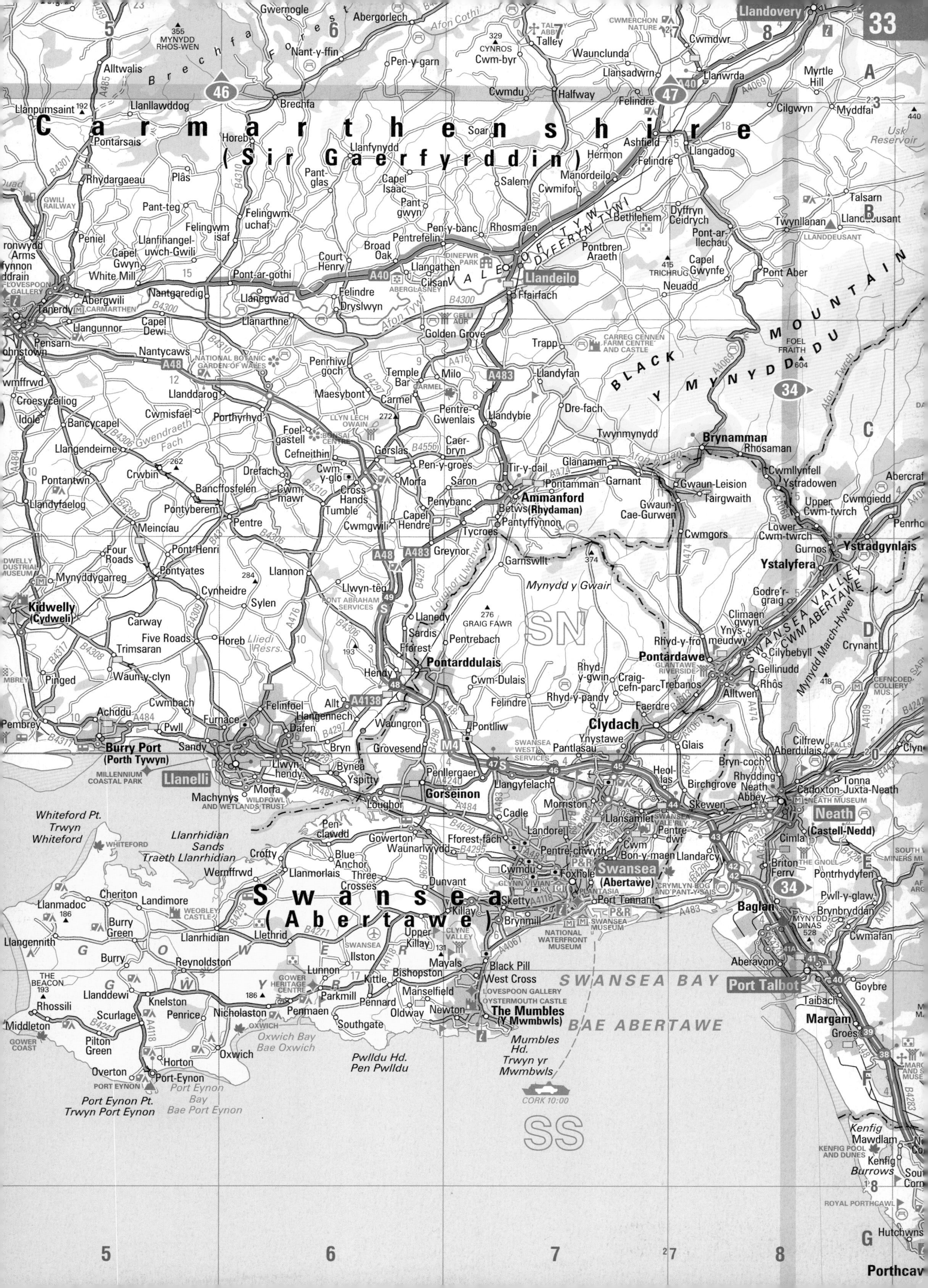
Llandovery
Carmarthenshire
(Sir Gaerfyrddin)
Swansea
(Abertawe)
Brechfa Forest
Gwernogle
Abergorlech
Afon Cothi
Talley
Cwmdwr
Nant-y-ffin
Pen-y-garn
Cynros
Cwm-byr
Wauncluda
Llansadwrn
Llanwrda
Myrtle Hill
Mynydd Rhos-Wen
Alltwalis
Cwmdu
Halfway
Felindre
Cilgwyn
Myddfai
Usk Reservoir
Llanpumsaint
Llanllawddog
Brechfa
Pontarsais
Horeb
Soar
Hermon
Ashfield
Llangadog
Llanfynydd
Rhydargaeau
Plâs
Pant-glas
Capel Isaac
Salem
Manordeilo
Cwmifor
Pant-teg
Felingwm uchaf
Felingwm isaf
Pant gwyn
Pen-y-banc
Rhosmaen
Bethlehem
Dyffryn Ceidrych
Talsarn
Twynllanan
Llanddeusant
Peniel
Llanfihangel-uwch-Gwili
Capel Gwyn
Pentrefelin
Broad Oak
Court Henry
Vale of Tywi
Dyffryn Tywi
Pontbren Araeth
Pont-ar-llechau
Dinefwr Park
Llangathen
Cilsan
Llandeilo
Trichrug
Capel Gwynfe
Pont Aber
White Mill
Pont-ar-gothi
Abergwili
Nantgaredig
Llanegwad
Felindre
Dryslwyn
Aberglasney
Ffairfach
Neuadd
Black Mountain
Y Mynydd Du
Tanerdy
Carmarthen
Llangunnor
Capel Dewi
Llanarthne
Afon Tywi
Gelli Aur
Golden Grove
Trapp
Carreg Cennen Farm Centre and Castle
Foel Fraith
Pensarn
Johnstown
Nantycaws
National Botanic Garden of Wales
Penrhiw-goch
Temple Bar
Milo
Llandyfan
Llanddarog
Maesybont
Carmel
Croesyceiliog
Idole
Bancycapel
Cwmisfael
Porthyrhyd
Foel-gastell
Llyn Llech Owain
Pentre-Gwenlais
Llandybie
Dre-fach
Gwendraeth Fach
Llangendeirne
Cefneithin
Gorslas
Caer-bryn
Twynmynydd
Brynamman
Rhosaman
Afon Aman
Crwbin
Drefach
Cwm-y-glo
Pen-y-groes
Tir-y-dail
Glanaman
Pontamman
Garnant
Cwmllynfell
Ystradowen
Abercraf
Pontantwn
Bancffosfelen
Cwm-mawr
Cross Hands
Morfa
Saron
Ammanford (Rhydaman)
Gwaun-Leision
Tairgwaith
Llandyfaelog
Pontyberem
Tumble
Penybanc
Betws
Pantyffynnon
Gwaun-Cae-Gurwen
Upper Cwm-twrch
Cwmgiedd
Meinciau
Pentre
Cwmgwili
Capel Hendre
Tycroes
Cwmgors
Lower Cwm-twrch
Gurnos
Ystradgynlais
Pont-Henri
Four Roads
Greynor
Garnswllt
Ystalyfera
Mynyddygarreg
Pontyates
Llannon
Llwyn-teg
Pont Abraham Services
Mynydd y Gwair
Kidwelly (Cydweli)
Cynheidre
Sylen
Loughor (Llwchwr)
Llanedy
Graig Fawr
SN
Godre'r-graig
Swansea Valley
Cwm Abertawe
Carway
Sardis
Pentrebach
Climaen gwyn
Ynys-meudwy
Five Roads
Trimsaran
Horeb
Lliedi Resrs.
Fforest
Pontarddulais
Rhyd-y-fro
Pontardawe
Glantawe Riverside
Cilybebyll
Crynant
Mynydd March-Hywel
Pinged
Waun-y-clyn
Hendy
Cwm-Dulais
Rhyd-y-gwin
Craig-cefn-parc
Trebanos
Gellinudd
Rhôs
Alltwen
Cefncoed Colliery Mus.
Cwmbach
Felinfoel
Allt
Llangennech
Felindre
Rhyd-y-pandy
Faerdre
Achddu
Pembrey
Pwll
Furnace
Dafen
Waungron
Pontlliw
Clydach
Burry Port (Porth Tywyn)
Sandy
Bryn
Grovesend
Swansea West Services
Pantlasau
Ynystawe
Glais
Cilfrew
Aberdulais
Millennium Coastal Park
Llanelli
Llwyn-hendy
Bynea
Yspitty
Penllergaer
Llangyfelach
Heol-las
Bryn-coch
Rhydding
Tonna
Machynys
Morfa
Wildfowl and Wetlands Trust
Loughor
Gorseinon
Morriston
Birchgrove
Neath Abbey
Cadoxton-Juxta-Neath
Neath Museum
Whiteford Pt.
Trwyn Whiteford
Whiteford
Pen-clawdd
Cadle
Llansamlet
Skewen
Neath (Castell-Nedd)
Llanrhidian Sands
Traeth Llanrhidian
Gowerton
Waunarlwydd
Fforest-fach
Landore
Pentre-dwr
Cimla
Crofty
Blue Anchor
Pentre-chwyth
Cwm
Bon-y-maen
Llandarcy
Briton Ferry
The Gnoll
Pontrhydyfen
Wernffrwd
Llanmorlais
Three Crosses
Cwmdu
Foxhole
Swansea (Abertawe)
Crymlyn Bog and Pant-y-Sais
Dunvant
Glynn Vivian
Plantasia
Port Tennant
Pwll-y-glaw
Cheriton
Llanmadoc
Landimore
Weobley Castle
Sketty
Baglan
Brynbryddan
Burry Green
Llanrhidian
Llethrid
Upper Killay
Clyne Valley
Brynmill
Swansea Museum
National Waterfront Museum
Mynydd Dinas
Cwmafan
Llangennith
Gower
Burry
Swansea
Killay
Ilston
Mayals
Black Pill
Aberavon
The Beacon
Reynoldston
Gower Heritage Centre
Lunnon
Kittle
Bishopston
West Cross
Swansea Bay
Port Talbot
Goybre
Rhossili
Llanddewi
Knelston
Parkmill
Mansefield
Lovespoon Gallery
Oystermouth Castle
Taibach
Middleton
Scurlage
Penrice
Nicholaston
Penmaen
Pennard
Oldway
Newton
The Mumbles (Y Mwmbwls)
Margam
Bae Abertawe
Gower Coast
Pilton Green
Oxwich
Southgate
Groes
Oxwich Bay
Bae Oxwich
Mumbles Hd.
Trwyn yr Mwmbwls
Horton
Pwlldu Hd.
Pen Pwlldu
Overton
Port-Eynon
Port Eynon
Port Eynon Bay
Bae Port Eynon
Port Eynon Pt.
Trwyn Port Eynon
Cork 10:00
SS
Kenfig
Mawdlam
Kenfig Pool and Dunes
Kenfig Burrows
Royal Porthcawl
Hutchwns
Porthcawl
A40
A48
A476
A483
A484
A485
A474
A4069
A4067
A4118
A4138
A4240
A4109
M4
B4300
B4301
B4310
B4306
B4309
B4317
B4308
B4311
B4297
B4296
B4295
B4271
B4247
B4556
B4620
B4290
B4283
46
47
34
5
6
7
8
A
B
C
D
E
F
G

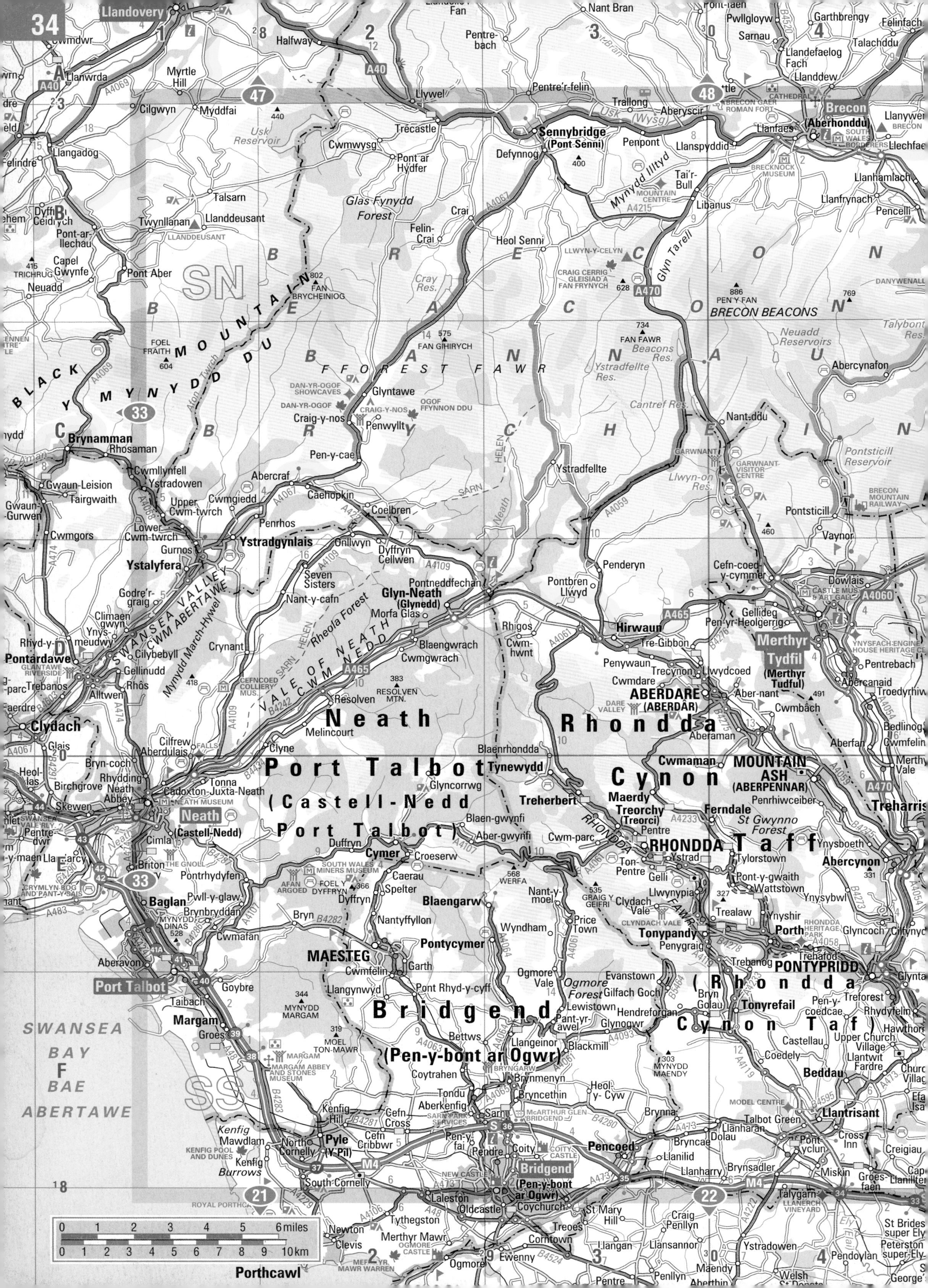
Llandovery
Cwmdwr
Llanwrda
Myrtle Hill
Halfway
Pentre-bach
Nant Bran
Pwllgloyw
Sarnau
Garthbrengy
Felinfach
Talachddu
Llandefaelog Fach
Llanddew
Llywel
Pentre'r-felin
Trallong
Aberyscir
Brecon
(Aberhonddu)
Cilgwyn
Myddfai
Usk Reservoir
Trecastle
Sennybridge
(Pont Senni)
Penpont
Llanspyddid
Llanfaes
Llanywern
Llechfaen
Llangadog
Cwmwysg
Pont ar Hydfer
Defynnog
Brecknock Museum
Tai'r-Bull
Llanhamlach
Llanfrynach
Pencelli
Mynydd Illtyd
Mountain Centre
Libanus
Talsarn
Glas Fynydd Forest
Crai
Felin-Crai
Heol Senni
Twynllanan
Llanddeusant
Pont-ar-llechau
Capel Gwynfe
Neuadd
Pont Aber
Cray Res.
Glyn Tarell
Llwyn-y-celyn
Craig Cerrig Gleisiad a Fan Frynych
Pen y Fan
Brecon Beacons
Fan Brycheiniog
Fan Gihirych
Fan Fawr
Beacons Res.
Ystradfellte Res.
Neuadd Reservoirs
Abercynafon
Talybont Res.
Foel Fraith
Black Mountain
Mynydd Du
Fforest Fawr
Brecon Beacons
Dan-yr-Ogof Showcaves
Glyntawe
Craig-y-nos
Ogof Ffynnon Ddu
Penwyllt
Cantref Res.
Nant-ddu
Brynamman
Rhosaman
Pen-y-cae
Garwnant Visitor Centre
Llwyn-on Res.
Pontsticill Reservoir
Ystradfellte
Cwmllynfell
Gwaun-Leision
Tairgwaith
Ystradowen
Abercraf
Caehopkin
Gwaun-Cae-Gurwen
Upper Cwm-twrch
Cwmgiedd
Coelbren
Brecon Mountain Railway
Pontsticill
Lower Cwm-twrch
Cwmgors
Penrhos
Vaynor
Gurnos
Ystradgynlais
Onllwyn
Dyffryn Cellwen
Ystalyfera
Seven Sisters
Penderyn
Cefn-coed-y-cymmer
Dowlais
Pontbren Llwyd
Pontneddfechan
Godre'r-graig
Nant-y-cafn
Glyn-Neath
(Glynedd)
Rheola Forest
Morfa Glas
Swansea Valley
Cwm Abertawe
Climaen gwyn
Ynys-meudwy
Rhigos
Hirwaun
Gellideg
Pen-yr-Heolgerrig
Merthyr Tydfil
(Merthyr Tudful)
Rhyd-y-fro
Pontardawe
Crynant
Mynydd March-Hywel
Vale of Neath
Cwm Nedd
Blaengwrach
Cwmgwrach
Cwm-hwnt
Tre-Gibbon
Penywaun
Trecynon
Llwydcoed
Pentrebach
Abercanaid
Troedyrhiw
Cilybebyll
Gellinudd
Trebanos
Alltwen
Rhôs
Resolven
Cwmdare
Aberdare
(Aberdâr)
Aber-nant
Cwmbach
Clydach
Neath
Melincourt
Rhondda
Aberaman
Bedlinog
Aberfan
Glais
Cilfrew
Aberdulais
Clyne
Blaenrhondda
Tynewydd
Cwmaman
Mountain Ash
(Aberpennar)
Merthyr Vale
Bryn-coch
Heol-las
Rhydding
Birchgrove
Neath Abbey
Tonna
Cadoxton-Juxta-Neath
Port Talbot
(Castell-Nedd Port Talbot)
Glyncorrwg
Cynon
Maerdy
Penrhiwceiber
Treharris
Skewen
Neath Museum
Neath
(Castell-Nedd)
Treherbert
Treorchy
(Treorci)
Ferndale
St Gwynno Forest
Blaen-gwynfi
Pentre
Cimla
Aber-gwynfi
Cwm-parc
Rhondda
Ynysboeth
Abercynon
Taf
Duffryn
Cymer
Croeserw
Ystrad
Tylorstown
Llansamlet
Briton Ferry
The Gnoll
Pontrhydyfen
South Wales Miners Museum
Caerau
Ton-Pentre
Gelli
Pont-y-gwaith
Wattstown
Crymlyn Bog and Pant-y-Sais
Afan Argoed
Foel y Dyffryn
Spelter
Werfa
Nant-y-moel
Graig y Geifri
Llwynypia
Baglan
Pwll-y-glaw
Dyffryn
Blaengarw
Clydach Vale
Trealaw
Ynysybwl
Brynbryddan
Nantyffyllon
Ynyshir
Mynydd Dinas
Bryn
Price Town
Tonypandy
Porth
Rhondda Heritage Park
Glyncoch
Cilfynydd
Cwmafan
Wyndham
Penygraig
Maesteg
Pontycymer
Trebanog
Pontypridd
Aberavon
Garth
Trehafod
Cwmfelin
Ogmore Vale
Port Talbot
Goybre
Llangynwyd
Pont Rhyd-y-cyff
Ogmore Forest
Evanstown
Gilfach Goch
Bryn Golau
Tonyrefail
Treforest
Pen-y-coedcae
Rhydyfelin
Taibach
Mynydd Margam
Bridgend
Lewistown
Hendreforgan
Pant-yr-awel
Glynogwr
Margam
Swansea Bay
Bae Abertawe
Groes
Moel Ton-Mawr
Bettws
Llangeinor
Blackmill
Hawthorn
Castellau
Upper Church Village
Llantwit Fardre
Margam Abbey and Stones Museum
(Pen-y-bont ar Ogwr)
Mynydd Maendy
Coedely
Coytrahen
Brynmenyn
Beddau
Bryncethin
Heol-y-Cyw
Tondu
Aberkenfig
Kenfig Hill
Cefn Cross
Sarn
Sarn Park Services
McArthur Glen Bridgend
Brynna
Model Centre
Llantrisant
Talbot Green
Llanharan
Kenfig
Mawdlam
North Cornelly
Pyle
(Y Pîl)
Cefn Cribbwr
Pen-y-fai
Coity
Coity Castle
Bryncae
Dolau
Pont-y-clun
Cross Inn
Creigiau
Kenfig Pool and Dunes
Kenfig Burrows
Pendre
Pencoed
Llanilid
South Cornelly
New Castle
Bridgend
(Pen-y-bont ar Ogwr)
Llanharry
Brynsadler
Miskin
Groes-faen
Talygarn
Llanerch Vineyard
Royal Porthcawl
Laleston
Oldcastle
Coychurch
St Mary Hill
Craig Penllyn
Newton
Tythegston
Treoes
Merthyr Mawr
Ogmore Castle
Cornton
Llangan
Llansannor
Ystradowen
Pendoylan
St Brides super Ely
Peterston super-Ely
Clevis
Merthyr Mawr Warren
Ogmore
Ewenny
Porthcawl
Maendy
Penllyn
Welsh St Donats
Aberthin
Pentre
SN
SS
0 1 2 3 4 5 6 miles
0 1 2 3 4 5 6 7 8 9 10 km
A40
A4069
A4067
A470
A4215
A4059
A465
A4109
A474
A4060
A4061
A4233
A4107
A4058
A4119
A4093
A4063
A4064
A48
A4229
A473
A4222
A4054
A4275
A4059
A4067
A4282
A4106
B4287
B4281
B4280
B4524
M4
33
47
48
21
22

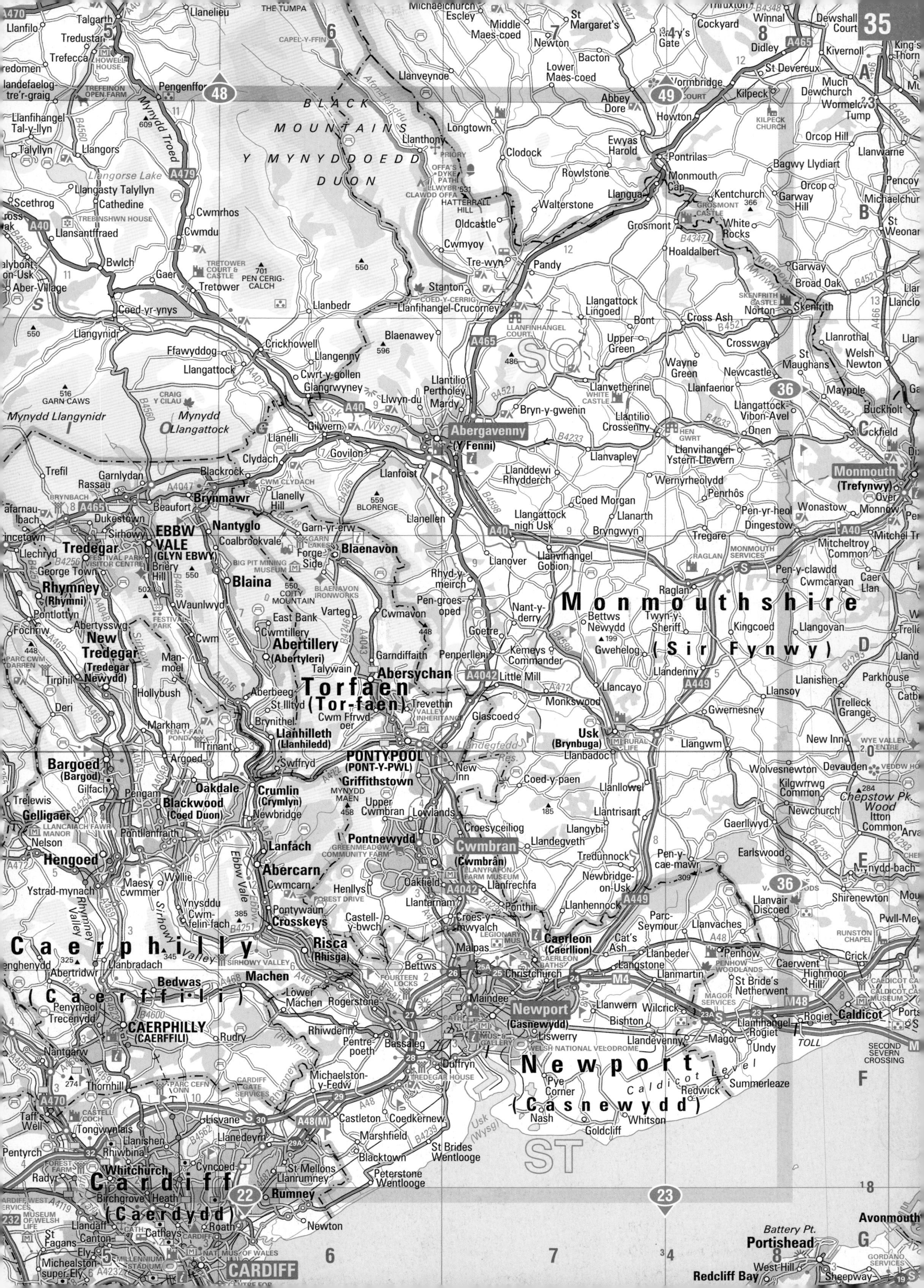
BLACK MOUNTAINS
Y MYNYDDOEDD DUON
Monmouthshire
(Sir Fynwy)
Torfaen
(Tor-faen)
Caerphilly
(Caerffili)
Newport
(Casnewydd)
Cardiff
(Caerdydd)
Abergavenny
(Y Fenni)
Monmouth
(Trefynwy)
Cwmbran
(Cwmbrân)
PONTYPOOL
(PONT-Y-PWL)
EBBW VALE
(GLYN EBWY)
Tredegar
Blaenavon
Blaina
Brynmawr
Nantyglo
Abertillery
(Abertyleri)
Abersychan
Griffithstown
Pontnewydd
Crumlin
(Crymlyn)
Oakdale
Blackwood
(Coed Duon)
Abercarn
Crosskeys
Risca
(Rhisga)
Rhymney
(Rhymni)
New Tredegar
(Tredegar Newydd)
Bargoed
Hengoed
Gelligaer
CAERPHILLY
(CAERFFILI)
Machen
Bedwas
Rogerstone
Bassaleg
Caerleon
(Caerllion)
Christchurch
Maindee
Usk
(Brynbuga)
Raglan
Caldicot
Magor
Portishead
Avonmouth
Whitchurch
Rumney
CARDIFF
Crickhowell
Llangattock
Gilwern
Govilon
Llanfoist
Pandy
Grosmont
Skenfrith
Pontrilas
Llanthony
Longtown
Talgarth
Llangorse Lake
Llangors
Bwlch
Tretower
Llangynidr
Beaufort
Llanelly Hill
Clydach
Mynydd Llangynidr
Mynydd Llangattock
Little Mill
Llancayo
Llandenny
Llangwm
Llanishen
Devauden
Wolvesnewton
Chepstow Pk. Wood
Llanvair Discoed
Shirenewton
Penhow
Caerwent
Llanmartin
Langstone
Bishton
Llanwern
Wilcrick
Rogiet
Undy
Redwick
Whitson
Goldcliff
Nash
Caldicot Level
SECOND SEVERN CROSSING
Battery Pt.
Redcliff Bay
St Brides Wentlooge
Peterstone Wentlooge
Marshfield
Castleton
Michaelston-y-Fedw
Lisvane
Llanedeyrn
Llanrumney
St Mellons
Rhiwbina
Llanishen
Tongwynlais
Taff's Well
Radyr
Llandaff
Canton
Cathays
Roath
Heath
Birchgrove
St Fagans
Ely
Michaelston-super-Ely
Newton
Pentyrch
Nantgarw
Thornhill
Rudry
Llanbradach
Abertridwr
Senghenydd
Trecenydd
Penyrheol
Ystrad-mynach
Nelson
Trelewis
Gilfach
Pengam
Pontllanfraith
Maesycwmmer
Wyllie
Ynysddu
Cwmfelinfach
Pontywaun
Cwmcarn
Newbridge
Llanhilleth
(Llanhiledd)
Swffryd
Aberbeeg
Cwmtillery
Six Bells
Llanover
Goetre
Penperlleni
Glascoed
Monkswood
Llanbadoc
Llantrisant
Llangybi
Llandegveth
Tredunnock
Newbridge-on-Usk
Llanhennock
Ponthir
Llanfrechfa
Llantarnam
Croesyceiliog
Malpas
Bettws
A40
A465
A4042
A449
A48
A48(M)
M4
M48
A470
A4232
A479
A4047
A466
48
49
36
22
23
S
SO
ST

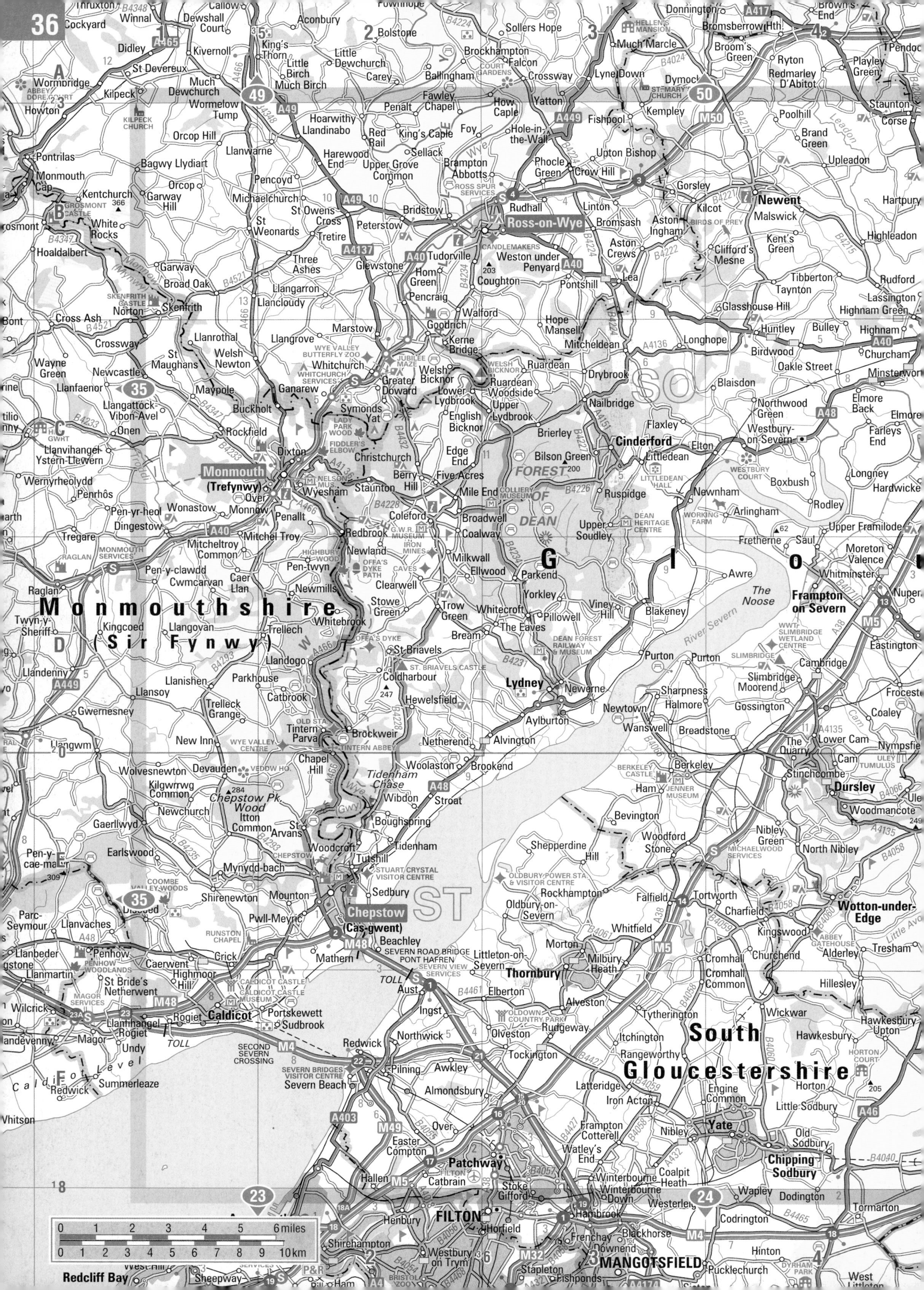

Cockyard
Winnal
Dewshall Court
Aconbury
Bolstone
Sollers Hope
Donnington
Bromsberrow Hth.
Much Marcle
Broom's Green
Ryton
Playley Green
Redmarley D'Abitot
Didley
Kivernoll
King's Thorn
Little Birch
Much Birch
Little Dewchurch
Carey
Brockhampton
Falcon
Crossway
Ballingham
Lyne Down
Dymock
Wormbridge
Kilpeck
St Devereux
Much Dewchurch
Wormelow Tump
Kilpeck Church
Howton
Penalt
Fawley Chapel
How Caple
Yatton
Kempley
Staunton
Corse
Poolhill
Brand Green
Orcop Hill
Llanwarne
Hoarwithy
Llandinabo
Red Rail
King's Caple
Foy
Hole-in-the-Wall
Fishpool
Pontrilas
Monmouth Cap
Bagwy Llydiart
Harewood End
Sellack
Upper Grove Common
Brampton Abbotts
Phocle Green
Upton Bishop
Crow Hill
Gorsley
Upleadon
Kentchurch
Garway Hill
Orcop
Pencoyd
Michaelchurch
Ross Spur Services
Rudhall
Linton
Kilcot
Newent
Hartpury
Grosmont Castle
White Rocks
St Owens Cross
St Weonards
Tretire
Peterstow
Bridstow
Ross-on-Wye
Bromsash
Aston Ingham
Birds of Prey
Malswick
Hoaldalbert
Garway
Broad Oak
Three Ashes
Glewstone
Tudorville
Candlemakers
Weston under Penyard
Aston Crews
Clifford's Mesne
Kent's Green
Highleadon
Hom Green
Coughton
Pontshill
Lea
Tibberton
Taynton
Rudford
Lassington
Skenfrith Castle
Norton
Skenfrith
Llangarron
Llancloudy
Pencraig
Walford
Hope Mansell
Glasshouse Hill
Highnam Green
Cross Ash
Crossway
Marstow
Goodrich
Kerne Bridge
Mitcheldean
Longhope
Huntley
Bulley
Highnam
Churcham
Llanrothal
Welsh Newton
Llangrove
Wye Valley Butterfly Zoo
Whitchurch
Jubilee Maze
Welsh Bicknor
Ruardean
Birdwood
Oakle Street
Wayne Green
Newcastle
St Maughans
Whitchurch Services
Greater Doward
Welsh Bicknor
Ruardean Woodside
Drybrook
Blaisdon
Minsterworth
Llanfaenor
Maypole
Ganarew
Lower Lydbrook
Upper Lydbrook
Nailbridge
Northwood Green
Elmore Back
Llangattock-Vibon-Avel
Buckholt
Symonds Yat
English Bicknor
Lady Park Wood
Flaxley
Westbury-on-Severn
Elmore
Farleys End
Llanvihangel-Ystern-Llewern
Onen
Rockfield
Fiddler's Elbow
Edge End
Brierley
Cinderford
Elton
Wernyrheolydd
Dixton
Monmouth (Trefynwy)
Nelson Mus.
Christchurch
Berry Hill
Five Acres
Bilson Green
Littledean
Littledean Hall
Westbury Court
Longney
Penrhôs
Pen-yr-heol
Wonastow
Over Monnow
Wyesham
Staunton
Mile End
Colliery Museum
Forest of Dean
Ruspidge
Newnham
Boxbush
Hardwicke
Dingestow
Penallt
Coleford
Broadwell
Upper Soudley
Dean Heritage Centre
Working Farm
Arlingham
Rodley
Tregare
Mitchel Troy
Redbrook
G.W.R. Museum
Coalway
Fretherne
Saul
Upper Framilode
Raglan
Monmouth Services
Mitcheltroy Common
Highbury Wood
Newland
Iron Mines
Milkwall
Moreton Valence
Pen-y-clawdd
Cwmcarvan
Caer Llan
Pen-twyn
Offa's Dyke Path
Caves
Clearwell
Ellwood
Parkend
Awre
Whitminster
Monmouthshire (Sir Fynwy)
Newmills
Stowe Green
Yorkley
The Noose
Frampton on Severn
Twyn-y-Sheriff
Kingcoed
Llangovan
Trellech
Whitebrook
Trow Green
Whitecroft
Pillowell
Viney Hill
Blakeney
Nupend
Offa's Dyke
Bream
The Eaves
St Briavels
Dean Forest Railway & Museum
River Severn
WWT Slimbridge Wetland Centre
Eastington
Llandenny
Llanishen
Parkhouse
Llandogo
St. Briavels Castle
Coldharbour
Lydney
Purton
Slimbridge
Cambridge
Llansoy
Catbrook
Hewelsfield
Newerne
Sharpness
Halmore
Moorend
Gossington
Frocester
Gwernesney
Trelleck Grange
Old Sta.
Tintern Parva
Brockweir
Aylburton
Newtown
Wanswell
Breadstone
Coaley
Llangwm
New Inn
Wye Valley Centre
Tintern Abbey
Netherend
Alvington
The Quarry
Lower Cam
Nympsfield
Chapel Hill
Woolaston
Brookend
Berkeley
Berkeley Castle
Jenner Museum
Cam
Uley Tumulus
Wolvesnewton
Devauden
Veddw Ho.
Tidenham Chase
Stinchcombe
Dursley
Kilgwrrwg Common
Chepstow Pk. Wood
Newchurch
Itton Common
Wibdon
Stroat
Ham
Woodmancote
Gaerllwyd
St Arvans
Boughspring
Bevington
Pen-y-cae-mawr
Earlswood
Chepstow Racecourse
Woodcroft
Tidenham
Shepperdine
Hill
Woodford
Stone
Nibley Green
North Nibley
Michaelwood Services
Mynydd-bach
Tutshill
Stuart Crystal Visitor Centre
Oldbury Power Sta. & Visitor Centre
Coombe Valley Woods
Shirenewton
Mounton
Sedbury
Rockhampton
Falfield
Tortworth
Charfield
Wotton-under-Edge
Parc-Seymour
Llanvaches
Pwll-Meyric
Chepstow (Cas-gwent)
Oldbury-on-Severn
Whitfield
Kingswood
Abbey Gatehouse
Tresham
Runston Chapel
Beachley
Morton
Alderley
Llanbeder
Penhow
Penhow Woodlands
Caerwent
Grick
Mathern
Severn Road Bridge Pont Hafren
Severn View Services
Littleton-on-Severn
Thornbury
Milbury Heath
Cromhall
Cromhall Common
Churchend
Llanmartin
St Bride's Netherwent
Highmoor Hill
Caldicot Castle
Caldicot Castle Museum
Toll
Aust
Elberton
Alveston
Hillesley
Magor Services
Wilcrick
Llanfihangel Rogiet
Rogiet
Caldicot
Portskewett
Sudbrook
Ingst
Oldown Country Park
Tytherington
Wickwar
Hawkesbury Upton
Magor
Undy
Redwick
Northwick
Olveston
Rudgeway
Itchington
South Gloucestershire
Hawkesbury
Horton Court
Second Severn Crossing
Pilning
Awkley
Tockington
Rangeworthy
Caldicot Level
Redwick
Summerleaze
Severn Bridges Visitor Centre
Severn Beach
Almondsbury
Latteridge
Iron Acton
Engine Common
Horton
Little Sodbury
Whitson
Over
Frampton Cotterell
Nibley
Yate
Old Sodbury
Easter Compton
Patchway
Watley's End
Chipping Sodbury
Hallen
Catbrain
Stoke Gifford
Winterbourne
Coalpit Heath
Winterbourne Down
Westerleigh
Wapley
Dodington
Tormarton
Henbury
Filton
Horfield
Hambrook
Codrington
Shirehampton
Frenchay
Blackhorse
Downend
Hinton
Westbury on Trym
Stapleton
Fishponds
Mangotsfield
Pucklechurch
Dyrham Park
Redcliff Bay
Sheepway
West Littleton
0 1 2 3 4 5 6 miles
0 1 2 3 4 5 6 7 8 9 10 km

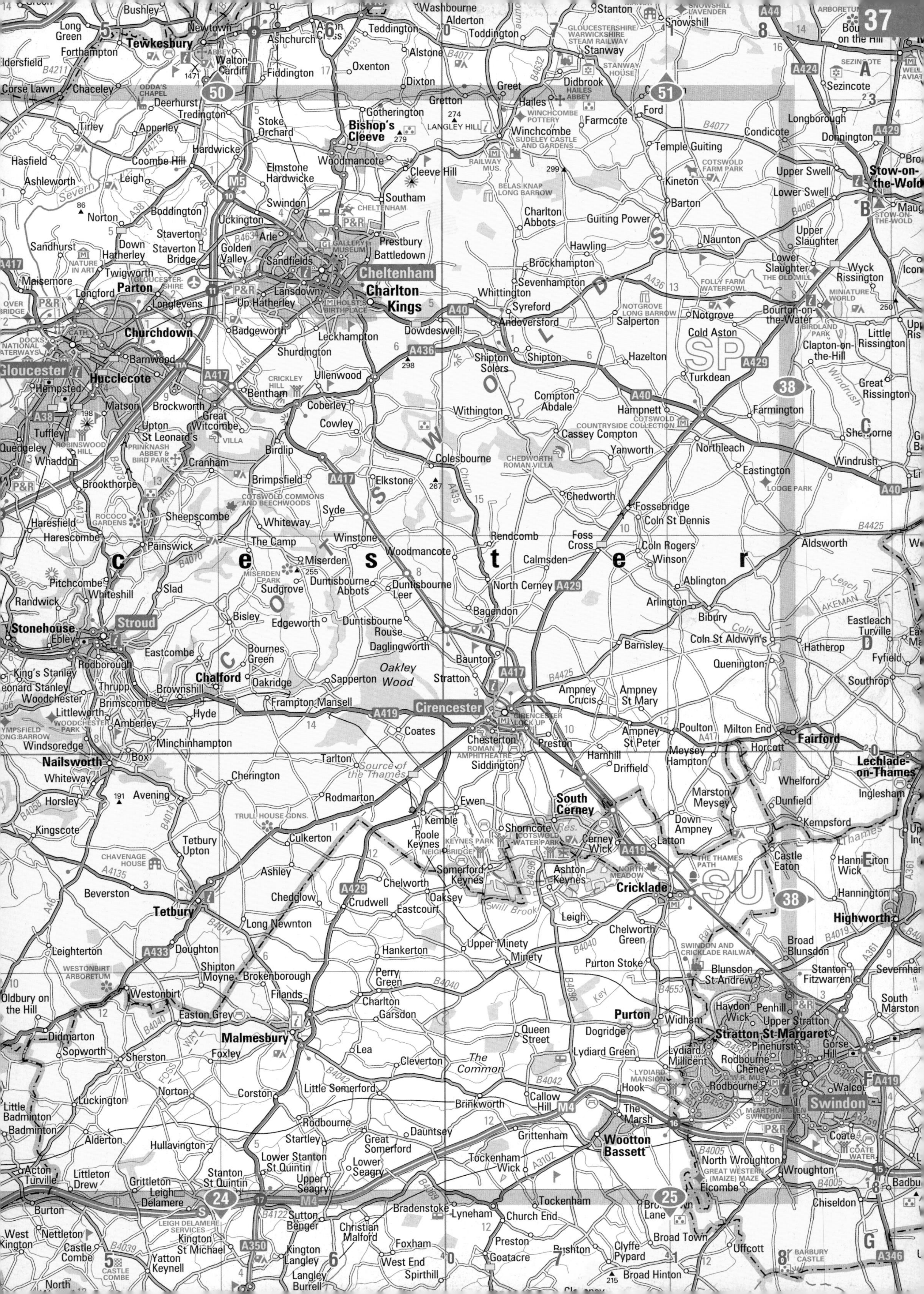
37
Tewkesbury
Cheltenham
Charlton Kings
Gloucester
Churchdown
Hucclecote
Stroud
Stonehouse
Nailsworth
Cirencester
South Cerney
Cricklade
Fairford
Lechlade-on-Thames
Highworth
Swindon
Stratton St Margaret
Purton
Wootton Bassett
Malmesbury
Tetbury
Chalford
Bishop's Cleeve
Winchcombe
Stow-on-the-Wold
Bourton-on-the-Water
Northleach
Bibury
Sezincote
Swindon and Cricklade Railway
Cotswold Water Park
Westonbirt Arboretum
Leigh Delamere Services

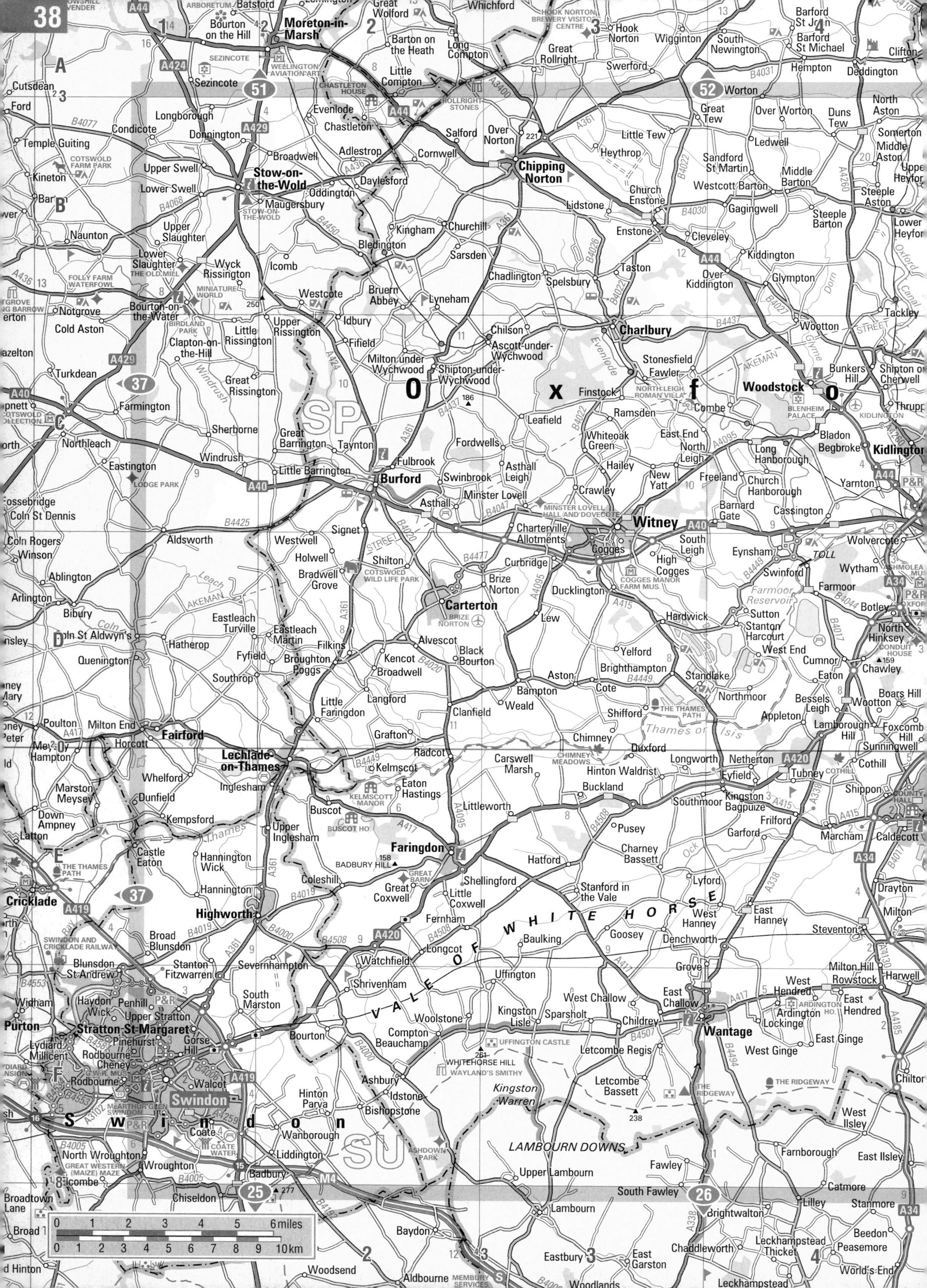

A44
Batsford
Bourton on the Hill
Moreton-in-Marsh
Great Wolford
Whichford
HOOK NORTON BREWERY VISITOR CENTRE
Hook Norton
Barford St John
Barford St Michael
Barton on the Heath
Long Compton
Great Rollright
Wigginton
South Newington
Clifton
Hempton
Deddington
A424
SEZINCOTE
WELLINGTON AVIATION ART
Sezincote
51
Little Compton
CHASTLETON HOUSE
ROLLRIGHT STONES
A3400
Swerford
B4031
52
Worton
Cutsdean
Ford
B4077
Condicote
Longborough
Donnington
A429
Evenlode
Chastleton
A44
Salford
Over Norton
Great Tew
Over Worton
Duns Tew
North Aston
Temple Guiting
COTSWOLD FARM PARK
Kineton
Upper Swell
Lower Swell
Broadwell
Adlestrop
Cornwell
Chipping Norton
Little Tew
Heythrop
Ledwell
Sandford St Martin
Somerton
Middle Aston
Upper Heyford
Stow-on-the-Wold
STOW-ON-THE-WOLD
Maugersbury
Oddington
Daylesford
Church Enstone
Westcott Barton
Middle Barton
Steeple Aston
Lidstone
B4030
Gagingwell
Steeple Barton
Lower Heyford
Naunton
Upper Slaughter
B4068
B4450
Kingham
Churchill
Enstone
Cleveley
Lower Slaughter
THE OLD MILL
Wyck Rissington
Icomb
Bledington
Sarsden
Kiddington
A436
FOLLY FARM WATERFOWL
Tasto n
A44
Over Kiddington
Glympton
Chadlington
Spelsbury
B4022
B4026
Notgrove
Cold Aston
Bourton-on-the-Water
MINIATURE WORLD
Westcote
Bruern Abbey
Lyneham
Tackley
BIRDLAND PARK
Clapton-on-the-Hill
Little Rissington
Upper Rissington
Idbury
Fifield
Chilson
Ascott-under-Wychwood
Charlbury
B4437
Wootton
B4027
Turkdean
A429
Windrush
Great Rissington
37
A424
Milton under Wychwood
Shipton-under-Wychwood
Stonesfield
Fawler
AKEMAN STREET
Evenlode
Bunkers Hill
Shipton on Cherwell
A40
Farmington
COTSWOLD COLLECTION
Northleach
SP
O x f o
Finstock
NORTH LEIGH ROMAN VILLA
Combe
Woodstock
BLENHEIM PALACE
KIDLINGTON
Thrupp
Sherborne
Great Barrington
Taynton
A361
B4437
Leafield
Ramsden
Whiteoak Green
East End
North Leigh
A4095
Long Hanborough
Bladon
Begbroke
Kidlington
Eastington
LODGE PARK
Windrush
Little Barrington
Fulbrook
Burford
Fordwells
Swinbrook
Asthall
Asthall Leigh
Hailey
New Yatt
Freeland
Church Hanborough
Yarnton
A44
P&R
Fossebridge
Coln St Dennis
A40
Asthall
Minster Lovell
MINSTER LOVELL HALL AND DOVECOTE
B4047
Crawley
Barnard Gate
Cassington
B4425
Aldsworth
Signet
B4020
Witney
A40
Charterville Allotments
Cogges
South Leigh
Eynsham
Wolvercote
TOLL
Coln Rogers
Winson
Westwell
Holwell
Shilton
COTSWOLD WILD LIFE PARK
Bradwell Grove
B4477
Curbridge
Brize Norton
High Cogges
COGGES MANOR FARM MUS.
Swinford
Wytham
Ablington
Arlington
Bibury
AKEMAN
Leach
Carterton
BRIZE NORTON
A4095
Ducklington
A415
B4449
Farmoor Reservoir
Farmoor
B4044
Botley
A34
Eastleach Turville
Eastleach Martin
Lew
Hardwick
Sutton
Stanton Harcourt
B4017
North Hinksey
Coln St Aldwyn's
D
Hatherop
Filkins
Alvescot
Black Bourton
Yelford
West End
Cumnor
CONDUIT HOUSE
159
Chawley
Quenington
Fyfield
Broughton Poggs
Kencot
Broadwell
B4020
Southrop
Aston
Brighthampton
B4449
Standlake
Eaton
Bampton
Cote
Northmoor
Bessels Leigh
Boars Hill
Wootton
Little Faringdon
Langford
Clanfield
Weald
Shifford
THE THAMES PATH
Appleton
Thames or Isis
Poulton
Milton End
Fairford
A417
Horcott
Meysey Hampton
Grafton
Chimney
Duxford
CHIMNEY MEADOWS
Lamborough Hill
Foxcombe Hill
Sunningwell
Lechlade-on-Thames
Radcot
B4449
Kelmscot
Carswell Marsh
Hinton Waldrist
Longworth
Netherton
A420
Tubney
Cothill
Fyfield
Whelford
Inglesham
KELMSCOTT MANOR
Eaton Hastings
Buckland
Southmoor
Kingston Bagpuize
A415
A338
Shippon
Marston Meysey
Dunfield
Buscot
Littleworth
A4095
B4508
Pusey
Frilford
A415
Down Ampney
Kempsford
Thames
BUSCOT HO.
A417
Upper Inglesham
Garford
Marcham
Caldecott
Latton
Faringdon
BADBURY HILL
158
Charney Bassett
Ock
A34
E
THE THAMES PATH
Castle Eaton
Hannington Wick
A361
GREAT BARN
Hatford
Lyford
Drayton
Coleshill
Shellingford
Stanford in the Vale
A338
Cricklade
37
Hannington
Great Coxwell
Little Coxwell
B4019
East Hanney
Milton
A419
Highworth
Fernham
V A L E O F W H I T E H O R S E
West Hanney
Steventon
SWINDON AND CRICKLADE RAILWAY
Broad Blunsdon
B4019
B4000
B4508
A420
B4508
Baulking
Goosey
Denchworth
A4130
Blunsdon St Andrew
Stanton Fitzwarren
A361
Sevenhampton
Watchfield
Longcot
A417
Grove
Milton Hill
Rowstock
Harwell
B4553
Widham
Haydon Wick
Penhill
P&R
Upper Stratton
Shrivenham
South Marston
Uffington
West Challow
East Challow
A417
West Hendred
ARDINGTON HO.
East Hendred
Ardington
Purton
Stratton St Margaret
Woolstone
Kingston Lisle
Sparsholt
Childrey
Wantage
Lockinge
A4185
Lydiard Millicent
Pinehurst
Rodbourne Cheney
Gorse Hill
Bourton
Compton Beauchamp
B4507
East Ginge
West Ginge
B4494
UFFINGTON CASTLE
261
WHITEHORSE HILL
WAYLAND'S SMITHY
Letcombe Regis
F
Rodbourne
Walcot
A419
B4000
Ashbury
Letcombe Bassett
THE RIDGEWAY
THE RIDGEWAY
Chilton
Swindon
Hinton Parva
Idstone
Kingston Warren
McARTHURGLEN SWINDON
Bishopstone
238
West Ilsley
S w i n d o n
P&R
A3102
B4553
A4259
Coate
COATE WATER
Wanborough
SU
LAMBOURN DOWNS
Farnborough
East Ilsley
B4005
North Wroughton
GREAT WESTERN (MAIZE) MAZE
Wroughton
Liddington
ASHDOWN PARK
Upper Lambourn
Fawley
Elcombe
B4005
Badbury
M4
25
277
South Fawley
26
Catmore
Broadtown Lane
Chiseldon
B4192
Lambourn
Lilley
Stanmore
A34
A338
Brightwalton
0 1 2 3 4 5 6 miles
0 1 2 3 4 5 6 7 8 9 10 km
Broad
Baydon
Leckhampstead Thicket
Beedon
Peasemore
Eastbury
East Garston
Chaddleworth
Hinton
Woodsend
Aldbourne
MEMBURY SERVICES
Woodlands
Leckhampstead
World's End

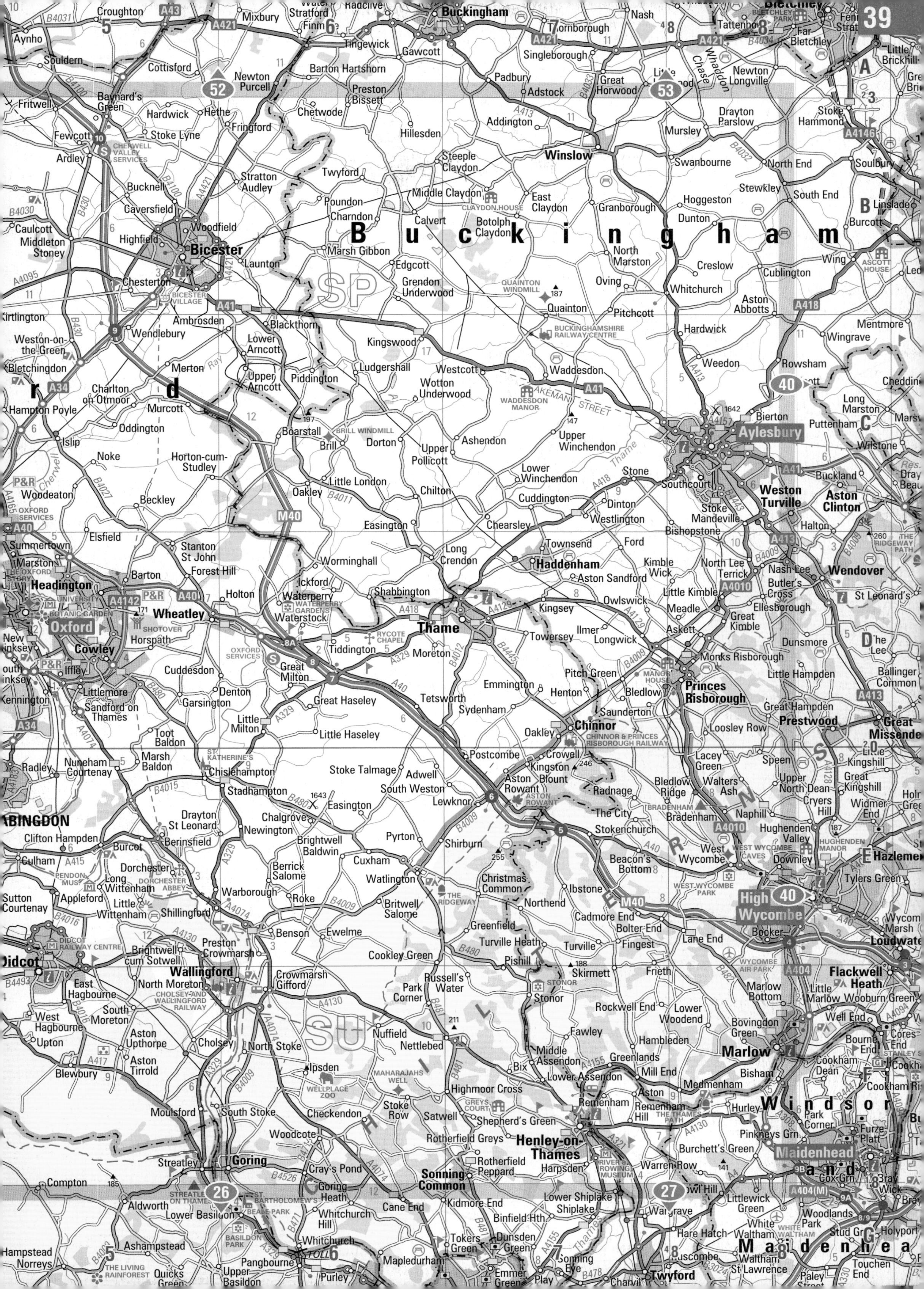
39
Croughton
Aynho
Souldern
Cottisford
Mixbury
Stratford
Finmere
Tingewick
Gawcott
Buckingham
Thornborough
Singleborough
Nash
Tattenhoe
Bletchley Park
Far Bletchley
Fenny Stratford
Little Brickhill
Newton Purcell
Barton Hartshorn
Preston Bissett
Padbury
Adstock
Great Horwood
Little Horwood
Whaddon Chase
Newton Longville
Fritwell
Baynard's Green
Hardwick
Hethe
Fringford
Chetwode
Hillesden
Addington
Mursley
Drayton Parslow
Stoke Hammond
Fewcott
Ardley
Stoke Lyne
Cherwell Valley Services
Winslow
Swanbourne
North End
Soulbury
Steeple Claydon
Twyford
Stratton Audley
Bucknell
Caversfield
Poundon
Middle Claydon
Claydon House
East Claydon
Granborough
Hoggeston
Stewkley
South End
Linslade
Charndon
Calvert
Botolph Claydon
Dunton
Burcott
Caulcott
Middleton Stoney
Woodfield
Highfield
Bicester
Launton
Marsh Gibbon
North Marston
Creslow
Cublington
Wing
Ascott House
Buckingham
SP
Chesterton
Bicester Village
Edgcott
Grendon Underwood
Quainton Windmill
Quainton
Oving
Whitchurch
Aston Abbotts
Pitchcott
Kirtlington
Ambrosden
Wendlebury
Blackthorn
Lower Arncott
Kingswood
Buckinghamshire Railway Centre
Hardwick
Mentmore
Wingrave
Weston-on-the-Green
Bletchingdon
Merton
Upper Arncott
Piddington
Ludgershall
Westcott
Wotton Underwood
Waddesdon
Waddesdon Manor
Weedon
Rowsham
Akeman Street
Hampton Poyle
Charlton on Otmoor
Murcott
Oddington
Islip
Boarstall
Brill Windmill
Brill
Dorton
Ashendon
Upper Pollicott
Upper Winchendon
Bierton
Aylesbury
Long Marston
Puttenham
Wilstone
Noke
Horton-cum-Studley
Little London
Oakley
Lower Winchendon
Chilton
Stone
Southcourt
Buckland
Weston Turville
Aston Clinton
Woodeaton
Oxford Services
Beckley
Cuddington
Dinton
Westlington
Stoke Mandeville
Easington
Chearsley
Bishopstone
Halton
The Ridgeway Path
Elsfield
Summertown
Marston
Stanton St John
Forest Hill
Townsend
Ford
Haddenham
Kimble Wick
Aston Sandford
North Lee
Terrick
Nash Lee
Wendover
Butler's Cross
Headington
The Oxford Story
Barton
Worminghall
Long Crendon
Ickford
Waterperry
Waterperry Gardens
Shabbington
Owlswick
Little Kimble
Meadle
Ellesborough
St Leonard's
Holton
Wheatley
Oxford
Botanic Garden
Shotover
Waterstock
Thame
Kingsey
Towersey
Ilmer
Longwick
Great Kimble
Askett
Horspath
Cowley
Iffley
Rycote Chapel
Tiddington
Moreton
Monks Risborough
Dunsmore
The Lee
Oxford Services
Great Milton
Cuddesdon
Littlemore
Sandford on Thames
Denton
Garsington
Kennington
Emmington
Henton
Pitch Green
Bledlow
Manor House
Princes Risborough
Little Hampden
Ballinger Common
Tetsworth
Sydenham
Great Haseley
Little Milton
Toot Baldon
Little Haseley
Saunderton
Chinnor
Oakley
Chinnor & Princes Risborough Railway
Loosley Row
Great Hampden
Prestwood
Great Missenden
Radley
Nuneham Courtenay
Marsh Baldon
St Katherine's
Chislehampton
Stoke Talmage
Adwell
Postcombe
Crowell
Kingston Blount
Lacey Green
Speen
Kingshill
Walters Ash
Great Kingshill
Stadhampton
South Weston
Lewknor
Aston Rowant
Radnage
Bledlow Ridge
Upper North Dean
Cryers Hill
Widmer End
Abingdon
Drayton St Leonard
Chalgrove
Easington
The City
Bradenham
Naphill
Hughenden Valley
Hughenden Manor
Clifton Hampden
Berinsfield
Newington
Brightwell Baldwin
Pyrton
Shirburn
Stokenchurch
Beacon's Bottom
West Wycombe
West Wycombe Caves
Downley
Hazlemere
Culham
Burcot
Dorchester
Long Wittenham
Dorchester Abbey
Pendon Mus
Berrick Salome
Cuxham
Watlington
Christmas Common
Ibstone
West Wycombe Park
Tylers Green
Sutton Courtenay
Appleford
Little Wittenham
Shillingford
Warborough
Roke
Britwell Salome
The Ridgeway
Northend
Cadmore End
Bolter End
High Wycombe
Booker
Loudwater
Wycombe Marsh
Benson
Ewelme
Greenfield
Turville Heath
Turville
Fingest
Lane End
Didcot
Didcot Railway Centre
Brightwell-cum-Sotwell
Preston Crowmarsh
Wallingford
Cookley Green
Pishill
Skirmett
Frieth
Wycombe Air Park
Flackwell Heath
North Moreton
East Hagbourne
Cholsey and Wallingford Railway
Crowmarsh Gifford
Park Corner
Russell's Water
Stonor
Marlow Bottom
Little Marlow
Wooburn Green
South Moreton
West Hagbourne
Upton
Aston Upthorpe
Cholsey
North Stoke
Nuffield
Nettlebed
SU
Rockwell End
Lower Woodend
Fawley
Hambleden
Bovingdon Green
Well End
Bourne End
Cores End
Marlow
Blewbury
Aston Tirrold
Ipsden
Maharajahs Well
Wellplace Zoo
Bix
Middle Assendon
Greenlands
Lower Assendon
Mill End
Medmenham
Cookham Dean
Bisham
Cookham
Cookham Rise
Moulsford
South Stoke
Checkendon
Stoke Row
Highmoor Cross
Greys Court
Satwell
Shepherd's Green
Remenham
Remenham Hill
The Thames Path
Hurley
Windsor
Park Corner
Pinkneys Green
Furze Platt
Woodcote
Rotherfield Greys
Henley-on-Thames
Goring
Streatley
Cray's Pond
Rotherfield Peppard
River & Rowing Museum
Harpsden
Warren Row
Burchett's Green
Maidenhead
Compton
Streatley on Thames
Goring Heath
Sonning Common
Aldworth
Lower Basildon
Beale Park
Whitchurch Hill
Cane End
Kidmore End
Lower Shiplake
Shiplake
Binfield Heath
Bowl Hill
Wargrave
Littlewick Green
White Waltham
Woodlands Park
Cox Green
Bray Wick
Holyport
Hampstead Norreys
Ashampstead
Basildon Park
Whitchurch
Pangbourne
Mapledurham
Tokers Green
Dunsden Green
Sonning Eye
Hare Hatch
Waltham St Lawrence
Ruscombe
Twyford
Stud Green
Maidenhead
Touchen End
Paley Street
The Living Rainforest
Quicks Green
Upper Basildon
Purley
Emmer Green
Play Hatch
Charvil
M40
A41
A34
A40
A4142
A413
A418
A4010
A404
A4155
A4130
A329
A4074
A421
A43
B4009
B4011
B4012
B480
B481
B4015
B4016
B4027
B4030
B4031
B4032
B4033
B4034
B4095
B4100
B4443
B4445
B4526
B4493
B478
B482
A4095
A4421
A4146
A4157
A4129
A4128
A4094
A415
A417
A4183
A404(M)
A4
A308
A321
B3024
52
53
40
26
27

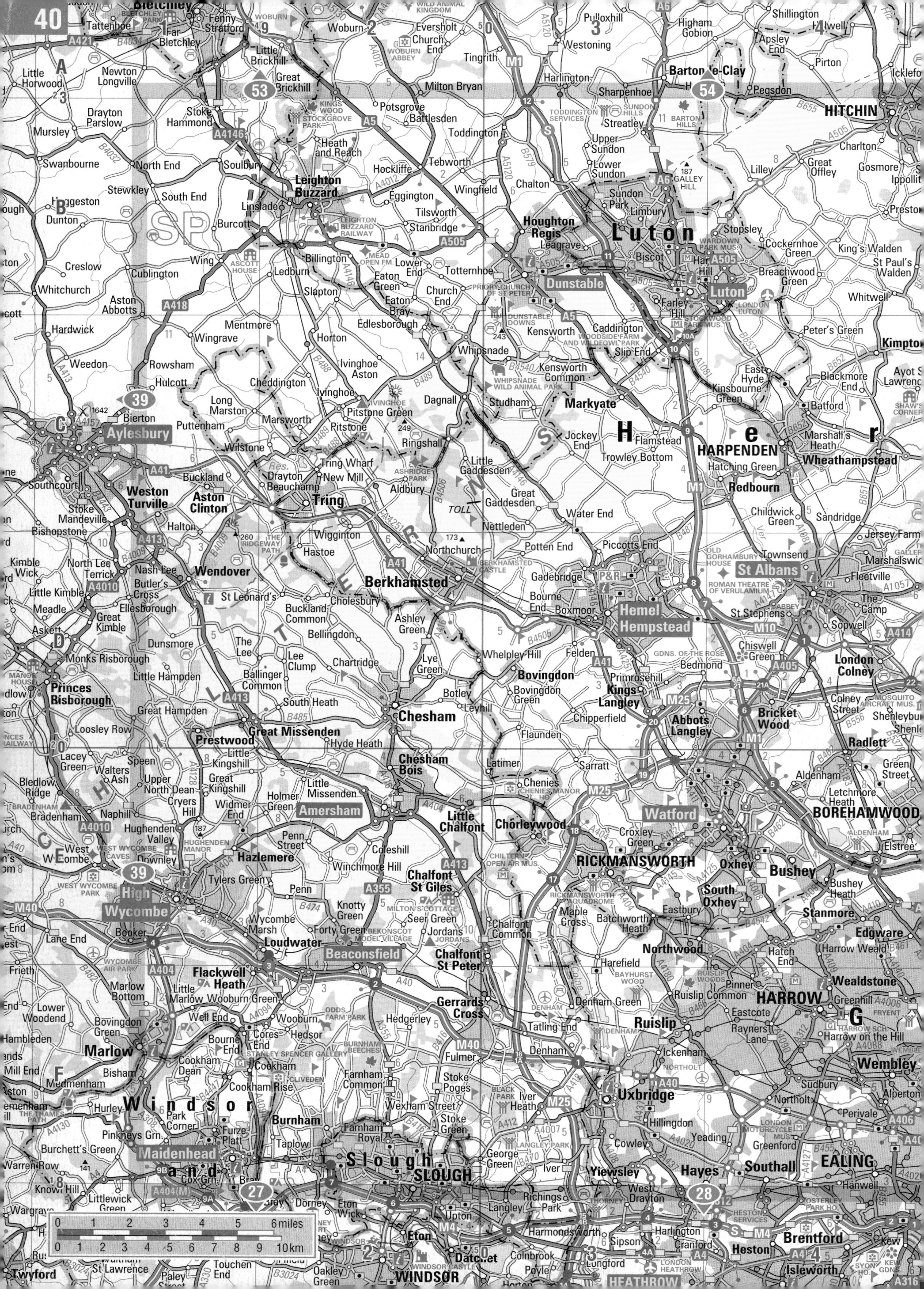
Bletchley
Fenny Stratford
Woburn
Tattenhoe
Far Bletchley
Little Brickhill
Great Brickhill
Eversholt
Church End
Pulloxhill
Westoning
Higham Gobion
Shillington
Apsley End
Pirton
Little Horwood
Newton Longville
Drayton Parslow
Mursley
Stoke Hammond
Potsgrove
Battlesden
Milton Bryan
Tingrith
Harlington
Barton-le-Clay
Sharpenhoe
Pegsdon
HITCHIN
Swanbourne
North End
Soulbury
Heath and Reach
Toddington
Upper Sundon
Lower Sundon
Streatley
Charlton
Great Offley
Gosmore
Lilley
Leighton Buzzard
Hockliffe
Tebworth
Wingfield
Chalton
Stewkley
South End
Linslade
Eggington
Tilsworth
Stanbridge
Houghton Regis
Sundon Park
Limbury
Luton
Stopsley
Cockernhoe Green
King's Walden
St Paul's Walden
Hoggeston
Dunton
Burcott
Leagrave
Biscot
Creslow
Wing
Billington
Lower End
Totternhoe
Dunstable
Whitchurch
Cublington
Ledburn
Eaton Green
Eaton Bray
Church End
Breachwood Green
Whitwell
Aston Abbotts
Slapton
Farley Hill
Hardwick
Mentmore
Wingrave
Horton
Edlesborough
Kensworth
Caddington
Slip End
Peter's Green
Kimpton
Weedon
Rowsham
Hulcott
Cheddington
Ivinghoe Aston
Whipsnade
Kensworth Common
East Hyde
Blackmore End
Long Marston
Ivinghoe
Dagnall
Studham
Markyate
Kinsbourne Green
Batford
Bierton
Aylesbury
Puttenham
Marsworth
Pitstone Green
Pitstone
Ringshall
Jockey End
Flamstead
Trowley Bottom
HARPENDEN
Marshall's Heath
Wheathampstead
Wilstone
Buckland
Drayton Beauchamp
Tring Wharf
New Mill
Little Gaddesden
Aldbury
Hatching Green
Redbourn
Southcourt
Weston Turville
Aston Clinton
Tring
Great Gaddesden
Childwick Green
Sandridge
Stoke Mandeville
Bishopstone
Halton
Wigginton
Hastoe
Nettleden
Water End
Potten End
Northchurch
Piccotts End
Townsend
St Albans
Jersey Farm
Marshalswick
Kimble Wick
North Lee
Terrick
Nash Lee
Wendover
Butler's Cross
Little Kimble
Berkhamsted
Gadebridge
Fleetville
Meadle
Ellesborough
St Leonard's
Buckland Common
Cholesbury
Bourne End
Boxmoor
Hemel Hempstead
St Stephens
The Camp
Great Kimble
Askett
Ashley Green
Bellingdon
Sopwell
Dunsmore
Monks Risborough
The Lee
Lee Clump
Chartridge
Lye Green
Whelpley Hill
Felden
Chiswell Green
Bedmond
London Colney
Little Hampden
Princes Risborough
Ballinger Common
Bovingdon
Bovingdon Green
Primrosehill
Kings Langley
Colney Street
Shenley
Great Hampden
South Heath
Botley
Leyhill
Chesham
Chipperfield
Abbots Langley
Bricket Wood
Loosley Row
Prestwood
Great Missenden
Hyde Heath
Flaunden
Radlett
Lacey Green
Speen
Little Kingshill
Chesham Bois
Latimer
Sarratt
Aldenham
Green Street
Walters Ash
Upper North Dean
Great Kingshill
Little Missenden
Chenies
Letchmore Heath
Bledlow Ridge
Bradenham
Naphill
Cryers Hill
Widmer End
Holmer Green
Amersham
Little Chalfont
Chorleywood
Watford
BOREHAMWOOD
Hughenden Valley
Penn Street
Croxley Green
West Wycombe
Downley
Hazlemere
Coleshill
RICKMANSWORTH
Oxhey
Bushey
Elstree
Tylers Green
Winchmore Hill
Chalfont St Giles
South Oxhey
Bushey Heath
High Wycombe
Penn
Knotty Green
Seer Green
Maple Cross
Batchworth Heath
Eastbury
Stanmore
Lane End
Booker
Wycombe Marsh
Forty Green
Jordans
Chalfont Common
Northwood
Edgware
Loudwater
Beaconsfield
Chalfont St Peter
Hatch End
Harrow Weald
Frieth
Flackwell Heath
Harefield
Wealdstone
Marlow Bottom
Little Marlow
Wooburn Green
Gerrards Cross
Pinner
Ruislip Common
HARROW
Greenhill
Lower Woodend
Well End
Hedgerley
Denham Green
Eastcote
Bovingdon Green
Cores End
Hedsor
Wooburn
Ruislip
Rayners Lane
Harrow on the Hill
Hambleden
Marlow
Bourne End
Tatling End
Denham
Fulmer
Cookham Dean
Cookham
Farnham Common
Stoke Poges
Ickenham
Wembley
Mill End
Medmenham
Bisham
Cookham Rise
Uxbridge
Sudbury
Alperton
Hurley
Windsor
Wexham Street
Iver Heath
Northolt
Perivale
Park Corner
Burnham
Stoke Green
Hillingdon
Pinkneys Grn.
Furze Platt
Farnham Royal
Cowley
Yeading
Greenford
Burchett's Green
Maidenhead
Taplow
Slough
George Green
Warren Row
Cox Grn.
Bray
SLOUGH
Iver
Yiewsley
Hayes
Southall
EALING
Knowl Hill
Littlewick Green
Dorney
Eton Wick
Langley
Richings Park
West Drayton
Hanwell
Wargrave
Upton
Harmondsworth
Sipson
Harlington
Cranford
Brentford
Eton
Datchet
Colnbrook
Heston
Kew
Twyford
St Lawrence
Touchen End
Oakley Green
WINDSOR
Poyle
Longford
Isleworth
HEATHROW
0 1 2 3 4 5 6 miles
0 1 2 3 4 5 6 7 8 9 10 km

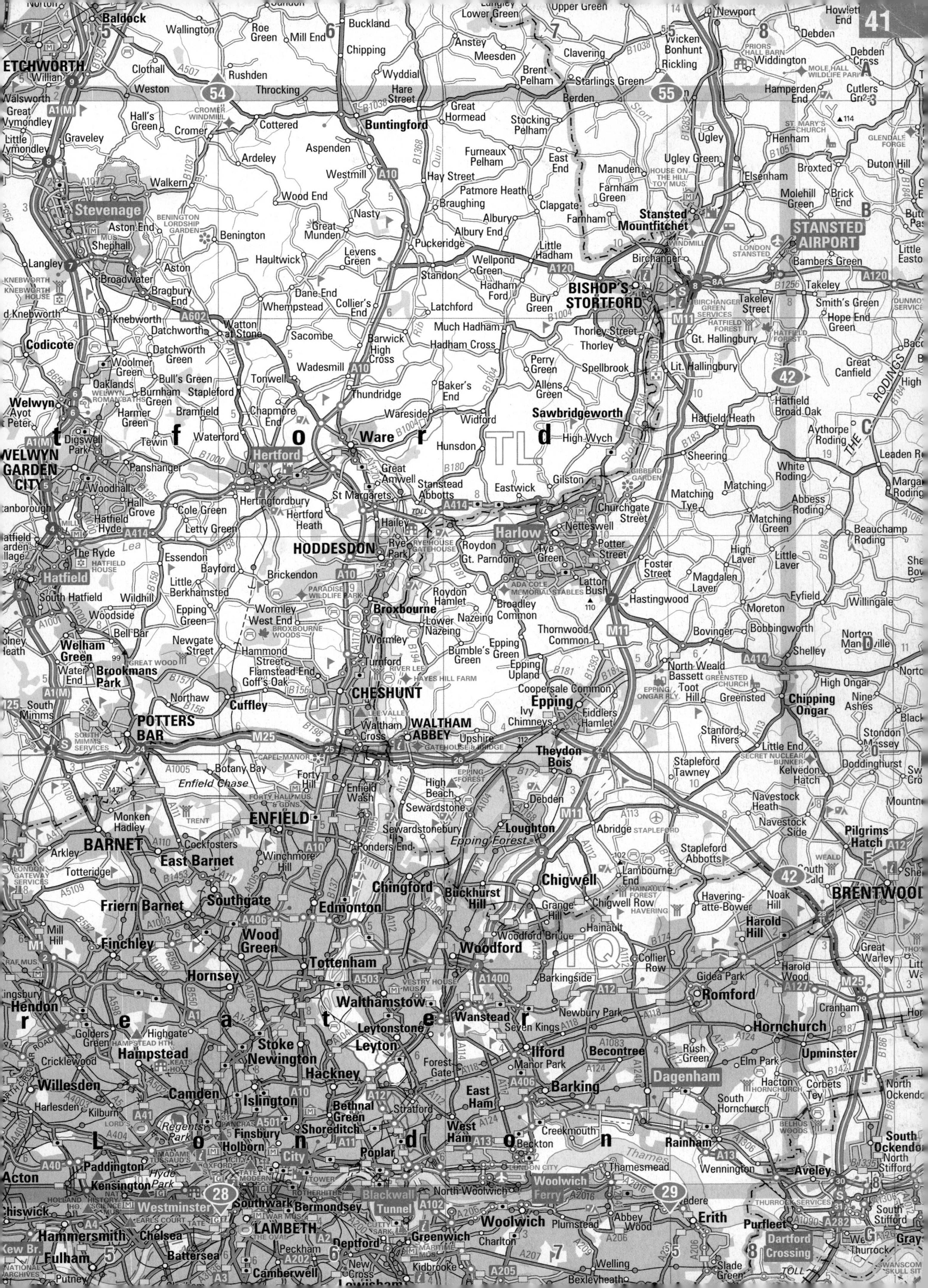
41
Baldock
Wallington
Roe Green
Mill End
Buckland
Lower Green
Upper Green
Newport
Howlett End
Letchworth
Willian
Clothall
Rushden
Chipping
Anstey
Meesden
Clavering
Wicken Bonhunt
Rickling
Debden
Widdington
Priors Hall Barn
Mole Hall Wildlife Park
Debden Cross
Weston
Throcking
Wyddial
Hare Street
Brent Pelham
Starlings Green
Berden
Hamperden End
Cutlers Green
Walsworth
Great Wymondley
Little Wymondley
Graveley
Hall's Green
Cromer Windmill
Cromer
Cottered
Buntingford
Great Hormead
Stocking Pelham
Ugley
St. Mary's Church
Henham
Glendale Forge
Aspenden
Ardeley
Westmill
Furneaux Pelham
East End
Ugley Green
Manuden
House on the Hill Toy Mus.
Elsenham
Broxted
Duton Hill
Walkern
Hay Street
Patmore Heath
Farnham Green
Molehill Green
Brick End
Stevenage
Wood End
Braughing
Clapgate
Benington Lordship Garden
Benington
Aston End
Nasty
Great Munden
Albury
Farnham
Stansted Mountfitchet
Stansted Airport
Shephall
Albury End
Levens Green
Puckeridge
Little Hadham
Windmill
London Stansted
Langley
Aston
Haultwick
Wellpond Green
Birchanger
Bambers Green
Knebworth
Knebworth House
Broadwater
Bragbury End
Dane End
Standon
Hadham Ford
Bishop's Stortford
Takeley
Whempstead
Collier's End
Latchford
Bury Green
Birchanger Green Services
Takeley Street
Smith's Green
Hope End Green
Datchworth
Watton at Stone
Sacombe
Much Hadham
Thorley Street
Thorley
Hatfield Forest
Gt. Hallingbury
Codicote
Datchworth Green
Barwick
High Cross
Hadham Cross
Wadesmill
Perry Green
Spellbrook
Lit. Hallingbury
Great Canfield
Woolmer Green
Oaklands
Welwyn Roman Baths
Bull's Green
Burnham Green
Stapleford
Tonwell
Thundridge
Baker's End
Allens Green
Welwyn
Ayot St Peter
Harmer Green
Bramfield
Chapmore End
Wareside
Widford
Sawbridgeworth
Hatfield Heath
Hatfield Broad Oak
Aythorpe Roding
The Rodings
Digswell Park
Tewin
Waterford
Ware
Hunsdon
High Wych
Sheering
Leaden Roding
Welwyn Garden City
Hertford
Panshanger
Great Amwell
Stanstead Abbotts
Eastwick
Gilston
Gibberd Garden
White Roding
Matching
Margaret Roding
Woodhall
Hertingfordbury
St Margarets
Matching Tye
Abbess Roding
Hall Grove
Cole Green
Hertford Heath
Hailey
Churchgate Street
Matching Green
Hatfield Hyde
Letty Green
Harlow
Netteswell
Beauchamp Roding
The Ryde
Essendon
Hoddesdon
Rye Park
Rye House Gatehouse
Roydon
Gt. Parndon
Tye Green
Potter Street
High Laver
Little Laver
Hatfield
Hatfield House
Bayford
Brickendon
Foster Street
Magdalen Laver
Little Berkhamsted
Paradise Wildlife Park
Roydon Hamlet
Ada Cole Memorial Stables
Latton Bush
South Hatfield
Wildhill
Broxbourne
Broadley Common
Hastingwood
Fyfield
Willingale
Woodside
Epping Green
Wormley West End
Broxbourne Woods
Lower Nazeing
Nazeing
Moreton
Bell Bar
Wormley
Thornwood Common
Bovinger
Bobbingworth
Norton Mandeville
Welham Green
Newgate Street
Hammond Street
Bumble's Green
Epping Green
Shelley
Great Wood
Turnford
North Weald Bassett
Water End
Brookmans Park
Flamstead End
Goff's Oak
River Lee
Hayes Hill Farm
Epping Upland
Greensted Church
High Ongar
Toot Hill
Cheshunt
Coopersale Common
Epping Ongar Rly.
Greensted
Chipping Ongar
Nine Ashes
South Mimms
Northaw
Cuffley
Epping
Fiddlers Hamlet
Potters Bar
Lee Valley
Waltham Cross
Waltham Abbey
Upshire
Ivy Chimneys
Stanford Rivers
Stondon Massey
South Mimms Services
Gatehouse & Bridge
Theydon Bois
Little End
Secret Nuclear Bunker
Capel Manor
Botany Bay
Stapleford Tawney
Kelvedon Hatch
Doddinghurst
Forty Hill
Enfield Chase
Forty Hall Mus. & Gdns.
Enfield Wash
Epping Forest
High Beach
Debden
Monken Hadley
Trent
Enfield
Sewardstone
Navestock Heath
Navestock Side
Barnet
Cockfosters
Sewardstonebury
Loughton
Abridge
Stapleford
Pilgrims Hatch
Arkley
East Barnet
Ponders End
Stapleford Abbotts
Totteridge
Winchmore Hill
Lambourne End
Weald
London Gateway Services
Chingford
Buckhurst Hill
Chigwell
South Weald
Brentwood
Friern Barnet
Southgate
Edmonton
Hainault Forest
Chigwell Row
Havering-atte-Bower
Noak Hill
Grange Hill
Mill Hill
Wood Green
Woodford Bridge
Hainault
Harold Hill
Finchley
Woodford
Collier Row
Great Warley
Tottenham
Hornsey
Vestry House Mus.
Barkingside
Gidea Park
Harold Wood
Hendon
Walthamstow
Romford
Wanstead
Newbury Park
Cranham
Golders Green
Highgate
Seven Kings
Hornchurch
Hampstead Hth.
Hampstead
Keats Ho.
Stoke Newington
Leytonstone
Leyton
Ilford
Becontree
Rush Green
Upminster
Cricklewood
Manor Park
Elm Park
Hackney
Forest Gate
Dagenham
Willesden
Camden
Barking
Hacton
Hornchurch
Corbets Tey
North Ockendon
Harlesden
Kilburn
Islington
East Ham
South Hornchurch
Lord's
Regent's Park
St. Pancras
Bethnal Green
Stratford
Creekmouth
Belhus Woods
Finsbury
Shoreditch
West Ham
Beckton
Rainham
South Ockendon
Paddington
Holborn
City
Poplar
Thames
North Stifford
Madame Tussaud's
Oxford
Tate Modern
London City
Thamesmead
Wennington
Aveley
Acton
Hyde Park
Kensington
Tower
Rotherhithe
Blackwall Tunnel
North Woolwich
Woolwich Ferry
Thurrock Services
Holland Ho.
Natural History Science Mus.
Westminster
Southwark
Bermondsey
Belvedere
Chiswick
Earls Court
Tate
War Mus.
Cutty Sark
Woolwich
Plumstead
Abbey Wood
Erith
Purfleet
South Stifford
Hammersmith
Chelsea
Lambeth
The Oval
Greenwich
Maritime Mus.
Charlton
Dartford Crossing
West Thurrock
Grays
Kew Br.
Fulham
Battersea
Peckham
Deptford
New Cross
Welling
Slade Green
Swanscombe Skull Site
National Archives
Putney
Camberwell
Lewisham
Kidbrooke
Bexleyheath
Toll
TL
TQ
Hertford
London
M25
M11
M1
A1(M)
54
55
42
28
29

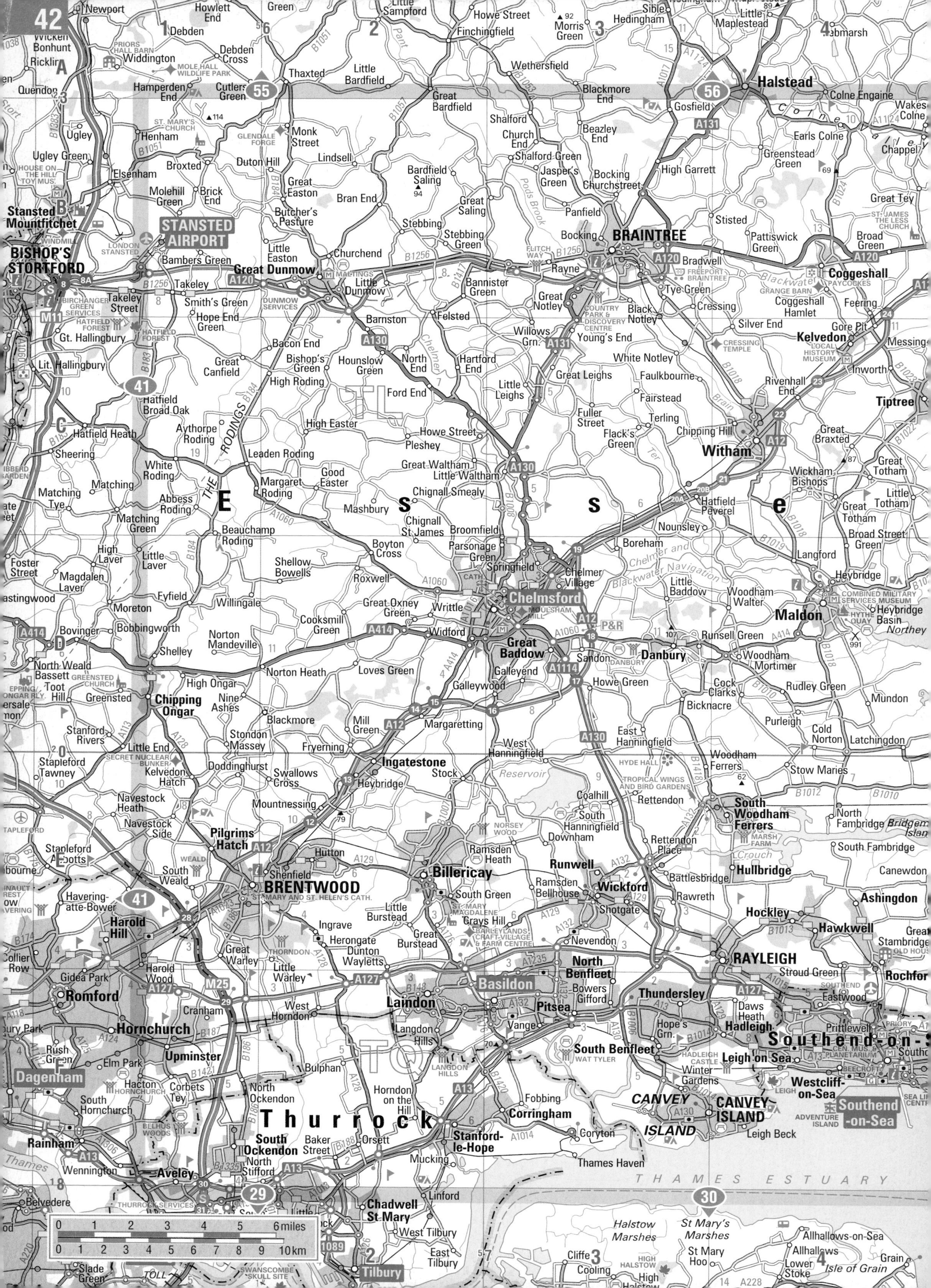

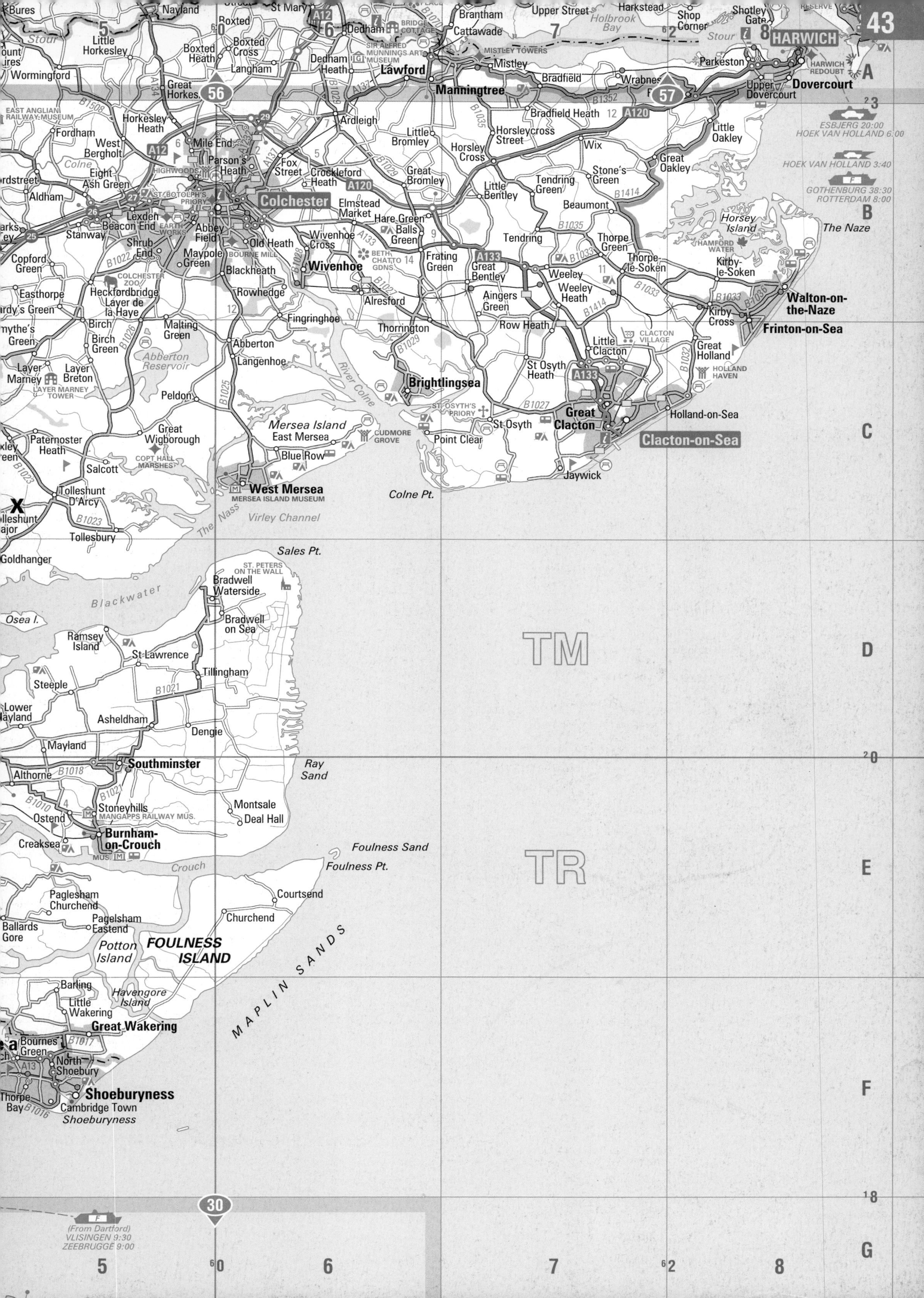
HARWICH
Dovercourt
Manningtree
Lawford
Colchester
Wivenhoe
Brightlingsea
Great Clacton
Clacton-on-Sea
Walton-on-the-Naze
Frinton-on-Sea
West Mersea
Mersea Island
Southminster
Burnham-on-Crouch
Great Wakering
Shoeburyness
FOULNESS ISLAND
MAPLIN SANDS
TM
TR
ESBJERG 20:00
HOEK VAN HOLLAND 6:00
HOEK VAN HOLLAND 3:40
GOTHENBURG 38:30
ROTTERDAM 8:00
(From Dartford)
VLISINGEN 9:30
ZEEBRUGGE 9:00
56
57
30

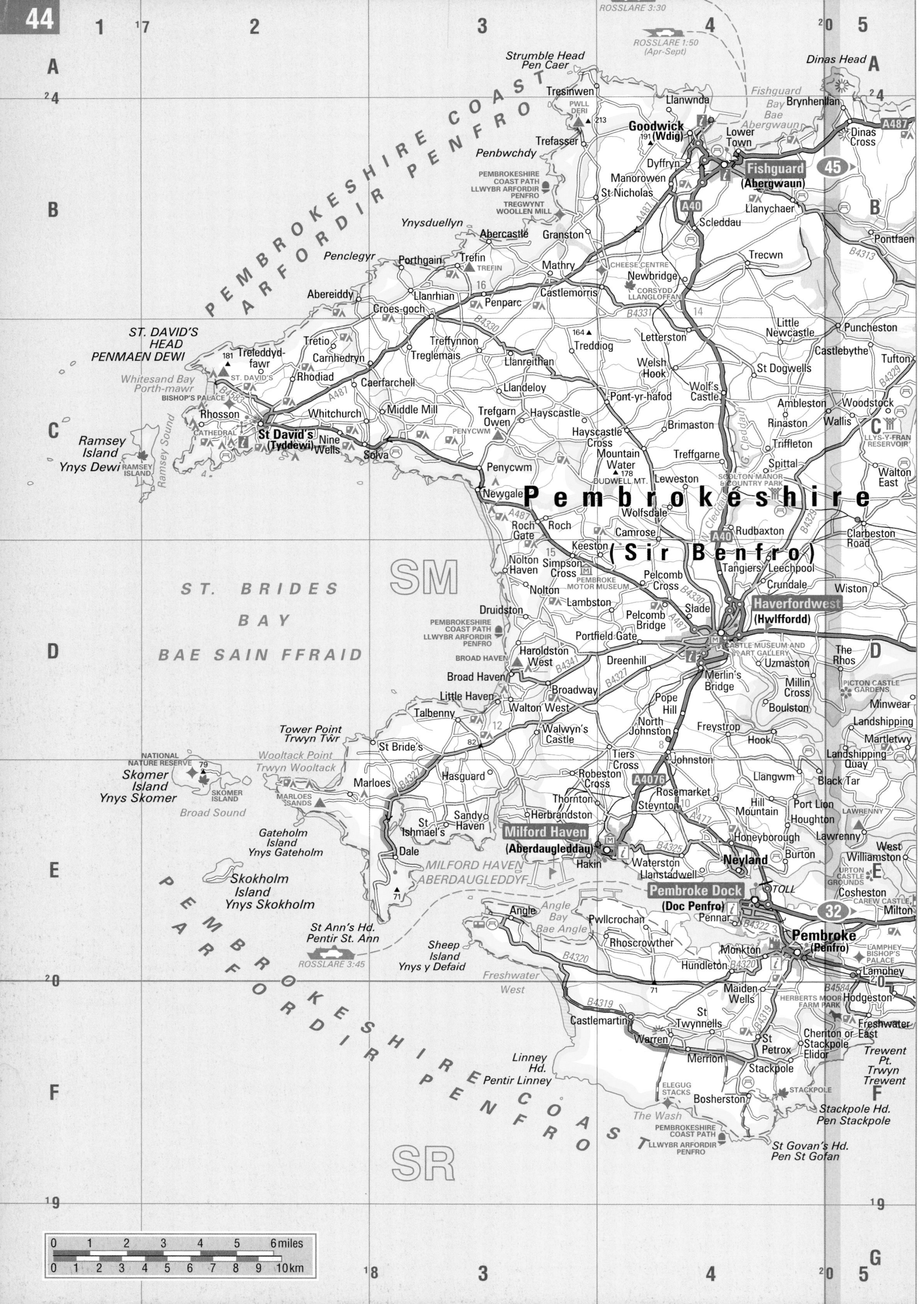

PEMBROKESHIRE COAST
ARFORDIR PENFRO
Strumble Head
Pen Caer
ROSSLARE 3:30
ROSSLARE 1:50 (Apr-Sept)
Dinas Head
Fishguard Bay
Bae Abergwaun
Tresinwen
Llanwnda
Goodwick (Wdig)
Lower Town
Brynhenllan
Dinas Cross
Trefasser
Penbwchdy
Dyffryn
Fishguard (Abergwaun)
Manorowen
St Nicholas
Llanychaer
Scleddau
Pontfaen
Ynysduellyn
Abercastle
Granston
Penclegyr
Porthgain
Trefin
Mathry
Trecwn
Newbridge
Abereiddy
Llanrhian
Penparc
Castlemorris
Croes-goch
Little Newcastle
Puncheston
ST. DAVID'S HEAD
PENMAEN DEWI
Tretio
Treleddyd-fawr
Treffynnon
Treglemais
Treddiog
Letterston
Castlebythe
Tufton
Carnhedryn
Llanreithan
Welsh Hook
St Dogwells
Whitesand Bay
Porth-mawr
Rhodiad
Caerfarchell
Llandeloy
Pont-yr-hafod
Wolf's Castle
Ambleston
Woodstock
Rhosson
Whitchurch
Middle Mill
Trefgarn Owen
Hayscastle
Brimaston
Rinaston
Wallis
Ramsey Island
Ynys Dewi
Ramsey Sound
St David's (Tyddewi)
Nine Wells
Solva
Hayscastle Cross
Mountain Water
Treffgarne
Triffleton
Spittal
Walton East
Penycwm
Leweston
Newgale
Pembrokeshire (Sir Benfro)
Wolfsdale
Roch Gate
Roch
Camrose
Rudbaxton
Clarbeston Road
Keeston
Tangiers
Leechpool
Nolton Haven
Simpson Cross
Pelcomb Cross
Crundale
Wiston
SM
ST. BRIDES BAY
BAE SAIN FFRAID
Nolton
Lambston
Slade
Haverfordwest (Hwlffordd)
Druidston
Pelcomb Bridge
Portfield Gate
Haroldston West
Dreenhill
The Rhos
Uzmaston
Broad Haven
Merlin's Bridge
Millin Cross
Broadway
Pope Hill
Boulston
Minwear
Little Haven
Walton West
Talbenny
North Johnston
Freystrop
Landshipping
Tower Point
Trwyn Twr
Walwyn's Castle
Martletwy
St Bride's
Hook
Landshipping Quay
Wooltack Point
Trwyn Wooltack
Tiers Cross
Johnston
Skomer Island
Ynys Skomer
Marloes
Hasguard
Robeston Cross
Llangwm
Black Tar
Rosemarket
Broad Sound
Thornton
Steynton
Hill Mountain
Port Lion
Houghton
Gateholm Island
Ynys Gateholm
St Ishmael's
Sandy Haven
Herbrandston
Milford Haven (Aberdaugleddau)
Honeyborough
Lawrenny
Dale
Hakin
Waterston
Neyland
Burton
West Williamston
Skokholm Island
Ynys Skokholm
MILFORD HAVEN
ABERDAUGLEDDYF
Llanstadwell
Pembroke Dock (Doc Penfro)
Cosheston
Milton
Angle
Angle Bay
Bae Angle
Pwllcrochan
Pennar
St Ann's Hd.
Pentir St. Ann
Rhoscrowther
Pembroke (Penfro)
Sheep Island
Ynys y Defaid
ROSSLARE 3:45
Monkton
Hundleton
Lamphey
Freshwater West
Maiden Wells
Hodgeston
Castlemartin
St Twynnells
Freshwater East
Warren
St Petrox
Chenton or Stackpole Elidor
Merrion
Trewent Pt.
Trwyn Trewent
Linney Hd.
Pentir Linney
Stackpole
Bosherston
The Wash
Stackpole Hd.
Pen Stackpole
St Govan's Hd.
Pen St Gofan
SR
0 1 2 3 4 5 6 miles
0 1 2 3 4 5 6 7 8 9 10 km

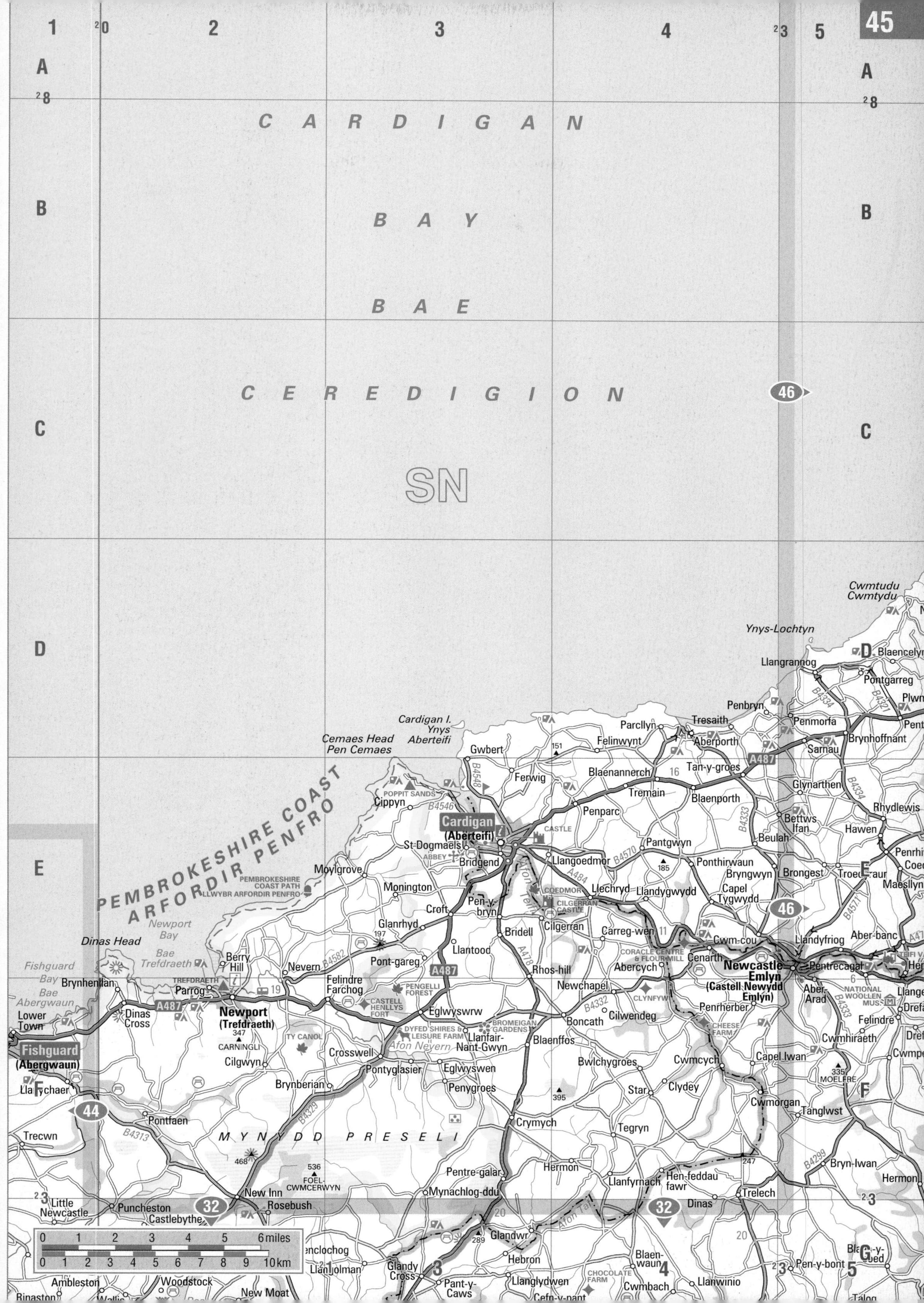
CARDIGAN BAY
BAE CEREDIGION
SN
Cwmtudu Cwmtydu
Ynys-Lochtyn
Llangrannog
Blaencelyn
Pontgarreg
Penbryn
Tresaith
Parcllyn
Aberporth
Penmorfa
Brynhoffnant
Sarnau
Cardigan I. Ynys Aberteifi
Cemaes Head Pen Cemaes
Gwbert
Felinwynt
Ferwig
Blaenannerch
Tan-y-groes
Tremain
Blaenporth
Glynarthen
Rhydlewis
Poppit Sands
Cippyn
Penparc
Bettws Ifan
Hawen
Cardigan (Aberteifi)
Castle
St Dogmaels
Abbey
Bridgend
Pantgwyn
Beulah
Llangoedmor
Ponthirwaun
Bryngwyn
Brongest
Troedyraur
Pembrokeshire Coast Arfordir Penfro
Pembrokeshire Coast Path Llwybr Arfordir Penfro
Moylgrove
Monington
Llechryd
Llandygwydd
Capel Tygwydd
Coedmor
Cilgerran Castle
Croft
Pen-y-bryn
Cilgerran
Bridell
Carreg-wen
Newport Bay
Dinas Head
Glanrhyd
Llantood
Cwm-cou
Llandyfriog
Aber-banc
Fishguard Bay Bae Abergwaun
Bae Trefdraeth
Berry Hill
Nevern
Pont-gareg
Coracle Centre & Flour Mill
Cenarth
Newcastle Emlyn (Castell Newydd Emlyn)
Pentrecagal
Brynhenllan
Trefdraeth
Parrog
Felindre Farchog
Pengelli Forest
Rhos-hill
Abercych
Newchapel
Clynfyw
Aber-Arad
National Woollen Mus.
Lower Town
Dinas Cross
Newport (Trefdraeth)
Castell Henllys Fort
Eglwyswrw
Boncath
Cilwendeg
Penrherber
Felindre
Dyfed Shires & Leisure Farm
Bromeigan Gardens
Cheese Farm
Carningli
Ty Canol
Llanfair-Nant-Gwyn
Blaenffos
Cwmhiraeth
Fishguard (Abergwaun)
Cilgwyn
Crosswell
Afon Nevern
Bwlchygroes
Cwmcych
Capel Iwan
Pontyglasier
Eglwyswen
Llanychaer
Brynberian
Penygroes
Star
Clydey
Moelfre
Cwmorgan
Tanglwst
44
Pontfaen
Crymych
Tegryn
Trecwn
Mynydd Preseli
Foel Cwmcerwyn
Pentre-galar
Hermon
Llanfyrnach
Hen-feddau fawr
Bryn-Iwan
Hermon
New Inn
Mynachlog-ddu
Trelech
Dinas
Little Newcastle
Puncheston
Castlebythe
Rosebush
32
46
A487
A484
A478
B4546
B4548
B4570
B4582
B4313
B4329
B4332
B4333
B4334
B4321
B4571
B4299
Glandwr
Afon Taf
Maenclochog
Llanjolman
Glandy Cross
Hebron
Blaen-waun
Pant-y-Caws
Llanglydwen
Chocolate Farm
Cwmbach
Llanwinio
Pen-y-bont
Blaen-y-coed
Ambleston
Woodstock
New Moat
0 1 2 3 4 5 6 miles
0 1 2 3 4 5 6 7 8 9 10 km

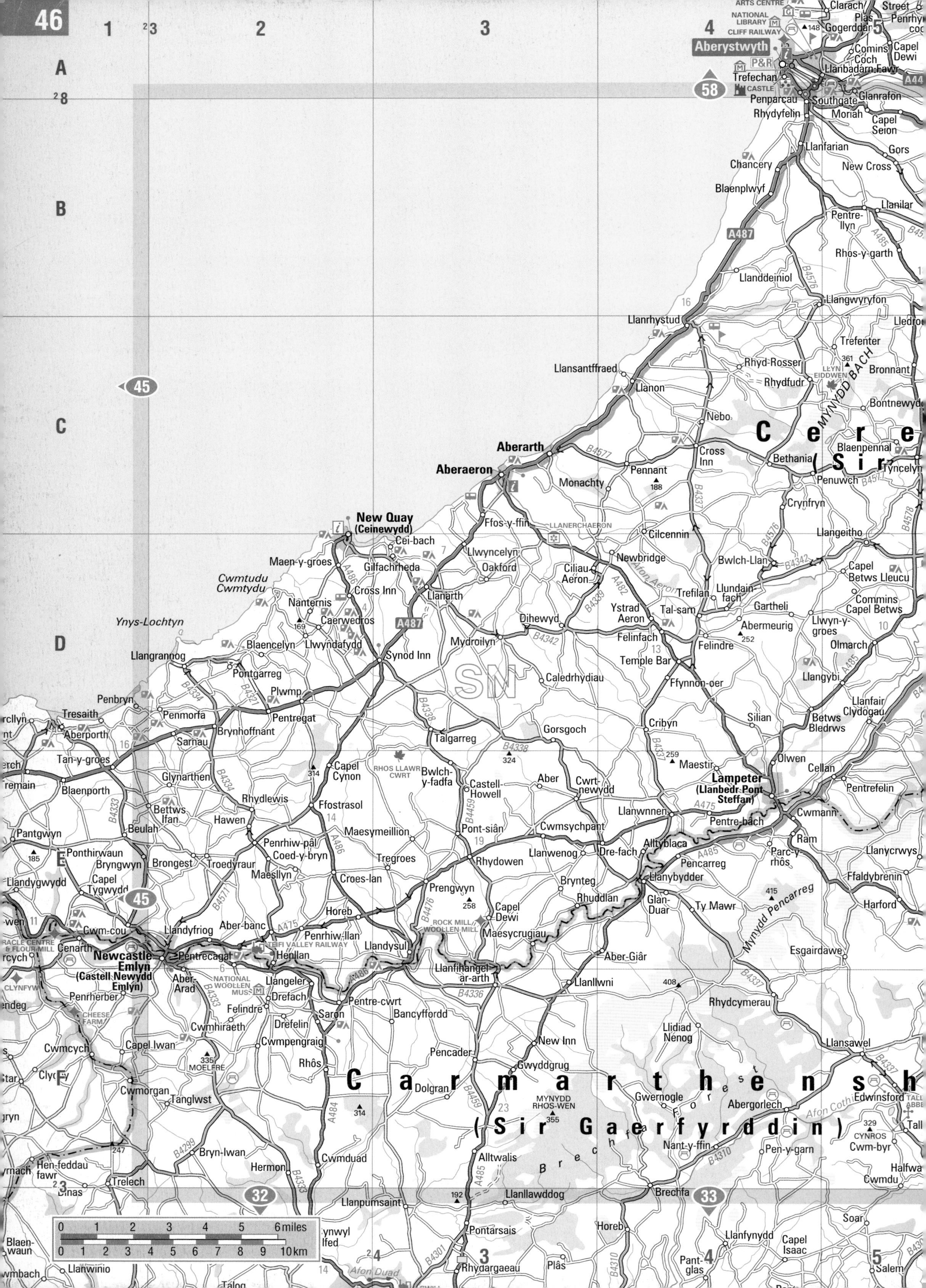
Aberystwyth
Llanrhystud
Llanon
Aberarth
Aberaeron
New Quay
(Ceinewydd)
Llangrannog
Aberporth
Newcastle
Emlyn
(Castell Newydd
Emlyn)
Lampeter
(Llanbedr Pont
Steffan)
Llandysul
Carmarthenshire
(Sir Gaerfyrddin)
Brechfa
0 1 2 3 4 5 6 miles
0 1 2 3 4 5 6 7 8 9 10 km

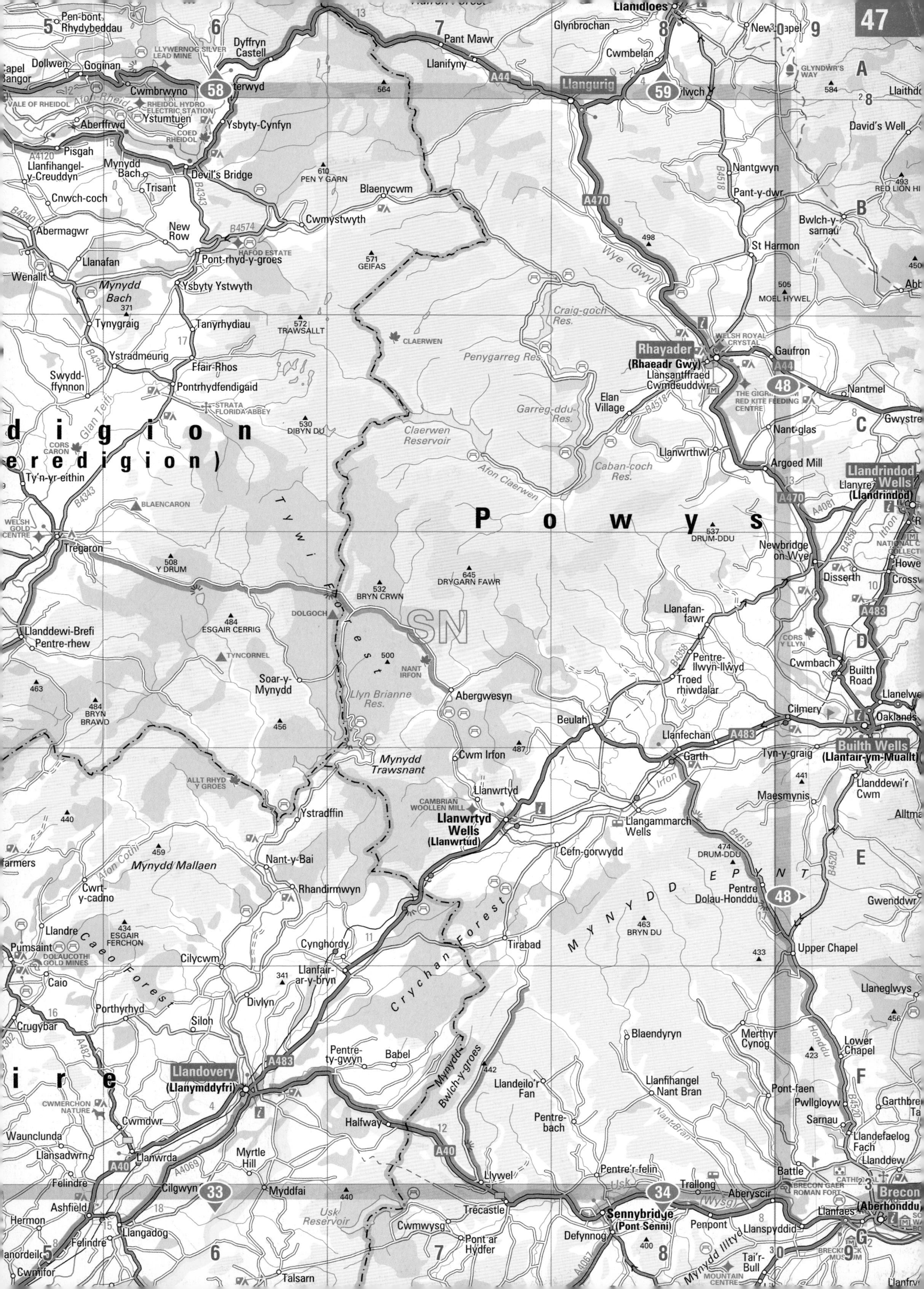
Llanidloes
Glynbrochan
Pen-bont Rhydybeddau
Dyffryn Castell
Pant Mawr
Llanifyny
Cwmbelan
Goginan
Dollwen
LLYWERNOG SILVER LEAD MINE
Cwmbrwyno
VALE OF RHEIDOL
RHEIDOL HYDRO ELECTRIC STATION
Ystumtuen
Aberffrwd
Ysbyty-Cynfyn
COED RHEIDOL
Llangurig
GLYNDWR'S WAY
David's Well
Pisgah
Llanfihangel-y-Creuddyn
Mynydd Bach
Trisant
Devil's Bridge
610 PEN Y GARN
Blaenycwm
Nantgwyn
Pant-y-dwr
493 RED LION HILL
Cnwch-coch
Abermagwr
New Row
Cwmystwyth
HAFOD ESTATE
Pont-rhyd-y-groes
Llanafan
Wenallt
571 GEIFAS
498
St Harmon
Bwlch-y-sarnau
Wye (Gwy)
505 MOEL HYWEL
Mynydd Bach
371
Ysbyty Ystwyth
Tynygraig
Tanyrhydiau
572 TRAWSALLT
Craig-goch Res.
Ystradmeurig
Ffair-Rhos
CLAERWEN
Penygarreg Res.
Rhayader (Rhaeadr Gwy)
WELSH ROYAL CRYSTAL
Gaufron
Swydd-ffynnon
Pontrhydfendigaid
STRATA FLORIDA ABBEY
Llansantffraed Cwmdeuddwr
THE GIGRIN FARM RED KITE FEEDING CENTRE
Nantmel
Elan Village
Garreg-ddu Res.
530 DIBYN DU
Claerwen Reservoir
Nant-glas
Gwystre
Ceredigion
CORS CARON
Llanwrthwl
Argoed Mill
Caban-coch Res.
Afon Claerwen
Llandrindod Wells (Llandrindod)
Llanyre
Ty'n-yr-eithin
BLAENCARON
Powys
537 DRUM-DDU
WELSH GOLD CENTRE
Tregaron
Newbridge on Wye
508 Y DRUM
645 DRYGARN FAWR
Disserth
Howey
Crossway
532 BRYN CRWN
Tywi Forest
DOLGOCH
SN
Llanafan-fawr
484 ESGAIR CERRIG
Llanddewi-Brefi
Pentre-rhew
TYNCORNEL
500
NANT IRFON
CORS Y LLYN
Pentre-llwyn-llwyd
Cwmbach
Builth Road
463
484 BRYN BRAWD
Soar-y-Mynydd
Llyn Brianne Res.
Abergwesyn
Troed rhiwdalar
456
Beulah
Cilmery
Oaklands
Llanelwedd
Llanfechan
487
Cwm Irfon
Mynydd Trawsnant
Garth
Tyn-y-graig
Builth Wells (Llanfair-ym-Muallt)
ALLT RHYD Y GROES
Llanwrtyd
441
Maesmynis
Llanddewi'r Cwm
CAMBRIAN WOOLLEN MILL
Llanwrtyd Wells (Llanwrtud)
Ystradffin
440
Llangammarch Wells
Alltmawr
459
Mynydd Mallaen
Nant-y-Bai
Cefn-gorwydd
474 DRUM-DDU
Farmers
Afon Cothi
Mynydd Epynt
Cwrt-y-cadno
Rhandirmwyn
Pentre Dolau-Honddu
Gwenddwr
Crychan Forest
463 BRYN DU
Llandre
434 ESGAIR FERCHON
Cynghordy
Tirabad
Upper Chapel
Pumsaint
DOLAUCOTHI GOLD MINES
Cilycwm
Caeo Forest
433
Caio
341
Llanfair-ar-y-bryn
Llaneglwys
Divlyn
Porthyrhyd
Siloh
Crugybar
Blaendyryn
Merthyr Cynog
456
Lower Chapel
Honddu
Pentre-ty-gwyn
Babel
423
Llandovery (Llanymddyfri)
Mynydd Bwlch-y-groes
442
Llandeilo'r Fan
Llanfihangel Nant Bran
Pont-faen
Pwllgloyw
Garthbrengy
CWMERCHON NATURE
Cwmdwr
Halfway
Pentre-bach
Sarnau
Wauncluda
Nant Brân
Llandefaelog Fach
Llansadwrn
Llanwrda
Myrtle Hill
Llanddew
Llywel
Pentre'r-felin
Battle
Felindre
Cilgwyn
Myddfai
440
Trallong
Aberyscir
BRECON GAER ROMAN FORT
CATHEDRAL
Brecon (Aberhonddu)
Ashfield
Usk Reservoir
Trecastle
Usk (Wysg)
Sennybridge (Pont Senni)
Penpont
Llanspyddid
Llanfaes
Hermon
Llangadog
Cwmwysg
Pont ar Hydfer
Defynnog
400
Felindre
Llanddeusant
Mynydd Illtyd
BRECKNOCK MUSEUM
Cwmifor
Talsarn
MOUNTAIN CENTRE
Tai'r-Bull
Llanfrynach
A44
A470
A4120
B4343
B4574
B4340
B4518
A4081
B4358
A483
B4519
B4520
A482
A40
A4069
A4067
58
59
48
33
34
A
B
C
D
E
F
G
5
6
7
8
9

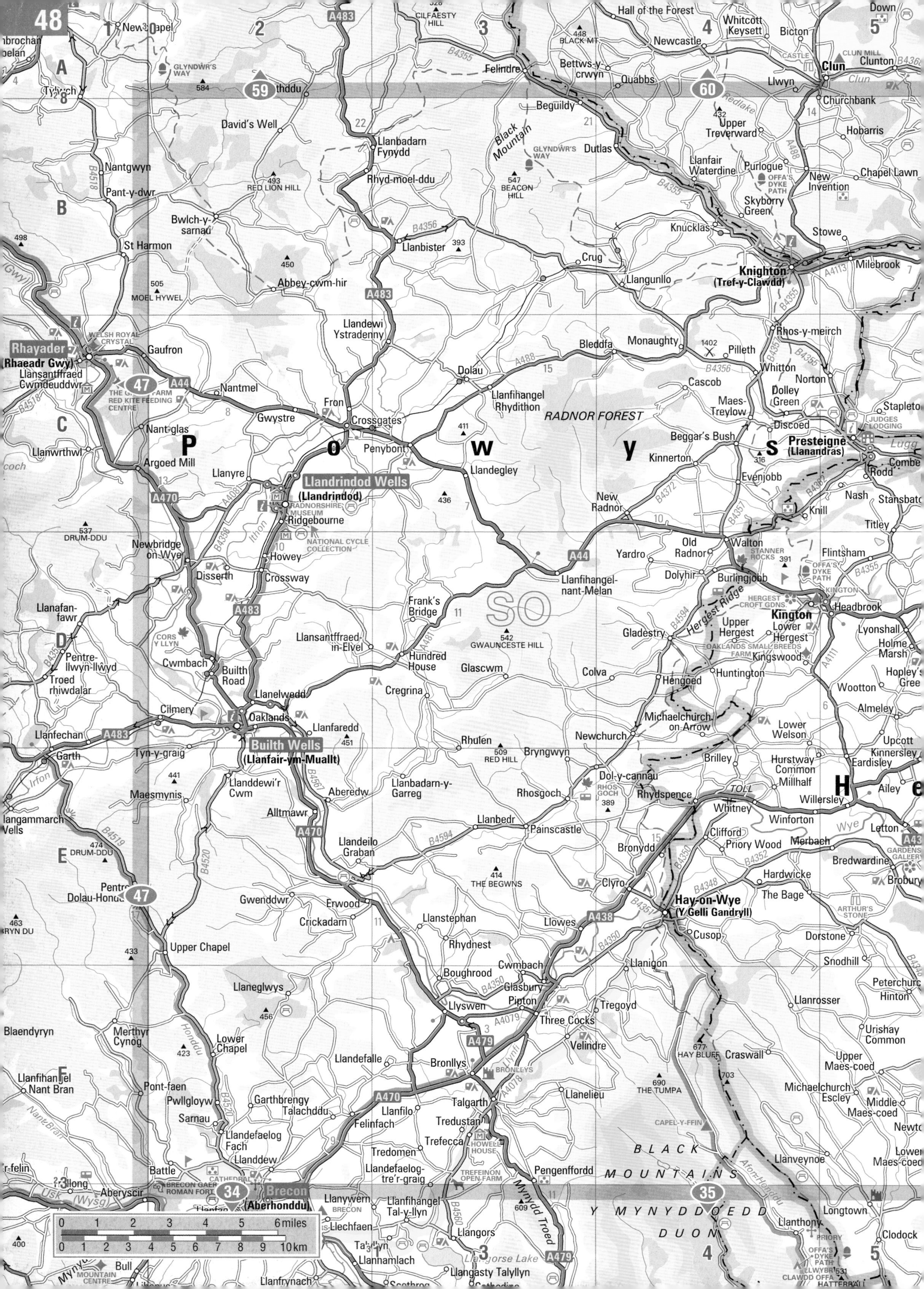

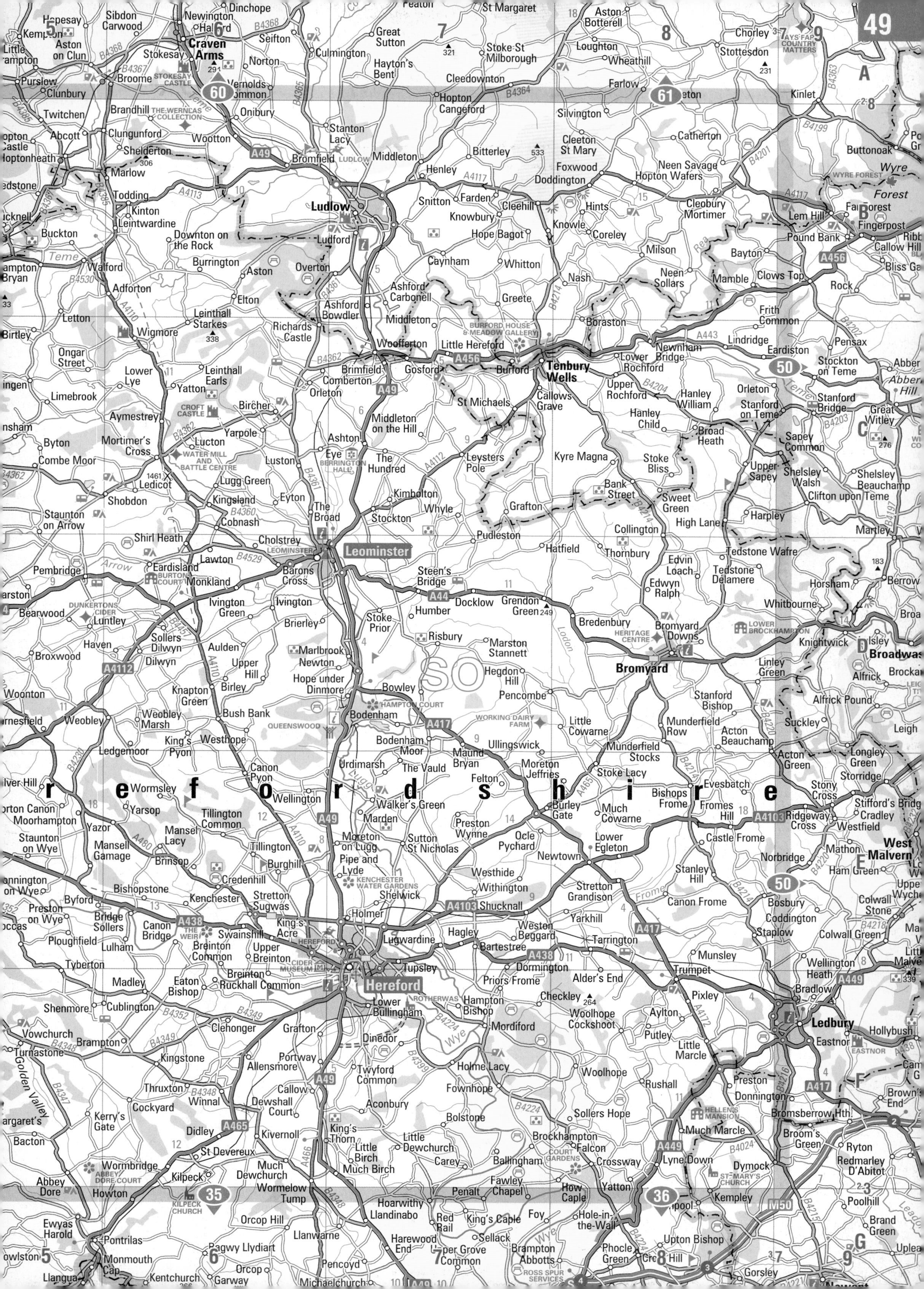

Hopesay
Kempton
Little Brampton
Sibdon Carwood
Newington
Dinchope
Halford
Craven Arms
Aston on Clun
Stokesay
Purslow
Clunbury
Broome
Stokesay Castle
Vernolds Common
Norton
Seifton
Culmington
Great Sutton
Feaon
St Margaret
Stoke St Milborough
Hayton's Bent
Cleedownton
Hopton Cangeford
Aston Botterell
Loughton
Wheathill
Farlow
Chorley
Stottesdon
Days Farm Country Matters
Kinlet
Twitchen
Brandhill
The Wernlas Collection
Onibury
Stanton Lacy
Silvington
Cleeton St Mary
Catherton
Hopton Castle
Hoptonheath
Abcott
Clungunford
Shelderton
Wootton
Bromfield
Ludlow
Middleton
Bitterley
Henley
Foxwood
Doddington
Neen Savage
Hopton Wafers
Buttonoak
Wyre Forest
Bedstone
Marlow
Todding
Kinton
Leintwardine
Bucknell
Buckton
Snitton
Farden
Cleehill
Knowbury
Hints
Knowle
Coreley
Cleobury Mortimer
Lem Hill
Far Forest
Fingerpost
Pound Bank
Callow Hill
Downton on the Rock
Ludford
Hope Bagot
Milson
Bayton
Teme
Walford
Burrington
Aston
Overton
Caynham
Whitton
Nash
Neen Sollars
Mamble
Clows Top
Bliss Gate
Rock
Brampton Bryan
Adforton
Elton
Ashford Carbonell
Greete
Ashford Bowdler
Letton
Leinthall Starkes
Wigmore
Richards Castle
Middleton
Burford House & Meadow Gallery
Boraston
Frith Common
Birtley
Ongar Street
Lower Lye
Leinthall Earls
Woofferton
Little Hereford
Brimfield
Gosford
Comberton
Burford
Tenbury Wells
Lower Rochford
Newnham Bridge
Lindridge
Eardiston
Pensax
Stockton on Teme
Limebrook
Yatton
Orleton
Upper Rochford
Hanley William
Orleton
Stanford Bridge
Stanford on Teme
Great Witley
Croft Castle
Bircher
Middleton on the Hill
St Michaels
Callows Grave
Hanley Child
Broad Heath
Aymestrey
Yarpole
Byton
Mortimer's Cross
Lucton
Water Mill and Battle Centre
Ashton
Eye
Berrington Hall
The Hundred
Leysters Pole
Kyre Magna
Stoke Bliss
Sapey Common
Upper Sapey
Shelsley Walsh
Shelsley Beauchamp
Clifton upon Teme
Combe Moor
Luston
Ledicot
Lugg Green
Kimbolton
Bank Street
Sweet Green
Staunton on Arrow
Shobdon
Kingsland
Eyton
Cobnash
The Broad
Stockton
Whyle
Grafton
High Lane
Harpley
Shirl Heath
Cholstrey
Leominster
Pudleston
Collington
Hatfield
Thornbury
Martley
Tedstone Wafre
Eardisland
Lawton
Barons Cross
Pembridge
Arrow
Burton Court
Monkland
Steen's Bridge
Edvin Loach
Tedstone Delamere
Edwyn Ralph
Horsham
Berrow
Dunkertons Cider
Ivington Green
Ivington
Docklow
Grendon Green
Bredenbury
Whitbourne
Bearwood
Luntley
Stoke Prior
Humber
Heritage Centre
Bromyard Downs
Lower Brockhampton
Sollers Dilwyn
Brierley
Risbury
Marston Stannett
Knightwick
Isley
Broadwas
Haven
Aulden
Broxwood
Dilwyn
Marlbrook
Newton
Upper Hill
Bromyard
Linley Green
Alfrick
Hope under Dinmore
Hegdon Hill
SO
Woonton
Knapton Green
Birley
Bowley
Pencombe
Stanford Bishop
Alfrick Pound
Hampton Court
Bodenham
Weobley
Weobley Marsh
Bush Bank
Queenswood
Working Dairy Farm
Little Cowarne
Munderfield Row
Acton Beauchamp
Suckley
Leigh
Ledgemoor
King's Pyon
Westhope
Bodenham Moor
Ullingswick
Munderfield Stocks
Acton Green
Longley Green
Urdimarsh
The Vauld
Maund Bryan
Moreton Jeffries
Stoke Lacy
Storridge
Canon Pyon
Felton
Evesbatch
Stony Cross
Wormsley
Wellington
Bishops Frome
Fromes Hill
Burley Gate
Much Cowarne
Ridgeway Cross
Stifford's Bridge
Cradley
Herefordshire
Yarsop
Tillington Common
Walker's Green
Marden
Preston Wynne
Lower Egleton
Westfield
Norton Canon
Moorhampton
Yazor
Mansel Lacy
Tillington
Moreton on Lugg
Sutton St Nicholas
Ocle Pychard
Castle Frome
Mathon
West Malvern
Staunton on Wye
Mansell Gamage
Brinsop
Burghill
Pipe and Lyde
Newtown
Norbridge
Ham Green
Credenhill
Kenchester Water Gardens
Westhide
Stanley Hill
Monnington on Wye
Bishopstone
Stretton Sugwas
Withington
Stretton Grandison
Upper Wyche
Byford
Kenchester
Shelwick
Shucknall
Canon Frome
Bosbury
Colwall Stone
Preston on Wye
Bridge Sollers
Canon Bridge
King's Acre
Holmer
Yarkhill
Coddington
Moccas
The Weir
Swainshill
Lugwardine
Hagley
Weston Beggard
Staplow
Colwall Green
Ploughfield
Lulham
Breinton Common
Upper Breinton
Hereford
Cider Museum
Bartestree
Tarrington
Munsley
Tyberton
Breinton
Tupsley
Dormington
Trumpet
Wellington Heath
Madley
Eaton Bishop
Ruckhall Common
Hereford
Rotherwas
Hampton Bishop
Priors Frome
Alder's End
Pixley
Bradlow
Ledbury
Shenmore
Cublington
Lower Bullingham
Checkley
Aylton
Vowchurch
Clehonger
Grafton
Mordiford
Woolhope Cockshoot
Putley
Eastnor
Hollybush
Turnastone
Brampton
Dinedor
Wye
Little Marcle
Golden Valley
Kingstone
Portway
Allensmore
Twyford Common
Holme Lacy
Woolhope
Rushall
Preston
Donnington
Thruxton
Callow
Winnal
Fownhope
Brown's End
Cockyard
Dewsall Court
Aconbury
Sollers Hope
Hellens Mansion
Bromsberrow Hth.
Margaret's
Kerry's Gate
Didley
Bolstone
Much Marcle
Bacton
Kivernoll
King's Thorn
Little Birch
Little Dewchurch
Brockhampton
Broom's Green
St Devereux
Much Birch
Carey
Falcon
Court Gardens
Crossway
Lyne Down
Ryton
Dymock
Redmarley D'Abitot
Wormbridge
Abbey Dore Court
Kilpeck
Much Dewchurch
Ballingham
St Mary's Church
Abbey Dore
Howton
Kilpeck Church
Wormelow Tump
Penalt
Fawley Chapel
How Caple
Yatton
Kempley
Poolhill
Orcop Hill
Hoarwithy
Llandinabo
Red Rail
King's Caple
Foy
Hole-in-the-Wall
Ewyas Harold
Pontrilas
Llanwarne
Harewood End
Sellack
Upton Bishop
Brand Green
Bowlston
Monmouth Cap
Bagwy Llydiart
Upper Grove Common
Brampton Abbotts
Phocle Green
Llangua
Kentchurch
Orcop
Garway
Pencoyd
Michaelchurch
Ross Spur Services
Gorsley

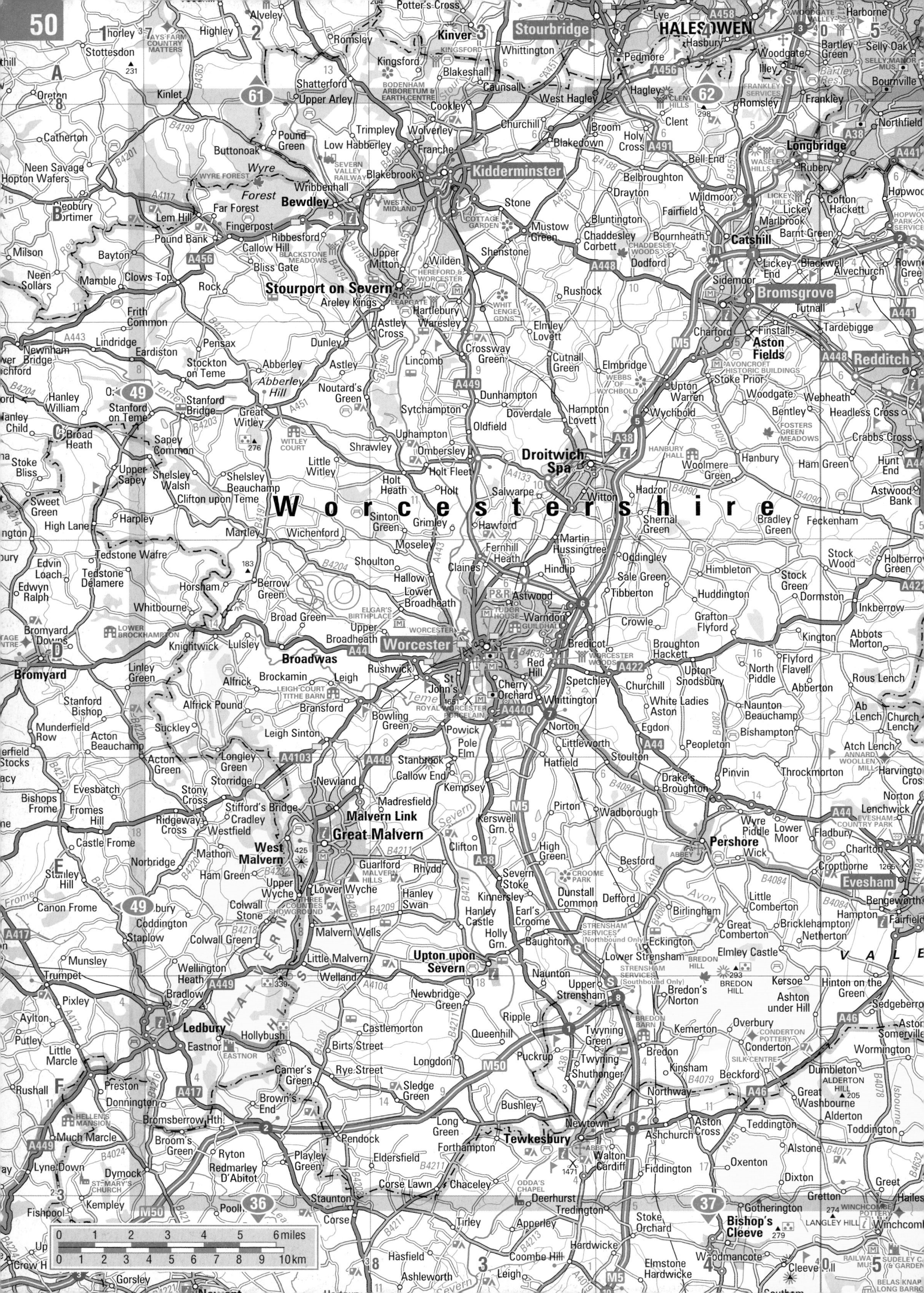
Thorley
Stottesdon
Highley
Alveley
Romsley
Potter's Cross
Kinver
Kingsford
Stourbridge
Whittington
Blakeshall
Caunsall
HALESOWEN
Hasbury
Pedmore
Harborne
Bartley Green
Selly Oak
Woodgate
Illey
Bournville
Oreton
Kinlet
Shatterford
Upper Arley
BODENHAM ARBORETUM & EARTH CENTRE
Cookley
West Hagley
Hagley
Clent Hills
Romsley
Frankley
Catherton
Buttonoak
Pound Green
Low Habberley
Trimpley
Wolverley
Franche
Churchill
Blakedown
Broom
Clent
Holy Cross
Northfield
Longbridge
Neen Savage
Hopton Wafers
Wyre Forest
Wribbenhall
Blakebrook
SEVERN VALLEY RAILWAY
Kidderminster
Belbroughton
Bell End
Rubery
Cleobury Mortimer
Lem Hill
Far Forest
Bewdley
WEST MIDLAND
Stone
Drayton
Fairfield
Wildmoor
Cofton Hackett
Lickey
Hopwood
Fingerpost
Pound Bank
Ribbesford
COTTAGE GARDEN
Mustow Green
Bluntington
Chaddesley Corbett
Bournheath
Marlbrook
Barnt Green
Catshill
Milson
Bayton
Callow Hill
BLACKSTONE MEADOWS
Upper Mitton
Shenstone
Dodford
Lickey End
Blackwell
Alvechurch
Rowney Green
Neen Sollars
Mamble
Clows Top
Bliss Gate
Rock
Stourport on Severn
Wilden
HEREFORD & WORCESTER
Rushock
Sidemoor
Bromsgrove
Areley Kings
Hartlebury
WHITLENGE GDNS
Frith Common
Astley Cross
Waresley
Elmley Lovett
Tutnall
Charford
Finstall
Tardebigge
Newnham Bridge
Lindridge
Eardiston
Pensax
Dunley
Astley
Lincomb
Crossway Green
Cutnall Green
Elmbridge
Aston Fields
Redditch
Stockton on Teme
Abberley
Abberley Hill
Noutard's Green
WEBBS OF WYCHBOLD
AVONCROFT HISTORIC BUILDINGS
Stoke Prior
Upton Warren
Woodgate
Webheath
Hanley William
Stanford Bridge
Stanford on Teme
Great Witley
Sytchampton
Dunhampton
Doverdale
Hampton Lovett
Wychbold
Bentley
Headless Cross
Hanley Child
Broad Heath
Sapey Common
WITLEY COURT
Uphampton
Oldfield
FOSTERS GREEN MEADOWS
Crabbs Cross
Stoke Bliss
Upper Sapey
Shrawley
Ombersley
Droitwich Spa
HANBURY HALL
Hanbury
Little Witley
Holt Fleet
Woolmere Green
Ham Green
Hunt End
Shelsley Walsh
Shelsley Beauchamp
Holt Heath
Holt
Salwarpe
Witton
Hadzor
Astwood Bank
Sweet Green
Clifton upon Teme
Worcestershire
High Lane
Harpley
Sinton Green
Grimley
Hawford
Shernal Green
Bradley Green
Feckenham
Martley
Wichenford
Martin Hussingtree
Tedstone Wafre
Moseley
Fernhill Heath
Oddingley
Stock Wood
Holberrow Green
Edvin Loach
Tedstone Delamere
Shoulton
Claines
Hindlip
Himbleton
Edwyn Ralph
Horsham
Berrow Green
Hallow
Lower Broadheath
Sale Green
Stock Green
Whitbourne
P&R
Astwood
Tibberton
Huddington
Dormston
TUDOR HOUSE
Warndon
Inkberrow
Bromyard Downs
LOWER BROCKHAMPTON
Broad Green
ELGAR'S BIRTHPLACE
Crowle
Grafton Flyford
Knightwick
Lulsley
Upper Broadheath
WORCESTER
GUILDHALL
Kington
Abbots Morton
Bromyard
Broadwas
Worcester
Bredicot
Broughton Hackett
Flyford Flavell
Linley Green
Rushwick
Red Hill
WORCESTER WOODS
Upton Snodsbury
North Piddle
Rous Lench
Alfrick
Brockamin
Leigh
St John's
Cherry Orchard
Spetchley
Churchill
Abberton
Stanford Bishop
LEIGH COURT TITHE BARN
Bransford
ROYAL WORCESTER PORCELAIN
Whittington
White Ladies Aston
Naunton Beauchamp
Ab Lench
Church Lench
Alfrick Pound
Bowling Green
Munderfield Row
Acton Beauchamp
Suckley
Leigh Sinton
Powick
Norton
Egdon
Bishampton
Pole Elm
Littleworth
Peopleton
Atch Lench
ANNARD WOOLLEN MILL
Harvington Cross
Acton Green
Longley Green
Stanbrook
Hatfield
Stoulton
Pinvin
Throckmorton
Storridge
Callow End
Kempsey
Drake's Broughton
Evesbatch
Stony Cross
Newland
Norton
Bishops Frome
Fromes Hill
Stifford's Bridge
Cradley
Madresfield
Pirton
Wadborough
Lenchwick
Ridgeway Cross
Westfield
Malvern Link
Great Malvern
Kerswell Grn.
Wyre Piddle
Lower Moor
Fladbury
EVESHAM COUNTRY PARK
Castle Frome
West Malvern
Clifton
High Green
Pershore
ABBEY
Charlton
Wick
Mathon
Norbridge
Guarlford
MALVERN HILLS
Rhydd
Besford
Cropthorne
Stanley Hill
Ham Green
Upper Wyche
Lower Wyche
Severn Stoke
CROOME PARK
Evesham
Hanley Swan
Kinnersley
Dunstall Common
Defford
Little Comberton
Bengeworth
Canon Frome
Colwall Stone
THREE COUNTIES SHOWGROUND
Hanley Castle
Earl's Croome
Birlingham
Avon
Hampton
Fairfield
Coddington
Great Comberton
Bricklehampton
Malvern Wells
Holly Grn.
STRENSHAM SERVICES (Northbound Only)
Eckington
Netherton
Staplow
Colwall Green
Baughton
Little Malvern
Upton upon Severn
Lower Strensham
Elmley Castle
VALE
Munsley
Wellington Heath
Welland
Naunton
STRENSHAM SERVICES (Southbound Only)
BREDON HILL
Kersoe
Hinton on the Green
Trumpet
Bradlow
Newbridge Green
Upper Strensham
Bredon's Norton
Ashton under Hill
Pixley
Sedgeberrow
Aylton
Ledbury
Hollybush
Castlemorton
Ripple
BREDON BARN
Kemerton
Overbury
CONDERTON POTTERY
Aston Somerville
Putley
Eastnor
Birts Street
Queenhill
Twyning Green
Bredon
Conderton
Wormington
Little Marcle
EASTNOR
Longdon
Puckrup
Twyning
Kinsham
SILK CENTRE
Dumbleton
ALDERTON HILL
Rushall
Preston
Camer's Green
Rye Street
Shuthonger
Beckford
Donnington
Sledge Green
Northway
Great Washbourne
Alderton
HELLENS MANSION
Brown's End
Bushley
Aston Cross
Teddington
Toddington
Bromsberrow Hth.
Long Green
Newtown
Ashchurch
Much Marcle
Broom's Green
Pendock
Forthampton
Tewkesbury
ABBEY
Alstone
Lyne Down
Ryton
Redmarley D'Abitot
Playley Green
Eldersfield
Walton Cardiff
Fiddington
Oxenton
Dymock
ST MARY'S CHURCH
Corse Lawn
Chaceley
ODDA'S CHAPEL
Dixton
Greet
Kempley
Staunton
Deerhurst
Tredington
Gretton
Gotherington
WINCHCOMBE POTTERY
Hailes
Fishpool
Pool Hill
Corse
Tirley
Apperley
Stoke Orchard
Bishop's Cleeve
LANGLEY HILL
Winchcombe
Hasfield
Coombe Hill
Hardwicke
Elmstone Hardwicke
Woodmancote
Cleeve Hill
SUDELEY CASTLE & GARDENS
BELAS KNAP LONG BARROW
Gorsley
Crow Hill
Ashleworth
Leigh
0 1 2 3 4 5 6 miles
0 1 2 3 4 5 6 7 8 9 10 km

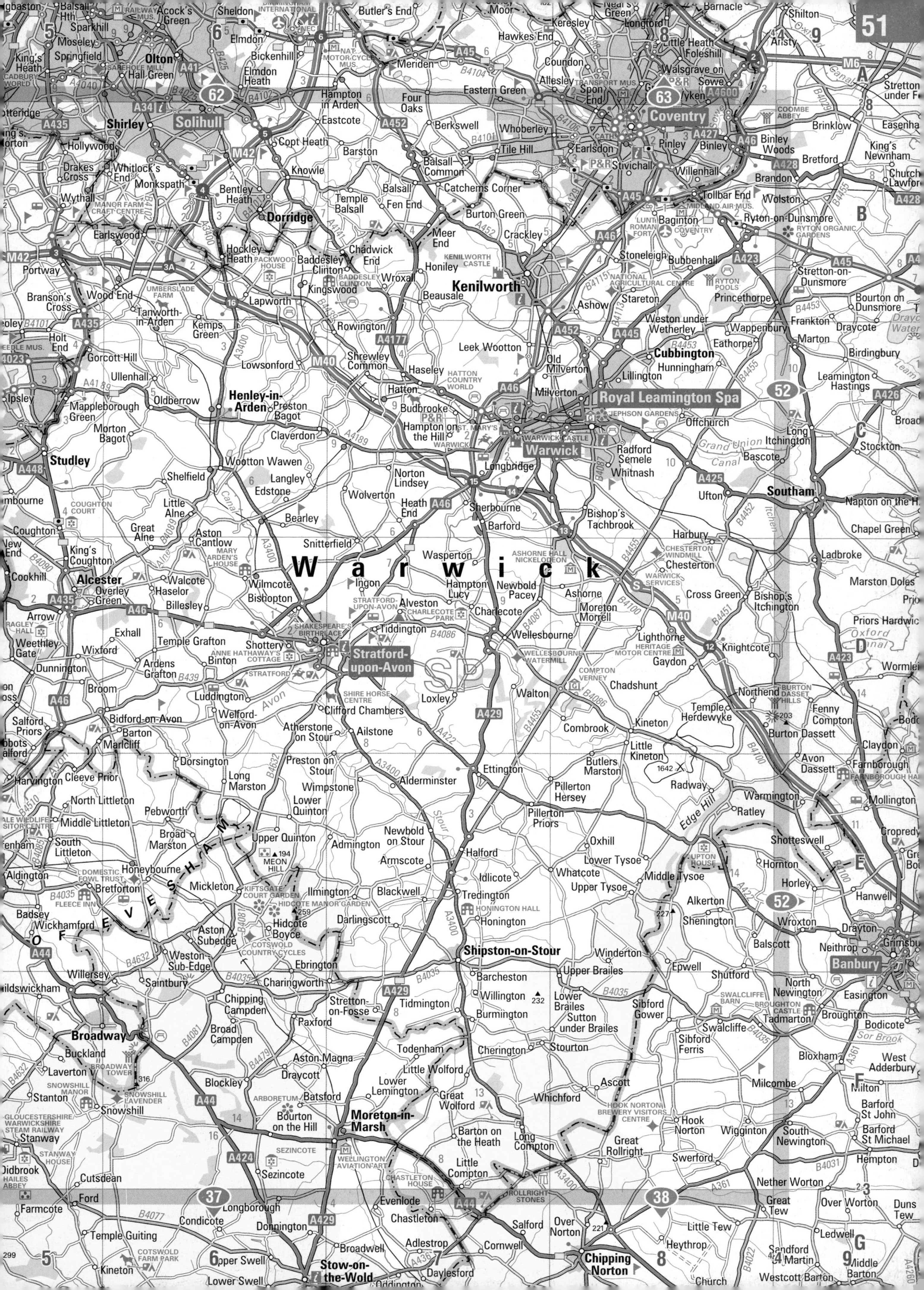

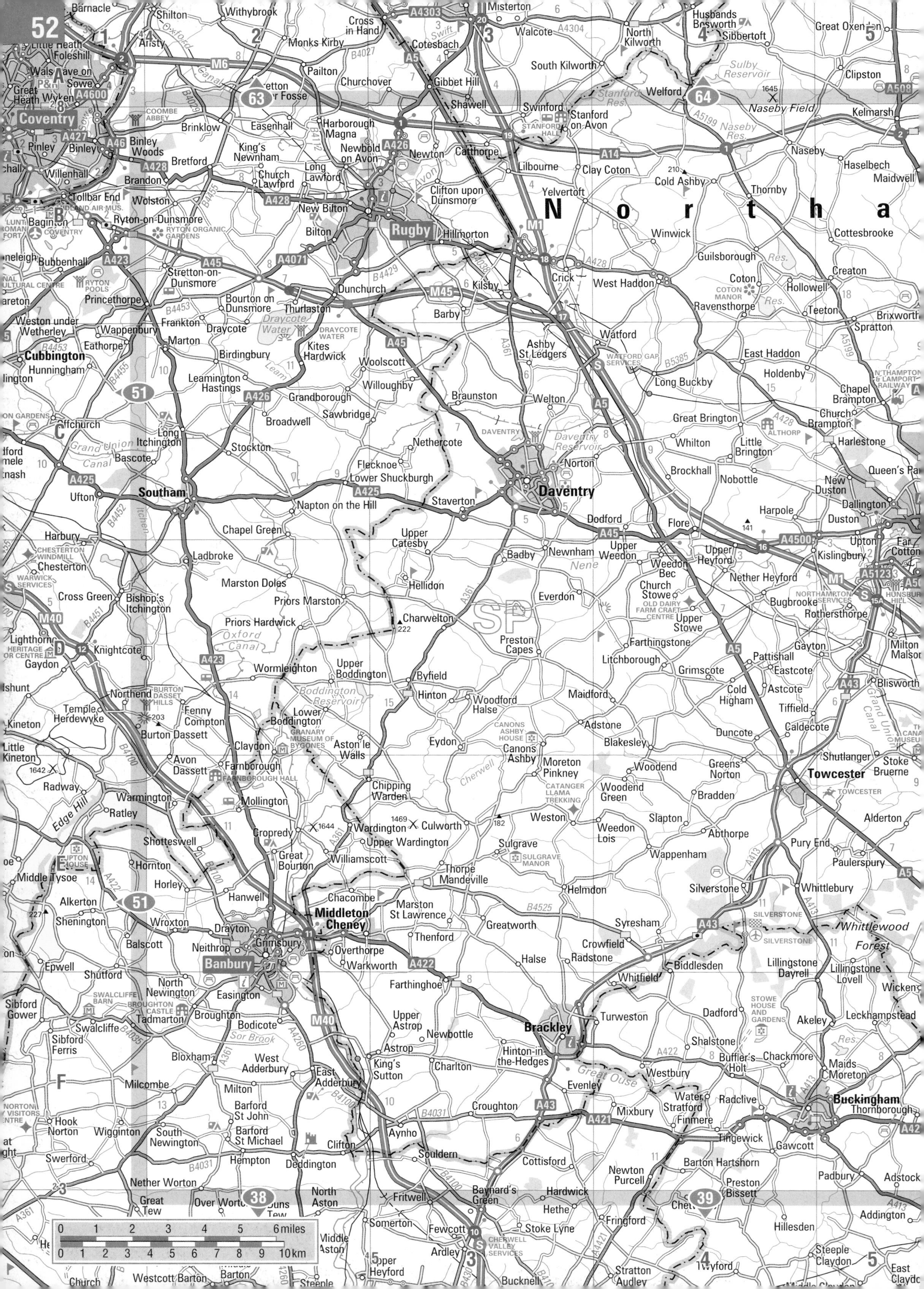
52
Northa
SP
Coventry
Rugby
Daventry
Southam
Banbury
Brackley
Towcester
Buckingham
Middleton Cheney
Barnacle
Shilton
Withybrook
Cross in Hand
Misterton
Walcote
Husbands Bosworth
Great Oxendon
Ansty
Monks Kirby
Cotesbach
North Kilworth
Sibbertoft
Little Heath
Foleshill
Pailton
Gibbet Hill
South Kilworth
Sulby Reservoir
Clipston
Churchover
Welford
Naseby Field
Shawell
Swinford
Stanford on Avon
Stanford Res.
Kelmarsh
Great Heath
Wyken
Sowe
Coombe Abbey
Brinklow
Easenhall
Harborough Magna
Newbold on Avon
Newton
Catthorpe
Naseby Res.
Naseby
Binley
Binley Woods
King's Newnham
Church Lawford
Long Lawford
Lilbourne
Clay Coton
Cold Ashby
Haselbech
Maidwell
Pinley
Willenhall
Bretford
Brandon
Wolston
Clifton upon Dunsmore
Yelvertoft
Thornby
Tollbar End
Baginton
Ryton-on-Dunsmore
Ryton Organic Gardens
New Bilton
Bilton
Hillmorton
Winwick
Cottesbrooke
Bubbenhall
Stretton-on-Dunsmore
Guilsborough
Creaton
Ryton Pools
Dunchurch
Kilsby
Crick
West Haddon
Coton
Hollowell
Princethorpe
Bourton on Dunsmore
Thurlaston
Barby
Coton Manor
Ravensthorpe
Teeton
Brixworth
Weston under Wetherley
Frankton
Draycote
Draycote Water
Watford
Spratton
Wappenbury
Marton
Kites Hardwick
Ashby St Ledgers
Watford Gap Services
Eathorpe
Birdingbury
Woolscott
Long Buckby
East Haddon
Cubbington
Hunningham
Leamington Hastings
Willoughby
Holdenby
Grandborough
Braunston
Welton
Chapel Brampton
Sawbridge
Broadwell
Great Brington
Church Brampton
Offchurch
Long Itchington
Grand Union Canal
Stockton
Nethercote
Daventry Reservoir
Whilton
Little Brington
Althorp
Harlestone
Bascote
Flecknoe
Lower Shuckburgh
Norton
Brockhall
Nobottle
New Duston
Queen's Park
Ufton
Napton on the Hill
Staverton
Dodford
Harpole
Dallington
Duston
Chapel Green
Upper Catesby
Flore
Upper Weedon
Upper Heyford
Upton
Harbury
Ladbroke
Badby
Newnham
Nene
Weedon Bec
Kislingbury
Chesterton Windmill
Chesterton
Hellidon
Nether Heyford
Warwick Services
Marston Doles
Church Stowe
Everdon
Cross Green
Bishop's Itchington
Priors Marston
Old Dairy Farm Craft Centre
Upper Stowe
Bugbrooke
Northampton Services
Rothersthorpe
Priors Hardwick
Charwelton
Preston Capes
Oxford Canal
Farthingstone
Gayton
Milton Malsor
Lighthorne
Heritage Motor Centre
Knightcote
Gaydon
Wormleighton
Upper Boddington
Byfield
Litchborough
Grimscote
Pattishall
Eastcote
Blisworth
Northend
Burton Dassett Hills
Boddington Reservoir
Hinton
Woodford Halse
Maidford
Cold Higham
Astcote
Temple Herdewycke
Fenny Compton
Lower Boddington
Adstone
Tiffield
Kineton
Burton Dassett
Granary Museum of Bygones
Aston le Walls
Eydon
Canons Ashby House
Canons Ashby
Blakesley
Duncote
Caldecote
Little Kineton
Claydon
Avon Dassett
Farnborough
Farnborough Hall
Moreton Pinkney
Woodend
Greens Norton
Shutlanger
Stoke Bruerne
Radway
Chipping Warden
Woodend Green
Bradden
Catanger Llama Trekking
Warmington
Mollington
Edge Hill
Ratley
Cropredy
Wardington
Culworth
Upper Wardington
Weston
Weedon Lois
Slapton
Abthorpe
Alderton
Shotteswell
Sulgrave
Sulgrave Manor
Great Bourton
Williamscott
Wappenham
Pury End
Paulerspury
Upton House
Hornton
Middle Tysoe
Horley
Thorpe Mandeville
Helmdon
Silverstone
Whittlebury
Alkerton
Hanwell
Chacombe
Marston St Lawrence
Shenington
Wroxton
Drayton
Greatworth
Syresham
Whittlewood Forest
Thenford
Crowfield
Lillingstone Dayrell
Lillingstone Lovell
Balscott
Neithrop
Grimsbury
Overthorpe
Warkworth
Halse
Radstone
Biddlesden
Epwell
Shutford
North Newington
Farthinghoe
Whitfield
Wicken
Swalcliffe Barn
Broughton Castle
Easington
Turweston
Dadford
Stowe House and Gardens
Akeley
Leckhampstead
Sibford Gower
Tadmarton
Broughton
Bodicote
Upper Astrop
Newbottle
Swalcliffe
Sibford Ferris
Sor Brook
Astrop
Shalstone
Bloxham
West Adderbury
King's Sutton
Charlton
Hinton-in-the-Hedges
Buffler's Holt
Chackmore
Westbury
Maids Moreton
Milcombe
East Adderbury
Evenley
Great Ouse
Milton
Water Stratford
Radclive
Thornborough
Barford St John
Croughton
Mixbury
Finmere
Hook Norton
Wiggington
South Newington
Barford St Michael
Clifton
Aynho
Tingewick
Gawcott
Swerford
Hempton
Deddington
Souldern
Cottisford
Barton Hartshorn
Padbury
Adstock
Newton Purcell
Preston Bissett
Nether Worton
North Aston
Fritwell
Baynard's Green
Hardwick
Hethe
Great Tew
Over Worton
Chetwode
Addington
Somerton
Fewcott
Stoke Lyne
Fringford
Hillesden
Middle Aston
Ardley
Cherwell Valley Services
Upper Heyford
Steeple Claydon
Twyford
East Claydon
Stratton Audley
Bucknell
Church
Westcott Barton
Middle Barton
Steeple
0 1 2 3 4 5 6 miles
0 1 2 3 4 5 6 7 8 9 10 km

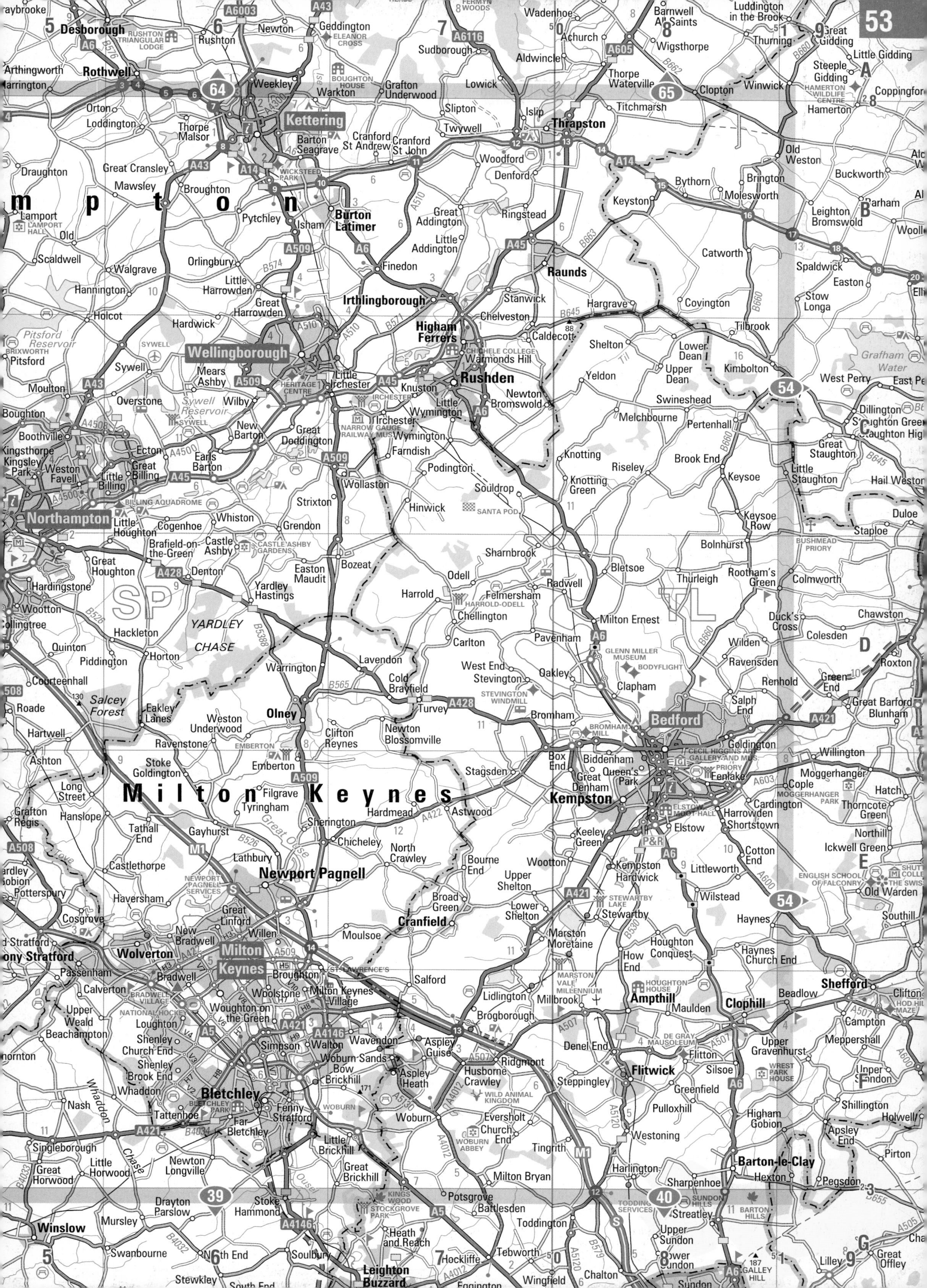
Desborough
Rothwell
Kettering
Thrapston
Burton Latimer
Irthlingborough
Higham Ferrers
Rushden
Raunds
Wellingborough
Northampton
Olney
Milton Keynes
Newport Pagnell
Wolverton
Bletchley
Bedford
Kempston
Ampthill
Flitwick
Clophill
Shefford
Barton-le-Clay
Leighton Buzzard
Winslow
Woburn
Cranfield
Geddington
Wadenhoe
Barnwell All Saints
Luddington in the Brook
Great Gidding
Thorpe Waterville
Clopton
Winwick
Titchmarsh
Islip
Woodford
Denford
Ringstead
Finedon
Isham
Pytchley
Broughton
Mawsley
Great Cransley
Draughton
Lamport
Scaldwell
Walgrave
Hannington
Holcot
Sywell
Moulton
Pitsford Reservoir
Brixworth
Pitsford
Mears Ashby
Wilby
Little Irchester
Knuston
Wymington
Farndish
Podington
Hinwick
Souldrop
Sharnbrook
Odell
Harrold
Felmersham
Radwell
Chellington
Carlton
Pavenham
Milton Ernest
Oakley
Clapham
Bromham
Stevington
Turvey
Lavendon
Cold Brayfield
Warrington
Newton Blossomville
Clifton Reynes
Emberton
Stagsden
Astwood
Hardmead
Sherington
Chicheley
North Crawley
Bourne End
Wootton
Upper Shelton
Lower Shelton
Marston Moretaine
Lidlington
Millbrook
Brogborough
Ridgmont
Husborne Crawley
Aspley Guise
Aspley Heath
Woburn Sands
Wavendon
Salford
Moulsoe
Broad Green
Keysoe
Riseley
Knotting
Knotting Green
Melchbourne
Swineshead
Pertenhall
Kimbolton
Tilbrook
Covington
Catworth
Keyston
Bythorn
Molesworth
Brington
Old Weston
Buckworth
Leighton Bromswold
Spaldwick
Easton
Stow Longa
Grafham Water
West Perry
Dillington
Great Staughton
Little Staughton
Hail Weston
Duloe
Staploe
Bushmead Priory
Colmworth
Bolnhurst
Thurleigh
Rootham's Green
Duck's Cross
Chawston
Colesden
Wilden
Ravensden
Renhold
Roxton
Great Barford
Blunham
Goldington
Willington
Moggerhanger
Cople
Cardington
Harrowden
Shortstown
Elstow
Kempston Hardwick
Stewartby
Wilstead
Houghton Conquest
Haynes
Haynes Church End
Cotton End
Littleworth
Maulden
Silsoe
Flitton
Greenfield
Pulloxhill
Westoning
Harlington
Sharpenhoe
Streatley
Upper Sundon
Toddington
Tebworth
Hockliffe
Heath and Reach
Potsgrove
Battlesden
Milton Bryan
Eversholt
Tingrith
Steppingley
Wild Animal Kingdom
Woburn Abbey
Great Brickhill
Little Brickhill
Fenny Stratford
Far Bletchley
Simpson
Walton
Woughton on the Green
Woolstone
Broughton
Bradwell
Great Linford
Willen
New Bradwell
Haversham
Castlethorpe
Hanslope
Long Street
Gayhurst
Lathbury
Tyringham
Filgrave
Stoke Goldington
Ravenstone
Weston Underwood
Eakley Lanes
Salcey Forest
Roade
Hartwell
Ashton
Yardley Chase
Yardley Hastings
Denton
Castle Ashby
Easton Maudit
Bozeat
Grendon
Strixton
Wollaston
Great Doddington
Earls Barton
Ecton
Great Billing
Little Billing
Weston Favell
Kingsthorpe
Boothville
Overstone
Sywell Reservoir
Cogenhoe
Whiston
Little Houghton
Brafield-on-the-Green
Great Houghton
Hardingstone
Wootton
Collingtree
Quinton
Piddington
Hackleton
Horton
Courteenhall
Grafton Regis
Potterspury
Cosgrove
Stony Stratford
Passenham
Calverton
Upper Weald
Beachampton
Loughton
Shenley Church End
Shenley Brook End
Whaddon
Nash
Tattenhoe
Singleborough
Great Horwood
Little Horwood
Newton Longville
Drayton Parslow
Stoke Hammond
Mursley
Swanbourne
Soulbury
Stewkley
Great Offley
Lilley
Pegsdon
Hexton
Pirton
Apsley End
Shillington
Higham Gobion
Upper Gravenhurst
Meppershall
Campton
Upper Stondon
Clifton
Beadlow
Southill
Old Warden
Ickwell Green
Northill
Thorncote Green
Hatch
Sandy
Great Gidding
Little Gidding
Steeple Gidding
Hamerton
Coppingford
Thurning
Wigsthorpe
Achurch
Aldwincle
Sudborough
Lowick
Slipton
Twywell
Grafton Underwood
Warkton
Weekley
Cranford St Andrew
Cranford St John
Barton Seagrave
Great Addington
Little Addington
Stanwick
Chelveston
Caldecott
Hargrave
Shelton
Lower Dean
Upper Dean
Yeldon
Newton Bromswold
Rushton
Newton
Orton
Loddington
Thorpe Malsor
Arthingworth
Harrington
Orlingbury
Little Harrowden
Great Harrowden
Hardwick
Irchester
Brook End
Biddenham
Great Denham
Box End
Queen's Park
Fenlake
Keeley Green
How End
Houghton House
Denel End
Wingfield
Chalton
Lower Sundon
Eggington
South End
Sundon
Galley Hill

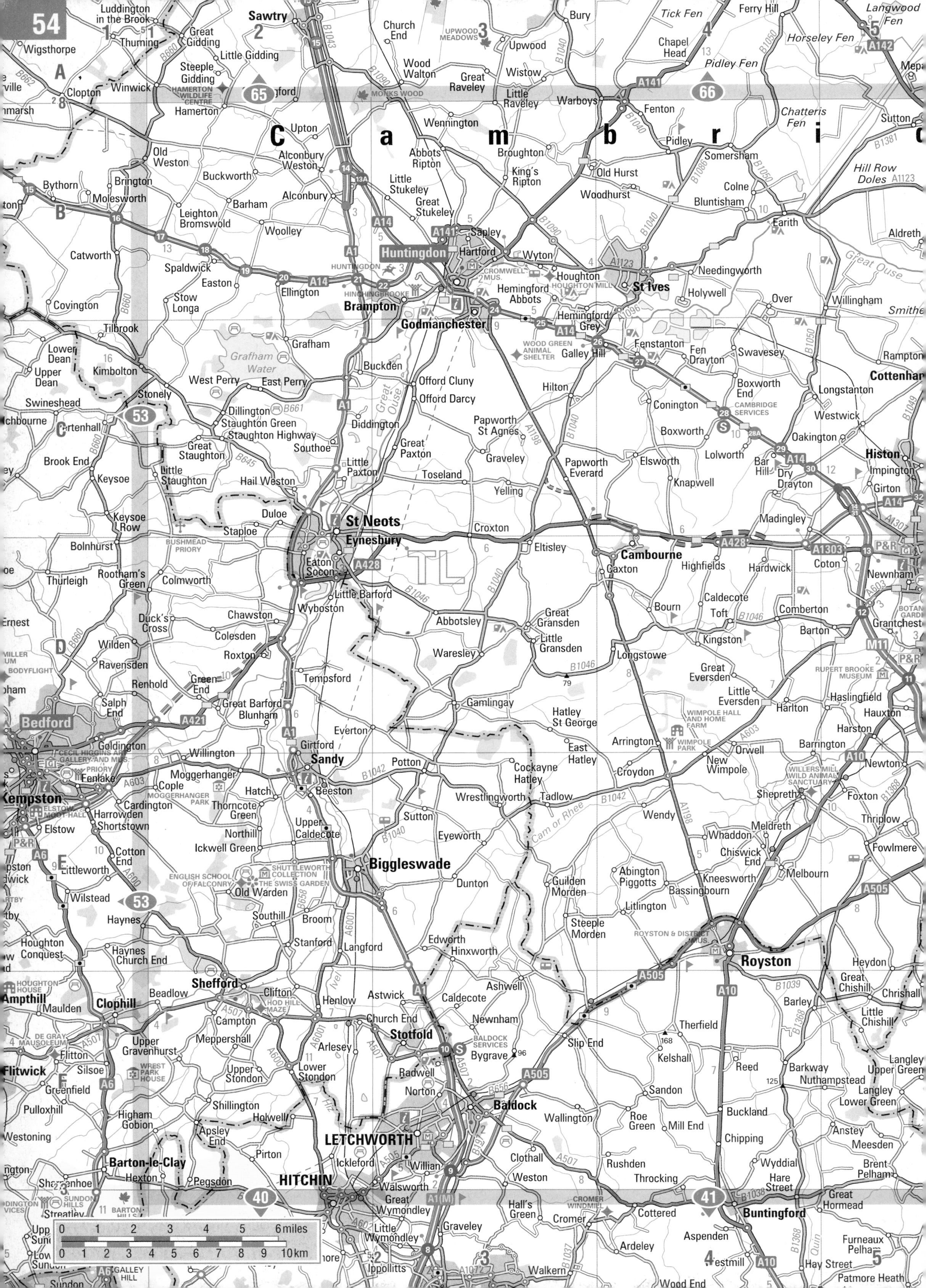

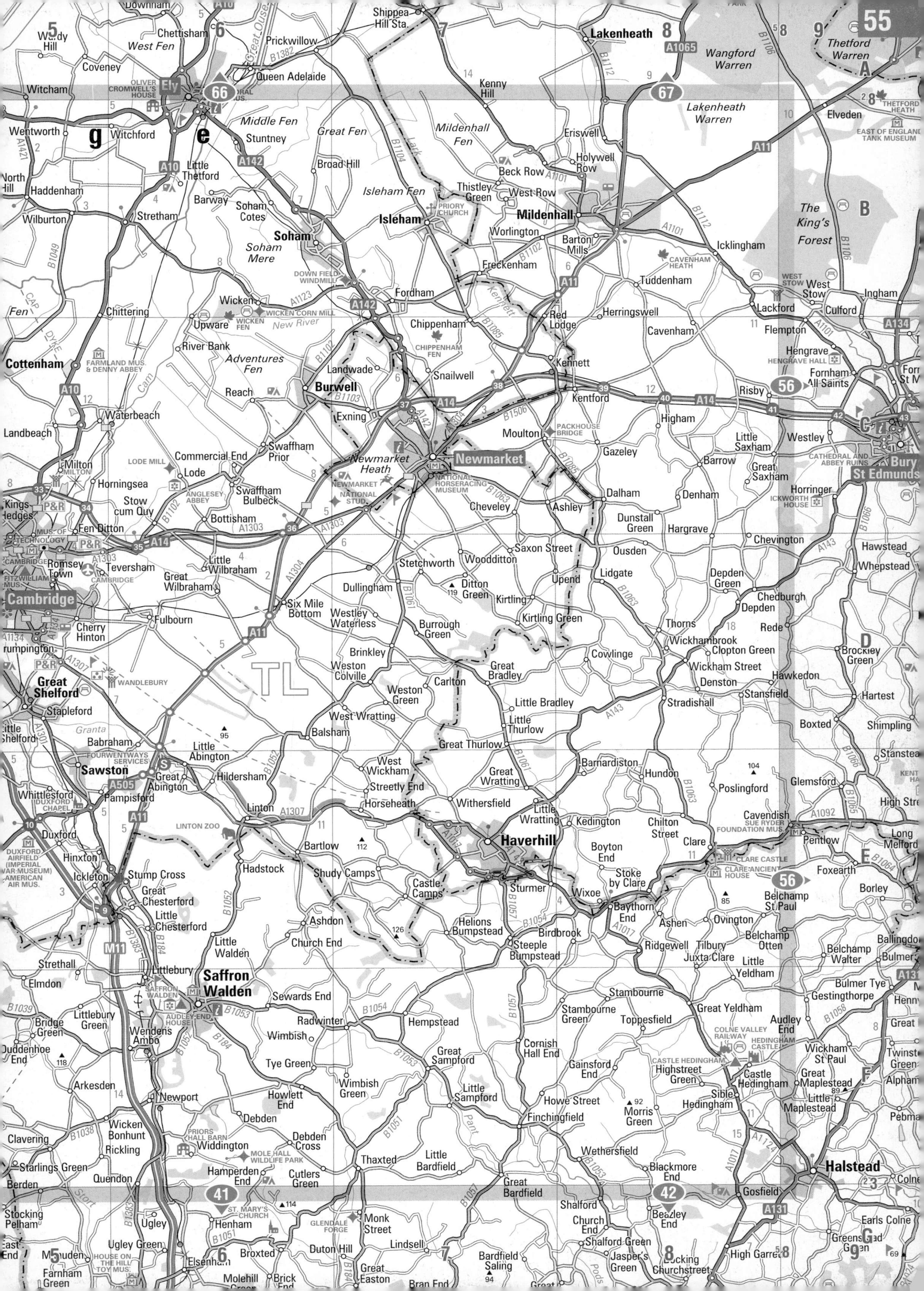

55
Downham
Chettisham
West Fen
Witchford
Witcham
Coveney
Wentworth
Ely
Oliver Cromwell's House
66
Queen Adelaide
Prickwillow
Great Ouse
B1382
Shippea Hill Sta.
Lakenheath
A1065
Wangford Warren
B1106
B1112
Thetford Warren
Kenny Hill
67
Lakenheath Warren
Elveden
Thetford Heath
East of England Tank Museum
Middle Fen
Great Fen
Stuntney
Mildenhall Fen
Eriswell
Holywell Row
Beck Row
A1101
A11
Little Thetford
A142
A10
Broad Hill
B1104
Lark
Isleham Fen
Thistley Green
West Row
North Hill
Haddenham
Barway
Soham Cotes
Priory Church
Isleham
Mildenhall
Wilburton
Stretham
Soham
Worlington
Barton Mills
The King's Forest
Soham Mere
Freckenham
Icklingham
Cavenham Heath
B1049
Down Field Windmill
A1123
Fordham
Tuddenham
West Stow
Ingham
Culford
Lackford
Wicken
Wicken Corn Mill
Wicken Fen
New River
Chittering
Upware
Chippenham
Kennett
Red Lodge
Herringswell
Cavenham
Flempton
A134
A1101
Cap Dyke
Fen
River Bank
Adventures Fen
Chippenham Fen
Kennett
Hengrave
Hengrave Hall
Fornham All Saints
Cottenham
Farmland Mus. & Denny Abbey
Landwade
Snailwell
B1102
B1085
Burwell
B1103
Reach
Exning
A14
B1506
Kentford
Higham
Risby
56
Waterbeach
Landbeach
Cam
Swaffham Prior
Newmarket Heath
Newmarket
National Horseracing Museum
Moulton
Packhouse Bridge
Gazeley
Little Saxham
Westley
Barrow
Bury St Edmunds
Cathedral and Abbey Ruins
Great Saxham
Lode Mill
Commercial End
Lode
Milton
Horningsea
Anglesey Abbey
Swaffham Bulbeck
Newmarket National Stud
B1063
Cheveley
Ashley
Dalham
Denham
Horringer
Ickworth House
Kings Hedges
Stow cum Quy
Bottisham
Fen Ditton
A1303
Dunstall Green
Hargrave
Chevington
B1066
Cambridge
Romsey Town
Teversham
Little Wilbraham
Great Wilbraham
A1304
Stetchworth
Woodditton
Saxon Street
Ousden
A143
Hawstead
Whepstead
Dullingham
Ditton Green
Upend
Lidgate
Depden Green
Chedburgh
Depden
Fitzwilliam Mus.
Cherry Hinton
Fulbourn
Six Mile Bottom
Westley Waterless
B1061
Burrough Green
Kirtling
Kirtling Green
Thorns
Rede
Trumpington
Brinkley
Wickhambrook
Clopton Green
Brockley Green
Great Shelford
Wandlebury
TL
Weston Colville
Carlton
Great Bradley
Cowlinge
Wickham Street
Denston
Hawkedon
Stapleford
Weston Green
Little Bradley
Stansfield
Hartest
Stradishall
Little Shelford
Granta
West Wratting
Little Thurlow
Boxted
Shimpling
Babraham
Balsham
Great Thurlow
Stanstead
Fourwentways Services
Little Abington
West Wickham
Barnardiston
Hundon
Sawston
Great Abington
Hildersham
Great Wratting
B1052
Poslingford
Glemsford
A505
Whittlesford
Duxford Chapel
Pampisford
Streetly End
Withersfield
Horseheath
Linton
A1307
Little Wratting
Kedington
Chilton Street
Cavendish
Sue Ryder Foundation Mus.
A1092
High Street
Long Melford
Linton Zoo
Haverhill
Duxford
Bartlow
Boyton End
Clare
Pentlow
Duxford Airfield (Imperial War Museum) American Air Mus.
Hinxton
Hadstock
Shudy Camps
Stoke by Clare
Clare Castle
Clare Ancient House
Foxearth
Ickleton
Stump Cross
Castle Camps
Sturmer
Wixoe
Borley
Great Chesterford
Baythorn End
Belchamp St Paul
Little Chesterford
Ashdon
Helions Bumpstead
Birdbrook
Ashen
Ovington
Belchamp Otten
Ballingdon
M11
Church End
Steeple Bumpstead
Ridgewell
Tilbury Juxta Clare
Belchamp Walter
Bulmer
Strethall
Little Walden
Little Yeldham
Elmdon
Littlebury
Saffron Walden
Bulmer Tye
Gestingthorpe
Sewards End
Stambourne
Audley End House
Littlebury Green
Radwinter
Hempstead
Stambourne Green
Toppesfield
Great Yeldham
Audley End
Bridge Green
Wendens Ambo
Wimbish
Colne Valley Railway
Hedingham Castle
Duddenhoe End
Great Sampford
Cornish Hall End
Castle Hedingham
Highstreet Green
Wickham St Paul
Tye Green
Gainsford End
Twinstead Green
Arkesden
Wimbish Green
Howlett End
Little Sampford
Sible Hedingham
Great Maplestead
Little Maplestead
Newport
Howe Street
Morris Green
Debden
Finchingfield
Wicken Bonhunt
Priors Hall Barn
Widdington
Debden Cross
Clavering
Rickling
Mole Hall Wildlife Park
Wethersfield
Starlings Green
Quendon
Thaxted
Little Bardfield
Blackmore End
Halstead
Berden
Hamperden End
Cutlers Green
Great Bardfield
Gosfield
41
42
St. Mary's Church
Stocking Pelham
Ugley
Henham
Monk Street
Shalford
Beazley End
Earls Colne
Glendale Forge
Church End
Ugley Green
Lindsell
Shalford Green
Greenstead Green
Manuden
House on the Hill Toy Mus.
Elsenham
Broxted
Duton Hill
Bardfield Saling
Jasper's Green
Gosling Churchstreet
High Garrett
Farnham Green
Molehill Green
Brick End
Great Easton
Bran End

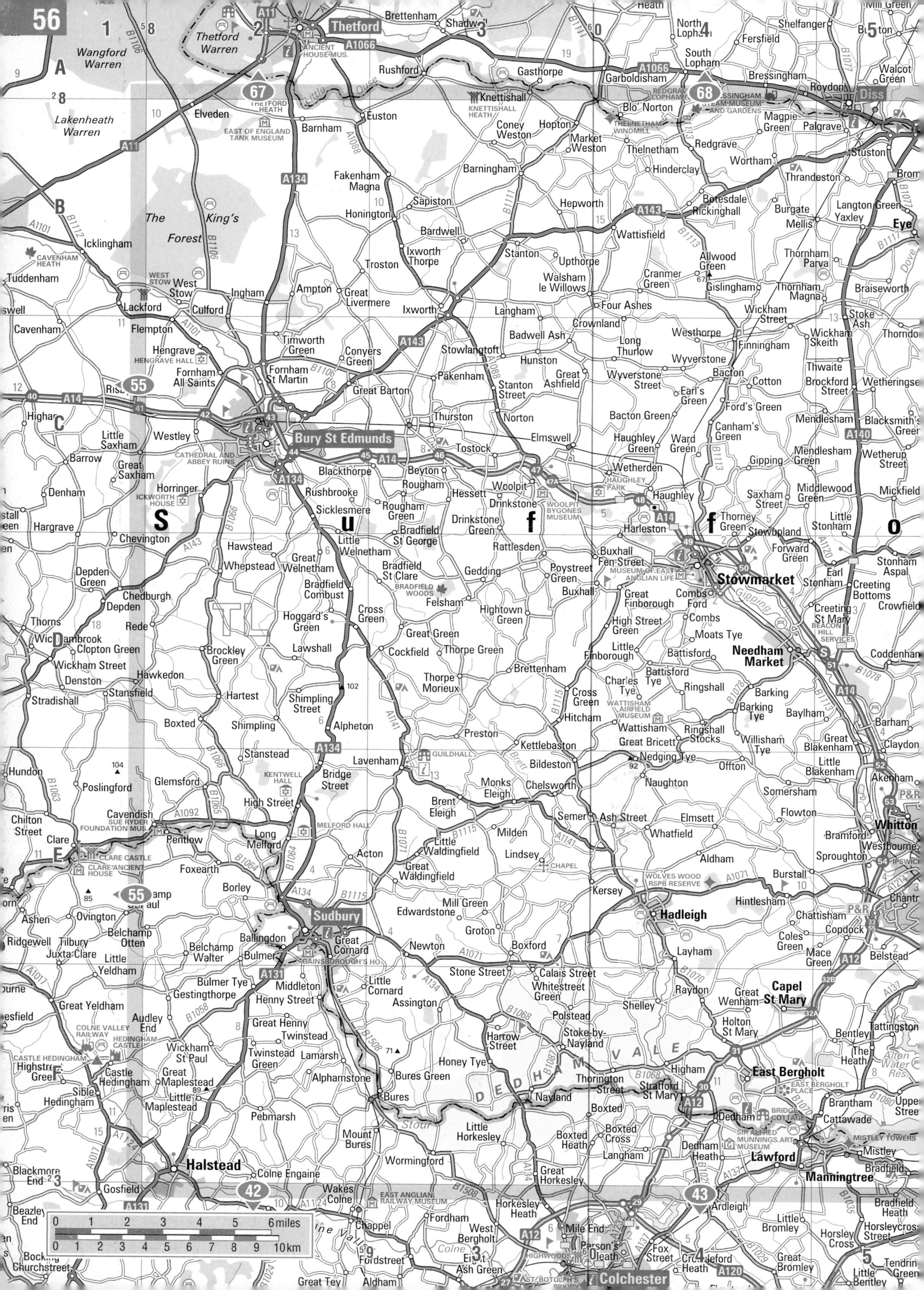
Thetford
Thetford Warren
Wangford Warren
Lakenheath Warren
Brettenham
Shadwell
Rushford
Ancient House Mus.
Elveden
Thetford Heath
East of England Tank Museum
Barnham
Euston
Gasthorpe
Knettishall
Knettishall Heath
Coney Weston
Hopton
Market Weston
Garboldisham
North Lopham
South Lopham
Redgrave
Blo' Norton
Thelnetham
Thelnetham Windmill
Hinderclay
Bressingham
Bressingham Steam Museum and Gardens
Fersfield
Shelfanger
Roydon
Diss
Walcot Green
Magpie Green
Palgrave
Wortham
Stuston
Thrandeston
Fakenham Magna
Sapiston
Honington
Barningham
Hepworth
Botesdale
Rickinghall
Burgate
Mellis
Langton Green
Yaxley
Eye
The King's Forest
Icklingham
Cavenham Heath
Tuddenham
West Stow
Lackford
Culford
Ingham
Ampton
Great Livermere
Troston
Bardwell
Ixworth Thorpe
Ixworth
Stanton
Upthorpe
Walsham le Willows
Wattisfield
Cranmer Green
Allwood Green
Gislingham
Thornham Parva
Thornham Magna
Braiseworth
Cavenham
Flempton
Hengrave
Hengrave Hall
Timworth Green
Conyers Green
Fornham All Saints
Fornham St Martin
Great Barton
Stowlangtoft
Langham
Badwell Ash
Crownland
Four Ashes
Long Thurlow
Westhorpe
Wyverstone
Wyverstone Street
Wickham Street
Finningham
Wickham Skeith
Stoke Ash
Thorndon
Pakenham
Hunston
Great Ashfield
Stanton Street
Norton
Bacton
Cotton
Thwaite
Brockford Street
Wetheringsett
Risby
Highar
Westley
Little Saxham
Barrow
Great Saxham
Bury St Edmunds
Cathedral and Abbey Ruins
Thurston
Tostock
Elmswell
Bacton Green
Earl's Green
Ford's Green
Canham's Green
Mendlesham
Blacksmith's Green
Haughley Green
Ward Green
Wetherden
Haughley
Haughley Park
Gipping
Mendlesham Green
Wetherup Street
Denham
Horringer
Ickworth House
Blackthorpe
Rushbrooke
Beyton
Rougham
Hessett
Woolpit
Drinkstone
Woolpit Bygones Museum
Sicklesmere
Rougham Green
Drinkstone Green
Saxham Street
Middlewood Green
Mickfield
Hargrave
Chevington
Little Welnetham
Bradfield St George
Rattlesden
Harleston
Thorney Green
Stowupland
Little Stonham
Hawstead
Whepstead
Great Welnetham
Bradfield St Clare
Bradfield Combust
Bradfield Woods
Felsham
Gedding
Buxhall
Fen Street
Poystreet Green
Museum of East Anglian Life
Stowmarket
Forward Green
Earl Stonham
Stonham Aspal
Creeting Bottoms
Depden Green
Chedburgh
Depden
Hightown Green
Great Finborough
Combs Ford
Combs
Creeting St Mary
Crowfield
Thorns
Wickhambrook
Clopton Green
Rede
Hoggard's Green
Cross Green
Brockley Green
Lawshall
Great Green
Cockfield
Thorpe Green
High Street Green
Moats Tye
Little Finborough
Battisford
Needham Market
Coddenham
Wickham Street
Denston
Stradishall
Stansfield
Hawkedon
Hartest
Shimpling Street
Thorpe Morieux
Brettenham
Charles Tye
Battisford Tye
Ringshall
Barking
Cross Green
Hitcham
Barking Tye
Baylham
Wattisham Airfield Museum
Wattisham
Ringshall Stocks
Willisham Tye
Barham
Boxted
Shimpling
Alpheton
Preston
Kettlebaston
Great Bricett
Nedging Tye
Offton
Great Blakenham
Claydon
Little Blakenham
Hundon
Poslingford
Stanstead
Kentwell Hall
Glemsford
Lavenham
Guildhall
Bridge Street
Bildeston
Monks Eleigh
Chelsworth
Naughton
Somersham
Akenham
High Street
Brent Eleigh
Flowton
Chilton Street
Cavendish
Sue Ryder Foundation Mus.
Clare
Pentlow
Long Melford
Melford Hall
Milden
Semer
Ash Street
Elmsett
Whatfield
Whitton
Bramford
Westbourne
Clare Castle
Clare Ancient House
Foxearth
Acton
Little Waldingfield
Great Waldingfield
Lindsey
Chapel
Aldham
Sproughton
Ipswich
Borley
Wolves Wood RSPB Reserve
Kersey
Burstall
Hadleigh
Hintlesham
Chantry
Ashen
Ovington
Sudbury
Edwardstone
Mill Green
Groton
Chattisham
Copdock
Ridgewell
Tilbury Juxta Clare
Belchamp Otten
Ballingdon
Great Cornard
Gainsborough's Ho.
Newton
Boxford
Layham
Coles Green
Mace Green
Belstead
Little Yeldham
Belchamp Walter
Bulmer
Stone Street
Calais Street
Whitestreet Green
Middleton
Little Cornard
Bulmer Tye
Gestingthorpe
Henny Street
Assington
Raydon
Great Wenham
Capel St Mary
Shelley
Great Yeldham
Audley End
Colne Valley Railway
Hedingham Castle
Great Henny
Twinstead
Polstead
Holton St Mary
Tattingston
Harrow Street
Stoke-by-Nayland
Bentley
Castle Hedingham
Highstreet Green
Wickham St Paul
Twinstead Green
Lamarsh
Honey Tye
Higham
The Heath
Alton Water Res.
Sible Hedingham
Great Maplestead
Little Maplestead
Alphamstone
Bures Green
Dedham Vale
Thorington Street
Stratford St Mary
East Bergholt
East Bergholt Place
Bures
Nayland
Boxted
Dedham
Bridge Cottage
Brantham
Upper Street
Cattawade
Pebmarsh
Stour
Little Horkesley
Boxted Heath
Boxted Cross
Sir Alfred Munnings Art Museum
Mistley Towers
Mount Bures
Dedham Heath
Langham
Lawford
Mistley
Manningtree
Halstead
Colne Engaine
Wormingford
Great Horkesley
Bradfield
Blackmore End
Gosfield
Wakes Colne
East Anglian Railway Museum
Horkesley Heath
Ardleigh
Bradfield Heath
Beazley End
Chappel
Fordham
West Bergholt
Mile End
Little Bromley
Horsley Cross
Horsleycross Street
Colne Valley
Colne
Eight Ash Green
Highwoods
Parson's Heath
Fox Street
Crockleford Heath
Great Bromley
Tendring Green
Bocking Churchstreet
Fordstreet
Aldham
Great Tey
St Botolph's Priory
Colchester
Little Bentley
0 1 2 3 4 5 6 miles
0 1 2 3 4 5 6 7 8 9 10 km

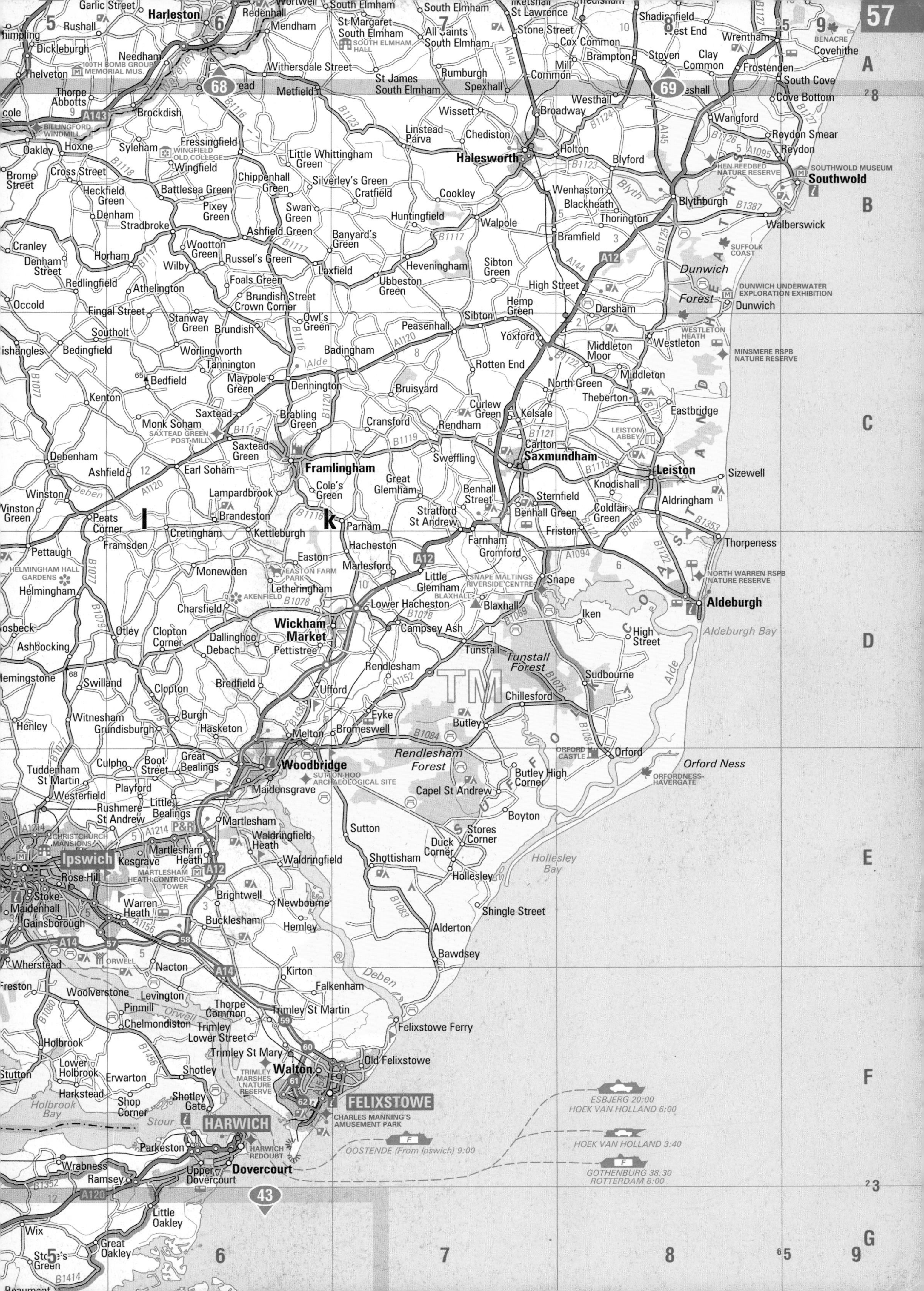
Garlic Street
Harleston
Redenhall
Wortwell
South Elmham
St Margaret South Elmham
South Elmham HALL
All Saints South Elmham
St Lawrence
Stone Street
Cox Common
Brampton
Shadingfield
West End
Wrentham
BENACRE
Covehithe
Rushall
Dickleburgh
Needham
100TH BOMB GROUP MEMORIAL MUS.
Thelveton
Mendham
Withersdale Street
St James South Elmham
Rumburgh
Spexhall
Mill Common
Stoven
Clay Common
Frostenden
South Cove
Cove Bottom
Thorpe Abbotts
Metfield
Westhall
Brockdish
BILLINGFORD WINDMILL
Oakley
Hoxne
Syleham
WINGFIELD OLD COLLEGE
Fressingfield
Wingfield
Wissett
Broadway
Wangford
Linstead Parva
Chediston
Holton
Halesworth
Reydon Smear
Reydon
Blyford
HEN REEDBED NATURE RESERVE
SOUTHWOLD MUSEUM
Southwold
Brome Street
Cross Street
Heckfield Green
Little Whittingham Green
Chippenhall Green
Silverley's Green
Battlesea Green
Cratfield
Cookley
Wenhaston
Blackheath
Blythburgh
Denham
Stradbroke
Pixey Green
Swan Green
Huntingfield
Walpole
Thorington
Walberswick
Ashfield Green
Banyard's Green
Bramfield
Cranley
Horham
Wootton Green
Russel's Green
SUFFOLK COAST
Denham Street
Wilby
Laxfield
Heveningham
Sibton Green
Dunwich
Redlingfield
Athelington
Foals Green
Ubbeston Green
High Street
Forest
DUNWICH UNDERWATER EXPLORATION EXHIBITION
Occold
Brundish Street
Crown Corner
Hemp Green
Darsham
Fingal Street
Stanway Green
Brundish
Owl's Green
Sibton
Peasenhall
Yoxford
WESTLETON HEATH
Westleton
Southolt
MINSMERE RSPB NATURE RESERVE
Bedingfield
Worlingworth
Badingham
Middleton Moor
Tannington
Rotten End
Middleton
Bedfield
Maypole Green
Dennington
Bruisyard
North Green
Theberton
Kenton
Saxtead
Brabling Green
Curlew Green
Kelsale
Eastbridge
Monk Soham
Cransford
Rendham
SAXTEAD GREEN POST MILL
LEISTON ABBEY
Carlton
Saxtead Green
Saxmundham
Debenham
Framlingham
Sweffling
Leiston
Sizewell
Ashfield
Earl Soham
Great Glemham
Knodishall
Benhall Street
Sternfield
Aldringham
Winston
Cole's Green
Lampardbrook
Coldfair Green
Winston Green
Brandeston
Stratford St Andrew
Benhall Green
Peats Corner
Parham
Friston
Cretingham
Kettleburgh
Farnham
Thorpeness
Pettaugh
Framsden
Hacheston
Gromford
HELMINGHAM HALL GARDENS
Easton
Monewden
EASTON FARM PARK
Marlesford
Little Glemham
SNAPE MALTINGS RIVERSIDE CENTRE
Snape
NORTH WARREN RSPB NATURE RESERVE
Helmingham
Letheringham
AKENFIELD
BLAXHALL
Blaxhall
Charsfield
Lower Hacheston
Aldeburgh
Iken
Gosbeck
Otley
Clopton Corner
Dallinghoo
Wickham Market
Campsey Ash
High Street
Aldeburgh Bay
Ashbocking
Debach
Pettistree
Tunstall
Tunstall Forest
Rendlesham
Hemingstone
Swilland
Clopton
Bredfield
Ufford
Sudbourne
Chillesford
Witnesham
Burgh
Eyke
Butley
Henley
Grundisburgh
Hasketon
Melton
Bromeswell
Culpho
Boot Street
Great Bealings
Woodbridge
Rendlesham Forest
ORFORD CASTLE
Orford
Orford Ness
Tuddenham St Martin
SUTTON HOO ARCHAEOLOGICAL SITE
Butley High Corner
ORFORDNESS-HAVERGATE
Westerfield
Playford
Maidensgrave
Capel St Andrew
Rushmere St Andrew
Little Bealings
Boyton
Martlesham
Sutton
Stores Corner
CHRISTCHURCH MANSIONS
Waldringfield Heath
Martlesham Heath
Waldringfield
Duck Corner
Ipswich
Kesgrave
Shottisham
Hollesley
Hollesley Bay
Rose Hill
MARTLESHAM HEATH CONTROL TOWER
Stoke
Brightwell
Maidenhall
Warren Heath
Newbourne
Shingle Street
Gainsborough
Bucklesham
Hemley
Alderton
Bawdsey
ORWELL
Wherstead
Nacton
Kirton
Freston
Falkenham
Woolverstone
Levington
Deben
Pinmill
Orwell
Thorpe Common
Trimley St Martin
Chelmondiston
Trimley Lower Street
Felixstowe Ferry
Holbrook
Trimley St Mary
Lower Holbrook
Walton
Old Felixstowe
Stutton
Erwarton
Shotley
TRIMLEY MARSHES NATURE RESERVE
Harkstead
Shotley Gate
FELIXSTOWE
Holbrook Bay
Shop Corner
CHARLES MANNING'S AMUSEMENT PARK
ESBJERG 20:00
HOEK VAN HOLLAND 6:00
Stour
HARWICH
Parkeston
HARWICH REDOUBT
OOSTENDE (From Ipswich) 9:00
HOEK VAN HOLLAND 3:40
Wrabness
Ramsey
Upper Dovercourt
Dovercourt
GOTHENBURG 38:30
ROTTERDAM 8:00
Little Oakley
Wix
Great Oakley
Stone's Green
Beaumont
TM
A
B
C
D
E
F
G
5
6
7
8
9
68
69
43

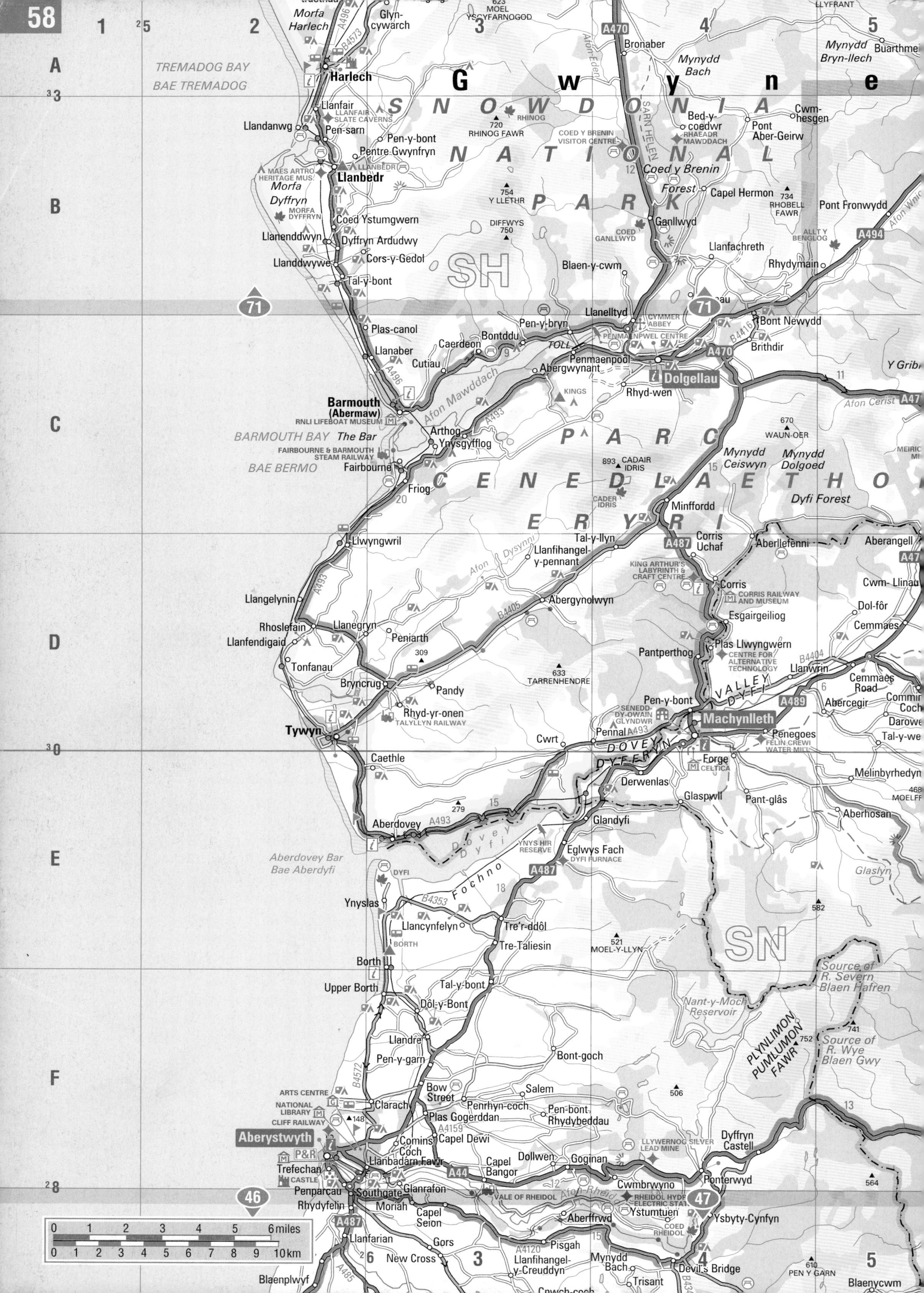

TREMADOG BAY
BAE TREMADOG
Morfa Harlech
Harlech
Glyn-cywarch
MOEL YSGYFARNOGOD
Bronaber
Mynydd Bach
LLYFRANT
Mynydd Bryn-llech
Buarthme
Gwynedd
SNOWDONIA NATIONAL PARK
Llanfair
LLANFAIR SLATE CAVERNS
Llandanwg
Pen-sarn
Pen-y-bont
Pentre Gwynfryn
RHINOG
720 RHINOG FAWR
COED Y BRENIN VISITOR CENTRE
SARN HELEN
Bed-y-coedwr
RHAEADR MAWDDACH
Pont Aber-Geirw
Cwm-hesgen
Coed y Brenin Forest
MAES ARTRO HERITAGE MUS.
Llanbedr
Morfa Dyffryn
MORFA DYFFRYN
Coed Ystumgwern
754 Y LLETHR
Capel Hermon
734 RHOBELL FAWR
Pont Fronwydd
DIFFWYS 750
Ganllwyd
COED GANLLWYD
Llanenddwyn
Dyffryn Ardudwy
Llanddwywe
Cors-y-Gedol
Tal-y-bont
SH
Blaen-y-cwm
Llanfachreth
ALLT Y BENGLOG
Rhydymain
A494
71
Plas-canol
Llanelltyd
CYMMER ABBEY
Pen-y-bryn
Bontddu
Caerdeon
Llanaber
Cutiau
TOLL
PENMAENPWEL CENTRE
Penmaenpool
Abergwynant
Dolgellau
A470
Bont Newydd
Brithdir
B4416
Y Grib
Rhyd-wen
KINGS
Afon Mawddach
Barmouth (Abermaw)
RNLI LIFEBOAT MUSEUM
A496
A493
Arthog
Ynysgyfflog
BARMOUTH BAY
The Bar
FAIRBOURNE & BARMOUTH STEAM RAILWAY
BAE BERMO
Fairbourne
Friog
PARC CENEDLAETHOL ERYRI
893 CADAIR IDRIS
CADER IDRIS
Mynydd Ceiswyn
Mynydd Dolgoed
670 WAUN-OER
Afon Cerist
Dyfi Forest
Minffordd
Tal-y-llyn
Corris Uchaf
A487
Aberllefenni
Aberangell
Llwyngwril
Afon Dysynni
Llanfihangel-y-pennant
KING ARTHUR'S LABYRINTH & CRAFT CENTRE
Corris
CORRIS RAILWAY AND MUSEUM
Cwm-Llinau
Llangelynin
Abergynolwyn
B4405
Dol-fôr
Esgairgeiliog
Rhoslefain
Llanegryn
Peniarth
Llanfendigaid
Cemmaes
Tonfanau
309
633 TARRENHENDRE
Pantperthog
Plas Llwyngwern
CENTRE FOR ALTERNATIVE TECHNOLOGY
Llanwrin
B4404
Cemmaes Road
Bryncrug
Pandy
Rhyd-yr-onen
TALYLLYN RAILWAY
VALLEY DYFI
Pen-y-bont
SENEDD-DY-OWAIN GLYNDWR
Machynlleth
A489
Abercegir
Commins Coch
Darowen
Tywyn
Cwrt
Pennal
Penegoes
FELIN CREWI WATER MILL
Tal-y-wern
DOVEY DYFFRYN
Caethle
Forge
CELTICA
Derwenlas
Melinbyrhedyn
Glaspwll
Pant-glâs
468 MOELFRE
279
Aberhosan
Aberdovey
Glandyfi
Dovey Dyfi
YNYS HIR RESERVE
Eglwys Fach
DYFI FURNACE
Aberdovey Bar
Bae Aberdyfi
DYFI
Fochno
Glaslyn
Ynyslas
B4353
Llancynfelyn
Tre'r-ddôl
582
BORTH
Tre-Taliesin
521 MOEL-Y-LLYN
SN
Borth
Source of R. Severn Blaen Hafren
Upper Borth
Tal-y-bont
Dôl-y-Bont
Nant-y-Moch Reservoir
PLYNLIMON PUMLUMON FAWR
752
741
Source of R. Wye Blaen Gwy
Llandre
Pen-y-garn
Bont-goch
B4572
Bow Street
Salem
506
ARTS CENTRE
Clarach
Penrhyn-coch
Pen-bont Rhydybeddau
NATIONAL LIBRARY
CLIFF RAILWAY
148
Plas Gogerddan
A4159
Aberystwyth
Comins Coch
Capel Dewi
LLYWERNOG SILVER LEAD MINE
Dyffryn Castell
P&R
Llanbadarn Fawr
Dollwen
Goginan
Trefechan
CASTLE
Capel Bangor
A44
Cwmbrwyno
Ponterwyd
564
Penparcau
Southgate
Glanrafon
VALE OF RHEIDOL
Afon Rheidol
RHEIDOL HYDRO ELECTRIC STN
46
47
Rhydyfelin
Moriah
Capel Seion
Aberffrwd
Ystumtuen
Ysbyty-Cynfyn
COED RHEIDOL
A487
Llanfarian
Gors
A4120
Pisgah
New Cross
Llanfihangel-y-Creuddyn
Mynydd Bach
610 PEN Y GARN
Devil's Bridge
A485
Blaenplwyf
Trisant
Blaenycwm
0 1 2 3 4 5 6 miles
0 1 2 3 4 5 6 7 8 9 10 km

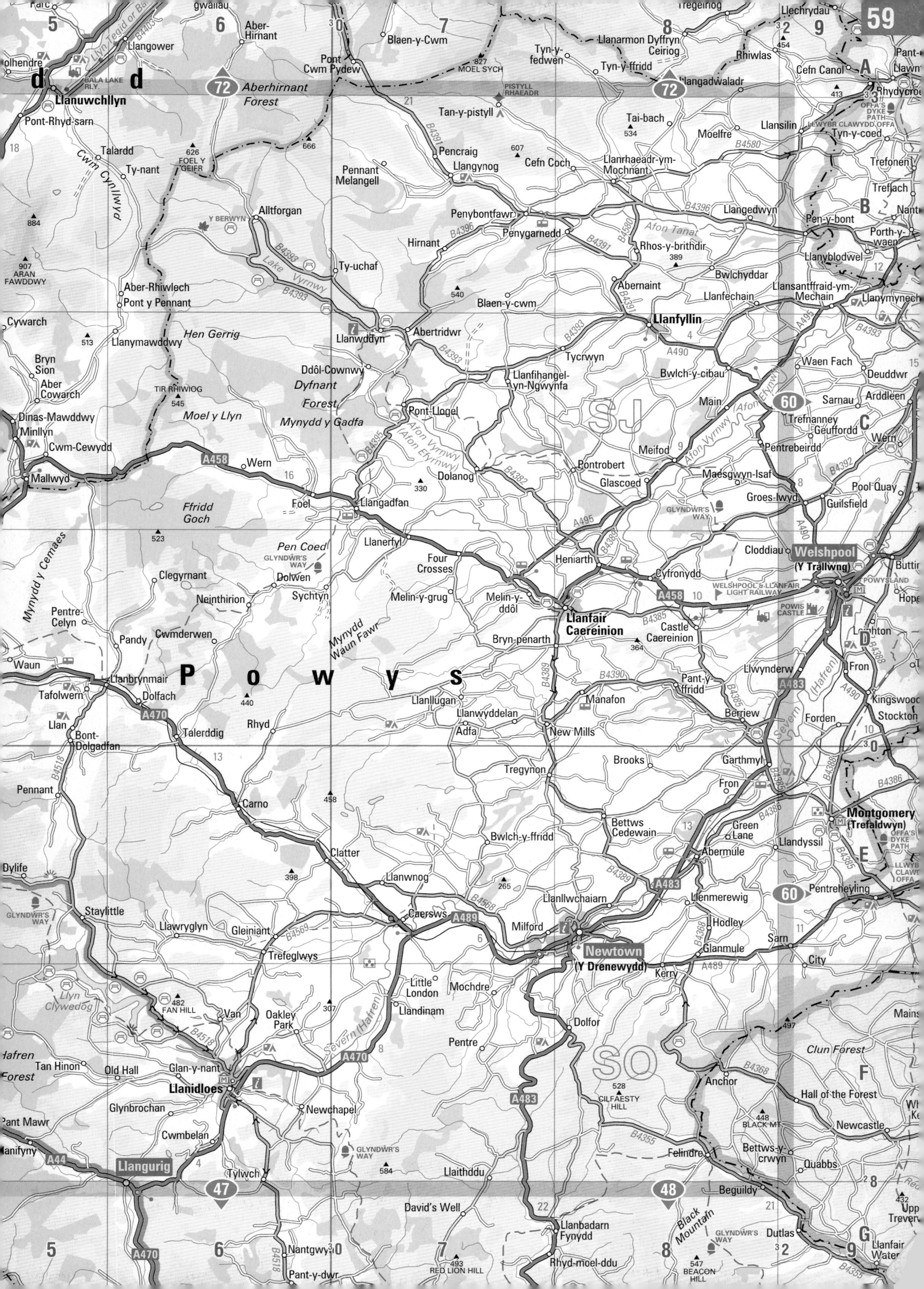
Llanuwchllyn
Pont-Rhyd-sarn
Llangower
Llyn Tegid or Bala
Bala Lake Rly.
Aber-Hirnant
Aberhirnant Forest
Pont Cwm Pydew
Blaen-y-Cwm
Moel Sych
Pistyll Rhaeadr
Tan-y-pistyll
Tyn-y-fedwen
Llanarmon Dyffryn Ceiriog
Tyn-y-fridd
Llangadwaladr
Llechrydau
Rhiwlas
Cefn Canol
Rhydycroesau
Offa's Dyke Path
Llwybr Clawdd Offa
Tyn-y-coed
Llansilin
Moelfre
Tai-bach
Trefonen
Treflach
Talardd
Ty-nant
Cwm Cynllwyd
Foel y Geifr
Pennant Melangell
Pencraig
Llangynog
Cefn Coch
Llanrhaeadr-ym-Mochnant
Llangedwyn
Pen-y-bont
Porth-y-waen
Llanyblodwel
Aran Fawddwy
Y Berwyn
Alltforgan
Penybontfawr
Penygarnedd
Hirnant
Afon Tanat
Rhos-y-brithdir
Lake Vyrnwy
Ty-uchaf
Aber-Rhiwlech
Pont y Pennant
Abernaint
Bwlchyddar
Llanfechain
Llansantffraid-ym-Mechain
Llanymynech
Blaen-y-cwm
Cywarch
Llanymawddwy
Hen Gerrig
Llanwddyn
Abertridwr
Llanfyllin
Bryn Sion
Aber Cowarch
Tir Rhiwiog
Ddôl-Cownwy
Dyfnant Forest
Tycrwyn
Bwlch-y-cibau
Waen Fach
Deuddwr
Llanfihangel-yn-Ngwynfa
Main
Sarnau
Arddleen
Trefnanney
Geuffordd
Wern
Dinas-Mawddwy
Minllyn
Moel y Llyn
Mynydd y Gadfa
Pont-Llogel
Afon Vyrnwy (Afon Efyrnwy)
Meifod
Pentrebeirdd
Cwm-Cewydd
Mallwyd
Wern
Dolanog
Pontrobert
Glascoed
Maesgwyn-Isaf
Groes-lwyd
Guilsfield
Pool Quay
Foel
Llangadfan
Ffridd Goch
Glyndŵr's Way
Llanerfyl
Pen Coed
Four Crosses
Heniarth
Cyfronydd
Cloddiau
Welshpool (Y Trallwng)
Buttington
Mynydd y Cemaes
Clegyrnant
Dolwen
Sychtyn
Melin-y-grug
Melin-y-ddôl
Llanfair Caereinion
Welshpool & Llanfair Light Railway
Powis Castle
Powysland
Hope
Neinthirion
Pentre-Celyn
Pandy
Cwmderwen
Mynydd Waun Fawr
Bryn-penarth
Castle Caereinion
Leighton
Waun
Llanbrynmair
Tafolwern
Dolfach
Powys
Llanllugan
Manafon
Pant-y-ffridd
Llwynderw
Fron
Kingswood
Llan
Bont-Dolgadfan
Talerddig
Rhyd
Llanwyddelan
Adfa
New Mills
Berriew
Forden
Stockton
Severn (Hafren)
Tregynon
Brooks
Garthmyl
Pennant
Carno
Fron
Montgomery (Trefaldwyn)
Bettws Cedewain
Green Lane
Llandyssil
Dylife
Bwlch-y-ffridd
Abermule
Clatter
Llanwnog
Llanllwchaiarn
Llanmerewig
Pentreheyling
Staylittle
Llawryglyn
Gleiniant
Caersws
Milford
Newtown (Y Drenewydd)
Hodley
Sarn
Glanmule
City
Trefeglwys
Kerry
Llyn Clywedog
Fan Hill
Van
Oakley Park
Little London
Mochdre
Llandinam
Dolfor
Mainstone
Clun Forest
Tan Hinon
Old Hall
Glan-y-nant
Llanidloes
Pentre
Anchor
Hall of the Forest
Glynbrochan
Newchapel
Cilfaesty Hill
Black Mt
Newcastle
Pant Mawr
Cwmbelan
Felindre
Bettws-y-crwyn
Quabbs
Llangurig
Tylwch
Llaithddu
Beguildy
David's Well
Black Mountain
Llanbadarn Fynydd
Dutlas
Llanfair Waterdine
Nantgwyn
Red Lion Hill
Rhyd-moel-ddu
Beacon Hill
Pant-y-dwr
SJ
SO

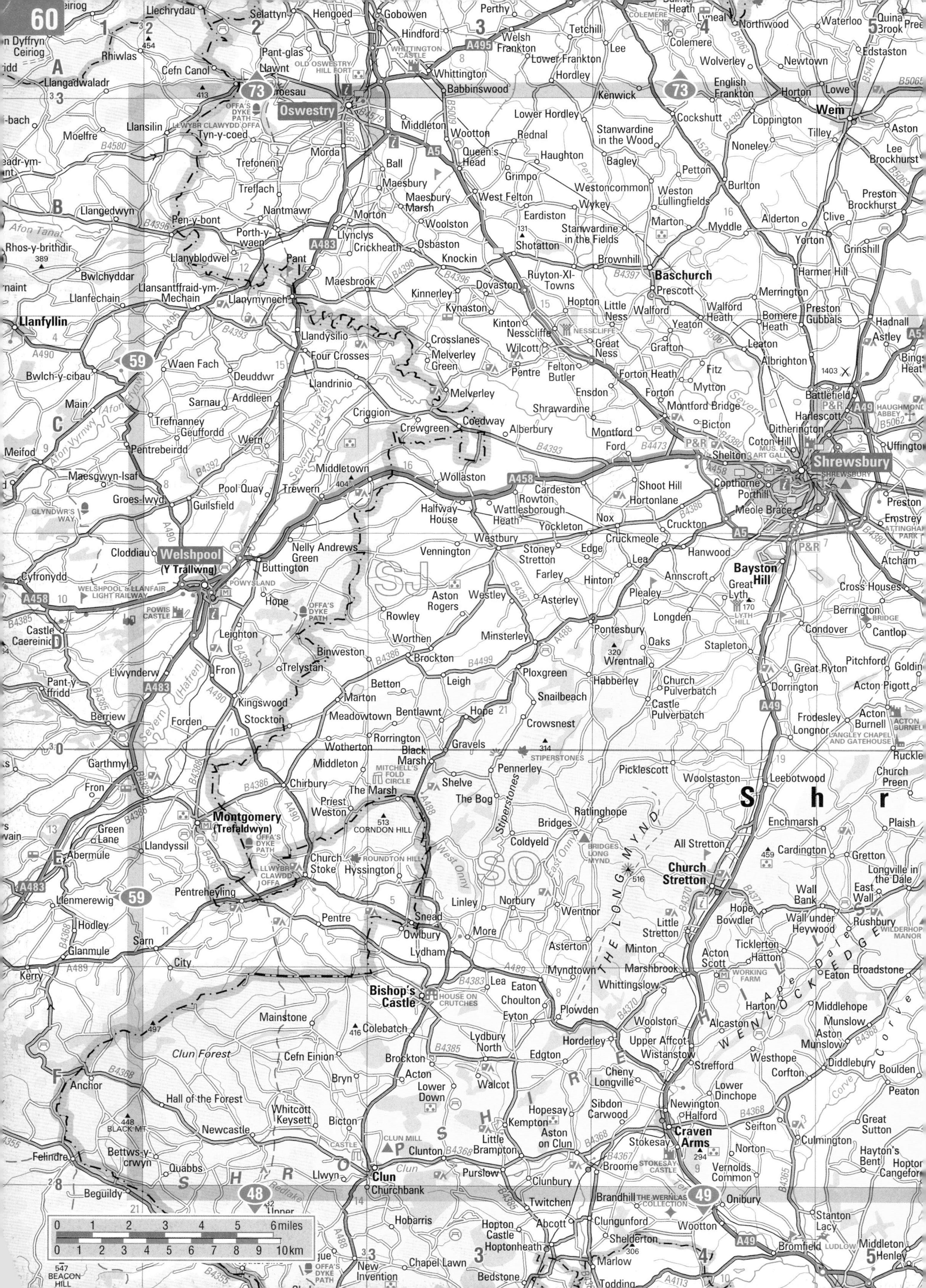
Oswestry
Welshpool
(Y Trallwng)
Montgomery
(Trefaldwyn)
Shrewsbury
Wem
Baschurch
Bishop's
Castle
Clun
Church
Stretton
Craven
Arms
Llanfyllin
Bayston
Hill
SJ
SO
73
59
48
49
0 1 2 3 4 5 6 miles
0 1 2 3 4 5 6 7 8 9 10 km

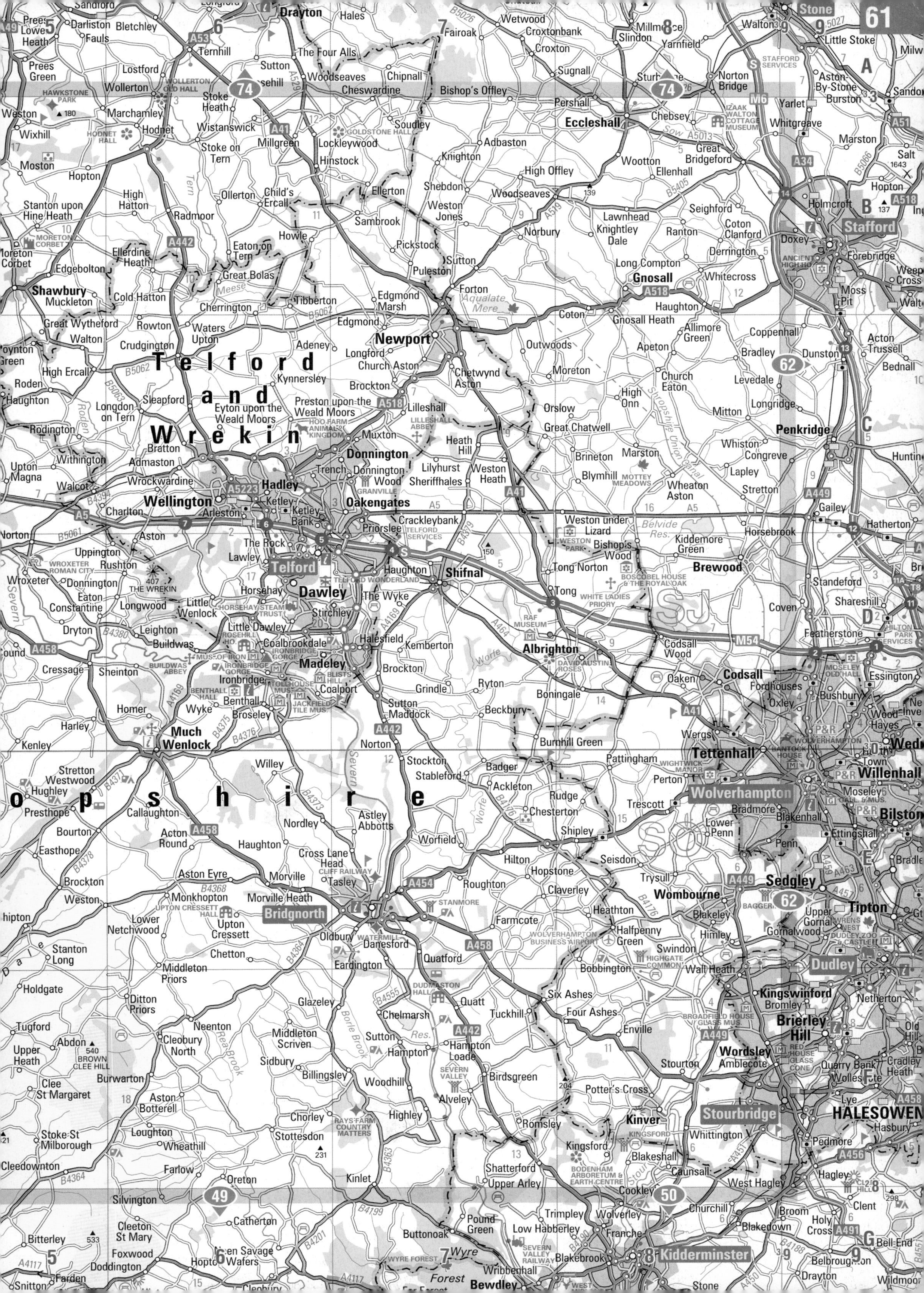
Telford and Wrekin
Shropshire
Drayton
Hales
Fairoak
Wetwood
Croxtonbank
Croxton
Millmeece
Slindon
Yarnfield
Walton
Stone
Little Stoke
Darliston
Bletchley
Fauls
Ternhill
Sutton
The Four Alls
Woodseaves
Chipnall
Cheswardine
Bishop's Offley
Sugnall
Sturbridge
Norton Bridge
Stafford Services
Aston-By-Stone
Burston
Sandon
Prees Green
Lostford
Wollerton
Wollerton Old Hall
Hawkstone Park
Stoke Heath
Pershall
Eccleshall
Chebsey
Izaak Walton Cottage Museum
Yarlet
Whitgreave
Marston
Weston
Wixhill
Marchamley
Hodnet
Hodnet Hall
Wistanswick
Millgreen
Goldstone Hall
Lockleywood
Soudley
Adbaston
Knighton
Wootton
Ellenhall
Great Bridgeford
Salt
Moston
Stoke on Tern
Hinstock
High Offley
Hopton
Hopton
Stanton upon Hine Heath
High Hatton
Radmoor
Ollerton
Child's Ercall
Ellerton
Shebdon
Woodseaves
Seighford
Holmcroft
Stafford
Sambrook
Weston Jones
Lawnhead
Knightley Dale
Ranton
Coton Clanford
Doxey
Moreton Corbet
Howle
Pickstock
Norbury
Derrington
Forebridge
Ellerdine Heath
Eaton on Tern
Sutton
Long Compton
Gnosall
Whitecross
Weeping Cross
Edgebolton
Puleston
Great Bolas
Forton
Aqualate Mere
Moss Pit
Shawbury
Muckleton
Cold Hatton
Tibberton
Edgmond Marsh
Haughton
Walton
Cherrington
Edgmond
Coton
Gnosall Heath
Allimore Green
Coppenhall
Acton Trussell
Great Wytheford
Rowton
Waters Upton
Newport
Outwoods
Apeton
Bradley
Dunston
Bednall
Walton
Crudgington
Adeney
Longford
Church Aston
Chetwynd Aston
Moreton
Church Eaton
Levedale
High Ercall
Roden
Kynnersley
Brockton
High Onn
Haughton
Sleapford
Longdon on Tern
Eyton upon the Weald Moors
Preston upon the Weald Moors
Lilleshall
Lilleshall Abbey
Orslow
Mitton
Longridge
Penkridge
Rodington
Hoo Farm Animal Kingdom
Great Chatwell
Whiston
Congreve
Huntington
Withington
Bratton
Muxton
Heath Hill
Brineton
Marston
Lapley
Upton Magna
Admaston
Donnington
Donnington Wood
Lilyhurst
Weston Heath
Blymhill
Motley Meadows
Wheaton Aston
Stretton
Walcot
Wrockwardine
Trench
Sheriffhales
Granville
Hadley
Wellington
Ketley
Oakengates
Gailey
Charlton
Arleston
Ketley Bank
Crackleybank
Priorslee
Telford Services
Weston under Lizard
Belvide Res.
Hatherton
Aston
Norton
Uppington
The Rock
Lawley
Weston Park
Bishop's Wood
Kiddemore Green
Horsebrook
Telford
Wroxeter Roman City
Rushton
Haughton
Shifnal
Tong Norton
Brewood
Wroxeter
Donnington
The Wrekin
Telford Wonderland
Boscobel House & The Royal Oak
Standeford
Eaton
Horsehay
Dawley
Tong
White Ladies Priory
Shareshill
Constantine
Longwood
Little Wenlock
Horsehay Steam Trust
The Wyke
Coven
Dryton
Leighton
Stirchley
Little Dawley
RAF Museum
Featherstone
Hilton Park Services
Rosehill Ho.
Buildwas
Coalbrookdale
Ironbridge Gorge
Halesfield
Kemberton
Albrighton
Codsall
Codsall Wood
Cressage
Sheinton
Buildwas Abbey
Mus. of Iron
Ironbridge
Madeley
Brockton
David Austin Roses
Oaken
Fordhouses
Moseley Old Hall
Essington
Benthall Hall
Tollhouse Mus.
Blists Hill
Coalport
Jackfield Tile Mus.
Grindle
Ryton
Boningale
Oxley
Bushbury
Wyke
Benthall
Broseley
Sutton Maddock
Beckbury
Homer
Harley
Much Wenlock
Wergs
Wood Hayes
Kenley
Norton
Burnhill Green
Tettenhall
Bantock House
Wolverhampton
Willenhall
Stretton Westwood
Hughley
Willey
Stockton
Stableford
Badger
Pattingham
Wightwick Manor
Perton
Moseley
Presthope
Callaughton
Astley Abbotts
Ackleton
Rudge
Chesterton
Trescott
Bradmore
Blakenhall
Bilston
Nordley
Bourton
Acton Round
Haughton
Cross Lane Head
Worfield
Shipley
Lower Penn
Penn
Ettingshall
Easthope
Cliff Railway
Hilton
Hopstone
Seisdon
Aston Eyre
Morville
Tasley
Roughton
Claverley
Trysull
Wombourne
Sedgley
Brockton
Monkhopton
Morville Heath
Weston
Upton Cressett Hall
Bridgnorth
Stanmore
Heathton
Tipton
Upper Gornal
Lower Netchwood
Upton Cressett
Farmcote
Halfpenny Green
Blakeley
Wrens Nest
Gornalwood
Oldbury
Watermill
Danesford
Wolverhampton Business Airport
Himley
Dudley Zoo & Castle
Stanton Long
Chetton
Eardington
Quatford
Swindon
Highgate Common
Dudley
Middleton Priors
Bobbington
Wall Heath
Holdgate
Dudmaston Hall
Glazeley
Quatt
Six Ashes
Kingswinford
Bromley
Netherton
Ditton Priors
Chelmarsh
Tuckhill
Four Ashes
Brierley Hill
Tugford
Neenton
Middleton Scriven
Enville
Broadfield House Glass Mus.
Abdon
Brown Clee Hill
Cleobury North
Sutton
Hampton
Hampton Loade
Upper Heath
Sidbury
Severn Valley
Stourton
Wordsley
Amblecote
Red House Glass Cone
Quarry Bank
Cradley Heath
Clee St Margaret
Burwarton
Billingsley
Woodhill
Birdsgreen
Wollescote
Aston Botterell
Alveley
Potter's Cross
Lye
Chorley
Highley
Rays Farm Country Matters
Kinver
Stourbridge
Halesowen
Loughton
Stottesdon
Romsley
Kinver
Whittington
Hasbury
Stoke St Milborough
Wheathill
Kingsford
Pedmore
Blakeshall
Cleedownton
Farlow
Shatterford
Upper Arley
Bodenham Arboretum & Earth Centre
Caunsall
Hagley
Oreton
Kinlet
Cookley
West Hagley
Clent
Silvington
Trimpley
Wolverley
Churchill
Broom
Catherton
Pound Green
Low Habberley
Blakedown
Holy Cross
Cleeton St Mary
Bitterley
Severn Valley Railway
Franche
Bell End
Foxwood
Buttonoak
Wyre Forest
Wyre
Blakebrook
Kidderminster
Belbroughton
Doddington
Hopton Wafers
Neen Savage
Wribbenhall
Farden
Snitton
Forest
Bewdley
Drayton
Wildmoor
Stone
Cleobury
M6
M54
A41
A53
A442
A518
A5223
A5
A458
A449
A454
A456
A491
A34
A51
A519
A4169
B5062
B4380
B4373
B4364
B4363
B4555
B4199
B4176
B5061
B4394
B4368
B4378
B4371
B4375
B4376
B4201
B4190
B5026
B5405
B5066
B5027
A5013
A4117
74
62
49
50
SJ
SO
Sow
Tern
Meese
Roden
Severn
Worfe
Borle Brook
Rea Brook
Stour
Shropshire Union Canal
Dale

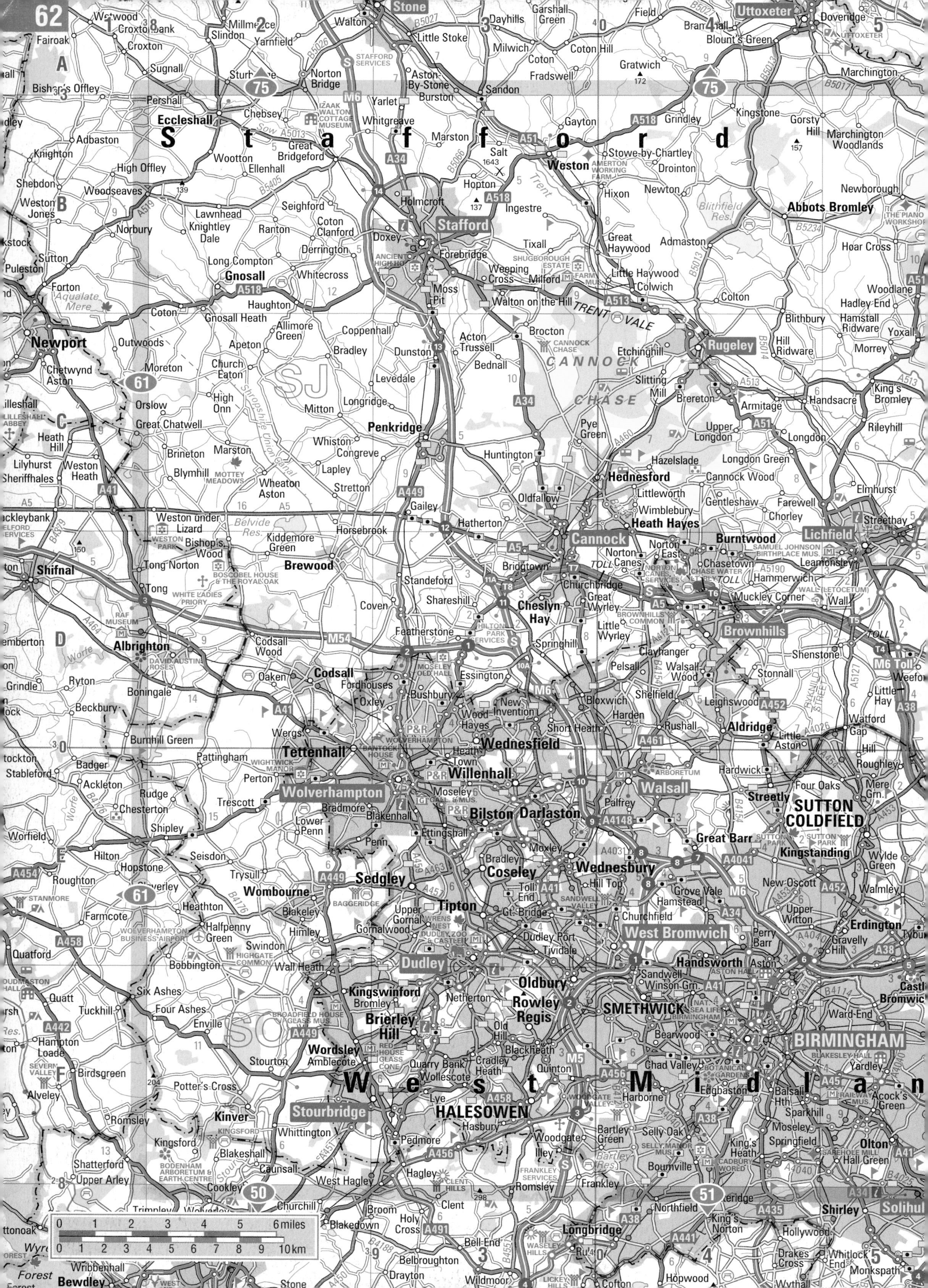
Stafford
West Midlan
Stone
Uttoxeter
Doveridge
Walton
Millmeece
Yarnfield
Slindon
Croxton
Fairoak
Sugnall
Bishop's Offley
Pershall
Eccleshall
Chebsey
Norton Bridge
Little Stoke
Dayhills
Milwich
Garshall Green
Coton
Coton Hill
Fradswell
Gratwick
Blount's Green
Marchington
Aston-By-Stone
Burston
Sandon
Yarlet
Whitgreave
Marston
Gayton
Grindley
Kingstone
Gorsty Hill
Marchington Woodlands
Adbaston
Knighton
High Offley
Wootton
Ellenhall
Great Bridgeford
Salt
Weston
Stowe-by-Chartley
Drointon
Hixon
Newton
Newborough
Abbots Bromley
Shebdon
Weston Jones
Woodseaves
Seighford
Lawnhead
Knightley Dale
Ranton
Coton Clanford
Holmcroft
Hopton
Ingestre
Blithfield Res.
Norbury
Derrington
Doxey
Forebridge
Tixall
Great Haywood
Admaston
Hoar Cross
Puleston
Sutton
Long Compton
Gnosall
Whitecross
Weeping Cross
Milford
Little Haywood
Colwich
Moss Pit
Walton on the Hill
Forton
Aqualate Mere
Haughton
Coton
Gnosall Heath
Allimore Green
Coppenhall
Brocton
Trent Vale
Colton
Woodlane
Hadley End
Blithbury
Hamstall Ridware
Yoxall
Newport
Outwoods
Apeton
Bradley
Dunston
Acton Trussell
Bednall
Cannock Chase
Etchinghill
Rugeley
Hill Ridware
Morrey
Chetwynd Aston
Moreton
Church Eaton
Levedale
Slitting Mill
Brereton
Armitage
Handsacre
King's Bromley
High Onn
Orslow
Mitton
Longridge
Penkridge
Pye Green
Upper Longdon
Longdon
Rileyhill
Great Chatwell
Heath Hill
Whiston
Congreve
Huntington
Hazelslade
Longdon Green
Brineton
Marston
Lapley
Lilyhurst
Weston Heath
Sheriffhales
Blymhill
Mottey Meadows
Wheaton Aston
Stretton
Hednesford
Cannock Wood
Elmhurst
Gailey
Oldfallow
Littleworth
Wimblebury
Gentleshaw
Farewell
Chorley
Weston under Lizard
Belvide Res.
Horsebrook
Hatherton
Heath Hayes
Burntwood
Lichfield
Streethay
Bishop's Wood
Kiddemore Green
Cannock
Norton East
Norton Canes
Chasetown
Leamonsley
Shifnal
Tong Norton
Brewood
Bridgtown
Hammerwich
Tong
Boscobel House & The Royal Oak
White Ladies Priory
Standeford
Churchbridge
Great Wyrley
Muckley Corner
Wall
Coven
Shareshill
Cheslyn Hay
Brownhills
Featherstone
Little Wyrley
Shenstone
Albrighton
Codsall Wood
Springhill
Clayhanger
Pelsall
Walsall Wood
Stonnall
Weeford
Grindle
Ryton
Oaken
Codsall
Fordhouses
Essington
Bushbury
Oxley
Boningale
Beckbury
Bloxwich
Shelfield
Leighswood
Little Hay
New Invention
Wood Hayes
Harden
Aldridge
Watford Gap
Wergs
Burnhill Green
Short Heath
Rushall
Little Aston
Tettenhall
Wednesfield
Hill
Badger
Pattingham
Heath Town
Hardwick
Roughley
Stableford
Perton
Willenhall
Walsall
Streetly
Four Oaks
Mere Grn.
Ackleton
Rudge
Wolverhampton
Moseley
Palfrey
Sutton Coldfield
Chesterton
Trescott
Bradmore
Bilston
Darlaston
Blakenhall
Lower Penn
Ettingshall
Great Barr
Kingstanding
Worfield
Shipley
Penn
Moxley
Wylde Green
Hilton
Seisdon
Bradley
Coseley
Wednesbury
Hopstone
Trysull
Sedgley
Hill Top
Grove Vale
Roughton
Wombourne
Tipton
Hamstead
New Oscott
Walmley
Heathton
Toll End
Churchfield
Upper Witton
Farmcote
Upper Gornal
Gt. Bridge
Erdington
Halfpenny Green
Blakeley
Himley
Gornalwood
West Bromwich
Perry Barr
Gravelly Hill
Quatford
Swindon
Dudley Port
Tividale
Bobbington
Wall Heath
Dudley
Handsworth
Aston
Oldbury
Sandwell
Winson Grn.
Castle Bromwich
Quatt
Six Ashes
Kingswinford
Netherton
Rowley Regis
Smethwick
Tuckhill
Four Ashes
Bromley
Brierley Hill
Ward End
Enville
Old Hill
Bearwood
Birmingham
Hampton Loade
Wordsley
Blackheath
Stourton
Amblecote
Quarry Bank
Cradley Heath
Quinton
Chad Valley
Yardley
Birdsgreen
Wollescote
Harborne
Edgbaston
Balsall Hth
Acock's Green
Alveley
Potter's Cross
Lye
Kinver
Stourbridge
Halesowen
Sparkhill
Romsley
Whittington
Hasbury
Woodgate
Bartley Green
Selly Oak
Moseley
Springfield
Olton
Kingsford
Pedmore
Illey
King's Heath
Hall Green
Blakeshall
Shatterford
Upper Arley
Caunsall
Hagley
West Hagley
Bournville
Cookley
Romsley
Frankley
Churchill
Clent
Northfield
Shirley
Solihull
Broom
Blakedown
Holy Cross
Longbridge
King's Norton
Hollywood
Bell End
Belbroughton
Drakes Cross
Whitlock's End
Monkspath
Wribbenhall
Bewdley
Drayton
Wildmoor
Hopwood
Cofton
Wythall
0 1 2 3 4 5 6 miles
0 1 2 3 4 5 6 7 8 9 10 km

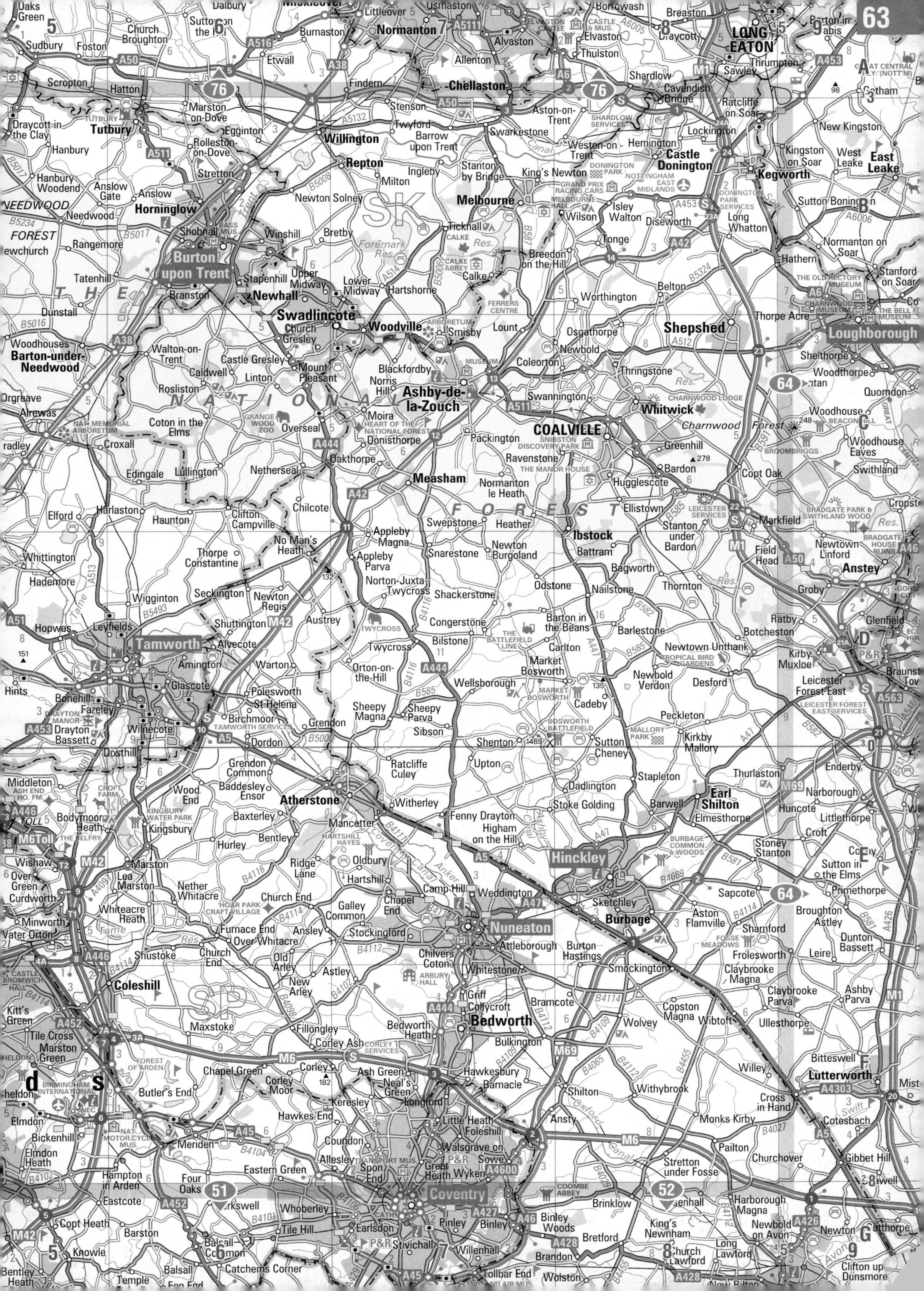
63
Oaks Green
Church Broughton
Sutton on the Hill
Burnaston
Littleover
Normanton
Osmaston
Alvaston
Elvaston Castle
Elvaston
Borrowash
Breaston
Draycott
Long Eaton
Thrumpton
Sawley
Sudbury
Foston
Etwall
Allenton
Thulston
Scropton
Hatton
Findern
Chellaston
Shardlow
Cavendish Bridge
Ratcliffe on Soar
Gotham
Marston on Dove
Stenson
Aston-on-Trent
Draycott in the Clay
Tutbury
Egginton
Willington
Twyford
Barrow upon Trent
Swarkestone
Weston-on-Trent
Hemington
Lockington
New Kingston
Hanbury
Rolleston-on-Dove
Castle Donington
Kingston on Soar
West Leake
East Leake
Stretton
Repton
Ingleby
Stanton by Bridge
King's Newton
Donington Park
Nottingham East Midlands
Kegworth
Hanbury Woodend
Anslow Gate
Anslow
Milton
Newton Solney
Melbourne
Grand Prix Racing Cars
Melbourne Hall
Wilson
Isley Walton
Diseworth
Long Whatton
Sutton Bonington
Needwood
Horninglow
Needwood Forest
Shobnall
Bass Mus.
Winshill
Bretby
Foremark Res.
Ticknall
Calke
Calke Abbey
Breedon on the Hill
Tonge
Normanton on Soar
Hathern
Newchurch
Rangemore
Burton upon Trent
Stapenhill
Upper Midway
Lower Midway
Hartshorne
Tatenhill
Branston
Newhall
Swadlincote
Woodville
Arboretum
Smisby
Ferrers Centre
Lount
Worthington
Belton
Stanford on Soar
The Old Rectory Museum
Charnwood Museum
The Bell Foundry Museum
Thorpe Acre
Loughborough
Dunstall
Church Gresley
Osgathorpe
Shepshed
Woodhouses
Barton-under-Needwood
Walton-on-Trent
Castle Gresley
Mount Pleasant
Blackfordby
Norris Hill
Ashby-de-la-Zouch
Coleorton
Newbold
Thringstone
Shelthorpe
Woodthorpe
Quorndon
Caldwell
Linton
Rosliston
Swannington
Whitwick
Charnwood Lodge
Orgreave
Alrewas
Grange Wood Zoo
Overseal
Moira
Heart of the National Forest
Coalville
Charnwood Forest
Woodhouse
Beacon Hill
Nat. Memorial Arboretum
Coton in the Elms
Donisthorpe
Packington
Snibston Discovery Park
Greenhill
Woodhouse Eaves
Broombriggs
Croxall
Ravenstone
Oakthorpe
The Manor House
Bardon
Swithland
Edingale
Lullington
Netherseal
Measham
Normanton le Heath
Hugglescote
Copt Oak
Chilcote
Forest
Ellistown
Leicester Services
Markfield
Bradgate Park & Swithland Wood
Cropston
Elford
Harlaston
Haunton
Clifton Campville
Swepstone
Heather
Stanton under Bardon
Appleby Magna
Ibstock
No Man's Heath
Appleby Parva
Snarestone
Newton Burgoland
Battram
Field Head
Newtown Linford
Bradgate House Ruins
Whittington
Thorpe Constantine
Bagworth
Anstey
Hademore
Norton-Juxta-Twycross
Odstone
Nailstone
Thornton
Groby
Wigginton
Seckington
Newton Regis
Shackerstone
Congerstone
Twycross
Barton in the Beans
Barlestone
Ratby
Glenfield
Hopwas
Leyfields
Shuttington
Austrey
Bilstone
The Battlefield Line
Botcheston
Tamworth
Alvecote
Carlton
Newtown Unthank
Kirby Muxloe
Amington
Warton
Orton-on-the-Hill
Market Bosworth
Tropical Bird Gardens
Newbold Verdon
Desford
Leicester Forest East
Hints
Glascote
Polesworth
St Helena
Wellsborough
Cadeby
Leicester Forest East Services
Bonehill
Fazeley
Drayton Manor
Drayton Bassett
Wilnecote
Birchmoor
Tamworth Services
Sheepy Magna
Sheepy Parva
Sibson
Grendon
Bosworth Battlefield
Mallory Park
Peckleton
Kirkby Mallory
Dosthill
Dordon
Shenton
Sutton Cheney
Enderby
Middleton
Ash End Ho. Fm.
Croft Farm
Grendon Common
Baddesley Ensor
Ratcliffe Culey
Upton
Stapleton
Thurlaston
Wood End
Kingsbury Water Park
Atherstone
Witherley
Dadlington
Earl Shilton
Narborough
Bodymoor Heath
Kingsbury
Baxterley
Mancetter
Fenny Drayton
Higham on the Hill
Stoke Golding
Barwell
Elmesthorpe
Huncote
Littlethorpe
M6 Toll
The Belfry
Hartshill Hayes
Bentley
Hurley
Oldbury
Ridge Lane
Stoney Stanton
Burbage Common & Woods
Croft
Cosby
Wishaw
Over Green
Marston
Lea Marston
Hartshill
Weddington
Hinckley
Sutton in the Elms
Curdworth
Nether Whitacre
Whiteacre Heath
Hoar Park Craft Village
Church End
Galley Common
Chapel End
Camp Hill
Sketchley
Burbage
Sapcote
Aston Flamville
Primethorpe
Broughton Astley
Minworth
Water Orton
Furnace End
Over Whitacre
Ansley
Stockingford
Nuneaton
Sharnford
Dunton Bassett
Castle Bromwich Hall
Shustoke
Church End
Old Arley
Astley
Chilvers Coton
Attleborough
Burton Hastings
Fosse Meadows
Frolesworth
Leire
Coleshill
New Arley
Arbury Hall
Whitestone
Smockington
Claybrooke Magna
Claybrooke Parva
Ashby Parva
Kitt's Green
Griff
Collycroft
Bramcote
Bedworth
Copston Magna
Wibtoft
Ullesthorpe
Tile Cross
Marston Green
Maxstoke
Fillongley
Bedworth Heath
Wolvey
Corley Ash
Corley Services
Bulkington
Bitteswell
Forest of Arden
Chapel Green
Corley
Corley Moor
Ash Green
Neal's Green
Hawkesbury
Barnacle
Willey
Lutterworth
Birmingham International
NEC
Butler's End
Keresley
Longford
Shilton
Withybrook
Cross in Hand
Misterton
Elmdon
Nat. Motorcycle Mus.
Hawkes End
Little Heath
Foleshill
Ansty
Monks Kirby
Cotesbach
Bickenhill
Meriden
Coundon
Walsgrave on Sowe
Pailton
Elmdon Heath
Allesley
Transport Mus.
Great Heath
Wyken
Stretton under Fosse
Churchover
Gibbet Hill
Hampton in Arden
Four Oaks
Eastern Green
Spon End
Coombe Abbey
Catthorpe
Eastcote
Berkswell
Whoberley
Coventry
Brinklow
Harborough Magna
Copt Heath
Barston
Tile Hill
Earlsdon
Pinley
Binley
Binley Woods
King's Newnham
Newbold on Avon
Newton
Knowle
Balsall Common
Stivichall
Willenhall
Bretford
Long Lawford
Church Lawford
Clifton upon Dunsmore
Bentley Heath
Temple Balsall
Balsall
Catchems Corner
Tollbar End
Brandon
Wolston
Midland Air Mus.
New Bilton

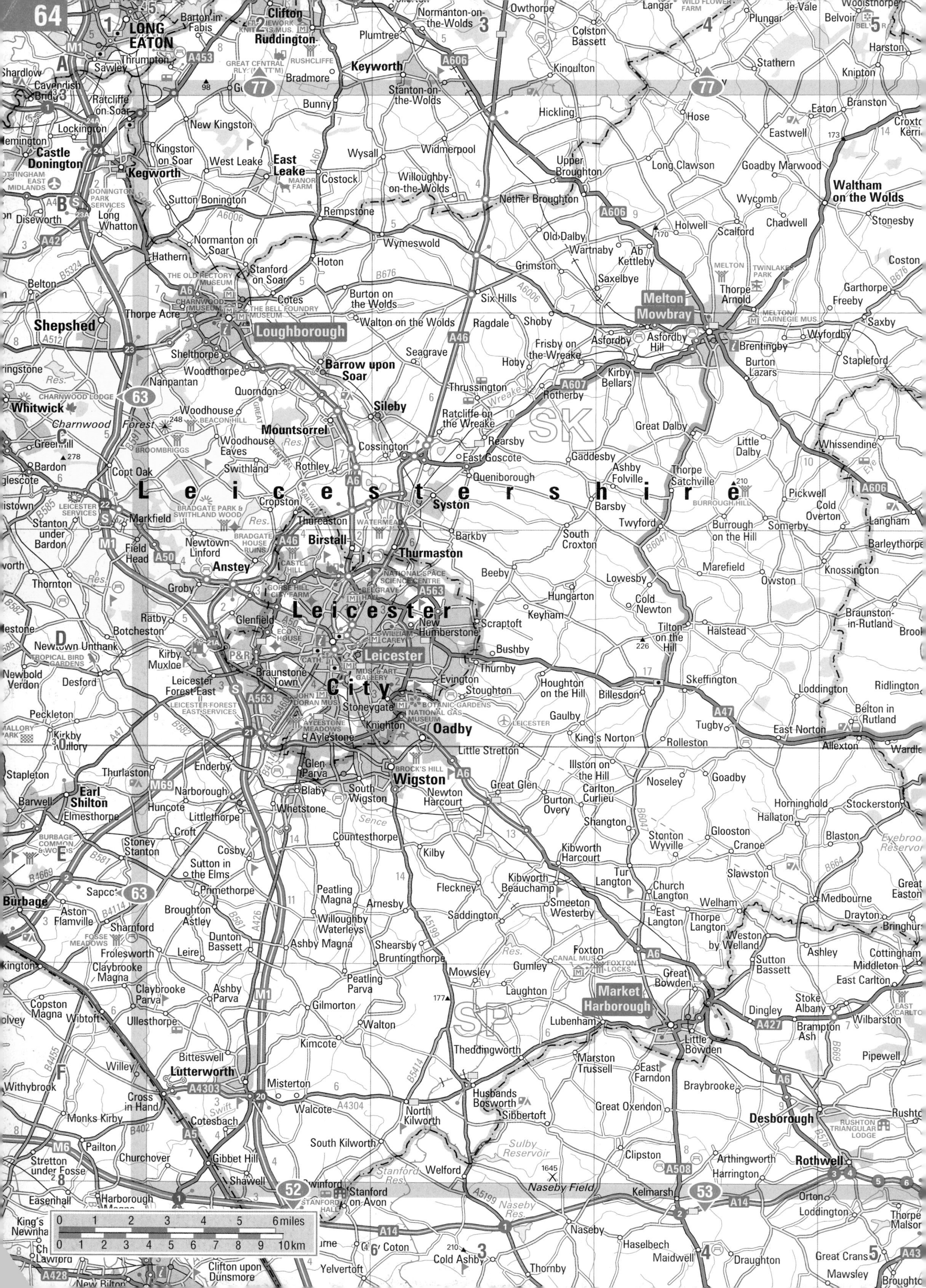

LONG EATON
Barton in Fabis
Clifton
Ruddington
Normanton-on-the-Wolds
Owthorpe
Colston Bassett
Langar
Plungar
le-Vale
Woolsthorpe
Belvoir
Harston
Sawley
Thrumpton
Plumtree
Keyworth
Bradmore
Kinoulton
Stathern
Knipton
Shardlow
Cavendish Bridge
Ratcliffe on Soar
GREAT CENTRAL RLY
RUSHCLIFFE
Stanton-on-the-Wolds
Bunny
Hickling
Hose
Eaton
Branston
Eastwell
Lockington
New Kingston
Widmerpool
Castle Donington
Kingston on Soar
West Leake
East Leake
Wysall
Upper Broughton
Long Clawson
Goadby Marwood
Waltham on the Wolds
Kegworth
Costock
Willoughby-on-the-Wolds
EAST MIDLANDS
DONINGTON PARK SERVICES
Sutton Bonington
Nether Broughton
Wycomb
Chadwell
Diseworth
Long Whatton
Rempstone
Stonesby
Holwell
Scalford
Normanton on Soar
Wymeswold
Old Dalby
Wartnaby
Ab Kettleby
Hathern
Hoton
Grimston
MELTON
TWINLAKES PARK
Coston
Belton
THE OLD RECTORY MUSEUM
Stanford on Soar
Saxelbye
Thorpe Arnold
Garthorpe
Freeby
CHARNWOOD MUSEUM
Cotes
Burton on the Wolds
Six Hills
Melton Mowbray
THE BELL FOUNDRY
Thorpe Acre
Loughborough
Walton on the Wolds
Ragdale
Shoby
Asfordby
Asfordby Hill
MELTON CARNEGIE MUS.
Saxby
Shepshed
Wyfordby
Brentingby
Shelthorpe
Seagrave
Frisby on the Wreake
Burton Lazars
Stapleford
Barrow upon Soar
Hoby
Kirby Bellars
Nanpantan
Woodthorpe
Thrussington
Rotherby
Quorndon
CHARNWOOD LODGE
Whitwick
Woodhouse
Sileby
Ratcliffe on the Wreake
Charnwood Forest
BEACON HILL
Mountsorrel
Great Dalby
Greenhill
Woodhouse Eaves
Cossington
Rearsby
Little Dalby
Whissendine
BROOMBRIGGS
East Goscote
Gaddesby
Bardon
Swithland
Rothley
Copt Oak
Queniborough
Ashby Folville
Thorpe Satchville
Leicestershire
Pickwell
Cold Overton
LEICESTER SERVICES
Stanton under Bardon
Markfield
BRADGATE PARK & SWITHLAND WOOD
Cropston
Syston
Barsby
BURROUGH HILL
Langham
Thurcaston
WATERMEAD
Twyford
Burrough on the Hill
Somerby
Barkby
South Croxton
Barleythorpe
Newtown Linford
BRADGATE HOUSE RUINS
Birstall
Field Head
Thurmaston
Marefield
Knossington
Owston
Thornton
Anstey
CASTLE HILL
NATIONAL SPACE SCIENCE CENTRE
Beeby
Lowesby
Groby
GORSE HILL CITY FARM
BELGRAVE HALL
Hungarton
Cold Newton
Leicester
Braunston-in-Rutland
Ratby
Glenfield
Keyham
Scraptoft
Botcheston
ECO HOUSE
New Humberstone
Tilton on the Hill
Halstead
Newtown Unthank
WILLIAM CAREY
Bushby
TROPICAL BIRD GARDENS
Kirby Muxloe
CATH.
Leicester City
Thurnby
Newbold Verdon
Desford
Braunstone Town
MUS & ART GALLERY
Evington
Houghton on the Hill
Billesdon
Skeffington
Leicester Forest East
Stoughton
Loddington
Ridlington
JOHN DORAN MUS
BOTANIC GARDENS
LEICESTER FOREST EAST SERVICES
Stoneygate
NATIONAL GAS MUSEUM
Gaulby
Belton in Rutland
Peckleton
AYLESTONE MEADOWS
Knighton
Oadby
Tugby
East Norton
Kirkby Mallory
Aylestone
King's Norton
Rolleston
Allexton
Little Stretton
Enderby
Wardle
Stapleton
Thurlaston
Glen Parva
BROCK'S HILL
Illston on the Hill
Goadby
Noseley
Earl Shilton
Narborough
Wigston
Great Glen
Carlton Curlieu
Barwell
Blaby
South Wigston
Newton Harcourt
Burton Overy
Hothorpe
Horninghold
Stockerston
Huncote
Elmesthorpe
Whetstone
Hallaton
Littlethorpe
Shangton
Sence
Croft
Stoney Stanton
BURBAGE COMMON & WOODS
Countesthorpe
Stonton Wyville
Glooston
Cranoe
Blaston
Eyebrook Reservoir
Cosby
Kibworth Harcourt
Kilby
Sutton in the Elms
Slawston
Tur Langton
Great Easton
Sapcote
Primethorpe
Peatling Magna
Fleckney
Kibworth Beauchamp
Church Langton
Welham
Medbourne
Burbage
Aston Flamville
Broughton Astley
Arnesby
Smeeton Westerby
East Langton
Thorpe Langton
Drayton
Saddington
Bringhurst
Sharnford
Willoughby Waterleys
Weston by Welland
FOSSE MEADOWS
Dunton Bassett
Frolesworth
Ashby Magna
Shearsby
Foxton
Ashley
Cottingham
Leire
Bruntingthorpe
CANAL MUS.
FOXTON LOCKS
Sutton Bassett
Middleton
Claybrooke Magna
Gumley
Great Bowden
East Carlton
Mowsley
Peatling Parva
Laughton
Market Harborough
Claybrooke Parva
Ashby Parva
Stoke Albany
Copston Magna
Gilmorton
Dingley
Wilbarston
Wibtoft
Ullesthorpe
Brampton Ash
Lubenham
Walton
Little Bowden
Kimcote
Theddingworth
Pipewell
Bitteswell
Willey
Marston Trussell
East Farndon
Lutterworth
Withybrook
Misterton
Braybrooke
Husbands Bosworth
Cross in Hand
Walcote
North Kilworth
Great Oxendon
Desborough
Monks Kirby
Sibbertoft
Cotesbach
RUSHTON TRIANGULAR LODGE
South Kilworth
Sulby Reservoir
Pailton
Clipston
Churchover
Gibbet Hill
Arthingworth
Rothwell
Welford
Stretton under Fosse
Stanford Res.
Harrington
Shawell
Naseby Field
Swinford
Kelmarsh
Stanford on Avon
Orton
Easenhall
Harborough Magna
STANFORD HALL
Naseby Res.
Loddington
King's Newnham
Thorpe Malsor
Coton
Naseby
Cold Ashby
Haselbech
Maidwell
Draughton
Great Cransley
Lawford
Clifton upon Dunsmore
Yelvertoft
Thornby
Mawsley
Broughton
New Bilton
SK
SP
0 1 2 3 4 5 6 miles
0 1 2 3 4 5 6 7 8 9 10 km

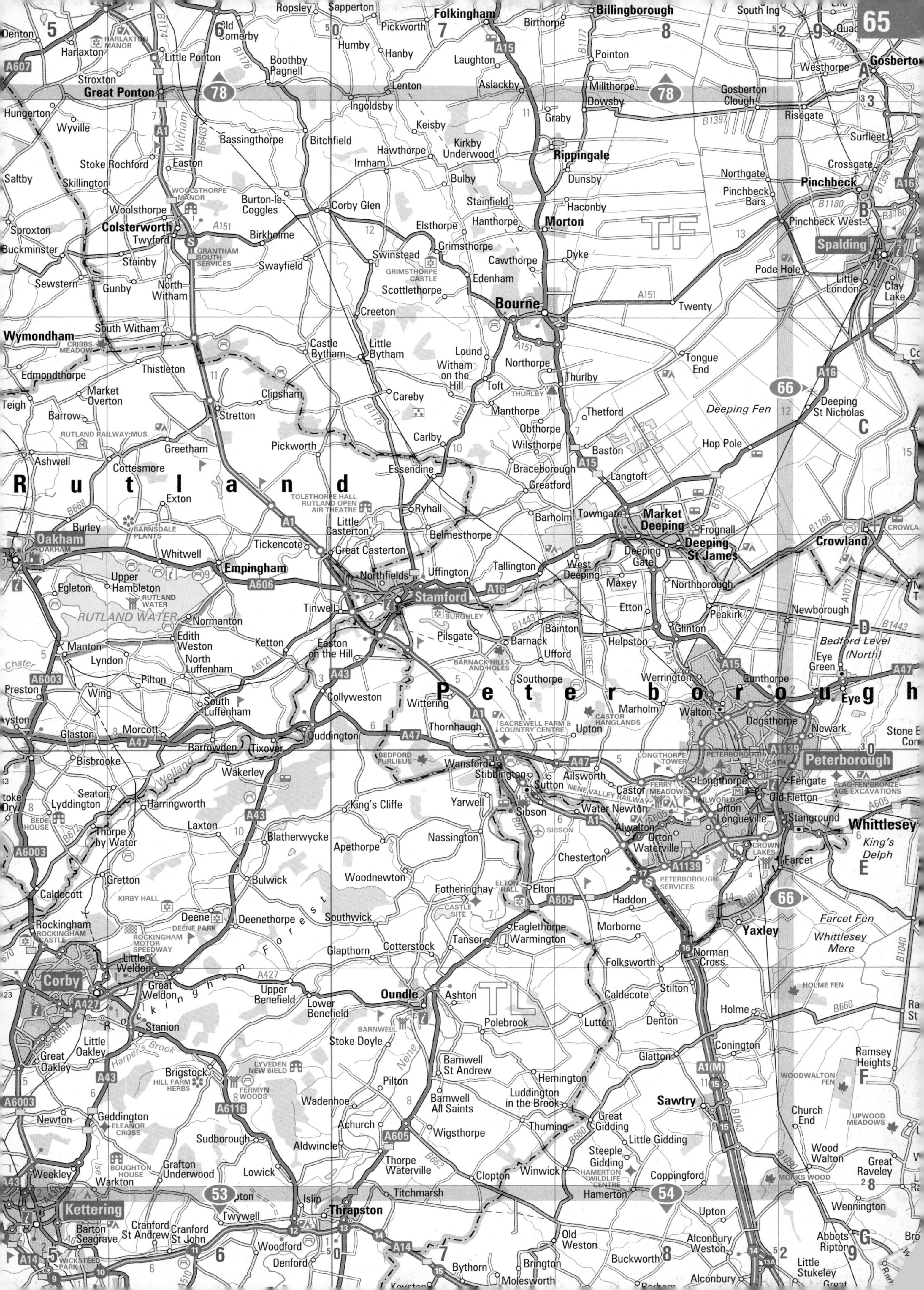
Rutland
Peterborough
Oakham
Stamford
Bourne
Market Deeping
Deeping St James
Spalding
Crowland
Peterborough
Whittlesey
Yaxley
Oundle
Corby
Kettering
Thrapston
Sawtry
Great Ponton
Colsterworth
Empingham
Rutland Water
Deeping Fen
Bedford Level (North)
Rockingham Forest
Farcet Fen
Whittlesey Mere
TF
TL
78
66
53
54

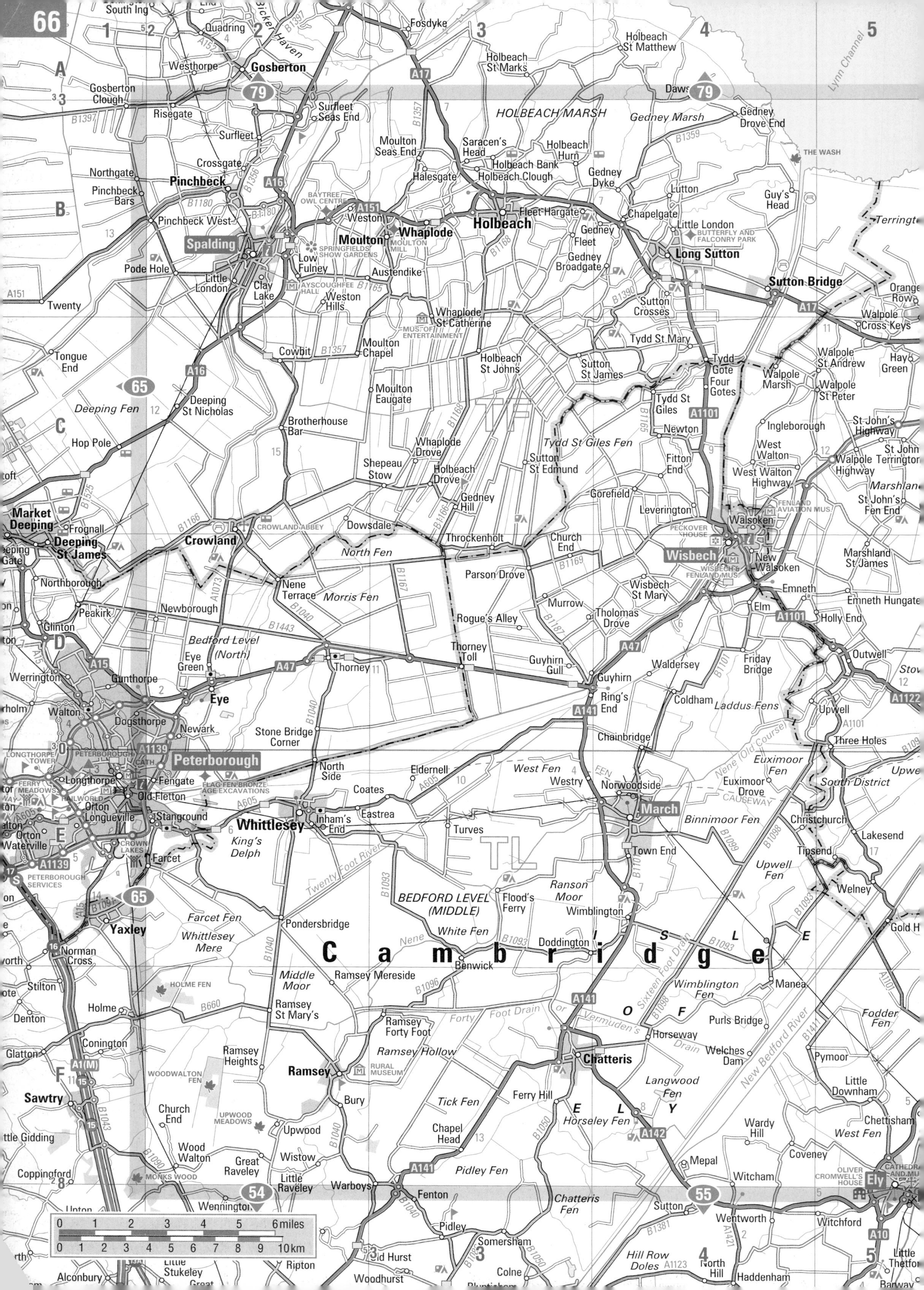
South Ing
Quadring
Bicker Haven
Fosdyke
Holbeach St Matthew
Westhorpe
Gosberton
Holbeach St Marks
A17
Lynn Channel
Gosberton Clough
79
Daws
Surfleet Seas End
Risegate
HOLBEACH MARSH
Gedney Marsh
Gedney Drove End
B1397
Surfleet
B1357
B1359
Moulton Seas End
Saracen's Head
Holbeach Hurn
THE WASH
Crossgate
Halesgate
Holbeach Bank
Holbeach Clough
Gedney Dyke
Northgate
Pinchbeck
B1356
A16
Lutton
Pinchbeck Bars
BAYTREE OWL CENTRE
A151
Guy's Head
B1180
Weston
Fleet Hargate
Chapelgate
Pinchbeck West
Moulton
Whaplode
Holbeach
Gedney
Little London
BUTTERFLY AND FALCONRY PARK
Terrington
Spalding
MOULTON MILL
Fleet
SPRINGFIELDS SHOW GARDENS
B1168
Long Sutton
Low Fulney
Gedney Broadgate
Pode Hole
Austendike
Little London
Clay Lake
AYSCOUGHFEE HALL
B1165
Sutton Bridge
Orange Row
A151
Twenty
Weston Hills
B1390
Sutton Crosses
A17
Whaplode St Catherine
Walpole Cross Keys
MUS. OF ENTERTAINMENT
Tydd St Mary
Cowbit
B1357
Moulton Chapel
Tongue End
Holbeach St Johns
Sutton St James
Tydd Gote
Walpole St Andrew
Hay Green
Four Gotes
Walpole Marsh
A16
Walpole St Peter
65
Moulton Eaugate
Tydd St Giles
Deeping St Nicholas
Deeping Fen
A1101
TF
Brotherhouse Bar
B1165
Newton
Ingleborough
St John's Highway
B1168
Tydd St Giles Fen
Hop Pole
Whaplode Drove
West Walton
St John
Sutton St Edmund
Fitton End
Walpole Highway
Terrington
Shepeau Stow
Holbeach Drove
West Walton Highway
Marshland
B1525
Gedney Hill
Gorefield
St John's Fen End
Market Deeping
Frognall
B1166
FENLAND AVIATION MUS.
Leverington
Walsoken
Deeping St James
Deeping Gate
Crowland
CROWLAND ABBEY
Dowsdale
Throckenholt
Church End
PECKOVER HOUSE
Wisbech
New Walsoken
Marshland St James
North Fen
B1169
WISBECH & FENLAND MUS.
Northborough
B1167
Parson Drove
Wisbech St Mary
A1073
Nene Terrace
Morris Fen
Emneth
Murrow
Emneth Hungate
Newborough
B1040
Tholomas Drove
Elm
Peakirk
Rogue's Alley
A1101
Holly End
B1187
Glinton
B1443
Bedford Level (North)
Thorney Toll
A47
Outwell
Eye Green
Guyhirn Gull
Friday Bridge
A15
A47
Thorney
B1101
Waldersey
Stow
Werrington
Gunthorpe
Guyhirn
Eye
Ring's End
Coldham
Laddus Fens
A1122
Walton
Dogsthorpe
B1040
Upwell
A141
A1101
Newark
Stone Bridge Corner
Chainbridge
Three Holes
A1139
Nene (Old Course)
LONGTHORPE TOWER
PETERBOROUGH CATH
Peterborough
North Side
Euximoor Fen
Eldernell
West Fen
Westry
Upwell
Longthorpe
Fengate
FLAG FEN BRONZE AGE EXCAVATIONS
A605
Norwoodside
Euximoor Drove
FERRY MEADOWS
Coates
CAUSEWAY
South District
RAILWORLD
Old Fletton
Orton Longueville
A605
March
Stanground
Whittlesey
Inham's End
Eastrea
Binnimoor Fen
Christchurch
Orton Waterville
Turves
Lakesend
King's Delph
TL
Town End
CROWN LAKES
Twenty Foot River
B1099
B1098
Tipsend
A1139
Farcet
B1101
Upwell Fen
PETERBOROUGH SERVICES
Ranson Moor
Welney
B1093
BEDFORD LEVEL (MIDDLE)
Flood's Ferry
B1091
65
Wimblington
A15
Farcet Fen
Yaxley
Pondersbridge
White Fen
Gold Hill
Whittlesey Mere
B1093
Doddington
ISLE
B1093
Nene
Norman Cross
B1040
Cambridge
Benwick
Sixteen Foot Drain
Middle Moor
Ramsey Mereside
Manea
Stilton
HOLME FEN
B1096
Wimblington Fen
B1098
A141
Holme
B660
Ramsey St Mary's
Forty Foot Drain
or Vermuden's Drain
OF
Purls Bridge
Fodder Fen
Denton
Ramsey Forty Foot
Horseway
New Bedford River
B1411
Conington
Ramsey Hollow
Welches Dam
Glatton
Ramsey Heights
Pymoor
Chatteris
A1(M)
WOODWALTON FEN
Ramsey
RURAL MUSEUM
Langwood Fen
Little Downham
Sawtry
Bury
Ferry Hill
Church End
Tick Fen
B1043
ELY
UPWOOD MEADOWS
Horseley Fen
Chettisham
Chapel Head
Wardy Hill
A142
B1050
West Fen
Little Gidding
Upwood
Wood Walton
Coveney
B1090
Wistow
Mepal
Great Raveley
B1040
Pidley Fen
Coppingford
OLIVER CROMWELL'S HOUSE
MONKS WOOD
Little Raveley
Witcham
Ely
A141
Warboys
Chatteris Fen
CATHEDRAL AND MUS
Wennington
54
Fenton
55
Upton
Sutton
Wentworth
Witchford
B1040
A1421
A10
Pidley
B1381
0 1 2 3 4 5 6 miles
0 1 2 3 4 5 6 7 8 9 10 km
Somersham
Hill Row Doles
Little Thetford
Old Hurst
B1050
A1123
North Hill
Ripton
Little Stukeley
Colne
Alconbury
Woodhurst
Haddenham
Barway
Great
Bluntisham

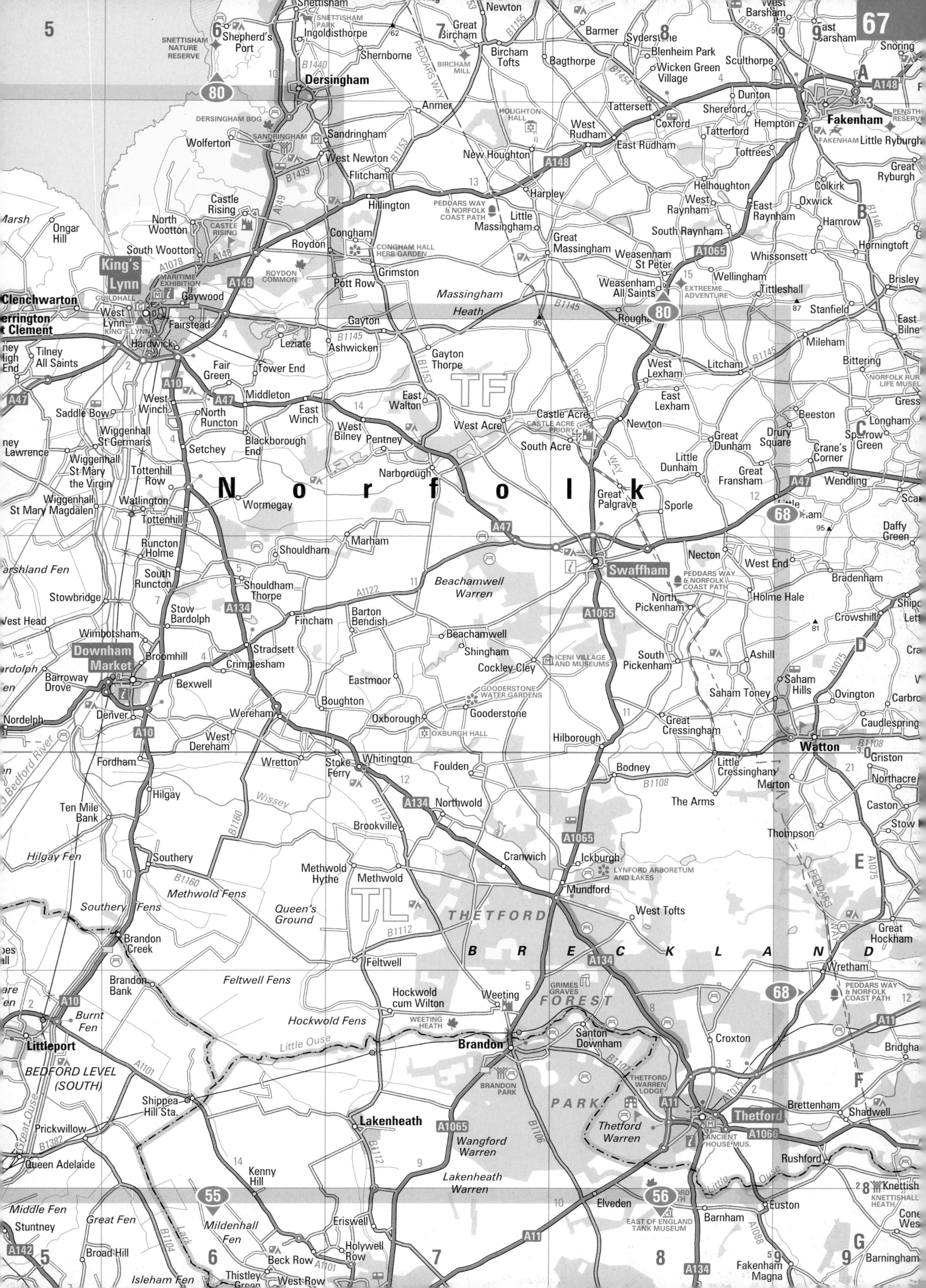

67
Snettisham
Snettisham Park
Ingoldisthorpe
Newton
Great Bircham
Barmer
West Barsham
East Barsham
Snoring
Snettisham Nature Reserve
Shepherd's Port
Shernborne
Bircham Mill
Bircham Tofts
Bagthorpe
Syderstone
Blenheim Park
Wicken Green Village
Sculthorpe
Dersingham
Dersingham Bog
Anmer
Houghton Hall
Tattersett
Coxford
Dunton
Shereford
Tatterford
Hempton
Fakenham
Little Ryburgh
Pensthorpe Reserve
Wolferton
Sandringham
West Newton
Flitcham
New Houghton
West Rudham
East Rudham
Toftrees
Great Ryburgh
Helhoughton
Colkirk
Oxwick
West Raynham
East Raynham
Hamrow
South Raynham
Horningtoft
Castle Rising
North Wootton
South Wootton
Ongar Hill
Hillington
Congham
Congham Hall Herb Garden
Roydon
Roydon Common
Peddars Way & Norfolk Coast Path
Little Massingham
Harpley
Great Massingham
Weasenham St Peter
Weasenham All Saints
Whissonsett
Wellingham
Extreme Adventure
Tittleshall
Brisley
Stanfield
East Bilney
King's Lynn
Maritime Exhibition
Guildhall
Gaywood
Grimston
Pott Row
Massingham Heath
Clenchwarton
Terrington St Clement
West Lynn
Fairstead
Gayton
Leziate
Ashwicken
Rougham
Hardwick
Tilney All Saints
Tower End
Fair Green
Gayton Thorpe
West Lexham
Litcham
Mileham
Bittering
Norfolk Rural Life Museum
Middleton
East Walton
East Lexham
Saddle Bow
West Winch
North Runcton
East Winch
Castle Acre
Castle Acre Priory
West Acre
Newton
Beeston
Longham
Gressenhall
Wiggenhall St Germans
Setchey
Blackborough End
West Bilney
Pentney
South Acre
Great Dunham
Drury Square
Sparrow Green
Crane's Corner
Tilney St Lawrence
Wiggenhall St Mary the Virgin
Tottenhill Row
Narborough
Little Dunham
Great Fransham
Wendling
Norfolk
Wiggenhall St Mary Magdalen
Watlington
Tottenhill
Wormegay
Great Palgrave
Sporle
Little Fransham
Scarning
Daffy Green
Runcton Holme
Shouldham
Marham
Necton
West End
Swaffham
Marshland Fen
South Runcton
Shouldham Thorpe
Beachamwell Warren
Peddars Way & Norfolk Coast Path
North Pickenham
Bradenham
Holme Hale
Shipdham
Stowbridge
Stow Bardolph
Fincham
Barton Bendish
Crowshill
West Head
Wimbotsham
Beachamwell
Shingham
Ashill
Downham Market
Broomhill
Stradsett
Crimplesham
Iceni Village and Museums
Cockley Cley
South Pickenham
Saham Hills
Barroway Drove
Bexwell
Eastmoor
Saham Toney
Ovington
Carbrooke
Nordelph
Denver
Wereham
Boughton
Oxborough
Gooderstone Water Gardens
Gooderstone
Great Cressingham
Caudlesprings
West Dereham
Oxburgh Hall
Hilborough
Watton
Griston
Fordham
Wretton
Stoke Ferry
Whitington
Foulden
Bodney
Little Cressingham
Merton
Northacre
Hilgay
Wissey
The Arms
Caston
Ten Mile Bank
Northwold
Brookville
Stow Bedon
Thompson
Hilgay Fen
Southery
Cranwich
Ickburgh
Lynford Arboretum and Lakes
Methwold Hythe
Methwold
Methwold Fens
Mundford
Southery Fens
Queen's Ground
Thetford
West Tofts
Peddars Way
Great Hockham
Brandon Creek
Breckland
Feltwell
Wretham
Feltwell Fens
Brandon Bank
Hockwold cum Wilton
Weeting
Grimes Graves
Forest
Peddars Way & Norfolk Coast Path
Littleport
Burnt Fen
Hockwold Fens
Weeting Heath
Little Ouse
Brandon
Santon Downham
Croxton
Bridgham
Bedford Level (South)
Thetford Warren Lodge
Brettenham
Shadwell
Shippea Hill Sta.
Brandon Park
Park
Thetford Warren
Thetford
Ancient House Mus.
Prickwillow
Lakenheath
Wangford Warren
Rushford
Queen Adelaide
Kenny Hill
Lakenheath Warren
Knettishall Heath
Middle Fen
Great Fen
Mildenhall Fen
Elveden
East of England Tank Museum
Euston
Barnham
Stuntney
Eriswell
Coney Weston
Broad Hill
Holywell Row
Beck Row
Barningham
Isleham Fen
Thistley Green
West Row
Fakenham Magna
Great Ouse
Ten Mile Bank
Bedford River
TF
TL
5
6
7
8
9
A
B
C
D
E
F
G
55
56
68
80
A10
A47
A134
A148
A149
A1065
A1066
A1075
A1088
A1101
A1122
A11
A142
A1078
B1145
B1153
B1155
B1454
B1355
B1439
B1440
B1146
B1108
B1106
B1107
B1112
B1160
B1104
B1382

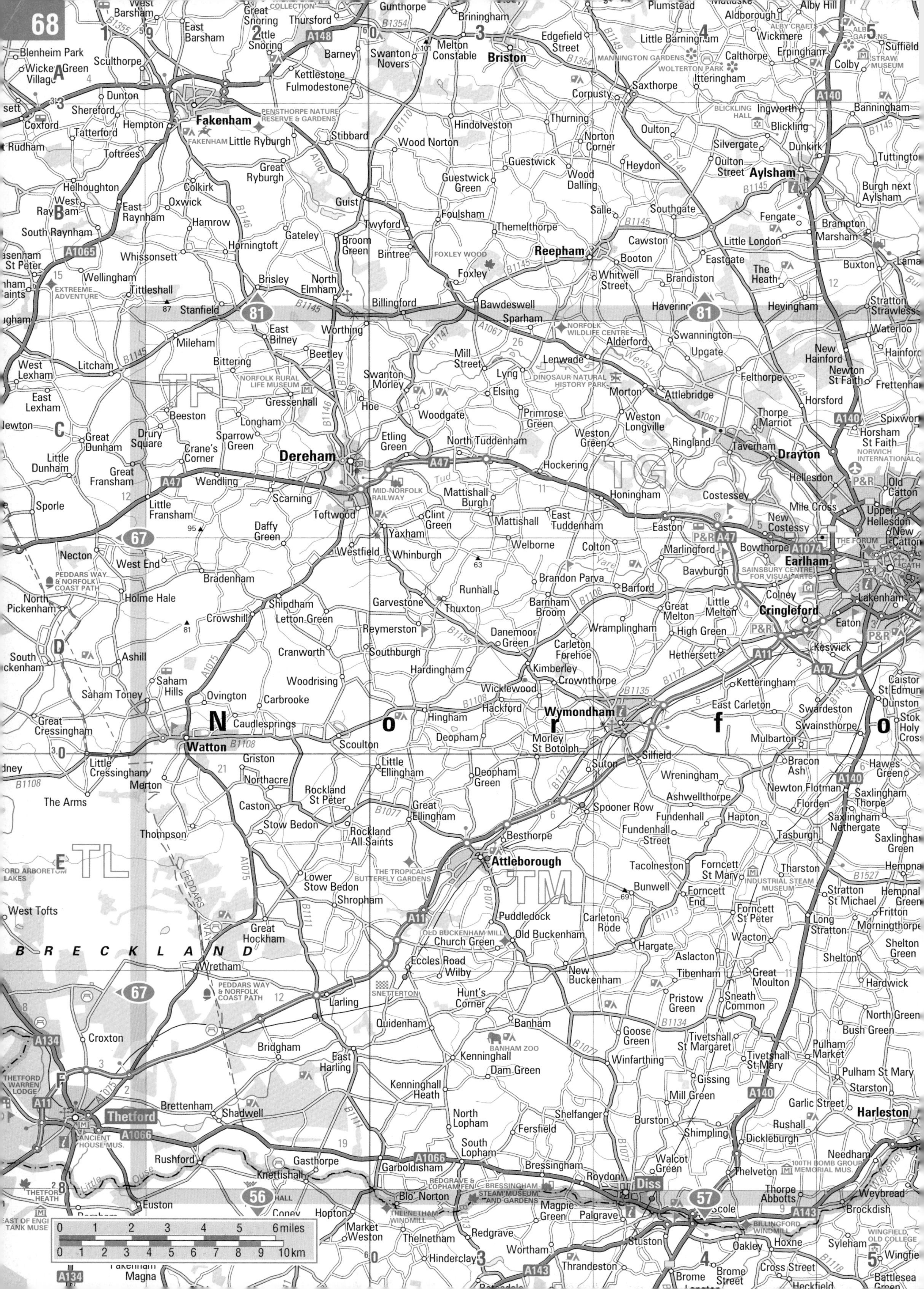
Fakenham
Dereham
Reepham
Aylsham
Drayton
Earlham
Cringleford
Wymondham
Watton
Attleborough
Thetford
Diss
Harleston
Norfolk
BRECKLAND
0 1 2 3 4 5 6 miles
0 1 2 3 4 5 6 7 8 9 10 km

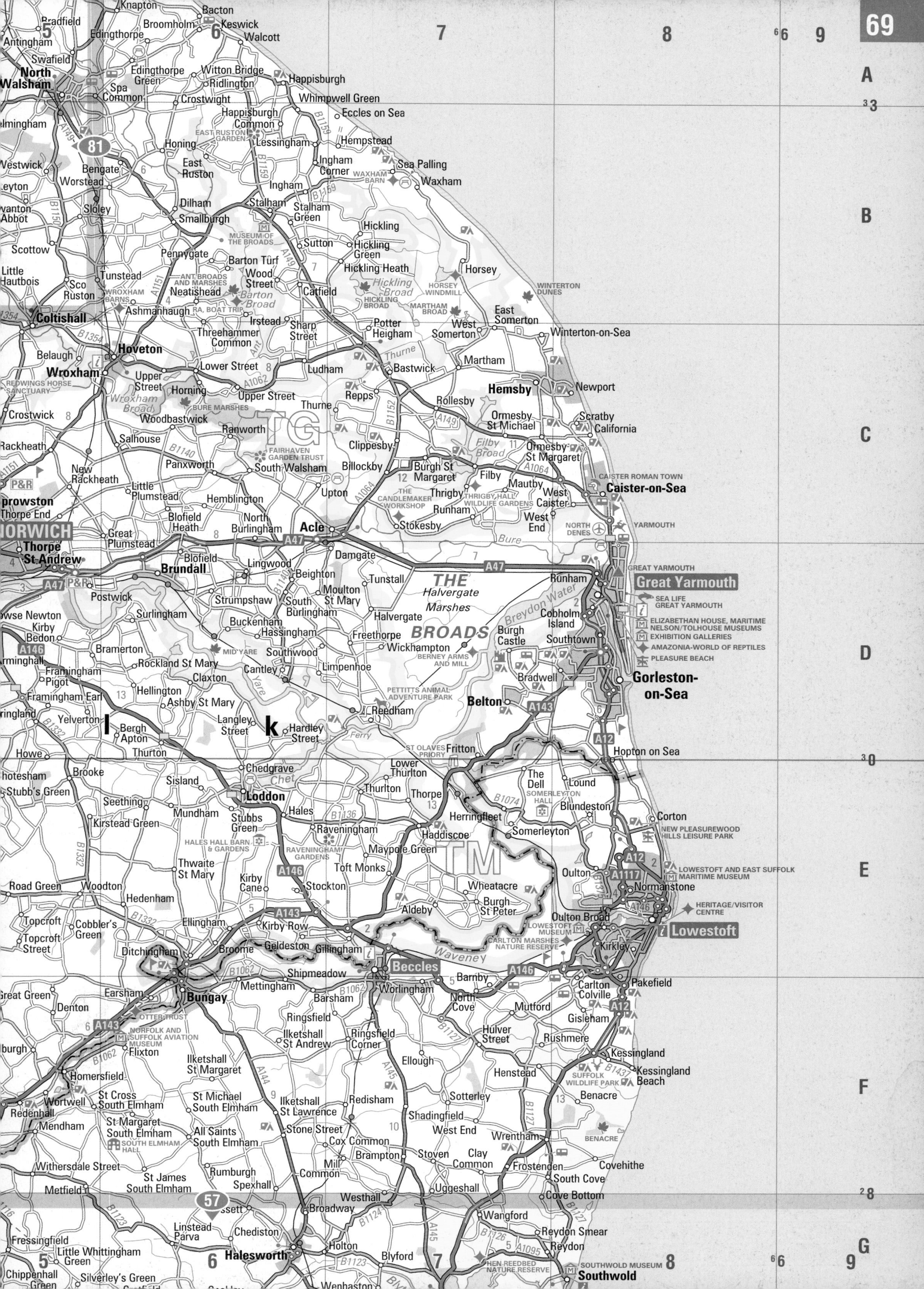
North Walsham
Coltishall
Hoveton
Wroxham
Happisburgh
Sea Palling
Hickling
Horsey
Winterton-on-Sea
Hemsby
Ludham
Acle
Caister-on-Sea
Great Yarmouth
Gorleston-on-Sea
NORWICH
Thorpe St Andrew
Brundall
Loddon
Beccles
Bungay
Lowestoft
Kessingland
Halesworth
Southwold
THE BROADS
Halvergate Marshes
Breydon Water
Hopton on Sea
Oulton Broad
Wrentham
Reydon
MUSEUM OF THE BROADS
CAISTER ROMAN TOWN
SEA LIFE GREAT YARMOUTH
ELIZABETHAN HOUSE, MARITIME
NELSON/TOLHOUSE MUSEUMS
EXHIBITION GALLERIES
AMAZONIA-WORLD OF REPTILES
PLEASURE BEACH
NEW PLEASUREWOOD HILLS LEISURE PARK
LOWESTOFT AND EAST SUFFOLK MARITIME MUSEUM
HERITAGE/VISITOR CENTRE
SOUTHWOLD MUSEUM
A47
A12
A146
A143
A1117
A144
A145
A1064
A149
TG
TM

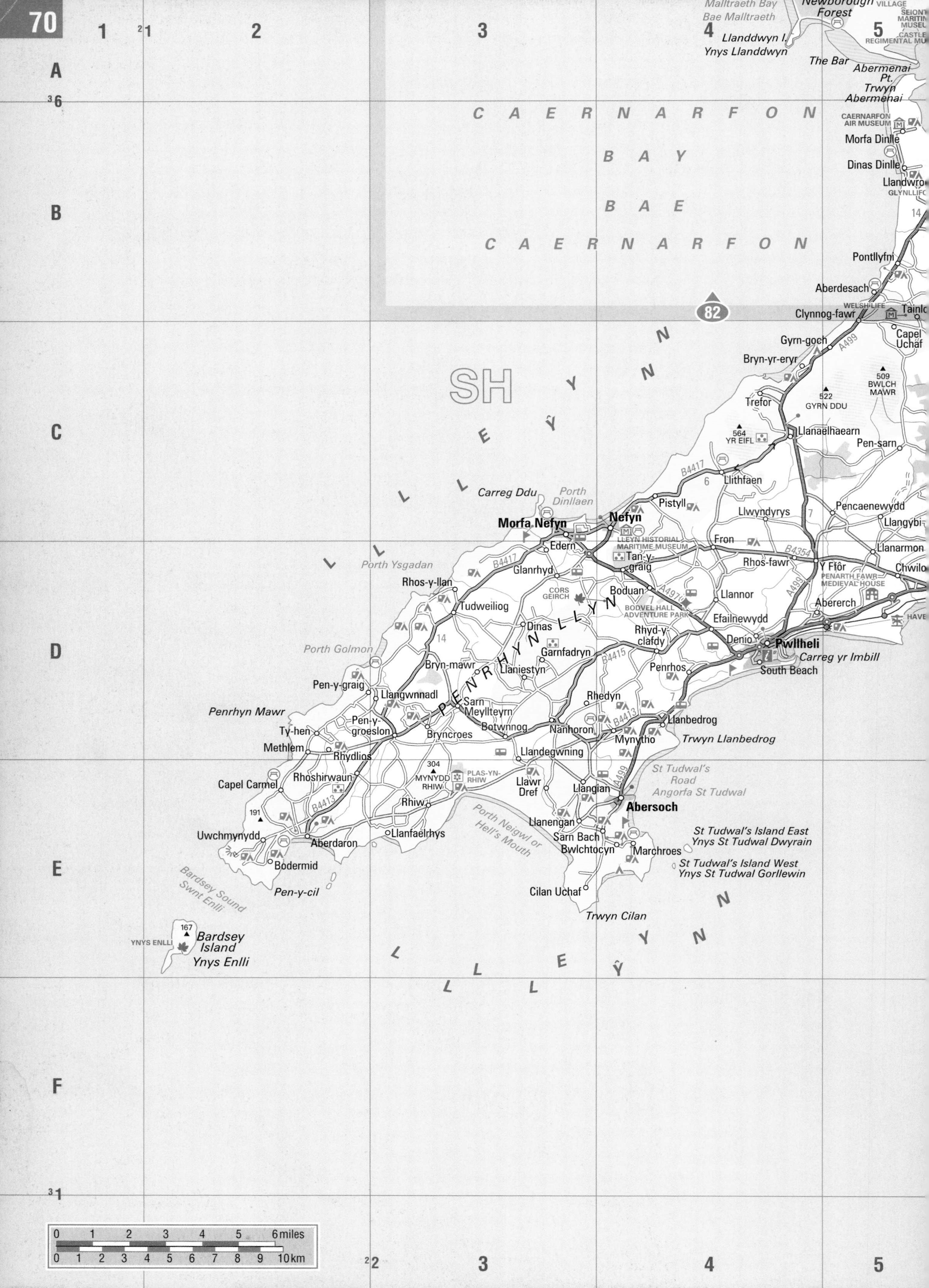

Malltraeth Bay
Bae Malltraeth
Newborough Forest
Llanddwyn I.
Ynys Llanddwyn
The Bar
Abermenai Pt.
Trwyn Abermenai
CAERNARFON AIR MUSEUM
Morfa Dinlle
Dinas Dinlle
Llandwrog
GLYNLLIFON
C A E R N A R F O N
B A Y
B A E
C A E R N A R F O N
Pontllyfni
Aberdesach
WELSHLIFE
Clynnog-fawr
Capel Uchaf
Gyrn-goch
A499
Bryn-yr-eryr
509 BWLCH MAWR
522 GYRN DDU
Trefor
SH
564 YR EIFL
Llanaelhaearn
Pen-sarn
B4417
Llithfaen
Carreg Ddu
Porth Dinllaen
Pistyll
Llwyndyrys
Pencaenewydd
Llangybi
Morfa Nefyn
Nefyn
LLEYN HISTORICAL MARITIME MUSEUM
Edern
Fron
B4354
Llanarmon
Porth Ysgadan
Tan-y-graig
Rhos-fawr
Y Ffôr
Chwilog
PENARTH FAWR MEDIEVAL HOUSE
Glanrhyd
Rhos-y-llan
CORS GEIRCH
Boduan
A497
Llannor
Abererch
Tudweiliog
BODVEL HALL ADVENTURE PARK
Efailnewydd
Dinas
Rhyd-y-clafdy
Denio
Pwllheli
Porth Golmon
Garnfadryn
B4415
Carreg yr Imbill
Bryn-mawr
Llaniestyn
Penrhos
South Beach
Pen-y-graig
Llangwnnadl
P E N R H Y N   L L Y N
Rhedyn
Penrhyn Mawr
Sarn Meyllteyrn
B4413
Llanbedrog
Ty-hen
Pen-y-groeslon
Botwnnog
Nanhoron
Mynytho
Trwyn Llanbedrog
Methlem
Bryncroes
Rhydlios
Llandegwning
304 MYNYDD RHIW
PLAS-YN-RHIW
St Tudwal's Road
Angorfa St Tudwal
Capel Carmel
Rhoshirwaun
Llawr Dref
Llangian
Abersoch
191
Rhiw
Porth Neigwl or Hell's Mouth
Llanengan
St Tudwal's Island East
Ynys St Tudwal Dwyrain
Uwchmynydd
Aberdaron
Llanfaelrhys
Sarn Bach
Bwlchtocyn
Marchroes
St Tudwal's Island West
Ynys St Tudwal Gorllewin
Bodermid
Bardsey Sound
Swnt Enlli
Pen-y-cil
Cilan Uchaf
Trwyn Cilan
167
YNYS ENLLI
Bardsey Island
Ynys Enlli
L L E Y N
L L E Ŷ N
L L E Ŷ N
82
0 1 2 3 4 5 6 miles
0 1 2 3 4 5 6 7 8 9 10 km

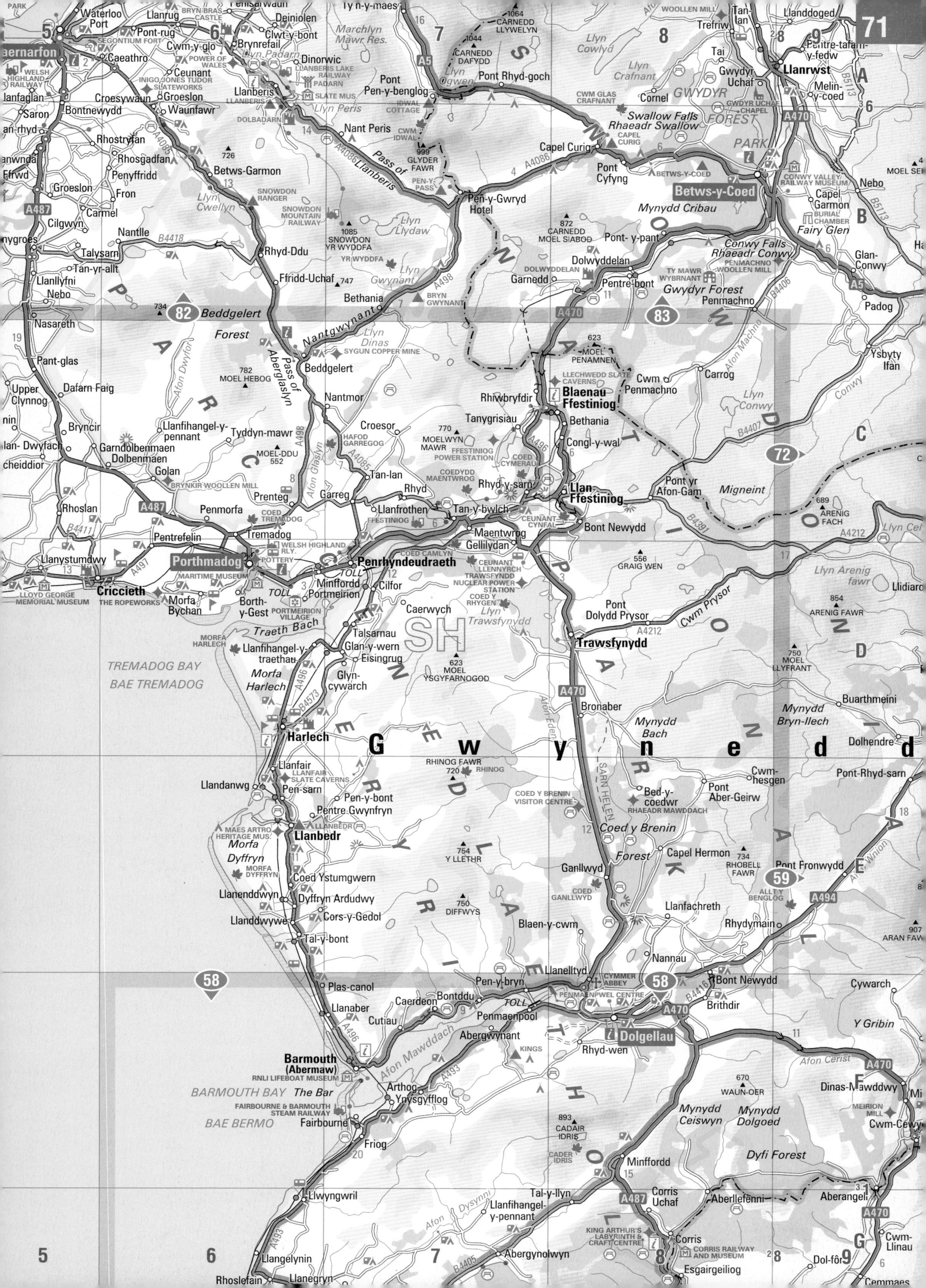
71
Caernarfon
Waterloo Port
Llanrug
Pont-rug
Bryn Bras Castle
Segontium Fort
Cwm-y-glo
Brynrefail
Clwt-y-bont
Deiniolen
Dinorwic
Caeathro
Power of Wales
Llyn Padarn
Llanberis Lake Railway
Padarn
Ceunant
Inigo Jones Tudor Slateworks
Welsh Highland Railway
Llanfaglan
Bontnewydd
Croesywaun
Groeslon
Waunfawr
Llanberis
Slate Mus.
Dolbadarn
Saron
Llanwnda
Rhostryfan
Rhosgadfan
Penyffridd
Betws-Garmon
Groeslon
Fron
Carmel
Cilgwyn
Nantlle
Talysarn
Tan-yr-allt
Llanllyfni
Nebo
Llyn Cwellyn
Snowdon Ranger
Snowdon Mountain Railway
Rhyd-Ddu
Ffridd-Uchaf
Llyn Peris
Nant Peris
Pass of Llanberis
Marchlyn Mawr Res.
Pont Pen-y-benglog
Idwal Cottage
Cwm Idwal
999 Glyder Fawr
Pen-y-Pass
1064 Carnedd Llywelyn
1044 Carnedd Dafydd
Llyn Ogwen
Pont Rhyd-goch
1085 Snowdon Yr Wyddfa
Yr Wyddfa
Llyn Llydaw
Llyn Gwynant
Pen-y-Gwryd Hotel
Bethania
Bryn Gwynant
Nantgwynant
Llyn Dinas
Sygun Copper Mine
Beddgelert
Beddgelert Forest
Pass of Aberglaslyn
782 Moel Hebog
Nasareth
Pant-glas
Upper Clynnog
Dafarn Faig
Bryncir
Llanfihangel-y-pennant
Tyddyn-mawr
Garndolbenmaen
Dolbenmaen
Moel-Ddu 552
Golan
Brynkir Woollen Mill
Rhoslan
Penmorfa
Prenteg
Tremadog
Coed Tremadog
Pentrefelin
Llanystumdwy
Porthmadog
Welsh Highland Rly.
Pottery
Maritime Museum
Criccieth
Lloyd George Memorial Museum
The Ropeworks
Morfa Bychan
Borth-y-Gest
Portmeirion Village
Portmeirion
Minffordd
Penrhyndeudraeth
Traeth Bach
Nantmor
Croesor
Hafod Garregog
Tan-lan
Garreg
Rhyd
Llanfrothen
Ffestiniog
Tan-y-bwlch
Maentwrog
Gellilydan
Coed Camlyn
Ceunant Llennyrch
Trawsfynydd Nuclear Power Station
Cilfor
Caerwych
Talsarnau
Glan-y-wern
Eisingrug
Glyn-cywarch
Llanfihangel-y-traethau
Morfa Harlech
Tremadog Bay
Bae Tremadog
Harlech
Llanfair
Llanfair Slate Caverns
Llandanwg
Pen-sarn
Pen-y-bont
Pentre Gwynfryn
Llanbedr
Maes Artro Heritage Mus.
Morfa Dyffryn
Coed Ystumgwern
Llanenddwyn
Dyffryn Ardudwy
Llanddwywe
Cors-y-Gedol
Tal-y-bont
Plas-canol
Llanaber
Barmouth (Abermaw)
RNLI Lifeboat Museum
Barmouth Bay
The Bar
Bae Bermo
Fairbourne & Barmouth Steam Railway
Fairbourne
Friog
Llwyngwril
Llangelynin
Rhoslefain
Llanegryn
770 Moelwyn Mawr
Ffestiniog Power Station
Tanygrisiau
Rhiwbryfdir
Blaenau Ffestiniog
Llechwedd Slate Caverns
623 Moel Penamnen
Bethania
Congl-y-wal
Coed Cymerau
Coedydd Maentwrog
Rhyd-y-sarn
Llan-Ffestiniog
Ceunant Cynfal
Bont Newydd
556 Graig Wen
Pont Dolydd Prysor
Cwm Prysor
Coed y Rhygen
Llyn Trawsfynydd
Trawsfynydd
623 Moel Ysgyfarnogod
SH
Gwynedd
Rhinog Fawr 720
Bronaber
Mynydd Bach
Sarn Helen
Coed y Brenin Visitor Centre
Bed-y-coedwr
Rhaeadr Mawddach
Pont Aber-Geirw
Cwm-hesgen
Coed y Brenin Forest
Capel Hermon
754 Y Llethr
750 Diffwys
Ganllwyd
Coed Ganllwyd
Blaen-y-cwm
Llanfachreth
Nannau
Llanelltyd
Cymmer Abbey
Pen-y-bryn
Bontddu
Caerdeon
Cutiau
Penmaenpool
Penmaenpwl Centre
Abergwynant
Afon Mawddach
Kings
Arthog
Ynysgyfflog
Dolgellau
Rhyd-wen
893 Cadair Idris
Cader Idris
Minffordd
Tal-y-llyn
Llanfihangel-y-pennant
Afon Dysynni
Abergynolwyn
King Arthur's Labyrinth & Craft Centre
Corris
Corris Uchaf
Corris Railway and Museum
Esgairgeiliog
Aberllefenni
Aberangell
Dyfi Forest
Mynydd Ceiswyn
Mynydd Dolgoed
670 Waun-Oer
Dinas-Mawddwy
Meirion Mill
Cwm-Cewydd
Cwm-Llinau
Dol-fôr
Cemmaes
Y Gribin
Afon Cerist
Cywarch
Brithdir
Bont Newydd
Rhydymain
Allt y Benglog
Pont Fronwydd
734 Rhobell Fawr
907 Aran Fawddwy
Pont-Rhyd-sarn
Dolhendre
Mynydd Bryn-llech
Buarthmeini
750 Moel Llyfrant
854 Arenig Fawr
Llyn Arenig fawr
Llidiardau
689 Arenig Fach
Llyn Celyn
Migneint
Pont yr Afon-Gam
Llyn Conwy
Cwm Penmachno
Carrog
Ysbyty Ifan
Padog
Penmachno
Gwydyr Forest
Ty Mawr Wybrnant
Penmachno Woollen Mill
Pentre-bont
Dolwyddelan
Garnedd
872 Carnedd Moel Siabod
Pont-y-pant
Mynydd Cribau
Betws-y-Coed
Conwy Valley Railway Museum
Capel Garmon
Burial Chamber
Fairy Glen
Conwy Falls Rhaeadr Conwy
Glan-Conwy
Nebo
Pont Cyfyng
Capel Curig
Swallow Falls Rhaeadr Swallow
Gwydyr Forest Park
Gwydyr Uchaf Chapel
Cwm Glas Crafnant
Cornel
Llyn Crafnant
Llyn Cowlyd
Gwydyr Uchaf
Llanrwst
Tai
Trefriw
Woollen Mill
Tan-lan
Llanddoged
Pentre-tafarn-y-fedw
Melin-y-coed
Moel Seisiog
Snowdonia National Park
Parc Cenedlaethol Eryri
82
83
72
59
58
A5
A470
A4086
A498
A487
A4085
A496
A497
B4418
B4411
B4573
A4212
B4391
B4407
B4406
B5113
A494
B4416
A493
B4405
Toll
5
6
7
8
9
A
B
C
D
E
F
G

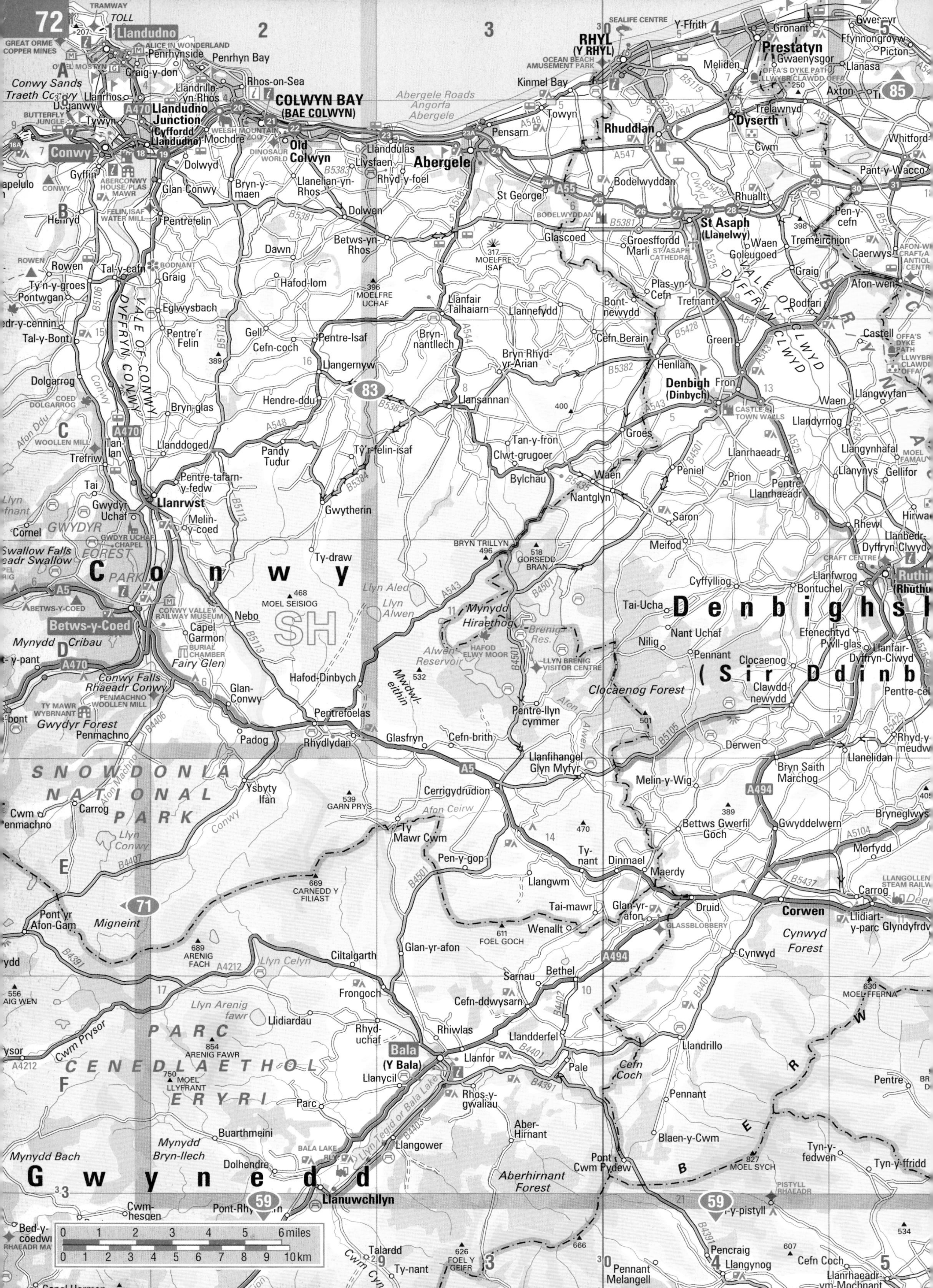
Llandudno
Great Orme Copper Mines
Alice in Wonderland
Penrhynside
Penrhyn Bay
Craig-y-don
Conwy Sands
Traeth Conwy
Llanrhos
Llandrillo-yn-Rhos
Rhos-on-Sea
Colwyn Bay
(Bae Colwyn)
Llandudno Junction
(Cyffordd Llandudno)
Deganwy
Butterfly Jungle
Tywyn
Mochdre
Welsh Mountain Zoo
Old Colwyn
Dinosaur World
Conwy
Gyffin
Aberconwy House/Plas Mawr
Dolwyd
Glan Conwy
Bryn-y-maen
Llanelian-yn-Rhos
Llysfaen
Llanddulas
Abergele
Rhyd-y-foel
Abergele Roads
Angorfa Abergele
Dolwen
Betws-yn-Rhos
Dawn
Felin Isaf Water Mill
Pentrefelin
Henryd
Rowen
Tal-y-cafn
Bodnant
Graig
Ty'n-y-groes
Pontwgan
Eglwysbach
Hafod-lom
Moelfre Uchaf
Tal-y-Bont
Pentre'r Felin
Vale of Conwy
Dyffryn Conwy
Gell
Cefn-coch
Pentre-Isaf
Llangernyw
Dolgarrog
Coed Dolgarrog
Hendre-ddu
Bryn-glas
Afon Ddu
Woollen Mill
Trefriw
Tan-lan
Llanddoged
Pandy Tudur
Ty'n-felin-isaf
Tai
Pentre-tafarn-y-fedw
Llanrwst
Gwydyr Uchaf
Gwytherin
Melin-y-coed
Cornel
Gwydyr Forest
Gwydyr Uchaf Chapel
Swallow Falls
Rhaeadr Ewynnol
Ty-draw
Conwy
Park
Betws-y-Coed
Conwy Valley Railway Museum
Capel Garmon
Burial Chamber
Nebo
Moel Seisiog
Llyn Aled
Llyn Alwen
SH
Mynydd Cribau
Fairy Glen
Conwy Falls
Rhaeadr Conwy
Penmachno Woollen Mill
Ty Mawr Wybrnant
Gwydyr Forest
Penmachno
Glan-Conwy
Hafod-Dinbych
Mwdwl-eithin
Pentrefoelas
Padog
Rhydlydan
Glasfryn
Cefn-brith
Snowdonia National Park
Ysbyty Ifan
Garn Prys
Cwm Penmachno
Carrog
Llyn Conwy
Afon Ceirw
Ty Mawr Cwm
Pen-y-gop
Carnedd y Filiast
Migneint
Pont yr Afon-Gam
Arenig Fach
Llyn Celyn
Ciltalgarth
Glan-yr-afon
Frongoch
Llyn Arenig fawr
Lllidiardau
Rhyd-uchaf
Arenig Fawr
Cwm Prysor
Parc Cenedlaethol Eryri
Moel Llyfrant
Bala
(Y Bala)
Llanycil
Parc
Buarthmeini
Mynydd Bryn-llech
Mynydd Bach
Dolhendre
Bala Lake Rly
Llyn Tegid or Bala Lake
Gwynedd
Llanuwchllyn
Pont-Rhyd-y-fen
Cwm-hesgen
Bed-y-coedwr
Rhaeadr Mawddach
Talardd
Cwm Cynllwyd
Ty-nant
Foel y Geifr
Rhyl
(Y Rhyl)
Sealife Centre
Ocean Beach Amusement Park
Kinmel Bay
Towyn
Pensarn
St George
Bodelwyddan
Rhuddlan
Y-Ffrith
Gronant
Prestatyn
Gwaenysgor
Meliden
Offa's Dyke Path
Llwybr Clawdd Offa
Dyserth
Trelawnyd
Cwm
Gwespyr
Ffynnongroyw
Picton
Llanasa
Axton
Whitford
Pant-y-Wacco
Glascoed
Moelfre Isaf
Groesffordd Marli
St Asaph Cathedral
St Asaph
(Llanelwy)
Waen
Goleugoed
Rhuallt
Tremeirchion
Pen-y-cefn
Caerwys
Afon-wen
Craft & Antique Centre
Plas-yn-Cefn
Bont-newydd
Trefnant
Llannefydd
Llanfair Talhaiarn
Bryn-nantllech
Vale of Clwyd
Dyffryn Clwyd
Bodfari
Cefn Berain
Bryn Rhyd-yr-Arian
Henllan
Green
Denbigh
(Dinbych)
Fron
Castle & Town Walls
Castell
Llangwyfan
Llansannan
Waen
Llandyrnog
Groes
Tan-y-fron
Clwt-grugoer
Llanrhaeadr
Llangynhafal
Moel Famau
Bylchau
Waen
Peniel
Prion
Pentre Llanrhaeadr
Llanynys
Gellifor
Nantglyn
Saron
Rhewl
Hirwaen
Bryn Trillyn
Gorsedd Bran
Meifod
Llanbedr-Dyffryn-Clwyd
Craft Centre
Ruthin
(Rhuthun)
Llanfwrog
Bontuchel
Cyffylliog
Tai-Ucha
Denbighshire
Nant Uchaf
Mynydd Hiraethog
Brenig Res.
Nilig
Pennant
Efenechtyd
Pwll-glas
Llanfair-Dyffryn-Clwyd
Alwen Reservoir
Hafod Elwy Moor
Llyn Brenig Visitor Centre
Clocaenog
(Sir Ddinbych)
Clocaenog Forest
Clawdd-newydd
Pentre-celyn
Pentre-llyn cymmer
Afon Alwen
Derwen
Rhyd-y-meudwy
Llanfihangel Glyn Myfyr
Llanelidan
Bryn Saith Marchog
Melin-y-Wig
Cerrigydrudion
Bryneglwys
Bettws Gwerfil Goch
Gwyddelwern
Ty-nant
Dinmael
Maerdy
Morfydd
Llangwm
Llangollen Steam Railway
Carrog
Druid
Corwen
Tai-mawr
Glan-yr-afon
Llidiart-y-parc
Glyndyfrdwy
Wenallt
Foel Goch
Glassblobbery
Cynwyd Forest
Cynwyd
Bethel
Sarnau
Moel Fferna
Cefn-ddwysarn
Rhiwlas
Llandderfel
Llandrillo
Llanfor
Pale
Cefn Coch
Berwyn
Pentre
Rhos-y-gwaliau
Pennant
Aber-Hirnant
Llangower
Blaen-y-Cwm
Pont Cwm Pydew
Aberhirnant Forest
Moel Sych
Tyn-y-fedwen
Tyn-y-ffridd
Pistyll Rhaeadr
Tyn-y-pistyll
Pencraig
Llangynog
Cefn Coch
Pennant Melangell
Llanrhaeadr-ym-Mochnant
Capel Hermon
0 1 2 3 4 5 6 miles
0 1 2 3 4 5 6 7 8 9 10 km
A
B
C
D
E
F
1
2
3
4
5
A55
A470
A5
A543
A548
A544
A547
A525
A494
A4212
A5104
A5151
B5381
B5382
B5113
B5106
B4406
B4407
B4391
B4501
B5435
B5105
B5428
B5429
B5437
B4401
B4402
B4403
B5384
83
85
71
59

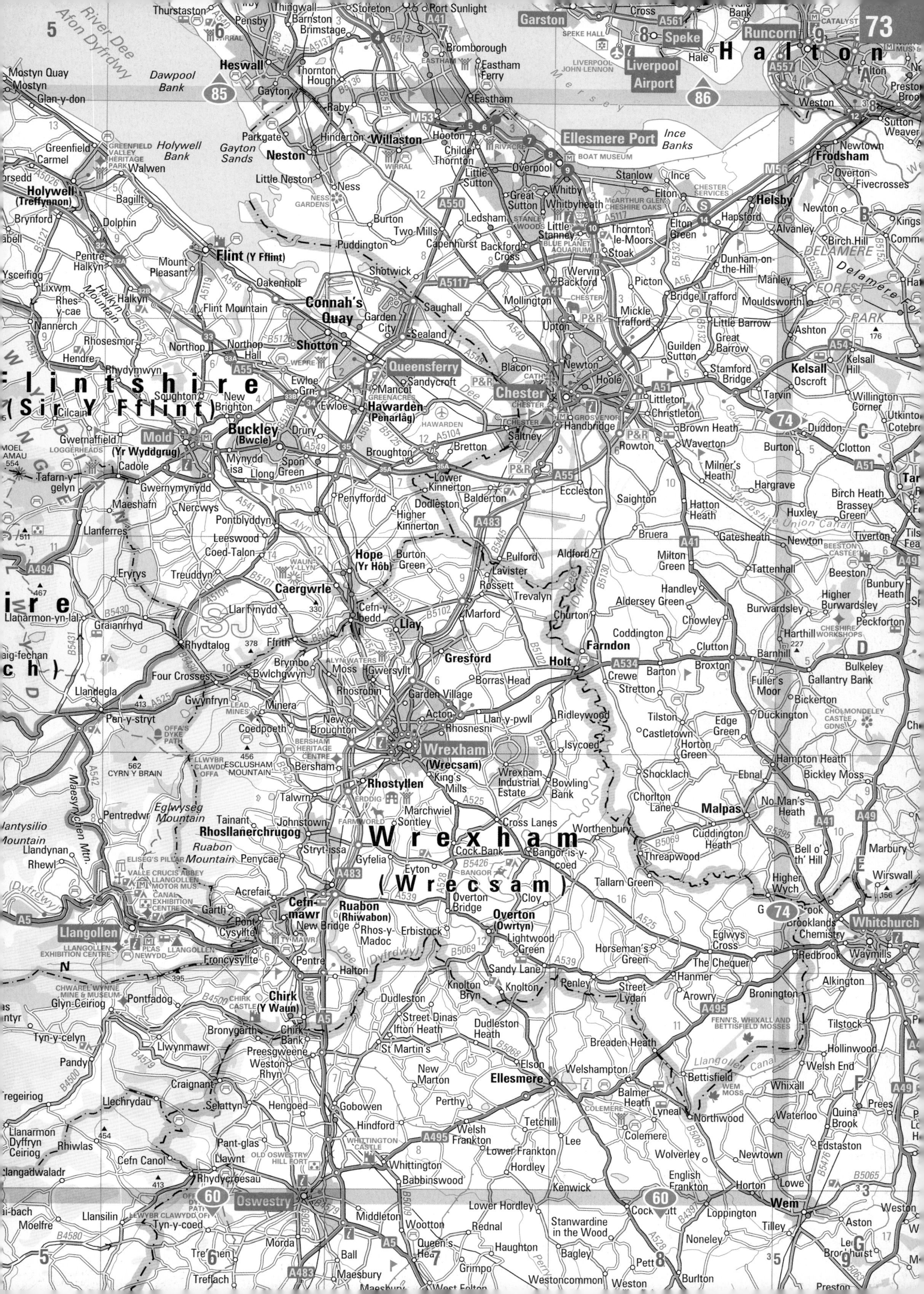
Flintshire
(Sir Y Fflint)
Wrexham
(Wrecsam)
Halton
Chester
Wrexham
Ellesmere Port
Liverpool Airport
Runcorn
Speke
Garston
Queensferry
Mold
Llangollen
Oswestry
Whitchurch
Ellesmere
Malpas
Frodsham
Helsby
Connah's Quay
Shotton
Flint (Y Fflint)
Holywell (Treffynnon)
Buckley (Bwcle)
Hawarden (Penarlâg)
Neston
Heswall
Willaston
Hope (Yr Hôb)
Caergwrle
Llay
Gresford
Holt
Farndon
Rhostyllen
Ruabon (Rhiwabon)
Chirk (Y Waun)
Overton (Owrtyn)
Wem
Kelsall
85
86
74
60

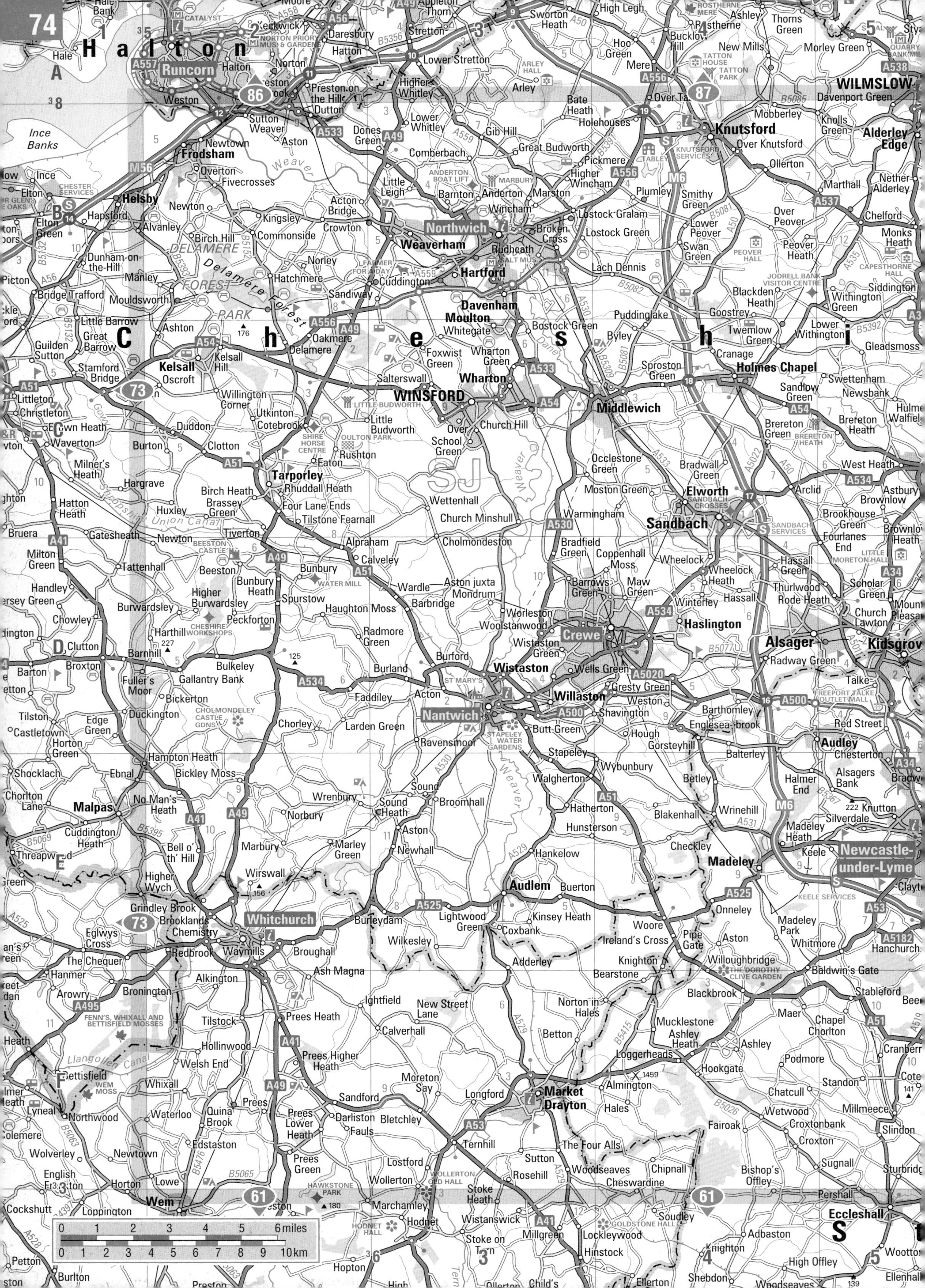

Halton
Runcorn
Halton
Hale
Weston
Norton
Daresbury
Hatton
Stretton
Lower Stretton
Appleton Thorn
Swinton Heath
High Legh
Hoo Green
Mere
Bucklow Hill
Rostherne
Ashley
Thorns Green
Morley Green
New Mills
Tatton House
Tatton Park
WILMSLOW
Davenport Green
Arley Hall
Arley
Higher Whitley
Preston on the Hill
Dutton
Sutton Weaver
Aston
Frodsham
Newtown
Ince Banks
Over Tabley
Bate Heath
Holehouses
Knutsford
Over Knutsford
Mobberley
Knolls Green
Alderley Edge
Lower Whitley
Dones Green
Comberbach
Gib Hill
Great Budworth
Pickmere
Higher Wincham
Tabley
Knutsford Services
Ollerton
Nether Alderley
Overton
Fivecrosses
Ince
Elton
Chester Services
Helsby
Hapsford
Elton Green
Newton
Alvanley
Kingsley
Acton Bridge
Crowton
Little Leigh
Anderton Boat Lift
Marbury
Barnton
Anderton
Marston
Plumley
Smithy Green
Marthall
Commonside
Birch Hill
Delamere Forest Park
Northwich
Wincham
Lostock Gralam
Lostock Green
Broken Cross
Lower Peover
Swan Green
Peover Hall
Over Peover
Peover Heath
Chelford
Monks Heath
Capesthorne Hall
Dunham-on-the-Hill
Manley
Norley
Weaverham
Rudheath
Salt Mus
Hartford
Lach Dennis
Jodrell Bank Visitor Centre
Siddington
Picton
Bridge Trafford
Mouldsworth
Hatchmere
Cuddington
Sandiway
Farmer Ted's Farm
Blackden Heath
Withington Green
Davenham
Moulton
Whitegate
Bostock Green
Puddinglake
Goostrey
Twemlow Green
Lower Withington
Little Barrow
Great Barrow
Guilden Sutton
Ashton
Delamere
Oakmere
Foxwist Green
Wharton Green
Byley
Cranage
Gleadsmoss
Stamford Bridge
Kelsall
Kelsall Hill
Oscroft
Salterswall
WINSFORD
Wharton
Sproston Green
Holmes Chapel
Swettenham
Newsbank
Sandlow Green
Littleton
Christleton
Willington Corner
Utkinton
Cotebrook
Little Budworth
Over
Church Hill
Middlewich
Cown Heath
Waverton
Duddon
Burton
Clotton
Shire Horse Centre
Oulton Park
Rushton
Eaton
School Green
Brereton Green
Brereton Heath
Milner's Heath
Tarporley
Occlestone Green
Bradwall Green
West Heath
Hargrave
Birch Heath
Rhuddall Heath
Brassey Green
Four Lane Ends
Tilstone Fearnall
Wettenhall
Church Minshull
Moston Green
Elwortth
Sandbach Crosses
Arclid
Astbury
Brownlow
Hatton Heath
Huxley
Warmingham
Sandbach
Sandbach Services
Brookhouse Green
Bruera
Gatesheath
Newton
Tiverton
Beeston Castle
Alpraham
Cholmondeston
Bradfield Green
Coppenhall Moss
Wheelock
Fourlanes End
Milton Green
Tattenhall
Beeston
Calveley
Bunbury
Water Mill
Wheelock Heath
Hassall Green
Little Moreton Hall
Handley
Bunbury Heath
Wardle
Aston juxta Mondrum
Barrows Green
Maw Green
Thurlwood
Rode Heath
Scholar Green
Higher Burwardsley
Burwardsley
Spurstow
Haughton Moss
Barbridge
Winterley
Hassall
Chowley
Cheshire Workshops
Peckforton
Worleston
Woolstanwood
Haslington
Church Lawton
Harthill
Radmore Green
Crewe
Wistaston Green
Clutton
Barnhill
Alsager
Kidsgrove
Barton
Broxton
Bulkeley
Burland
Burford
Wistaston
Wells Green
Radway Green
Fuller's Moor
Gallantry Bank
St Mary's
Gresty Green
Talke
Bickerton
Faddiley
Acton
Willaston
Weston
Freeport Talke Outlet Mall
Tilston
Duckington
Cholmondeley Castle Gdns
Nantwich
Shavington
Barthomley
Castletown
Edge Green
Chorley
Larden Green
Butt Green
Englesea-brook
Red Street
Horton Green
Stapeley Water Gardens
Hough
Gorsteyhill
Audley
Hampton Heath
Ravensmoor
Chesterton
Shocklach
Ebnal
Bickley Moss
Stapeley
Wybunbury
Balterley
Chorlton Lane
No Man's Heath
Walgherton
Betley
Halmer End
Alsagers Bank
Malpas
Wrenbury
Sound
Broomhall
Sound Heath
Hatherton
Wrinehill
Knutton
Silverdale
Cuddington Heath
Norbury
Aston
Blakenhall
Madeley Heath
Threapwood
Bell o' th' Hill
Marbury
Marley Green
Newhall
Hunsterson
Checkley
Keele
Newcastle-under-Lyme
Hankelow
Madeley
Higher Wych
Wirswall
Audlem
Buerton
Keele Services
Clayton
Grindley Brook
Brooklands
Chemistry
Whitchurch
Burleydam
Lightwood Green
Kinsey Heath
Onneley
Madeley Park
Eglwys Cross
Coxbank
Woore
Ireland's Cross
Pipe Gate
Aston
Whitmore
Hanchurch
Redbrook
Waymills
Broughall
Wilkesley
The Chequer
Adderley
Knighton
Willoughbridge
The Dorothy Clive Garden
Baldwin's Gate
Hanmer
Ash Magna
Bearstone
Alkington
Arowry
Bronington
Blackbrook
Stableford
Fenn's, Whixall and Bettisfield Mosses
Ightfield
New Street Lane
Norton in Hales
Maer
Chapel Chorlton
Tilstock
Prees Heath
Calverhall
Mucklestone
Ashley Heath
Ashley
Hollinwood
Betton
Welsh End
Prees Higher Heath
Loggerheads
Podmore
Bettisfield
Whixall
Wem Moss
Moreton Say
Hookgate
Almington
Standon
Lyneal
Waterloo
Quina Brook
Prees
Sandford
Longford
Market Drayton
Chatcull
Northwood
Prees Lower Heath
Darliston
Bletchley
Fauls
Hales
Wetwood
Millmeece
Fairoak
Croxtonbank
Slindon
Colemere
Wolverley
Edstaston
Ternhill
The Four Alls
Croxton
Newtown
Sutton
Woodseaves
Chipnall
Sugnall
Prees Green
Lostford
Rosehill
Cheswardine
Bishop's Offley
English Frankton
Horton
Lowe
Hawkstone Park
Wollerton Old Hall
Wollerton
Stoke Heath
Pershall
Cockshutt
Loppington
Wem
Marchamley
Hodnet Hall
Hodnet
Wistanswick
Goldstone Hall
Soudley
Eccleshall
Stoke on Tern
Millgreen
Lockleywood
Adbaston
Petton
Burlton
Hopton
Hinstock
Knighton
High Offley
Wootton
Woodseaves
Shebdon
Ellerton
Child's Ercall
Ellenhall
Weaver
Delamere Forest
Shropshire Union Canal
Llangollen Canal
Dane
SJ
Cheshire
M6
M56
A56
A49
A50
A51
A54
A41
A53
A525
A530
A533
A534
A556
A559
A5020
A500
A529
A495
A557
A537
A538
A5182
A34
0 1 2 3 4 5 6 miles
0 1 2 3 4 5 6 7 8 9 10 km

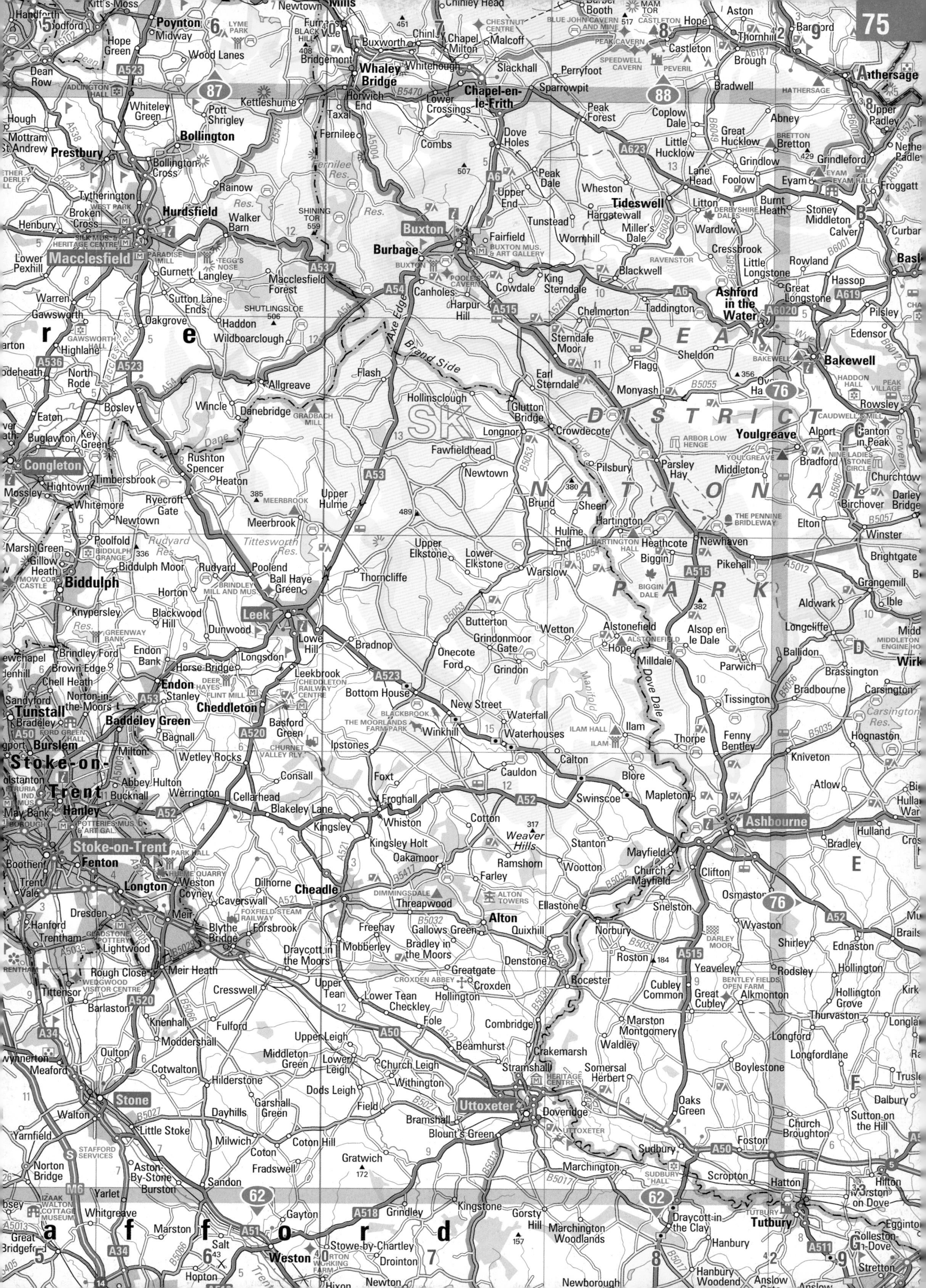
Handforth
Bramhall
Poynton
Lyme Park
Newtown
New Mills
Chinley Head
Barber Booth
Mam Tor
Aston
Hope
Bamford
Hope Green
Midway
Wood Lanes
Furness Vale
Buxworth
Chinley
Chapel Milton
Malcoff
Blue John Cavern and Mine
Peak Cavern
Castleton
Thornhill
Brough
Dean Row
Adlington Hall
Bridgemont
Whaley Bridge
Whitehough
Slackhall
Perryfoot
Speedwell Cavern
Peveril
Bradwell
Hathersage
Whiteley Green
Pott Shrigley
Kettleshume
Horwich End
Taxal
Lower Crossings
Chapel-en-le-Frith
Sparrowpit
Peak Forest
Coplow Dale
Abney
Upper Padley
Hough
Mottram St Andrew
Prestbury
Bollington
Fernilee
Fernilee Res.
Combs
Dove Holes
Great Hucklow
Little Hucklow
Bretton
Grindleford
Nether Padley
Bollington Cross
Rainow
Peak Dale
Wheston
Lane Head
Foolow
Grindlow
Eyam
Eyam Hall
Froggatt
Tytherington
Broken Cross
West Park
Hurdsfield
Walker Barn
Shining Tor
Upper End
Tideswell
Hargatewall
Litton
Derbyshire Dales
Burnt Heath
Stoney Middleton
Calver
Curbar
Henbury
Silk Mus. & Heritage Centre
Macclesfield
Buxton
Fairfield
Buxton Mus. & Art Gallery
Burbage
Tunstead
Wormhill
Miller's Dale
Wardlow
Cressbrook
Rowland
Lower Pexhill
Paradise Mill
Tegg's Nose
Gurnett
Langley
Macclesfield Forest
Poole's Cavern
Cowdale
King Sterndale
Ravenstor
Blackwell
Little Longstone
Great Longstone
Hassop
Warren
Sutton Lane Ends
Canholes
Harpur Hill
Chelmorton
Taddington
Ashford in the Water
Pilsley
Gawsworth
Gawsworth Hall
Oakgrove
Haddon
Shutlingsloe
Wildboarclough
Axe Edge
Brand Side
Sterndale Moor
Flagg
Sheldon
Peak
Edensor
Bakewell
Highlane
North Rode
Flash
Earl Sterndale
Monyash
Over Haddon
Haddon Hall
Peak Village
Rowsley
Eaton
Bosley
Wincle
Allgreave
Danebridge
Gradbach Mill
Hollinsclough
Glutton Bridge
Crowdecote
District
Caudwell's Mill
Alport
Youlgreave
Stanton in Peak
Buglawton
Key Green
Arbor Low Henge
Parsley Hay
Middleton
Bradford
Nine Ladies Stone Circle
Congleton
Rushton Spencer
Longnor
Fawfieldhead
Newtown
Pilsbury
Churchtown
Mossley
Hightown
Timbersbrook
Heaton
National
Darley Bridge
Whitemore
Ryecroft Gate
Meerbrook
Upper Hulme
Brund
Sheen
Birchover
Hartington
The Pennine Bridleway
Elton
Winster
Poolfold
Biddulph Grange
Rudyard Res.
Tittesworth Res.
Upper Elkstone
Lower Elkstone
Hulme End
Hartington Hall
Heathcote
Newhaven
Brightgate
Marsh Green
Gillow Heath
Biddulph Moor
Rudyard
Poolend
Biggin
Pikehall
Mow Cop Castle
Biddulph
Horton
Brindley Mill and Mus.
Ball Haye Green
Thorncliffe
Warslow
Biggin Dale
Park
Grangemill
Ible
Knypersley
Blackwood Hill
Leek
Aldwark
Greenway Bank
Dunwood
Butterton
Wetton
Alstonefield
Alsop en le Dale
Longcliffe
Middleton Engine Ho.
Brindley Ford
Endon Bank
Lowe Hill
Bradnop
Grindonmoor Gate
Onecote Ford
Hope
Ballidon
Newchapel
Brown Edge
Horse Bridge
Longsdon
Leekbrook
Cheddleton Railway Centre
Grindon
Milldale
Parwich
Wirksworth
Chell Heath
Endon
Deer Hayes
Flint Mill
Bottom House
Dove Dale
Manifold
Brassington
Sandyford
Norton-in-the-Moors
Stanley
Cheddleton
Blackbrook
New Street
Bradbourne
Carsington
Tunstall
Bradeley
Baddeley Green
The Moorlands Farm Park
Winkhill
Waterfall
Waterhouses
Ilam Hall
Ilam
Tissington
Carsington Res.
Burslem
Bagnall
Basford Green
Churnet Valley Rly.
Thorpe
Fenny Bentley
Hognaston
Stoke-on-Trent
Milton
Wetley Rocks
Ipstones
Calton
Cauldon
Kniveton
Abbey Hulton
Consall
Foxt
Blore
Swinscoe
Mapleton
Atlow
Etruria Ind. Mus.
Hanley
Bucknall
Werrington
Cellarhead
Froghall
Blakeley Lane
Kingsley
Whiston
Cotton
Weaver Hills
Ashbourne
Hulland
Potteries Mus. & Art Gal.
Park Hall
Kingsley Holt
Oakamoor
Stanton
Mayfield
Bradley
Boothen
Fenton
Hulme Quarry
Weston Coyney
Dilhorne
Cheadle
Ramshorn
Farley
Wootton
Church Mayfield
Clifton
Osmaston
Trent Vale
Longton
Caverswall
Dimmingsdale
Threapwood
Alton Towers
Ellastone
Snelston
Hanford
Trentham
Dresden
Meir
Foxfield Steam Railway
Blythe Bridge
Forsbrook
Freehay
Gallows Green
Alton
Quixhill
Norbury
Wyaston
Shirley
Brailsford
Gladstone Pottery
Lightwood
Draycott in the Moors
Mobberley
Bradley in the Moors
Denstone
Roston
Darley Moor
Ednaston
Trentham
Rough Close
Meir Heath
Wedgwood Visitor Centre
Greatgate
Croxden Abbey
Croxden
Rocester
Yeaveley
Rodsley
Hollington
Tittensor
Barlaston
Cresswell
Upper Tean
Lower Tean
Checkley
Hollington
Cubley Common
Great Cubley
Bentley Fields Open Farm
Alkmonton
Hollington Grove
Thurvaston
Knenhall
Fulford
Fole
Combridge
Marston Montgomery
Longford
Moddershall
Upper Leigh
Beamhurst
Crakemarsh
Waldley
Longfordlane
Oulton
Middleton Green
Lower Leigh
Church Leigh
Stramshall
Heritage Centre
Somersal Herbert
Boylestone
Swynnerton
Meaford
Cotwalton
Hilderstone
Withington
Dods Leigh
Uttoxeter
Doveridge
Oaks Green
Dalbury
Stone
Walton
Dayhills
Garshall Green
Field
Bramshall
Blount's Green
Church Broughton
Sutton on the Hill
Yarnfield
Little Stoke
Milwich
Coton Hill
Coton
Stafford Services
Sudbury
Foston
Norton Bridge
Aston-By-Stone
Burston
Fradswell
Gratwich
Marchington
Sudbury Hall
Scropton
Hatton
Hilton
Egginton
Sandon
Yarlet
Whitgreave
Izaak Walton Cottage Museum
Gayton
Grindley
Kingstone
Gorsty Hill
Marchington Woodlands
Draycott-in-the-Clay
Tutbury
Rolleston-on-Dove
Stafford
Great Bridgeford
Marston
Salt
Weston
Stowe-by-Chartley
Amerton Working Farm
Drointon
Hanbury
Hanbury Woodend
Anslow
Stretton
Hopton
Hixon
Newton
Newborough
Sk

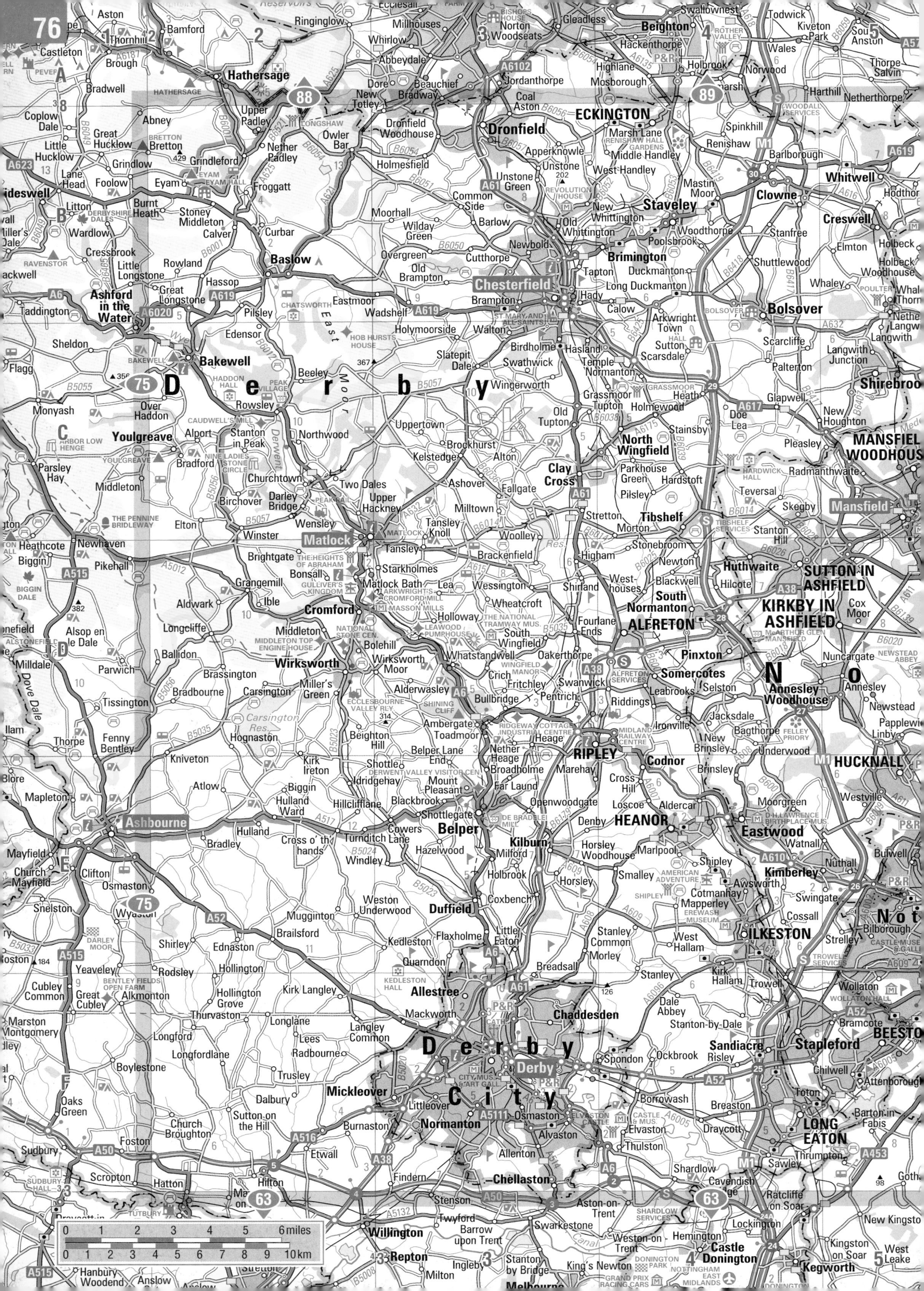

Aston
Bamford
Ringinglow
Millhouses
Norton
Woodseats
Gleadless
Beighton
Swallownest
Todwick
Kiveton Park
South Anston
Thornhill
Castleton
Brough
Hathersage
Whirlow
Abbeydale
Dore
Beauchief
Bradway
Jordanthorpe
Hackenthorpe
Highlane
Mosborough
Holbrook
Norwood
Wales
Thorpe Salvin
Bradwell
Upper Padley
New Totley
Coal Aston
ECKINGTON
Harthill
Netherthorpe
Coplow Dale
Abney
Nether Padley
Owler Bar
Dronfield Woodhouse
Dronfield
Marsh Lane
Spinkhill
Great Hucklow
Bretton
Little Hucklow
Grindleford
Holmesfield
Apperknowle
Unstone
Middle Handley
West Handley
Renishaw
Barlborough
Grindlow
Lane Head
Foolow
Eyam
Froggatt
Unstone Green
Mastin Moor
Whitwell
Clowne
Tideswell
Litton
Burnt Heath
Stoney Middleton
Calver
Common Side
Moorhall
Barlow
New Whittington
Old Whittington
Staveley
Creswell
Hodthorpe
Wardlow
Curbar
Wildey Green
Woodthorpe
Poolsbrook
Stanfree
Holbeck
Elmton
Cressbrook
Little Longstone
Rowland
Baslow
Overgreen
Old Brampton
Cutthorpe
Newbold
Brimington
Tapton
Duckmanton
Long Duckmanton
Shuttlewood
Whaley
Holbeck Woodhouse
Hassop
Great Longstone
Ashford in the Water
Taddington
Pilsley
Eastmoor
Wadshelf
Brampton
Chesterfield
Hady
Calow
Arkwright Town
Bolsover
Sheldon
Edensor
Holymoorside
Walton
Birdholme
Hasland
Sutton Scarsdale
Scarcliffe
Langwith Junction
Langwith
Flagg
Bakewell
East Moor
Slatepit Dale
Swathwick
Temple Normanton
Palterton
Shirebrook
Monyash
Over Haddon
Beeley
Rowsley
Wingerworth
Grassmoor
Heath
Glapwell
Youlgreave
Alport
Stanton in Peak
Northwood
Uppertown
Old Tupton
Tupton
Holmewood
Doe Lea
New Houghton
Brockhurst
Stainsby
Pleasley
MANSFIELD WOODHOUSE
Parsley Hay
Bradford
Kelstedge
Alton
North Wingfield
Clay Cross
Parkhouse Green
Hardstoft
Radmanthwaite
Middleton
Churchtown
Two Dales
Ashover
Fallgate
Pilsley
Teversal
Birchover
Darley Bridge
Upper Hackney
Milltown
Skegby
Mansfield
Elton
Wensley
Tansley Knoll
Stretton
Morton
Tibshelf
Stanton Hill
Heathcote
Newhaven
Winster
Matlock
Tansley
Woolley
Brackenfield
Higham
Stonebroom
Biggin
Pikehall
Brightgate
Starkholmes
Newton
Huthwaite
SUTTON IN ASHFIELD
Bonsall
Matlock Bath
Lea
Wessington
Shirland
Westhouses
Blackwell
Hilcote
Grangemill
Ible
Wheatcroft
South Normanton
KIRKBY IN ASHFIELD
Cox Moor
Aldwark
Cromford
Holloway
Fourlane Ends
ALFRETON
Alsop en le Dale
Longcliffe
Middleton
South Wingfield
Bolehill
Milldale
Ballidon
Wirksworth
Wirksworth Moor
Whatstandwell
Oakerthorpe
Pinxton
Nuncargate
Parwich
Brassington
Crich
Fritchley
Swanwick
Somercotes
Annesley Woodhouse
Annesley
Bradbourne
Carsington
Miller's Green
Alderwasley
Leabrooks
Selston
Tissington
Bullbridge
Pentrich
Riddings
Newstead
Dove Dale
Carsington Res.
Ambergate
Toadmoor
Jacksdale
Ironville
Bagthorpe
Papplewick
Linby
Ilam
Thorpe
Fenny Bentley
Hognaston
Beighton Hill
Heage
New Brinsley
Kniveton
Kirk Ireton
Shottle
Belper Lane End
Nether Heage
RIPLEY
Codnor
Underwood
HUCKNALL
Blore
Idridgehay
Broadholme
Marehay
Brinsley
Mapleton
Atlow
Biggin
Mount Pleasant
Far Laund
Cross Hill
Hulland Ward
Blackbrook
Openwoodgate
Loscoe
Aldercar
Moorgreen
Westville
Ashbourne
Hillcliffe Lane
Shottlegate
Denby
HEANOR
Eastwood
Hulland
Cowers Lane
Belper
Kilburn
Horsley Woodhouse
Marlpool
Watnall
Mayfield
Bradley
Cross o' th' hands
Turnditch
Hazelwood
Milford
Bulwell
Church Mayfield
Clifton
Windley
Holbrook
Smalley
Shipley
Nuthall
Kimberley
Osmaston
Horsley
Cotmanhay
Awsworth
Mapperley
Swingate
Snelston
Wyaston
Weston Underwood
Duffield
Coxbench
Cossall
Mugginton
Little Eaton
Stanley Common
ILKESTON
Strelley
Bilborough
Brailsford
Flaxholme
Shirley
Ednaston
Kedleston
West Hallam
Morley
Boston
Yeaveley
Rodsley
Quarndon
Breadsall
Kirk Hallam
Trowell
Hollington
Stanley
Cubley Common
Great Cubley
Alkmonton
Hollington Grove
Kirk Langley
Allestree
Dale Abbey
Wollaton
Marston Montgomery
Thurvaston
Mackworth
Chaddesden
Longlane
Langley Common
Stanton-by-Dale
Bramcote
Longford
Lees
BEESTON
Longfordlane
Radbourne
Derby
Spondon
Ockbrook
Sandiacre
Risley
Stapleford
Boylestone
Trusley
Derby City
Chilwell
Attenborough
Oaks Green
Dalbury
Mickleover
Borrowash
Toton
Littleover
Breaston
Barton in Fabis
Church Broughton
Sutton on the Hill
Burnaston
Normanton
Osmaston
Elvaston
Draycott
LONG EATON
Foston
Alvaston
Thulston
Sudbury
Etwall
Allenton
Thrumpton
Scropton
Hatton
Hilton
Findern
Chellaston
Shardlow
Cavendish Bridge
Sawley
Gotham
Stenson
Aston-on-Trent
Ratcliffe on Soar
Twyford
Swarkestone
Lockington
New Kingston
Willington
Barrow upon Trent
Weston-on-Trent
Hemington
Kingston on Soar
Repton
Milton
Ingleby
Stanton by Bridge
King's Newton
Castle Donington
Kegworth
West Leake
Hanbury Woodend
Anslow
Melbourne
Derby
Notts
SK
0 1 2 3 4 5 6 miles
0 1 2 3 4 5 6 7 8 9 10 km

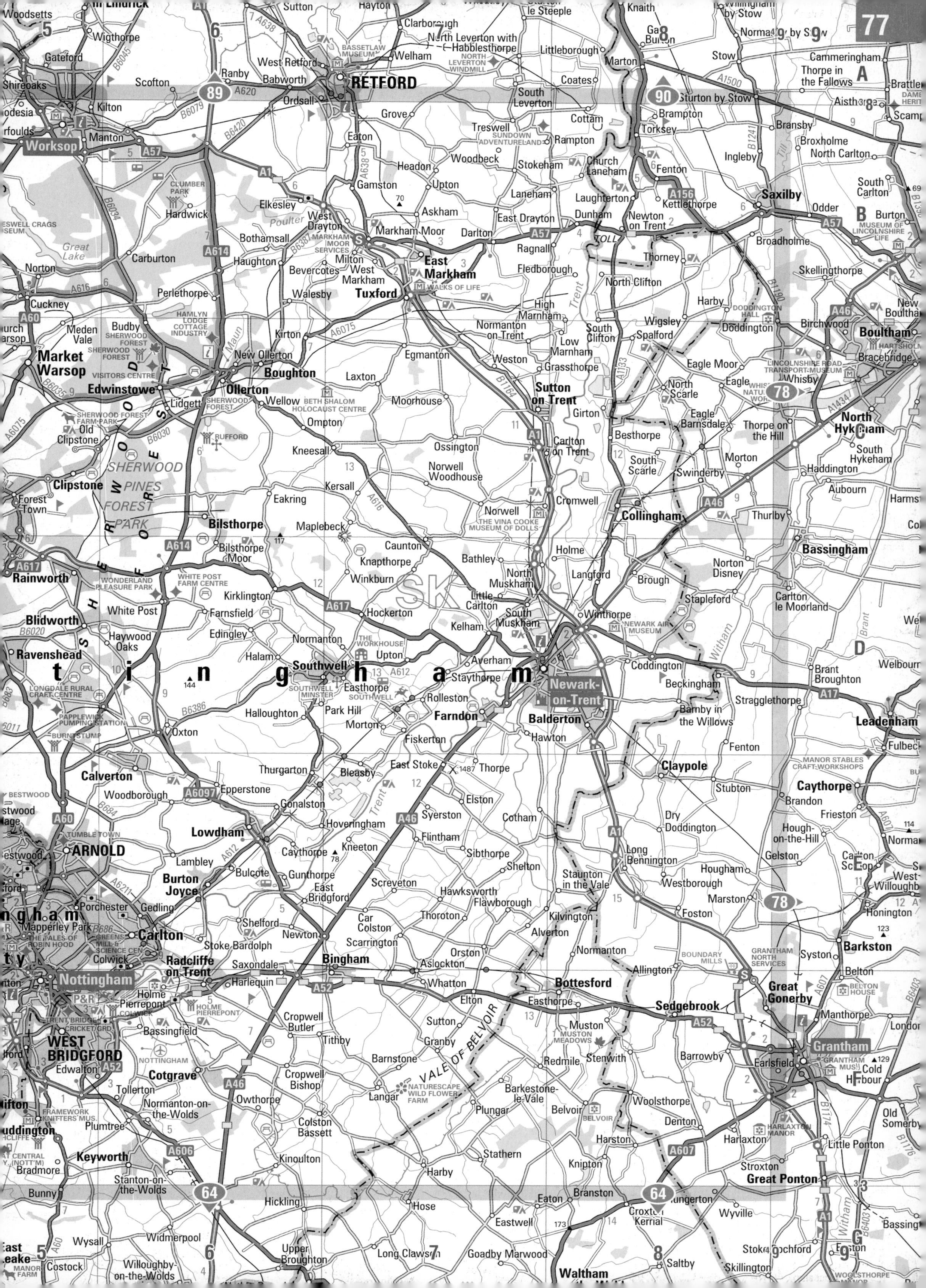
RETFORD
Worksop
Market Warsop
Edwinstowe
Ollerton
Boughton
Tuxford
East Markham
Sutton on Trent
Saxilby
Collingham
Southwell
Newark-on-Trent
Balderton
Farndon
Bingham
Nottingham
WEST BRIDGFORD
ARNOLD
Carlton
Cotgrave
Keyworth
Radcliffe on Trent
Bottesford
Grantham
Great Gonerby
North Hykeham
Boultham
Bassingham
Caythorpe
Claypole
Calverton
Lowdham
Bilsthorpe
Clipstone
Rainworth
Blidworth
Ravenshead
Gamston
Elkesley
West Drayton
Laxton
Cromwell
Long Bennington
Sedgebrook
Barkston
Great Ponton
Leadenham
SHERWOOD FOREST
VALE OF BELVOIR
Nottingham
Trent
Witham
89
90
78
64

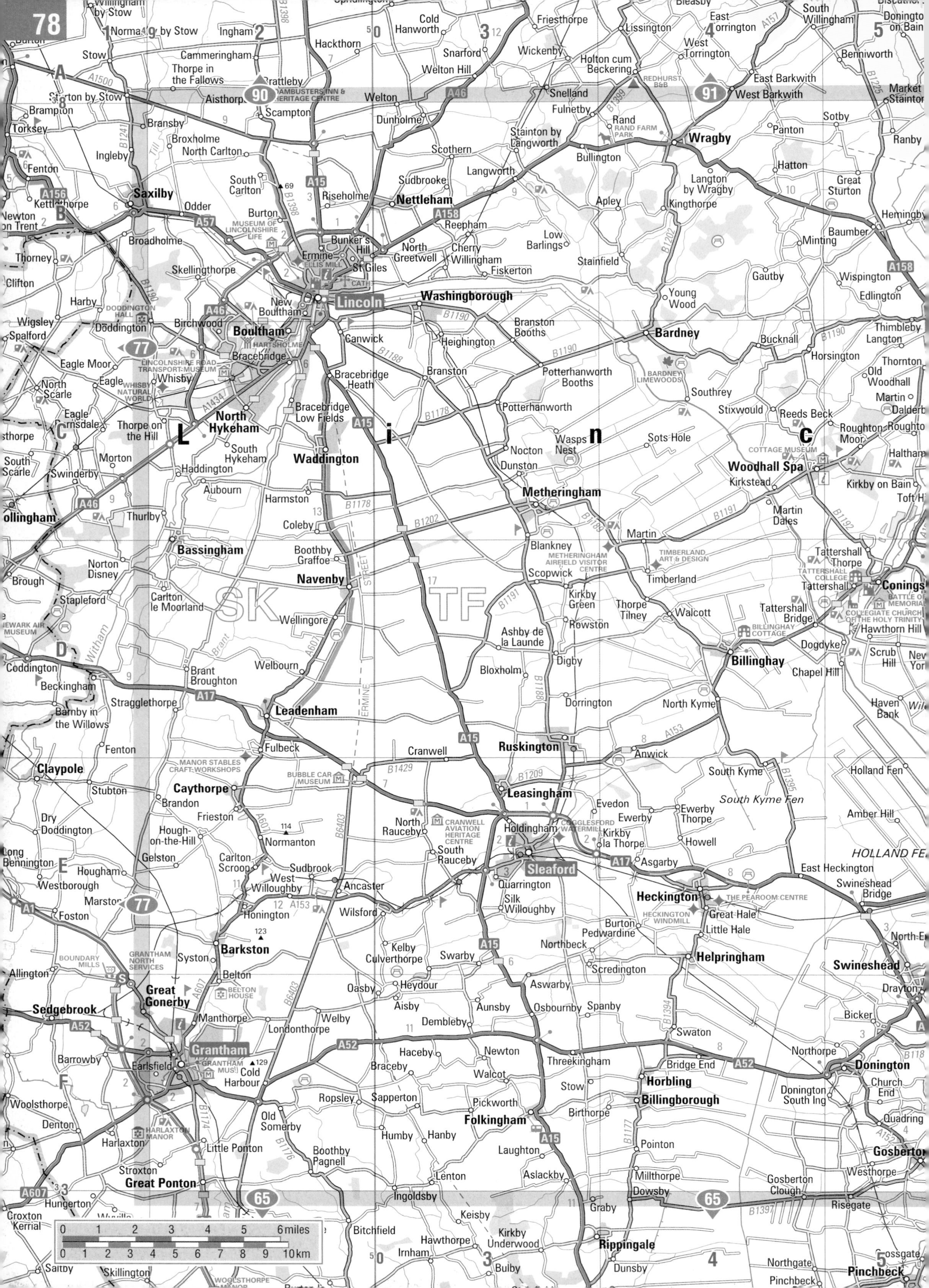
Normanby by Stow
Ingham
Cold Hanworth
Hackthorn
Friesthorpe
Lissington
East Torrington
West Torrington
South Willingham
Donington on Bain
Stow
Cammeringham
Snarford
Wickenby
Holton cum Beckering
Benniworth
Thorpe in the Fallows
Brattleby
Welton Hill
REDHURST B&B
East Barkwith
Sturton by Stow
Aisthorpe
DAMBUSTERS INN & HERITAGE CENTRE
Welton
Snelland
West Barkwith
Market Stainton
Brampton
Scampton
Dunholme
Fulnetby
Rand
RAND FARM PARK
Sotby
Torksey
Bransby
Stainton by Langworth
Wragby
Panton
Ranby
Broxholme
North Carlton
Scothern
Bullington
Ingleby
Fenton
Langworth
Hatton
South Carlton
Sudbrooke
Langton by Wragby
Great Sturton
Saxilby
Riseholme
Nettleham
Kettlethorpe
Odder
Apley
Kingthorpe
Hemingby
Newton on Trent
Burton
Reepham
Baumber
MUSEUM OF LINCOLNSHIRE LIFE
Low Barlings
Minting
Broadholme
Bunker's Hill
North Greetwell
Cherry Willingham
Thorney
Ermine
ELLIS MILL
St Giles
Stainfield
Skellingthorpe
Fiskerton
Gautby
Wispington
Clifton
CATH
Washingborough
Young Wood
Edlington
Harby
New Boultham
Lincoln
DODDINGTON HALL
Wigsley
Birchwood
Boultham
Branston Booths
Bardney
Thimbleby
Langton
Doddington
Spalford
Canwick
HARTSHOLME
Heighington
Bucknall
Horsington
Thornton
LINCOLNSHIRE ROAD TRANSPORT MUSEUM
Bracebridge
Eagle Moor
Branston
Potterhanworth Booths
BARDNEY LIMEWOODS
Old Woodhall
Bracebridge Heath
Eagle
Whisby
WHISBY NATURAL WORLD
North Scarle
Southrey
Martin
Potterhanworth
Stixwould
Reeds Beck
Dalderby
Bracebridge Low Fields
Eagle Barnsdale
North Hykeham
Roughton Moor
Roughton
Thorpe on the Hill
Wasps Nest
Sots Hole
Lincoln
Morton
South Hykeham
Nocton
COTTAGE MUSEUM
Haltham
South Scarle
Waddington
Swinderby
Haddington
Dunston
Woodhall Spa
Kirkstead
Kirkby on Bain
Aubourn
Metheringham
Toft Hill
Harmston
Martin Dales
Collingham
Thurlby
Coleby
Martin
Blankney
METHERINGHAM AIRFIELD VISITOR CENTRE
TIMBERLAND ART & DESIGN
Tattershall Thorpe
Bassingham
Boothby Graffoe
Norton Disney
Navenby
Scopwick
Timberland
TATTERSHALL COLLEGE
Tattershall
Coningsby
Brough
Carlton le Moorland
SK
TF
Kirkby Green
Thorpe Tilney
Walcott
Tattershall Bridge
BATTLE OF BRITAIN MEMORIAL FLIGHT
Stapleford
COLLEGIATE CHURCH OF THE HOLY TRINITY
NEWARK AIR MUSEUM
Wellingore
Rowston
BILLINGHAY COTTAGE
Hawthorn Hill
Ashby de la Launde
Dogdyke
Coddington
Welbourn
Brant Broughton
Bloxholm
Digby
Billinghay
Scrub Hill
New York
Chapel Hill
Beckingham
Stragglethorpe
Leadenham
Dorrington
North Kyme
Haven Bank
Barnby in the Willows
Fenton
Ruskington
Anwick
Fulbeck
Cranwell
Claypole
MANOR STABLES CRAFT WORKSHOPS
BUBBLE CAR MUSEUM
South Kyme
Holland Fen
Stubton
Caythorpe
Leasingham
South Kyme Fen
Brandon
Evedon
Ewerby Thorpe
Ewerby
Amber Hill
Dry Doddington
Friston
North Rauceby
CRANWELL AVIATION HERITAGE CENTRE
Holdingham
COGGLESFORD WATERMILL
Hough-on-the-Hill
Normanton
Kirkby la Thorpe
Howell
HOLLAND FEN
Long Bennington
Gelston
Carlton Scroop
South Rauceby
Sleaford
Asgarby
East Heckington
Hougham
Sudbrook
Quarrington
Swineshead Bridge
Westborough
West Willoughby
Ancaster
Heckington
THE PEAROOM CENTRE
Marston
Silk Willoughby
Foston
Honington
Wilsford
HECKINGTON WINDMILL
Great Hale
Burton Pedwardine
Little Hale
North End
Barkston
Kelby
Northbeck
Helpringham
Swineshead
BOUNDARY MILLS
GRANTHAM NORTH SERVICES
Syston
Culverthorpe
Swarby
Allington
Scredington
Belton
Heydour
Aswarby
Drayton
BELTON HOUSE
Great Gonerby
Oasby
Sedgebrook
Manthorpe
Aisby
Aunsby
Osbournby
Spanby
Bicker
Welby
Dembleby
Londonthorpe
Swaton
Haceby
Newton
Northorpe
Barrowby
Threekingham
Grantham
Braceby
Bridge End
Donington
Earlsfield
GRANTHAM MUS.
Cold Harbour
Walcot
Horbling
Church End
Woolsthorpe
Ropsley
Sapperton
Pickworth
Stow
Billingborough
Donington South Ing
Folkingham
Birthorpe
Denton
Quadring
Old Somerby
HARLAXTON MANOR
Harlaxton
Humby
Hanby
Little Ponton
Boothby Pagnell
Laughton
Pointon
Gosberton
Stroxton
Millthorpe
Westhorpe
Lenton
Aslackby
Gosberton Clough
Great Ponton
Dowsby
Hungerton
Ingoldsby
Graby
Risegate
Croxton Kerrial
Keisby
Bitchfield
Hawthorpe
Kirkby Underwood
Rippingale
Irnham
Bulby
Dunsby
Northgate
Gossgate
Pinchbeck
Saltby
Skillington
0 1 2 3 4 5 6 miles
0 1 2 3 4 5 6 7 8 9 10 km

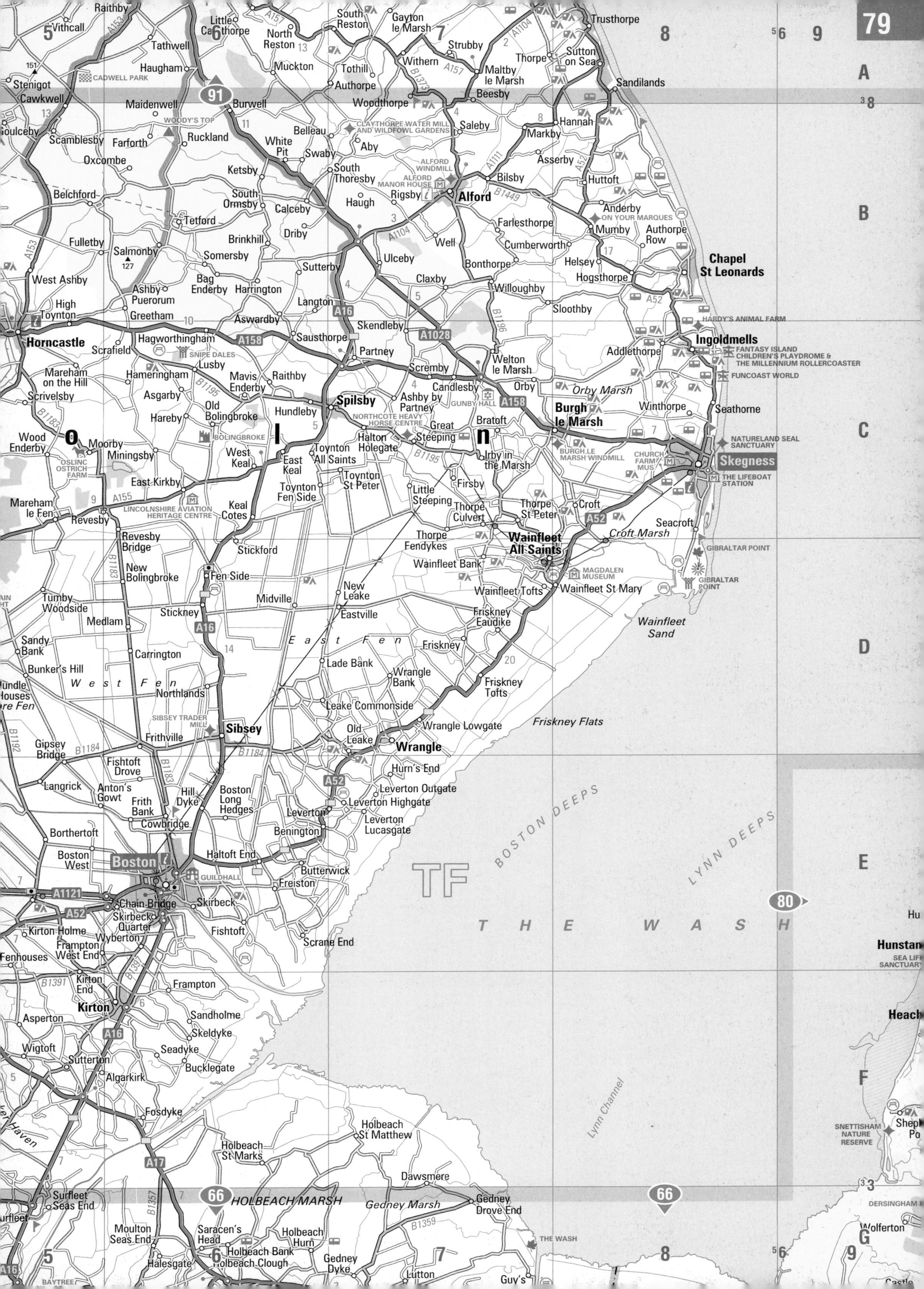

79
Raithby
Vithcall
Little Cadthorpe
South Reston
Gayton le Marsh
Trusthorpe
North Reston
Tathwell
Strubby
Sutton on Sea
Haugham
Muckton
Withern
Thorpe
Maltby le Marsh
Stenigot
CADWELL PARK
Tothill
Authorpe
Sandilands
Cawkwell
Maidenwell
Burwell
Woodthorpe
Beesby
Hannah
WOODY'S TOP
Saleby
Goulceby
Scamblesby
Farforth
Ruckland
Belleau
CLAYTHORPE WATER MILL AND WILDFOWL GARDENS
Markby
White Pit
Swaby
Aby
Oxcombe
Asserby
Ketsby
South Thoresby
ALFORD WINDMILL
Bilsby
Huttoft
ALFORD MANOR HOUSE
Belchford
South Ormsby
Rigsby
Alford
Haugh
Calceby
Tetford
Anderby
ON YOUR MARQUES
Farlesthorpe
Brinkhill
Driby
Mumby
Authorpe Row
Fulletby
Well
Salmonby
Cumberworth
Somersby
Ulceby
Chapel St Leonards
Helsey
Bonthorpe
Sutterby
Hogsthorpe
West Ashby
Bag Enderby
Claxby
Ashby Puerorum
Harrington
Willoughby
High Toynton
Langton
Sloothby
Greetham
HARDY'S ANIMAL FARM
Aswardby
Horncastle
Skendleby
Ingoldmells
Hagworthingham
Sausthorpe
FANTASY ISLAND CHILDREN'S PLAYDROME & THE MILLENNIUM ROLLERCOASTER
Scrafield
Addlethorpe
SNIPE DALES
Partney
Lusby
FUNCOAST WORLD
Mareham on the Hill
Hameringham
Mavis Enderby
Raithby
Scremby
Welton le Marsh
Candlesby
Orby
Orby Marsh
Scrivelsby
Asgarby
Ashby by Partney
GUNBY HALL
Winthorpe
Spilsby
Seathorne
Old Bolingbroke
Hundleby
Burgh le Marsh
Hareby
NORTHCOTE HEAVY HORSE CENTRE
Bratoft
Great Steeping
Wood Enderby
Moorby
BOLINGBROKE
Halton Holegate
NATURELAND SEAL SANCTUARY
Toynton All Saints
Skegness
Miningsby
West Keal
East Keal
BURGH LE MARSH WINDMILL
CHURCH FARM MUS.
OSLINC OSTRICH FARM
Irby in the Marsh
THE LIFEBOAT STATION
Toynton St Peter
Firsby
East Kirkby
Little Steeping
Toynton Fen Side
Mareham le Fen
Croft
LINCOLNSHIRE AVIATION HERITAGE CENTRE
Keal Cotes
Thorpe Culvert
Thorpe St Peter
Revesby
Seacroft
Croft Marsh
Thorpe Fendykes
Wainfleet All Saints
Revesby Bridge
Stickford
GIBRALTAR POINT
Wainfleet Bank
New Bolingbroke
MAGDALEN MUSEUM
Fen Side
GIBRALTAR POINT
New Leake
Wainfleet Tofts
Wainfleet St Mary
Tumby Woodside
Midville
Eastville
Friskney Eaudike
Stickney
Wainfleet Sand
Medlam
East Fen
Sandy Bank
Friskney
Carrington
Bunker's Hill
Lade Bank
Wrangle Bank
West Fen
Friskney Tofts
Northlands
Leake Commonside
SIBSEY TRADER MILL
Sibsey
Wrangle Lowgate
Friskney Flats
Frithville
Old Leake
Wrangle
Gipsey Bridge
Fishtoft Drove
Hurn's End
Langrick
Anton's Gowt
Boston Long Hedges
Leverton Outgate
Hill Dyke
Leverton Highgate
Frith Bank
BOSTON DEEPS
Cowbridge
Leverton
Leverton Lucasgate
Borthertoft
Benington
LYNN DEEPS
Boston West
Boston
Haltoft End
Butterwick
GUILDHALL
TF
Freiston
Chain Bridge
Skirbeck
80
Skirbeck Quarter
THE WASH
Kirton Holme
Wyberton
Fishtoft
Frampton West End
Scrane End
Hunstanton
Fenhouses
SEA LIFE SANCTUARY
Kirton End
Frampton
Kirton
Sandholme
Asperton
Skeldyke
Heacham
Wigtoft
Seadyke
Sutterton
Bucklegate
Algarkirk
Lynn Channel
Fosdyke
Holbeach St Matthew
SNETTISHAM NATURE RESERVE
Holbeach St Marks
Dawsmere
Surfleet Seas End
HOLBEACH MARSH
Gedney Marsh
Gedney Drove End
DERSINGHAM
Surfleet
Moulton Seas End
Saracen's Head
Holbeach Hurn
THE WASH
Wolferton
Holbeach Bank
Gedney Dyke
Halesgate
Holbeach Clough
Lutton
Guy's
BAYTREE

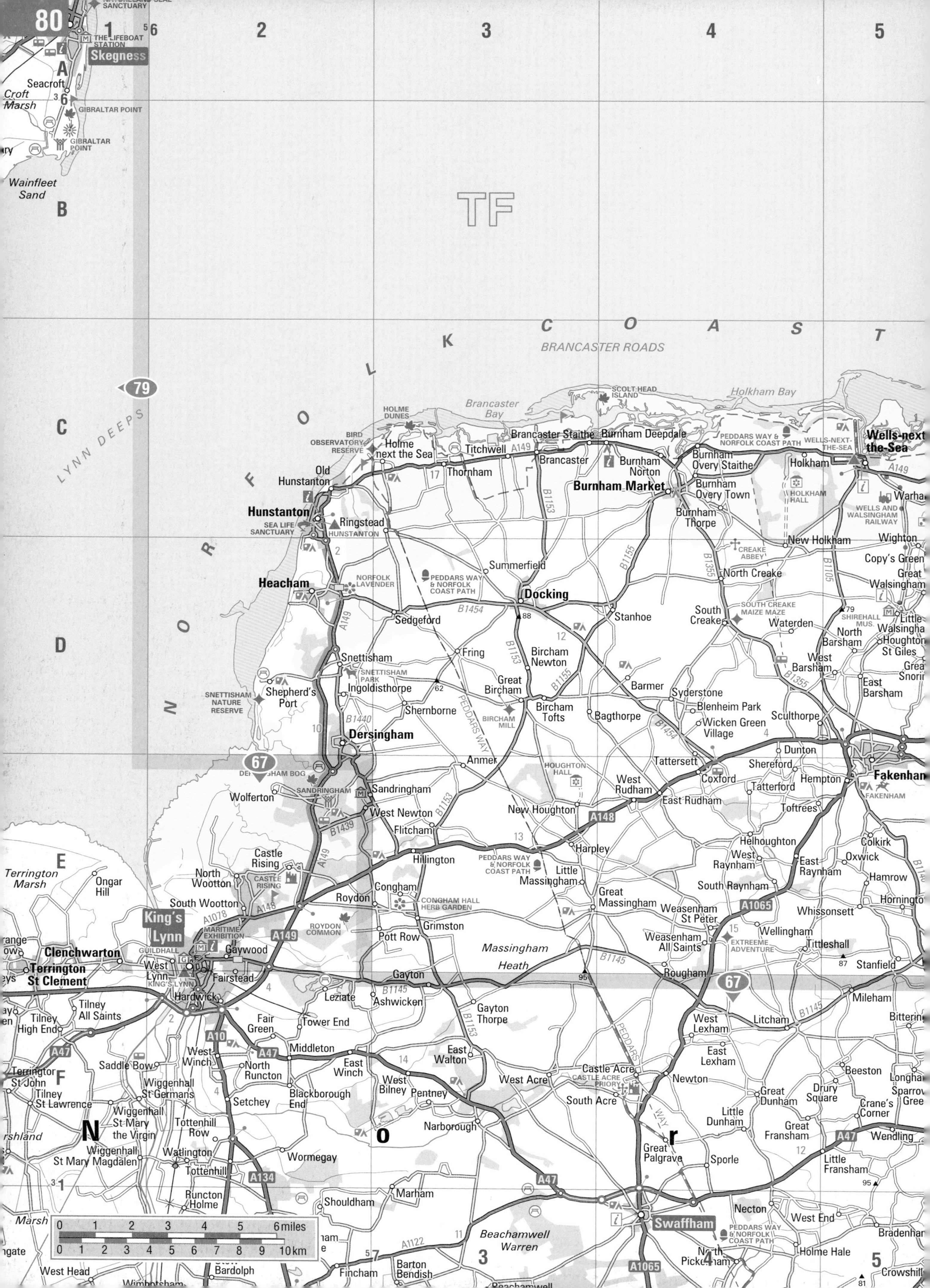

TF

NORFOLK COAST

BRANCASTER ROADS

LYNN DEEPS

NORFOLK

Skegness

THE LIFEBOAT STATION

Seacroft

Croft Marsh

GIBRALTAR POINT

GIBRALTAR POINT

Wainfleet Sand

79

Holme next the Sea

HOLME DUNES

BIRD OBSERVATORY RESERVE

Old Hunstanton

Thornham

Titchwell

A149

SCOLT HEAD ISLAND

Holkham Bay

Brancaster Staithe

Burnham Deepdale

PEDDARS WAY & NORFOLK COAST PATH

WELLS-NEXT-THE-SEA

Wells-next-the-Sea

Brancaster

Burnham Norton

Burnham Overy Staithe

Holkham

A149

Warha

Hunstanton

SEA LIFE SANCTUARY

Ringstead

HUNSTANTON

Burnham Market

Burnham Overy Town

HOLKHAM HALL

New Holkham

Wighton

WELLS AND WALSINGHAM RAILWAY

Copy's Green

Heacham

NORFOLK LAVENDER

Summerfield

B1153

Burnham Thorpe

CREAKE ABBEY

North Creake

Great Walsingham

Sedgeford

PEDDARS WAY & NORFOLK COAST PATH

Docking

B1454

88

Stanhoe

SOUTH CREAKE MAIZE MAZE

South Creake

SHIREHALL MUS.

Little Walsingha

Snettisham

SNETTISHAM PARK

Fring

Bircham Newton

12

Waterden

North Barsham

Houghton St Giles

Grea Snori

SNETTISHAM NATURE RESERVE

Shepherd's Port

Ingoldisthorpe

62

Great Bircham

B1155

Barmer

Syderstone

Blenheim Park

West Barsham

B1355

East Barsham

Shernborne

BIRCHAM MILL

Bircham Tofts

Bagthorpe

Wicken Green Village

Sculthorpe

Dersingham

PEDDARS WAY

Anmer

HOUGHTON HALL

West Rudham

Dunton

67

DERSINGHAM BOG

SANDRINGHAM

Sandringham

Tattersett

B1454

Shereford

Hempton

Fakenham

Wolferton

West Newton

B1153

New Houghton

Coxford

Tatterford

FAKENHAM

East Rudham

Toftrees

Flitcham

A148

Helhoughton

Colkirk

Terrington Marsh

Ongar Hill

Castle Rising

Hillington

PEDDARS WAY & NORFOLK COAST PATH

Harpley

13

West Raynham

Oxwick

North Wootton

CASTLE RISING

Congham

Little Massingham

South Raynham

East Raynham

Hamrow

Horningto

South Wootton

Roydon

CONGHAM HALL HERB GARDEN

Great Massingham

Weasenham St Peter

A1065

Whissonsett

King's Lynn

MARITIME EXHIBITION

A1078

ROYDON COMMON

Grimston

Weasenham All Saints

Wellingham

Tittleshall

Clenchwarton

GUILDHALL

Gaywood

Pott Row

Massingham Heath

B1145

EXTREME ADVENTURE

15

87

Stanfield

Terrington St Clement

WEST LYNN

KING'S LYNN

Fairstead

Gayton

95

Rougham

67

Tilney All Saints

Hardwick

4

Leziate

Ashwicken

B1145

Mileham

Tilney High End

A47

Fair Green

Tower End

Gayton Thorpe

West Lexham

Litcham

B1145

Bitterin

Terrington St John

A10

Saddle Bow

A47

Middleton

14

East Walton

East Lexham

Tilney St Lawrence

West Winch

East Winch

West Bilney

Pentney

West Acre

Castle Acre

CASTLE ACRE PRIORY

Newton

Great Dunham

Drury Square

Beeston

Longha

Wiggenhall St Germans

North Runcton

Blackborough End

West Bilney

Pentney

Narborough

Narborough

WAY

Little Dunham

Great Fransham

Crane's Gree

Sparrov

N

Setchey

South Acre

r

Sporle

Great Palgrave

Little Fransham

A47

Wendling

Wiggenhall St Mary the Virgin

Watlington

Wormegay

O

Great Palgrave

95

Wiggenhall St Mary Magdalen

Tottenhill Row

Tottenhill

A134

Runcton Holme

Shouldham

Marham

A47

Necton

West End

Bradenha

Marsh

Swaffham

PEDDARS WAY & NORFOLK COAST PATH

Holme Hale

West Head

Bardolph

A1122

Beachamwell Warren

Fincham

Barton Bendish

North Picke ham

A1065

Crowshil

Wimbotsham

West

81

0 1 2 3 4 5 6 miles

0 1 2 3 4 5 6 7 8 9 10km

1   2   3   4   5

A   B   C   D   E   F

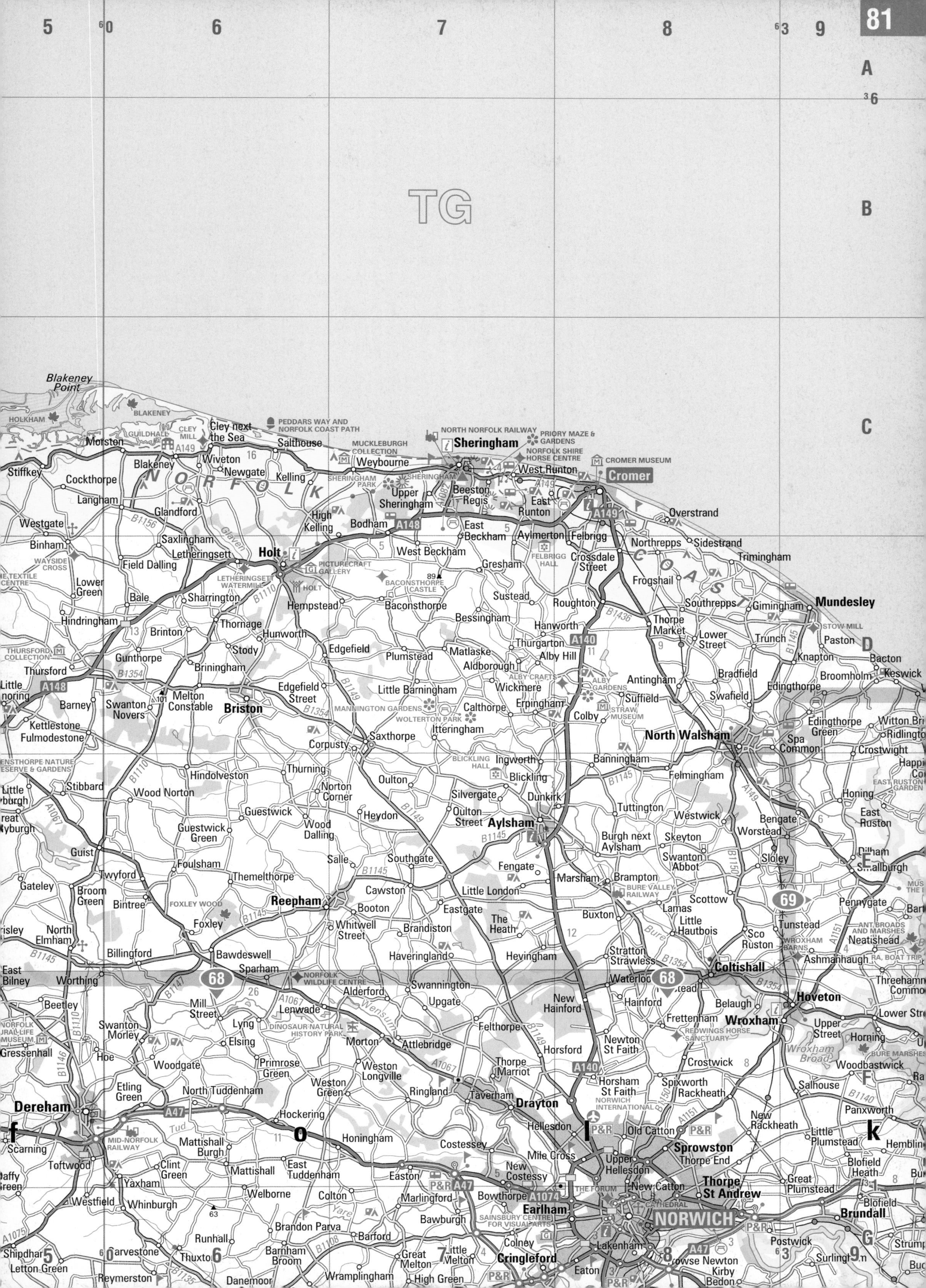
5
6
7
8
9
A
B
C
D
E
F
G
TG
Blakeney Point
HOLKHAM
BLAKENEY
CLEY MILL
GUILDHALL
Cley next the Sea
PEDDARS WAY AND NORFOLK COAST PATH
Morston
Salthouse
MUCKLEBURGH COLLECTION
NORTH NORFOLK RAILWAY
Sheringham
PRIORY MAZE & GARDENS
NORFOLK SHIRE HORSE CENTRE
CROMER MUSEUM
Cromer
Stiffkey
Blakeney
Wiveton
Newgate
Kelling
Weybourne
SHERINGHAM PARK
SHERINGHAM
Upper Sheringham
Beeston Regis
West Runton
East Runton
Overstrand
NORFOLK
COAST
Cockthorpe
Langham
Glandford
High Kelling
Bodham
A148
East Beckham
Aylmerton
Felbrigg
FELBRIGG HALL
Crossdale Street
Northrepps
Sidestrand
Trimingham
Westgate
Binham
Saxlingham
Letheringsett
Holt
West Beckham
Gresham
Field Dalling
WAYSIDE CROSS
TEXTILE CENTRE
LETHERINGSETT WATERMILL
PICTURECRAFT GALLERY
HOLT
BACONSTHORPE CASTLE
Frogshall
Lower Green
Bale
Sharrington
Hempstead
Baconsthorpe
Sustead
Roughton
Southrepps
Gimingham
Mundesley
Hindringham
Thornage
Bessingham
Hanworth
Thorpe Market
Lower Street
Trunch
STOW MILL
Paston
Brinton
Hunworth
Stody
Edgefield
Plumstead
Matlaske
Thurgarton
A140
Alby Hill
Aldborough
Knapton
Bacton
THURSFORD COLLECTION
Gunthorpe
Briningham
ALBY CRAFTS
ALBY GARDENS
Antingham
Bradfield
Broomholm
Keswick
Thursford
Edgefield Street
Little Barningham
Wickmere
Suffield
Swafield
Edingthorpe
Little Snoring
Barney
Swanton Novers
Melton Constable
Briston
MANNINGTON GARDENS
Calthorpe
WOLTERTON PARK
Erpingham
Colby
STRAW MUSEUM
Itteringham
Kettlestone
Fulmodestone
Saxthorpe
Corpusty
North Walsham
Spa Common
Edingthorpe Green
Witton Bridge
Ridlington
Crostwight
Banningham
BLICKLING HALL
Ingworth
Blickling
PENSTHORPE NATURE RESERVE & GARDENS
Hindolveston
Thurning
Felmingham
Stibbard
Wood Norton
Norton Corner
Oulton
Silvergate
Dunkirk
EAST RUSTON GARDEN
Honing
Little Ryburgh
Great Ryburgh
Guestwick
Heydon
Oulton Street
Aylsham
Tuttington
Westwick
East Ruston
Bengate
Worstead
Guestwick Green
Wood Dalling
Burgh next Aylsham
Skeyton
Swanton Abbot
Dilham
Smallburgh
Sloley
Guist
Foulsham
Salle
Southgate
Fengate
Marsham
Brampton
BURE VALLEY RAILWAY
Gateley
Twyford
Themelthorpe
Cawston
Little London
Lamas
Scottow
Pennygate
Broom Green
Bintree
FOXLEY WOOD
Reepham
Booton
Eastgate
The Heath
Buxton
Little Hautbois
Tunstead
Foxley
Whitwell Street
Brandiston
Sco Ruston
ANT BROADS AND MARSHES
Neatishead
North Elmham
Billingford
Bawdeswell
Haveringland
Hevingham
Stratton Strawless
Coltishall
WROXHAM BARNS
Ashmanhaugh
East Bilney
Worthing
Sparham
NORFOLK WILDLIFE CENTRE
Swannington
Waterloo
Belaugh
Hoveton
Threehammer Common
Beetley
Mill Street
Alderford
Upgate
New Hainford
Hainford
Frettenham
Wroxham
Lower Street
Swanton Morley
Lyng
Lenwade
DINOSAUR NATURAL HISTORY PARK
Felthorpe
REDWINGS HORSE SANCTUARY
Upper Street
Horning
NORFOLK RURAL LIFE MUSEUM
Elsing
Morton
Attlebridge
Newton St Faith
Horsford
Wroxham Broad
Gressenhall
Hoe
Woodgate
Primrose Green
Weston Longville
Thorpe Marriot
Crostwick
Woodbastwick
Etling Green
North Tuddenham
Weston Green
Ringland
Taverham
Horsham St Faith
Spixworth
Rackheath
Salhouse
Dereham
Hockering
Drayton
NORWICH INTERNATIONAL
New Rackheath
Panxworth
A47
Hellesdon
Old Catton
P&R
MID-NORFOLK RAILWAY
Scarning
Mattishall Burgh
Honingham
Costessey
Sprowston
Little Plumstead
Hemblington
Toftwood
Clint Green
East Tuddenham
Mile Cross
Upper Hellesdon
Thorpe End
Blofield Heath
Yaxham
Mattishall
Easton
New Costessey
Thorpe St Andrew
Great Plumstead
Westfield
Whinburgh
Welborne
Colton
Marlingford
Bowthorpe
A1074
THE FORUM
New Catton
Earlham
CATHEDRAL
Blofield
Brundall
Brandon Parva
Bawburgh
SAINSBURY CENTRE FOR VISUAL ARTS
NORWICH
Runhall
Barford
Colney
Postwick
Shipdham
Garvestone
Thuxton
Barnham Broom
Great Melton
Little Melton
Cringleford
Lakenham
Surlingham
Letton Green
Reymerston
Danemoor
Wramplingham
High Green
Eaton
Trowse Newton
Kirby Bedon

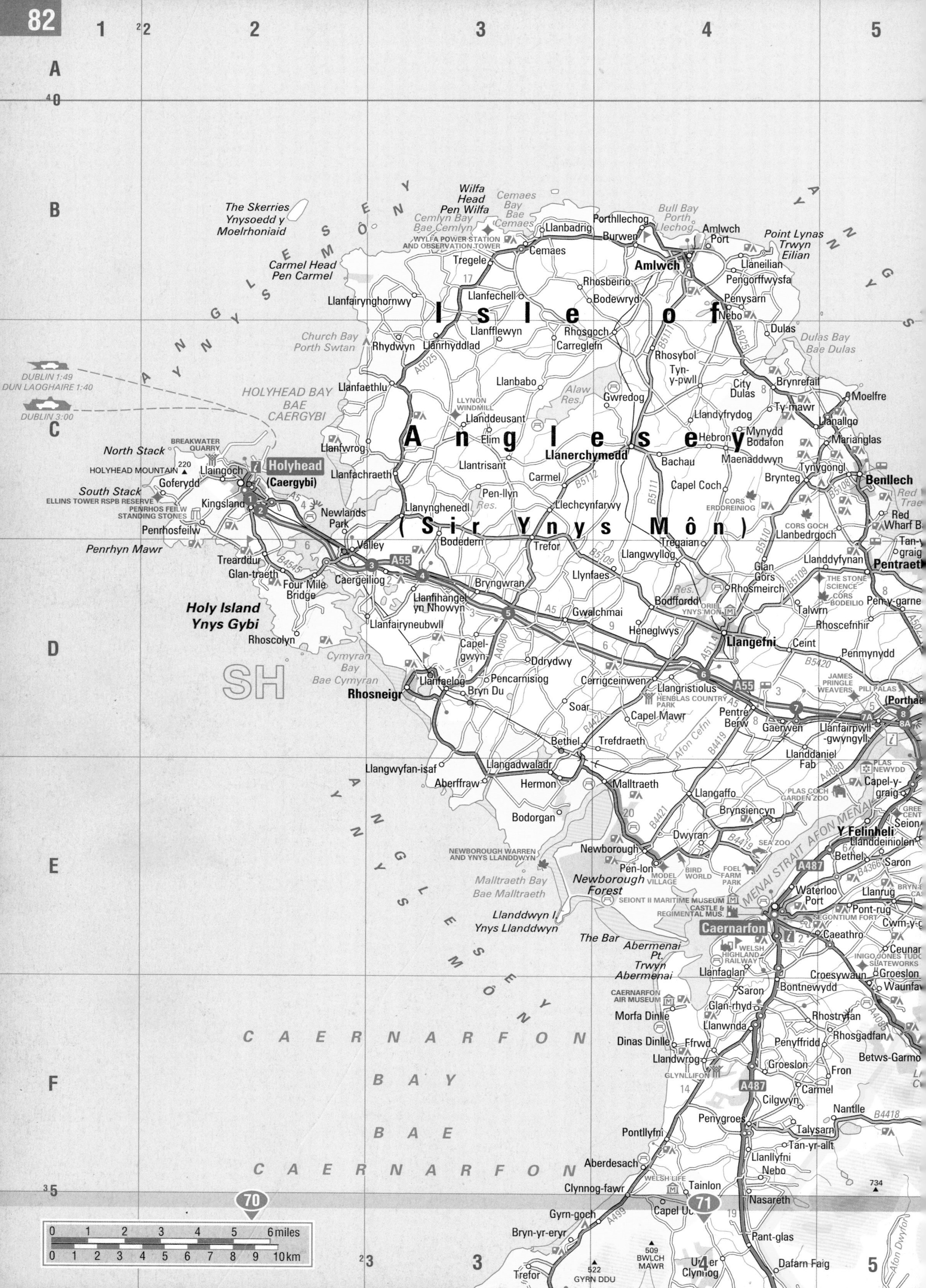
Isle of Anglesey
(Sir Ynys Môn)
Holyhead
(Caergybi)
Holy Island
Ynys Gybi
Amlwch
Llangefni
Llanerchymedd
Benllech
Caernarfon
Rhosneigr
Y Felinheli
The Skerries
Ynysoedd y
Moelrhoniaid
Carmel Head
Pen Carmel
Wylfa Head
Pen Wilfa
Cemaes Bay
Bae Cemaes
Cemlyn Bay
Bae Cemlyn
WYLFA POWER STATION
AND OBSERVATION TOWER
Bull Bay
Porth Llechog
Point Lynas
Trwyn
Eilian
Church Bay
Porth Swtan
Dulas Bay
Bae Dulas
HOLYHEAD BAY
BAE
CAERGYBI
DUBLIN 1:49
DUN LAOGHAIRE 1:40
DUBLIN 3:00
North Stack
South Stack
HOLYHEAD MOUNTAIN
ELLINS TOWER RSPB RESERVE
PENRHOS FEILW
STANDING STONES
BREAKWATER
QUARRY
Penrhyn Mawr
Cymyran Bay
Bae Cymyran
Malltraeth Bay
Bae Malltraeth
Newborough
Forest
NEWBOROUGH WARREN
AND YNYS LLANDDWYN
Llanddwyn I.
Ynys Llanddwyn
The Bar
Abermenai
Pt.
Trwyn
Abermenai
MENAI STRAIT AFON MENAI
CAERNARFON
BAY
BAE
CAERNARFON
ANGLESEY SEA
MÔR YNYS MÔN
SH
A55
A5
A5025
A487
A499
A4080
B5111
B5112
B5109
B5110
B5420
B4419
B4421
B4422
B4545
B5108
B4418
B4366
SEIONT II MARITIME MUSEUM
CASTLE &
REGIMENTAL MUS.
SEGONTIUM FORT
WELSH
HIGHLAND
RAILWAY
INIGO JONES TUDOR
SLATEWORKS
CAERNARFON
AIR MUSEUM
GLYNLLIFON
WELSH LIFE
LLYNON
WINDMILL
CORS
ERDDREINIOG
CORS GOCH
THE STONE
SCIENCE
CORS
BODEILIO
ORIEL
YNYS MÔN
HENBLAS COUNTRY
PARK
JAMES
PRINGLE
WEAVERS
PLAS
NEWYDD
PLAS COCH
GARDEN ZOO
SEA ZOO
BIRD
WORLD
FOEL
FARM
PARK
MODEL
VILLAGE
Alaw Res.
Afon Cefni
Afon Dwyfor
Llanbadrig
Porthllechog
Burwen
Amlwch Port
Cemaes
Tregele
Llaneilian
Pengorffwysfa
Rhosbeirio
Bodewryd
Llanfechell
Llanfairynghornwy
Penysarn
Nebo
Dulas
Rhosgoch
Carreglefn
Llanfflewyn
Rhydwyn
Llanrhyddlad
Rhosybol
Tyn-y-pwll
City Dulas
Brynrefail
Moelfre
Ty-mawr
Llanallgo
Marianglas
Llanbabo
Gwredog
Llanfaethlu
Llanddeusant
Llandyfrydog
Mynydd Bodafon
Hebron
Elim
Llanfwrog
Bachau
Maenaddwyn
Tynygongl
Llantrisant
Carmel
Capel Coch
Brynteg
Llanfachraeth
Pen-llyn
Llechcynfarwy
Llanynghenedl
Red Wharf Bay
Llanbedrgoch
Llaingoch
Goferydd
Kingsland
Newlands Park
Penrhosfeilw
Valley
Bodedern
Trefor
Tregaian
Llangwyllog
Tan-y-graig
Llanddyfnan
Pentraeth
Trearddur
Glan-traeth
Four Mile Bridge
Caergeiliog
Bryngwran
Llynfaes
Glan Gors
Rhosmeirch
Llanfihangel yn Nhowyn
Bodffordd
Talwrn
Pen-y-garnedd
Gwalchmai
Llanfairyneubwll
Heneglwys
Rhoscefnhir
Rhoscolyn
Capel-gwyn
Ddrydwy
Ceint
Penmynydd
Llanfaelog
Pencarnisiog
Bryn Du
Cerrigceinwen
Llangristiolus
Pili Palas
Porthaethwy
Soar
Capel Mawr
Pentre Berw
Gaerwen
Llanfairpwll-gwyngyll
Bethel
Trefdraeth
Llanddaniel Fab
Llangwyfan-isaf
Llangadwaladr
Aberffraw
Hermon
Malltraeth
Capel-y-graig
Llangaffo
Brynsiencyn
Bodorgan
Seion
Llanddeiniolen
Dwyran
Newborough
Pen-lon
Saron
Llanrug
Waterloo Port
Pont-rug
Cwm-y-glo
Caeathro
Ceunant
Llanfaglan
Croesywaun
Groeslon
Bontnewydd
Waunfawr
Saron
Glan-rhyd
Morfa Dinlle
Rhostryfan
Llanwnda
Dinas Dinlle
Ffrwd
Penyffridd
Rhosgadfan
Llandwrog
Betws-Garmon
Groeslon
Fron
Carmel
Cilgwyn
Nantlle
Penygroes
Talysarn
Pontllyfni
Tan-yr-allt
Llanllyfni
Aberdesach
Nebo
Clynnog-fawr
Tainlon
Nasareth
Capel Uchaf
Gyrn-goch
Bryn-yr-eryr
Pant-glas
509
BWLCH
MAWR
522
GYRN DDU
734
Trefor
Uwchmynydd
Clynnog
Dafarn Faig
0 1 2 3 4 5 6 miles
0 1 2 3 4 5 6 7 8 9 10 km
70
71

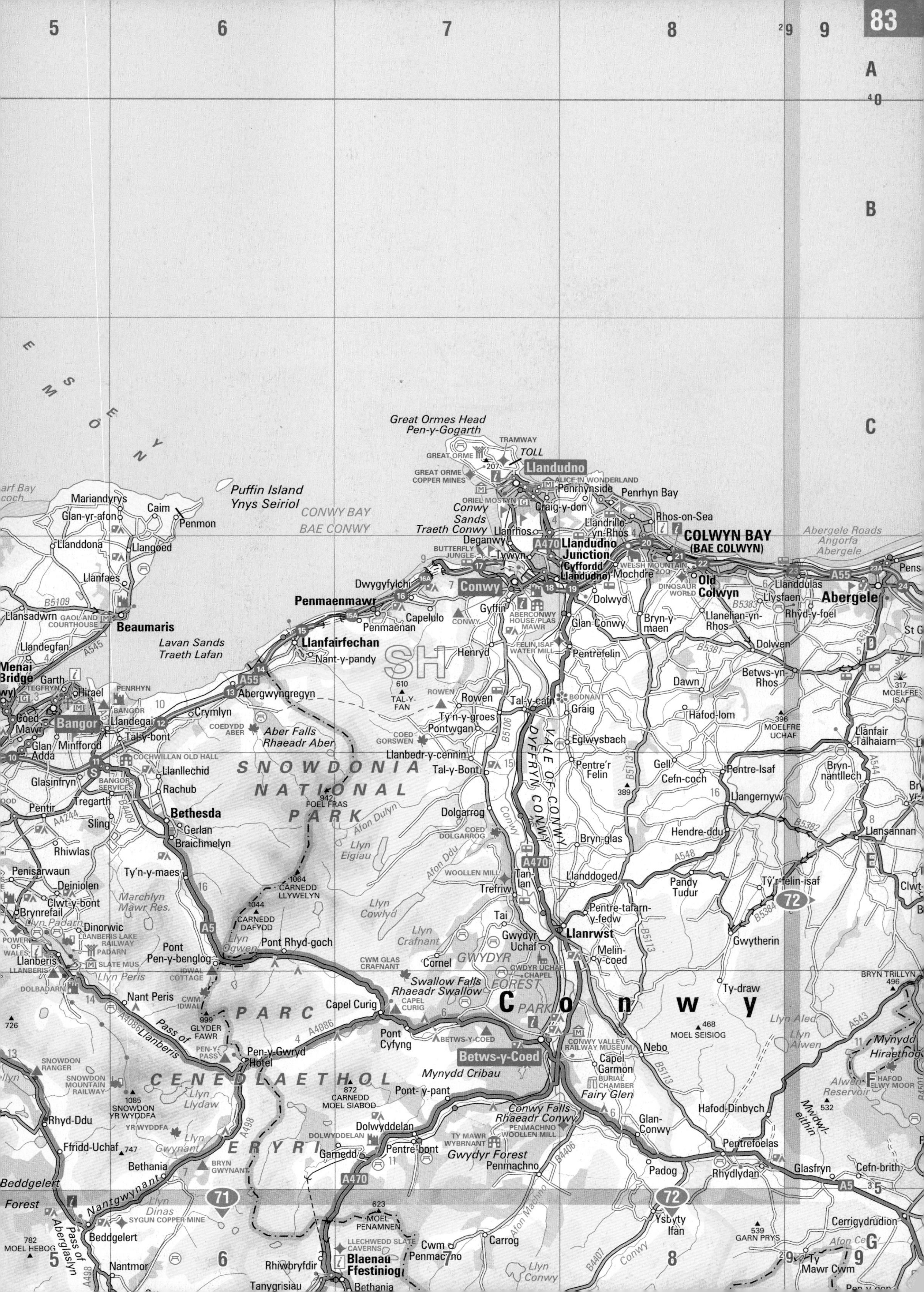

5
6
7
8
9
A
B
C
D
E
F
G
Great Ormes Head
Pen-y-Gogarth
TRAMWAY
TOLL
GREAT ORME
207
Llandudno
GREAT ORME COPPER MINES
ALICE IN WONDERLAND
Penrhynside
Penrhyn Bay
ORIEL MOSTYN
Craig-y-don
Puffin Island
Ynys Seiriol
CONWY BAY
BAE CONWY
Conwy Sands
Traeth Conwy
Llandrillo-yn-Rhos
Rhos-on-Sea
COLWYN BAY
(BAE COLWYN)
Abergele Roads
Angorfa Abergele
Llanrhos
Deganwy
BUTTERFLY JUNGLE
Tywyn
Llandudno Junction
(Cyffordd Llandudno)
WELSH MOUNTAIN ZOO
Mochdre
Old Colwyn
DINOSAUR WORLD
Llanddulas
Llysfaen
Abergele
Rhyd-y-foel
Pens
A55
A470
Mariandyrys
Glan-yr-afon
Caim
Penmon
Llanddona
Llangoed
Llanfaes
B5109
Llansadwrn
GAOL AND COURTHOUSE
Beaumaris
Llandegfan
A545
Lavan Sands
Traeth Lafan
Menai Bridge
Garth
Hirael
PENRHYN
Bangor
Coed Mawr
Glan Adda
Minffordd
Llandegai
Tal-y-bont
Crymlyn
Abergwyngregyn
Dwygyfylchi
Penmaenmawr
Conwy
Gyffin
Capelulo
Penmaenan
Llanfairfechan
Nant-y-pandy
CONWY
ABERCONWY HOUSE/PLAS MAWR
FELIN ISAF WATER MILL
Henryd
Glan Conwy
Pentrefelin
Dolwyd
Bryn-y-maen
Llanelian-yn-Rhos
Dolwen
B5381
B5383
Dawn
Betws-yn-Rhos
MOELFRE ISAF
317
SH
610
TAL-Y-FAN
ROWEN
Rowen
Tal-y-cafn
BODNANT
Graig
Ty'n-y-groes
Pontwgan
COEDYDD ABER
Aber Falls
Rhaeadr Aber
COED GORSWEN
Hafod-lom
396
MOELFRE UCHAF
Llanfair Talhaiarn
COCHWILLAN OLD HALL
Llanllechid
Glasinfryn
BANGOR SERVICES
Rachub
Tregarth
B4409
Pentir
A4244
Sling
SNOWDONIA NATIONAL PARK
942
FOEL FRAS
Llanbedr-y-cennin
Tal-y-Bont
B5106
VALE OF CONWY
DYFFRYN CONWY
Eglwysbach
Pentre'r Felin
B5113
389
Gell
Cefn-coch
Pentre-Isaf
Bryn-nantllech
A544
Llangernyw
Bethesda
Gerlan
Braichmelyn
Afon Dulyn
Llyn Eigiau
Dolgarrog
COED DOLGARROG
Conwy
Bryn-glas
Hendre-ddu
B5382
Llansannan
Rhiwlas
Afon Ddu
WOOLLEN MILL
A470
A548
Penisarwaun
Deiniolen
Ty'n-y-maes
Marchlyn Mawr Res.
1064
CARNEDD LLYWELYN
Trefriw
Tan-lan
Llanddoged
Pandy Tudur
Tŷ'r-felin-isaf
Clwt-y-bont
Brynrefail
Llyn Padarn
Dinorwic
1044
CARNEDD DAFYDD
Llyn Cowlyd
Pentre-tafarn-y-fedw
B5384
72
POWER OF WALES
LLANBERIS LAKE RAILWAY
PADARN
A5
Llyn Ogwen
Pont Rhyd-goch
Tai
Llanrwst
Gwytherin
Llanberis
SLATE MUS.
Pont Pen-y-benglog
IDWAL COTTAGE
Llyn Crafnant
Gwydyr Uchaf
Melin-y-coed
B5113
DOLBADARN
Llyn Peris
CWM GLAS CRAFNANT
Cornel
GWYDYR
GWDYR UCHAF CHAPEL
FOREST
BRYN TRILLYN
496
Nant Peris
CWM IDWAL
Swallow Falls
Rhaeadr Swallow
Capel Curig
CAPEL CURIG
PARK
Conwy
Ty-draw
Llyn Aled
726
999
GLYDER FAWR
PARC
A4086
Pont Cyfyng
BETWS-Y-COED
CONWY VALLEY RAILWAY MUSEUM
468
MOEL SEISIOG
Llyn Alwen
A543
Mynydd Hiraethog
Pass of Llanberis
PEN-Y-PASS
Pen-y-Gwryd Hotel
Betws-y-Coed
Nebo
Capel Garmon
BURIAL CHAMBER
SNOWDON RANGER
SNOWDON MOUNTAIN RAILWAY
CENEDLAETHOL
Mynydd Cribau
B5113
Alwen Reservoir
HAFOD ELWY MOOR
872
CARNEDD MOEL SIABOD
Pont-y-pant
Fairy Glen
532
1085
SNOWDON
YR WYDDFA
Llyn Llydaw
Conwy Falls
Rhaeadr Conwy
PENMACHNO WOOLLEN MILL
Glan-Conwy
Hafod-Dinbych
Mwdwl-eithin
Rhyd-Ddu
YR WYDDFA
A498
Dolwyddelan
DOLWYDDELAN
TY MAWR WYBRNANT
Ffridd-Uchaf
747
Llyn Gwynant
ERYRI
Garnedd
Pentre-bont
Gwydyr Forest
B4406
Pentrefoelas
Bethania
BRYN GWYNANT
A470
Penmachno
Padog
Rhydlydan
Glasfryn
Cefn-brith
A5
Beddgelert
Forest
71
Nantgwynant
Llyn Dinas
SYGUN COPPER MINE
623
MOEL PENAMNEN
Afon Machno
72
Ysbyty Ifan
539
GARN PRYS
Cerrigydrudion
Afon Ce
782
MOEL HEBOG
Beddgelert
Pass of Aberglaslyn
LLECHWEDD SLATE CAVERNS
Blaenau Ffestiniog
Cwm Penmachno
Carrog
B4407
Conwy
Llyn Conwy
Ty Mawr Cwm
A498
Nantmor
Rhiwbryfdir
Tanygrisiau
Bethania

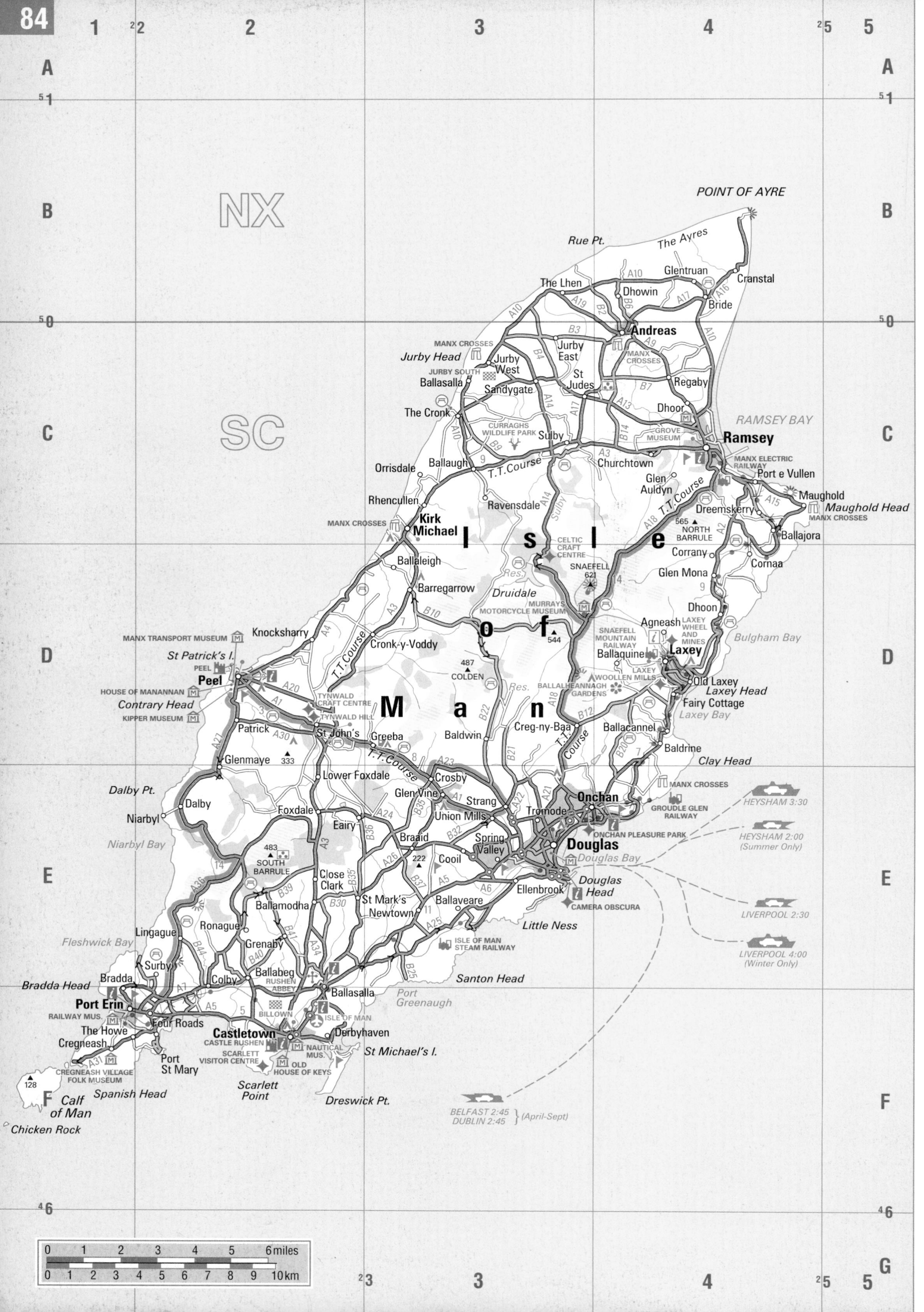
NX
SC
Isle of Man
POINT OF AYRE
Rue Pt.
The Ayres
Glentruan
Cranstal
The Lhen
Dhowin
Bride
Andreas
MANX CROSSES
Jurby Head
Jurby West
Jurby East
JURBY SOUTH
Ballasalla
Sandygate
St Judes
Regaby
Dhoor
The Cronk
CURRAGHS WILDLIFE PARK
Sulby
GROVE MUSEUM
RAMSEY BAY
Ramsey
MANX ELECTRIC RAILWAY
Port e Vullen
Maughold
Maughold Head
Orrisdale
Ballaugh
T.T.Course
Churchtown
Glen Auldyn
Rhencullen
Ravensdale
Dreemskerry
Kirk Michael
565 NORTH BARRULE
Ballajora
CELTIC CRAFT CENTRE
Corrany
Cornaa
Ballaleigh
SNAEFELL 621
Glen Mona
Barregarrow
Druidale
MURRAYS MOTORCYCLE MUSEUM
Dhoon
MANX TRANSPORT MUSEUM
Knocksharry
Agneash
LAXEY WHEEL AND MINES
SNAEFELL MOUNTAIN RAILWAY
Bulgham Bay
St Patrick's I.
Cronk-y-Voddy
544
Ballaquine
Laxey
PEEL
Peel
487 COLDEN
LAXEY WOOLLEN MILLS
Old Laxey
HOUSE OF MANANNAN
Laxey Head
Contrary Head
TYNWALD CRAFT CENTRE
BALLALHEANNAGH GARDENS
Fairy Cottage
KIPPER MUSEUM
TYNWALD HILL
Laxey Bay
Patrick
St John's
Greeba
Baldwin
Creg-ny-Baa
Ballacannel
Glenmaye
333
Baldrine
Clay Head
Lower Foxdale
Crosby
Dalby Pt.
MANX CROSSES
Glen Vine
Strang
Onchan
HEYSHAM 3:30
Dalby
GROUDLE GLEN RAILWAY
Niarbyl
Foxdale
Union Mills
Tromode
Eairy
ONCHAN PLEASURE PARK
HEYSHAM 2:00 (Summer Only)
Braaid
Spring Valley
Douglas
Niarbyl Bay
483 SOUTH BARRULE
222
Cooil
Douglas Bay
Close Clark
Ellenbrook
Douglas Head
CAMERA OBSCURA
Ballamodha
St Mark's
Newtown
Ballaveare
LIVERPOOL 2:30
Ronague
Little Ness
Lingague
Fleshwick Bay
Grenaby
ISLE OF MAN STEAM RAILWAY
LIVERPOOL 4:00 (Winter Only)
Surby
Bradda
Colby
Ballabeg
RUSHEN ABBEY
Santon Head
Bradda Head
Ballasalla
Port Greenaugh
Port Erin
BILLOWN
ISLE OF MAN
RAILWAY MUS.
Four Roads
The Howe
Castletown
Derbyhaven
Cregneash
CASTLE RUSHEN
NAUTICAL MUS.
St Michael's I.
SCARLETT VISITOR CENTRE
Port St Mary
OLD HOUSE OF KEYS
CREGNEASH VILLAGE FOLK MUSEUM
128
Scarlett Point
Calf of Man
Spanish Head
Dreswick Pt.
BELFAST 2:45
DUBLIN 2:45
(April-Sept)
Chicken Rock
0 1 2 3 4 5 6 miles
0 1 2 3 4 5 6 7 8 9 10 km

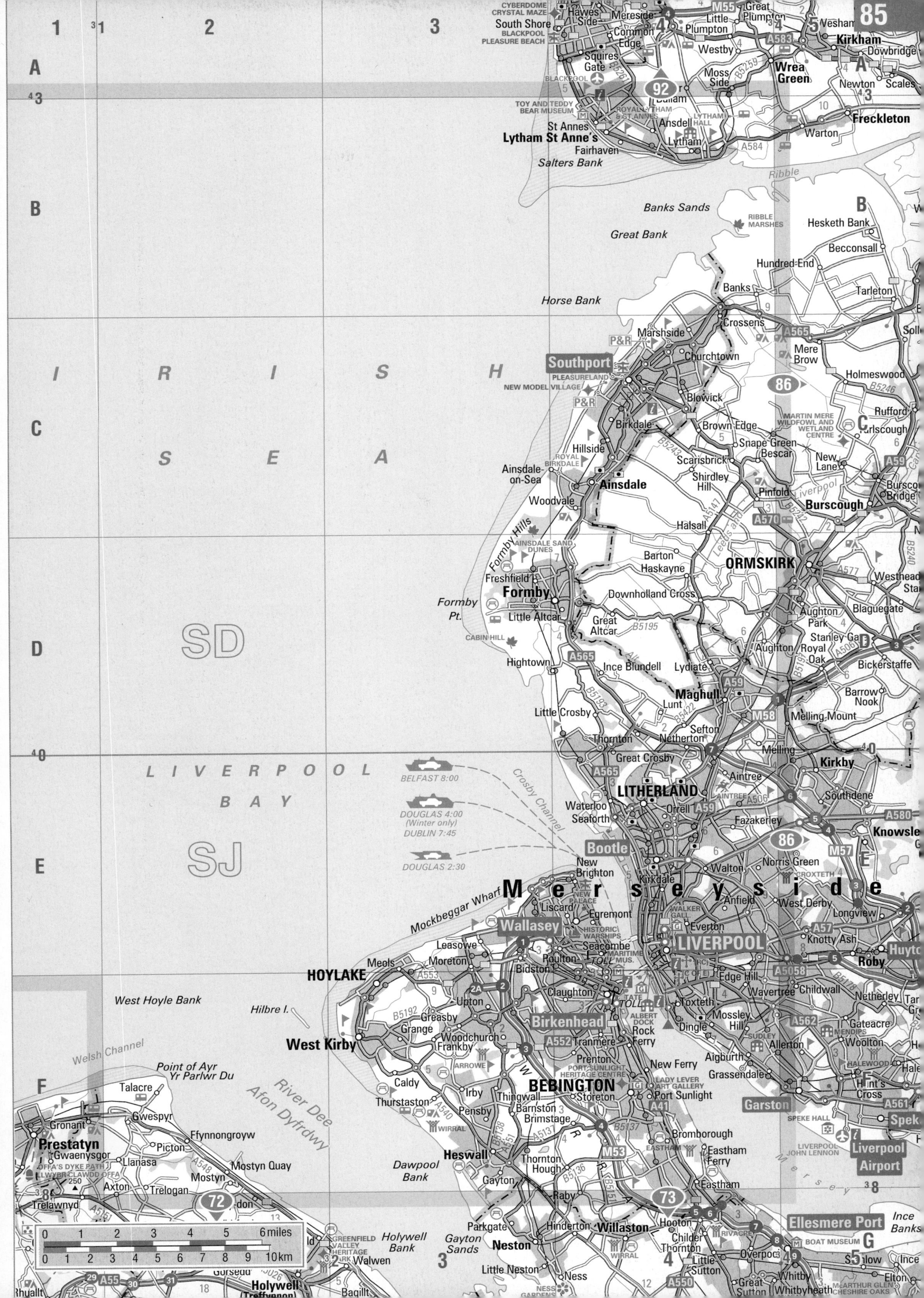

85
IRISH SEA
LIVERPOOL BAY
SD
SJ
Merseyside
Blackpool Pleasure Beach
South Shore
Squires Gate
Lytham St Anne's
St Annes
Ansdell
Lytham
Fairhaven
Salters Bank
Warton
Freckleton
Kirkham
Wrea Green
Westby
Little Plumpton
Great Plumpton
Newton
Scales
Dowbridge
Ribble
Banks Sands
Great Bank
Ribble Marshes
Hesketh Bank
Becconsall
Hundred End
Tarleton
Banks
Horse Bank
Crossens
Marshside
Churchtown
Southport
Pleasureland
New Model Village
Mere Brow
Holmeswood
Rufford
Martin Mere Wildfowl and Wetland Centre
Blowick
Birkdale
Brown Edge
Snape Green
Bescar
Scarisbrick
Hillside
Royal Birkdale
Ainsdale-on-Sea
Ainsdale
Shirdley Hill
Pinfold
New Lane
Burscough
Woodvale
Halsall
Formby Hills
Ainsdale Sand Dunes
Freshfield
Formby
Formby Pt.
Little Altcar
Barton
Haskayne
Ormskirk
Downholland Cross
Great Altcar
Aughton Park
Blaguegate
Westhead
Cabin Hill
Hightown
Ince Blundell
Lydiate
Aughton
Royal Oak
Bickerstaffe
Maghull
Lunt
Little Crosby
Barrow Nook
Melling Mount
Sefton
Netherton
Thornton
Great Crosby
Melling
Kirkby
Belfast 8:00
Douglas 4:00 (Winter only)
Dublin 7:45
Douglas 2:30
Crosby Channel
Aintree
Litherland
Southdene
Waterloo
Seaforth
Orrell
Fazakerley
Knowsley
Bootle
Walton
Norris Green
Croxteth
New Brighton
Kirkdale
Anfield
West Derby
Mockbeggar Wharf
Liscard
Egremont
Everton
Longview
Wallasey
Historic Warships
Leasowe
Seacombe
Liverpool
Knotty Ash
Roby
Meols
Moreton
Poulton
Maritime Mus.
Hoylake
Bidston
Edge Hill
Wavertree
Childwall
Claughton
Netherley
West Hoyle Bank
Hilbre I.
Upton
Toxteth
Greasby
Birkenhead
Albert Dock
Mossley Hill
Dingle
Gateacre
Grange
Woodchurch
Rock Ferry
Tranmere
Allerton
Woolton
West Kirby
Frankby
Sudley
Welsh Channel
Point of Ayr
Yr Parlwr Du
Arrowe
Prenton
Port Sunlight Heritage Centre
New Ferry
Aigburth
Grassendale
Halewood
Caldy
Bebington
Lady Lever Art Gallery
Hunt's Cross
Talacre
River Dee
Afon Dyfrdwy
Irby
Thingwall
Storeton
Port Sunlight
Garston
Thurstaston
Barnston
Speke Hall
Gwespyr
Pensby
Brimstage
Gronant
Gwaenysgor
Prestatyn
Ffynnongroyw
Picton
Bromborough
Liverpool John Lennon
Liverpool Airport
Llanasa
Heswall
Eastham
Eastham Ferry
Offa's Dyke Path
Mostyn Quay
Mostyn
Dawpool Bank
Thornton Hough
Axton
Trelogan
Gayton
Trelawnyd
Raby
Ellesmere Port
Ince Banks
Boat Museum
Parkgate
Hinderton
Willaston
Hooton
Childer Thornton
Rivacre
Overpool
Greenfield Valley Heritage Park
Holywell Bank
Gayton Sands
Neston
Walwen
Little Sutton
Little Neston
Ness
Ness Gardens
Great Sutton
Whitby
Whitbyheath
McArthur Glen Cheshire Oaks
Holywell (Treffynnon)
Gorsedd
Bagillt
Rhuallt
Elton
0 1 2 3 4 5 6 miles
0 1 2 3 4 5 6 7 8 9 10 km

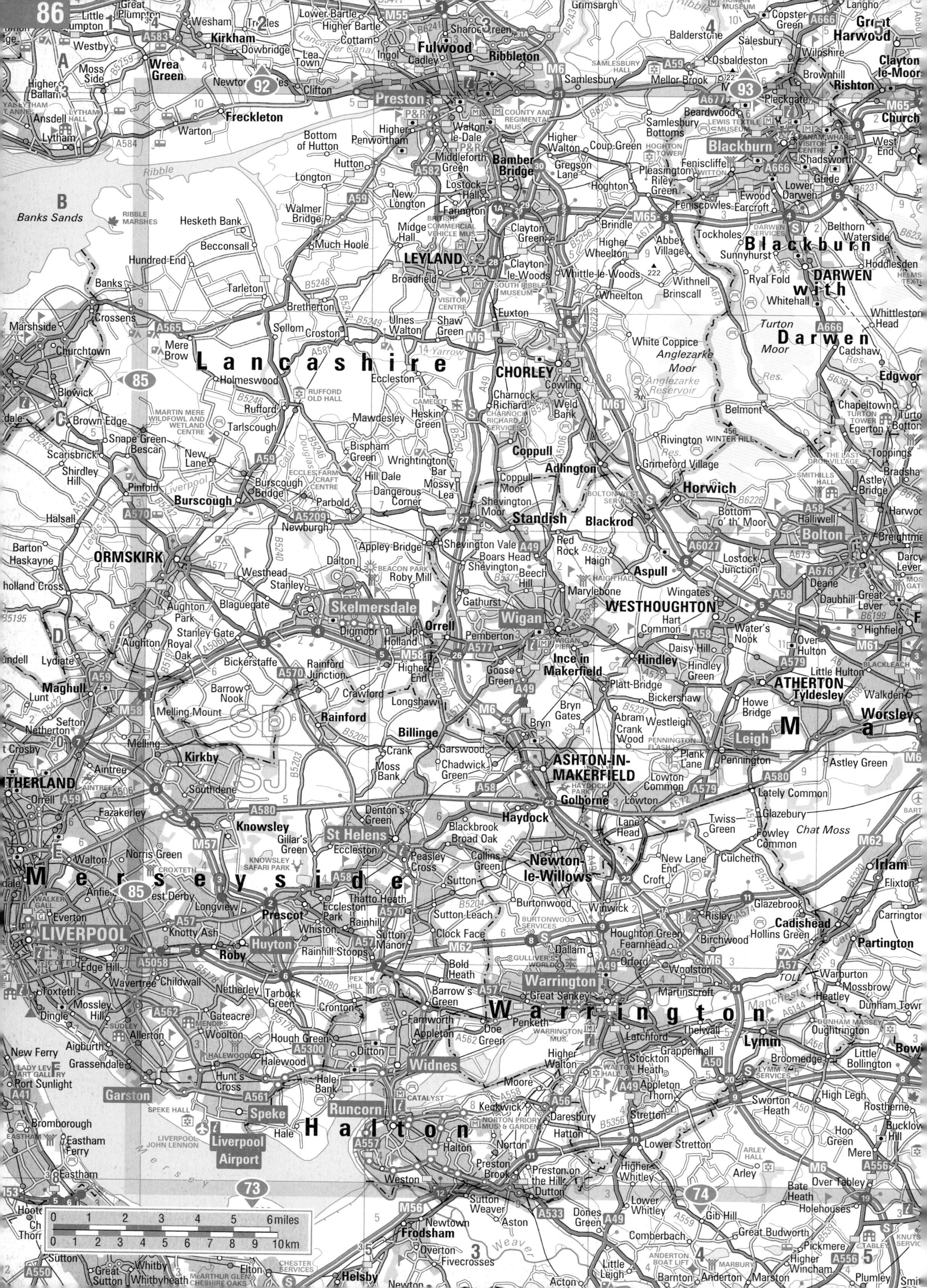

Lancashire
Merseyside
Warrington
Halton
Blackburn with Darwen
Preston
Fulwood
Ribbleton
Kirkham
Wrea Green
Lytham
Freckleton
Warton
Banks Sands
Ribble
Hesketh Bank
Much Hoole
Longton
Leyland
Bamber Bridge
Blackburn
Darwen
Chorley
Euxton
Croston
Tarleton
Banks
Crossens
Churchtown
Holmeswood
Rufford
Mawdesley
Eccleston
Coppull
Adlington
Horwich
Bolton
Standish
Blackrod
Aspull
Westhoughton
Wigan
Orrell
Skelmersdale
Ormskirk
Burscough
Parbold
Newburgh
Appley Bridge
Shevington
Ince in Makerfield
Hindley
Atherton
Tyldesley
Leigh
Ashton-in-Makerfield
Golborne
Haydock
Billinge
Rainford
Newton-le-Willows
St Helens
Knowsley
Kirkby
Maghull
Lydiate
Aughton
Melling
Crosby
Prescot
Huyton
Roby
Liverpool
Everton
Garston
Speke
Liverpool Airport
Hale
Widnes
Runcorn
Frodsham
Helsby
Daresbury
Stretton
Lymm
Partington
Cadishead
Irlam
Culcheth
Birchwood
Woolston
Thelwall
Grappenhall
Appleton
Great Sankey
Penketh
Rainhill
Whiston
Cronton
Hough Green
Halewood
Woolton
Allerton
Childwall
Wavertree
Toxteth
Dingle
Aigburth
Bromborough
Eastham
Port Sunlight
Great Sutton
Whitby
Elton
Comberbach
Great Budworth
Pickmere
Plumley
Rostherne
Bucklow Hill
Little Leigh
Barnton
Anderton
Marston
Acton
Weaver
Mersey
Chat Moss
Anglezarke Moor
Turton Moor
Rivington
Belmont
Egerton
Edgworth
Great Harwood
Clayton-le-Moors
Rishton
Church
Samlesbury
Mellor Brook
Osbaldeston
Salesbury
Wilpshire
Balderstone
Grimsargh
Ribble Marshes
Martin Mere Wildfowl and Wetland Centre
Rufford Old Hall
Knowsley Safari Park
Croxteth
Speke Hall
Norton Priory Museum & Gardens
Gulliver's World
Warrington Mus.
Catalyst
Anderton Boat Lift
Lady Lever Art Gallery
Haydock Park
Camelot
M6
M55
M65
M61
M58
M57
M62
M56
A59
A49
A580
A57
A56
0 1 2 3 4 5 6 miles
0 1 2 3 4 5 6 7 8 9 10 km

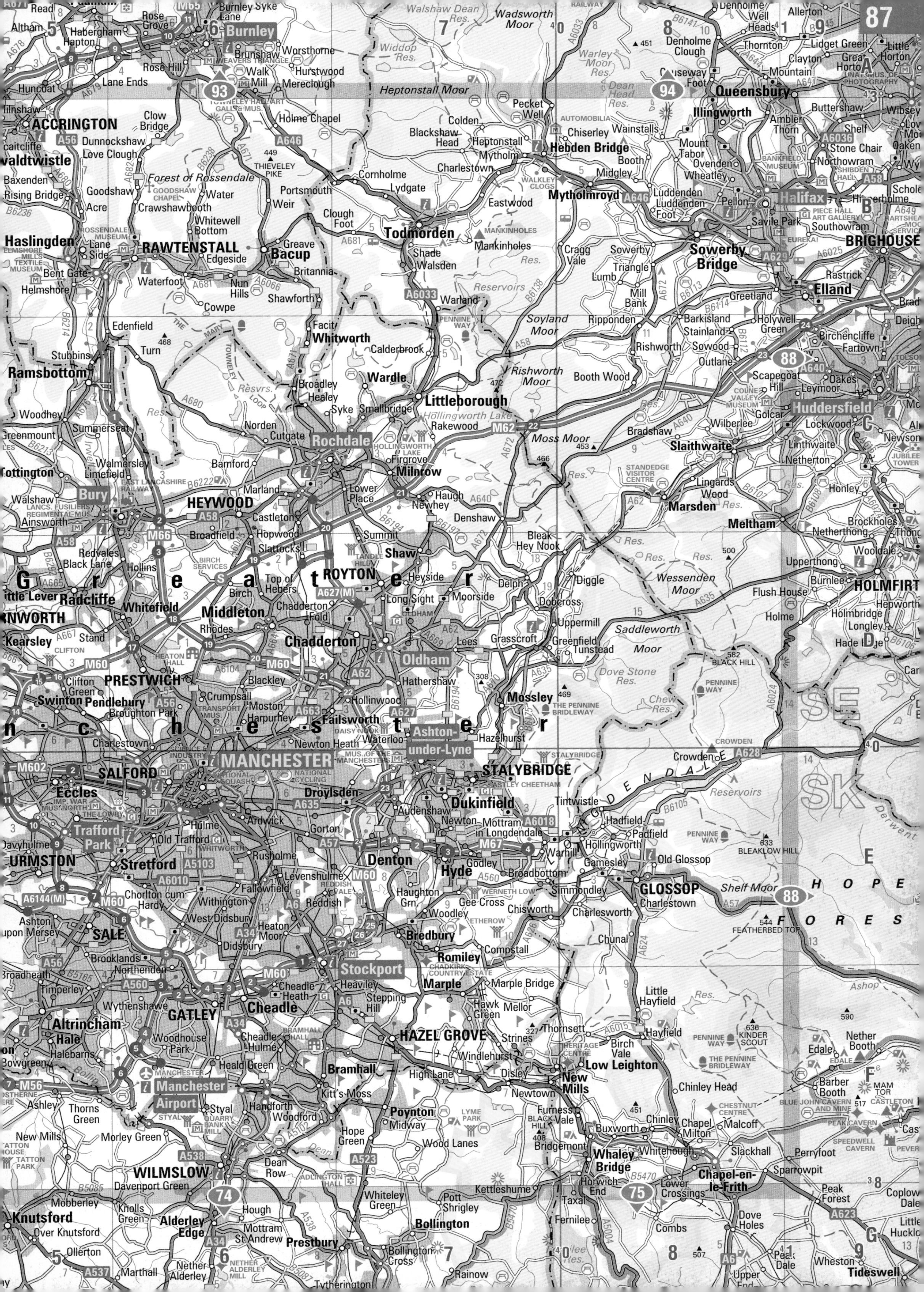
Burnley
Accrington
Oswaldtwistle
Haslingden
Rawtenstall
Bacup
Forest of Rossendale
Helmshore
Edenfield
Ramsbottom
Whitworth
Wardle
Littleborough
Todmorden
Walsden
Hebden Bridge
Heptonstall
Heptonstall Moor
Mytholmroyd
Halifax
Queensbury
Illingworth
Sowerby Bridge
Brighouse
Elland
Ripponden
Soyland Moor
Rishworth Moor
Booth Wood
Huddersfield
Slaithwaite
Marsden
Meltham
Holmfirth
Wessenden Moor
Saddleworth Moor
Rochdale
Milnrow
Heywood
Bury
Tottington
Radcliffe
Whitefield
Middleton
Royton
Shaw
Chadderton
Oldham
Prestwich
Swinton
Pendlebury
Salford
Eccles
Manchester
Trafford Park
Urmston
Stretford
Sale
Altrincham
Hale
Manchester Airport
Wilmslow
Knutsford
Alderley Edge
Prestbury
Bollington
Poynton
Bramhall
Cheadle
Gatley
Stockport
Hazel Grove
Marple
Romiley
Bredbury
Hyde
Denton
Dukinfield
Stalybridge
Ashton-under-Lyne
Droylsden
Mossley
Hollingworth
Glossop
Shelf Moor
Longdendale
Crowden
Bleaklow Hill
Kinder Scout
Hayfield
New Mills
Whaley Bridge
Chapel-en-le-Frith
Edale
Castleton
Tideswell
Hope Forest
Greater Manchester
SE
SK

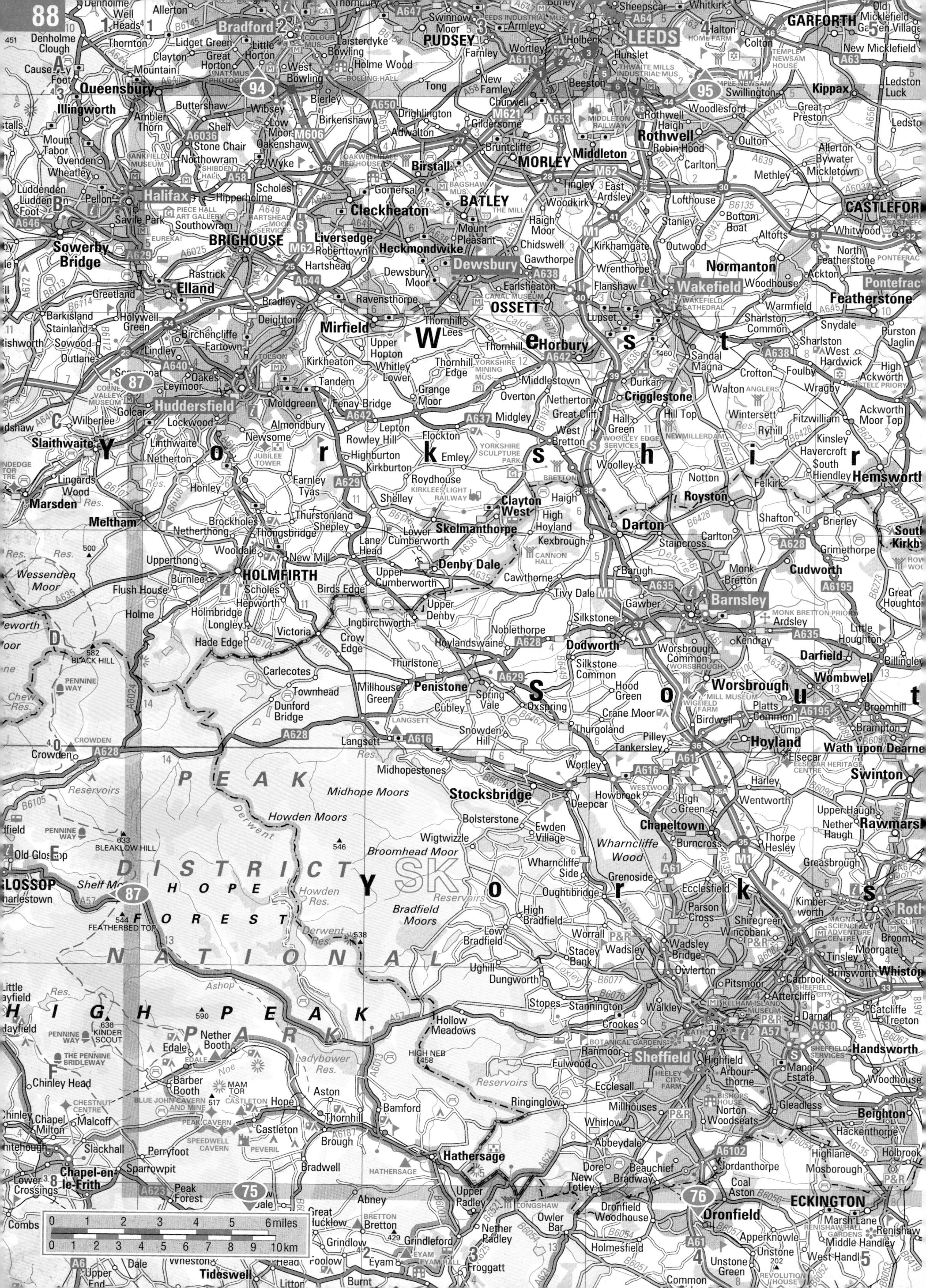

Denholme
Well Heads
Allerton
Bradford
Thornbury
Swinnow Moor
PUDSEY
Armley
Sheepscar
Whitkirk
LEEDS
Halton
GARFORTH
Garforth Village
Denholme Clough
Thornton
Lidget Green
Little Horton
Laisterdyke
Bowling
Farnley
Wortley
Holbeck
Hunslet
Colton
New Micklefield
Causeway Foot
Clayton
Great Horton
West Bowling
Holme Wood
Temple Newsam House
Queensbury
Mountain
Bolling Hall
Tong
New Farnley
Beeston
Thwaite Mills Industrial Mus.
Swillington
Kippax
Ledston Luck
Illingworth
Buttershaw
Wibsey
Bierley
Birkenshaw
Drighlington
Churwell
Gildersome
Rothwell
Woodlesford
Great Preston
Ledston
Ambler Thorn
Shelf
Low Moor
Adwalton
Middleton Railway
Haigh
Mount Tabor
Stone Chair
Oakenshaw
Bruntcliffe
Rothwell
Robin Hood
Oulton
Allerton Bywater
Ovenden
Northowram
Wyke
Oakwell Hall Red House
Birstall
MORLEY
Middleton
Carlton
Mickletown
Wheatley
Shibden Hall
Bankfield Museum
Scholes
Gomersal
Bagshaw Mus.
Tingley
East Ardsley
Methley
Luddenden
Luddenden Foot
Pellon
Halifax
Hipperholme
Cleckheaton
BATLEY
Woodkirk
Lofthouse
Castleford
Savile Park
Piece Hall Art Gallery
Southowram
Hartshead Moor Services
Liversedge
The Mill
Haigh Moor
Stanley
Bottom Boat
Whitwood
Sowerby Bridge
Eureka!
BRIGHOUSE
Roberttown
Heckmondwike
Mount Pleasant
Chidswell
Kirkhamgate
Outwood
Altofts
North Featherstone
Pontefract
Rastrick
Hartshead
Dewsbury
Gawthorpe
Wrenthorpe
Normanton
Ackton
Elland
Dewsbury Moor
Earlsheaton
Flanshaw
Wakefield
Woodhouse
Greetland
Bradley
Ravensthorpe
Canal Museum
OSSETT
Wakefield Cathedral
Featherstone
Barkisland
Stainland
Holywell Green
Deighton
Mirfield
Thornhill Lees
Lupset
Warmfield
Sharlston Common
Snydale
Purston Jaglin
Rishworth
Sowood
Birchencliffe
Fartown
Upper Hopton
Thornhill
Horbury
Sandal Magna
Sharlston
West Hardwick
High Ackworth
Outlane
Lindley
Tolson
Kirkheaton
Whitley Lower
Thornhill Edge
Yorkshire Mining Mus.
Middlestown
Durkar
Crofton
Foulby
Scapegoat Hill
Oakes
Leymoor
Tandem
Grange Moor
Overton
Netherton
Crigglestone
Walton
Wragby
Nostell Priory
Colne Valley Museum
Golcar
Huddersfield
Moldgreen
Fenay Bridge
Midgley
Great Cliff
Hill Top
Anglers
Wintersett
Ackworth Moor Top
Wilberlee
Lockwood
Almondbury
Lepton
Hall Green
West Bretton
Newmillerdam
Ryhill
Fitzwilliam
Slaithwaite
Linthwaite
Newsome
Rowley Hill
Flockton
Yorkshire Sculpture Park
Woolley Edge Services
Kinsley
Havercroft
Netherton
Jubilee Tower
Highburton
Emley
Woolley
South Hiendley
Hemsworth
Kirkburton
Roydhouse
Notton
Lingards Wood
Honley
Farnley Tyas
Kirklees Light Railway
Bretton
Royston
Felkirk
Marsden
Shelley
Clayton West
Haigh
Meltham
Brockholes
Thurstonland
Skelmanthorpe
High Hoyland
Darton
Shafton
Brierley
South Kirkby
Netherthong
Thongsbridge
Shepley
Lower Cumberworth
Lane Head
Kexbrough
Staincross
Carlton
Grimethorpe
Wessenden Moor
Upperthong
Wooldale
New Mill
Cannon Hall
Denby Dale
Monk Bretton
Cudworth
Burnlee
HOLMFIRTH
Upper Cumberworth
Cawthorne
Barugh
Flush House
Scholes
Birds Edge
Tivy Dale
Gawber
Barnsley
Great Houghton
Holme
Holmbridge
Hepworth
Upper Denby
Silkstone
Monk Bretton Priory
Ardsley
Longley
Victoria
Ingbirchworth
Noblethorpe
Little Houghton
Hade Edge
Crow Edge
Hoylandswaine
Dodworth
Worsbrough Common
Kendray
Darfield
Black Hill
Thurlstone
Silkstone Common
Billingley
Pennine Way
Carlecotes
Millhouse Green
Penistone
Hood Green
Worsbrough
Wombwell
Chew Res.
Townhead
Spring Vale
Mill Museum
Wigfield Farm
Dunford Bridge
Cubley
Oxspring
Crane Moor
Platts Common
Broomhill
Langsett
Snowden Hill
Thurgoland
Birdwell
Jump
Brampton
Crowden
Langsett
Pilley
Tankersley
Hoyland
Wath upon Dearne
Midhopestones
Wortley
Elsecar
Elsecar Heritage Centre
Swinton
PEAK
Midhope Moors
Stocksbridge
Howbrook
Westwood
Harley
Reservoirs
Deepcar
High Green
Wentworth
Howden Moors
Bolsterstone
Upper Haugh
Ewden Village
Chapeltown
Nether Haugh
Rawmarsh
Pennine Way
Wigtwizzle
Wharncliffe Wood
Burncross
Thorpe Hesley
Bleaklow Hill
Broomhead Moor
Old Glossop
DISTRICT
Wharncliffe Side
Greasbrough
GLOSSOP
Shelf Moor
HOPE
Howden Res.
SK
Oughtibridge
Grenoside
Ecclesfield
Kimberworth
Charlestown
Reservoirs
Parson Cross
FOREST
Bradfield Moors
High Bradfield
Shiregreen
Rotherham
Featherbed Top
Magna Science Adventure Centre
Wincobank
Broom
Derwent Res.
Low Bradfield
Worrall
Wadsley
Wadsley Bridge
Moorgate
NATIONAL
Stacey Bank
Tinsley
Owlerton
Brinsworth
Whiston
Ughill
Dungworth
Loxley
Pitsmoor
Carbrook
Hayfield
Ashop
Attercliffe
HIGH PEAK
Stopes
Stannington
Walkley
Kelham Island Museum
Darnall
Catcliffe
Treeton
Kinder Scout
Nether Booth
Hollow Meadows
Crookes
Sheffield City Airport
Edale
Broomhill
Botanical Gardens
Handsworth
Ladybower Res.
High Neb
Ranmoor
Sheffield
Highfield
Sheffield Services
Manor Estate
The Pennine Bridleway
Arbourthorne
Chinley Head
Barber Booth
Mam Tor
Fulwood
Woodhouse
Heeley City Farm
Chestnut Centre
Aston
Reservoirs
Ecclesall
Bishops House
Gleadless
Beighton
Blue John Cavern and Mine
Castleton
Hope
Bamford
Millhouses
Norton
Woodseats
Chinley
Chapel Milton
Malcoff
Peak Cavern
Thornhill
Castleton
Ringinglow
Whirlow
Hackenthorpe
Chinley
Speedwell Cavern
Peveril
Brough
Abbeydale
Highlane
Whitehough
Slackhall
Perryfoot
Hathersage
Holbrook
Sparrowpit
Bradwell
Hathersage
Dore
Beauchief
Jordanthorpe
Mosborough
Chapel-en-le-Frith
Lower Crossings
Peak Forest
New Totley
Bradway
Coal Aston
Upper Padley
Longshaw
Dronfield
ECKINGTON
Combs
Abney
Dronfield Woodhouse
Marsh Lane
Great Hucklow
Bretton
Owler Bar
Renishaw Hall Gardens
Renishaw
Nether Padley
Apperknowle
Middle Handley
Grindlow
Grindleford
Holmesfield
Unstone
West Handley
Foolow
Eyam
Eyam Hall
Froggatt
Unstone Green
Revolution House
Upper End
Dale
Wheston
Tideswell
Burnt
Litton
Common
Yorkshire
West
South Yorkshire
0 1 2 3 4 5 6 miles
0 1 2 3 4 5 6 7 8 9 10 km

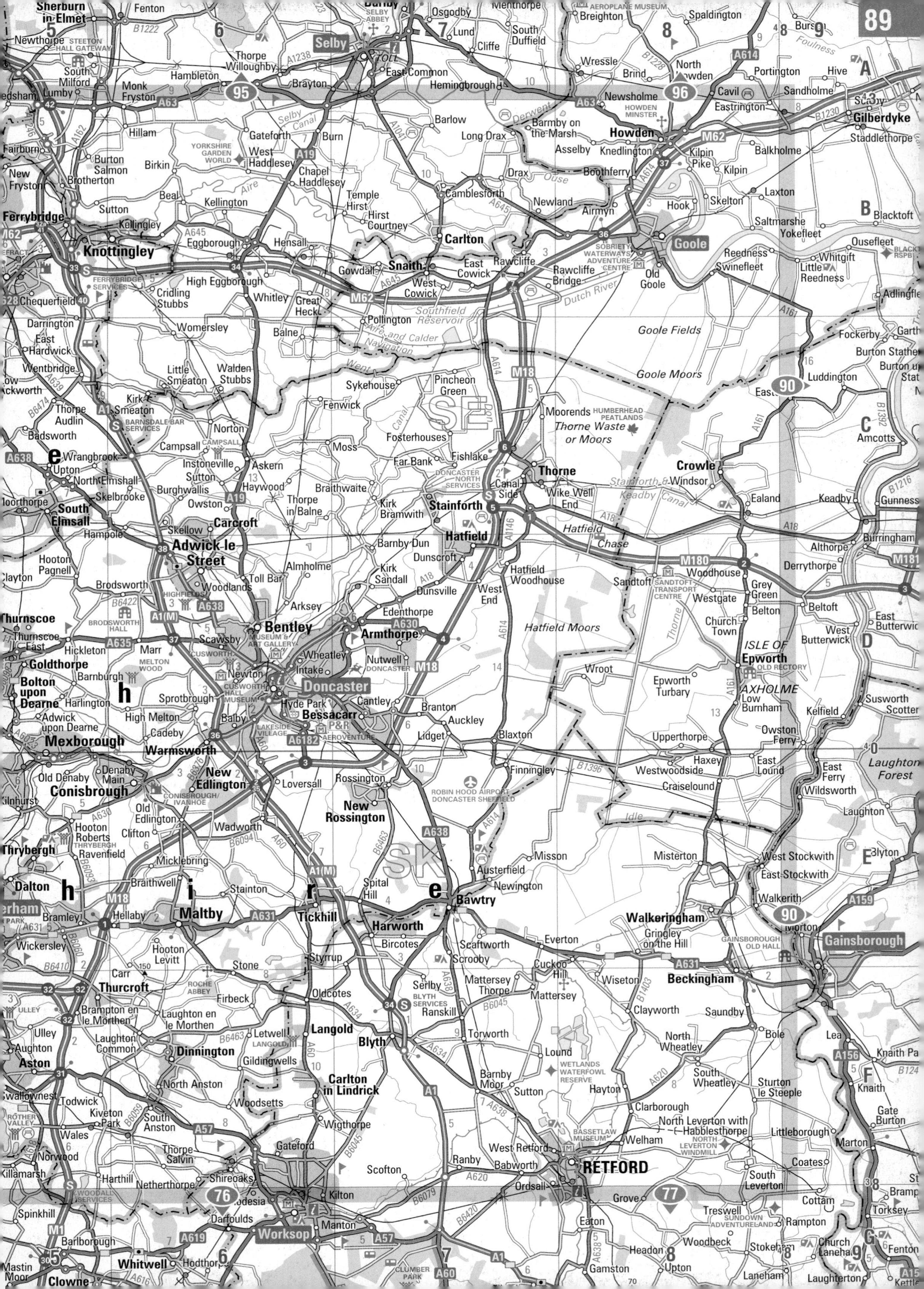
Sherburn in Elmet
Fenton
Selby
Osgodby
Menthorpe
Breighton
Spaldington
Newthorpe
Thorpe Willoughby
Lund
Cliffe
South Duffield
Wressle
North Howden
Portington
Hive
South Milford
Hambleton
East Common
Brind
Monk Fryston
Brayton
Hemingbrough
Newsholme
Cavil
Sandholme
Lumby
Eastrington
Gilberdyke
Staddlethorpe
Barlow
Barmby on the Marsh
Howden
Howden Minster
Hillam
Gateforth
Burn
Long Drax
Asselby
Knedlington
Kilpin Pike
Balkholme
Fairburn
Burton Salmon
Birkin
West Haddlesey
Chapel Haddlesey
Drax
Boothferry
Kilpin
Brotherton
Temple Hirst
Camblesforth
Newland
Hook
Skelton
Laxton
Beal
Kellington
Hirst Courtney
Airmyn
Saltmarshe
Yokefleet
Blacktoft
Ferrybridge
Sutton
Kellingley
Carlton
Goole
Knottingley
Eggborough
Hensall
Reedness
Whitgift
Ousefleet
Snaith
East Cowick
Rawcliffe
Rawcliffe Bridge
Swinefleet
Little Reedness
Gowdall
West Cowick
Old Goole
High Eggborough
Chequerfield
Cridling Stubbs
Whitley
Great Heck
Pollington
Southfield Reservoir
Adlingfleet
Darrington
Womersley
Balne
Aire and Calder Navigation
Goole Fields
East Hardwick
Fockerby
Garthorpe
Wentbridge
Little Smeaton
Walden Stubbs
Pincheon Green
Goole Moors
Burton Stather
Ackworth
Kirk Smeaton
Sykehouse
Fenwick
Luddington
Thorpe Audlin
Moorends
Humberhead Peatlands
Thorne Waste or Moors
Badsworth
Norton
Fosterhouses
Amcotts
Campsall
Moss
Fishlake
Thorne
Crowle
Wrangbrook
Upton
Instoneville
Askern
Far Bank
Doncaster North Services
Canal Side
Stainforth & Keadby Canal
Windsor
North Elmsall
Sutton
Burghwallis
Haywood
Braithwaite
Wike Well End
Ealand
Keadby
Gunness
South Elmsall
Skelbrooke
Owston
Thorpe in Balne
Kirk Bramwith
Stainforth
Hampole
Skellow
Carcroft
Hatfield
Hatfield Chase
Burringham
Adwick le Street
Barnby Dun
Dunscroft
Althorpe
Hooton Pagnell
Almholme
Kirk Sandall
Hatfield Woodhouse
Sandtoft
Woodhouse
Derrythorpe
Clayton
Brodsworth
Woodlands
Toll Bar
Dunsville
West End
Sandtoft Transport Centre
Grey Green
Westgate
Belton
Beltoft
Thurnscoe
Arksey
Edenthorpe
Church Town
East Butterwick
Thurnscoe East
Hickleton
Marr
Scawsby
Bentley
Armthorpe
Hatfield Moors
West Butterwick
Goldthorpe
Barnburgh
Melton Wood
Cusworth
Wheatley
Nutwell
Isle of Axholme
Epworth
Old Rectory
Bolton upon Dearne
Newton
Intake
Doncaster
Wroot
Epworth Turbary
Susworth
Scotter
Harlington
Sprotbrough
Hyde Park
Cantley
Branton
Low Burnham
Kelfield
Adwick upon Dearne
High Melton
Balby
Bessacarr
Auckley
Owston Ferry
Mexborough
Cadeby
Lakeside Village
Lidget
Blaxton
Upperthorpe
Warmsworth
Aeroventure
Haxey
East Lound
Laughton Forest
Old Denaby
Denaby Main
New Edlington
Loversall
Rossington
Finningley
Westwoodside
East Ferry
Conisbrough
Conisbrough Ivanhoe
Robin Hood Airport Doncaster Sheffield
Craiseland
Wildsworth
Old Edlington
New Rossington
Idle
Laughton
Hooton Roberts
Wadworth
Clifton
Thrybergh
Ravenfield
Micklebring
Misson
Misterton
West Stockwith
Blyton
East Stockwith
Dalton
Braithwell
Stainton
Spital Hill
Austerfield
Newington
Walkerith
Bramley
Hellaby
Maltby
Tickhill
Bawtry
Harworth
Walkeringham
Morton
Wickersley
Hooton Levitt
Bircotes
Scaftworth
Everton
Gringley on the Hill
Gainsborough
Gainsborough Old Hall
Styrrup
Scrooby
Carr
Stone
Cuckoo Hill
Wiseton
Beckingham
Thurcroft
Roche Abbey
Oldcotes
Serlby
Mattersey Thorpe
Mattersey
Firbeck
Blyth Services
Ranskill
Clayworth
Saundby
Brampton en le Morthen
Laughton en le Morthen
Ulley
Letwell
Langold
Torworth
Bole
Lea
Aughton
Laughton Common
Dinnington
Blyth
North Wheatley
Aston
Gildingwells
Lound
Wetlands Waterfowl Reserve
Knaith Park
Swallownest
North Anston
Carlton in Lindrick
Barnby Moor
Sutton
Hayton
South Wheatley
Sturton le Steeple
Knaith
Todwick
Kiveton Park
Woodsetts
Clarborough
Gate Burton
Rother Valley
South Anston
Wigthorpe
North Leverton with Habblesthorpe
Wales
Gateford
Bassetlaw Museum
Welham
North Leverton Windmill
Littleborough
Marton
Norwood
Thorpe Salvin
West Retford
Killamarsh
Shireoaks
Scofton
Ranby
Babworth
Retford
Coates
South Leverton
Harthill
Netherthorpe
Kilton
Ordsall
Grove
Torksey
Woodall Services
Rhodesia
Cottam
Spinkhill
Darfoulds
Worksop
Manton
Eaton
Treswell
Sundown Adventureland
Rampton
Barlborough
Church Laneham
Woodbeck
Mastin Moor
Whitwell
Hodthorpe
Clumber Park
Headon
Upton
Stokeham
Fenton
Clowne
Gamston
Laneham
Laughterton
Kettlethorpe

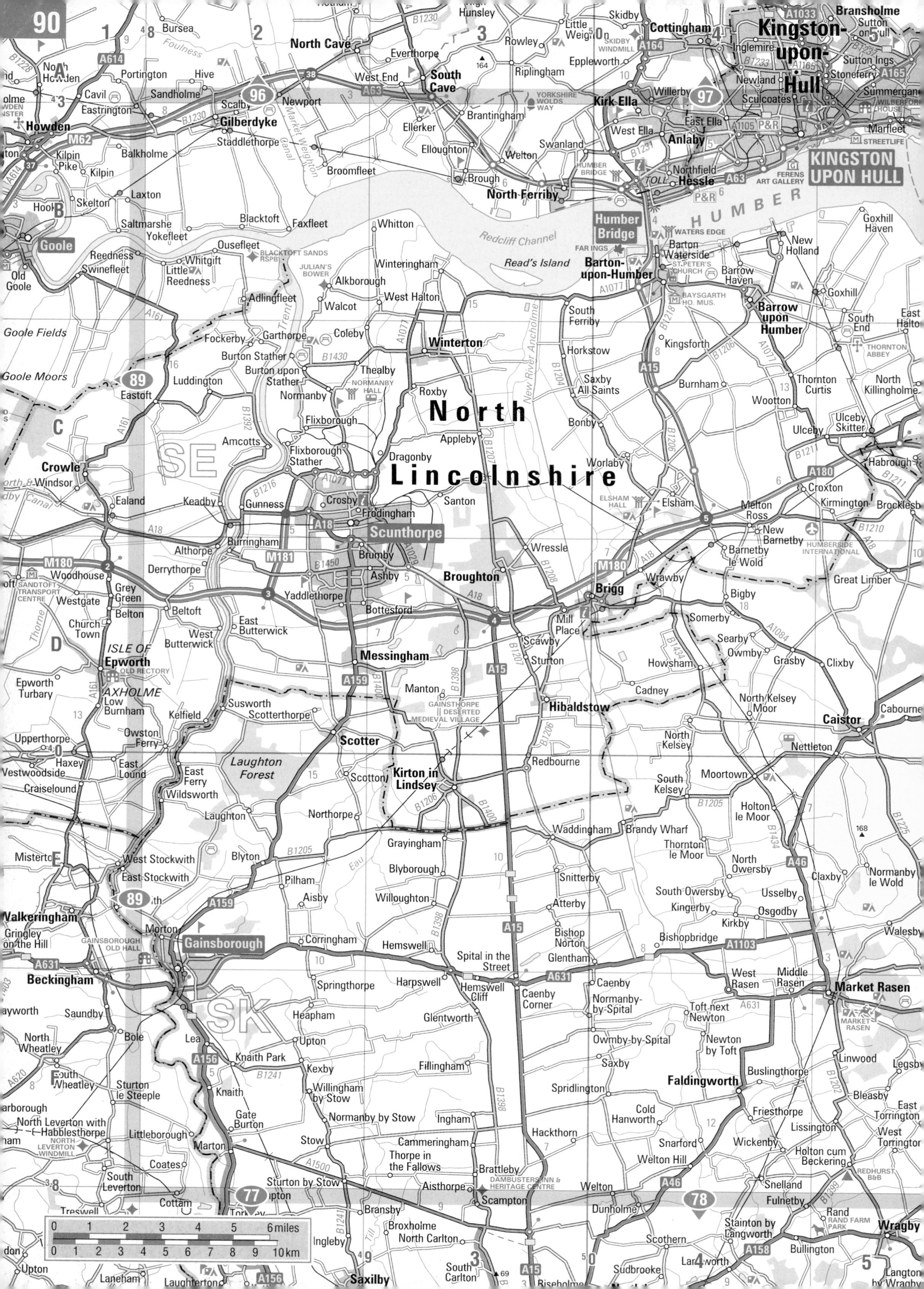
Bursea
Foulness
North Cave
Hunsley
Rowley
Little Weighton
Skidby
SKIDBY WINDMILL
Cottingham
Kingston-upon-Hull
Bransholme
Sutton on Hull
Inglemire
Sutton Ings
Newland
Stoneferry
Summergangs
Everthorpe
Eppleworth
Riplingham
North Howden
Portington
Hive
West End
South Cave
Cavil
Sandholme
Eastrington
Scalby
Newport
Gilberdyke
YORKSHIRE WOLDS WAY
Kirk Ella
Willerby
Sculcoates
WILBERFORCE HOUSE
Marfleet
STREETLIFE
Howden
Brantingham
Ellerker
East Ella
West Ella
Anlaby
Staddlethorpe
Market Weighton Canal
Elloughton
Swanland
Kilpin Pike
Kilpin
Balkholme
Broomfleet
Welton
HUMBER BRIDGE
Northfield
Hessle
TOLL
KINGSTON UPON HULL
FERENS ART GALLERY
Brough
North Ferriby
Laxton
Skelton
Hook
Saltmarshe
Yokefleet
Blacktoft
Faxfleet
Whitton
HUMBER
Goxhill Haven
Goole
Humber Bridge
WATERS EDGE
New Holland
Redcliff Channel
Barton Waterside
Ousefleet
BLACKTOFT SANDS RSPB
FAR INGS
ST PETER'S CHURCH
Reedness
Whitgift
Little Reedness
Swinefleet
Old Goole
JULIAN'S BOWER
Read's Island
Barton-upon-Humber
Barrow Haven
Winteringham
Alkborough
Adlingfleet
Walcot
West Halton
BAYSGARTH HO. MUS.
Goxhill
Barrow upon Humber
South Ferriby
South End
East Halton
Goole Fields
Fockerby
Garthorpe
Coleby
Winterton
Kingsforth
Horkstow
THORNTON ABBEY
Burton Stather
Burton upon Stather
Thealby
NORMANBY HALL
Goole Moors
Eastoft
Luddington
Normanby
Roxby
Saxby All Saints
Burnham
Thornton Curtis
North Killingholme
Wootton
North Lincolnshire
New River Ancholme
Flixborough
Bonby
Ulceby
Ulceby Skitter
Amcotts
Appleby
Flixborough Stather
Dragonby
Worlaby
Habrough
Crowle
North & Windsor
Ealand
Keadby
Gunness
Crosby
Frodingham
Santon
ELSHAM HALL
Elsham
Croxton
Melton Ross
Kirmington
Brocklesby
Scunthorpe
Burringham
Althorpe
Brumby
Wressle
New Barnetby
Barnetby le Wold
HUMBERSIDE INTERNATIONAL
Woodhouse
SANDTOFT TRANSPORT CENTRE
Derrythorpe
Grey Green
Westgate
Ashby
Broughton
Brigg
Wrawby
Great Limber
Belton
Beltoft
Yaddlethorpe
Bigby
Church Town
East Butterwick
West Butterwick
Bottesford
Mill Place
Somerby
Scawby
Searby
Owmby
Grasby
Clixby
ISLE OF AXHOLME
Epworth
OLD RECTORY
Messingham
Sturton
Howsham
Epworth Turbary
Manton
Cadney
Low Burnham
Susworth
Scotterthorpe
Kelfield
GAINSTHORPE DESERTED MEDIEVAL VILLAGE
Hibaldstow
North Kelsey Moor
Caistor
Cabourne
Owston Ferry
Upperthorpe
Scotter
North Kelsey
Nettleton
Haxey
East Lound
Laughton Forest
Redbourne
Westwoodside
East Ferry
Scotton
Kirton in Lindsey
South Kelsey
Moortown
Craiseland
Wildsworth
Holton le Moor
Laughton
Northorpe
Waddingham
Brandy Wharf
Grayingham
Thornton le Moor
Misterton
West Stockwith
Blyton
North Owersby
Normanby le Wold
Blyborough
East Stockwith
Pilham
Snitterby
Claxby
Aisby
South Owersby
Usselby
Willoughton
Atterby
Kingerby
Osgodby
Walkeringham
Kirkby
Morton
Gringley on the Hill
GAINSBOROUGH OLD HALL
Gainsborough
Corringham
Hemswell
Bishop Norton
Bishopbridge
Walesby
Spital in the Street
Glentham
Beckingham
Springthorpe
Harpswell
Hemswell Cliff
Caenby
Caenby Corner
West Rasen
Middle Rasen
Market Rasen
Normanby-by-Spital
Toft next Newton
MARKET RASEN
Saundby
Heapham
Glentworth
North Wheatley
Bole
Lea
Upton
Owmby-by-Spital
Newton by Toft
Knaith Park
Fillingham
Saxby
Linwood
South Wheatley
Sturton le Steeple
Kexby
Buslingthorpe
Knaith
Willingham by Stow
Spridlington
Faldingworth
Bleasby
Gate Burton
Cold Hanworth
North Leverton with Habblesthorpe
Normanby by Stow
Ingham
Friesthorpe
East Torrington
NORTH LEVERTON WINDMILL
Littleborough
Stow
Hackthorn
Lissington
Marton
Cammeringham
Snarford
Wickenby
West Torrington
Coates
Thorpe in the Fallows
Welton Hill
Holton cum Beckering
South Leverton
Brattleby
Sturton by Stow
DAMBUSTERS INN & HERITAGE CENTRE
REDHURST B&B
Aisthorpe
Welton
Snelland
Cottam
Scampton
Dunholme
Fulnetby
Treswell
Bransby
Rand
RAND FARM PARK
Wragby
Broxholme
Stainton by Langworth
North Carlton
Scothern
Ingleby
Bullington
Upton
Laneham
Laughterton
Saxilby
South Carlton
Sudbrooke
Langworth
Langton by Wragby
SE
SK
0 1 2 3 4 5 6 miles
0 1 2 3 4 5 6 7 8 9 10 km

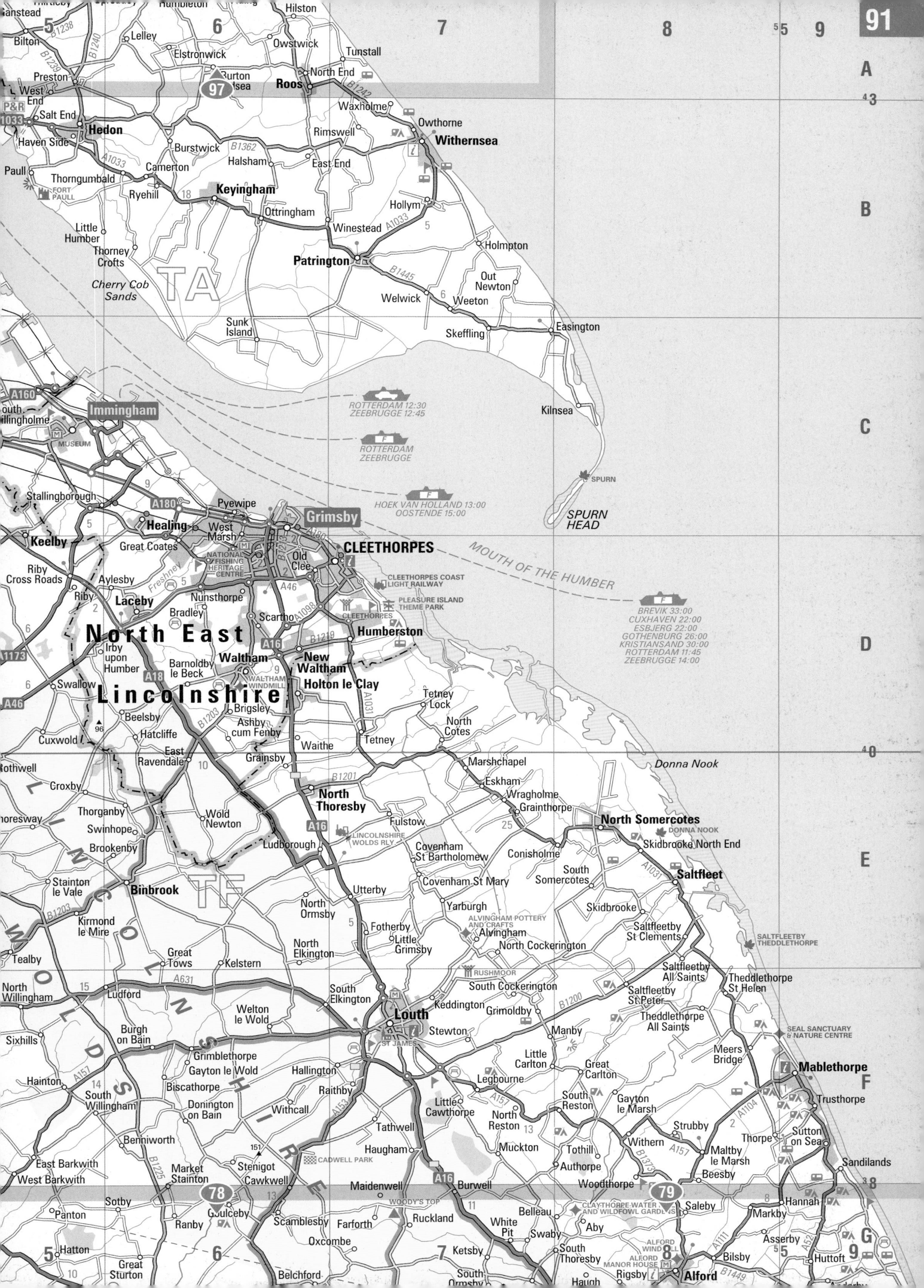

Hilston
Lelley
Owstwick
Tunstall
Bilton
Elstronwick
Preston
Burton Pidsea
North End
Roos
West End
Waxholme
Salt End
Hedon
Owthorne
Rimswell
Haven Side
Withernsea
Burstwick
Halsham
East End
Paull
Camerton
Thorngumbald
FORT PAULL
Ryehill
Keyingham
Hollym
Ottringham
Little Humber
Winestead
Holmpton
Thorney Crofts
Patrington
Cherry Cob Sands
Out Newton
Welwick
Weeton
Sunk Island
Skeffling
Easington
ROTTERDAM 12:30
ZEEBRUGGE 12:45
Immingham
MUSEUM
ROTTERDAM
ZEEBRUGGE
Kilnsea
SPURN
Stallingborough
HOEK VAN HOLLAND 13:00
OOSTENDE 15:00
Pyewipe
Healing
Grimsby
SPURN HEAD
Keelby
West Marsh
CLEETHORPES
MOUTH OF THE HUMBER
Great Coates
NATIONAL FISHING HERITAGE CENTRE
Old Clee
Riby Cross Roads
Aylesby
CLEETHORPES COAST LIGHT RAILWAY
Riby
Laceby
Nunsthorpe
PLEASURE ISLAND THEME PARK
Bradley
Scartho
CLEETHORPES
BREVIK 33:00
CUXHAVEN 22:00
ESBJERG 22:00
GOTHENBURG 26:00
KRISTIANSAND 30:00
ROTTERDAM 11:45
ZEEBRUGGE 14:00
North East Lincolnshire
Humberston
Irby upon Humber
Barnoldby le Beck
Waltham
New Waltham
Swallow
WALTHAM WINDMILL
Holton le Clay
Tetney Lock
Brigsley
Beelsby
Ashby cum Fenby
North Cotes
Hatcliffe
Waithe
Tetney
Cuxwold
East Ravendale
Grainsby
Marshchapel
Donna Nook
Rothwell
Eskham
Croxby
North Thoresby
Wragholme
Grainthorpe
Thorganby
Wold Newton
Fulstow
North Somercotes
DONNA NOOK
Swinhope
LINCOLNSHIRE WOLDS RLY.
Skidbrooke North End
Brookenby
Ludborough
Covenham St Bartholomew
Conisholme
Saltfleet
Stainton le Vale
Binbrook
Covenham St Mary
South Somercotes
Utterby
North Ormsby
Yarburgh
Skidbrooke
Kirmond le Mire
Fotherby
ALVINGHAM POTTERY AND CRAFTS
Alvingham
Saltfleetby St Clements
Little Grimsby
SALTFLEETBY THEDDLETHORPE
Tealby
Great Tows
Kelstern
North Elkington
North Cockerington
RUSHMOOR
Saltfleetby All Saints
Theddlethorpe St Helen
North Willingham
Ludford
South Elkington
South Cockerington
Saltfleetby St Peter
Keddington
Grimoldby
Theddlethorpe All Saints
Welton le Wold
Louth
Sixhills
Burgh on Bain
Stewton
Manby
SEAL SANCTUARY & NATURE CENTRE
ST JAMES
Little Carlton
Meers Bridge
Grimblethorpe
Great Carlton
Mablethorpe
Gayton le Wold
Hallington
Legbourne
Hainton
Biscathorpe
Raithby
South Reston
Gayton le Marsh
Trusthorpe
South Willingham
Little Cawthorpe
Donington on Bain
Withcall
North Reston
Strubby
Tathwell
Sutton on Sea
Withern
Thorpe
Benniworth
Maltby le Marsh
Muckton
Tothill
Haugham
Sandilands
East Barkwith
CADWELL PARK
Authorpe
Beesby
Stenigot
Market Stainton
West Barkwith
Woodthorpe
Cawkwell
Burwell
Maidenwell
Hannah
WOODY'S TOP
Sotby
Saleby
Belleau
CLAYTHORPE WATER AND WILDFOWL GARDENS
Markby
Goulceby
Panton
Scamblesby
Ruckland
Farforth
White Pit
Ranby
Aby
Swaby
Asserby
Oxcombe
ALFORD WINDMILL
Hatton
Ketsby
South Thoresby
Bilsby
ALFORD MANOR HOUSE
Huttoft
Great Sturton
Belchford
Rigsby
Alford
South Ormsby
Haugh

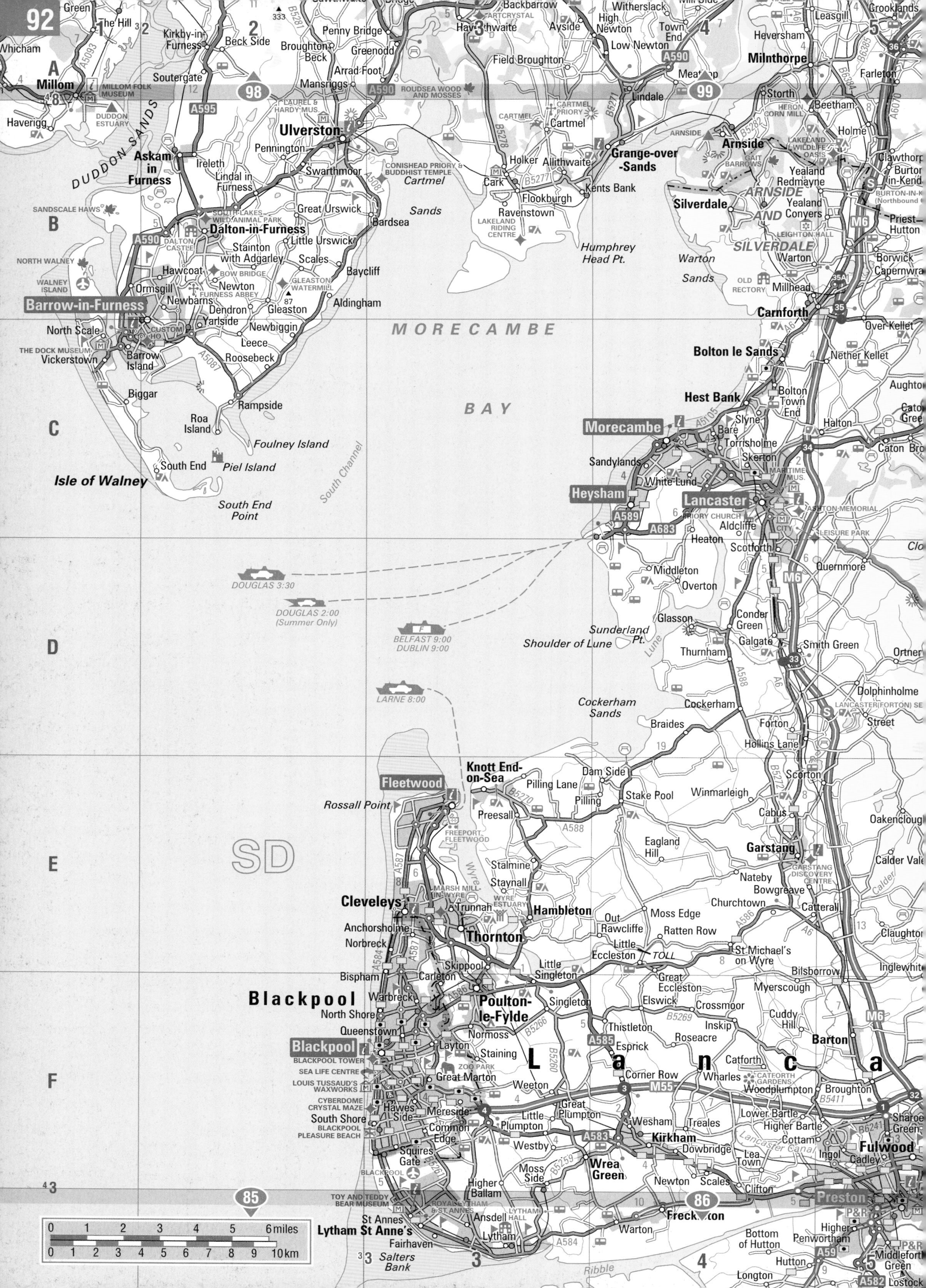
Green
The Hill
Whicham
Kirkby-in-Furness
Beck Side
Broughton Beck
Penny Bridge
Greenodd
Arrad Foot
Mansriggs
Haverthwaite
Backbarrow
Ayside
Witherslack
High Newton
Low Newton
Town End
Leasgill
Crooklands
Heversham
Milnthorpe
Farleton
Millom
MILLOM FOLK MUSEUM
Haverigg
DUDDON ESTUARY
DUDDON SANDS
Soutergate
A595
A590
98
99
ROUDSEA WOOD AND MOSSES
LAUREL & HARDY MUS.
Ulverston
Field Broughton
Lindale
Meathop
Storth
HERON CORN MILL
Beetham
Holme
CARTMEL PRIORY
CARTMEL
Cartmel
Grange-over-Sands
Allithwaite
Holker
Cark
Flookburgh
Kents Bank
Ravenstown
LAKELAND RIDING CENTRE
ARNSIDE
Arnside
LAKELAND WILDLIFE OASIS
GAIT BARROWS
Clawthorpe
Burton-in-Kendal
Yealand Redmayne
Yealand Conyers
ARNSIDE AND SILVERDALE
Silverdale
LEIGHTON HALL
Priest Hutton
Warton
Borwick
Capernwray
Millhead
OLD RECTORY
Carnforth
Over Kellet
Nether Kellet
Bolton le Sands
Bolton Town End
Hest Bank
Aughton
Halton
Caton
Slyne
Bare
Torrisholme
Skerton
Morecambe
Sandylands
White Lund
Heysham
Lancaster
MARITIME MUS.
PRIORY CHURCH
ASHTON MEMORIAL
LEISURE PARK
Aldcliffe
Heaton
Scotforth
Quernmore
Middleton
Overton
Glasson
Conder Green
Galgate
Smith Green
Ortner
Thurnham
Sunderland Pt.
Shoulder of Lune
Lune
Cockerham Sands
Cockerham
Dolphinholme
Forton
LANCASTER (FORTON) SE
Street
Braides
Hollins Lane
Scorton
Dam Side
Stake Pool
Pilling Lane
Pilling
Winmarleigh
Cabus
Oakenclough
Garstang
GARSTANG DISCOVERY CENTRE
Calder Vale
Eagland Hill
Nateby
Bowgreave
Churchtown
Catterall
Claughton
Askam in Furness
Ireleth
Pennington
Swarthmoor
Lindal in Furness
CONISHEAD PRIORY & BUDDHIST TEMPLE
Cartmel Sands
SANDSCALE HAWS
SOUTH LAKES WILD ANIMAL PARK
Dalton-in-Furness
DALTON CASTLE
Great Urswick
Bardsea
Little Urswick
Stainton with Adgarley
Scales
Baycliff
Humphrey Head Pt.
Warton Sands
NORTH WALNEY
WALNEY ISLAND
Hawcoat
BOW BRIDGE
Ormsgill
Newton
FURNESS ABBEY
GLEASTON WATERMILL
Newbarns
Dendron
Gleaston
Aldingham
Barrow-in-Furness
North Scale
Yarlside
CUSTOM HO
Newbiggin
THE DOCK MUSEUM
Vickerstown
Barrow Island
Leece
Roosebeck
MORECAMBE BAY
Biggar
Rampside
Roa Island
Foulney Island
South End
Piel Island
Isle of Walney
South Channel
South End Point
DOUGLAS 3:30
DOUGLAS 2:00 (Summer Only)
BELFAST 9:00 DUBLIN 9:00
LARNE 8:00
Knott End-on-Sea
Fleetwood
Rossall Point
Preesall
FREEPORT FLEETWOOD
SD
Stalmine
Staynall
Wyre
MARSH MILL-IN-WYRE
WYRE ESTUARY
Cleveleys
Trunnah
Hambleton
Anchorsholme
Thornton
Out Rawcliffe
Moss Edge
Ratten Row
Norbreck
Little Eccleston
TOLL
St Michael's on Wyre
Skippool
Little Singleton
Bilsborrow
Inglewhite
Bispham
Carleton
Great Eccleston
Myerscough
Blackpool
Warbreck
Poulton-le-Fylde
Singleton
Elswick
Crossmoor
North Shore
Thistleton
Cuddy Hill
Queenstown
Normoss
Inskip
Roseacre
Barton
Blackpool
BLACKPOOL TOWER
Layton
Staining
Esprick
SEA LIFE CENTRE
ZOO PARK
Lancashire
Catforth
LOUIS TUSSAUD'S WAXWORKS
Great Marton
Corner Row
Wharles
CATFORTH GARDENS
Woodplumpton
Broughton
CYBERDOME CRYSTAL MAZE
Hawes Side
Weeton
M55
Mereside
Little Plumpton
Great Plumpton
Lower Bartle
Sharoe Green
South Shore
BLACKPOOL PLEASURE BEACH
Common Edge
Wesham
Treales
Higher Bartle
Kirkham
Cottam
Fulwood
Westby
Dowbridge
Ingol
Cadley
Lancaster Canal
Squires Gate
BLACKPOOL
Moss Side
Wrea Green
Lea Town
Higher Ballam
Newton
Scales
Clifton
Preston
TOY AND TEDDY BEAR MUSEUM
ROYAL LYTHAM & ST ANNES
LYTHAM HALL
St Annes
Lytham St Anne's
Ansdell
Lytham
Freckleton
Warton
Fairhaven
Salters Bank
Bottom of Hutton
Higher Penwortham
Middleforth Green
Hutton
Longton
Lostock
Ribble
85
86
M6
A6
A588
A589
A683
A585
A583
A584
A586
A587
A5087
B5269
B5411
0 1 2 3 4 5 6 miles
0 1 2 3 4 5 6 7 8 9 10 km

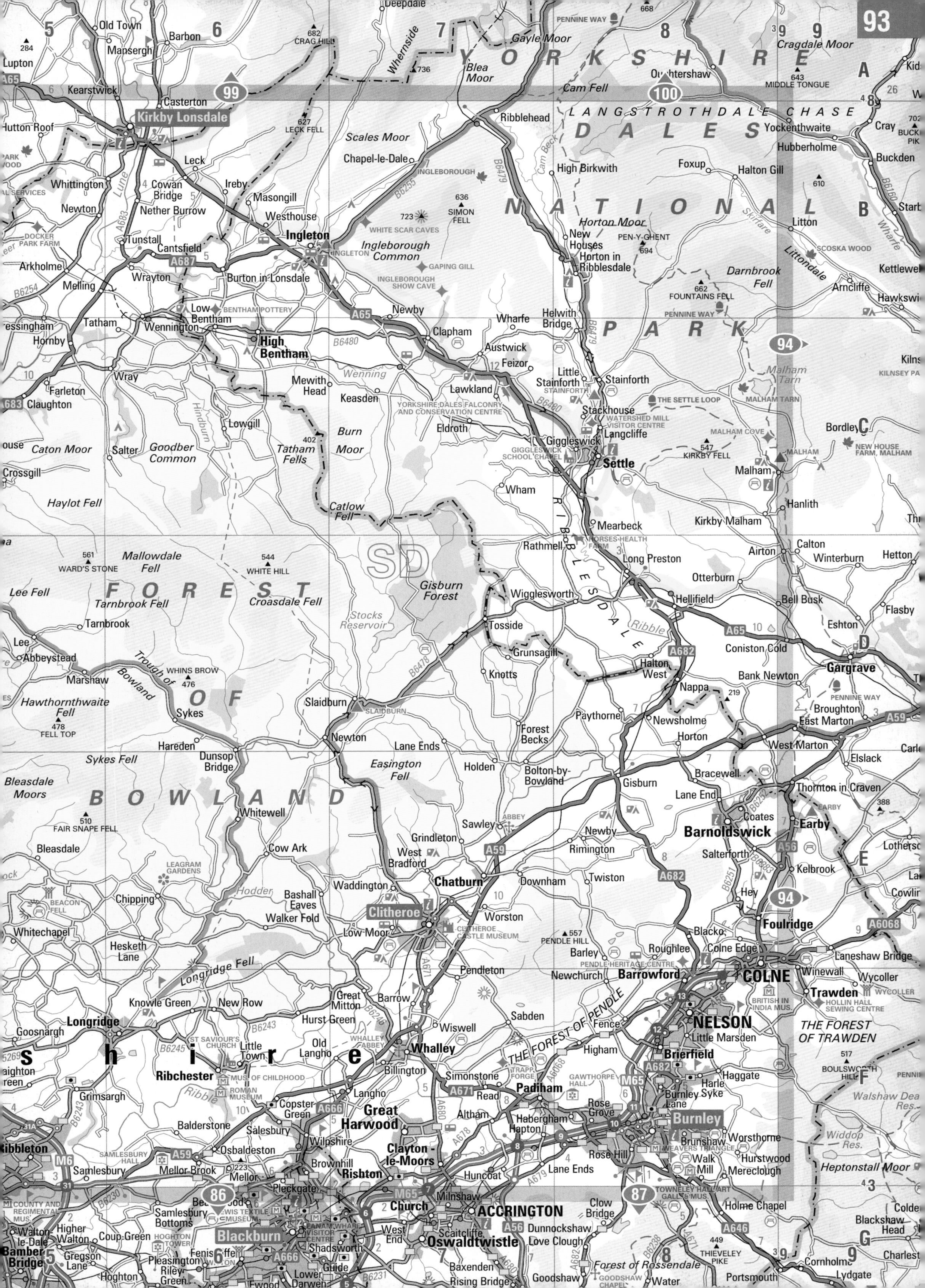
Old Town
Barbon
Mansergh
682 CRAG HILL
Deepdale
Whernside
736
Blea Moor
Gayle Moor
PENNINE WAY
668
Cragdale Moor
YORKSHIRE
Oughtershaw
643 MIDDLE TONGUE
Cam Fell
Lupton
284
Kearstwick
Casterton
99
100
Kirkby Lonsdale
Hutton Roof
627 LECK FELL
Ribblehead
LANGSTROTHDALE CHASE
DALES
Yockenthwaite
Cray
Hubberholme
Buckden
Scales Moor
Chapel-le-Dale
INGLEBOROUGH
Leck
Cam Beck
High Birkwith
Foxup
Halton Gill
610
Whittington
Cowan Bridge
Ireby
Masongill
636 SIMON FELL
723
Newton
Nether Burrow
Westhouse
NATIONAL
Horton Moor
Litton
WHITE SCAR CAVES
DOCKER PARK FARM
Tunstall
Cantsfield
Ingleton
INGLETON
Ingleborough Common
New Houses
PEN-Y-GHENT
694
Horton in Ribblesdale
SCOSKA WOOD
Littondale
Kettlewell
Arkholme
A687
GAPING GILL
Darnbrook Fell
Wrayton
Burton in Lonsdale
INGLEBOROUGH SHOW CAVE
662 FOUNTAINS FELL
Arncliffe
Melling
B6254
Low Bentham
BENTHAM POTTERY
A65
Newby
Helwith Bridge
PENNINE WAY
Tatham
Wennington
Wharfe
Hornby
High Bentham
Clapham
Austwick
PARK
94
Feizor
B6480
Wenning
Malham Tarn
Farleton
Wray
Mewith Head
Lawkland
Little Stainforth
Stainforth
Claughton
Keasden
YORKSHIRE DALES FALCONRY AND CONSERVATION CENTRE
THE SETTLE LOOP
MALHAM TARN
Lowgill
Hindburn
Stackhouse
WATERSHED MILL VISITOR CENTRE
Langcliffe
402
Burn Moor
Eldroth
Giggleswick
MALHAM COVE
Bordley
Caton Moor
Salter
Goodber Common
Tatham Fells
GIGGLESWICK SCHOOL CHAPEL
547 KIRKBY FELL
NEW HOUSE FARM, MALHAM
Crossgill
Settle
Malham
Haylot Fell
Catlow Fell
Wham
RIBBLESDALE
Hanlith
Kirkby Malham
Mearbeck
HORSES HEALTH FARM
Rathmell
SD
561 WARD'S STONE
Mallowdale Fell
544 WHITE HILL
Long Preston
Airton
Calton
Winterburn
Hetton
FOREST
Gisburn Forest
Otterburn
Lee Fell
Tarnbrook Fell
Croasdale Fell
Wigglesworth
Hellifield
Bell Busk
Flasby
Tarnbrook
Stocks Reservoir
Tosside
Ribble
A65
Eshton
Lee
Abbeystead
Trough of Bowland
Grunsagill
Coniston Cold
Gargrave
WHINS BROW 476
Knotts
Halton West
A682
Bank Newton
Marshaw
OF
B6478
Nappa
219
PENNINE WAY
Hawthornthwaite Fell
Slaidburn
SLAIDBURN
Paythorne
Broughton
478 FELL TOP
Sykes
Newsholme
East Marton
A59
Forest Becks
Hareden
Newton
Lane Ends
Horton
West Marton
Elslack
Sykes Fell
Dunsop Bridge
Easington Fell
Holden
Bolton-by-Bowland
Bracewell
Bleasdale Moors
BOWLAND
Gisburn
Lane End
Thornton in Craven
Whitewell
ABBEY
Coates
Earby
EARBY
388
510 FAIR SNAPE FELL
Sawley
Barnoldswick
Grindleton
Newby
Rimington
Salterforth
A56
Lothersdale
Bleasdale
Cow Ark
West Bradford
A59
LEAGRAM GARDENS
Kelbrook
Chatburn
Downham
Twiston
A682
Hodder
Bashall Eaves
Waddington
Hey
94
BEACON FELL
Chipping
Walker Fold
Clitheroe
Worston
Foulridge
A6068
Whitechapel
Low Moor
CLITHEROE CASTLE MUSEUM
557 PENDLE HILL
Blacko
Hesketh Lane
Barley
Roughlee
Colne Edge
Laneshaw Bridge
Longridge Fell
A671
Pendleton
PENDLE HERITAGE CENTRE
Newchurch
Barrowford
COLNE
Winewall
Wycoller
Knowle Green
New Row
Great Mitton
Barrow
BRITISH IN INDIA MUS.
Trawden
WYCOLLER
HOLLIN HALL SEWING CENTRE
Goosnargh
Longridge
B6243
Hurst Green
Sabden
NELSON
THE FOREST OF PENDLE
Fence
Wiswell
THE FOREST OF TRAWDEN
B6245
ST SAVIOUR'S CHURCH
Little Town
Old Langho
WHALLEY ABBEY
Whalley
Higham
Little Marsden
Brierfield
517 BOULSWORTH HILL
Ribchester
MUS. OF CHILDHOOD
Billington
Simonstone
TRAPP FORGE
GAWTHORPE HALL
A682
M65
Haggate
ROMAN MUSEUM
Ribble
Grimsargh
Langho
A671
Read
Padiham
Harle Syke
Burnley Lane
Walshaw Dean Res.
B6243
Copster Green
A666
Great Harwood
Altham
Habergham
Rose Grove
Burnley
Balderstone
Salesbury
Hapton
Brunshaw
Worsthorne
Widdop Res.
Ribbleton
Wilpshire
Clayton-le-Moors
A678
A680
WEAVERS' TRIANGLE
Walk Mill
Hurstwood
M6
SAMLESBURY HALL
A59
Osbaldeston
Brownhill
Rose Hill
Lane Ends
Samlesbury
Mellor Brook
223
Mellor
Rishton
Huncoat
Mereclough
Heptonstall Moor
A679
B6230
86
Pleckgate
M65
Milnshaw
87
TOWNELEY HALL ART GALLERY & MUS.
COUNTY AND REGIMENTAL MUS.
Beardwood
LEWIS TEXTILE MUSEUM
Church
ACCRINGTON
Clow Bridge
Holme Chapel
Samlesbury Bottoms
Higher Walton
Walton-le-Dale
Coup Green
HOGHTON TOWER
Blackburn
EANAM WHARF VISITOR CENTRE
West End
Oswaldtwistle
Scaitcliffe
A56
Dunnockshaw
Love Clough
A646
Colden
Blackshaw Head
Bamber Bridge
Gregson Lane
Feniscowles
Pleasington
Riley Green
Hoghton
A666
Shadsworth
Guide
Lower Darwen
Ewood
B6231
Baxenden
Rising Bridge
A680
A682
Goodshaw
GOODSHAW CHAPEL
Forest of Rossendale
B6238
A671
Water
449 THIEVELEY PIKE
Portsmouth
Cornholme
Lydgate
Charlestown

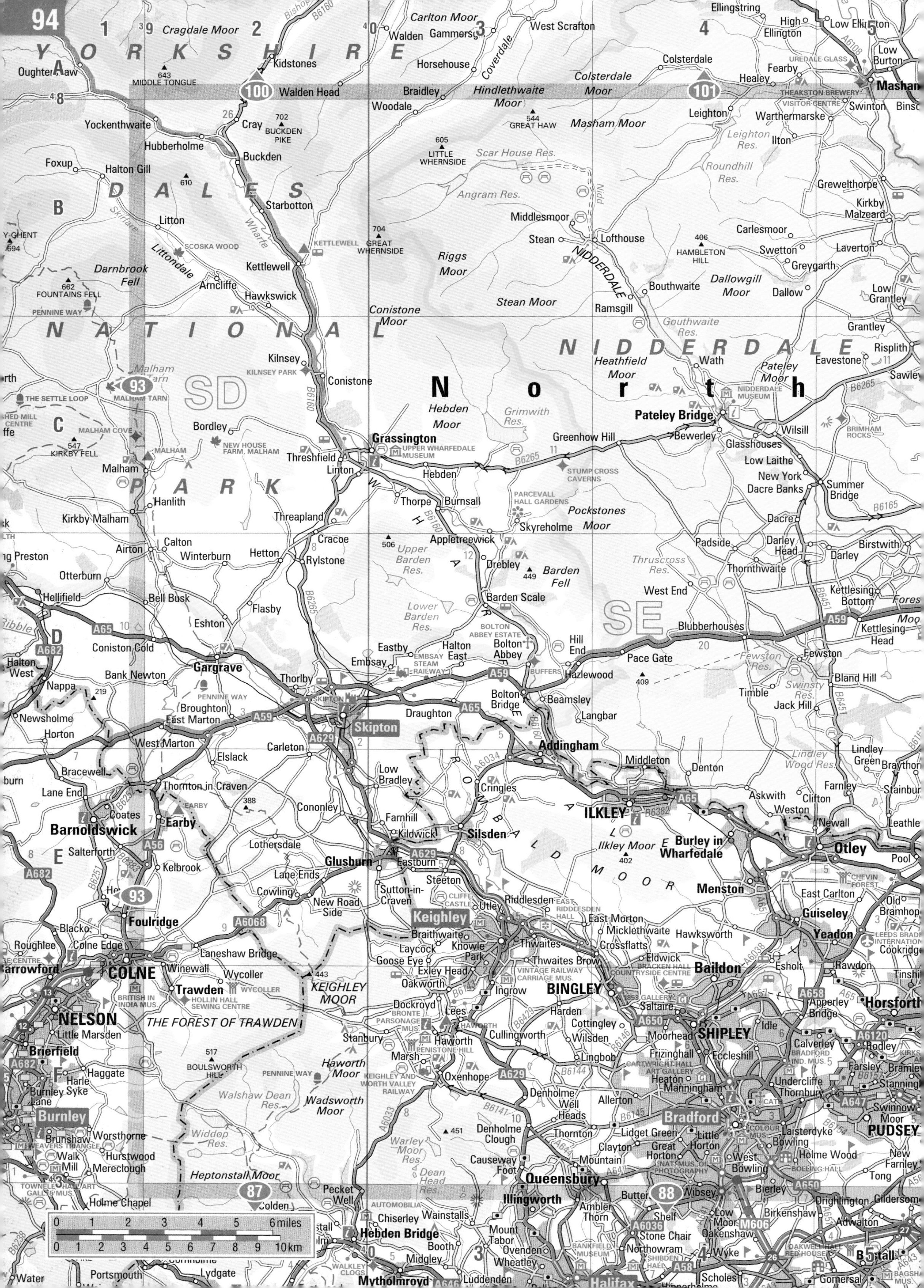

YORKSHIRE DALES NATIONAL PARK
NIDDERDALE
North
SD
SE
Cragdale Moor
Carlton Moor
West Scrafton
Ellingstring
High Ellington
Low Ellington
Low Burton
Masham
Kidstones
Walden
Gammersgill
Horsehouse
Coverdale
Colsterdale
Colsterdale Moor
Fearby
Healey
Walden Head
Braidley
Hindlethwaite Moor
Swinton
Woodale
Warthermarske
Leighton
Yockenthwaite
Cray
Buckden Pike
Great Haw
Masham Moor
Leighton Res.
Ilton
Hubberholme
Buckden
Little Whernside
Scar House Res.
Roundhill Res.
Foxup
Halton Gill
Grewelthorpe
Angram Res.
Kirkby Malzeard
Starbotton
Litton
Middlesmoor
Carlesmoor
Stean
Lofthouse
Laverton
Great Whernside
Kettlewell
Swetton
Hambleton Hill
Riggs Moor
Greygarth
Littondale
Scoska Wood
Nidderdale
Darnbrook Fell
Fountains Fell
Arncliffe
Bouthwaite
Dallowgill Moor
Dallow
Low Grantley
Hawkswick
Stean Moor
Pennine Way
Conistone Moor
Ramsgill
Gouthwaite Res.
Grantley
Risplith
Heathfield Moor
Wath
Pateley Moor
Eavestone
Kilnsey
Kilnsey Park
Malham Tarn
Conistone
Sawley
The Settle Loop
Nidderdale Museum
Hebden Moor
Grimwith Res.
Pateley Bridge
Bordley
Malham Cove
Kirkby Fell
New House Farm, Malham
Grassington
Upper Wharfedale Museum
Greenhow Hill
Bewerley
Wilsill
Brimham Rocks
Glasshouses
Malham
Threshfield
Linton
Hebden
Stump Cross Caverns
Low Laithe
New York
Dacre Banks
Summer Bridge
Hanlith
Thorpe
Burnsall
Parcevall Hall Gardens
Pockstones Moor
Kirkby Malham
Threapland
Skyreholme
Dacre
Calton
Cracoe
Appletreewick
Padside
Darley Head
Birstwith
Airton
Winterburn
Hetton
Rylstone
Upper Barden Res.
Drebley
Barden Fell
Thruscross Res.
Darley
Long Preston
Thornthwaite
Otterburn
West End
Kettlesing Bottom
Hellifield
Bell Busk
Flasby
Barden Scale
Lower Barden Res.
Eshton
Bolton Abbey Estate
Bolton Abbey
Blubberhouses
Kettlesing Head
Coniston Cold
Halton East
Eastby
Hill End
Pace Gate
Fewston
Fewston Res.
Halton West
Embsay
Embsay Steam Railway
Buffers
Hazlewood
Bank Newton
Gargrave
Thorlby
Bland Hill
Nappa
Pennine Way
Swinsty Res.
Timble
Broughton
Skipton
Draughton
Bolton Bridge
Beamsley
Jack Hill
Newsholme
East Marton
Langbar
Horton
West Marton
Carleton
Addingham
Lindley Green
Elslack
Middleton
Denton
Lindley Wood Res.
Braythorn
Bracewell
Low Bradley
Rombalds Moor
Cringles
Farnley
Stainburn
Lane End
Thornton in Craven
Earby
Askwith
Clifton
Coates
Ilkley
Weston
Newall
Leathley
Barnoldswick
Cononley
Farnhill
Kildwick
Silsden
Ilkley Moor
Burley in Wharfedale
Otley
Salterforth
Lothersdale
Pool
Kelbrook
Glusburn
Eastburn
Lane Ends
Steeton
Chevin Forest
Cowling
Sutton-in-Craven
Menston
East Carlton
Old Bramhope
New Road Side
Cliffe Castle
Riddlesden
East Riddlesden Hall
Utley
Guiseley
Foulridge
Keighley
East Morton
Micklethwaite
Hawksworth
Yeadon
Leeds Bradford International
Cookridge
Blacko
Braithwaite
Roughlee
Colne Edge
Laneshaw Bridge
Laycock
Knowle Park
Thwaites
Crossflatts
Eldwick
Bracken Hall Countryside Centre
Goose Eye
Exley Head
Thwaites Brow
Baildon
Esholt
Rawdon
Barrowford
Colne
Winewall
Wycoller
Oakworth
Vintage Railway Carriage Mus.
Tinshill
Trawden
British in India Mus.
Hollin Hall Sewing Centre
Keighley Moor
Ingrow
Bingley
1853 Gallery
Saltaire
Apperley Bridge
Horsforth
Nelson
Dockroyd
Brontë Parsonage Mus.
Lees
Harden
Shipley
Idle
Little Marsden
The Forest of Trawden
Haworth
Cottingley
Wilsden
Moorhead
Calverley
Rodley
Stanbury
Penistone Hill
Cullingworth
Brierfield
Haworth Moor
Marsh
Lingbob
Frizinghall
Eccleshill
Bradford Ind. Mus.
Farsley
Bramley
Boulsworth Hill
Keighley and Worth Valley Railway
Oxenhope
Cartwright Hall Art Gallery
Heaton
Manningham
Undercliffe
Thornbury
Stanningley
Harle Syke
Haggate
Burnley
Walshaw Dean Res.
Wadsworth Moor
Denholme
Well Heads
Allerton
Bradford
Swinnow Moor
Pudsey
Brunshaw
Worsthorne
Widdop Res.
Denholme Clough
Thornton
Lidget Green
Little Horton
Colour Mus.
Laisterdyke
Bowling
Weavers Triangle
Hurstwood
Warley Moor Res.
Clayton
Great Horton
Holme Wood
New Farnley
Walk Mill
Mereclough
Causeway Foot
Mountain
Nat. Mus. of Photography
West Bowling
Bolling Hall
Tong
Towneley Hall Art Gall. & Mus.
Heptonstall Moor
Dean Head Res.
Queensbury
Wibsey
Bierley
Holme Chapel
Colden
Pecket Well
Illingworth
Butter Shelf
Drighlington
Gildersome
Automobilia
Chiserley
Wainstalls
Ambler Thorn
Low Moor
Birkenshaw
Hebden Bridge
Mount Tabor
Stone Chair
Oakenshaw
Adwalton
Ovenden
Booth
Bankfield Museum
Northowram
Oakwell Hall Red House
Wheatley
Shibden Hall
Wyke
Birstall
Portsmouth
Midgley
Lydgate
Walkley Clogs
Mytholmroyd
Luddenden
Halifax
Hipperholme
Scholes
Gomersal
Water
Uredale Glass
Theakston Brewery Visitor Centre
Middle Tongue
0 1 2 3 4 5 6 miles
0 1 2 3 4 5 6 7 8 9 10 km

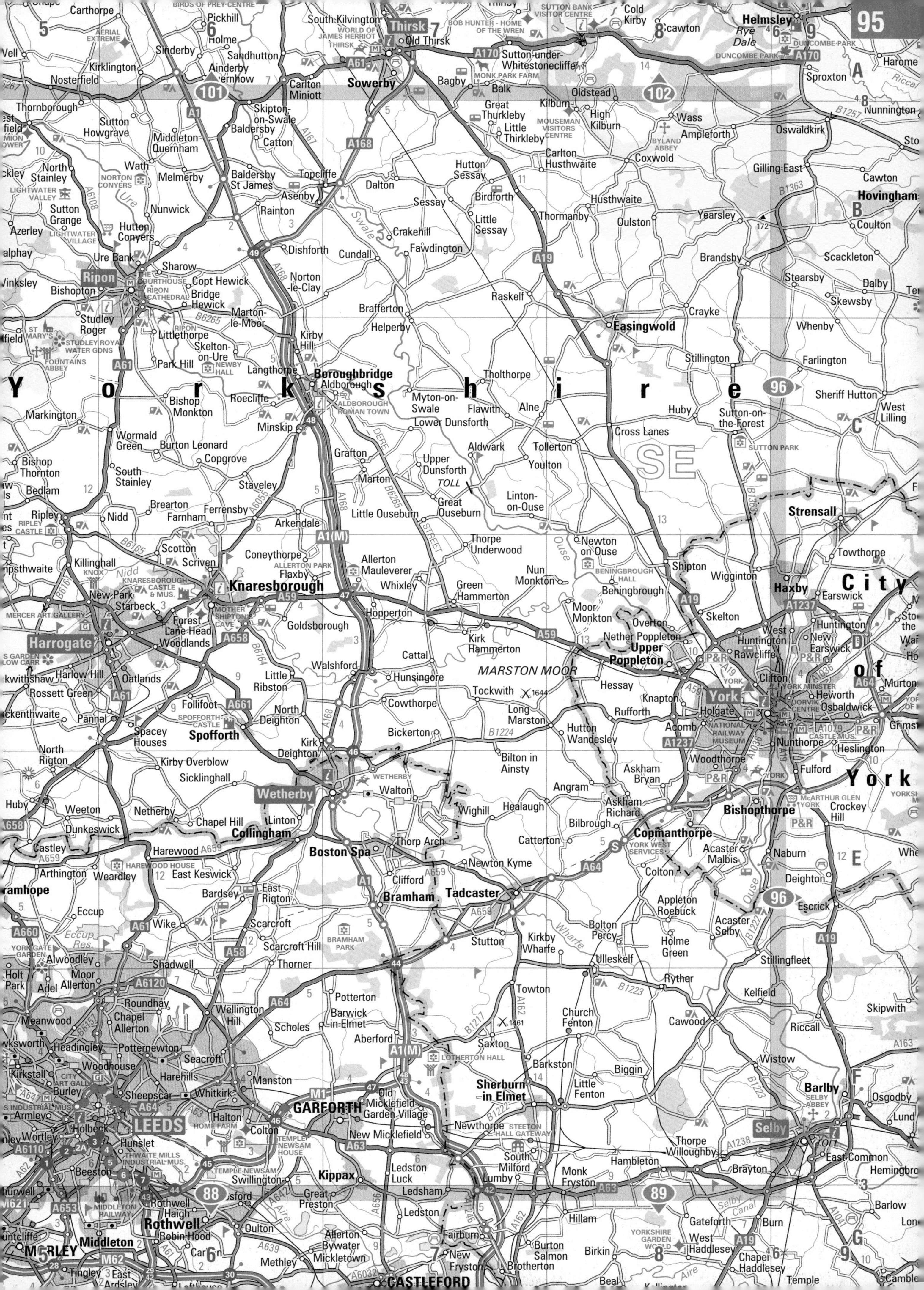
Yorkshire
City of York
SE
Thirsk
Helmsley
Ripon
Harrogate
Knaresborough
Wetherby
York
Selby
LEEDS
GARFORTH
Easingwold
Boroughbridge
Tadcaster
Sowerby
Carthorpe
Pickhill
Sinderby
Holme
Sandhutton
Ainderby Quernhow
Kirklington
Nosterfield
Carlton Miniott
South Kilvington
Old Thirsk
Bagby
Balk
Sutton-under-Whitestonecliffe
Cold Kirby
Scawton
Rye Dale
Harome
Sproxton
Oldstead
Kilburn
High Kilburn
Wass
Ampleforth
Oswaldkirk
Nunnington
Coxwold
Byland Abbey
Mouseman Visitors Centre
Great Thirkleby
Little Thirkleby
Carlton Husthwaite
Husthwaite
Gilling East
Cawton
Hovingham
Coulton
Yearsley
Oulston
Thormanby
Birdforth
Little Sessay
Sessay
Hutton Sessay
Dalton
Topcliffe
Asenby
Rainton
Baldersby St James
Baldersby
Skipton-on-Swale
Catton
Thornborough
Sutton Howgrave
Middleton Quernham
Wath
Melmerby
North Stainley
Norton Conyers
Lightwater Valley
Sutton Grange
Nunwick
Azerley
Hutton Conyers
Ure Bank
Sharow
Copt Hewick
Bishopton
Bridge Hewick
Marton-le-Moor
Norton-le-Clay
Dishforth
Cundall
Crakehill
Fawdington
Brafferton
Helperby
Raskelf
Brandsby
Scackleton
Stearsby
Dalby
Skewsby
Crayke
Whenby
Stillington
Farlington
Sheriff Hutton
West Lilling
Huby
Sutton-on-the-Forest
Sutton Park
Tholthorpe
Myton-on-Swale
Flawith
Alne
Lower Dunsforth
Aldwark
Tollerton
Youlton
Cross Lanes
Upper Dunsforth
Linton-on-Ouse
Strensall
Towthorpe
Newton on Ouse
Beningbrough Hall
Beningbrough
Shipton
Wigginton
Haxby
Earswick
Nun Monkton
Moor Monkton
Overton
Skelton
Nether Poppleton
Upper Poppleton
Huntington
New Earswick
Rawcliffe
Clifton
Hessay
Knapton
Rufforth
Acomb
Holgate
National Railway Museum
Jorvik Centre
York Minster
Heworth
Osbaldwick
Murton
Heslington
Nunthorpe
Fulford
Woodthorpe
Askham Bryan
Askham Richard
Bishopthorpe
Copmanthorpe
Crockey Hill
Acaster Malbis
Naburn
Deighton
Escrick
Colton
Appleton Roebuck
Acaster Selby
Bolton Percy
Holme Green
Stillingfleet
Ryther
Kelfield
Cawood
Riccall
Skipwith
Wistow
Barlby
Osgodby
Selby Abbey
Thorpe Willoughby
Brayton
East Common
Hemingbrough
Barlow
Burn
Gateforth
West Haddlesey
Chapel Haddlesey
Temple
Camblesforth
Hambleton
Studley Roger
Studley Royal Water Gdns
Fountains Abbey
Littlethorpe
Skelton-on-Ure
Newby Hall
Langthorpe
Kirby Hill
Aldborough
Aldborough Roman Town
Park Hill
Markington
Bishop Monkton
Roecliffe
Minskip
Wormald Green
Burton Leonard
Copgrove
Bishop Thornton
South Stainley
Staveley
Grafton
Marton
Great Ouseburn
Little Ouseburn
Arkendale
Ferrensby
Brearton
Farnham
Bedlam
Ripley
Ripley Castle
Nidd
Killinghall
Scotton
Scriven
Coneythorpe
Allerton Park
Allerton Mauleverer
Flaxby
Whixley
Green Hammerton
Thorpe Underwood
New Park
Starbeck
Forest Lane Head
Woodlands
Mother Shipton's Cave
Goldsborough
Hopperton
Kirk Hammerton
Marston Moor
Cattal
Walshford
Hunsingore
Cowthorpe
Tockwith
Long Marston
Hutton Wandesley
Bickerton
Bilton in Ainsty
Harlow Hill
Oatlands
Rossett Green
Pannal
Little Ribston
North Deighton
Follifoot
Spofforth Castle
Spofforth
Spacey Houses
Kirk Deighton
North Rigton
Kirby Overblow
Sicklinghall
Walton
Angram
Wighill
Healaugh
Bilbrough
Catterton
Newton Kyme
Thorp Arch
Boston Spa
Clifford
Bramham
Bramham Park
Linton
Collingham
Huby
Weeton
Dunkeswick
Netherby
Chapel Hill
Castley
Harewood
Harewood House
East Keswick
Arthington
Weardley
Bramhope
Eccup
Eccup Res.
Bardsey
East Rigton
Scarcroft
Scarcroft Hill
Thorner
Wike
Shadwell
Alwoodley
Moor Allerton
Adel
Holt Park
Roundhay
Chapel Allerton
Meanwood
Headingley
Potternewton
Woodhouse
Kirkstall
Burley
Harehills
Seacroft
Manston
Whitkirk
Sheepscar
Halton
Colton
Temple Newsam House
Armley
Wortley
Holbeck
Hunslet
Beeston
Thwaite Mills Industrial Mus.
Middleton Railway
Rothwell
Rothwell Haigh
Robin Hood
Middleton
Morley
Tingley
East Ardsley
Carlton
Oulton
Swillington
Great Preston
Kippax
Allerton Bywater
Methley
Mickletown
Castleford
Ledston
Ledston Luck
Ledsham
Fairburn
New Fryston
Brotherton
Burton Salmon
Birkin
Beal
Hillam
Monk Fryston
Lumby
South Milford
Newthorpe
Steeton Hall Gateway
Old Micklefield
Micklefield Garden Village
New Micklefield
Lotherton Hall
Aberford
Barwick-in-Elmet
Scholes
Potterton
Wellington Hill
Sherburn in Elmet
Little Fenton
Biggin
Barkston
Saxton
Church Fenton
Towton
Ulleskelf
Kirkby Wharfe
Stutton
Grimston
Yorkshire Garden World
Mercer Art Gallery
Marston Moor
A1(M)
A1
A19
A59
A61
A64
A168
A170
A658
A661
A1237
M1
M62
101
102
88
89
96

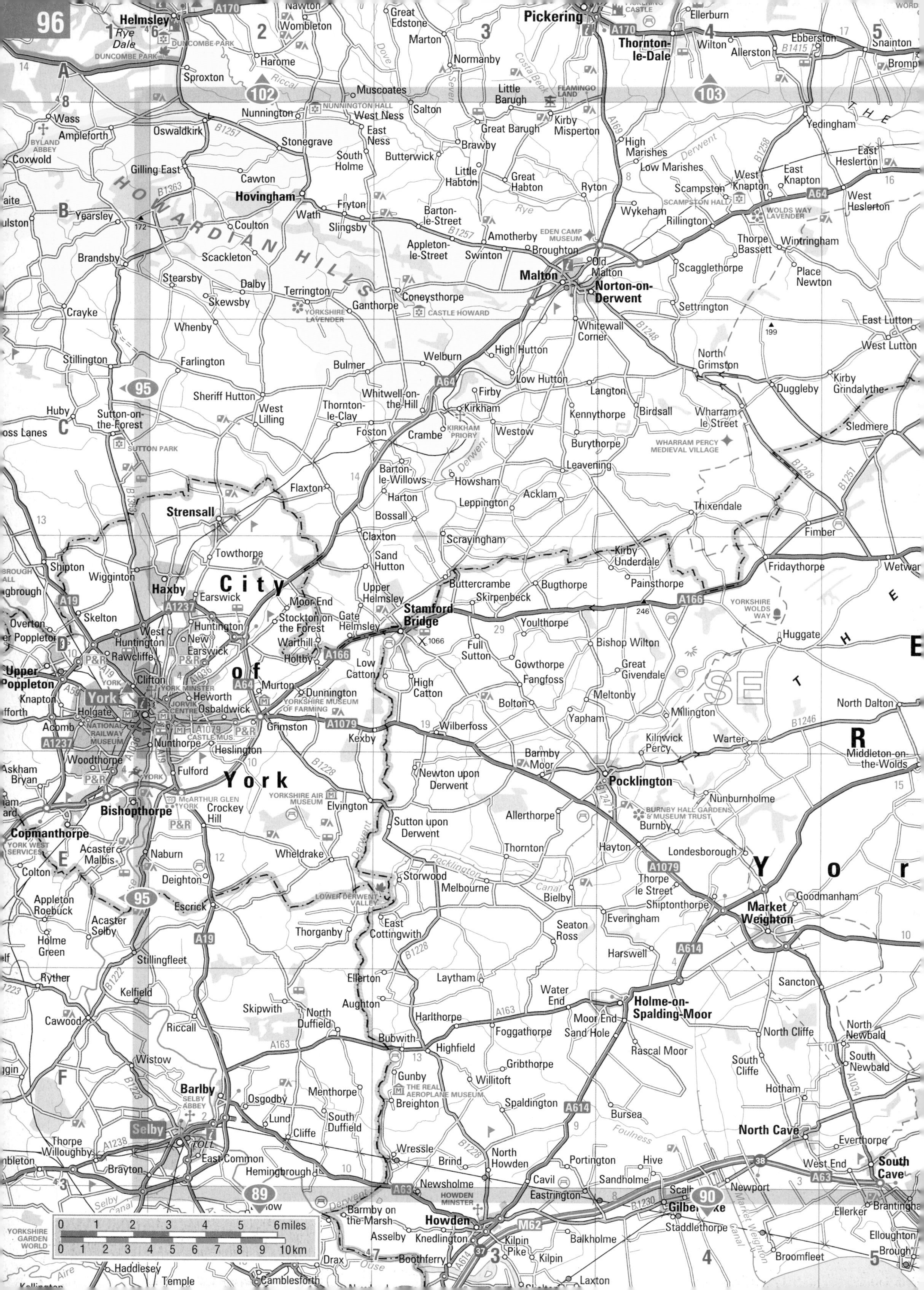
Helmsley
Pickering
Thornton-le-Dale
Malton
Norton-on-Derwent
Hovingham
HOWARDIAN HILLS
Strensall
Haxby
City of York
York
Stamford Bridge
Pocklington
Market Weighton
Holme-on-Spalding-Moor
Bishopthorpe
Copmanthorpe
Barlby
Selby
Howden
North Cave
South Cave
Gilberdyke
102
103
95
89
90
0 1 2 3 4 5 6 miles
0 1 2 3 4 5 6 7 8 9 10 km

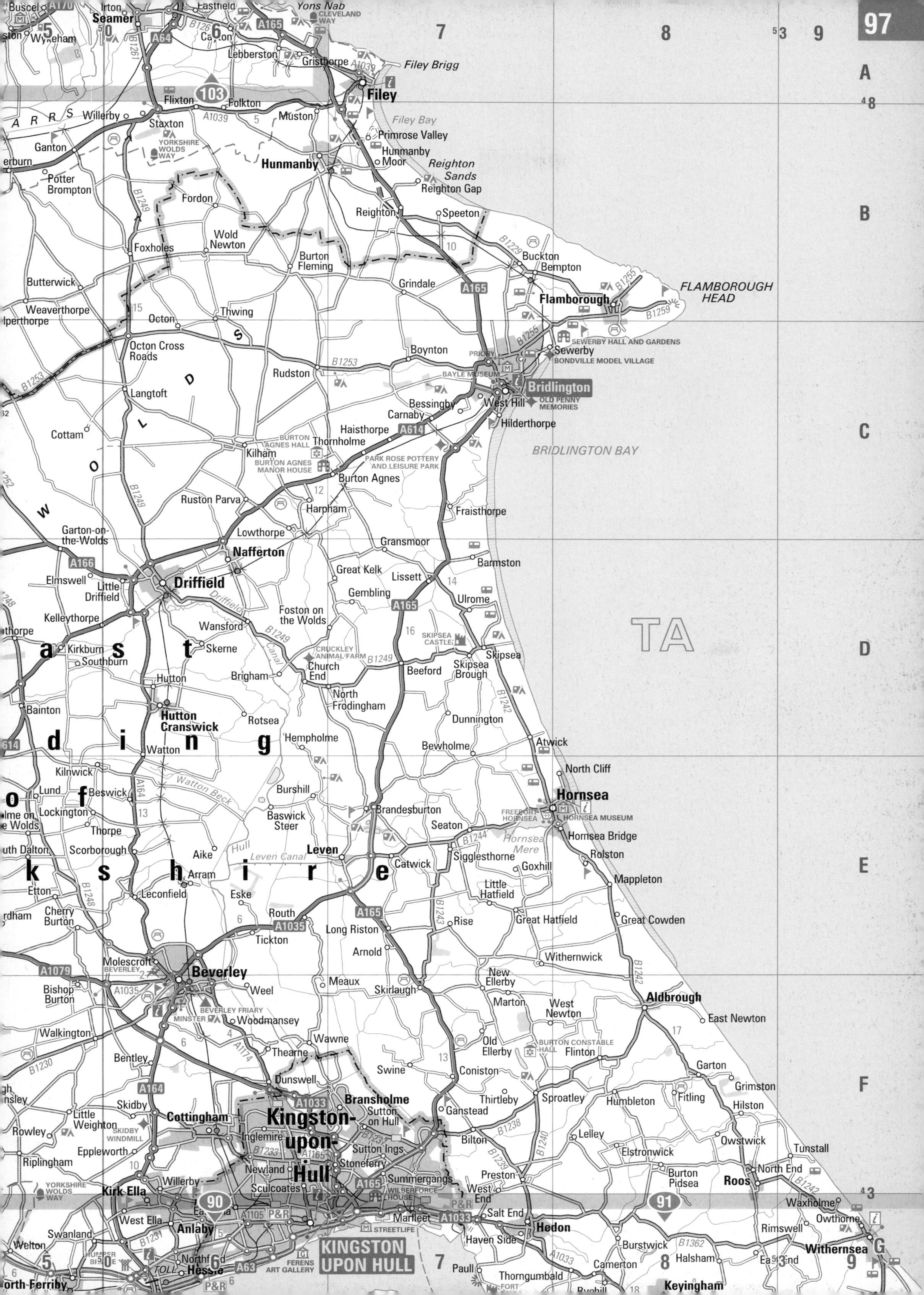
Seamer
Filey Brigg
Filey
Filey Bay
Primrose Valley
Hunmanby
Hunmanby Moor
Reighton Sands
Reighton Gap
Reighton
Speeton
Buckton
Bempton
Flamborough
FLAMBOROUGH HEAD
SEWERBY HALL AND GARDENS
Sewerby
BONDVILLE MODEL VILLAGE
Bridlington
OLD PENNY MEMORIES
Hilderthorpe
BRIDLINGTON BAY
Fraisthorpe
Barmston
Ulrome
Skipsea
SKIPSEA CASTLE
TA
Atwick
North Cliff
Hornsea
HORNSEA MUSEUM
Hornsea Bridge
Rolston
Mappleton
Great Cowden
Aldbrough
East Newton
Garton
Grimston
Hilston
Owstwick
Tunstall
Roos
Waxholme
Owthorne
Withernsea
Rimswell
Keyingham
Hedon
Driffield
Nafferton
Beverley
Kingston-upon-Hull
KINGSTON UPON HULL
Cottingham
Hessle
Anlaby
Leven
Brandesburton
Rudston
Boynton
Grindale
Burton Fleming
Wold Newton
Foxholes
Thwing
Octon
Langtoft
Kilham
Burton Agnes
Harpham
Lowthorpe
Gransmoor
Lissett
Beeford
Hutton Cranswick
Watton
Skirlaugh
Sproatley
Flinton
Swine
Dunswell
Woodmansey
Walkington
Skidby
Willerby
Kirk Ella
Swanland
North Ferriby
Paull
Thorngumbald
Burstwick
Halsham
YORKSHIRE WOLDS WAY

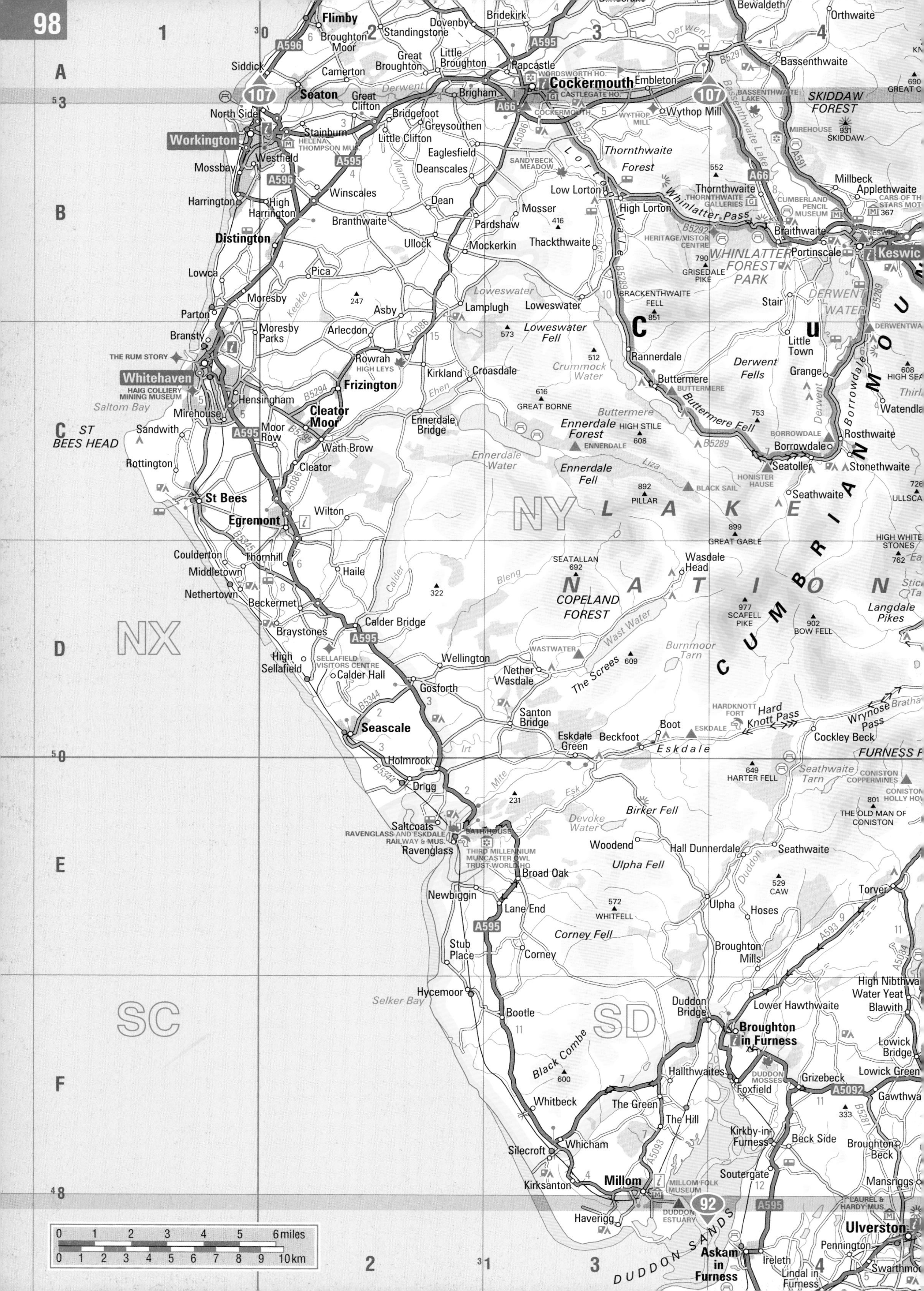

Flimby
Workington
Cockermouth
Whitehaven
Cleator Moor
Egremont
St Bees
Seascale
Ravenglass
Millom
Broughton in Furness
Ulverston
Askam in Furness
Keswick
Distington
Seaton
Frizington
LAKE DISTRICT NATIONAL PARK
CUMBRIAN MOUNTAINS
Ennerdale Water
Wast Water
Buttermere
Crummock Water
Loweswater
Bassenthwaite Lake
Derwent Water
SKIDDAW FOREST
Whinlatter Forest Park
COPELAND FOREST
SCAFELL PIKE
GREAT GABLE
PILLAR
Black Combe
DUDDON SANDS
Selker Bay
Saltom Bay
ST BEES HEAD
NX
NY
SC
SD

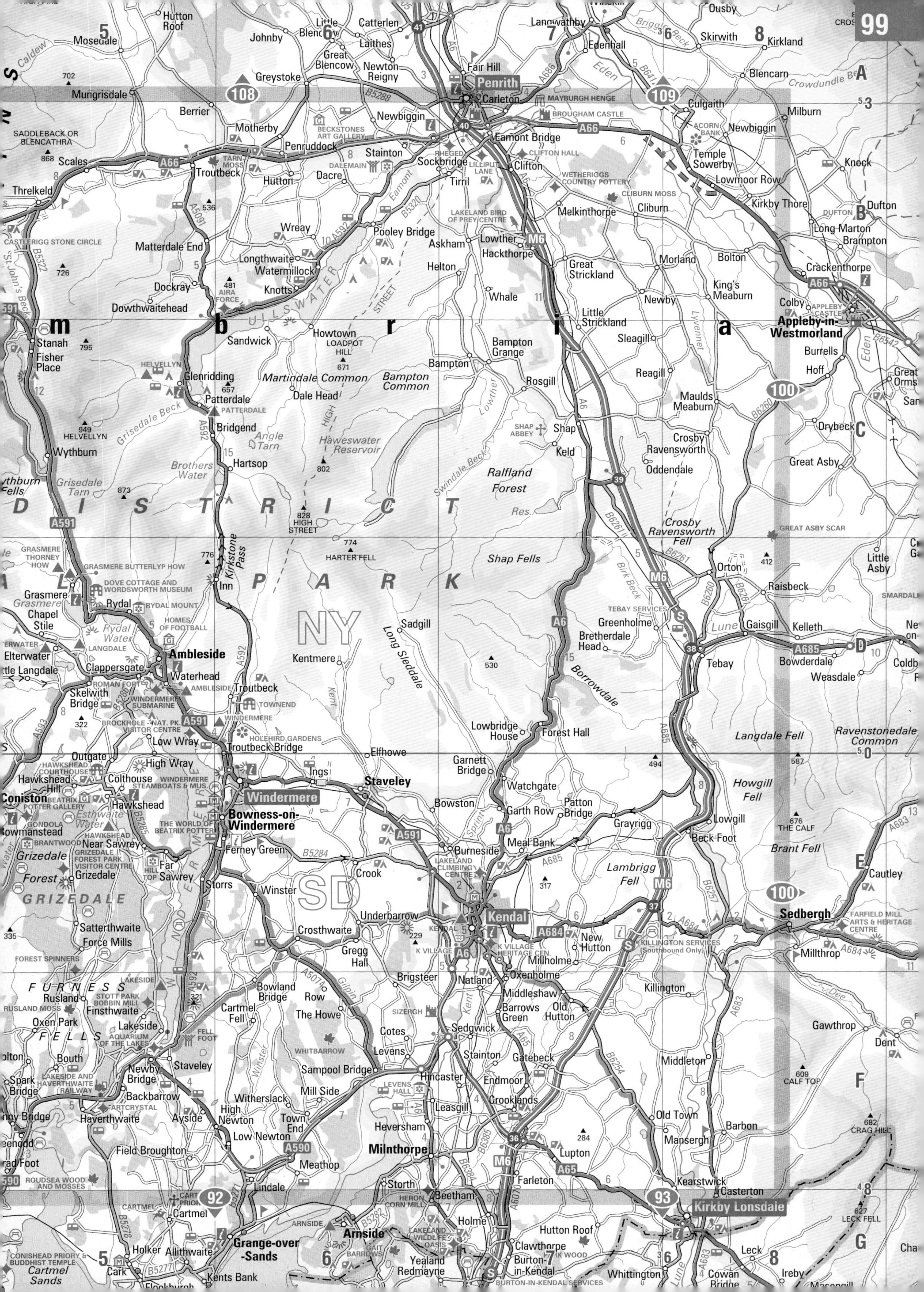
99
Penrith
Kendal
Windermere
Bowness-on-Windermere
Ambleside
Appleby-in-Westmorland
Kirkby Lonsdale
Sedbergh
Staveley
Milnthorpe
Grange-over-Sands
Arnside
Coniston
Hawkshead
Grasmere
Rydal
Glenridding
Patterdale
Pooley Bridge
Shap
Orton
Tebay
Kirkby Thore
Temple Sowerby
Langwathby
Edenhall
Greystoke
Mungrisdale
Threlkeld
Troutbeck
Lowther
Askham
Clifton
Eamont Bridge
Carleton
Newbiggin
Stainton
Dacre
Morland
Great Strickland
Little Strickland
Bampton
Bampton Grange
Rosgill
Keld
Crosby Ravensworth
Maulds Meaburn
King's Meaburn
Colby
Burrells
Hoff
Drybeck
Great Asby
Raisbeck
Kelleth
Gaisgill
Greenholme
Bretherdale Head
Sadgill
Kentmere
Ings
Burneside
Crook
Winster
Crosthwaite
Underbarrow
Natland
Oxenholme
Sedgwick
Levens
Heversham
Beetham
Holme
Burton-in-Kendal
Lupton
Barbon
Mansergh
Casterton
Killington
Middleton
Lowgill
Grayrigg
Cartmel
Lindale
Newby Bridge
Lakeside
Haverthwaite
Grizedale
Satterthwaite
Far Sawrey
Near Sawrey
Storrs
Ullswater
Haweswater Reservoir
Shap Fells
Howgill Fells
Lake District National Park
NY
SD
M6
A6
A66
A591
A592
A590
A65
A683
A684
A685
108
109
92
93
100

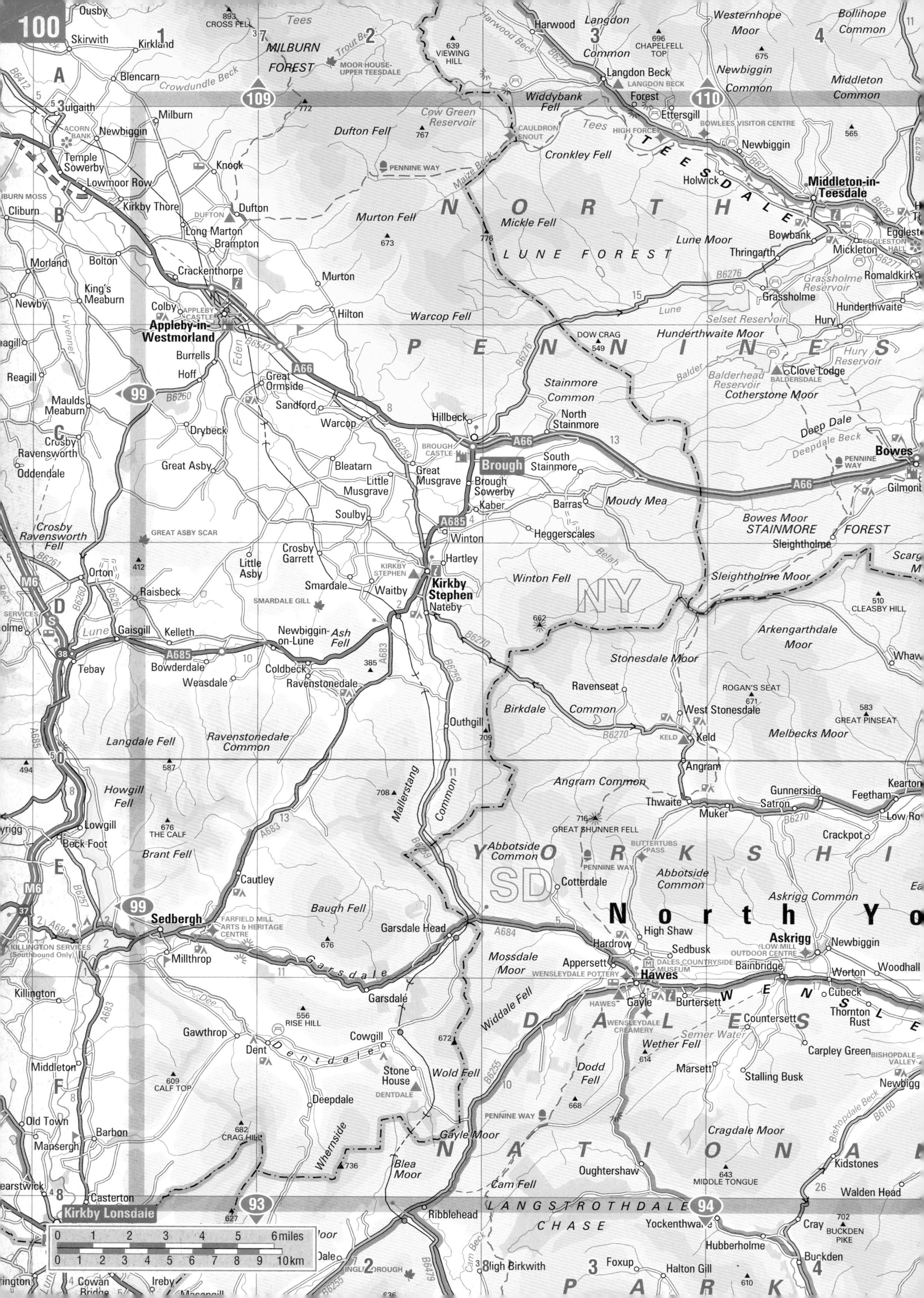
Ousby
Skirwith
Kirkland
893
CROSS FELL
Tees
MILBURN
FOREST
Trout Beck
MOOR HOUSE-
UPPER TEESDALE
Crowdundle Beck
109
772
Blencarn
Culgaith
ACORN
BANK
Newbiggin
Milburn
Temple
Sowerby
Knock
Lowmoor Row
Kirkby Thore
IBURN MOSS
Cliburn
DUFTON
Dufton
Long Marton
Brampton
Morland
Bolton
Crackenthorpe
King's
Meaburn
Newby
Colby
APPLEBY
CASTLE
Appleby-in-
Westmorland
Burrells
Hoff
Eden
B6542
A66
Reagill
99
B6260
Maulds
Meaburn
Crosby
Ravensworth
Oddendale
Drybeck
Great Asby
Great
Ormside
Sandford
Warcop
Bleatarn
Little
Musgrave
Soulby
Crosby
Ravensworth
Fell
GREAT ASBY SCAR
412
Orton
Raisbeck
M6
SERVICES
Tebay
Lune
Gaisgill
Kelleth
A685
Bowderdale
Weasdale
Little
Asby
Crosby
Garrett
Smardale
SMARDALE GILL
Waitby
Newbiggin-
on-Lune
Ash
Fell
Coldbeck
Ravenstonedale
385
Langdale Fell
Ravenstonedale
Common
494
587
Howgill
Fell
Lowgill
Beck Foot
676
THE CALF
Brant Fell
Cautley
Sedbergh
FARFIELD MILL
ARTS & HERITAGE
CENTRE
KILLINGTON SERVICES
(Southbound Only)
Millthrop
Killington
Garsdale
Dee
Gawthrop
Dent
Dentdale
556
RISE HILL
Middleton
609
CALF TOP
Deepdale
Old Town
Barbon
682
CRAG HILL
Mansergh
Whernside
736
Casterton
Kirkby Lonsdale
93
627
Cowan
Bridge
Ireby
Dufton Fell
767
Cow Green
Reservoir
PENNINE WAY
Maize Beck
Murton Fell
673
Murton
Hilton
Warcop Fell
639
VIEWING
HILL
Harwood Beck
Harwood
Langdon
Common
696
CHAPELFELL
TOP
Langdon Beck
LANGDON BECK
Widdybank
Fell
CAULDRON
SNOUT
Forest
Ettersgill
HIGH FORCE
Cronkley Fell
TEESDALE
Westernhope
Moor
675
Newbiggin
Common
110
BOWLEES VISITOR CENTRE
Newbiggin
Holwick
Bollihope
Common
Middleton
Common
565
Middleton-in-
Teesdale
NORTH
Mickle Fell
776
LUNE FOREST
Lune Moor
Bowbank
Thringarth
Mickleton
EGGLESTON
HALL
Eggleston
Romaldkirk
B6276
Grassholme
Reservoir
Grassholme
15
Lune
Selset Reservoir
Hury
Hunderthwaite
Hury
Reservoir
DOW CRAG
549
Hunderthwaite Moor
PENNINES
Balder
Balderhead
Reservoir
Clove Lodge
BALDERSDALE
Cotherstone Moor
Stainmore
Common
North
Stainmore
Hillbeck
Deep Dale
Deepdale Beck
BROUGH
CASTLE
Brough
A66
13
South
Stainmore
Bowes
PENNINE
WAY
Gilmonby
Great
Musgrave
Brough
Sowerby
Kaber
Barras
Moudy Mea
Bowes Moor
STAINMORE FOREST
Sleightholme
A685
Winton
Heggerscales
Hartley
Belah
KIRKBY
STEPHEN
Kirkby
Stephen
Nateby
Winton Fell
NY
Sleightholme Moor
510
CLEASBY HILL
662
B6270
Arkengarthdale
Moor
Stonesdale Moor
Ravenseat
ROGAN'S SEAT
671
583
GREAT PINSEAT
Birkdale
Common
West Stonesdale
Outhgill
709
KELD
Keld
Melbecks Moor
Angram
Angram Common
Mallerstang
Common
708
Thwaite
Muker
Gunnerside
Satron
Feetham
Low Row
Crackpot
716
GREAT SHUNNER FELL
BUTTERTUBS
PASS
Abbotside
Common
YORKSHIRE
PENNINE WAY
Abbotside
Common
SD
Cotterdale
Askrigg Common
North Yorks
Baugh Fell
676
Garsdale Head
A684
Mossdale
Moor
High Shaw
Hardrow
Sedbusk
Askrigg
Newbiggin
LOW MILL
OUTDOOR CENTRE
Appersett
DALES COUNTRYSIDE
MUSEUM
WENSLEYDALE POTTERY
Hawes
Bainbridge
Worton
Woodhall
Gayle
Burtersett
Cubeck
Thornton
Rust
HAWES
WENSLEYDALE
CREAMERY
Widdale Fell
DALES
WENSLEYDALE
Countersett
Semer Water
Cowgill
672
Wether Fell
614
Carpley Green
BISHOPDALE
VALLEY
Stone
House
DENTDALE
Wold Fell
B6255
Dodd
Fell
Marsett
Stalling Busk
Newbiggin
PENNINE WAY
668
Bishopdale Beck
B6160
Cragdale Moor
Gayle Moor
NATIONAL
Blea
Moor
Oughtershaw
643
MIDDLE TONGUE
Kidstones
Cam Fell
26
Walden Head
Ribblehead
LANGSTROTHDALE
94
CHASE
Yockenthwaite
702
BUCKDEN
PIKE
Cray
Hubberholme
Buckden
Cam Beck
B6479
INGLEBOROUGH
Gearstones
High Birkwith
Foxup
Halton Gill
610
PARK
0 1 2 3 4 5 6 miles
0 1 2 3 4 5 6 7 8 9 10 km

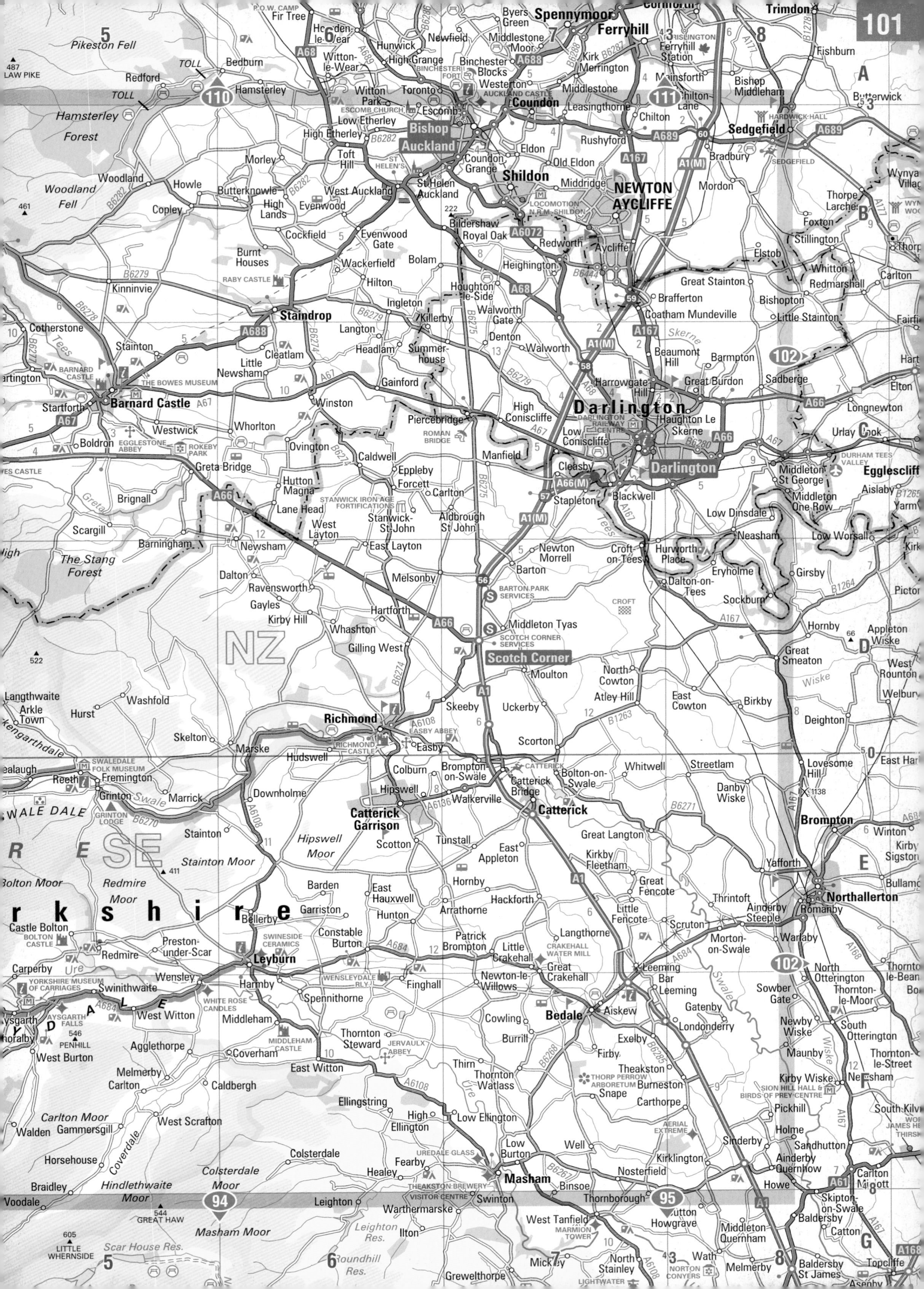
5
Pikeston Fell
487
LAW PIKE
P.O.W. CAMP
Fir Tree
Howden-le-Wear
6
Byers Green
Spennymoor
Ferryhill
Cornforth
Trimdon
Hunwick
Newfield
Middlestone Moor
7
A688
Kirk Merrington
ISLINGTON
Ferryhill Station
8
Fishburn
B1278
A177
Witton-le-Wear
High Grange
Binchester Blocks
BINCHESTER FORT
Westerton
AUCKLAND CASTLE
Middlestone
Mainsforth
Bishop Middleham
A
Bedburn
TOLL
Redford
TOLL
110
Hamsterley
Witton Park
Toronto
Coundon
Leasingthorne
111
Chilton Lane
Butterwick
ESCOMB CHURCH
Escomb
Chilton
HARDWICK HALL
Hamsterley Forest
Low Etherley
Bishop Auckland
High Etherley
B6282
A689
60
Sedgefield
A689
Rushyford
Morley
Toft Hill
ST HELEN'S
Coundon Grange
Eldon
Old Eldon
A167
A1(M)
Bradbury
SEDGEFIELD
Woodland
Woodland Fell
Howle
Butterknowle
West Auckland
St Helen Auckland
Shildon
Middridge
NEWTON AYCLIFFE
Mordon
Wynyard Village
461
B6282
Copley
High Lands
Evenwood
LOCOMOTION N.R.M. SHILDON
Thorpe Larches
222
Bildershaw
A177
B
Foxton
Cockfield
Evenwood Gate
Royal Oak
A6072
Redworth
Aycliffe
Stillington
Burnt Houses
Wackerfield
Bolam
Heighington
Elstob
Whitton
Thorpe
RABY CASTLE
Hilton
B6444
Great Stainton
Redmarshall
Carlton
B6279
Kinninvie
Houghton-le-Side
A68
59
Brafferton
Bishopton
Ingleton
Killerby
Walworth Gate
Coatham Mundeville
Little Stainton
Fairfield
B6278
Staindrop
B6279
B6275
Cotherstone
Langton
A167
Skerne
Denton
Stainton
A688
Headlam
Summerhouse
Walworth
A1(M)
Beaumont Hill
Barmpton
102
Tees
B6277
Cleatlam
BARNARD CASTLE
Little Newsham
58
Harrowgate Hill
Great Burdon
Sadberge
Elton
Hartburn
THE BOWES MUSEUM
A67
Gainford
B6279
Romaldkirk
Startforth
Barnard Castle
A67
Winston
High Coniscliffe
Darlington
A66
Longnewton
A67
Westwick
Whorlton
Piercebridge
DARLINGTON RAILWAY CENTRE
Haughton Le Skerne
Urlay Nook
C
Boldron
EGGLESTONE ABBEY
ROKEBY PARK
Ovington
ROMAN BRIDGE
A67
Low Coniscliffe
B6280
A66
A67
BOWES CASTLE
Greta Bridge
B6274
Caldwell
Manfield
Cleasby
Darlington
Middleton St George
DURHAM TEES VALLEY
Egglescliffe
Eppleby
A66(M)
Aislaby
Hutton Magna
Forcett
B6275
Blackwell
Middleton One Row
Yarm
Brignall
Greta
STANWICK IRON AGE FORTIFICATIONS
Carlton
57
Stapleton
A167
Low Dinsdale
A66
Lane Head
Stanwick-St-John
Aldbrough St John
A1(M)
Tees
Neasham
Low Worsall
Scargill
West Layton
12
East Layton
Newton Morrell
Croft-on-Tees
Hurworth Place
Kirklevington
Barningham
Newsham
Barton
Eryholme
Girsby
The Stang Forest
Dalton
Melsonby
56
BARTON PARK SERVICES
Dalton-on-Tees
B1264
Picton
Ravensworth
CROFT
Gayles
Sockburn
Kirby Hill
Hartforth
A167
A66
Middleton Tyas
Hornby
Appleton Wiske
Whashton
SCOTCH CORNER SERVICES
66
D
NZ
522
Gilling West
Scotch Corner
Great Smeaton
Moulton
West Rounton
North Cowton
Wiske
B6274
Atley Hill
Welbury
Langthwaite
Washfold
A1
East Cowton
Birkby
Arkle Town
Hurst
Skeeby
Uckerby
Richmond
A6108
EASBY ABBEY
Deighton
Arkengarthdale
Skelton
Marske
RICHMOND CASTLE
Easby
B1263
Scorton
Hudswell
SWALEDALE FOLK MUSEUM
Colburn
Brompton-on-Swale
CATTERICK
Bolton-on-Swale
Whitwell
Streetlam
Lovesome Hill
East Harlsey
Healaugh
Reeth
Fremington
Catterick Bridge
Danby Wiske
Grinton
Swale
Marrick
Downholme
Hipswell
Walkerville
Catterick
1138
SWALE DALE
GRINTON LODGE
B6270
A6108
Catterick Garrison
A6136
B6271
A167
Brompton
Winton
Stainton
Hipswell Moor
Scotton
Tunstall
Great Langton
Kirby Sigston
R E
SE
Stainton Moor
411
East Appleton
Kirkby Fleetham
Yafforth
E
Bolton Moor
Redmire Moor
Barden
Hornby
Great Fencote
Bullamoor
East Hauxwell
Hackforth
A1
Thrintoft
Northallerton
Yorkshire
Bellerby
Garriston
Arrathorne
Little Fencote
Ainderby Steeple
Romanby
Castle Bolton
BOLTON CASTLE
Hunton
Scruton
Preston-under-Scar
SWINESIDE CERAMICS
Constable Burton
Patrick Brompton
Langthorne
Morton-on-Swale
Warlaby
Redmire
A684
Little Crakehall
CRAKEHALL WATER MILL
Leeming Bar
102
North Otterington
Carperby
Ure
Leyburn
Great Crakehall
A684
Thornton-le-Beans
YORKSHIRE MUSEUM OF CARRIAGES
Wensley
Harmby
WENSLEYDALE RLY
Finghall
Newton-le-Willows
Leeming
Sowber Gate
Thornton-le-Moor
Swinithwaite
WHITE ROSE CANDLES
Spennithorne
Swale
Aysgarth
West Witton
Cowling
Bedale
Aiskew
Gatenby
DALE
AYSGARTH FALLS
546
PENHILL
Middleham
Newby Wiske
South Otterington
Thoralby
Burrill
Londonderry
Agglethorpe
MIDDLEHAM CASTLE
Thornton Steward
JERVAULX ABBEY
Exelby
Maunby
Thornton-le-Street
West Burton
Coverham
Firby
East Witton
10
Thirn
Theakston
Wiske
Melmerby
Thornton Watlass
THORP PERROW ARBORETUM
Burneston
Kirby Wiske
Newsham
F
Carlton
Caldbergh
B6268
B6285
SION HILL HALL & BIRDS OF PREY CENTRE
Snape
A6108
Carthorpe
Ellingstring
Pickhill
South Kilvington
Carlton Moor
High Ellington
Low Ellington
A167
Walden
Gammersgill
West Scrafton
AERIAL EXTREME
JAMES HERRIOT
Well
Sinderby
Holme
Coverdale
Low Burton
Sandhutton
Colsterdale
UREDALE GLASS
Kirklington
Horsehouse
Fearby
Ainderby Quernhow
Colsterdale Moor
Healey
Masham
B6267
Nosterfield
Carlton Miniott
Braidley
Hindlethwaite Moor
THEAKSTON BREWERY VISITOR CENTRE
Binsoe
Howe
A61
Voodale
94
Leighton
Swinton
Thornborough
95
Sutton Howgrave
Skipton-on-Swale
544
GREAT HAW
Warthermarske
West Tanfield
Middleton Quernham
Baldersby
Masham Moor
Leighton Res.
Ilton
MARMION TOWER
Catton
G
605
LITTLE WHERNSIDE
Scar House Res.
6
Roundhill Res.
7
Mickley
North Stainley
Wath
8
Baldersby St James
Topcliffe
A168
5
Grewelthorpe
NORTON CONYERS
Melmerby
LIGHTWATER
Asenby
A6108
A1
3

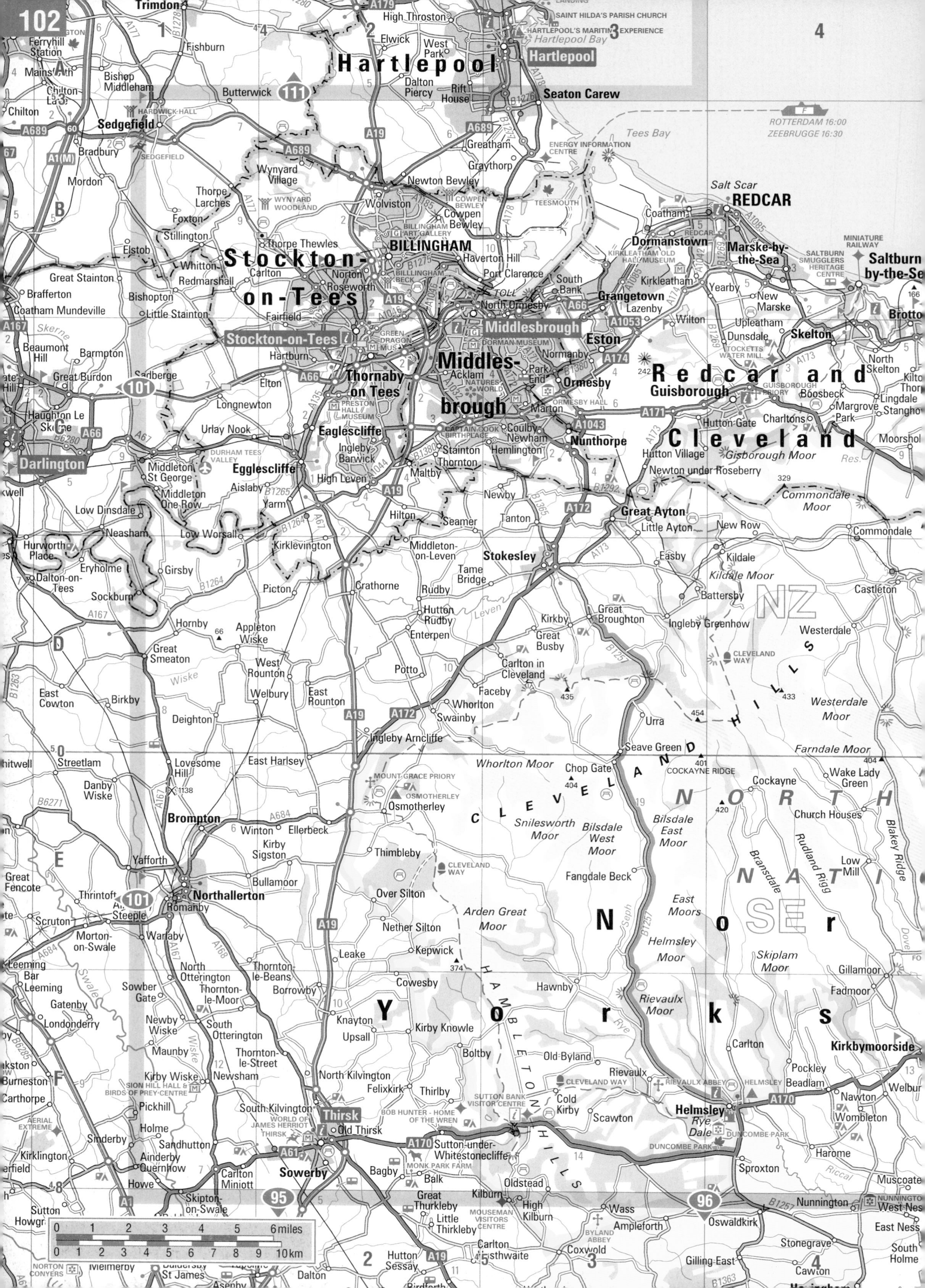

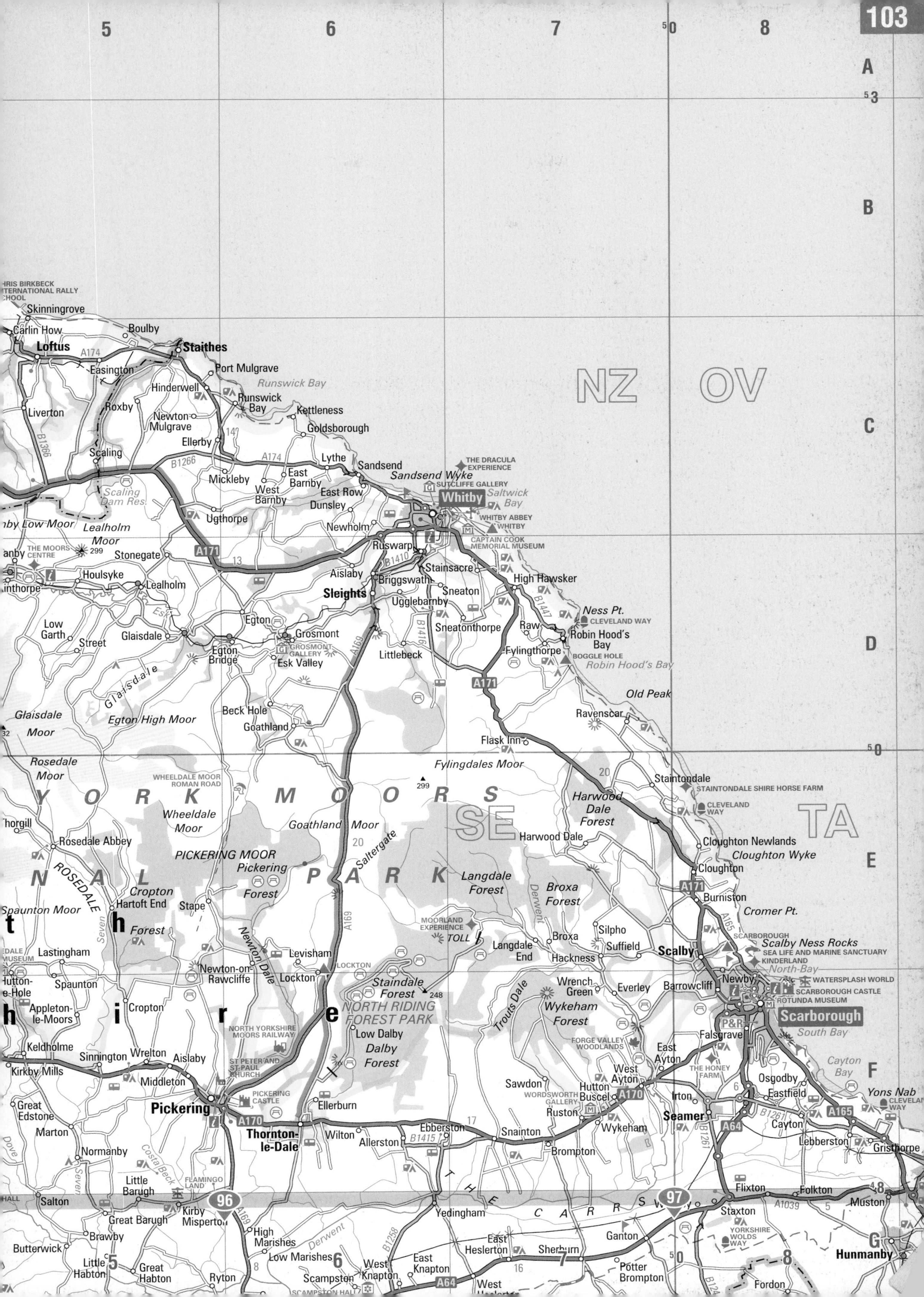
5
6
7
8
A
B
C
D
E
F
G
NZ
OV
SE
TA
Skinningrove
Carlin How
Boulby
Loftus
Staithes
A174
Easington
Port Mulgrave
Runswick Bay
Hinderwell
Runswick Bay
Kettleness
Liverton
Roxby
Newton Mulgrave
Goldsborough
B1366
Ellerby
Scaling
B1266
A174
Lythe
Sandsend
THE DRACULA EXPERIENCE
Sandsend Wyke
Mickleby
East Barnby
SUTCLIFFE GALLERY
Whitby
Saltwick Bay
Scaling Dam Res.
West Barnby
East Row
Dunsley
WHITBY ABBEY
YHA WHITBY
Lealholm Moor
Ugthorpe
Newholm
CAPTAIN COOK MEMORIAL MUSEUM
THE MOORS CENTRE
299
Stonegate
A171
13
Ruswarp
B1410
Stainsacre
Houlsyke
Lealholm
Aislaby
Briggswath
High Hawsker
Sneaton
Sleights
Ugglebarnby
Ness Pt.
CLEVELAND WAY
Low Garth
Egton
B1416
B1447
Sneatonthorpe
Raw
Robin Hood's Bay
Glaisdale
Street
Grosmont
GROSMONT GALLERY
A169
Littlebeck
Fylingthorpe
BOGGLE HOLE
Robin Hood's Bay
Egton Bridge
Esk Valley
Glaisdale
A171
Old Peak
Glaisdale Moor
Egton High Moor
Beck Hole
Ravenscar
Goathland
Flask Inn
Rosedale Moor
Fylingdales Moor
20
Staintondale
STAINTONDALE SHIRE HORSE FARM
WHEELDALE MOOR ROMAN ROAD
299
YORK MOORS
Harwood Dale Forest
CLEVELAND WAY
Wheeldale Moor
Goathland Moor
Harwood Dale
Rosedale Abbey
20
Saltergate
Cloughton Newlands
Cloughton Wyke
PICKERING MOOR
Pickering Forest
ROSEDALE
NAL PARK
Langdale Forest
Cloughton
Cropton
Hartoft End
Broxa Forest
A171
Burniston
Spaunton Moor
Stape
Derwent
Cromer Pt.
MOORLAND EXPERIENCE
TOLL
Forest
Newton Dale
A169
Silpho
A165
SCARBOROUGH
Scalby Ness Rocks
Broxa
SEA LIFE AND MARINE SANCTUARY
Lastingham
Levisham
Langdale End
Suffield
Scalby
KINDERLAND
Hackness
North Bay
Newton-on-Rawcliffe
LOCKTON
Lockton
Staindale Forest
Wrench Green
Newby
WATERSPLASH WORLD
Spaunton
248
Everley
Barrowcliff
SCARBOROUGH CASTLE
NORTH RIDING FOREST PARK
Trouts Dale
ROTUNDA MUSEUM
Appleton-le-Moors
Cropton
Wykeham Forest
Scarborough
P&R
South Bay
NORTH YORKSHIRE MOORS RAILWAY
Low Dalby
FORGE VALLEY WOODLANDS
Falsgrave
Keldholme
Dalby Forest
East Ayton
Sinnington
Wrelton
Aislaby
ST PETER AND ST PAUL CHURCH
Cayton Bay
Kirkby Mills
THE HONEY FARM
West Ayton
Osgodby
Middleton
Sawdon
Hutton Buscel
A170
Yons Nab
CLEVELAND WAY
PICKERING CASTLE
Irton
Eastfield
Great Edstone
WORDSWORTH GALLERY
Pickering
Ellerburn
Ruston
Seamer
B1261
A165
Marton
A170
Thornton-le-Dale
Wilton
Ebberston
17
Snainton
Wykeham
A64
Cayton
Allerston
B1415
Brompton
B1261
Lebberston
Gristhorpe
Normanby
Costa Beck
Little Barugh
FLAMINGO LAND
Flixton
Folkton
48
Salton
96
97
THE CARRS
A1039
Muston
Kirby Misperton
Yedingham
Staxton
Great Barugh
A169
High Marishes
Derwent
B1258
YORKSHIRE WOLDS WAY
Brawby
East Heslerton
Ganton
Butterwick
Low Marishes
Sherburn
Hunmanby
Little Habton
Great Habton
West Knapton
East Knapton
16
Potter Brompton
Ryton
Scampston
SCAMPSTON HALL
A64
West Heslerton
Fordon

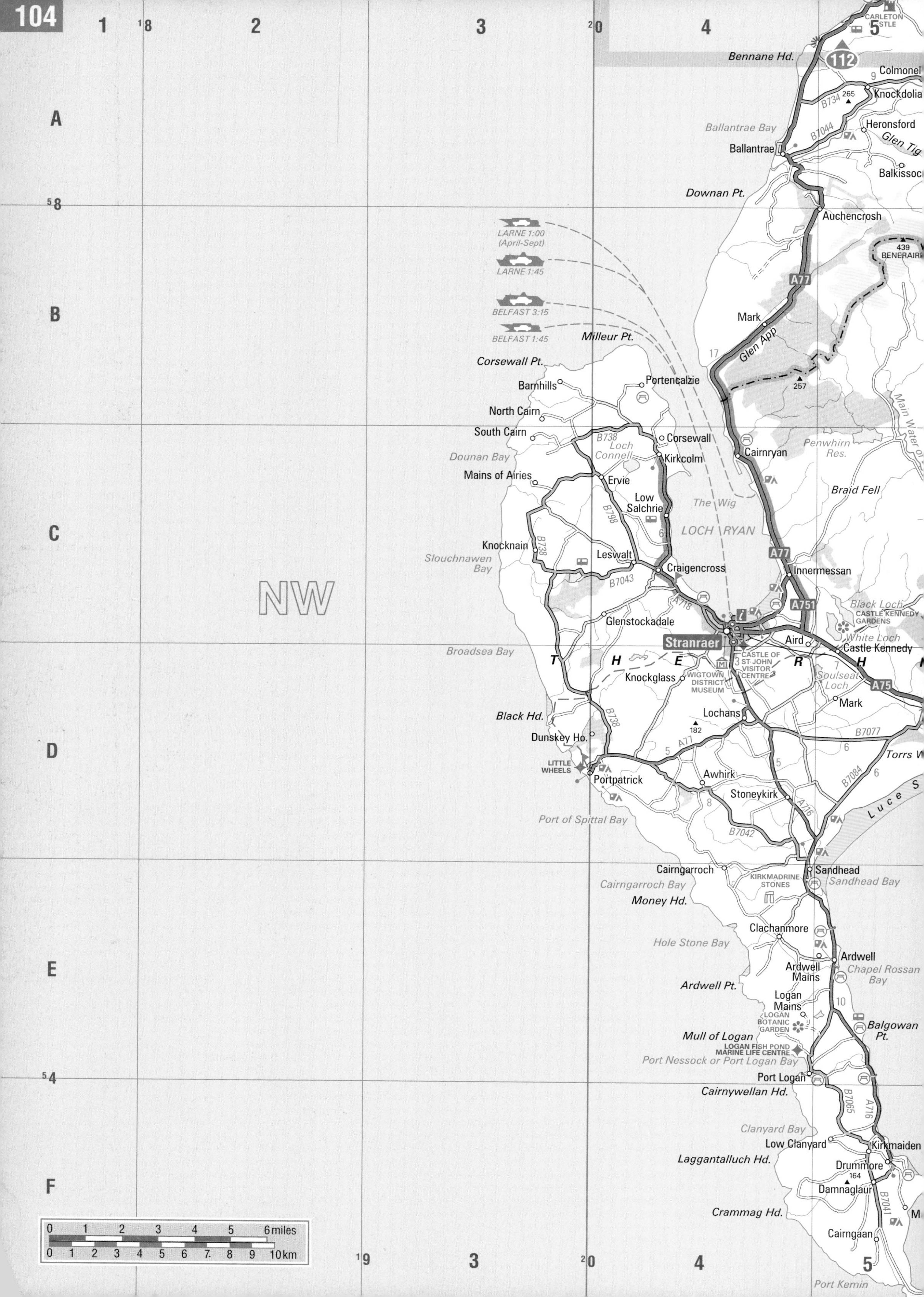

1 **2** **3** **4** **5**

A

B

C

NW

D

E

F

CARLETON CSTLE

Bennane Hd. 112

Colmonel

9

B734 265 Knockdolia

Heronsford

B7044 Glen Tig

Ballantrae Bay

Ballantrae

Balkissoc

Downan Pt.

Auchencrosh

439 BENERAIR

A77

Mark

257

17 Glen App

Corsewall Pt.

Milleur Pt.

Barnhills Portencalzie

North Cairn

Penwhirn Res.

South Cairn Corsewall

B738 Kirkcolm

Loch Connell

Cairnryan

Dounan Bay

Mains of Airies Ervie

Braid Fell

Low Salchrie

The Wig

B798

LOCH RYAN

Knocknain B738 Leswalt

A77

Slouchnawen Bay B7043 Craigencross Innermessan

A718

Black Loch

CASTLE KENNEDY GARDENS

Glenstockadale

White Loch

Broadsea Bay

Stranraer Aird Castle Kennedy

T   **H**   **E**   **R**   **H**

CASTLE OF ST JOHN VISITOR CENTRE

Knockglass WIGTOWN DISTRICT MUSEUM Soulseat Loch

A75

Black Hd. Mark

Dunskey Ho. 182 Lochans

B7077

LITTLE WHEELS 5 A77 5 6

Portpatrick Awhirk 5 Torrs W

Stoneykirk A716 6

Port of Spittal Bay 8 Luce S

B7042

Cairngarroch Sandhead

KIRKMADRINE STONES Sandhead Bay

Cairngarroch Bay

Money Hd.

Clachanmore

Hole Stone Bay

Ardwell

Ardwell Mains Chapel Rossan Bay

Ardwell Pt.

Logan Mains 10

LOGAN BOTANIC GARDEN Balgowan Pt.

Mull of Logan

LOGAN FISH POND MARINE LIFE CENTRE

Port Nessock or Port Logan Bay

Port Logan

Cairnywellan Hd.

B7065 A716

Clanyard Bay

Low Clanyard Kirkmaiden

Laggantalluch Hd.

Drummore

164

Damnaglaur B7041 M

Crammag Hd.

Cairngaan

0 1 2 3 4 5 6 miles
0 1 2 3 4 5 6 7 8 9 10km

Port Kemin

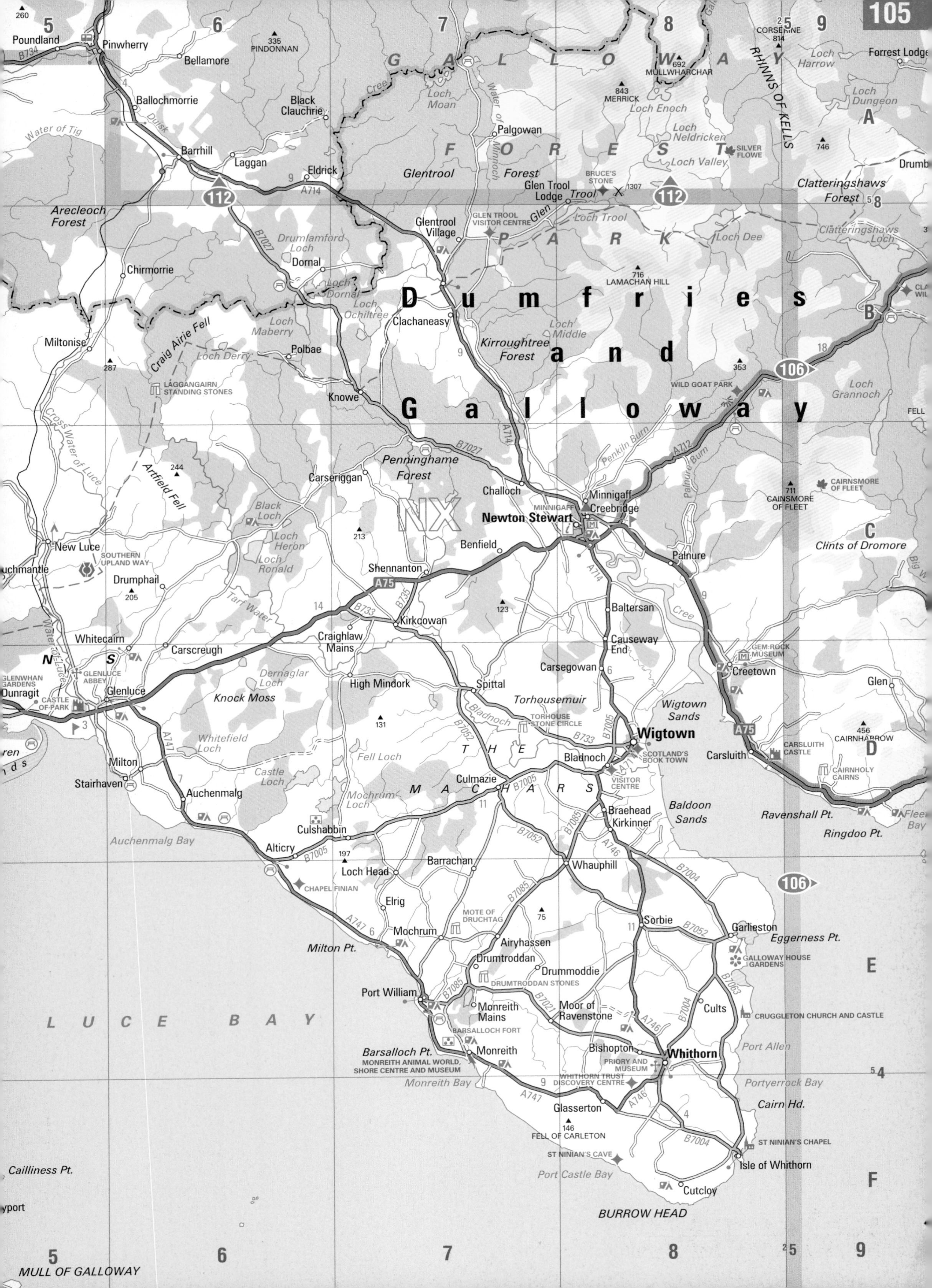
Dumfries and Galloway
GALLOWAY FOREST PARK
Poundland
Pinwherry
Bellamore
PINDONNAN
Ballochmorrie
Black Clauchrie
Barrhill
Laggan
Eldrick
Arecleoch Forest
Glentrool
Glentrool Village
Glen Trool Lodge
Loch Trool
GLEN TROOL VISITOR CENTRE
BRUCE'S STONE
Palgowan
Loch Moan
MERRICK
MULLWHARCHAR
Loch Enoch
Loch Neldricken
Loch Valley
SILVER FLOWE
RHINNS OF KELLS
CORSERINE
Loch Harrow
Forrest Lodge
Loch Dungeon
Clatteringshaws Forest
Clatteringshaws Loch
Loch Dee
LAMACHAN HILL
Drumlamford Loch
Dornal
Loch Dornal
Chirmorrie
Loch Ochiltree
Clachaneasy
Loch Maberry
Miltonise
Craig Airie Fell
Loch Derry
Polbae
LAGGANGAIRN STANDING STONES
Loch Middle
Kirroughtree Forest
Knowe
WILD GOAT PARK
Loch Grannoch
Cross Water of Luce
Artfield Fell
Penninghame Forest
Carseriggan
Challoch
Minnigaff
Creebridge
Newton Stewart
CAIRNSMORE OF FLEET
Black Loch
Loch Heron
Loch Ronald
New Luce
SOUTHERN UPLAND WAY
Drumphail
Benfield
Shennanton
Palnure
Clints of Dromore
Tarf Water
Kirkcowan
Baltersan
Causeway End
Whitecairn
Carscreugh
Craighlaw Mains
Cree
GEM ROCK MUSEUM
Creetown
GLENWHAN GARDENS
Dunragit
CASTLE OF PARK
GLENLUCE ABBEY
Glenluce
Knock Moss
Dernaglar Loch
High Mindork
Spittal
Torhousemuir
Carsegowan
TORHOUSE STONE CIRCLE
Wigtown Sands
Wigtown
SCOTLAND'S BOOK TOWN
Glen
CAIRNHARROW
Whitefield Loch
Fell Loch
Bladnoch
Carsluith
CARSLUITH CASTLE
CAIRNHOLY CAIRNS
Milton
Stairhaven
Castle Loch
Culmazie
THE MACHARS
VISITOR CENTRE
Auchenmalg
Mochrum Loch
Braehead
Kirkinner
Baldoon Sands
Ravenshall Pt.
Ringdoo Pt.
Culshabbin
Auchenmalg Bay
Alticry
Barrachan
Loch Head
Whauphill
CHAPEL FINIAN
Elrig
MOTE OF DRUCHTAG
Sorbie
Garlieston
Eggerness Pt.
Mochrum
Milton Pt.
Airyhassen
GALLOWAY HOUSE GARDENS
Drumtroddan
Drummoddie
DRUMTRODDAN STONES
Port William
Monreith Mains
Moor of Ravenstone
Cults
CRUGGLETON CHURCH AND CASTLE
LUCE BAY
BARSALLOCH FORT
Barsalloch Pt.
Monreith
Bishopton
Whithorn
Port Allen
MONREITH ANIMAL WORLD, SHORE CENTRE AND MUSEUM
PRIORY AND MUSEUM
WHITHORN TRUST DISCOVERY CENTRE
Monreith Bay
Portyerrock Bay
Glasserton
Cairn Hd.
FELL OF CARLETON
ST NINIAN'S CHAPEL
ST NINIAN'S CAVE
Isle of Whithorn
Port Castle Bay
Cailliness Pt.
Cutcloy
BURROW HEAD
MULL OF GALLOWAY
NX
A75
A714
A712
A747
A746
B7027
B7052
B7005
B7085
B7004
B7063
B7021
B733
B735
B734
112
106

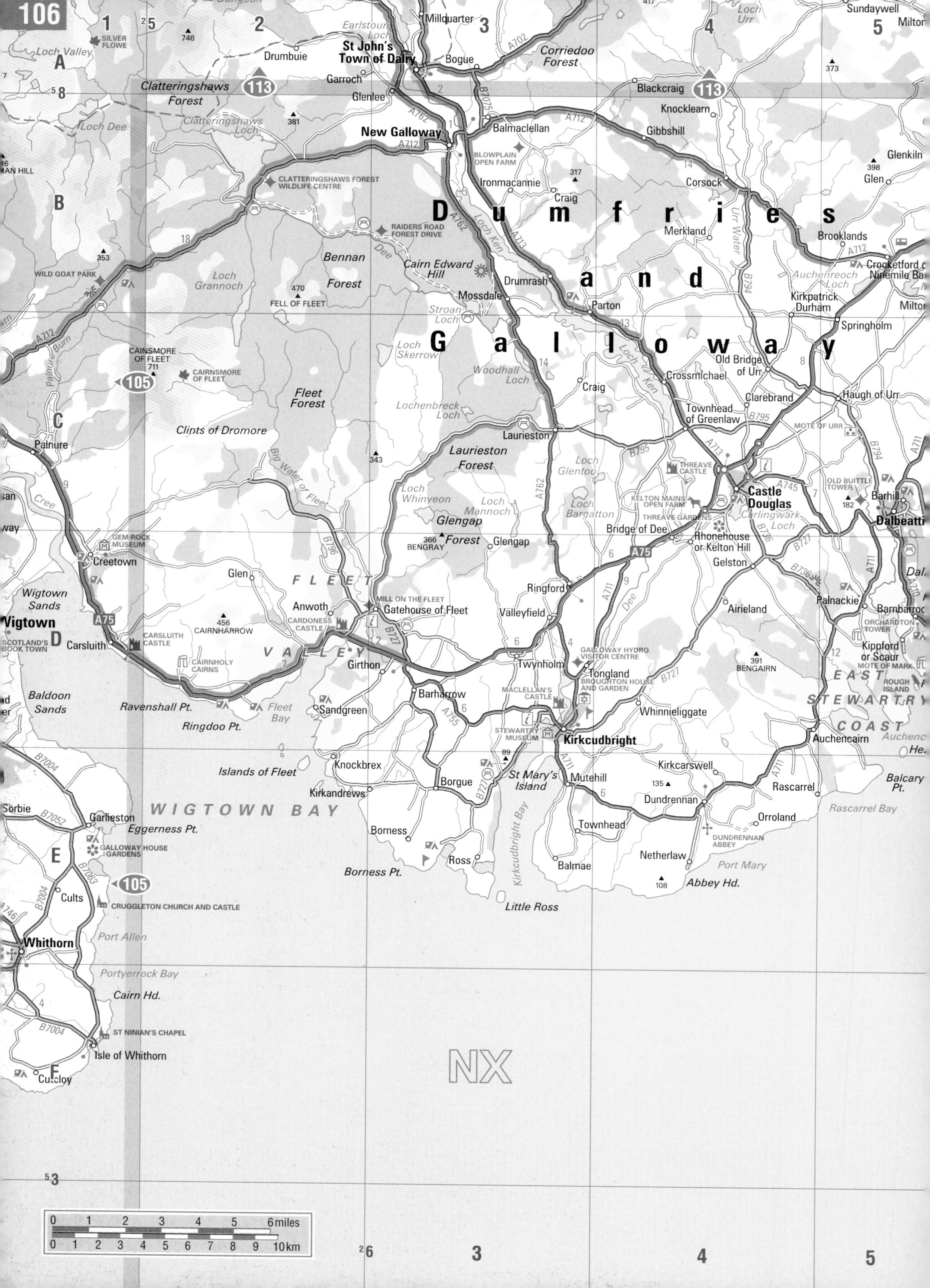

Dumfries and Galloway
St John's Town of Dalry
Millquarter
Earlstoun Loch
Corriedoo Forest
Sundaywell
Milton
Loch Urr
Loch Valley
SILVER FLOWE
746
Drumbuie
Garroch
Bogue
Glenlee
373
Clatteringshaws Forest
113
Blackcraig
Knocklearn
Loch Dee
Clatteringshaws Loch
381
New Galloway
Balmaclellan
Gibbshill
BLOWPLAIN OPEN FARM
Glenkiln
398
Glen
AN HILL
CLATTERINGSHAWS FOREST WILDLIFE CENTRE
317
Ironmacannie
Craig
Corsock
RAIDERS ROAD FOREST DRIVE
Merkland
Urr Water
Brooklands
A712
A762
A713
Loch Ken
Bennan Forest
Cairn Edward Hill
Crocketford or Ninemile Bar
Auchenreoch Loch
353
WILD GOAT PARK
Loch Grannoch
470
FELL OF FLEET
Drumrash
Mossdale
Parton
Kirkpatrick Durham
Stroan Loch
Springholm
Milton
Loch Skerrow
Old Bridge of Urr
CAINSMORE OF FLEET 711
CAIRNSMORE OF FLEET
105
Woodhall Loch
Craig
Crossmichael
Clarebrand
Haugh of Urr
Palnure Burn
Fleet Forest
Lochenbreck Loch
Townhead of Greenlaw
B795
MOTE OF URR
Clints of Dromore
Laurieston
Palnure
Laurieston Forest
343
Big Water of Fleet
Loch Glentoo
THREAVE CASTLE
Castle Douglas
OLD BUITTLE TOWER
A745
B794
Cree
Loch Whinyeon
Loch Mannoch
Loch Bargatton
KELTON MAINS OPEN FARM
THREAVE GARDENS
Carlingwark Loch
Barhill
182
Dalbeattie
GEM ROCK MUSEUM
Glengap Forest
366 BENGRAY
Glengap
Bridge of Dee
Rhonehouse or Kelton Hill
Creetown
B796
A75
Gelston
B727
B736
A711
Wigtown Sands
Glen
FLEET
Ringford
Dee
Palnackie
Wigtown
Anworth
MILL ON THE FLEET
Gatehouse of Fleet
Valleyfield
Airieland
Barnbarroch
SCOTLAND'S BOOK TOWN
Carsluith
CARSLUITH CASTLE
456 CAIRNHARROW
CARDONESS CASTLE
ORCHARDTON TOWER
VALLEY
GALLOWAY HYDRO VISITOR CENTRE
Kippford or Scaur
MOTE OF MARK
CAIRNHOLY CAIRNS
Girthon
Twynholm
Tongland
391 BENGAIRN
BROUGHTON HOUSE AND GARDEN
EAST STEWARTRY COAST
ROUGH ISLAND
Baldoon Sands
Ravenshall Pt.
Fleet Bay
Barharrow
MACLELLAN'S CASTLE
Whinnieliggate
Sandgreen
A755
Ringdoo Pt.
STEWARTRY MUSEUM
Kirkcudbright
Auchencairn
Auchencairn Bay
Hestan Island
B7004
Knockbrex
89
Kirkcarswell
Islands of Fleet
St Mary's Isle
Mutehill
135
Rascarrel
Balcary Pt.
Sorbie
Kirkandrews
Borgue
Dundrennan
B7052
Garlieston
WIGTOWN BAY
Kirkcudbright Bay
Townhead
Orroland
Rascarrel Bay
Eggerness Pt.
GALLOWAY HOUSE GARDENS
Borness
DUNDRENNAN ABBEY
B7063
Netherlaw
Port Mary
Ross
Balmae
Borness Pt.
Abbey Hd.
108
Cults
CRUGGLETON CHURCH AND CASTLE
Little Ross
Port Allen
Whithorn
Portyerrock Bay
Cairn Hd.
ST NINIAN'S CHAPEL
Isle of Whithorn
Cutcloy
NX
0 1 2 3 4 5 6 miles
0 1 2 3 4 5 6 7 8 9 10 km

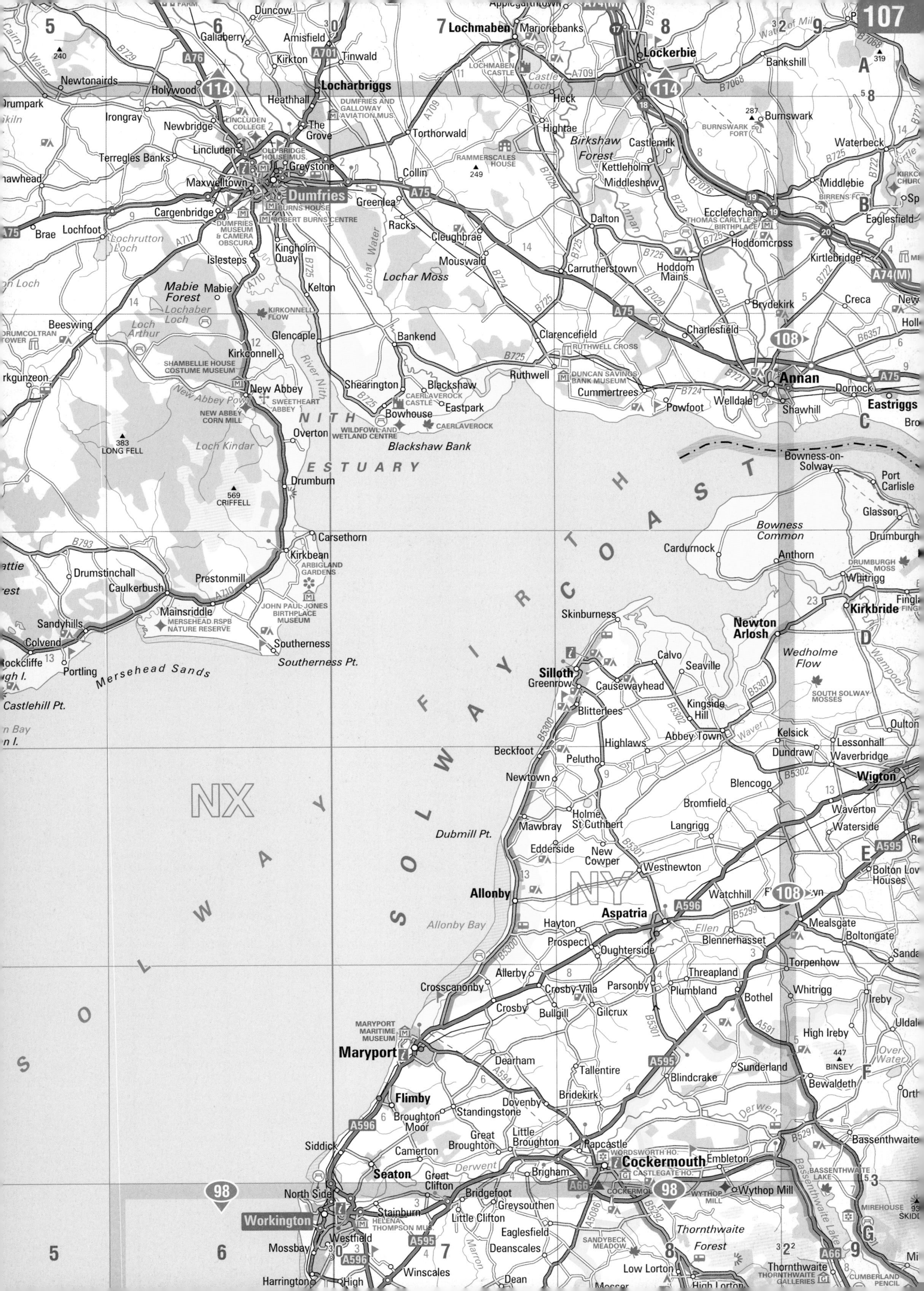
Lochmaben
Lockerbie
Locharbriggs
Dumfries
Annan
Eastriggs
Silloth
Kirkbride
Newton Arlosh
Wigton
Aspatria
Allonby
Maryport
Flimby
Seaton
Workington
Cockermouth
NITH ESTUARY
SOLWAY FIRTH
SOLWAY COAST
NX
NY
Lochar Moss
Mabie Forest
Birkshaw Forest
Blackshaw Bank
Mersehead Sands
Southerness Pt.
Dubmill Pt.
Allonby Bay
Bowness Common
Wedholme Flow
Thornthwaite Forest
Bassenthwaite Lake
569 CRIFFELL
383 LONG FELL
447 BINSEY
Ecclefechan
Gretna
Kirkbean
New Abbey
Glencaple
Ruthwell
Clarencefield
Carrutherstown
Bowness-on-Solway
Port Carlisle
Abbey Town
Dearham
Bothel
Plumbland
Mealsgate
Torpenhow
Brigham
Papcastle
Embleton
Wythop Mill
Harrington
Great Clifton
Little Clifton
Eaglesfield
Deanscales
Low Lorton

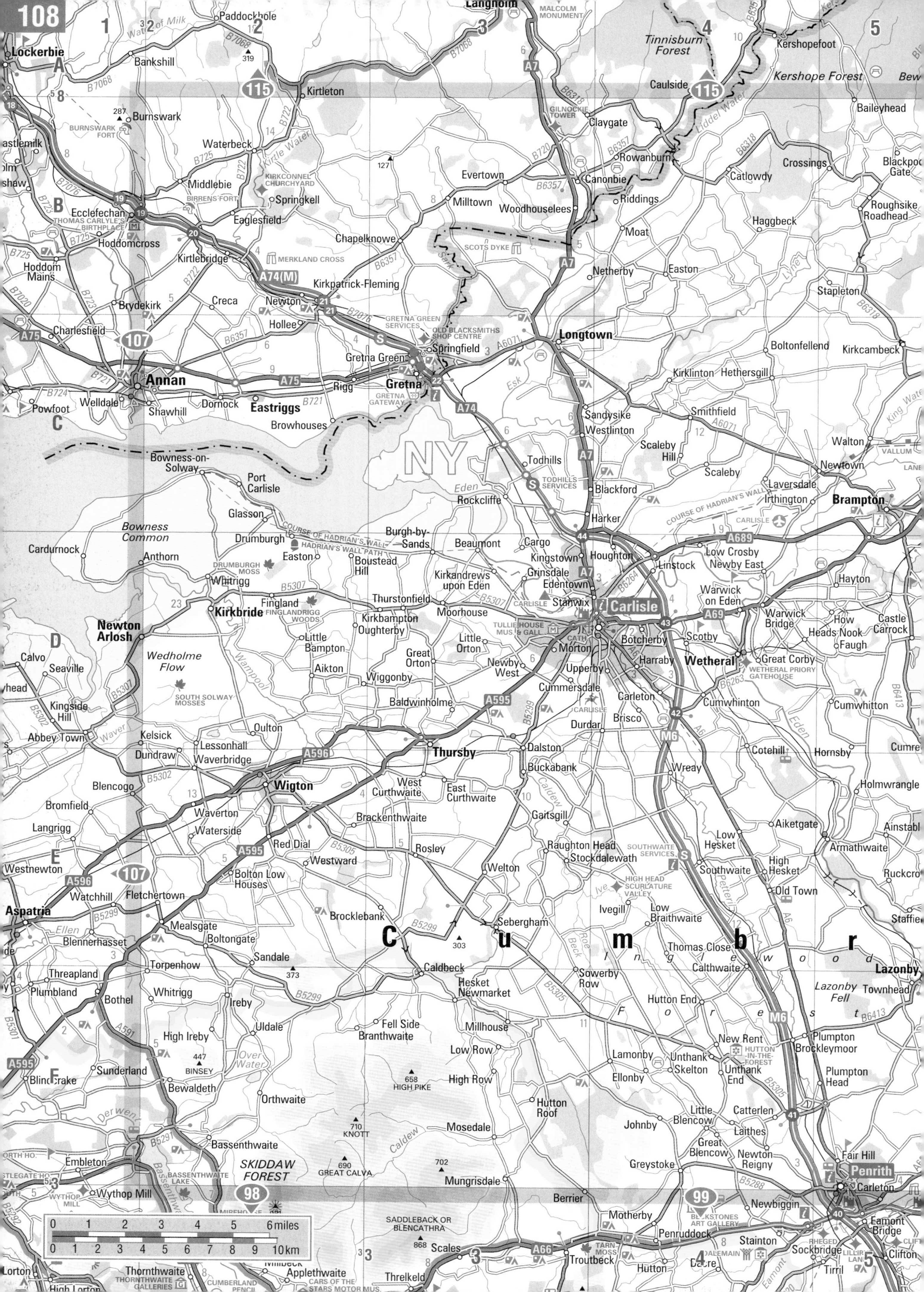
Lockerbie
Paddockhole
Langholm
Malcolm Monument
Tinnisburn Forest
Kershopefoot
Kershope Forest
Bankshill
Kirtleton
Caulside
Baileyhead
Burnswark
Burnswark Fort
Claygate
Gilnockie Tower
Waterbeck
Rowanburn
Crossings
Blackpool Gate
Catlowdy
Middlebie
Kirkconnel Churchyard
Evertown
Canonbie
Birrens Fort
Springkell
Milltown
Woodhouselees
Riddings
Roughsike
Roadhead
Ecclefechan
Thomas Carlyle's Birthplace
Eaglesfield
Haggbeck
Moat
Hoddomcross
Chapelknowe
Scots Dyke
Kirtlebridge
Merkland Cross
Hoddom Mains
Netherby
Easton
Stapleton
Kirkpatrick-Fleming
Brydekirk
Creca
Newton
Gretna Green Services
Old Blacksmiths Shop Centre
Charlesfield
Hollee
Springfield
Longtown
Boltonfellend
Kirkcambeck
Gretna Green
Annan
Rigg
Gretna
Gretna Gateway
Kirklinton
Hethersgill
Powfoot
Welldale
Shawhill
Dornock
Eastriggs
Browhouses
Sandysike
Westlinton
Smithfield
Scaleby Hill
Walton
Vallum
NY
Bowness-on-Solway
Todhills
Todhills Services
Scaleby
Newtown
Port Carlisle
Eden
Rockcliffe
Blackford
Laversdale
Irthington
Brampton
Glasson
Course of Hadrian's Wall
Carlisle
Harker
Bowness Common
Drumburgh
Hadrian's Wall Path
Burgh-by-Sands
Beaumont
Cargo
Houghton
Low Crosby
Newby East
Cardurnock
Anthorn
Easton
Boustead Hill
Kingstown
Linstock
Hayton
Drumburgh Moss
Whitrigg
Kirkandrews upon Eden
Grinsdale
Edentown
Warwick on Eden
Fingland
Finglandrigg Woods
Thurstonfield
Stanwix
Carlisle
Warwick Bridge
How
Castle Carrock
Kirkbride
Kirkbampton
Moorhouse
Tullie House Mus & Gall
Cath
Heads Nook
Newton Arlosh
Oughterby
Little Bampton
Little Orton
Morton
Botcherby
Scotby
Faugh
Calvo
Wedholme Flow
Great Orton
Newby West
Harraby
Wetheral
Great Corby
Wetheral Priory Gatehouse
Seaville
Aikton
Wiggonby
Upperby
South Solway Mosses
Baldwinholme
Cummersdale
Carleton
Cumwhinton
Cumwhitton
Kingside Hill
Durdar
Brisco
Oulton
Abbey Town
Kelsick
Lessonhall
Dalston
Cotehill
Hornsby
Cumrew
Dundraw
Waverbridge
Thursby
Wreay
Buckabank
Blencogo
Wigton
West Curthwaite
East Curthwaite
Holmwrangle
Bromfield
Waverton
Brackenthwaite
Gaitsgill
Aiketgate
Ainstable
Langrigg
Waterside
Red Dial
Raughton Head
Stockdalewath
Southwaite Services
Low Hesket
Armathwaite
Westnewton
Westward
Rosley
Welton
High Hesket
Southwaite
Ruckcroft
Bolton Low Houses
High Head Sculpture Valley
Old Town
Watchhill
Fletchertown
Aspatria
Mealsgate
Brocklebank
Sebergham
Ivegill
Low Braithwaite
Staffield
Blennerhasset
Boltongate
Sandale
Thomas Close
Calthwaite
Cumbria
Inglewood Forest
Lazonby
Threapland
Torpenhow
Caldbeck
Sowerby Row
Lazonby Fell
Townhead
Plumbland
Bothel
Whitrigg
Ireby
Hesket Newmarket
Hutton End
Uldale
Fell Side
Branthwaite
Millhouse
New Rent
Hutton-in-the-Forest
Plumpton
Brockleymoor
High Ireby
Low Row
Lamonby
Unthank
Skelton
Unthank End
Binsey
Over Water
Blindcrake
Sunderland
High Pike
High Row
Ellonby
Plumpton Head
Bewaldeth
Orthwaite
Hutton Roof
Little Blencow
Catterlen
Knott
Mosedale
Johnby
Laithes
Bassenthwaite
Great Blencow
Newton Reigny
Fair Hill
Embleton
Skiddaw Forest
Great Calva
Greystoke
Penrith
Bassenthwaite Lake
Wythop Mill
Mungrisdale
Carleton
Mirehouse
Berrier
Newbiggin
Motherby
Blencathra
Saddleback or Blencathra
Blakstones Art Gallery
Eamont Bridge
Penruddock
Rheged
Stainton
Scales
Tarn Moss
Dalemain
Sockbridge
Lillip Lane
Clifton
Thornthwaite
Thornthwaite Galleries
Troutbeck
Hutton
Dacre
Tirril
Lorton
High Lorton
Applethwaite
Cars of the Stars Motor Mus.
Cumberland Pencil
Threlkeld
0 1 2 3 4 5 6 miles
0 1 2 3 4 5 6 7 8 9 10 km

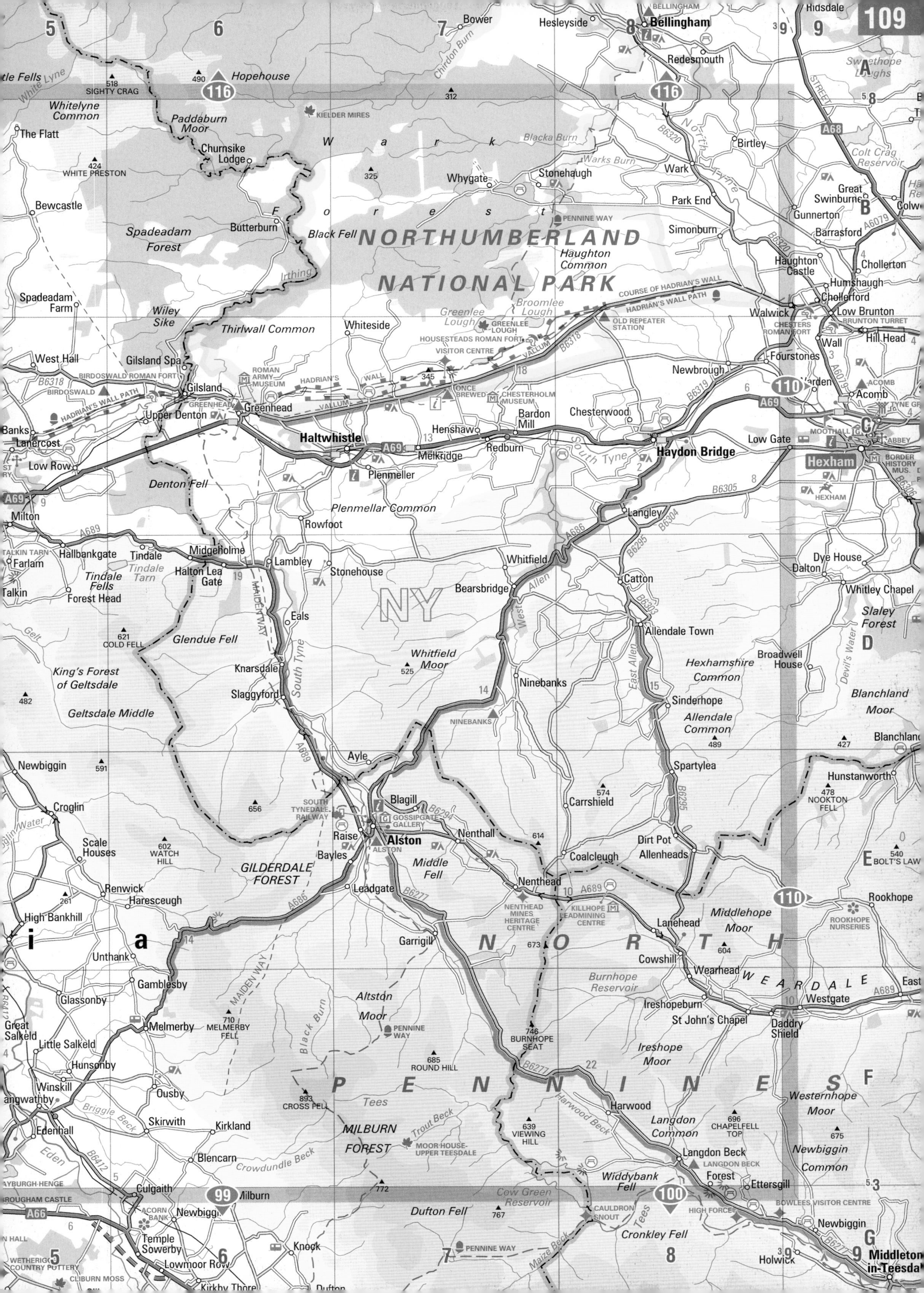
NORTHUMBERLAND
NATIONAL PARK
NORTH PENNINES
Wark Forest
WEARDALE
NY
Bower
Hesleyside
Bellingham
Ridsdale
Hopehouse
SIGHTY CRAG
Whitelyne Common
Paddaburn Moor
KIELDER MIRES
The Flatt
Churnsike Lodge
WHITE PRESTON
Blacka Burn
Warks Burn
Stonehaugh
Whygate
Wark
Birtley
Redesmouth
Colt Crag Reservoir
Great Swinburne
Gunnerton
Barrasford
Chollerton
Bewcastle
Butterburn
Black Fell
Spadeadam Forest
Park End
Simonburn
Haughton Common
Haughton Castle
Humshaugh
Chollerford
PENNINE WAY
Irthing
Spadeadam Farm
Wiley Sike
Thirlwall Common
Whiteside
Greenlee Lough
Broomlee Lough
GREENLEE LOUGH
HOUSESTEADS ROMAN FORT
VISITOR CENTRE
COURSE OF HADRIAN'S WALL
HADRIAN'S WALL PATH
OLD REPEATER STATION
Walwick
CHESTERS ROMAN FORT
Low Brunton
BRUNTON TURRET
Hill Head
Wall
Fourstones
West Hall
Gilsland Spa
BIRDOSWALD ROMAN FORT
BIRDOSWALD
ROMAN ARMY MUSEUM
VALLUM
ONCE BREWED
CHESTERHOLM MUSEUM
Newbrough
Warden
ACOMB
Acomb
Gilsland
GREENHEAD
Greenhead
Upper Denton
Banks
Lanercost
Haltwhistle
Henshaw
Bardon Mill
Chesterwood
Melkridge
Redburn
Haydon Bridge
Low Gate
MOOTHALL
Hexham
BORDER HISTORY MUS.
ABBEY
Low Row
Plenmeller
South Tyne
Denton Fell
HEXHAM
Milton
Plenmellar Common
Rowfoot
Langley
TALKIN TARN
Farlam
Hallbankgate
Tindale
Midgeholme
Tindale Tarn
Halton Lea Gate
Lambley
Stonehouse
Whitfield
Catton
Dye House
Dalton
Whitley Chapel
Talkin
Tindale Fells
Forest Head
Bearsbridge
MAIDEN WAY
Eals
West Allen
Allendale Town
Slaley Forest
COLD FELL
Glendue Fell
Whitfield Moor
Broadwell House
Hexhamshire Common
Devil's Water
King's Forest of Geltsdale
Knarsdale
Ninebanks
East Allen
Sinderhope
Allendale Common
Blanchland Moor
Geltsdale Middle
Slaggyford
NINEBANKS
Blanchland
Newbiggin
Ayle
Spartylea
Hunstanworth
NOOKTON FELL
Croglin
SOUTH TYNEDALE RAILWAY
Blagill
GOSSIPGATE GALLERY
Carrshield
Scale Houses
WATCH HILL
Raise
Alston
ALSTON
Nenthall
Dirt Pot
Allenheads
Coalcleugh
BOLT'S LAW
GILDERDALE FOREST
Bayles
Middle Fell
Nenthead
Renwick
Harescough
Leadgate
NENTHEAD MINES HERITAGE CENTRE
KILLHOPE LEADMINING CENTRE
Middlehope Moor
Rookhope
ROOKHOPE NURSERIES
High Bankhill
Garrigill
Lanehead
Unthank
Cowshill
Wearhead
Gamblesby
Burnhope Reservoir
Glassonby
Altston Moor
Ireshopeburn
Westgate
St John's Chapel
Daddry Shield
Great Salkeld
Melmerby
MELMERBY FELL
Little Salkeld
BURNHOPE SEAT
Ireshope Moor
Hunsonby
ROUND HILL
Black Burn
Winskill
Ousby
Langwathby
CROSS FELL
Tees
Harwood
Westernhope Moor
Brigg!e Beck
Edenhall
Skirwith
Kirkland
MILBURN FOREST
Trout Beck
VIEWING HILL
Harwood Beck
Langdon Common
CHAPELFELL TOP
Newbiggin Common
MOOR HOUSE-UPPER TEESDALE
Eden
Blencarn
Crowdundle Beck
Langdon Beck
LANGDON BECK
Widdybank Fell
Forest
Ettersgill
Culgaith
Milburn
Cow Green Reservoir
HIGH FORCE
BOWLEES VISITOR CENTRE
ACORN BANK
Newbiggin
Dufton Fell
CAULDRON SNOUT
Temple Sowerby
Knock
Cronkley Fell
Middleton-in-Teesdale
Lowmoor Row
Maize Beck
Holwick
WETHERIGG COUNTRY POTTERY
CLIBURN MOSS
Kirkby Thore
Dufton
A69
A689
A686
B6318
B6320
B6319
B6305
B6304
B6295
B6303
B6294
B6277
B6412
A6079
A68
A66
116
110
99
100

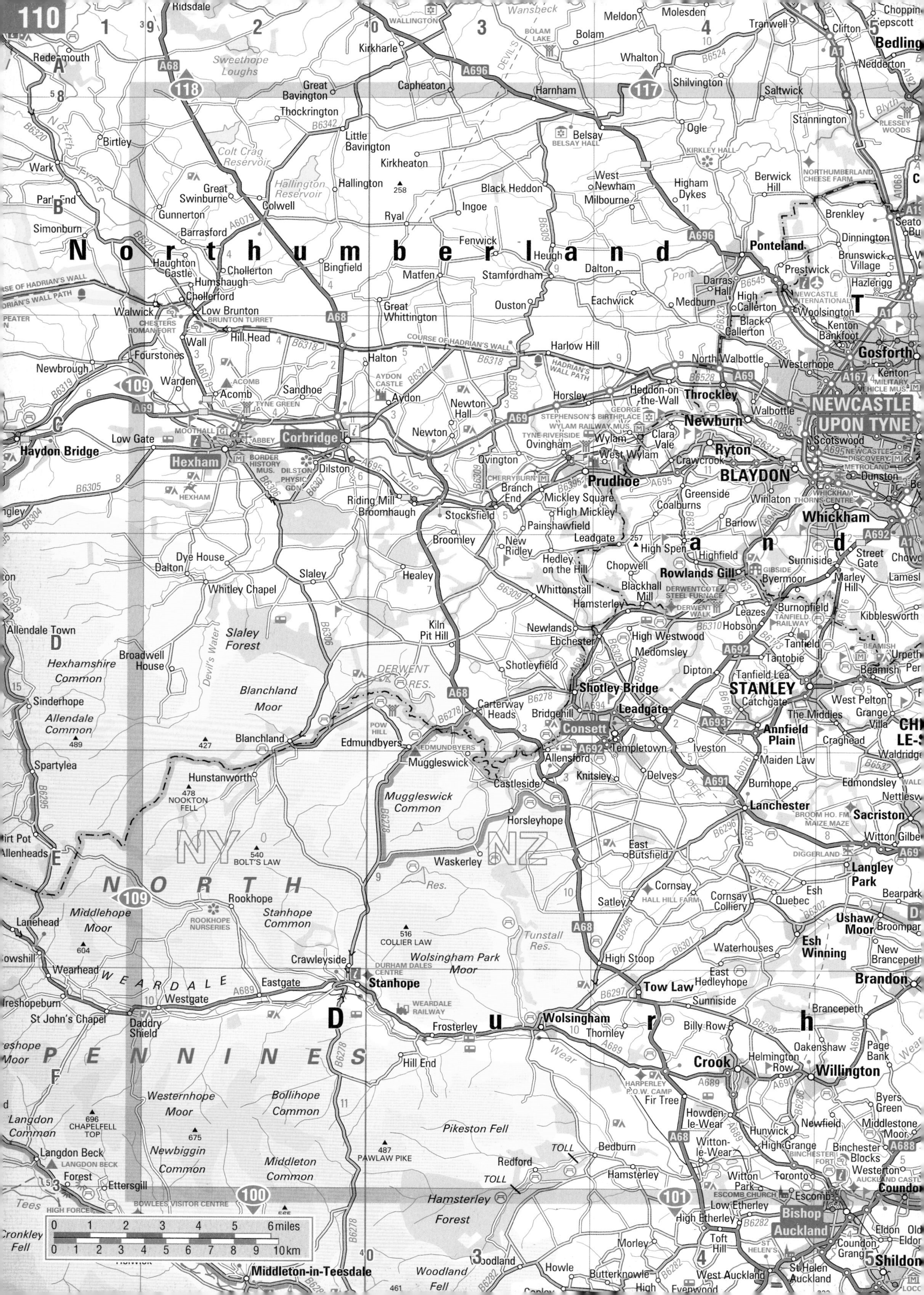

110
Northumberland
Durham
NORTH PENNINES
NEWCASTLE UPON TYNE
Hexham
Corbridge
Consett
Bishop Auckland
STANLEY
BLAYDON
Prudhoe
Ponteland
Gosforth
Newburn
Ryton
Throckley
Whickham
Crook
Willington
Stanhope
Wolsingham
Tow Law
Lanchester
Shotley Bridge
Leadgate
Haydon Bridge
Middleton-in-Teesdale
Shildon
Sacriston
Brandon
Esh Winning
Ushaw Moor
Langley Park
Annfield Plain
Rowlands Gill
Bedlington
Kirkharle
Capheaton
Great Bavington
Thockrington
Little Bavington
Kirkheaton
Hallington
Colwell
Great Swinburne
Gunnerton
Barrasford
Chollerton
Humshaugh
Chollerford
Walwick
Low Brunton
Wall
Fourstones
Newbrough
Warden
Acomb
Hill Head
Halton
Aydon
Sandhoe
Low Gate
Dilston
Riding Mill
Broomhaugh
Stocksfield
Bywell
Ovington
Ovingham
Wylam
Horsley
Heddon-on-the-Wall
Matfen
Stamfordham
Great Whittington
Ouston
Harlow Hill
Dalton
Eachwick
Medburn
Belsay
Harnham
Bolam
Meldon
Molesden
Whalton
Shilvington
Ogle
Saltwick
Stannington
Berwick Hill
Higham Dykes
Milbourne
West Newham
Black Heddon
Ingoe
Ryal
Fenwick
Heugh
Bingfield
Wark
Birtley
Simonburn
Redesmouth
Slaley
Whitley Chapel
Dye House
Healey
Broomley
New Ridley
Hedley on the Hill
Whittonstall
Kiln Pit Hill
Newlands
Ebchester
Medomsley
Hamsterley
Blanchland
Edmundbyers
Muggleswick
Castleside
Allensford
Carterway Heads
Hunstanworth
Allendale Town
Sinderhope
Allenheads
Rookhope
Eastgate
Westgate
Daddry Shield
St John's Chapel
Wearhead
Frosterley
Hill End
Thornley
Billy Row
Sunniside
Satley
Cornsay
Cornsay Colliery
Quebec
Esh
Burnhope
Maiden Law
Delves
Iveston
Knitsley
Dipton
Tanfield
Tantobie
Burnopfield
Byermoor
Sunniside
Marley Hill
Greenside
Coalburns
Barlow
Winlaton
Crawcrook
Clara Vale
Mickley Square
High Mickley
Painshawfield
Leadgate
High Spen
Highfield
Chopwell
Blackhall Mill
Hobson
Leazes
Catchgate
Templetown
Craghead
Edmondsley
Witton Gilbert
Helmington Row
Fir Tree
Howden-le-Wear
Witton-le-Wear
Hunwick
High Grange
Newfield
Toronto
Escomb
Low Etherley
High Etherley
Toft Hill
West Auckland
St Helen Auckland
Bedburn
Hamsterley
Redford
Hamsterley Forest
Woodland
Eldon
Coundon
Westerton
Byers Green
Page Bank
Brancepeth
New Brancepeth
Weardale
Tunstall Res.
Derwent Res.
Slaley Forest
Blanchland Moor
Muggleswick Common
Stanhope Common
Wolsingham Park Moor
Pikeston Fell
Bollihope Common
Westernhope Moor
Newbiggin Common
Middleton Common
Middlehope Moor
Hexhamshire Common
Allendale Common
Langdon Common
Sweethope Loughs
Colt Crag Reservoir
Hallington Reservoir
NY
NZ
A68
A69
A696
A692
A693
A691
A689
A1
0 1 2 3 4 5 6 miles
0 1 2 3 4 5 6 7 8 9 10 km

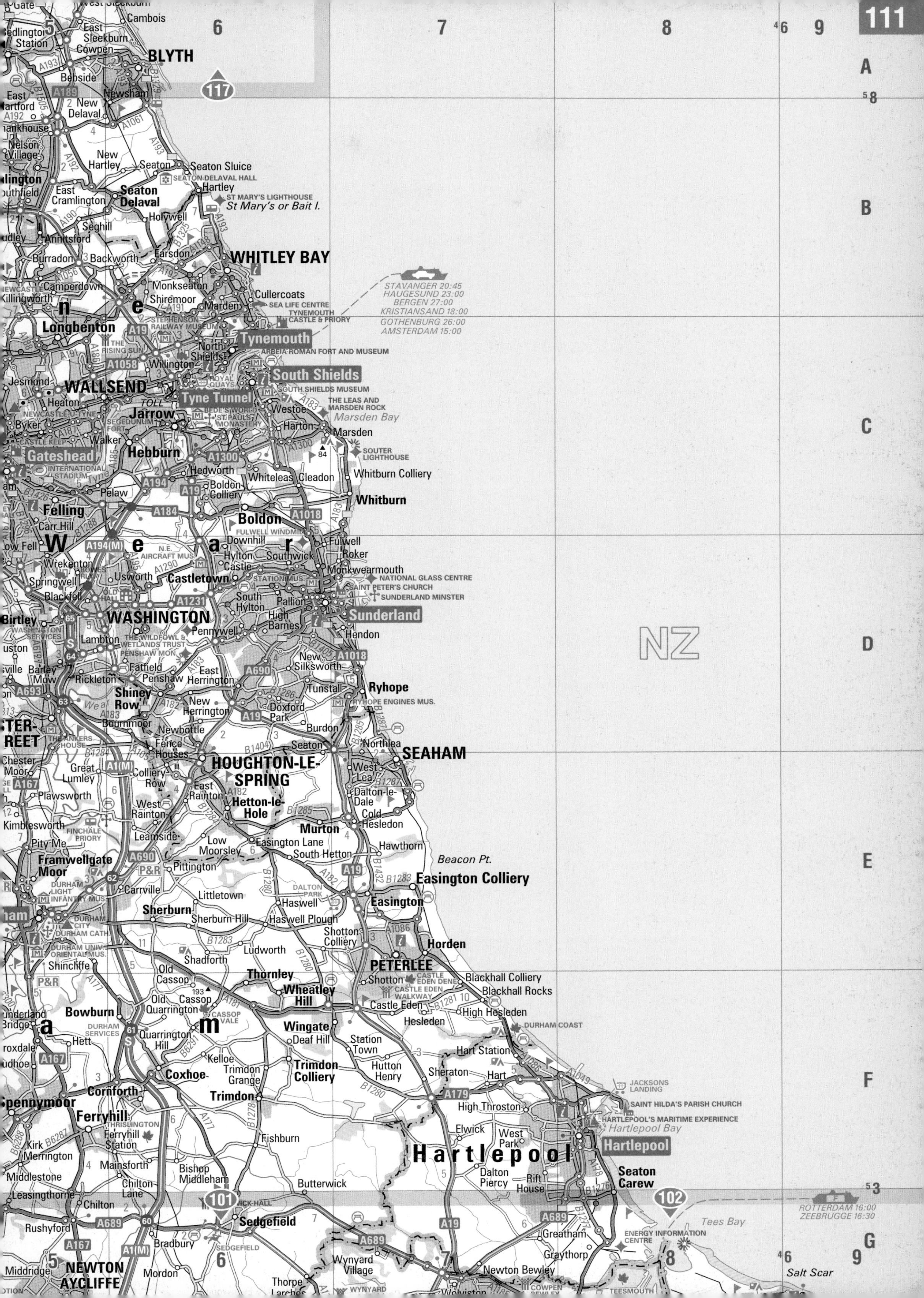
6
7
8
9
A
B
C
D
E
F
G
117
101
102
NZ
BLYTH
Cambois
East Sleekburn
Cowpen
Bebside
Newsham
New Delaval
New Hartley
Seaton
Seaton Sluice
SEATON DELAVAL HALL
Hartley
ST MARY'S LIGHTHOUSE
St Mary's or Bait I.
East Cramlington
Seaton Delaval
Holywell
Seghill
Annitsford
Burradon
Backworth
Earsdon
WHITLEY BAY
Camperdown
Monkseaton
Shiremoor
Killingworth
Cullercoats
SEA LIFE CENTRE
TYNEMOUTH CASTLE & PRIORY
Marden
STAVANGER 20:45
HAUGESUND 23:00
BERGEN 27:00
KRISTIANSAND 18:00
GOTHENBURG 26:00
AMSTERDAM 15:00
Longbenton
STEPHENSON RAILWAY MUSEUM
Tynemouth
THE RISING SUN
North Shields
ARBEIA ROMAN FORT AND MUSEUM
Willington
South Shields
Jesmond
WALLSEND
ROYAL QUAYS
SOUTH SHIELDS MUSEUM
Heaton
Tyne Tunnel
TOLL
Jarrow
BEDE'S WORLD
ST PAUL'S MONASTERY
Westoe
THE LEAS AND MARSDEN ROCK
Marsden Bay
Harton
Marsden
SEGEDUNUM FORT
Byker
Walker
CASTLE KEEP
Hebburn
SOUTER LIGHTHOUSE
Gateshead
INTERNATIONAL STADIUM
Hedworth
Whiteleas
Cleadon
Whitburn Colliery
Boldon Colliery
Pelaw
Whitburn
Felling
Boldon
Carr Hill
FULWELL WINDMILL
Downhill
Fulwell
N.E. AIRCRAFT MUS.
Hylton Castle
Southwick
Roker
Wrekenton
Monkwearmouth
Springwell
Usworth
Castletown
STATION MUS.
NATIONAL GLASS CENTRE
SAINT PETER'S CHURCH
SUNDERLAND MINSTER
Blackfell
South Hylton
Pallion
Birtley
WASHINGTON
High Barnes
Sunderland
WASHINGTON SERVICES
Pennywell
Hendon
Lambton
THE WILDFOWL & WETLANDS TRUST
PENSHAW MON.
New Silksworth
Fatfield
Penshaw
East Herrington
Rickleton
Shiney Row
Tunstall
Ryhope
RYHOPE ENGINES MUS.
New Herrington
Doxford Park
Bournmoor
Newbottle
Burdon
Fence Houses
Seaton
Northlea
SEAHAM
Great Lumley
Colliery Row
HOUGHTON-LE-SPRING
West Lea
Chester Moor
Plawsworth
East Rainton
Dalton-le-Dale
West Rainton
Hetton-le-Hole
Cold Hesledon
Kimblesworth
FINCHALE PRIORY
Murton
Pity Me
Leamside
Low Moorsley
Easington Lane
Hawthorn
South Hetton
Beacon Pt.
Framwellgate Moor
Pittington
Easington Colliery
DURHAM LIGHT INFANTRY MUS.
Carrville
DALTON PARK
Littletown
Easington
Haswell
Sherburn
Sherburn Hill
Haswell Plough
DURHAM CITY
DURHAM CATH.
Shotton Colliery
Horden
DURHAM UNIV. ORIENTAL MUS.
Shadforth
Ludworth
Shincliffe
PETERLEE
Old Cassop
Thornley
Shotton
CASTLE EDEN DENE
Blackhall Colliery
Blackhall Rocks
Cassop
Wheatley Hill
CASTLE EDEN WALKWAY
Castle Eden
Old Quarrington
CASSOP VALE
High Hesleden
Bowburn
Hesleden
DURHAM COAST
DURHAM SERVICES
Wingate
Quarrington Hill
Deaf Hill
Station Town
Hett
Hart Station
Kelloe
Trimdon Grange
Trimdon Colliery
Hutton Henry
Sheraton
Hart
JACKSONS LANDING
Coxhoe
Cornforth
Trimdon
Spennymoor
SAINT HILDA'S PARISH CHURCH
High Throston
HARTLEPOOL'S MARITIME EXPERIENCE
Ferryhill
THRISLINGTON
Hartlepool Bay
Elwick
West Park
Ferryhill Station
Fishburn
Hartlepool
Kirk Merrington
Mainsforth
Middlestone
Bishop Middleham
Dalton Piercy
Rift House
Seaton Carew
Chilton Lane
Butterwick
Leasingthorne
Chilton
NICK HALL
Sedgefield
ROTTERDAM 16:00
ZEEBRUGGE 16:30
Rushyford
Tees Bay
ENERGY INFORMATION CENTRE
Greatham
Bradbury
SEDGEFIELD
Graythorp
Wynyard Village
Middridge
NEWTON AYCLIFFE
Mordon
Newton Bewley
Salt Scar
Thorpe Larches
WYNYARD
COWPEN BEWLEY
TEESMOUTH
A189
A193
A192
A1061
A190
B1325
A191
A1058
A19
A187
A185
A1300
A194
A184
A1018
A183
A194(M)
A1290
A1231
A690
A1018
A693
A182
A1(M)
A167
A181
B1404
A182
A1086
A179
A1049
A177
B1280
A689
A19
P&R

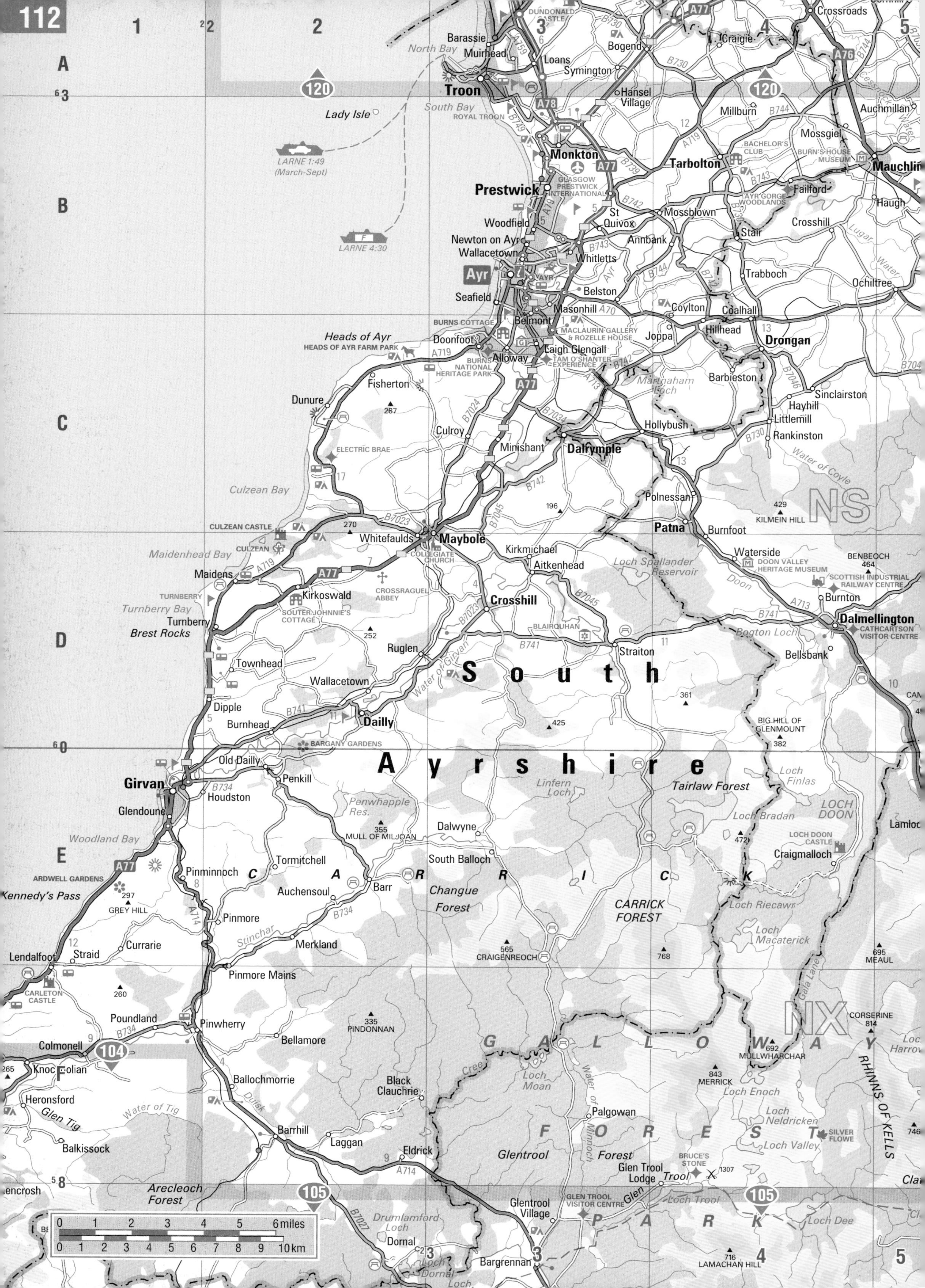

North Bay
South Bay
Lady Isle
LARNE 1:49
(March-Sept)
LARNE 4:30
Barassie
Muirhead
Loans
Symington
Troon
ROYAL TROON
Dundonald Castle
Bogend
Craigie
Crossroads
Hansel Village
Millburn
Auchmillan
Mossgiel
BACHELOR'S CLUB
BURN'S HOUSE MUSEUM
Mauchline
Monkton
Tarbolton
Prestwick
GLASGOW PRESTWICK INTERNATIONAL
AYR GORGE WOODLANDS
Failford
Haugh
Woodfield
St Quivox
Mossblown
Crosshill
Newton on Ayr
Wallacetown
Annbank
Stair
Whitletts
Ayr
Trabboch
Ochiltree
Seafield
Belston
Masonhill
Coylton
Coalhall
BURNS COTTAGE
Belmont
Hillhead
Drongan
Heads of Ayr
HEADS OF AYR FARM PARK
Doonfoot
MACLAURIN GALLERY & ROZELLE HOUSE
Joppa
Laigh Glengall
Alloway
BURNS NATIONAL HERITAGE PARK
TAM O'SHANTER EXPERIENCE
Martnaham Loch
Barbieston
Fisherton
Dunure
Sinclairston
Hayhill
Littlemill
Rankinston
Hollybush
Culroy
Minishant
Dalrymple
ELECTRIC BRAE
Water of Coyle
Culzean Bay
Polnessan
Patna
Burnfoot
KILMEIN HILL
NS
CULZEAN CASTLE
CULZEAN
Whitefaulds
Maybole
COLLEGIATE CHURCH
Kirkmichael
Aitkenhead
Maidenhead Bay
Maidens
Waterside
DOON VALLEY HERITAGE MUSEUM
BENBEOCH
SCOTTISH INDUSTRIAL RAILWAY CENTRE
Loch Spallander Reservoir
Doon
Kirkoswald
CROSSRAGUEL ABBEY
TURNBERRY
Turnberry Bay
Turnberry
Brest Rocks
SOUTER JOHNNIE'S COTTAGE
Crosshill
Burnton
Dalmellington
CATHCARTSON VISITOR CENTRE
BLAIRQUHAN
Bogton Loch
Ruglen
Straiton
Bellsbank
Townhead
South
Wallacetown
Water of Girvan
Dipple
Burnhead
Dailly
BIG HILL OF GLENMOUNT
BARGANY GARDENS
Old Dailly
Ayrshire
Girvan
Penkill
Houdston
Glendoune
Linfern Loch
Tairlaw Forest
Loch Finlas
Penwhapple Res.
MULL OF MILJOAN
Dalwyne
Loch Bradan
LOCH DOON
Woodland Bay
LOCH DOON CASTLE
Craigmalloch
Lamloch
South Balloch
ARDWELL GARDENS
Pinminnoch
Tormitchell
CARRICK
Kennedy's Pass
GREY HILL
Auchensoul
Barr
Changue Forest
CARRICK FOREST
Loch Riecawr
Pinmore
Stinchar
Loch Macaterick
Lendalfoot
Straid
Currarie
Merkland
CRAIGENREOCH
MEAUL
CARLETON CASTLE
Pinmore Mains
Gala Lane
Poundland
Pinwherry
PINDONNAN
NX
CORSERINE
Colmonell
Bellamore
GALLOWAY
MULLWHARCHAR
Knockdolian
Ballochmorrie
Black Clauchrie
Loch Moan
MERRICK
Loch Enoch
RHINNS OF KELLS
Heronsford
Glen Tig
Water of Tig
Duisk
Palgowan
Water of Minnoch
Loch Neldricken
Barrhill
FOREST
SILVER FLOWE
Balkissock
Laggan
Eldrick
Glentrool
Forest
Loch Valley
BRUCE'S STONE
Glen Trool Lodge
Trool
Arecleoch Forest
GLEN TROOL VISITOR CENTRE
Glentrool Village
Loch Trool
PARK
Loch Dee
Drumlamford Loch
Dornal
Loch Dornal
Bargrennan
LAMACHAN HILL
0 1 2 3 4 5 6 miles
0 1 2 3 4 5 6 7 8 9 10 km

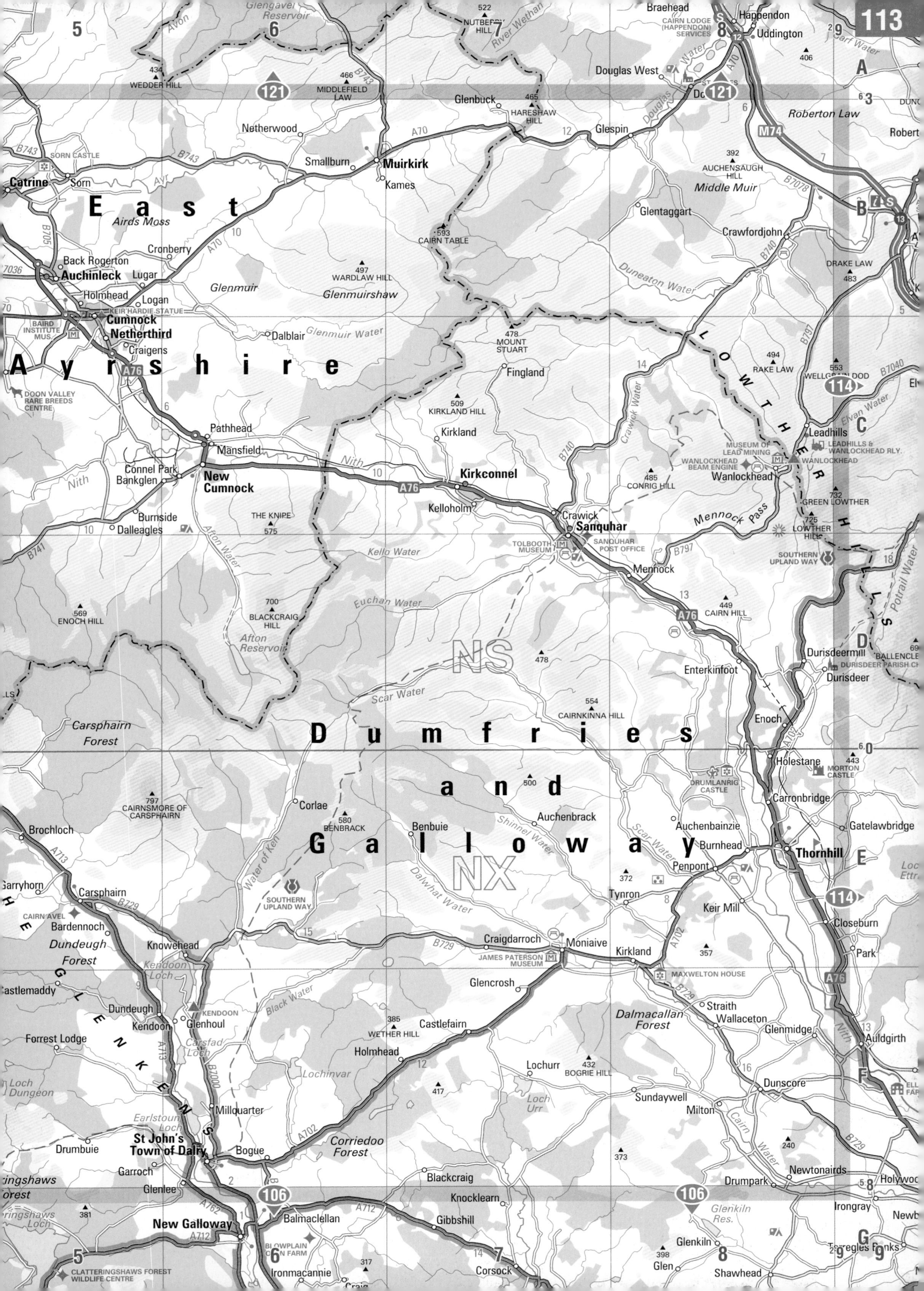
113
East Ayrshire
Dumfries and Galloway
NS
NX
LOWTHER HILLS
THE GLENKENS
Glengavel Reservoir
Avon
434 WEDDER HILL
466 MIDDLEFIELD LAW
522 NUTBERRY HILL
River Wethan
Braehead
CAIRN LODGE (HAPPENDON) SERVICES
Happendon
Uddington
Douglas West
Douglas Water
406
Roberton Law
Robert
Glenbuck
465 HARESHAW HILL
Netherwood
Glespin
M74
392 AUCHENSAUGH HILL
Middle Muir
SORN CASTLE
Catrine
Sorn
Smallburn
Muirkirk
Kames
Glentaggart
Airds Moss
Crawfordjohn
Cronberry
593 CAIRN TABLE
Back Rogerton
Auchinleck
Lugar
497 WARDLAW HILL
Glenmuir
Glenmuirshaw
Duneaton Water
DRAKE LAW 483
Holmhead
Logan
KEIR HARDIE STATUE
BAIRD INSTITUTE MUS.
Cumnock
Netherthird
Craigens
Dalblair
Glenmuir Water
478 MOUNT STUART
494 RAKE LAW
553 WELLGRAIN DOD
Fingland
DOON VALLEY RARE BREEDS CENTRE
509 KIRKLAND HILL
Crawick Water
Elvan Water
Leadhills
LEADHILLS & WANLOCKHEAD RLY.
MUSEUM OF LEAD MINING
WANLOCKHEAD BEAM ENGINE
WANLOCKHEAD
Wanlockhead
Pathhead
Mansfield
Kirkland
Connel Park
Bankglen
New Cumnock
Nith
Kirkconnel
485 CONRIG HILL
732 GREEN LOWTHER
Kelloholm
Burnside
Dalleagles
THE KNIPE 575
Crawick
Sanquhar
Mennock Pass
725 LOWTHER HILL
TOLBOOTH MUSEUM
SANQUHAR POST OFFICE
Kello Water
SOUTHERN UPLAND WAY
Afton Water
Mennock
Potrail Water
569 ENOCH HILL
700 BLACKCRAIG HILL
Euchan Water
449 CAIRN HILL
Afton Reservoir
478
Durisdeermill
DURISDEER PARISH CH
Durisdeer
BALLENCLE
Enterkinfoot
Scar Water
554 CAIRNKINNA HILL
Carsphairn Forest
Enoch
443 MORTON CASTLE
Holestane
500
797 CAIRNSMORE OF CARSPHAIRN
Corlae
580 BENBRACK
DRUMLANRIG CASTLE
Carronbridge
Benbuie
Auchenbrack
Auchenbainzie
Gatelawbridge
Brochloch
Shinnel Water
Burnhead
Thornhill
Water of Ken
Penpont
372
Garryhorn
Carsphairn
SOUTHERN UPLAND WAY
Tynron
Dalwhat Water
Keir Mill
CAIRN AVEL
Bardennoch
Closeburn
Dundeugh Forest
Knowehead
Craigdarroch
Moniaive
Kirkland
357
Park
Kendoon Loch
JAMES PATERSON MUSEUM
MAXWELTON HOUSE
Castlemaddy
Glencrosh
Black Water
Dundeugh
KENDOON
Straith
Kendoon
Glenhoul
Dalmacallan Forest
Wallaceton
385 WETHER HILL
Castlefairn
Glenmidge
Forrest Lodge
Carsfad Loch
Auldgirth
Holmhead
Lochurr
432 BOGRIE HILL
Loch Dungeon
Lochinvar
417
Dunscore
Loch Urr
Sundaywell
Milton
Cairn Water
Millquarter
Earlstoun Loch
Corriedoo Forest
240
St John's Town of Dalry
Drumbuie
Bogue
373
Garroch
Blackcraig
Newtonairds
Drumpark
Holywood
Glenlee
Knocklearn
Clatteringshaws Forest
381
Glenkiln Res.
Irongray
New Galloway
Balmaclellan
Gibbshill
Newb
BLOWPLAIN OPEN FARM
Glenkiln
Terregles Banks
CLATTERINGSHAWS FOREST WILDLIFE CENTRE
317
Corsock
398
Glen
Shawhead
Ironmacannie
A70
A76
A713
A702
A762
A712
B743
B705
B741
B729
B7000
B740
B797
B7078
B7040
121
114
106

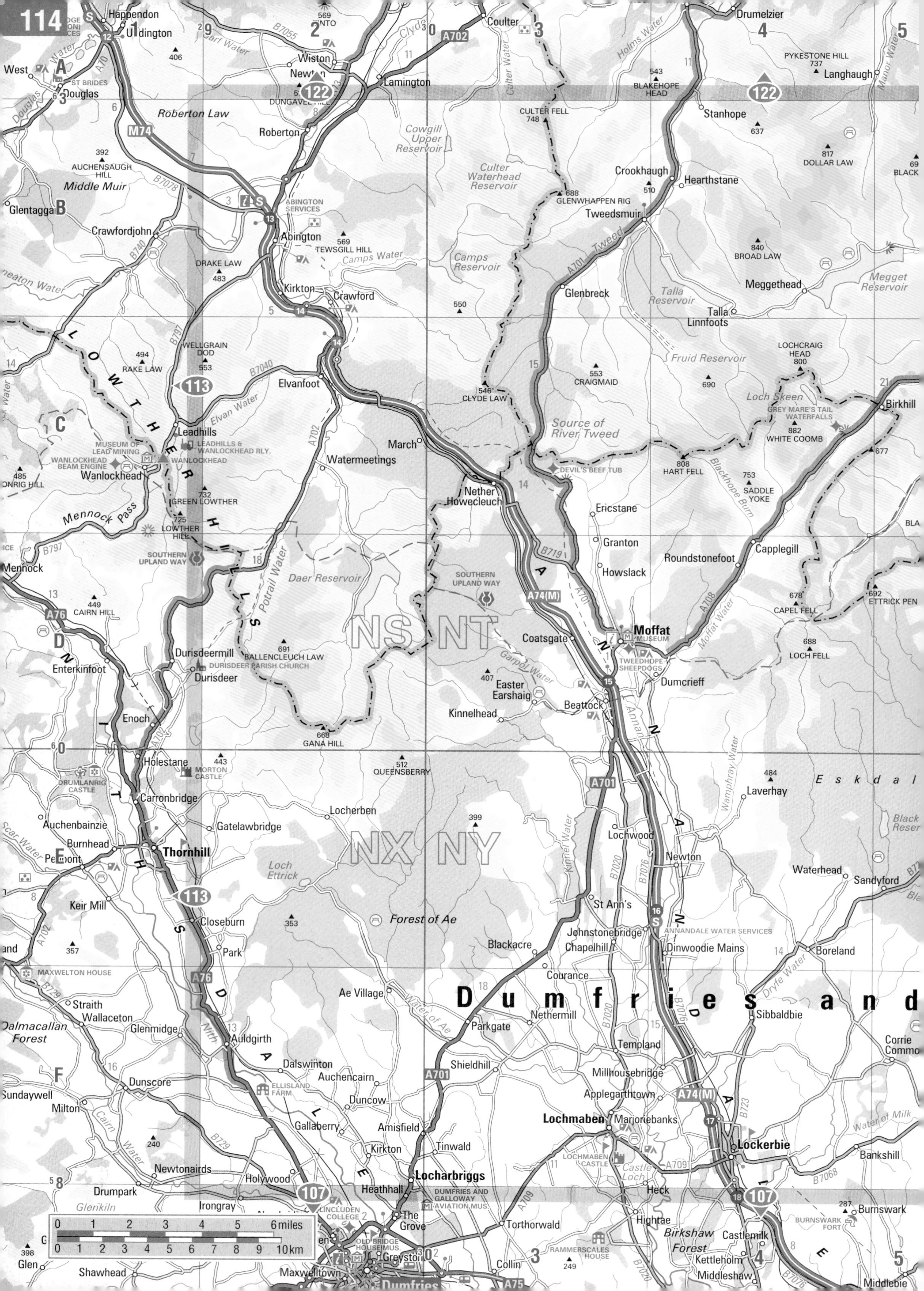

Happendon
Uddington
Coulter
Drumelzier
Wiston
Newton
Lamington
Douglas
Roberton Law
Roberton
Abington
Crawfordjohn
Crawford
Kirkton
Elvanfoot
Leadhills
Wanlockhead
Tweedsmuir
Crookhaugh
Hearthstane
Stanhope
Glenbreck
Meggethead
Talla Linnfoots
Birkhill
March
Watermeetings
Nether Howecleuch
Ericstane
Granton
Howslack
Roundstonefoot
Capplegill
Moffat
Coatsgate
Beattock
Dumcrieff
Kinnelhead
Easter Earshaig
Durisdeermill
Durisdeer
Enterkinfoot
Enoch
Holestane
Carronbridge
Thornhill
Gatelawbridge
Locherben
Laverhay
Lochwood
Newton
Waterhead
Sandyford
St Ann's
Johnstonebridge
Chapelhill
Dinwoodie Mains
Boreland
Blackacre
Courance
Closeburn
Park
Keir Mill
Ae Village
Parkgate
Nethermill
Sibbaldbie
Templand
Auldgirth
Dalswinton
Auchencairn
Shieldhill
Millhousebridge
Applegarthtown
Dunscore
Duncow
Lochmaben
Marjoriebanks
Lockerbie
Gallaberry
Amisfield
Kirkton
Tinwald
Bankshill
Newtonairds
Holywood
Locharbriggs
Heathhall
Heck
Drumpark
Irongray
The Grove
Torthorwald
Hightae
Burnswark
Castlemilk
Kettleholm
Middleshaw
Shawhead
Maxwelltown
Dumfries
Collin
Middlebie
Dumfries and
LOWTHER HILLS
NITHSDALE
ANNANDALE
Daer Reservoir
Forest of Ae
Loch Ettrick
Talla Reservoir
Fruid Reservoir
Loch Skeen
Source of River Tweed
Camps Reservoir
Culter Waterhead Reservoir
Cowgill Upper Reservoir
Birkshaw Forest
Middle Muir
Mennock Pass
Mennock
Eskdal
NS NT
NX NY
CULTER FELL 748
HART FELL 808
WHITE COOMB 882
BROAD LAW 840
DOLLAR LAW 817
QUEENSBERRY 512
GANA HILL 668
BALLENCLEUCH LAW 691
GREEN LOWTHER 732
LOWTHER HILL 725
LOCH FELL 688
CAPEL FELL 678
0 1 2 3 4 5 6 miles
0 1 2 3 4 5 6 7 8 9 10 km

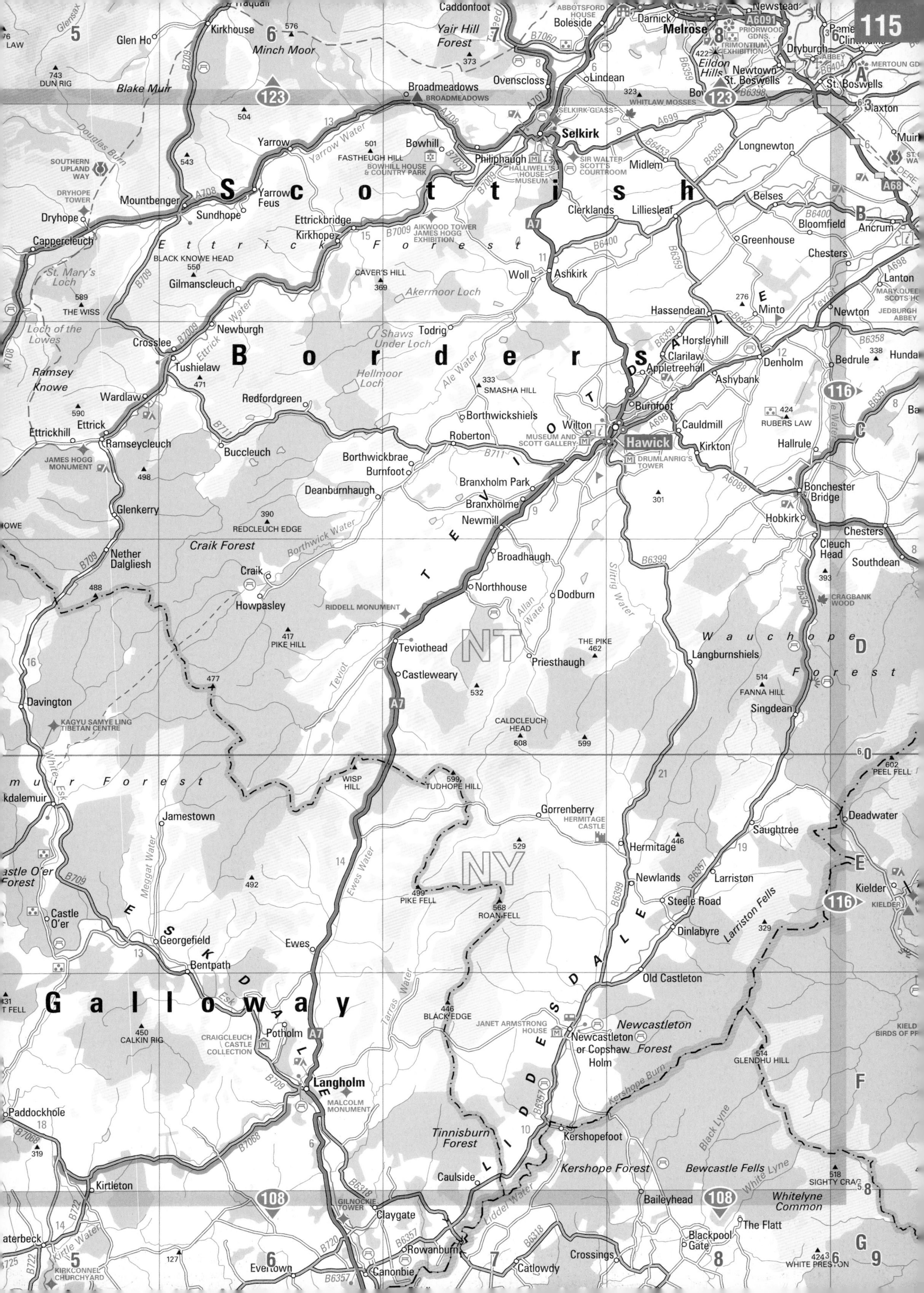
Scottish Borders
Dumfries and Galloway
Ettrick Forest
Selkirk
Hawick
Melrose
St. Boswells
Newtown St. Boswells
Ancrum
Denholm
Langholm
Newcastleton or Copshaw Holm
Canonbie
Teviothead
Yarrow
Ettrickbridge
Ashkirk
Lilliesleaf
Kielder
Craik Forest
Wauchope Forest
Newcastleton Forest
Kershope Forest
Tinnisburn Forest
Eskdalemuir Forest
TEVIOTDALE
LIDDESDALE
ESKDALE
NT
NY
A7
A68
A698
A699
A708
A6088
A6091
B709
B711
B6357
B6399
123
116
108

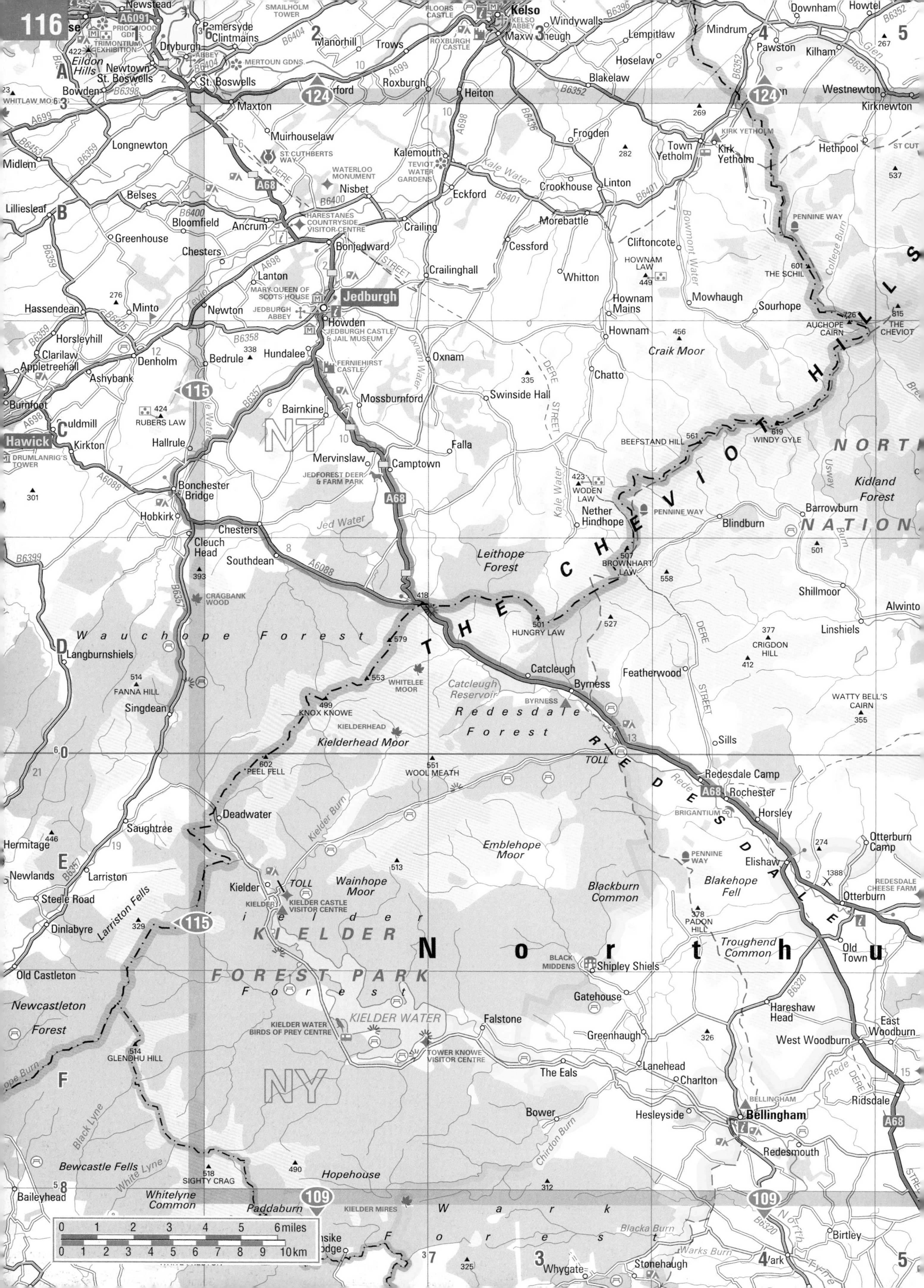
Newstead
Pomersyde
Clintmains
Dryburgh
Eildon Hills
Newtown St. Boswells
St. Boswells
Bowden
Maxton
Longnewton
Midlem
Muirhouselaw
Lilliesleaf
Belses
Bloomfield
Ancrum
Greenhouse
Chesters
Lanton
Minto
Hassendean
Newton
Horsleyhill
Clarilaw
Appletreehall
Denholm
Ashybank
Burnfoot
Cauldmill
Hawick
Kirkton
Bedrule
Hundalee
Hallrule
Bonchester Bridge
Hobkirk
Cleuch Head
Chesters
Southdean
Langburnshiels
Singdean
Saughtree
Hermitage
Newlands
Larriston
Steele Road
Dinlabyre
Old Castleton
Newcastleton Forest
Bewcastle Fells
Baileyhead
Whitelyne Common
Paddaburn
Manorhill
Trows
Roxburgh
Heiton
Kelso
Maxwheugh
Windywalls
Lempitlaw
Hoselaw
Blakelaw
Frogden
Kalemouth
Nisbet
Eckford
Crailing
Bonjedward
Crailinghall
Jedburgh
Howden
Oxnam
Mossburnford
Bairnkine
Mervinslaw
Camptown
Falla
Swinside Hall
Crookhouse
Linton
Morebattle
Cessford
Whitton
Town Yetholm
Kirk Yetholm
Cliftoncote
Hownam Mains
Hownam
Mowhaugh
Sourhope
Chatto
Craik Moor
Nether Hindhope
Mindrum
Pawston
Downham
Howtel
Kilham
Westnewton
Kirknewton
Hethpool
Blindburn
Barrowburn
Shillmoor
Alwinton
Linshiels
Kidland Forest
Leithope Forest
Catcleugh
Byrness
Featherwood
Redesdale Forest
Sills
Redesdale Camp
Rochester
Horsley
Elishaw
Otterburn
Otterburn Camp
Old Town
Blakehope Fell
Troughend Common
Blackburn Common
Emblehope Moor
Wainhope Moor
Kielder
Kielderhead Moor
Deadwater
KIELDER FOREST PARK
Kielder Water
Falstone
Gatehouse
Greenhaugh
Lanehead
Charlton
The Eals
Shipley Shiels
Hareshaw Head
West Woodburn
East Woodburn
Ridsdale
Bellingham
Hesleyside
Redesmouth
Bower
Hopehouse
Birtley
Stonehaugh
Whygate
Wark
THE CHEVIOT HILLS
NORTHUMBERLAND NATIONAL PARK
Wauchope Forest
Kielder Forest
Wark Forest
North
NT
NY
A68
A698
A699
A6088
A6091
B6357
B6358
B6359
B6400
B6401
B6404
B6405
B6352
B6320
124
115
109
0 1 2 3 4 5 6 miles
0 1 2 3 4 5 6 7 8 9 10 km

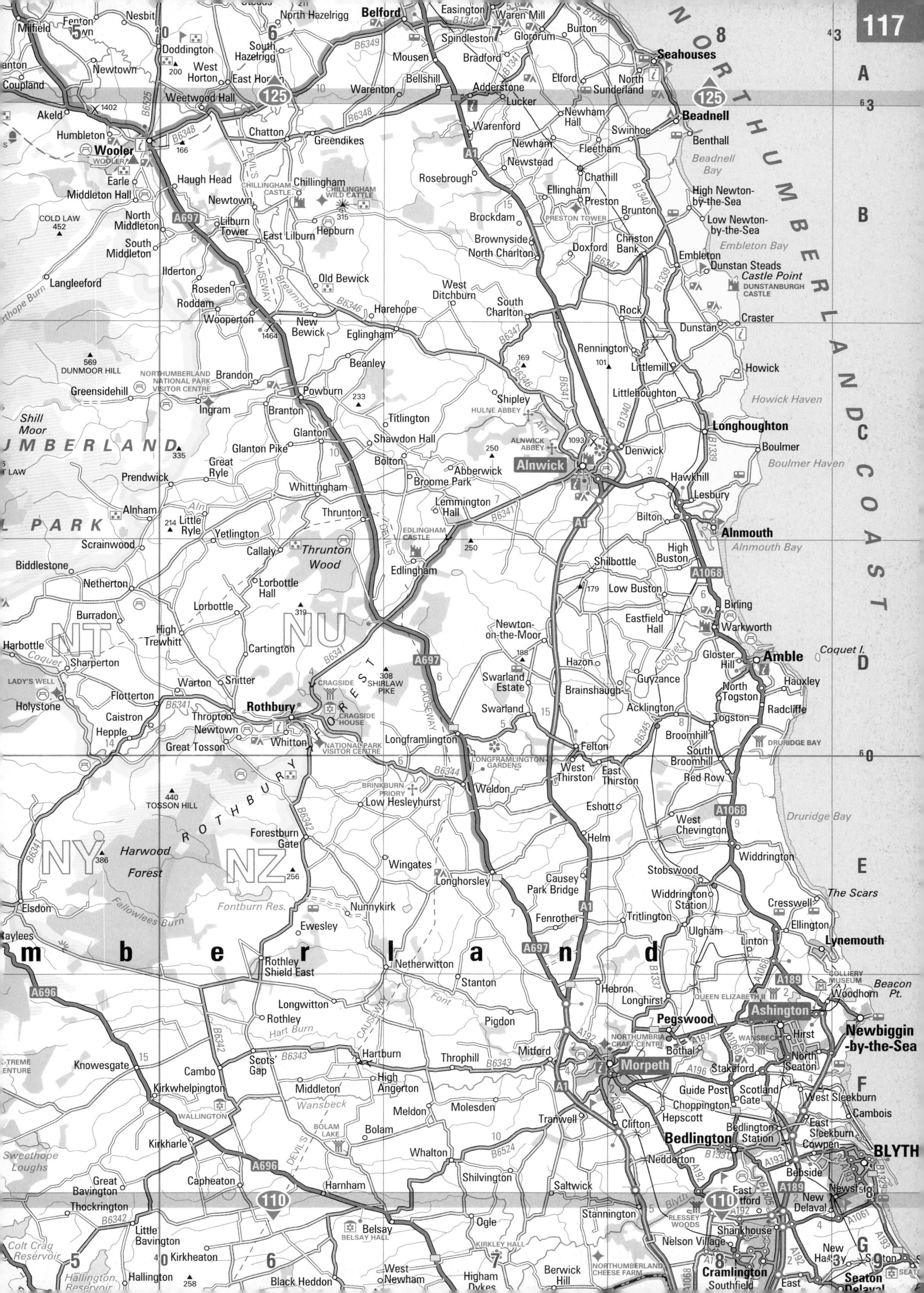

NORTHUMBERLAND COAST
Belford
Seahouses
Beadnell
Wooler
Chillingham
Chatton
Alnwick
Longhoughton
Alnmouth
Amble
Warkworth
Rothbury
Longframlington
Felton
Widdrington
Lynemouth
Ashington
Newbiggin-by-the-Sea
Morpeth
Bedlington
BLYTH
Cramlington
Seaton Delaval
Pegswood
Elsdon
Harwood Forest
Thrunton Wood
Rothbury Forest
Embleton
Craster
Howick
Boulmer
Hauxley
Cresswell
Belsay
Kirkwhelpington
Cambo
Hartburn
Mitford
Whalton
Stannington
Ellingham
Bamburgh
Coquet I.
Druridge Bay
Alnmouth Bay
Embleton Bay
Beadnell Bay
125
110

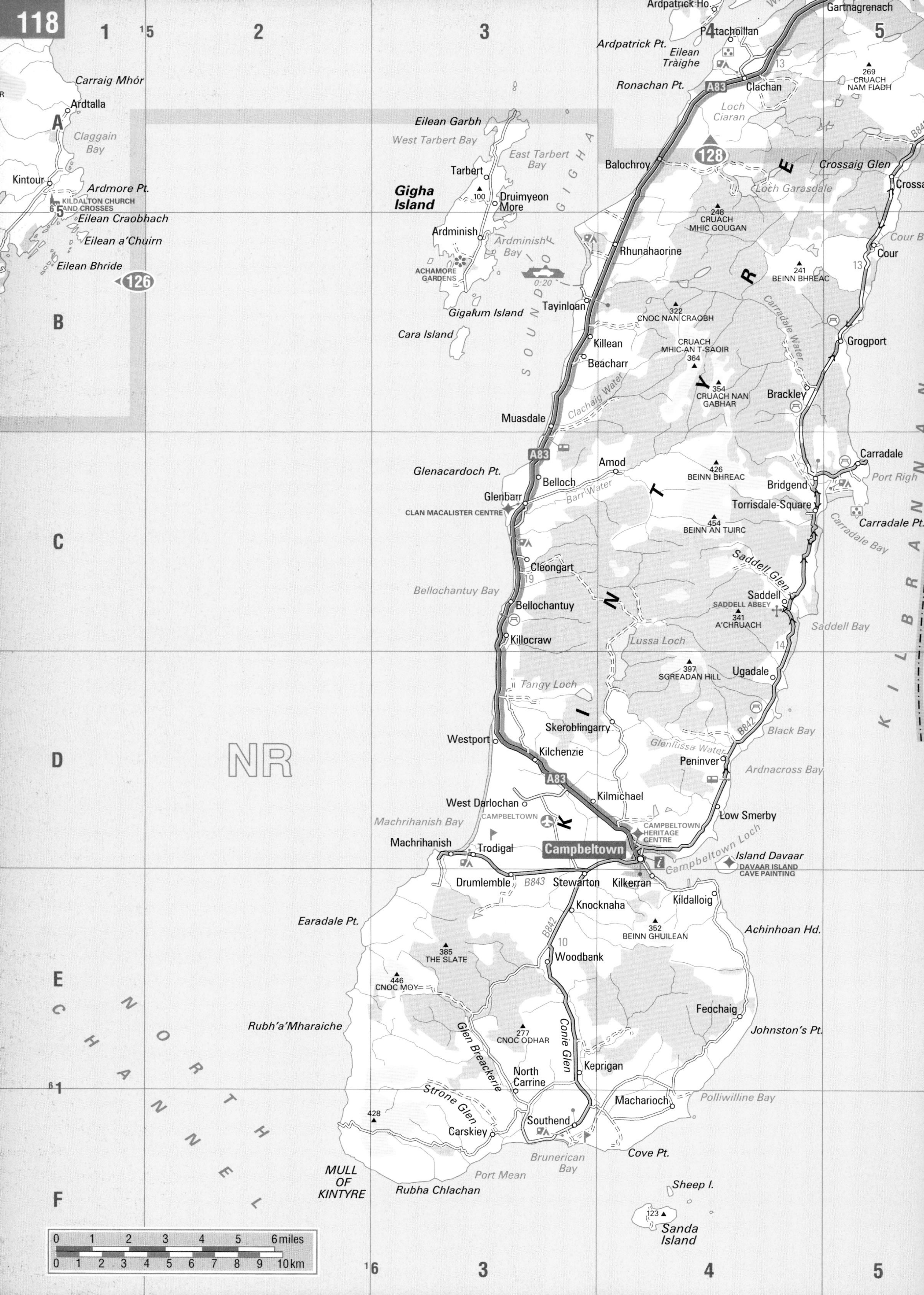

Ardpatrick Ho.
Gartnagrenach
Altachoillan
Ardpatrick Pt.
Eilean Tràighe
Ronachan Pt.
A83
Clachan
269 CRUACH NAM FIADH
Loch Ciaran
Carraig Mhór
Ardtalla
Claggain Bay
Eilean Garbh
West Tarbert Bay
East Tarbert Bay
128
Balochroy
Crossaig Glen
Tarbert
Gigha Island
100
Druimyeon More
Loch Garasdale
Kintour
Ardmore Pt.
KILDALTON CHURCH AND CROSSES
Eilean Craobhach
Eilean a'Chuirn
Eilean Bhride
126
Ardminish
Ardminish Bay
248 CRUACH MHIC GOUGAN
Rhunahaorine
Cour
ACHAMORE GARDENS
0:20
241 BEINN BHREAC
Gigalum Island
Tayinloan
322 CNOC NAN CRAOBH
SOUND OF GIGHA
Cara Island
Killean
Beacharr
CRUACH MHIC-AN T-SAOIR 364
Carradale Water
Grogport
354 CRUACH NAN GABHAR
Brackley
Clachaig Water
Muasdale
A83
Amod
426 BEINN BHREAC
Carradale
Port Righ
Glenacardoch Pt.
Belloch
Barr Water
Glenbarr
CLAN MACALISTER CENTRE
Bridgend
Torrisdale-Square
454 BEINN AN TUIRC
Carradale Pt.
Carradale Bay
Cleongart
Saddell Glen
Bellochantuy Bay
Bellochantuy
Saddell
SADDELL ABBEY
341 A'CHRUACH
Saddell Bay
Killocraw
Lussa Loch
397 SGREADAN HILL
Ugadale
Tangy Loch
Skeroblingarry
B842
Black Bay
Westport
Kilchenzie
Glenlussa Water
Peninver
Ardnacross Bay
NR
A83
Kilmichael
West Darlochan
Low Smerby
Machrihanish Bay
CAMPBELTOWN
CAMPBELTOWN HERITAGE CENTRE
Machrihanish
Trodigal
Campbeltown
Campbeltown Loch
Island Davaar
DAVAAR ISLAND CAVE PAINTING
Drumlemble
B843
Stewarton
Kilkerran
Kildalloig
Knocknaha
Earadale Pt.
352 BEINN GHUILEAN
Achinhoan Hd.
B842
385 THE SLATE
Woodbank
446 CNOC MOY
Feochaig
Rubh'a'Mharaiche
277 CNOC ODHAR
Johnston's Pt.
Glen Breackerie
Conie Glen
Keprigan
North Carrine
Macharioch
Polliwilline Bay
Strone Glen
428
Southend
Carskiey
Cove Pt.
Bruneran Bay
Port Mean
MULL OF KINTYRE
Rubha Chlachan
Sheep I.
123
Sanda Island
NORTH CHANNEL
KINTYRE
KILBRANNAN
0 1 2 3 4 5 6 miles
0 1 2 3 4 5 6 7 8 9 10 km

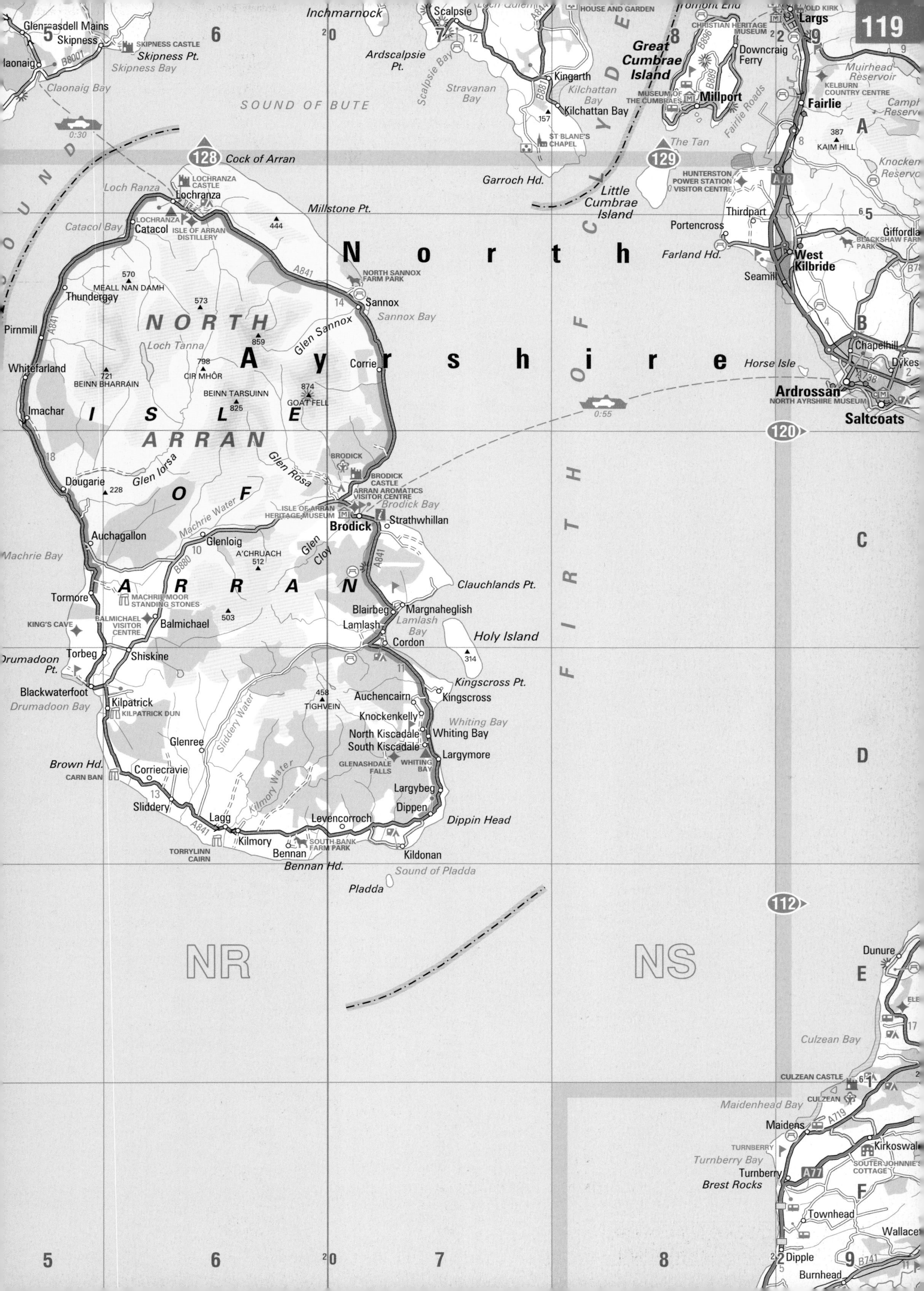
North Ayrshire
ISLE OF ARRAN
NORTH ARRAN
ARRAN
SOUND OF BUTE
FIRTH OF CLYDE
Brodick
Lamlash
Lochranza
Catacol
Sannox
Corrie
Blackwaterfoot
Whiting Bay
Kildonan
Holy Island
Pladda
Great Cumbrae Island
Little Cumbrae Island
Millport
Largs
Fairlie
West Kilbride
Ardrossan
Saltcoats
Turnberry
Maidens
Dunure
Culzean Bay
Goat Fell
Cock of Arran
NR
NS

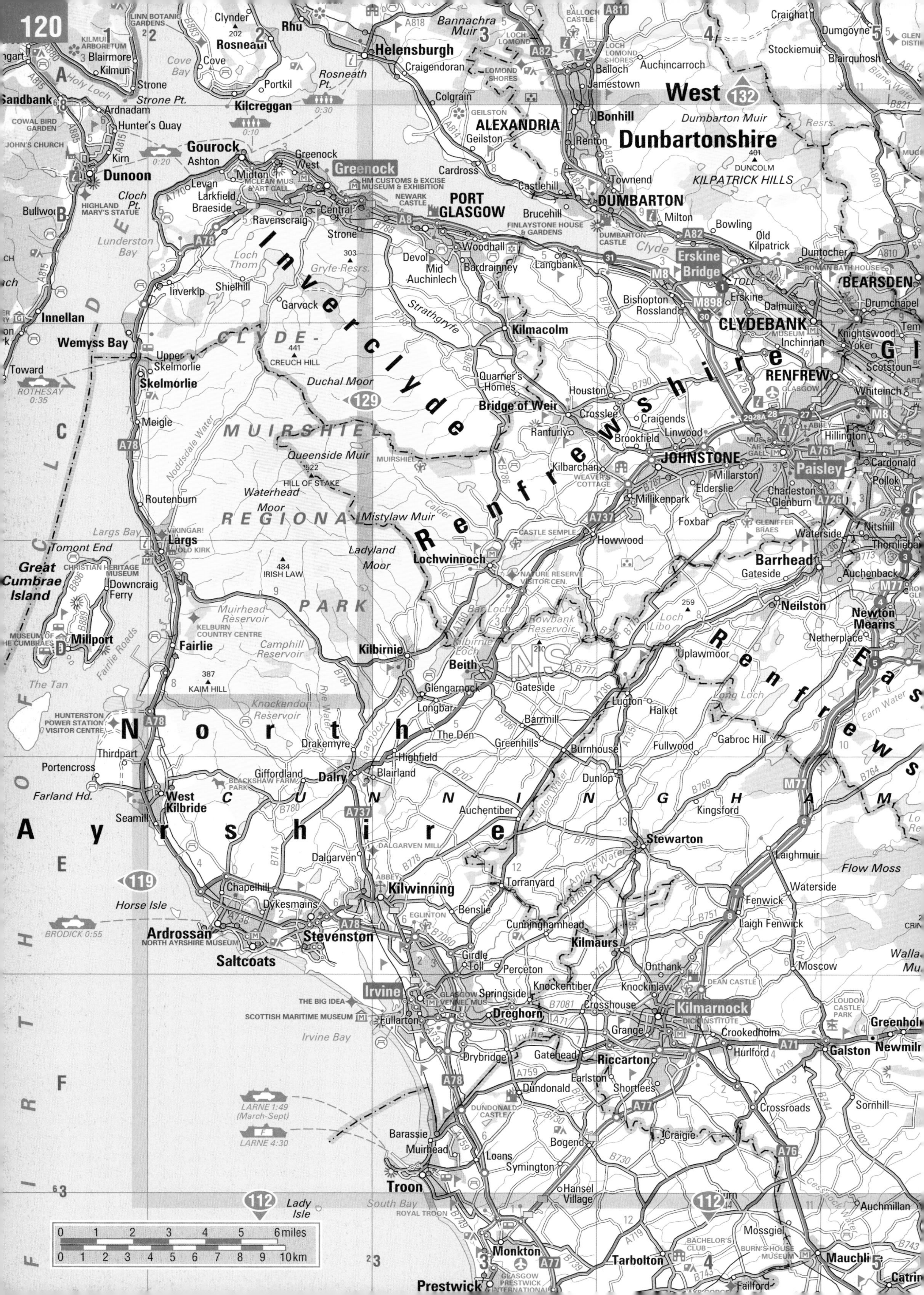
West Dunbartonshire
Inverclyde
Renfrewshire
East Renfrewshire
North Ayrshire
CUNNINGHAME
FIRTH OF CLYDE
CLYDE-MUIRSHIEL REGIONAL PARK
Helensburgh
Craigendoran
Rhu
Rosneath
Rosneath Pt.
Clynder
Cove
Cove Bay
Portkil
Kilcreggan
Kilmun
Blairmore
Strone
Strone Pt.
Holy Loch
Sandbank
Ardnadam
Hunter's Quay
Kirn
Dunoon
Cowal Bird Garden
Highland Mary's Statue
Bullwood
Innellan
Toward
Gourock
Ashton
Cloch Pt.
Levan
Larkfield
Braeside
Midton
Greenock West
Greenock
HM Customs & Excise Museum & Exhibition
Newark Castle
Port Glasgow
Ravenscraig
Central
Strone
Lunderston Bay
Inverkip
Shielhill
Loch Thom
Gryfe Resrs.
Garvock
Wemyss Bay
Upper Skelmorlie
Skelmorlie
ROTHESAY 0:35
Meigle
Creuch Hill
Duchal Moor
Muirshiel
Queenside Muir
Hill of Stake
Waterhead Moor
Noddsdale Water
Routenburn
Largs Bay
Largs
Vikingar!
Old Kirk
Tomont End
Great Cumbrae Island
Christian Heritage Museum
Downcraig Ferry
Millport
Museum of the Cumbraes
Irish Law
Muirhead Reservoir
Kelburn Country Centre
Fairlie
Fairlie Roads
Camphill Reservoir
Kaim Hill
The Tan
Hunterston Power Station Visitor Centre
Knockendon Reservoir
Rye Water
Thirdpart
Portencross
Farland Hd.
West Kilbride
Seamill
Blackshaw Farm Park
Giffordland
Dalry
Blairland
Drakemyre
Highfield
Garnock
Kilbirnie
Beith
Glengarnock
Longbar
The Den
Gateside
Barrmill
Greenhills
Lochwinnoch
Ladyland Moor
Mistylaw Muir
Castle Semple
Nature Reserve Visitor Cen.
Barr Loch
Kilbirnie Loch
Rowbank Reservoir
Howwood
Alexandria
Geilston
Colgrain
Cardross
Castlehill
Dumbarton
Dumbarton Castle
Bonhill
Renton
Jamestown
Balloch
Balloch Castle
Loch Lomond Shores
Auchincarroch
Dumbarton Muir
Kilpatrick Hills
Duncolm
Townend
Milton
Bowling
Old Kilpatrick
Duntocher
Roman Bath House
Bearsden
Drumchapel
Clydebank
Dalmuir
Erskine
Erskine Bridge
Bishopton
Rossland
Inchinnan
Renfrew
Glasgow
Knightswood
Yoker
Scotstoun
Whiteinch
Hillington
Cardonald
Pollok
Paisley
Abbey
Johnstone
Millarston
Elderslie
Linwood
Brookfield
Craigends
Crosslee
Houston
Bridge of Weir
Ranfurly
Quarrier's Homes
Kilmacolm
Strathgryfe
Kilbarchan
Weaver's Cottage
Milliken park
Foxbar
Gleniffer Braes
Charleston
Glenburn
Nitshill
Waterside
Thornliebank
Barrhead
Gateside
Auchenback
Neilston
Newton Mearns
Netherplace
Loch Libo
Uplawmoor
Long Loch
Lugton
Halket
Burnhouse
Fullwood
Gabroc Hill
Earn Water
Dunlop
Kingsford
Auchentiber
Lugton Water
Stewarton
Laighmuir
Flow Moss
Waterside
Fenwick
Laigh Fenwick
Moscow
Torranyard
Annick Water
Benslie
Cunninghamhead
Kilmaurs
Onthank
Knockinlaw
Dean Castle
Kilmarnock
Dick Institute
Crookedholm
Hurlford
Galston
Newmilns
Greenholm
Loudoun Castle Park
Riccarton
Grange
Crosshouse
Knockentiber
Springside
Dreghorn
Perceton
Girdle Toll
Irvine
Glasgow Vennel Mus.
The Big Idea
Scottish Maritime Museum
Fullarton
Irvine Bay
Drybridge
Gatehead
Earlston
Shortlees
Dundonald
Dundonald Castle
Crossroads
Sornhill
Craigie
Bogend
Symington
Loans
Barassie
Muirhead
Troon
Hansel Village
South Bay
Royal Troon
Lady Isle
Monkton
Prestwick
Glasgow Prestwick International
Tarbolton
Bachelor's Club
Burns House Museum
Mossgiel
Mauchline
Auchmillan
Failford
Kilwinning
Abbey
Eglinton
Dalgarven
Dalgarven Mill
Chapelhill
Dykesmains
Ardrossan
North Ayrshire Museum
Stevenston
Saltcoats
Horse Isle
BRODICK 0:55
LARNE 1:49 (March-Sept)
LARNE 4:30
Craighat
Dumgoyne
Stockiemuir
Blairquhosh
Bannachra Muir
Loch Lomond
Lomond Shores
Finlaystone House & Gardens
Woodhall
Devol
Mid Auchinlech
Bardrainney
Langbank
Brucehill
Clyde
Gare Loch
Cessnock Water
0:20
0:10
0:30
129
119
132
112
NS
0 1 2 3 4 5 6 miles
0 1 2 3 4 5 6 7 8 9 10 km

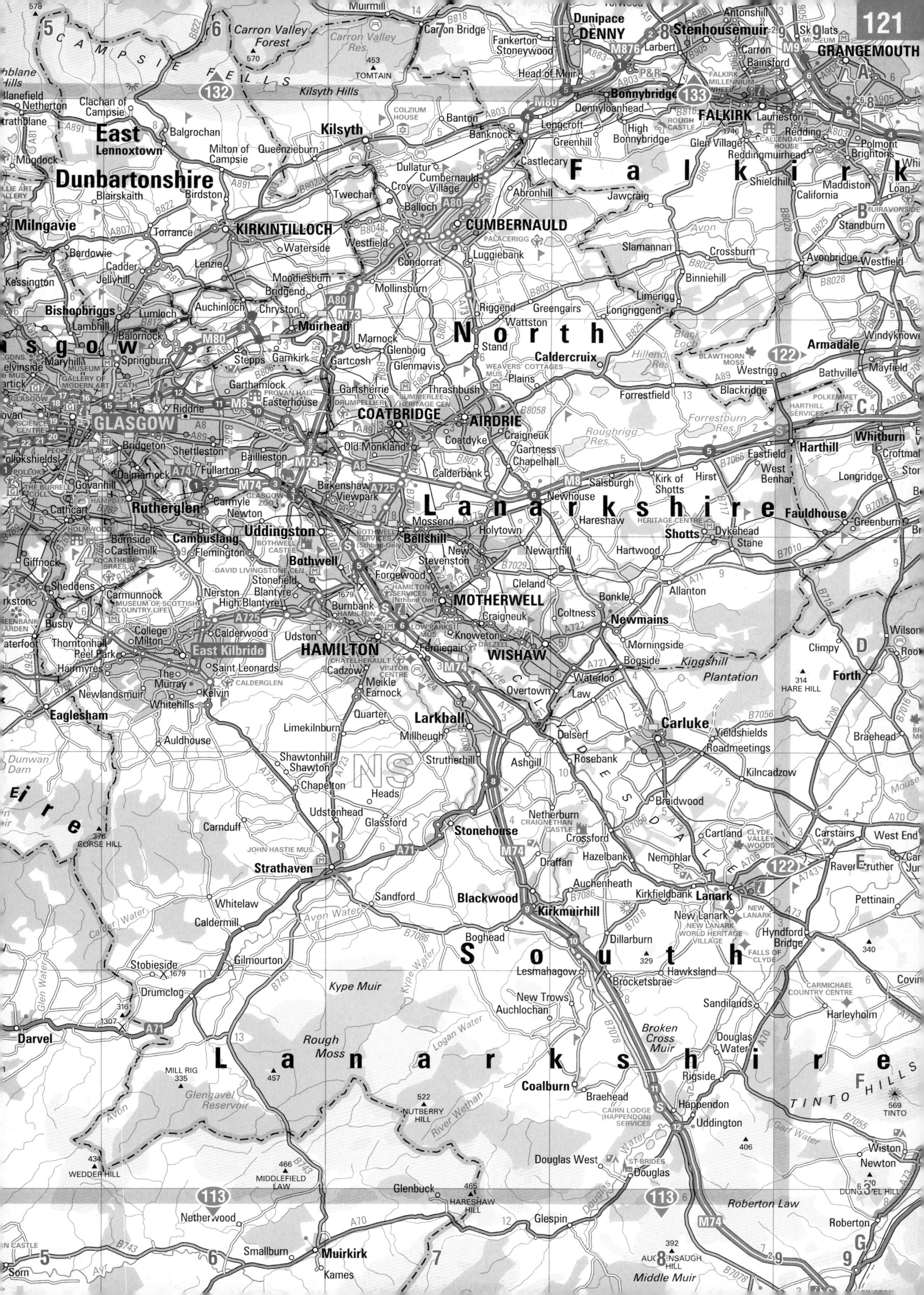
Campsie Fells
Carron Valley Forest
Carron Valley Res.
Tomtain
Kilsyth Hills
Muirmill
Carron Bridge
Dunipace
Denny
Fankerton
Stoneywood
Head of Muir
Stenhousemuir
Larbert
Carron
Bainsford
Skinflats
Grangemouth
Falkirk Millennium Wheel
Bonnybridge
Falkirk
Laurieston
Redding
Polmont
Brightons
Dennyloanhead
High Bonnybridge
Rough Castle
Glen Village
Callendar House
Reddingmuirhead
Blanefield
Netherton
Strathblane
Clachan of Campsie
Mugdock
East Dunbartonshire
Lennoxtown
Balgrochan
Milton of Campsie
Queenzieburn
Kilsyth
Colzium House
Banton
Banknock
Longcroft
Greenhill
Castlecary
Falkirk
Shieldhill
Maddiston
California
Standburn
Muiravonside
Blairskaith
Birdston
Twechar
Dullatur
Croy
Cumbernauld Village
Balloch
Abronhill
Jawcraig
Milngavie
Torrance
Kirkintilloch
Waterside
Westfield
Cumbernauld
Palacerigg
Luggiebank
Condorrat
Avon
Slamannan
Crossburn
Avonbridge
Westfield
Bardowie
Cadder
Lenzie
Jellyhill
Kessington
Moodiesburn
Bridgend
Mollinsburn
Binniehill
Limerigg
Bishopbriggs
Lumloch
Auchinloch
Chryston
Muirhead
Riggend
Greengairs
Longriggend
Lambhill
Balornock
Marnock
Glenboig
Wattston
North
Stand
Black Loch
Armadale
Windyknowe
Glasgow
Maryhill
Springburn
Stepps
Garnkirk
Gartcosh
Glenmavis
Caldercruix
Hillend Res.
Blawthorn Moss
Westrigg
Bathville
Mayfield
Gallery of Modern Art
Garthamlock
Provan Hall
Gartsherrie
Summerlee Heritage Cen.
Drumpellier
Thrashbush
Weavers' Cottages Mus.
Plains
Forrestfield
Blackridge
Polkemmet
Harthill Services
Riddrie
Easterhouse
Coatbridge
Airdrie
Roughrigg Res.
Forrestburn Res.
Harthill
Whitburn
Croftmalloch
Science Centre
Glasgow
Bridgeton
Shettleston
Old Monkland
Coatdyke
Craigneuk
Gartness
Chapelhall
Eastfield
Hirst
Longridge
Pollokshields
People's Palace
Pollok
Dalmarnock
Fullarton
Baillieston
Calderbank
Kirk of Shotts
Salsburgh
West Benhar
The Burrell Coll.
Govanhill
Hampden
Rutherglen
Carmyle
Glasgow Zoo
Birkenshaw
Viewpark
Newhouse
Lanarkshire
Fauldhouse
Cathcart
Newton
Mossend
Hareshaw
Heritage Centre
Shotts
Dykehead
Stane
Greenburn
Holmwood
Burnside
Cambuslang
Uddingston
Bothwell Services
Bellshill
Holytown
Bothwell Castle
Castlemilk
Flemington
New Stevenston
Newarthill
Hartwood
Giffnock
Cathkin Braes
Bothwell
David Livingstone Cen.
Forgewood
Cleland
Allanton
Sheddens
Carmunnock
Stonefield
Hamilton Services
Bonkle
Nerston
Blantyre
Motherwell
Coltness
Newmains
Museum of Scottish Country Life
High Blantyre
Burnbank
Craigneuk
Busby
College Milton
Calderwood
Udston
Low Parks Mus.
Knowetop
Dalzell
Morningside
Wilsontown
Thorntonhall
Peel Park
East Kilbride
Hamilton
Ferniegair
Wishaw
Bogside
Kingshill Plantation
Climpy
Forth
Hairmyres
Saint Leonards
Chatelherault
Cadzow
Visitor Centre
Waterloo
Hare Hill
The Murray
Calderglen
Meikle Earnock
Overtown
Law
Newlandsmuir
Kelvin
Whitehills
Eaglesham
Quarter
Larkhall
Carluke
Yieldshields
Braehead
Limekilnburn
Millheugh
Dalserf
Roadmeetings
Auldhouse
Dunwan Dam
Shawtonhill
Shawton
Struthérhill
Ashgill
Rosebank
Kilncadzow
Chapelton
Heads
Braidwood
Udstonhead
Glassford
Netherburn
Craignethan Castle
Cartland
Clyde Valley Woods
Carstairs
West End
Carnduff
Stonehouse
Crossford
Corse Hill
John Hastie Mus.
Hazelbank
Nemphlar
Strathaven
Draffan
Auchenheath
Kirkfieldbank
Lanark
Carnwath
Pettinain
Whitelaw
Sandford
Blackwood
Kirkmuirhill
New Lanark
New Lanark World Heritage Village
Calder Water
Caldermill
Avon Water
Boghead
Dillarburn
Hyndford Bridge
Falls of Clyde
South
Stobieside
Gilmourton
Lesmahagow
Hawksland
Brocketsbrae
Kype Muir
Kype Water
Carmichael Country Centre
Covington
Drumclog
New Trows
Auchlochan
Sandilands
Harleyholm
Darvel
Rough Moss
Logan Water
Broken Cross Muir
Douglas Water
Lanarkshire
Mill Rig
Glengavel Reservoir
Coalburn
Braehead
Rigside
Tinto Hills
Tinto
Nutberry Hill
River Wethan
Cairn Lodge (Happendon) Services
Happendon
Uddington
Garf Water
Wedder Hill
Middlefield Law
Douglas West
St Brides
Douglas
Wiston
Newton
Dungavel Hill
Glenbuck
Hareshaw Hill
Roberton Law
Netherwood
Glespin
Roberton
Smallburn
Muirkirk
Auchensaugh Hill
Sorn
Kames
Middle Muir
Ayr

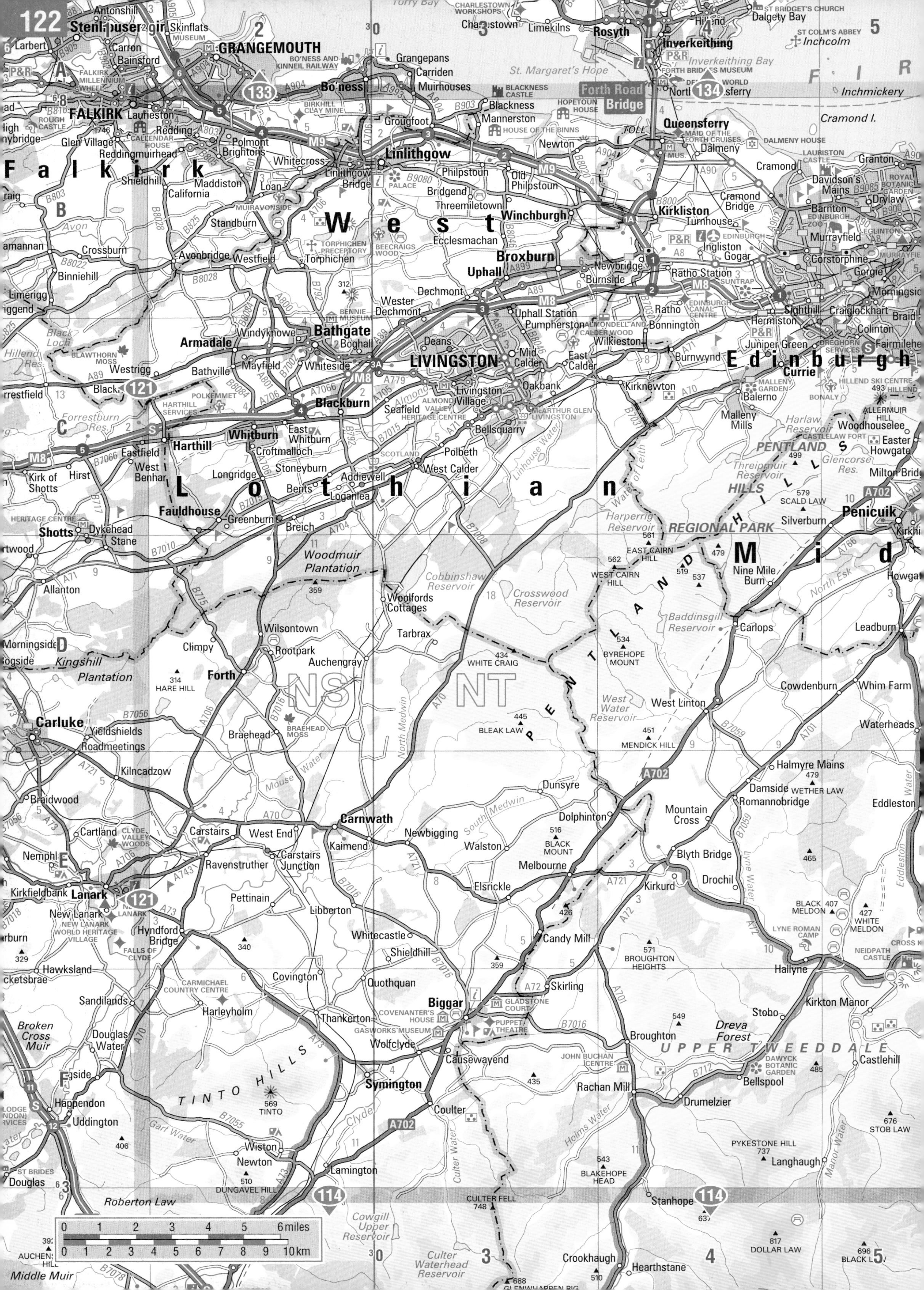
Antonshill
Skinflats
Larbert
Carron
GRANGEMOUTH
Bainsford
BO'NESS AND KINNEIL RAILWAY
Grangepans
Carriden
FALKIRK
Bo'ness
Muirhouses
Charlestown
Limekilns
Rosyth
Inverkeithing
Dalgety Bay
ST BRIDGET'S CHURCH
ST COLM'S ABBEY
Inchcolm
Inverkeithing Bay
St. Margaret's Hope
FORTH BRIDGES MUSEUM
BLACKNESS CASTLE
Forth Road Bridge
Blackness
HOPETOUN HOUSE
Inchmickery
Cramond I.
Laurieston
ROUGH CASTLE
Redding
Polmont
Brightons
Reddingmuirhead
Glen Village
CALLENDAR HOUSE
BIRKHILL CLAY MINE
Grougfoot
Mannerston
HOUSE OF THE BINNS
Queensferry
MAID OF THE FORTH CRUISES
Dalmeny
DALMENY HOUSE
Newton
Linlithgow
Whitecross
Linlithgow Bridge
PALACE
Philpstoun
Old Philpstoun
Cramond
Granton
LAURISTON CASTLE
Davidson's Mains
ROYAL BOTANIC GARDEN
Falkirk
Shieldhill
Maddiston
California
Loan
MUIRAVONSIDE
Bridgend
Threemiletown
Winchburgh
Kirkliston
Cramond Bridge
Turnhouse
Barnton
Drylaw
EDINBURGH ZOO
Murrayfield
West
Standburn
Avon
Crossburn
TORPHICHEN PRECEPTORY
BEECRAIGS WOOD
Ecclesmachan
Ingliston
Gogar
Corstorphine
Avonbridge
Westfield
Torphichen
Broxburn
Uphall
Newbridge
Burnside
Ratho Station
SUNTRAP
Gorgie
Binniehill
Limerigg
Dechmont
Wester Dechmont
Uphall Station
Ratho
EDINBURGH CANAL CENTRE
Sighthill
Craiglockhart
Hermiston
Bonnington
Pumpherston
ALMONDELL AND CALDER WOOD
Wilkieston
Juniper Green
Colinton
Fairmilehead
Black Loch
Windyknowe
Bathgate
Armadale
Boghall
BLAWTHORN MOSS
Deans
LIVINGSTON
Mid Calder
East Calder
Burnwynd
Edinburgh
Currie
Westrigg
Bathville
Mayfield
Whiteside
Blackburn
Seafield
Livingston Village
Oakbank
Kirknewton
MALLENY GARDEN
Balerno
BONALY
HILLEND SKI CENTRE
Forrestburn Res.
HARTHILL SERVICES
POLKEMMET
ALMOND VALLEY HERITAGE CENTRE
MCARTHUR GLEN LIVINGSTON
Bellsquarry
Malleny Mills
Harlaw Reservoir
Woodhouselee
ALLERMUIR HILL
CASTLELAW FORT
Easter Howgate
Harthill
Whitburn
East Whitburn
Croftmalloch
Eastfield
Polbeth
West Calder
Threipmuir Reservoir
Glencorse Res.
Milton Bridge
PENTLAND
Kirk of Shotts
Hirst
West Benhar
Longridge
Stoneyburn
Addiewell
Bents
Loganlea
Lothian
HILLS
SCALD LAW
Penicuik
HERITAGE CENTRE
Shotts
Dykehead
Fauldhouse
Greenburn
Breich
Harperrig Reservoir
REGIONAL PARK
Silverburn
Stane
EAST CAIRN HILL
WEST CAIRN HILL
Nine Mile Burn
Mid
Allanton
Woodmuir Plantation
Cobbinshaw Reservoir
Crosswood Reservoir
North Esk
Howgate
Woolfords Cottages
Baddinsgill Reservoir
Carlops
Leadburn
Morningside
Kingshill Plantation
Climpy
Wilsontown
Rootpark
Tarbrax
Auchengray
WHITE CRAIG
BYREHOPE MOUNT
Forth
HARE HILL
NS
NT
PENTLAND
Cowdenburn
Whim Farm
West Water Reservoir
West Linton
Carluke
Yieldshields
Roadmeetings
BRAEHEAD MOSS
Braehead
BLEAK LAW
MENDICK HILL
Waterheads
Kilncadzow
North Medwin
Mouse Water
Halmyre Mains
WETHER LAW
Damside
Romannobridge
Braidwood
Dunsyre
Dolphinton
Mountain Cross
Eddleston
Cartland
CLYDE VALLEY WOODS
Carstairs
West End
Carnwath
Newbigging
South Medwin
Kaimend
Walston
BLACK MOUNT
Blyth Bridge
Nemphlar
Carstairs Junction
Ravenstruther
Melbourne
Drochil
Kirkfieldbank
Lanark
Pettinain
Elsrickle
Kirkurd
Lyne Water
New Lanark
NEW LANARK WORLD HERITAGE VILLAGE
Libberton
BLACK MELDON
WHITE MELDON
LYNE ROMAN CAMP
Hyndford Bridge
FALLS OF CLYDE
Whitecastle
Candy Mill
BROUGHTON HEIGHTS
Hawksland
Shieldhill
NEIDPATH CASTLE
Hallyne
Covington
CARMICHAEL COUNTRY CENTRE
Quothquan
Skirling
Sandilands
Harleyholm
Biggar
GLADSTONE COURT
Kirkton Manor
Thankerton
COVENANTER'S HOUSE
GASWORKS MUSEUM
PUPPET THEATRE
Stobo
Broken Cross Muir
Douglas Water
Broughton
Dreva Forest
UPPER TWEEDDALE
Wolfclyde
Causewayend
JOHN BUCHAN CENTRE
DAWYCK BOTANIC GARDEN
Castlehill
TINTO HILLS
Symington
Rachan Mill
Bellspool
Drumelzier
Happendon
TINTO
Coulter
Holms Water
STOB LAW
Uddington
Garf Water
Clyde
Culter Water
PYKESTONE HILL
Wiston
Langhaugh
Manor Water
Newton
BLAKEHOPE HEAD
ST BRIDES
Douglas
Lamington
DUNGAVEL HILL
Roberton Law
CULTER FELL
Stanhope
Cowgill Upper Reservoir
DOLLAR LAW
BLACK LAW
AUCHENSHILL
Culter Waterhead Reservoir
Crookhaugh
Hearthstone
Middle Muir
GLENWHAPPEN RIG
0 1 2 3 4 5 6 miles
0 1 2 3 4 5 6 7 8 9 10 km

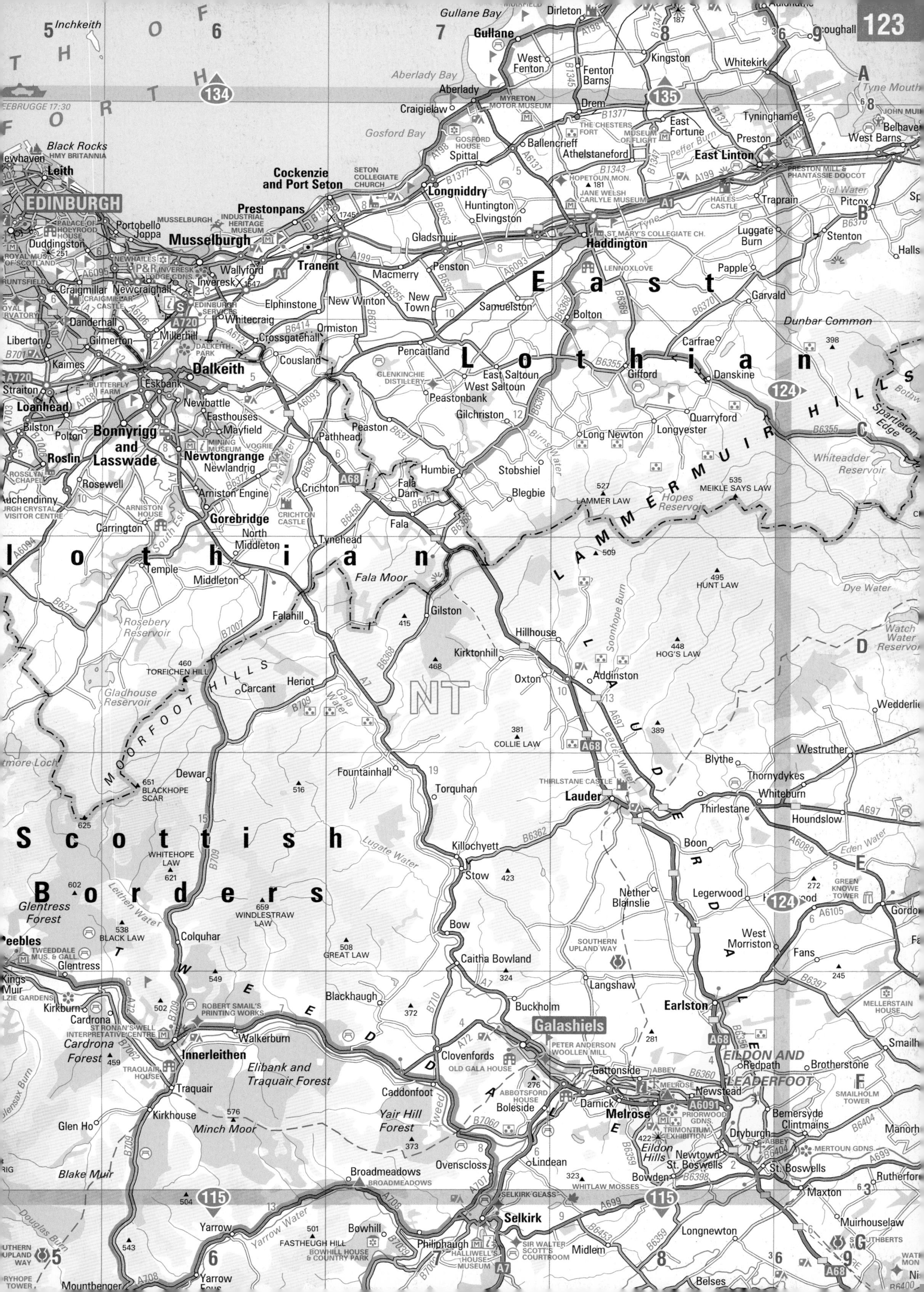

Inchkeith
F O R T H
134
135
124
115
Gullane Bay
Gullane
Dirleton
Kingston
Whitekirk
West Fenton
Fenton Barns
Aberlady Bay
Aberlady
Tyne Mouth
Craigielaw
MYRETON MOTOR MUSEUM
Drem
Tyninghame
Belhaven
West Barns
Gosford Bay
GOSFORD HOUSE
Spittal
Ballencrieff
THE CHESTERS FORT
MUSEUM OF FLIGHT
East Fortune
Athelstaneford
Preston
East Linton
PRESTON MILL & PHANTASSIE DOOCOT
Black Rocks
HMY BRITANNIA
Newhaven
Leith
EDINBURGH
Cockenzie and Port Seton
SETON COLLEGIATE CHURCH
Longniddry
HOPETOUN MON.
JANE WELSH CARLYLE MUSEUM
HAILES CASTLE
Traprain
Biel Water
Pitcox
Prestonpans
Huntington
Elvingston
PALACE OF HOLYROODHOUSE
Portobello
Joppa
MUSSELBURGH
INDUSTRIAL HERITAGE MUSEUM
Musselburgh
Gladsmuir
ST MARY'S COLLEGIATE CH.
Haddington
Luggate Burn
Stenton
Duddingston
ROYAL MUSEUM OF SCOTLAND
NEWHAILES
INVERESK LODGE GDNS.
Wallyford
Inveresk
Tranent
Penston
Macmerry
LENNOXLOVE
Papple
Craigmillar
Newcraighall
CRAIGMILLAR CASTLE
EDINBURGH SERVICES
Elphinstone
New Winton
New Town
Samuelston
East
Bolton
Garvald
Whitecraig
Danderhall
Liberton
Gilmerton
Millerhill
Crossgatehall
Ormiston
DALKEITH PARK
Dunbar Common
Carfrae
Kaimes
Dalkeith
Cousland
Pencaitland
Lothian
Gifford
Danskine
Straiton
Eskbank
BUTTERFLY FARM
GLENKINCHIE DISTILLERY
East Saltoun
West Saltoun
Peastonbank
Loanhead
Newbattle
Easthouses
Mayfield
Gilchriston
Quarryford
Longyester
Spartleton Edge
Bilston
Polton
Bonnyrigg and Lasswade
MINING MUSEUM
VOGRIE
Pathhead
Peaston
Long Newton
Roslin
ROSSLYN CHAPEL
Newtongrange
Newlandrig
Humbie
Stobshiel
LAMMERMUIR HILLS
Whiteadder Reservoir
Rosewell
Arniston Engine
Crichton
Fala Dam
Blegbie
527 LAMMER LAW
535 MEIKLE SAYS LAW
Hopes Reservoir
Auchendinny
EDINBURGH CRYSTAL VISITOR CENTRE
ARNISTON HOUSE
Gorebridge
CRICHTON CASTLE
Fala
Carrington
North Middleton
Tynehead
Temple
Middleton
Fala Moor
509
495 HUNT LAW
Dye Water
Gilston
415
Falahill
Rosebery Reservoir
Watch Water Reservoir
Hillhouse
Kirktonhill
468
448 HOG'S LAW
460 TORFICHEN HILL
Heriot
Carcant
MOORFOOT HILLS
Gladhouse Reservoir
Oxton
Addinston
NT
Gala Water
Soonhope Burn
Wedderlie
381 COLLIE LAW
389
Leader Water
LAUDERDALE
Westruther
Blythe
Thornydykes
Dewar
Fountainhall
516
Torquhan
651 BLACKHOPE SCAR
THIRLSTANE CASTLE
Lauder
Whiteburn
Thirlestane
Houndslow
625
Scottish Borders
Killochyett
Lugate Water
Boon
Eden Water
WHITEHOPE LAW 621
Stow
423
272
GREEN KNOWE TOWER
602
Glentress Forest
659 WINDLESTRAW LAW
Nether Blainslie
Legerwood
Gordon
Leithen Water
538 BLACK LAW
Bow
Peebles
TWEEDDALE MUS. & GALL.
Colquhar
508 GREAT LAW
SOUTHERN UPLAND WAY
West Morriston
Fans
Glentress
Caitha Bowland
549
324
Langshaw
245
Kings Muir
KAILZIE GARDENS
TWEEDDALE
Blackhaugh
MELLERSTAIN HOUSE
Kirkburn
Cardrona
502
ROBERT SMAIL'S PRINTING WORKS
372
Buckholm
Earlston
ST RONAN'S WELL INTERPRETATIVE CENTRE
Walkerburn
Galashiels
Cardrona Forest
459
Innerleithen
Clovenfords
PETER ANDERSON WOOLLEN MILL
281
EILDON AND LEADERFOOT
Redpath
Brotherstone
Smailholm
TRAQUAIR HOUSE
Elibank and Traquair Forest
OLD GALA HOUSE
Gattonside
ABBEY
MELROSE
Newstead
SMAILHOLM TOWER
Traquair
Caddonfoot
276
ABBOTSFORD HOUSE
Boleside
Darnick
Melrose
PRIORWOOD GDNS.
TRIMONTIUM EXHIBITION
Bemersyde
Clintmains
Kirkhouse
576
Minch Moor
Yair Hill Forest
Tweed
422
Eildon Hills
Dryburgh
ABBEY
Manorhill
Glen Ho
373
MERTOUN GDNS.
Lindean
Newtown St. Boswells
St. Boswells
Blake Muir
Ovenscloss
Bowden
Rutherford
Broadmeadows
BROADMEADOWS
323 WHITLAW MOSSES
Maxton
504
SELKIRK GLASS
Selkirk
Yarrow Water
Muirhouselaw
Yarrow
501 FASTHEUGH HILL
Bowhill
Philiphaugh
SIR WALTER SCOTT'S COURTROOM
Longnewton
ST CUTHBERTS WAY
543
BOWHILL HOUSE & COUNTRY PARK
HALLIWELL'S HOUSE MUSEUM
Midlem
Douglas Burn
SOUTHERN UPLAND WAY
Yarrow Feus
Mountbenger
Belses
A
B
C
D
E
F
G
5
6
7
8
9

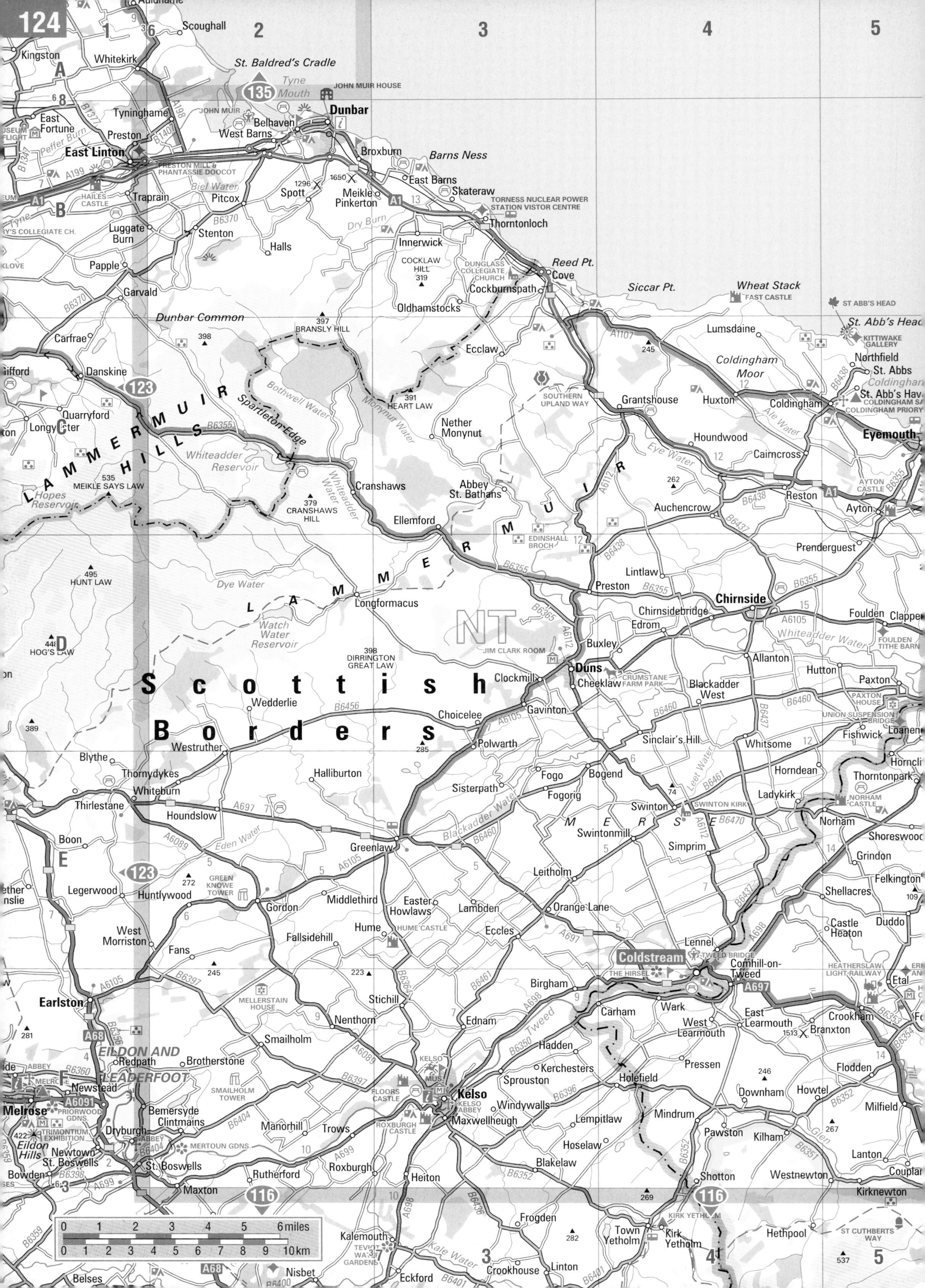

Dunbar
Eyemouth
Chirnside
Duns
Coldstream
Kelso
Melrose
Earlston
East Linton
Scottish Borders
LAMMERMUIR HILLS
MERSE
0 1 2 3 4 5 6 miles
0 1 2 3 4 5 6 7 8 9 10 km

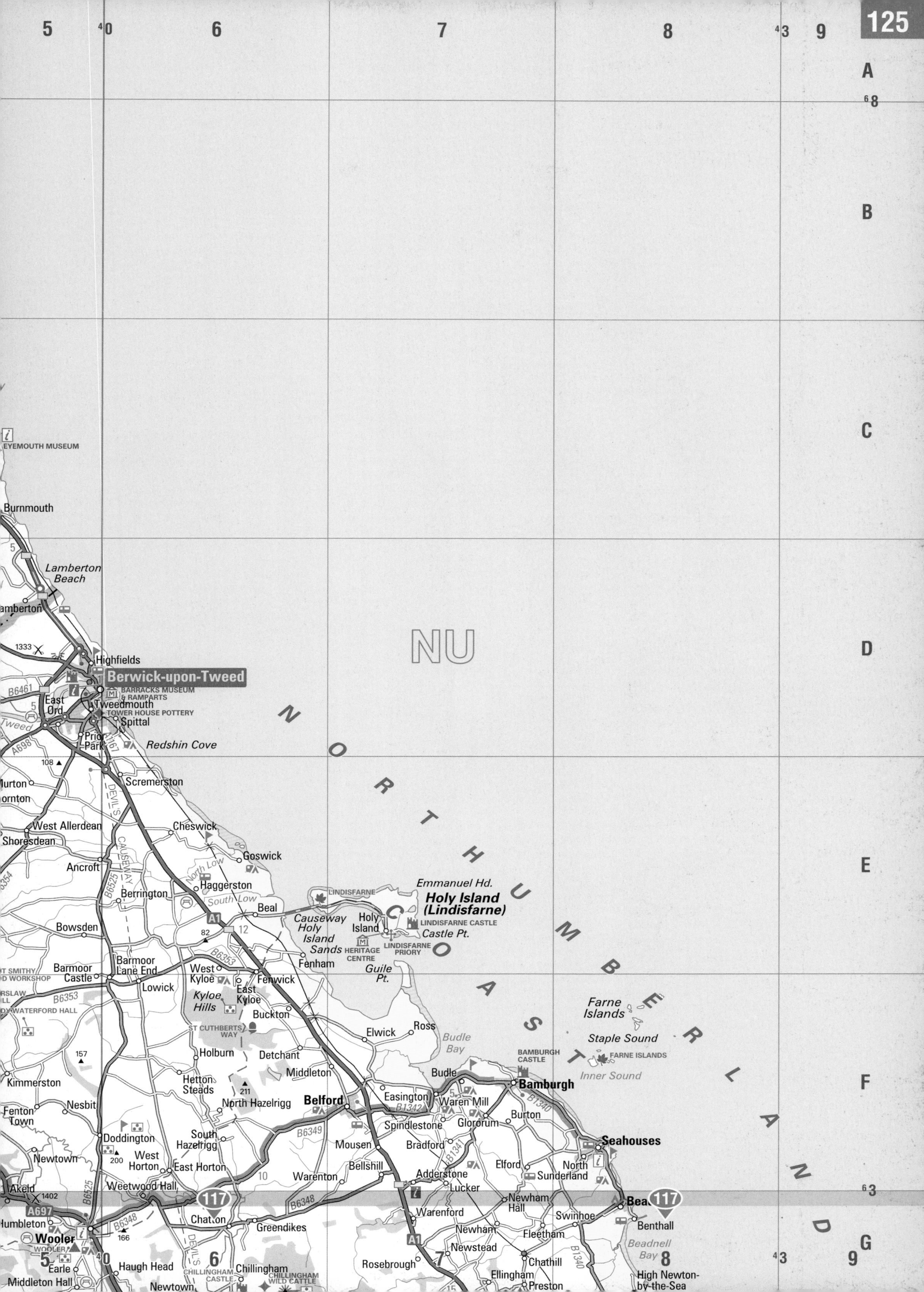
NU
NORTHUMBERLAND COAST
Berwick-upon-Tweed
Highfields
Tweedmouth
Spittal
East Ord
Prior Park
Redshin Cove
Lamberton Beach
Burnmouth
EYEMOUTH MUSEUM
BARRACKS MUSEUM & RAMPARTS
TOWER HOUSE POTTERY
Scremerston
Cheswick
Goswick
Haggerston
North Low
South Low
Beal
Berrington
Ancroft
West Allerdean
Shoresdean
Bowsden
Barmoor Lane End
Barmoor Castle
Lowick
West Kyloe
East Kyloe
Kyloe Hills
Fenwick
Fenham
Buckton
ST CUTHBERTS WAY
Holburn
Detchant
Middleton
Hetton Steads
North Hazelrigg
South Hazelrigg
Doddington
West Horton
East Horton
Weetwood Hall
Belford
Easington
Spindlestone
Mousen
Bradford
Bellshill
Warenton
Adderstone
Lucker
Warenford
Waren Mill
Glororum
Budle
Budle Bay
Elwick
Ross
Bamburgh
BAMBURGH CASTLE
Burton
Seahouses
North Sunderland
Elford
Newham Hall
Newham
Swinhoe
Benthall
Beadnell Bay
Fleetham
Newstead
Chathill
Ellingham
Preston
High Newton-by-the-Sea
Rosebrough
Chatton
Greendikes
Chillingham
CHILLINGHAM CASTLE
CHILLINGHAM WILD CATTLE
Haugh Head
Newtown
Wooler
Earle
Middleton Hall
Akeld
Humbleton
Kimmerston
Nesbit
Fenton Town
Holy Island (Lindisfarne)
Emmanuel Hd.
LINDISFARNE
LINDISFARNE CASTLE
LINDISFARNE PRIORY
HERITAGE CENTRE
Castle Pt.
Guile Pt.
Causeway
Holy Island Sands
Farne Islands
FARNE ISLANDS
Staple Sound
Inner Sound
DEVIL'S CAUSEWAY
A1
A697
A698
B6525
B6353
B6349
B6348
B6461
B1340
B1341
B1342
117

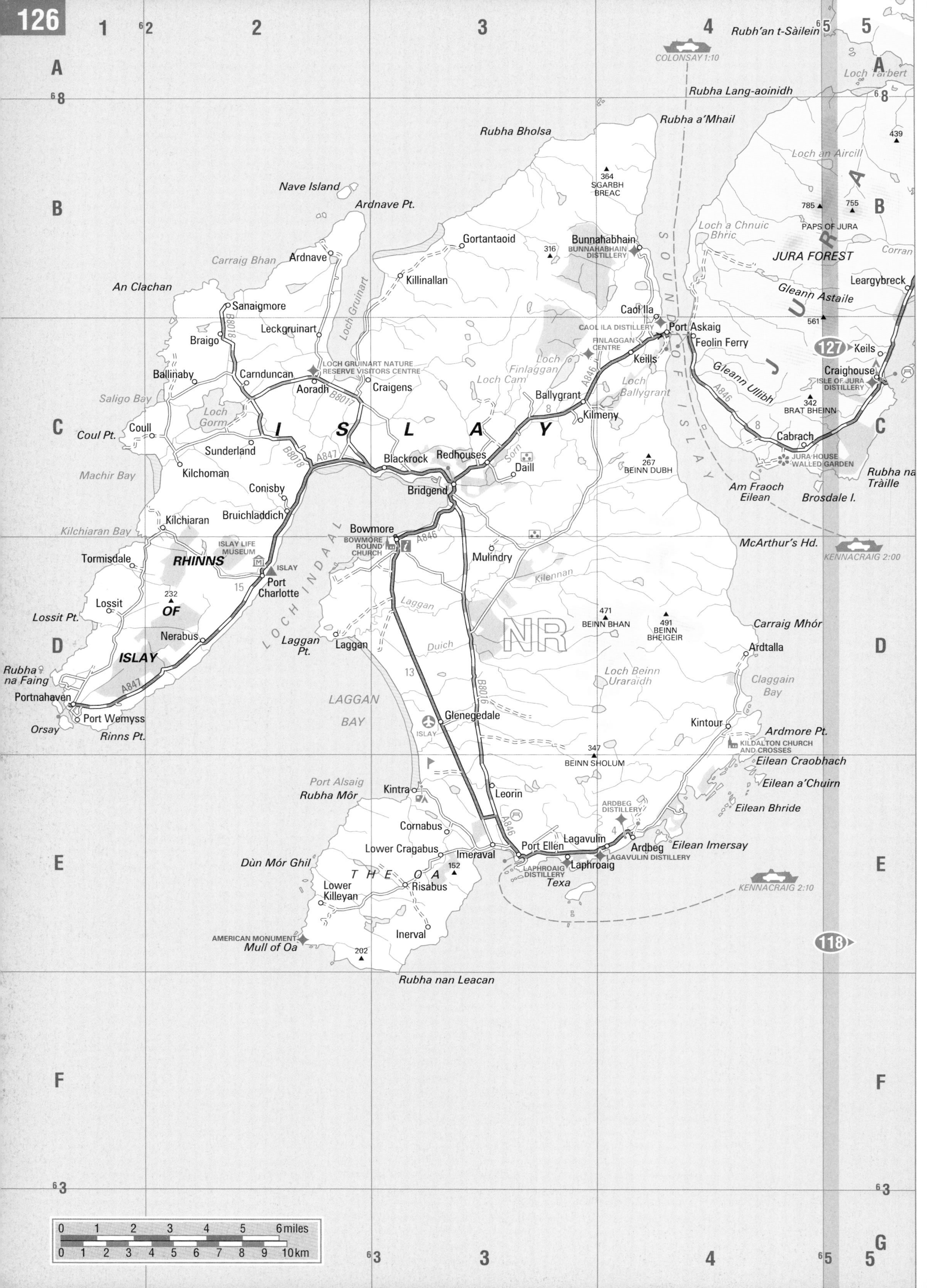
COLONSAY 1:10
Rubh'an t-Sàilein
Loch Tarbert
Rubha Lang-aoinidh
Rubha a'Mhail
Rubha Bholsa
Loch an Aircill
364
SGARBH BREAC
Nave Island
Ardnave Pt.
785
755
PAPS OF JURA
Loch a Chnuic Bhric
JURA FOREST
Corran
Gortantaoid
316
Bunnahabhain
BUNNAHABHAIN DISTILLERY
Carraig Bhan
Ardnave
Killinallan
Leargybreck
An Clachan
Gleann Astaile
Sanaigmore
Caol Ila
CAOL ILA DISTILLERY
Port Askaig
Feolin Ferry
561
Leckgruinart
Loch Gruinart
Braigo
B8018
FINLAGGAN CENTRE
Keills
Keils
LOCH GRUINART NATURE RESERVE VISITORS CENTRE
Loch Finlaggan
Ballinaby
Carnduncan
Craigens
Loch Cam
Gleann Ullibh
Craighouse
ISLE OF JURA DISTILLERY
Aoradh
B8017
Loch Ballygrant
Ballygrant
Saligo Bay
Loch Gorm
A846
342
BRAT BHEINN
Kilmeny
Coull
I S L A Y
Coul Pt.
Cabrach
Sunderland
B8018
A847
Blackrock
Redhouses
Sorn
Daill
JURA HOUSE WALLED GARDEN
267
BEINN DUBH
Rubha na Tràille
Kilchoman
Machir Bay
Am Fraoch Eilean
Brosdale I.
Conisby
Bridgend
Bruichladdich
Kilchiaran
Kilchiaran Bay
Bowmore
BOWMORE ROUND CHURCH
McArthur's Hd.
KENNACRAIG 2:00
ISLAY LIFE MUSEUM
Tormisdale
RHINNS
Mulindry
ISLAY
Kilennan
Port Charlotte
LOCH INDAAL
232
OF
Lossit
Laggan
471
BEINN BHAN
491
BEINN BHEIGEIR
Carraig Mhór
Lossit Pt.
NR
Nerabus
Laggan Pt.
Laggan
Duich
Ardtalla
Rubha na Faing
ISLAY
A847
B8016
Loch Beinn Uraraidh
Claggain Bay
Portnahaven
LAGGAN
Port Wemyss
BAY
Glenegedale
Kintour
Orsay
Rinns Pt.
ISLAY
Ardmore Pt.
KILDALTON CHURCH AND CROSSES
347
BEINN SHOLUM
Eilean Craobhach
Port Alsaig
Eilean a'Chuirn
Rubha Mòr
Kintra
Leorin
ARDBEG DISTILLERY
Eilean Bhride
Cornabus
Lagavulin
Ardbeg
Eilean Imersay
Lower Cragabus
Imeraval
Port Ellen
Dùn Mór Ghil
LAGAVULIN DISTILLERY
T H E O A
152
LAPHROAIG DISTILLERY
Laphroaig
Lower Killeyan
Risabus
Texa
KENNACRAIG 2:10
Inerval
118
AMERICAN MONUMENT
Mull of Oa
202
Rubha nan Leacan
127
0 1 2 3 4 5 6 miles
0 1 2 3 4 5 6 7 8 9 10 km

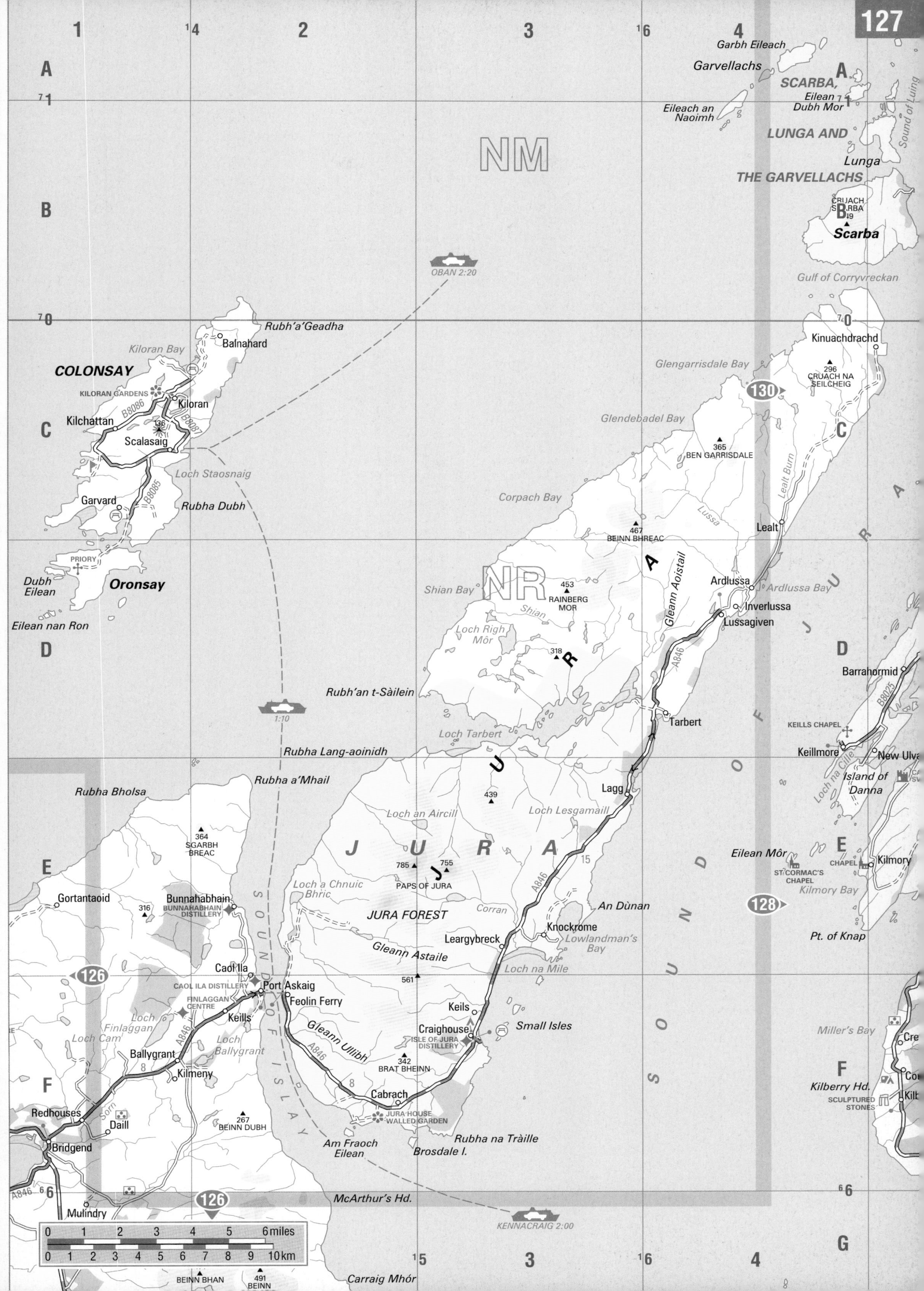
NM
NR
Garbh Eileach
Garvellachs
Eileach an Naoimh
SCARBA, LUNGA AND THE GARVELLACHS
Eilean Dubh Mor
Lunga
Sound of Luing
CRUACH SCARBA 449
Scarba
OBAN 2:20
Gulf of Corryvreckan
Rubh'a'Geadha
Balnahard
Kiloran Bay
COLONSAY
KILORAN GARDENS
Kiloran
Kilchattan
Scalasaig
B8086
B8087
B8085
136
Loch Staosnaig
Garvard
Rubha Dubh
PRIORY
Dubh Eilean
Oronsay
Eilean nan Ron
Kinuachdrachd
Glengarrisdale Bay
296 CRUACH NA SEILCHEIG
130
Glendebadel Bay
365 BEN GARRISDALE
Lealt Burn
Corpach Bay
467 BEINN BHREAC
Lussa
Lealt
Gleann Aoistail
Ardlussa
Ardlussa Bay
Inverlussa
Lussagiven
Shian Bay
453 RAINBERG MOR
Shian
Loch Righ Mòr
318
A846
Barrahormid
B8025
Rubh'an t-Sàilein
1:10
Tarbert
Loch Tarbert
KEILLS CHAPEL
Keillmore
New Ulva
Rubha Lang-aoinidh
Rubha a'Mhail
Rubha Bholsa
Lagg
439
Loch na Cille
Island of Danna
Loch an Aircill
Loch Lesgamaill
364 SGARBH BREAC
JURA
785
755
PAPS OF JURA
Eilean Mòr
ST CORMAC'S CHAPEL
CHAPEL
Kilmory
Kilmory Bay
Loch a Chnuic Bhric
Gortantaoid
316
Bunnahabhain
BUNNAHABHAIN DISTILLERY
JURA FOREST
Corran
An Dùnan
128
Knockrome
Lowlandman's Bay
Leargybreck
Pt. of Knap
Gleann Astaile
SOUND OF JURA
SOUND OF ISLAY
126
Caol Ila
CAOL ILA DISTILLERY
Port Askaig
Feolin Ferry
Loch na Mile
561
FINLAGGAN CENTRE
Loch Finlaggan
Keills
Loch Cam
Loch Ballygrant
Gleann Ullibh
Keils
Craighouse
ISLE OF JURA DISTILLERY
Small Isles
Miller's Bay
Ballygrant
Kilmeny
342 BRAT BHEINN
Kilberry Hd.
SCULPTURED STONES
Cabrach
Redhouses
Sorn
Daill
267 BEINN DUBH
JURA HOUSE WALLED GARDEN
Bridgend
Am Fraoch Eilean
Brosdale I.
Rubha na Tràille
A846
McArthur's Hd.
Mulindry
KENNACRAIG 2:00
0 1 2 3 4 5 6 miles
0 1 2 3 4 5 6 7 8 9 10 km
BEINN BHAN
491 BEINN
Carraig Mhór

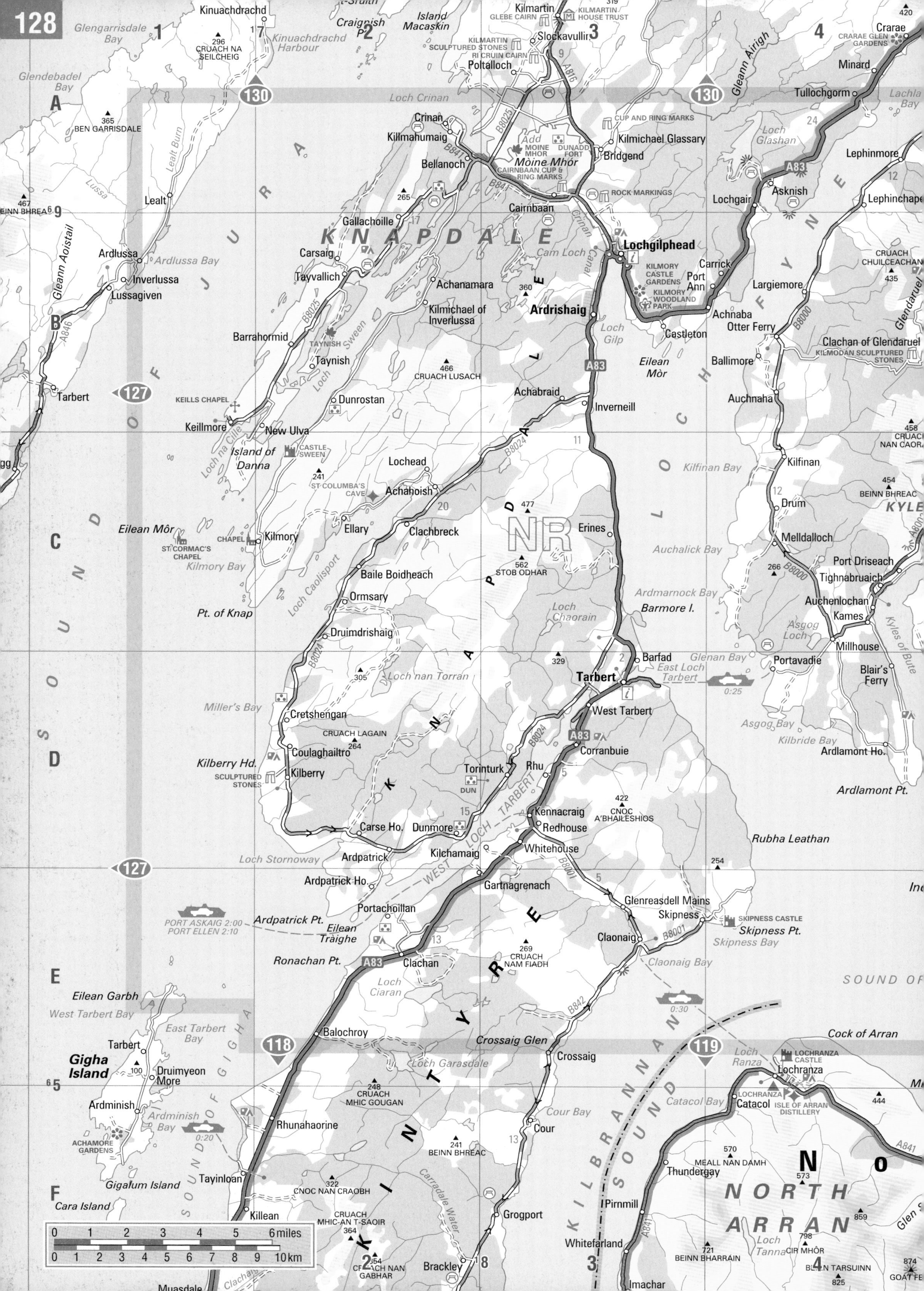
Kinuachdrachd
Glengarrisdale Bay
296 CRUACH NA SEILCHEIG
Kinuachdrachd Harbour
Craignish
Island Macaskin
Kilmartin
GLEBE CAIRN
KILMARTIN HOUSE TRUST
KILMARTIN SCULPTURED STONES
RI CRUIN CAIRN
Slockavullin
Poltalloch
Crarae
CRARAE GLEN GARDENS
Minard
Gleann Airigh
Glendebadel Bay
Tullochgorm
Lachla Bay
Loch Crinan
365 BEN GARRISDALE
Crinan
Killmahumaig
CUP AND RING MARKS
Kilmichael Glassary
Bridgend
MOINE MHOR
DUNADD FORT
Mòine Mhór
CAIRNBAAN CUP & RING MARKS
Bellanoch
Loch Glashan
Lephinmore
Lealt Burn
Lussa
Lealt
467
265
ROCK MARKINGS
Cairnbaan
Lochgair
Asknish
Lephinchapel
Gallachoille
KNAPDALE
Carsaig
Crinan Canal
Cam Loch
Lochgilphead
Ardlussa
Ardlussa Bay
Gleann Aoistail
Inverlussa
Lussagiven
Tayvallich
Achanamara
KILMORY CASTLE GARDENS
KILMORY WOODLAND PARK
Port Ann
Carrick
Largiemore
CRUACH CHUILCEACHAN
435
360
Ardrishaig
Kilmichael of Inverlussa
Achnaba
Otter Ferry
Castleton
Barrahormid
TAYNISH
Loch Sween
Loch Gilp
Clachan of Glendaruel
KILMODAN SCULPTURED STONES
Taynish
466 CRUACH LUSACH
Eilean Mòr
Ballimore
Glendaruel
Tarbert
KEILLS CHAPEL
Dunrostan
Achabraid
Inverneill
Auchnaha
Keillmore
New Ulva
Loch na Cille
CASTLE SWEEN
Island of Danna
458
Lochead
Kilfinan
Kilfinan Bay
241
ST COLUMBA'S CAVE
Achahoish
454 BEINN BHREAC
KYLE
Drum
477
Eilean Mór
CHAPEL
ST CORMAC'S CHAPEL
Kilmory
Ellary
Clachbreck
NR
Erines
Melldalloch
Auchalick Bay
Kilmory Bay
Loch Caolisport
562 STOB ODHAR
266
Port Driseach
Tighnabruaich
Baile Boidheach
Ormsary
Ardmarnock Bay
Barmore I.
Auchenlochan
Kames
Pt. of Knap
Loch Chaorain
Asgog Loch
Kyles of Bute
Millhouse
Druimdrishaig
329
Barfad
Glenan Bay
Portavadie
East Loch Tarbert
Blair's Ferry
305
Loch nan Torran
Tarbert
0:25
Miller's Bay
West Tarbert
Cretshengan
CRUACH LAGAIN 264
Asgog Bay
Kilbride Bay
Ardlamont Ho.
Corranbuie
Coulaghailtro
Kilberry Hd.
SCULPTURED STONES
Kilberry
Torinturk
DUN
Rhu
422 CNOC A'BHAILESHIOS
Ardlamont Pt.
Kennacraig
Redhouse
Carse Ho.
Dunmore
WEST LOCH TARBERT
Rubha Leathan
Loch Stornoway
Ardpatrick
Kilchamaig
Whitehouse
254
Ardpatrick Ho.
Gartnagrenach
Glenreasdell Mains
Skipness
SKIPNESS CASTLE
Skipness Pt.
Skipness Bay
Portachoillan
PORT ASKAIG 2:00
PORT ELLEN 2:10
Ardpatrick Pt.
Eilean Traighe
269 CRUACH NAM FIADH
Claonaig
Claonaig Bay
Ronachan Pt.
Clachan
Loch Ciaran
SOUND OF
Eilean Garbh
West Tarbert Bay
East Tarbert Bay
0:30
Balochroy
Crossaig Glen
Cock of Arran
Tarbert
Gigha Island
100
Druimyeon More
Loch Garasdale
Crossaig
Loch Ranza
LOCHRANZA CASTLE
Lochranza
248 CRUACH MHIC GOUGAN
LOCHRANZA
ISLE OF ARRAN DISTILLERY
Catacol
Catacol Bay
444
Ardminish
Ardminish Bay
SOUND OF GIGHA
Cour Bay
Rhunahaorine
Cour
0:20
ACHAMORE GARDENS
241 BEINN BHREAC
570 MEALL NAN DAMH
Thundergay
KILBRANNAN SOUND
KINTYRE
Gigalum Island
Tayinloan
322 CNOC NAN CRAOBH
573
NORTH ARRAN
Cara Island
Carradale Water
Pirnmill
859
Killean
CRUACH MHIC-AN T-SAOIR 364
Grogport
Glen
0 1 2 3 4 5 6 miles
0 1 2 3 4 5 6 7 8 9 10 km
Whitefarland
Loch Tanna
798 CIR MHÒR
721 BEINN BHARRAIN
654 CRUACH NAN GABHAR
Brackley
BEINN TARSUINN 825
874 GOAT FELL
Imachar
Muasdale
A816 A83 A846 A841 A8003 B8025 B841 B8024 B8000 B8001 B842
130 127 118 119

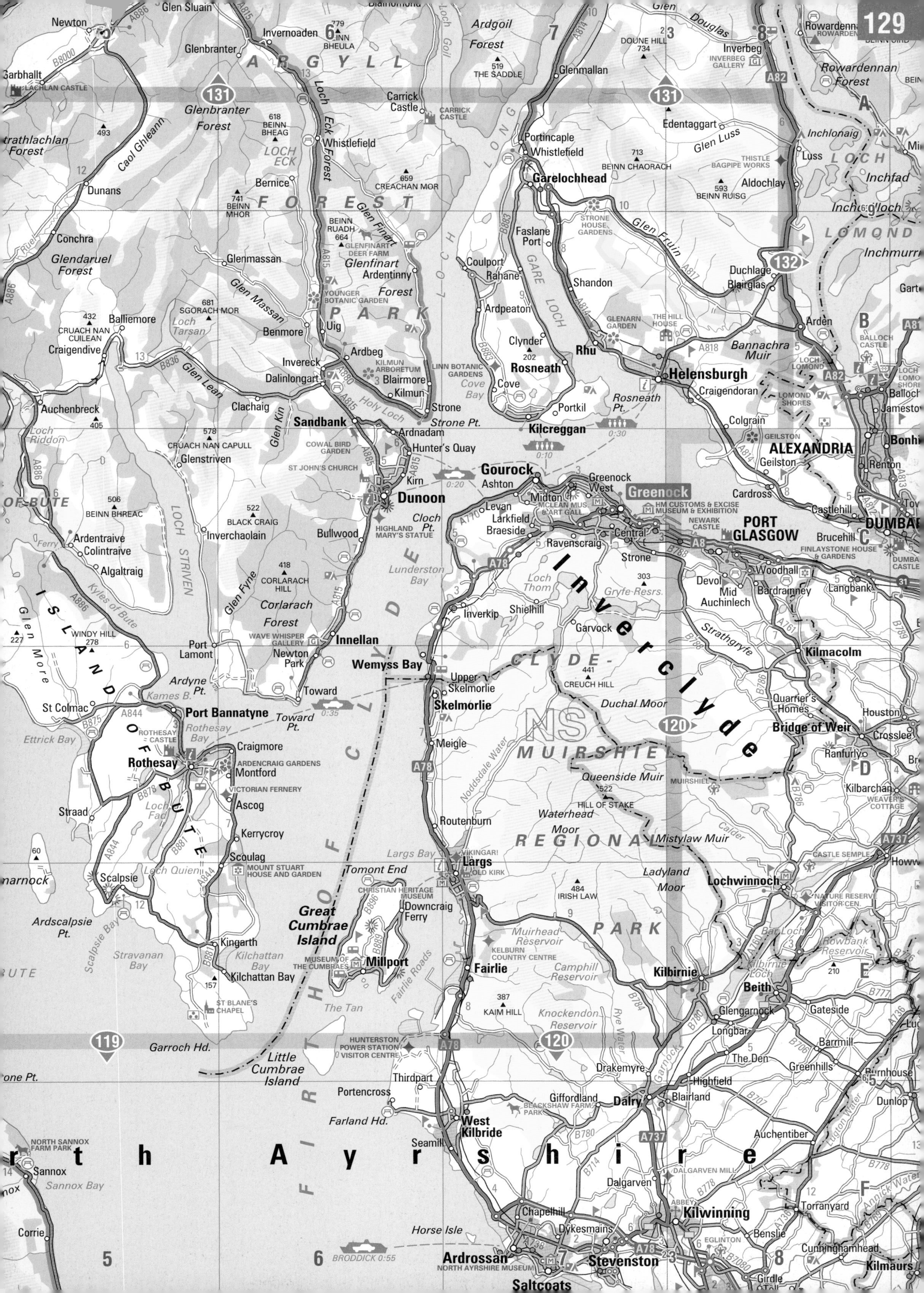

ARGYLL
FOREST
PARK
Inverclyde
CLYDE-MUIRSHIEL REGIONAL PARK
North Ayrshire
FIRTH OF CLYDE
ISLAND OF BUTE
Dunoon
Gourock
Greenock
PORT GLASGOW
Helensburgh
ALEXANDRIA
Rothesay
Largs
Millport
Great Cumbrae Island
Little Cumbrae Island
Kilbirnie
Beith
Dalry
Kilwinning
Ardrossan
Saltcoats
Stevenston
West Kilbride
Fairlie
Skelmorlie
Wemyss Bay
Inverkip
Kilmacolm
Bridge of Weir
Lochwinnoch
Garelochhead
Rhu
Rosneath
Kilcreggan
Cove
Sandbank
Innellan
Port Bannatyne
Loch Eck
Loch Long
Gare Loch
Loch Striven
Kyles of Bute
BRODDICK 0:55

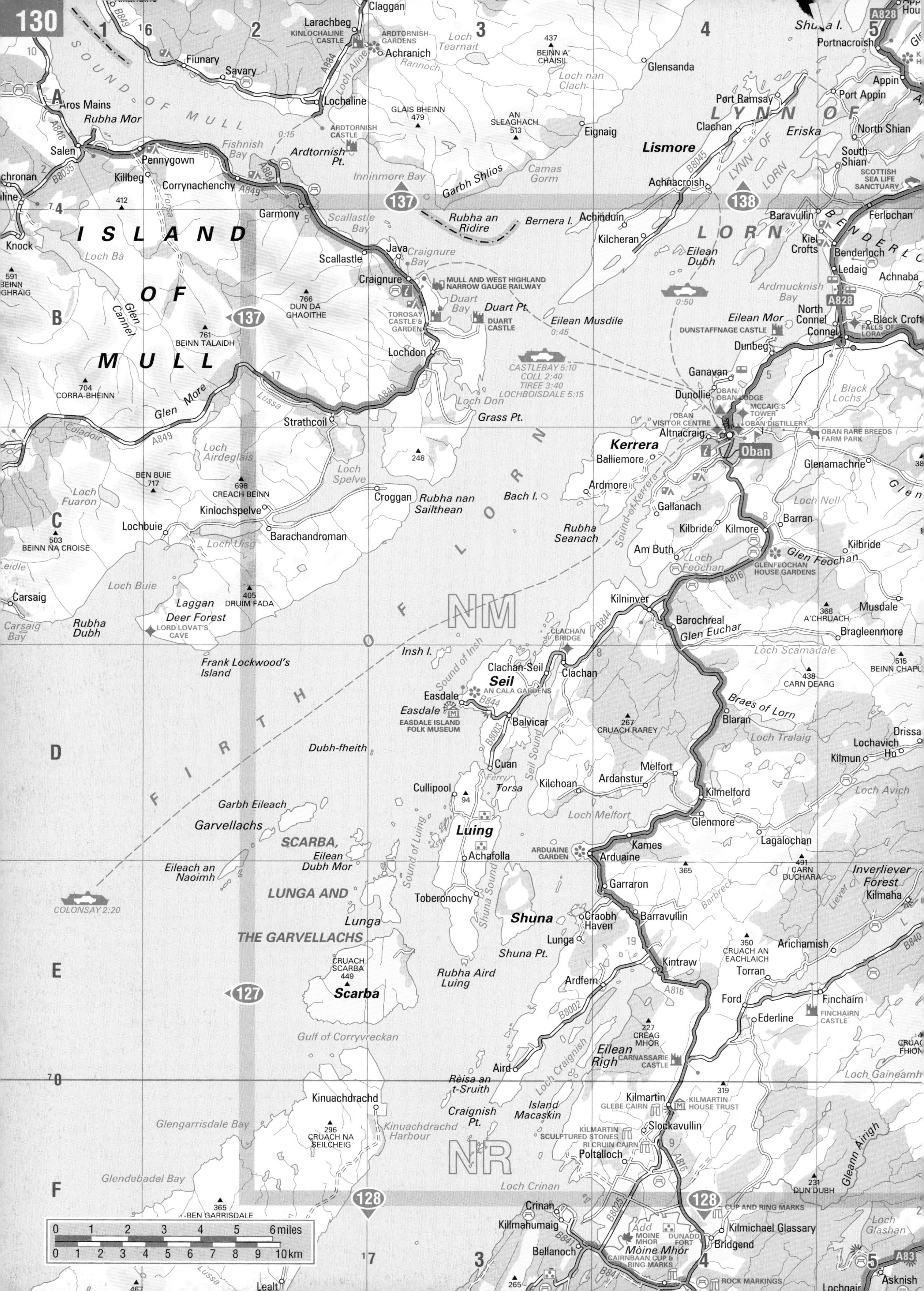
Claggan
Larachbeg
KINLOCHALINE CASTLE
ARDTORNISH GARDENS
Achranich
Loch Tearnait
Rannoch
437
BEINN A' CHAISIL
Glensanda
Loch nan Clach
Shuna I.
Portnacroish
A828
SOUND OF MULL
Fiunary
Savary
Loch Aline
A884
Lochaline
Aros Mains
Rubha Mor
A848
GLAIS BHEINN
479
AN SLEAGHACH
513
Eignaig
Port Ramsay
Clachan
LYNN OF LORN
Eriska
Appin
Port Appin
North Shian
South Shian
Lismore
B8045
SCOTTISH SEA LIFE SANCTUARY
Salen
B8035
Pennygown
Fishnish Bay
0:15
ARDTORNISH CASTLE
Ardtornish Pt.
Killbeg
Corrynachenchy
A849
Garbh Shlios
Camas Gorm
Achnacroish
Inninmore Bay
137
138
412
Torsa
Garmony
Scallastle Bay
Rubha an Ridire
Bernera I.
Achinduin
LORN
Baravullin
BENDERLOCH
Ferlochan
Kiel Crofts
Benderloch
Ledaig
Achnaba
ISLAND OF MULL
Knock
Loch Bà
Scallastle
Java
Craignure Bay
Kilcheran
Eilean Dubh
Craignure
MULL AND WEST HIGHLAND NARROW GAUGE RAILWAY
Ardmucknish Bay
0:50
591 BEINN CHRAIG
Glen Cannel
766
DUN DA GHAOITHE
TOROSAY CASTLE & GARDEN
Duart Bay
Duart Pt.
DUART CASTLE
Eilean Musdile
0:45
Eilean Mor
North Connel
Connel
Black Croft
FALLS OF LORA
DUNSTAFFNAGE CASTLE
Dunbeg
761
BEINN TALAIDH
Lochdon
CASTLEBAY 5:10
COLL 2:40
TIREE 3:40
LOCHBOISDALE 5:15
Ganavan
Dunollie
OBAN/OBAN LODGE
MCCAIG'S TOWER
OBAN DISTILLERY
OBAN VISITOR CENTRE
704
CORRA-BHEINN
Glen More
17
Lussa
Loch Don
Grass Pt.
Black Lochs
Strathcoil
Coladoir
A849
Altnacraig
Oban
OBAN RARE BREEDS FARM PARK
Kerrera
Balliemore
Glenamachrie
Loch Airdeglais
248
Loch Spelve
BEN BUIE
717
698
CREACH BEINN
Ardmore
Sound of Kerrera
Glen Lonan
Loch Nell
Loch Fuaron
Kinlochspelve
Croggan
Rubha nan Sailthean
Bach I.
Gallanach
Barran
Lochbuie
Barachandroman
Loch Uisg
Rubha Seanach
Kilbride
Kilmore
503
BEINN NA CROISE
Am Buth
Loch Feochan
Glen Feochan
Kilbride
GLENFEOCHAN HOUSE GARDENS
A816
Loch Buie
405
DRUIM FADA
NM
Carsaig
Laggan
Deer Forest
LORD LOVAT'S CAVE
Kilninver
368
A'CHRUACH
Musdale
Carsaig Bay
Rubha Dubh
B844
Barochreal
Glen Euchar
Bragleenmore
CLACHAN BRIDGE
Insh I.
Sound of Insh
Loch Scamadale
515
BEINN CHAPULL
Frank Lockwood's Island
Clachan-Seil
Seil
Clachan
AN CALA GARDENS
438
CARN DEARG
FIRTH OF LORN
Easdale
Easdale
EASDALE ISLAND FOLK MUSEUM
B8003
Balvicar
267
CRUACH RAREY
Braes of Lorn
Blaran
Loch Tralaig
Dubh-fheith
Seil Sound
Lochavich
Kilmun
Cuan
Ferry
Torsa
Melfort
Ardanstur
Kilchoan
Kilmelford
Loch Avich
Cullipool
94
Garbh Eileach
Garvellachs
Loch Melfort
Glenmore
Luing
SCARBA, Eilean Dubh Mor
LUNGA AND THE GARVELLACHS
Sound of Luing
Achafolla
ARDUAINE GARDEN
Arduaine
Kames
Lagalochan
Eileach an Naoimh
365
491
CARN DUCHARA
Inverliever Forest
Kilmaha
Garraron
Toberonochy
Shuna Sound
Barbreck
COLONSAY 2:20
Lunga
Shuna
Craobh Haven
Barravullin
Lunga
19
Shuna Pt.
350
CRUACH AN EACHLAICH
Arichamish
Torran
Kintraw
CRUACH SCARBA
449
Scarba
Rubha Aird Luing
Ardfern
127
A816
Ford
Finchairn
FINCHAIRN CASTLE
Ederline
B8002
227
CREAG MHOR
Gulf of Corryvreckan
Eilean Righ
CARNASSARIE CASTLE
Loch Craignish
Aird
Rèisa an t-Sruith
Loch Gaineamh
Kinuachdrachd
319
Kilmartin
GLEBE CAIRN
KILMARTIN HOUSE TRUST
Craignish Pt.
Island Macaskin
296
CRUACH NA SEILCHEIG
Kinuachdrachd Harbour
Glengarrisdale Bay
KILMARTIN SCULPTURED STONES
RI CRUIN CAIRN
Slockavullin
NR
Poltalloch
Gleann Airigh
Glendebadel Bay
231
DUN DUBH
Loch Crinan
128
128
365
BEN GARRISDALE
Crinan
CUP AND RING MARKS
Kilmahumaig
B8025
Add
MOINE MHOR
DUNADD FORT
Kilmichael Glassary
Bridgend
Loch Glashan
Bellanoch
B841
Mòine Mhòr
CAIRNBAAN CUP & RING MARKS
265
Lussa
ROCK MARKINGS
Lochgair
Asknish
Lealt
0 1 2 3 4 5 6 miles
0 1 2 3 4 5 6 7 8 9 10 km

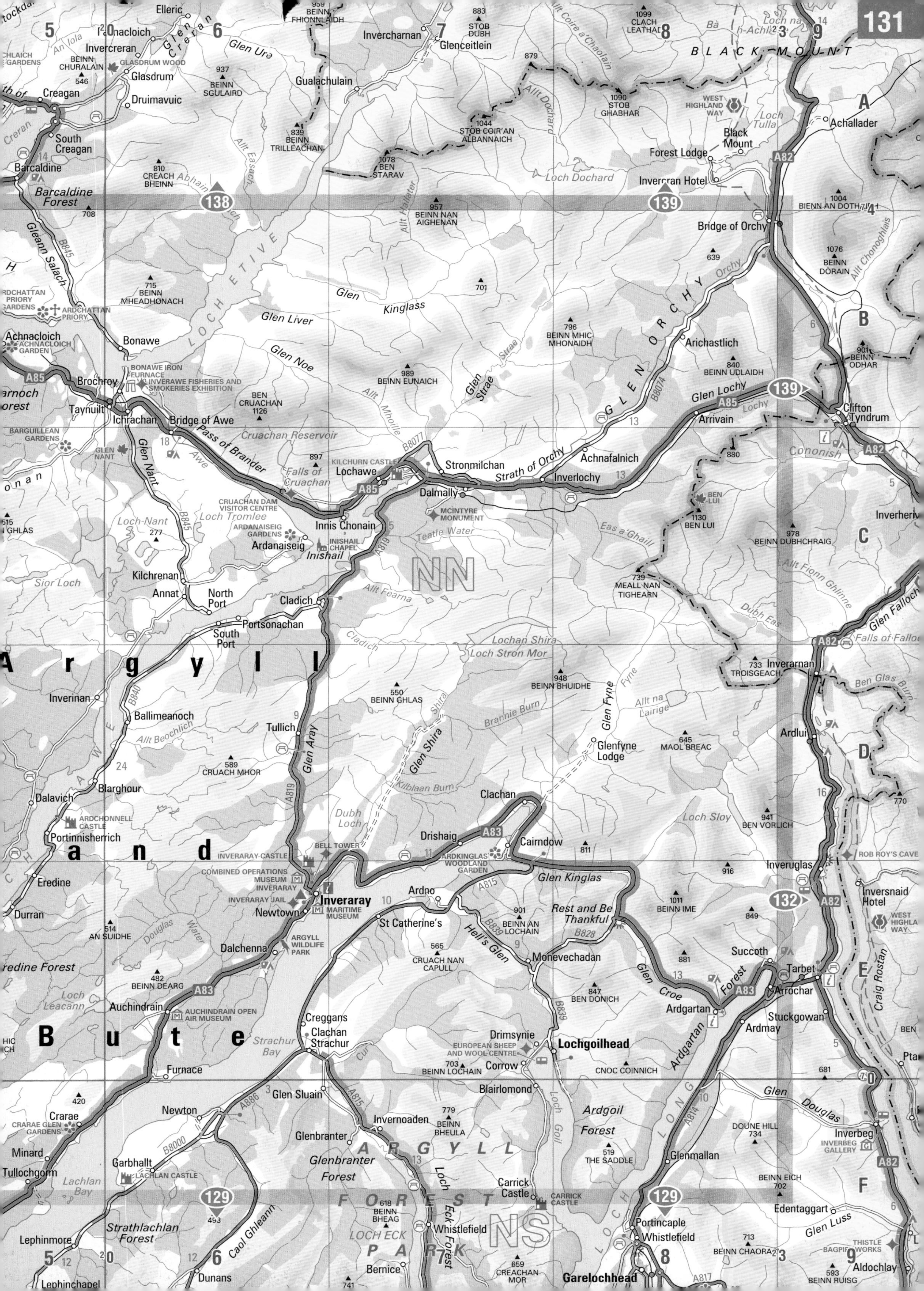
Argyll and Bute
NN
NS
BLACK MOUNT
LOCH ETIVE
GLEN ORCHY
Loch Tulla
Loch Dochard
Bridge of Orchy
Tyndrum
Dalmally
Lochawe
Inveraray
Arrochar
Tarbet
Lochgoilhead
Strachur
Taynuilt
Bonawe
Glen Kinglas
Glen Fyne
Glen Shira
Glen Aray
Loch Sloy
BEN LUI
BEN VORLICH
BEINN IME
ARGYLL FOREST PARK
Garelochhead
Whistlefield
Portincaple
Ardlui
Inverarnan
Crianlarich
A82
A85
A83
A819
A815
A886
A814
B8074
B8077
B828
B839
B840
B845
B8000
138
139
132
129

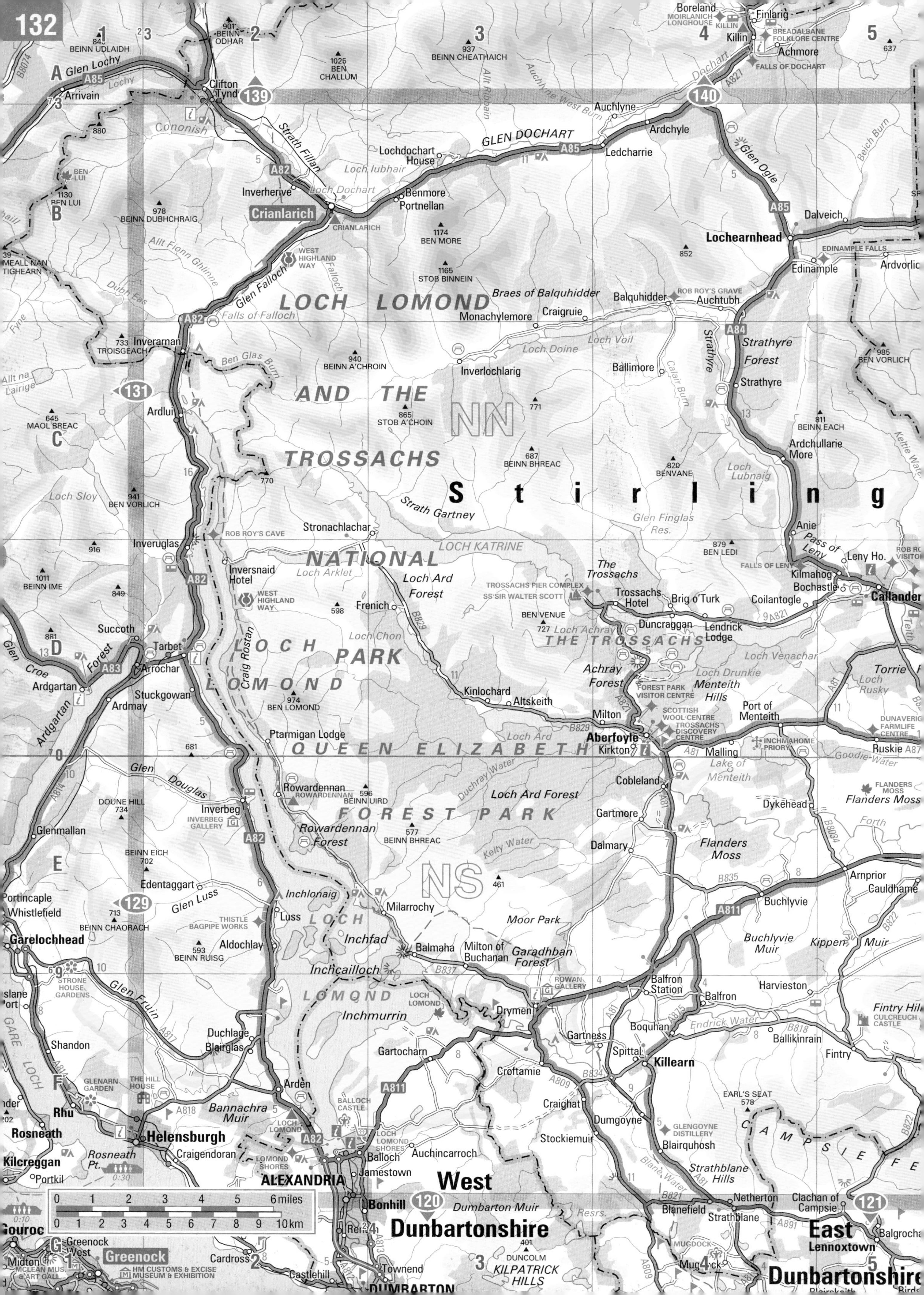
LOCH LOMOND AND THE TROSSACHS NATIONAL PARK
Stirling
West Dunbartonshire
East Dunbartonshire
NN
NS
139
140
131
129
120
121
Glen Lochy
Arrivain
Clifton
Tyndrum
BEINN UDLAIDH
BEINN ODHAR
BEN CHALLUM
BEINN CHEATHAICH
Boreland
MOIRLAICH LONGHOUSE
Killin
Finlarig
BREADALBANE FOLKLORE CENTRE
Achmore
FALLS OF DOCHART
Auchlyne
Ardchyle
GLEN DOCHART
Ledcharrie
Glen Ogle
Lochdochart House
Loch Iubhair
Strath Fillan
Inverherive
Loch Dochart
Benmore
Portnellan
Crianlarich
BEN MORE
STOB BINNEIN
BEN LUI
BEINN DUBHCHRAIG
MEALL NAN TIGHEARN
WEST HIGHLAND WAY
Glen Falloch
Falls of Falloch
Dalveich
Lochearnhead
EDINAMPLE FALLS
Edinample
Ardvorlich
Braes of Balquhidder
Balquhidder
ROB ROY'S GRAVE
Auchtubh
Monachylemore
Craigruie
Loch Voil
Loch Doine
Inverlochlarig
Ballimore
Strathyre
Strathyre Forest
BEN VORLICH
Inverarnan
TROISGEACH
BEINN A'CHROIN
Ardlui
MAOL BREAC
STOB A'CHOIN
BEINN BHREAC
BENVANE
BEINN EACH
Ardchullarie More
Loch Lubnaig
Loch Sloy
Strath Gartney
Glen Finglas Res.
Stronachlachar
LOCH KATRINE
Inveruglas
ROB ROY'S CAVE
Inversnaid Hotel
Loch Arklet
Loch Ard Forest
BEN LEDI
Anie
Pass of Leny
Leny Ho.
FALLS OF LENY
Kilmahog
Bochastle
Callander
Coilantogle
The Trossachs
TROSSACHS PIER COMPLEX
SS SIR WALTER SCOTT
Trossachs Hotel
Brig o'Turk
BEN VENUE
Loch Achray
Duncraggan
Lendrick Lodge
BEINN IME
Frenich
Loch Chon
THE TROSSACHS
Loch Venachar
Succoth
Tarbet
Arrochar
Glen Croe
Ardgartan
Ardgartan Forest
Craig Rostan
Achray Forest
Loch Drunkie
Menteith Hills
Torrie
Loch Rusky
Stuckgowan
Ardmay
BEN LOMOND
Kinlochard
Altskeith
FOREST PARK VISITOR CENTRE
SCOTTISH WOOL CENTRE
TROSSACHS DISCOVERY CENTRE
Milton
Aberfoyle
Kirkton
Port of Menteith
Ptarmigan Lodge
QUEEN ELIZABETH FOREST PARK
Loch Ard
INCHMAHOME PRIORY
Malling
Lake of Menteith
Ruskie
Goodie Water
DUNAVERIG FARMLIFE CENTRE
Glen Douglas
Rowardennan
BEINN UIRD
Duchray Water
Cobleland
FLANDERS MOSS
Dykehead
Flanders Moss
Loch Ard Forest
DOUNE HILL
Inverbeg
INVERBEG GALLERY
Gartmore
Glenmallan
Rowardennan Forest
BEINN BHREAC
Dalmary
Kelty Water
Forth
BEINN EICH
Edentaggart
Inchlonaig
Milarrochy
Arnprior
Cauldhame
Portincaple
Whistlefield
Glen Luss
Luss
THISTLE BAGPIPE WORKS
Moor Park
Buchlyvie
BEINN CHAORACH
Inchfad
Balmaha
Milton of Buchanan
Garadhban Forest
Buchlyvie Muir
Kippen
Muir
Garelochhead
Aldochlay
BEINN RUISG
Inchcailloch
STRONE HOUSE GARDENS
Glen Fruin
LOCH LOMOND
Inchmurrin
ROWAN GALLERY
Balfron Station
Balfron
Harvieston
Fintry Hills
CULCREUCH CASTLE
Drymen
Endrick Water
Boquhan
Ballikinrain
Duchlage
Blairglas
Gartness
Shandon
GARE LOCH
Gartocharn
Spittal
Killearn
Fintry
Croftamie
GLENARN GARDEN
THE HILL HOUSE
Arden
EARL'S SEAT
Rhu
BALLOCH CASTLE
Craighat
Bannachra Muir
Dumgoyne
GLENGOYNE DISTILLERY
CAMPSIE FELLS
Rosneath
Helensburgh
LOCH LOMOND SHORES
Balloch
Auchincarroch
Stockiemuir
Blairquhosh
Kilcreggan
Rosneath Pt.
Craigendoran
Strathblane Hills
Portkil
ALEXANDRIA
Jamestown
Blane Water
Bonhill
Dumbarton Muir
Resrs.
Blanefield
Netherton
Strathblane
Clachan of Campsie
Balgrochan
Gourock
Greenock West
Greenock
Renton
Lennoxtown
Midton
MCLEAN MUS. & ART GALL.
HM CUSTOMS & EXCISE MUSEUM & EXHIBITION
Cardross
Castlehill
Townend
DUNCOLM
KILPATRICK HILLS
MUGDOCK
Mugdock
DUMBARTON
A85
A82
A827
A84
A821
A81
A83
A814
A817
A818
A811
A809
A875
A873
A891
B829
B837
B835
B834
B821
B822
B818
B8034
B8074
0 1 2 3 4 5 6 miles
0 1 2 3 4 5 6 7 8 9 10 km

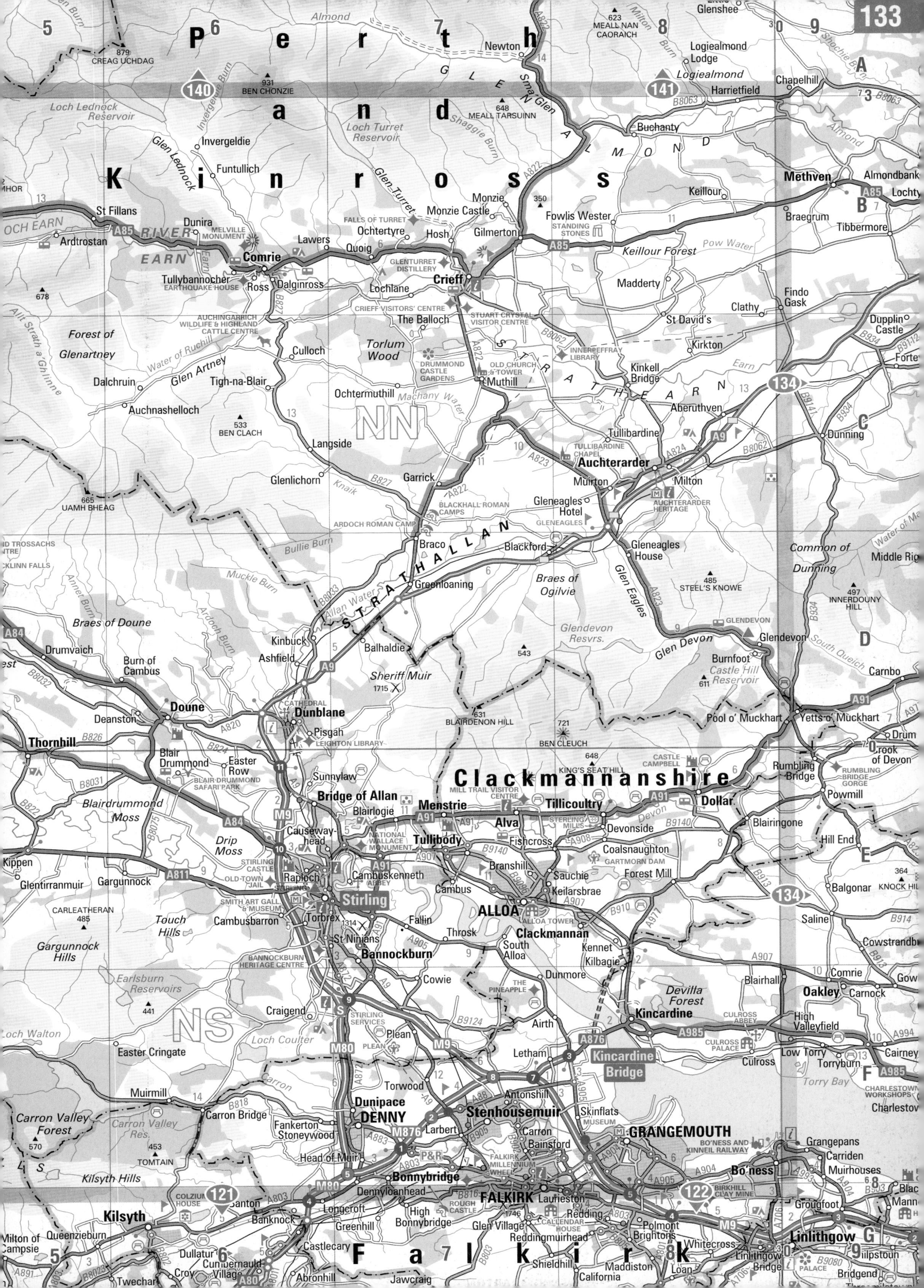
Perth and Kinross
Clackmannanshire
Falkirk
Stirling
Crieff
Comrie
Auchterarder
Dunblane
Doune
Bridge of Allan
Alloa
Tillicoultry
Dollar
Alva
Menstrie
Tullibody
Bannockburn
Denny
Stenhousemuir
Grangemouth
Falkirk
Bo'ness
Linlithgow
Kilsyth
Kincardine
Methven
Muthill
Braco
Blackford
Greenloaning
Thornhill
Kippen
Strathallan
Strathearn
Glen Almond
Glen Devon
Sheriff Muir
Ben Cleuch
Ben Chonzie
Kincardine Bridge
Carron Valley Forest
Kilsyth Hills
Loch Turret Reservoir
Glendevon Resvrs.
NN
NS

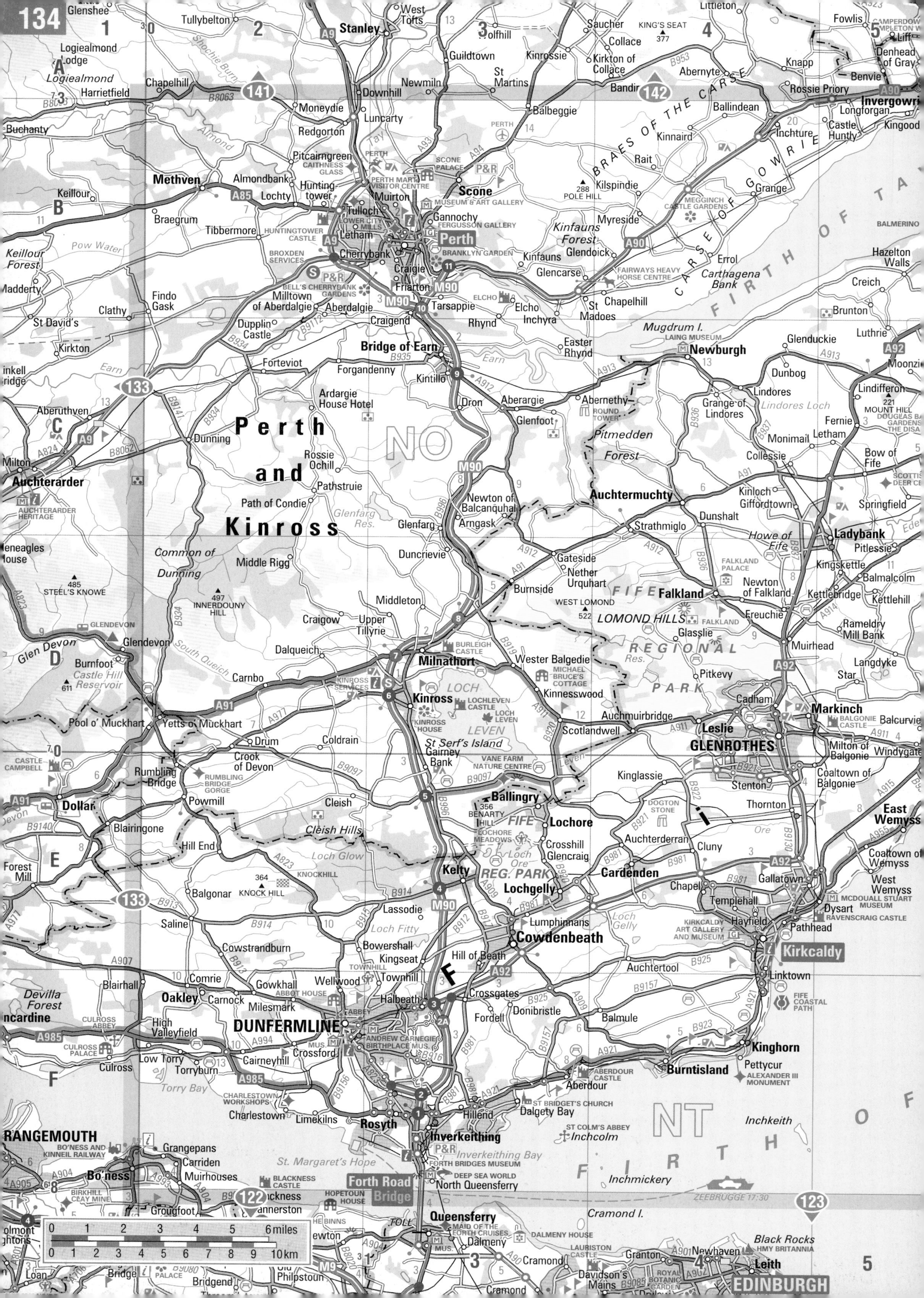
Glenshee
Tullybelton
Stanley
West Tofts
Saucher
KING'S SEAT 377
Littleton
Fowlis
Logiealmond Lodge
Logiealmond
Guildtown
Kinrossie
Collace
Kirkton of Collace
Abernyte
Knapp
Denhead of Gray
Benvie
Harrietfield
Chapelhill
141
Newmiln
St Martins
Bandir
142
Rossie Priory
Invergowrie
Longforgan
Kingoodie
Downhill
Moneydie
Luncarty
Balbeggie
Ballindean
Buchanty
Redgorton
BRAES OF THE CARSE
Kinnaird
Inchture
Castle Huntly
Almond
Pitcairngreen
Methven
Almondbank
Huntingtower
Lochty
Scone
Rait
Kilspindie
Grange
CARSE OF GOWRIE
Keillour
Muirton
Tulloch
288 POLE HILL
MEGGINCH CASTLE GARDENS
Braegrum
Tibbermore
Letham
Gannochy
Perth
FERGUSSON GALLERY
Kinfauns Forest
Myreside
Glendoick
BALMERINO
Keillour Forest
Pow Water
HUNTINGTOWER CASTLE
BROXDEN SERVICES
Cherrybank
BRANKLYN GARDEN
Kinfauns
Glencarse
Errol
Carthagena Bank
FIRTH OF TAY
Hazelton Walls
Madderty
Findo Gask
Milltown of Aberdalgie
Aberdalgie
Craigie
Friarton
FAIRWAYS HEAVY HORSE CENTRE
Creich
Clathy
St David's
Tarsappie
Elcho
Inchyra
St Madoes
Chapelhill
Brunton
Dupplin Castle
Craigend
Rhynd
Mugdrum I.
Luthrie
Kirkton
Bridge of Earn
Easter Rhynd
Newburgh
LAING MUSEUM
Glenduckie
Forteviot
Forgandenny
Kintillo
Earn
Dunbog
Lindores
Moonzie
133
Aberuthven
Ardargie House Hotel
Dron
Aberargie
Abernethy
ROUND TOWER
Grange of Lindores
Lindores Loch
Lindifferon
221 MOUNT HILL
DOUGLAS BARS GARDENS
Fernie
Letham
Dunning
Perth and Kinross
NO
Glenfoot
Pitmedden Forest
Monimail
Collessie
Bow of Fife
Milton
Auchterarder
AUCHTERARDER HERITAGE
Rossie Ochill
Pathstruie
Path of Condie
Glenfarg Res.
Glenfarg
Newton of Balcanquhal
Arngask
Auchtermuchty
Kinloch
Giffordtown
Springfield
Strathmiglo
Dunshalt
Ladybank
Howe of Fife
Pitlessie
Gleneagles House
Kinross
Common of Dunning
Middle Rigg
Duncrievie
Gateside
Nether Urquhart
FALKLAND PALACE
Kingskettle
Balmalcolm
485 STEEL'S KNOWE
497 INNERDOUNY HILL
Burnside
FIFE
Falkland
Newton of Falkland
Kettlebridge
Kettlehill
Middleton
WEST LOMOND 522
LOMOND HILLS
FALKLAND
Freuchie
Rameldry Mill Bank
Glendevon
GLENDEVON
Glen Devon
Craigow
Upper Tillyrie
Glasslie
Muirhead
Dalqueich
BURLEIGH CASTLE
REGIONAL PARK
Burnfoot
Castle Hill Reservoir
611
South Queich
Carnbo
Milnathort
Wester Balgedie
MICHAEL BRUCE'S COTTAGE
Pitkevy
Langdyke
Star
KINROSS SERVICES
LOCH LEVEN
LOCHLEVEN CASTLE
Kinnesswood
Cadham
Markinch
Balcurvie
BALGONIE CASTLE
Pool o' Muckhart
Yetts o' Muckhart
KINROSS HOUSE
Auchmuirbridge
Scotlandwell
Leslie
GLENROTHES
Milton of Balgonie
Windygates
Drum
Coldrain
St Serf's Island
Gairney Bank
CASTLE CAMPBELL
Crook of Devon
VANE FARM NATURE CENTRE
Kinglassie
Stenton
Coaltown of Balgonie
Rumbling Bridge
RUMBLING BRIDGE GORGE
Ballingry
356 BENARTY HILL
DOGTON STONE
Thornton
Dollar
Powmill
Cleish
FIFE
Lochore
East Wemyss
Blairingone
Cleish Hills
LOCHORE MEADOWS
Crosshill
Glencraig
Auchterderran
Cluny
Forest Mill
Hill End
Loch Glow
Loch Ore
REG. PARK
Cardenden
Coaltown of Wemyss
364 KNOCK HILL
KNOCKHILL
Kelty
Lochgelly
Chapel
Gallatown
West Wemyss
Balgonar
Lassodie
Templehall
Dysart
MCDOUALL STUART MUSEUM
RAVENSCRAIG CASTLE
Saline
Loch Fitty
Lumphinnans
Loch Gelly
Hayfield
Pathhead
KIRKCALDY ART GALLERY AND MUSEUM
Cowstrandburn
Bowershall
Kingseat
Cowdenbeath
Kirkcaldy
TOWNHILL
Hill of Beath
Auchtertool
Blairhall
Comrie
Gowkhall
Wellwood
Townhill
F
Linktown
Devilla Forest
Kincardine
Oakley
Carnock
ABBOT HOUSE
Halbeath
Crossgates
FIFE COASTAL PATH
CULROSS ABBEY
Milesmark
Fordell
Donibristle
Balmule
High Valleyfield
DUNFERMLINE
ABBEY
ANDREW CARNEGIE BIRTHPLACE MUS.
CULROSS PALACE
Culross
Low Torry
Torryburn
Cairneyhill
Crossford
Kinghorn
Burntisland
Pettycur
ALEXANDER III MONUMENT
ABERDOUR CASTLE
Aberdour
Torry Bay
CHARLESTOWN WORKSHOPS
Charlestown
Limekilns
Rosyth
Hillend
ST BRIDGET'S CHURCH
Dalgety Bay
NT
Inchkeith
FIRTH OF FORTH
GRANGEMOUTH
BO'NESS AND KINNEIL RAILWAY
Grangepans
Carriden
Muirhouses
Bo'ness
BIRKHILL CLAY MINE
Inverkeithing
Inverkeithing Bay
ST COLM'S ABBEY
Inchcolm
St. Margaret's Hope
FORTH BRIDGES MUSEUM
DEEP SEA WORLD
North Queensferry
Forth Road Bridge
BLACKNESS CASTLE
HOPETOUN HOUSE
Inchmickery
ZEEBRUGGE 17:30
122
123
Grougfoot
Cramond I.
Queensferry
MAID OF THE FORTH CRUISES
DALMENY HOUSE
Dalmeny
Black Rocks
HMY BRITANNIA
LAURISTON CASTLE
Granton
Newhaven
Leith
Cramond
Davidson's Mains
ROYAL BOTANIC GARDEN
EDINBURGH
Bridgend
Philpstoun
Loan
0 1 2 3 4 5 6 miles
0 1 2 3 4 5 6 7 8 9 10 km

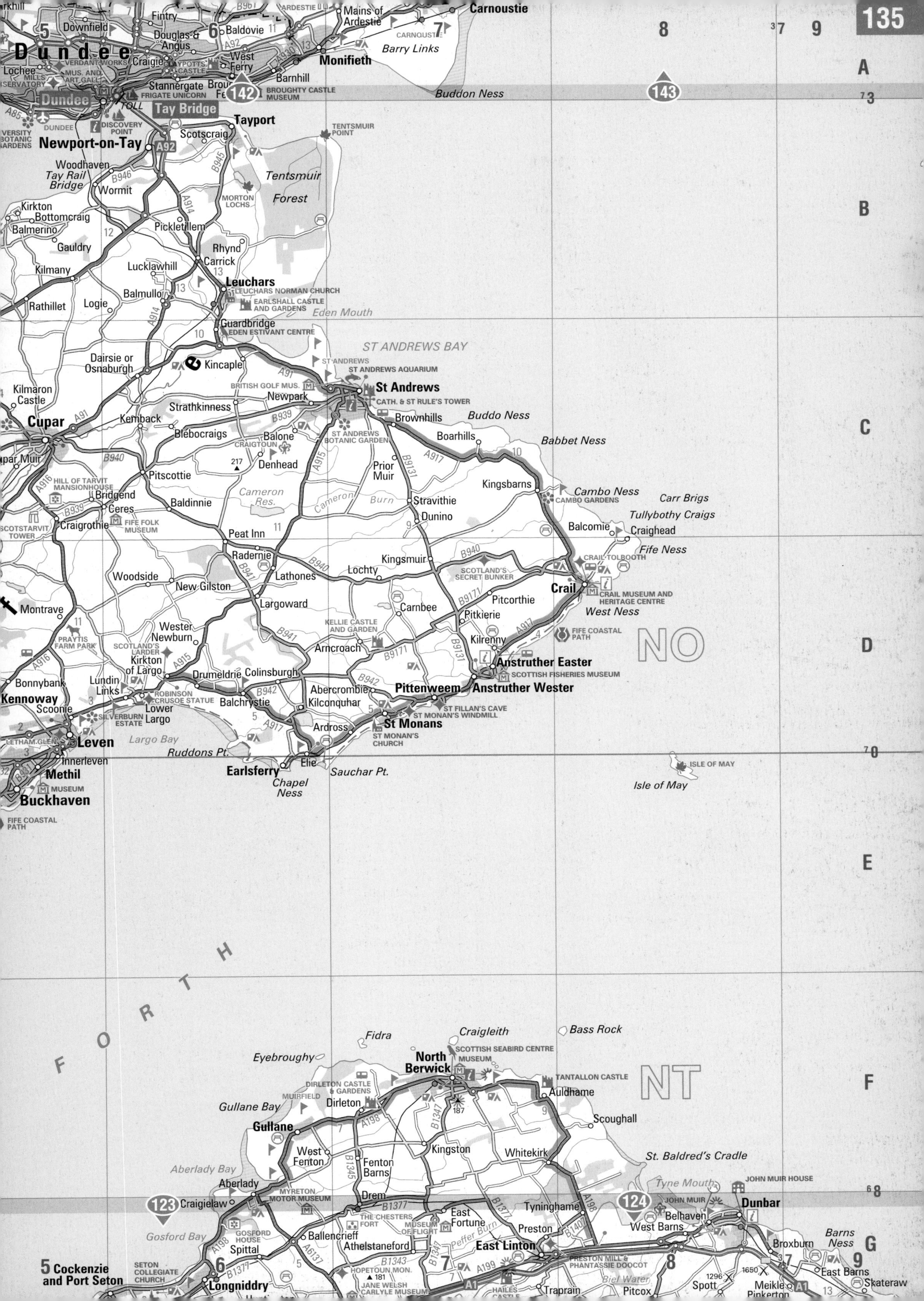
Dundee
Downfield
Fintry
Douglas & Angus
Baldovie
Mains of Ardestie
Carnoustie
Barry Links
Monifieth
West Ferry
Craigie
Lochee
Barnhill
Broughty Castle Museum
Frigate Unicorn
Buddon Ness
Tay Bridge
Tayport
Scotscraig
Tentsmuir Point
Newport-on-Tay
Woodhaven
Tay Rail Bridge
Wormit
Tentsmuir Forest
Morton Lochs
Kirkton
Bottomcraig
Balmerino
Pickletillem
Gauldry
Rhynd
Carrick
Kilmany
Lucklawhill
Leuchars
Leuchars Norman Church
Earlshall Castle and Gardens
Balmullo
Rathillet
Logie
Eden Mouth
Guardbridge
Eden Estivant Centre
St Andrews Bay
Dairsie or Osnaburgh
Kincaple
St Andrews Aquarium
British Golf Mus.
St Andrews
Cath. & St Rule's Tower
Kilmaron Castle
Newpark
Strathkinness
Brownhills
Buddo Ness
Cupar
Kemback
Blebocraigs
Balone
Craigtoun
Boarhills
Babbet Ness
St Andrews Botanic Garden
Denhead
Prior Muir
Hill of Tarvit Mansionhouse
Pitscottie
Bridgend
Ceres
Cameron Res.
Kingsbarns
Cambo Ness
Cambo Gardens
Carr Brigs
Stravithie
Baldinnie
Dunino
Tullybothy Craigs
Scotstarvit Tower
Craigrothie
Fife Folk Museum
Peat Inn
Balcomie
Craighead
Fife Ness
Radernie
Kingsmuir
Crail Tolbooth
Woodside
Lathones
Lochty
Scotland's Secret Bunker
New Gilston
Crail
Crail Museum and Heritage Centre
Montrave
Largoward
Carnbee
Pitcorthie
West Ness
Pitkierie
Kellie Castle and Garden
Wester Newburn
Praytis Farm Park
Scotland's Larder
Fife Coastal Path
Kilrenny
NO
Arncroach
Kirkton of Largo
Anstruther Easter
Scottish Fisheries Museum
Bonnybank
Lundin Links
Drumeldrie
Colinsburgh
Abercrombie
Pittenweem
Anstruther Wester
Kennoway
Robinson Crusoe Statue
Balchrystie
Kilconquhar
Scoonie
Lower Largo
St Fillan's Cave
St Monan's Windmill
Silverburn Estate
Ardross
St Monans
St Monan's Church
Leven
Largo Bay
Letham Glen
Ruddons Pt.
Isle of May
Innerleven
Elie
Methil
Earlsferry
Chapel Ness
Sauchar Pt.
Buckhaven
Museum
FORTH
Fidra
Craigleith
Bass Rock
Scottish Seabird Centre
Eyebroughy
North Berwick
Museum
Tantallon Castle
NT
Dirleton Castle & Gardens
Muirfield
Auldhame
Gullane Bay
Dirleton
Scoughall
Gullane
Kingston
Whitekirk
West Fenton
Fenton Barns
St. Baldred's Cradle
Aberlady Bay
Aberlady
Tyne Mouth
John Muir House
Myreton Motor Museum
Drem
John Muir
Dunbar
Craigielaw
Tyninghame
Belhaven
The Chesters Fort
East Fortune
Museum of Flight
West Barns
Gosford House
Ballencrieff
Preston
Barns Ness
Gosford Bay
Athelstaneford
Broxburn
Peffer Burn
East Linton
Spittal
Preston Mill & Phantassie Doocot
East Barns
Cockenzie and Port Seton
Seton Collegiate Church
Hopetoun Mon.
Jane Welsh Carlyle Museum
Biel Water
Longniddry
Hailes Castle
Traprain
Pitcox
Spott
Meikle Pinkerton
Skateraw

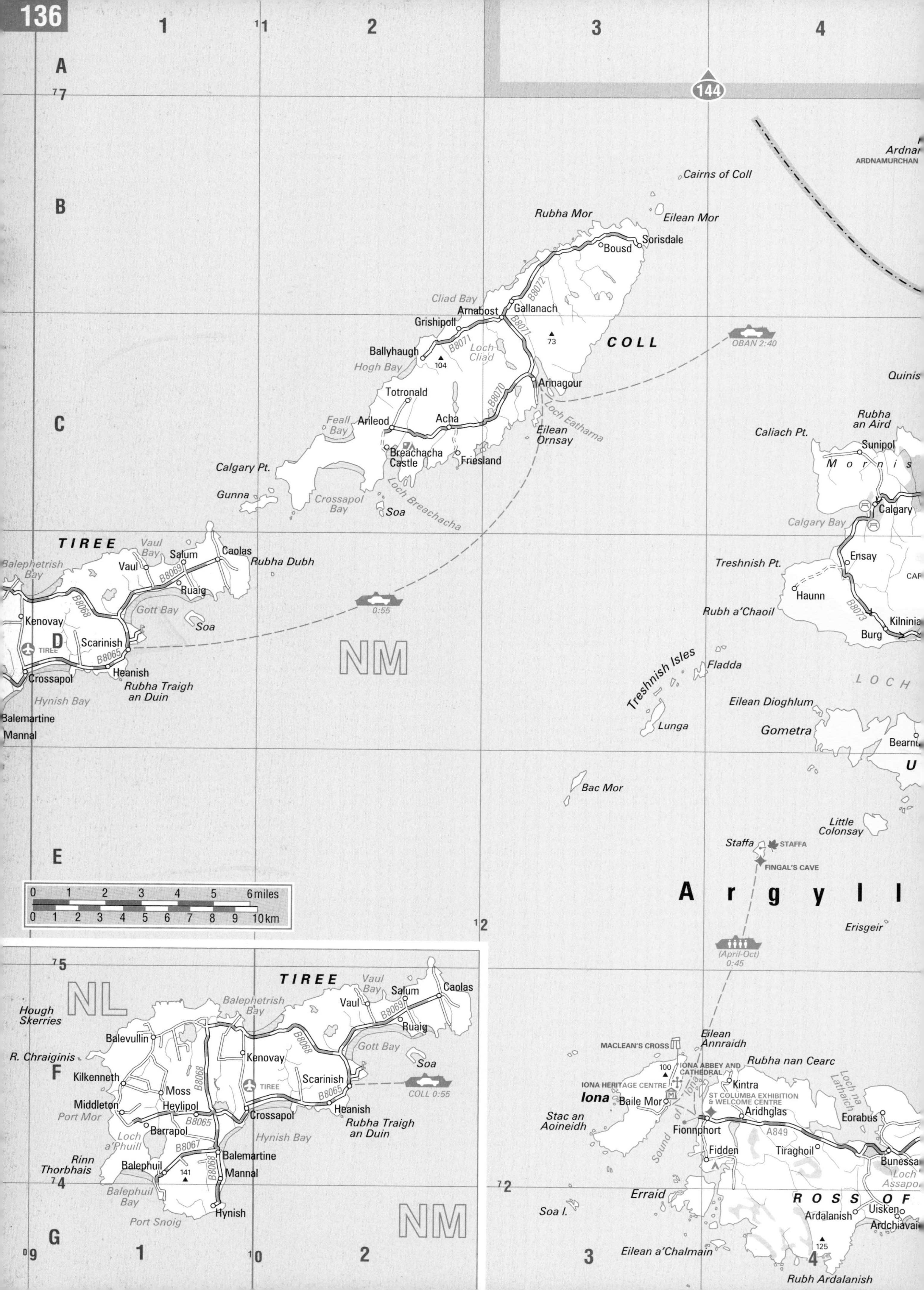

COLL
Cairns of Coll
Eilean Mor
Rubha Mor
Sorisdale
Bousd
Cliad Bay
Arnabost
Gallanach
Grishipoll
Ballyhaugh
Loch Cliad
Hogh Bay
Arinagour
Totronald
Feall Bay
Arileod
Acha
Breachacha Castle
Friesland
Loch Eatharna
Eilean Ornsay
Calgary Pt.
Gunna
Crossapol Bay
Soa
Loch Breachacha
OBAN 2:40
TIREE
Vaul Bay
Salum
Caolas
Vaul
Rubha Dubh
Balephetrish Bay
Ruaig
Gott Bay
Kenovay
Scarinish
Crossapol
Heanish
Rubha Traigh an Duin
Hynish Bay
Balemartine
Mannal
0:55
NM
Ardnamurchan
ARDNAMURCHAN
Quinish
Rubha an Aird
Caliach Pt.
Sunipol
Mornish
Calgary
Calgary Bay
Ensay
Treshnish Pt.
Haunn
Rubh a'Chaoil
Kilninian
Burg
Treshnish Isles
Fladda
LOCH
Eilean Dioghlum
Lunga
Gometra
Bearnus
Bac Mor
Little Colonsay
Staffa
STAFFA
FINGAL'S CAVE
Argyll
Erisgeir
(April-Oct) 0:45
Eilean Annraidh
MACLEAN'S CROSS
IONA ABBEY AND CATHEDRAL
Rubha nan Cearc
IONA HERITAGE CENTRE
Iona
Baile Mor
Kintra
ST COLUMBA EXHIBITION & WELCOME CENTRE
Aridhglas
Loch na Lathaich
Stac an Aoineidh
Sound of Iona
Fionnphort
Eorabus
A849
Fidden
Tiraghoil
Bunessan
Loch Assapol
Erraid
ROSS OF MULL
Soa I.
Ardalanish
Uisken
Ardchiavaig
Eilean a'Chalmain
Rubh Ardalanish
0 1 2 3 4 5 6 miles
0 1 2 3 4 5 6 7 8 9 10 km
NL
Hough Skerries
Balevullin
R. Chraiginis
Kilkenneth
Moss
Middleton
Heylipol
Port Mor
Barrapol
Loch a'Phuill
Rinn Thorbhais
Balephuil
Balephuil Bay
Port Snoig
Hynish
TIREE
COLL 0:55

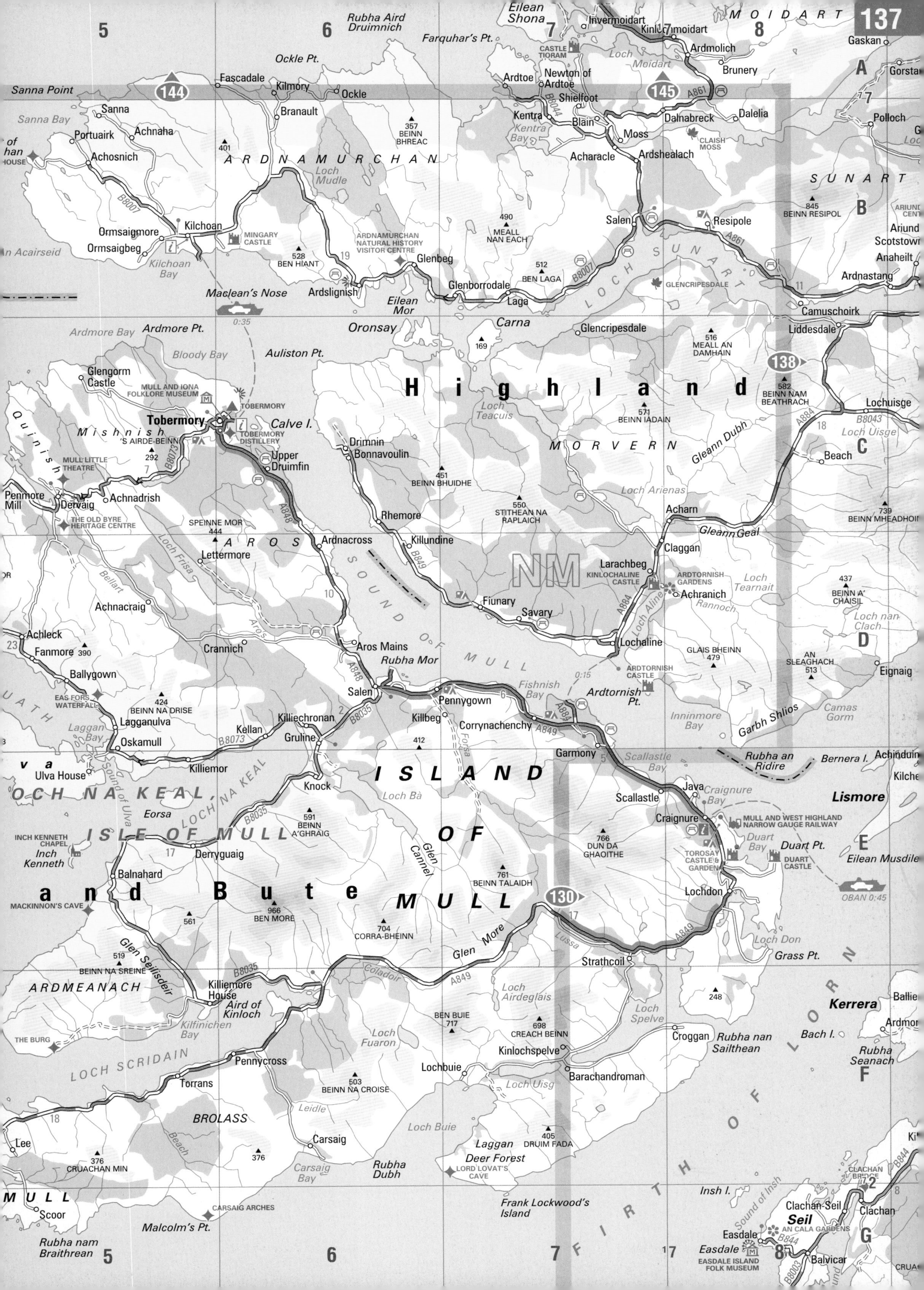

Eilean Shona
Invermoidart
Kinlochmoidart
MOIDART
Rubha Aird Druimnich
Farquhar's Pt.
Castle Tioram
Loch Moidart
Ardmolich
Brunery
Gaskan
Gorstan
Ockle Pt.
Sanna Point
Fascadale
Kilmory
Ockle
Ardtoe
Newton of Ardtoe
Shielfoot
Sanna
Sanna Bay
Branault
357 Beinn Bhreac
Kentra
Kentra Bay
Blain
Moss
Dalnabreck
Dalelia
Polloch
Portuairk
Achnaha
Achosnich
401
ARDNAMURCHAN
Loch Mudle
Acharacle
Ardshealach
Claish Moss
SUNART
845 Beinn Resipol
Ormsaigmore
Ormsaigbeg
Kilchoan
Kilchoan Bay
Mingary Castle
Ardnamurchan Natural History Visitor Centre
490 Meall nan Each
Salen
Resipole
Ariundle Centre
Ariundle
Scotstown
Anaheilt
528 Ben Hiant
Glenbeg
512 Ben Laga
LOCH SUNART
Glencripesdale
Ardnastang
Maclean's Nose
Ardslignish
Eilean Mor
Glenborrodale
Laga
Camuschoirk
Liddesdale
Ardmore Bay
Ardmore Pt.
Oronsay
Carna
169
Glencripesdale
516 Meall an Damhain
Bloody Bay
Auliston Pt.
Glengorm Castle
Mull and Iona Folklore Museum
Tobermory
Highland
582 Beinn nam Beathrach
Lochuisge
Loch Teacuis
571 Beinn Iadain
Loch Uisge
Mishnish
'S Airde-Beinn
Tobermory Distillery
Calve I.
Drimnin
Bonnavoulin
MORVERN
Gleann Dubh
Beach
Quinish
292
Mull Little Theatre
Upper Druimfin
451 Beinn Bhuidhe
Loch Arienas
Penmore Mill
Dervaig
Achnadrish
The Old Byre Heritage Centre
Rhemore
550 Stithean na Raplaich
Acharn
739 Beinn Mheadhoin
Speinne Mor
444
AROS
Lettermore
Ardnacross
Killundine
Gleann Geal
Claggan
Loch Frisa
SOUND OF MULL
NM
Larachbeg
Kinlochaline Castle
Ardtornish Gardens
Loch Tearnait
437 Beinn a' Chaisil
Bellart
Achnacraig
Fiunary
Savary
Achranich
Rannoch
Loch Aline
Loch nan Clach
Achleck
Fanmore
390
Crannich
Aros Mains
Lochaline
Glais Bheinn 479
An Sleaghach 513
Eignaig
Ballygown
Rubha Mor
Ardtornish Castle
Eas Fors Waterfall
424 Beinn na Drise
Salen
Pennygown
Fishnish Bay
Ardtornish Pt.
Laggan Bay
Lagganulva
Kellan
Killiechronan
Killbeg
Corrynachenchy
Inninmore Bay
Garbh Shlios
Camas Gorm
Oskamull
Gruline
412
Forsa
Garmony
Scallastle Bay
Rubha an Ridire
Bernera I.
Achinduin
Ulva
Ulva House
Killiemor
Sound of Ulva
LOCH NA KEAL
Knock
ISLAND OF MULL
Loch Bà
Java
Craignure Bay
Scallastle
Kilcheran
Lismore
Eorsa
591 Beinn a' Ghraig
Craignure
Mull and West Highland Narrow Gauge Railway
Inch Kenneth Chapel
Inch Kenneth
ISLE OF MULL
Derryguaig
Glen Cannel
766 Dun da Ghaoithe
Duart Bay
Duart Pt.
Torosay Castle & Garden
Duart Castle
Eilean Musdile
Balnahard
Argyll and Bute
761 Beinn Talaidh
Lochdon
Mackinnon's Cave
561
966 Ben More
704 Corra-Bheinn
Glen More
Oban 0:45
Glen Seilisdeir
519 Beinn na Sreine
Lussa
Loch Don
Grass Pt.
Strathcoil
ARDMEANACH
Killiemore House
Aird of Kinloch
Coladoir
Loch Airdeglais
248
Ballie
Kerrera
Kilfinichen Bay
Ben Buie 717
698 Creach Beinn
Loch Spelve
Ardmore
The Burg
Loch Fuaron
Croggan
Rubha nan Sailthean
Bach I.
LOCH SCRIDAIN
Kinlochspelve
Rubha Seanach
Pennycross
Torrans
Lochbuie
Barachandroman
503 Beinn na Croise
Loch Uisg
Leidle
BROLASS
Loch Buie
Lee
Beach
376 Cruachan Min
376
Carsaig
Carsaig Bay
Laggan Deer Forest
405 Druim Fada
Rubha Dubh
Lord Lovat's Cave
FIRTH OF LORN
Clachan Bridge
Insh I.
Sound of Insh
MULL
Scoor
Carsaig Arches
Frank Lockwood's Island
Clachan-Seil
Clachan
Seil
An Cala Gardens
Rubha nam Braithrean
Malcolm's Pt.
Easdale
Easdale Island Folk Museum
Balvicar
5
6
7
8
A
B
C
D
E
F
G

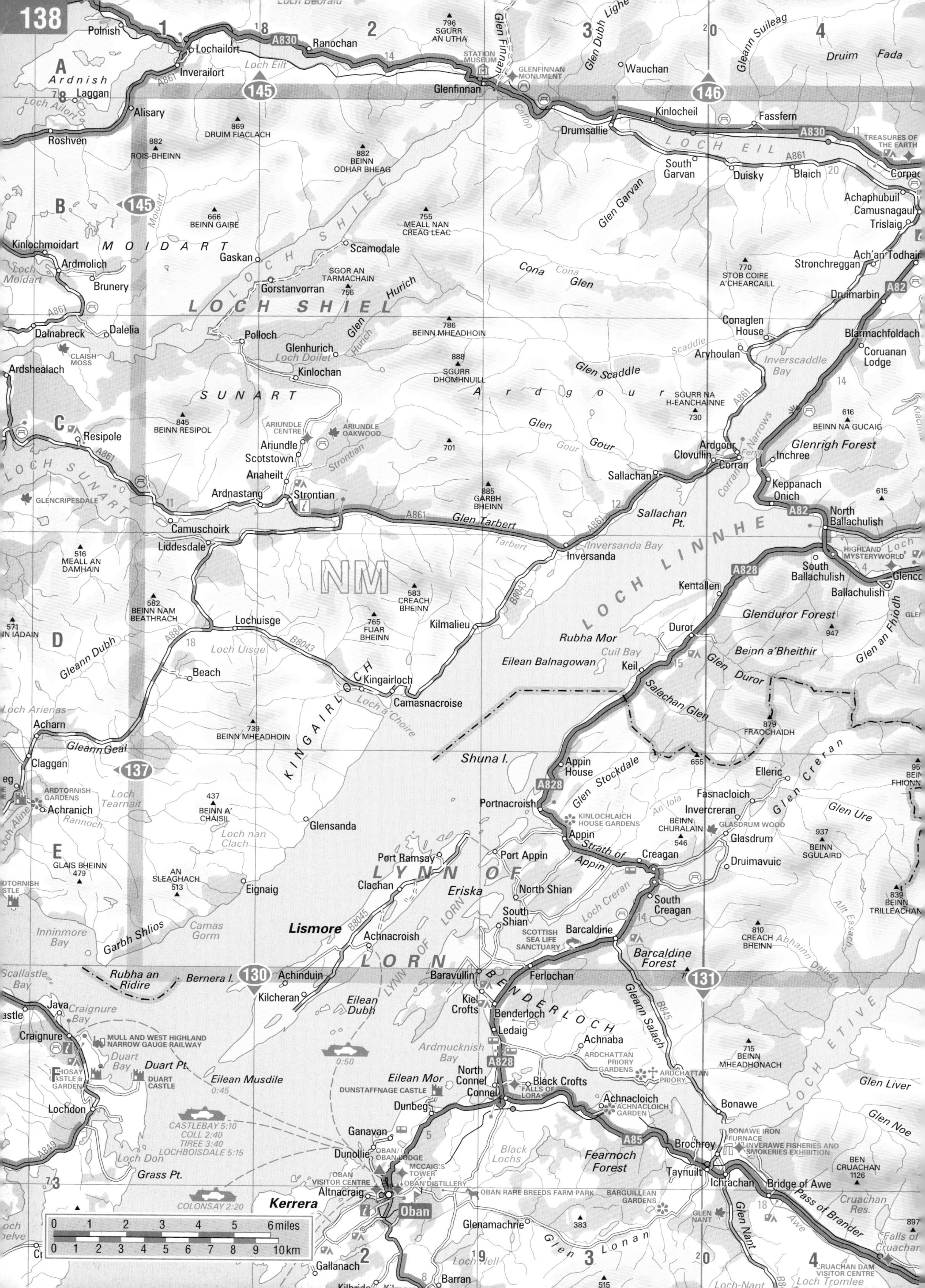

Polnish
Lochailort
Inveralilort
Ardnish
Laggan
Loch Ailort
Alisary
Roshven
A830
Ranochan
Loch Eilt
145
796
SGURR AN UTHA
STATION MUSEUM
Glen Finnan
GLENFINNAN MONUMENT
Glenfinnan
Glen Dubh Lighe
Wauchan
Gleann Suileag
Druim Fada
146
Kinlocheil
Fassfern
Drumsallie
LOCH EIL
TREASURES OF THE EARTH
Corpach
South Garvan
Duisky
Blaich
Callop
869
DRUIM FIACLACH
882
ROIS-BHEINN
882
BEINN ODHAR BHEAG
666
BEINN GAIRE
755
MEALL NAN CREAG LEAC
Glen Garvan
Achaphubuil
Camusnagaul
Trislaig
Kinlochmoidart
MOIDART
Ardmolich
Loch Moidart
Brunery
Gaskan
Scamodale
Gorstanvorran
SGOR AN TARMACHAIN
756
LOCH SHIEL
Glen Hurich
Cona Glen
770
STOB COIRE A'CHEARCAILL
Stronchreggan
Ach'an Todhair
Druimarbin
A82
Dalnabreck
Dalelia
CLAISH MOSS
Polloch
Glenhurich
Loch Doilet
786
BEINN MHEADHOIN
Conaglen House
Blarmachfoldach
Coruanan Lodge
Aryhoulan
Inverscaddle Bay
Ardshealach
Kinlochan
888
SGURR DHOMHNUILL
Glen Scaddle
SUNART
Ardgour
SGURR NA H-EANCHAINNE
730
616
BEINN NA GUCAIG
Resipole
845
BEINN RESIPOL
ARIUNDLE CENTRE
ARIUNDLE OAKWOOD
Ariundle
Scotstown
Anaheilt
Glen Gour
701
Ardgour
Clovullin
Corran
Corran Narrows
Glenrigh Forest
Inchree
LOCH SUNART
Sallachan
Strontian
Ardnastang
GLENCRIPESDALE
885
GARBH BHEINN
Keppanach
Onich
615
North Ballachulish
Sallachan Pt.
A861
Glen Tarbert
Camuschoirk
Liddesdale
Inversanda Bay
Inversanda
LOCH LINNHE
HIGHLAND MYSTERYWORLD
South Ballachulish
Ballachulish
Glencoe
516
MEALL AN DAMHAIN
NM
583
CREACH BHEINN
A828
Kentallen
582
BEINN NAM BEATHRACH
765
FUAR BHEINN
Kilmalieu
Glenduror Forest
Lochuisge
Loch Uisge
B8043
A884
Rubha Mor
Duror
947
Gleann Dubh
Cuil Bay
Beinn a'Bheithir
Glen an Fhiodh
Eilean Balnagowan
Keil
Glen Duror
Beach
Kingairloch
Camasnacroise
Loch a'Choire
Salachan Glen
Loch Arienas
Acharn
739
BEINN MHEADHOIN
KINGAIRLOCH
879
FRAOCHAIDH
Gleann Geal
Claggan
137
Shuna I.
Appin House
655
Glen Stockdale
Elleric
Glen Creran
ARDTORNISH GARDENS
Achranich
Loch Tearnait
437
BEINN A' CHAISIL
Portnacroish
Fasnacloich
Invercreran
Glen Ure
KINLOCHLAICH HOUSE GARDENS
BEINN CHURALAIN
546
GLASDRUM WOOD
Glasdrum
937
BEINN SGULAIRD
Glensanda
Loch nan Clach
Appin
Strath of Appin
Creagan
Druimavuic
GLAIS BHEINN
479
Port Ramsay
Port Appin
LYNN OF LORN
AN SLEAGHACH
513
Eignaig
Clachan
Eriska
North Shian
Loch Creran
South Creagan
839
BEINN TRILLEACHAN
Lismore
South Shian
Barcaldine
SCOTTISH SEA LIFE SANCTUARY
810
CREACH BHEINN
Inninmore Bay
Garbh Shlios
Camas Gorm
Achnacroish
B8045
Barcaldine Forest
Scallastle Bay
Rubha an Ridire
Bernera I.
130
Achinduin
LORN
Baravullin
Ferlochan
131
Kilcheran
Eilean Dubh
Kiel Crofts
Benderloch
Ledaig
BENDERLOCH
Gleann Salach
B845
Java
Craignure Bay
Craignure
MULL AND WEST HIGHLAND NARROW GAUGE RAILWAY
Achnaba
715
BEINN MHEADHONACH
Duart Bay
Duart Pt.
DUART CASTLE
Ardmucknish Bay
A828
ARDCHATTAN PRIORY GARDENS
ARDCHATTAN PRIORY
Glen Liver
Eilean Musdile
Eilean Mor
North Connel
Black Crofts
DUNSTAFFNAGE CASTLE
FALLS OF LORA
Connel
Achnacloich
ACHNACLOICH GARDEN
Bonawe
LOCH ETIVE
Glen Noe
Lochdon
Dunbeg
CASTLEBAY 5:10
COLL 2:40
TIREE 3:40
LOCHBOISDALE 5:15
Ganavan
A85
BONAWE IRON FURNACE
Brochroy
INVERAWE FISHERIES AND SMOKERIES EXHIBITION
Loch Don
Dunollie
OBAN LODGE
Black Lochs
Fearnoch Forest
A849
MCCAIG'S TOWER
Taynuilt
BEN CRUACHAN
1126
Grass Pt.
OBAN VISITOR CENTRE
OBAN DISTILLERY
Ichrachan
Bridge of Awe
Cruachan Res.
Altnacraig
OBAN RARE BREEDS FARM PARK
BARGUILLEAN GARDENS
Pass of Brander
COLONSAY 2:20
Kerrera
Oban
383
GLEN NANT
Glen Nant
Glenamachrie
Glen Lonan
Falls of Cruachan
0 1 2 3 4 5 6 miles
0 1 2 3 4 5 6 7 8 9 10 km
Gallanach
CRUACHAN DAM VISITOR CENTRE
Barran
Loch Nell
Loch Tromlee
Kilbride
515

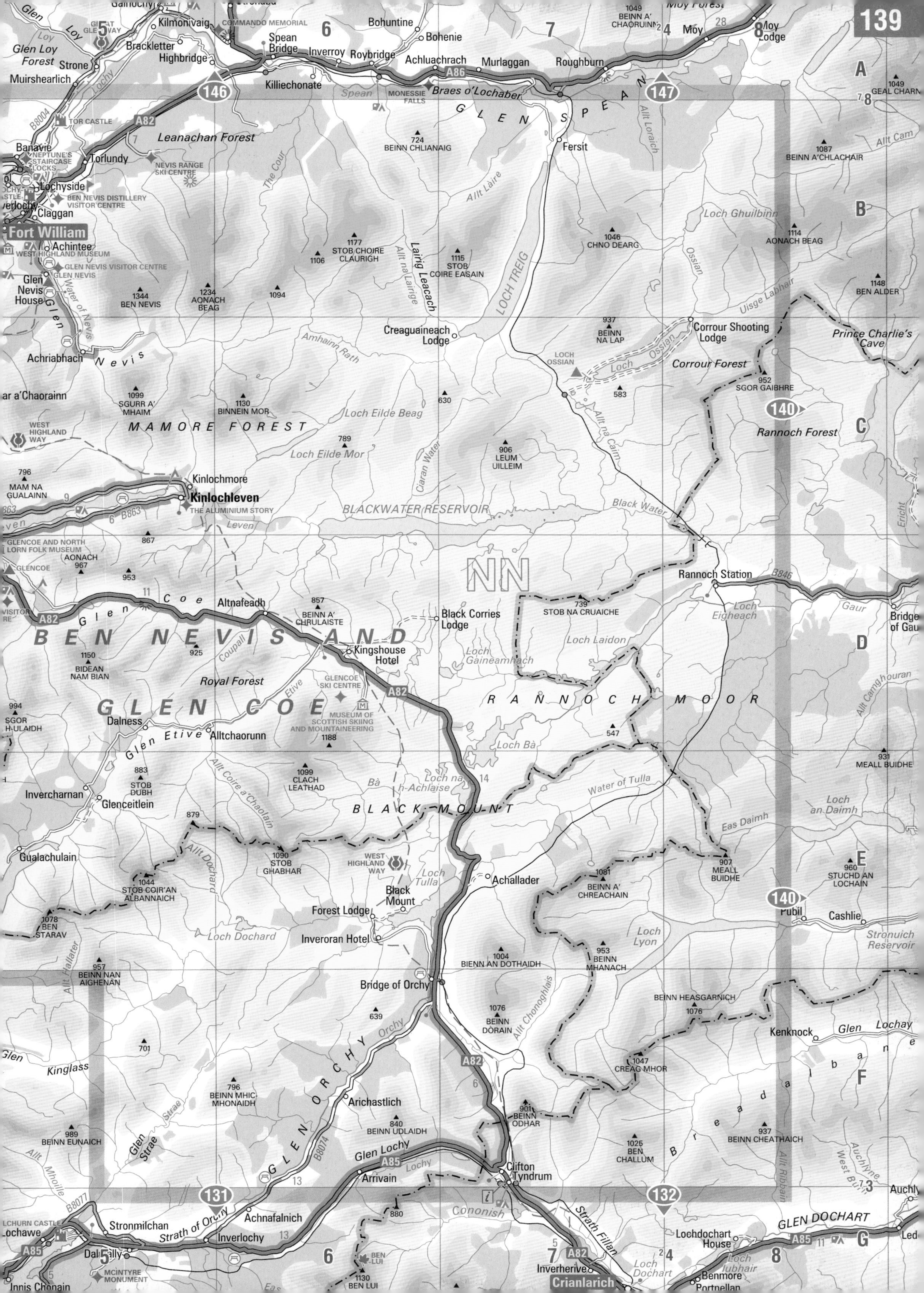
Fort William
Kinlochleven
Kilmonivaig
Spean Bridge
Roybridge
Inverroy
Bohuntine
Bohenie
Achluachrach
Murlaggan
Roughburn
Moy
Moy Lodge
Brackletter
Highbridge
Strone
Muirshearlich
Glen Loy Forest
Killiechonate
Braes o'Lochaber
GLEN SPEAN
Banavie
Torlundy
Lochyside
Claggan
Achintee
Glen Nevis House
Achriabhach
Leanachan Forest
NEVIS RANGE SKI CENTRE
BEN NEVIS DISTILLERY VISITOR CENTRE
WEST HIGHLAND MUSEUM
GLEN NEVIS VISITOR CENTRE
TOR CASTLE
COMMANDO MEMORIAL
MONESSIE FALLS
Fersit
724 BEINN CHLIANAIG
1087 BEINN A'CHLACHAIR
1049 GEAL CHARN
1344 BEN NEVIS
1234 AONACH BEAG
1094
1106
1177 STOB CHOIRE CLAURIGH
1115 STOB COIRE EASAIN
Lairig Leacach
LOCH TREIG
1046 CHNO DEARG
Loch Ghuilbinn
1114 AONACH BEAG
1148 BEN ALDER
937 BEINN NA LAP
Creaguaineach Lodge
Corrour Shooting Lodge
Corrour Forest
Loch Ossian
Prince Charlie's Cave
952 SGOR GAIBHRE
Rannoch Forest
1099 SGURR A' MHAIM
1130 BINNEIN MOR
MAMORE FOREST
630
583
Loch Eilde Beag
789
Loch Eilde Mor
906 LEUM UILLEIM
796 MAM NA GUALAINN
Kinlochmore
THE ALUMINIUM STORY
BLACKWATER RESERVOIR
Black Water
GLENCOE AND NORTH LORN FOLK MUSEUM
867
967 AONACH
953
NN
Rannoch Station
Loch Eigheach
Bridge of Gaur
739 STOB NA CRUAICHE
Altnafeadh
857 BEINN A' CHRULAISTE
Black Corries Lodge
BEN NEVIS AND
GLEN COE
925
1150 BIDEAN NAM BIAN
Kingshouse Hotel
Royal Forest
GLENCOE SKI CENTRE
MUSEUM OF SCOTTISH SKIING AND MOUNTAINEERING
Loch Laidon
Loch Gaineamhach
RANNOCH MOOR
Dalness
Alltchaorunn
Glen Etive
1188
547
Loch Bà
931 MEALL BUIDHE
883 STOB DUBH
1099 CLACH LEATHAD
Inverchарnan
Glenceitlein
BLACK MOUNT
Water of Tulla
Loch an Daimh
879
Gualachulain
1090 STOB GHABHAR
WEST HIGHLAND WAY
Loch Tulla
Achallader
1081 BEINN A' CHREACHAIN
907 MEALL BUIDHE
960 STUCHD AN LOCHAIN
1044 STOB COIR'AN ALBANNAICH
Black Mount
Forest Lodge
Inveroran Hotel
Loch Dochard
1078 BEN STARAV
Pubil
Cashlie
Stronuich Reservoir
957 BEINN NAN AIGHENAN
1004 BIENN AN DOTHAIDH
953 BEINN MHANACH
Loch Lyon
Bridge of Orchy
BEINN HEASGARNICH 1076
639
1076 BEINN DORAIN
Kenknock
Glen Lochay
701
Glen Kinglass
1047 CREAG MHOR
796 BEINN MHIC-MHONAIDH
Arichastlich
GLEN ORCHY
901 BEINN ODHAR
840 BEINN UDLAIDH
Breadalbane
937 BEINN CHEATHAICH
989 BEINN EUNAICH
1025 BEN CHALLUM
Glen Strae
Glen Lochy
Clifton
Tyndrum
Arrivain
Auchlyne
Stronmilchan
Strath of Orchy
Achnafalnich
880
Cononish
Strath Fillan
GLEN DOCHART
Lochawe
Inverlochy
Dalmally
Lochdochart House
Loch Iubhair
Benmore
Portnellan
Loch Dochart
Inverherive
Crianlarich
BEN LUI
1130 BEN LUI
MCINTYRE MONUMENT
Innis Chonain
A82
A86
A85
B8004
B863
B846
B8074
B8077
146
147
140
131
132
A
B
C
D
E
F
G
5
6
7
8

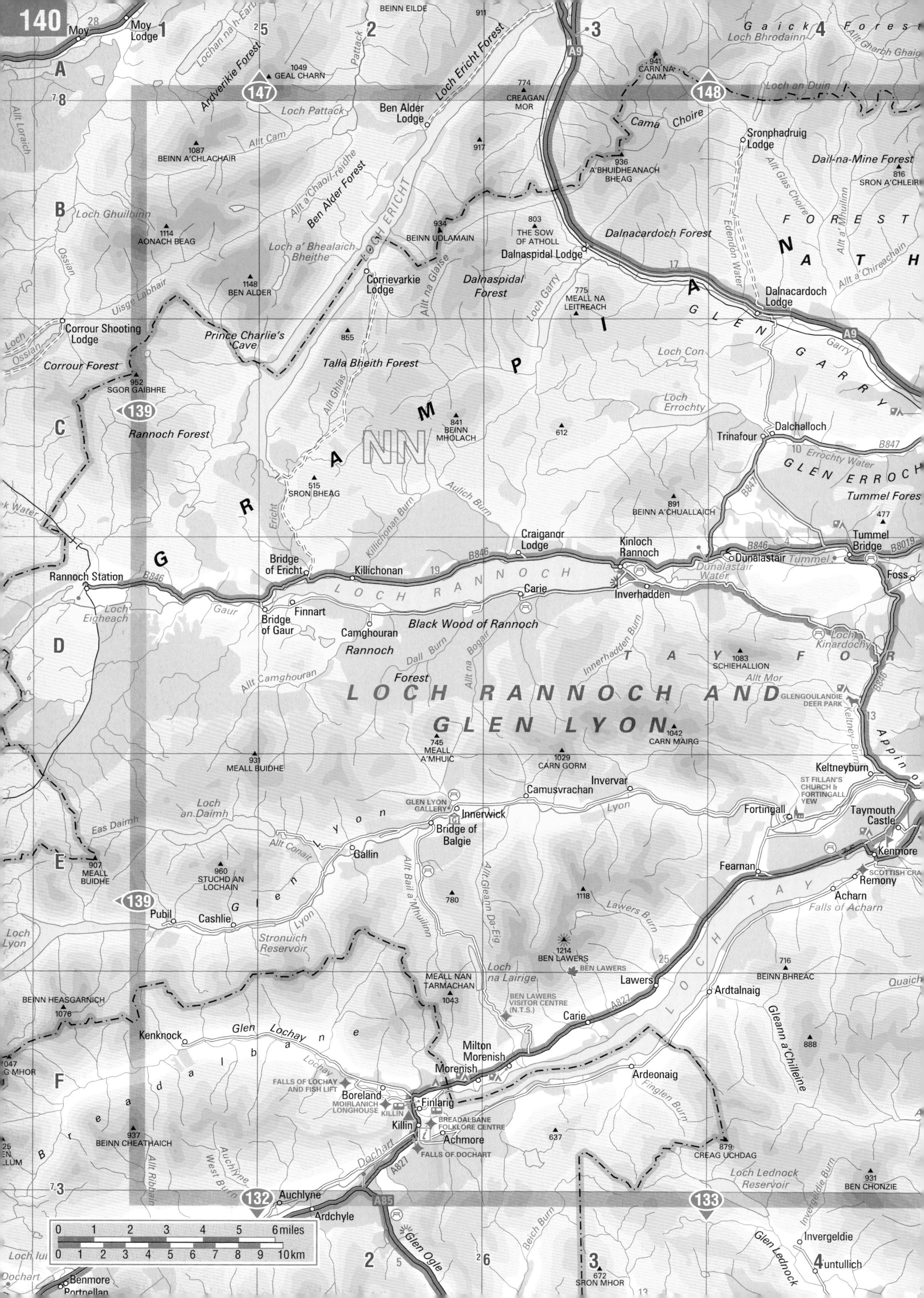
Moy
Moy Lodge
BEINN EILDE
911
Lochan na h-Earba
Ardverikie Forest
1049 GEAL CHARN
Pattack
Loch Ericht Forest
147
148
A9
941 CARN NA CAIM
Gaick Forest
Loch Bhrodainn
Allt Gharbh Ghaig
Loch an Duin
774 CREAGAN MOR
Loch Pattack
Ben Alder Lodge
Cama Choire
Allt Loraich
Allt Cam
1087 BEINN A'CHLACHAIR
917
936 A'BHUIDHEANACH BHEAG
Sronphadruig Lodge
Dail-na-Mine Forest
816 SRON A'CHLEIRICH
Allt a'Chaoil-réidhe
Ben Alder Forest
Loch Ghuilbinn
1114 AONACH BEAG
LOCH ERICHT
934 BEINN UDLAMAIN
803 THE SOW OF ATHOLL
Dalnaspidal Lodge
Dalnacardoch Forest
Allt Glas Choire
Edendon Water
FOREST OF ATHOLL
Allt a'Mhuilinn
Allt a'Chireachain
Loch a'Bhealaich Bheithe
Ossian
Corrievarkie Lodge
Allt na Glaise
Dalnaspidal Forest
Loch Garry
775 MEALL NA LEITREACH
Dalnacardoch Lodge
1148 BEN ALDER
Uisge Labhair
17
Loch Ossian
Corrour Shooting Lodge
Prince Charlie's Cave
855
Corrour Forest
Talla Bheith Forest
GLEN GARRY
Garry
Loch Con
952 SGOR GAIBHRE
139
GRAMPIAN
Loch Errochty
Allt Ghlas
841 BEINN MHOLACH
612
Rannoch Forest
Trinafour
Dalchalloch
B847
NN
10
Errochty Water
GLEN ERROCHTY
515 SRON BHEAG
Aulich Burn
Killichonan Burn
891 BEINN A'CHUALLAICH
Tummel Forest
477
Ericht
Craiganor Lodge
Kinloch Rannoch
Tummel Bridge
B846
B8019
Bridge of Ericht
Killichonan
19
Dunalastair
Loch Tummel
Dunalastair Water
Rannoch Station
LOCH RANNOCH
Carie
Inverhadden
Foss
Loch Eigheach
Gaur
Bridge of Gaur
Finnart
Camghouran
Black Wood of Rannoch
Loch Kinardochy
Rannoch
Dall Burn
Allt na Bogair
Innerhadden Burn
TAY FOREST
1083 SCHIEHALLION
Allt Camghouran
Forest
Allt Mor
LOCH RANNOCH AND GLEN LYON
GLENGOULANDIE DEER PARK
Keltney Burn
13
1042 CARN MAIRG
745 MEALL A'MHUIC
931 MEALL BUIDHE
1029 CARN GORM
Keltneyburn
Appin of Dull
Loch an Daimh
Invervar
Camusvrachan
ST FILLAN'S CHURCH & FORTINGALL YEW
GLEN LYON GALLERY
Innerwick
Lyon
Fortingall
Taymouth Castle
Eas Daimh
Bridge of Balgie
Allt Conait
Gallin
Glen Lyon
Kenmore
907 MEALL BUIDHE
960 STUCHD AN LOCHAIN
Allt Bail a'Mhuilinn
Allt Gleann Da-Eig
780
1118
Fearnan
SCOTTISH CRANNOG CENTRE
Remony
Acharn
Falls of Acharn
LOCH TAY
Pubil
Cashlie
Lawers Burn
Loch Lyon
Stronuich Reservoir
1214 BEN LAWERS
BEN LAWERS
25
716 BEINN BHREAC
Quaich
MEALL NAN TARMACHAN
1043
Loch na Lairige
Lawers
Ardtalnaig
BEINN HEASGARNICH
1076
BEN LAWERS VISITOR CENTRE (N.T.S.)
Carie
A827
Gleann a'Chilleine
Kenknock
Glen Lochay
Breadalbane
Milton Morenish
888
Morenish
Ardeonaig
FALLS OF LOCHAY AND FISH LIFT
Boreland
Finglen Burn
MOIRLANICH LONGHOUSE
KILLIN
Finlarig
Killin
BREADALBANE FOLKLORE CENTRE
937 BEINN CHEATHAICH
Achmore
637
879 CREAG UCHDAG
FALLS OF DOCHART
Dochart
A827
Allt Ribhain
West Burn
Auchlyne
Loch Lednock Reservoir
Invergeldie Burn
931 BEN CHONZIE
Auchlyne
132
133
A85
Ardchyle
Glen Ogle
Beich Burn
Glen Lednock
Invergeldie
0 1 2 3 4 5 6 miles
0 1 2 3 4 5 6 7 8 9 10 km
Loch Iubhair
Dochart
Benmore
Portnellan
672 SRON MHOR
Untullich
A
B
C
D
E
F
1
2
3
4

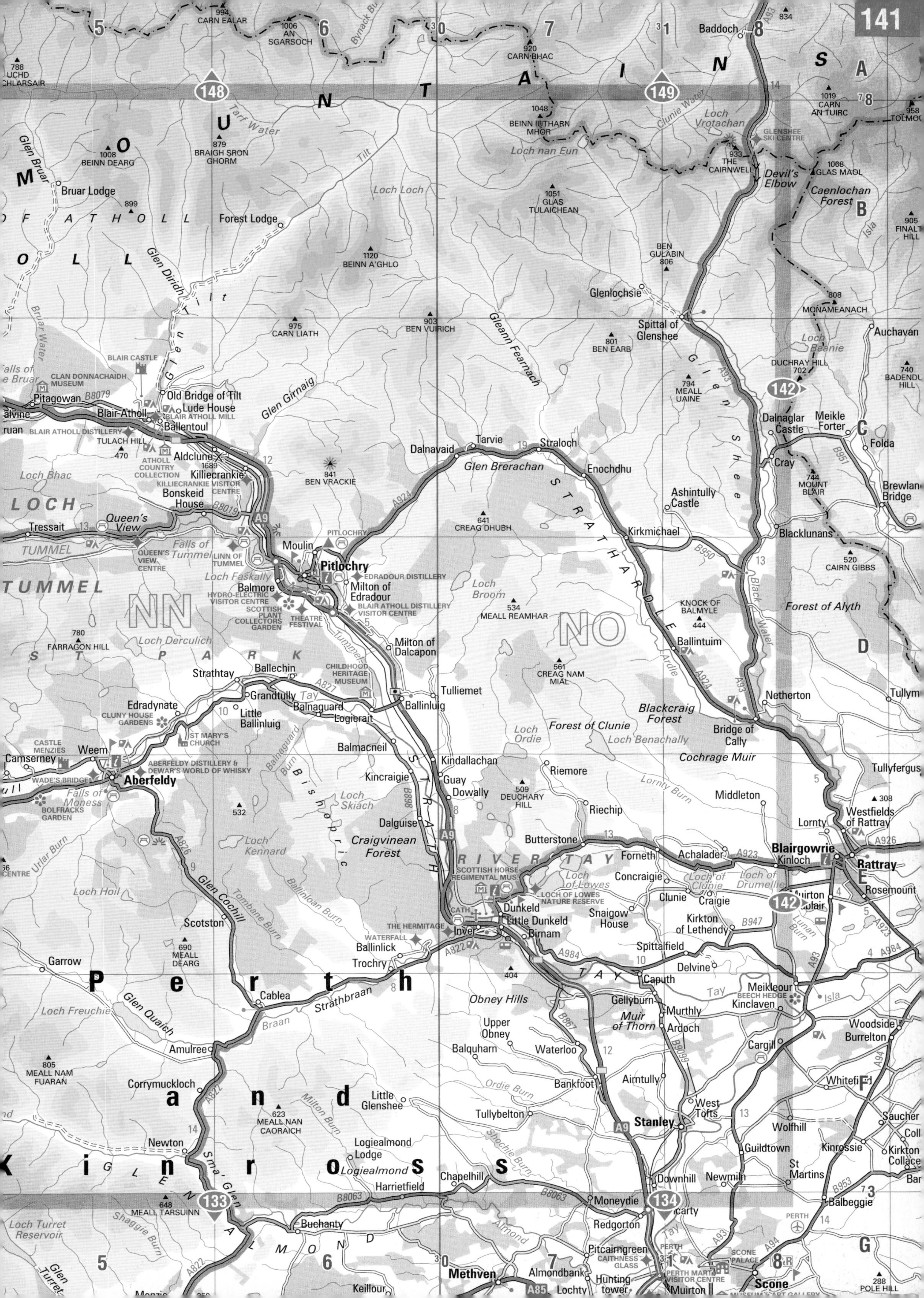

994 CARN EALAR
1006 AN SGARSOCH
Bynack Burn
920 CARN BHAC
Baddoch
834
788 UCHD CHLARSAIR
148
149
M O U N T A I N S
1048 BEINN IUTHARN MHOR
Clunie Water
Loch Vrotachan
GLENSHEE SKI CENTRE
1019 CARN AN TUIRC
958 TOLMOU
Tarf Water
879 BRAIGH SRON GHORM
1008 BEINN DEARG
Glen Bruar
Bruar Lodge
899
Loch nan Eun
933 THE CAIRNWELL
Devil's Elbow
1068 GLAS MAOL
Caenlochan Forest
Tilt
Loch Loch
1051 GLAS TULAICHEAN
F O R E S T O F A T H O L L
Forest Lodge
905 FINALTY HILL
Isla
Glen Diridh
1120 BEINN A'GHLO
BEN GULABIN 806
Glen Tilt
Glenlochsie
808 MONAMEANACH
Bruar Water
975 CARN LIATH
903 BEN VUIRICH
Gleann Fearnach
801 BEN EARB
Spittal of Glenshee
Loch Beanie
Auchavan
BLAIR CASTLE
CLAN DONNACHAIDH MUSEUM
Glen Girnaig
794 MEALL UAINE
Glen Shee
DUCHRAY HILL 702
740 BADENDU HILL
142
Pitagowan
B8079
Old Bridge of Tilt
Lude House
BLAIR ATHOLL MILL
Blair Atholl
Ballentoul
BLAIR ATHOLL DISTILLERY
TULACH HILL
470
ATHOLL COUNTRY COLLECTION
Aldclune
1689
Killiecrankie
KILLIECRANKIE VISITOR CENTRE
Bonskeid House
B8019
841 BEN VRACKIE
Tarvie
Dalnavaid
Straloch
Glen Brerachan
Enochdhu
A924
Dalnaglar Castle
Meikle Forter
Folda
Cray
B951
744 MOUNT BLAIR
Brewlands Bridge
Ashintully Castle
Loch Bhac
LOCH TUMMEL
Tressait
Queen's View
Falls of Tummel
QUEEN'S VIEW CENTRE
LINN OF TUMMEL
A9
641 CREAG DHUBH
Kirkmichael
Blacklunans
STRATHARDLE
B950
520 CAIRN GIBBS
Moulin
PITLOCHRY
Pitlochry
EDRADOUR DISTILLERY
Milton of Edradour
Loch Faskally
Balmore
HYDRO-ELECTRIC VISITOR CENTRE
SCOTTISH PLANT COLLECTORS GARDEN
THEATRE FESTIVAL
BLAIR ATHOLL DISTILLERY VISITOR CENTRE
Loch Broom
534 MEALL REAMHAR
KNOCK OF BALMYLE 444
Forest of Alyth
NN
NO
Black Water
780 FARRAGON HILL
Loch Derculich
TUMMEL
Milton of Dalcapon
Ballintuim
STRATHTAY
Strathtay
Ballechin
CHILDHOOD HERITAGE MUSEUM
561 CREAG NAM MIAL
Ardle
A924
Netherton
Tullymet
Tulliemet
Ballinluig
Grandtully
Tay
A827
Edradynate
CLUNY HOUSE GARDENS
Little Ballinluig
Balnaguard
Logierait
Blackcraig Forest
Forest of Clunie
Loch Ordie
Loch Benachally
Bridge of Cally
CASTLE MENZIES
Weem
ST MARY'S CHURCH
Camserney
Balmacneil
Cochrage Muir
Kindallachan
Riemore
Tullyfergus
WADE'S BRIDGE
Aberfeldy
ABERFELDY DISTILLERY & DEWAR'S WORLD OF WHISKY
Falls of Moness
BOLFRACKS GARDEN
Balnaguard Burn
Bishopric
Kincraigie
Loch Skiach
B898
Guay
Dowally
509 DEUCHARY HILL
Lornty Burn
Middleton
308
Westfields of Rattray
Lornty
532
Riechip
Dalguise
Craigvinean Forest
Loch Kennard
A826
Urlar Burn
RIVER TAY
Butterstone
Forneth
Achalader
A923
Blairgowrie
Kinloch
Rattray
A926
Glen Cochill
SCOTTISH HORSE REGIMENTAL MUSEUM
Loch of Lowes
LOCH OF LOWES NATURE RESERVE
Concraigie
Loch of Clunie
Loch of Drumellie
Muirton of Ballied
Rosemount
Loch Hoil
Tombane Burn
Ballinloan Burn
Dunkeld
Clunie
Craigie
Lunan Burn
Scotston
THE HERMITAGE
Inver
Little Dunkeld
Birnam
Snaigow House
Kirkton of Lethendy
B947
A923
690 MEALL DEARG
WATERFALL
Ballinlick
A822
A984
Spittalfield
Delvine
A984
Garrow
Trochry
404
Caputh
A93
Perth and Kinross
Cablea
Strathbraan
Obney Hills
Gellyburn
Tay
Meikleour
BEECH HEDGE
Isla
Kinclaven
Glen Quaich
Loch Freuchie
Braan
Muir of Thorn
Murthly
Ardoch
Upper Obney
B867
Woodside
Burrelton
Amulree
Balquharn
Waterloo
Cargill
805 MEALL NAM FUARAN
B9099
A94
Corrymuckloch
Airntully
Ordie Burn
Bankfoot
Whitefield
Little Glenshee
Milton Burn
623 MEALL NAN CAORAICH
West Tofts
Tullybelton
A9
Stanley
Saucher
Wolfhill
Collace
Newton
Shochie Burn
Guildtown
Kinrossie
Kirkton of Collace
Logiealmond Lodge
Logiealmond
Sma' Glen
Glen Almond
Chapelhill
Downhill
Newmill
St Martins
Harrietfield
B8063
B953
648 MEALL TARSUINN
133
134
Moneydie
Luncarty
Balbeggie
Loch Turret Reservoir
Shaggie Burn
Buchanty
Almond
Redgorton
PERTH
Glen Turret
Pitcairngreen
CAITHNESS GLASS
PERTH
SCONE PALACE
Methven
Almondbank
Huntingtower
PERTH MART VISITOR CENTRE
Scone
288 POLE HILL
A85
Lochty
Keillour
Muirton
A822
A93
A94

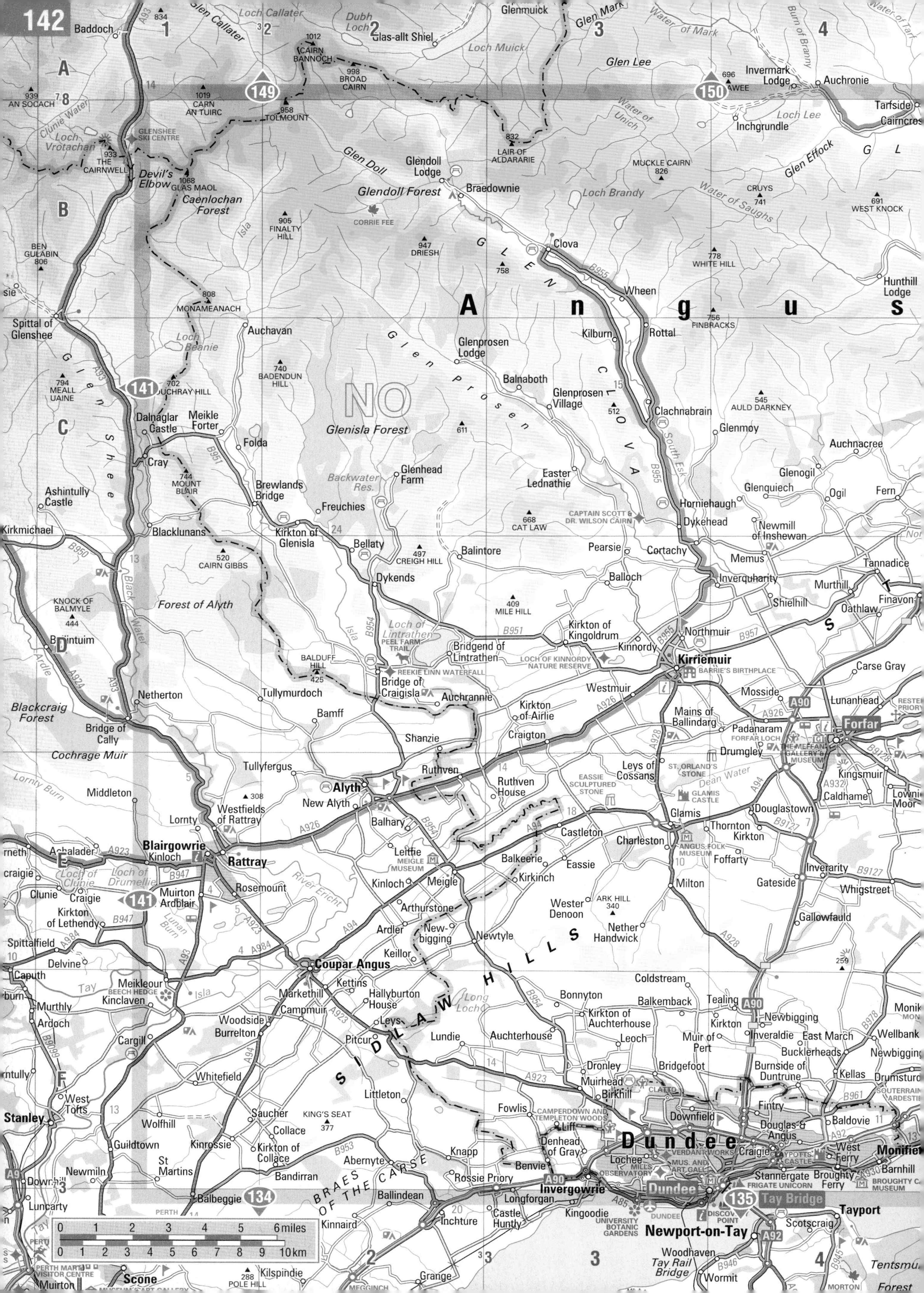

Baddoch
834
1
Glen Callater
Loch Callater
2
Dubh Loch
Glas-allt Shiel
1012 CAIRN BANNOCH
Glenmuick
Glen Mark
3
Water of Mark
Burn of Branny
Water of Tarf
4
Loch Muick
Glen Lee
A
939 AN SOCACH
998 BROAD CAIRN
1019 CARN AN TUIRC
149
958 TOLMOUNT
696 CAWEE
Invermark Lodge
Auchronie
150
Tarfside
Cairncross
Clunie Water
Loch Vrotachan
GLENSHEE SKI CENTRE
933 THE CAIRNWELL
Devil's Elbow
1068 GLAS MAOL
Caenlochan Forest
Water of Unich
832 LAIR OF ALDARARIE
Loch Lee
Inchgrundle
Glen Effock
Glen Doll
Glendoll Lodge
Braedownie
Glendoll Forest
CORRIE FEE
MUCKLE CAIRN 826
Loch Brandy
Water of Saughs
CRUYS 741
691 WEST KNOCK
B
Isla
905 FINALTY HILL
947 DRIESH
758
Clova
778 WHITE HILL
BEN GULABIN 806
808 MONAMEANACH
B955
Wheen
Hunthill Lodge
Spittal of Glenshee
Loch Beanie
Auchavan
Angus
756 FINBRACKS
Kilburn
Rottal
Glenprosen Lodge
Glen Prosen
Glen Clova
Glen Shee
794 MEALL UAINE
A93
740 BADENDUN HILL
141
702 DUCHRAY HILL
NO
Balnaboth
Glenprosen Village
512
545 AULD DARKNEY
C
Dalnaglar Castle
Meikle Forter
Folda
Glenisla Forest
611
Clachnabrain
Glenmoy
Auchnacree
Cray
B951
744 MOUNT BLAIR
Backwater Res.
Glenhead Farm
South Esk
Easter Lednathie
Glenogil
Ashintully Castle
Brewlands Bridge
Freuchies
Glenquiech
Ogil
Fern
668 CAT LAW
CAPTAIN SCOTT & DR. WILSON CAIRN
Horniehaugh
Dykehead
Newmill of Inshewan
Kirkmichael
Blacklunans
Kirkton of Glenisla
Bellaty
497 CREIGH HILL
Balintore
Pearsie
Cortachy
Memus
Tannadice
B950
520 CAIRN GIBBS
Dykends
Balloch
Inverquharity
Murthill
Finavon
Shielhill
Oathlaw
KNOCK OF BALMYLE 444
Forest of Alyth
Black Water
409 MILE HILL
Kirkton of Kingoldrum
Northmuir
B957
Loch of Lintrathen
PEEL FARM TRAIL
B954
Bridgend of Lintrathen
LOCH OF KINNORDY NATURE RESERVE
Kinnordy
Kirriemuir
BARRIE'S BIRTHPLACE
D
Ardle
A924
BALDUFF HILL 425
REEKIE LINN WATERFALL
Bridge of Craigisla
Tullymurdoch
Carse Gray
Netherton
Auchrannie
Westmuir
Kirkton of Airlie
A926
Mosside
Lunanhead
Blackcraig Forest
Bridge of Cally
Bamff
Mains of Ballindarg
A928
Padanaram
FORFAR LOCH
A90
Forfar
THE MEFFAN GALLERY & MUSEUM
Shanzie
Craigton
Drumgley
Cochrage Muir
Tullyfergus
Ruthven
Leys of Cossans
ST. ORLAND'S STONE
Dean Water
Kingsmuir
Lornty Burn
Middleton
308
Alyth
Ruthven House
EASSIE SCULPTURED STONE
GLAMIS CASTLE
A94
A932
Caldhame
Lownie Moor
Westfields of Rattray
New Alyth
Balhary
Glamis
Douglastown
Lornty
B9127
Thornton
Kirkton
Castleton
Charleston
ANGUS FOLK MUSEUM
Foffarty
Blairgowrie
Rattray
Kinloch
A923
E
Achalader
Loch of Clunie
Loch of Drumellie
B947
Leitfie
MEIGLE MUSEUM
Balkeerie
Eassie
Inverarity
Craigie
Clunie
Muirton of Ardblair
Rosemount
River Ericht
Kinloch
Meigle
Kirkinch
Milton
Gateside
Whigstreet
Kirkton of Lethendy
Lunan Burn
Arthurstone
Wester Denoon
ARK HILL 340
Gallowfauld
Spittalfield
A984
Ardler
New-bigging
Newtyle
Nether Handwick
Delvine
Caputh
Tay
Coupar Angus
Keillor
259
Meikleour
BEECH HEDGE
Kinclaven
Kettins
Coldstream
Murthly
Ardoch
Markethill
Hallyburton House
Long Loch
Bonnyton
Balkemback
Tealing
Monikie
Woodside
Burrelton
Campmuir
Leys
Kirkton of Auchterhouse
Kirkton
Newbigging
Inveraldie
East March
Wellbank
Cargill
Pitcur
Lundie
Auchterhouse
Leoch
Muir of Pert
Bucklerheads
Newbigging
B9099
SIDLAW HILLS
Dronley
Bridgefoot
Burnside of Duntrune
Kellas
Drumsturdy
F
Whitefield
Muirhead
Birkhill
CLATTO
Stanley
West Tofts
Littleton
Fowlis
CAMPERDOWN AND TEMPLETON WOODS
Downfield
Fintry
SOUTERRAIN ARDESTIE
B961
Wolfhill
Saucher
KING'S SEAT 377
Collace
Liff
Baldovie
Guildtown
Kinrossie
Kirkton of Collace
Knapp
Denhead of Gray
Dundee
Craigie
Douglas & Angus
West Ferry
Monifieth
St Martins
Abernyte
B953
Lochee
VERDANT WORKS
MUS. AND ART GALL.
MILLS OBSERVATORY
BROUGHTY CASTLE
Newmiln
Bandirran
Benvie
Rossie Priory
A90
Invergowrie
Stannergate
Broughty Ferry
FRIGATE UNICORN
BROUGHTY CASTLE MUSEUM
Barnhill
Dowhill
Balbeggie
134
BRAES OF THE CARSE
Ballindean
Longforgan
Kingoodie
A85
Dundee
DISCOVERY POINT
135
Tay Bridge
Tayport
Luncarty
PERTH
Inchture
Castle Huntly
UNIVERSITY BOTANIC GARDENS
Newport-on-Tay
Scotscraig
A92
0 1 2 3 4 5 6 miles
0 1 2 3 4 5 6 7 8 9 10 km
Kinnaird
PERTH MART VISITOR CENTRE
Scone
288 POLE HILL
Kilspindie
Woodhaven
Tay Rail Bridge
B946
Wormit
B945
Tentsmuir Forest
Muirton
MUSEUM & ART GALLERY
Grange
MEGGINCH
MORTON

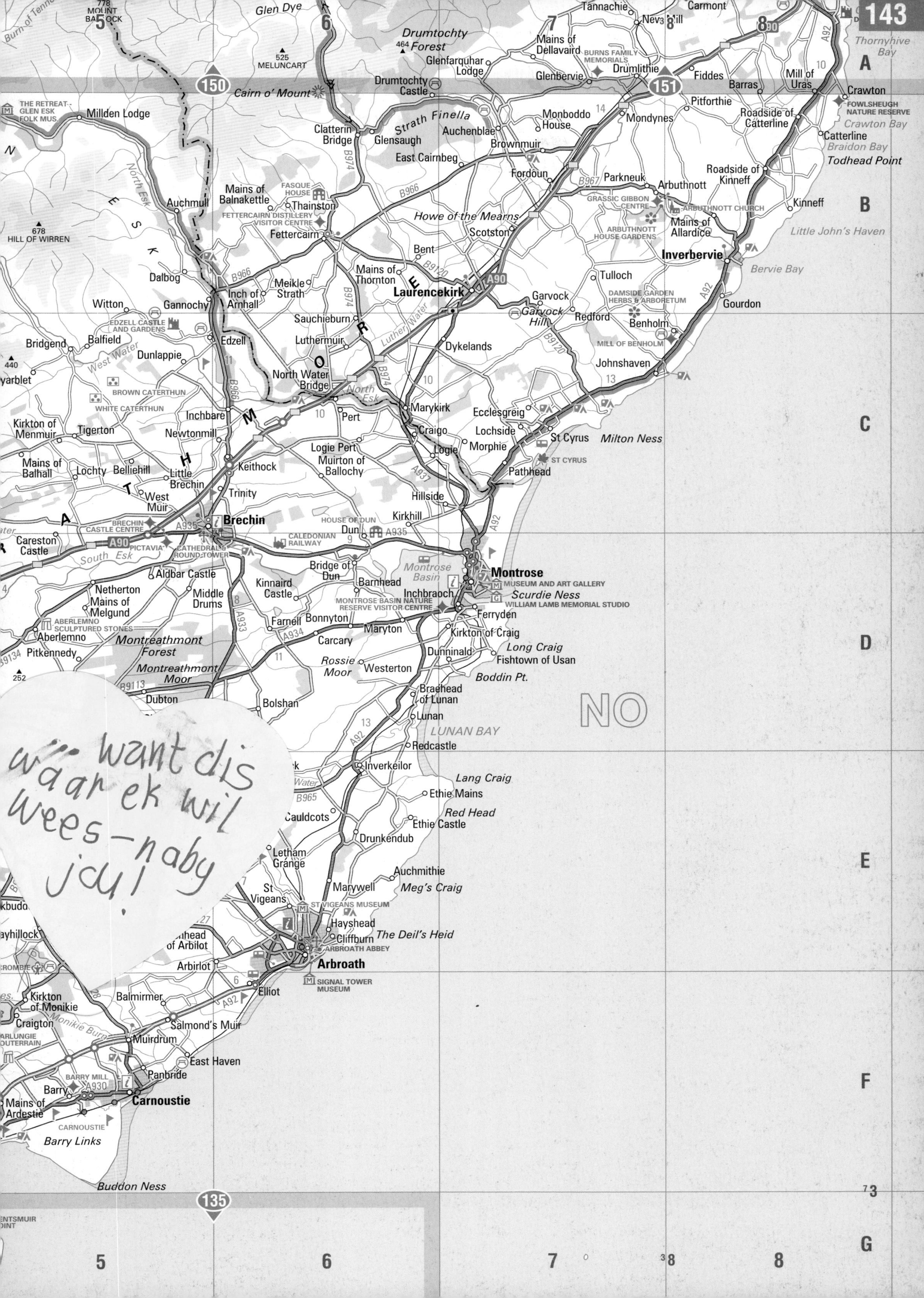
143
Glen Dye
778 MOUNT BATTOCK
Drumtochty Forest
464
525 MELUNCART
Tannachie
Carmont
Newbigging
Mains of Dellavaird
BURNS FAMILY MEMORIALS
Drumlithie
Glenfarquhar Lodge
Glenbervie
Thornyhive Bay
150
Cairn o' Mount
Drumtochty Castle
151
Fiddes
Barras
Mill of Uras
Crawton
FOWLSHEUGH NATURE RESERVE
THE RETREAT GLEN ESK FOLK MUS.
Millden Lodge
Strath Finella
Monboddo House
Pitforthie
Mondynes
Roadside of Catterline
Crawton Bay
Catterline
Braidon Bay
Todhead Point
Clatterin Bridge
Glensaugh
Auchenblae
Brownmuir
East Cairnbeg
Fordoun
Roadside of Kinneff
Parkneuk
Arbuthnott
Kinneff
Mains of Balnakettle
FASQUE HOUSE
Thainston
Auchmull
FETTERCAIRN DISTILLERY VISITOR CENTRE
Fettercairn
GRASSIC GIBBON CENTRE
ARBUTHNOTT CHURCH
Howe of the Mearns
Scotston
ARBUTHNOTT HOUSE GARDENS
Mains of Allardice
678 HILL OF WIRREN
Little John's Haven
Bent
Inverbervie
Bervie Bay
Mains of Thornton
Dalbog
Meikle Strath
Laurencekirk
Tulloch
Inch of Arnhall
Garvock
DAMSIDE GARDEN HERBS & ARBORETUM
Gourdon
Witton
Gannochy
EDZELL CASTLE AND GARDENS
Sauchieburn
Garvock Hill
Redford
Benholm
Bridgend
Balfield
Edzell
Luthermuir
Luther Water
Dykelands
MILL OF BENHOLM
West Water
Dunlappie
Johnshaven
440
Tarryblet
North Water Bridge
BROWN CATERTHUN
North Esk
WHITE CATERTHUN
Pert
Marykirk
Ecclesgreig
Kirkton of Menmuir
Tigerton
Inchbare
Newtonmill
Craigo
Lochside
St Cyrus
Milton Ness
Logie Pert
Logie
Morphie
Mains of Balhall
Lochty
Belliehill
Keithock
Muirton of Ballochy
ST CYRUS
Little Brechin
Pathhead
West Muir
Trinity
Hillside
Brechin
BRECHIN CASTLE CENTRE
HOUSE OF DUN
Kirkhill
Careston Castle
PICTAVIA
CATHEDRAL & ROUND TOWER
Dun
CALEDONIAN RAILWAY
South Esk
Montrose Basin
Montrose
MUSEUM AND ART GALLERY
Aldbar Castle
Bridge of Dun
Netherton
Mains of Melgund
Middle Drums
Kinnaird Castle
Barnhead
Inchbraoch
Scurdie Ness
WILLIAM LAMB MEMORIAL STUDIO
MONTROSE BASIN NATURE RESERVE VISITOR CENTRE
Ferryden
ABERLEMNO SCULPTURED STONES
Aberlemno
Farnell
Bonnyton
Maryton
Kirkton of Craig
Montreathmont Forest
Pitkennedy
Carcary
Dunninald
Long Craig
Fishtown of Usan
Rossie Moor
Westerton
252
Montreathmont Moor
Boddin Pt.
Dubton
Braehead of Lunan
Bolshan
NO
Lunan
LUNAN BAY
Redcastle
Inverkeilor
Lang Craig
Ethie Mains
Cauldcots
Red Head
Ethie Castle
Drunkendub
Letham Grange
Auchmithie
Marywell
Meg's Craig
St Vigeans
ST VIGEANS MUSEUM
Hayshead
Cliffburn
The Deil's Heid
ARBROATH ABBEY
Arbroath
SIGNAL TOWER MUSEUM
Arbirlot
Elliot
Balmirmer
Kirkton of Monikie
Craigton
Monikie Burn
Salmond's Muir
Muirdrum
East Haven
Panbride
BARRY MILL
Barry
Carnoustie
Mains of Ardestie
CARNOUSTIE
Barry Links
Buddon Ness
135
A B C D E F G
5 6 7 8
want dis waar ek wil wees - naby jou!

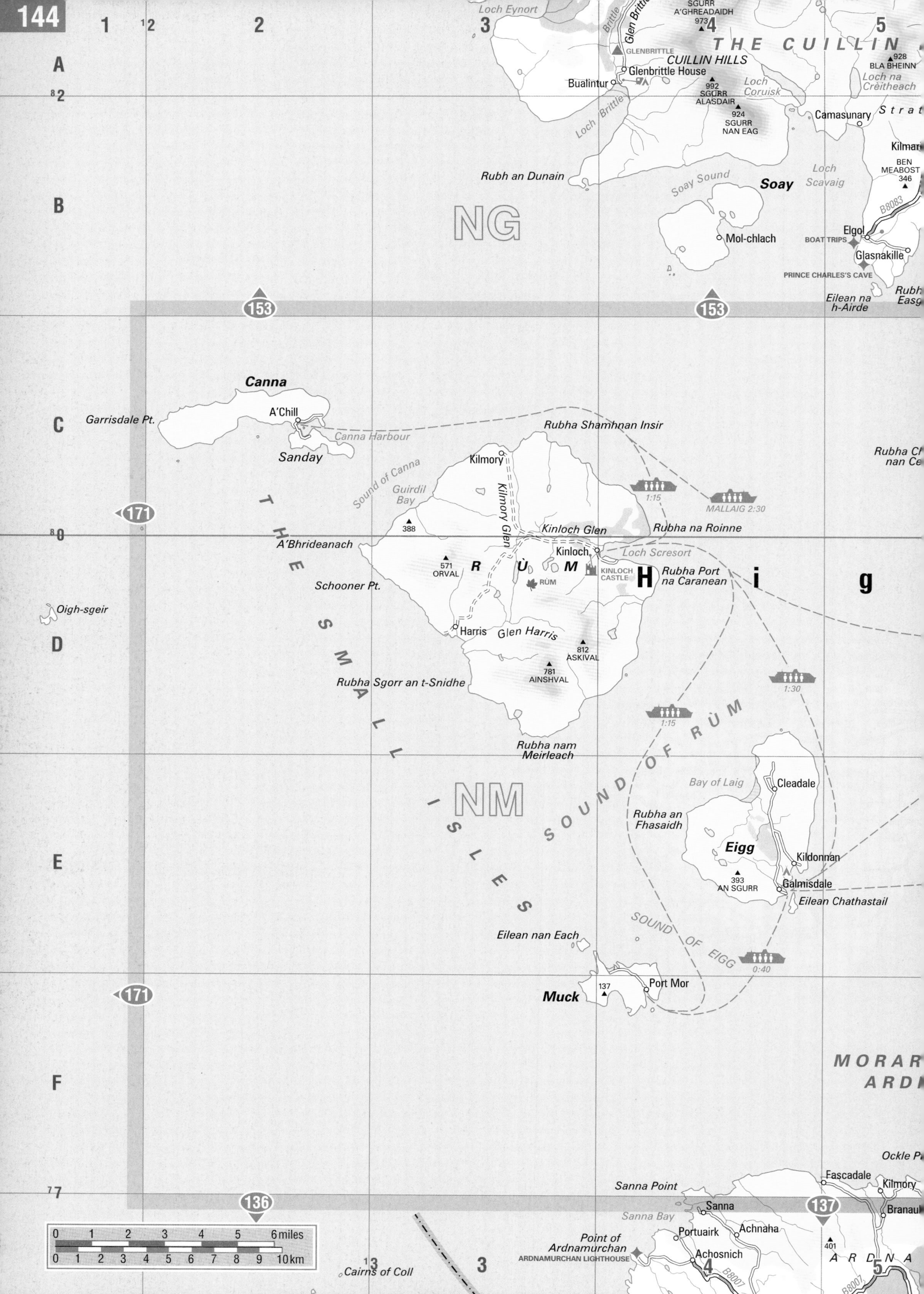

1   2   2   3   4   5

A

8 2

THE CUILLIN

SGURR
A'GHREADAIDH
973 4

Glen Brittle
Glenbrittle
CUILLIN HILLS
Glenbrittle House
928
BLA BHEINN
Loch na
Crèitheach
Bualintur
992
SGURR
ALASDAIR
Loch
Coruisk
924
SGURR
NAN EAG
Camasunary   Strat
Kilmar

B

Rubh an Dunain
Soay Sound
Soay
Loch
Scavaig
BEN
MEABOST
346
Mol-chlach
BOAT TRIPS
Elgol
B8083
Glasnakille
NG
PRINCE CHARLES'S CAVE
Eilean na
h-Airde
Rubh
Easg

153   153

Canna

C

Garrisdale Pt.
A'Chill
Rubha Shamhnan Insir
Rubha C
nan Ce
Canna Harbour
Kilmory
Sanday
Kilmory Glen
1:15
Sound of Canna
Guirdil
Bay
MALLAIG 2:30

171

8 0
A'Bhrideanach
388
Kinloch Glen
Rubha na Roinne
Kinloch
571
ORVAL
R   Ù   M
Loch Scresort
Schooner Pt.
RÙM
KINLOCH
CASTLE
H   i   g
Rubha Port
na Caranean
Oigh-sgeir

D

Harris
Glen Harris
812
ASKIVAL
1:30
T H E   S M A L L
Rubha Sgorr an t-Snidhe
781
AINSHVAL
SOUND   OF   RÙM
1:15

Rubha nam
Meirleach

E

I S L E S
Bay of Laig
Cleadale
NM
Rubha an
Fhasaidh
Eigg
Kildonnan
393
AN SGURR
Galmisdale
Eilean nan Each
Eilean Chathastail
SOUND   OF   EIGG
0:40

Muck
137
Port Mor

171

F

MORAR
ARDN

7 7

Ockle P
Fascadale
Kilmory
Sanna Point
Branau
137
Sanna
136
Sanna Bay
Portuairk
Achnaha
Point of
Ardnamurchan
ARDNAMURCHAN LIGHTHOUSE
Achosnich
401
A R D N A
Cairns of Coll
3
4
5

0 1 2 3 4 5 6miles
0 1 2 3 4 5 6 7 8 9 10km

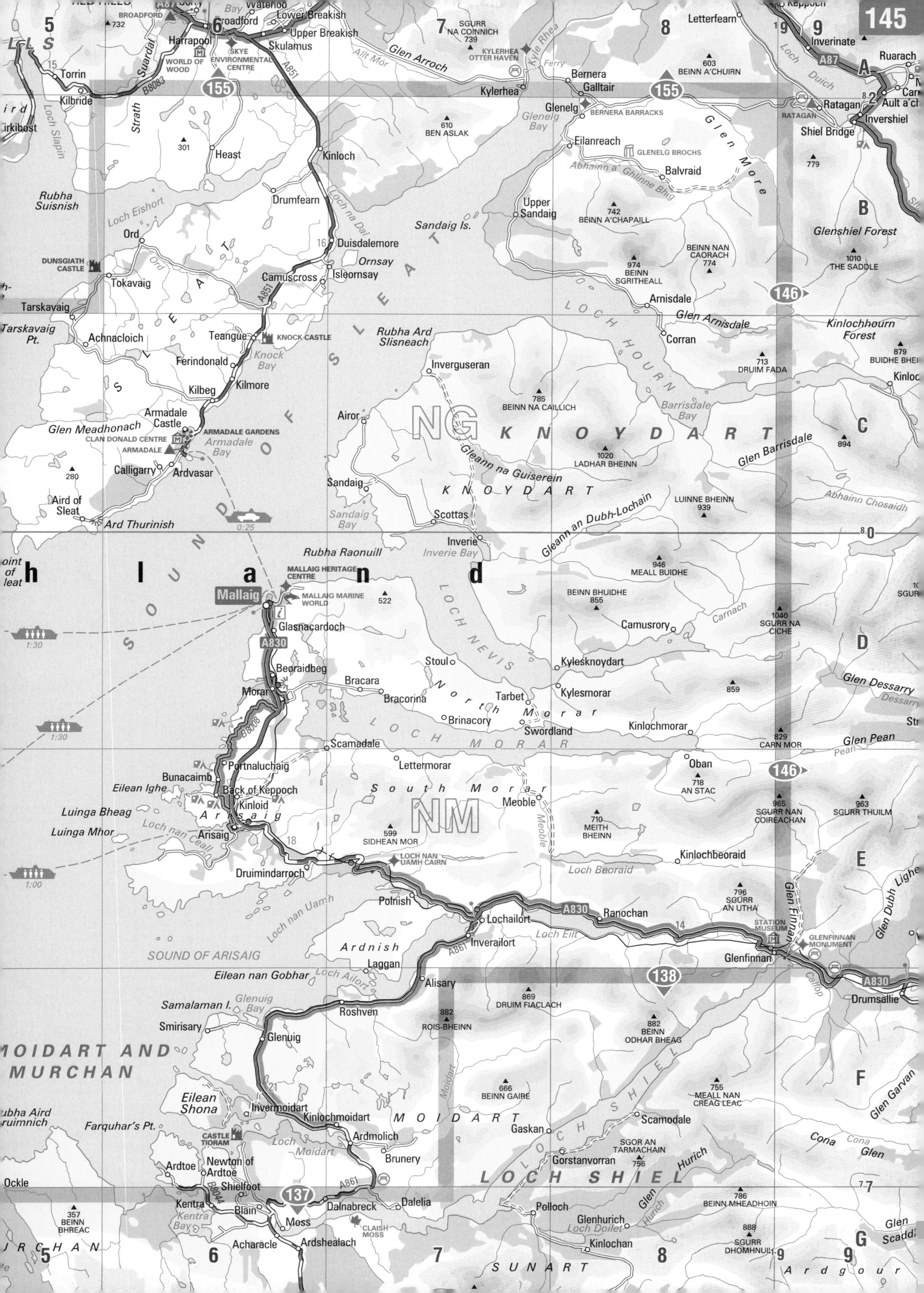
Broadford
Harrapool
Upper Breakish
Skulamus
Lower Breakish
Waterloo
Glen Arroch
Kylerhea
Kylerhea Otter Haven
Skye Environmental Centre
World of Wood
Torrin
Kilbride
Strath
Suardal
Loch Slapin
Heast
Kinloch
Drumfearn
Loch Eishort
Rubha Suisnish
Ord
Dunsgiath Castle
Tokavaig
Tarskavaig
Tarskavaig Pt.
Achnacloich
Duisdalemore
Isleornsay
Ornsay
Camuscross
Teangue
Knock Castle
Knock Bay
Ferindonald
Kilmore
Kilbeg
Armadale Castle
Armadale Gardens
Clan Donald Centre
Armadale
Armadale Bay
Glen Meadhonach
Calligarry
Ardvasar
Aird of Sleat
Ard Thurinish
Sound of Sleat
Sandaig Is.
Rubha Ard Slisneach
Letterfearn
Inverinate
Ruarach
Loch Duich
Ratagan
Shiel Bridge
Invershiel
Bernera
Galltair
Glenelg
Glenelg Bay
Bernera Barracks
Eilanreach
Glenelg Brochs
Balvraid
Glen More
Upper Sandaig
Beinn a'Chapaill
Beinn a'Chuirn
Ben Aslak
Sgurr na Coinnich
Glenshiel Forest
The Saddle
Beinn nan Caorach
Beinn Sgritheall
Arnisdale
Glen Arnisdale
Corran
Loch Hourn
Kinlochhourn Forest
Druim Fada
Inverguseran
Beinn na Caillich
Barrisdale Bay
Airor
Knoydart
Ladhar Bheinn
Glen Barrisdale
Gleann na Guiserein
Sandaig
Sandaig Bay
Scottas
Luinne Bheinn
Gleann an Dubh-Lochain
Abhainn Chosaidh
Inverie
Inverie Bay
Rubha Raonuill
Highland
Mallaig
Mallaig Heritage Centre
Mallaig Marine World
Meall Buidhe
Beinn Bhuidhe
Loch Nevis
Camusrory
Sgurr na Ciche
Glasnacardoch
Beoraidbeg
Stoul
Kylesknoydart
Kylesmorar
Glen Dessarry
Morar
Bracara
Bracorina
Tarbet
North Morar
Brinacory
Swordland
Kinlochmorar
Loch Morar
Carn Mor
Glen Pean
Scamadale
Lettermorar
Oban
An Stac
Portnaluchaig
Bunacaimb
Eilean Ighe
Back of Keppoch
Kinloid
South Morar
Meoble
Meith Bheinn
Sgurr nan Coireachan
Sgurr Thuilm
Luinga Bheag
Luinga Mhor
Arisaig
Loch nan Ceall
Sidhean Mor
Loch nan Uamh Cairn
Kinlochbeoraid
Loch Beoraid
Druimindarroch
Polnish
Lochailort
Ranochan
Sgurr an Utha
Station Museum
Glenfinnan
Glenfinnan Monument
Glen Finnan
Glen Dubh Lighe
Loch nan Uamh
Inverailort
Loch Eilt
Ardnish
Sound of Arisaig
Laggan
Eilean nan Gobhar
Loch Ailort
Alisary
Druim Fiaclach
Drumsallie
Callop
Samalaman I.
Glenuig Bay
Roshven
Rois-Bheinn
Beinn Odhar Bheag
Smirisary
Glenuig
Moidart and Ardnamurchan
Eilean Shona
Invermoidart
Kinlochmoidart
Moidart
Beinn Gaire
Meall nan Creag Leac
Glen Garvan
Rubha Aird Druimnich
Farquhar's Pt.
Castle Tioram
Loch Moidart
Ardmolich
Gaskan
Scamodale
Sgor an Tarmachain
Gorstanvorran
Cona Glen
Brunery
Ardtoe
Newton of Ardtoe
Shielfoot
Loch Shiel
Glen Hurich
Ockle
Kentra
Kentra Bay
Blain
Dalnabreck
Dalelia
Polloch
Beinn Mheadhoin
Beinn Bhreac
Moss
Claish Moss
Glenhurich
Loch Doilet
Acharacle
Ardshealach
Kinlochan
Sgurr Dhomhnuill
Sunart
Ardgour
Glen Scaddle

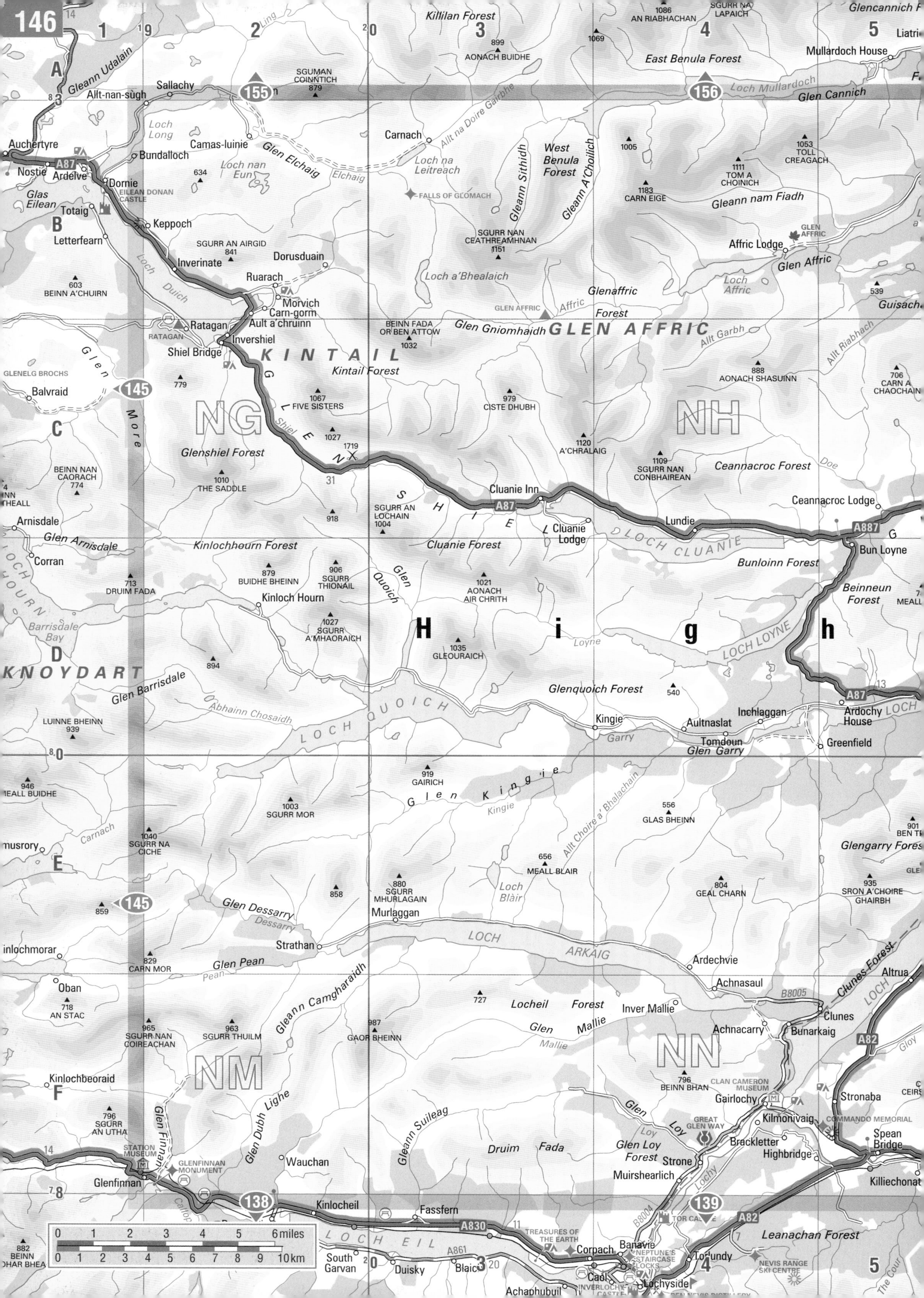

Killilan Forest
AN RIABHACHAN
SGURR NA LAPAICH
Glencannich
Mullardoch House
East Benula Forest
AONACH BUIDHE
Gleann Udalain
Allt-nan-sùgh
Sallachy
SGUMAN COINNTICH
155
156
Loch Mullardoch
Glen Cannich
Carnach
Loch Long
Camas-luinie
Glen Elchaig
Loch na Leitreach
West Benula Forest
Gleann Sithidh
Gleann A'Choilich
TOLL CREAGACH
TOM A CHOINICH
CARN EIGE
Gleann nam Fiadh
Auchertyre
Bundalloch
Loch nan Eun
Nostie
Ardelve
Dornie
EILEAN DONAN CASTLE
Glas Eilean
Totaig
FALLS OF GLOMACH
Letterfearn
Keppoch
SGURR AN AIRGID
SGURR NAN CEATHREAMHNAN
Affric Lodge
GLEN AFFRIC
Glen Affric
Inverinate
Dorusduain
Loch a'Bhealaich
Loch Affric
Loch Duich
Ruarach
Morvich
BEINN A'CHUIRN
Glenaffric Forest
Guisachan
Carn-gorm
Ratagan
Ault a'chruinn
BEINN FADA OR BEN ATTOW
Glen Gniomhaidh
GLEN AFFRIC
Allt Garbh
Allt Riabhach
RATAGAN
Invershiel
Shiel Bridge
KINTAIL
Kintail Forest
AONACH SHASUINN
CARN A CHAOCHAIN
GLENELG BROCHS
Glen More
Balvraid
145
FIVE SISTERS
CISTE DHUBH
NG
NH
Glen Shiel
C
A'CHRALAIG
Glenshiel Forest
SGURR NAN CONBHAIREAN
Ceannacroc Forest
BEINN NAN CAORACH
THE SADDLE
Cluanie Inn
A87
Ceannacroc Lodge
SGURR AN LOCHAIN
Cluanie Lodge
Lundie
Arnisdale
Glen Arnisdale
Kinlochhourn Forest
Cluanie Forest
LOCH CLUANIE
A887
Bun Loyne
Corran
BUIDHE BHEINN
SGURR THIONAIL
Glen Quoich
AONACH AIR CHRITH
Bunloinn Forest
DRUIM FADA
Kinloch Hourn
Beinneun Forest
LOCH HOURN
Barrisdale Bay
SGURR A'MHAORAICH
Highland
GLEOURAICH
Loyne
LOCH LOYNE
D
KNOYDART
Glen Barrisdale
Glenquoich Forest
Abhainn Chosaidh
LOCH QUOICH
Kingie
Aultnaslat
Inchlaggan
Ardochy House
LUINNE BHEINN
Garry
Tomdoun
Glen Garry
Greenfield
MEALL BUIDHE
GAIRICH
Glen Kingie
SGURR MOR
Allt Choire a' Bhalachain
GLAS BHEINN
Carnach
SGURR NA CICHE
BEN TEE
Glengarry Forest
E
MEALL BLAIR
Loch Blàir
SGURR MHURLAGAIN
GEAL CHARN
SRON A'CHOIRE GHAIRBH
Glen Dessarry
Murlaggan
Strathan
LOCH ARKAIG
Clunes Forest
Kinlochmorar
CARN MOR
Glen Pean
Ardechvie
Oban
AN STAC
Gleann Camgharaidh
Achnasaul
Altrua
Locheil Forest
Inver Mallie
B8005
Clunes
SGURR NAN COIREACHAN
SGURR THUILM
GAOR BHEINN
Glen Mallie
Achnacarry
Bunarkaig
A82
NM
NN
Kinlochbeoraid
F
BEINN BHAN
CLAN CAMERON MUSEUM
Gairlochy
Stronaba
SGURR AN UTHA
Glen Finnan
Glen Dubh Lighe
Gleann Suileag
Glen Loy
GREAT GLEN WAY
Kilmonivaig
COMMANDO MEMORIAL
Spean Bridge
STATION MUSEUM
GLENFINNAN MONUMENT
Wauchan
Druim Fada
Glen Loy Forest
Strone
Brackletter
Highbridge
Muirshearlich
Glenfinnan
Killiechonate
138
Kinlocheil
Fassfern
139
A830
TREASURES OF THE EARTH
Corpach
Banavie
NEPTUNE'S STAIRCASE LOCKS
TOR CASTLE
Leanachan Forest
LOCH EIL
A861
South Garvan
Duisky
Blaich
Caol
Tomundy
NEVIS RANGE SKI CENTRE
BEINN
Achaphubuil
INVERLOCHY CASTLE
Lochyside
0 1 2 3 4 5 6 miles
0 1 2 3 4 5 6 7 8 9 10 km

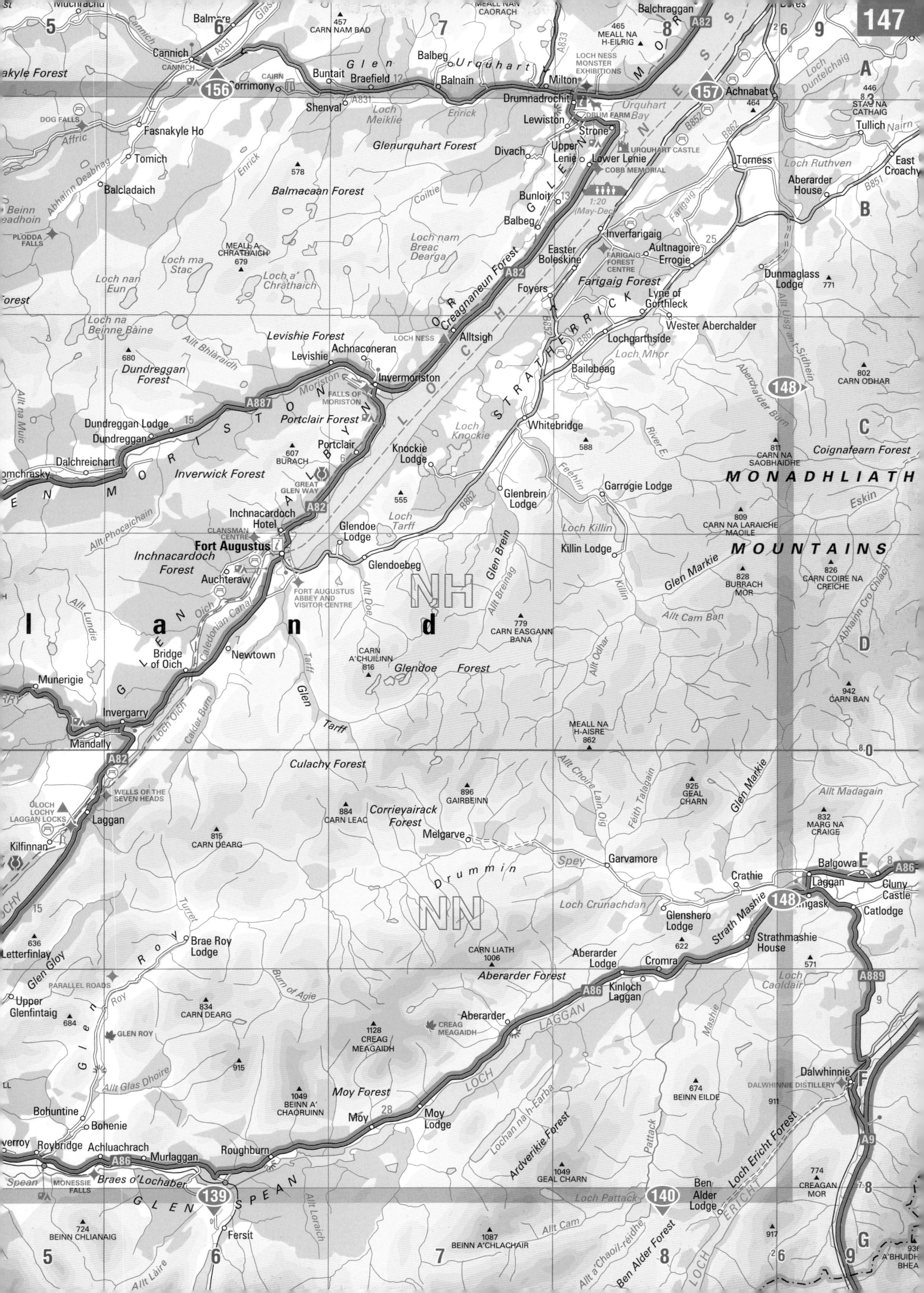
Cannich
Balmore
Glen Urquhart
Buntait
Braefield
Balbeg
Balnain
Milton
Drumnadrochit
Corrimony
Shenval
Loch Meiklie
Enrick
Lewiston
Strone
Urquhart Bay
Achnabat
Balchraggan
MEALL NA H-EILRIG
LOCH NESS MONSTER EXHIBITIONS
URQUHART CASTLE
Upper Lenie
Lower Lenie
COBB MEMORIAL
Divach
Glenurquhart Forest
Fasnakyle Ho
Tomich
DOG FALLS
Affric
Balcladaich
Balmacaan Forest
PLODDA FALLS
MEALL A CHRATHAICH
Loch ma Stac
Loch nan Eun
Loch a' Chràthaich
Loch nam Breac Dearga
Bunloit
Balbeg
Inverfarigaig
FARIGAIG FOREST CENTRE
Aultnagoire
Errogie
Easter Boleskine
Foyers
Farigaig Forest
Lyne of Gorthleck
Torness
Loch Ruthven
Aberarder House
Tullich
East Croachy
Dunmaglass Lodge
Creagnaneun Forest
Alltsigh
LOCH NESS
Loch na Beinne Bàine
Levishie Forest
Levishie
Achnaconeran
Invermoriston
FALLS OF MORISTON
Dundreggan Forest
Dundreggan Lodge
Dundreggan
Dalchreichart
Portclair Forest
Portclair
BURACH
Inverwick Forest
GREAT GLEN WAY
Wester Aberchalder
Lochgarthside
Loch Mhor
Bailebeag
Whitebridge
Loch Knockie
Knockie Lodge
STRATHERRICK
LOCH NESS
GLEN MORISTON
CARN NA SAOBHAIDHE
Coignafearn Forest
MONADHLIATH MOUNTAINS
CARN ODHAR
Glenbrein Lodge
Garrogie Lodge
Loch Killin
Killin Lodge
Inchnacardoch Hotel
CLANSMAN CENTRE
Fort Augustus
Inchnacardoch Forest
Auchteraw
FORT AUGUSTUS ABBEY AND VISITOR CENTRE
Glendoe Lodge
Glendoebeg
Loch Tarff
CARN NA LARAICHE MAOILE
BURRACH MOR
CARN COIRE NA CREICHE
Glen Markie
Allt Cam Ban
Highland
NH
Bridge of Oich
Newtown
Caledonian Canal
CARN EASGANN BANA
CARN A'CHUILINN
Glendoe Forest
Munerigie
Invergarry
Mandally
CARN BAN
MEALL NA H-AISRE
Culachy Forest
WELLS OF THE SEVEN HEADS
LOCH LOCHY
LAGGAN LOCKS
Laggan
Kilfinnan
CARN DEARG
CARN LEAC
Corrieyairack Forest
GAIRBEINN
Melgarve
GEAL CHARN
MARG NA CRAIGE
Garvamore
Spey
Drummin
Loch Crunachdan
Crathie
Balgowan
Laggan
Cluny Castle
Catlodge
Glenshero Lodge
Strath Mashie
Strathmashie House
NN
Letterfinlay
Glen Gloy
Brae Roy Lodge
Glen Roy
PARALLEL ROADS
Upper Glenfintaig
CARN DEARG
GLEN ROY
CARN LIATH
Aberarder Lodge
Cromra
Aberarder Forest
Kinloch Laggan
Loch Caoldair
Aberarder
CREAG MEAGAIDH
LOCH LAGGAN
Mashie
Allt Glas Dhoire
Dalwhinnie
DALWHINNIE DISTILLERY
BEINN EILDE
Bohuntine
Bohenie
BEINN A' CHAORUINN
Moy Forest
Moy
Moy Lodge
Roybridge
Achluachrach
Murlaggan
Roughburn
MONESSIE FALLS
Braes o'Lochaber
GLEN SPEAN
Ardverikie Forest
Lochan na h-Earba
GEAL CHARN
Pattack
Loch Pattack
Ben Alder Lodge
Loch Ericht Forest
CREAGAN MOR
BEINN CHLIANAIG
Fersit
Allt Loraich
BEINN A'CHLACHAIR
Ben Alder Forest
Allt Làire
LOCH ERICHT
A'BHUIDH BHEA
A82
A831
A833
A887
A86
A889
A9
B852
B862
B851
156
157
148
139
140

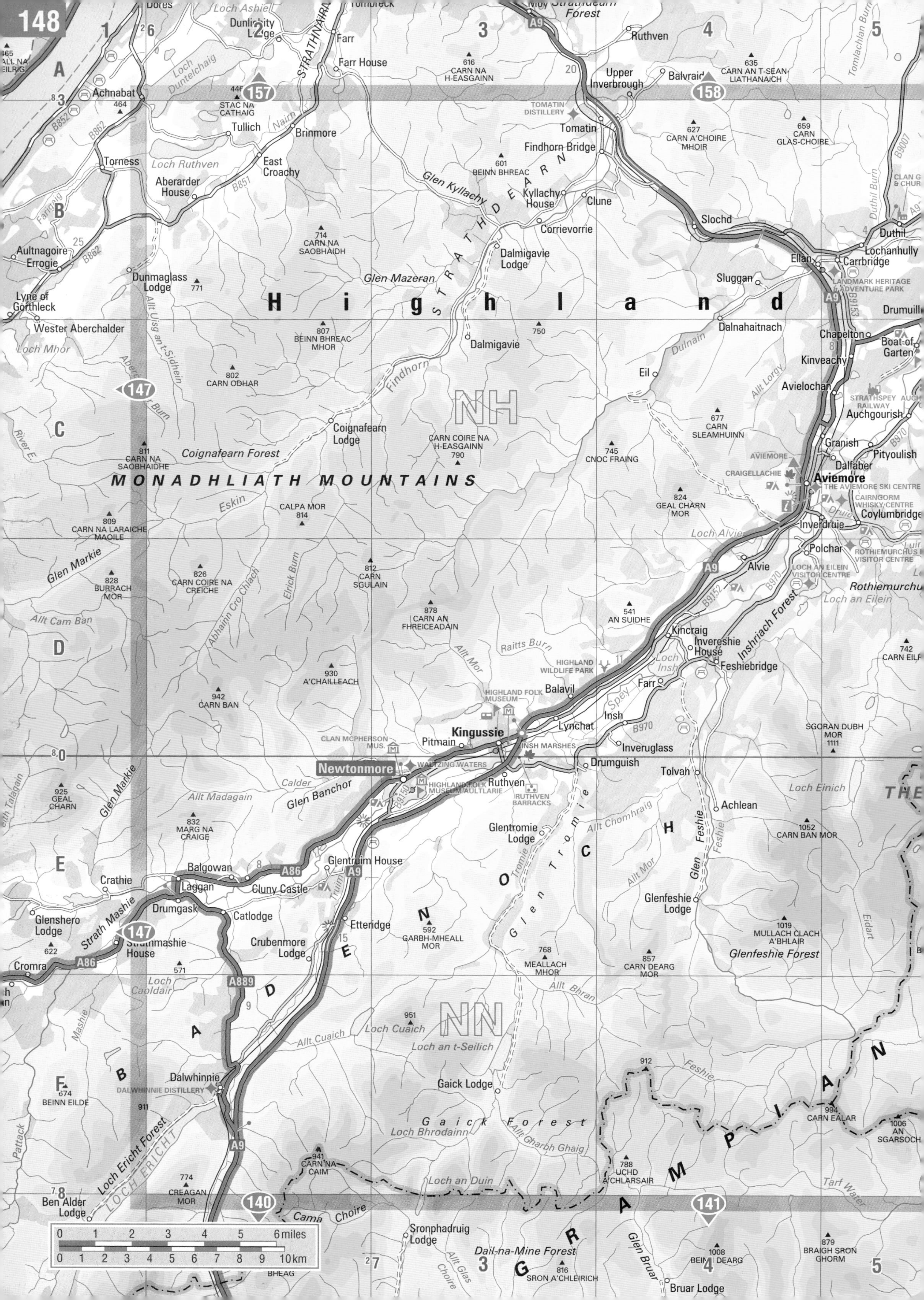

Highland
MONADHLIATH MOUNTAINS
GRAMPIAN
Aviemore
Kingussie
Newtonmore
Dalwhinnie
Tomatin
Carrbridge
Laggan
Balgowan
Crathie
Feshiebridge
Kincraig
Coylumbridge
Inverdruie
Glen Banchor
Glen Markie
Strathdearn
Glen Tromie
Glen Feshie
Gaick Forest
Coignafearn Forest
Glenfeshie Forest
Loch Ericht Forest
Gaick Lodge
Ben Alder Lodge
Bruar Lodge
Findhorn Bridge
Slochd
Aultnagoire
Errogie
Aberarder House
Torness
Tullich
Brinmore
East Croachy
Dunmaglass Lodge
Coignafearn Lodge
Dalmigavie Lodge
Dalmigavie
Kyllachy House
Clune
Corrievorrie
Ruthven
Balvraid
Upper Inverbrough
Farr
Farr House
Achnabat
Dunlichity Lodge
Dalnahaitnach
Sluggan
Ellan
Duthil
Lochanhully
Chapelton
Boat of Garten
Kinveachy
Avielochan
Auchgourish
Granish
Dalfaber
Pityoulish
Alvie
Polchar
Rothiemurchus
Invereshie House
Balavil
Lynchat
Insh
Inveruglass
Drumguish
Tolvah
Achlean
Glentromie Lodge
Glenfeshie Lodge
Glentruim House
Cluny Castle
Etteridge
Crubenmore Lodge
Catlodge
Drumgask
Strathmashie House
Glenshero Lodge
Cromra
Sronphadruig Lodge
Pitmain
Ruthven Barracks
Highland Folk Museum
Highland Wildlife Park
Insh Marshes
Waltzing Waters
Clan McPherson Mus.
Dalwhinnie Distillery
Tomatin Distillery
The Aviemore Ski Centre
Cairngorm Whisky Centre
Rothiemurchus Visitor Centre
Loch an Eilein Visitor Centre
Landmark Heritage & Adventure Park
Strathspey Railway
A9
A86
A889
B851
B862
B852
B9152
B970
B9153
NH
NN
157
158
147
140
141
0 1 2 3 4 5 6 miles
0 1 2 3 4 5 6 7 8 9 10 km

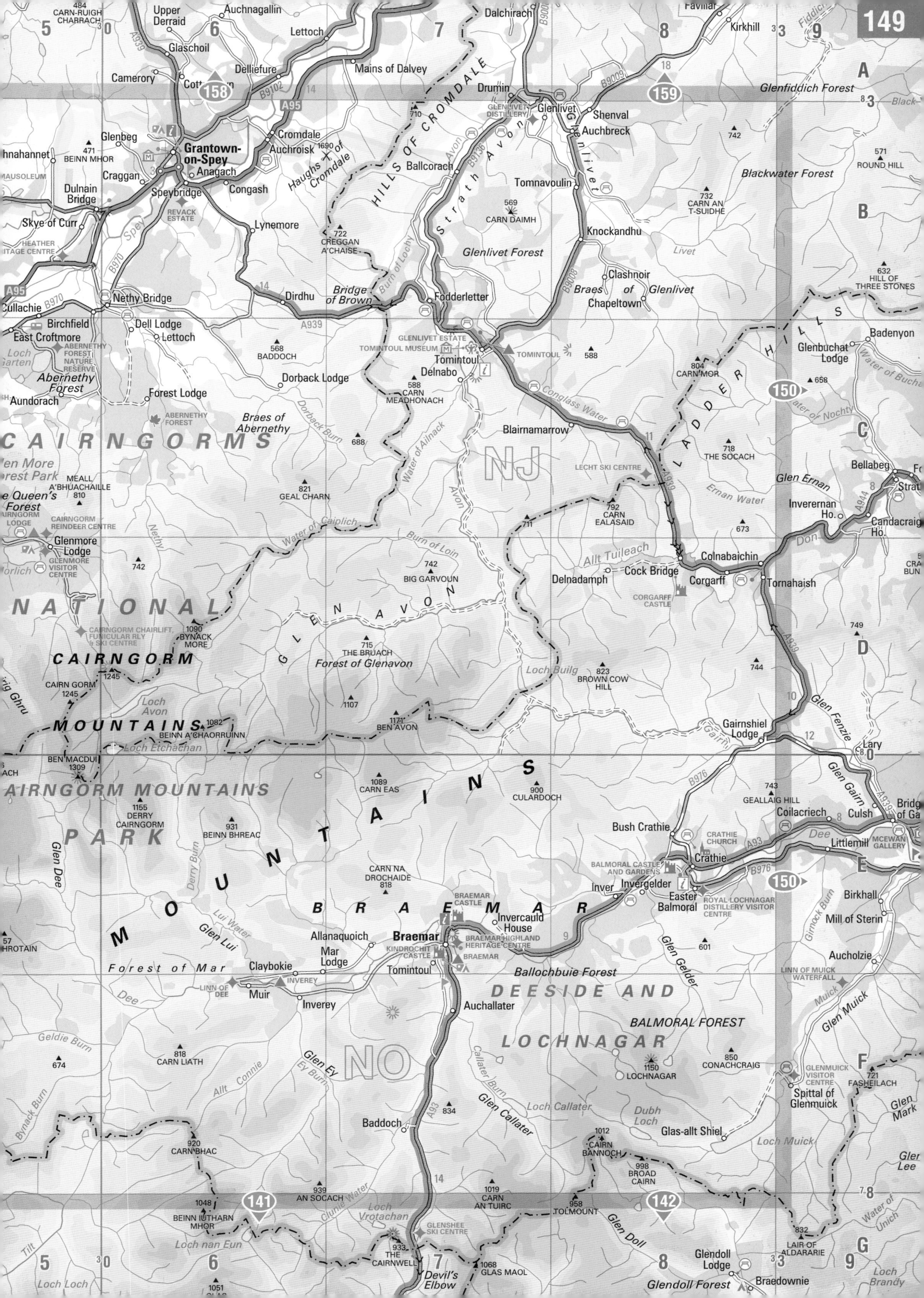
CARN-RUIGH CHARRACH
Upper Derraid
Auchnagallin
Lettoch
Dalchirach
Favillar
Kirkhill
Glaschoil
Dellefure
Mains of Dalvey
Camerory
HILLS OF CROMDALE
Drumin
158
159
Glenfiddich Forest
GLENLIVET DISTILLERY
Glenlivet
Shenval
Glenbeg
Grantown-on-Spey
Cromdale
Auchroisk
Auchbreck
BEINN MHOR
Haughs of Cromdale
Anagach
Craggan
Ballcorach
Strath Avon
Glenlivet
ROUND HILL
MAUSOLEUM
Dulnain Bridge
Speybridge
Congash
Tomnavoulin
Blackwater Forest
CARN AN T-SUIDHE
REVACK ESTATE
CARN DAIMH
Skye of Curr
Lynemore
Knockandhu
CREGGAN A'CHAISE
Glenlivet Forest
Livet
Spey
Burn of Lochy
Clashnoir
HILL OF THREE STONES
Braes of Glenlivet
Chapeltown
Bridge of Brown
Fodderletter
Dirdhu
Nethy Bridge
Cullachie
Birchfield
Dell Lodge
Lettoch
East Croftmore
ABERNETHY FOREST NATURE RESERVE
GLENLIVET ESTATE
TOMINTOUL MUSEUM
Tomintoul
TOMINTOUL
BADDOCH
Delnabo
Loch Garten
CARN MOR
Badenyon
Glenbuchat Lodge
Abernethy Forest
Dorback Lodge
CARN MEADHONACH
LADDER HILLS
150
Aundorach
Forest Lodge
Conglass Water
Water of Buchat
Water of Nochty
ABERNETHY FOREST
Braes of Abernethy
Dorback Burn
Water of Ailnack
Blairnamarrow
CAIRNGORMS
Glen More Forest Park
THE SOCACH
LECHT SKI CENTRE
NJ
Bellabeg
MEALL A'BHUACHAILLE
GEAL CHARN
Glen Ernan
Ernan Water
The Queen's Forest
CAIRNGORM REINDEER CENTRE
Avon
CARN EALASAID
Inverernan Ho.
Candacraig Ho.
Water of Caiplich
Glenmore Lodge
GLENMORE VISITOR CENTRE
Nethy
Burn of Loin
BIG GARVOUN
Allt Tuileach
Cock Bridge
Delnadamph
Colnabaichin
Corgarff
Tornahaish
Don
CORGARFF CASTLE
NATIONAL
CAIRNGORM CHAIRLIFT, FUNICULAR RLY & SKI CENTRE
BYNACK MORE
GLEN AVON
THE BRUACH
CAIRNGORM
Forest of Glenavon
Loch Builg
BROWN COW HILL
Glen Fenzie
CAIRN GORM
Loch Avon
MOUNTAINS
BEINN A'CHAORRUINN
BEN AVON
Gairnshiel Lodge
Gairn
Lary
Loch Etchachan
BEN MACDUI
CAIRNGORM MOUNTAINS
CARN EAS
CULARDOCH
MOUNTAINS
Glen Gairn
GEALLAIG HILL
DERRY CAIRNGORM
BEINN BHREAC
Bush Crathie
Coilacriech
Culsh
PARK
CRATHIE CHURCH
Crathie
Dee
Littlemill
MCEWAN GALLERY
Glen Dee
Derry Burn
CARN NA DROCHAIDE
BALMORAL CASTLE AND GARDENS
Inver
Invergelder
Easter Balmoral
ROYAL LOCHNAGAR DISTILLERY VISITOR CENTRE
Birkhall
BRAEMAR CASTLE
BRAEMAR
Invercauld House
Mill of Sterin
Lui Water
Glen Lui
Allanaquoich
Braemar
BRAEMAR HIGHLAND HERITAGE CENTRE
KINDROCHIT CASTLE
Glen Gelder
Aucholzie
Mar Lodge
Claybokie
Tomintoul
Ballochbuie Forest
Forest of Mar
INVEREY
LINN OF DEE
Muir
Inverey
DEESIDE AND
LINN OF MUICK WATERFALL
Auchallater
Muick
Glen Muick
Dee
BALMORAL FOREST
Geldie Burn
CARN LIATH
LOCHNAGAR
Glen Ey
Ey Burn
NO
Callater Burn
LOCHNAGAR
CONACHCRAIG
GLENMUICK VISITOR CENTRE
FASHEILACH
Allt Connie
Spittal of Glenmuick
Bynack Burn
Baddoch
A93
Glen Callater
Loch Callater
Dubh Loch
Glen Mark
Glas-allt Shiel
Loch Muick
CARN BHAC
CAIRN BANNOCH
BROAD CAIRN
Glen Lee
AN SOCACH
Clunie Water
CARN AN TUIRC
141
142
BEINN IUTHARN MHOR
Loch Vrotachan
TOLMOUNT
Glen Doll
Water of Unich
GLENSHEE SKI CENTRE
LAIR OF ALDARARIE
Loch nan Eun
Tilt
THE CAIRNWELL
Glendoll Lodge
GLAS MAOL
Devil's Elbow
Loch Loch
Glendoll Forest
Braedownie
Loch Brandy

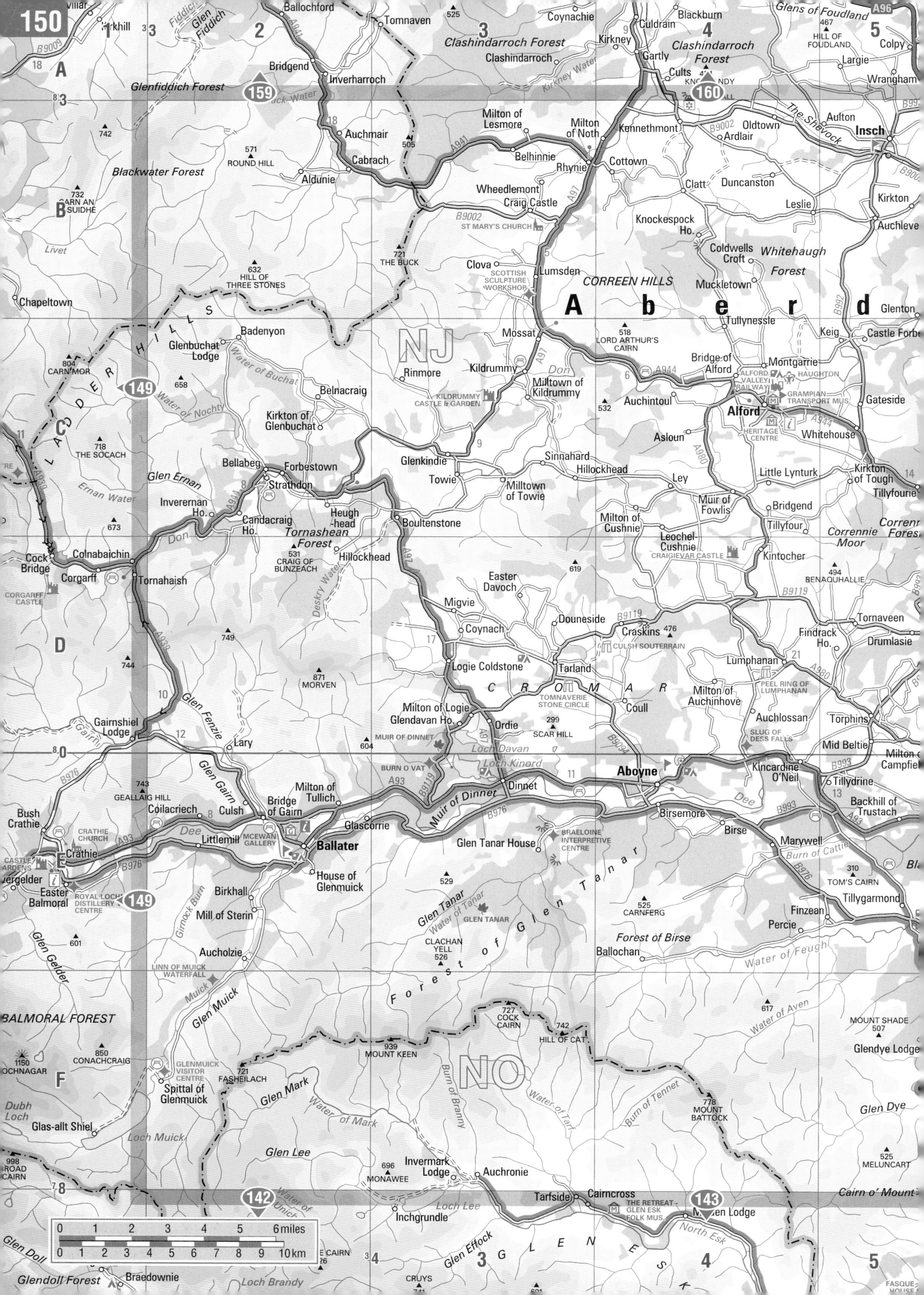
Ballochford
Tomnaven
Coynachie
Blackburn
Glens of Foudland
Culdrain
Kirkney
Gartly
Clashindarroch Forest
Clashindarroch
Glen Fiddich
Bridgend
Inverharroch
Cults
Glenfiddich Forest
159
160
Largie
Wrangham
Colpy
HILL OF FOUDLAND
Milton of Lesmore
Milton of Noth
Kennethmont
Oldtown
Ardlair
Aulton
Insch
The Shevock
Auchmair
ROUND HILL
Belhinnie
Cabrach
Rhynie
Cottown
Aldunie
Blackwater Forest
Clatt
Duncanston
Wheedlemont
Craig Castle
Leslie
Kirkton
CARN AN SUIDHE
ST MARY'S CHURCH
Knockespock Ho.
Auchleven
Livet
THE BUCK
Coldwells Croft
Whitehaugh Forest
Clova
SCOTTISH SCULPTURE WORKSHOP
Lumsden
CORREEN HILLS
HILL OF THREE STONES
Muckletown
Chapeltown
Aberd
Glenton
LADDER HILLS
Mossat
Tullynessle
LORD ARTHUR'S CAIRN
Keig
Castle Forbes
Badenyon
Glenbuchat Lodge
NJ
Bridge of Alford
Montgarrie
CARN MOR
Water of Buchat
Rinmore
Kildrummy
Milltown of Kildrummy
ALFORD VALLEY RAILWAY
HAUGHTON
149
Water of Nochty
Belnacraig
KILDRUMMY CASTLE & GARDEN
Auchintoul
GRAMPIAN TRANSPORT MUS
Gateside
Kirkton of Glenbuchat
Alford
HERITAGE CENTRE
Whitehouse
THE SOCACH
Asloun
Glenkindie
Sinnahard
Hillockhead
Bellabeg
Forbestown
Little Lynturk
Kirkton of Tough
Glen Ernan
Strathdon
Towie
Milltown of Towie
Ley
Tillyfourie
Ernan Water
Muir of Fowlis
Bridgend
Inverernan Ho.
Heugh-head
Boultenstone
Milton of Cushnie
Candacraig Ho.
Tornashean Forest
Tillyfour
Corrennie Moor
Correnn Fores
Leochel-Cushnie
Cock Bridge
Colnabaichin
CRAIG OF BUNZEACH
Hillockhead
CRAIGIEVAR CASTLE
Kintocher
Corgarff
Tornahaish
CORGARFF CASTLE
Easter Davoch
BENAQUHALLIE
Deskry Water
Migvie
Douneside
Tornaveen
Coynach
Craskins
Findrack Ho.
Drumlasie
CULSH SOUTERRAIN
Logie Coldstone
Tarland
Lumphanan
MORVEN
CROMAR
PEEL RING OF LUMPHANAN
TOMNAVERIE STONE CIRCLE
Milton of Auchinhove
Glen Fenzie
Milton of Logie
Coull
Glendavan Ho.
Auchlossan
Torphins
Gairnshiel Lodge
Ordie
SCAR HILL
SLUG OF DESS FALLS
Lary
MUIR OF DINNET
Mid Beltie
Loch Davan
Loch Kinord
Milton of Campfield
BURN O VAT
Aboyne
Kincardine O'Neil
Glen Gairn
Dinnet
Tillydrine
GEALLAIG HILL
Milton of Tullich
Muir of Dinnet
Backhill of Trustach
Bush
Crathie
Coilacriech
Bridge of Gairn
Culsh
Birsemore
CRATHIE CHURCH
Glascorrie
Birse
Dee
Littlemill
MCEWAN GALLERY
Ballater
Glen Tanar House
BRAELOINE INTERPRETIVE CENTRE
Marywell
Burn of Cattie
Crathie
House of Glenmuick
TOM'S CAIRN
Easter Balmoral
ROYAL LOCHNAGAR DISTILLERY CENTRE
Birkhall
Glen Tanar
Water of Tanar
GLEN TANAR
CARNFERG
Tillygarmond
Mill of Sterin
Finzean
Percie
Girnock Burn
Forest of Glen Tanar
Forest of Birse
Glen Gelder
Aucholzie
CLACHAN YELL
Ballochan
Water of Feugh
LINN OF MUICK WATERFALL
Glen Muick
Water of Aven
BALMORAL FOREST
COCK CAIRN
MOUNT SHADE
HILL OF CAT
Glendye Lodge
CONACHCRAIG
MOUNT KEEN
LOCHNAGAR
GLENMUICK VISITOR CENTRE
FASHEILACH
NO
Burn of Branny
Water of Tarf
Burn of Tennet
MOUNT BATTOCK
Spittal of Glenmuick
Glen Mark
Water of Mark
Glen Dye
Dubh Loch
Glas-allt Shiel
Loch Muick
Glen Lee
MELUNCART
ROAD CAIRN
MONAWEE
Invermark Lodge
Auchronie
Cairn o' Mount
142
Water of Unich
Tarfside
Cairncross
THE RETREAT - GLEN ESK FOLK MUS.
143
Millden Lodge
Loch Lee
Inchgrundle
North Esk
0 1 2 3 4 5 6 miles
0 1 2 3 4 5 6 7 8 9 10 km
Glen Doll
Glen Effock
GLEN ESK
Glendoll Forest
Braedownie
Loch Brandy
CRUYS
FASQUE HOUSE

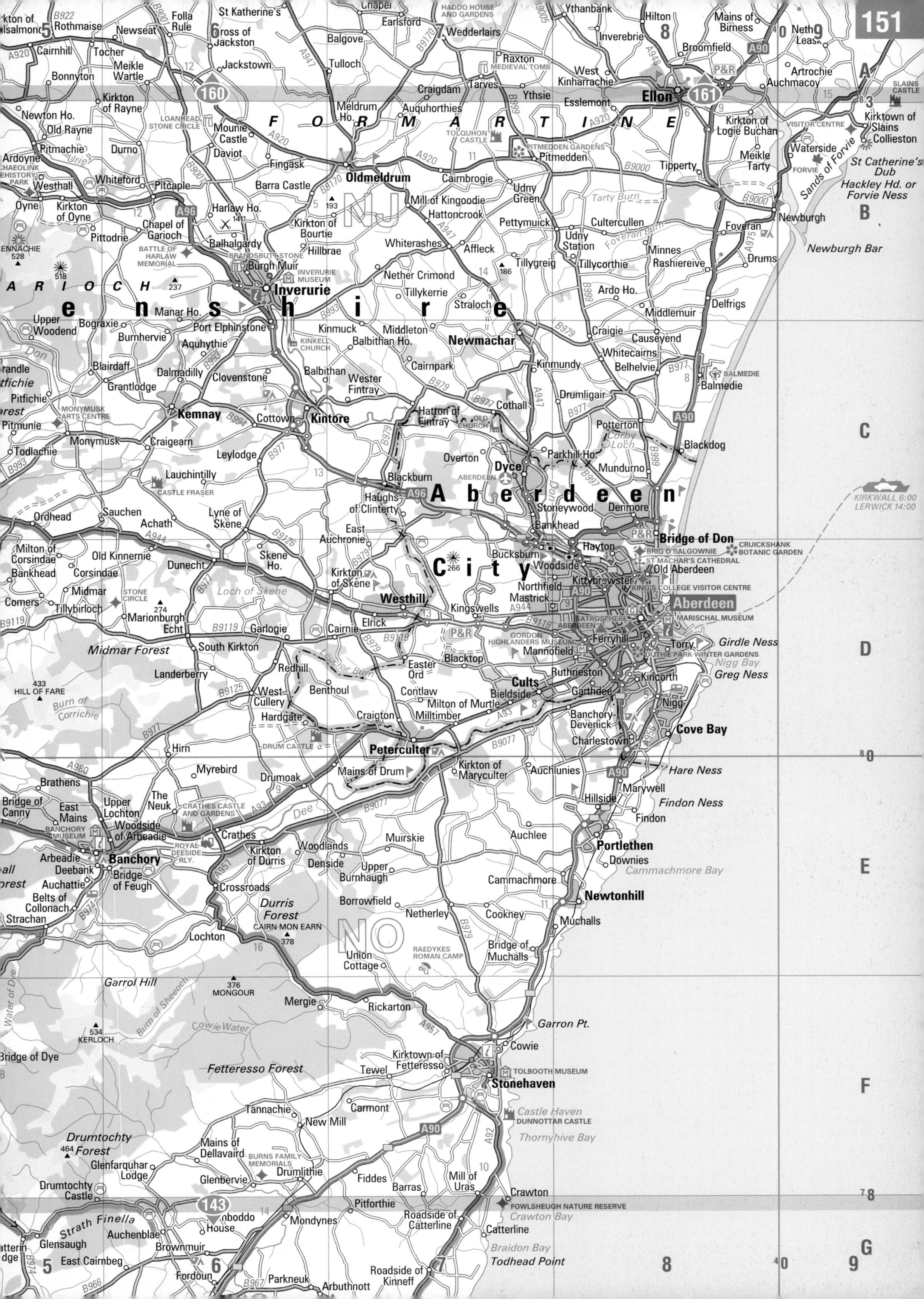

FORMARTINE
Aberdeenshire
GARIOCH
Aberdeen City
NJ
NO
Ellon
Oldmeldrum
Inverurie
INVERURIE MUSEUM
Kintore
Kemnay
Newmachar
Dyce
ABERDEEN
Westhill
Aberdeen
Bridge of Don
Cults
Peterculter
Banchory
Portlethen
Newtonhill
Stonehaven
Cove Bay
Balmedie
Newburgh
Pitmedden
Tarves
Udny Green
Ythsie
Esslemont
Raxton
Wedderlairs
Earlsford
Balgove
Tulloch
Chapel
HADDO HOUSE AND GARDENS
Ythanbank
Hilton
Mains of Birness
Inverebrie
Broomfield
Neth Leask
Artrochie
Auchmacoy
West Kinharrachie
SLAINS CASTLE
Kirktown of Slains
Collieston
Waterside
VISITOR CENTRE
FORVIE
St Catherine's Dub
Sands of Forvie
Hackley Hd. or Forvie Ness
Kirkton of Logie Buchan
Meikle Tarty
Tipperty
Foveran
Drums
Newburgh Bar
Minnes
Rashierieve
Tillycorthie
Udny Station
Cultercullen
Pettymuick
Tillygreig
Affleck
Ardo Ho.
Delfrigs
Middlemuir
Craigie
Causeyend
Whitecairns
Belhelvie
BALMEDIE
Kinmundy
Drumligair
Potterton
Corby Loch
Blackdog
Parkhill Ho.
Mundurno
Denmore
Stoneywood
Bankhead
Hayton
BRIG O' BALGOWNIE
CRUICKSHANK BOTANIC GARDEN
ST MACHAR'S CATHEDRAL
Old Aberdeen
KING'S COLLEGE VISITOR CENTRE
MARISCHAL MUSEUM
SATROSPHERE
Kittybrewster
Woodside
Bucksburn
Northfield
Mastrick
Kingswells
Ferryhill
Torry
Girdle Ness
DUTHIE PARK WINTER GARDENS
Nigg Bay
Greg Ness
Kincorth
Nigg
Garthdee
Ruthrieston
Mannofield
GORDON HIGHLANDERS MUSEUM
Bieldside
Banchory-Devenick
Charlestown
Hare Ness
Maryculter
Kirkton of Maryculter
Auchlunies
Hillside
Findon Ness
Findon
Auchlee
Downies
Cammachmore Bay
Cammachmore
Cookney
Muchalls
Bridge of Muchalls
Netherley
RAEDYKES ROMAN CAMP
Garron Pt.
Cowie
TOLBOOTH MUSEUM
Castle Haven
DUNNOTTAR CASTLE
Thornyhive Bay
Crawton
FOWLSHEUGH NATURE RESERVE
Crawton Bay
Catterline
Braidon Bay
Todhead Point
KIRKWALL 6:00
LERWICK 14:00
Skene Ho.
Lyne of Skene
Kirkton of Skene
Loch of Skene
East Auchronie
Elrick
Cairnie
Garlogie
Echt
Marionburgh
South Kirkton
Midmar Forest
Landerberry
HILL OF FARE
Burn of Corrichie
West Cullery
Hardgate
DRUM CASTLE
Mains of Drum
Drumoak
Myrebird
Hirn
Brathens
Bridge of Canny
East Mains
Upper Lochton
The Neuk
CRATHES CASTLE AND GARDENS
Woodside of Arbeadie
Crathes
ROYAL DEESIDE RLY.
BANCHORY MUSEUM
Arbeadie
Deebank
Bridge of Feugh
Auchattie
Belts of Collonach
Strachan
Kirkton of Durris
Woodlands
Denside
Muirskie
Upper Burnhaugh
Crossroads
Durris Forest
CAIRN MON EARN
Borrowfield
Lochton
Union Cottage
Garrol Hill
MONGOUR
Mergie
Rickarton
KERLOCH
Cowie Water
Bridge of Dye
Fetteresso Forest
Kirktown of Fetteresso
Tewel
Tannachie
Carmont
New Mill
Drumtochty Forest
Mains of Dellavaird
BURNS FAMILY MEMORIALS
Drumlithie
Glenbervie
Glenfarquhar Lodge
Drumtochty Castle
Fiddes
Barras
Mill of Uras
Pitforthie
Mondynes
Roadside of Catterline
Strath Finella
Glensaugh
Auchenblae
Brownmuir
East Cairnbeg
Fordoun
Parkneuk
Arbuthnott
Roadside of Kinneff
Redhill
Benthoul
Contlaw
Easter Ord
Blacktop
Milton of Murtle
Milltimber
Craigton
Blackburn
Haughs of Clinterty
Overton
Hatton of Fintray
Cothall
Cairnpark
Wester Fintray
Balbithan
Middleton
Balbithan Ho.
Kinmuck
KINKELL CHURCH
Tillykerrie
Straloch
Nether Crimond
Whiterashes
Hattoncrook
Mill of Kingoodie
Cairnbrogie
Craigdam
Auquhorthies
Meldrum Ho.
Fingask
Barra Castle
Kirkton of Bourtie
Hillbrae
Balhalgardy
Harlaw Ho.
BATTLE OF HARLAW MEMORIAL
BRANDSBUTT STONE
Burgh Muir
Manar Ho.
Port Elphinstone
Aquhythie
Clovenstone
Dalmadilly
Blairdaff
Grantlodge
Cottown
Leylodge
Craigearn
Monymusk
MONYMUSK ARTS CENTRE
Pitmunie
Todlachie
Lauchintilly
CASTLE FRASER
Sauchen
Achath
Ordhead
Milton of Corsindae
Corsindae
Old Kinnernie
Dunecht
Bankhead
Midmar
STONE CIRCLE
Tillybirloch
Comers
Upper Woodend
Bograxie
Burnhervie
Chapel of Garioch
Pittodrie
Kirkton of Oyne
Oyne
Westhall
Whiteford
Pitcaple
Daviot
Mounie Castle
LOANHEAD STONE CIRCLE
Durno
Pitmachie
Old Rayne
Newton Ho.
Kirkton of Rayne
Bonnyton
Meikle Wartle
Tocher
Cairnhill
Rothmaise
Newseat
Folla Rule
St Katherine's
Cross of Jackston
Jackstown
TOLQUHON CASTLE
PITMEDDEN GARDENS
Tarty Burn
Foveran Burn
Leuchar Burn
Dee
Don
A90
A96
A947
A920
A944
A93
A980
A957
A92
A956
A975
B9000
B979
B977
B9119
B9077
B993
160
161
143

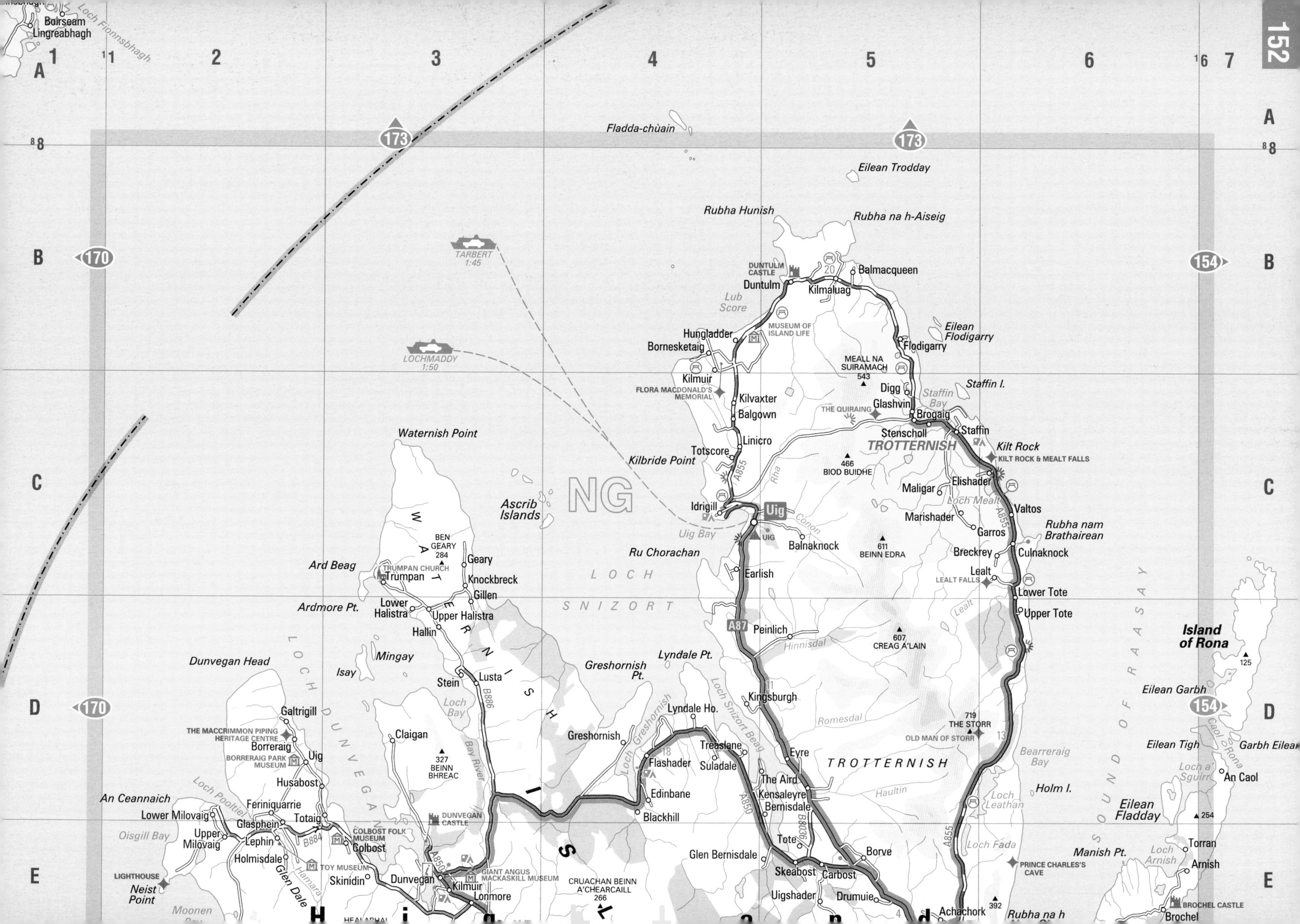
Boirseam
Lingreabhagh
Loch Fionnsbhagh
Fladda-chùain
Eilean Trodday
Rubha Hunish
Rubha na h-Aiseig
TARBERT 1:45
LOCHMADDY 1:50
DUNTULM CASTLE
Duntulm
Balmacqueen
Kilmaluag
Lub Score
MUSEUM OF ISLAND LIFE
Eilean Flodigarry
Flodigarry
Hungladder
Bornesketaig
Kilmuir
FLORA MACDONALD'S MEMORIAL
MEALL NA SUIRAMACH 543
Digg
Staffin Bay
Staffin I.
Kilvaxter
Balgown
THE QUIRAING
Glashvin
Brogaig
Staffin
Stenscholl
TROTTERNISH
Kilt Rock
KILT ROCK & MEALT FALLS
Waternish Point
Linicro
Totscore
Kilbride Point
466 BIOD BUIDHE
A855
Rha
Elishader
Maligar
Loch Mealt
Valtos
NG
Ascrib Islands
Idrigill
Uig
Conon
Uig Bay
UIG
Marishader
Garros
Rubha nam Brathairean
Balnaknock
611 BEINN EDRA
Breckrey
Culnaknock
Ru Chorachan
BEN GEARY 284
Geary
Ard Beag
TRUMPAN CHURCH
Trumpan
Knockbreck
LOCH
Earlish
Lealt
LEALT FALLS
Lower Tote
Gillen
SNIZORT
Lower Halistra
Upper Halistra
Ardmore Pt.
Upper Tote
A87
Peinlich
WATERNISH
Hallin
Hinnisdal
607 CREAG A'LAIN
Island of Rona
125
Mingay
Lyndale Pt.
Dunvegan Head
Isay
Stein
Lusta
Greshornish Pt.
Kingsburgh
Eilean Garbh
LOCH DUNVEGAN
Loch Bay
B886
Lyndale Ho.
Loch Snizort Beag
Romesdal
Galtrigill
Claigan
Greshornish
Loch Greshornish
719 THE STORR
OLD MAN OF STORR
THE MACCRIMMON PIPING HERITAGE CENTRE
Borreraig
Treaslane
Eyre
Eilean Tigh
Garbh Eilean
Caol Rona
SOUND OF RAASAY
BORRERAIG PARK MUSEUM
Uig
327 BEINN BHREAC
Bay River
Flashader
Suladale
TROTTERNISH
Bearreraig Bay
Loch a' Sguirr
An Caol
Husabost
The Aird
Kensaleyre
Haultin
Holm I.
An Ceannaich
Loch Pooltiel
Feriniquarrie
Edinbane
Bernisdale
Loch Leathan
Eilean Fladday
Lower Milovaig
Glasphein
Totaig
DUNVEGAN CASTLE
Blackhill
A850
254
Oisgill Bay
Upper Milovaig
Lephin
B884
COLBOST FOLK MUSEUM
Colbost
B8036
Tote
Torran
Holmisdale
Loch Fada
Manish Pt.
Loch Arnish
Glen Bernisdale
Borve
Arnish
LIGHTHOUSE
Neist Point
Glen Dale
Hamara
TOY MUSEUM
Skinidin
Dunvegan
GIANT ANGUS MACKASKILL MUSEUM
Kilmuir
Skeabost
Carbost
PRINCE CHARLES'S CAVE
Lonmore
CRUACHAN BEINN A'CHEARCAILL 266
Uigshader
Drumuie
392
BROCHEL CASTLE
Moonen Bay
Achachork
Rubha na h
Brochel
170
173
154

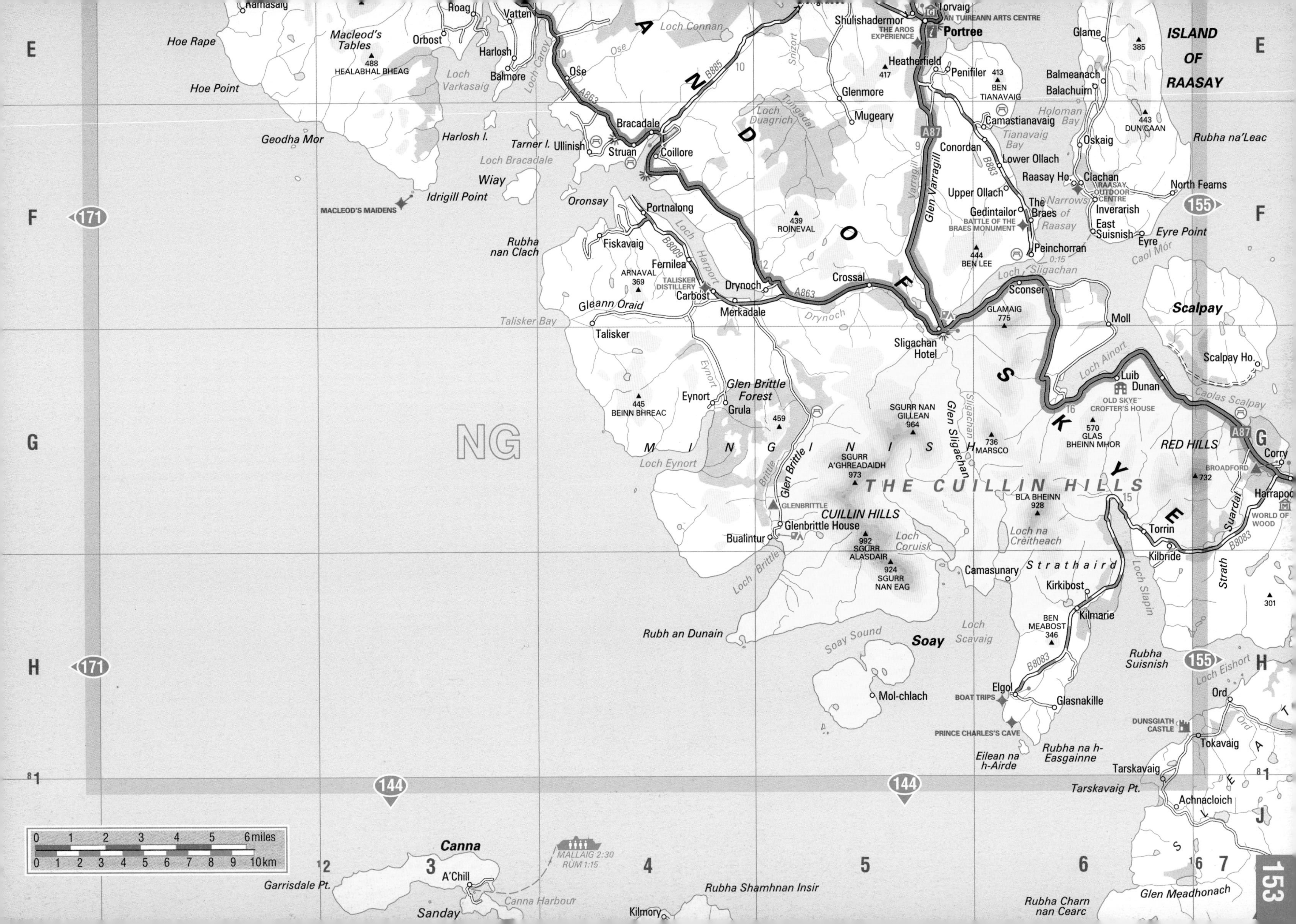
ISLAND OF RAASAY
Rubha na'Leac
North Fearns
Eyre Point
Eyre
Caol Mòr
DUN CAAN
443
385
Glame
Balmeanach
Balachuirn
Oskaig
Clachan
RAASAY OUTDOOR CENTRE
Inverarish
East Suisnish
Holoman Bay
Tianavaig Bay
The Narrows of Raasay
Raasay Ho.
Lower Ollach
Camastianavaig
BEN TIANAVAIG
413
Penifiler
Portree
AN TUIREANN ARTS CENTRE
Heatherfield
Conordan
Upper Ollach
Gedintailor
The Braes
BATTLE OF THE BRAES MONUMENT
Peinchorran
BEN LEE
444
Sconser
Loch Sligachan
GLAMAIG
775
Moll
Scalpay
Scalpay Ho.
Caolas Scalpay
Loch Ainort
Luib
Dunan
OLD SKYE CROFTER'S HOUSE
GLAS BHEINN MHOR
570
RED HILLS
BROADFORD
732
Corry
Harrapool
WORLD OF WOOD
Suardal
Strath
301
Torrin
Kilbride
Loch Slapin
Strathaird
Kilmarie
Kirkibost
BEN MEABOST
346
Glasnakille
Elgol
BOAT TRIPS
PRINCE CHARLES'S CAVE
Eilean na h-Airde
Rubha na h-Easgainne
Rubha Suisnish
DUNSGIATH CASTLE
Tokavaig
Ord
Loch Eishort
Achnacloich
Tarskavaig
Tarskavaig Pt.
Glen Meadhonach
Rubha Charn nan Cearc
SLEAT
BLA BHEINN
928
Loch na Crèitheach
MARSCO
736
Sligachan
Glen Sligachan
Sligachan Hotel
Glen Varragill
THE CUILLIN HILLS
SKYE
SGURR NAN GILLEAN
964
SGURR A'GHREADAIDH
973
SGURR ALASDAIR
992
SGURR NAN EAG
924
CUILLIN HILLS
Loch Coruisk
Camasunary
Loch Scavaig
Soay
Soay Sound
Mol-chlach
Glenbrittle House
GLENBRITTLE
Glen Brittle
Loch Brittle
Bualintur
Rubh an Dunain
MINGINISH
Glen Brittle Forest
459
Grula
Eynort
Loch Eynort
BEINN BHREAC
445
Talisker
Gleann Oraid
Talisker Bay
Carbost
TALISKER DISTILLERY
Fernilea
ARNAVAL
369
Fiskavaig
Portnalong
Loch Harport
Drynoch
Merkadale
Crossal
Drynoch
ROINEVAL
439
Loch Duagrich
Tungadal
Glenmore
Mugeary
417
Shulishadermor
THE AROS EXPERIENCE
Snizort
Loch Connan
Coillore
Bracadale
Struan
Ullinish
Tarner I.
Oronsay
Loch Bracadale
Ose
Loch Caroy
Vatten
Harlosh
Balmore
Harlosh I.
Wiay
Rubha nan Clach
Idrigill Point
MACLEOD'S MAIDENS
Roag
Orbost
Loch Varkasaig
Macleod's Tables
HEALABHAL BHEAG
488
Geodha Mor
Ramasaig
Hoe Rape
Hoe Point
NG
MALLAIG 2:30
RUM 1:15
Canna Harbour
Canna
A'Chill
Sanday
Garrisdale Pt.
Rubha Shamhnan Insir
Kilmory
A863
A87
B885
B883
B8009
B8083
155
171
144
E
F
G
H
J
3
4
5
6
7
12
81
0 1 2 3 4 5 6 miles
0 1 2 3 4 5 6 7 8 9 10km

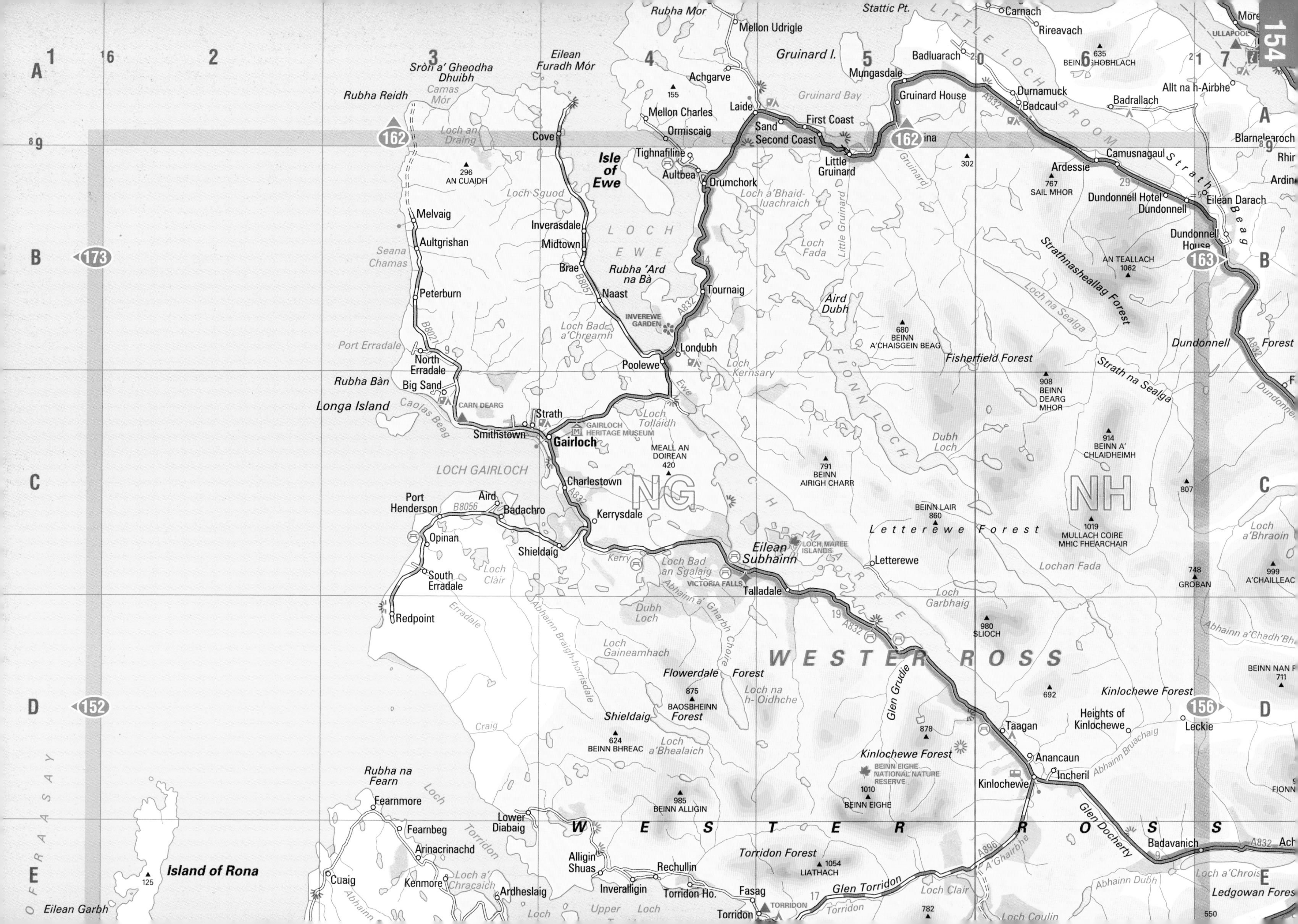

Rubha Mor
Mellon Udrigle
Static Pt.
Carnach
Rireavach
Little Loch Broom
Ullapool
Sròn a' Gheodha Dhuibh
Eilean Furadh Mór
Rubha Reidh
Camas Mór
Gruinard I.
Gruinard Bay
Badluarach
Mungasdale
Gruinard House
Durnamuck
Badcaul
Badrallach
Allt na h-Airbhe
Achgarve
Mellon Charles
Ormiscaig
Laide
Sand
Second Coast
First Coast
Little Gruinard
Cove
Loch an Draing
Isle of Ewe
Tighnafiline
Aultbea
Drumchork
Camusnagaul
Ardessie
767 Sail Mhor
Dundonnell Hotel
Dundonnell
Dundonnell House
Eilean Darach
Strath Beag
Blarnalearoch
296 An Cuaidh
Loch Sguod
Loch a'Bhaid-luachraich
Loch Fada
Little Gruinard
Melvaig
Aultgrishan
Seana Chamas
Peterburn
Inverasdale
Midtown
Brae
Naast
Loch Ewe
Rubha 'Ard na Bà
Tournaig
Aird Dubh
An Teallach 1062
Strathnasheallag Forest
Loch na Sealga
Inverewe Garden
Loch Bad a'Chreamh
Londubh
Poolewe
Loch Kernsary
680 Beinn a'Chaisgein Beag
Fisherfield Forest
Dundonnell Forest
Strath na Sealga
Port Erradale
North Erradale
Rubha Bàn
Big Sand
Longa Island
Caolas Beag
Carn Dearg
Strath
Smithstown
Gairloch
Gairloch Heritage Museum
Loch Tollaidh
Meall an Doirean 420
Fionn Loch
908 Beinn Dearg Mhor
914 Beinn a' Chlaidheimh
Dubh Loch
791 Beinn Airigh Charr
Loch Gairloch
Charlestown
NG
NH
Port Henderson
Aird
Badachro
Kerrysdale
Beinn Lair 860
Letterewe Forest
1019 Mullach Coire Mhic Fhearchair
Loch a'Bhraoin
Opinan
Shieldaig
Eilean Subhainn
Loch Maree Islands
Loch Maree
Letterewe
Lochan Fada
748 Groban
999 A'Chailleach
South Erradale
Loch Clàir
Loch Bad an Sgalaig
Victoria Falls
Talladale
Loch Garbhaig
Redpoint
Erradale
Abhainn Braigh-horrisdale
Dubh Loch
Abhainn a' Gharbh Choire
980 Slioch
Abhainn a'Chadh'Bhe
Loch Gaineamhach
Wester Ross
Flowerdale Forest
875 Baosbheinn Forest
Loch na h-Oidhche
Glen Grudie
692
Kinlochewe Forest
Beinn nan F 711
Craig
Shieldaig
624 Beinn Bhreac
Loch a'Bhealaich
878
Taagan
Heights of Kinlochewe
Leckie
Anancaun
Beinn Eighe National Nature Reserve
Incheril
Abhainn Bruachaig
Kinlochewe
Rubha na Fearn
Fearnmore
Loch Torridon
985 Beinn Alligin
1010 Beinn Eighe
Fionn
Lower Diabaig
Fearnbeg
Arinacrinachd
Glen Docherty
Badavanich
Alligin Shuas
Torridon Forest
1054 Liathach
A'Ghairbhe
Island of Rona
125
Cuaig
Kenmore
Loch a' Chracaich
Ardheslaig
Rechullin
Inveralligin
Torridon Ho.
Fasag
Torridon
Glen Torridon
Loch Clair
Abhainn Dubh
Loch a'Chrois
Ledgowan Forest
Eilean Garbh
Upper Loch Torridon
782
Loch Coulin
Raasay
A832
A896
B8021
B8056
B8057
162
163
173
152
156

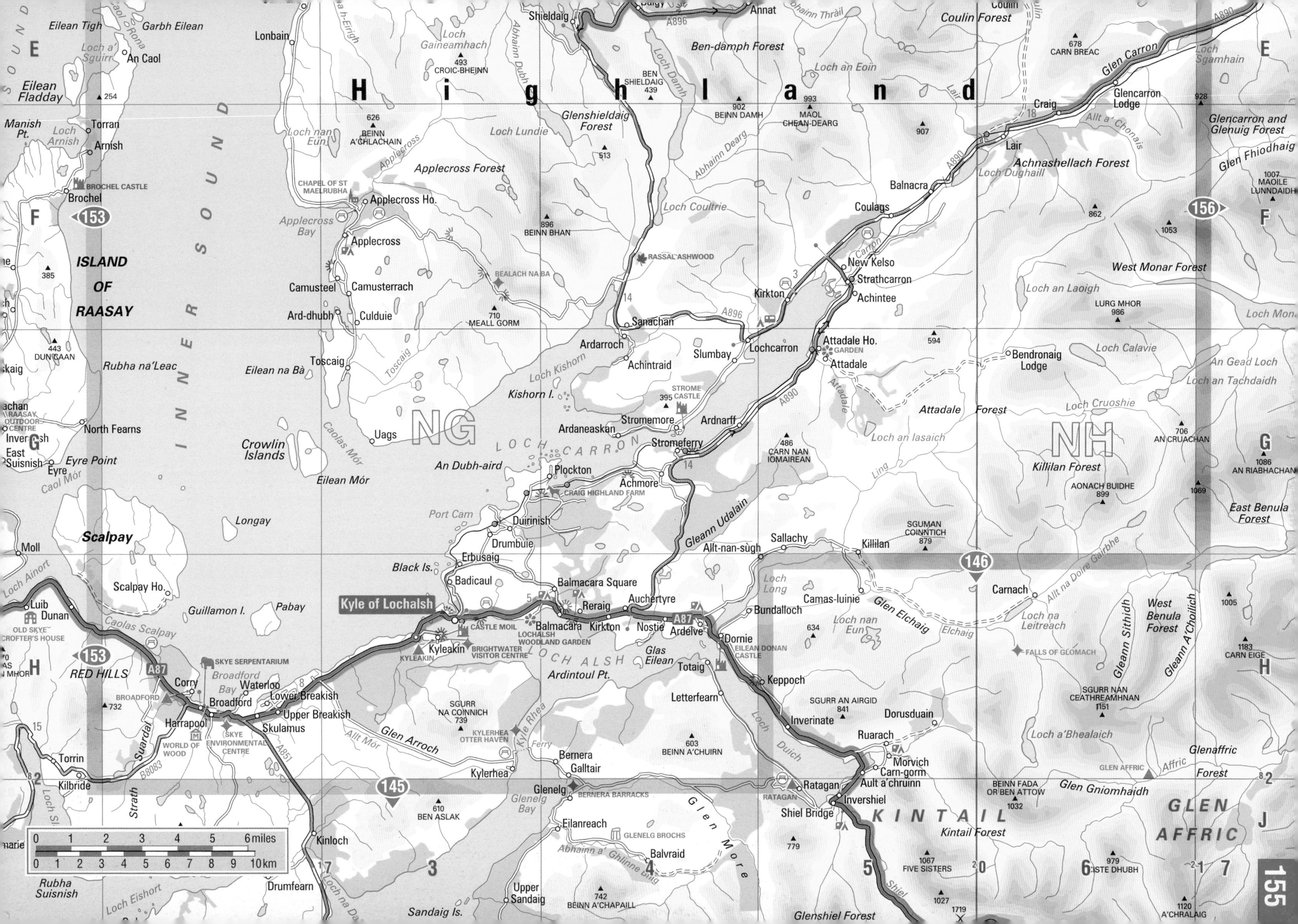

Highland
INNER SOUND
ISLAND OF RAASAY
Scalpay
Kyle of Lochalsh
LOCH CARRON
LOCH ALSH
KINTAIL
GLEN AFFRIC
NG
NH
Applecross
Applecross Forest
Applecross Ho.
Shieldaig
Ben-damph Forest
Coulin Forest
Lochcarron
Strathcarron
Achnashellach Forest
West Monar Forest
Attadale Forest
Killilan Forest
West Benula Forest
East Benula Forest
Glen Elchaig
Dornie
EILEAN DONAN CASTLE
Plockton
Balmacara
Kyleakin
Broadford
Glenelg
Shiel Bridge
Kintail Forest
Glenshiel Forest
Glen Arroch
RED HILLS
Crowlin Islands
Longay
Pabay
Guillamon I.
Lower Breakish
Upper Breakish
Skulamus
Harrapool
Corry
Kinloch
Drumfearn
Torrin
Kilbride
Luib
Dunan
Moll
Brochel
BROCHEL CASTLE
Arnish
Torran
An Caol
Eilean Tigh
Garbh Eilean
Eilean Fladday
Manish Pt.
North Fearns
Eyre Point
Scalpay Ho.
Toscaig
Camusteel
Camusterrach
Culduie
Ard-dhubh
Uags
Eilean Mór
Eilean na Bà
Rubha na'Leac
Lonbain
Sandaig Is.
Upper Sandaig
Eilanreach
Balvraid
Bernera
Galltair
Kylerhea
Letterfearn
Totaig
Ratagan
Invershiel
Ault a'chruinn
Carn-gorm
Morvich
Ruarach
Dorusduain
Inverinate
Keppoch
Bundalloch
Sallachy
Killilan
Camas-luinie
Carnach
Bendronaig Lodge
Attadale Ho.
Attadale
Achintee
New Kelso
Coulags
Balnacra
Lair
Craig
Glencarron Lodge
Glen Carron
Glencarron and Glenuig Forest
Kirkton
Slumbay
Ardnarff
Stromeferry
Stromemore
Achmore
Ardaneaskan
Achintraid
Sanachan
Ardarroch
Kishorn I.
Duirinish
Drumbuie
Erbusaig
Badicaul
Balmacara Square
Reraig
Auchertyre
Nostie
Ardelve
Black Is.
An Dubh-aird
Annat
Loch Duich
Glen More
Glen Gniomhaidh
Glenaffric Forest
Strath Suardal
SKYE SERPENTARIUM
CRAIG HIGHLAND FARM
STROME CASTLE
RASSAL ASHWOOD
BEALACH NA BA
FALLS OF GLOMACH
BERNERA BARRACKS
GLENELG BROCHS
FIVE SISTERS
BEN ASLAK
BEINN BHAN
MEALL GORM
0 1 2 3 4 5 6 miles
0 1 2 3 4 5 6 7 8 9 10 km

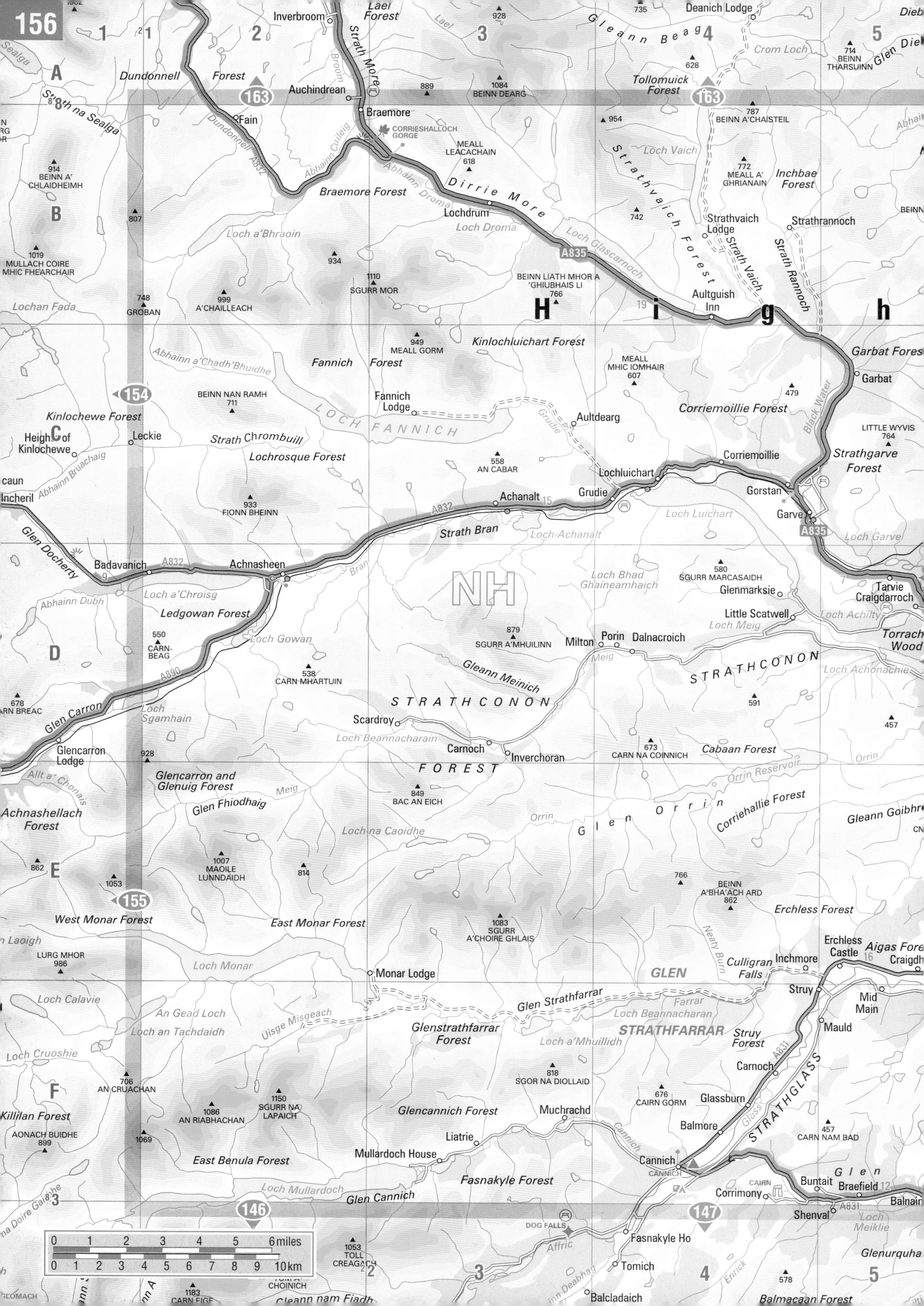

Inverbroom
Lael Forest
Strath More
Deanich Lodge
Gleann Beag
Dundonnell Forest
Auchindrean
Braemore
Fain
CORRIESHALLOCH GORGE
BEINN DEARG
Tollomuick Forest
Crom Loch
BEINN THARSUINN
Glen Diebidale
Strath na Sealga
BEINN A' CHLAIDHEIMH
MEALL LEACACHAIN
BEINN A'CHAISTEIL
Loch Vaich
MEALL A' GHRIANAIN
Inchbae Forest
Braemore Forest
Dirrie More
Lochdrum
Loch Droma
Strathvaich Lodge
Strathrannoch
Strath Vaich
Strath Rannoch
Strathvaich Forest
Loch a'Bhraoin
MULLACH COIRE MHIC FHEARCHAIR
SGURR MOR
BEINN LIATH MHOR A 'GHIUBHAIS LI
Loch Glascarnoch
A835
Aultguish Inn
A'CHAILLEACH
GROBAN
Lochan Fada
Highland
Kinlochluichart Forest
MEALL GORM
Fannich Forest
MEALL MHIC IOMHAIR
Garbat Forest
Garbat
154
BEINN NAN RAMH
Fannich Lodge
LOCH FANNICH
Aultdearg
Corriemoillie Forest
Kinlochewe Forest
Heights of Kinlochewe
Leckie
Strath Chrombuill
Lochrosque Forest
AN CABAR
LITTLE WYVIS
Strathgarve Forest
Corriemoillie
Lochluichart
Grudie
Achanalt
Gorstan
Garve
Incheril
Glen Docherty
FIONN BHEINN
A832
Strath Bran
Loch Achanalt
Loch Luichart
Loch Garve
Badavanich
Achnasheen
NH
Loch Bhad Ghaineamhaich
SGURR MARCASAIDH
Glenmarksie
Tarvie
Craigdarroch
Loch a'Chroisg
Abhainn Dubh
Ledgowan Forest
Little Scatwell
Loch Achilty
Loch Meig
Torrachilty Wood
CARN-BEAG
Loch Gowan
SGURR A'MHUILINN
Milton
Porin
Dalnacroich
STRATHCONON
Loch Achonachie
Gleann Meinich
CARN MHARTUIN
A890
Glen Carron
Loch Sgamhain
STRATHCONON FOREST
Scardroy
Loch Beannacharain
Carnoch
Inverchoran
CARN NA COINNICH
Cabaan Forest
Orrin Reservoir
Glencarron Lodge
Glencarron and Glenuig Forest
Allt a' Chonais
Achnashellach Forest
Glen Fhiodhaig
BAC AN EICH
Glen Orrin
Corriehallie Forest
Gleann Goibhre
Loch na Caoidhe
MAOILE LUNNDAIDH
BEINN A'BHA'ACH ARD
Erchless Forest
155
West Monar Forest
East Monar Forest
SGURR A'CHOIRE GHLAIS
Neaty Burn
Erchless Castle
Aigas Forest
Craigdhu
LURG MHOR
Loch Monar
Monar Lodge
GLEN
Culligran Falls
Inchmore
Struy
Mid Main
Loch Calavie
Glen Strathfarrar
An Gead Loch
Loch an Tachdaidh
Uisge Misgeach
Glenstrathfarrar Forest
Loch Beannacharan
STRATHFARRAR
Struy Forest
Mauld
Loch a'Mhuillidh
Loch Cruoshie
AN CRUACHAN
SGOR NA DIOLLAID
Carnoch
A831
STRATHGLASS
CAIRN GORM
Glassburn
Killilan Forest
AN RIABHACHAN
SGURR NA LAPAICH
Glencannich Forest
Muchrachd
Balmore
CARN NAM BAD
AONACH BUIDHE
Liatrie
East Benula Forest
Mullardoch House
Cannich
Fasnakyle Forest
Loch Mullardoch
Glen Cannich
Buntait
Glen
Braefield
Corrimony
Balnain
146
147
DOG FALLS
Shenval
Loch Meiklie
Fasnakyle Ho
Affric
Glenurquhart
TOLL CREAGACH
Tomich
Balcladaich
Balmacaan Forest
CARN EIGE
Gleann nam Fiadh
0 1 2 3 4 5 6 miles
0 1 2 3 4 5 6 7 8 9 10 km

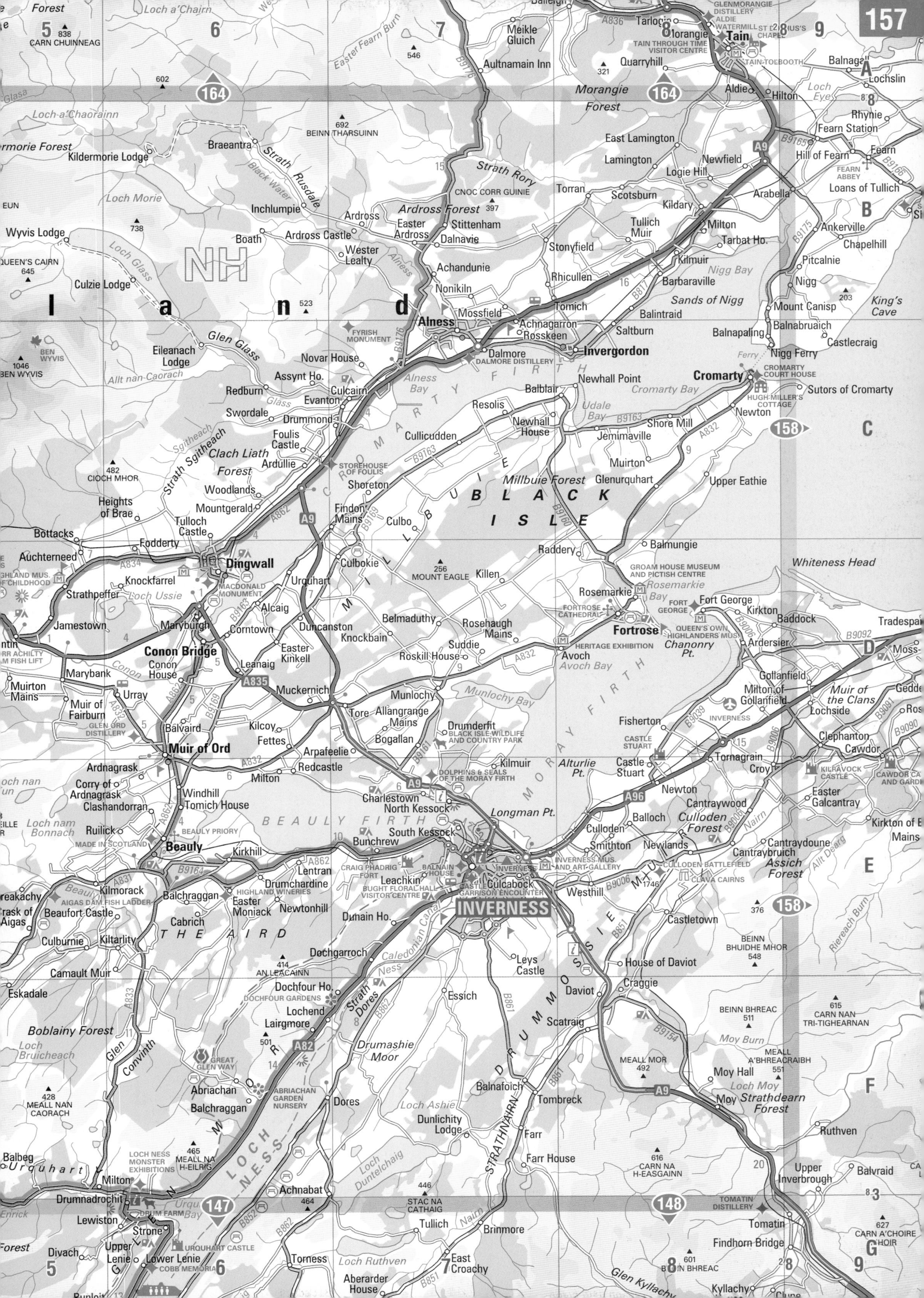

NH
Tain
Tarlogie
Morangie
Meikle Gluich
Aultnamain Inn
Quarryhill
Morangie Forest
Aldie
Hilton
Balnagall
Lochslin
Loch Eye
Rhynie
Fearn Station
Hill of Fearn
Fearn
Fearn Abbey
Loans of Tullich
East Lamington
Lamington
Newfield
Logie Hill
Strath Rory
Cnoc Corr Guinie
Torran
Scotsburn
Kildary
Arabella
Ardross Forest
Stittenham
Ardross
Easter Ardross
Dalnavie
Tullich Muir
Milton
Tarbat Ho.
Ankerville
Chapelhill
Stonyfield
Kilmuir
Nigg Bay
Pitcalnie
Nigg
Barbaraville
Sands of Nigg
Mount Canisp
King's Cave
Achandunie
Rhicullen
Nonikiln
Tomich
Balintraid
Balnabruaich
Balnapaling
Castlecraig
Nigg Ferry
Alness
Mossfield
Achnagarron
Rosskeen
Saltburn
Invergordon
Dalmore
Dalmore Distillery
Fyrish Monument
Novar House
Cromarty Firth
Newhall Point
Cromarty
Cromarty Court House
Sutors of Cromarty
Hugh Miller's Cottage
Cromarty Bay
Balblair
Udale Bay
Resolis
Newhall House
Shore Mill
Newton
Jemimaville
Cullicudden
Muirton
Glenurquhart
Upper Eathie
Alness Bay
Assynt Ho.
Redburn
Culcairn
Evanton
Swordale
Drummond
Foulis Castle
Ardullie
Storehouse of Foulis
Shoreton
Clach Liath Forest
Strath Sgitheach
Cioch Mhor
Woodlands
Mountgerald
Heights of Brae
Findon Mains
Culbo
Millbuie Forest
Black Isle
Millbuie
Tulloch Castle
Bottacks
Fodderty
Dingwall
Auchterneed
Strathpeffer
Knockfarrel
Loch Ussie
Macdonald Monument
Culbokie
Urquhart
Mount Eagle
Killen
Raddery
Balmungie
Groam House Museum and Pictish Centre
Rosemarkie
Rosemarkie Bay
Fortrose Cathedral
Fortrose
Whiteness Head
Fort George
Kirkton
Baddock
Tradespark
Queen's Own Highlanders Mus.
Chanonry Pt.
Ardersier
Alcaig
Jamestown
Maryburgh
Corntown
Duncanston
Knockbain
Belmaduthy
Rosehaugh Mains
Suddie
Roskill House
Avoch
Avoch Bay
Heritage Exhibition
Conon Bridge
Conon House
Easter Kinkell
Leanaig
Marybank
Muirton Mains
Muir of Fairburn
Urray
Glen Ord Distillery
Balvaird
Muckernich
Munlochy
Munlochy Bay
Tore
Allangrange Mains
Kilcoy
Fettes
Drumderfit
Black Isle Wildlife and Country Park
Bogallan
Arpafeelie
Redcastle
Muir of Ord
Ardnagrask
Corry of Ardnagrask
Milton
Kilmuir
Dolphins & Seals of the Moray Firth
Moray Firth
Alturlie Pt.
Castle Stuart
Fisherton
Inverness
Gollanfield
Milton of Gollanfield
Muir of the Clans
Lochside
Clephanton
Cawdor
Kilravock Castle
Tornagrain
Croy
Newton
Easter Galcantray
Windhill
Tomich House
Clashandorran
Charlestown
North Kessock
Longman Pt.
Beauly Firth
Loch nam Bonnach
Ruilick
Beauly Priory
Made in Scotland
Beauly
Bunchrew
South Kessock
Balloch
Culloden
Cantraywood
Culloden Forest
Smithton
Newlands
Kirkhill
Lentran
Craig Phadrig Fort
Balnain House
Leachkin
Bught Floral Hall Visitor Centre
Castle Garrison Encounter
Culcabock
Inverness Mus. and Art Gallery
Culloden Battlefield
Clava Cairns
Cantraydoune
Cantraybruich
Assich Forest
Westhill
Kilmorack
Aigas Dam Fish Ladder
Balchraggan
Highland Wineries
Drumchardine
Easter Moniack
Newtonhill
Beaufort Castle
Crask of Aigas
Cabrich
The Aird
Culburnie
Kiltarlity
Dunain Ho.
Castletown
Caledonian Canal
Camault Muir
Dochgarroch
An Leacainn
Leys Castle
House of Daviot
Beinn Bhuidhe Mhor
Eskadale
Dochfour Ho.
Dochfour Gardens
Strath Dores
Essich
Daviot
Craggie
Lochend
Lairgmore
Drumashie Moor
Drummossie Muir
Scatraig
Beinn Bhreac
Carn nan Tri-Tighearnan
Boblainy Forest
Loch Bruicheach
Glen Convinth
Great Glen Way
Moy Burn
Meall Mor
Meall a'Bhreacraibh
Abriachan
Abriachan Garden Nursery
Balchraggan
Dores
Balnafoich
Tombreck
Moy Hall
Loch Moy
Moy
Strathdearn Forest
Meall nan Caorach
Loch Ashie
Dunlichity Lodge
Strathnairn
Farr
Ruthven
Balbeg
Urquhart
Loch Ness Monster Exhibitions
Meall na h-Eilrig
Loch Ness
Loch Duntelchaig
Farr House
Carn na h-Easgainn
Upper Inverbrough
Balvraid
Milton
Drumnadrochit
Drum Farm
Urquhart Bay
Achnabat
Stac na Cathaig
Tomatin Distillery
Tomatin
Lewiston
Strone
Urquhart Castle
Tullich
Brinmore
Carn a'Choire Mhoir
Divach
Upper Lenie
Lower Lenie
Torness
Loch Ruthven
East Croachy
Aberarder House
Findhorn Bridge
Kyllachy
Glen Kyllachy
Wyvis Lodge
Culzie Lodge
Kildermorie Lodge
Loch Morie
Braeantra
Strath Rusdale
Inchlumpie
Boath
Ardross Castle
Wester Lealty
Beinn Tharsuinn
Loch a'Chairn
Carn Chuinneag
Easter Fearn Burn
Loch a'Chaorainn
Glen Glass
Eileanach Lodge
Allt nan Caorach
Ben Wyvis
Queen's Cairn
164
158
147
148
A9
A82
A835
A96

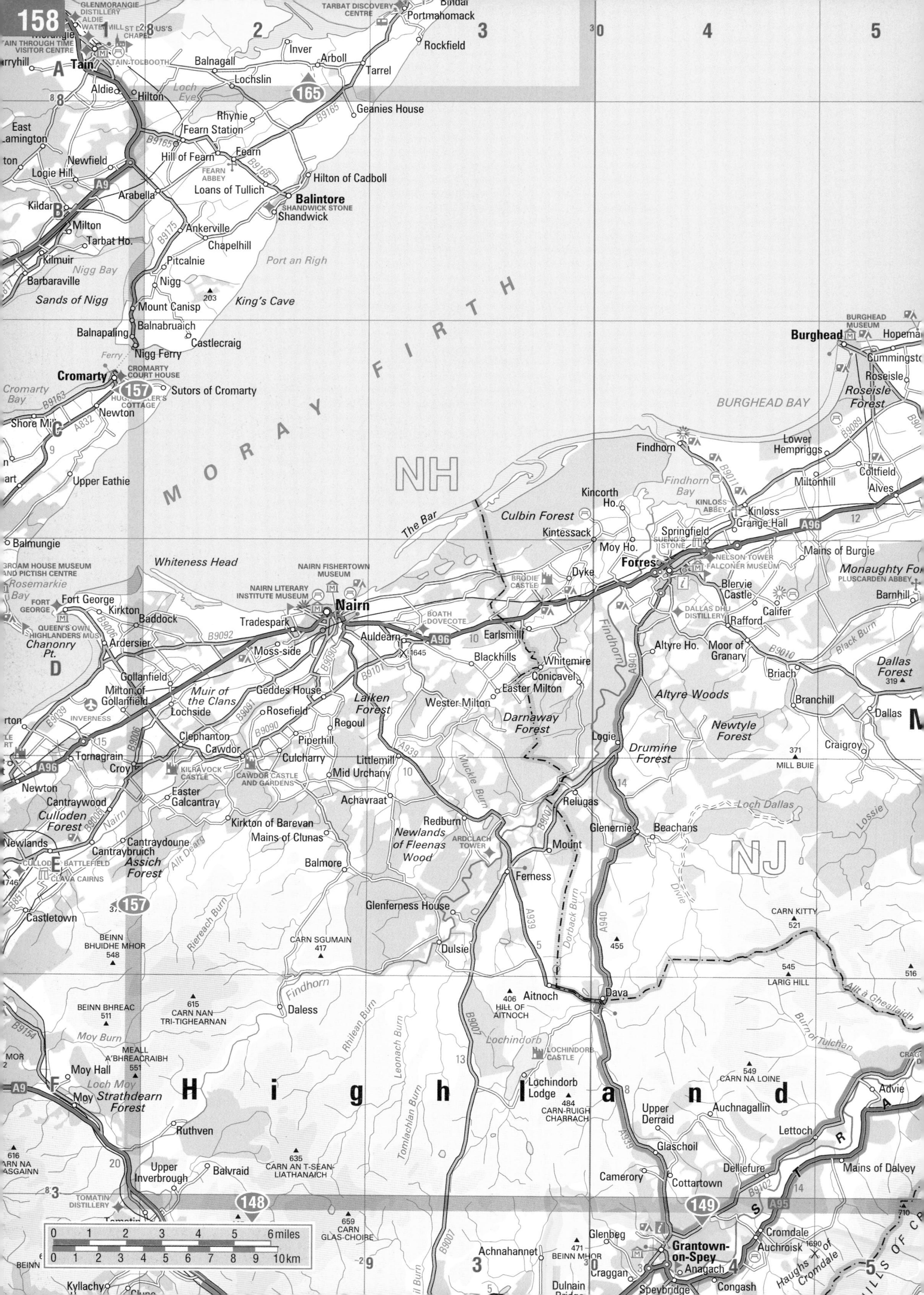
Tain
Portmahomack
Balintore
Cromarty
MORAY FIRTH
NH
NJ
Burghead
Findhorn
Forres
Nairn
Fort George
Culbin Forest
Darnaway Forest
Highland
Grantown-on-Spey
Dava
Lochindorb
Cawdor
Ardersier
Moy
0 1 2 3 4 5 6 miles
0 1 2 3 4 5 6 7 8 9 10 km

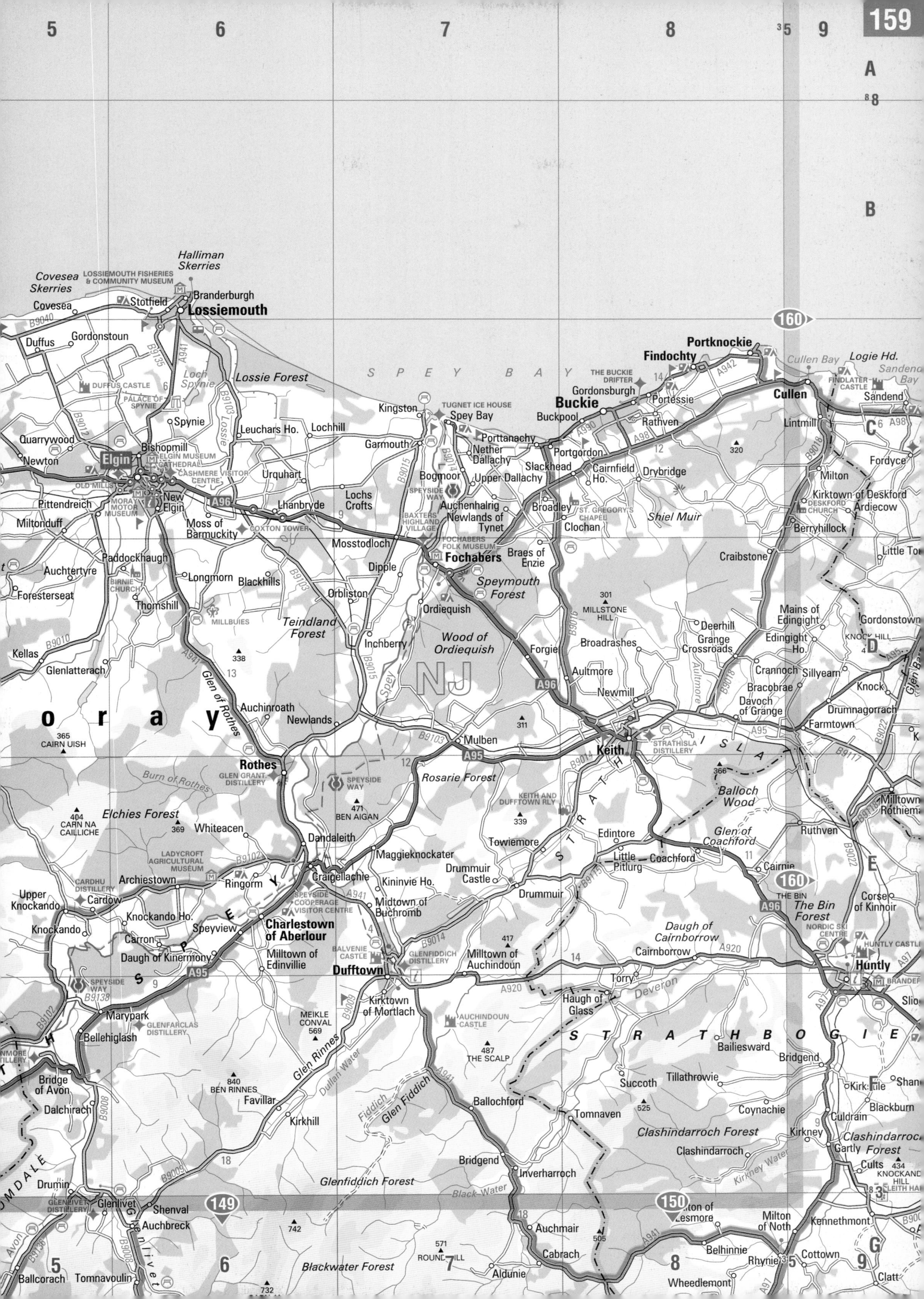

Halliman Skerries
Covesea Skerries
LOSSIEMOUTH FISHERIES & COMMUNITY MUSEUM
Covesea
Stotfield
Branderburgh
Lossiemouth
Duffus
Gordonstoun
Loch Spynie
Lossie Forest
DUFFUS CASTLE
PALACE OF SPYNIE
Spynie
Quarrywood
Newton
Bishopmill
Elgin
ELGIN MUSEUM
CATHEDRAL
CASHMERE VISITOR CENTRE
OLD MILLS
Pittendreich
MORAY MOTOR MUSEUM
New Elgin
Miltonduff
Leuchars Ho.
Lochhill
Urquhart
Lhanbryde
Moss of Barmuckity
COXTON TOWER
Paddockhaugh
Auchtertyre
BIRNIE CHURCH
Foresterseat
Longmorn
Blackhills
Thomshill
MILLBUIES
Kellas
Glenlatterach
Teindland Forest
Glen of Rothes
Auchinroath
Newlands
Moray
365 CAIRN UISH
Rothes
GLEN GRANT DISTILLERY
Burn of Rothes
404 CARN NA CAILLICHE
Elchies Forest
Whiteacen
LADYCROFT AGRICULTURAL MUSEUM
CARDHU DISTILLERY
Archiestown
Ringorm
Upper Knockando
Cardow
Knockando
Knockando Ho.
Carron
Speyview
Daugh of Kinermony
SPEYSIDE WAY
Marypark
GLENFARCLAS DISTILLERY
Bellehiglash
Bridge of Avon
Dalchirach
840 BEN RINNES
Favillar
Kirkhill
Glen Rinnes
Dullan Water
Drumin
GLENLIVET DISTILLERY
Glenlivet
Shenval
Auchbreck
Ballcorach
Tomnavoulin
Glenlivet
SPEY BAY
Kingston
TUGNET ICE HOUSE
Spey Bay
Garmouth
Porttanachy
Nether Dallachy
Upper Dallachy
Bogmoor
SPEYSIDE WAY
Lochs Crofts
Auchenhalrig
Newlands of Tynet
BAXTERS HIGHLAND VILLAGE
Mosstodloch
FOCHABERS FOLK MUSEUM
Fochabers
Dipple
Orbliston
Speymouth Forest
Ordiequish
Wood of Ordiequish
Inchberry
NJ
Mulben
Rosarie Forest
SPEYSIDE WAY
471 BEN AIGAN
Dandaleith
Maggieknockater
Craigellachie
Kininvie Ho.
SPEYSIDE COOPERAGE VISITOR CENTRE
Midtown of Buchromb
Charlestown of Aberlour
Milltown of Edinvillie
BALVENIE CASTLE
GLENFIDDICH DISTILLERY
Dufftown
Milltown of Auchindoun
Kirktown of Mortlach
MEIKLE CONVAL 569
AUCHINDOUN CASTLE
487 THE SCALP
Glen Fiddich
Ballochford
Bridgend
Inverharroch
Glenfiddich Forest
Black Water
Auchmair
Cabrach
571 ROUND HILL
Aldunie
Blackwater Forest
THE BUCKIE DRIFTER
Gordonsburgh
Buckie
Buckpool
Findochty
Portknockie
Portessie
Rathven
Portgordon
Slackhead
Cairnfield Ho.
Drybridge
Broadley
ST. GREGORY'S CHAPEL
Clochan
Shiel Muir
Braes of Enzie
301 MILLSTONE HILL
Deerhill
Broadrashes
Grange Crossroads
Forgie
Aultmore
Newmill
Keith
STRATHISLA DISTILLERY
STRATH ISLA
KEITH AND DUFFTOWN RLY
Towiemore
Edintore
Little Pitlurg
Coachford
Drummuir Castle
Drummuir
Balloch Wood
Glen of Coachford
Daugh of Cairnborrow
Cairnborrow
Torry
Deveron
Haugh of Glass
STRATHBOGIE
Bailiesward
Succoth
Tillathrowie
Tomnaven
Clashindarroch Forest
Clashindarroch
Kirkney Water
Milton of Lesmore
Belhinnie
Wheedlemont
Rhynie
Cullen Bay
Logie Hd.
Sandend Bay
FINDLATER CASTLE
Sandend
Cullen
Lintmill
Fordyce
Milton
Kirktown of Deskford
DESKFORD CHURCH
Ardiecow
Berryhillock
Craibstone
Little Tor
Mains of Edingight
Gordonstown
Edingight Ho.
KNOCK HILL
Crannoch
Sillyearn
Bracobrae
Knock
Davoch of Grange
Drumnagorrach
Farmtown
Glen Barry
Milltown of Rothiemay
Ruthven
Cairnie
THE BIN
The Bin Forest
NORDIC SKI CENTRE
Corse of Kinnoir
HUNTLY CASTLE
Huntly
BRANDER
Slioch
Bridgend
Kirkhill
Shanquhar
Blackburn
Coynachie
Culdrain
Kirkney
Gartly
Clashindarroch Forest
Cults
434 KNOCKANDHILL
LEITH HALL
Milton of Noth
Kennethmont
Cottown
Clatt
160
149
150

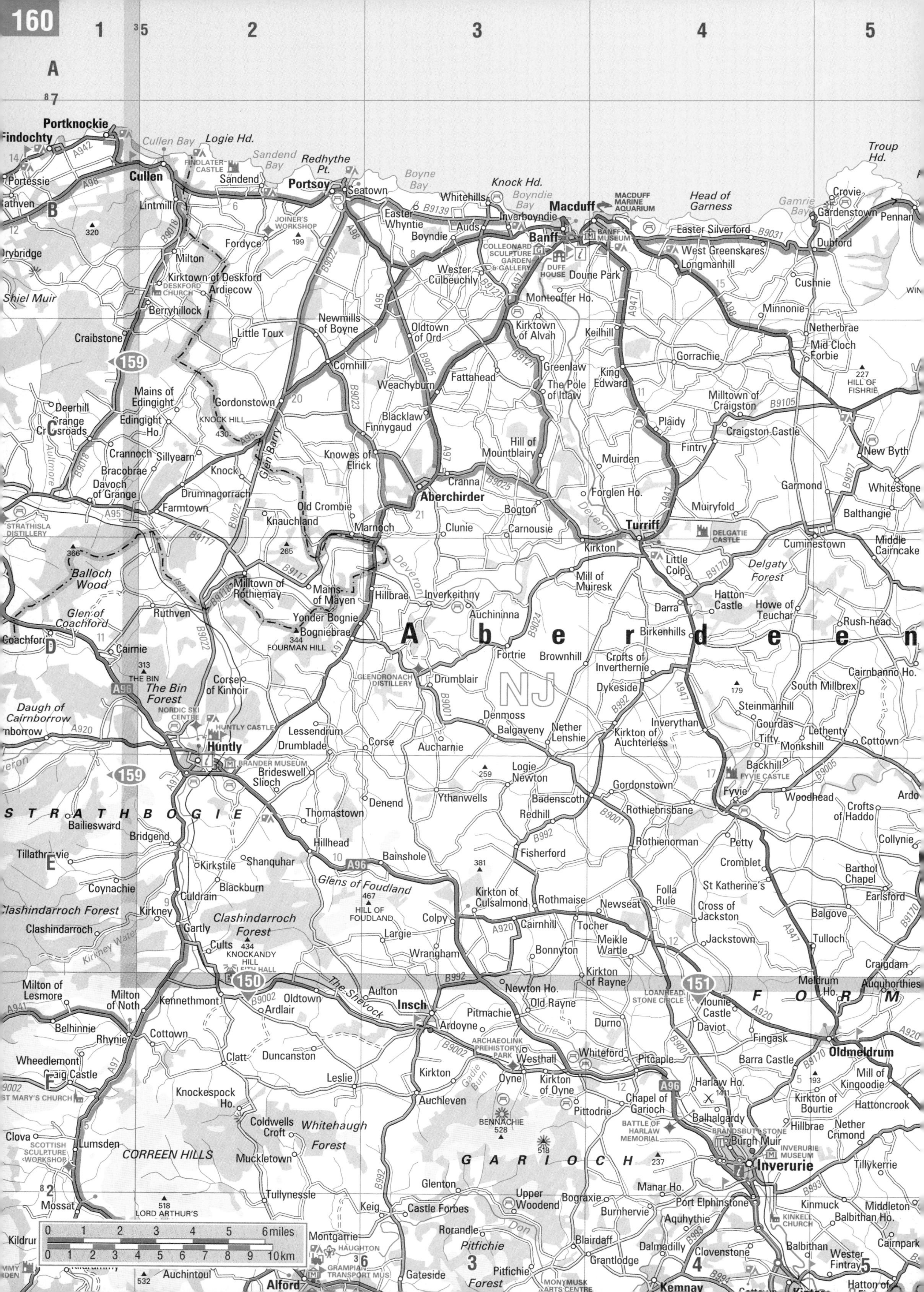

1
2
3
4
5
A
B
C
D
E
F
Portknockie
Findochty
Cullen Bay
Logie Hd.
Sandend Bay
Redhythe Pt.
Boyne Bay
Knock Hd.
Boyndie Bay
Head of Garness
Gamrie Bay
Troup Hd.
Portessie
Cullen
Findlater Castle
Sandend
Portsoy
Seatown
Whitehills
Macduff
Macduff Marine Aquarium
Crovie
Gardenstown
Pennan
Rathven
Lintmill
Joiner's Workshop
Easter Whyntie
Inverboyndie
Banff
Banff Museum
Easter Silverford
Dubford
Drybridge
Fordyce
Boyndie
Auds
Colleonard Sculpture Garden & Gallery
Duff House
West Greenskares
Longmanhill
Milton
Kirktown of Deskford
Deskford Church
Ardiecow
Wester Culbeuchly
Doune Park
Cushnie
Shiel Muir
Berryhillock
Montcoffer Ho.
Minnonie
Craibstone
Little Toux
Newmills of Boyne
Oldtown of Ord
Kirktown of Alvah
Keilhill
Netherbrae
Mid Cloch Forbie
Cornhill
Greenlaw
Gorrachie
Hill of Fishrie
Mains of Edingight
Gordonstown
Weachyburn
Fattahead
The Pole of Itlaw
King Edward
Milltown of Craigston
Deerhill
Grange Crossroads
Edingight Ho.
Knock Hill
Blacklaw
Finnygaud
Plaidy
Craigston Castle
Crannoch
Sillyearn
Hill of Mountblairy
Fintry
New Byth
Bracobrae
Knock
Knowes of Elrick
Muirden
Davoch of Grange
Drumnagorrach
Cranna
Aberchirder
Forglen Ho.
Garmond
Whitestone
Glen Barry
Farmtown
Old Crombie
Bogton
Muiryfold
Balthangie
Strathisla Distillery
Knauchland
Marnoch
Clunie
Carnousie
Turriff
Delgatie Castle
Cuminestown
Middle Cairncake
Balloch Wood
Kirkton
Little Colp
Delgaty Forest
Milltown of Rothiemay
Mains of Mayen
Hillbrae
Inverkeithny
Mill of Muiresk
Darra
Hatton Castle
Howe of Teuchar
Glen of Coachford
Ruthven
Yonder Bognie
Bogniebrae
Auchininna
Rush-head
Coachford
Cairnie
Fourman Hill
Fortrie
Brownhill
Birkenhills
Aberdeen
The Bin
The Bin Forest
Corse of Kinnoir
Glendronach Distillery
Drumblair
Crofts of Inverthernie
Cairnbanno Ho.
Daugh of Cairnborrow
Nordic Ski Centre
Huntly Castle
Dykeside
South Millbrex
NJ
Steinmanhill
Cairnborrow
Huntly
Lessendrum
Drumblade
Corse
Denmoss
Balgaveny
Nether Lenshie
Inverythan
Kirkton of Auchterless
Gourdas
Tifty
Lethenty
Monkshill
Cottown
Brander Museum
Brideswell
Slioch
Aucharnie
Logie Newton
Backhill
Fyvie Castle
Gordonstown
Fyvie
Woodhead
Strathbogie
Denend
Ythanwells
Badenscoth
Rothiebrisbane
Crofts of Haddo
Bailiesward
Thomastown
Redhill
Bridgend
Hillhead
Rothienorman
Petty
Collynie
Tillathrowie
Bainshole
Fisherford
Cromblet
Barthol Chapel
Kirkstile
Shanquhar
Glens of Foudland
St Katherine's
Coynachie
Blackburn
Culdrain
Hill of Foudland
Kirkton of Culsalmond
Rothmaise
Newseat
Folla Rule
Cross of Jackston
Earlsford
Clashindarroch Forest
Kirkney
Colpy
Cairnhill
Tocher
Balgove
Clashindarroch
Gartly
Largie
Meikle Wartle
Jackstown
Tulloch
Kirkney Water
Cults
Knockandy Hill
Wrangham
Bonnyton
Craigdam
Milton of Lesmore
Kennethmont
Oldtown
Aulton
Newton Ho.
Kirkton of Rayne
Loanhead Stone Circle
Meldrum Ho.
Auquhorthies
Milton of Noth
Ardlair
The Shevock
Insch
Pitmachie
Old Rayne
Mounie Castle
Formartine
Belhinnie
Ardoyne
Durno
Daviot
Rhynie
Cottown
Archaeolink Prehistory Park
Urie
Fingask
Oldmeldrum
Wheedlemont
Clatt
Duncanston
Westhall
Whiteford
Pitcaple
Barra Castle
Craig Castle
St Mary's Church
Leslie
Kirkton
Oyne
Kirkton of Oyne
Harlaw Ho.
Mill of Kingoodie
Knockespock Ho.
Auchleven
Gadie Burn
Chapel of Garioch
Kirkton of Bourtie
Hattoncrook
Pittodrie
Balhalgardy
Battle of Harlaw Memorial
Coldwells Croft
Whitehaugh Forest
Bennachie
Brandsbutt Stone
Hillbrae
Nether Crimond
Clova
Scottish Sculpture Workshop
Lumsden
Correen Hills
Muckletown
Garioch
Burgh Muir
Inverurie Museum
Inverurie
Tillykerrie
Glenton
Manar Ho.
Mossat
Tullynessle
Upper Woodend
Bograxie
Port Elphinstone
Kinmuck
Middleton
Lord Arthur's
Keig
Castle Forbes
Burnhervie
Aquhythie
Kinkell Church
Balbithan Ho.
Rorandle
Don
Kildrummy
Montgarrie
Haughton
Pitfichie
Blairdaff
Dalmadilly
Clovenstone
Balbithan
Wester Fintray
Cairnpark
Grampian Transport Mus
Auchintoul
Alford
Gateside
Pitfichie Forest
Grantlodge
Monymusk Arts Centre
Kemnay
Hatton of
0 1 2 3 4 5 6 miles
0 1 2 3 4 5 6 7 8 9 10 km
159
150
151
A942
A98
B9018
B9022
B9023
B9025
B9139
A95
A97
B9121
A947
B9031
B9105
B9027
B9117
A96
B9024
B9001
B992
B9170
B9005
A920
A941
B9002
B8170
B993

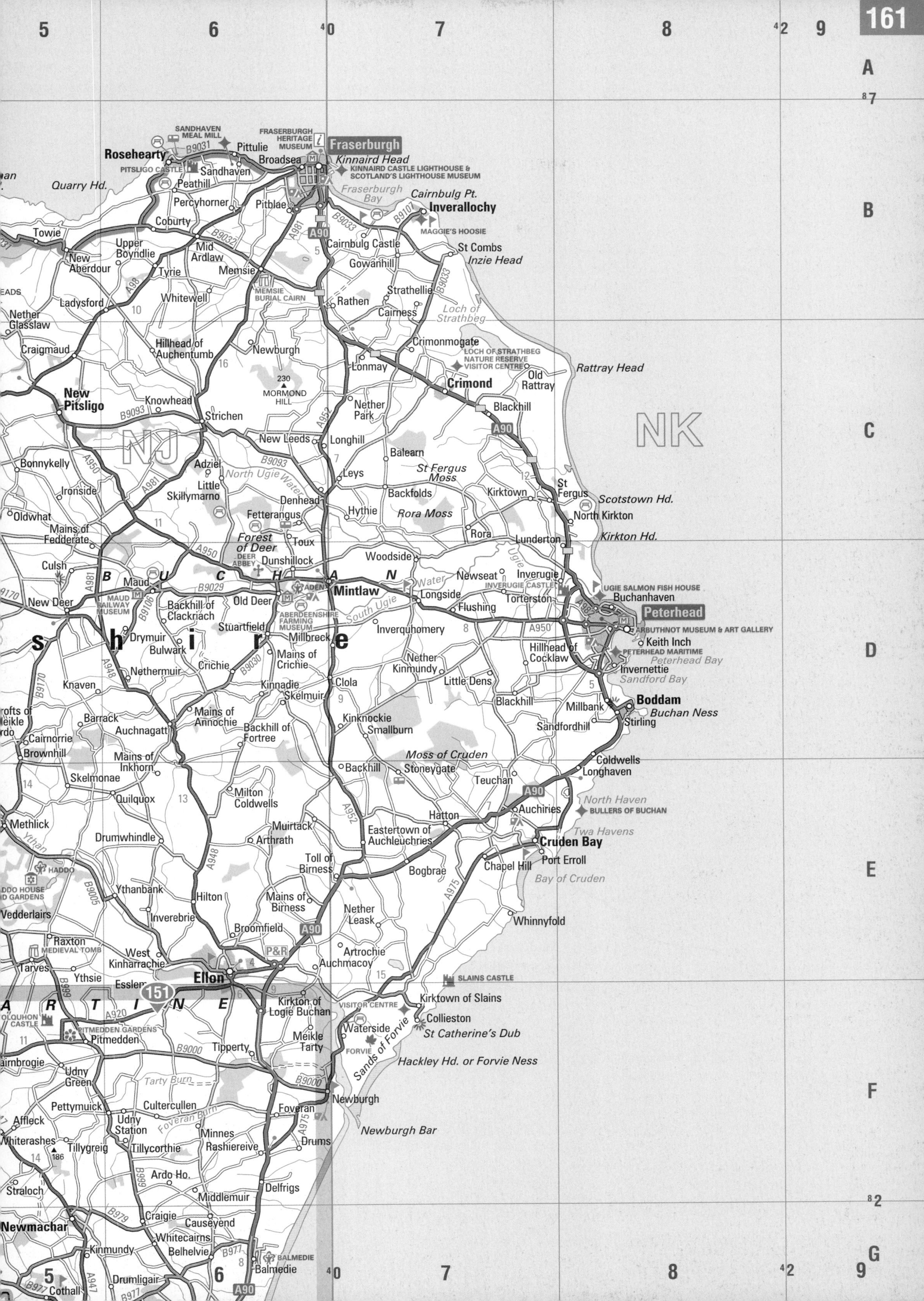

Fraserburgh
Kinnaird Head
KINNAIRD CASTLE LIGHTHOUSE & SCOTLAND'S LIGHTHOUSE MUSEUM
FRASERBURGH HERITAGE MUSEUM
SANDHAVEN MEAL MILL
Rosehearty
Pittulie
Broadsea
PITSLIGO CASTLE
Sandhaven
Peathill
Quarry Hd.
Percyhorner
Pitblae
Fraserburgh Bay
Cairnbulg Pt.
Inverallochy
MAGGIE'S HOOSIE
Coburty
Towie
New Aberdour
Upper Boyndlie
Mid Ardlaw
Tyrie
Memsie
MEMSIE BURIAL CAIRN
Cairnbulg Castle
Gowanhill
St Combs
Inzie Head
Ladysford
Whitewell
Rathen
Strathellie
Cairness
Loch of Strathbeg
Nether Glasslaw
Craigmaud
Hillhead of Auchentumb
Newburgh
Crimonmogate
LOCH OF STRATHBEG NATURE RESERVE VISITOR CENTRE
Lonmay
Rattray Head
Old Rattray
Crimond
230 MORMOND HILL
New Pitsligo
Knowhead
Strichen
Nether Park
Blackhill
NJ
NK
New Leeds
Longhill
Balearn
Bonnykelly
Adziel
North Ugie Water
St Fergus Moss
Leys
Little Skillymarno
Ironside
Denhead
Backfolds
Kirktown
St Fergus
Scotstown Hd.
Oldwhat
Fetterangus
Hythie
Rora Moss
North Kirkton
Mains of Fedderate
Forest of Deer
Toux
Rora
Lunderton
Kirkton Hd.
DEER ABBEY
Dunshillock
Woodside
Culsh
Maud
MAUD RAILWAY MUSEUM
B U C H A N
Mintlaw
ADEN
Newseat
Inverugie
INVERUGIE CASTLE
UGIE SALMON FISH HOUSE
Buchanhaven
New Deer
Backhill of Clackriach
Old Deer
Longside
Flushing
Torterston
Peterhead
ABERDEENSHIRE FARMING MUSEUM
Stuartfield
South Ugie
Millbreck
Inverquhomery
ARBUTHNOT MUSEUM & ART GALLERY
Keith Inch
s h i r e
Drymuir
Bulwark
Mains of Crichie
Nether Kinmundy
Hillhead of Cocklaw
PETERHEAD MARITIME
Peterhead Bay
Nethermuir
Crichie
Invernettie
Sandford Bay
Knaven
Kinnadie
Clola
Little Dens
Skelmuir
Blackhill
Millbank
Boddam
Buchan Ness
Crofts of Meikle Ardo
Barrack
Mains of Annochie
Auchnagatt
Backhill of Fortree
Kinknockie
Smallburn
Sandfordhill
Stirling
Cairnorrie
Brownhill
Mains of Inkhorn
Moss of Cruden
Backhill
Stoneygate
Coldwells
Longhaven
Skelmonae
Teuchan
Quilquox
Milton Coldwells
North Haven
Auchiries
BULLERS OF BUCHAN
Hatton
Methlick
Ythan
Drumwhindle
Muirtack
Arthrath
Eastertown of Auchleuchries
Twa Havens
Cruden Bay
HADDO
HADDO HOUSE AND GARDENS
Toll of Birness
Bogbrae
Chapel Hill
Port Erroll
Bay of Cruden
Ythanbank
Hilton
Mains of Birness
Vedderlairs
Inverebrie
Nether Leask
Whinnyfold
Broomfield
Raxton
MEDIEVAL TOMB
West Kinharrachie
Tarves
Artrochie
Auchmacoy
Ythsie
Ellon
P&R
SLAINS CASTLE
Esslemont
151
F O R M A R T I N E
Kirkton of Logie Buchan
VISITOR CENTRE
Kirktown of Slains
Collieston
THOLQUHON CASTLE
PITMEDDEN GARDENS
Pitmedden
Waterside
St Catherine's Dub
Meikle Tarty
Tipperty
FORVIE
Sands of Forvie
Hackley Hd. or Forvie Ness
Cairnbrogie
Udny Green
Tarty Burn
Newburgh
Pettymuick
Culter Cullen
Foveran
Foveran Burn
Affleck
Udny Station
Minnes
Whiterashes
186
Tillygreig
Tillycorthie
Rashiereive
Drums
Newburgh Bar
Ardo Ho.
Straloch
Delfrigs
Middlemuir
Craigie
Newmachar
Causeyend
Whitecairns
Kinmundy
Belhelvie
BALMEDIE
Balmedie
Drumligair
Cothall
A90
A98
A981
A952
A950
A948
A975
A920
A947
B9031
B9032
B9033
B9107
B9093
B9029
B9030
B9106
B9170
B9005
B999
B9000
B979
B977
5
6
7
8
9
A
B
C
D
E
F
G

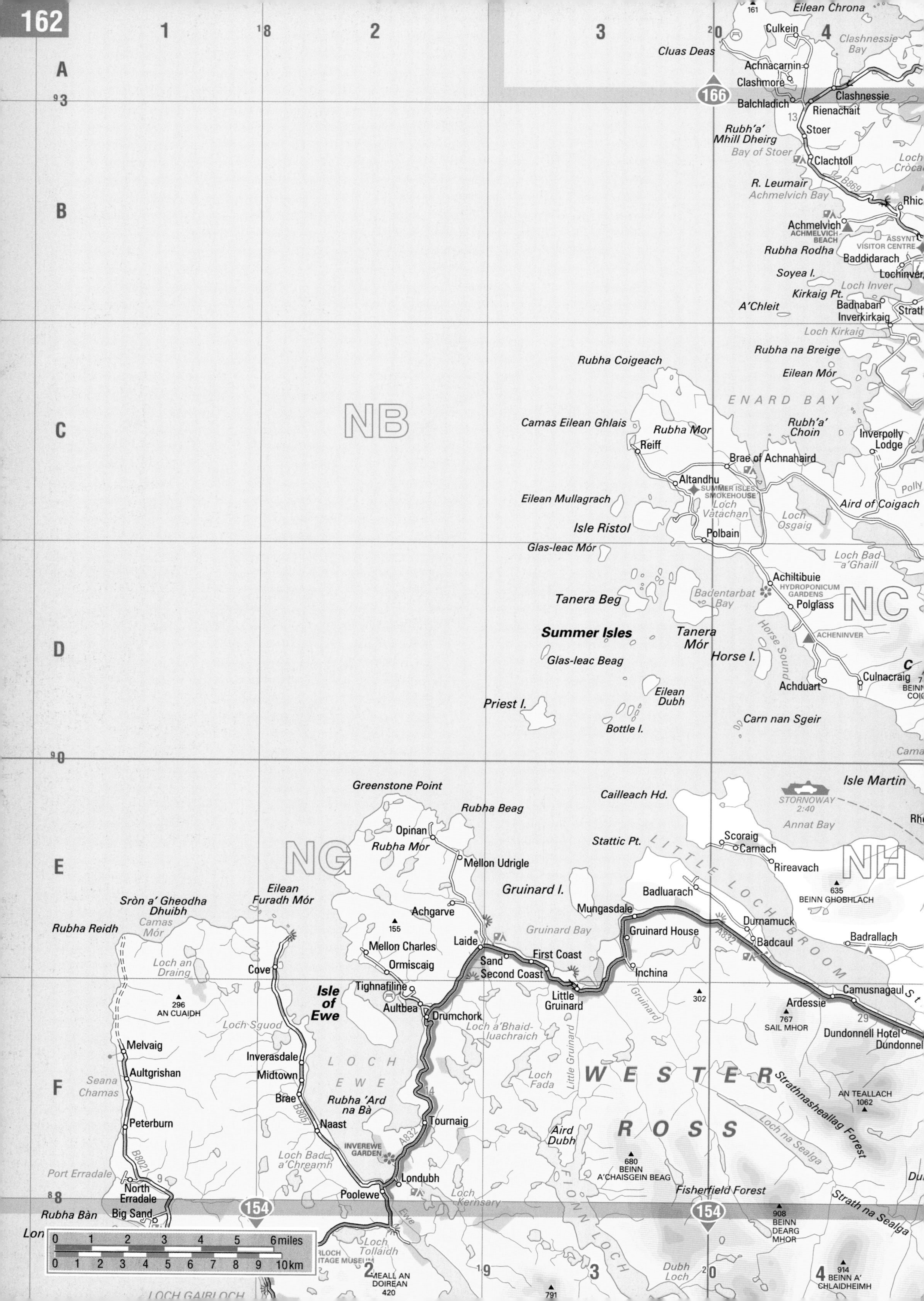
Eilean Chrona
Culkein
Clashnessie Bay
Cluas Deas
Achnacarnin
Clashmore
Clashnessie
Balchladich
Rienachait
Stoer
Rubh'a' Mhill Dheirg
Bay of Stoer
Clachtoll
Loch Cròcach
R. Leumair
Achmelvich Bay
Achmelvich
ACHMELVICH BEACH
ASSYNT VISITOR CENTRE
Rubha Rodha
Baddidarach
Lochinver
Soyea I.
Loch Inver
Kirkaig Pt.
A'Chleit
Badnaban
Inverkirkaig
Loch Kirkaig
Rubha na Breige
Rubha Coigeach
Eilean Mór
ENARD BAY
NB
Camas Eilean Ghlais
Rubha Mor
Rubh'a' Choin
Inverpolly Lodge
Reiff
Brae of Achnahaird
Altandhu
SUMMER ISLES SMOKEHOUSE
Eilean Mullagrach
Loch Vatachan
Loch Osgaig
Aird of Coigach
Isle Ristol
Polbain
Glas-leac Mór
Loch Bad a'Ghaill
Achiltibuie
HYDROPONICUM GARDENS
Tanera Beg
Badentarbat Bay
Polglass
NC
Summer Isles
Tanera Mór
Horse Sound
ACHENINVER
Horse I.
Glas-leac Beag
Culnacraig
Achduart
Eilean Dubh
Priest I.
Bottle I.
Carn nan Sgeir
Isle Martin
Greenstone Point
Cailleach Hd.
STORNOWAY 2:40
Rubha Beag
Annat Bay
Opinan
Rubha Mor
Stattic Pt.
Scoraig
Carnach
Rireavach
NG
Mellon Udrigle
LITTLE LOCH BROOM
NH
Gruinard I.
Badluarach
635 BEINN GHOBHLACH
Eilean Furadh Mór
Sròn a' Gheodha Dhuibh
Achgarve
Mungasdale
Camas Mór
155
Gruinard Bay
Dundonnell
Rubha Reidh
Gruinard House
Durnamuck
Badcaul
Badrallach
Laide
Mellon Charles
Sand
First Coast
Loch an Draing
Cove
Ormiscaig
Second Coast
Inchina
Tighnafiline
Isle of Ewe
Little Gruinard
302
Camusnagaul
296 AN CUAIDH
Aultbea
Ardessie
Drumchork
Loch Sguod
Loch a'Bhaid-luachraich
767 SAIL MHOR
Melvaig
Dundonnell Hotel
Inverasdale
LOCH EWE
Aultgrishan
Midtown
Loch Fada
WESTER ROSS
Strathnasheallag Forest
Seana Chamas
Brae
Rubha 'Ard na Bà
AN TEALLACH 1062
Peterburn
Naast
Tournaig
Aird Dubh
Loch na Sealga
INVEREWE GARDEN
Loch Bad a'Chreamh
680 BEINN A'CHAISGEIN BEAG
Port Erradale
North Erradale
Londubh
Loch Kernsary
Fisherfield Forest
Strath na Sealga
Poolewe
Rubha Bàn
Big Sand
908 BEINN DEARG MHOR
Loch Tollaidh
FIONN LOCH
0 1 2 3 4 5 6 miles
0 1 2 3 4 5 6 7 8 9 10 km
MEALL AN DOIREAN 420
Dubh Loch
914 BEINN A' CHLAIDHEIMH
791
LOCH GAIRLOCH
166
154

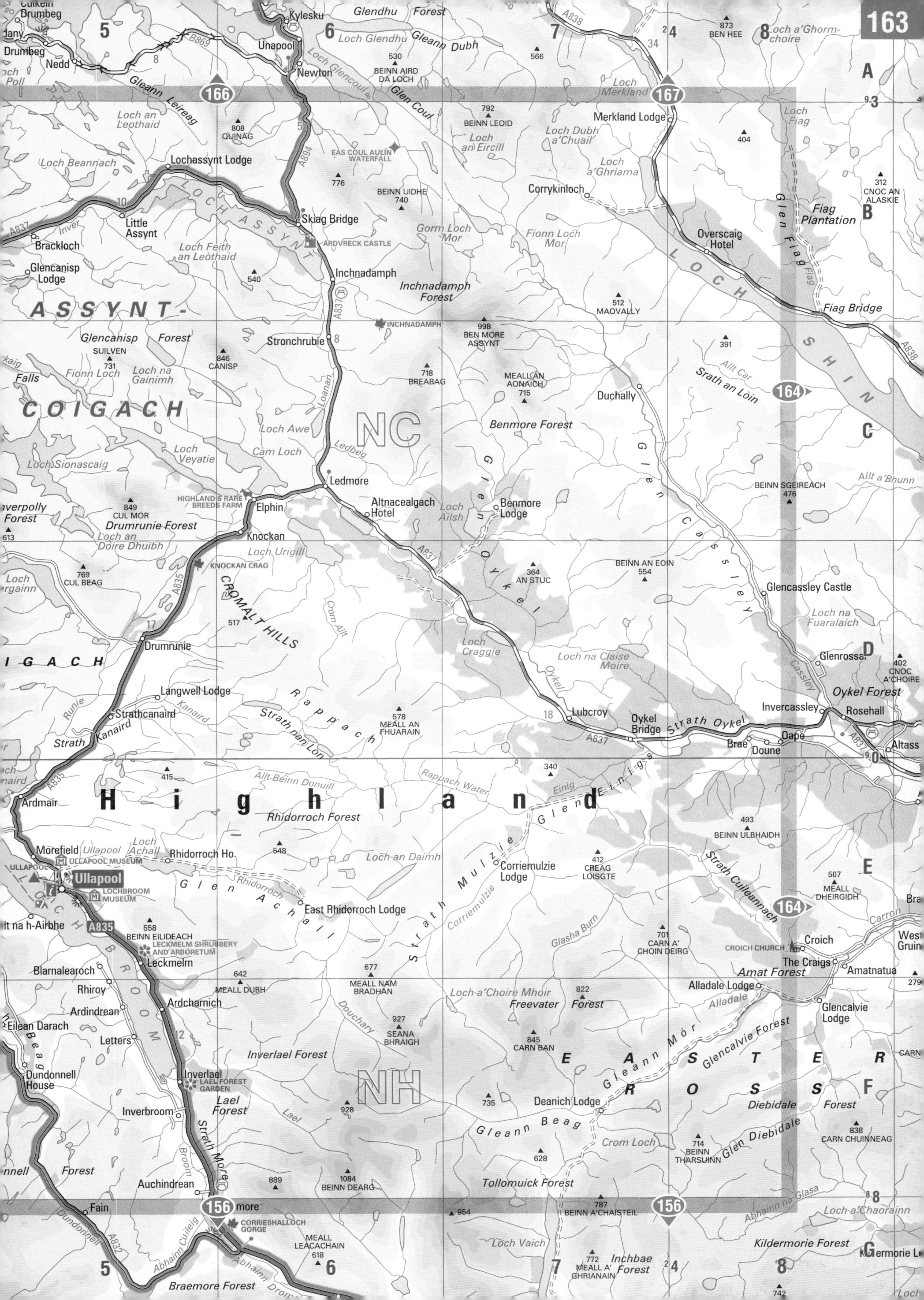
Drumbeg
Nedd
Kylesku
Unapool
Newton
Glendhu Forest
Loch Glendhu
Gleann Dubh
Loch Glencoul
Glen Coul
Gleann Leireag
Loch an Leothaid
808 QUINAG
Loch Beannach
Lochassynt Lodge
LOCH ASSYNT
Little Assynt
Brackloch
Skiag Bridge
ARDVRECK CASTLE
Loch Feith an Leothaid
Glencanisp Lodge
Inchnadamph
Inchnadamph Forest
EAS COUL AULIN WATERFALL
776
BEINN UIDHE 740
530 BEINN AIRD DA LOCH
566
792 BEINN LEOID
Loch an Eircill
Gorm Loch Mor
Fionn Loch Mor
Loch Merkland
Merkland Lodge
Loch Dubh a'Chuail
Loch a'Ghriama
Corrykinloch
Overscaig Hotel
LOCH SHIN
Fiag Bridge
Glen Fiag
Loch Fiag
Fiag Plantation
873 BEN HEE
Loch a'Ghorm-choire
404
312 CNOC AN ALASKIE
512 MAOVALLY
391
Strath an Loin
Allt Car
ASSYNT-COIGACH
Glencanisp Forest
SUILVEN 731
Fionn Loch
Loch na Gainimh
846 CANISP
Stronchrubie
INCHNADAMPH
998 BEN MORE ASSYNT
718 BREABAG
MEALL AN AONAICH 715
Duchally
Benmore Forest
NC
Loch Awe
Cam Loch
Loch Veyatie
Loch Sionascaig
Ledmore
Ledbeg
Altnacealgach Hotel
Loch Ailsh
Benmore Lodge
Glen Oykel
Glen Cassley
BEINN SGEIREACH 476
Allt a'Bhunn
HIGHLAND & RARE BREEDS FARM
Elphin
849 CUL MOR
Drumrunie Forest
Loch an Doire Dhuibh
Knockan
Loch Urigill
KNOCKAN CRAG
769 CUL BEAG
CROMALT HILLS
517
Crom Allt
364 AN STUC
BEINN AN EOIN 554
Glencassley Castle
Loch na Fuaralaich
Loch Craggie
Loch na Claise Moire
Drumrunie
Glenrossal
402 CNOC A'CHOIRE
Oykel Forest
Langwell Lodge
Strathcanaird
Strath Kanaird
Rappach
Strath nan Lon
578 MEALL AN FHUARAIN
Lubcroy
Oykel Bridge
Strath Oykel
Invercassley
Rosehall
Brae
Doune
Oape
Altass
Ardmair
415
Allt Beinn Donuill
Rappach Water
340
Einig
Glen Einig
Highland
Rhidorroch Forest
493 BEINN ULBHAIDH
Morefield
Loch Achall
Rhidorroch Ho.
548
Loch an Daimh
Corriemulzie Lodge
412 CREAG LOISGTE
Strath Mulzie
Strath Cuileannach
ULLAPOOL MUSEUM
Ullapool
LOCHBROOM MUSEUM
Glen Achall
East Rhidorroch Lodge
507 MEALL DHEIRGIDH
Allt na h-Airbhe
558 BEINN EILIDEACH
LECKMELM SHRUBBERY AND ARBORETUM
Leckmelm
Glasha Burn
701 CARN A' CHOIN DEIRG
CROICH CHURCH
Croich
The Craigs
Amatnatua
Amat Forest
Carron
Blarnalearoch
Rhiroy
Ardindrean
Ardcharnich
642 MEALL DUBH
677 MEALL NAM BRADHAN
Loch a'Choire Mhoir
Freevater Forest
822
Alladale Lodge
Glencalvie Lodge
Eilean Darach
Letters
LOCH BROOM
927 SEANA BHRAIGH
845 CARN BAN
Gleann Mor
Glencalvie Forest
EASTER ROSS
Dundonnell House
Inverlael
LAEL FOREST GARDEN
Inverlael Forest
NH
735
Deanich Lodge
Inverbroom
Lael Forest
928
Gleann Beag
Diebidale Forest
Glen Diebidale
838 CARN CHUINNEAG
Crom Loch
714 BEINN THARSUINN
628
Strath More
Forest
Auchindrean
889
1084 BEINN DEARG
Tollomuick Forest
Fain
954
787 BEINN A'CHAISTEIL
Abhainn na Glasa
Loch a'Chaorainn
CORRIESHALLOCH GORGE
MEALL LEACACHAIN 618
Loch Vaich
772 MEALL A' GHRIANAIN
Inchbae Forest
Kildermorie Forest
Braemore Forest
A837
A838
A835
A894
A832
B869
166
167
164
156
A
B
C
D
E
F
G
5
6
7
8

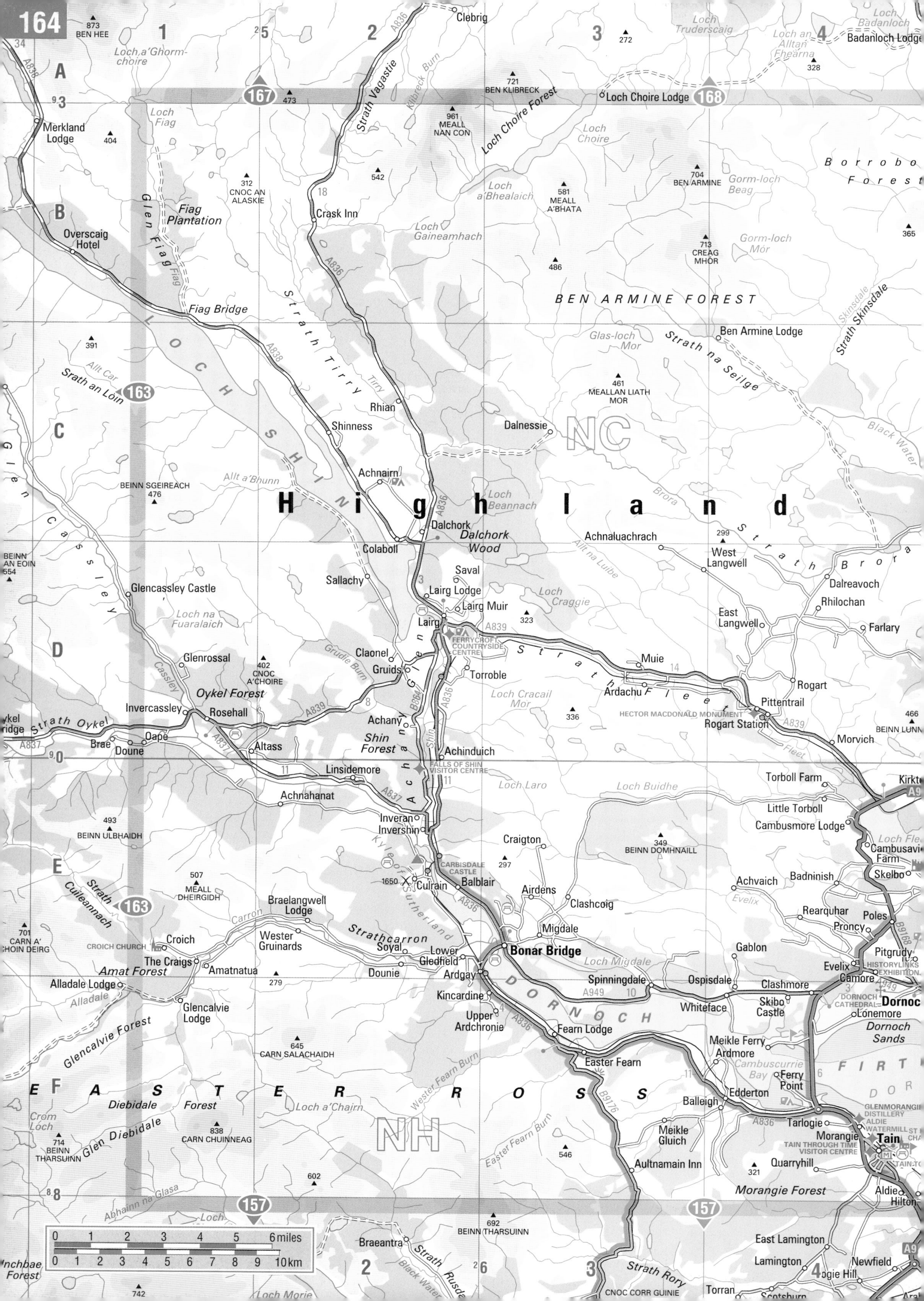
Highland
NC
NH
BEN HEE 873
Loch a'Ghorm-choire
Clebrig
A836
Loch Truderscaig
Loch Badanloch
Loch an Alltan Fhèarna
Badanloch Lodge
328
272
167
473
721 BEN KLIBRECK
Loch Choire Lodge
168
Merkland Lodge
404
Loch Fiag
Strath Vagastie
Kilbreck Burn
961 MEALL NAN CON
Loch Choire Forest
Loch Choire
312 CNOC AN ALASKIE
542
Glen Fiag
Fiag Plantation
Crask Inn
Loch a'Bhealaich
581 MEALL A'BHATA
704 BEN ARMINE
Gorm-loch Beag
Borrobol Forest
Overscaig Hotel
Loch Gaineamhach
713 CREAG MHÒR
Gorm-loch Mòr
365
486
BEN ARMINE FOREST
Fiag Bridge
LOCH SHIN
Strath Tirry
A838
Ben Armine Lodge
Glas-loch Mor
Strath na Seilge
Strath Skinsdale
Skinsdale
391
Allt Car
Srath an Lòin
163
461 MEALLAN LIATH MOR
Rhian
Shinness
Dalnessie
Black Water
Glen Cassley
Achnairn
Allt a'Bhunn
BEINN SGEIREACH 476
Loch Beannach
Brora
Dalchork
Dalchork Wood
Colaboll
Achnaluachrach
299
West Langwell
Strath Brora
BEINN AN EOIN 554
Saval
Sallachy
Allt na Luibe
Dalreavoch
Glencassley Castle
Lairg Lodge
Loch Craggie
Rhilochan
Lairg Muir
Loch na Fuaralaich
Lairg
323
East Langwell
Farlary
A839
FERRYCROFT COUNTRYSIDE CENTRE
Grudie Burn
Claonel
Strath Fleet
Glenrossal
402 CNOC A'CHOIRE
Gruids
Torroble
Muie
Rogart
Cassley
Oykel Forest
Loch Cracail Mor
Ardachu
Invercassley
Rosehall
Achany
336
HECTOR MACDONALD MONUMENT
Pittentrail
Rogart Station
466 BEINN LUNN
Strath Oykel
B864
A836
A837
Oape
Brae
Doune
Altass
Shin Forest
Glen Achany
Achinduich
Morvich
Fleet
Linsidemore
FALLS OF SHIN VISITOR CENTRE
Shin
Torboll Farm
Loch Laro
Loch Buidhe
Achnahanat
Little Torboll
493 BEINN ULBHAIDH
Inveran
Invershin
Cambusmore Lodge
Craigton
349 BEINN DOMHNAILL
Loch Fleet
Cambusavie Farm
Kyle of Sutherland
CARBISDALE CASTLE
297
Skelbo
E
507 MEALL DHEIRGIDH
1650
Culrain
Balblair
Airdens
Achvaich
Badninish
Strath Cuileannach
Clashcoig
Evelix
Braelangwell Lodge
Rearquhar
Poles
701 CARN A' CHOIN DEIRG
Carron
Migdale
Proncy
Wester Gruinards
Strathcarron
Croich
CROICH CHURCH
Soyal
Lower Gledfield
Bonar Bridge
Gablon
Pitgrudy
The Craigs
Amatnatua
Loch Migdale
Evelix
HISTORYLINKS EXHIBITION
Amat Forest
Dounie
279
Ardgay
Spinningdale
Ospisdale
Clashmore
Camore
Alladale Lodge
A949
DORNOCH CATHEDRAL
Dornoch
Alladale
Kincardine
Skibo Castle
Lonemore
Glencalvie Lodge
Upper Ardchronie
DORNOCH FIRTH
Whiteface
Dornoch Sands
Glencalvie Forest
645 CARN SALACHAIDH
Fearn Lodge
Meikle Ferry
Ardmore
Wester Fearn Burn
Easter Fearn
Cambuscurrie Bay
Ferry Point
EASTER ROSS
Diebidale Forest
Loch a'Chairn
B9176
Edderton
Balleigh
Crom Loch
GLENMORANGIE DISTILLERY
ALDIE WATERMILL
Glen Diebidale
838 CARN CHUINNEAG
Meikle Gluich
Tarlogie
Morangie
Tain
714 BEINN THARSUINN
Easter Fearn Burn
546
TAIN THROUGH TIME VISITOR CENTRE
Aultnamain Inn
Quarryhill
321
602
Morangie Forest
Abhainn na Glasa
157
Aldie
Hilton
692 BEINN THARSUINN
Braeantra
Strath Rusdale
East Lamington
0 1 2 3 4 5 6 miles
0 1 2 3 4 5 6 7 8 9 10km
Inchbae Forest
Black Water
Strath Rory
Lamington
Newfield
Hill
742
Loch Morie
CNOC CORR GUINIE
Torran
Scotsburn
A9
A B C D E F
1 2 3 4

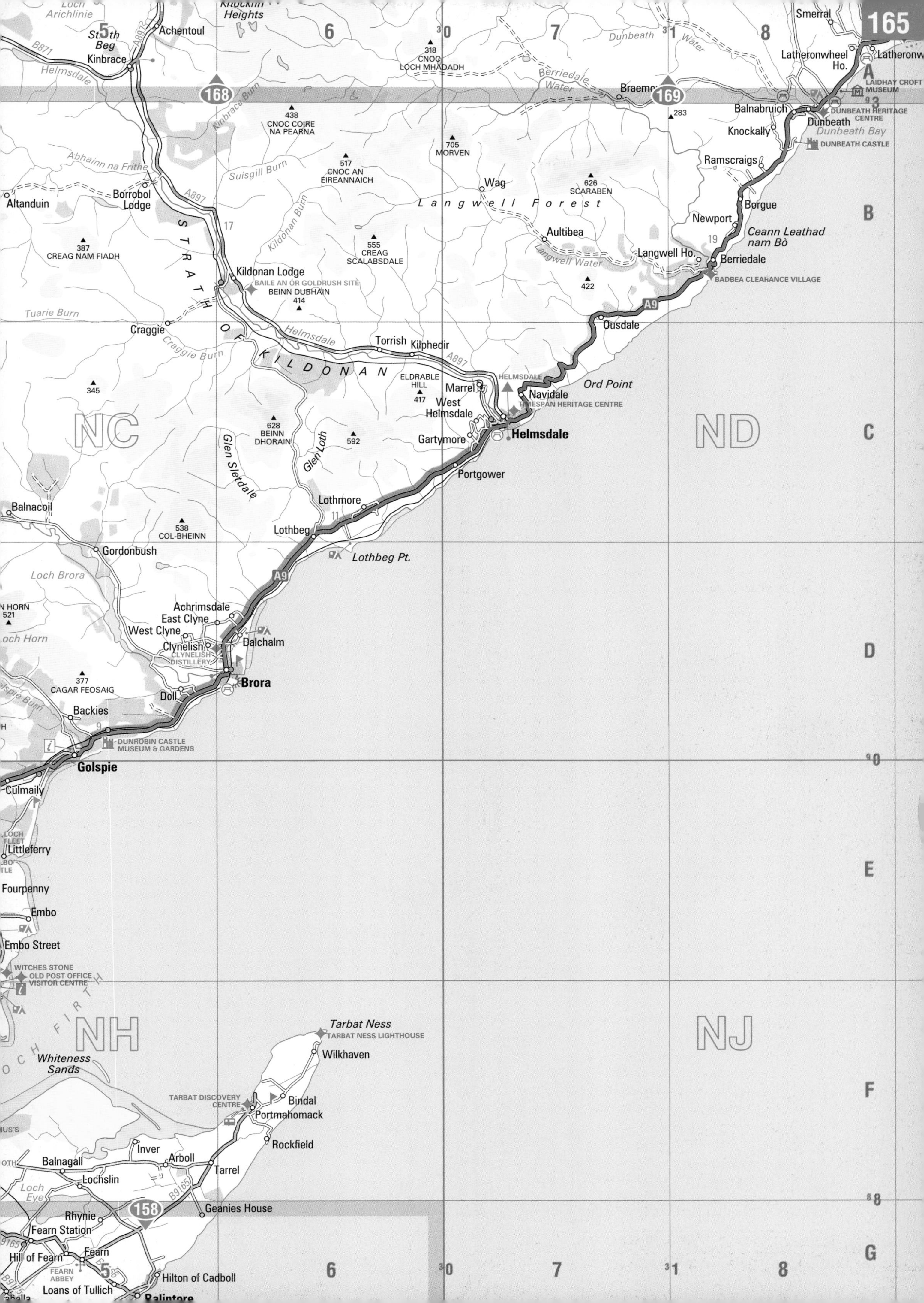

Loch Arichlinie
Knockfin Heights
Smerral
Latheronwheel Ho.
Latheronw

St 5th Beg
Achentoul
Dunbeath Water
Laidhay Croft Museum
A

B871
Kinbrace
6
0
7
Braemo
169
Balnabruich
Dunbeath
DUNBEATH HERITAGE CENTRE

Helmsdale
168
Berriedale Water
283
Knockally
Dunbeath Bay
DUNBEATH CASTLE

318
CNOC LOCH MHADADH
Ramscraigs

438
CNOC COIRE NA PEARNA
Newport
Borgue
B

Altanduin
Borrobol Lodge
A897
517
CNOC AN EIREANNAICH
705
MORVEN
Langwell Ho.
19
Ceann Leathad nam Bò

387
CREAG NAM FIADH
17
Wag
626
SCARABEN
Langwell Water
Berriedale

Kildonan Lodge
555
CREAG SCALABSDALE
Aultibea
422
BADBEA CLEARANCE VILLAGE

Tuarie Burn
BAILE AN ÒR GOLDRUSH SITE
BEINN DUBHAIN
414
Ousdale
A9

Craggie
Craggie Burn
Helmsdale
Torrish
Kilphedir
A897

345
STRATH OF KILDONAN
ELDRABLE HILL 417
Marrel
HELMSDALE
Navidale
Ord Point

NC
628
BEINN DHORAIN
592
West Helmsdale
TIMESPAN HERITAGE CENTRE
ND
C

Glen Sletdale
Glen Loth
Gartymore
Helmsdale

Balnacoil
538
COL-BHEINN
Portgower

Gordonbush
Lothmore
Lothbeg
11

N HORN 521
Lothbeg Pt.

Loch Brora
Achrimsdale
East Clyne
West Clyne
Clynelish
Dalchalm
A9
D

och Horn
CLYNELISH DISTILLERY

377
CAGAR FEOSAIG
Brora

Backies
Doll
DUNROBIN CASTLE MUSEUM & GARDENS
0

Gaspie Burn
9
Golspie

Culmaily
LOCH FLEET

Littleferry

Fourpenny
E

Embo

Embo Street

WITCHES STONE
OLD POST OFFICE
VISITOR CENTRE

Tarbat Ness
TARBAT NESS LIGHTHOUSE

NH
Whiteness Sands
Wilkhaven
NJ
F

TARBAT DISCOVERY CENTRE
Bindal
Portmahomack

Balnagall
Inver
Arboll
Rockfield

Lochslin
Tarrel

Loch Eye
Rhynie
158
Geanies House
8

Fearn Station
Fearn
7
1
8
G

Hill of Fearn
FEARN ABBEY
5
Hilton of Cadboll

Loans of Tullich
Balintore
6
0
7
1
8

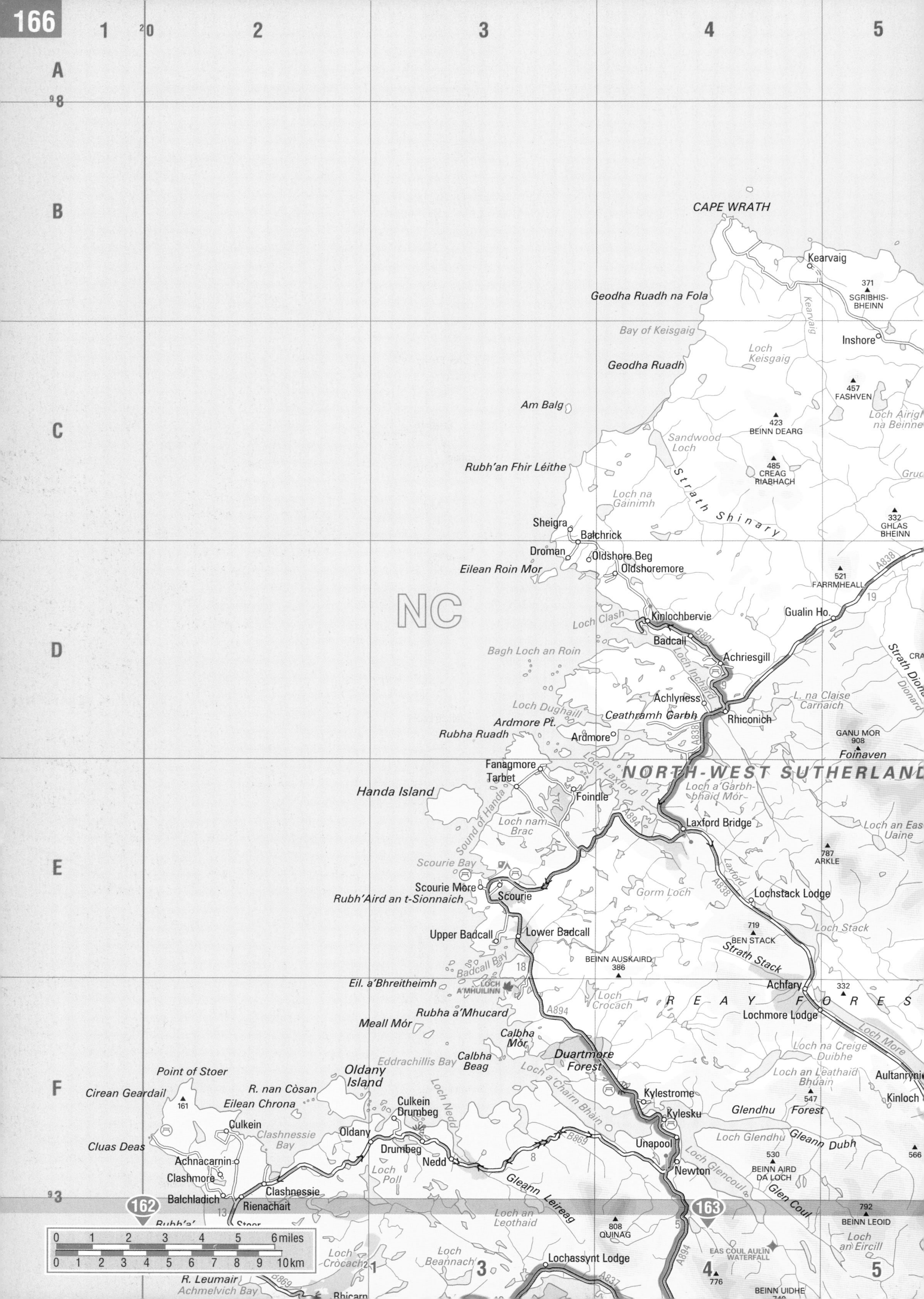
1
2
3
4
5
A
B
C
D
E
F
CAPE WRATH
Kearvaig
371
SGRIBHIS-BHEINN
Geodha Ruadh na Fola
Bay of Keisgaig
Kearvaig
Inshore
Loch Keisgaig
Geodha Ruadh
457
FASHVEN
Am Balg
423
BEINN DEARG
Loch Airigh na Beinne
Sandwood Loch
485
CREAG RIABHACH
Rubh'an Fhir Léithe
Strath Shinary
Loch na Gainimh
Sheigra
Balchrick
332
GHLAS BHEINN
Droman
Oldshore Beg
Oldshoremore
Eilean Roin Mor
521
FARRMHEALL
A838
NC
Kinlochbervie
Loch Clash
Gualin Ho.
Badcall
B801
Bagh Loch an Roin
Loch Inchard
Achriesgill
Strath Dionard
Achlyness
L. na Claise Carnaich
Loch Dughaill
Ceathramh Garbh
Rhiconich
Ardmore Pt.
Rubha Ruadh
Ardmore
GANU MOR
908
Foinaven
Fanagmore
Tarbet
NORTH-WEST SUTHERLAND
Loch Laxford
Loch a'Garbh-bhaid Mór
Handa Island
Foindle
Sound of Handa
A894
Laxford Bridge
Loch nam Brac
Loch an Eas Uaine
787
ARKLE
Scourie Bay
Laxford
Scourie More
Scourie
Gorm Loch
A838
Lochstack Lodge
Rubh'Aird an t-Sionnaich
719
BEN STACK
Loch Stack
Upper Badcall
Lower Badcall
Strath Stack
BEINN AUSKAIRD
386
Badcall Bay
Achfary
332
Eil. a'Bhreitheimh
LOCH A'MHUILINN
Loch Crocach
REAY FOREST
A894
Rubha a'Mhucard
Lochmore Lodge
Meall Mór
Calbha Mór
Loch More
Calbha Beag
Duartmore Forest
Loch na Creige Duibhe
Eddrachillis Bay
Point of Stoer
Oldany Island
Loch a'Chairn Bhàin
Loch an Leathaid Bhuain
Aultanrynie
Cirean Geardail
161
R. nan Còsan
Loch Nedd
Kylestrome
547
Eilean Chrona
Kinloch
Culkein Drumbeg
Kylesku
Glendhu
Forest
Culkein
Clashnessie Bay
Oldany
Loch Glendhu
Gleann Dubh
Cluas Deas
Drumbeg
B869
Unapool
Achnacarnin
Nedd
Loch Poll
Gleann Leireag
Newton
Loch Glencoul
530
BEINN AIRD DA LOCH
Clashmore
Glen Coul
Clashnessie
Balchladich
Rienachait
162
163
Loch an Leothaid
792
BEINN LEOID
808
QUINAG
0 1 2 3 4 5 6 miles
0 1 2 3 4 5 6 7 8 9 10 km
Loch Beannach
Loch Cròcach
Lochassynt Lodge
EAS COUL AULIN WATERFALL
Loch an Eircill
R. Leumair
Achmelvich Bay
A837
A894
776
BEINN UIDHE

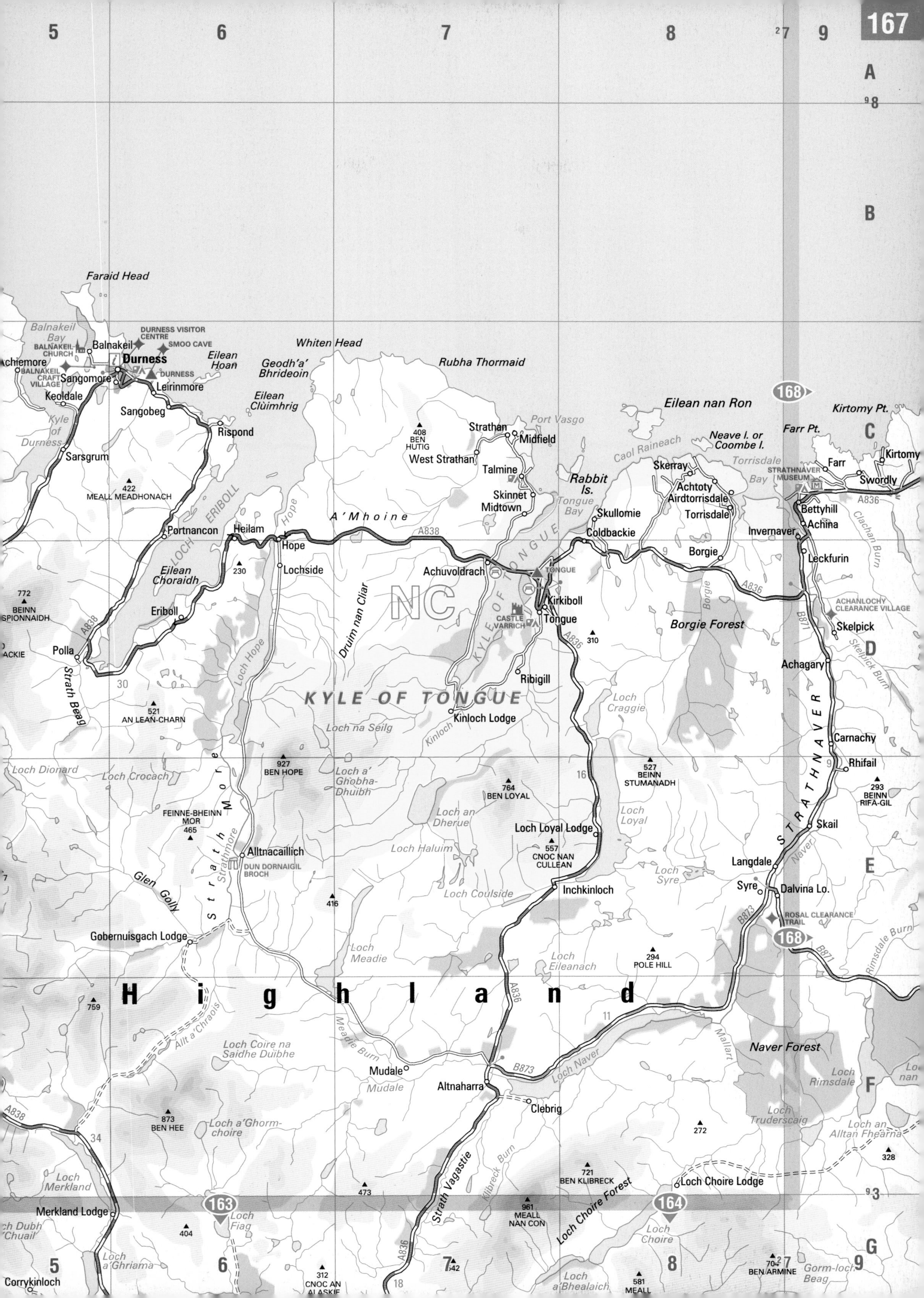
Faraid Head
Balnakeil Bay
Balnakeil
Durness
DURNESS VISITOR CENTRE
SMOO CAVE
Sangomore
Leirinmore
Keoldale
Sangobeg
Rispond
Kyle of Durness
Sarsgrum
Eilean Hoan
Geodh'a' Bhrideoin
Eilean Clùimhrig
Whiten Head
Rubha Thormaid
MEALL MEADHONACH
LOCH ERIBOLL
Portnancon
Heilam
Hope
Lochside
Eilean Choraidh
Eriboll
Polla
Strath Beag
BEN HUTIG
Strathan
Midfield
Port Vasgo
West Strathan
Talmine
Skinnet
Midtown
A'Mhoine
Rabbit Is.
Tongue Bay
Eilean nan Ron
Caol Raineach
Skerray
Achtoty
Airdtorrisdale
Torrisdale
Skullomie
Coldbackie
Borgie
Neave I. or Coombe I.
Torrisdale Bay
Farr Pt.
Kirtomy Pt.
Farr
Kirtomy
Swordly
STRATHNAVER MUSEUM
Bettyhill
Achina
Invernaver
Leckfurin
Achuvoldrach
TONGUE
Kirkiboll
Tongue
CASTLE VARRICH
KYLE OF TONGUE
Druim nan Cliar
Borgie Forest
ACHANLOCHY CLEARANCE VILLAGE
Skelpick
Achagary
Ribigill
Kinloch Lodge
Loch Craggie
Loch na Seilg
BEN HOPE
Loch a' Ghobha-Dhuibh
BEN LOYAL
BEINN STUMANADH
Carnachy
Rhifail
BEINN RIFA-GIL
STRATHNAVER
Loch Dionard
Loch Crocach
FEINNE-BHEINN MOR
Strath More
Alltnacaillich
DUN DORNAIGIL BROCH
Loch an Dherue
Loch Loyal Lodge
Loch Loyal
CNOC NAN CULLEAN
Skail
Langdale
Syre
Dalvina Lo.
Loch Syre
Inchkinloch
Loch Haluim
Loch Coulside
Glen Golly
Gobernuisgach Lodge
ROSAL CLEARANCE TRAIL
Loch Meadie
Loch Eileanach
POLE HILL
Rimsdale Burn
Highland
Allt a'Chraois
Loch Coire na Saidhe Duibhe
Meadie Burn
Mudale
Altnaharra
Loch Naver
Naver Forest
Mallart
Loch Rimsdale
Clebrig
BEN HEE
Loch a'Ghorm-choire
Loch Truderscaig
Loch an Alltan Fhearna
Loch Merkland
Merkland Lodge
BEN KLIBRECK
Loch Choire Lodge
Strath Vagastie
Kilbreck Burn
MEALL NAN CON
Loch Choire Forest
Loch Fiag
Loch Choire
Loch a'Ghriama
CNOC AN ALASKIE
Loch a'Bhealaich
MEALL
BEN ARMINE
Gorm-loch Beag
Corrykinloch
NC

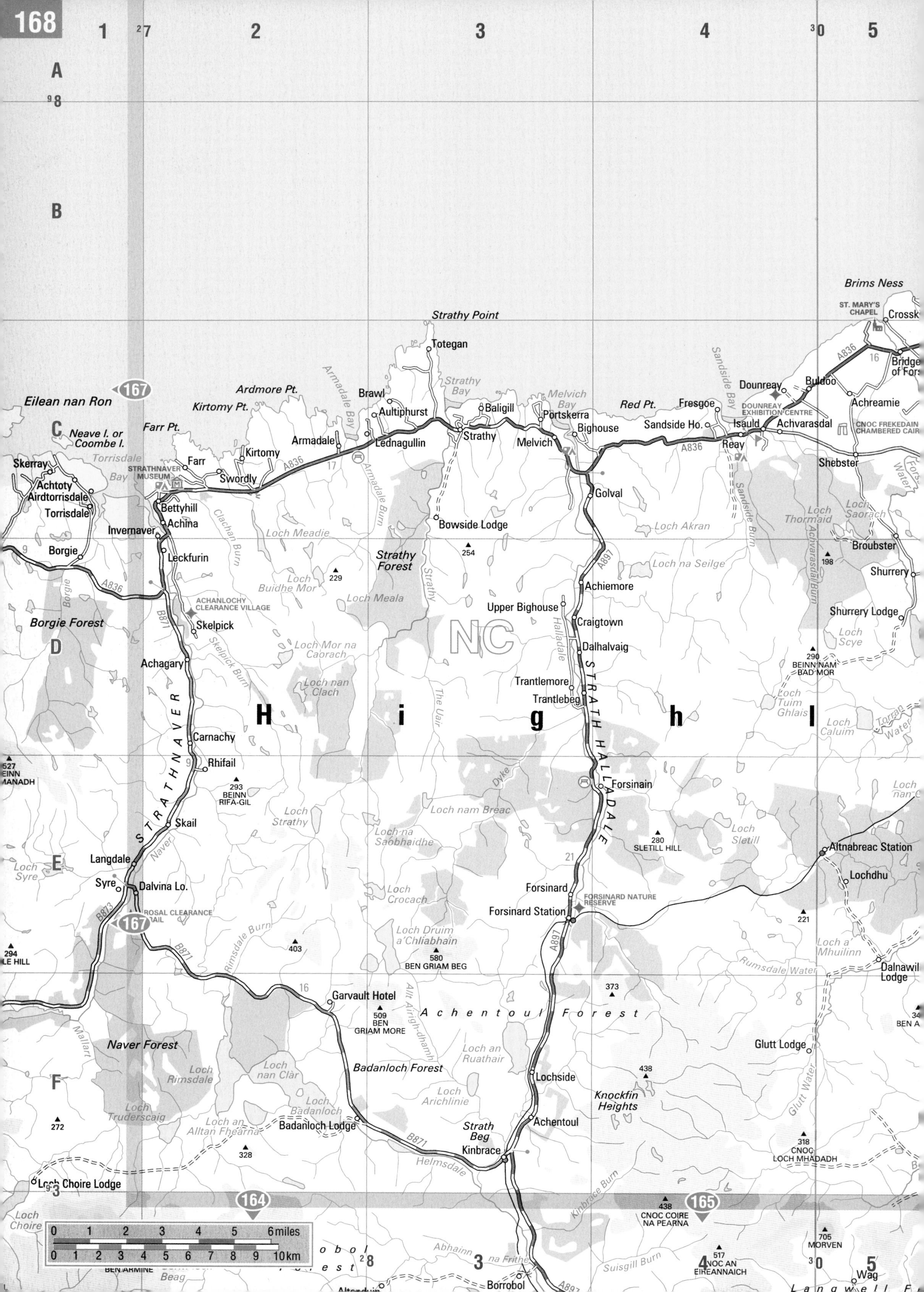
Eilean nan Ron
Neave I. or Coombe I.
Skerray
Achtoty
Airdtorrisdale
Torrisdale
Torrisdale Bay
Farr Pt.
Kirtomy Pt.
Ardmore Pt.
Farr
Swordly
Kirtomy
Armadale
Brawl
Aultiphurst
Lednagullin
Strathy Point
Totegan
Strathy Bay
Baligill
Strathy
Melvich Bay
Portskerra
Melvich
Bighouse
Red Pt.
Fresgoe
Sandside Ho.
Isauld
Reay
Dounreay
DOUNREAY EXHIBITION CENTRE
Achvarasdal
Buldoo
Achreamie
CNOC FREKEDAIN CHAMBERED CAIR
Brims Ness
ST. MARY'S CHAPEL
Crossk
Bridge of For
Shebster
STRATHNAVER MUSEUM
Bettyhill
Achina
Invernaver
Borgie
Leckfurin
Bowside Lodge
Golval
Loch Akran
Loch Meadie
Strathy Forest
Loch Buidhe Mor
Loch Meala
Loch na Seilge
Achiemore
Broubster
Shurrery
Shurrery Lodge
Borgie Forest
ACHANLOCHY CLEARANCE VILLAGE
Skelpick
Upper Bighouse
Craigtown
Dalhalvaig
Loch Mor na Caorach
Loch nan Clach
NC
Achagary
Trantlemore
Trantlebeg
STRATH HALLADALE
BEINN NAM BAD MOR
H i g h l
Carnachy
Rhifail
BEINN RIFA-GIL
STRATHNAVER
Forsinain
Loch Strathy
Loch nam Breac
Loch na Saobhaidhe
SLETILL HILL
Loch Sletill
Skail
Langdale
Syre
Dalvina Lo.
Altnabreac Station
Lochdhu
Forsinard
Forsinard Station
FORSINARD NATURE RESERVE
Loch Crocach
Loch Druim a'Chliabhain
BEN GRIAM BEG
Rumsdale Water
Dalnawil Lodge
Garvault Hotel
BEN GRIAM MORE
Achentoul Forest
Glutt Lodge
Naver Forest
Loch Rimsdale
Loch nan Clàr
Badanloch Forest
Loch an Ruathair
Lochside
Knockfin Heights
Loch Arichlinie
Loch Badanloch
Loch Truderscaig
Loch an Alltan Fhearna
Badanloch Lodge
Strath Beg
Achentoul
Kinbrace
Helmsdale
CNOC LOCH MHADADH
Loch Choire Lodge
CNOC COIRE NA PEARNA
0 1 2 3 4 5 6 miles
0 1 2 3 4 5 6 7 8 9 10 km
MORVEN
NOC AN EIREANNAICH
Borrobol
Wag
A836
A897
B871
B873

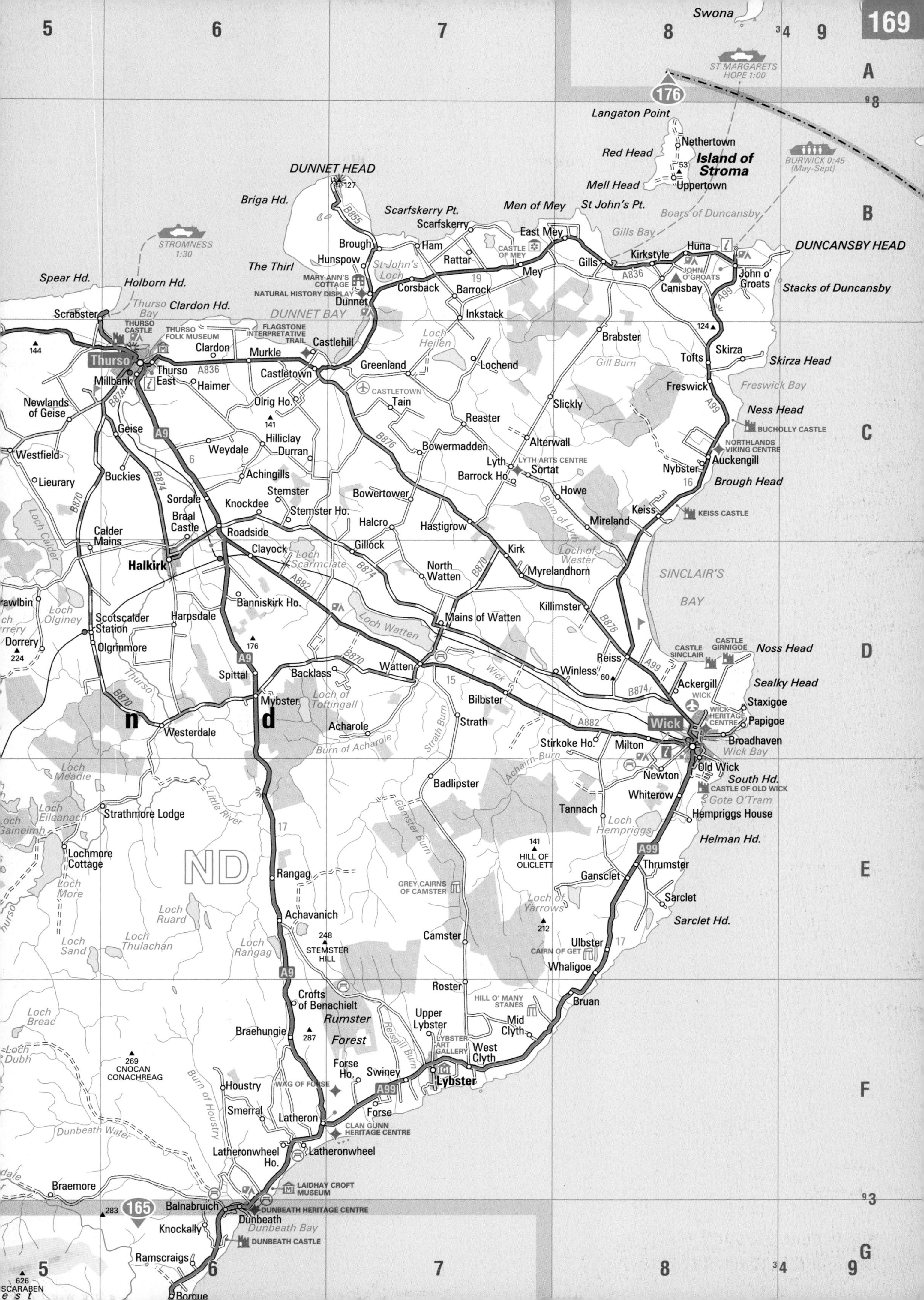

DUNNET HEAD
DUNCANSBY HEAD
Island of Stroma
Swona
Thurso
Wick
Halkirk
Lybster
Dunbeath
John o' Groats
Castletown
Keiss
Watten
SINCLAIR'S BAY
Dunnet Bay
Freswick Bay
Wick Bay
Dunbeath Bay
Loch Watten
Loch Calder
Stacks of Duncansby
Noss Head
Sealky Head
Brough Head
Ness Head
Skirza Head
Helman Hd.
Sarclet Hd.
South Hd.
Clardon Hd.
Holborn Hd.
Spear Hd.
Briga Hd.
Scarfskerry Pt.
St John's Pt.
Men of Mey
Mell Head
Red Head
Langaton Point
ST MARGARETS HOPE 1:00
BURWICK 0:45 (May-Sept)
STROMNESS 1:30
CASTLE OF MEY
MARY-ANN'S COTTAGE
NATURAL HISTORY DISPLAY
FLAGSTONE INTERPRETATIVE TRAIL
THURSO CASTLE
THURSO FOLK MUSEUM
CASTLETOWN
LYTH ARTS CENTRE
NORTHLANDS VIKING CENTRE
BUCHOLLY CASTLE
KEISS CASTLE
CASTLE SINCLAIR
CASTLE GIRNIGOE
WICK HERITAGE CENTRE
CASTLE OF OLD WICK
GREY CAIRNS OF CAMSTER
CAIRN OF GET
HILL O' MANY STANES
LYBSTER ART GALLERY
WAG OF FORSE
CLAN GUNN HERITAGE CENTRE
LAIDHAY CROFT MUSEUM
DUNBEATH HERITAGE CENTRE
DUNBEATH CASTLE
HILL OF OLICLETT
STEMSTER HILL
CNOCAN CONACHREAG
SCARABEN
Rumster Forest
ND
A9
A99
A836
A882
B874
B876
B870
B855
176
165

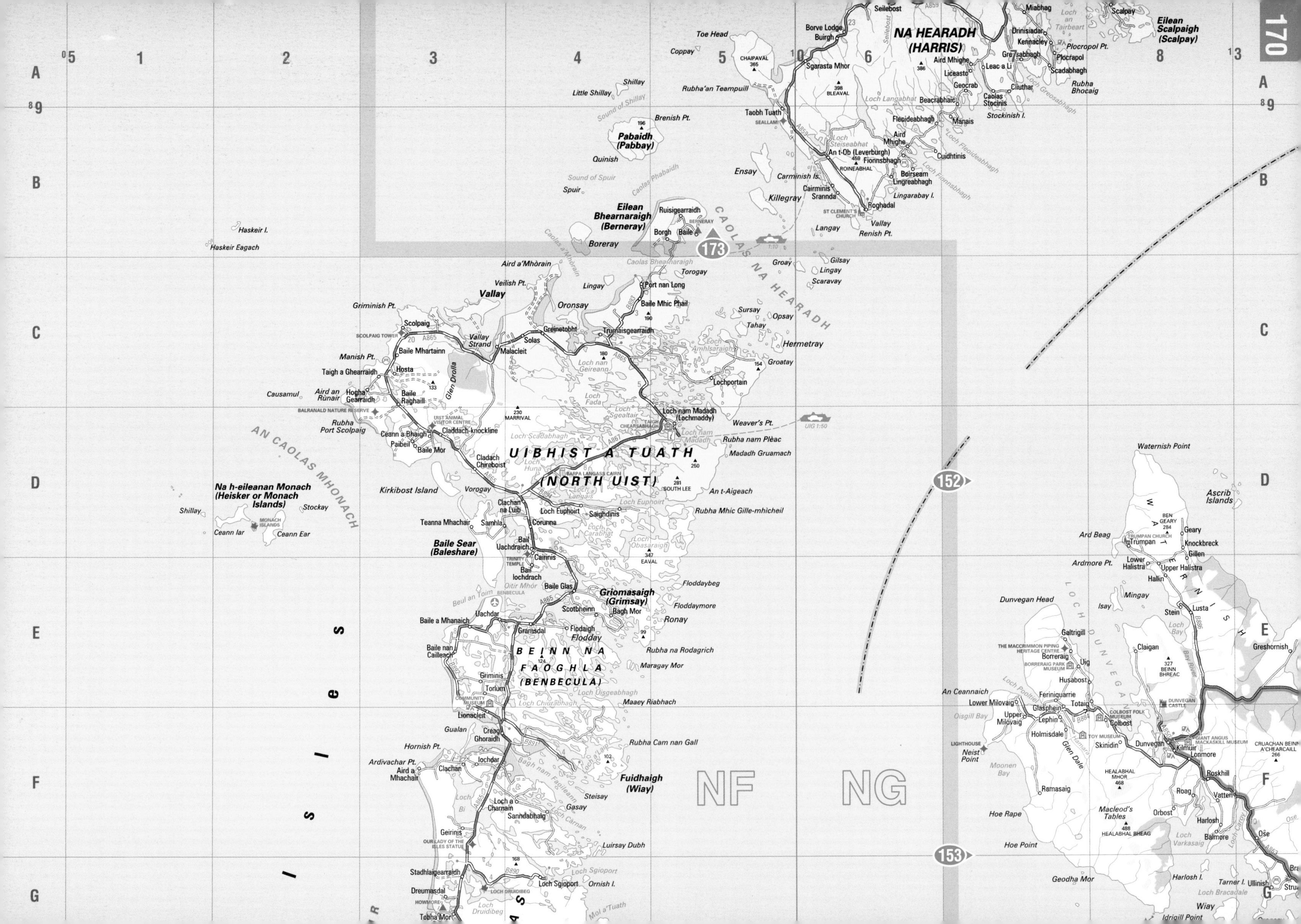

NA HEARADH (HARRIS)
Eilean Scalpaigh (Scalpay)
Scalpay
Miabhag
Drinisiadar
Kennacley
Plocropol Pt.
Plocrapol
Greosabhagh
Scadabhagh
Rubha Bhocaig
Aird Mhighe
Liceasto
Leac a Li
Geocrab
Cliuthar
Caolas Stocinis
Stockinish I.
Beacrabhaic
Fleoideabhagh
Manais
Aird Mhighe
Cuidhtinis
An t-Ob (Leverburgh)
Fionnsbhagh
ROINEABHAL
Boirseam
Lingreabhagh
Lingarabay I.
Roghadal
Vallay
Renish Pt.
ST CLEMENT'S CHURCH
Cairminis
Srannda
Carminish Is.
Killegray
Langay
Seilebost
Borve Lodge
Buirgh
Sgarasta Mhor
BLEAVAL
Taobh Tuath
SEALLAM!
CHAIPAVAL
Toe Head
Coppay
Rubha'an Teampuill
Shillay
Little Shillay
Sound of Shillay
Brenish Pt.
Pabaidh (Pabbay)
Quinish
Sound of Spuir
Spuir
Ensay
Eilean Bhearnaraigh (Berneray)
Ruisigearraidh
BERNERAY
Borgh
Baile
Boreray
CAOLAS NA HEARADH
Caolas Bhearnaraigh
Gilsay
Lingay
Scaravay
Groay
Torogay
Port nan Long
Baile Mhic Phail
Lingay
Oronsay
Aird a'Mhòrain
Veilish Pt.
Vallay
Griminish Pt.
Scolpaig
SCOLPAIG TOWER
Baile Mhartainn
Vallay Strand
Solas
Greinetobht
Trumaisgearraidh
Malacleit
Sursay
Tahay
Opsay
Hermetray
Groatay
Lochportain
Manish Pt.
Hosta
Taigh a Ghearraidh
Baile Raghaill
Glen Drolla
Causamul
Aird an Rùnair
Hogha Gearraidh
BALRANALD NATURE RESERVE
Rubha Port Scolpaig
MARRIVAL
Loch nan Geireann
Loch Fada
Loch Sgealtair
Loch nam Madadh (Lochmaddy)
Weaver's Pt.
UIG 1:50
Rubha nam Plèac
Madadh Gruamach
Ceann a Bhaigh
Claddach-knockline
Paibeil
Baile Mor
Cladach Chireboist
Loch Scadabhagh
UIBHIST A TUATH (NORTH UIST)
BARPA LANGASS CAIRN
SOUTH LEE
An t-Aigeach
AN CAOLAS MHONACH
Na h-eileanan Monach (Heisker or Monach Islands)
Shillay
Stockay
MONACH ISLANDS
Ceann Iar
Ceann Ear
Kirkibost Island
Vorogay
Clachan na Luib
Loch Euphoirt
Saighdinis
Rubha Mhic Gille-mhicheil
Teanna Mhachair
Samhla
Corunna
Baile Sear (Baleshare)
Baile Uachdraich
Cairinis
TRINITY TEMPLE
Baile Iochdrach
EAVAL
Oitir Mhòr
Baile Glas
Floddaybeg
Griomasaigh (Grimsay)
Floddaymore
Beul an Toim
BENBECULA
Uachdar
Scotbheinn
Bagh Mor
Ronay
Baile a Mhanaich
Gramsdal
Flodaigh
Flodday
BEINN NA FAOGHLA (BENBECULA)
Rubha na Rodagrich
Baile nan Cailleach
Maragay Mor
Griminis
Torlum
Loch Uisgeabhagh
COMMUNITY MUSEUM
Loch Chiarabhagh
Maaey Riabhach
Lionacleit
Gualan
Creag Ghoraidh
Rubha Cam nan Gall
Hornish Pt.
Iochdar
Ardivachar Pt.
Aird a Mhachair
Clachan
Bagh nam Faoileann
Fuidhaigh (Wiay)
Steisay
Loch a Charnain
Gasay
Sanndabhaig
Loch Carnan
Geirinis
OUR LADY OF THE ISLES STATUE
Luirsay Dubh
Stadhlaigearraidh
Loch Sgioport
Ornish I.
Dreumasdal
LOCH DRUIDIBEG
HOWMORE
Tobha Mor
Loch Druidibeg
Mol a'Tuath
Haskeir I.
Haskeir Eagach
NF
NG
152
153
173
Waterish Point
Ascrib Islands
WATERNISH
BEN GEARY
Geary
Knockbreck
Gillen
Ard Beag
TRUMPAN CHURCH
Trumpan
Ardmore Pt.
Lower Halistra
Upper Halistra
Hallin
Mingay
Isay
Dunvegan Head
LOCH DUNVEGAN
Stein
Lusta
Loch Bay
Bay River
Greshornish
Galtrigill
THE MACCRIMMON PIPING HERITAGE CENTRE
Borreraig
BORRERAIG PARK MUSEUM
Uig
Claigan
BEINN BHREAC
Husabost
DUNVEGAN CASTLE
An Ceannaich
Feriniquarrie
Lower Milovaig
Glasphein
Totaig
COLBOST FOLK MUSEUM
Upper Milovaig
Lephin
Colbost
Oisgill Bay
Holmisdale
TOY MUSEUM
GIANT ANGUS MACKASKILL MUSEUM
LIGHTHOUSE
Neist Point
Skinidin
Dunvegan
Kilmuir
Lonmore
CRUACHAN BEINN A'CHEARCAILL
Glen Dale
Moonen Bay
HEALABHAL MHOR
Roskhill
Ramasaig
Roag
Vatten
Hoe Rape
Macleod's Tables
Orbost
HEALABHAL BHEAG
Harlosh
Loch Varkasaig
Balmore
Ose
Hoe Point
Geodha Mor
Harlosh I.
Tarner I.
Ullinish
Loch Bracadale
Wiay
Idrigill Point
Isles

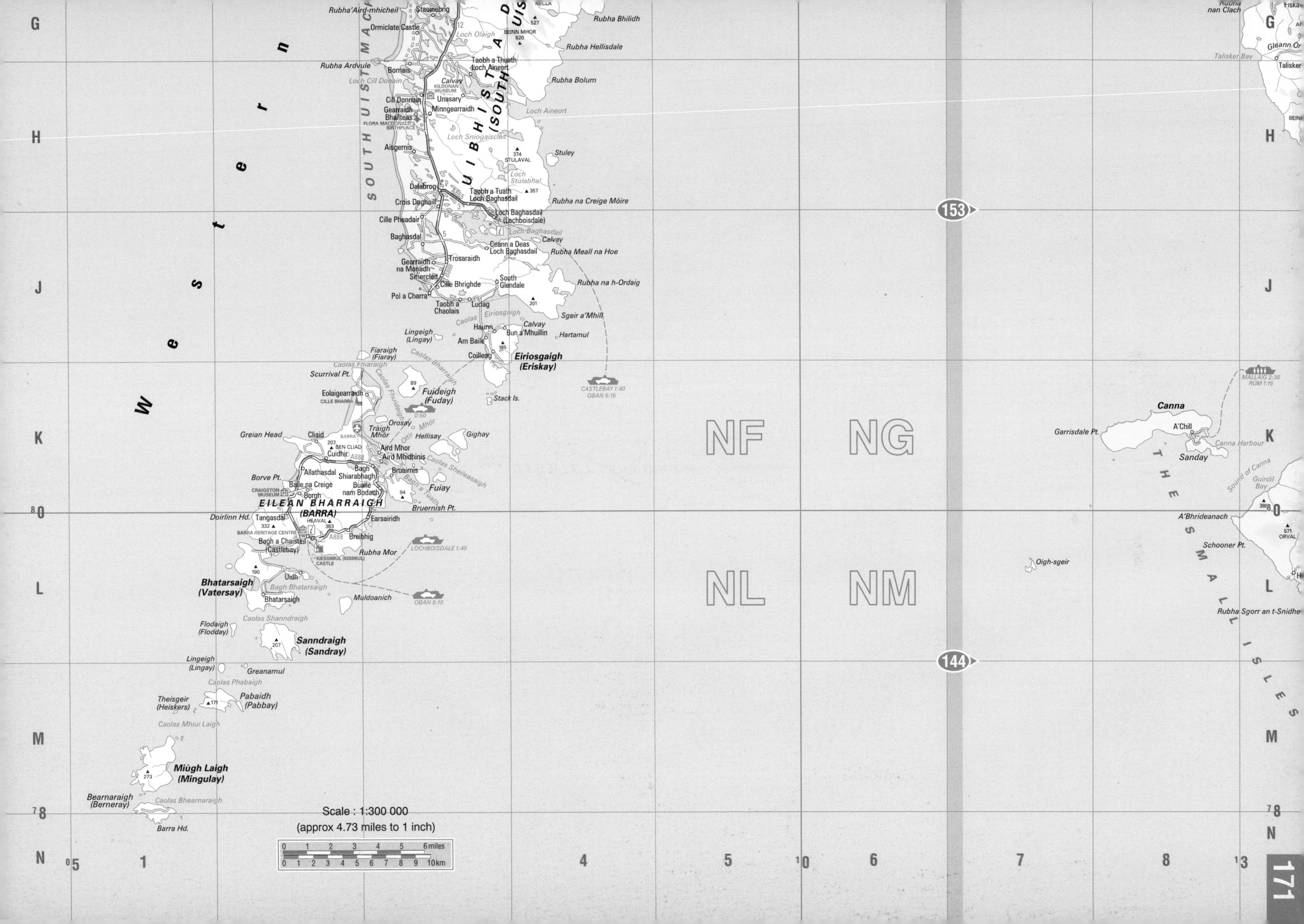

Western
SOUTH UIST
UIBHIST A DEAS (SOUTH UIST)
Rubha Aird-mhicheil
Staoinebrig
Ormiclate Castle
Loch Olaigh
BEINN MHOR 620
527
Rubha Bhilidh
Rubha Hellisdale
Rubha Ardvule
Bornais
Taobh a Thuath Loch Aineort
Rubha Bolum
Loch Cill Donain
Calvay
KILDONAN MUSEUM
Cill Donnain
Unasary
Gearraidh Bhailteas
Minngearraidh
FLORA MACDONALD'S BIRTHPLACE
Loch Aineort
Loch Sniogaisgleit
Aisgernis
374 STULAVAL
Stuley
Loch Stùlabhal
Dalabrog
Taobh a Tuath Loch Baghasdail
357
Crois Dughaill
Rubha na Creige Móire
Cille Pheadair
Loch Baghasdail (Lochboisdale)
Loch Baghasdail
Calvay
Baghasdal
Ceann a Deas Loch Baghasdail
Rubha Meall na Hoe
Gearraidh na Monadh
Trosaraidh
Smercleit
Cille Bhrighde
South Glendale
Rubha na h-Ordaig
Pol a Charra
Taobh a Chaolais
Ludag
201
Caolas Eiriosgaigh
Sgeir a'Mhill
Lingeigh (Lingay)
Haunn
Calvay
Bun a'Mhuillin
Hartamul
Am Baile
185
Fiaraigh (Fiaray)
Coilleag
Eiriosgaigh (Eriskay)
Caolas Fhiaraigh
Caolas Bharraigh
Scurrival Pt.
89
CASTLEBAY 1:40 OBAN 5:15
Eolaigearraidh
Fuideigh (Fuday)
CILLE BHARRA
Caolas Fhuideigh
Stack Is.
0:50
Orosay
Tràigh Mhòr
Oitir Mhòr
Hellisay
Gighay
Greian Head
Cliaid
BARRA
207
BEN CLIAD
Cuidhir
A888
Aird Mhor
Aird Mhidhinis
Caolas Sheileasaigh
Bagh Shiarabhagh
Bruairnis
Borve Pt.
Allathasdal
Baile na Creige
Buaile nam Bodach
Fuiay
CRAIGSTON MUSEUM
Borgh
94
Bagh a Tuath
EILEAN BHARRAIGH (BARRA)
Bruernish Pt.
Doirlinn Hd.
Tangasdal
HEAVAL
Earsairidh
332
383
BARRA HERITAGE CENTRE
A888
Breibhig
Bagh a Chaisteil (Castlebay)
LOCHBOISDALE 1:40
Rubha Mor
KIESSIMUL (KISIMUL) CASTLE
190
Uidh
Bhatarsaigh (Vatersay)
Bagh Bhatarsaigh
Bhatarsaigh
Muldoanich
OBAN 5:10
Caolas Shanndraigh
Flodaigh (Flodday)
207
Sanndraigh (Sandray)
Lingeigh (Lingay)
Greanamul
Caolas Phabaigh
Theisgeir (Heiskers)
171
Pabaidh (Pabbay)
Caolas Mhiui Laigh
273
Miùgh Laigh (Mingulay)
Bearnaraigh (Berneray)
Caolas Bhearnaraigh
Barra Hd.
Scale : 1:300 000
(approx 4.73 miles to 1 inch)
0 1 2 3 4 5 6 miles
0 1 2 3 4 5 6 7 8 9 10 km
153
144
NF
NG
NL
NM
MALLAIG 2:30 RUM 1:15
Canna
A'Chill
Garrisdale Pt.
Canna Harbour
Sanday
Sound of Canna
Guirdil Bay
THE SMALL ISLES
388
A'Bhrideanach
571 ORVAL
Schooner Pt.
Oigh-sgeir
Rubha Sgorr an t-Snidhe
Rubha nan Clach
Talisker Bay
Talisker
Gleann Or
G
H
J
K
L
M
N
5
1
4
5
10
6
7
8
13
80
78

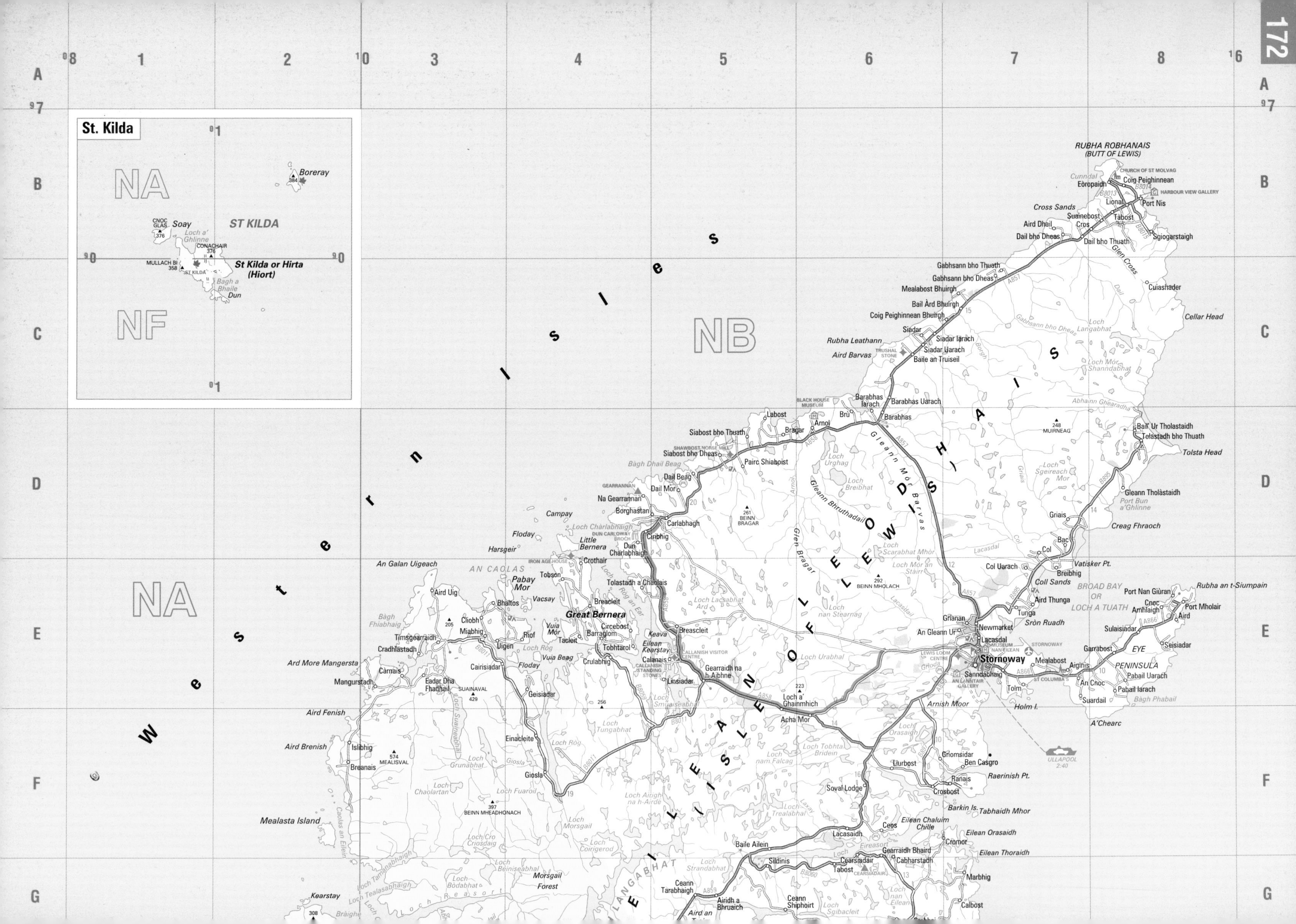

St. Kilda

ST KILDA

Soay

CNOC
GLAS
376

*St Kilda or Hirta
(Hiort)*

MULLACH BÌ
358

Boreray
384

CONACHAIR

Loch a'
Ghlinne

Bagh a
Bhaile
Dùn

RUBHA ROBHANAIS
(BUTT OF LEWIS)

CHURCH OF ST MOLVAG
HARBOUR VIEW GALLERY
Coig Peighinnean
Port Nis
Lional
Tabost
Eoropaidh
Cros
Sgiogarstaigh
Suaineabost
Dail bho Thuath
Aird Dhail
Dail bho Dheas
Cross Sands
Glen Cross

Cellar Head
Cuashader

Bail' Ur Tholastaidh
Tolstadh bho Thuath
Tolsta Head

Gleann Tholastaidh
Creag Fhraoch

Rubha an t-Siumpain
Port Mholair
Port Nan Giùran
Aird
Cnoc
Amhlaidh
Seisiadar
Pabail Uarach
Bagh Phabail
Pabail Iarach

Gabhsann bho Thuath
Gabhsann bho Dheas
Mealabost Bhuirgh
Bail Àrd Bhuirgh
Coig Peighinnean Bhuirgh
Siadar
Siadar Iarach
Siadar Uarach
Baile an Truiseil
Barabhas Uarach

Abhainn Ghearadha
Loch Mòr Shanndabhat
Loch Sgeireach Mòr
Griais

Vatisker Pt.
Bac
Col
Braibhig
Aird Thunga
Tunga
Sròn Ruadh
Newmarket

BROAD BAY
OR
LOCH A TUATH

PENINSULA
EYE
Garrabost
Aignis
An Cnoc
A'Chearc
Suardail

Rubha Leathann
Aird Barvas
Barabhas
Iarach
Barabhas
Brù
Arnol
Bragar
Labost
Pàirc Shiabost

TRISHAL
STONE
BLACK HOUSE
MUSEUM

Gleann Mòr Barvas
Loch Urghag
Loch Breibhat
Gleann Bhudhladail
Glen Bragar

BENN
BHRAGAR
261

ISLE OF LEWIS

Loch Mòr an
Starr
Loch Scarabhat
Mòr
292
BENN MHOLACH
Loch nan Urabhail

An Gleann Ur
Grianan

STORNOWAY
Mealabost
ST COLUMBA
Laxdale
Sanndabhig
Tolm
Holm I.

ARNISH AN LANNTAIR
GALLERY
ARTS
CENTRE

Arnish Mòr

ULLAPOOL 2:40

Gress

Col Uarach
Lacasdal

A'Gearraidh na
h-Aibhne

223

Loch a'
Ghainmhich
Achamòr

Raerinish Pt.
Ben Casgro
Griomsidar
Ranais
Crosbost

Eilean Orasaidh
Barkin Is Tabhaidh Mhor
Eilean Thoraidh
Marbhig
Cromor

Siabost bho Thuath
Siabost bho Dheas
Dail Beag
Dail Mòr
Carlabhagh
Na Gearrannan

SHAWBOST NORSE MILL
DUN CARLOWAY
BROCH

Breasclett
GALLSON VISITOR
CENTRE
Linsiadar

Soval Lodge
Liurbost

Keose
Lacasaidh
Cearsiadar
Tabost
Ceann Shiphoirt

Loch Tròlabhat
Loch Bridhin
Loch Trealabhat

SLèibhte
Siltinis

Borghastan
Cùrabhig
Dun
Charlabhaigh

IRON AGE HOUSE
DUN
Crothair
Little
Bernera

Calanais
Eilean
Kearstaigh

CALLANISH
STANDING
STONES

Garynahine

Tobhta Uarach
Tolastadh a' Chaolais
Breacleit
Crulabhig

Great Bernera
Barraglom
Kirkibost
Tobhtarol

AN CAOLAS
Vacasay
Pabay
Mòr
Bhaltos
Floday
Miabhig
Riof
Ungen

Loch Ròg
Loch Fuarbhill

266

Loch Sgìollar

Baile Ailein

Ceann Tarabhaigh
Àird a
Bhruaich

LANGABHAT
Loch Langabhat
Loch Sgìodar
Loch Tungabhat

Loch Airigh
na h-Airde

Einacleite
Giosla

Floday
Geisiadar

Campay
Harsgeir

Floday

AN GALAN UIGEACH
Aird Uig
Cliobh
205
Crabhlastadh
Timsgearraidh
Carnais

Ard Mòr Mangersta
Mangurstadh

Loch Ròg

Loch Morsgail

MORSGAIL
FOREST

Loch
Sgaire

Loch
Chlàrtan

Bagh
Fhlabhaig
MEALISVAL
574
BEINN MHEADHONACH
SUAINAVAL
429
397
Loch
Grunabhat
Isbihig
Breanais

Aird Brenish
Aird Fenish

Mealasta Island

388

Ceos

Loch Roaig

Loch Coirgeabhal

Loch Bhrollum

Caolas an Eilein

Kearstay

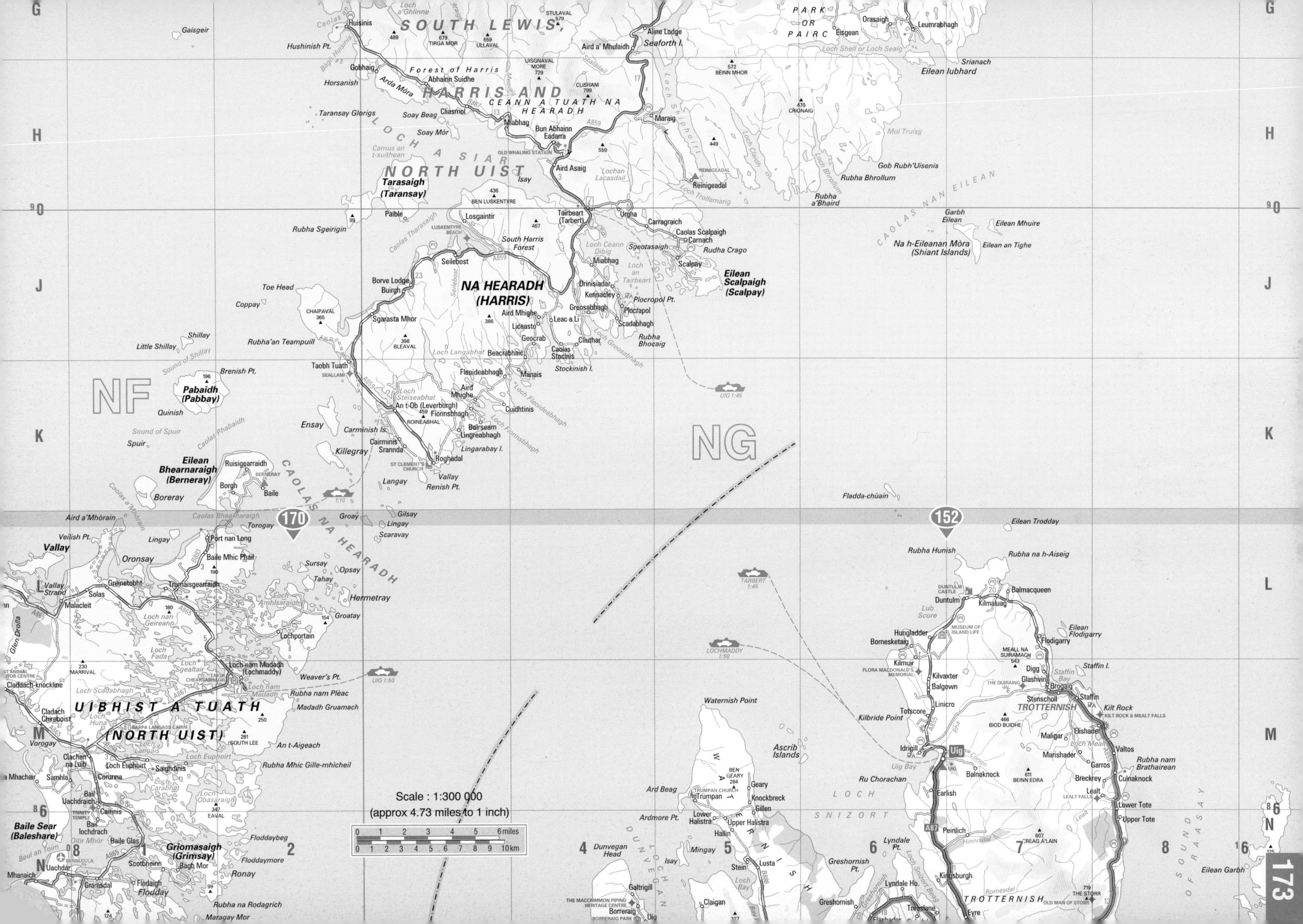

SOUTH LEWIS
HARRIS AND
CEANN A TUATH NA HEARADH
NORTH UIST
LOCH A SIAR
NA HEARADH (HARRIS)
UIBHIST A TUATH (NORTH UIST)
TROTTERNISH
WATERNISH
PARK OR PAIRC
Forest of Harris
South Harris Forest
Eilean Scalpaigh (Scalpay)
Tarasaigh (Taransay)
Eilean Bhearnaraigh (Berneray)
Pabaidh (Pabbay)
Griomasaigh (Grimsay)
Baile Sear (Baleshare)
Na h-Eileanan Mòra (Shiant Islands)
Eilean Iubhard
Eilean Mhuire
Eilean an Tighe
Garbh Eilean
Ascrib Islands
Eilean Flodigarry
Eilean Trodday
Fladda-chùain
Staffin I.
Seaforth I.
Loch Seaforth
Loch Shell or Loch Sealg
Loch Snizort
Loch Dunvegan
Sound of Raasay
Sound of Shillay
Sound of Spuir
CAOLAS NA HEARADH
CAOLAS NAN EILEAN
Huisinis
Tairbeart (Tarbert)
An t-Ob (Leverburgh)
Roghadal
Seilebost
Borve Lodge
Scalpay
Loch nam Madadh (Lochmaddy)
Baile Mhic Phail
Port nan Long
Lochportain
Uig
Staffin
Duntulm
Kilmuir
Balmacqueen
Flodigarry
Kilt Rock
Waternish Point
Dunvegan Head
Rubha Hunish
Rubha na h-Aiseig
Weaver's Pt.
Toe Head
Renish Pt.
NF
NG
170
152
Scale : 1:300 000
(approx 4.73 miles to 1 inch)

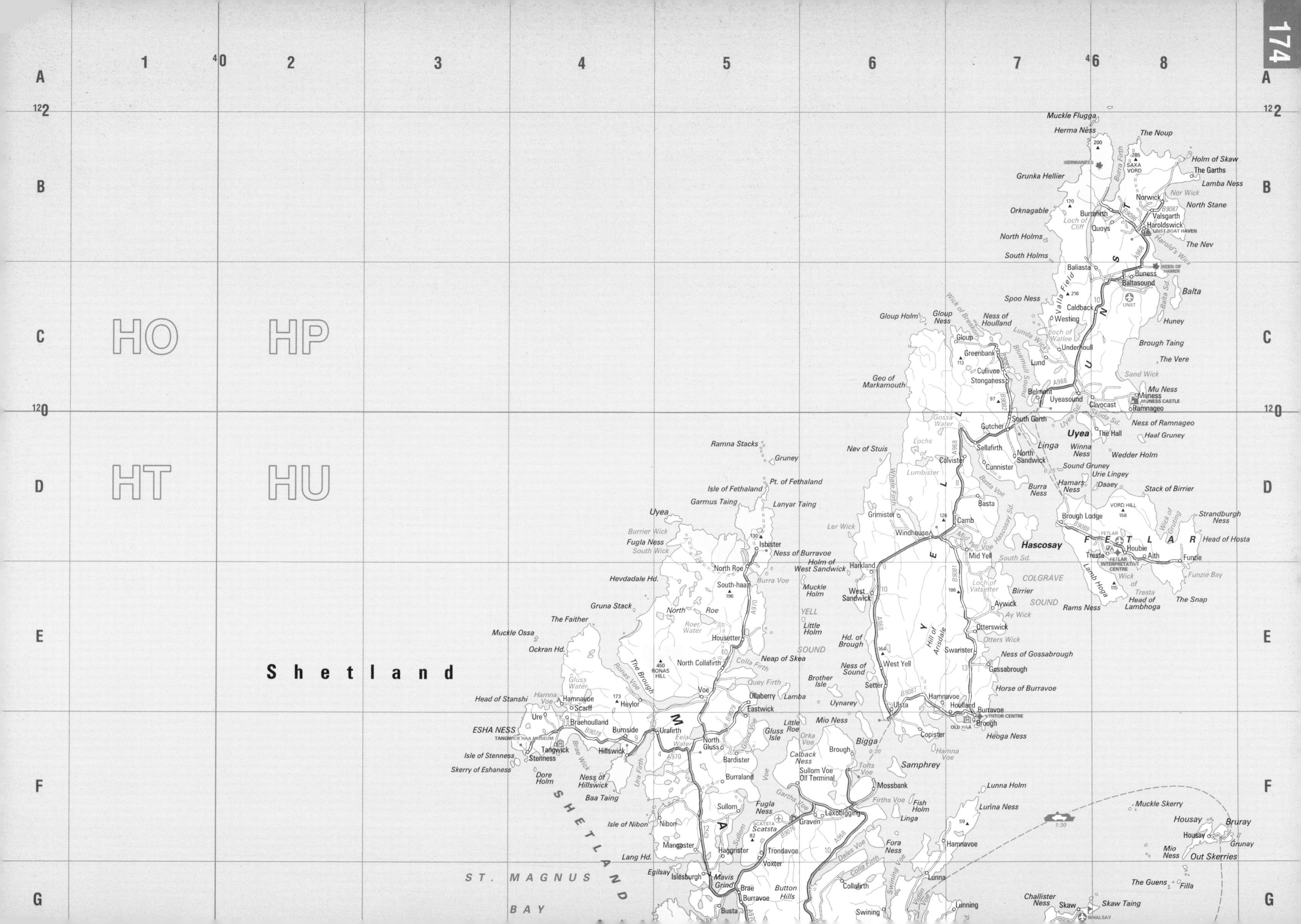

Shetland
HO
HP
HT
HU
UNST
YELL
FETLAR
MAINLAND
Muckle Flugga
Herma Ness
The Noup
Holm of Skaw
The Garths
Lamba Ness
Norwick
Nor Wick
North Stane
Valsgarth
Haroldswick
Burrafirth
Burra Firth
Saxa Vord
Hermaness
Grunka Hellier
Orknagable
Loch of Cliff
Quoys
North Holms
South Holms
The Nev
Harold's Wick
Baliasta
Keen of Hamar
Buness
Baltasound
Balta
Balta Sd.
Valla Field
Spoo Ness
Caldback
Westing
Huney
Loch of Watlee
Underhoull
Brough Taing
The Vere
Sand Wick
Lund
Lunda Wick
Bluemull Sound
Belmont
Uyeasound
Clivocast
Muness
Muness Castle
Mu Ness
Ramnageo
Ness of Ramnageo
Haaf Gruney
Uyea
Uyea Sd.
Skuda Sd.
The Hall
Wedder Holm
Winna Ness
Linga
Sound Gruney
Urie Lingey
Daaey
Stack of Birrier
Hamars Ness
Burra Ness
Gloup Holm
Gloup Ness
Gloup
Wick of Breakon
Ness of Houlland
Greenbank
Cullivoe
Stonganess
Geo of Markamouth
South Garth
Gutcher
Gossa Water
Sellafirth
North Sandwick
Cunnister
Colvister
Basta Voe
Basta
Lochs of Lumbister
Nev of Stuis
Whale Firth
Grimister
Windhouse
Camb
Mid Yell
Mid Yell Voe
Hascosay
Hascosay Sd.
South Sd.
COLGRAVE SOUND
Brough Lodge
Vord Hill
Wick of Gruting
Strandburgh Ness
Head of Hosta
Fetlar Interpretative Centre
Tresta
Houbie
Aith
Funzie
Funzie Bay
Lamb Hoga
Wick of Tresta
Head of Lambhoga
The Snap
Rams Ness
Birrier
Loch of Vatsetter
Aywick
Ay Wick
Otterswick
Otters Wick
Swarister
Ness of Gossabrough
Gossabrough
Horse of Burravoe
Hill of Arisdale
Harkland
West Sandwick
Ler Wick
Hd. of Brough
Ness of Sound
West Yell
Setter
Hamnavoe
Houlland
Burravoe
Old Haa
Brough
Visitor Centre
Ulsta
Copister
Heoga Ness
Hamna Voe
Ramna Stacks
Gruney
Pt. of Fethaland
Isle of Fethaland
Garmus Taing
Lanyar Taing
Uyea
Burrier Wick
Fugla Ness
South Wick
Isbister
Ness of Burravoe
Holm of West Sandwick
Muckle Holm
Little Holm
YELL SOUND
North Roe
Burra Voe
South-haa
Hevdadale Hd.
Gruna Stack
The Faither
North Roe
Roer Water
Housetter
Muckle Ossa
Ockran Hd.
Ronas Hill
North Collafirth
Colla Firth
Neap of Skea
Quey Firth
Brother Isle
The Brough
Ronas Voe
Gluss Water
Head of Stanshi
Hamna Voe
Hamnavoe
Heylor
Voe
Ollaberry
Lamba
Uynarey
Eastwick
Ure
Scarff
Braehoulland
ESHA NESS
Tangwick Haa Museum
Tangwick
Burnside
Urafirth
Eela Water
Mio Ness
Little Roe
Gluss Isle
Orka Voe
Bigga
Isle of Stenness
Stenness
Hillswick
Brae Wick
North Gluss
Gluss Voe
Bardister
Calback Ness
Sullom Voe Oil Terminal
Brough
Tofts Voe
Samphrey
Skerry of Eshaness
Dore Holm
Ness of Hillswick
Ura Firth
Burraland
Baa Taing
Sullom
Fugla Ness
Garths Voe
Mossbank
Firths Voe
Fish Holm
Linga
Lunna Holm
Lunna Ness
Muckle Skerry
Housay
Bruray
Grunay
Out Skerries
Mio Ness
Isle of Nibon
Nibon
Scatsta
Graven
Laxobigging
Mangaster
Lang Hd.
Haggrister
Sullom Voe
Trondavoe
Voxter
Fora Ness
Hamnavoe
Dales Voe
Egilsay
Islesburgh
Mavis Grind
Brae
Burravoe
Busta
Button Hills
Colla Firth
Collafirth
Swining Voe
Swining
Lunna
Vidlin Voe
Lunning
The Guens
Filla
Challister Ness
Skaw
Skaw Taing
Whalsay
SHETLAND
ST. MAGNUS BAY

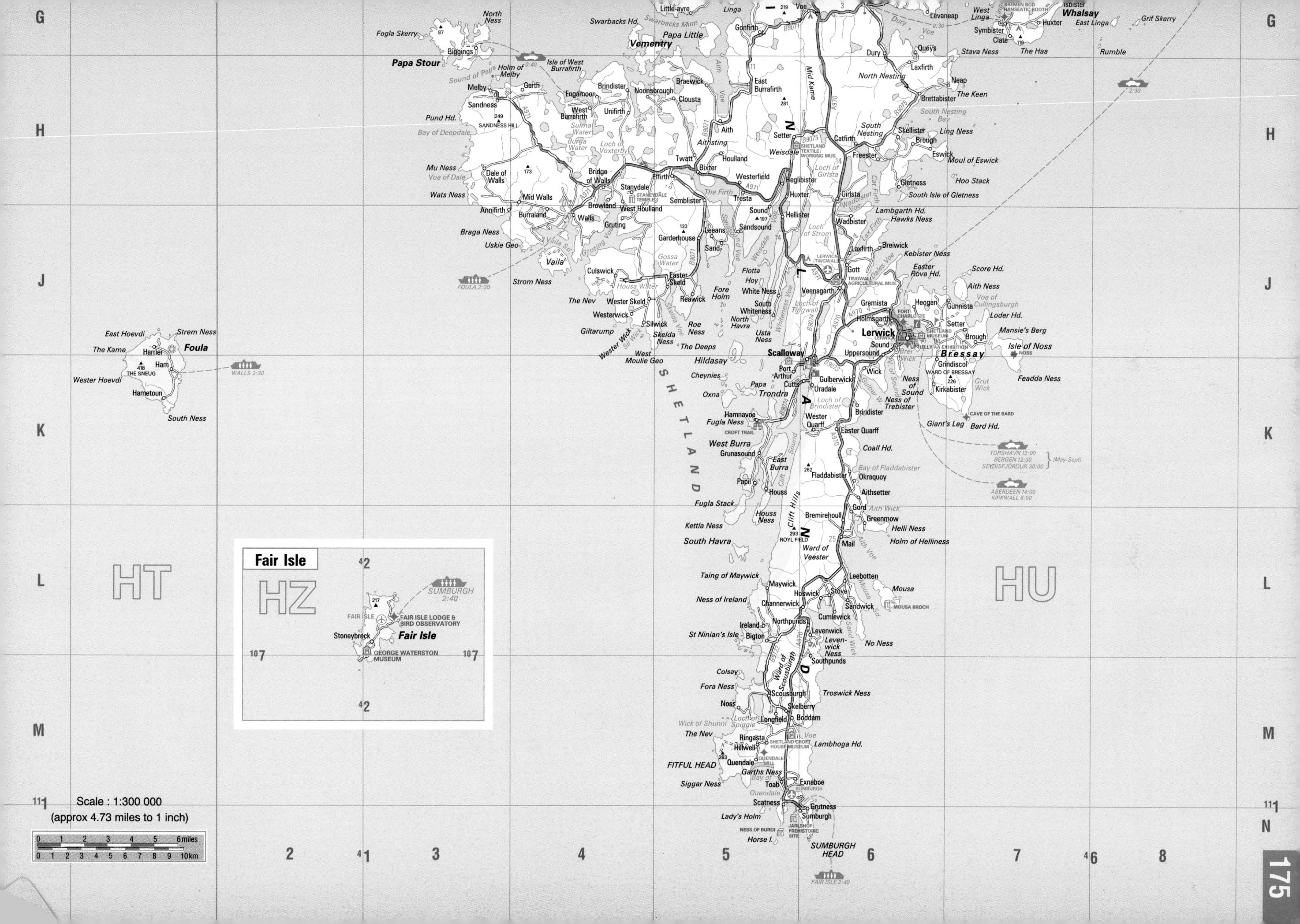

SHETLAND
Lerwick
Scalloway
Bressay
Isle of Noss
Whalsay
Papa Stour
Vementry
Papa Little
Foula
Vaila
Trondra
West Burra
East Burra
Mousa
Fair Isle
HT
HZ
HU
Sumburgh Head
Fitful Head
Stoneybreck
Fair Isle Lodge & Bird Observatory
George Waterston Museum
Sumburgh 2:40
Walls 2:30
Foula 2:30
Fair Isle 2:40
Aberdeen 14:00
Kirkwall 6:00
Torshavn 12:00
Bergen 12:30
Seydisfjördur 30:00
(May-Sept)
Scale : 1:300 000
(approx 4.73 miles to 1 inch)

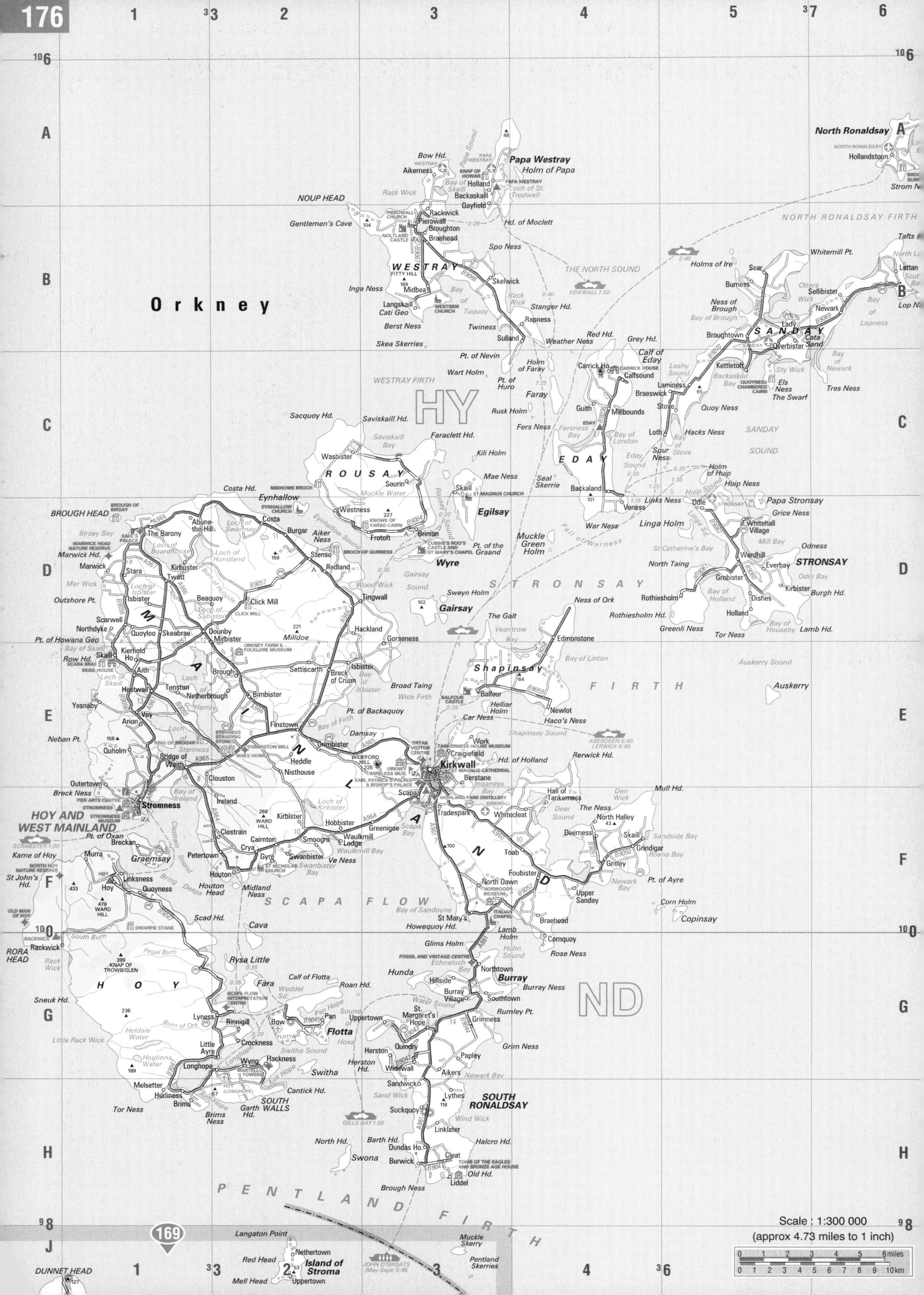
Orkney
HY
ND
Papa Westray
Westray
Rousay
Egilsay
Wyre
Gairsay
Eday
Sanday
North Ronaldsay
Stronsay
Papa Stronsay
Shapinsay
Auskerry
Kirkwall
Stromness
HOY AND WEST MAINLAND
Hoy
Graemsay
Flotta
Burray
SOUTH RONALDSAY
SOUTH WALLS
Swona
Island of Stroma
SCAPA FLOW
PENTLAND FIRTH
STRONSAY FIRTH
WESTRAY FIRTH
NORTH RONALDSAY FIRTH
Copinsay
Scale : 1:300 000
(approx 4.73 miles to 1 inch)

169

Aberdeen

Bath

Birmingham

0 Miles ¼

A4040 OUTER RING ROAD
A41 WOLVERHAMPTON M5
A34 WALSALL M6
A38(M) TO M6
A5127 SUTTON COLDFIELD
A47 CASTLE BROMWICH M6
A457 DUDLEY
A456 KIDDERMINSTER M5
A4540 RING ROAD
A38 BROMSGROVE
A441 REDDITCH
A41 STRATFORD-UPON-AVON (A34, A3400) M42
A45 COVENTRY, AIRPORT & NEC M42

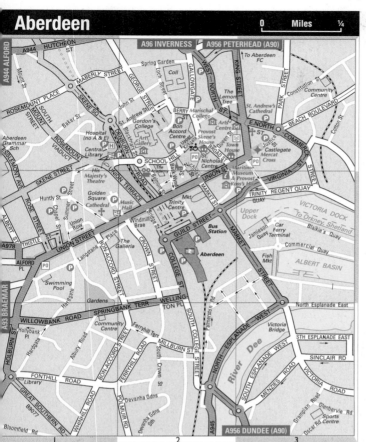

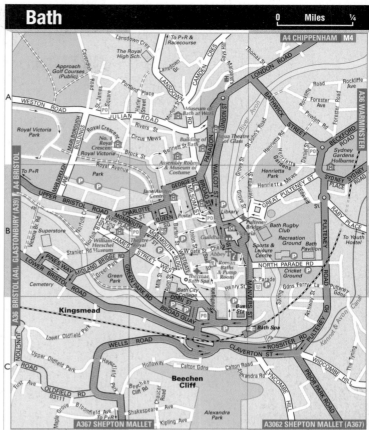

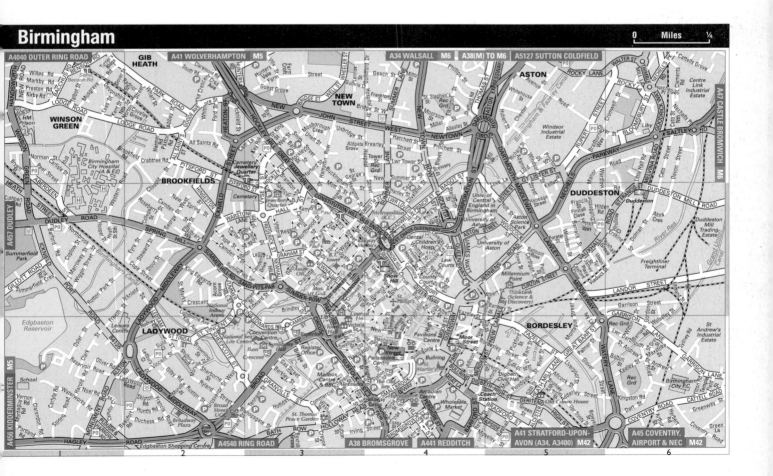

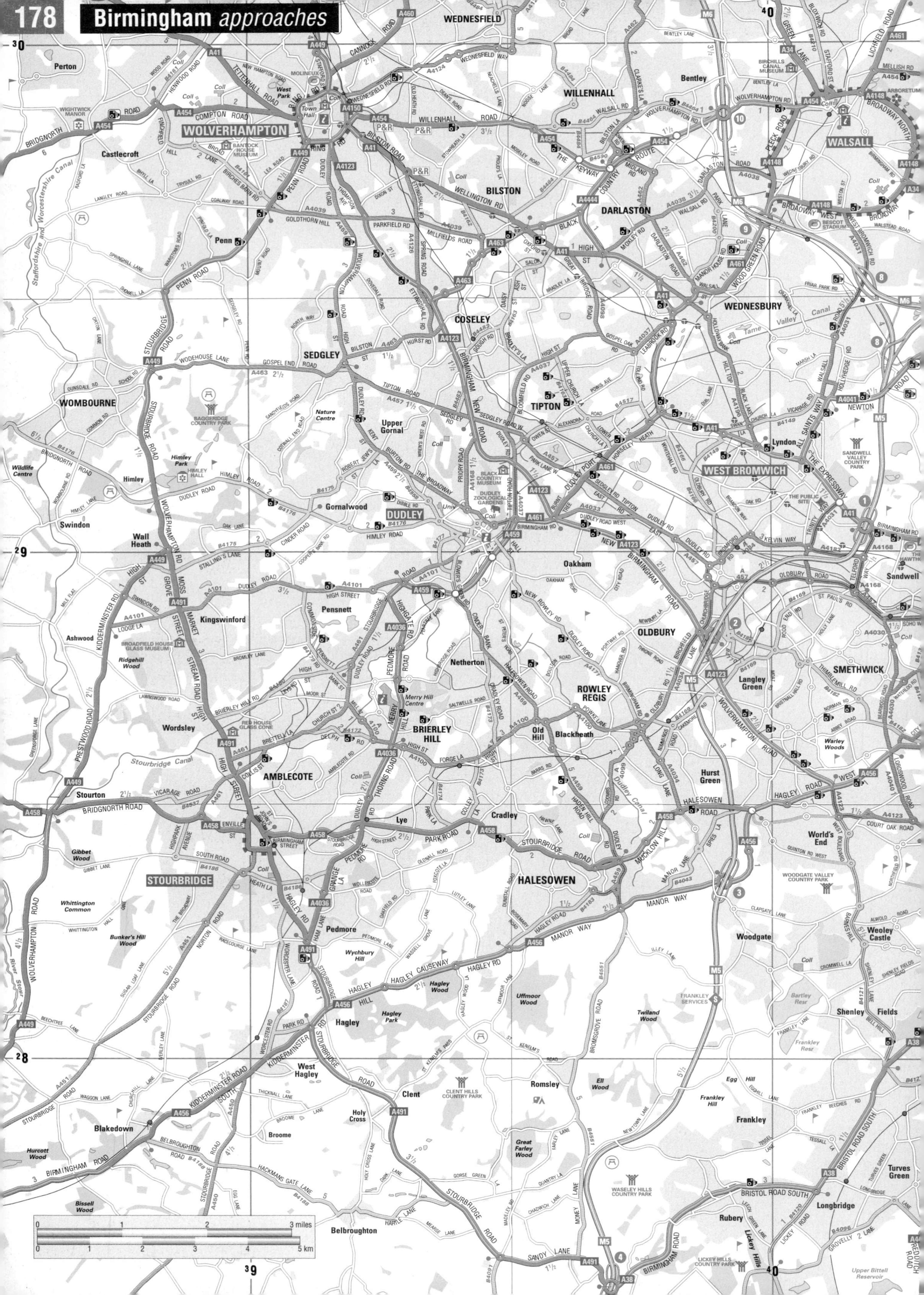
WOLVERHAMPTON
WALSALL
WEDNESFIELD
WILLENHALL
Bentley
BILSTON
DARLASTON
WEDNESBURY
COSELEY
SEDGLEY
TIPTON
WOMBOURNE
Upper Gornal
DUDLEY
WEST BROMWICH
Gornalwood
Himley
Swindon
Wall Heath
Oakham
Kingswinford
Pensnett
OLDBURY
SMETHWICK
Netherton
ROWLEY REGIS
Ashwood
BRIERLEY HILL
Wordsley
Blackheath
Old Hill
AMBLECOTE
Hurst Green
Stourton
Lye
Cradley
STOURBRIDGE
HALESOWEN
Pedmore
Woodgate
Hagley
West Hagley
Clent
Romsley
Blakedown
Broome
Frankley
Rubery
Longbridge
Belbroughton
0 1 2 3 miles
0 1 2 3 4 5 km

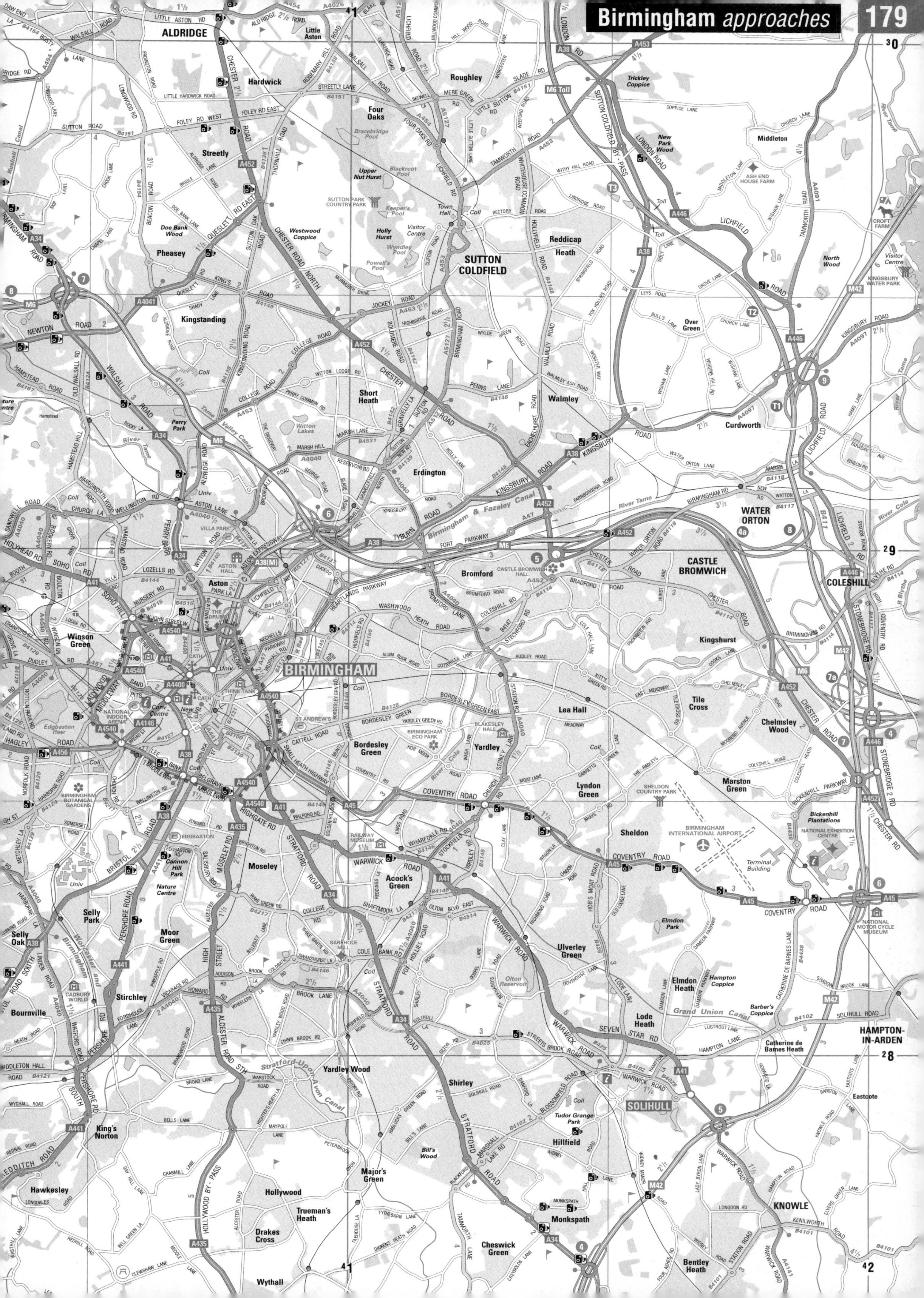
ALDRIDGE
Little Aston
Hardwick
Roughley
Four Oaks
Streetly
Upper Nut Hurst
SUTTON PARK COUNTRY PARK
Doe Bank Wood
Westwood Coppice
Holly Hurst
Pheasey
SUTTON COLDFIELD
Reddicap Heath
Trickley Coppice
New Park Wood
Middleton
ASH END HOUSE FARM
CROFT FARM
North Wood
KINGSBURY WATER PARK
Kingstanding
Over Green
Short Heath
Walmley
Curdworth
Perry Park
Witton Lakes
Erdington
WATER ORTON
CASTLE BROMWICH
COLESHILL
Bromford
CASTLE BROMWICH HALL
Aston
ASTON HALL
Winson Green
Kingshurst
BIRMINGHAM
Lea Hall
Tile Cross
Chelmsley Wood
Bordesley Green
BIRMINGHAM ECO PARK
Yardley
Lyndon Green
Marston Green
SHELDON COUNTRY PARK
BIRMINGHAM BOTANICAL GARDENS
Sheldon
BIRMINGHAM INTERNATIONAL AIRPORT
Bickenhill Plantations
NATIONAL EXHIBITION CENTRE
Moseley
RAILWAY MUSEUM
Acock's Green
Cannon Hill Park
Nature Centre
Selly Park
Moor Green
Selly Oak
Elmdon Park
NATIONAL MOTOR CYCLE MUSEUM
Ulverley Green
Olton Reservoir
Stirchley
CADBURY WORLD
Bournville
Elmdon Heath
Hampton Coppice
Barber's Coppice
Lode Heath
HAMPTON-IN-ARDEN
Catherine de Barnes Heath
Yardley Wood
Shirley
SOLIHULL
Tudor Grange Park
Eastcote
King's Norton
Hillfield
Bill's Wood
Major's Green
Hawkesley
Hollywood
Trueman's Heath
Monkspath
KNOWLE
Drakes Cross
Cheswick Green
Bentley Heath
Wythall

Blackpool

0 Miles ¼

A584 FLEETWOOD (A587)

A586 LANCASTER (A6)

A583 PRESTON

M55

A584 LYTHAM ST. ANNE'S

A5099

North Station

Bus Sta

Town Hall

Winter Gdns Theatre & Opera House

Blackpool Tower

Louis Tussaud's Waxworks

North Pier

Central Pier

Revoe

Tram Depot

Coach Station

To South Station

Blackpool F.C.

Recreation Ground

To South Pier & Pleasure Beach

Bournemouth

0 Miles ¼

A347 FERNDOWN

A338 RINGWOOD

A338 POOLE (A35)

A35 CHRISTCHURCH

Meyrick Park

Recreation Ground

Dean Park Cricket Ground

Horseshoe Common

Bournemouth Station

Coach Station

Town Hall

The Triangle

Public Library

Bournemouth International Centre

Pier Approach

Oceanarium

Bournemouth Pier

Pier Theatre

Russell Cotes Art Gallery & Museum

College & Library (private)

Poole Bay

Bradford

0 Miles ¼

A6037 KEIGHLEY (A650)

A658 HARROGATE (A61)

A647 LEEDS

A650 WAKEFIELD

M62, M1

A641 HUDDERSFIELD

M606, M62

A647 HALIFAX

Forster Square Retail Park

Bradford Forster Sq

Inland Revenue

Cathedral

St. Mary's Church (RC)

Bradford Playhouse

Colour Museum

Kirkgate Centre

Wool Exch.

Centenary Square

City Hall

Law Courts

St. George's Hall

Redevelopment Area

Bus Station

Bradford Interchange

Alhambra

Nat. Mus. of Photography Film & Television

Ice Rink

Jacob's Well Municipal Offices

University of Bradford

Bradford College

St. Lukes Hospital

To Bolling Hall

Brighton

0 Miles ¼

A23 CRAWLEY

M23

A270 WORTHING (A27)

A259 WORTHING

A270 LEWES (A27)

To Booth Museum

To Withdean Stadium Park & Ride

To Engineerium

Library (temp.)

St. Bartholomew's

Brighton

Toy & Model Museum

Albert Rd Royal Alexandra Hosp

St. Nicholas'

Clock Tower

Churchill Square Shopping Centre

Brighton Centre

Theatre Royal

The Dome

Royal Pavilion

Art Gallery & Museum

The Lanes

Town Hall

University of Brighton

Fruit & Veg Market (Wholesale)

West Pier (Closed to the public)

Palace Pier

Sea Life Centre

Volk's Electric Railway

To Brighton Marina

To Royal Sussex Hospital (A & E)

Paddling Pool

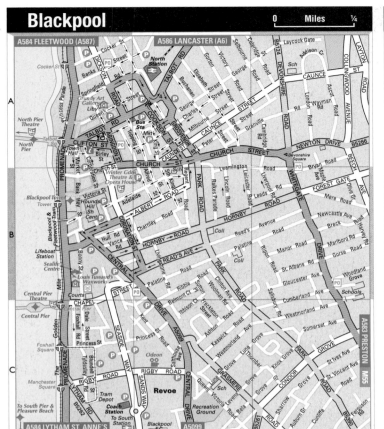

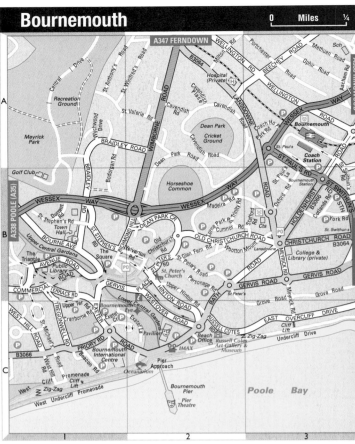

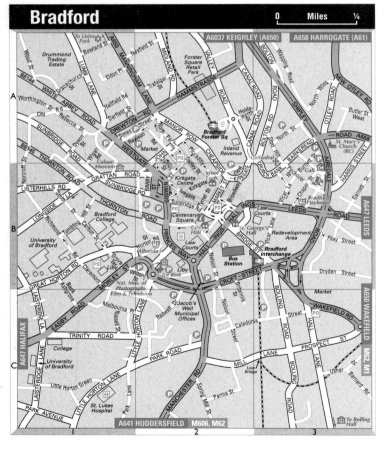

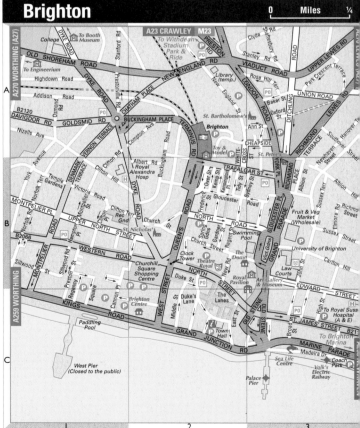

Bristol

0 Miles ¼

A4018 TO M5

A38 TO M5

A4032 TO M32 & M4

A432 MANGOTSFIELD

A420 CHIPPENHAM

A4 AVONMOUTH & M5

A370 WESTON SUPER MARE

A38 TAUNTON

A37 SHEPTON MALLET

A4 BATH

To Bristol Zoo Gardens

To Clifton Suspension Bridge

CLIFTON

Broadcasting House

Bristol Grammar School

University of Bristol

Cabot Tower

Bristol Cathedral

City of Bristol College

SS Great Britain & The Matthew

Maritime Heritage Centre

Floating Harbour

River Avon (New Cut)

Bristol Temple Meads

St. Mary Redcliffe

Castle Park

The Mall Galleries

Cumberland Basin

Bristol Marina

Millennium Square

The Lloyds' Building

Amphitheatre

Industrial Museum

General Hospital

Bedminster Bridge

Greville Smyth Park

The Tobacco Factory

Bristol Royal Infirmary (A & E)

Children's Hospital

St. Michael's Maternity

Cambridge

0 Miles ¼

Canterbury

0 Miles ¼

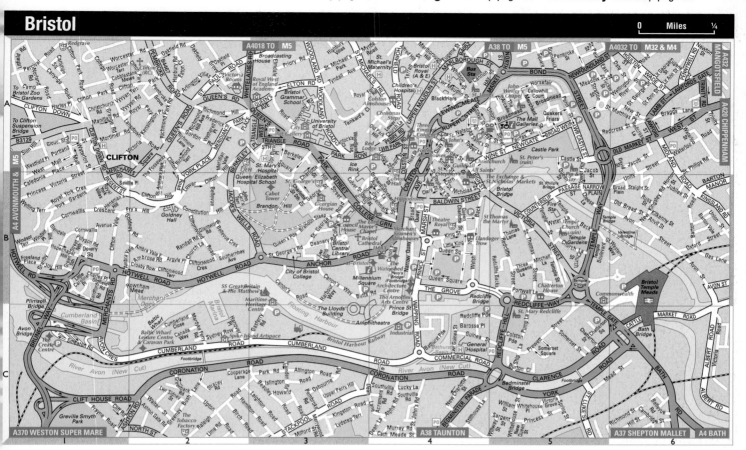

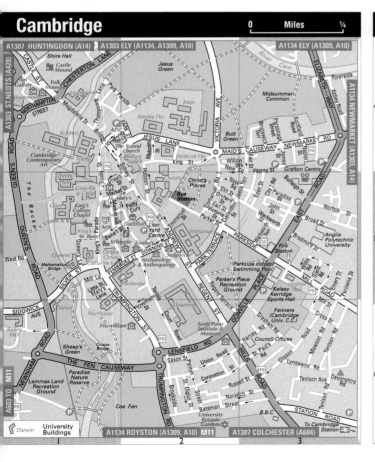

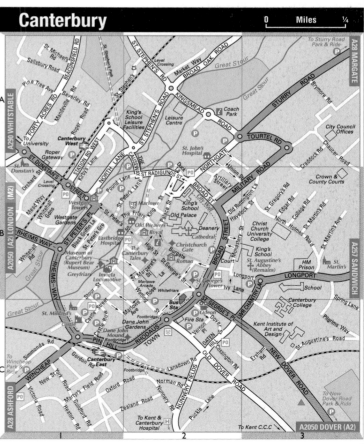

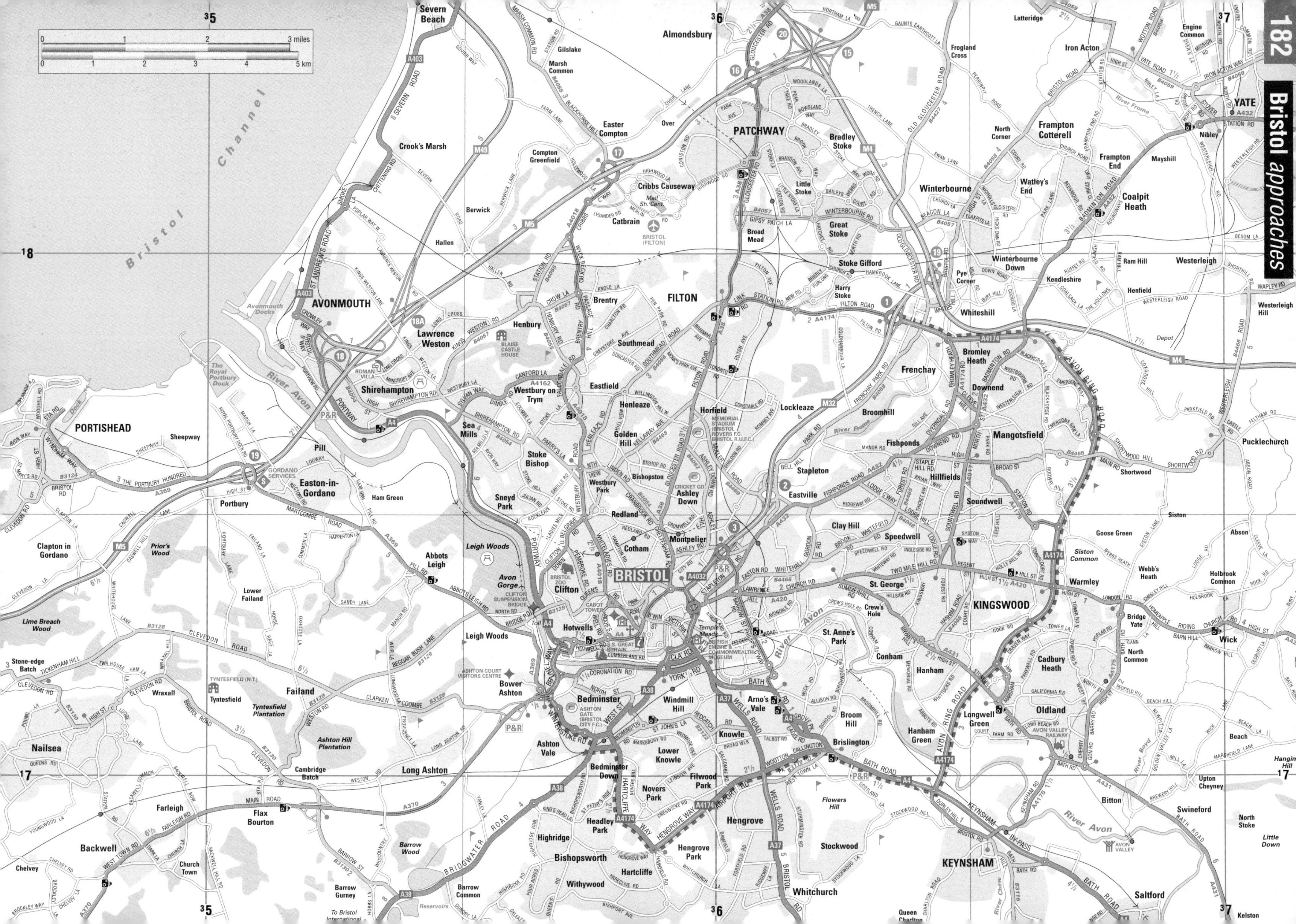

Severn Beach
Almondsbury
Gilslake
Marsh Common
Easter Compton
Over
Patchway
Bradley Stoke
Crook's Marsh
Compton Greenfield
Cribbs Causeway
Catbrain
Berwick
Hallen
Bristol Channel
Avonmouth
Little Stoke
Great Stoke
Broad Mead
Stoke Gifford
Harry Stoke
Filton
Brentry
Henbury
Lawrence Weston
Southmead
Shirehampton
Westbury on Trym
Eastfield
Henleaze
Horfield
Lockleaze
Frenchay
Broomhill
Portishead
Sheepway
Pill
Sea Mills
Golden Hill
Stoke Bishop
Bishopston
Stapleton
Fishponds
Easton-in-Gordano
Portbury
Ham Green
Sneyd Park
Westbury Park
Ashley Down
Eastville
Redland
Montpelier
Cotham
Clay Hill
Speedwell
Clapton in Gordano
Prior's Wood
Abbots Leigh
Leigh Woods
Avon Gorge
Clifton
Bristol
Lower Failand
Lime Breach Wood
Hotwells
St. George
Crew's Hole
St. Anne's Park
Conham
Stone-edge Batch
Wraxall
Tyntesfield
Tyntesfield Plantation
Failand
Bower Ashton
Bedminster
Windmill Hill
Arno's Vale
Broom Hill
Nailsea
Ashton Hill Plantation
Ashton Vale
Knowle
Brislington
Cambridge Batch
Long Ashton
Bedminster Down
Lower Knowle
Filwood Park
Novers Park
Farleigh
Flax Bourton
Headley Park
Highridge
Hengrove
Flowers Hill
Backwell
Barrow Wood
Bishopsworth
Hengrove Park
Stockwood
Chelvey
Church Town
Barrow Gurney
Barrow Common
Hartcliffe
Withywood
Whitchurch
Latteridge
Frogland Cross
Iron Acton
Engine Common
Yate
Nibley
North Corner
Frampton Cotterell
Frampton End
Mayshill
Winterbourne
Watley's End
Coalpit Heath
Winterbourne Down
Pye Corner
Ram Hill
Westerleigh
Kendleshire
Henfield
Whiteshill
Westerleigh Hill
Bromley Heath
Downend
Mangotsfield
Pucklechurch
Shortwood
Hillfields
Soundwell
Siston
Goose Green
Abson
Siston Common
Webb's Heath
Holbrook Common
Warmley
Kingswood
Bridge Yate
Wick
North Common
Cadbury Heath
Hanham
Longwell Green
Oldland
Hanham Green
Beach
Hanging Hill
Upton Cheyney
Bitton
Swineford
North Stoke
Little Down
Keynsham
Saltford
Kelston
Queen Charlton
River Avon
River Frome
M4
M5
M32
M49
Avon Ring Road

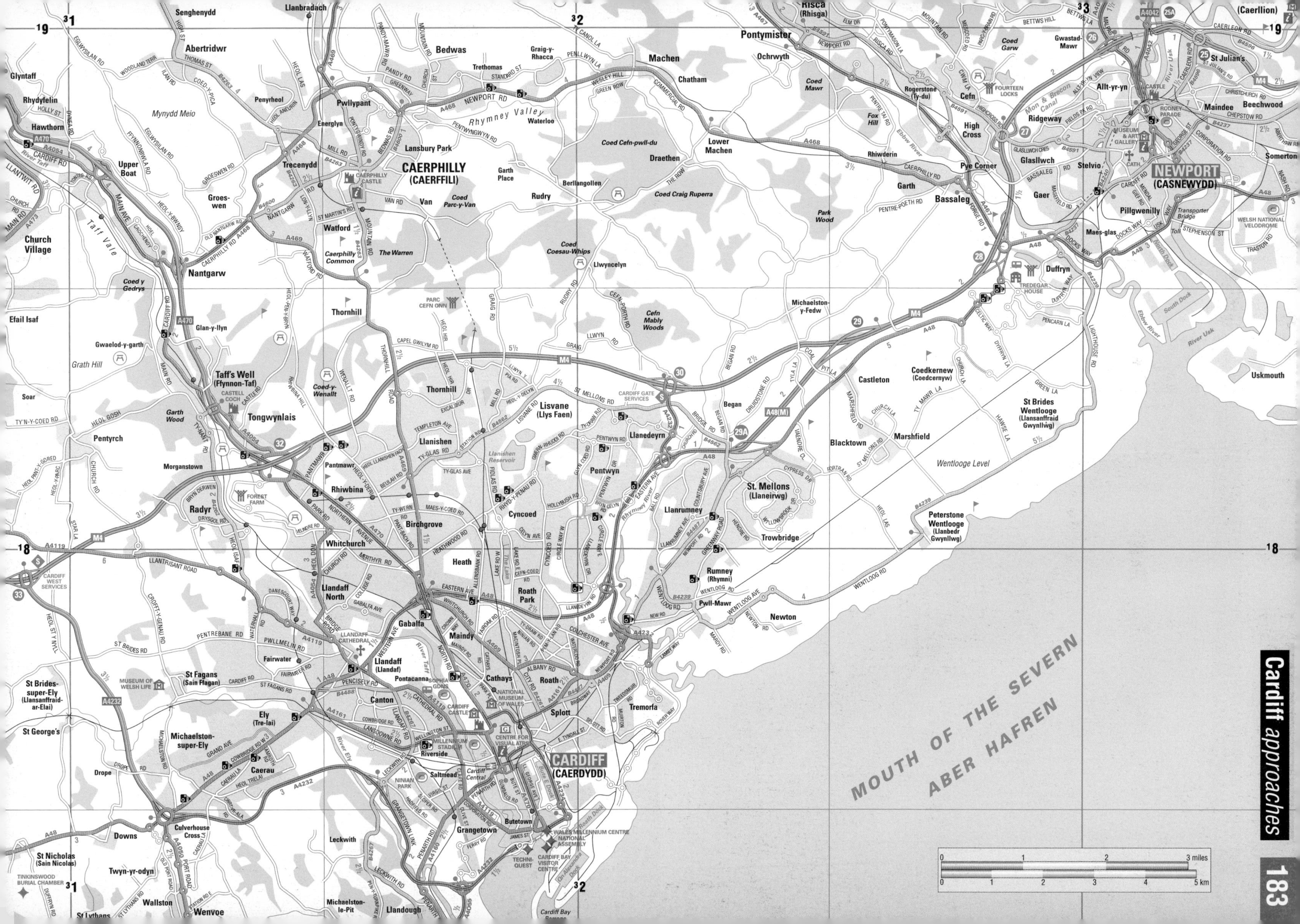
NEWPORT (CASNEWYDD)
CARDIFF (CAERDYDD)
CAERPHILLY (CAERFFILI)
MOUTH OF THE SEVERN
ABER HAFREN
Wentlooge Level
Rhymney Valley
Taff Vale
St Julian's
Maindee
Beechwood
Somerton
Uskmouth
Pillgwenlly
Maes-glas
Stelvio
Allt-yr-yn
Ridgeway
Glasllwch
Gaer
Duffryn
Bassaleg
Pye Corner
High Cross
Cefn
Rogerstone (Ty-du)
Rhiwderin
Garth
Coedkernew (Coedcernyw)
Castleton
Marshfield
Blacktown
St Brides Wentlooge (Llansanffraid Gwynllŵg)
Peterstone Wentlooge (Llanbedr Gwynllŵg)
Michaelston-y-Fedw
St. Mellons (Llaneirwg)
Trowbridge
Newton
Rumney (Rhymni)
Pwll-Mawr
Llanrumney
Began
Lower Machen
Machen
Draethen
Risca (Rhisga)
Pontymister
Ochrwyth
Chatham
Llanedeyrn
Pentwyn
Tremorfa
Splott
Roath
Roath Park
Cyncoed
Lisvane (Llys Faen)
Llanishen
Thornhill
Heath
Cathays
Maindy
Gabalfa
Birchgrove
Rhiwbina
Whitchurch
Llandaff North
Llandaff (Llandaf)
Pontcanna
Canton
Riverside
Grangetown
Butetown
Llandough
Leckwith
Michaelston-le-Pit
Ely (Tre-lai)
Caerau
Fairwater
St Fagans (Sain Ffagan)
Michaelston-super-Ely
Culverhouse Cross
Wenvoe
Wallston
Twyn-yr-odyn
Downs
Drope
St George's
St Brides-super-Ely (Llansanffraid-ar-Elai)
St Nicholas (Sain Nicolas)
Radyr
Morganstown
Pentyrch
Tongwynlais
Taff's Well (Ffynnon-Taf)
Nantgarw
Groes-wen
Glan-y-llyn
Gwaelod-y-garth
Upper Boat
Church Village
Efail Isaf
Soar
Rhydyfelin
Glyntaff
Hawthorn
Abertridwr
Senghenydd
Llanbradach
Penyrheol
Trecenydd
Energlyn
Pwllypant
Watford
Van
Lansbury Park
Bedwas
Trethomas
Waterloo
Graig-y-Rhacca
Rudry
Llwyncelyn
Berllangollen
Caerphilly Common
The Warren
Garth Wood
Coed Cefn-pwll-du
Coed Craig Ruperra
Cefn Mably Woods
Mynydd Meio
Grath Hill

Cardiff / Caerdydd

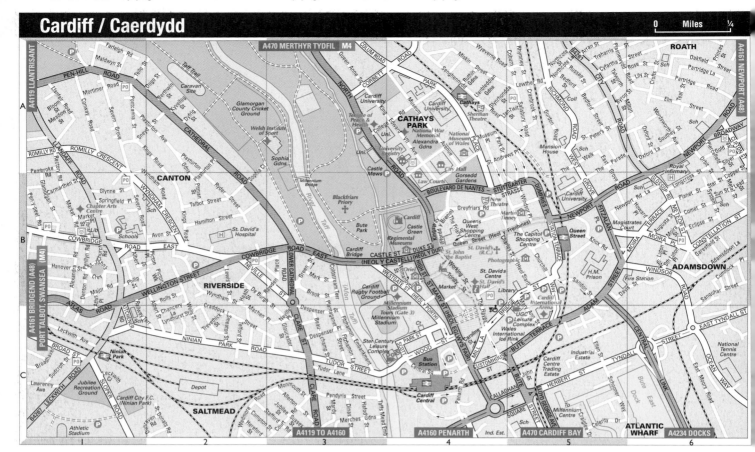

Cheltenham

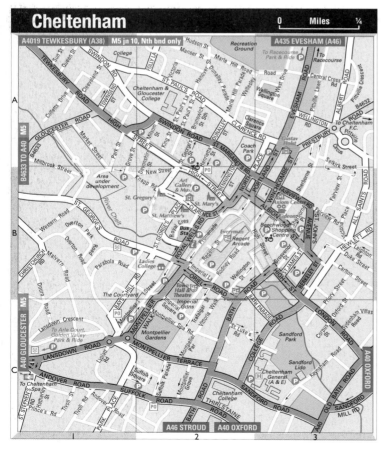

Chester

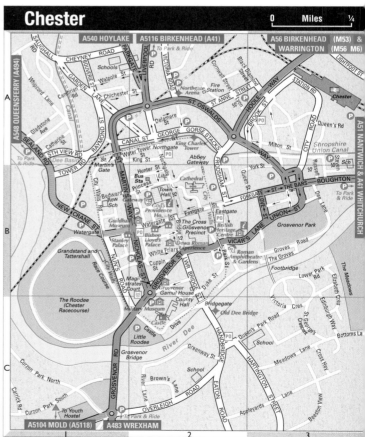

Colchester road map page 43 • **Coventry** road map page 51 • **Derby** road map page 76 • **Durham** road map page 111

185

Colchester

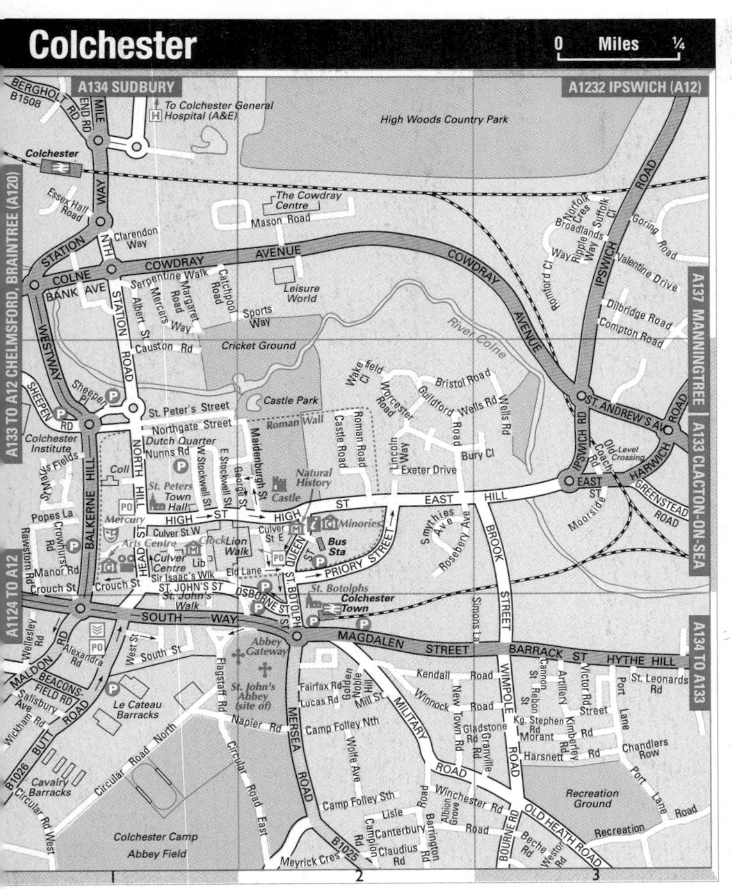

Coventry

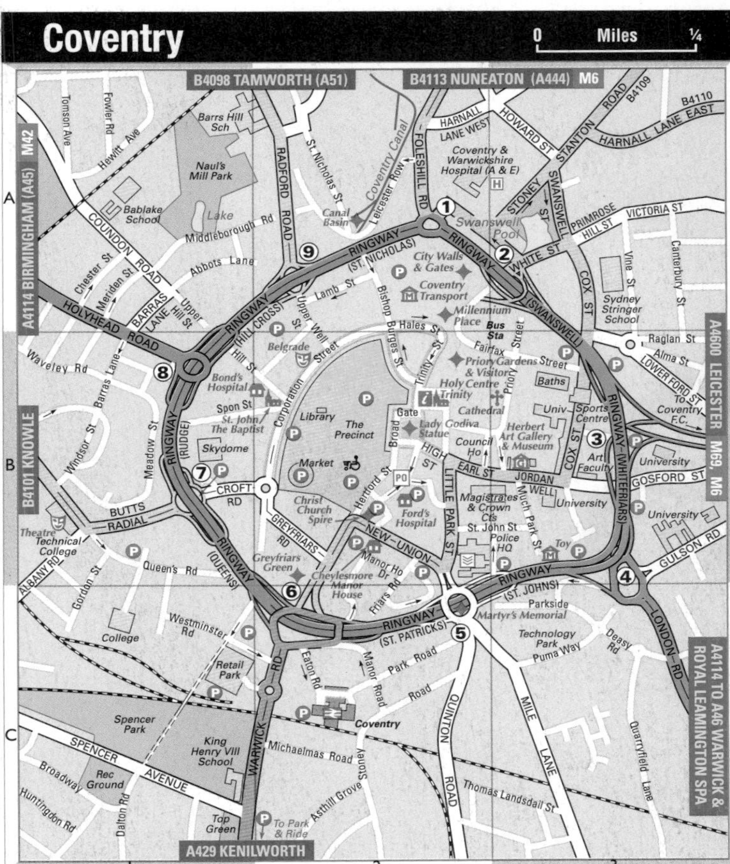

Derby

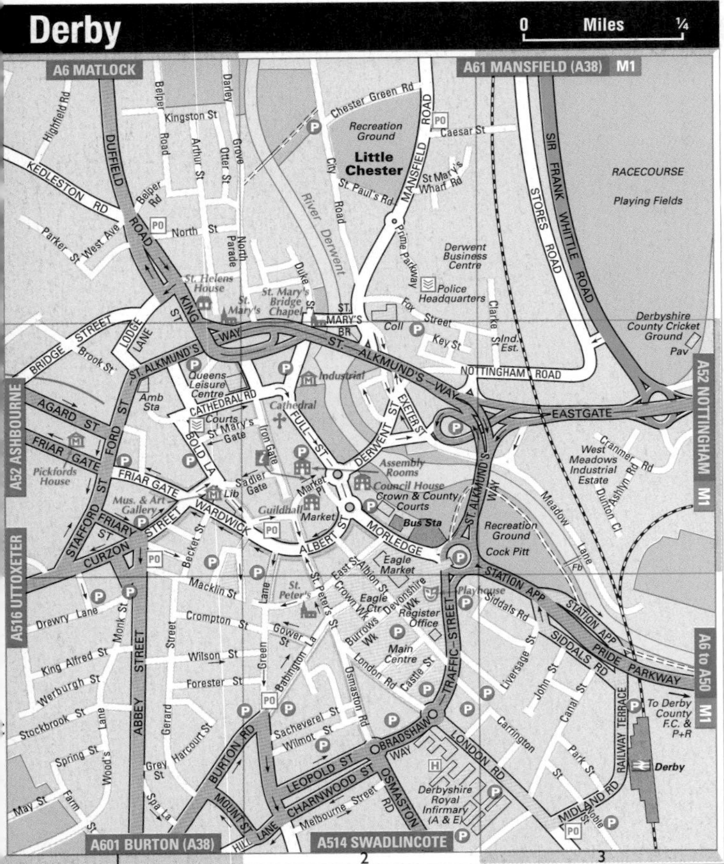

Durham

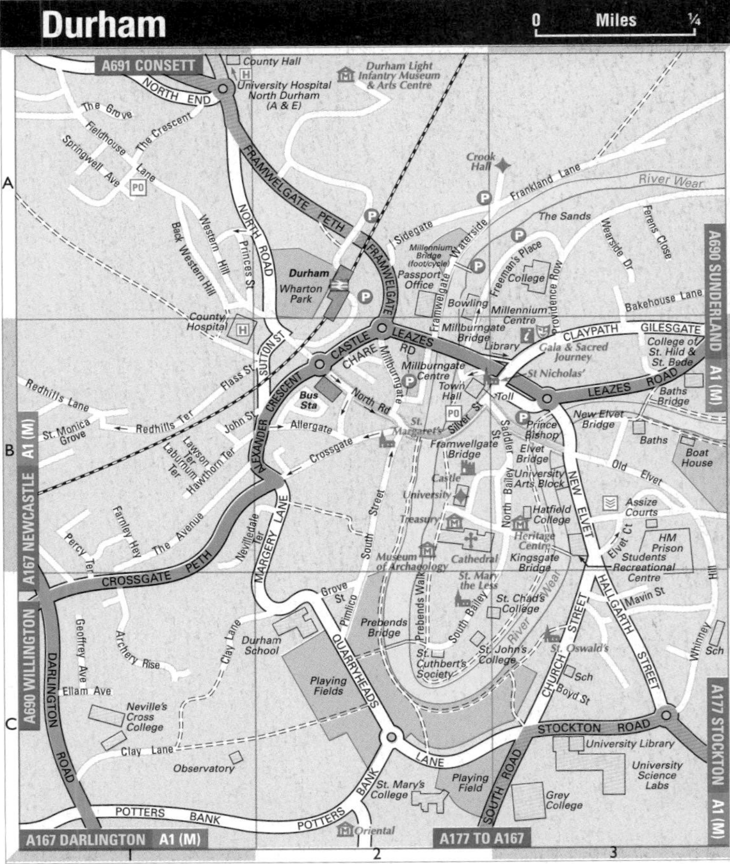

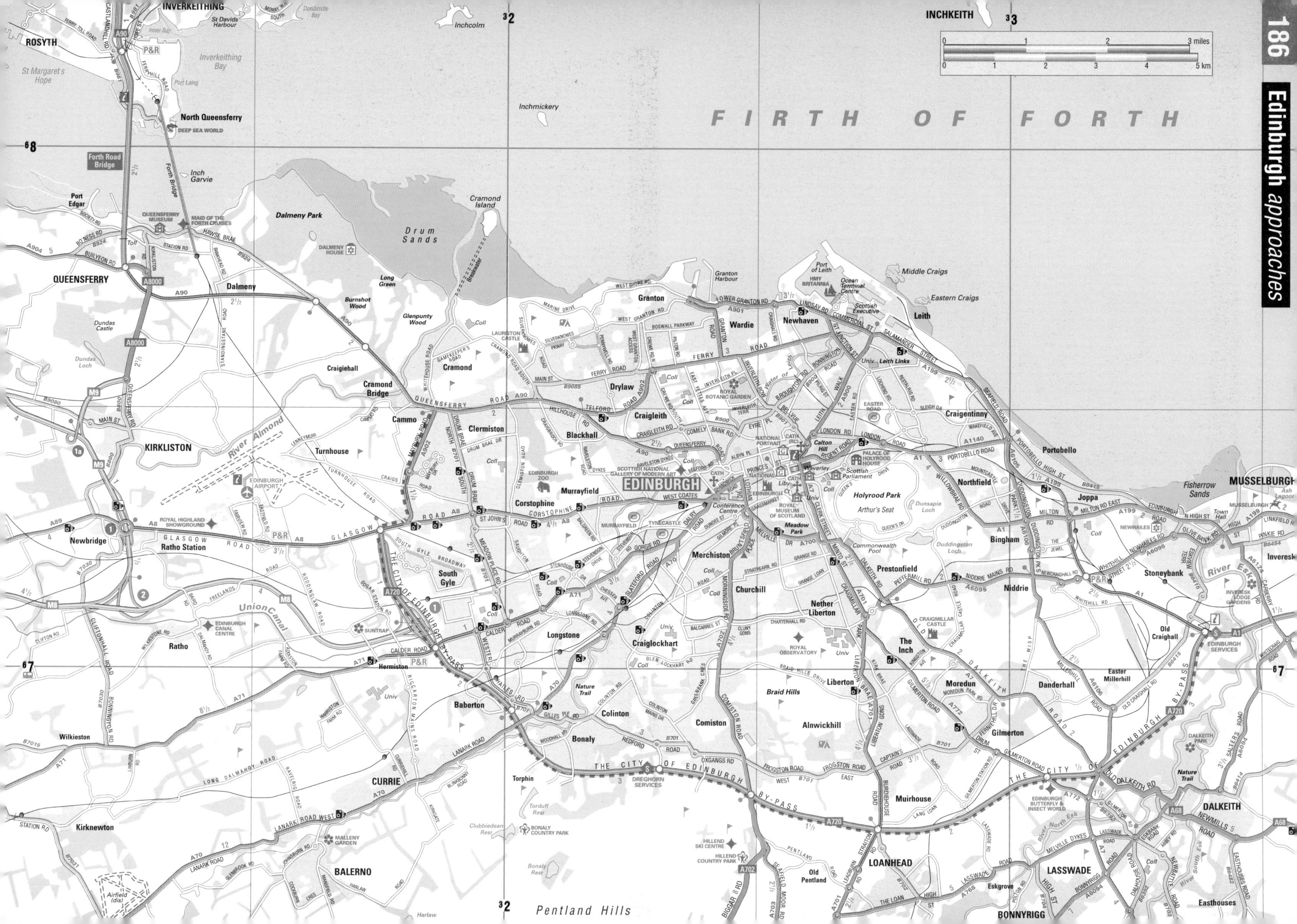

FIRTH OF FORTH
EDINBURGH
INCHKEITH
Inchcolm
Inchmickery
Cramond Island
Drum Sands
Middle Craigs
Eastern Craigs
Leith
Newhaven
Granton
Wardie
Granton Harbour
Port of Leith
HMY Britannia
Ocean Terminal Centre
Scottish Executive
Leith Links
Portobello
Joppa
Musselburgh
Fisherrow Sands
River Esk
Inveresk Lodge Gardens
Newhailes
Stoneybank
Old Craighall
Edinburgh Services
Easter Millerhill
Danderhall
Niddrie
Bingham
Northfield
Craigentinny
Holyrood Park
Arthur's Seat
Duddingston Loch
Dunsapie Loch
Commonwealth Pool
Prestonfield
Craigmillar Castle
The Inch
Moredun
Gilmerton
Nether Liberton
Liberton
Alnwickhill
Braid Hills
Royal Observatory
Calton Hill
Waverley
Palace of Holyroodhouse
Scottish Parliament
National Portrait Gallery
Royal Museum of Scotland
Meadow Park
Conference Centre
Royal Botanic Garden
Scottish National Gallery of Modern Art
Edinburgh Zoo
Churchill
Merchiston
Craiglockhart
Colinton
Comiston
Bonaly
Longstone
Murrayfield
Corstophine
Blackhall
Craigleith
Drylaw
Clermiston
Cramond
Lauriston Castle
Cammo
Cramond Bridge
Craigiehall
Turnhouse
Edinburgh Airport
River Almond
Dalmeny
Dalmeny Park
Dalmeny House
Long Green
Burnshot Wood
Glenpunty Wood
Queensferry
Dundas Castle
Dundas Loch
Kirkliston
Newbridge
Royal Highland Showground
Ratho Station
Ratho
Edinburgh Canal Centre
Union Canal
Suntrap
Hermiston
South Gyle
Baberton
Nature Trail
Currie
Balerno
Malleny Garden
Kirknewton
Wilkieston
Torphin
Dreghorn Services
Torduff Resr
Clubbiedean Resr
Bonaly Rest
Bonaly Country Park
Hillend Ski Centre
Hillend Country Park
Pentland Hills
Old Pentland
Loanhead
Muirhouse
Edinburgh Butterfly & Insect World
Lasswade
Eskgrove
Bonnyrigg
Dalkeith
Dalkeith Park
Newmills
Easthouses
Forth Bridge
Forth Road Bridge
Queensferry Museum
Maid of the Forth Cruises
North Queensferry
Deep Sea World
Inverkeithing
Inverkeithing Bay
St Davids Harbour
Port Laing
Rosyth
St Margaret's Hope
Port Edgar
Inch Garvie
Airfield (dis)
THE CITY OF EDINBURGH BY-PASS
A1
A7
A8
A68
A70
A71
A90
A199
A702
A720
A772
A8000
M8
M9
B701
0 1 2 3 miles
0 1 2 3 4 5 km

Edinburgh

0 Miles ¼

A900 LEITH
A1 BERWICK UPON TWEED
A90 FORTH ROAD BRIDGE & PERTH (M90)
A8 GLASGOW & STIRLING (M8) (M9)
A71 KILMARNOCK
A702 CARLISLE & M74
TO A7
A7 GALASHIELS & JEDBURGH (A68)

Glasgow

0 Miles ¼

A82 ERSKINE BRIDGE
A81 BEARSDEN
A879 MILNGAVIE (A807)
A803 KIRKINTILLOCH
M8 EDINBURGH
M73, M74
A814 CLYDEBANK
A8 PAISLEY (A761)
A89 AIRDRIE
A749
M8 GREENOCK
M77
A77 KILMARNOCK
A730 RUTHERGLEN
A728
A74

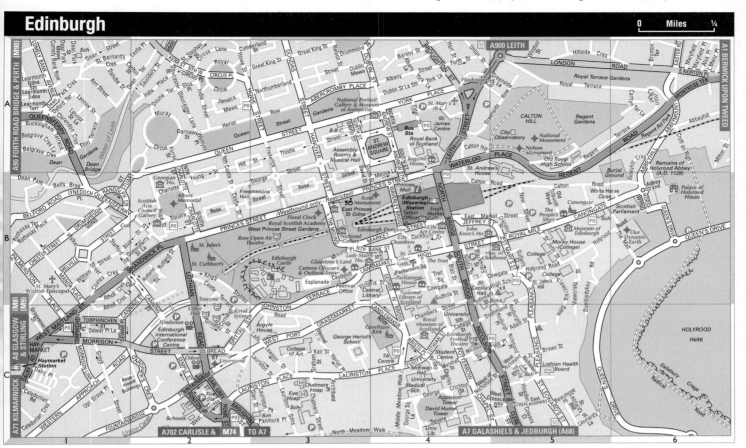

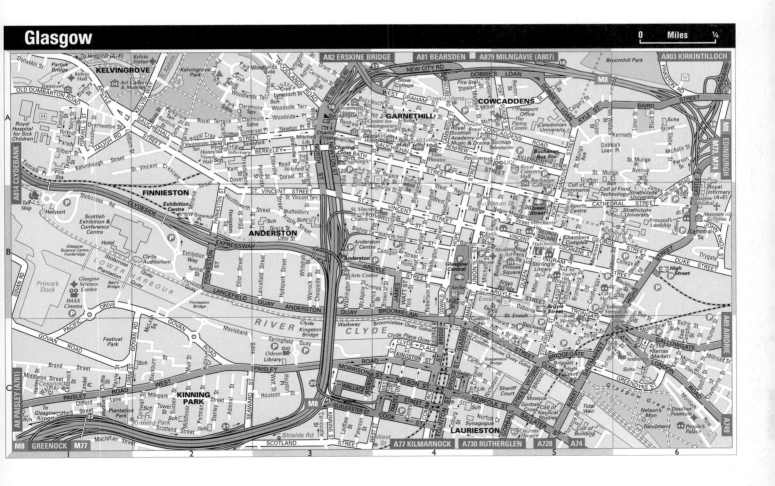

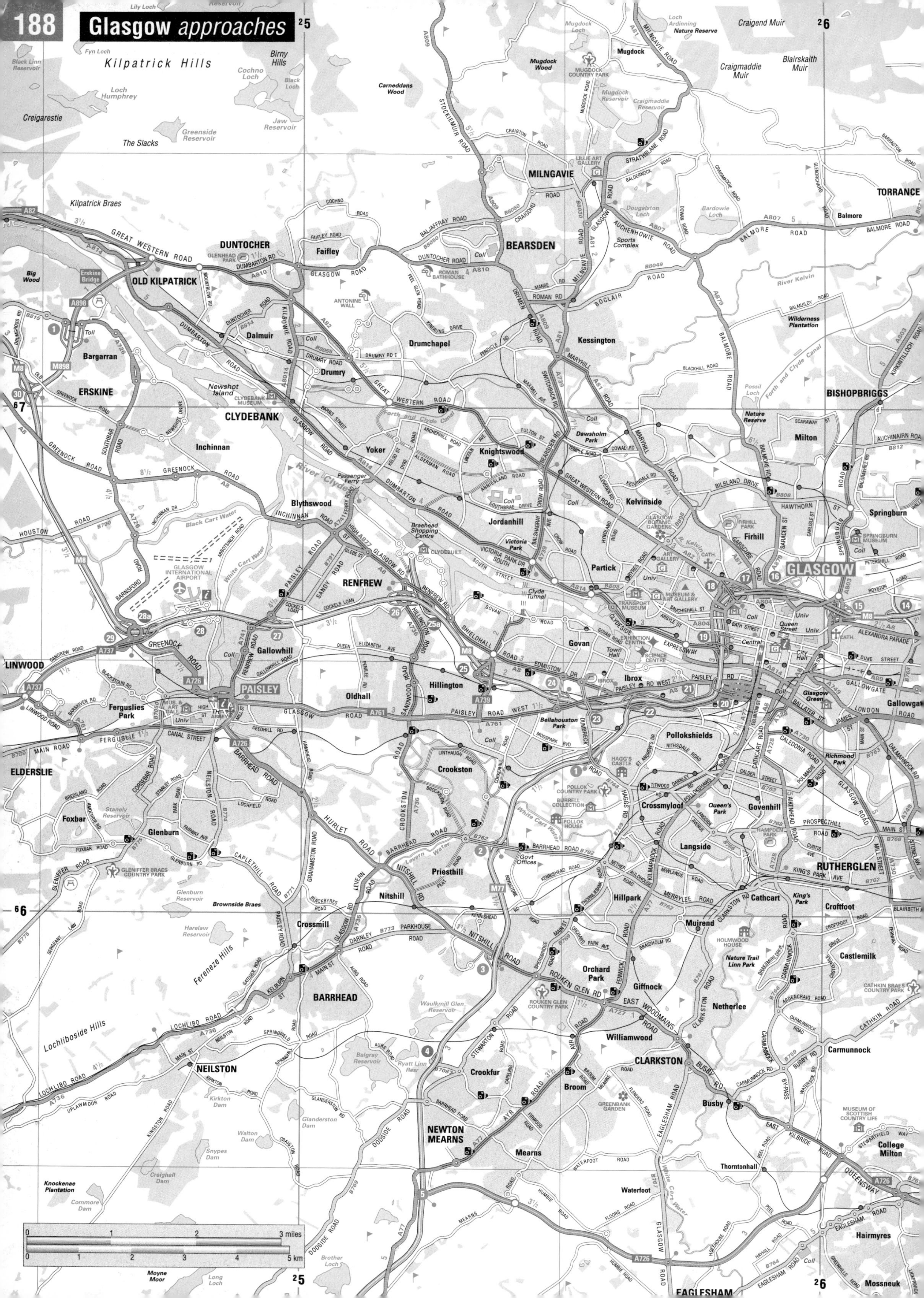

Kilpatrick Hills
Milngavie
Bearsden
Torrance
Duntocher
Faifley
Old Kilpatrick
Dalmuir
Drumchapel
Kessington
Bargarran
Erskine
Drumry
Bishopbriggs
Clydebank
Inchinnan
Yoker
Knightswood
Milton
Springburn
Kelvinside
Blythswood
Jordanhill
Firhill
Partick
Renfrew
Glasgow
Govan
Linwood
Gallowhill
Paisley
Ibrox
Oldhall
Hillington
Ferguslie Park
Elderslie
Crookston
Pollokshields
Foxbar
Glenburn
Crossmyloof
Govanhill
Langside
Rutherglen
Priesthill
Nitshill
Hillpark
Cathcart
Croftfoot
Crossmill
Muirend
Castlemilk
Orchard Park
Barrhead
Giffnock
Netherlee
Williamwood
Carmunnock
Neilston
Clarkston
Crookfur
Broom
Busby
Newton Mearns
Mearns
College Milton
Thorntonhall
Waterfoot
Hairmyres
Mossneuk
Eaglesham
3 miles
5 km

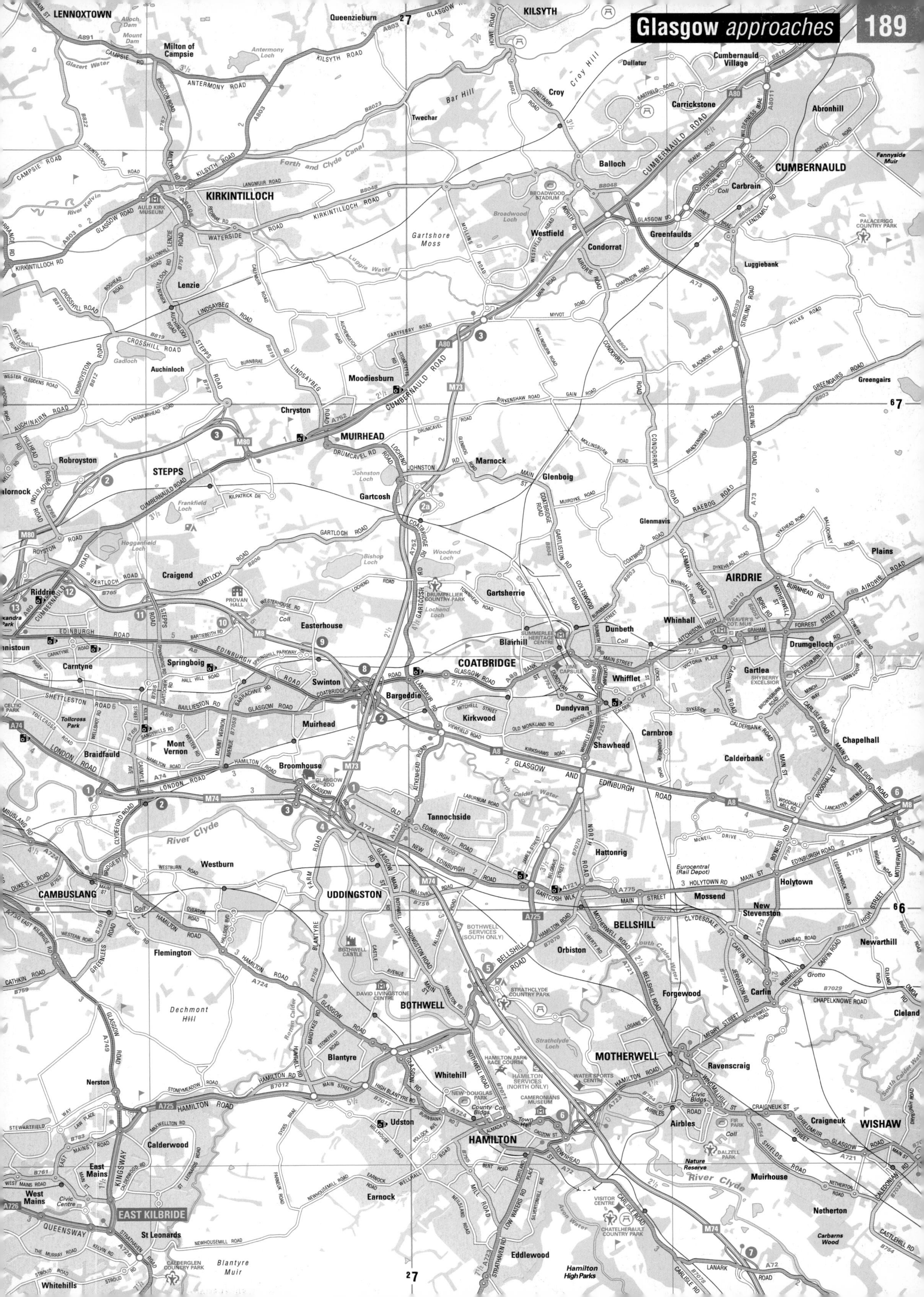
LENNOXTOWN
Queenzieburn
KILSYTH
Milton of Campsie
Antermony Loch
Dullatur
Cumbernauld Village
Croy
Bar Hill
Twechar
Carrickstone
Abronhill
Balloch
CUMBERNAULD
Fannyside Muir
Forth and Clyde Canal
KIRKINTILLOCH
AULD KIRK MUSEUM
BROADWOOD STADIUM
Carbrain
Broadwood Loch
Westfield
Greenfaulds
Gartshore Moss
Condorrat
PALACERIGG COUNTRY PARK
Luggiebank
Lenzie
Gadloch
Auchinloch
Moodiesburn
Greengairs
Chryston
MUIRHEAD
Robroyston
STEPPS
Johnston Loch
Marnock
Glenboig
Gartcosh
Frankfield Loch
Glenmavis
Hogganfield Loch
Bishop Loch
Woodend Loch
Plains
Craigend
AIRDRIE
Riddrie
DRUMPELLIER COUNTRY PARK
Gartsherrie
PROVAN HALL
Lochend Loch
Easterhouse
Dunbeth
Whinhall
SUMMERLEE HERITAGE CENTRE
Blairhill
WEAVER'S COT. MUS
Drumgelloch
Carntyne
Springboig
COATBRIDGE
TIME CAPSULE
Whifflet
Swinton
Gartlea
SHYBERRY EXCELSIOR
Bargeddie
Kirkwood
Dundyvan
Tollcross Park
Muirhead
Carnbroe
Mont Vernon
Shawhead
Chapelhall
Braidfauld
Calderbank
Broomhouse
GLASGOW ZOO
North Calder Water
Tannochside
River Clyde
Westburn
Hattonrig
Eurocentral (Rail Depot)
Holytown
CAMBUSLANG
UDDINGSTON
Mossend
New Stevenston
BELLSHILL
Flemington
BOTHWELL SERVICES (SOUTH ONLY)
BOTHWELL CASTLE
Orbiston
Newarthill
South Calder Water
Grotto
DAVID LIVINGSTONE CENTRE
STRATHCLYDE COUNTRY PARK
Carfin
Dechmont Hill
BOTHWELL
Forgewood
Cleland
Blantyre
Strathclyde Loch
MOTHERWELL
Ravenscraig
Nerston
Whitehill
HAMILTON PARK RACE COURSE
HAMILTON SERVICES (NORTH ONLY)
WATER SPORTS CENTRE
NEW DOUGLAS PARK
CAMERONIANS MUSEUM
County Bldgs
Civic Bldgs
Calderwood
Udston
Town Hall
Airbles
FIR PARK
Craigneuk
WISHAW
HAMILTON
DALZELL PARK
Nature Reserve
East Mains
Muirhouse
West Mains
Civic Centre
Earnock
VISITOR CENTRE
Netherton
EAST KILBRIDE
Carbarns Wood
St Leonards
CHATELHERAULT COUNTRY PARK
Eddlewood
Avon Water
CALDERGLEN COUNTRY PARK
Blantyre Muir
Hamilton High Parks
Whitehills
M80
M73
M8
M74
A80
A8
A73
A725
A721
A724
A749
A726
A72
27
67
66

190

Exeter road map page 10 • **Gloucester** road map page 37 • **Hull** road map page 90 • **Ipswich** road map page 57

Exeter

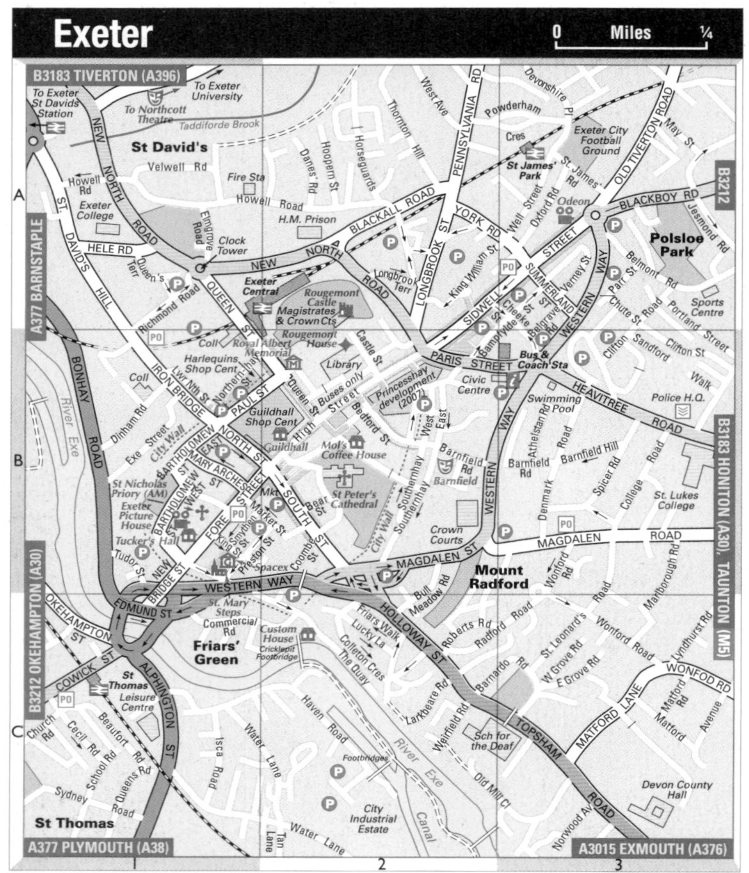

Gloucester

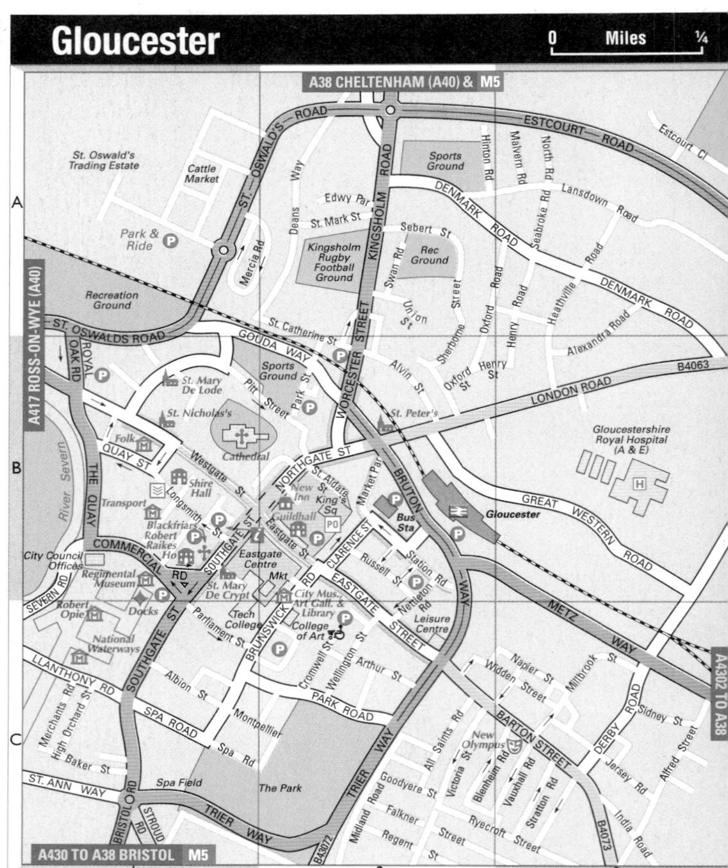

Hull

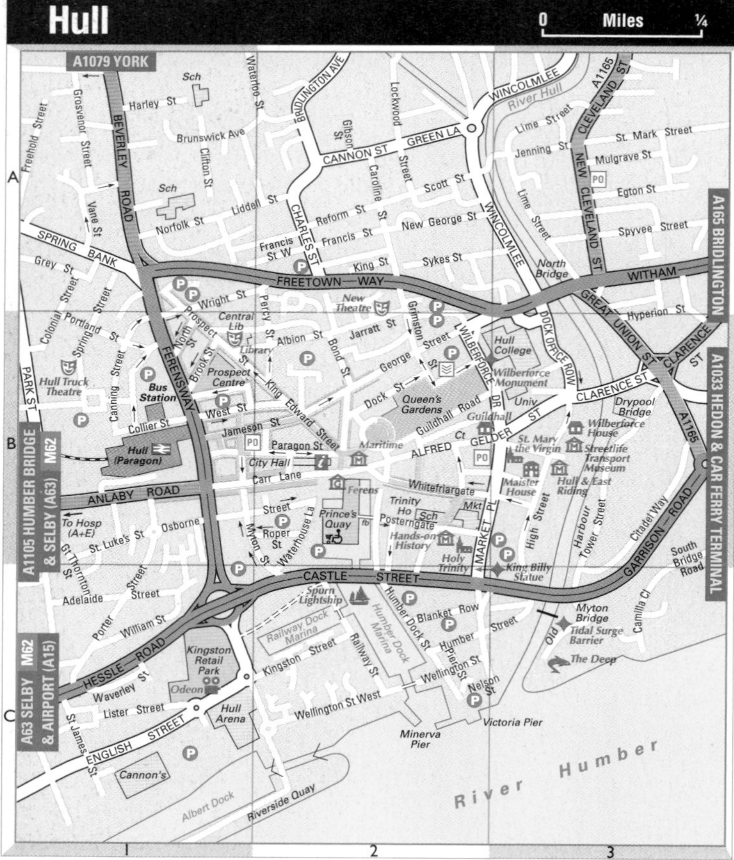

Ipswich

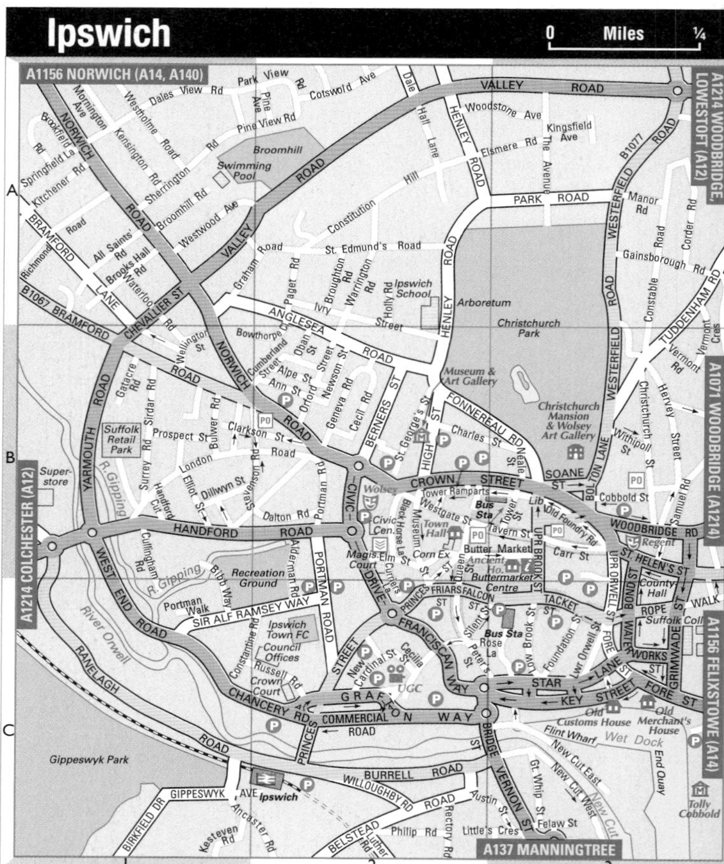

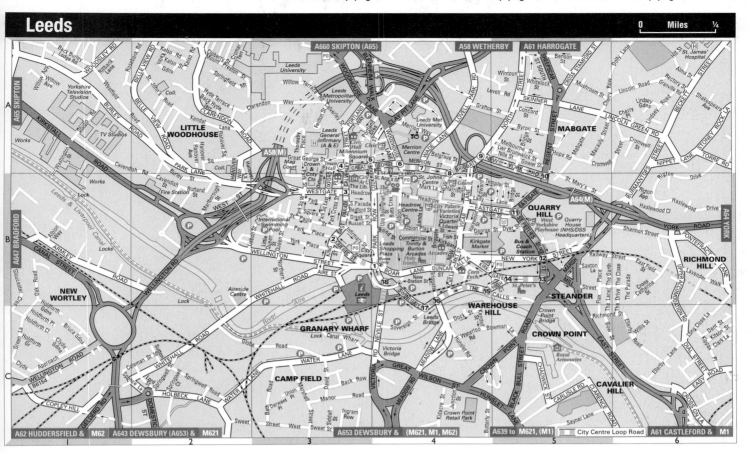

Leeds

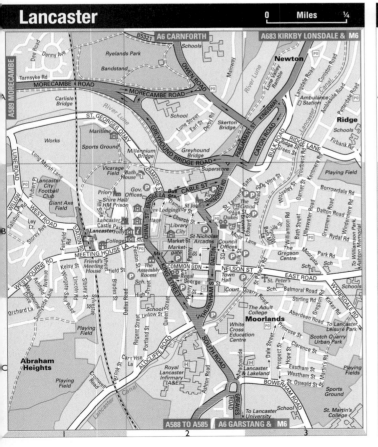

Lancaster

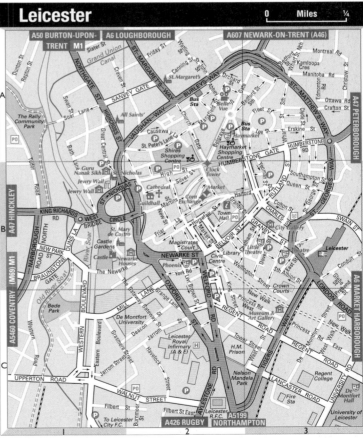

Leicester

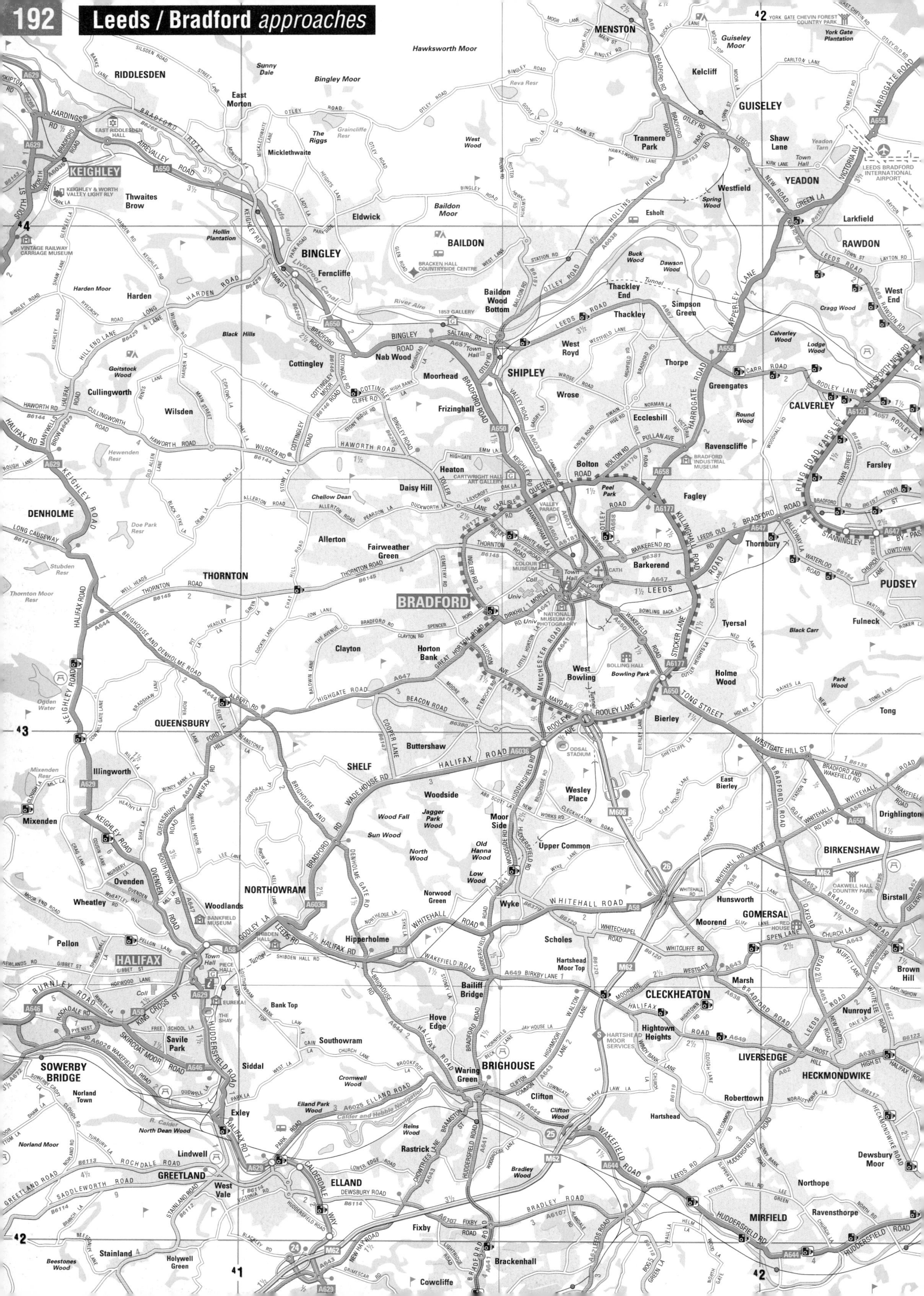
BRADFORD
KEIGHLEY
HALIFAX
RIDDLESDEN
BINGLEY
BAILDON
SHIPLEY
MENSTON
GUISELEY
YEADON
RAWDON
CALVERLEY
PUDSEY
DENHOLME
THORNTON
QUEENSBURY
NORTHOWRAM
SHELF
BRIGHOUSE
CLECKHEATON
GOMERSAL
BIRKENSHAW
LIVERSEDGE
HECKMONDWIKE
MIRFIELD
ELLAND
GREETLAND
SOWERBY BRIDGE
LEEDS BRADFORD INTERNATIONAL AIRPORT
Hawksworth Moor
Bingley Moor
Baildon Moor
Harden Moor
Cottingley
Cullingworth
Wilsden
Allerton
Clayton
Heaton
Daisy Hill
Frizinghall
Thackley
Idle
Eccleshill
Fagley
Thornbury
Farsley
Tyersal
Bierley
Tong
Wyke
Low Moor
Illingworth
Mixenden
Ovenden
Wheatley
Pellon
Savile Park
Southowram
Hipperholme
Bailiff Bridge
Rastrick
Fixby
Stainland
West Vale
Holywell Green
Lindwell
Exley
Norland Town
Ravensthorpe
Robertown
Hartshead
Scholes
Drighlington
Birstall
Nunroyd
Brown Hill
Dewsbury Moor
Northorpe
Brackenhall
Cowcliffe

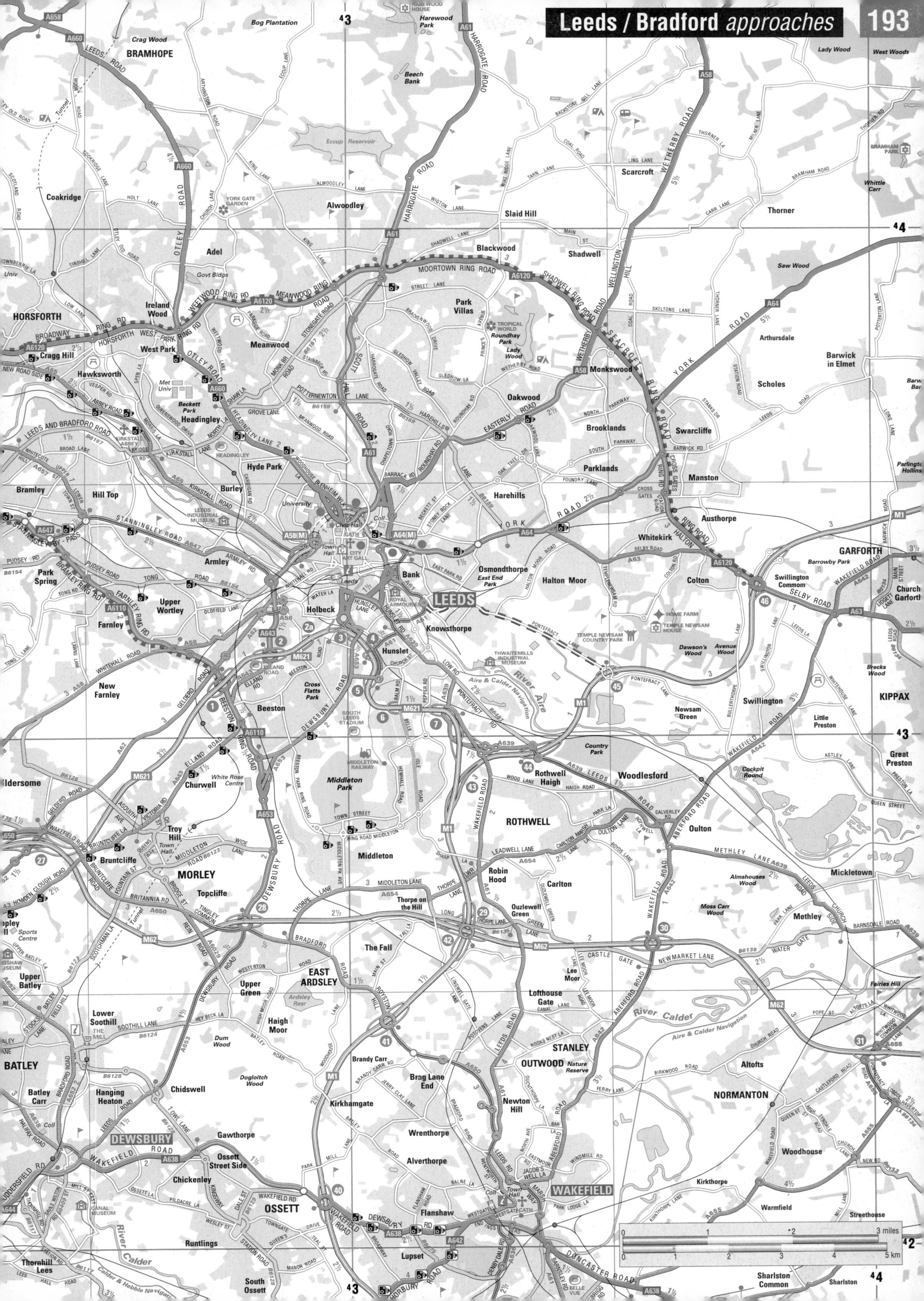
Bog Plantation
Harewood House
Harewood Park
Crag Wood
BRAMHOPE
Lady Wood
West Woods
Beech Bank
Eccup Reservoir
Bramham Park
Scarcroft
Whittle Carr
Coakridge
York Gate Garden
Alwoodley
Slaid Hill
Thorner
Adel
Blackwood
Shadwell
Saw Wood
Govt Bldgs
Ireland Wood
HORSFORTH
Meanwood
Park Villas
Tropical World
Roundhay Park
Lady Wood
West Park
Cragg Hill
Hawksworth
Monkswood
Arthursdale
Barwick in Elmet
Scholes
Met Univ
Beckett Park
Headingley
Oakwood
Brooklands
Swarcliffe
Kirkstall Abbey
Hyde Park
Parklands
Manston
Bramley
Hill Top
Burley
Harehills
University
Leeds Industrial Museum
Civic Hall
Austhorpe
Whitekirk
Armley
Town Hall
City Art Gall
Osmondthorpe
East End Park
Halton Moor
Colton
GARFORTH
Barrowby Park
Swillington Common
Church Garforth
Park Spring
Upper Wortley
Holbeck
Bank
LEEDS
Royal Armouries
Farnley
Knowsthorpe
Home Farm
Temple Newsam House
Temple Newsam Country Park
Dawson's Wood
Avenue Wood
Hunslet
Thwaitemills Industrial Museum
Brecks Wood
New Farnley
Cross Flatts Park
River Aire
Aire & Calder Navigation
KIPPAX
Beeston
South Leeds Stadium
Newsam Green
Swillington
Little Preston
Country Park
Great Preston
Middleton Railway
Middleton Park
Rothwell Haigh
Woodlesford
Cockpit Round
Gildersome
Churwell
White Rose Centre
ROTHWELL
Oulton
Troy Hill
Town Hall
Bruntcliffe
Middleton
MORLEY
Robin Hood
Carlton
Almshouses Wood
Mickletown
Topcliffe
Thorpe on the Hill
Ouzlewell Green
Moss Carr Wood
Methley
Sports Centre
The Fall
Lee Moor
EAST ARDSLEY
Upper Green
Ardsley Resr
Lofthouse Gate
Fairies Hill
Upper Batley
Lower Soothill
Haigh Moor
River Calder
The Mill
Dum Wood
STANLEY
OUTWOOD
Nature Reserve
BATLEY
Brandy Carr
Altofts
Dogloitch Wood
Bragg Lane End
NORMANTON
Batley Carr
Hanging Heaton
Chidswell
Kirkhamgate
Newton Hill
DEWSBURY
Gawthorpe
Wrenthorpe
Woodhouse
Ossett Street Side
Alverthorpe
Chickenley
Kirkthorpe
OSSETT
WAKEFIELD
Canal Museum
Flanshaw
Warmfield
Streethouse
Runtlings
Lupset
Thornhill Lees
South Ossett
Belle Vue
Sharlston Common
Sharlston
0 1 2 3 miles
0 1 2 3 4 5 km

Liverpool

0 Miles ¼

A5036 TO A565 · A565 SOUTHPORT · A5038 KIRKDALE · A59 PRESTON M57 & M58 & KINGSWAY TUNNEL · A580 TO A59 · A5049 WEST DERBY

A57 WARRINGTON · A5047 TO M62 & MANCHESTER

A5036 TO A562 · A561 GARSTON · A5038 TO A561

RIVER MERSEY

Lincoln

0 Miles ¼

Middlesbrough

0 Miles ¼

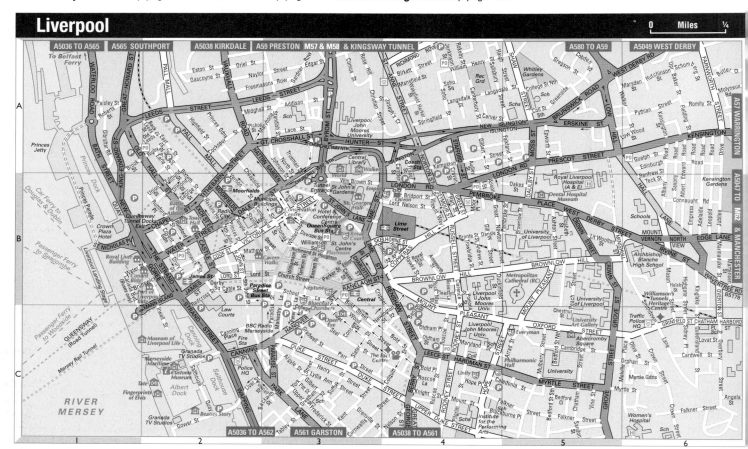

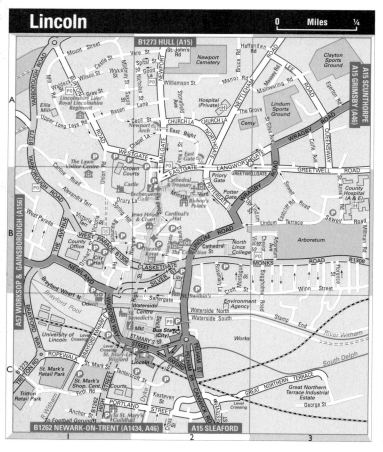

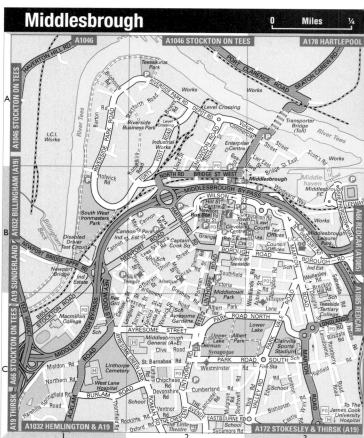

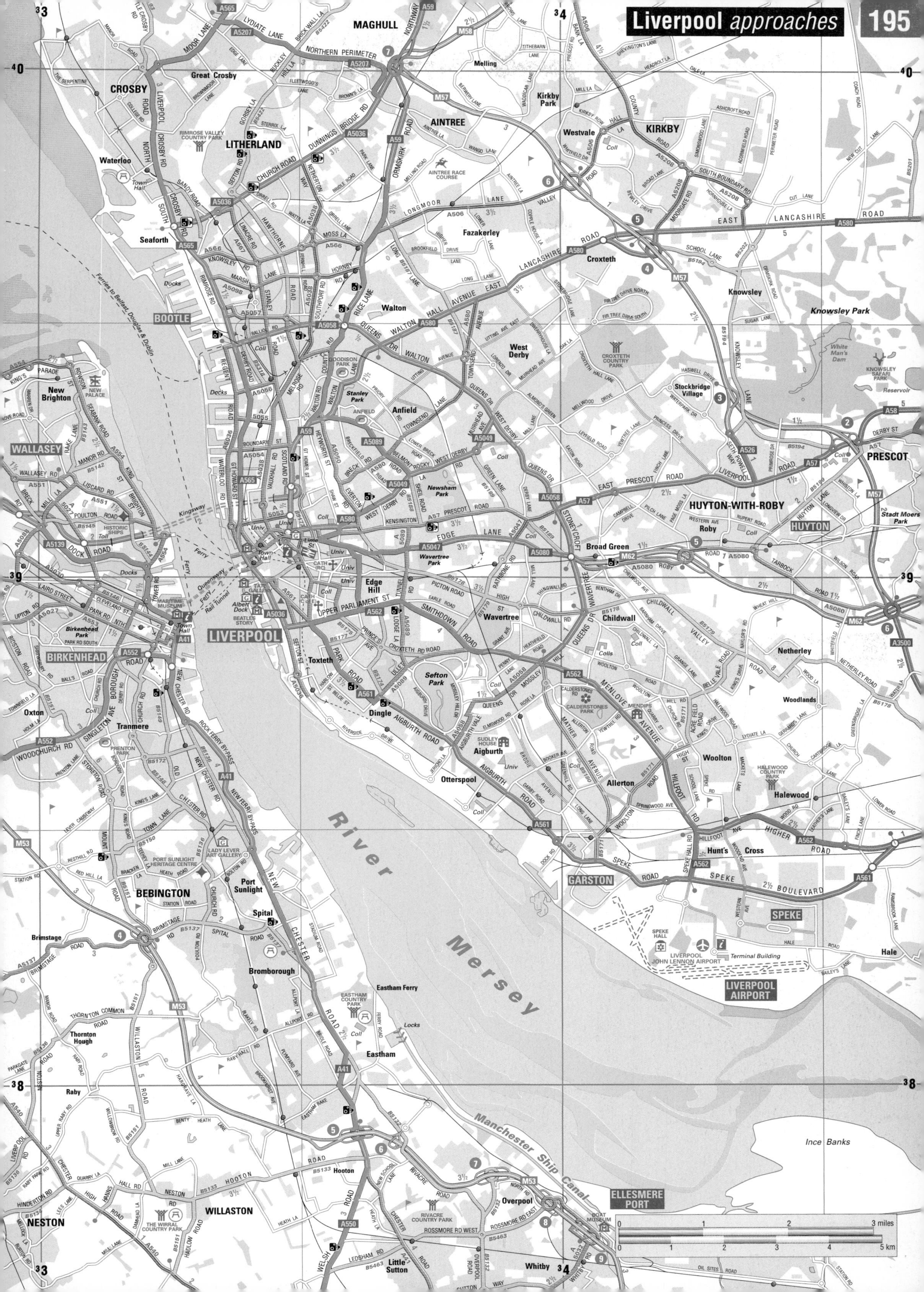
LIVERPOOL
BIRKENHEAD
BOOTLE
WALLASEY
CROSBY
LITHERLAND
MAGHULL
AINTREE
KIRKBY
PRESCOT
HUYTON-WITH-ROBY
GARSTON
SPEKE
LIVERPOOL AIRPORT
ELLESMERE PORT
BEBINGTON
NESTON
WILLASTON
River Mersey
Manchester Ship Canal
Knowsley Park
Ince Banks

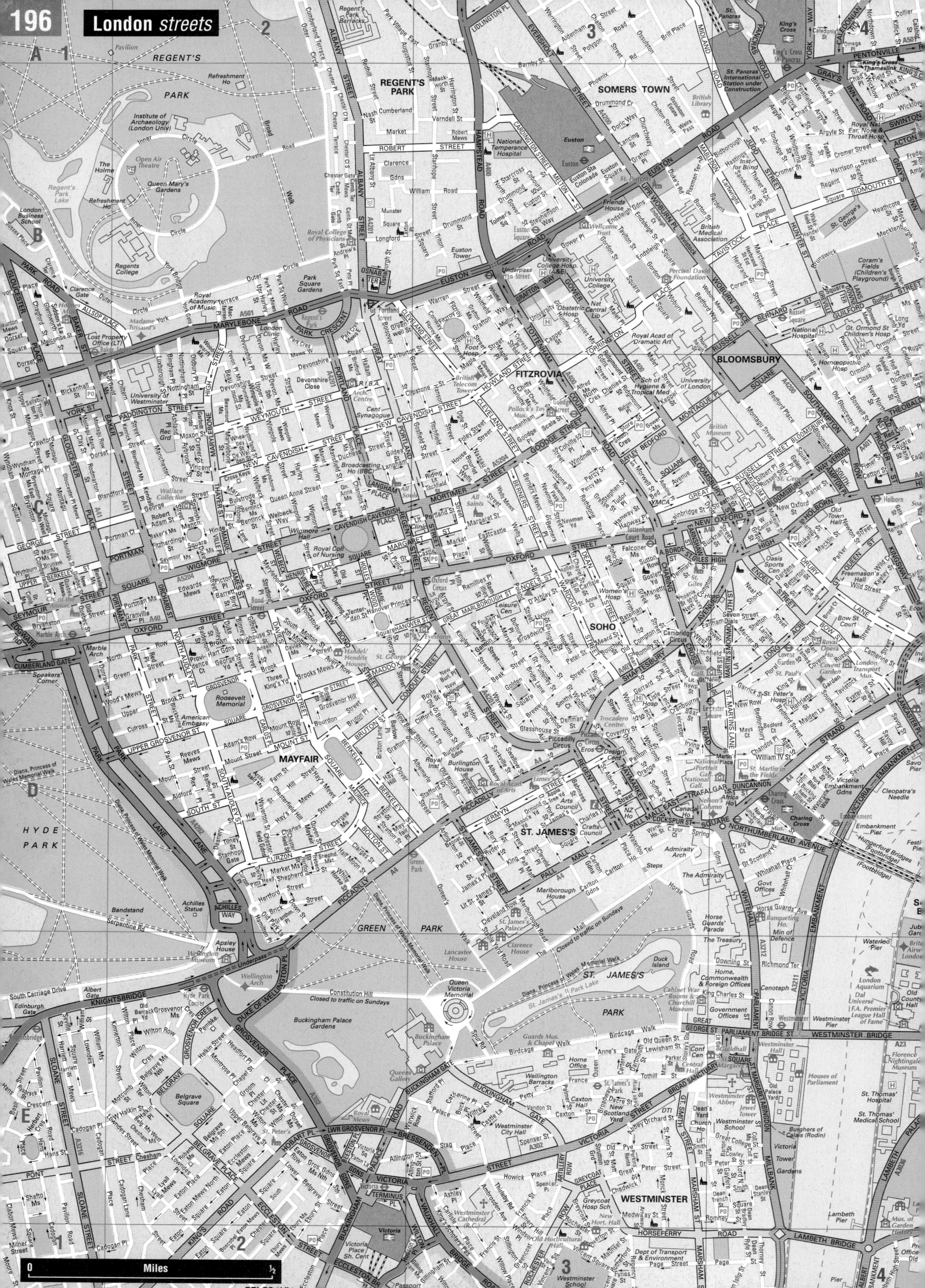
REGENT'S PARK
REGENT'S PARK
SOMERS TOWN
BLOOMSBURY
FITZROVIA
SOHO
MAYFAIR
ST. JAMES'S
HYDE PARK
GREEN PARK
ST. JAMES'S PARK
WESTMINSTER
Queen Mary's Gardens
Open Air Theatre
Regent's Park Lake
London Business School
Regents College
Madame Tussaud's
University of Westminster
Wallace Collection
Broadcasting Ho (BBC)
Royal Coll of Nursing
British Telecom Tower
Euston
St. Pancras
King's Cross
St. Pancras International Station under Construction
British Library
University College Hosp. (A&E)
University College
Royal Acad of Dramatic Art
University of London
British Museum
Coram's Fields (Children's Playground)
Great Ormond St Children's Hosp
Trocadero Centre
Piccadilly Circus
National Portrait Gall.
National Gall.
Trafalgar Square
Nelson's Column
Charing Cross
Royal Opera Ho
London Transport Mus.
Covent Garden
Burlington House
Royal Acad. of Arts
Marble Arch
Speakers' Corner
Roosevelt Memorial
American Embassy
Apsley House
Wellington Museum
Wellington Arch
Buckingham Palace
Buckingham Palace Gardens
Queen Victoria Memorial
Clarence House
St. James's Palace
Lancaster House
Marlborough House
Horse Guards' Parade
The Admiralty
Admiralty Arch
Downing St
Cabinet War Rooms & Churchill Museum
Westminster Abbey
Houses of Parliament
Westminster Bridge
Lambeth Bridge
London Aquarium
County Hall
St. Thomas' Hospital
Westminster Cathedral (R.C.)
Victoria
Cleopatra's Needle
Waterloo Pier
Westminster Pier
Embankment Pier
Hungerford Bridges (Footbridge)
Guards Mus. & Chapel
Wellington Barracks
Queen's Gallery
Royal Mews
Westminster City Hall
New Scotland Yard
Dept of Transport & Environment
Achilles Statue
Bandstand
Serpentine Rd
Constitution Hill
Closed to traffic on Sundays
Diana, Princess of Wales Memorial Walk
OXFORD STREET
REGENT STREET
PICCADILLY
PARK LANE
MARYLEBONE ROAD
EUSTON ROAD
KNIGHTSBRIDGE
SHAFTESBURY AVENUE
CHARING CROSS ROAD
TOTTENHAM COURT ROAD
NEW OXFORD STREET
HIGH HOLBORN
KINGSWAY
STRAND
VICTORIA EMBANKMENT
WHITEHALL
VICTORIA STREET
Miles
0
½

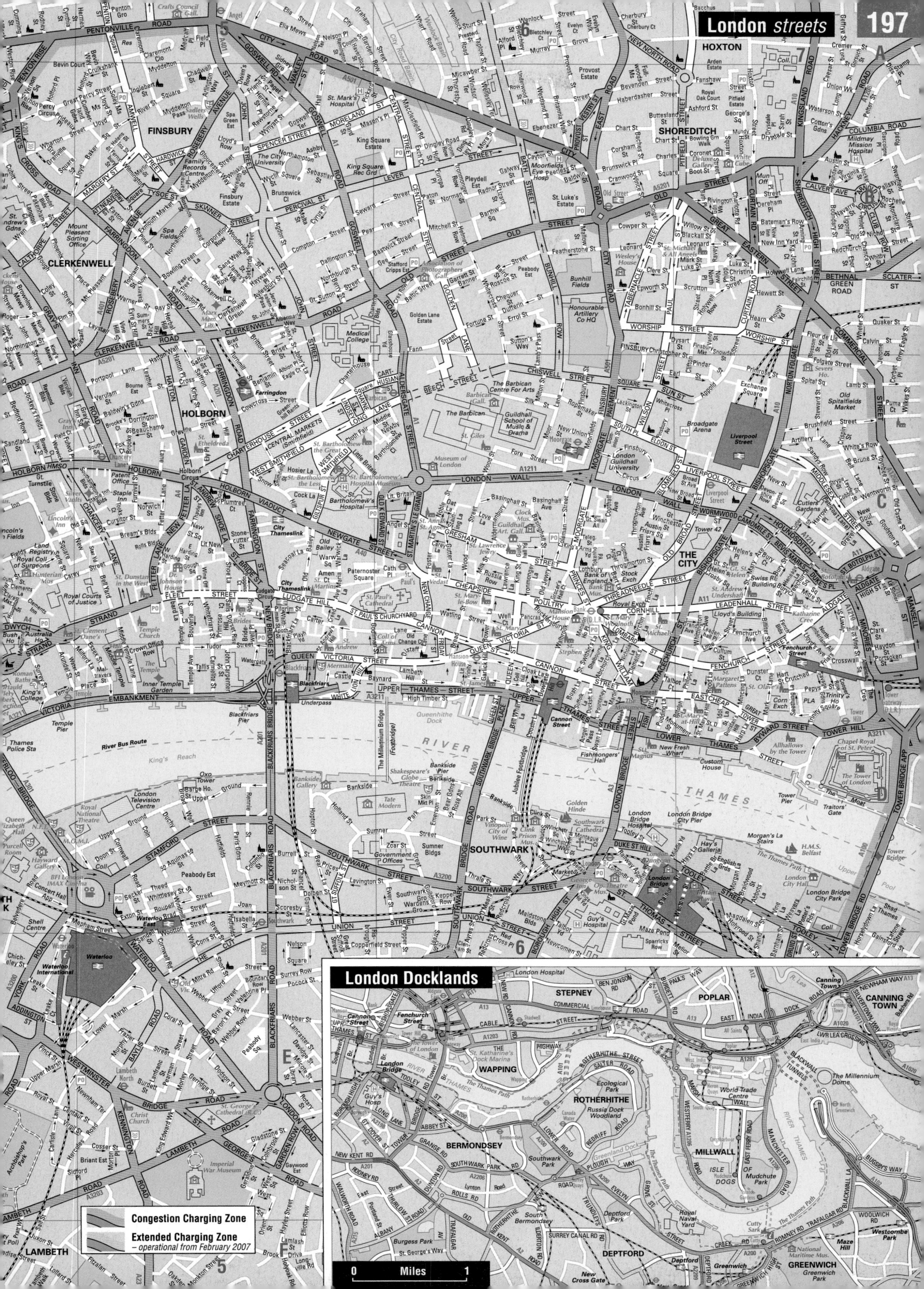
London streets
197
HOXTON
SHOREDITCH
FINSBURY
CLERKENWELL
HOLBORN
THE CITY
SOUTHWARK
LAMBETH
BETHNAL GREEN ROAD
PENTONVILLE ROAD
CITY ROAD
OLD STREET
GOSWELL ROAD
FARRINGDON ROAD
CLERKENWELL ROAD
LONDON WALL
HOLBORN VIADUCT
NEWGATE STREET
CHEAPSIDE
FLEET STREET
STRAND
LUDGATE HILL
CANNON STREET
UPPER THAMES STREET
LOWER THAMES STREET
VICTORIA EMBANKMENT
BISHOPSGATE
COMMERCIAL STREET
LIVERPOOL STREET
FENCHURCH STREET
EASTCHEAP
LEADENHALL STREET
TOWER HILL
TOWER BRIDGE APP
TOWER BRIDGE RD
LONDON BRIDGE
SOUTHWARK BRIDGE
BLACKFRIARS BRIDGE
BLACKFRIARS ROAD
SOUTHWARK STREET
STAMFORD STREET
UNION STREET
BOROUGH HIGH ST
TOOLEY STREET
WATERLOO ROAD
WESTMINSTER BRIDGE ROAD
KENNINGTON ROAD
LAMBETH ROAD
ST. GEORGE'S ROAD
LONDON ROAD
RIVER THAMES
River Bus Route
King's Reach
Queenhithe Dock
Liverpool Street
Farringdon
City Thameslink
Blackfriars
Cannon Street
Fenchurch Street
London Bridge
Waterloo
Waterloo East
Waterloo International
The Barbican
Barbican Centre For Arts
Museum of London
St. Paul's Cathedral
Bank of England
Royal Exch
Monument
The Tower of London
Traitors' Gate
H.M.S. Belfast
Tate Modern
Shakespeare's Globe Theatre
The Millennium Bridge (footbridge)
Southwark Cathedral
Guy's Hospital
Imperial War Museum
Royal National Theatre
London Television Centre
Oxo Tower
Bunhill Fields
Honourable Artillery Co HQ
Temple
Inner Temple Garden
Royal Courts of Justice
Lincoln's Inn
Gray's Inn
Mount Pleasant Sorting Office
London Docklands
STEPNEY
POPLAR
CANNING TOWN
WAPPING
ROTHERHITHE
BERMONDSEY
MILLWALL
ISLE OF DOGS
DEPTFORD
GREENWICH
The Millennium Dome
World Trade Centre
Mudchute Park
Southwark Park
Deptford Park
Royal Naval Yard
National Maritime Mus.
Greenwich Park
Cutty Sark
Ecological Park
Russia Dock Woodland
St. Katharine's Dock Marina
Burgess Park
0 Miles 1
Congestion Charging Zone
Extended Charging Zone
– operational from February 2007

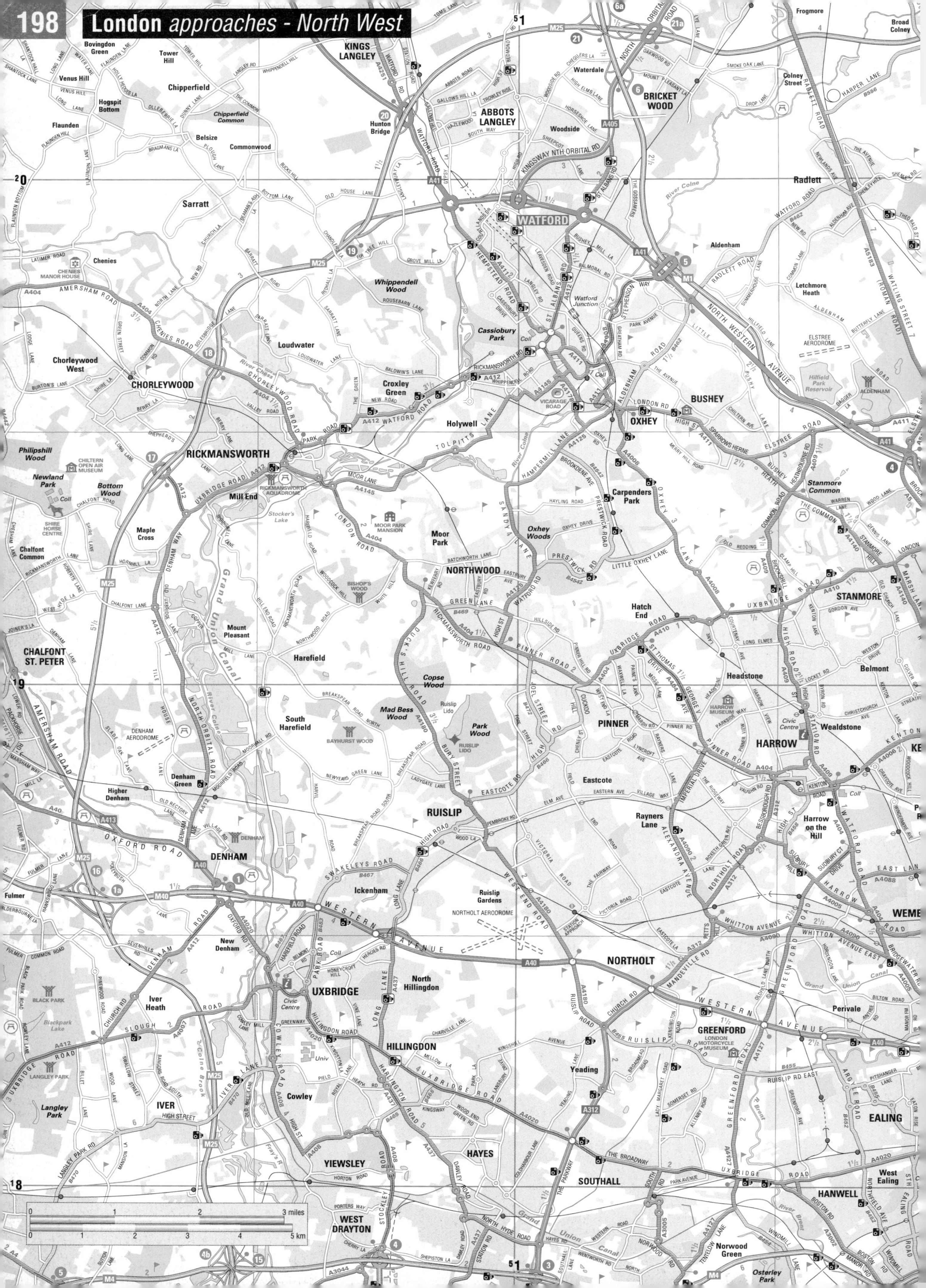
KINGS LANGLEY
ABBOTS LANGLEY
BRICKET WOOD
WATFORD
Radlett
Aldenham
Bovingdon Green
Tower Hill
Venus Hill
Chipperfield
Hogspit Bottom
Flaunden
Hunton Bridge
Belsize
Commonwood
Sarratt
Chenies
Waterdale
Woodside
Colney Street
Frogmore
Broad Colney
Letchmore Heath
ELSTREE AERODROME
Hilfield Park Reservoir
Whippendell Wood
Cassiobury Park
Watford Junction
Loudwater
Chorleywood West
CHORLEYWOOD
Croxley Green
Holywell
OXHEY
BUSHEY
Philipshill Wood
CHILTERN OPEN AIR MUSEUM
RICKMANSWORTH
Newland Park
Bottom Wood
Mill End
RICKMANSWORTH AQUADROME
Stocker's Lake
MOOR PARK MANSION
Moor Park
Carpenters Park
Oxhey Woods
Stanmore Common
Maple Cross
Chalfont Common
NORTHWOOD
BISHOP'S WOOD
STANMORE
Mount Pleasant
Harefield
Hatch End
CHALFONT ST. PETER
Grand Union Canal
Copse Wood
Mad Bess Wood
Ruislip Lido
Headstone
HARROW MUSEUM
Belmont
South Harefield
BAYHURST WOOD
DENHAM AERODROME
Park Wood
RUISLIP LIDO
PINNER
HARROW
Wealdstone
Denham Green
Higher Denham
Eastcote
RUISLIP
Rayners Lane
Harrow on the Hill
DENHAM
Ickenham
Ruislip Gardens
NORTHOLT AERODROME
Fulmer
New Denham
NORTHOLT
UXBRIDGE
North Hillingdon
BLACK PARK
Iver Heath
Blackpark Lake
GREENFORD
LONDON MOTORCYCLE MUSEUM
Perivale
HILLINGDON
LANGLEY PARK
Langley Park
IVER
Cowley
Yeading
EALING
YIEWSLEY
HAYES
SOUTHALL
West Ealing
HANWELL
WEST DRAYTON
Norwood Green
Osterley Park
M25
M1
M40
M4
A40
A41
A404
A412
A4020
WESTERN AVENUE
NORTH ORBITAL ROAD
UXBRIDGE ROAD
0 1 2 3 miles
0 1 2 3 4 5 km

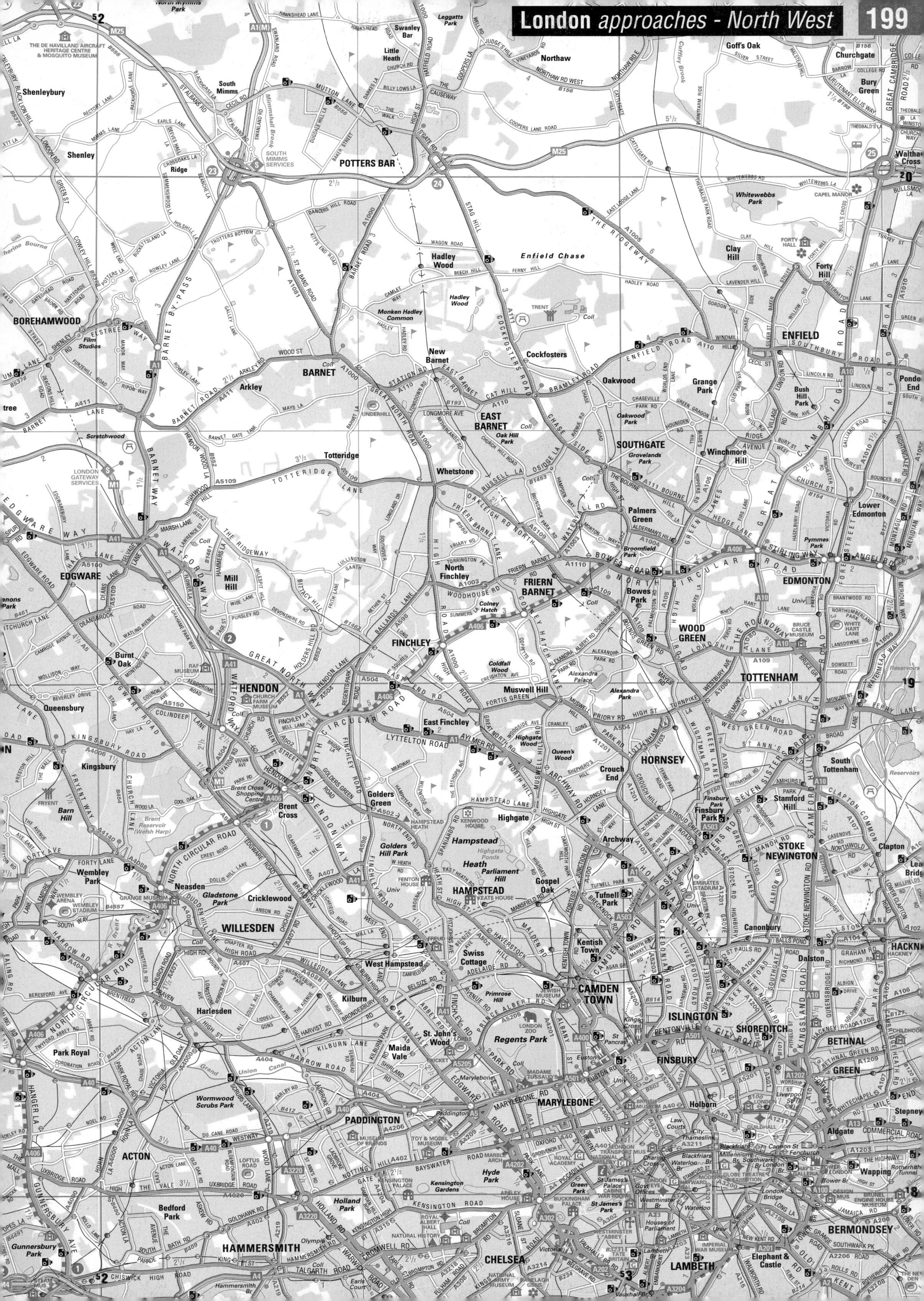

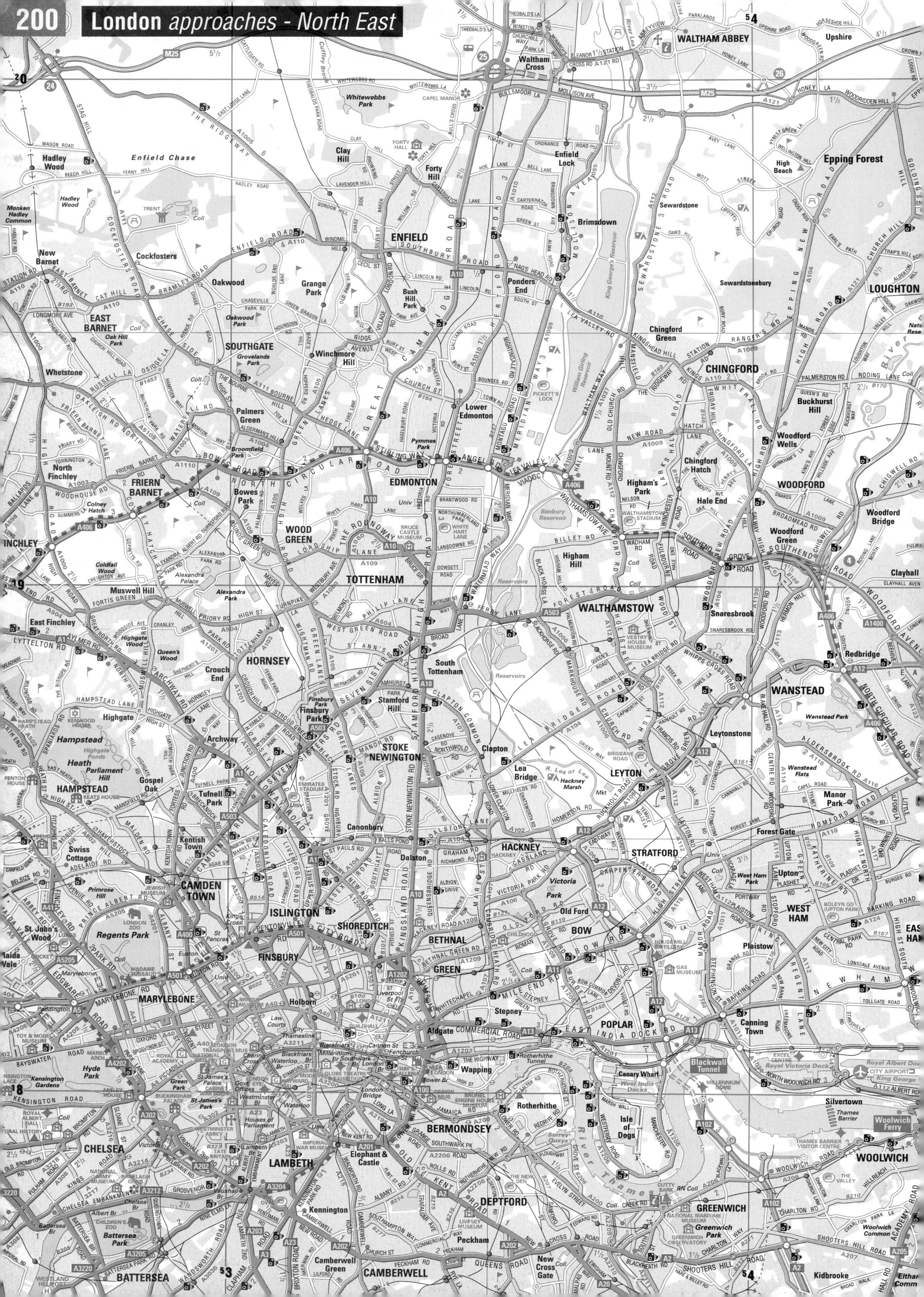

WALTHAM ABBEY
Upshire
Waltham Cross
Whitewebbs Park
Enfield Chase
Hadley Wood
Clay Hill
Forty Hill
Enfield Lock
Epping Forest
High Beach
Sewardstone
Monken Hadley Common
Brimsdown
ENFIELD
Cockfosters
New Barnet
Oakwood
Grange Park
Bush Hill Park
Ponders End
Sewardstonebury
LOUGHTON
EAST BARNET
SOUTHGATE
Winchmore Hill
Chingford Green
CHINGFORD
Whetstone
Palmers Green
Lower Edmonton
Buckhurst Hill
Woodford Wells
North Finchley
FRIERN BARNET
EDMONTON
Chingford Hatch
Higham's Park
Hale End
WOODFORD
Woodford Bridge
Woodford Green
WOOD GREEN
Higham Hill
Muswell Hill
TOTTENHAM
WALTHAMSTOW
Snaresbrook
Clayhall
East Finchley
HORNSEY
Crouch End
South Tottenham
Redbridge
WANSTEAD
Highgate
Hampstead
Stamford Hill
Finsbury Park
Archway
STOKE NEWINGTON
Clapton
Leytonstone
HAMPSTEAD
Gospel Oak
Tufnell Park
Lea Bridge
LEYTON
Manor Park
Kentish Town
Canonbury
Swiss Cottage
Dalston
HACKNEY
STRATFORD
Forest Gate
Upton
CAMDEN TOWN
Victoria Park
ISLINGTON
SHOREDITCH
BETHNAL GREEN
BOW
Old Ford
Plaistow
WEST HAM
St. John's Wood
Regents Park
FINSBURY
MARYLEBONE
Holborn
Stepney
POPLAR
Canning Town
Aldgate
Wapping
Hyde Park
Canary Wharf
Silvertown
Rotherhithe
Isle of Dogs
BERMONDSEY
CHELSEA
LAMBETH
Elephant & Castle
WOOLWICH
Kennington
DEPTFORD
GREENWICH
Peckham
Camberwell Green
CAMBERWELL
New Cross Gate
Kidbrooke
BATTERSEA
Blackwall Tunnel
Woolwich Ferry

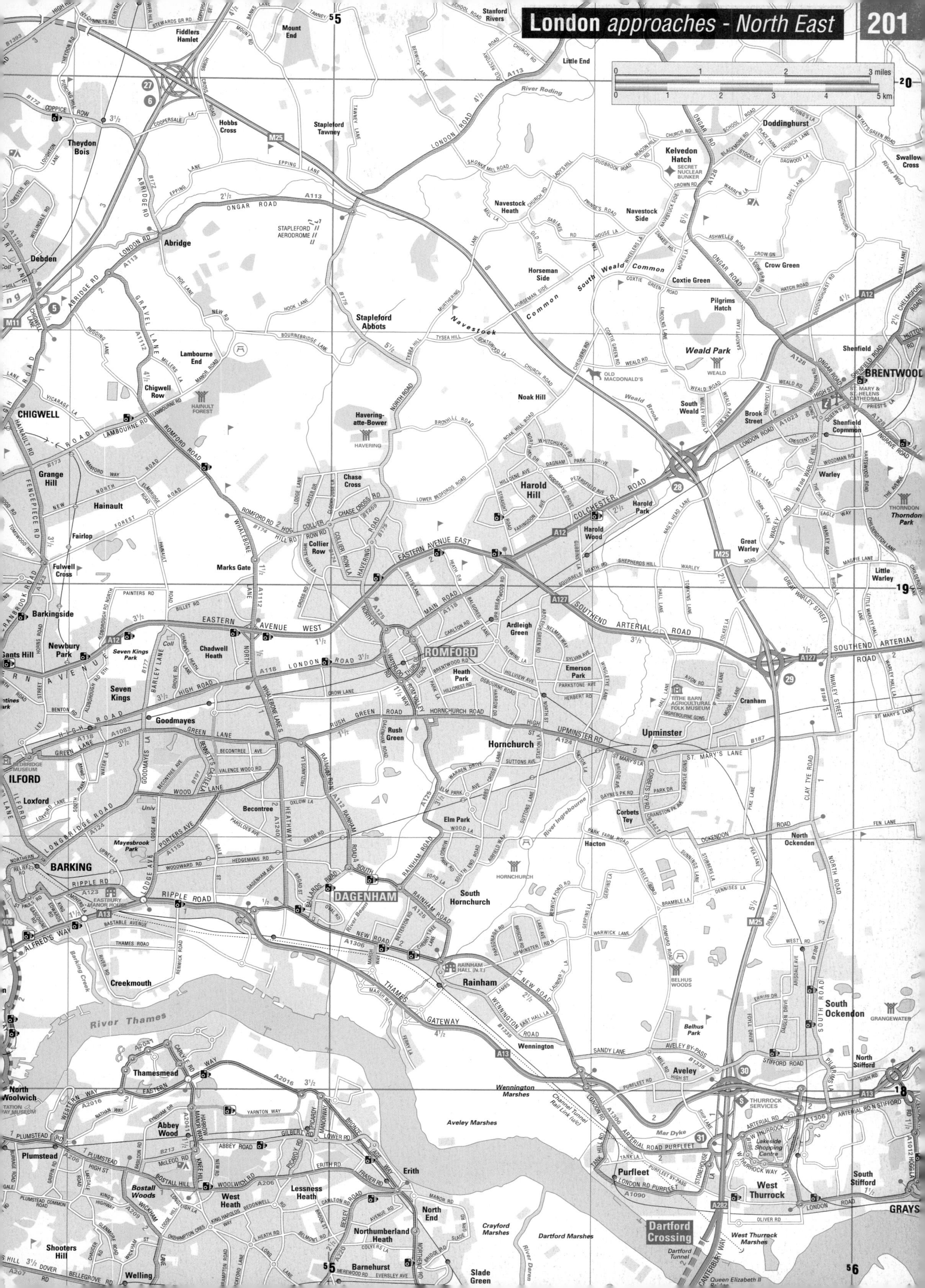
Mount End
Stanford Rivers
Fiddlers Hamlet
Little End
Theydon Bois
Hobbs Cross
Stapleford Tawney
Doddinghurst
Kelvedon Hatch
Swallows Cross
Navestock Heath
Navestock Side
Abridge
Debden
Horseman Side
Crow Green
Coxtie Green
Pilgrims Hatch
Stapleford Abbots
Lambourne End
Weald Park
Shenfield
BRENTWOOD
Chigwell Row
Noak Hill
CHIGWELL
South Weald
Brook Street
Havering-atte-Bower
Shenfield Common
Grange Hill
Chase Cross
Harold Hill
Warley
Hainault
Harold Park
Thorndon Park
Fairlop
Collier Row
Harold Wood
Great Warley
Marks Gate
Fulwell Cross
Little Warley
Barkingside
Ardleigh Green
Newbury Park
Chadwell Heath
ROMFORD
Seven Kings Park
Seven Kings
Heath Park
Emerson Park
Cranham
Goodmayes
Rush Green
Hornchurch
Upminster
ILFORD
Loxford
Becontree
Elm Park
Corbets Tey
BARKING
Hacton
North Ockendon
Mayesbrook Park
DAGENHAM
South Hornchurch
Creekmouth
Rainham
River Thames
South Ockendon
Belhus Park
Wennington
Thamesmead
Aveley
North Stifford
North Woolwich
Wennington Marshes
Aveley Marshes
Abbey Wood
Plumstead
Mar Dyke
Erith
Purfleet
West Thurrock
South Stifford
Bostall Woods
West Heath
Lessness Heath
North End
GRAYS
Crayford Marshes
Dartford Marshes
Northumberland Heath
Dartford Crossing
West Thurrock Marshes
Shooters Hill
Barnehurst
Welling
Slade Green
M25
M11
A12
A13
A127
River Roding
Dartford Tunnel

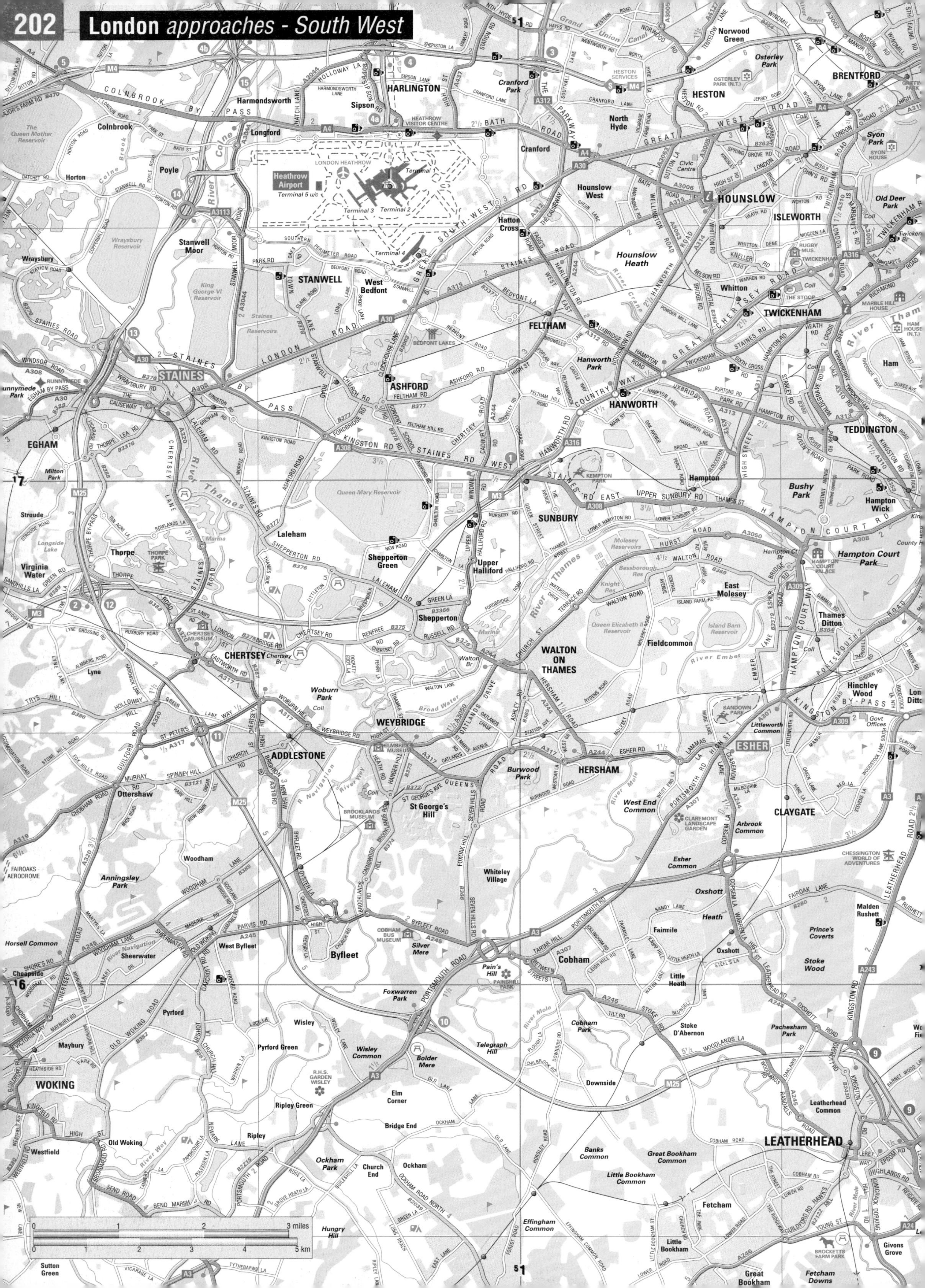

HARLINGTON
Harmondsworth
Sipson
Colnbrook
Longford
Cranford Park
Cranford
North Hyde
Norwood Green
Osterley Park
BRENTFORD
HESTON
Heathrow Airport
LONDON HEATHROW
Terminal 1
Terminal 2
Terminal 3
Terminal 4
Terminal 5 u/c
HEATHROW VISITOR CENTRE
Horton
Poyle
Stanwell Moor
Wraysbury
Wraysbury Reservoir
King George VI Reservoir
Staines Reservoirs
The Queen Mother Reservoir
STANWELL
West Bedfont
Hatton Cross
Hounslow West
HOUNSLOW
ISLEWORTH
Syon Park
Old Deer Park
Hounslow Heath
Whitton
TWICKENHAM
FELTHAM
BEDFONT LAKES
STAINES
Runnymede Park
EGHAM
Milton Park
ASHFORD
Hanworth Park
HANWORTH
Ham
TEDDINGTON
Queen Mary Reservoir
KEMPTON PARK
Hampton
Bushy Park
Hampton Wick
SUNBURY
Laleham
Stroude
Thorpe
THORPE PARK
Virginia Water
Longside Lake
Shepperton Green
Upper Halliford
Molesey Reservoirs
Hampton Court Park
Bessborough Res
Knight Res
East Molesey
Thames Ditton
Shepperton
Queen Elizabeth II Reservoir
Island Barn Reservoir
CHERTSEY
CHERTSEY MUSEUM
Lyne
WALTON ON THAMES
Fieldcommon
Hinchley Wood
Woburn Park
WEYBRIDGE
SANDOWN PARK
Littleworth Common
ADDLESTONE
Burwood Park
HERSHAM
ESHER
ELMBRIDGE MUSEUM
Ottershaw
St George's Hill
BROOKLANDS MUSEUM
West End Common
CLAREMONT LANDSCAPE GARDEN
Arbrook Common
CLAYGATE
Woodham
Anningsley Park
FAIROAKS AERODROME
Whiteley Village
Esher Common
CHESSINGTON WORLD OF ADVENTURES
Oxshott
Heath
Malden Rushett
Horsell Common
West Byfleet
Sheerwater
COBHAM BUS MUSEUM
Silver Mere
Byfleet
Fairmile
Cobham
Prince's Coverts
Stoke Wood
Pain's Hill
PAINSHILL PARK
Little Heath
Foxwarren Park
Pyrford
Wisley
Cobham Park
Stoke D'Abernon
Pachesham Park
Maybury
Pyrford Green
Wisley Common
Telegraph Hill
Bolder Mere
WOKING
R.H.S. GARDEN WISLEY
Elm Corner
Downside
Leatherhead Common
Ripley Green
Bridge End
Old Woking
Ripley
LEATHERHEAD
Westfield
Ockham Park
Church End
Ockham
Banks Common
Great Bookham Common
Little Bookham Common
Fetcham
Effingham Common
Hungry Hill
Little Bookham
BROCKETTS FARM PARK
Givons Grove
Sutton Green
Great Bookham
Fetcham Downs
M25
M3
M4
A3
A30
A308
A316
0 1 2 3 miles
0 1 2 3 4 5 km

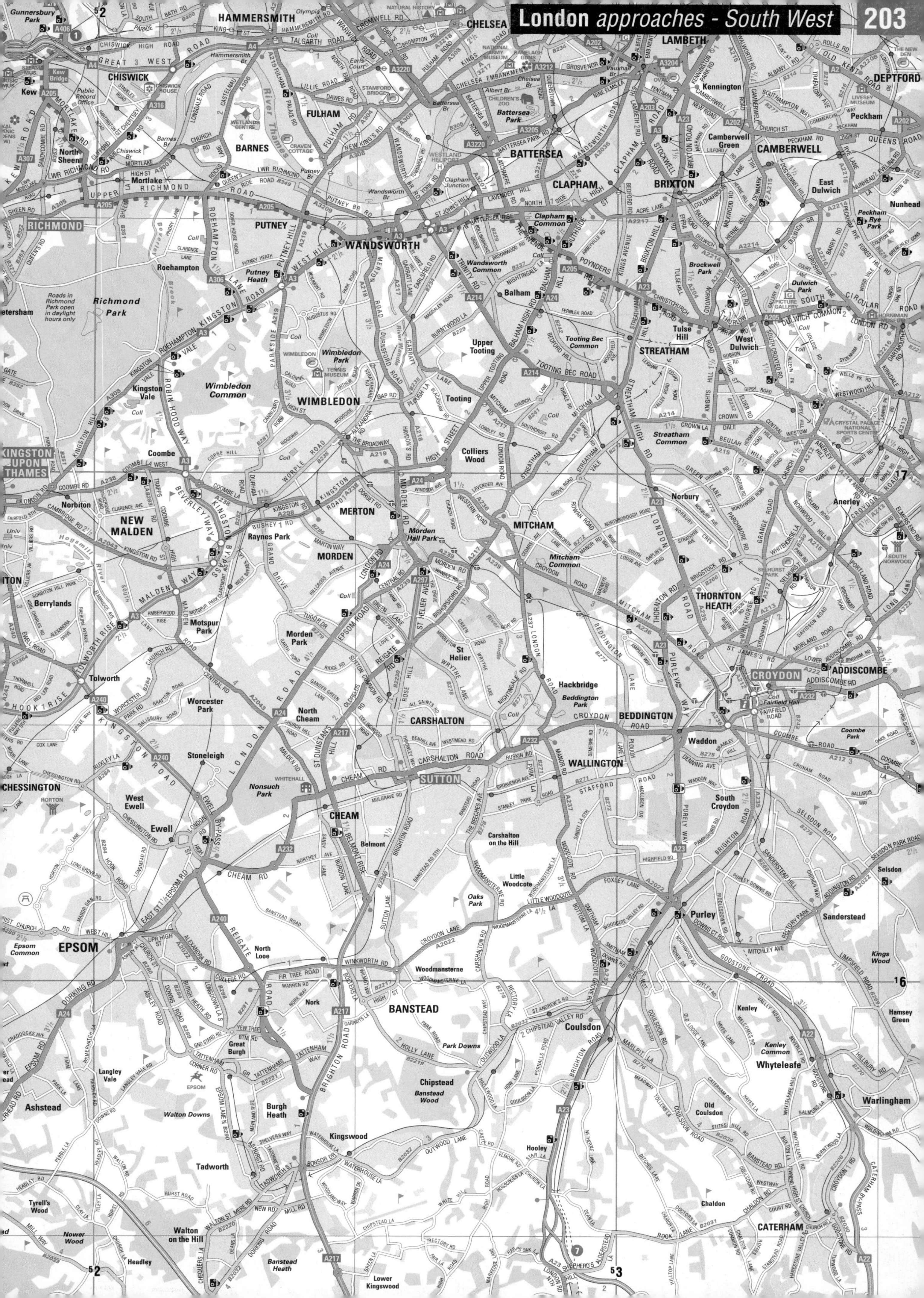
HAMMERSMITH
CHELSEA
LAMBETH
DEPTFORD
CHISWICK
FULHAM
Kennington
Peckham
BARNES
BATTERSEA
CAMBERWELL
CLAPHAM
BRIXTON
RICHMOND
PUTNEY
WANDSWORTH
East Dulwich
Nunhead
Roehampton
Richmond Park
Balham
Upper Tooting
STREATHAM
Wimbledon Common
WIMBLEDON
Tooting
Kingston Vale
KINGSTON UPON THAMES
Coombe
Colliers Wood
NEW MALDEN
MERTON
MITCHAM
Norbury
Raynes Park
MORDEN
THORNTON HEATH
Anerley
Berrylands
Motspur Park
Morden Park
St Helier
CROYDON
ADDISCOMBE
Tolworth
Worcester Park
Hackbridge
North Cheam
CARSHALTON
BEDDINGTON
Waddon
Stoneleigh
SUTTON
WALLINGTON
CHESSINGTON
West Ewell
Ewell
CHEAM
South Croydon
Belmont
Carshalton on the Hill
Little Woodcote
Purley
Sanderstead
EPSOM
North Looe
Woodmansterne
Nork
BANSTEAD
Coulsdon
Kenley
Whyteleafe
Langley Vale
Great Burgh
Chipstead
Warlingham
Ashtead
Walton Downs
Burgh Heath
Kingswood
Hooley
Old Coulsdon
Tadworth
Chaldon
CATERHAM
Walton on the Hill
Headley
Banstead Heath
Lower Kingswood

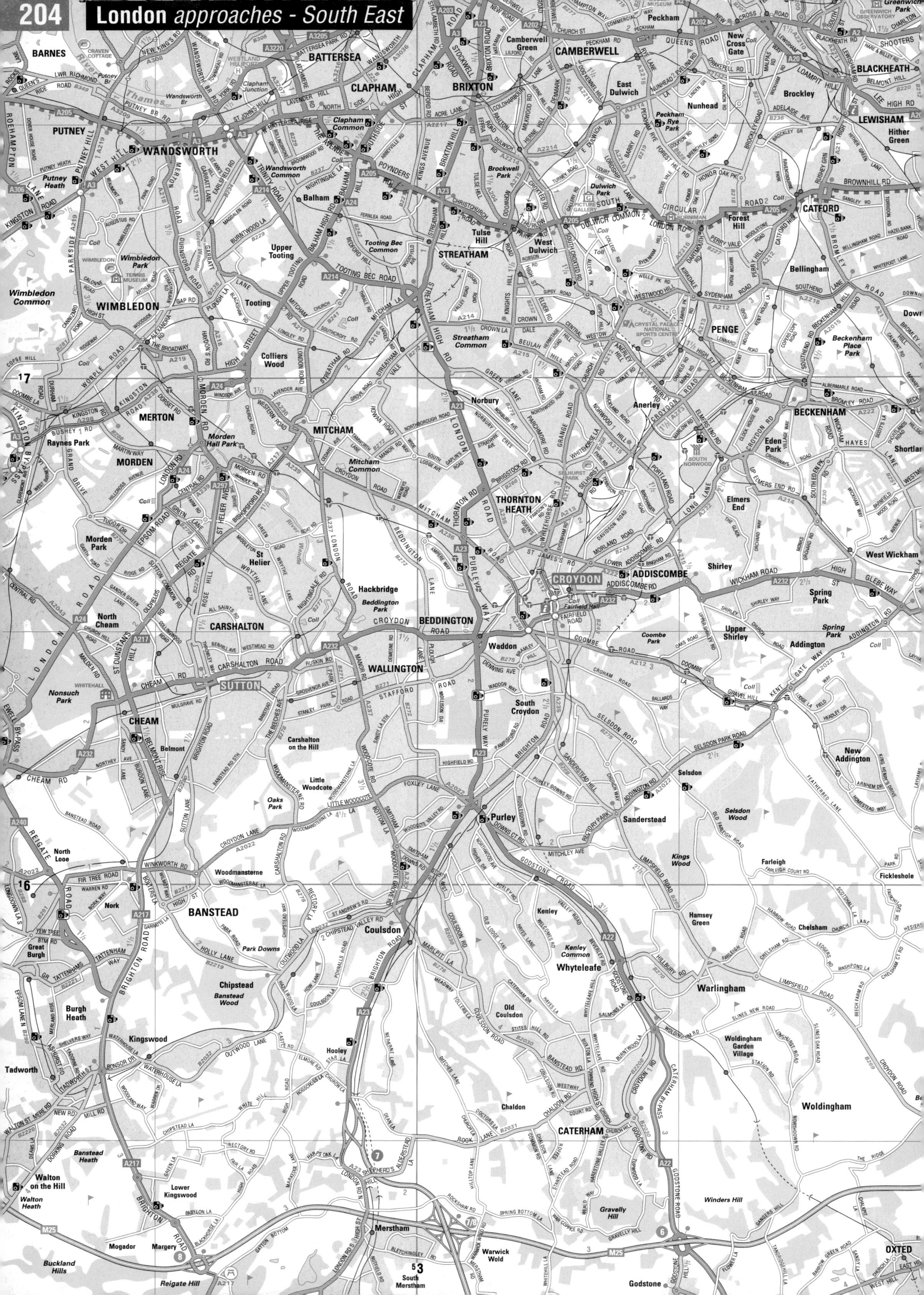
BARNES
PUTNEY
WANDSWORTH
BATTERSEA
CLAPHAM
BRIXTON
CAMBERWELL
Peckham
New Cross Gate
BLACKHEATH
LEWISHAM
Brockley
Nunhead
East Dulwich
Dulwich Park
West Dulwich
Forest Hill
CATFORD
Bellingham
Balham
Upper Tooting
Tooting
Tooting Bec Common
STREATHAM
Tulse Hill
Wimbledon Park
Wimbledon Common
WIMBLEDON
Colliers Wood
Streatham Common
PENGE
Beckenham Place Park
Norbury
Anerley
BECKENHAM
MERTON
MITCHAM
Mitcham Common
Raynes Park
MORDEN
Morden Hall Park
THORNTON HEATH
Eden Park
Elmers End
Shortlands
Morden Park
St Helier
Hackbridge
Beddington Park
CROYDON
ADDISCOMBE
Shirley
West Wickham
Spring Park
North Cheam
CARSHALTON
BEDDINGTON
Waddon
Upper Shirley
Addington
WALLINGTON
SUTTON
Nonsuch Park
CHEAM
Belmont
Carshalton on the Hill
South Croydon
New Addington
Little Woodcote
Oaks Park
Purley
Sanderstead
Selsdon
Selsdon Wood
North Looe
Woodmansterne
Kings Wood
Farleigh
Fickleshole
Nork
BANSTEAD
Coulsdon
Kenley
Hamsey Green
Chelsham
Great Burgh
Park Downs
Kenley Common
Whyteleafe
Warlingham
Chipstead
Banstead Wood
Burgh Heath
Old Coulsdon
Woldingham Garden Village
Kingswood
Hooley
Tadworth
Chaldon
Woldingham
CATERHAM
Banstead Heath
Walton on the Hill
Walton Heath
Lower Kingswood
Winders Hill
Gravelly Hill
Merstham
Mogador
Margery
Warwick Wold
OXTED
Buckland Hills
Reigate Hill
South Merstham
Godstone

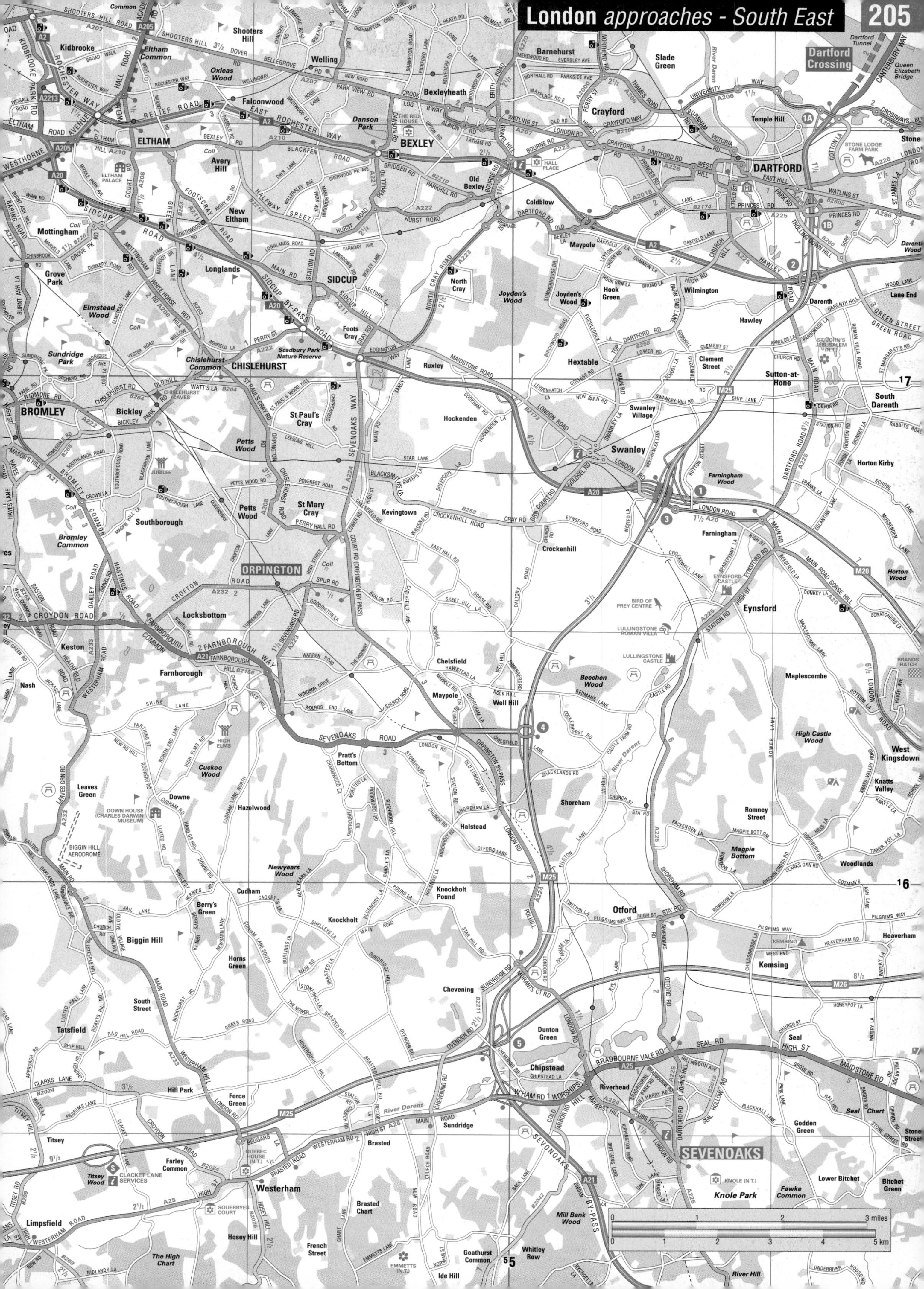
Kidbrooke
Shooters Hill
Eltham Common
Welling
Barnehurst
Slade Green
Dartford Tunnel
Dartford Crossing
Queen Elizabeth Bridge
Oxleas Wood
Falconwood
Bexleyheath
Crayford
Temple Hill
Danson Park
THE RED HOUSE
BEXLEY
ELTHAM
ELTHAM PALACE
Avery Hill
Old Bexley
HALL PLACE
DARTFORD
STONE LODGE FARM PARK
Stone
New Eltham
Coldblow
Mottingham
Maypole
Darenth Wood
Longlands
SIDCUP
Grove Park
North Cray
Joyden's Wood
Hook Green
Wilmington
Darenth
Lane End
Elmstead Wood
Foots Cray
Hawley
Sundridge Park
Scadbury Park Nature Reserve
Chislehurst Common
CHISLEHURST
Ruxley
Hextable
Clement Street
ST JOHN'S JERUSALEM
Sutton-at-Hone
CHISLEHURST CAVES
BROMLEY
Bickley
St Paul's Cray
Hockenden
Swanley Village
South Darenth
Petts Wood
Swanley
JUBILEE
Farningham Wood
Horton Kirby
Southborough
Petts Wood
St Mary Cray
Kevingtown
Farningham
Bromley Common
Crockenhill
ORPINGTON
EYNSFORD CASTLE
Horton Wood
BIRD OF PREY CENTRE
Eynsford
Locksbottom
LULLINGSTONE ROMAN VILLA
Keston
LULLINGSTONE CASTLE
Chelsfield
Farnborough
Beechen Wood
Maplescombe
BRANDS HATCH
Nash
Maypole
Well Hill
HIGH ELMS
Pratt's Bottom
High Castle Wood
West Kingsdown
Cuckoo Wood
Leaves Green
Downe
Shoreham
Knatts Valley
DOWN HOUSE (CHARLES DARWIN MUSEUM)
Hazelwood
Romney Street
Halstead
BIGGIN HILL AERODROME
Magpie Bottom
Newyears Wood
Woodlands
Cudham
Knockholt Pound
Berry's Green
Knockholt
Otford
Biggin Hill
Heaverham
Horns Green
KEMSING
Kemsing
Chevening
South Street
Dunton Green
Tatsfield
Seal
Chipstead
Hill Park
Force Green
Riverhead
River Darent
Sundridge
Seal Chart
Titsey
Godden Green
Stone Street
Brasted
QUEBEC HOUSE (N.T.)
Farley Common
SEVENOAKS
Titsey Wood
CLACKET LANE SERVICES
Westerham
KNOLE (N.T.)
Knole Park
Fawke Common
Lower Bitchet
Bitchet Green
SQUERRYES COURT
Brasted Chart
Mill Bank Wood
Limpsfield
Hosey Hill
French Street
Goathurst Common
Whitley Row
The High Chart
EMMETTS (N.T.)
Ide Hill
River Hill
0 1 2 3 miles
0 1 2 3 4 5 km
M25
M20
M26
A20
A2
A21
A25
A225

Manchester

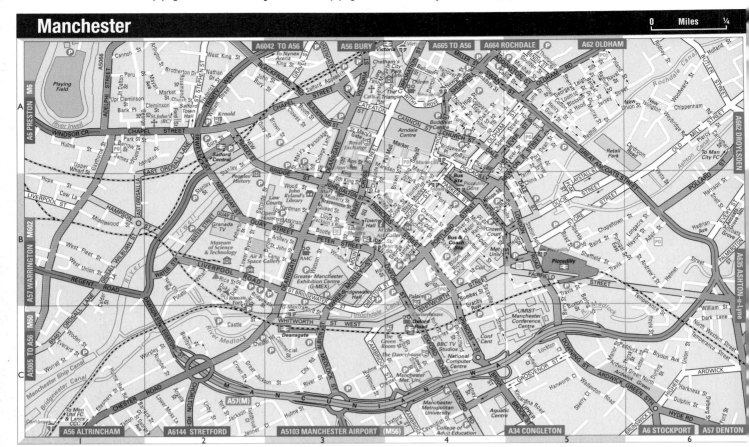

Milton Keynes

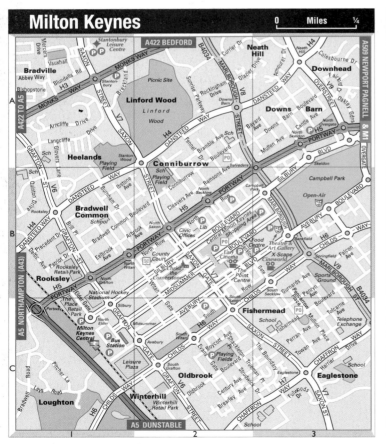

Northampton

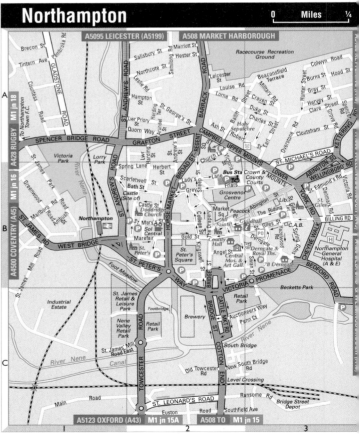

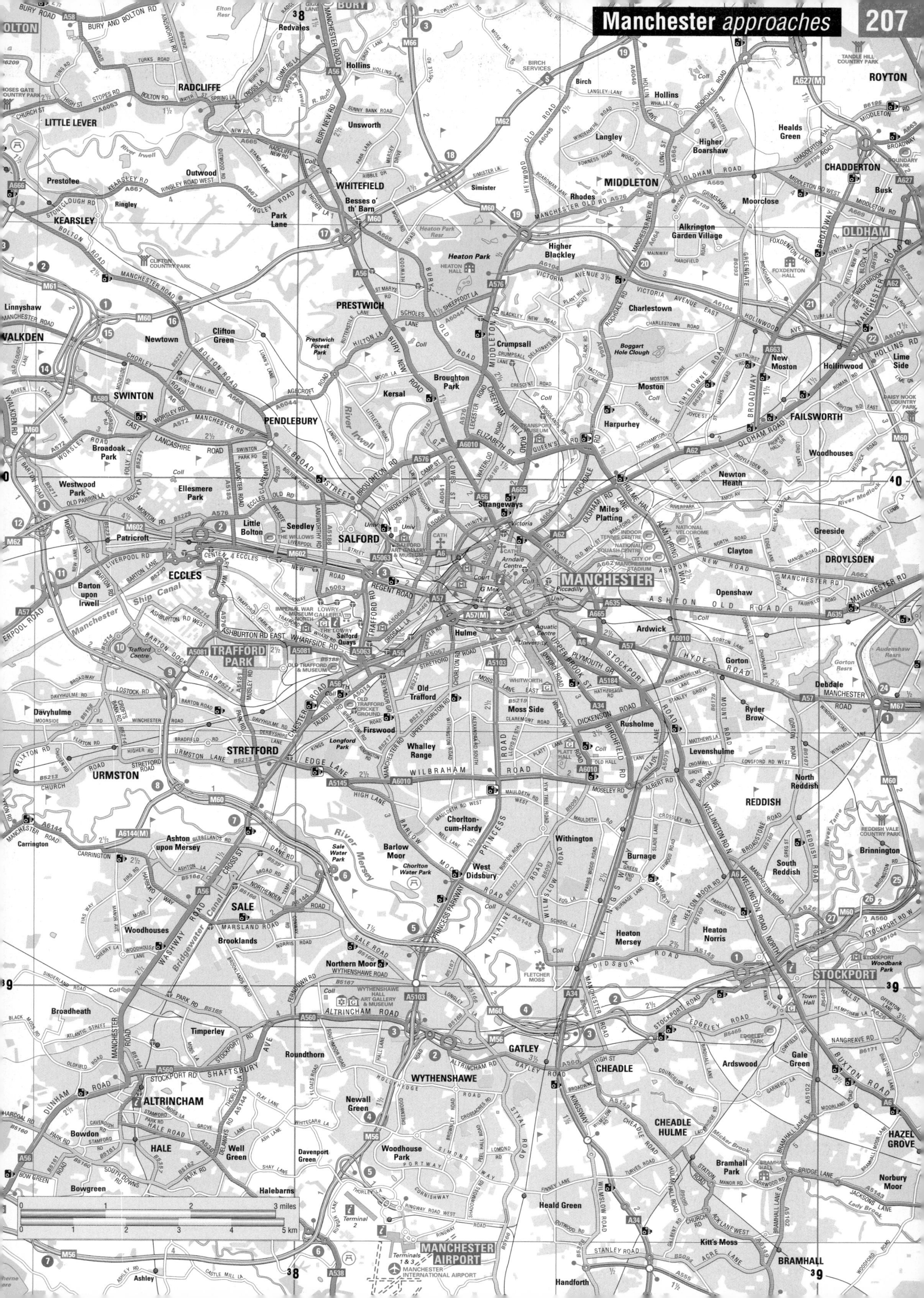
MANCHESTER
SALFORD
STOCKPORT
OLDHAM
BURY
BOLTON
MANCHESTER AIRPORT
TRAFFORD PARK
ALTRINCHAM
SALE
STRETFORD
URMSTON
ECCLES
SWINTON
PRESTWICH
WHITEFIELD
MIDDLETON
CHADDERTON
FAILSWORTH
DROYLSDEN
REDDISH
CHEADLE
CHEADLE HULME
GATLEY
WYTHENSHAWE
HALE
BRAMHALL
HAZEL GROVE
ROYTON
RADCLIFFE
KEARSLEY
WALKDEN
LITTLE LEVER
PENDLEBURY
0 1 2 3 miles
0 1 2 3 4 5 km

Newcastle upon Tyne

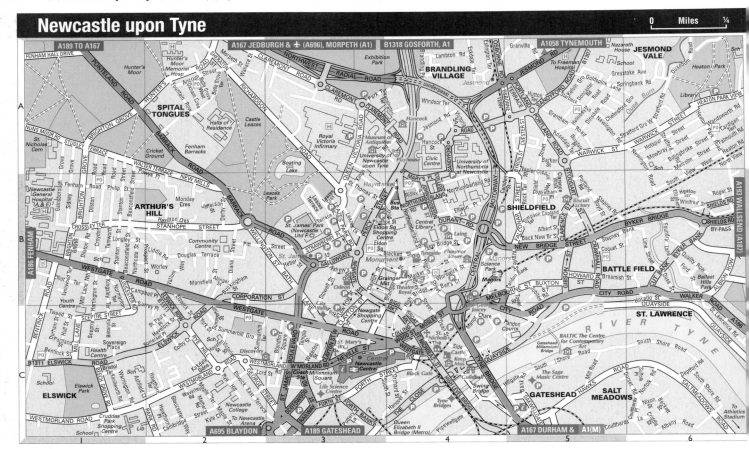

Norwich

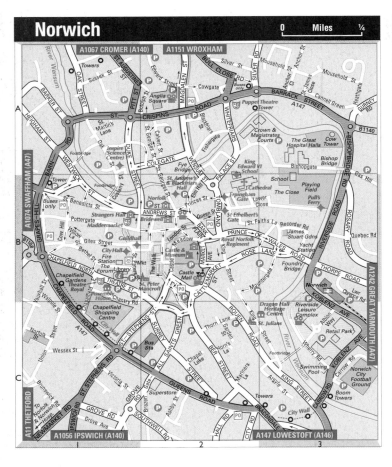

Oxford

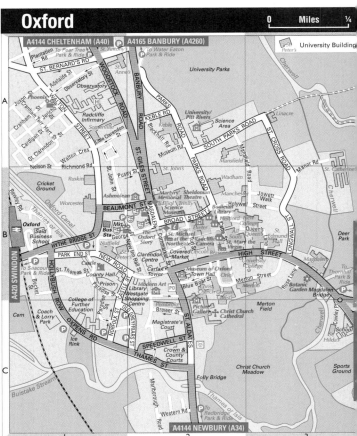

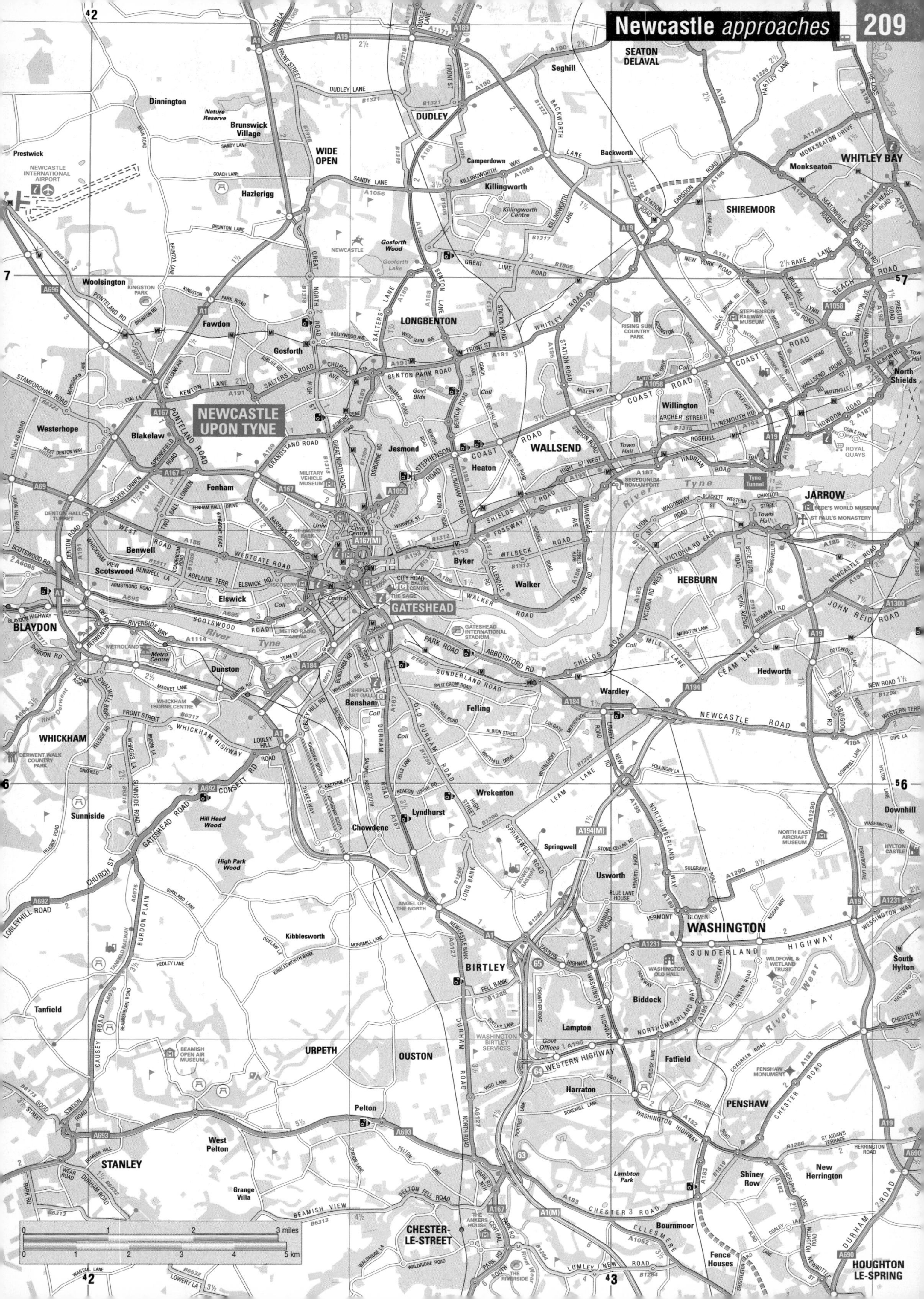
SEATON DELAVAL
Seghill
Dinnington
Nature Reserve
Brunswick Village
DUDLEY
WIDE OPEN
Prestwick
NEWCASTLE INTERNATIONAL AIRPORT
Hazlerigg
Camperdown
Killingworth
Killingworth Centre
Backworth
WHITLEY BAY
Monkseaton
SHIREMOOR
Gosforth Wood
Gosforth Lake
Woolsington
KINGSTON PARK
LONGBENTON
STEPHENSON RAILWAY MUSEUM
RISING SUN COUNTRY PARK
Fawdon
Gosforth
North Shields
Westerhope
Blakelaw
NEWCASTLE UPON TYNE
Jesmond
Govt Blds
Willington
WALLSEND
Town Hall
ROYAL QUAYS
Heaton
MILITARY VEHICLE MUSEUM
Fenham
SEGEDUNUM ROMAN FORT
Tyne Tunnel
JARROW
BEDE'S WORLD MUSEUM
ST PAUL'S MONASTERY
DENTON HALL TURRET
Civic Centre
Benwell
Scotswood
Byker
HEBBURN
Walker
Elswick
DISCOVERY
CITY ROAD
BALTIC CENTRE
THE SAGE
GATESHEAD
BLAYDON
METRO RADIO ARENA
GATESHEAD INTERNATIONAL STADIUM
River Tyne
METROLAND
Metro Centre
Dunston
Hedworth
Wardley
WHICKHAM THORNS CENTRE
SHIPLEY ART GALL
Bensham
Felling
WHICKHAM
DERWENT WALK COUNTRY PARK
LOBLEY HILL
Wrekenton
Sunniside
Hill Head Wood
Lyndhurst
Chowdene
Downhill
Springwell
NORTH EAST AIRCRAFT MUSEUM
HYLTON CASTLE
High Park Wood
Usworth
BLUE LANE HOUSE
BOWES RAILWAY
ANGEL OF THE NORTH
VERMONT
GLOVER
WASHINGTON
Kibblesworth
BIRTLEY
WASHINGTON OLD HALL
WILDFOWL & WETLAND TRUST
South Hylton
Tanfield
TANFIELD RAILWAY
Biddock
River Wear
Lampton
WASHINGTON BIRTLEY SERVICES
Govt Offices
BEAMISH OPEN AIR MUSEUM
URPETH
OUSTON
Fatfield
PENSHAW MONUMENT
Harraton
PENSHAW
Pelton
West Pelton
STANLEY
Lambton Park
Shiney Row
New Herrington
Grange Villa
THE ANKERS HOUSE
CHESTER-LE-STREET
THE RIVERSIDE
Bournmoor
Fence Houses
HOUGHTON LE-SPRING
0 1 2 3 miles
0 1 2 3 4 5 km

210

Nottingham road map page 77 • **Plymouth** road map page 6 • **Portsmouth** road map page 15 • **Preston** road map page 86

Nottingham

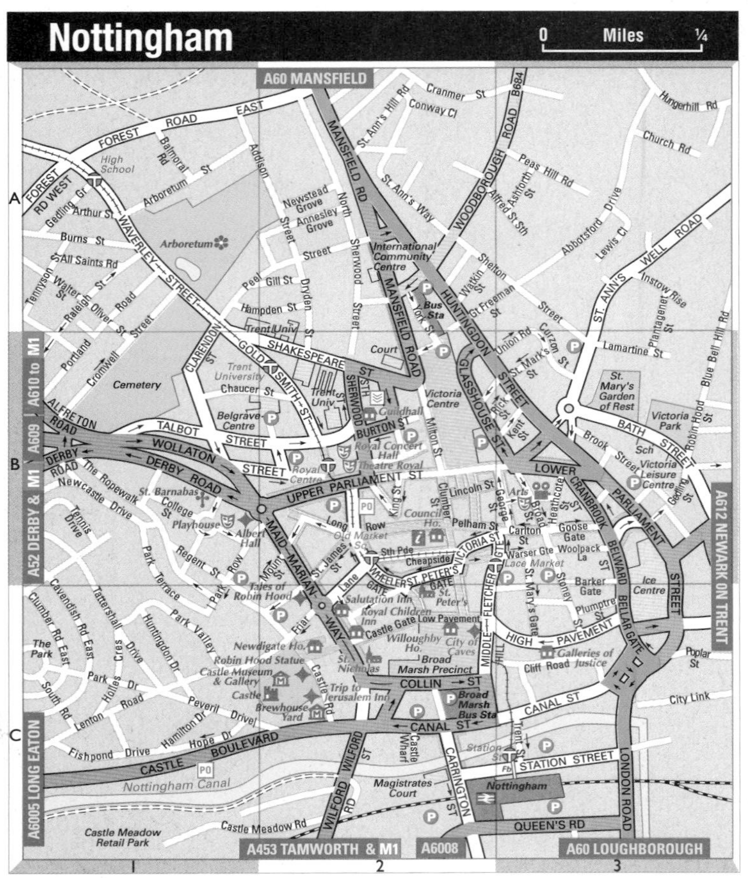

Plymouth

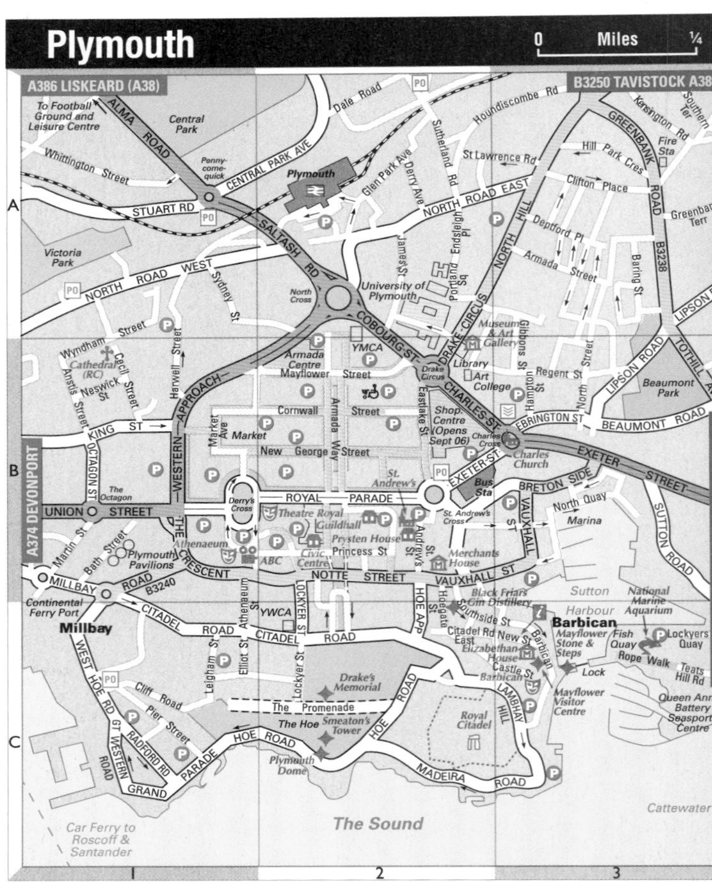

Portsmouth

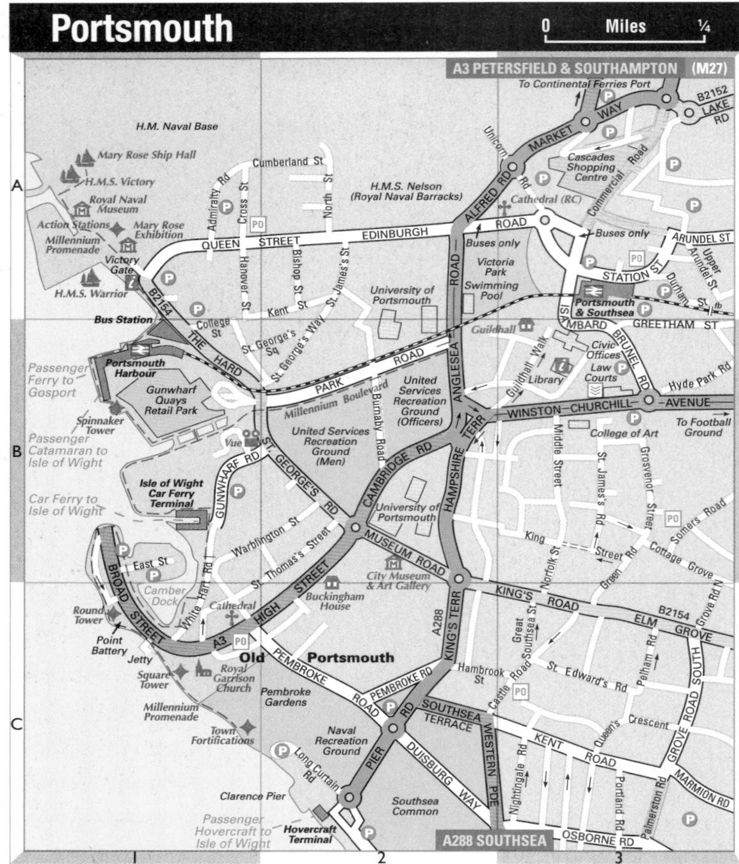

Preston

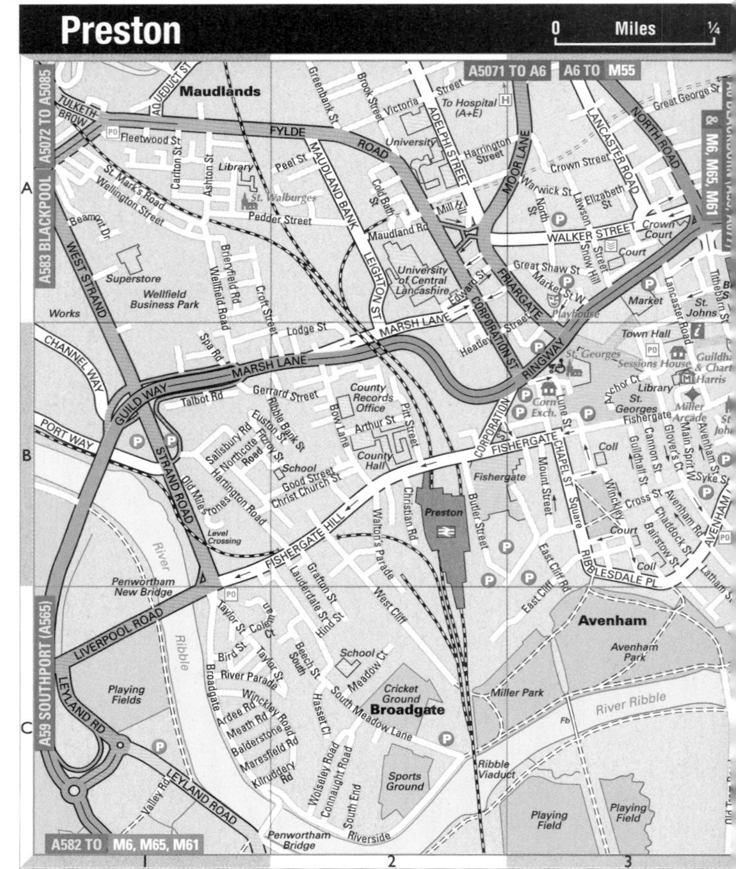

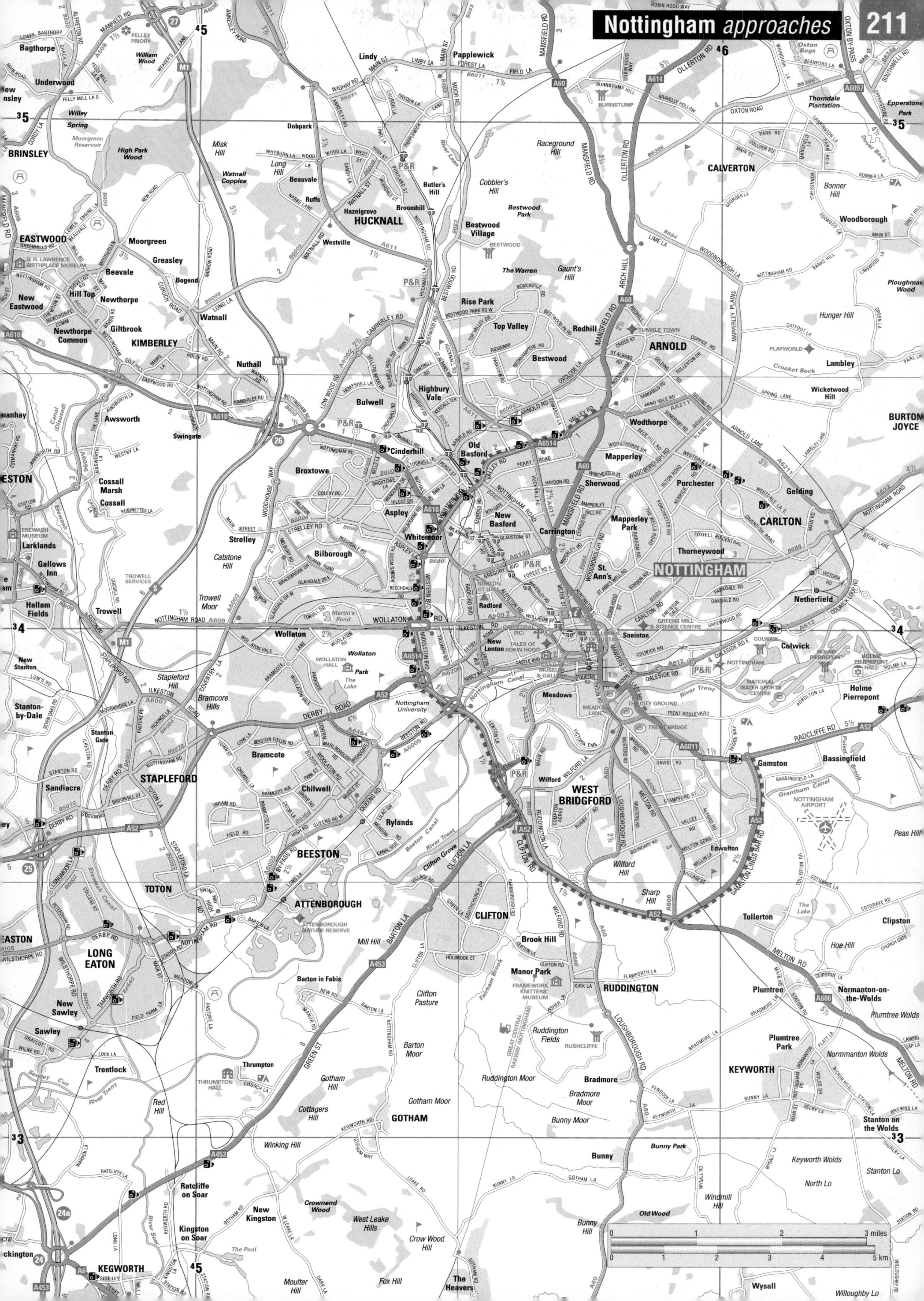
NOTTINGHAM
HUCKNALL
EASTWOOD
KIMBERLEY
ARNOLD
CALVERTON
CARLTON
WEST BRIDGFORD
BEESTON
STAPLEFORD
LONG EATON
ATTENBOROUGH
CLIFTON
RUDDINGTON
GOTHAM
KEYWORTH
KEGWORTH
BRINSLEY
Bulwell
Sherwood
Mapperley
Gedling
Netherfield
Colwick
Wollaton
Bramcote
Chilwell
Toton
Sandiacre
Trowell
Strelley
Aspley
Basford
Radford
Lenton
Sneinton
Wilford
Edwalton
Gamston
Tollerton
Plumtree
Bradmore
Bunny
Thrumpton
Barton in Fabis
Ratcliffe on Soar
Kingston on Soar
Sawley
Trent Lock
Nottingham Airport
Nottingham University
Wollaton Park
River Trent
Grantham Canal
Nottingham Canal
Beeston Canal
0 1 2 3 miles
0 1 2 3 4 5 km

Reading

Reading
0 Miles ¼
A4155 HENLEY ON THAMES, OXFORD (A4074)
A329 OXFORD
A4155 TO A4
A4 NEWBURY M4
A33 BASINGSTOKE (M4)
A327 ALDERSHOT
A4 MAIDENHEAD, A329 WOKINGHAM, M4
Caversham Rd
Vastern Road
Christchurch Playing Fields
Hill's Meadow
View Island
River Thames
Sports Ground
King's Meadow Recreation Ground
Superstore
Napier Road
Reading
Station Hill
Forbury Road
Forbury Retail Park
Kenavon Drive
Forbury Gardens
Abbot's Walk
Abbey Ruins
HM Prison
Riverside
River Kennet
Gas Works Rd
King's Road
Orts Road
Technical College
To Loddon Bridge Park & Ride
The Oracle Shopping Centre
Queen's Road
London Road
Eldon Terrace
Erleigh Road
Inner Distribution Rd
Castle Hill
St. Giles
Crown St
Southampton Street
Silver St
Mount Pleasant
Old Reading University
Royal Berks Hosp (A & E)
Museum of English Rural Life
Playing Field
Berkeley Avenue
Elgar Road
Addington Road
Morgan Road
Allcroft Road
To Madejski Stadium Park & Ride

Salisbury

Salisbury
0 Miles ¼
A360 DEVIZES
A345 AMESBURY
A338 BASINGSTOKE (A30) (M3)
A36 WARMINSTER
A3094 YEOVIL (A30)
A354 BLANDFORD FORUM
A338 RINGWOOD
Devizes Road
Churchill Way West
Churchill Way North
London Rd
Wilton Road
To Police Station
Salisbury
Churchfields Road
Fisherton Street
Mill Road
Crane Bridge Rd
River Nadder
River Avon
Playhouse
City Hall
The Maltings
Library
Guildhall
Poultry Cross
Bus Sta
Blue Boar Row
Milford St
Winchester St
House of John A'Port
Hall of John Halle
New Canal
Queen Elizabeth Gdns
Church House
Mompesson House (N.T.)
The Wardrobe
North Canonry
Medieval Hall & Discover Salisbury
Salisbury & South Wilts.
St. Mary's Cathedral
Chapter House
Bishop's Palace
South Canonry
South Gate
De Vaux Pl
St. Nicholas Hospital
Churchill Way South
Southampton Rd
Winston Churchill Gardens
Harnham Mill
Cricket Grd
Harnham Road
New Harnham Rd
New Bridge Road
To Salisbury General Hospital (A & E)
Sports Ground
Britford Lane
Navigation Channel
College of Further Education
St. Martins
School
Council House
Arts Centre

Sheffield

0 Miles ¼

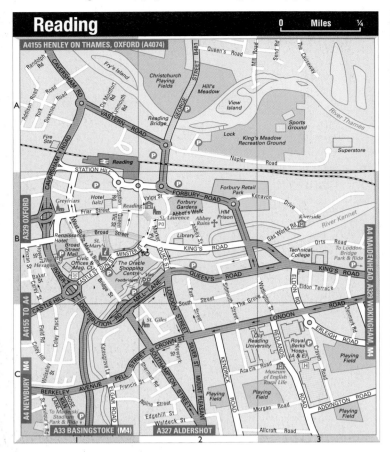

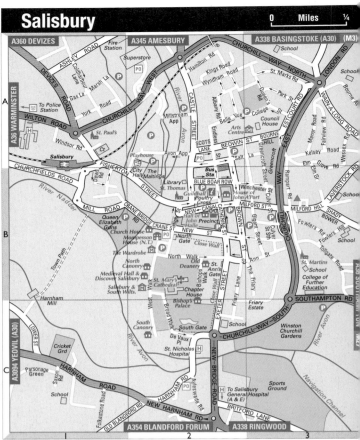

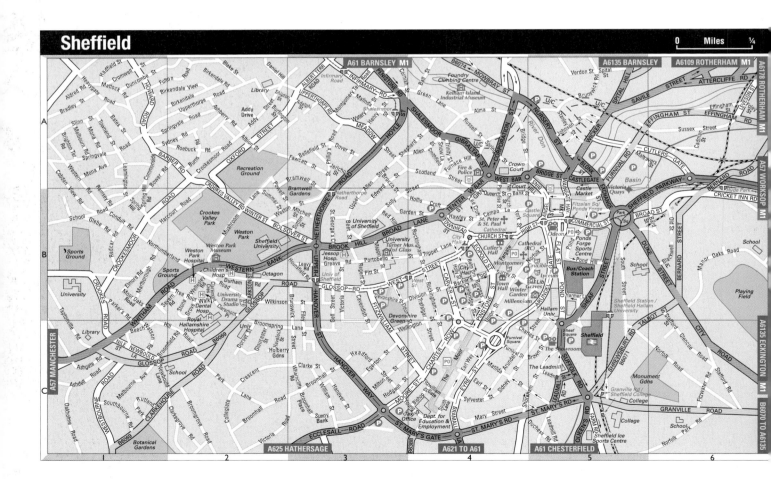

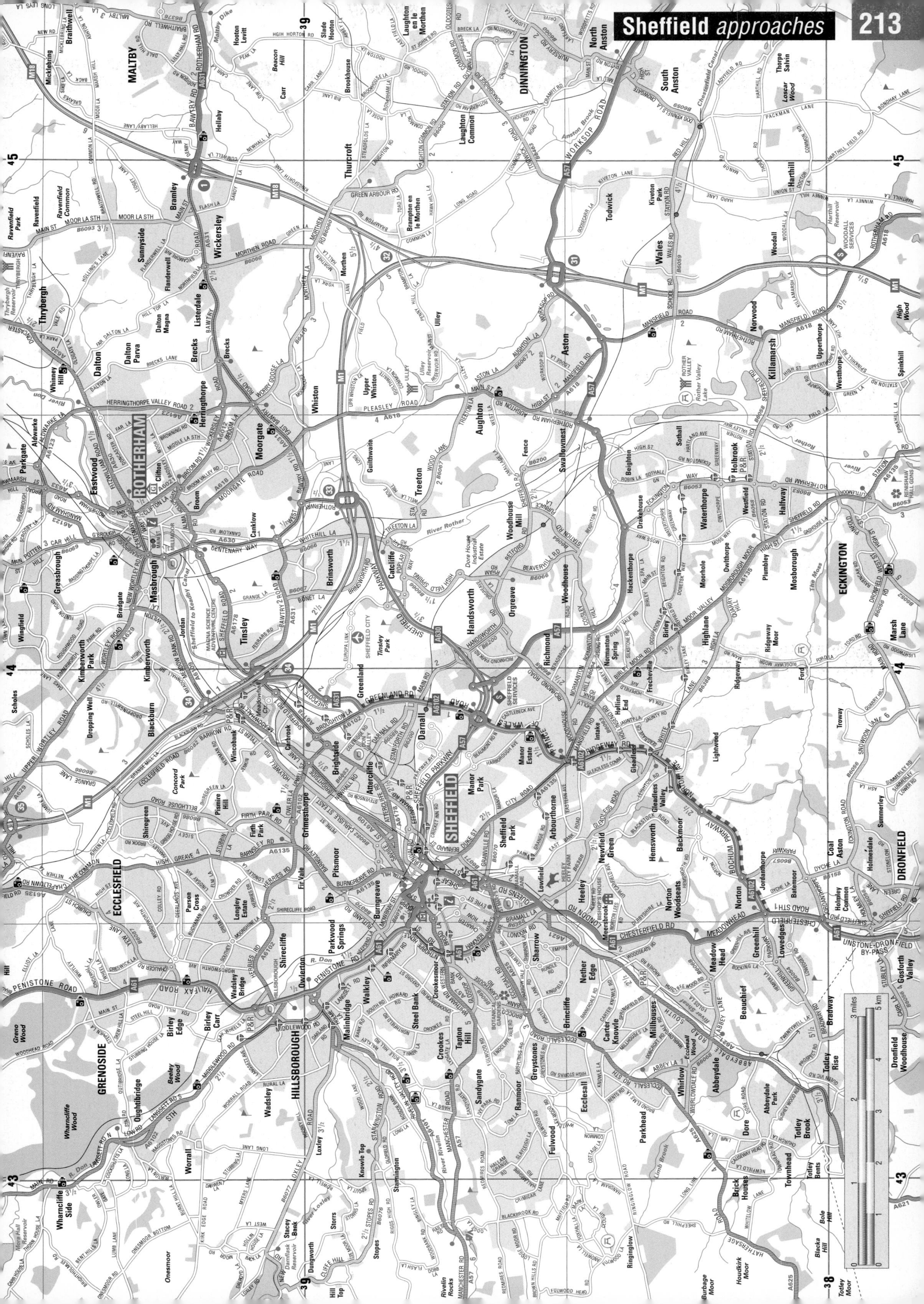

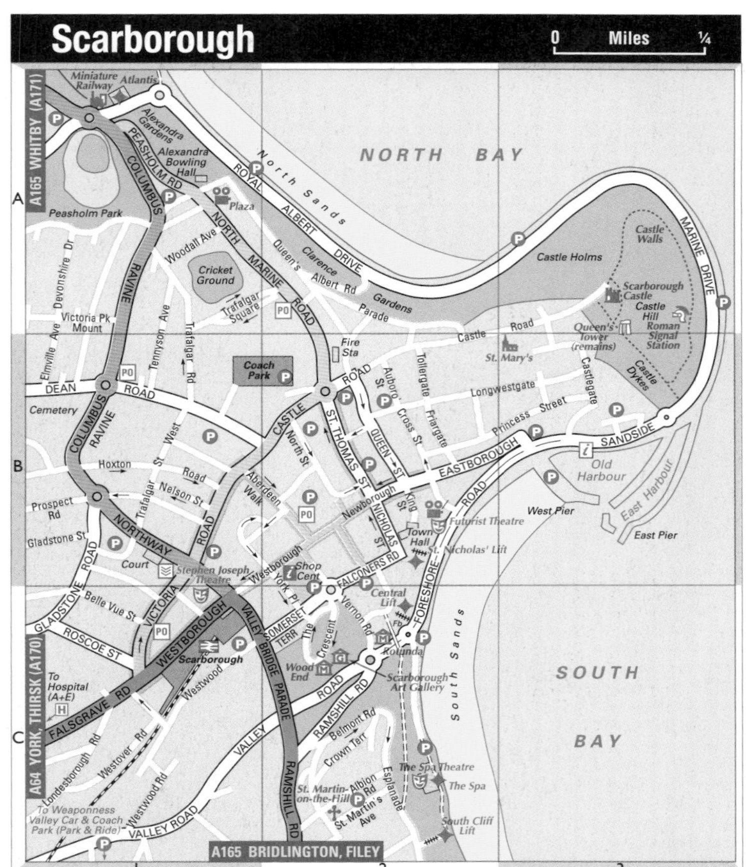

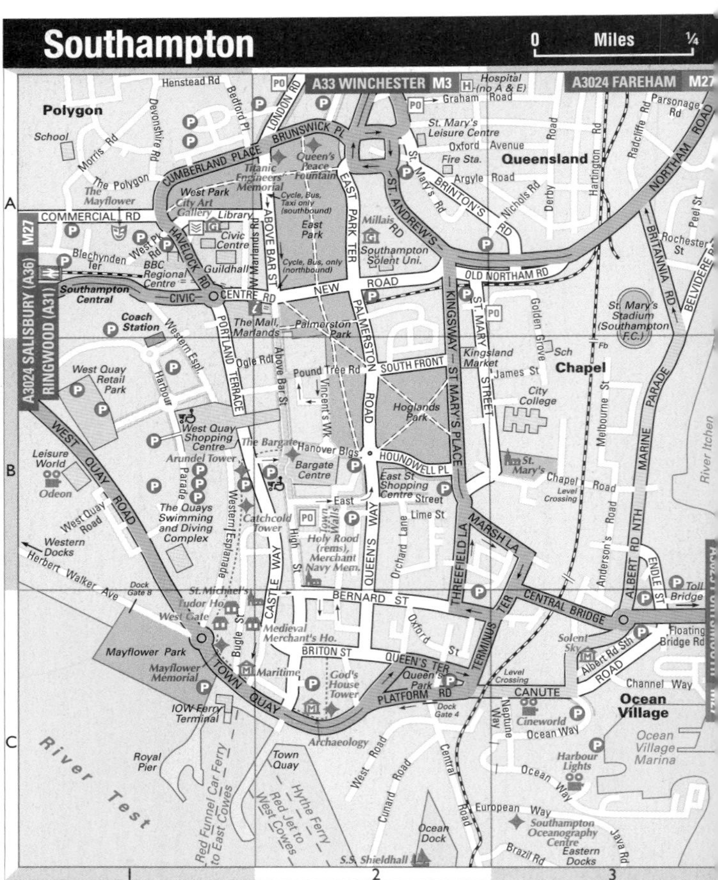

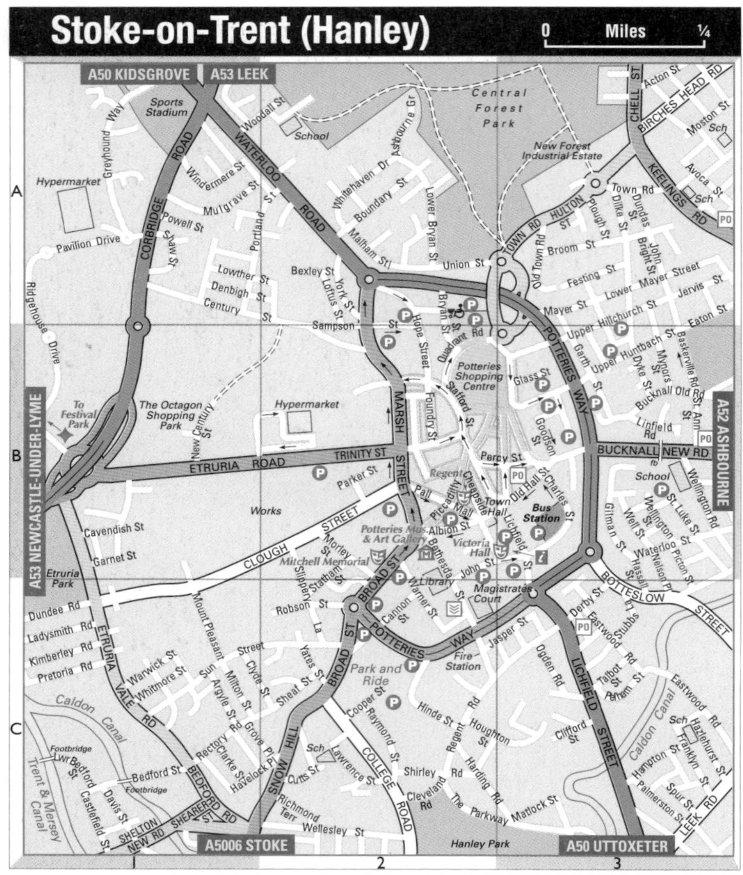

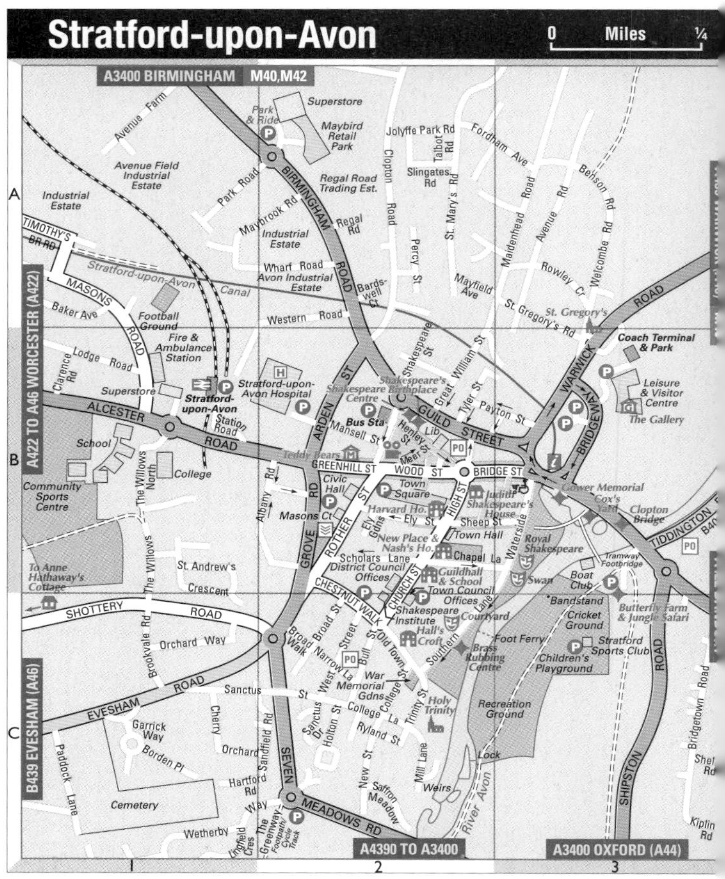

Sunderland road map page 111 • **Swansea** road map page 33 • **Telford** road map page 61 • **Torquay** road map page 7

215

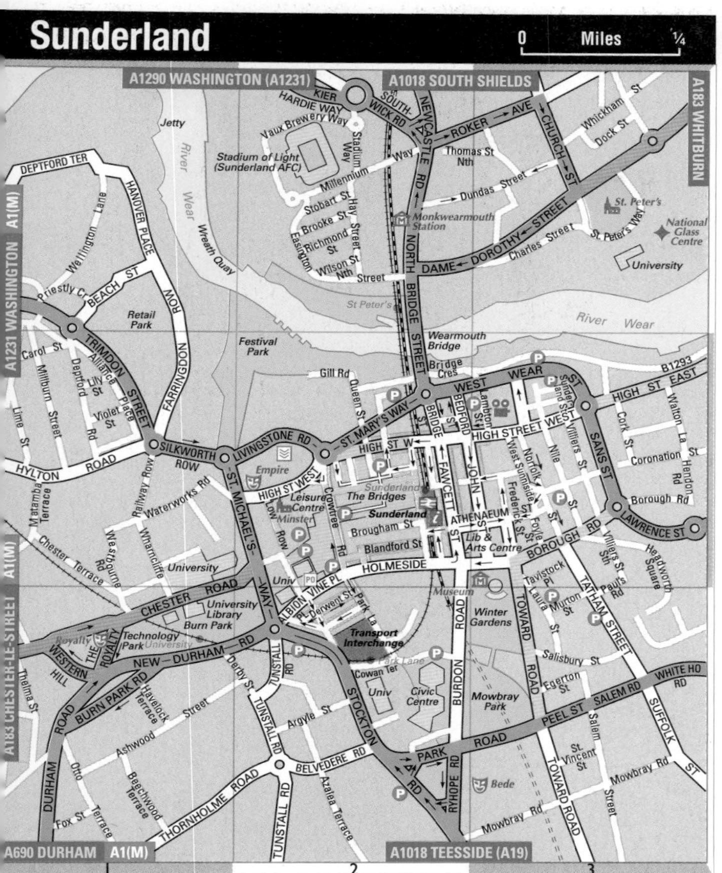

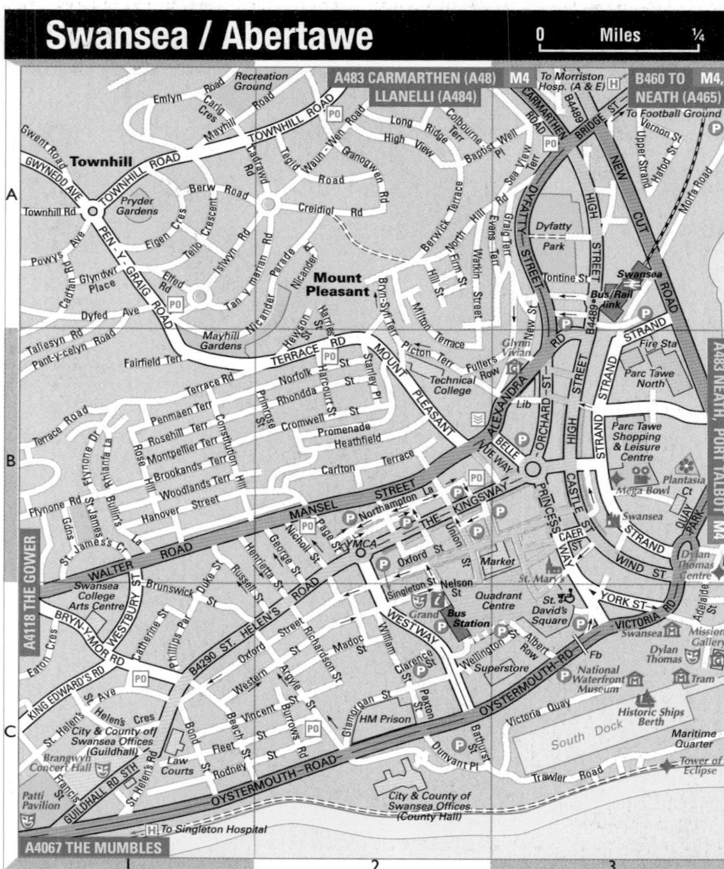

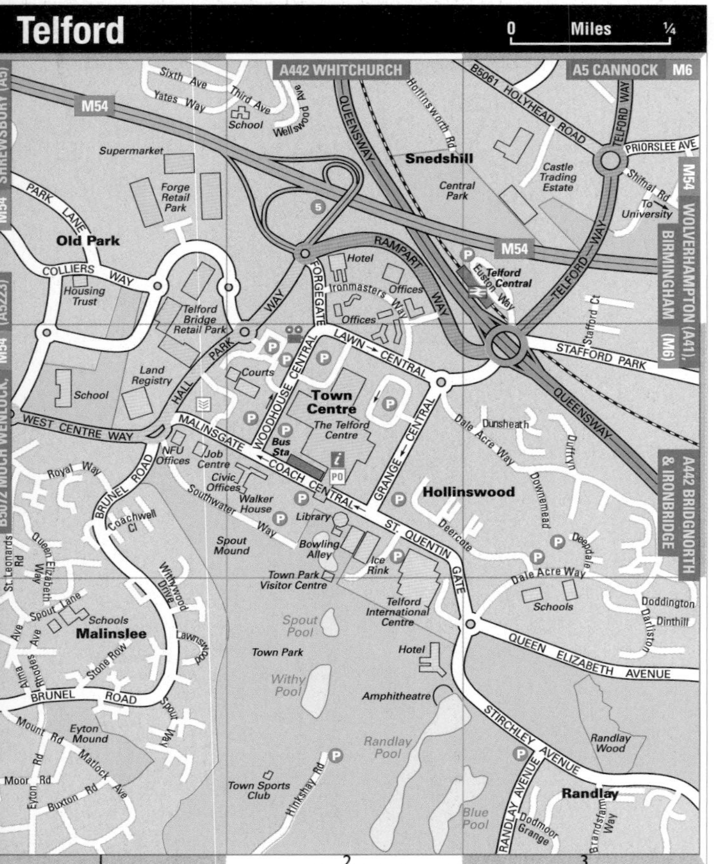

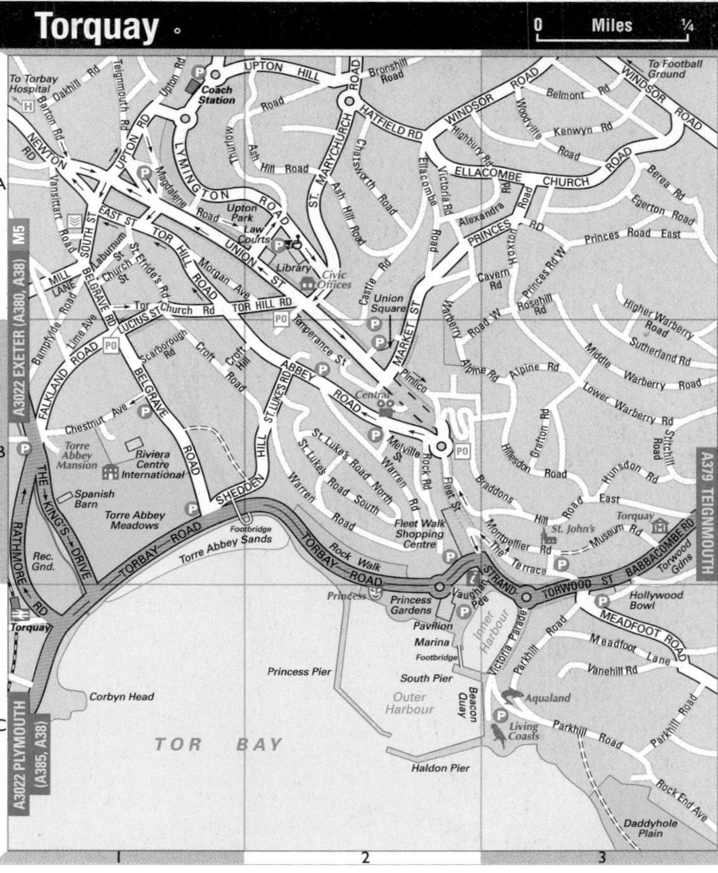

216

Winchester road map page 15 • **Windsor** road map page 27 • **Worcester** road map page 50 • **York** road map page 95

Winchester

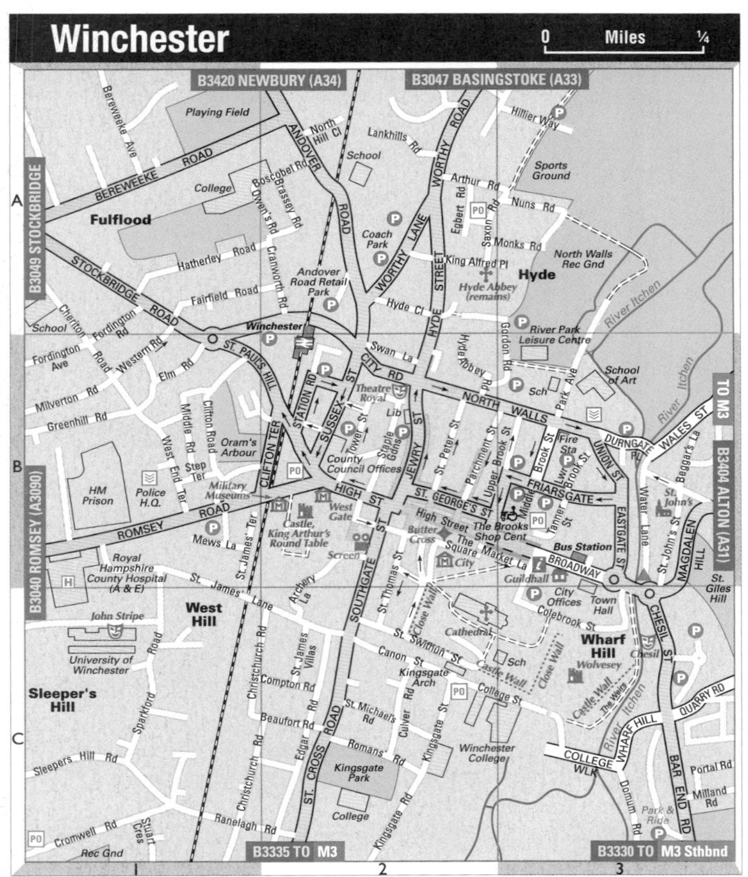

Windsor

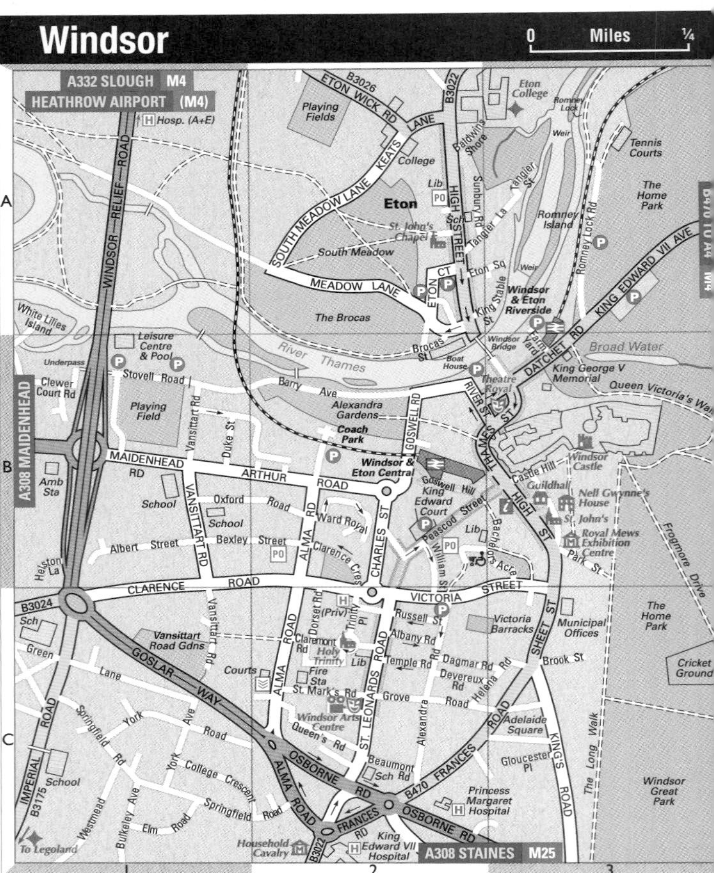

Worcester

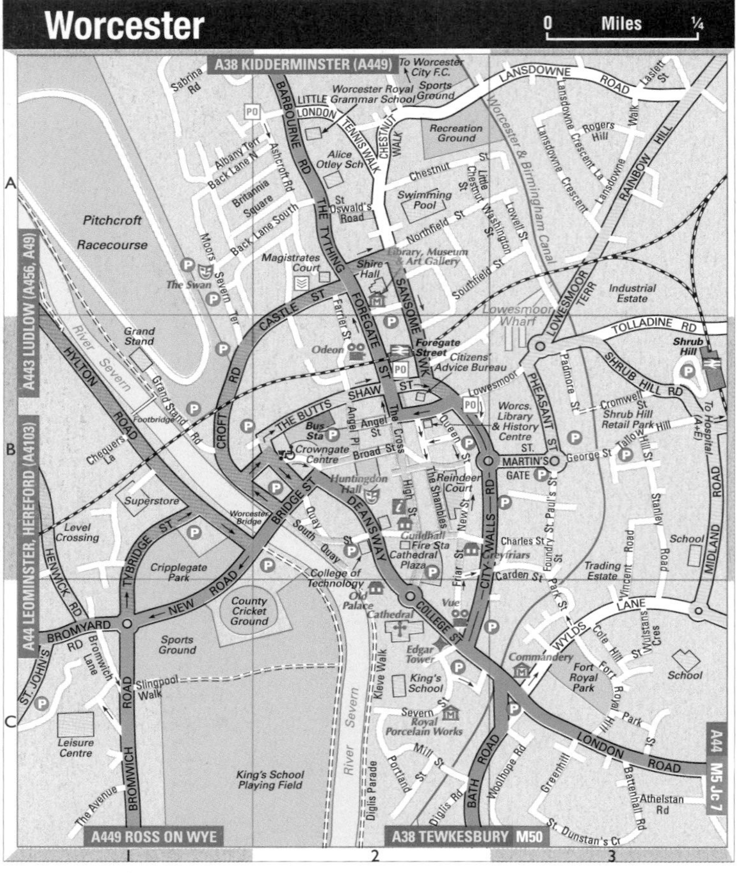

York

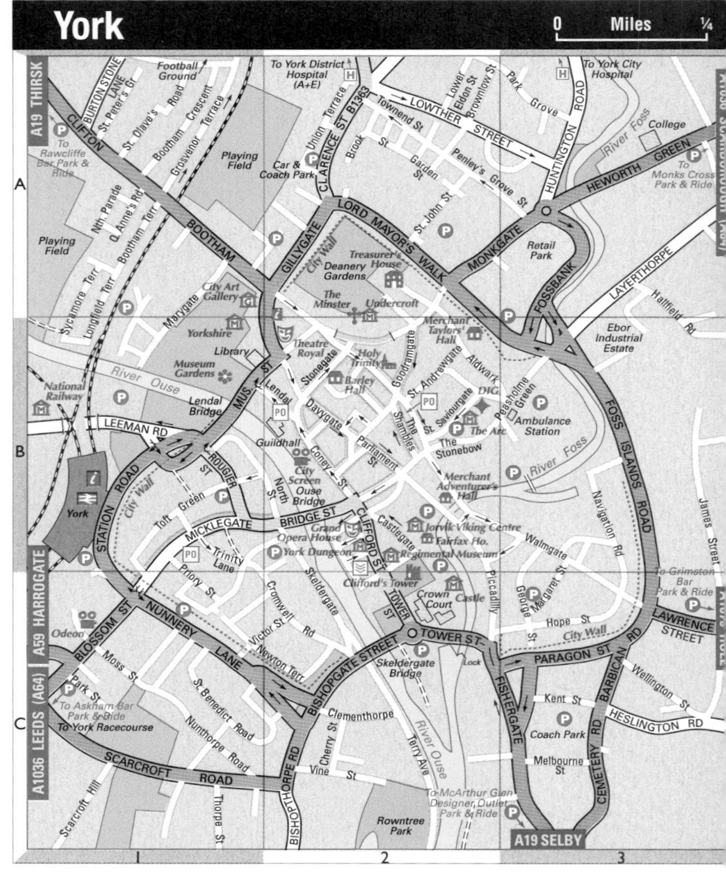

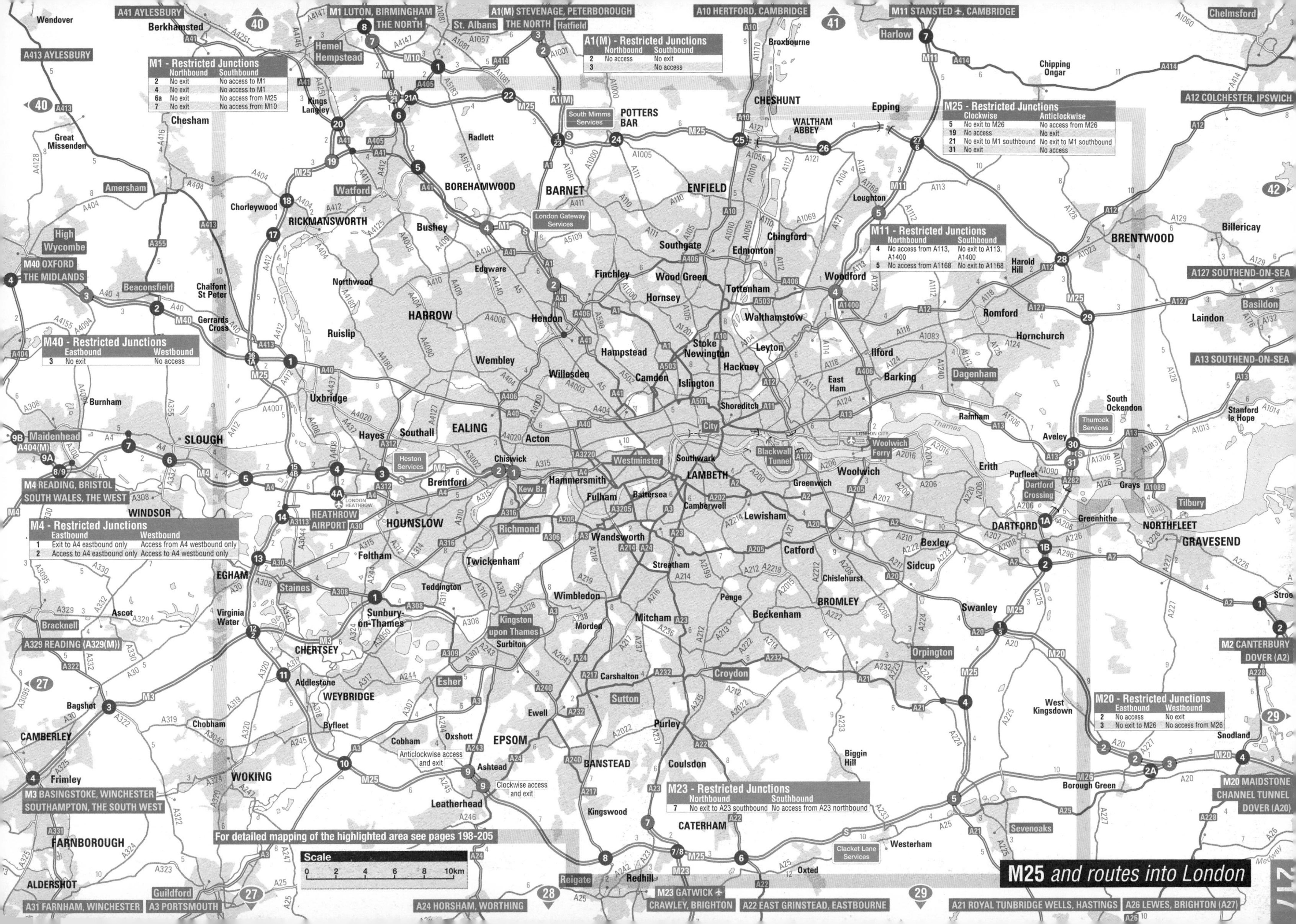

217
M25 and routes into London
M1 - Restricted Junctions
Northbound | Southbound
2 No exit | No access to M1
4 No exit | No access to M1
6a No exit | No access from M25
7 No exit | No access from M10
A1(M) - Restricted Junctions
Northbound | Southbound
2 No access | No exit
3 | No access
M25 - Restricted Junctions
Clockwise | Anticlockwise
5 No exit to M26 | No access from M26
19 No access | No exit
21 No exit to M1 southbound | No exit to M1 southbound
31 No exit | No access
M11 - Restricted Junctions
Northbound | Southbound
4 No access from A113, A1400 | No exit to A113, A1400
5 No access from A1168 | No exit to A1168
M40 - Restricted Junctions
Eastbound | Westbound
3 No exit | No access
M4 - Restricted Junctions
Eastbound | Westbound
1 Exit to A4 eastbound only | Access from A4 westbound only
2 Access to A4 eastbound only | Access to A4 westbound only
M23 - Restricted Junctions
Northbound | Southbound
7 No exit to A23 southbound | No access from A23 northbound
M20 - Restricted Junctions
Eastbound | Westbound
2 No access | No exit
3 No exit to M26 | No access from M26
Scale
0 2 4 6 8 10km
For detailed mapping of the highlighted area see pages 198-205
Clockwise access and exit
Anticlockwise access and exit
A41 AYLESBURY
M1 LUTON, BIRMINGHAM THE NORTH
A1(M) STEVENAGE, PETERBOROUGH THE NORTH
A10 HERTFORD, CAMBRIDGE
M11 STANSTED, CAMBRIDGE
A12 COLCHESTER, IPSWICH
A127 SOUTHEND-ON-SEA
A13 SOUTHEND-ON-SEA
M2 CANTERBURY DOVER (A2)
M20 MAIDSTONE CHANNEL TUNNEL DOVER (A20)
A26 LEWES, BRIGHTON (A27)
A21 ROYAL TUNBRIDGE WELLS, HASTINGS
A22 EAST GRINSTEAD, EASTBOURNE
M23 GATWICK CRAWLEY, BRIGHTON
A24 HORSHAM, WORTHING
A3 PORTSMOUTH
A31 FARNHAM, WINCHESTER
M3 BASINGSTOKE, WINCHESTER SOUTHAMPTON, THE SOUTH WEST
A329 READING (A329(M))
M4 READING, BRISTOL, SOUTH WALES, THE WEST
M40 OXFORD THE MIDLANDS
A413 AYLESBURY
South Mimms Services
London Gateway Services
Heston Services
Thurrock Services
Clacket Lane Services
HEATHROW AIRPORT
Dartford Crossing
Blackwall Tunnel
Woolwich Ferry
WATFORD
BOREHAMWOOD
BARNET
ENFIELD
CHESHUNT
WALTHAM ABBEY
BRENTWOOD
HARROW
EALING
HOUNSLOW
SLOUGH
WINDSOR
LAMBETH
BROMLEY
DARTFORD
GRAVESEND
NORTHFLEET
EPSOM
BANSTEAD
CATERHAM
WOKING
WEYBRIDGE
CHERTSEY
EGHAM
RICKMANSWORTH
CAMBERLEY
FARNBOROUGH
ALDERSHOT

M60 and routes into Manchester and Liverpool

Restricted Junctions

M6	Northbound	Southbound
20	No exit to M56 eastbound	No access from M56 westbound
24	No exit	No access
25	No access from A49	No exit

M53	Northbound	Southbound
11	No exit to M56 westbound	No exit to M56 westbound

M56	Eastbound	Westbound
2	No exit	No access
4	No exit	No access
7		No access
8	No exit or access	No exit
9	No access from M6 northbound	No access to M6 southbound
15	No exit to M53	No access from M53 northbound

M57	Northbound	Southbound
3	No exit	No access
5	No exit	No access

M58	Eastbound	Westbound
1	No exit	No access

M60	Clockwise	Anticlockwise
2	No exit	No access
3	No exit to A34 northbound	No exit to A34 northbound
4	No access to M56	No exit to M56
5	No exit to A5103 southbound	No exit to A5103 northbound
14	No exit to A580	No access from A580
16	No exit	No access
20	No access	No exit
22		No access
25	No access	
26		No exit or access
27	No exit	No access

M61	Northbound	Southbound
2	No access from A580 eastbound	No exit to A580 westbound
3	No access from A580 eastbound No access from A666 southbound	No exit to A580 westbound

M66	Northbound	Southbound
1	No access	No exit

M67	Eastbound	Westbound
1a	No access	No exit
2	No exit	No access

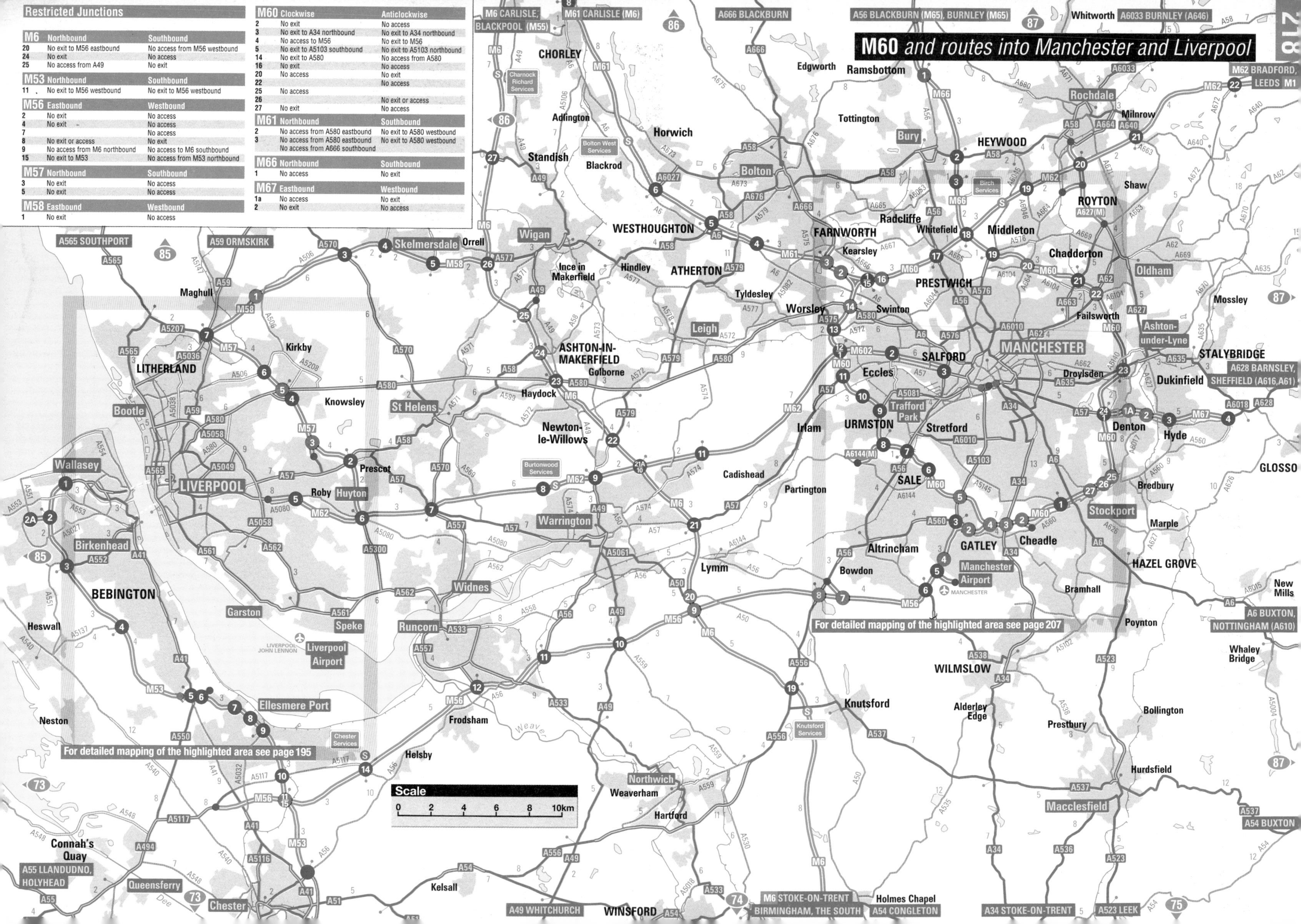

Heathrow Airport (London)

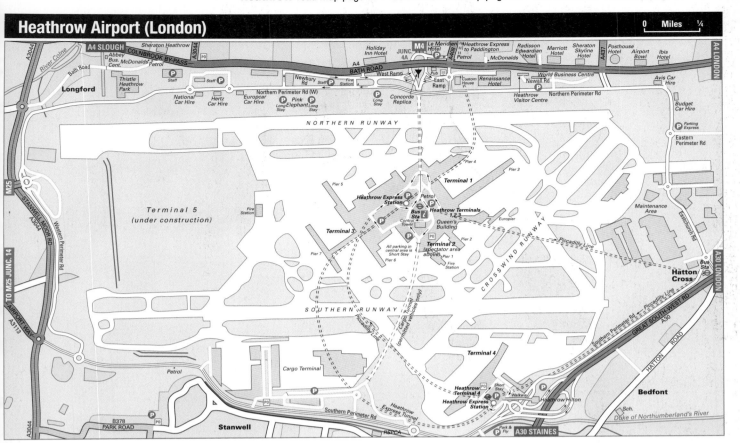

0   Miles   ¼

Gatwick Airport (London)

0   Miles   ¼

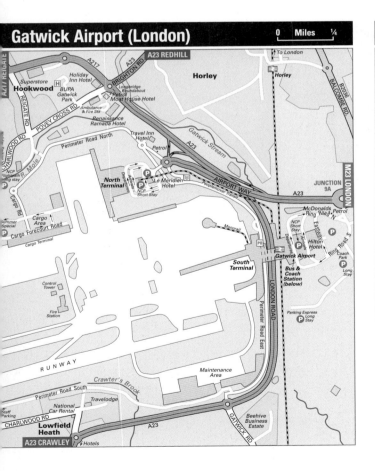

Manchester Airport

0   Miles   ¼

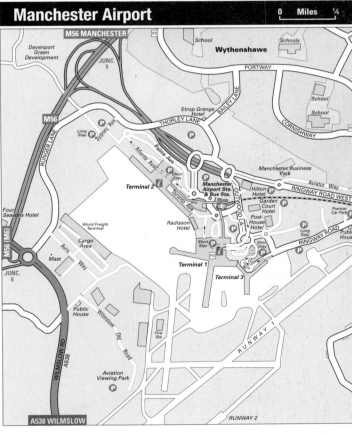

220

Dover road map page 31 • **Felixstowe** road map page 57 • **Portsmouth** road map page 15 • **Southampton** road map page 14

Port of Dover

0 Miles ¼

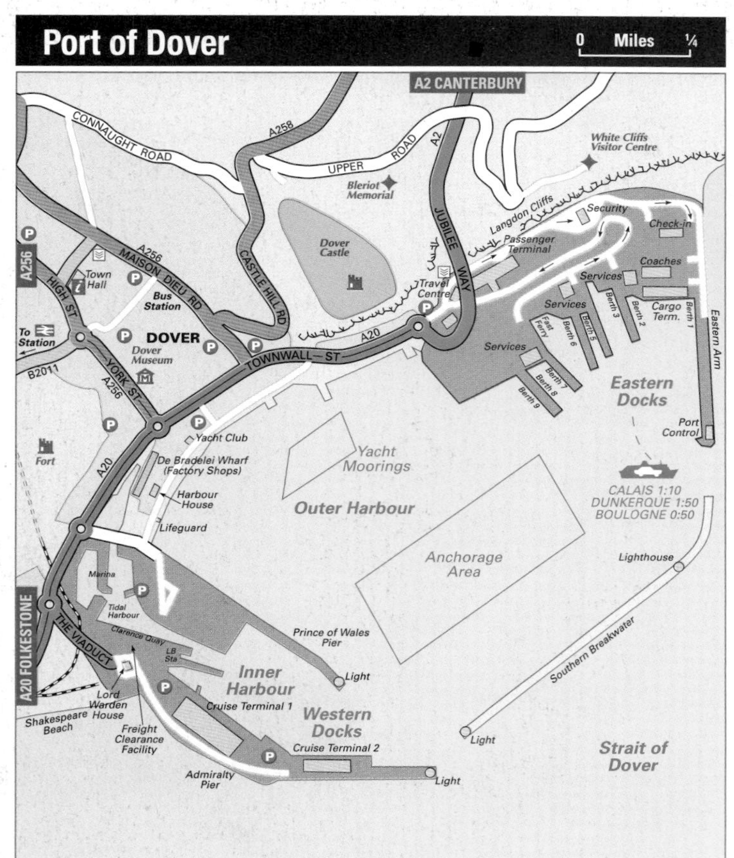

Port of Felixstowe

0 Miles ¼

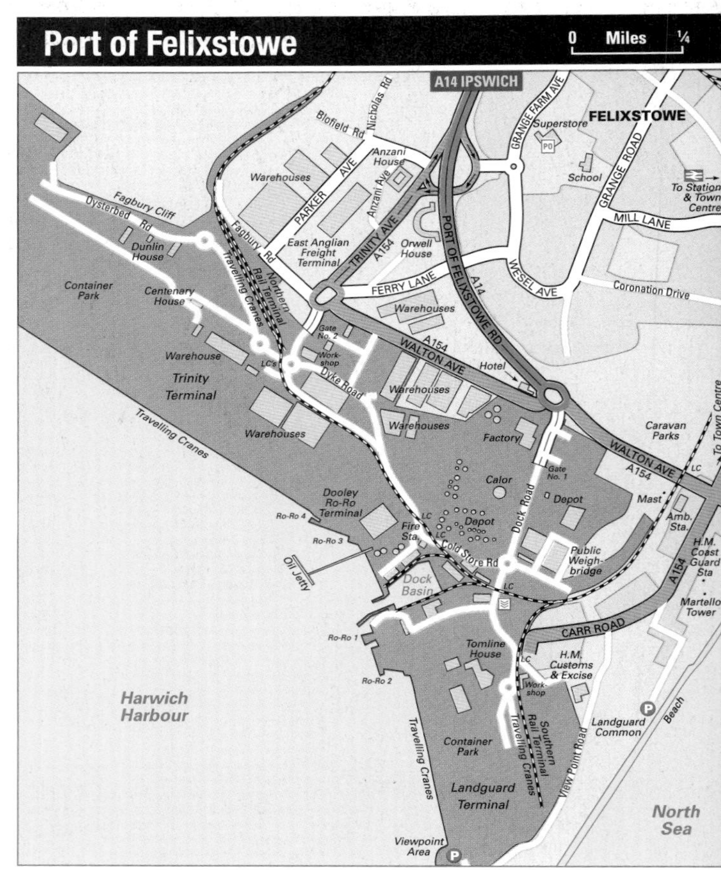

Portsmouth-Continental Ferry Port

0 Miles ¼

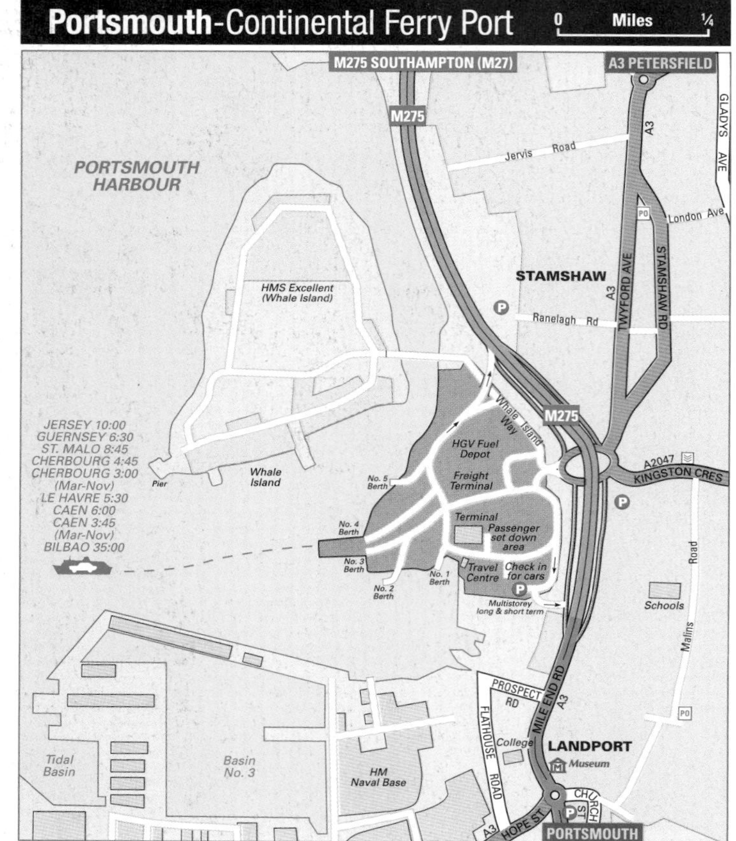

Port of Southampton

0 Miles 1

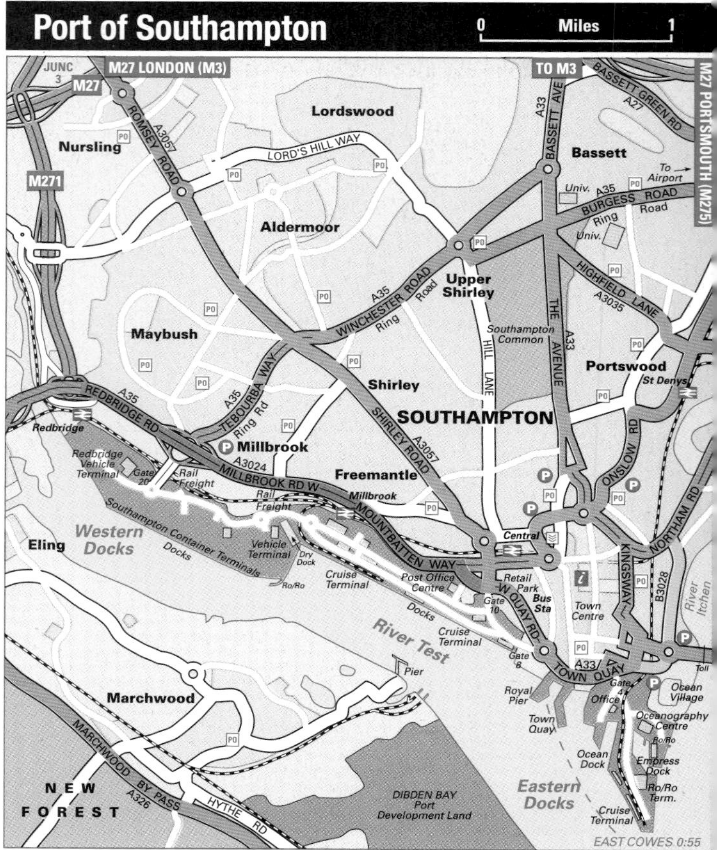

Boulogne

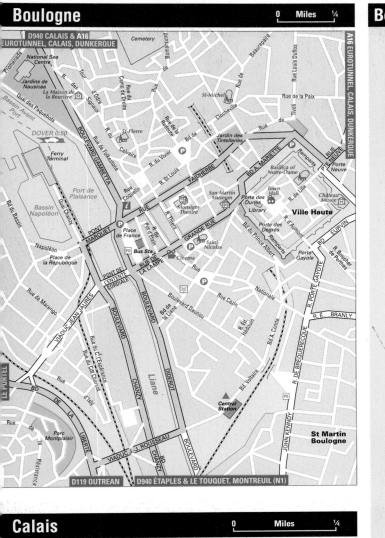

Calais

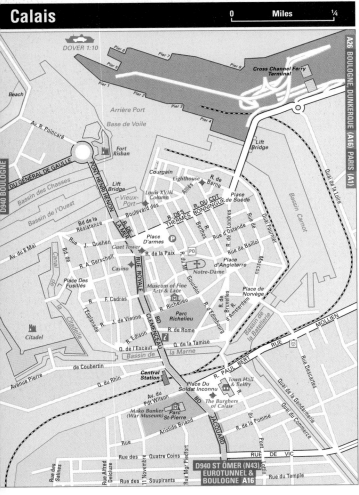

Boulogne and Calais *approaches*

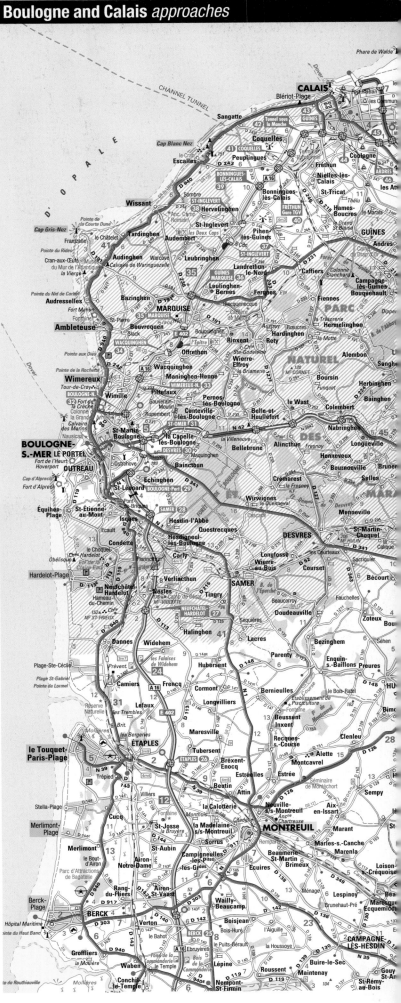

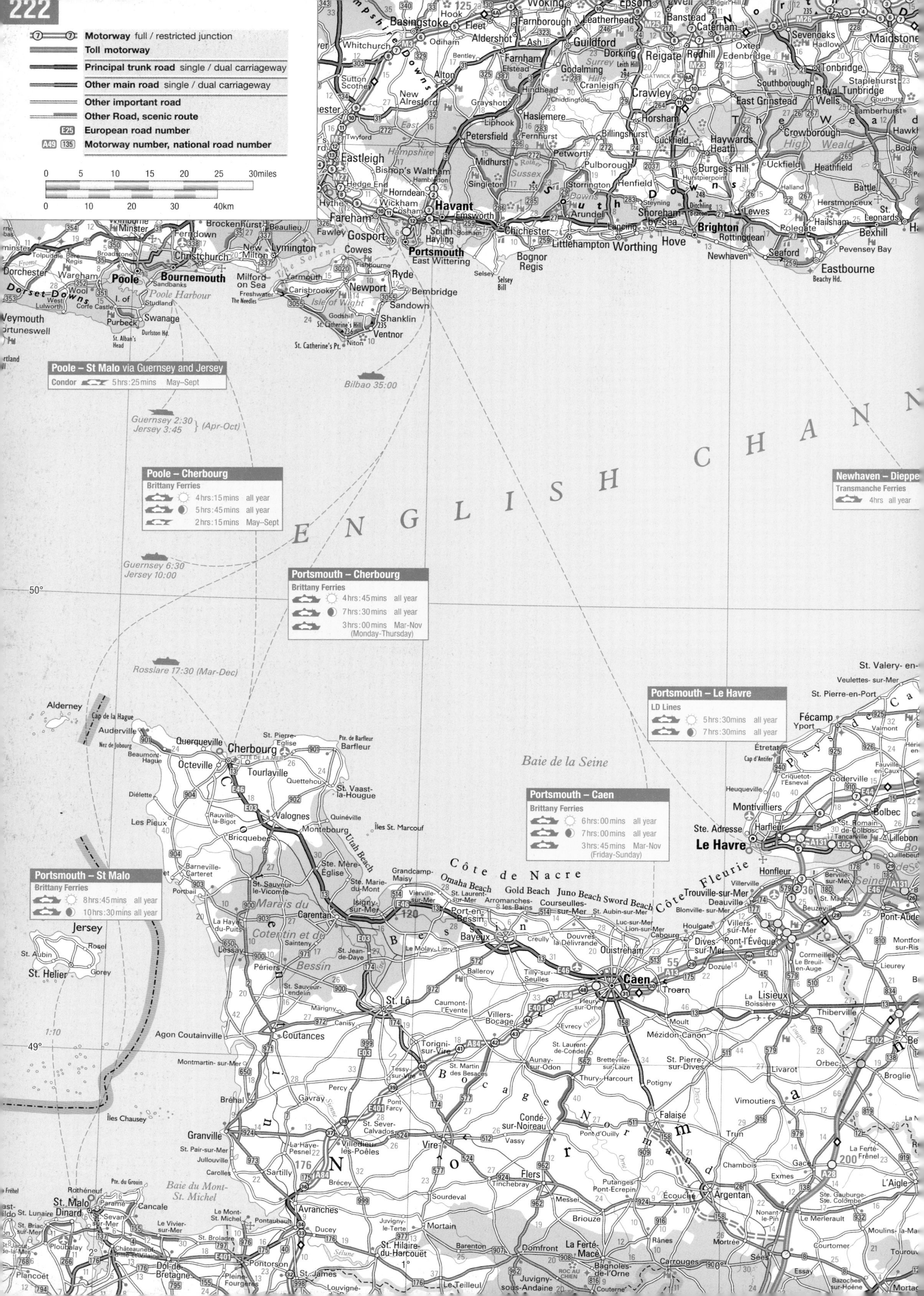
Motorway full / restricted junction
Toll motorway
Principal trunk road single / dual carriageway
Other main road single / dual carriageway
Other important road
Other Road, scenic route
E25 European road number
A49 135 Motorway number, national road number
0 5 10 15 20 25 30miles
0 10 20 30 40km
Poole – St Malo via Guernsey and Jersey
Condor 5hrs:25mins May–Sept
Bilbao 35:00
Guernsey 2:30
Jersey 3:45
(Apr-Oct)
Poole – Cherbourg
Brittany Ferries
4hrs:15mins all year
5hrs:45mins all year
2hrs:15mins May–Sept
Guernsey 6:30
Jersey 10:00
Portsmouth – Cherbourg
Brittany Ferries
4hrs:45mins all year
7hrs:30mins all year
3hrs:00mins Mar-Nov (Monday-Thursday)
Rosslare 17:30 (Mar-Dec)
Newhaven – Dieppe
Transmanche Ferries
4hrs all year
Portsmouth – Le Havre
LD Lines
5hrs:30mins all year
7hrs:30mins all year
Portsmouth – Caen
Brittany Ferries
6hrs:00mins all year
7hrs:00mins all year
3hrs:45mins Mar-Nov (Friday-Sunday)
Portsmouth – St Malo
Brittany Ferries
8hrs:45mins all year
10hrs:30mins all year
ENGLISH CHANN
Baie de la Seine
Côte de Nacre
Côte Fleurie
Baie du Mont-St. Michel
50°
49°
Basingstoke
Guildford
Reigate
Sevenoaks
Maidstone
Farnham
Crawley
Horsham
East Grinstead
Royal Tunbridge Wells
Petersfield
Haywards Heath
Eastleigh
Havant
Portsmouth
Chichester
Worthing
Brighton
Lewes
Eastbourne
Newhaven
Hastings
Bournemouth
Poole
Christchurch
Lymington
Dorchester
Weymouth
Swanage
Newport
Ryde
Cowes
Sandown
Shanklin
Ventnor
Isle of Wight
Alderney
Jersey
St. Helier
Cherbourg
Valognes
Carentan
St. Lô
Coutances
Granville
Avranches
Bayeux
Caen
Le Havre
Honfleur
Deauville
Lisieux
Falaise
Argentan
Vire
Flers
St. Malo
Dinard
Fécamp
Omaha Beach
Gold Beach
Juno Beach
Sword Beach
Utah Beach

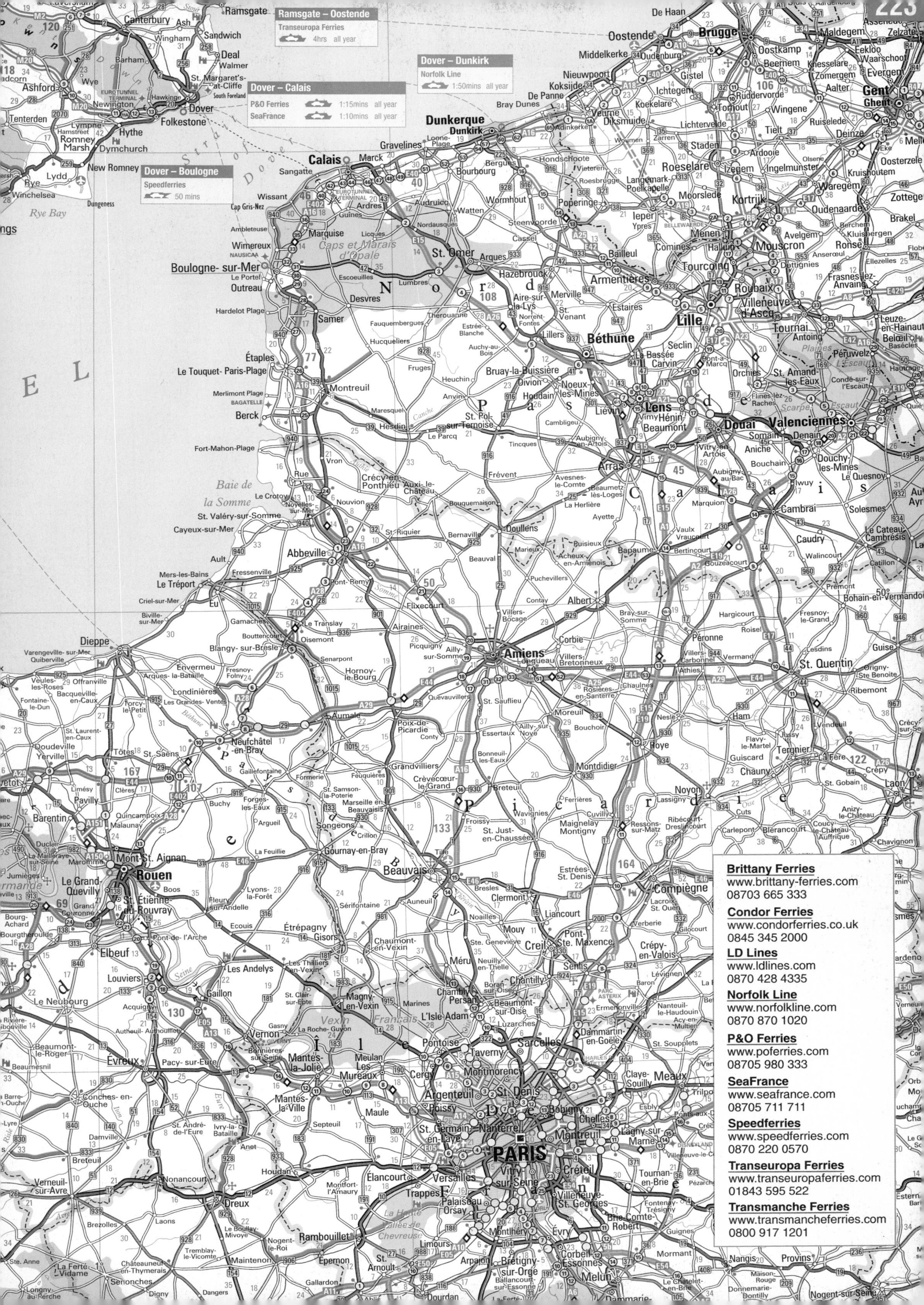

Ramsgate – Oostende
Transeuropa Ferries
4hrs all year

Dover – Dunkirk
Norfolk Line
1:50mins all year

Dover – Calais
P&O Ferries 1:15mins all year
SeaFrance 1:10mins all year

Dover – Boulogne
Speedferries
50 mins

Counties and unitary authorities

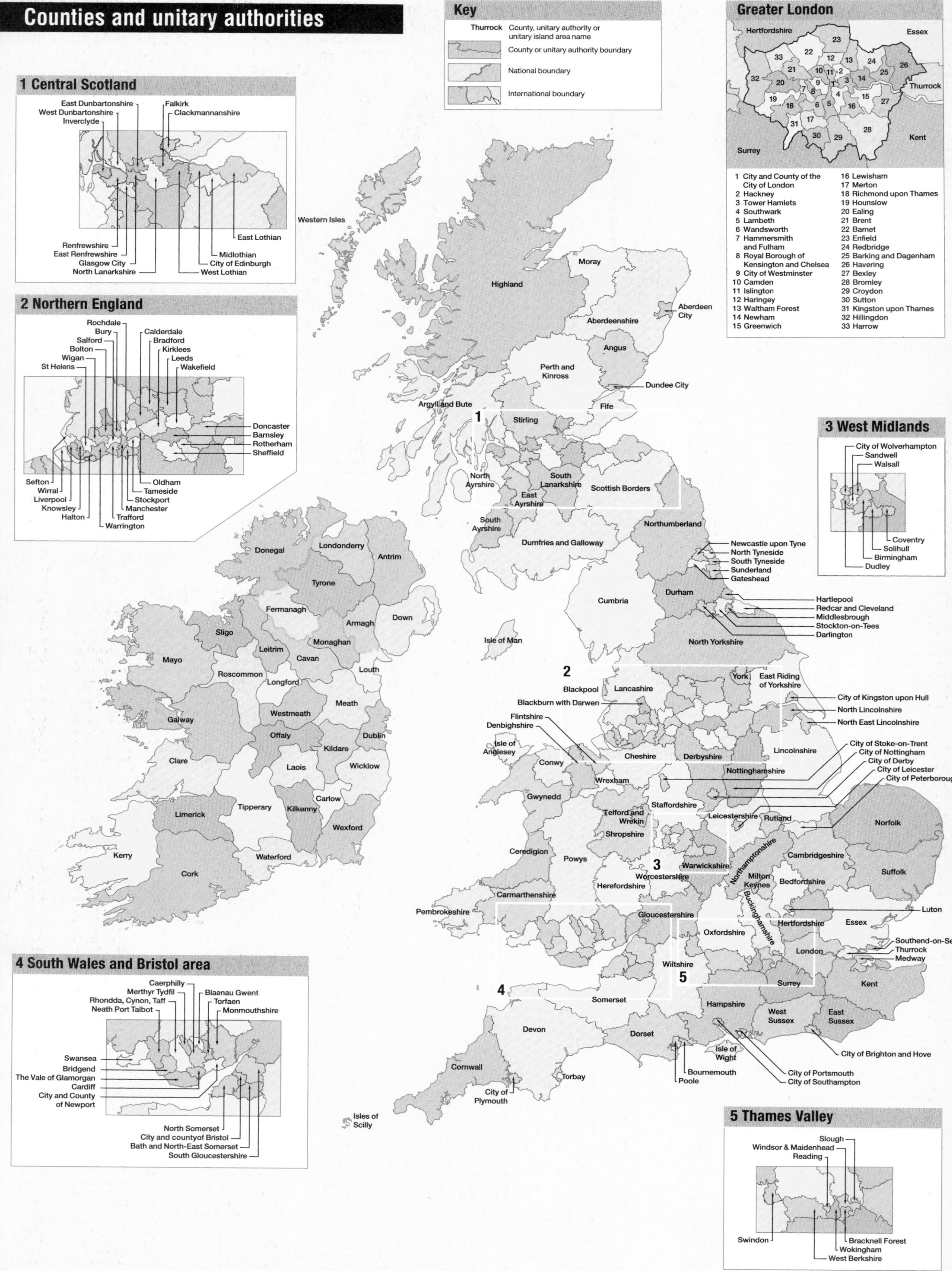

1 Central Scotland

East Dunbartonshire
West Dunbartonshire
Inverclyde
Falkirk
Clackmannanshire

Renfrewshire
East Renfrewshire
Glasgow City
North Lanarkshire
Midlothian
City of Edinburgh
West Lothian
East Lothian

2 Northern England

Rochdale
Bury
Salford
Bolton
Wigan
St Helens
Calderdale
Bradford
Kirklees
Leeds
Wakefield

Doncaster
Barnsley
Rotherham
Sheffield

Sefton
Wirral
Liverpool
Knowsley
Halton
Oldham
Tameside
Stockport
Manchester
Trafford
Warrington

4 South Wales and Bristol area

Caerphilly
Merthyr Tydfil
Rhondda, Cynon, Taff
Neath Port Talbot
Blaenau Gwent
Torfaen
Monmouthshire

Swansea
Bridgend
The Vale of Glamorgan
Cardiff
City and County
of Newport

North Somerset
City and county of Bristol
Bath and North-East Somerset
South Gloucestershire

Greater London

Hertfordshire
Essex
Thurrock
Surrey
Kent

1 City and County of the City of London
2 Hackney
3 Tower Hamlets
4 Southwark
5 Lambeth
6 Wandsworth
7 Hammersmith and Fulham
8 Royal Borough of Kensington and Chelsea
9 City of Westminster
10 Camden
11 Islington
12 Haringey
13 Waltham Forest
14 Newham
15 Greenwich
16 Lewisham
17 Merton
18 Richmond upon Thames
19 Hounslow
20 Ealing
21 Brent
22 Barnet
23 Enfield
24 Redbridge
25 Barking and Dagenham
26 Havering
27 Bexley
28 Bromley
29 Croydon
30 Sutton
31 Kingston upon Thames
32 Hillingdon
33 Harrow

3 West Midlands

City of Wolverhampton
Sandwell
Walsall
Coventry
Solihull
Birmingham
Dudley

5 Thames Valley

Slough
Windsor & Maidenhead
Reading
Swindon
Bracknell Forest
Wokingham
West Berkshire

Western Isles

Highland

Moray

Aberdeenshire

Aberdeen City

Angus

Perth and Kinross

Dundee City

Argyll and Bute

Fife

Stirling

North Ayrshire

South Lanarkshire

East Ayrshire

Scottish Borders

South Ayrshire

Dumfries and Galloway

Northumberland

Newcastle upon Tyne
North Tyneside
South Tyneside
Sunderland
Gateshead

Cumbria

Durham

Hartlepool
Redcar and Cleveland
Middlesbrough
Stockton-on-Tees
Darlington

Isle of Man

North Yorkshire

York

East Riding of Yorkshire

Blackpool
Lancashire

Blackburn with Darwen

City of Kingston upon Hull
North Lincolnshire
North East Lincolnshire

Flintshire
Denbighshire

Isle of Anglesey

Conwy

Cheshire

Derbyshire

Lincolnshire

Gwynedd

Wrexham

Nottinghamshire

City of Stoke-on-Trent
City of Nottingham
City of Derby
City of Leicester
City of Peterborough

Staffordshire

Telford and Wrekin

Shropshire

Leicestershire
Rutland

Norfolk

Ceredigion

Powys

Warwickshire

Worcestershire

Herefordshire

Northamptonshire

Milton Keynes

Cambridgeshire

Bedfordshire

Suffolk

Carmarthenshire

Pembrokeshire

Buckinghamshire

Gloucestershire

Oxfordshire

Hertfordshire

Essex

Luton

London

Southend-on-Sea
Thurrock
Medway

Wiltshire

Surrey

Kent

Somerset

Hampshire

West Sussex

East Sussex

Devon

Dorset

Isle of Wight

City of Brighton and Hove

Cornwall

Torbay

City of Plymouth

Bournemouth
Poole

City of Portsmouth
City of Southampton

Isles of Scilly

Donegal

Londonderry

Antrim

Tyrone

Fermanagh

Armagh

Down

Sligo

Monaghan

Mayo

Leitrim

Cavan

Roscommon

Longford

Louth

Meath

Galway

Westmeath

Offaly

Dublin

Kildare

Wicklow

Clare

Laois

Carlow

Limerick

Tipperary

Kilkenny

Wexford

Kerry

Waterford

Cork

How to use the index

Example

Adlestrop Glos **38** B2

- grid square
- page number
- county or unitary authority

Places of special interest are highlighted in magenta

Abbreviations used in the index

Aberdeen	Aberdeen City
Aberds	Aberdeenshire
Ald	Alderney
Anglesey	Isle of Anglesey
Angus	Angus
Argyll	Argyll and Bute
Bath	Bath and North East Somerset
Beds	Bedfordshire
Bl Gwent	Blaenau Gwent
Blkburn	Blackburn with Darwen
Blkpool	Blackpool
Bmouth	Bournemouth
Borders	Scottish Borders
Brack	Bracknell
Bridgend	Bridgend
Brighton	City of Brighton and Hove
Bristol	City and County of Bristol
Bucks	Buckinghamshire
Caerph	Caerphilly
Cambs	Cambridgeshire
Cardiff	Cardiff
Carms	Carmarthenshire
Ceredig	Ceredigion
Ches	Cheshire
Clack	Clackmannanshire
Conwy	Conwy
Corn	Cornwall
Cumb	Cumbria
Darl	Darlington
Denb	Denbighshire
Derby	City of Derby
Derbys	Derbyshire
Devon	Devon
Dorset	Dorset
Dumfries	Dumfries and Galloway
Dundee	Dundee City
Durham	Durham
E Ayrs	East Ayrshire
E Dunb	East Dunbartonshire
E Loth	East Lothian
E Renf	East Renfrewshire
E Sus	East Sussex
E Yorks	East Riding of Yorkshire
Edin	City of Edinburgh
Essex	Essex
Falk	Falkirk
Fife	Fife
Flint	Flintshire
Glasgow	City of Glasgow
Glos	Gloucesterhire
Gtr Man	Greater Manchester
Guern	Guernsey
Gwyn	Gwynedd
Halton	Halton
Hants	Hampshire
Hereford	Herefordshire
Herts	Hertfordshire
Highld	Highland
Hrtlpl	Hartlepool
Hull	Hull
I o M	Isle of Man
I o W	Isle of Wight
Invclyd	Inverclyde
Jersey	Jersey
Kent	Kent
Lancs	Lancashire
Leicester	City of Leicester
Leics	Leicestershire
Lincs	Lincolnshire
London	Greater London
Luton	Luton
M Keynes	Milton Keynes
M Tydf	Merthyr Tydfil
M'bro	Middlesbrough
Medway	Medway
Mers	Merseyside
Midloth	Midlothian
Mon	Monmouthshire
Moray	Moray
N Ayrs	North Ayrshire
N Lincs	North Lincolnshire
N Lnrk	North Lanarkshire
N Som	North Somerset
N Yorks	North Yorkshire
NE Lincs	North East Lincolnshire
Neath	Neath Port Talbot
Newport	City and County of Newport
Norf	Norfolk
Northants	Northamptonshire
Northumb	Northumberland
Nottingham	City of Nottingham
Notts	Nottinghamshire
Orkney	Orkney
Oxon	Oxfordshire
P'boro	Peterborough
Pembs	Pembrokeshire
Perth	Perth and Kinross
Plym	Plymouth
Poole	Poole
Powys	Powys
Ptsmth	Portsmouth
Reading	Reading
Redcar	Redcar and Cleveland
Renfs	Renfrewshire
Rhondda	Rhondda Cynon Taff
Rutland	Rutland
S Ayrs	South Ayrshire
S Glos	South Gloucestershire
S Lnrk	South Lanarkshire
S Yorks	South Yorkshire
Scilly	Scilly
Shetland	Shetland
Shrops	Shropshire
Slough	Slough
Som	Somerset
Soton	Southampton
Staffs	Staffordshire
Sthend	Southend-on-Sea
Stirl	Stirling
Stockton	Stockton-on-Tees
Stoke	Stoke-on-Trent
Suff	Suffolk
Sur	Surrey
Swansea	Swansea
T & W	Tyne and Wear
Telford	Telford and Wrekin
Thamesdown	Thamesdown
Thurrock	Thurrock
Torbay	Torbay
Torf	Torfaen
V Glam	The Vale of Glamorgan
W Berks	West Berkshire
W Dunb	West Dunbartonshire
W Isles	Western Isles
W Loth	West Lothian
W Mid	West Midlands
W Sus	West Sussex
W Yorks	West Yorkshire
Warks	Warwickshire
Warr	Warrington
Wilts	Wiltshire
Windsor	Windsor and Maidenhead
Wokingham	Wokingham
Worcs	Worcestershire
Wrex	Wrexham
York	City of York

A

Ab Kettleby Leics 64 B4
Ab Lench Worcs 50 D5
Abbas Combe Som 12 B5
Abberley Worcs 50 C2
Abberton Essex 43 C6
Abberton Worcs 50 D4
Abberwick Northumb 117 C7
Abbess Roding Essex 42 C1
Abbey Devon 11 C6
Abbey-cwm-hir Powys 48 B2
Abbey Dore Hereford 49 F5
Abbey Field Essex 43 B5
Abbey Hulton Stoke 75 E6
Abbey St Bathans Borders 124 C3
Abbey Town Cumb 107 D8
Abbey Village Lancs 86 B4
Abbey Wood London 29 B5
Abbeydale S Yorks 88 F4
Abbeystead Lancs 93 D5
Abbots Bickington Devon 9 C5
Abbots Bromley Staffs 62 B4
Abbots Langley Herts 40 D3
Abbots Leigh N Som 23 B7
Abbots Morton Worcs 50 D5
Abbots Ripton Cambs 54 B3
Abbots Salford Warks 51 D5
Abbotsbury Dorset 12 F3
Abbotsbury Sub Tropical Gardens Dorset 12 F3
Abbotsford House Borders 123 F8
Abbotsham Devon 9 B6
Abbotskerswell Devon 7 C6
Abbotsley Cambs 54 D3
Abbotswood Hants 14 B4
Abbotts Ann Hants 25 E8
Abcott Shrops 49 B5
Abdon Shrops 61 F5
Aber Ceredig 46 E3
Aber-Arad Carms 46 F2
Aber-banc Ceredig 46 E2
Aber Cowarch Gwyn 59 C5
Aber-Giâr Carms 46 E4
Aber-gwynfi Neath 34 E2
Aber-Hirnant Gwyn 72 F3
Aber-nant Rhondda 34 D4
Aber-Rhiwlech Gwyn 59 B6
Aber-Village Powys 35 B5
Aberaeron Ceredig 46 C3
Aberaman Rhondda 34 D4
Aberangell Gwyn 58 C5
Aberarder Highld 147 F7
Aberarder House Highld 148 B2
Aberarder Lodge Highld 147 F8
Aberargie Perth 134 C3
Aberarth Ceredig 46 C3
Aberavon Neath 33 E8
Aberbeeg Bl Gwent 35 D6
Abercanaid M Tydf 34 D4
Abercarn Caerph 35 E6
Abercastle Pembs 44 B3
Abercegir Powys 58 D5
Aberchirder Aberds 160 C3
Aberconwy House, Conwy Conwy 83 D7
Abercraf Powys 34 C2
Abercrombie Fife 135 D7
Abercych Pembs 45 E4
Abercynafon Powys 34 C4
Abercynon Rhondda 34 E4
Aberdalgie Perth 134 B2
Aberdâr = Aberdare Rhondda 34 D3
Aberdare = Aberdâr Rhondda 34 D3
Aberdaron Gwyn 70 E2
Aberdaugleddau = Milford Haven Pembs 44 E4
Aberdeen Aberdeen 151 D8
Aberdeen Airport Aberdeen 151 C7
Aberdesach Gwyn 82 F4
Aberdour Fife 134 F3
Aberdovey Gwyn 58 E3
Aberdulais Neath 34 D1
Aberedw Powys 48 E2
Abereiddy Pembs 44 B2
Abererch Gwyn 70 D4
Aberfan M Tydf 34 D4
Aberfeldy Perth 141 E5
Aberffraw Anglesey 82 E3
Aberffrwd Ceredig 47 B5
Aberford W Yorks 95 F7
Aberfoyle Stirl 132 D4
Abergavenny = Y Fenni Mon 35 C6
Abergele Conwy 72 B3
Abergorlech Carms 46 F4
Abergwaun = Fishguard Pembs 44 B4
Abergwesyn Powys 47 D7
Abergwili Carms 33 B5
Abergwynant Gwyn 58 C3
Abergwyngregyn Gwyn 83 D6
Abergynolwyn Gwyn 58 D3
Aberhonddu = Brecon Powys 34 B4
Aberhosan Powys 58 E5
Aberkenfig Bridgend 34 F2
Aberlady E Loth 135 F6
Aberlemno Angus 143 D5
Aberllefenni Gwyn 58 D4
Abermagwr Ceredig 47 B5
Abermaw = Barmouth Gwyn 58 C3
Abermeurig Ceredig 46 D4
Abermule Powys 59 E8
Abernaint Powys 59 B8
Abernant Carms 32 B4
Abernethy Perth 134 C3
Abernyte Perth 142 F2
Aberpennar = Mountain Ash Rhondda 34 E4
Aberporth Ceredig 45 D4
Abersoch Gwyn 70 E4
Abersychan Torf 35 D6
Abertawe = Swansea Swansea 33 E7
Aberteifi = Cardigan Ceredig 45 E3
Aberthin V Glam 22 B2
Abertillery = Abertyleri Bl Gwent 35 D6
Abertridwr Caerph 35 F5
Abertridwr Powys 59 C7
Abertyleri = Abertillery Bl Gwent 35 D6
Abertysswg Caerph 35 D5
Aberuthven Perth 133 C8
Aberyscir Powys 34 B3
Aberystwyth Ceredig 58 F2
Abhainn Suidhe W Isles 173 H3
Abingdon Oxon 38 E4
Abinger Common Sur 28 E2
Abinger Hammer Sur 27 E8
Abington S Lnrk 114 B2
Abington Piggotts Cambs 54 E4
Ablington Glos 37 D8
Ablington Wilts 25 E6
Abney Derbys 75 B8
Aboyne Aberds 150 E4
Abram Gtr Man 86 D4
Abriachan Highld 157 F6
Abridge Essex 41 E7
Abronhill N Lnrk 121 B7
Abson S Glos 24 B2
Abthorpe Northants 52 E4
Abune-the-Hill Orkney 176 D1
Aby Lincs 79 B7
Acaster Malbis York 95 E8
Acaster Selby N Yorks 95 E8
Accrington Lancs 87 B5
Acha Argyll 136 C2
Acha Mor W Isles 172 F6
Achabraid Argyll 128 B3
Achachork Highld 152 E5
Achafolla Argyll 130 D3
Achagary Highld 168 D2
Achahoish Argyll 128 C2
Achalader Perth 141 E8
Achallader Argyll 139 E7
Ach'an Todhair Highld 138 B4
Achanalt Highld 156 C3
Achanamara Argyll 128 B2
Achandunie Highld 157 B7
Achany Highld 164 D2
Achaphubuil Highld 138 B4
Acharacle Highld 137 B7
Acharn Highld 137 C8
Acharn Perth 140 E4
Acharole Highld 169 D7
Achath Aberds 151 C6
Achavanich Highld 169 E6
Achavraat Highld 158 E3
Achddu Carms 33 D5
Achduart Highld 162 D4
Achentoul Highld 168 F3
Achfary Highld 166 F4
Achgarve Highld 162 E2
Achiemore Highld 167 C5
Achiemore Highld 168 D3
A'Chill Highld 144 C2
Achiltibuie Highld 162 D4
Achina Highld 168 C2
Achinduich Highld 164 D2
Achinduin Argyll 130 B4
Achingills Highld 169 C6
Achintee Highld 139 B5
Achintee Highld 155 F5
Achintraid Highld 155 G4
Achlean Highld 148 E4
Achleck Argyll 137 D5
Achluachrach Highld 147 F5
Achlyness Highld 166 D4
Achmelvich Highld 162 B4
Achmore Highld 155 G4
Achmore Stirl 140 F2
Achnaba Argyll 130 B5
Achnaba Argyll 128 B4
Achnabat Highld 157 F6
Achnacarnin Highld 166 F2
Achnacarry Highld 146 F4
Achnacloich Argyll 131 B5
Achnacloich Highld 145 C5
Achnaconeran Highld 147 C7
Achnacraig Argyll 137 D5
Achnacroish Argyll 138 E2
Achnadrish Argyll 137 C5
Achnafalnich Argyll 131 C8
Achnagarron Highld 157 C7
Achnaha Highld 137 B5
Achnahanat Highld 164 E2
Achnahannet Highld 149 B5
Achnairn Highld 164 C2
Achnaluachrach Highld 164 D3
Achnasaul Highld 146 F4
Achnasheen Highld 156 D2
Achosnich Highld 137 B5
Achranich Highld 137 D8
Achreamie Highld 168 C5
Achriabhach Highld 139 C5
Achriesgill Highld 166 D4
Achrimsdale Highld 165 D6
Achtoty Highld 167 C8
Achurch Northants 65 F7
Achuvoldrach Highld 167 D7
Achvaich Highld 164 E4
Achvarasdal Highld 168 C4
Ackergill Highld 169 D8
Acklam M'bro 102 C2
Acklam N Yorks 96 C3
Ackleton Shrops 61 E7
Acklington Northumb 117 D8
Ackton W Yorks 88 B5
Ackworth Moor Top W Yorks 88 C5
Acle Norf 69 C7
Acock's Green W Mid 62 F5
Acol Kent 31 C7
Acomb Northumb 110 C2
Acomb York 95 D8
Aconbury Hereford 49 F7
Acre Lancs 87 B5
Acre Street W Sus 15 E8
Acrefair Wrex 73 E6
Acton Ches 74 D3
Acton Dorset 13 G7
Acton London 41 F5
Acton Shrops 60 F3
Acton Suff 56 E2
Acton Wrex 73 D7
Acton Beauchamp Hereford 49 D8
Acton Bridge Ches 74 B2
Acton Burnell Shrops 60 D5
Acton Green Hereford 49 D8
Acton Pigott Shrops 60 D5
Acton Round Shrops 61 E6
Acton Scott Shrops 60 F4
Acton Trussell Staffs 62 C3
Acton Turville S Glos 37 F5
Adbaston Staffs 61 B7
Adber Dorset 12 B3
Adderley Shrops 74 E3
Adderstone Northumb 125 F7
Addiewell W Loth 122 C2
Addingham W Yorks 94 E3
Addington Bucks 39 B7
Addington London 28 C4
Addington Kent 29 D7
Addinston Borders 123 D8
Addiscombe London 28 C4
Addlestone Sur 27 C8
Addlethorpe Lincs 79 C8
Adel W Yorks 95 F5
Adeney Telford 61 C7
Adfa Powys 59 D7
Adforton Hereford 49 B6
Adisham Kent 31 D6
Adlestrop Glos 38 B2
Adlingfleet E Yorks 90 B2
Adlington Lancs 86 C4
Admaston Staffs 62 B4
Admaston Telford 61 C6
Admington Warks 51 E7
Adstock Bucks 52 F5
Adstone Northants 52 D3
Adversane W Sus 16 B4
Advie Highld 158 F5
Adwalton W Yorks 88 B3
Adwell Oxon 39 E6
Adwick le Street S Yorks 89 D6
Adwick upon Dearne S Yorks 89 D5
Adziel Aberds 161 C6
Ae Village Dumfries 114 F2
Affleck Aberds 151 B7
Affpuddle Dorset 13 E6
Affric Lodge Highld 146 B4
Afon-wen Flint 72 B5
Afton I o W 14 F4
Agglethorpe N Yorks 101 F5
Agneash I o M 84 D4
Aigburth Mers 85 F4
Aiginis W Isles 172 E7
Aike E Yorks 97 E6
Aikerness Orkney 176 A3
Aikers Orkney 176 G3
Aiketgate Cumb 108 E4
Aikton Cumb 108 D2
Ailey Hereford 48 E5
Ailstone Warks 51 D7
Ailsworth P'boro 65 E8
Ainderby Quernhow N Yorks 102 F1
Ainderby Steeple N Yorks 101 E8
Aingers Green Essex 43 B7
Ainsdale Mers 85 C4
Ainsdale-on-Sea Mers 85 C4
Ainstable Cumb 108 E5
Ainsworth Gtr Man 87 C5
Ainthorpe N Yorks 103 D5
Aintree Mers 85 E4
Aintree Racecourse Mers 85 E8
Aird Argyll 130 E3
Aird Dumfries 104 C4
Aird Highld 154 C3
Aird W Isles 172 E8
Aird a Mhachair W Isles 170 F3
Aird a'Mhulaidh W Isles 173 G4
Aird Asaig W Isles 173 H4
Aird Dhail W Isles 172 B7
Aird Mhidhinis W Isles 171 K3
Aird Mhighe W Isles 173 J4
Aird Mhighe W Isles 173 K3
Aird Mhor W Isles 171 K3
Aird of Sleat Highld 145 C5
Aird Thunga W Isles 172 E7
Aird Uig W Isles 172 E3
Airdens Highld 164 E3
Airdrie N Lnrk 121 C7
Airdtorrisdale Highld 167 C8
Airidh a Bhruaich W Isles 172 G5
Airieland Dumfries 106 D4
Airmyn E Yorks 89 B8
Airntully Perth 141 F7
Airor Highld 145 C7
Airth Falk 133 F7
Airton N Yorks 94 D2
Airyhassen Dumfries 105 E7
Aisby Lincs 90 E2
Aisby Lincs 78 F3
Aisgernis W Isles 171 H3
Aiskew N Yorks 101 F7
Aislaby N Yorks 103 F5
Aislaby N Yorks 103 D6
Aislaby Stockton 102 C2
Aisthorpe Lincs 78 A2
Aith Orkney 176 E1
Aith Shetland 175 H5
Aith Shetland 174 D8
Aithsetter Shetland 175 K6
Aitkenhead S Ayrs 112 D3
Aitnoch Highld 158 F3
Akeld Northumb 117 B5
Akeley Bucks 52 F5
Akenham Suff 56 E5
Albaston Corn 6 B2
Alberbury Shrops 60 C3
Albert Dock, Liverpool Mers 85 F8
Albourne W Sus 17 C6
Albrighton Shrops 60 C4
Albrighton Shrops 62 D2
Alburgh Norf 69 F5
Albury Herts 41 B7
Albury Sur 27 E8
Albury End Herts 41 B7
Alby Hill Norf 81 D7
Alcaig Highld 157 D6
Alcaston Shrops 60 F4
Alcester Warks 51 D5
Alciston E Sus 18 E2
Alcombe Som 21 E8
Alcombe Wilts 24 C3
Alconbury Cambs 54 B2
Alconbury Weston Cambs 54 B2
Aldbar Castle Angus 143 D5
Aldborough Norf 81 D7
Aldborough N Yorks 95 C7
Aldbourne Wilts 25 B7
Aldbrough E Yorks 97 F8
Aldbrough St John N Yorks 101 C7
Aldbury Herts 40 C2
Aldcliffe Lancs 92 C4
Aldclune Perth 141 C6
Aldeburgh Suff 57 D8
Aldeby Norf 69 E7
Aldenham Herts 40 E4
Alderbury Wilts 14 B2
Aldercar Derbys 76 E4
Alderford Norf 68 C4
Alderholt Dorset 14 C2
Alderley Glos 36 E4
Alderley Edge Ches 74 B5
Aldermaston W Berks 26 C3
Aldermaston Wharf W Berks 26 C4
Alderminster Warks 51 E7
Alderney Airport Ald 16
Alder's End Hereford 49 E8
Aldersey Green Ches 73 D8
Aldershot Hants 27 D6
Alderton Glos 50 F5
Alderton Northants 52 E5
Alderton Shrops 60 B4
Alderton Suff 57 E7
Alderton Wilts 37 F5
Alderwasley Derbys 76 D3
Aldfield N Yorks 95 C5
Aldford Ches 73 D8
Aldham Essex 43 B5
Aldham Suff 56 E4
Aldie Highld 164 F4
Aldingbourne W Sus 16 D3
Aldingham Cumb 92 B2
Aldington Kent 19 B7
Aldington Worcs 51 E5
Aldington Frith Kent 19 B7
Aldochlay Argyll 132 E2
Aldreth Cambs 54 B5
Aldridge W Mid 62 D4
Aldringham Suff 57 C8
Aldsworth Glos 38 C1
Aldunie Moray 150 B2
Aldwark Derbys 76 D2
Aldwark N Yorks 95 C7
Aldwick W Sus 16 E3
Aldwincle Northants 65 F7
Aldworth W Berks 26 B3
Alexandria W Dunb 120 B3
Alfardisworthy Devon 8 C4
Alfington Devon 11 E6
Alfold Sur 27 F8
Alfold Bars W Sus 27 F8
Alfold Crossways Sur 27 F8
Alford Aberds 150 C4
Alford Lincs 79 B7
Alford Som 23 F8
Alfreton Derbys 76 D4
Alfrick Worcs 50 D2
Alfrick Pound Worcs 50 D2
Alfriston E Sus 18 E2
Algaltraig Argyll 129 C5
Algarkirk Lincs 79 F5
Alhampton Som 23 F8
Aline Lodge W Isles 173 G4
Alisary Highld 145 F7
Alkborough N Lincs 90 B2
Alkerton Oxon 51 E8
Alkham Kent 31 E6
Alkington Shrops 74 F2
Alkmonton Derbys 75 F8
All Cannings Wilts 25 C5
All Saints Church, Godshill I o W 15 F6
All Saints South Elmham Suff 69 F6
All Stretton Shrops 60 E4
Alladale Lodge Highld 163 F8
Allaleigh Devon 7 D6
Allanaquoich Aberds 149 E7
Allangrange Mains Highld 157 D7
Allanton Borders 124 D4
Allanton N Lnrk 121 D8
Allathasdal W Isles 171 K2
Allendale Town Northumb 109 D8
Allenheads Northumb 109 E8
Allens Green Herts 41 C7
Allensford Durham 110 D3
Allensmore Hereford 49 F6
Allenton Derby 76 F3
Aller Som 12 B2
Allerby Cumb 107 F7
Allerford Som 21 E8
Allerston N Yorks 103 F6
Allerthorpe E Yorks 96 E3
Allerton Mers 86 F2
Allerton W Yorks 94 F4
Allerton Bywater W Yorks 88 B5
Allerton Mauleverer N Yorks 95 D7
Allesley W Mid 63 F7
Allestree Derby 76 F3
Allet Corn 3 B6
Allexton Leics 64 D5
Allgreave Ches 75 C6
Allhallows Medway 30 B2
Allhallows-on-Sea Medway 30 B2
Alligin Shuas Highld 154 E4
Allimore Green Staffs 62 C2
Allington Lincs 77 E8
Allington Wilts 25 F7
Allington Wilts 25 C5
Allithwaite Cumb 92 B3
Alloa Clack 133 E7
Allonby Cumb 107 E7
Alloway S Ayrs 112 C3
Allt Carms 33 D6
Allt na h-Airbhe Highld 163 E5
Allt-nan-sùgh Highld 146 B2
Alltchaorunn Highld 139 D5
Alltforgan Powys 59 B6
Alltmawr Powys 48 E2
Alltnacaillich Highld 167 E6
Alltsigh Highld 147 C7
Alltwalis Carms 46 F3
Alltwen Neath 33 D8
Alltyblaca Ceredig 46 E4
Allwood Green Suff 56 B4
Almeley Hereford 48 D5
Almer Dorset 13 E7
Almholme S Yorks 89 D6
Almington Staffs 74 F4
Alminstone Cross Devon 8 B5
Almondbank Perth 134 B2
Almondbury W Yorks 88 C2
Almondsbury S Glos 36 F3
Alne N Yorks 95 C7
Alness Highld 157 C7
Alnham Northumb 117 C5
Alnmouth Northumb 117 C8
Alnwick Northumb 117 C7
Alperton London 40 F4
Alphamstone Essex 56 F2
Alpheton Suff 56 D2
Alphington Devon 10 E4
Alport Derbys 76 C2
Alpraham Ches 74 D2
Alresford Essex 43 B6
Alrewas Staffs 63 C5
Alsager Ches 74 D4
Alsagers Bank Staffs 74 E5
Alsop en le Dale Derbys 75 D8
Alston Cumb 109 E7
Alston Devon 11 D8
Alstone Glos 50 F4
Alstonefield Staffs 75 D8
Alswear Devon 10 B2
Altandhu Highld 162 C3
Altanduin Highld 165 B5
Altarnun Corn 8 F4
Altass Highld 164 D1
Alterwall Highld 169 C7
Altham Lancs 93 F7
Althorne Essex 43 E5
Althorp House, Great Brington Northants 52 C4
Althorpe N Lincs 90 D2
Alticry Dumfries 105 D6
Altnabreac Station Highld 168 E5
Altnacealgach Hotel Highld 163 C6
Altnacraig Argyll 130 C4
Altnafeadh Highld 139 D6
Altnaharra Highld 167 F7
Altofts W Yorks 88 B4
Alton Derbys 76 C3
Alton Hants 26 F5
Alton Staffs 75 E7
Alton Pancras Dorset 12 D5
Alton Priors Wilts 25 C6
Alton Towers Staffs 75 E7
Altrincham Gtr Man 87 F5
Altrua Highld 146 F5
Altskeith Stirl 132 D3
Altyre Ho. Moray 158 D4
Alva Clack 133 E7
Alvanley Ches 73 B8
Alvaston Derby 76 F3
Alvechurch Worcs 50 B5
Alvecote Warks 63 D6
Alvediston Wilts 13 B7
Alveley Shrops 61 F7
Alverdiscott Devon 9 B7
Alverstoke Hants 15 E7
Alverstone I o W 15 F6
Alverton Notts 77 E7
Alves Moray 158 C5
Alvescot Oxon 38 D2
Alveston S Glos 36 F3
Alveston Warks 51 D7
Alvie Highld 148 D4
Alvingham Lincs 91 E7
Alvington Glos 36 D3
Alwalton Cambs 65 E8
Alweston Dorset 12 C4
Alwinton Northumb 116 D5
Alwoodley W Yorks 95 E5
Alyth Perth 142 E2
Am Baile W Isles 171 J3
Am Buth Argyll 130 C4
Amatnatua Highld 164 E1
Amber Hill Lincs 78 E5
Ambergate Derbys 76 D3
Amberley Glos 37 D5
Amberley W Sus 16 C4
Amble Northumb 117 D8
Amblecote W Mid 62 F2
Ambler Thorn W Yorks 87 B8
Ambleside Cumb 99 D5
Ambleston Pembs 44 C5
Ambrosden Oxon 39 C6
Amcotts N Lincs 90 C2
American Adventure, Ilkeston Derbys 76 E4
American Air Museum, Duxford Cambs 55 E5
Amersham Bucks 40 E2
Amerton Working Farm, Stowe-by-Chartley Staffs 62 B3
Amesbury Wilts 25 E6
Amington Staffs 63 D6
Amisfield Dumfries 114 F2
Amlwch Anglesey 82 B4
Amlwch Port Anglesey 82 B4
Ammanford = Rhydaman Carms 33 C7
Amod Argyll 118 C4
Amotherby N Yorks 96 B3
Ampfield Hants 14 B5
Ampleforth N Yorks 95 B8
Ampney Crucis Glos 37 D7
Ampney St Mary Glos 37 D7
Ampney St Peter Glos 37 D7
Amport Hants 25 E7
Ampthill Beds 53 F8
Ampton Suff 56 B2
Amroth Pembs 32 D2
Amulree Perth 141 F5
An Caol Highld 155 E2
An Cnoc W Isles 172 E7
An Gleann Ur W Isles 172 E7
An t-Ob = Leverburgh W Isles 173 K3
Anagach Highld 149 B6
Anaheilt Highld 138 C2
Anancaun Highld 154 D6
Ancaster Lincs 78 E2
Anchor Shrops 59 F8
Anchorsholme Blkpool 92 E3
Ancroft Northumb 125 E5
Ancrum Borders 116 B2
Anderby Lincs 79 B8
Anderson Dorset 13 E6
Anderton Ches 74 B3
Andover Hants 25 E8
Andover Down Hants 25 E8
Andoversford Glos 37 C7
Andreas I o M 84 C4
Anfield Mers 85 E4
Angersleigh Som 11 C6

Angle Pembs 44 E3
Angmering W Sus 16 D4
Angram N Yorks 95 E8
Angram N Yorks 100 E3
Anie Stirl 132 C4
Ankerville Highld 158 B2
Anlaby E Yorks 90 B4
Anmer Norf 80 E3
Anna Valley Hants 25 E8
Annan Dumfries 107 C8
Annat Argyll 131 C6
Annat Highld 155 E4
Annbank S Ayrs 112 B4
Anne Hathaway's Cottage, Stratford-upon-Avon Warks 51 D6
Annesley Notts 76 D5
Annesley Woodhouse Notts 76 D4
Annfield Plain Durham 110 D4
Annifirth Shetland 175 J3
Annitsford T & W 111 B5
Annscroft Shrops 60 D4
Ansdell Lancs 85 B4
Ansford Som 23 F8
Ansley Warks 63 E6
Anslow Staffs 63 B6
Anslow Gate Staffs 63 B5
Anstey Herts 54 F5
Anstey Leics 64 D2
Anstruther Easter Fife 135 D7
Anstruther Wester Fife 135 D7
Ansty Hants 26 E5
Ansty Warks 63 F7
Ansty Wilts 13 B7
Ansty W Sus 17 B6
Anthill Common Hants 15 C7
Anthorn Cumb 107 D8
Antingham Norf 81 D8
Anton's Gowt Lincs 79 E5
Antonshill Falk 133 F7
Antony Corn 5 D8
Anwick Lincs 78 D4
Anwoth Dumfries 106 D2
Aoradh Argyll 126 C2
Apes Hall Cambs 67 E5
Apethorpe Northants 65 E7
Apeton Staffs 62 C2
Apley Lincs 78 B4
Apperknowle Derbys 76 B3
Apperley Glos 37 B5
Apperley Bridge W Yorks 94 F4
Appersett N Yorks 100 E3
Appin Argyll 138 E3
Appin House Argyll 138 E3
Appleby N Lincs 90 C3
Appleby-in-Westmorland Cumb 100 B1
Appleby Magna Leics 63 D7
Appleby Parva Leics 63 D7
Applecross Highld 155 F3
Applecross Ho. Highld 155 F3
Appledore Devon 20 F3
Appledore Devon 11 C5
Appledore Kent 19 C6
Appledore Heath Kent 19 B6
Appleford Oxon 39 E5
Applegarthtown Dumfries 114 F4
Appleshaw Hants 25 E8
Applethwaite Cumb 98 B4
Appleton Halton 86 F3
Appleton Oxon 38 D4
Appleton-le-Moors N Yorks 103 F5
Appleton-le-Street N Yorks 96 B3
Appleton Roebuck N Yorks 95 E8
Appleton Thorn Warr 86 F4
Appleton Wiske N Yorks 102 D1
Appletreehall Borders 115 C8
Appletreewick N Yorks 94 C3
Appley Som 11 B5
Appley Bridge Lancs 86 D3
Apse Heath I o W 15 F6
Apsley End Beds 54 F2
Apuldram W Sus 16 D2
Aquhythie Aberds 151 C6
Arabella Highld 158 B2
Arbeadie Aberds 151 E5
Arbeia Roman Fort and Museum T & W 111 C6
Arberth = Narberth Pembs 32 C2
Arbirlot Angus 143 E6
Arboll Highld 165 F5
Arborfield Wokingham 27 C5
Arborfield Cross Wokingham 27 C5
Arborfield Garrison Wokingham 27 C5
Arbour-thorne S Yorks 88 F4
Arbroath Angus 143 E6
Arbuthnott Aberds 143 B7
Archiestown Moray 159 E6
Arclid Ches 74 C4
Ard-dhubh Highld 155 F3
Ardachu Highld 164 D3
Ardalanish Argyll 136 G4
Ardanaiseig Argyll 131 C6
Ardaneaskan Highld 155 G4
Ardanstur Argyll 130 D4
Ardargie House Hotel Perth 134 C2
Ardarroch Highld 155 G4
Ardbeg Argyll 126 E4
Ardbeg Argyll 129 B6
Ardbeg Distillery, Port Ellen Argyll 126 E4
Ardcharnich Highld 163 F5
Ardchiavaig Argyll 136 G4
Ardchullarie More Stirl 132 C4
Ardchyle Stirl 132 B4
Arddleen Powys 60 C2
Ardechvie Highld 146 E4
Ardeley Herts 41 B6
Ardelve Highld 155 H4
Arden Argyll 132 F2
Ardens Grafton Warks 51 D6
Ardentinny Argyll 129 B6
Ardentraive Argyll 129 C5
Ardeonaig Stirl 140 F3
Ardersier Highld 157 D8
Ardessie Highld 162 F4
Ardfern Argyll 130 E4
Ardgartan Argyll 131 E8
Ardgay Highld 164 E2
Ardgour Highld 138 C4
Ardheslaig Highld 154 E3
Ardiecow Moray 160 B2
Ardindrean Highld 163 F5
Ardingly W Sus 17 B7
Ardington Oxon 38 F4
Ardlair Aberds 150 B4
Ardlamont Ho. Argyll 128 D4
Ardleigh Essex 43 B6
Ardler Perth 142 E2
Ardley Oxon 39 B5
Ardlui Argyll 132 C2
Ardlussa Argyll 127 D4
Ardmair Highld 163 E5
Ardmay Argyll 131 E8
Ardminish Argyll 118 B3
Ardmolich Highld 145 F7
Ardmore Argyll 130 C3
Ardmore Highld 166 D4
Ardmore Highld 164 F4
Ardnacross Argyll 137 D6
Ardnadam Argyll 129 C6
Ardnagrask Highld 157 E6
Ardnarff Highld 155 G4
Ardnastang Highld 138 C2
Ardnave Argyll 126 B2
Ardno Argyll 131 E7
Ardo Aberds 160 E5
Ardo Ho. Aberds 151 B8
Ardoch Perth 141 F7
Ardochy House Highld 146 D5
Ardoyne Aberds 151 B5
Ardpatrick Argyll 128 D2
Ardpatrick Ho. Argyll 128 E2
Ardpeaton Argyll 129 B7
Ardrishaig Argyll 128 B3
Ardross Fife 135 D7
Ardross Highld 157 B7
Ardross Castle Highld 157 B7
Ardrossan N Ayrs 120 E2
Ardshealach Highld 137 B7
Ardsley S Yorks 88 D4
Ardslignish Highld 137 B6
Ardtalla Argyll 126 D4
Ardtalnaig Perth 140 F4
Ardtoe Highld 145 F6
Ardtrostan Perth 133 B5
Arduaine Argyll 130 D3
Ardullie Highld 157 C6
Ardvasar Highld 145 C6
Ardvorlich Perth 132 B5
Ardwell Dumfries 104 E5
Ardwell Mains Dumfries 104 E5
Ardwick Gtr Man 87 E6
Areley Kings Worcs 50 B3
Arford Hants 27 F6
Argoed Caerph 35 E5
Argoed Mill Powys 47 C8
Argyll & Sutherland Highlanders Museum (See Stirling Castle) Stirl 133 E6
Arichamish Argyll 130 E5
Arichastlich Argyll 131 B8
Aridhglas Argyll 136 F4
Arileod Argyll 136 C2
Arinacrinachd Highld 154 E3
Arinagour Argyll 136 C3
Arion Orkney 176 E1
Arisaig Highld 145 E6
Ariundle Highld 138 C2
Arkendale N Yorks 95 C6
Arkesden Essex 55 F5
Arkholme Lancs 93 B5
Arkle Town N Yorks 101 D5
Arkley London 41 E5
Arksey S Yorks 89 D6
Arkwright Town Derbys 76 B4
Arle Glos 37 B6
Arlecdon Cumb 98 C2
Arlesey Beds 54 F2
Arleston Telford 61 C6
Arley Ches 86 F4
Arlingham Glos 36 C4
Arlington Devon 20 E5
Arlington E Sus 18 E2
Arlington Glos 37 D8
Arlington Court Devon 20 E5
Armadale Highld 168 C2
Armadale W Loth 122 C2
Armadale Castle Highld 145 C6
Armathwaite Cumb 108 E5
Arminghall Norf 69 D5
Armitage Staffs 62 C4
Armley W Yorks 95 F5
Armscote Warks 51 E7
Armthorpe S Yorks 89 D7
Arnabost Argyll 136 C3
Arncliffe N Yorks 94 B2
Arncroach Fife 135 D7
Arne Dorset 13 F7
Arnesby Leics 64 E3
Arngask Perth 134 C3
Arnisdale Highld 145 B8
Arnish Highld 152 E6
Arniston Engine Midloth 123 C6
Arnol W Isles 172 D6
Arnold E Yorks 97 E7
Arnold Notts 77 E5
Arnolfini Gallery Bristol 23 B7
Arnprior Stirl 132 E5
Arnside Cumb 92 B4
Aros Mains Argyll 137 D6
Arowry Wrex 73 F8
Arpafeelie Highld 157 D7
Arrad Foot Cumb 99 F5
Arram E Yorks 97 E6
Arrathorne N Yorks 101 E7
Arreton I o W 15 F6
Arrington Cambs 54 D4
Arrivain Argyll 131 B8
Arrochar Argyll 131 E8
Arrow Warks 51 D5
Arthington W Yorks 95 E5
Arthingworth Northants 64 F4
Arthog Gwyn 58 C3
Arthrath Aberds 161 E6
Arthurstone Perth 142 E2
Artrochie Aberds 161 E7
Arundel W Sus 16 D4
Arundel Castle W Sus 16 D4
Aryhoulan Highld 138 C4
Asby Cumb 98 B2
Ascog Argyll 129 D6
Ascot Windsor 27 C7
Ascot Racecourse Windsor 27 C7
Ascott Warks 51 F8
Ascott-under-Wychwood Oxon 38 C3
Asenby N Yorks 95 B6
Asfordby Leics 64 C4
Asfordby Hill Leics 64 C4
Asgarby Lincs 78 E4
Asgarby Lincs 79 C6
Ash Kent 29 C6
Ash Kent 31 D6
Ash Som 12 B2
Ash Sur 27 D6
Ash Bullayne Devon 10 D2
Ash Green Warks 63 F7
Ash Magna Shrops 74 F2
Ash Mill Devon 10 B2
Ash Priors Som 11 B6
Ash Street Suff 56 E4
Ash Thomas Devon 10 C5
Ash Vale Sur 27 D6
Ashampstead W Berks 26 B3
Ashbocking Suff 57 D5
Ashbourne Derbys 75 E8
Ashbrittle Som 11 B5
Ashburton Devon 7 C5
Ashbury Devon 9 E7
Ashbury Oxon 38 F2
Ashby N Lincs 90 D3
Ashby by Partney Lincs 79 C7
Ashby cum Fenby NE Lincs 91 D6
Ashby de la Launde Lincs 78 D3
Ashby-de-la-Zouch Leics 63 C7
Ashby Folville Leics 64 C4
Ashby Magna Leics 64 E2
Ashby Parva Leics 64 F2
Ashby Puerorum Lincs 79 B6
Ashby St Ledgers Northants 52 C3
Ashby St Mary Norf 69 D6
Ashchurch Glos 50 F4
Ashcombe Devon 7 B7
Ashcott Som 23 F6
Ashdon Essex 55 E6
Ashe Hants 26 E3
Asheldham Essex 43 D5
Ashen Essex 55 E8
Ashendon Bucks 39 C7
Ashfield Carms 33 B7
Ashfield Stirl 133 D6
Ashfield Suff 57 C6
Ashfield Green Suff 57 B6
Ashfold Crossways W Sus 17 B6
Ashford Devon 20 F4
Ashford Hants 14 C2
Ashford Kent 30 E4
Ashford Sur 27 B8
Ashford Bowdler Shrops 49 B7
Ashford Carbonell Shrops 49 B7
Ashford Hill Hants 26 C3
Ashford in the Water Derbys 75 C8
Ashgill S Lnrk 121 E7
Ashill Devon 11 C5
Ashill Norf 67 D8
Ashill Som 11 C8
Ashingdon Essex 42 E4
Ashington Northumb 117 F8
Ashington Som 12 B3
Ashington W Sus 16 C5
Ashintully Castle Perth 141 C8
Ashkirk Borders 115 B7
Ashlett Hants 15 D5
Ashleworth Glos 37 B5
Ashley Cambs 55 C7
Ashley Ches 87 F5
Ashley Devon 9 C8
Ashley Dorset 14 D2
Ashley Glos 37 E6
Ashley Hants 14 E3
Ashley Hants 25 F8
Ashley Northants 64 E4
Ashley Staffs 74 F4
Ashley Green Bucks 40 D2
Ashley Heath Dorset 14 D2
Ashley Heath Staffs 74 F4
Ashmanhaugh Norf 69 B6
Ashmansworth Hants 26 D2
Ashmansworthy Devon 8 C5
Ashmore Dorset 13 C7
Ashorne Warks 51 D8
Ashover Derbys 76 C3
Ashow Warks 51 B8
Ashprington Devon 7 D6
Ashreigney Devon 9 C8
Ashstead Sur 28 D2
Ashton Ches 74 C2
Ashton Corn 2 D5
Ashton Hants 15 C6
Ashton Hereford 49 C7
Ashton Invclyd 129 C7
Ashton Northants 53 E5
Ashton Northants 65 F7
Ashton Common Wilts 24 D3
Ashton-In-Makerfield Gtr Man 86 E3
Ashton Keynes Wilts 37 E7
Ashton under Hill Worcs 50 F4
Ashton-under-Lyne Gtr Man 87 E7
Ashton upon Mersey Gtr Man 87 E5
Ashurst Hants 14 C4
Ashurst Kent 18 B2
Ashurst W Sus 17 C5
Ashurstwood W Sus 28 F5
Ashwater Devon 9 E5
Ashwell Herts 54 F3
Ashwell Rutland 65 C5
Ashwell Som 11 C8
Ashwellthorpe Norf 68 E4
Ashwick Som 23 E8
Ashwicken Norf 67 C7
Ashybank Borders 115 C8
Askam in Furness Cumb 92 B2
Askern S Yorks 89 C6
Askerswell Dorset 12 E3
Askett Bucks 39 D8
Askham Cumb 99 B7
Askham Notts 77 B7
Askham Bryan York 95 E8
Askham Richard York 95 E8
Asknish Argyll 128 A4
Askrigg N Yorks 100 E4
Askwith N Yorks 94 E4
Aslackby Lincs 78 F3
Aslacton Norf 68 E4
Aslockton Notts 77 F7
Asloun Aberds 150 C4
Aspatria Cumb 107 E8
Aspenden Herts 41 B6
Asperton Lincs 79 F5
Aspley Guise Beds 53 F7
Aspley Heath Beds 53 F7
Aspull Gtr Man 86 D4
Asselby E Yorks 89 B8
Asserby Lincs 79 B7
Assington Suff 56 F3
Assynt Ho. Highld 157 C6
Astbury Ches 74 C5
Astcote Northants 52 D4
Asterley Shrops 60 D3
Asterton Shrops 60 E3
Asthall Oxon 38 C2
Asthall Leigh Oxon 38 C3
Astley Shrops 60 C5
Astley Warks 63 F7
Astley Worcs 50 C2
Astley Abbotts Shrops 61 E7
Astley Bridge Gtr Man 86 C5
Astley Cross Worcs 50 C3
Astley Green Gtr Man 86 E5
Aston Ches 74 E3
Aston Ches 74 B2
Aston Derbys 88 F2
Aston Hereford 49 B6
Aston Herts 41 B5
Aston Oxon 38 D3
Aston Shrops 60 B5
Aston Staffs 74 E4
Aston S Yorks 89 F5
Aston Telford 61 D6
Aston W Mid 62 F4
Aston Wokingham 39 F7
Aston Abbotts Bucks 39 B8
Aston Botterell Shrops 61 F6
Aston-By-Stone Staffs 75 F6
Aston Cantlow Warks 51 D6
Aston Clinton Bucks 40 C1
Aston Crews Hereford 36 B3
Aston Cross Glos 50 F4
Aston End Herts 41 B5
Aston Eyre Shrops 61 E6
Aston Fields Worcs 50 C4
Aston Flamville Leics 63 E8
Aston Ingham Hereford 36 B3
Aston juxta Mondrum Ches 74 D3
Aston le Walls Northants 52 D2
Aston Magna Glos 51 F6
Aston Munslow Shrops 60 F5
Aston on Clun Shrops 60 F3
Aston-on-Trent Derbys 63 B8
Aston Rogers Shrops 60 D3
Aston Rowant Oxon 39 E7
Aston Sandford Bucks 39 D7
Aston Somerville Worcs 50 F5
Aston Subedge Glos 51 E6
Aston Tirrold Oxon 39 F5
Aston Upthorpe Oxon 39 F5
Astrop Northants 52 F3
Astwick Beds 54 F3
Astwood M Keynes 53 E7
Astwood Worcs 50 D3
Astwood Bank Worcs 50 C5
Aswarby Lincs 78 F3
Aswardby Lincs 79 B6
Atch Lench Worcs 50 D5
Atcham Shrops 60 D5
Athelhampton Dorset 13 E5
Athelington Suff 57 B6
Athelney Som 11 B8
Athelstaneford E Loth 123 B8
Atherington Devon 9 B7
Atherstone Warks 63 E7
Atherstone on Stour Warks 51 D7
Atherton Gtr Man 86 D4
Atley Hill N Yorks 101 D7
Atlow Derbys 76 E2
Attadale Highld 155 G5
Attadale Ho. Highld 155 G5
Attenborough Notts 76 F5
Atterby Lincs 90 E3
Attercliffe S Yorks 88 F4
Attleborough Norf 68 E3
Attleborough Warks 63 E7
Attlebridge Norf 68 C4
Atwick E Yorks 97 D7
Atworth Wilts 24 C3
Aubourn Lincs 78 C2
Auchagallon N Ayrs 119 C5
Auchallater Aberds 149 F7
Aucharnie Aberds 160 D3
Auchattie Aberds 151 E5
Auchavan Angus 142 C1
Auchbreck Moray 149 B8
Auchenback E Renf 120 D5
Auchenbainzie Dumfries 113 E8
Auchenblae Aberds 143 B7
Auchenbrack Dumfries 113 E7
Auchenbreck Argyll 129 B5
Auchencairn Dumfries 106 D4
Auchencairn Dumfries 114 F2
Auchencairn N Ayrs 119 D7
Auchencrosh S Ayrs 104 B5
Auchencrow Borders 124 C4
Auchendinny Midloth 123 C5
Auchengray S Lnrk 122 D2
Auchenhalrig Moray 159 C7
Auchenheath S Lnrk 121 E8
Auchenlochan Argyll 128 C4
Auchenmalg Dumfries 105 D6
Auchensoul S Ayrs 112 E2
Auchentiber N Ayrs 120 E3
Auchertyre Highld 155 H4
Auchgourish Highld 148 C5
Auchincarroch W Dunb 132 F3
Auchindrain Argyll 131 E6
Auchindrean Highld 163 F5
Auchininna Aberds 160 D3
Auchinleck E Ayrs 113 B5
Auchinloch N Lnrk 121 B6
Auchinroath Moray 159 D6
Auchintoul Aberds 150 C4
Auchiries Aberds 161 E7
Auchlee Aberds 151 E7
Auchleven Aberds 150 B5
Auchlochan S Lnrk 121 F8
Auchlossan Aberds 150 D4
Auchlunies Aberds 151 E7
Auchlyne Stirl 132 B4
Auchmacoy Aberds 161 E6
Auchmair Moray 150 B2
Auchmantle Dumfries 105 C5
Auchmillan E Ayrs 112 B5
Auchmithie Angus 143 E6
Auchmuirbridge Fife 134 D4
Auchmull Angus 143 B5
Auchnacree Angus 142 C4
Auchnagallin Highld 158 F4
Auchnagatt Aberds 161 D6
Auchnaha Argyll 128 B4
Auchnashelloch Perth 133 C6
Aucholzie Aberds 150 E2
Auchrannie Angus 142 D2
Auchroisk Highld 149 B6
Auchronie Angus 150 F3
Auchterarder Perth 133 C8
Auchteraw Highld 147 D6
Auchterderran Fife 134 E4
Auchterhouse Angus 142 F3
Auchtermuchty Fife 134 C4
Auchterneed Highld 157 D5
Auchtertool Fife 134 E4
Auchtertyre Moray 159 D5
Auchtubh Stirl 132 B4
Auckengill Highld 169 C8
Auckley S Yorks 89 D7
Audenshaw Gtr Man 87 E7
Audlem Ches 74 E3
Audley Staffs 74 D4
Audley End Essex 56 F2
Audley End House Essex 55 F6
Auds Aberds 160 B3
Aughton E Yorks 96 F3
Aughton Lancs 85 D4
Aughton Lancs 93 C5
Aughton S Yorks 89 F5
Aughton Wilts 25 D7
Aughton Park Lancs 86 D2
Auldearn Highld 158 D3
Aulden Hereford 49 D6
Auldgirth Dumfries 114 F2
Auldhame E Loth 135 F7
Auldhouse S Lnrk 121 D6
Ault a'chruinn Highld 146 B2
Aultanrynie Highld 166 F5
Aultbea Highld 162 F2
Aultdearg Highld 156 C3
Aultgrishan Highld 154 B3
Aultguish Inn Highld 156 B4
Aultibea Highld 165 B7
Aultiphurst Highld 168 C3
Aultmore Moray 159 D8
Aultnagoire Highld 147 B8
Aultnamain Inn Highld 164 F3
Aultnaslat Highld 146 D4
Aulton Aberds 150 B5
Aundorach Highld 149 C5
Aunsby Lincs 78 F3
Auquhorthies Aberds 151 B7
Aust S Glos 36 F2
Austendike Lincs 66 B2
Austerfield S Yorks 89 E7
Austrey Warks 63 D6
Austwick N Yorks 93 C7
Authorpe Lincs 91 F8
Authorpe Row Lincs 79 B8
Avebury Wilts 25 C6
Aveley Thurrock 42 F1
Avening Glos 37 E5
Averham Notts 77 D7
Aveton Gifford Devon 6 E4
Avielochan Highld 148 C5
Aviemore Highld 148 C4
Avington Hants 26 F3
Avington W Berks 25 C8
Avoch Highld 157 D8
Avon Hants 14 E2
Avon Dassett Warks 52 E2
Avonbridge Falk 122 B2
Avonmouth Bristol 23 B7
Avonwick Devon 6 D5
Awbridge Hants 14 B4
Awhirk Dumfries 104 D4
Awkley S Glos 36 F2
Awliscombe Devon 11 D6
Awre Glos 36 D4
Awsworth Notts 76 E4
Axbridge Som 23 D6
Axford Hants 26 E4
Axford Wilts 25 B7
Axminster Devon 11 E7
Axmouth Devon 11 E7
Axton Flint 85 F2
Aycliff Kent 31 E7
Aycliffe Durham 101 B7
Aydon Northumb 110 C3
Aylburton Glos 36 D3
Ayle Northumb 109 E7
Aylesbeare Devon 10 E5
Aylesbury Bucks 39 C8
Aylesby NE Lincs 91 D6
Aylesford Kent 29 D8
Aylesham Kent 31 D6
Aylestone Leicester 64 D2
Aylmerton Norf 81 D7
Aylsham Norf 81 E7
Aylton Hereford 49 F8
Aymestrey Hereford 49 C6
Aynho Northants 52 F3
Ayot St Lawrence Herts 40 C4
Ayot St Peter Herts 41 C5
Ayr S Ayrs 112 B3
Ayr Racecourse S Ayrs 112 B3
Aysgarth N Yorks 101 F5
Ayside Cumb 99 F5
Ayston Rutland 65 D5
Aythorpe Roding Essex 42 C1
Ayton Borders 124 C5
Aywick Shetland 174 E7
Azerley N Yorks 95 B5

B

Babbacombe Torbay 7 C7
Babbinswood Shrops 73 F7
Babcary Som 12 B3
Babel Carms 47 F7
Babell Flint 73 B5
Babraham Cambs 55 D6
Babworth Notts 89 F7
Bac W Isles 172 D7
Bachau Anglesey 82 C4
Back of Keppoch Highld 145 E6
Back Rogerton E Ayrs 113 B5
Backaland Orkney 176 C4
Backaskaill Orkney 176 A3
Backbarrow Cumb 99 F5
Backe Carms 32 C3
Backfolds Aberds 161 C7
Backford Ches 73 B8
Backford Cross Ches 73 B7
Backhill Aberds 160 E4
Backhill Aberds 161 E7
Backhill of Clackriach Aberds 161 D6
Backhill of Fortree Aberds 161 D6
Backhill of Trustach Aberds 150 E5
Backies Highld 165 D5
Backlass Highld 169 D7
Backwell N Som 23 C6
Backworth T & W 111 B6
Bacon End Essex 42 C2
Baconsthorpe Norf 81 D7
Bacton Hereford 49 F5
Bacton Norf 81 D9
Bacton Suff 56 C4
Bacton Green Suff 56 C4
Bacup Lancs 87 B6
Badachro Highld 154 C3
Badanloch Lodge Highld 168 F2
Badavanich Highld 156 D2
Badbury Thamesdown 38 F1
Badby Northants 52 D3
Badcall Highld 166 D4
Badcaul Highld 162 E4
Baddeley Green Stoke 75 D6
Baddesley Clinton Warks 51 B7
Baddesley Clinton Hall Warks 51 B7
Baddesley Ensor Warks 63 E6
Baddidarach Highld 162 B4
Baddoch Aberds 149 F7
Baddock Highld 157 D8
Badenscoth Aberds 160 E4
Badenyon Aberds 150 C2
Badger Shrops 61 E7
Badger's Mount Kent 29 C5
Badgeworth Glos 37 C6
Badgworth Som 23 D5
Badicaul Highld 155 H3
Badingham Suff 57 C7
Badlesmere Kent 30 D4
Badlipster Highld 169 E7
Badluarach Highld 162 E3
Badminton S Glos 37 F5
Badnaban Highld 162 B4
Badninish Highld 164 E4
Badrallach Highld 162 E4
Badsey Worcs 51 E5
Badshot Lea Sur 27 E6
Badsworth W Yorks 89 C5
Badwell Ash Suff 56 C3
Bae Colwyn = Colwyn Bay Conwy 83 D8
Bag Enderby Lincs 79 B6
Bagby N Yorks 102 F2
Bagendon Glos 37 D7
Bagh a Chaisteil = Castlebay W Isles 171 L2
Bagh Mor W Isles 170 E4
Bagh Shiarabhagh W Isles 171 K3
Baghasdal W Isles 171 J3
Bagillt Flint 73 B6
Baginton Warks 51 B8
Baglan Neath 33 E8
Bagley Shrops 60 B4
Bagnall Staffs 75 D6
Bagnor W Berks 26 C2
Bagshot Sur 27 C7
Bagshot Wilts 25 C8
Bagthorpe Norf 80 D3
Bagthorpe Notts 76 D4
Bagworth Leics 63 D8
Bagwy Llydiart Hereford 35 B8
Bail Àrd Bhuirgh W Isles 172 C7
Bail Uachdraich W Isles 170 D4
Baildon W Yorks 94 F4
Baile W Isles 173 K2
Baile a Mhanaich W Isles 170 E3
Baile Ailein W Isles 172 F5
Baile an Truiseil W Isles 172 C6
Baile Boidheach Argyll 128 C2
Baile Glas W Isles 170 E4
Baile Mhartainn W Isles 170 C3
Baile Mhic Phail W Isles 170 C4
Baile Mor Argyll 136 F3
Baile Mor W Isles 170 D3
Baile na Creige W Isles 171 K2
Baile nan Cailleach W Isles 170 E3
Baile Raghaill W Isles 170 C3
Bailebeag Highld 147 C8
Baileyhead Cumb 108 B5
Bailiesward Aberds 159 F8
Baillieston Glasgow 121 C6
Bail'lochdrach W Isles 170 E4
Bail'Ur Tholastaidh W Isles 172 D8
Bainbridge N Yorks 100 E4
Bainsford Falk 133 F7
Bainshole Aberds 160 E3
Bainton E Yorks 97 D5
Bainton P'boro 65 D7
Bairnkine Borders 116 C2
Baker Street Thurrock 42 F2
Baker's End Herts 41 C6
Bakewell Derbys 76 C2
Bala = Y Bala Gwyn 72 F3
Balachuirn Highld 153 E6
Balavil Highld 148 D3
Balbeg Highld 147 B7
Balbeg Highld 157 F5
Balbeggie Perth 134 B3
Balbithan Aberds 151 C6
Balbithan Ho. Aberds 151 C7
Balblair Highld 157 C8
Balblair Highld 164 E2
Balby S Yorks 89 D6
Balchladich Highld 166 F2
Balchraggan Highld 157 F6
Balchraggan Highld 157 E6
Balchrick Highld 166 D3
Balchrystie Fife 135 D6
Balcladaich Highld 147 B5
Balcombe W Sus 28 F4
Balcombe Lane W Sus 28 F4
Balcomie Fife 135 C8
Balcurvie Fife 134 D5
Baldersby N Yorks 95 B6
Baldersby St James N Yorks 95 B6
Balderstone Lancs 93 F6
Balderton Ches 73 C7
Balderton Notts 77 D8
Baldhu Corn 3 B6
Baldinnie Fife 135 C6
Baldock Herts 54 F3
Baldovie Dundee 142 F4
Baldrine I o M 84 D4
Baldslow E Sus 18 D4
Baldwin I o M 84 D3
Baldwinholme Cumb 108 D3
Baldwin's Gate Staffs 74 E4
Bale Norf 81 D6
Balearn Aberds 161 C7
Balemartine Argyll 136 F1
Balephuil Argyll 136 F1
Balerno Edin 122 C4
Balevullin Argyll 136 F1
Balfield Angus 143 C5
Balfour Orkney 176 E3
Balfron Stirl 132 F4
Balfron Station Stirl 132 F4
Balgaveny Aberds 160 D3
Balgavies Angus 143 D5
Balgonar Fife 134 E2
Balgove Aberds 160 E5
Balgowan Highld 148 E2
Balgown Highld 152 C4
Balgrochan E Dunb 121 B6
Balgy Highld 155 E4
Balhaldie Stirl 133 D7
Balhalgardy Aberds 151 B6
Balham London 28 B3
Balhary Perth 142 E2
Baliasta Shetland 174 C8
Baligill Highld 168 C3
Balintore Angus 142 D2
Balintore Highld 158 B2
Balintraid Highld 157 B8
Balk N Yorks 102 F2
Balkeerie Angus 142 E3
Balkemback Angus 142 F3
Balkholme E Yorks 89 B8
Balkissock S Ayrs 104 A5
Ball Shrops 60 B3
Ball Haye Green Staffs 75 D6
Ball Hill Hants 26 C2
Ballabeg I o M 84 E2
Ballacannel I o M 84 D4
Ballachulish Highld 138 D4
Ballajora I o M 84 C4
Ballaleigh I o M 84 D3
Ballamodha I o M 84 E2
Ballantrae S Ayrs 104 A4
Ballaquine I o M 84 D4
Ballards Gore Essex 43 E5
Ballasalla I o M 84 C3
Ballasalla I o M 84 E2
Ballater Aberds 150 E2
Ballaugh I o M 84 C3
Ballaveare I o M 84 E3
Ballcorach Moray 149 B7
Ballechin Perth 141 D6
Balleigh Highld 164 F4
Ballencrieff E Loth 123 B7
Ballentoul Perth 141 C5
Ballidon Derbys 76 D2
Balliemore Argyll 129 B5
Balliemore Argyll 130 C4
Ballikinrain Stirl 132 F4
Ballimeanoch Argyll 131 D6
Ballimore Argyll 128 B4
Ballimore Stirl 132 C4
Ballinaby Argyll 126 C2
Ballindean Perth 134 B4
Ballingdon Suff 56 E2
Ballinger Common Bucks 40 D2
Ballingham Hereford 49 F7
Ballingry Fife 134 E3
Ballinlick Perth 141 E6
Ballinluig Perth 141 D6
Ballintuim Perth 141 D8
Balloch Angus 142 D3
Balloch Highld 157 E8
Balloch N Lnrk 121 B7
Balloch W Dunb 132 F2
Ballochan Aberds 150 E4
Ballochford Moray 159 F7
Ballochmorrie S Ayrs 112 F2
Balls Cross W Sus 16 B3
Balls Green Essex 43 B6
Ballygown Argyll 137 D5
Ballygrant Argyll 126 C3
Ballyhaugh Argyll 136 C2
Balmacara Highld 155 H4
Balmacara Square Highld 155 H4
Balmaclellan Dumfries 106 B3
Balmacneil Perth 141 D6
Balmacqueen Highld 152 B5
Balmae Dumfries 106 E3
Balmaha Stirl 132 E3
Balmalcolm Fife 134 D5
Balmeanach Highld 153 E6
Balmedie Aberds 151 C8
Balmer Heath Shrops 73 F8
Balmerino Fife 135 B5
Balmerlawn Hants 14 D4
Balmichael N Ayrs 119 C6
Balmirmer Angus 143 F5
Balmoral Castle and Gardens Aberds 149 E8
Balmore Highld 153 E3
Balmore Highld 156 F4
Balmore Highld 158 E2
Balmore Perth 141 D6
Balmule Fife 134 F4
Balmullo Fife 135 B6
Balmungie Highld 157 D8
Balnaboth Angus 142 C3
Balnabruaich Highld 157 C8
Balnabruich Highld 165 B8
Balnacoil Highld 165 C5
Balnacra Highld 155 F5
Balnafoich Highld 157 F7
Balnagall Highld 165 F5
Balnaguard Perth 141 D6
Balnahard Argyll 127 C2
Balnahard Argyll 137 E5
Balnain Highld 157 F5
Balnakeil Highld 167 C5
Balnaknock Highld 152 C5
Balnapaling Highld 157 C8
Balne N Yorks 89 C6
Balochroy Argyll 128 E2
Balone Fife 135 C6
Balornock Glasgow 121 C6
Balquharn Perth 141 F7
Balquhidder Stirl 132 B4
Balsall W Mid 51 B7
Balsall Common W Mid 51 B7
Balsall Heath W Mid 62 F4
Balscott Oxon 51 E8
Balsham Cambs 55 D6
Baltasound Shetland 174 C8

Balterley Staffs 74 D4
Baltersan Dumfries 105 C8
Balthangie Aberds 160 C5
Baltonsborough Som 23 F7
Balvaird Highld 157 D6
Balvicar Argyll 130 D3
Balvraid Highld 145 B8
Balvraid Highld 158 F2
Bamber Bridge Lancs 86 B3
Bambers Green Essex 42 B1
Bamburgh Northumb 125 F7
Bamburgh Castle Northumb 125 F7
Bamff Perth 142 D2
Bamford Derbys 88 F3
Bamford Gtr Man 87 C6
Bampton Cumb 99 C7
Bampton Devon 10 B4
Bampton Oxon 38 D3
Bampton Grange Cumb 99 C7
Banavie Highld 139 B5
Banbury Oxon 52 E2
Bancffosfelen Carms 33 C5
Banchory Aberds 151 E5
Banchory-Devenick Aberds 151 D8
Bancycapel Carms 33 C5
Bancyfelin Carms 32 C4
Bancyffordd Carms 46 F3
Bandirran Perth 142 F2
Banff Aberds 160 B3
Bangor Gwyn 83 D5
Bangor-is-y-coed Wrex 73 E7
Bangor on Dee Racecourse Wrex 73 E7
Banham Norf 68 F3
Banham Zoo, Diss Norf 68 F3
Bank Hants 14 D3
Bank Newton N Yorks 94 D2
Bank Street Worcs 49 C8
Bankend Dumfries 107 C7
Bankfoot Perth 141 F7
Bankglen E Ayrs 113 C6
Bankhead Aberdeen 151 C7
Bankhead Aberds 151 D5
Banknock Falk 121 B7
Banks Cumb 109 C5
Banks Lancs 85 B4
Bankshill Dumfries 114 F4
Banningham Norf 81 E8
Banniskirk Ho. Highld 169 D6
Bannister Green Essex 42 B2
Bannockburn Stirl 133 E7
Banstead Sur 28 D3
Bantham Devon 6 E4
Banton N Lnrk 121 B7
Banwell N Som 23 D5
Banyard's Green Suff 57 B6
Bapchild Kent 30 C3
Bar Hill Cambs 54 C4
Barabhas W Isles 172 D6
Barabhas Iarach W Isles 172 D6
Barabhas Uarach W Isles 172 C6
Barachandroman Argyll 130 C2
Barassie S Ayrs 120 F3
Baravullin Argyll 130 B4
Barbaraville Highld 157 B8
Barber Booth Derbys 88 F2
Barbieston S Ayrs 112 C4
Barbon Cumb 99 F8
Barbridge Ches 74 D3
Barbrook Devon 21 E6
Barby Northants 52 B3
Barcaldine Argyll 138 E3
Barcaldine Sea Life Centre Argyll 130 A5
Barcheston Warks 51 F7
Barcombe E Sus 17 C8
Barcombe Cross E Sus 17 C8
Barden N Yorks 101 E6
Barden Scale N Yorks 94 D3
Bardennoch Dumfries 113 E5
Bardfield Saling Essex 42 B2
Bardister Shetland 174 F5
Bardney Lincs 78 C4
Bardon Leics 63 C8
Bardon Mill Northumb 109 C7
Bardowie E Dunb 121 B5
Bardrainney Invclyd 120 B3
Bardsea Cumb 92 B3
Bardsey W Yorks 95 E6
Bardwell Suff 56 B3
Bare Lancs 92 C4
Barfad Argyll 128 D3
Barford Norf 68 D4
Barford Warks 51 C7
Barford St John Oxon 52 F2
Barford St Martin Wilts 25 F5
Barford St Michael Oxon 52 F2
Barfreston Kent 31 D6
Bargod = Bargoed Caerph 35 E5
Bargoed = Bargod Caerph 35 E5
Bargrennan Dumfries 105 B7
Barham Cambs 54 B2
Barham Kent 31 D6
Barham Suff 56 D5
Barharrow Dumfries 106 D3
Barhill Dumfries 106 C5
Barholm Lincs 65 C7
Barkby Leics 64 D3
Barkestone-le-Vale Leics 77 F7
Barkham Wokingham 27 C5
Barking London 41 F7
Barking Suff 56 D4
Barking Tye Suff 56 D4
Barkingside London 41 F7
Barkisland W Yorks 87 C8
Barkston Lincs 78 E2
Barkston N Yorks 95 F7
Barkway Herts 54 F4
Barlaston Staffs 75 F5
Barlavington W Sus 16 C3
Barlborough Derbys 76 B4
Barlby N Yorks 96 F2
Barlestone Leics 63 D8
Barley Herts 54 F4
Barley Lancs 93 E8
Barley Mow T & W 111 D5
Barleythorpe Rutland 64 D5
Barling Essex 43 F5
Barlow Derbys 76 B3
Barlow N Yorks 89 B7
Barlow T & W 110 C4
Barmby Moor E Yorks 96 E3
Barmby on the Marsh E Yorks 89 B7
Barmer Norf 80 D4
Barmoor Castle Northumb 125 F5
Barmoor Lane End Northumb 125 F6
Barmouth = Abermaw Gwyn 58 C3
Barmpton Darl 101 C8
Barmston E Yorks 97 D7
Barnack P'boro 65 D7
Barnacle Warks 63 F7
Barnard Castle Durham 101 C5
Barnard Gate Oxon 38 C4
Barnardiston Suff 55 E8
Barnbarroch Dumfries 106 D5
Barnburgh S Yorks 89 D5
Barnby Suff 69 F7
Barnby Dun S Yorks 89 D7
Barnby in the Willows Notts 77 D8
Barnby Moor Notts 89 F7
Barnes Street Kent 29 E7
Barnet London 41 E5
Barnetby le Wold N Lincs 90 D4
Barney Norf 81 D5
Barnham Suff 56 B2
Barnham W Sus 16 D3
Barnham Broom Norf 68 D3
Barnhead Angus 143 D6
Barnhill Ches 73 D8
Barnhill Dundee 142 F4
Barnhill Moray 158 D5
Barnhills Dumfries 104 B3
Barningham Durham 101 C5
Barningham Suff 56 B3
Barnoldby le Beck NE Lincs 91 D6
Barnoldswick Lancs 93 E8
Barns Green W Sus 16 B5
Barnsley Glos 37 D7
Barnsley S Yorks 88 D4
Barnstaple Devon 20 F4
Barnston Essex 42 C2
Barnston Mers 85 F3
Barnstone Notts 77 F7
Barnt Green Worcs 50 B5
Barnton Ches 74 B3
Barnton Edin 122 B4
Barnwell All Saints Northants 65 F7
Barnwell St Andrew Northants 65 F7
Barnwood Glos 37 C5
Barochreal Argyll 130 C4
Barons Cross Hereford 49 D6
Barr S Ayrs 112 E2
Barra Airport W Isles 171 K2
Barra Castle Aberds 151 B6
Barrachan Dumfries 105 E7
Barrack Aberds 161 D5
Barraglom W Isles 172 E4
Barrahormid Argyll 128 B2
Barran Argyll 130 C4
Barrapol Argyll 136 F1
Barras Aberds 151 F7
Barras Cumb 100 C3
Barrasford Northumb 110 B2
Barravullin Argyll 130 E4
Barregarrow I o M 84 D3
Barrhead E Renf 120 D4
Barrhill S Ayrs 112 F2
Barrington Cambs 54 E4
Barrington Som 11 C8
Barripper Corn 2 C5
Barrmill N Ayrs 120 D3
Barrock Highld 169 B7
Barrock Ho. Highld 169 C7
Barrow Lancs 93 F7
Barrow Rutland 65 C5
Barrow Suff 55 C8
Barrow Green Kent 30 C3
Barrow Gurney N Som 23 C7
Barrow Haven N Lincs 90 B4
Barrow-in-Furness Cumb 92 C2
Barrow Island Cumb 92 C1
Barrow Nook Lancs 86 D2
Barrow Street Wilts 24 F3
Barrow upon Humber N Lincs 90 B4
Barrow upon Soar Leics 64 C2
Barrow upon Trent Derbys 63 B7
Barroway Drove Norf 67 D5
Barrowburn Northumb 116 C4
Barrowby Lincs 77 F8
Barrowcliff N Yorks 103 F8
Barrowden Rutland 65 D6
Barrowford Lancs 93 F8
Barrows Green Ches 74 D3
Barrows Green Cumb 99 F7
Barrow's Green Mers 86 F3
Barry Angus 143 F5
Barry = Y Barri V Glam 22 C3
Barry Island V Glam 22 C3
Barsby Leics 64 C3
Barsham Suff 69 F6
Barston W Mid 51 B7
Bartestree Hereford 49 E7
Barthol Chapel Aberds 160 E5
Barthomley Ches 74 D4
Bartley Hants 14 C4
Bartley Green W Mid 62 F4
Bartlow Cambs 55 E6
Barton Cambs 54 D5
Barton Ches 73 D8
Barton Glos 37 B8
Barton Lancs 85 D4
Barton Lancs 92 F5
Barton N Yorks 101 D7
Barton Oxon 39 D5
Barton Torbay 7 C7
Barton Warks 51 D6
Barton Bendish Norf 67 D7
Barton Hartshorn Bucks 52 F4
Barton in Fabis Notts 76 F5
Barton in the Beans Leics 63 D7
Barton-le-Clay Beds 53 F8
Barton-le-Street N Yorks 96 B3
Barton-le-Willows N Yorks 96 C3
Barton Mills Suff 55 B8
Barton on Sea Hants 14 E3
Barton on the Heath Warks 51 F7
Barton St David Som 23 F7
Barton Seagrave Northants 53 B6
Barton Stacey Hants 26 E2
Barton Turf Norf 69 B6
Barton-under-Needwood Staffs 63 C5
Barton-upon-Humber N Lincs 90 B4
Barton Waterside N Lincs 90 B4
Barugh S Yorks 88 D4
Barway Cambs 55 B6
Barwell Leics 63 E8
Barwick Herts 41 C6
Barwick Som 12 C3
Barwick in Elmet W Yorks 95 F6
Baschurch Shrops 60 B4
Bascote Warks 52 C2
Basford Green Staffs 75 D6
Bashall Eaves Lancs 93 E6
Bashley Hants 14 E3
Basildon Essex 42 F3
Basingstoke Hants 26 D4
Baslow Derbys 76 B2
Bason Bridge Som 22 E5
Bassaleg Newport 35 F6
Bassenthwaite Cumb 108 F2
Bassett Soton 14 C5
Bassingbourn Cambs 54 E4
Bassingfield Notts 77 F6
Bassingham Lincs 78 C2
Bassingthorpe Lincs 65 B6
Basta Shetland 174 D7
Baston Lincs 65 C8
Bastwick Norf 69 C7
Baswick Steer E Yorks 97 E6
Batchworth Heath Herts 40 E3
Batcombe Dorset 12 D4
Batcombe Som 23 F8
Bate Heath Ches 74 B3
Bateman's, Burwash E Sus 18 C3
Batford Herts 40 C4
Bath Bath 24 C2
Bath Abbey Bath 24 C2
Bath Racecourse Bath 24 C2
Bathampton Bath 24 C2
Bathealton Som 11 B5
Batheaston Bath 24 C2
Bathford Bath 24 C2
Bathgate W Loth 122 C2
Bathley Notts 77 D7
Bathpool Corn 5 B7
Bathpool Som 11 B7
Bathville W Loth 122 C2
Batley W Yorks 88 B3
Batsford Glos 51 F6
Battersby N Yorks 102 D3
Battersea London 28 B3
Battisborough Cross Devon 6 E3
Battisford Suff 56 D4
Battisford Tye Suff 56 D4
Battle E Sus 18 D4
Battle Powys 48 F2
Battle Abbey E Sus 18 D4
Battledown Glos 37 B6
Battlefield Shrops 60 C5
Battlesbridge Essex 42 E3
Battlesden Beds 40 B2
Battlesea Green Suff 57 B6
Battleton Som 10 B4
Battram Leics 63 D8
Battramsley Hants 14 E4
Baughton Worcs 50 E3
Baughurst Hants 26 D3
Baulking Oxon 38 E3
Baumber Lincs 78 B5
Baunton Glos 37 D7
Baverstock Wilts 24 F5
Bawburgh Norf 68 D4
Bawdeswell Norf 81 E6
Bawdrip Som 22 F5
Bawdsey Suff 57 E7
Bawtry S Yorks 89 E7
Baxenden Lancs 87 B5
Baxterley Warks 63 E6
Baybridge Hants 15 B6
Baycliff Cumb 92 B2
Baydon Wilts 25 B7
Bayford Herts 41 D6
Bayford Som 12 B5
Bayles Cumb 109 E7
Baylham Suff 56 D5
Baynard's Green Oxon 39 B5
Bayston Hill Shrops 60 D4
Baythorn End Essex 55 E8
Bayton Worcs 49 B8
Beach Highld 138 D1
Beachampton Bucks 53 F5
Beachamwell Norf 67 D7
Beachans Moray 158 E4
Beacharr Argyll 118 B3
Beachborough Kent 19 B8
Beachley Glos 36 E2
Beacon Devon 11 D6
Beacon End Essex 43 B5
Beacon Hill Sur 27 F6
Beacon's Bottom Bucks 39 E7
Beaconsfield Bucks 40 F2
Beacrabhaic W Isles 173 J4
Beadlam N Yorks 102 F4
Beadlow Beds 54 F2
Beadnell Northumb 117 B8
Beaford Devon 9 C7
Beal Northumb 125 E6
Beal N Yorks 89 B6
Beale Park, Goring W Berks 26 B4
Beamhurst Staffs 75 F7
Beaminster Dorset 12 D2
Beamish Durham 110 D5
Beamish Open Air Museum, Stanley Durham 110 D5
Beamsley N Yorks 94 D3
Bean Kent 29 B6
Beanacre Wilts 24 C4
Beanley Northumb 117 C6
Beaquoy Orkney 176 D2
Bear Cross Bmouth 13 E8
Beardwood Blkburn 86 B4
Beare Green Sur 28 E2
Bearley Warks 51 C6
Bearnus Argyll 136 D4
Bearpark Durham 110 E5
Bearsbridge Northumb 109 D7
Bearsden E Dunb 120 B5
Bearsted Kent 29 D8
Bearstone Shrops 74 F4
Bearwood Hereford 49 D5
Bearwood Poole 13 E8
Bearwood W Mid 62 F4
Beattock Dumfries 114 D3
Beauchamp Roding Essex 42 C1
Beauchief S Yorks 88 F4
Beaufort Bl Gwent 35 C5
Beaufort Castle Highld 157 E6
Beaulieu Hants 14 D4
Beauly Highld 157 E6
Beaumaris Anglesey 83 D6
Beaumaris Castle Anglesey 83 D6
Beaumont Cumb 108 D3
Beaumont Essex 43 B7
Beaumont Hill Darl 101 C7
Beausale Warks 51 B7
Beauworth Hants 15 B6
Beaworthy Devon 9 E6
Beazley End Essex 42 B3
Bebington Mers 85 F4
Bebside Northumb 117 F8
Beccles Suff 69 E7
Becconsall Lancs 86 B2
Beck Foot Cumb 99 E8
Beck Hole N Yorks 103 D6
Beck Row Suff 55 B7
Beck Side Cumb 98 F4
Beckbury Shrops 61 D7
Beckenham London 28 C4
Beckermet Cumb 98 D2
Beckfoot Cumb 98 D3
Beckfoot Cumb 107 E7
Beckford Worcs 50 F4
Beckhampton Wilts 25 C5
Beckingham Lincs 77 D8
Beckingham Notts 89 F8
Beckington Som 24 D3
Beckley E Sus 19 C5
Beckley Hants 14 E3
Beckley Oxon 39 C5
Beckton London 41 F7
Beckwithshaw N Yorks 95 D5
Becontree London 41 F7
Bed-y-coedwr Gwyn 71 E8
Bedale N Yorks 101 F7
Bedburn Durham 110 F4
Bedchester Dorset 13 C6
Beddau Rhondda 34 F4
Beddgelert Gwyn 71 C6
Beddingham E Sus 17 D8
Beddington London 28 C4
Bedfield Suff 57 C6
Bedford Beds 53 D8
Bedham W Sus 16 B4
Bedhampton Hants 15 D8
Bedingfield Suff 57 C5
Bedlam N Yorks 95 C5
Bedlington Northumb 117 F8
Bedlington Station Northumb 117 F8
Bedlinog M Tydf 34 D4
Bedminster Bristol 23 B7
Bedmond Herts 40 D3
Bednall Staffs 62 C3
Bedrule Borders 116 C2
Bedstone Shrops 49 B5
Bedwas Caerph 35 F5
Bedworth Warks 63 F7
Bedworth Heath Warks 63 F7
Beeby Leics 64 D3
Beech Hants 26 F4
Beech Staffs 75 F5
Beech Hill Gtr Man 86 D3
Beech Hill W Berks 26 C4
Beechingstoke Wilts 25 D5
Beedon W Berks 26 B2
Beeford E Yorks 97 D7
Beeley Derbys 76 C2
Beelsby NE Lincs 91 D6
Beenham W Berks 26 C3
Beeny Corn 8 E3
Beer Devon 11 F7
Beer Hackett Dorset 12 C3
Beercrocombe Som 11 B8
Beesands Devon 7 E6
Beesby Lincs 91 F8
Beeson Devon 7 E6
Beeston Beds 54 E2
Beeston Ches 74 D2
Beeston Norf 68 C2
Beeston Notts 76 F5
Beeston W Yorks 95 F5
Beeston Castle Ches 74 D2
Beeston Regis Norf 81 C7
Beeswing Dumfries 107 C5
Beetham Cumb 92 B4
Beetley Norf 68 C2
Begbroke Oxon 38 C4
Begelly Pembs 32 D2
Beggar's Bush Powys 48 C4
Beguildy Powys 48 B3
Beighton Norf 69 D6
Beighton S Yorks 88 F5
Beighton Hill Derbys 76 D2
Beith N Ayrs 120 D3
Bekesbourne Kent 31 D5
Bekonscot Model Village, Beaconsfield Bucks 40 C2
Belaugh Norf 69 C5
Belbroughton Worcs 50 B4
Belchamp Otten Essex 56 E2
Belchamp St Paul Essex 55 E8
Belchamp Walter Essex 56 E2
Belchford Lincs 79 B5
Belford Northumb 125 F7
Belhaven E Loth 124 B2
Belhelvie Aberds 151 C8
Belhinnie Aberds 150 B3
Bell Bar Herts 41 D5
Bell Busk N Yorks 94 D2
Bell End Worcs 50 B4
Bell o'th'Hill Ches 74 E2
Bellabeg Aberds 150 C2
Bellamore S Ayrs 112 F2
Bellanoch Argyll 128 A2
Bellaty Angus 142 D2
Belleau Lincs 79 B7
Bellehiglash Moray 159 F5
Bellerby N Yorks 101 E6
Bellever Devon 6 B4
Belliehill Angus 143 C5
Bellingdon Bucks 40 D2
Bellingham Northumb 116 F4
Belloch Argyll 118 C3
Bellochantuy Argyll 118 C3
Bells Yew Green E Sus 18 B3
Bellsbank E Ayrs 112 D4
Bellshill N Lnrk 121 C7
Bellshill Northumb 125 F7
Bellspool Borders 122 F4
Bellsquarry W Loth 122 C3
Belmaduthy Highld 157 D7
Belmesthorpe Rutland 65 C7
Belmont Blkburn 86 C4
Belmont London 28 C3
Belmont S Ayrs 112 B3
Belmont Shetland 174 C7
Belnacraig Aberds 150 C2
Belowda Corn 4 C4
Belper Derbys 76 E3
Belper Lane End Derbys 76 E3
Belsay Northumb 110 B4
Belsay Hall Northumb 110 B3
Belses Borders 115 B8
Belsford Devon 7 D5
Belstead Suff 56 E5
Belston S Ayrs 112 B3
Belstone Devon 9 E8
Belthorn Lancs 86 B5
Beltinge Kent 31 C5
Beltoft N Lincs 90 D2
Belton Leics 63 B8
Belton Lincs 78 F2
Belton N Lincs 89 D8
Belton Norf 69 D7
Belton House, Grantham Lincs 78 F2
Belton in Rutland Rutland 64 D5
Beltring Kent 29 E7
Belts of Collonach Aberds 151 E5
Belvedere London 29 B5
Belvoir Leics 77 F8
Belvoir Castle Leics 77 F8
Bembridge I o W 15 F7
Bemersyde Borders 123 F8
Bemerton Wilts 25 F6
Bempton E Yorks 97 B7
Ben Alder Lodge Highld 140 B2
Ben Armine Lodge Highld 164 C4
Ben Casgro W Isles 172 F7
Benacre Suff 69 F8
Benbecula Airport W Isles 170 E3
Benbuie Dumfries 113 E7
Benderloch Argyll 130 B5
Bendronaig Lodge Highld 155 G6
Benenden Kent 18 B5
Benfield Dumfries 105 C7
Bengate Norf 69 B6
Bengeworth Worcs 50 E5
Benhall Green Suff 57 C7
Benhall Street Suff 57 C7
Benholm Aberds 143 C8
Beningbrough N Yorks 95 D8
Beningbrough Hall N Yorks 95 D8
Benington Herts 41 B5
Benington Lincs 79 E6
Benllech Anglesey 82 C5
Benmore Argyll 129 B6
Benmore Stirl 132 B3
Benmore Lodge Highld 163 C7
Bennacott Corn 8 E4
Bennan N Ayrs 119 D6
Benniworth Lincs 91 F6
Benover Kent 29 E8
Bensham T & W 110 C5
Benslie N Ayrs 120 E3
Benson Oxon 39 E6
Bent Aberds 143 B6
Bent Gate Lancs 87 B5
Benthall Northumb 117 B8
Benthall Shrops 61 D6
Bentham Glos 37 C6
Benthoul Aberdeen 151 D7
Bentlawnt Shrops 60 D3
Bentley E Yorks 97 F6
Bentley Hants 27 E5
Bentley Suff 56 F5
Bentley S Yorks 89 D6
Bentley Warks 63 E6
Bentley Worcs 50 C4
Bentley Heath W Mid 51 B6
Benton Devon 21 F5
Bentpath Dumfries 115 E6
Bents W Loth 122 C2
Bentworth Hants 26 E4
Benvie Dundee 142 F3
Benwick Cambs 66 E3
Beoley Worcs 51 C5
Beoraidbeg Highld 145 D6
Bepton W Sus 16 C2
Berden Essex 41 B7
Bere Alston Devon 6 C2
Bere Ferrers Devon 6 C2
Bere Regis Dorset 13 E6
Berepper Corn 3 D5
Bergh Apton Norf 69 D6
Berinsfield Oxon 39 E5
Berkeley Glos 36 E3
Berkhamsted Herts 40 D2
Berkley Som 24 E3
Berkswell W Mid 51 B7
Bermondsey London 28 B4
Bernera Highld 155 H4
Bernice Argyll 129 A6
Bernisdale Highld 152 D5
Berrick Salome Oxon 39 E6
Berriedale Highld 165 B8
Berrier Cumb 99 B5
Berriew Powys 59 D8
Berrington Northumb 125 E6
Berrington Shrops 60 D5
Berrow Som 22 D5
Berrow Green Worcs 50 D2
Berry Down Cross Devon 20 E4
Berry Hill Glos 36 C2
Berry Hill Pembs 45 E2
Berry Pomeroy Devon 7 C6
Berryhillock Moray 160 B2
Berrynarbor Devon 20 E4
Bersham Wrex 73 E7
Berstane Orkney 176 E3
Berwick E Sus 18 E2
Berwick Bassett Wilts 25 B5
Berwick Hill Northumb 110 B4
Berwick St James Wilts 25 F5
Berwick St John Wilts 13 B7
Berwick St Leonard Wilts 24 F4
Berwick-upon-Tweed Northumb 125 D5
Bescar Lancs 85 C4
Besford Worcs 50 E4
Bessacarr S Yorks 89 D7
Bessels Leigh Oxon 38 D4
Bessingby E Yorks 97 C7
Bessingham Norf 81 D7
Bestbeech Hill E Sus 18 B3
Besthorpe Norf 68 E3
Besthorpe Notts 77 C8
Bestwood Nottingham 77 E5
Bestwood Village Notts 77 E5
Beswick E Yorks 97 E6
Betchworth Sur 28 E3
Beth Shalom Holocaust Centre, Laxton Notts 77 C7
Bethania Ceredig 46 C4
Bethania Gwyn 83 F6
Bethania Gwyn 71 C8
Bethel Anglesey 82 D3
Bethel Gwyn 82 E5
Bethel Gwyn 72 F3
Bethersden Kent 30 E3
Bethesda Gwyn 83 E6
Bethesda Pembs 32 C1
Bethlehem Carms 33 B7
Bethnal Green London 41 F6
Betley Staffs 74 E4
Betsham Kent 29 B7
Betteshanger Kent 31 D7
Bettiscombe Dorset 11 E8
Bettisfield Wrex 73 F8
Betton Shrops 60 D3
Betton Shrops 74 F3
Bettws Bridgend 34 F3
Bettws Newport 35 E6
Bettws Cedewain Powys 59 E8
Bettws Gwerfil Goch Denb 72 E4
Bettws Ifan Ceredig 46 E2
Bettws Newydd Mon 35 D7
Bettws-y-crwyn Shrops 60 F2
Bettyhill Highld 168 C2
Betws Carms 33 C7
Betws Bledrws Ceredig 46 D4
Betws-Garmon Gwyn 82 F5
Betws-y-Coed Conwy 83 F7
Betws-yn-Rhos Conwy 72 B3
Beulah Ceredig 45 E4
Beulah Powys 47 D8
Bevendean Brighton 17 D7
Bevercotes Notts 77 B6
Beverley E Yorks 97 F6
Beverley Minster E Yorks 97 F6
Beverley Racecourse E Yorks 97 E6
Beverston Glos 37 E5
Bevington Glos 36 E3
Bewaldeth Cumb 108 F2
Bewcastle Cumb 109 B5
Bewdley Worcs 50 B2
Bewerley N Yorks 94 C4
Bewholme E Yorks 97 D7
Bexhill E Sus 18 E4
Bexley London 29 B5
Bexleyheath London 29 B5
Bexwell Norf 67 D6
Beyton Suff 56 C3
Bhaltos W Isles 172 E3
Bhatarsaigh W Isles 171 L2
Bibury Glos 37 D8
Bicester Oxon 39 B5
Bickenhall Som 11 C7
Bickenhill W Mid 63 F5
Bicker Lincs 78 F5
Bickershaw Gtr Man 86 D4
Bickerstaffe Lancs 86 D2
Bickerton Ches 74 D2
Bickerton N Yorks 95 D7
Bickington Devon 7 B5
Bickington Devon 20 F4
Bickleigh Devon 10 D4
Bickleigh Devon 6 C3
Bickleton Devon 20 F4
Bickley London 28 C5
Bickley Moss Ches 74 E2
Bicknacre Essex 42 D3
Bicknoller Som 22 F3
Bicknor Kent 30 D2
Bickton Hants 14 C2
Bicton Shrops 60 C4
Bicton Shrops 60 F2
Bicton Park Gardens Devon 11 F5
Bidborough Kent 29 E6
Biddenden Kent 19 B5
Biddenham Beds 53 E8
Biddestone Wilts 24 B3
Biddisham Som 23 D5
Biddlesden Bucks 52 E4
Biddlestone Northumb 117 D5
Biddulph Staffs 75 D5
Biddulph Moor Staffs 75 D6
Bideford Devon 9 B6
Bidford-on-Avon Warks 51 D6
Bidston Mers 85 E3
Bielby E Yorks 96 E3
Bieldside Aberdeen 151 D7
Bierley I o W 15 G6
Bierley W Yorks 94 F4
Bierton Bucks 39 C8
Big Pit National Mining Museum, Blaenavon Torf 35 D6
Big Sand Highld 154 C3
Bigbury Devon 6 E4
Bigbury on Sea Devon 6 E4
Bigby Lincs 90 D4
Biggar Cumb 92 C1
Biggar S Lnrk 122 F3
Biggin Derbys 75 D8
Biggin Derbys 76 E2
Biggin N Yorks 95 F8
Biggin Hill London 28 D5
Biggings Shetland 175 G3
Biggleswade Beds 54 E2
Bighouse Highld 168 C3
Bighton Hants 26 F4
Bignor W Sus 16 C3
Bigton Shetland 175 L5
Bilberry Corn 4 C5
Bilborough Nottingham 76 E5
Bilbrook Som 22 E2
Bilbrough N Yorks 95 E8
Bilbster Highld 169 D7
Bildershaw Durham 101 B7
Bildeston Suff 56 E3
Billericay Essex 42 E2
Billesdon Leics 64 D4
Billesley Warks 51 D6
Billingborough Lincs 78 F4
Billinge Mers 86 D3
Billingford Norf 81 E6
Billingham Stockton 102 B2
Billinghay Lincs 78 D4
Billingley S Yorks 88 D5
Billingshurst W Sus 16 B4
Billingsley Shrops 61 F7
Billington Beds 40 B2
Billington Lancs 93 F7
Billockby Norf 69 C7
Billown Motor Racing Circuit I o M 84 F2
Billy Row Durham 110 F4
Bilsborrow Lancs 92 F5
Bilsby Lincs 79 B7
Bilsham W Sus 16 D3
Bilsington Kent 19 B7
Bilson Green Glos 36 C3
Bilsthorpe Notts 77 C6
Bilsthorpe Moor Notts 77 D6
Bilston Midloth 123 C5
Bilston W Mid 62 E3
Bilstone Leics 63 D7
Bilting Kent 30 E4
Bilton E Yorks 97 F7
Bilton Northumb 117 C8
Bilton Warks 52 B2
Bilton in Ainsty N Yorks 95 E7
Bimbister Orkney 176 E2
Binbrook Lincs 91 E6
Binchester Blocks Durham 110 F5
Bincombe Dorset 12 F4
Bindal Highld 165 F6
Binegar Som 23 E8
Binfield Brack 27 B6
Binfield Heath Oxon 26 B5
Bingfield Northumb 110 B2
Bingham Notts 77 F7
Bingley W Yorks 94 F4
Bings Heath Shrops 60 C5
Binham Norf 81 D5
Binley Hants 26 D2
Binley W Mid 51 B8
Binley Woods Warks 51 B8
Binniehill Falk 121 B8
Binsoe N Yorks 94 B5
Binstead I o W 15 E6
Binsted Hants 27 E5
Binton Warks 51 D6
Bintree Norf 81 E6
Binweston Shrops 60 D3
Birch Essex 43 C5
Birch Gtr Man 87 D6
Birch Green Essex 43 C5
Birch Heath Ches 74 C2
Birch Hill Ches 74 B2
Birch Vale Derbys 87 F8
Bircham Newton Norf 80 D3
Bircham Tofts Norf 80 D3
Birchanger Essex 41 B8
Birchencliffe W Yorks 88 C2
Bircher Hereford 49 C6
Birchfield Highld 149 B5
Birchgrove Cardiff 22 B3
Birchgrove Swansea 33 E8
Birchington Kent 31 C6
Birchmoor Warks 63 D6
Birchover Derbys 76 C2
Birchwood Lincs 78 C2
Birchwood Warr 86 E4
Bircotes Notts 89 E7
Birdbrook Essex 55 E8
Birdforth N Yorks 95 B7
Birdham W Sus 16 E2
Birdholme Derbys 76 C3
Birdingbury Warks 52 C2
Birdland Park, Bourton-on-the-Water Glos 38 B1
Birdlip Glos 37 C6
Birds Edge W Yorks 88 D3
Birdsall N Yorks 96 C4
Birdsgreen Shrops 61 F7
Birdsmoor Gate Dorset 11 D8
Birdston E Dunb 121 B6
Birdwell S Yorks 88 D4
Birdwood Glos 36 C4
Birdworld and Underwaterworld, Farnham Hants 27 E6
Birgham Borders 124 F3
Birkby N Yorks 101 D8
Birkdale Mers 85 C4
Birkenhead Mers 85 F4
Birkenhills Aberds 160 D4
Birkenshaw N Lnrk 121 C6
Birkenshaw W Yorks 88 B3
Birkhall Aberds 150 E2
Birkhill Angus 142 F3
Birkhill Dumfries 114 C5
Birkholme Lincs 65 B6
Birkin N Yorks 89 B6
Birley Hereford 49 D6
Birling Kent 29 C7
Birling Northumb 117 D8
Birling Gap E Sus 18 F2
Birlingham Worcs 50 E4
Birmingham W Mid 62 F4
Birmingham Botanical Gardens W Mid 62 F4
Birmingham International Airport W Mid 63 F5
Birmingham Museum and Art Gallery W Mid 62 F4
Birmingham Museum of Science and Technology W Mid 62 F4
Birnam Perth 141 E7
Birse Aberds 150 E4
Birsemore Aberds 150 E4
Birstall Leics 64 D2
Birstall W Yorks 88 B3
Birstwith N Yorks 94 D5
Birthorpe Lincs 78 F4
Birtley Hereford 49 C5
Birtley Northumb 109 B8
Birtley T & W 111 D5
Birts Street Worcs 50 F2
Bisbrooke Rutland 65 E5
Biscathorpe Lincs 91 F6
Biscot Luton 40 B3
Bish Mill Devon 10 B2
Bisham Windsor 39 F8
Bishampton Worcs 50 D4
Bishop Auckland Durham 101 B7
Bishop Burton E Yorks 97 F5
Bishop Middleham Durham 111 F6
Bishop Monkton N Yorks 95 C6
Bishop Norton Lincs 90 E3
Bishop Sutton Bath 23 D7
Bishop Thornton N Yorks 95 C5

Bratton Clovelly Devon 9 E6
Bratton Fleming Devon 20 F5
Bratton Seymour Som 12 B4
Braughing Herts 41 B6
Braunston Northants 52 C3
Braunston-in-Rutland Rutland 64 D5
Braunstone Town Leics 64 D2
Braunton Devon 20 F3
Brawby N Yorks 96 B3
Brawl Highld 168 C3
Brawlbin Highld 169 D5
Bray Windsor 27 B7
Bray Shop Corn 5 B8
Bray Wick Windsor 27 B6
Braybrooke Northants 64 F4
Braye Ald 16
Brayford Devon 21 F5
Braystones Cumb 98 D2
Braythorn N Yorks 94 E5
Brayton N Yorks 95 F9
Brazacott Corn 8 E4
Breach Kent 30 C2
Breachacha Castle Argyll 136 C2
Breachwood Green Herts 40 B4
Breacleit W Isles 172 E4
Breaden Heath Shrops 73 F8
Breadsall Derbys 76 F3
Breadstone Glos 36 D4
Breage Corn 2 D5
Breakachy Highld 157 E5
Bream Glos 36 D3
Breamore Hants 14 C2
Brean Som 22 D4
Breanais W Isles 172 F2
Brearton N Yorks 95 C6
Breascleit W Isles 172 E5
Breaston Derbys 76 F4
Brechfa Carms 46 F4
Brechin Angus 143 C5
Breck of Cruan Orkney 176 E2
Breckan Orkney 176 F1
Breckrey Highld 152 C6
Brecon = Aberhonddu Powys 34 B4
Brecon Beacons Mountain Centre Powys 34 B3
Bredbury Gtr Man 87 E7
Brede E Sus 18 D5
Bredenbury Hereford 49 D8
Bredfield Suff 57 D6
Bredgar Kent 30 C2
Bredhurst Kent 29 C8
Bredicot Worcs 50 D4
Bredon Worcs 50 F4
Bredon's Norton Worcs 50 F4
Bredwardine Hereford 48 E5
Breedon on the Hill Leics 63 B8
Breibhig W Isles 171 L2
Breibhig W Isles 172 E7
Breich W Loth 122 C2
Breightmet Gtr Man 86 D5
Breighton E Yorks 96 F3
Breinton Hereford 49 F6
Breinton Common Hereford 49 E6
Breiwick Shetland 175 J6
Bremhill Wilts 24 B4
Bremirehoull Shetland 175 L6
Brenchley Kent 29 E7
Brendon Devon 21 E6
Brenkley T & W 110 B5
Brent Eleigh Suff 56 E3
Brent Knoll Som 22 D5
Brent Pelham Herts 54 F5
Brentford London 28 B2
Brentingby Leics 64 C4
Brentwood Essex 42 E1
Brenzett Kent 19 C7
Brereton Staffs 62 C4
Brereton Green Ches 74 C4
Brereton Heath Ches 74 C5
Bressingham Norf 68 F3
Bretby Derbys 63 B6
Bretford Warks 52 B2
Bretforton Worcs 51 E5
Bretherdale Head Cumb 99 D7
Bretherton Lancs 86 B2
Brettabister Shetland 175 H6
Brettenham Norf 68 F2
Brettenham Suff 56 D3
Bretton Derbys 76 B2
Bretton Flint 73 C7
Brewer Street Sur 28 D4
Brewlands Bridge Angus 142 C1
Brewood Staffs 62 D2
Briach Moray 158 D4
Briants Puddle Dorset 13 E6
Brick End Essex 42 B1
Brickendon Herts 41 D6
Bricket Wood Herts 40 D4
Bricklehampton Worcs 50 E4
Bride I o M 84 B4
Bridekirk Cumb 107 F8
Bridell Pembs 45 E3
Bridestowe Devon 9 F7
Brideswell Aberds 160 E2
Bridford Devon 10 F3
Bridfordmills Devon 10 F3
Bridge Kent 31 D5
Bridge End Lincs 78 F4
Bridge Green Essex 55 F5
Bridge Hewick N Yorks 95 B6
Bridge of Alford Aberds 150 C4
Bridge of Allan Stirl 133 E6
Bridge of Avon Moray 159 F5
Bridge of Awe Argyll 131 C6
Bridge of Balgie Perth 140 E2
Bridge of Cally Perth 141 D8
Bridge of Canny Aberds 151 E5
Bridge of Craigisla Angus 142 D2
Bridge of Dee Dumfries 106 D4
Bridge of Don Aberdeen 151 C8
Bridge of Dun Angus 143 D6
Bridge of Dye Aberds 151 F5
Bridge of Earn Perth 134 C3
Bridge of Ericht Perth 140 D2
Bridge of Feugh Aberds 151 E6
Bridge of Forss Highld 168 C5
Bridge of Gairn Aberds 150 E2
Bridge of Gaur Perth 140 D2
Bridge of Muchalls Aberds 151 E7
Bridge of Oich Highld 147 D6
Bridge of Orchy Argyll 131 B8
Bridge of Waith Orkney 176 E1
Bridge of Walls Shetland 175 H4
Bridge of Weir Renfs 120 C3
Bridge Sollers Hereford 49 E6
Bridge Street Suff 56 E2
Bridge Trafford Ches 73 B8
Bridge Yate S Glos 23 B8
Bridgefoot Angus 142 F3
Bridgefoot Cumb 98 B2
Bridgehampton Som 12 B3
Bridgehill Durham 110 D3
Bridgemary Hants 15 D6
Bridgemont Derbys 87 F8
Bridgend Aberds 160 E2
Bridgend Aberds 150 C4
Bridgend Angus 143 C5
Bridgend Argyll 128 A3
Bridgend Argyll 126 C3
Bridgend Argyll 118 C4
Bridgend Cumb 99 C5
Bridgend Fife 135 C5
Bridgend Moray 159 F7
Bridgend N Lnrk 121 B6
Bridgend Pembs 45 E3
Bridgend W Loth 122 B3
Bridgend = Pen-y-bont ar Ogwr Bridgend 21 B8
Bridgend of Lintrathen Angus 142 D2
Bridgerule Devon 8 D4
Bridges Shrops 60 E3
Bridgeton Glasgow 121 C6
Bridgetown Corn 8 F5
Bridgetown Som 21 F8
Bridgham Norf 68 F2
Bridgnorth Shrops 61 E7
Bridgnorth Cliff Railway Shrops 61 E7
Bridgtown Staffs 62 D3
Bridgwater Som 22 F5
Bridlington E Yorks 97 C7
Bridport Dorset 12 E2
Bridstow Hereford 36 B2
Brierfield Lancs 93 F8
Brierley Glos 36 C3
Brierley Hereford 49 D6
Brierley S Yorks 88 C5
Brierley Hill W Mid 62 F3
Briery Hill Bl Gwent 35 D5
Brig o'Turk Stirl 132 D4
Brigg N Lincs 90 D4
Briggswath N Yorks 103 D6
Brigham Cumb 107 F7
Brigham E Yorks 97 D6
Brighouse W Yorks 88 B2
Brighstone I o W 14 F5
Brightgate Derbys 76 D2
Brighthampton Oxon 38 D3
Brightling E Sus 18 C3
Brightlingsea Essex 43 C6
Brighton Brighton 17 D7
Brighton Corn 4 D4
Brighton Hill Hants 26 E4
Brighton Museum and Art Gallery Brighton 17 D7
Brighton Racecourse Brighton 17 D7
Brighton Sea Life Centre Brighton 17 D7
Brightons Falk 122 B2
Brightwalton W Berks 26 B2
Brightwell Suff 57 E6
Brightwell Baldwin Oxon 39 E6
Brightwell cum Sotwell Oxon 39 E5
Brignall Durham 101 C5
Brigsley NE Lincs 91 D6
Brigsteer Cumb 99 F6
Brigstock Northants 65 F6
Brill Bucks 39 C6
Brilley Hereford 48 E4
Brimaston Pembs 44 C4
Brimfield Hereford 49 C7
Brimington Derbys 76 B4
Brimley Devon 7 B5
Brimpsfield Glos 37 C6
Brimpton W Berks 26 C3
Brims Orkney 176 H1
Brimscombe Glos 37 D5
Brimstage Mers 85 F4
Brinacory Highld 145 D7
Brind E Yorks 96 F3
Brindister Shetland 175 H4
Brindister Shetland 175 K6
Brindle Lancs 86 B4
Brindley Ford Staffs 75 D5
Brineton Staffs 62 C2
Bringhurst Leics 64 E5
Brington Cambs 53 B8
Brinian Orkney 176 D3
Briningham Norf 81 D6
Brinkhill Lincs 79 B6
Brinkley Cambs 55 D7
Brinklow Warks 52 B2
Brinkworth Wilts 37 F7
Brinmore Highld 148 B2
Brinscall Lancs 86 B4
Brinsea N Som 23 C6
Brinsley Notts 76 E4
Brinsop Hereford 49 E6
Brinsworth S Yorks 88 F5
Brinton Norf 81 D6
Brisco Cumb 108 D4
Brisley Norf 81 E5
Brislington Bristol 23 B8
Bristol Bristol 23 B7
Bristol City Museum and Art Gallery Bristol 23 B7
Bristol International Airport N Som 23 C7
Bristol Zoo Bristol 23 B7
Briston Norf 81 D6
Britannia Lancs 87 B6
Britford Wilts 14 B2
Brithdir Gwyn 58 C4
British Legion Village Kent 29 D8
British Museum London 41 F5
Briton Ferry Neath 33 E8
Britwell Salome Oxon 39 E6
Brixham Torbay 7 D7
Brixton Devon 6 D3
Brixton London 28 B4
Brixton Deverill Wilts 24 F3
Brixworth Northants 52 B5
Brize Norton Oxon 38 D3
Broad Blunsdon Thamesdown 38 E1
Broad Campden Glos 51 F6
Broad Chalke Wilts 13 B8
Broad Green Beds 53 E7
Broad Green Essex 42 B4
Broad Green Worcs 50 D2
Broad Haven Pembs 44 D3
Broad Heath Worcs 49 C8
Broad Hill Cambs 55 B6
Broad Hinton Wilts 25 B6
Broad Laying Hants 26 C2
Broad Marston Worcs 51 E6
Broad Oak Carms 33 B6
Broad Oak Cumb 98 E3
Broad Oak Dorset 12 E2
Broad Oak Dorset 13 C5
Broad Oak E Sus 18 D5
Broad Oak E Sus 18 C3
Broad Oak Hereford 36 B1
Broad Oak Mers 86 E3
Broad Street Kent 30 D2
Broad Street Green Essex 42 D4
Broad Town Wilts 25 B5
Broadbottom Gtr Man 87 E7
Broadbridge W Sus 16 D2
Broadbridge Heath W Sus 28 F2
Broadclyst Devon 10 E4
Broadfield Gtr Man 87 C6
Broadfield Lancs 86 B3
Broadfield Pembs 32 D2
Broadfield W Sus 28 F3
Broadford Highld 155 H2
Broadford Bridge W Sus 16 B4
Broadhaugh Borders 115 D7
Broadhaven Highld 169 D8
Broadheath Gtr Man 87 F5
Broadhembury Devon 11 D6
Broadhempston Devon 7 C6
Broadholme Derbys 76 E3
Broadholme Lincs 77 B8
Broadland Row E Sus 18 D5
Broadlay Carms 32 D4
Broadley Lancs 87 C6
Broadley Moray 159 C7
Broadley Common Essex 41 D7
Broadmayne Dorset 12 F5
Broadmeadows Borders 123 F7
Broadmere Hants 26 E4
Broadmoor Pembs 32 D1
Broadoak Kent 31 C5
Broadrashes Moray 159 D8
Broadsea Aberds 161 B6
Broadstairs Kent 31 C7
Broadstone Poole 13 E8
Broadstone Shrops 60 F5
Broadtown Lane Wilts 25 B5
Broadview Gardens, Hadlow Kent 29 E7
Broadwas Worcs 50 D2
Broadwater Herts 41 B5
Broadwater W Sus 16 D5
Broadway Carms 32 D3
Broadway Pembs 44 D3
Broadway Som 11 C8
Broadway Suff 57 B7
Broadway Worcs 51 F5
Broadwell Glos 38 B2
Broadwell Glos 36 C2
Broadwell Oxon 38 D2
Broadwell Warks 52 C2
Broadwell House Northumb 110 D2
Broadwey Dorset 12 F4
Broadwindsor Dorset 12 D2
Broadwood Kelly Devon 9 D8
Broadwoodwidger Devon 9 F6
Brobury Hereford 48 E5
Brochel Highld 152 E6
Brochloch Dumfries 113 E5
Brochroy Argyll 131 B6
Brockamin Worcs 50 D2
Brockbridge Hants 15 C7
Brockdam Northumb 117 B7
Brockdish Norf 57 B6
Brockenhurst Hants 14 D4
Brocketsbrae S Lnrk 121 F8
Brockford Street Suff 56 C5
Brockhall Northants 52 C4
Brockham Sur 28 E2
Brockhampton Glos 37 B7
Brockhampton Hereford 49 F7
Brockhole -National Park Visitor Centre, Windermere Cumb 99 D5
Brockholes W Yorks 88 C2
Brockhurst Derbys 76 C3
Brockhurst Hants 15 D7
Brocklebank Cumb 108 E3
Brocklesby Lincs 90 C5
Brockley N Som 23 C6
Brockley Green Suff 56 D2
Brockleymoor Cumb 108 F4
Brockton Shrops 60 F3
Brockton Shrops 61 E5
Brockton Shrops 60 D3
Brockton Shrops 61 D7
Brockton Telford 61 C7
Brockweir Glos 36 D2
Brockwood Hants 15 B7
Brockworth Glos 37 C5
Brocton Staffs 62 C3
Brodick N Ayrs 119 C7
Brodick Castle N Ayrs 119 C7
Brodsworth S Yorks 89 D6
Brogaig Highld 152 C5
Brogborough Beds 53 F7
Broken Cross Ches 74 B3
Broken Cross Ches 75 B5
Brokenborough Wilts 37 F6
Bromborough Mers 85 F4
Brome Suff 56 B5
Brome Street Suff 57 B5
Bromeswell Suff 57 D7
Bromfield Cumb 107 E8
Bromfield Shrops 49 B6
Bromham Beds 53 D8
Bromham Wilts 24 C4
Bromley London 28 C5
Bromley W Mid 62 F3
Bromley Common London 28 C5
Bromley Green Kent 19 B6
Brompton Medway 29 C8
Brompton N Yorks 102 E1
Brompton N Yorks 103 F7
Brompton-on-Swale N Yorks 101 E7
Brompton Ralph Som 22 F2
Brompton Regis Som 21 F8
Bromsash Hereford 36 B3
Bromsberrow Heath Glos 50 F2
Bromsgrove Worcs 50 B4
Bromyard Hereford 49 D8
Bromyard Downs Hereford 49 D8
Bronaber Gwyn 71 D8
Brongest Ceredig 46 E2
Bronington Wrex 73 F8
Bronllys Powys 48 F3
Bronnant Ceredig 46 C5
Bronte Parsonage Museum, Keighley W Yorks 94 F3
Bronwydd Arms Carms 33 B5
Bronydd Powys 48 E4
Bronygarth Shrops 73 F6
Brook Carms 32 D3
Brook Hants 14 C3
Brook Hants 14 B4
Brook I o W 14 F4
Brook Kent 30 E4
Brook Sur 27 F7
Brook Sur 27 E8
Brook End Beds 53 C8
Brook Hill Hants 14 C3
Brook Street Kent 29 E6
Brook Street Kent 19 B6
Brook Street W Sus 17 B7
Brooke Norf 69 E5
Brooke Rutland 64 D5
Brookenby Lincs 91 E6
Brookend Glos 36 E2
Brookfield Renfs 120 C4
Brookhouse Lancs 92 C5
Brookhouse Green Ches 74 C5
Brookland Kent 19 C6
Brooklands Dumfries 106 B5
Brooklands Gtr Man 87 E5
Brooklands Shrops 74 E2
Brookmans Park Herts 41 D5
Brooks Powys 59 E8
Brooks Green W Sus 16 B5
Brookthorpe Glos 37 C5
Brookville Norf 67 E7
Brookwood Sur 27 D7
Broom Beds 54 E2
Broom S Yorks 88 E5
Broom Warks 51 D5
Broom Worcs 50 B4
Broom Green Norf 81 E5
Broom Hill Dorset 13 D8
Broome Norf 69 E6
Broome Shrops 60 F4
Broome Park Northumb 117 C7
Broomedge Warr 86 F5
Broomer's Corner W Sus 16 B5
Broomfield Aberds 161 E6
Broomfield Essex 42 C3
Broomfield Kent 30 D2
Broomfield Kent 31 C5
Broomfield Som 22 F4
Broomfleet E Yorks 90 B2
Broomhall Ches 74 E3
Broomhall Windsor 27 C7
Broomhaugh Northumb 110 C3
Broomhill Norf 67 D6
Broomhill Northumb 117 D8
Broomhill S Yorks 88 D5
Broomholm Norf 81 D9
Broomley Northumb 110 C3
Broompark Durham 110 E5
Broom's Green Hereford 50 F2
Broomy Lodge Hants 14 C3
Brora Highld 165 D6
Broseley Shrops 61 D6
Brotherhouse Bar Lincs 66 C2
Brotherstone Borders 124 F2
Brotherton N Yorks 89 B5
Brotton Redcar 102 C4
Broubster Highld 168 C5
Brough Cumb 100 C2
Brough Derbys 88 F2
Brough E Yorks 90 B3
Brough Highld 169 B7
Brough Notts 77 D8
Brough Orkney 176 E2
Brough Shetland 174 F6
Brough Shetland 174 G7
Brough Shetland 174 F7
Brough Shetland 175 J7
Brough Shetland 175 H6
Brough Lodge Shetland 174 D7
Brough Sowerby Cumb 100 C2
Broughall Shrops 74 E2
Broughton Borders 122 F4
Broughton Cambs 54 B3
Broughton Flint 73 C7
Broughton Hants 25 F8
Broughton Lancs 92 F5
Broughton M Keynes 53 E6
Broughton N Lincs 90 D3
Broughton Northants 53 B6
Broughton N Yorks 94 D2
Broughton N Yorks 96 B3
Broughton Orkney 176 B3
Broughton Oxon 52 F2
Broughton V Glam 21 B8
Broughton Astley Leics 64 E2
Broughton Beck Cumb 98 F4
Broughton Common Wilts 24 C3
Broughton Gifford Wilts 24 C3
Broughton Hackett Worcs 50 D4
Broughton in Furness Cumb 98 F4
Broughton Mills Cumb 98 E4
Broughton Moor Cumb 107 F7
Broughton Park Gtr Man 87 D6
Broughton Poggs Oxon 38 D2
Broughtown Orkney 176 B5
Broughty Ferry Dundee 142 F4
Browhouses Dumfries 108 C2
Browland Shetland 175 H4
Brown Candover Hants 26 F3
Brown Edge Lancs 85 C4
Brown Edge Staffs 75 D6
Brown Heath Ches 73 C8
Brownhill Aberds 161 D5
Brownhill Aberds 160 D3
Brownhill Blkburn 93 F6
Brownhill Shrops 60 B4
Brownhills Fife 135 C7
Brownhills W Mid 62 D4
Brownlow Ches 74 C5
Brownlow Heath Ches 74 C5
Brownmuir Aberds 143 B7
Brown's End Glos 50 F2
Brownshill Glos 37 D5
Brownston Devon 6 D4
Brownyside Northumb 117 B7
Broxa N Yorks 103 E7
Broxbourne Herts 41 D6
Broxburn E Loth 124 B2
Broxburn W Loth 122 B3
Broxholme Lincs 78 B2
Broxted Essex 42 B1
Broxton Ches 73 D8
Broxwood Hereford 49 D5
Broyle Side E Sus 17 C8
Brù W Isles 172 D6
Bruairnis W Isles 171 K3
Bruan Highld 169 F8
Bruar Lodge Perth 141 B5
Brucehill W Dunb 120 B3
Bruera Ches 73 C8
Bruern Abbey Oxon 38 B2
Bruichladdich Argyll 126 C2
Bruisyard Suff 57 C7
Brumby N Lincs 90 D2
Brund Staffs 75 C8
Brundall Norf 69 D6
Brundish Suff 57 C6
Brundish Street Suff 57 B6
Brunery Highld 145 F7
Brunshaw Lancs 93 F8
Brunswick Village T & W 110 B5
Bruntcliffe W Yorks 88 B3
Bruntingthorpe Leics 64 E3
Brunton Fife 134 B5
Brunton Northumb 117 B8
Brunton Wilts 25 D7
Brushford Devon 9 D8
Brushford Som 10 B4
Bruton Som 23 F8
Bryanston Dorset 13 D6
Brydekirk Dumfries 107 B8
Bryher Scilly 2 E3
Brymbo Wrex 73 D6
Brympton Som 12 C3
Bryn Carms 33 D6
Bryn Gtr Man 86 D3
Bryn Neath 34 E2
Bryn Shrops 60 F2
Bryn-coch Neath 33 E8
Bryn Du Anglesey 82 D3
Bryn Gates Gtr Man 86 D3
Bryn-glas Conwy 83 E8
Bryn Golau Rhondda 34 F3
Bryn-Iwan Carms 46 F2
Bryn-mawr Gwyn 70 D3
Bryn-nantllech Conwy 72 C3
Bryn-penarth Powys 59 D8
Bryn Rhyd-yr-Arian Conwy 72 C3
Bryn Saith Marchog Denb 72 D4
Bryn Sion Gwyn 59 C5
Bryn-y-gwenin Mon 35 C7
Bryn-y-maen Conwy 83 D8
Bryn-yr-eryr Gwyn 70 C4
Brynamman Carms 33 C8
Brynberian Pembs 45 F3
Brynbryddan Neath 34 E1
Brynbuga = Usk Mon 35 D7
Bryncae Rhondda 34 F3
Bryncethin Bridgend 34 F3
Bryncir Gwyn 71 C5
Bryncroes Gwyn 70 D3
Bryncrug Gwyn 58 D3
Bryneglwys Denb 72 E5
Brynford Flint 73 B5
Bryngwran Anglesey 82 D3
Bryngwyn Ceredig 45 E4
Bryngwyn Mon 35 D7
Bryngwyn Powys 48 E3
Brynhenllan Pembs 45 F2
Brynhoffnant Ceredig 46 D2
Brynithel Bl Gwent 35 D6
Brynmawr Bl Gwent 35 C5
Brynmenyn Bridgend 34 F3
Brynmill Swansea 33 E7
Brynna Rhondda 34 F3
Brynrefail Anglesey 82 C4
Brynrefail Gwyn 83 E5
Brynsadler Rhondda 34 F4
Brynsiencyn Anglesey 82 E4
Brynteg Anglesey 82 C4
Brynteg Ceredig 46 E3
Buaile nam Bodach W Isles 171 K3
Bualintur Highld 153 G5
Buarthmeini Gwyn 72 F2
Bubbenhall Warks 51 B8
Bubwith E Yorks 96 F3
Buccleuch Borders 115 C6
Buchanhaven Aberds 161 D8
Buchanty Perth 133 B8
Buchlyvie Stirl 132 E4
Buckabank Cumb 108 E3
Buckden Cambs 54 C2
Buckden N Yorks 94 B2
Buckenham Norf 69 D6
Buckerell Devon 11 D6
Buckfast Devon 6 C5
Buckfast Abbey, Buckfastleigh Devon 6 C5
Buckfastleigh Devon 6 C5
Buckhaven Fife 135 E5
Buckholm Borders 123 F7
Buckholt Mon 36 C2
Buckhorn Weston Dorset 13 B5
Buckhurst Hill Essex 41 E7
Buckie Moray 159 C8
Buckies Highld 169 C6
Buckingham Bucks 52 F4
Buckingham Palace London 28 B3
Buckland Bucks 40 C1
Buckland Devon 6 E4
Buckland Glos 51 F5
Buckland Hants 14 E4
Buckland Herts 54 F4
Buckland Kent 31 E7
Buckland Oxon 38 E3
Buckland Sur 28 D3
Buckland Abbey Devon 6 C2
Buckland Brewer Devon 9 B6
Buckland Common Bucks 40 D2
Buckland Dinham Som 24 D2
Buckland Filleigh Devon 9 D6
Buckland in the Moor Devon 6 B5
Buckland Monachorum Devon 6 C2
Buckland Newton Dorset 12 D4
Buckland St Mary Som 11 C7
Bucklebury W Berks 26 B3
Bucklegate Lincs 79 F6
Bucklerheads Angus 142 F4
Bucklers Hard Hants 14 E5
Bucklesham Suff 57 E6
Buckley = Bwcle Flint 73 C6
Bucklow Hill Ches 86 F5
Buckminster Leics 65 B5
Bucknall Lincs 78 C4
Bucknall Stoke 75 E6
Bucknell Oxon 39 B5
Bucknell Shrops 49 B5
Buckpool Moray 159 C8
Buck's Cross Devon 8 B5
Bucks Green W Sus 27 F8
Bucks Horn Oak Hants 27 E6
Buck's Mills Devon 9 B5
Bucksburn Aberdeen 151 D7
Buckskin Hants 26 D4
Buckton E Yorks 97 B7
Buckton Hereford 49 B5
Buckton Northumb 125 F6
Buckworth Cambs 54 B2
Budbrooke Warks 51 C7
Budby Notts 77 C6
Budd's Titson Corn 8 D4
Bude Corn 8 D4
Budlake Devon 10 E4
Budle Northumb 125 F7
Budleigh Salterton Devon 11 F5
Budock Water Corn 3 C6
Buerton Ches 74 E3
Buffler's Holt Bucks 52 F4
Bugbrooke Northants 52 D4
Buglawton Ches 75 C5
Bugle Corn 4 D5
Bugley Wilts 24 E3
Bugthorpe E Yorks 96 D3
Buildwas Shrops 61 D6
Builth Road Powys 48 D2
Builth Wells = Llanfair-ym-Muallt Powys 48 D2
Buirgh W Isles 173 J3
Bulby Lincs 65 B7
Bulcote Notts 77 E6
Buldoo Highld 168 C4
Bulford Wilts 25 E6
Bulford Camp Wilts 25 E6
Bulkeley Ches 74 D2
Bulkington Warks 63 F7
Bulkington Wilts 24 D4
Bulkworthy Devon 9 C5
Bull Hill Hants 14 E4
Bullamoor N Yorks 102 E1
Bullbridge Derbys 76 D3
Bullbrook Brack 27 C6
Bulley Glos 36 C4
Bullgill Cumb 107 F7
Bullington Hants 26 E2
Bullington Lincs 78 B3
Bull's Green Herts 41 C5
Bullwood Argyll 129 C6
Bulmer Essex 56 E2
Bulmer N Yorks 96 C2
Bulmer Tye Essex 56 F2
Bulphan Thurrock 42 F2
Bulverhythe E Sus 18 E4
Bulwark Aberds 161 D6
Bulwell Nottingham 76 E5
Bulwick Northants 65 E6
Bumble's Green Essex 41 D7
Bun Abhainn Eadarra W Isles 173 H4
Bun a'Mhuillin W Isles 171 J3
Bun Loyne Highld 146 D5
Bunacaimb Highld 145 E6
Bunarkaig Highld 146 F4
Bunbury Ches 74 D2
Bunbury Heath Ches 74 D2
Bunchrew Highld 157 E7
Bundalloch Highld 155 H4
Buness Shetland 174 C8
Bunessan Argyll 136 F4
Bungay Suff 69 F6
Bunker's Hill Lincs 78 B2
Bunker's Hill Lincs 79 D5
Bunkers Hill Oxon 38 C4
Bunloit Highld 147 B8
Bunnahabhain Argyll 126 B4
Bunny Notts 64 B2
Buntait Highld 156 F4
Buntingford Herts 41 B6
Bunwell Norf 68 E4
Burbage Derbys 75 B7
Burbage Leics 63 E8
Burbage Wilts 25 C7
Burchett's Green Windsor 39 F8
Burcombe Wilts 25 F5
Burcot Oxon 39 E5
Burcott Bucks 40 B1
Burdon T & W 111 D6
Bures Suff 56 F3
Bures Green Suff 56 F3
Burford Ches 74 D3
Burford Oxon 38 C2
Burford Shrops 49 C7
Burg Argyll 136 D4
Burgar Orkney 176 D2
Burgate Hants 14 C2
Burgate Suff 56 B4
Burgess Hill W Sus 17 C7
Burgh Suff 57 D6
Burgh-by-Sands Cumb 108 D3
Burgh Castle Norf 69 D7
Burgh Heath Sur 28 D3
Burgh le Marsh Lincs 79 C8
Burgh Muir Aberds 151 B6
Burgh next Aylsham Norf 81 E8
Burgh on Bain Lincs 91 F6
Burgh St Margaret Norf 69 C7
Burgh St Peter Norf 69 E7
Burghclere Hants 26 C2
Burghead Moray 158 C5
Burghfield W Berks 26 C4
Burghfield Common W Berks 26 C4
Burghfield Hill W Berks 26 C4
Burghill Hereford 49 E6
Burghwallis S Yorks 89 C6
Burham Kent 29 C8
Buriton Hants 15 B8
Burland Ches 74 D3
Burlawn Corn 4 B4
Burleigh Brack 27 C6
Burlescombe Devon 11 C5
Burleston Dorset 13 E5
Burley Hants 14 D3
Burley Rutland 65 C5
Burley W Yorks 95 F5
Burley Gate Hereford 49 E7
Burley in Wharfedale W Yorks 94 E4
Burley Lodge Hants 14 D3
Burley Street Hants 14 D3
Burleydam Ches 74 E3
Burlingjobb Powys 48 D4
Burlow E Sus 18 D2
Burlton Shrops 60 B4
Burmarsh Kent 19 B7
Burmington Warks 51 F7
Burn N Yorks 89 B6
Burn of Cambus Stirl 133 D6
Burnaston Derbys 76 F2
Burnbank S Lnrk 121 D7
Burnby E Yorks 96 E4
Burncross S Yorks 88 E4
Burneside Cumb 99 E7
Burness Orkney 176 B5
Burneston N Yorks 101 F8
Burnett Bath 23 C8
Burnfoot Borders 115 C7
Burnfoot Borders 115 C8
Burnfoot E Ayrs 112 D4
Burnfoot Perth 133 D8
Burnham Bucks 40 F2
Burnham N Lincs 90 C4
Burnham Deepdale Norf 80 C4
Burnham Green Herts 41 C5
Burnham Market Norf 80 C4
Burnham Norton Norf 80 C4
Burnham-on-Crouch Essex 43 E5
Burnham-on-Sea Som 22 E5
Burnham Overy Staithe Norf 80 C4
Burnham Overy Town Norf 80 C4
Burnham Thorpe Norf 80 C4
Burnhead Dumfries 113 E8
Burnhead S Ayrs 112 D2
Burnhervie Aberds 151 C6
Burnhill Green Staffs 61 D7
Burnhope Durham 110 E4
Burnhouse N Ayrs 120 D3
Burniston N Yorks 103 E8
Burnlee W Yorks 88 D2
Burnley Lancs 93 F8
Burnley Lane Lancs 93 F8
Burnmouth Borders 125 C5
Burnopfield Durham 110 D4
Burnsall N Yorks 94 C3
Burnside Angus 143 D5
Burnside E Ayrs 113 C5
Burnside Fife 134 D3
Burnside Shetland 174 F4
Burnside S Lnrk 121 C6
Burnside W Loth 122 B3
Burnside of Duntrune Angus 142 F4
Burnswark Dumfries 107 B8
Burnt Heath Derbys 76 B2
Burnt Houses Durham 101 B6
Burnt Yates N Yorks 95 C5
Burntcommon Sur 27 D8
Burnthouse Corn 3 C6
Burntisland Fife 134 F4
Burnton E Ayrs 112 D4
Burntwood Staffs 62 D4
Burnwynd Edin 122 C4
Burpham Sur 27 D8
Burpham W Sus 16 D4
Burradon Northumb 117 D5
Burradon T & W 111 B5
Burrafirth Shetland 174 B8
Burraland Shetland 174 F5
Burraland Shetland 175 J4
Burras Corn 3 C5
Burravoe Shetland 174 G5
Burravoe Shetland 174 F7
Burray Village Orkney 176 G3
Burrells Cumb 100 C1
Burrelton Perth 142 F2
Burridge Devon 20 F4
Burridge Hants 15 C6
Burrill N Yorks 101 F7
Burringham N Lincs 90 D2
Burrington Devon 9 C8
Burrington Hereford 49 B6
Burrington N Som 23 D6
Burrough Green Cambs 55 D7
Burrough on the Hill Leics 64 C4
Burrow-bridge Som 11 B8
Burrowhill Sur 27 C7
Burry Swansea 33 E5
Burry Green Swansea 33 E5
Burry Port = Porth Tywyn Carms 33 D5
Burscough Lancs 86 C2
Burscough Bridge Lancs 86 C2
Bursea E Yorks 96 F4
Burshill E Yorks 97 E6
Bursledon Hants 15 D5
Burslem Stoke 75 E5
Burstall Suff 56 E4
Burstock Dorset 12 D2
Burston Norf 68 F4
Burston Staffs 75 F6
Burstow Sur 28 E4
Burstwick E Yorks 91 B6
Burtersett N Yorks 100 F3
Burtle Som 23 E5
Burton Ches 73 B7
Burton Ches 74 C2
Burton Dorset 14 E2
Burton Lincs 78 B2
Burton Northumb 125 F7
Burton Pembs 44 E4
Burton Som 22 E3
Burton Wilts 24 B3
Burton Agnes E Yorks 97 C7
Burton Bradstock Dorset 12 F2
Burton Dassett Warks 51 D8

Burton Fleming E Yorks 97 B6
Burton Green W Mid 51 B7
Burton Green Wrex 73 D7
Burton Hastings Warks 63 E8
Burton-in-Kendal Cumb 92 B5
Burton in Lonsdale N Yorks 93 B6
Burton Joyce Notts 77 E6
Burton Latimer Northants 53 B7
Burton Lazars Leics 64 C4
Burton-le-Coggles Lincs 65 B6
Burton Leonard N Yorks 95 C6
Burton on the Wolds Leics 64 B2
Burton Overy Leics 64 E3
Burton Pedwardine Lincs 78 E4
Burton Pidsea E Yorks 97 F8
Burton Salmon N Yorks 89 B5
Burton Stather N Lincs 90 C2
Burton upon Stather N Lincs 90 C2
Burton upon Trent Staffs 63 B6
Burtonwood Warr 86 E3
Burwardsley Ches 74 D2
Burwarton Shrops 61 F6
Burwash E Sus 18 C3
Burwash Common E Sus 18 C3
Burwash Weald E Sus 18 C3
Burwell Cambs 55 C6
Burwell Lincs 79 B6
Burwen Anglesey 82 B4
Burwick Orkney 176 H3
Bury Cambs 66 F2
Bury Gtr Man 87 C6
Bury Som 10 B4
Bury W Sus 16 C4
Bury Green Herts 41 B7
Bury St Edmunds Suff 56 C2
Burythorpe N Yorks 96 C3
Busby E Renf 121 D5
Buscot Oxon 38 E2
Bush Bank Hereford 49 D6
Bush Crathie Aberds 149 E8
Bush Green Norf 68 F5
Bushbury W Mid 62 D3
Bushby Leics 64 D3
Bushey Herts 40 E4
Bushey Heath Herts 40 E4
Bushley Worcs 50 F3
Bushton Wilts 25 B5
Buslingthorpe Lincs 90 F4
Busta Shetland 174 G5
Butcher's Cross E Sus 18 C2
Butcher's Pasture Essex 42 B2
Butcombe N Som 23 C7
Butetown Cardiff 22 B3
Butleigh Som 23 F7
Butleigh Wootton Som 23 F7
Butler's Cross Bucks 39 D8
Butler's End Warks 63 F6
Butlers Marston Warks 51 E8
Butley Suff 57 D7
Butley High Corner Suff 57 E7
Butt Green Ches 74 D3
Butterburn Cumb 109 B6
Buttercrambe N Yorks 96 D3
Butterknowle Durham 101 B6
Butterleigh Devon 10 D4
Buttermere Cumb 98 C3
Buttermere Wilts 25 C8
Buttershaw W Yorks 88 B2
Butterstone Perth 141 E7
Butterton Staffs 75 D7
Butterwick Durham 102 B1
Butterwick Lincs 79 E6
Butterwick N Yorks 96 B3
Butterwick N Yorks 97 B5
Buttington Powys 60 D2
Buttonoak Shrops 50 B2
Butt's Green Hants 14 B4
Buttsash Hants 14 D5
Buxhall Suff 56 D4
Buxhall Fen Street Suff 56 D4
Buxley Borders 124 D4
Buxted E Sus 17 B8
Buxton Derbys 75 B7
Buxton Norf 81 E8
Buxworth Derbys 87 F8
Bwcle = Buckley Flint 73 C6
Bwlch Powys 35 B5
Bwlch-Llan Ceredig 46 D4
Bwlch-y-cibau Powys 59 C8
Bwlch-y-fadfa Ceredig 46 E3
Bwlch-y-ffridd Powys 59 E7
Bwlch-y-sarnau Powys 48 B2
Bwlchgwyn Wrex 73 D6
Bwlchnewydd Carms 32 B4
Bwlchtocyn Gwyn 70 E4
Bwlchyddar Powys 59 B8
Bwlchygroes Pembs 45 F4
Byermoor T & W 110 D4
Byers Green Durham 110 F5
Byfield Northants 52 D3
Byfleet Sur 27 C8
Byford Hereford 49 E5
Bygrave Herts 54 F3
Byker T & W 111 C5
Bylchau Conwy 72 C3
Byley Ches 74 C4
Bynea Carms 33 E6
Byrness Northumb 116 D3
Bythorn Cambs 53 B8
Byton Hereford 49 C5
Byworth W Sus 16 B3

C

Cabharstadh W Isles 172 F6
Cablea Perth 141 F6
Cabourne Lincs 90 D5
Cabrach Argyll 127 F2
Cabrach Moray 150 B2
Cabrich Highld 157 E6
Cabus Lancs 92 E4
Cackle Street E Sus 17 B8
Cadbury Devon 10 D4
Cadbury Barton Devon 9 C8
Cadbury World, Bournville W Mid 62 F4
Cadder E Dunb 121 B6
Caddington Beds 40 C3
Caddonfoot Borders 123 F7
Cade Street E Sus 18 C3
Cadeby Leics 63 D8
Cadeby S Yorks 89 D6
Cadeleigh Devon 10 D4
Cadgwith Corn 3 E6
Cadham Fife 134 D4
Cadishead Gtr Man 86 E5
Cadle Swansea 33 E7
Cadley Lancs 92 F5
Cadley Wilts 25 D7
Cadley Wilts 25 C7
Cadmore End Bucks 39 E7
Cadnam Hants 14 C3
Cadney N Lincs 90 D4
Cadole Flint 73 C6
Cadoxton V Glam 22 C3
Cadoxton-Juxta-Neath Neath 34 E1
Cadshaw Blkburn 86 C5
Cadwell Park Motor Racing Circuit Lincs 91 F6
Cadzow S Lnrk 121 D7
Caeathro Gwyn 82 E4
Caehopkin Powys 34 C2
Caenby Lincs 90 F4
Caenby Corner Lincs 90 F3
Caer-bryn Carms 33 C6
Caer Llan Mon 36 D1
Caerau Bridgend 34 E2
Caerau Cardiff 22 B3
Caerdeon Gwyn 58 C3
Caerdydd = Cardiff Cardiff 22 B3
Caerfarchell Pembs 44 C2
Caerffili = Caerphilly Caerph 35 F5
Caerfyrddin = Carmarthen Carms 33 B5
Caergeiliog Anglesey 82 D3
Caergwrle Flint 73 D7
Caergybi = Holyhead Anglesey 82 C2
Caerleon = Caerllion Newport 35 E7
Caerllion = Caerleon Newport 35 E7
Caernarfon Gwyn 82 E4
Caernarfon Castle Gwyn 82 E4
Caerphilly = Caerffili Caerph 35 F5
Caersws Powys 59 E7
Caerwedros Ceredig 46 D2
Caerwent Mon 36 E1
Caerwych Gwyn 71 D7
Caerwys Flint 72 B5
Caethle Gwyn 58 E3
Caim Anglesey 83 C6
Caio Carms 47 F5
Cairinis W Isles 170 D4
Cairisiadar W Isles 172 E3
Cairminis W Isles 173 K3
Cairnbaan Argyll 128 A3
Cairnbanno Ho. Aberds 160 D5
Cairnborrow Aberds 159 E8
Cairnbrogie Aberds 151 B7
Cairnbulg Castle Aberds 161 B7
Cairncross Angus 142 B4
Cairncross Borders 124 C4
Cairndow Argyll 131 D7
Cairness Aberds 161 B7
Cairneyhill Fife 134 F2
Cairnfield Ho. Moray 159 C8
Cairngaan Dumfries 104 F5
Cairngarroch Dumfries 104 E4
Cairnhill Aberds 160 E3
Cairnie Aberds 159 E8
Cairnie Aberds 151 D7
Cairnorrie Aberds 161 D5
Cairnpark Aberds 151 C7
Cairnryan Dumfries 104 C4
Cairnton Orkney 176 F2
Caister-on-Sea Norf 69 C8
Caistor Lincs 90 D5
Caistor St Edmund Norf 68 D5
Caistron Northumb 117 D5
Caitha Bowland Borders 123 E7
Caithness Glass, Perth Perth 134 B2
Calais Street Suff 56 F3
Calanais W Isles 172 E5
Calbost W Isles 172 G7
Calbourne I o W 14 F5
Calceby Lincs 79 B6
Calcot Row W Berks 26 B4
Calcott Kent 31 C5
Caldback Shetland 174 C8
Caldbeck Cumb 108 F3
Caldbergh N Yorks 101 F5
Caldecote Cambs 54 D4
Caldecote Cambs 65 F8
Caldecote Herts 54 F3
Caldecote Northants 52 D4
Caldecott Northants 53 C7
Caldecott Oxon 38 E4
Caldecott Rutland 65 E5
Calder Bridge Cumb 98 D2
Calder Hall Cumb 98 D2
Calder Mains Highld 169 D5
Calder Vale Lancs 92 E5
Calderbank N Lnrk 121 C7
Calderbrook Gtr Man 87 C7
Caldercruix N Lnrk 121 C8
Caldermill S Lnrk 121 E6
Calderwood S Lnrk 121 D6
Caldhame Angus 142 E4
Caldicot Mon 36 F1
Caldwell Derbys 63 C6
Caldwell N Yorks 101 C6
Caldy Mers 85 F3
Caledrhydiau Ceredig 46 D3
Calfsound Orkney 176 C4
Calgary Argyll 136 C4
Califer Moray 158 D4
California Falk 122 B2
California Norf 69 C8
Calke Derbys 63 B7
Callakille Highld 155 E2
Callaly Northumb 117 D6
Callander Stirl 132 D5
Callaughton Shrops 61 E6
Callestick Corn 4 D2
Calligarry Highld 145 C6
Callington Corn 5 C8
Callow Hereford 49 F6
Callow End Worcs 50 E3
Callow Hill Wilts 37 F7
Callow Hill Worcs 50 B2
Callows Grave Worcs 49 C7
Calmore Hants 14 C4
Calmsden Glos 37 D7
Calne Wilts 24 B5
Calow Derbys 76 B4
Calshot Hants 15 D5
Calstock Corn 6 C2
Calstone Wellington Wilts 24 C5
Calthorpe Norf 81 D7
Calthwaite Cumb 108 E4
Calton N Yorks 94 D2
Calton Staffs 75 D8
Calveley Ches 74 D2
Calver Derbys 76 B2
Calver Hill Hereford 49 E5
Calverhall Shrops 74 F3
Calverleigh Devon 10 C4
Calverley W Yorks 94 F5
Calvert Bucks 39 B6
Calverton M Keynes 53 F5
Calverton Notts 77 E6
Calvine Perth 141 C5
Calvo Cumb 107 D8
Cam Glos 36 E4
Camas-luinie Highld 146 B2
Camasnacroise Highld 138 D2
Camastianavaig Highld 153 F6
Camasunary Highld 153 H6
Camault Muir Highld 157 E6
Camb Shetland 174 D7
Camber E Sus 19 D6
Camberley Sur 27 C6
Camberwell London 28 B4
Camblesforth N Yorks 89 B7
Cambo Northumb 117 F6
Cambois Northumb 117 F9
Camborne Corn 3 B5
Cambourne Cambs 54 D4
Cambridge Cambs 55 D5
Cambridge Glos 36 D4
Cambridge Airport Cambs 55 D5
Cambridge Town Sthend 43 F5
Cambus Clack 133 E7
Cambusavie Farm Highld 164 E4
Cambusbarron Stirl 133 E6
Cambuskenneth Stirl 133 E7
Cambuslang S Lnrk 121 C6
Cambusmore Lodge Highld 164 E4
Camden London 41 F5
Camelford Corn 8 F3
Camelot Theme Park, Chorley Lancs 86 C3
Camelsdale W Sus 27 F6
Camerory Highld 158 F4
Camer's Green Worcs 50 F2
Camerton Bath 23 D8
Camerton Cumb 107 F7
Camerton E Yorks 91 B6
Camghouran Perth 140 D2
Cammachmore Aberds 151 E8
Cammeringham Lincs 90 F3
Camore Highld 164 E4
Camp Hill Warks 63 E7
Campbeltown Argyll 118 D4
Campbeltown Airport Argyll 118 D3
Camperdown T & W 111 B5
Campmuir Perth 142 F2
Campsall S Yorks 89 C6
Campsey Ash Suff 57 D7
Campton Beds 54 F2
Camptown Borders 116 C2
Camrose Pembs 44 C4
Camserney Perth 141 E5
Camster Highld 169 E7
Camuschoirk Highld 138 C1
Camuscross Highld 145 B6
Camusnagaul Highld 138 B4
Camusnagaul Highld 162 F4
Camusrory Highld 145 D8
Camusteel Highld 155 F3
Camusterrach Highld 155 F3
Camusvrachan Perth 140 E3
Canada Hants 14 C3
Canadia E Sus 18 D4
Canal Side S Yorks 89 C7
Candacraig Ho. Aberds 150 C2
Candlesby Lincs 79 C7
Candy Mill S Lnrk 122 E3
Cane End Oxon 26 B4
Canewdon Essex 42 E4
Canford Bottom Dorset 13 D8
Canford Cliffs Poole 13 F8
Canford Magna Poole 13 E8
Canham's Green Suff 56 C4
Canholes Derbys 75 B7
Canisbay Highld 169 B8
Cann Dorset 13 B6
Cann Common Dorset 13 B6
Cannard's Grave Som 23 E8
Cannich Highld 156 F4
Cannington Som 22 F4
Cannock Staffs 62 D3
Cannock Wood Staffs 62 C4
Canon Bridge Hereford 49 E6
Canon Frome Hereford 49 E8
Canon Pyon Hereford 49 E6
Canonbie Dumfries 108 B3
Canons Ashby Northants 52 D3
Canonstown Corn 2 C4
Canterbury Kent 30 D5
Canterbury Cathedral Kent 30 D5
Canterbury Tales Kent 30 D5
Cantley Norf 69 D6
Cantley S Yorks 89 D7
Cantlop Shrops 60 D5
Canton Cardiff 22 B3
Cantraybruich Highld 157 E8
Cantraydoune Highld 157 E8
Cantraywood Highld 157 E8
Cantsfield Lancs 93 B6
Canvey Island Essex 42 F3
Canwick Lincs 78 C2
Canworthy Water Corn 8 E4
Caol Highld 139 B5
Caol Ila Argyll 126 B4
Caolas Argyll 136 F2
Caolas Scalpaigh W Isles 173 J5
Caolas Stocinis W Isles 173 J4
Capel Sur 28 E2
Capel Bangor Ceredig 58 F3
Capel Betws Lleucu Ceredig 46 D5
Capel Carmel Gwyn 70 E2
Capel Coch Anglesey 82 C4
Capel Curig Conwy 83 F7
Capel Cynon Ceredig 46 E2
Capel Dewi Ceredig 46 E3
Capel Dewi Ceredig 58 F3
Capel Dewi Carms 33 B5
Capel Garmon Conwy 83 F8
Capel-gwyn Anglesey 82 D3
Capel Gwyn Carms 33 B5
Capel Gwynfe Carms 33 B8
Capel Hendre Carms 33 C6
Capel Hermon Gwyn 71 E8
Capel Isaac Carms 33 B6
Capel Iwan Carms 45 F4
Capel le Ferne Kent 31 F6
Capel Llanilltern Cardiff 34 F4
Capel Mawr Anglesey 82 D4
Capel St Andrew Suff 57 E7
Capel St Mary Suff 56 F4
Capel Seion Ceredig 46 B5
Capel Tygwydd Ceredig 45 E4
Capel Uchaf Gwyn 70 C5
Capel-y-graig Gwyn 82 E5
Capelulo Conwy 83 D7
Capenhurst Ches 73 B7
Capernwray Lancs 92 B5
Capheaton Northumb 117 F6
Cappercleuch Borders 115 B5
Capplegill Dumfries 114 D4
Capton Devon 7 D6
Caputh Perth 141 F7
Car Colston Notts 77 E7
Carbis Bay Corn 2 C4
Carbost Highld 153 F4
Carbost Highld 152 E5
Carbrook S Yorks 88 F4
Carbrooke Norf 68 D2
Carburton Notts 77 B6
Carcant Borders 123 D6
Carcary Angus 143 D6
Carclaze Corn 4 D5
Carcroft S Yorks 89 C6
Cardenden Fife 134 E4
Cardeston Shrops 60 C3
Cardiff = Caerdydd Cardiff 22 B3
Cardiff Bay Barrage Cardiff 22 B3
Cardiff Castle Cardiff 22 B3
Cardiff International Airport V Glam 22 C2
Cardigan = Aberteifi Ceredig 45 E3
Cardington Beds 53 E8
Cardington Shrops 60 E5
Cardinham Corn 5 C6
Cardonald Glasgow 120 C5
Cardow Moray 159 E5
Cardrona Borders 123 F6
Cardross Argyll 120 B3
Cardurnock Cumb 107 D8
Careby Lincs 65 C7
Careston Castle Angus 143 D5
Carew Pembs 32 D1
Carew Cheriton Pembs 32 D1
Carew Newton Pembs 32 D1
Carey Hereford 49 F7
Carfrae E Loth 123 C8
Cargenbridge Dumfries 107 B6
Cargill Perth 142 F1
Cargo Cumb 108 D3
Cargreen Corn 6 C2
Carham Northumb 124 F4
Carhampton Som 22 E2
Carharrack Corn 3 B6
Carie Perth 140 F3
Carie Perth 140 D3
Carines Corn 4 D2
Carisbrooke I o W 15 F5
Carisbrooke Castle I o W 15 F5
Cark Cumb 92 B3
Carlabhagh W Isles 172 D5
Carland Cross Corn 4 D3
Carlby Lincs 65 C7
Carlecotes S Yorks 88 D2
Carlesmoor N Yorks 94 B4
Carleton Cumb 99 B7
Carleton Cumb 108 D4
Carleton Lancs 92 F3
Carleton N Yorks 94 E2
Carleton Forehoe Norf 68 D3
Carleton Rode Norf 68 E4
Carlin How Redcar 103 C5
Carlingcott Bath 23 D8
Carlisle Cumb 108 D4
Carlisle Airport Cumb 108 C4
Carlisle Cathedral Cumb 108 D3
Carlisle Racecourse Cumb 108 D3
Carlops Borders 122 D4
Carlton Beds 53 D7
Carlton Cambs 55 D7
Carlton Leics 63 D7
Carlton Notts 77 E6
Carlton N Yorks 102 F4
Carlton N Yorks 89 B7
Carlton N Yorks 101 F5
Carlton N Yorks 101 C6
Carlton Stockton 102 B1
Carlton Suff 57 C7
Carlton S Yorks 88 C4
Carlton W Yorks 88 B4
Carlton Colville Suff 69 F8
Carlton Curlieu Leics 64 E3
Carlton Husthwaite N Yorks 95 B7
Carlton in Cleveland N Yorks 102 D3
Carlton in Lindrick Notts 89 F6
Carlton le Moorland Lincs 78 D2
Carlton Miniott N Yorks 102 F1
Carlton on Trent Notts 77 C7
Carlton Scroop Lincs 78 E2
Carluke S Lnrk 121 D8
Carmarthen = Caerfyrddin Carms 33 B5
Carmel Anglesey 82 C3
Carmel Carms 33 C6
Carmel Flint 73 B5
Carmel Guern 16
Carmel Gwyn 82 F4
Carmont Aberds 151 F7
Carmunnock Glasgow 121 D6
Carmyle Glasgow 121 C6
Carmyllie Angus 143 E5
Carn-gorm Highld 146 B2
Carnaby E Yorks 97 C7
Carnach Highld 162 E4
Carnach Highld 146 B3
Carnach W Isles 173 J5
Carnachy Highld 168 D2
Càrnais W Isles 172 E3
Carnbee Fife 135 D7
Carnbo Perth 134 D2
Carnbrea Corn 3 B5
Carnduff S Lnrk 121 E6
Carnduncan Argyll 126 C2
Carne Corn 3 C8
Carnforth Lancs 92 B4
Carnhedryn Pembs 44 C3
Carnhell Green Corn 2 C5
Carnkie Corn 3 C6
Carnkie Corn 3 C5
Carno Powys 59 E6
Carnoch Highld 156 F4
Carnoch Highld 156 D3
Carnock Fife 134 F2
Carnon Downs Corn 3 B6
Carnousie Aberds 160 C3
Carnoustie Angus 143 F5
Carnwath S Lnrk 122 E2
Carnyorth Corn 2 C2
Carperby N Yorks 101 F5
Carpley Green N Yorks 100 F4
Carr S Yorks 89 E6
Carr Hill T & W 111 C5
Carradale Argyll 118 C5
Carragraich W Isles 173 J4
Carrbridge Highld 148 B5
Carrefour Selous Jersey 17
Carreg-wen Pembs 45 E4
Carreglefn Anglesey 82 C3
Carrick Argyll 128 B4
Carrick Fife 135 B6
Carrick Castle Argyll 129 A6
Carrick Ho. Orkney 176 C4
Carriden Falk 134 F2
Carrington Gtr Man 86 E5
Carrington Lincs 79 D6
Carrington Midloth 123 C6
Carrog Conwy 71 C8
Carrog Denb 72 E5
Carron Falk 133 F7
Carron Moray 159 E6
Carron Bridge N Lnrk 133 F6
Carronbridge Dumfries 113 E8
Carrshield Northumb 109 E8
Carrutherstown Dumfries 107 B8
Carrville Durham 111 E6
Carsaig Argyll 137 F6
Carsaig Argyll 128 B2
Carscreugh Dumfries 105 D6
Carse Gray Angus 142 D4
Carse Ho. Argyll 128 D2
Carsegowan Dumfries 105 D8
Carseriggan Dumfries 105 C7
Carsethorn Dumfries 107 D6
Carshalton London 28 C3
Carsington Derbys 76 D2
Carskiey Argyll 118 F3
Carsluith Dumfries 105 D8
Carsphairn Dumfries 113 E5
Carstairs S Lnrk 122 E2
Carstairs Junction S Lnrk 122 E2
Carswell Marsh Oxon 38 E3
Carter's Clay Hants 14 B4
Carterton Oxon 38 D2
Carterway Heads Northumb 110 D3
Carthew Corn 4 D5
Carthorpe N Yorks 101 F8
Cartington Northumb 117 D6
Cartland S Lnrk 121 E8
Cartmel Cumb 92 B3
Cartmel Fell Cumb 99 F6
Cartmel Racecourse Cumb 92 B3
Carway Carms 33 D5
Cary Fitzpaine Som 12 B3
Cas-gwent = Chepstow Mon 36 E2
Cascob Powys 48 C4
Cashlie Perth 140 E1
Cashmere Visitor Centre, Elgin Moray 159 E6
Cashmoor Dorset 13 C7
Casnewydd = Newport Newport 35 F7
Cassey Compton Glos 37 C7
Cassington Oxon 38 C4
Cassop Durham 111 F6
Castell Denb 72 C5
Castell Coch Cardiff 35 F5
Castell-Howell Ceredig 46 E3
Castell-Nedd = Neath Neath 33 E8
Castell Newydd Emlyn = Newcastle Emlyn Carms 46 E2
Castell-y-bwch Torf 35 E6
Castellau Rhondda 34 F4
Casterton Cumb 93 B6
Castle Acre Norf 67 C8
Castle Ashby Northants 53 D6
Castle Bolton N Yorks 101 E5
Castle Bromwich W Mid 62 F5
Castle Bytham Lincs 65 C6
Castle Caereinion Powys 59 D8
Castle Camps Cambs 55 E7
Castle Carrock Cumb 108 D5
Castle Cary Som 23 F8
Castle Combe Wilts 24 B3
Castle Combe Motor Racing Circuit Wilts 24 B3
Castle Donington Leics 63 B8
Castle Douglas Dumfries 106 C4
Castle Drogo, Exeter Devon 10 E2
Castle Eaton Thamesdown 37 E8
Castle Eden Durham 111 F7
Castle Forbes Aberds 150 C5
Castle Frome Hereford 49 E8
Castle Green Sur 27 C7
Castle Gresley Derbys 63 C6
Castle Heaton Northumb 124 E5
Castle Hedingham Essex 55 F8
Castle Hill Kent 29 E7
Castle Howard, Malton N Yorks 96 B3
Castle Huntly Perth 134 B5
Castle Kennedy Dumfries 104 D5
Castle O'er Dumfries 115 E5
Castle Pulverbatch Shrops 60 D4
Castle Rising Norf 67 B6
Castle Stuart Highld 157 E8
Castlebay = Bagh a Chaisteil W Isles 171 L2
Castlebythe Pembs 32 B1
Castlecary N Lnrk 121 B7
Castlecraig Highld 158 C2
Castlefairn Dumfries 113 F7
Castleford W Yorks 88 B5
Castlehill Borders 122 F5
Castlehill Highld 169 C6
Castlehill W Dunb 120 B3
Castlemaddy Dumfries 113 F5
Castlemartin Pembs 44 F4
Castlemilk Dumfries 107 B8
Castlemilk Glasgow 121 D6
Castlemorris Pembs 44 B4
Castlemorton Worcs 50 F2
Castleside Durham 110 E3
Castlethorpe M Keynes 53 E6
Castleton Angus 142 E3
Castleton Argyll 128 B3
Castleton Derbys 88 F2
Castleton Gtr Man 87 C6
Castleton Newport 35 F6
Castleton N Yorks 102 D4
Castletown Ches 73 D8
Castletown Highld 169 C6
Castletown Highld 157 E8
Castletown I o M 84 F2
Castletown T & W 111 D6
Castleweary Borders 115 D7
Castley N Yorks 95 E5
Caston Norf 68 E2
Castor P'boro 65 E8
Catacol N Ayrs 119 B6
Catbrain S Glos 36 F2
Catbrook Mon 36 D2
Catchall Corn 2 D3
Catchems Corner W Mid 51 B7
Catchgate Durham 110 D4
Catcleugh Northumb 116 D3
Catcliffe S Yorks 88 F5
Catcott Som 23 F5
Caterham Sur 28 D4
Catfield Norf 69 B6
Catfirth Shetland 175 H6
Catford London 28 B4
Catforth Lancs 92 F4
Cathays Cardiff 22 B3
Cathcart Glasgow 121 C5
Cathedine Powys 35 B5
Catherington Hants 15 C7
Catherton Shrops 49 B8
Catlodge Highld 148 E2
Catlowdy Cumb 108 B4
Catmore W Berks 38 F4
Caton Lancs 92 C5
Caton Green Lancs 92 C5
Catrine E Ayrs 113 B5
Cat's Ash Newport 35 E7
Catsfield E Sus 18 D4
Catshill Worcs 50 B4
Cattal N Yorks 95 D7
Cattawade Suff 56 F5
Catterall Lancs 92 E4
Catterick N Yorks 101 E7
Catterick Bridge N Yorks 101 E7
Catterick Garrison N Yorks 101 E6
Catterick Racecourse N Yorks 101 E7
Catterlen Cumb 108 F4
Catterline Aberds 143 B8
Catterton N Yorks 95 E8
Catthorpe Leics 52 B3
Cattistock Dorset 12 E3
Catton Northumb 109 D8
Catton N Yorks 95 B6
Catwick E Yorks 97 E7
Catworth Cambs 53 B8
Caudlesprings Norf 68 D2
Caudwell's Mill, Matlock Derbys 76 C2
Caulcott Oxon 39 B5
Cauldcots Angus 143 E6
Cauldhame Stirl 132 E5
Cauldmill Borders 115 C8
Cauldon Staffs 75 E7
Caulkerbush Dumfries 107 D6
Caulside Dumfries 115 F7
Caunsall Worcs 62 F2
Caunton Notts 77 D7
Causeway End Dumfries 105 C8
Causeway Foot W Yorks 94 F3
Causeway-head Stirl 133 E6
Causewayend S Lnrk 122 F3
Causewayhead Cumb 107 D8
Causey Park Bridge Northumb 117 E7
Causeyend Aberds 151 C8
Cautley Cumb 100 E1
Cavendish Suff 56 E2
Cavendish Bridge Leics 63 B8
Cavenham Suff 55 C8
Caversfield Oxon 39 B5
Caversham Reading 26 B5
Caverswall Staffs 75 E6
Cavil E Yorks 96 F3
Cawdor Highld 158 D2
Cawdor Castle and Gardens Highld 158 E2
Cawkwell Lincs 79 B5
Cawood N Yorks 95 F8
Cawsand Corn 6 D2
Cawston Norf 81 E7
Cawthorne S Yorks 88 D3
Cawthorpe Lincs 65 B7
Cawton N Yorks 96 B2
Caxton Cambs 54 D4
Caynham Shrops 49 B7
Caythorpe Lincs 78 E2
Caythorpe Notts 77 E6
Cayton N Yorks 103 F8
Ceann a Bhaigh W Isles 170 D3
Ceann a Deas Loch Baghasdail W Isles 171 J3
Ceann Shiphoirt W Isles 172 G5
Ceann Tarabhaigh W Isles 172 G5
Ceannacroc Lodge Highld 146 C5
Cearsiadair W Isles 172 F6
Cefn Berain Conwy 72 C3
Cefn-brith Conwy 72 D3
Cefn Canol Powys 73 F6
Cefn-coch Conwy 83 E8
Cefn Coch Powys 59 B8
Cefn-coed-y-cymmer M Tydf 34 D4
Cefn Cribbwr Bridgend 34 F2
Cefn Cross Bridgend 34 F2
Cefn-ddwysarn Gwyn 72 F3
Cefn Einion Shrops 60 F2
Cefn-gorwydd Powys 47 E8
Cefn-mawr Wrex 73 E6
Cefn-y-bedd Flint 73 D7
Cefn-y-pant Carms 32 B2
Cefneithin Carms 33 C6
Cei-bach Ceredig 46 D3
Ceinewydd = New Quay Ceredig 46 D2
Ceint Anglesey 82 D4
Cellan Ceredig 46 E5
Cellarhead Staffs 75 E6
Cemaes Anglesey 82 B3
Cemmaes Powys 58 D5
Cemmaes Road Powys 58 D5
Cenarth Carms 45 E4
Cenin Gwyn 71 C5
Central Invclyd 129 C7
Ceos W Isles 172 F6
Ceres Fife 135 C6
Cerne Abbas Dorset 12 D4
Cerney Wick Glos 37 E7
Cerrigceinwen Anglesey 82 D4
Cerrigydrudion Conwy 72 E3
Cessford Borders 116 B3
Ceunant Gwyn 82 E5
Chaceley Glos 50 F3
Chacewater Corn 3 B6
Chackmore Bucks 52 F4
Chacombe Northants 52 E2
Chad Valley W Mid 62 F4
Chadderton Gtr Man 87 D7
Chadderton Fold Gtr Man 87 D6
Chaddesden Derby 76 F3
Chaddesley Corbett Worcs 50 B3
Chaddleworth W Berks 26 B2
Chadlington Oxon 38 B3
Chadshunt Warks 51 D8
Chadwell Leics 64 B4
Chadwell St Mary Thurrock 29 B7
Chadwick End W Mid 51 B7
Chadwick Green Mers 86 E3
Chaffcombe Som 11 C8
Chagford Devon 10 F2
Chailey E Sus 17 C7
Chain Bridge Lincs 79 E6
Chainbridge Cambs 66 D4
Chainhurst Kent 29 E8
Chalbury Dorset 13 D8
Chalbury Common Dorset 13 D8
Chaldon Sur 28 D4
Chaldon Herring or Dorset 13 F5
Chale I o W 15 G5
Chale Green I o W 15 G5
Chalfont Common Bucks 40 E3
Chalfont St Giles Bucks 40 E2
Chalfont St Peter Bucks 40 E3
Chalford Glos 37 D5
Chalgrove Oxon 39 E6
Chalk Kent 29 B7
Challacombe Devon 21 E5
Challoch Dumfries 105 C7
Challock Kent 30 D4
Chalton Beds 40 B3
Chalton Hants 15 C8
Chalvington E Sus 18 E2
Chancery Ceredig 46 B4
Chandler's Ford Hants 14 B5
Channel Tunnel Kent 19 B8
Channerwick Shetland 175 L6
Chantry Som 24 E2
Chantry Suff 56 E5
Chapel Fife 134 E4
Chapel Allerton Som 23 D6
Chapel Allerton W Yorks 95 F6
Chapel Amble Corn 4 B4
Chapel Brampton Northants 52 C5
Chapel Chorlton Staffs 74 F5
Chapel-en-le-Frith Derbys 87 F8
Chapel End Warks 63 E7
Chapel Green Warks 63 F6
Chapel Green Warks 52 C2
Chapel Haddlesey N Yorks 89 B6
Chapel Head Cambs 66 F3
Chapel Hill Aberds 161 E7
Chapel Hill Lincs 78 D5
Chapel Hill Mon 36 E2
Chapel Hill N Yorks 95 E6
Chapel Lawn Shrops 48 B5
Chapel-le-Dale N Yorks 93 B7
Chapel Milton Derbys 87 F8
Chapel of Garioch Aberds 151 B6
Chapel Row W Berks 26 C3
Chapel St Leonards Lincs 79 B8
Chapel Stile Cumb 99 D5
Chapelgate Lincs 66 B4
Chapelhall N Lnrk 121 C7
Chapelhill Dumfries 114 E3
Chapelhill Highld 158 B2
Chapelhill N Ayrs 120 E2
Chapelhill Perth 134 B4
Chapelhill Perth 141 F7
Chapelknowe Dumfries 108 B3
Chapelton Angus 143 E6
Chapelton Devon 9 B7
Chapelton Highld 148 C5
Chapelton S Lnrk 121 E6
Chapeltown Blkburn 86 C5
Chapeltown Moray 149 B8
Chapeltown S Yorks 88 E4
Chapmans Well Devon 9 E5
Chapmanslade Wilts 24 E3
Chapmore End Herts 41 C6
Chappel Essex 42 B4
Chard Som 11 D8
Chardstock Devon 11 D8
Charfield S Glos 36 E4
Charford Worcs 50 C4
Charing Kent 30 E3
Charing Cross Dorset 14 C2

Colebrook Devon 10 D5
Colebrooke Devon 10 E2
Coleby Lincs 78 C2
Coleby N Lincs 90 C2
Coleford Devon 10 D2
Coleford Glos 36 C2
Coleford Som 23 E8
Colehill Dorset 13 D8
Coleman's Hatch E Sus 29 F5
Colemere Shrops 73 F8
Colemore Hants 26 F5
Coleorton Leics 63 C8
Colerne Wilts 24 B3
Cole's Green Suff 57 C6
Coles Green Suff 56 E4
Colesbourne Glos 37 C6
Colesden Beds 54 D2
Coleshill Bucks 40 E2
Coleshill Oxon 38 E2
Coleshill Warks 63 F6
Colestocks Devon 11 D5
Colgate W Sus 28 F3
Colgrain Argyll 129 B8
Colinsburgh Fife 135 D6
Colinton Edin 122 C5
Colintraive Argyll 129 C5
Colkirk Norf 80 E5
Collace Perth 142 F2
Collafirth Shetland 174 G6
Collaton St Mary Torbay 7 D6
College Milton S Lnrk 121 D6
Collessie Fife 134 C4
Collier Row London 41 E8
Collier Street Kent 29 E8
Collier's End Herts 41 B6
Collier's Green Kent 18 B4
Colliery Row T & W 111 E6
Collieston Aberds 161 F7
Collin Dumfries 107 B7
Collingbourne Ducis Wilts 25 D7
Collingbourne Kingston Wilts 25 D7
Collingham Notts 77 C8
Collingham W Yorks 95 E6
Collington Hereford 49 C8
Collingtree Northants 53 D5
Collins Green Warr 86 E3
Colliston Angus 143 E6
Collycroft Warks 63 F7
Collynie Aberds 160 E5
Collyweston Northants 65 D6
Colmonell S Ayrs 104 A5
Colmworth Beds 54 D2
Coln Rogers Glos 37 D7
Coln St Aldwyn's Glos 37 D8
Coln St Dennis Glos 37 C7
Colnabaichin Aberds 149 D8
Colnbrook Slough 27 B8
Colne Cambs 54 B4
Colne Lancs 93 E8
Colne Edge Lancs 93 E8
Colne Engaine Essex 56 F2
Colney Norf 68 D4
Colney Heath Herts 41 D5
Colney Street Herts 40 D4
Colpy Aberds 160 E3
Colquhar Borders 123 E6
Colsterdale N Yorks 101 F6
Colsterworth Lincs 65 B6
Colston Bassett Notts 77 F6
Coltfield Moray 158 C5
Colthouse Cumb 99 E5
Coltishall Norf 69 C5
Coltness N Lnrk 121 D8
Colton Cumb 99 F5
Colton Norf 68 D4
Colton N Yorks 95 E8
Colton Staffs 62 B4
Colton W Yorks 95 F6
Colva Powys 48 D4
Colvend Dumfries 107 D5
Colvister Shetland 174 D7
Colwall Green Hereford 50 E2
Colwall Stone Hereford 50 E2
Colwell Northumb 110 B2
Colwich Staffs 62 B4
Colwick Notts 77 E6
Colwinston V Glam 21 B8
Colworth W Sus 16 D3
Colwyn Bay = Bae Colwyn Conwy 83 D8
Colyford Devon 11 E7
Colyton Devon 11 E7
Combe Hereford 48 C5
Combe Oxon 38 C4
Combe W Berks 25 C8
Combe Common Sur 27 F7
Combe Down Bath 24 C2
Combe Florey Som 22 F3
Combe Hay Bath 24 D2
Combe Martin Devon 20 E4
Combe Moor Hereford 49 C5
Combe Raleigh Devon 11 D6
Combe St Nicholas Som 11 C8
Combeinteignhead Devon 7 B7
Comberbach Ches 74 B3
Comberton Cambs 54 D4
Comberton Hereford 49 C6
Combpyne Devon 11 E7
Combridge Staffs 75 F7
Combrook Warks 51 D8
Combs Derbys 75 B7
Combs Suff 56 D4
Combs Ford Suff 56 D4
Combwich Som 22 E4
Comers Aberds 151 D5
Comins Coch Ceredig 58 F3
Commercial End Cambs 55 C6
Commins Capel Betws Ceredig 46 D5
Commins Coch Powys 58 D5
Common Edge Blkpool 92 F3
Common Side Derbys 76 B3
Commondale N Yorks 102 C4
Commonmoor Corn 5 C7
Commonside Ches 74 B2
Compstall Gtr Man 87 E7
Compton Devon 7 C6
Compton Hants 15 B5
Compton Sur 27 E6
Compton Sur 27 E7
Compton W Berks 26 B3
Compton Wilts 25 D6
Compton W Sus 15 C8
Compton Abbas Dorset 13 C6
Compton Abdale Glos 37 C7
Compton Acres Poole 13 F8
Compton Bassett Wilts 24 B5
Compton Beauchamp Oxon 38 F2
Compton Bishop Som 23 D5
Compton Chamberlayne Wilts 13 B8
Compton Dando Bath 23 C8
Compton Dundon Som 23 F6
Compton Martin Bath 23 D7
Compton Pauncefoot Som 12 B4
Compton Valence Dorset 12 E3
Comrie Fife 134 F2
Comrie Perth 133 B6
Conaglen House Highld 138 C4
Conchra Argyll 129 B5
Concraigie Perth 141 E8
Conder Green Lancs 92 D4
Conderton Worcs 50 F4
Condicote Glos 38 B1
Condorrat N Lnrk 121 B7
Condover Shrops 60 D4
Coney Weston Suff 56 B3
Coneyhurst W Sus 16 B5
Coneysthorpe N Yorks 96 B3
Coneythorpe N Yorks 95 D6
Conford Hants 27 F6
Congash Highld 149 B6
Congdon's Shop Corn 5 B7
Congerstone Leics 63 D7
Congham Norf 80 E3
Congl-y-wal Gwyn 71 C8
Congleton Ches 75 C5
Congresbury N Som 23 C6
Congreve Staffs 62 C3
Conicavel Moray 158 D3
Coningsby Lincs 78 D5
Conington Cambs 65 F8
Conington Cambs 54 C4
Conisbrough S Yorks 89 E6
Conisby Argyll 126 C2
Conisholme Lincs 91 E8
Coniston Cumb 99 E5
Coniston E Yorks 97 F7
Coniston Cold N Yorks 94 D2
Conistone N Yorks 94 C2
Connah's Quay Flint 73 C6
Connel Argyll 130 B5
Connel Park E Ayrs 113 C6
Connor Downs Corn 2 C4
Conon Bridge Highld 157 D6
Conon House Highld 157 D6
Cononley N Yorks 94 E2
Conordan Highld 153 F6
Consall Staffs 75 E6
Consett Durham 110 D4
Constable Burton N Yorks 101 E6
Constantine Corn 3 D6
Constantine Bay Corn 4 B3
Contin Highld 157 D5
Contlaw Aberdeen 151 D7
Conwy Conwy 83 D7
Conwy Castle Conwy 83 D7
Conyer Kent 30 C3
Conyers Green Suff 56 C2
Cooden E Sus 18 E4
Cooil I o M 84 E3
Cookbury Devon 9 D6
Cookham Windsor 40 F1
Cookham Dean Windsor 40 F1
Cookham Rise Windsor 40 F1
Cookhill Worcs 51 D5
Cookley Suff 57 B7
Cookley Worcs 62 F2
Cookley Green Oxon 39 E6
Cookney Aberds 151 E7
Cookridge W Yorks 95 E5
Cooksbridge E Sus 17 C8
Cooksmill Green Essex 42 D2
Coolham W Sus 16 B5
Cooling Medway 29 B8
Coombe Corn 8 C4
Coombe Corn 4 D4
Coombe Hants 15 B7
Coombe Wilts 25 D6
Coombe Bissett Wilts 14 B2
Coombe Hill Glos 37 B5
Coombe Keynes Dorset 13 F6
Coombes W Sus 17 D5
Coopersale Common Essex 41 D7
Cootham W Sus 16 C4
Copdock Suff 56 E5
Copford Green Essex 43 B5
Copgrove N Yorks 95 C6
Copister Shetland 174 F6
Cople Beds 54 E2
Copley Durham 101 B5
Coplow Dale Derbys 75 B8
Copmanthorpe York 95 E8
Coppathorne Corn 8 D4
Coppenhall Staffs 62 C3
Coppenhall Moss Ches 74 D4
Copperhouse Corn 2 C4
Coppingford Cambs 65 F8
Copplestone Devon 10 D2
Coppull Lancs 86 C3
Coppull Moor Lancs 86 C3
Copsale W Sus 17 B5
Copshaw Holm = Newcastleton Borders 115 F7
Copster Green Lancs 93 F6
Copston Magna Warks 63 F8
Copt Heath W Mid 51 B6
Copt Hewick N Yorks 95 B6
Copt Oak Leics 63 C8
Copthorne Shrops 60 C4
Copthorne W Sus 28 F4
Copy's Green Norf 80 D5
Copythorne Hants 14 C4
Corbets Tey London 42 F1
Corbridge Northumb 110 C2
Corby Northants 65 F5
Corby Glen Lincs 65 B6
Cordon N Ayrs 119 C7
Coreley Shrops 49 B8
Cores End Bucks 40 F2
Corfe Som 11 C7
Corfe Castle Dorset 13 F7
Corfe Castle Dorset 13 F7
Corfe Mullen Dorset 13 E7
Corfton Shrops 60 F4
Corgarff Aberds 149 D8
Corhampton Hants 15 B7
Corlae Dumfries 113 E6
Corley Warks 63 F7
Corley Ash Warks 63 F6
Corley Moor Warks 63 F6
Cornaa I o M 84 D4
Cornabus Argyll 126 E3
Cornel Conwy 83 E7
Corner Row Lancs 92 F4
Corney Cumb 98 E3
Cornforth Durham 111 F6
Cornhill Aberds 160 C2
Cornhill-on-Tweed Northumb 124 F4
Cornholme W Yorks 87 B7
Cornish Cyder Farm, Truro Corn 4 D2
Cornish Hall End Essex 55 F7
Cornquoy Orkney 176 G4
Cornsay Durham 110 E4
Cornsay Colliery Durham 110 E4
Corntown Highld 157 D6
Corntown V Glam 21 B8
Cornwell Oxon 38 B2
Cornwood Devon 6 D4
Cornworthy Devon 7 D6
Corpach Highld 138 B4
Corpusty Norf 81 D7
Corran Highld 138 C4
Corran Highld 145 C8
Corranbuie Argyll 128 D3
Corrany I o M 84 D4
Corrie N Ayrs 119 B7
Corrie Common Dumfries 114 F5
Corriecravie N Ayrs 119 D6
Corriemoillie Highld 156 C4
Corriemulzie Lodge Highld 163 E7
Corrievarkie Lodge Perth 140 B2
Corrievorrie Highld 148 B3
Corrimony Highld 156 F4
Corringham Lincs 90 E2
Corringham Thurrock 42 F3
Corris Gwyn 58 D4
Corris Uchaf Gwyn 58 D4
Corrour Shooting Lodge Highld 139 C8
Corrow Argyll 131 E7
Corry Highld 155 H2
Corry of Ardnagrask Highld 157 E6
Corrykinloch Highld 163 B7
Corrymuckloch Perth 141 F5
Corrynachenchy Argyll 137 D7
Cors-y-Gedol Gwyn 71 E6
Corsback Highld 169 B7
Corscombe Dorset 12 D3
Corse Aberds 160 D3
Corse Glos 36 B4
Corse Lawn Worcs 50 F3
Corse of Kinnoir Aberds 160 D2
Corsewall Dumfries 104 C4
Corsham Wilts 24 B3
Corsindae Aberds 151 D5
Corsley Wilts 24 E3
Corsley Heath Wilts 24 E3
Corsock Dumfries 106 B4
Corston Bath 23 C8
Corston Wilts 37 F6
Corstorphine Edin 122 B4
Cortachy Angus 142 D3
Corton Suff 69 E8
Corton Wilts 24 E4
Corton Denham Som 12 B4
Coruanan Lodge Highld 138 C4
Corunna W Isles 170 D4
Corwen Denb 72 E4
Coryton Devon 9 F6
Coryton Thurrock 42 F3
Cosby Leics 64 E2
Coseley W Mid 62 E3
Cosgrove Northants 53 E5
Cosham Ptsmth 15 D7
Cosheston Pembs 32 D1
Cossall Notts 76 E4
Cossington Leics 64 C3
Cossington Som 23 E5
Costa Orkney 176 D2
Costessey Norf 68 C4
Costock Notts 64 B2
Coston Leics 64 B5
Cote Oxon 38 D3
Cotebrook Ches 74 C2
Cotehele House Corn 6 C2
Cotehill Cumb 108 D4
Cotes Cumb 99 F6
Cotes Leics 64 B2
Cotes Staffs 74 F5
Cotesbach Leics 64 F2
Cotgrave Notts 77 F6
Cothall Aberds 151 C7
Cotham Notts 77 E7
Cothelstone Som 22 F3
Cotherstone Durham 101 C5
Cothill Oxon 38 E4
Cotleigh Devon 11 D7
Cotmanhay Derbys 76 E4
Cotmaton Devon 11 F6
Coton Cambs 54 D5
Coton Northants 52 B4
Coton Staffs 62 B2
Coton Staffs 75 F6
Coton Clanford Staffs 62 B2
Coton Hill Shrops 60 C4
Coton Hill Staffs 75 F6
Coton in the Elms Derbys 63 C6
Cotswold Wild Life Park, Burford Oxon 38 D2
Cott Devon 7 C5
Cottam E Yorks 97 C5
Cottam Lancs 92 F5
Cottam Notts 77 B8
Cottartown Highld 158 F4
Cottenham Cambs 54 C5
Cotterdale N Yorks 100 E3
Cottered Herts 41 B6
Cotteridge W Mid 50 B5
Cotterstock Northants 65 E7
Cottesbrooke Northants 52 B5
Cottesmore Rutland 65 C6
Cotteylands Devon 10 C4
Cottingham E Yorks 97 F6
Cottingham Northants 64 E5
Cottingley W Yorks 94 F4
Cottisford Oxon 52 F3
Cotton Staffs 75 E7
Cotton Suff 56 C4
Cotton End Beds 53 E8
Cottown Aberds 150 B4
Cottown Aberds 151 C6
Cottown Aberds 160 D5
Cotwalton Staffs 75 F6
Couch's Mill Corn 5 D6
Coughton Hereford 36 B2
Coughton Warks 51 C5
Coulaghailtro Argyll 128 D2
Coulags Highld 155 F5
Coulby Newham M'bro 102 C3
Coulderton Cumb 98 D1
Coulin Highld 155 E6
Coull Aberds 150 D4
Coull Argyll 126 C2
Coulport Argyll 129 B7
Coulsdon London 28 D3
Coulston Wilts 24 D4
Coulter S Lnrk 122 F3
Coulton N Yorks 96 B2
Cound Shrops 61 D5
Coundon Durham 101 B7
Coundon W Mid 63 F7
Coundon Grange Durham 101 B7
Countersett N Yorks 100 F4
Countess Wilts 25 E6
Countess Wear Devon 10 F4
Countesthorpe Leics 64 E2
Countisbury Devon 21 E6
County Oak W Sus 28 F3
Coup Green Lancs 86 B3
Coupar Angus Perth 142 E2
Coupland Northumb 124 F5
Cour Argyll 118 B5
Courance Dumfries 114 E3
Court-at-Street Kent 19 B7
Court Henry Carms 33 B6
Courteenhall Northants 53 D5
Courtsend Essex 43 E6
Courtway Som 22 F4
Cousland Midloth 123 C6
Cousley Wood E Sus 18 B3
Cove Argyll 129 B7
Cove Borders 124 B3
Cove Devon 10 C4
Cove Hants 27 D6
Cove Highld 162 E2
Cove Bay Aberdeen 151 D8
Cove Bottom Suff 57 B8
Covehithe Suff 69 F8
Coven Staffs 62 D3
Coveney Cambs 66 F4
Covenham St Bartholomew Lincs 91 E7
Covenham St Mary Lincs 91 E7
Coventry W Mid 51 B8
Coventry Airport Warks 51 B8
Coventry Cathedral W Mid 51 B8
Coverack Corn 3 E6
Coverham N Yorks 101 F6
Covesea Moray 159 B5
Covington Cambs 53 B8
Covington S Lnrk 122 F2
Cow Ark Lancs 93 E6
Cowan Bridge Lancs 93 B6
Cowbeech E Sus 18 D3
Cowbit Lincs 66 C2
Cowbridge Lincs 79 E6
Cowbridge Som 21 E8
Cowbridge = Y Bont-Faen V Glam 21 B8
Cowdale Derbys 75 B7
Cowden Kent 29 E5
Cowdenbeath Fife 134 E3
Cowdenburn Borders 122 D5
Cowers Lane Derbys 76 E3
Cowes I o W 15 E5
Cowesby N Yorks 102 F2
Cowfold W Sus 17 B6
Cowgill Cumb 100 F2
Cowie Aberds 151 F7
Cowie Stirl 133 F7
Cowley Devon 10 E4
Cowley Glos 37 C6
Cowley London 40 F3
Cowley Oxon 39 D5
Cowleymoor Devon 10 C4
Cowling Lancs 86 C3
Cowling N Yorks 94 E2
Cowling N Yorks 101 F7
Cowlinge Suff 55 D8
Cowpe Lancs 87 B6
Cowpen Northumb 117 F8
Cowpen Bewley Stockton 102 B2
Cowplain Hants 15 C7
Cowshill Durham 109 E8
Cowstrandburn Fife 134 E2
Cowthorpe N Yorks 95 D7
Cox Common Suff 69 F6
Cox Green Windsor 27 B6
Cox Moor Notts 76 D5
Coxbank Ches 74 E3
Coxbench Derbys 76 E3
Coxford Norf 80 E4
Coxford Soton 14 C4
Coxheath Kent 29 D8
Coxhill Kent 31 E6
Coxhoe Durham 111 F6
Coxley Som 23 E7
Coxwold N Yorks 95 B8
Coychurch Bridgend 21 B8
Coylton S Ayrs 112 B4
Coylumbridge Highld 148 C5
Coynach Aberds 150 D3
Coynachie Aberds 159 F8
Coytrahen Bridgend 34 F2
Crabadon Devon 7 D5
Crabbs Cross Worcs 50 C5
Crabtree W Sus 17 B6
Crackenthorpe Cumb 100 B1
Crackington Haven Corn 8 E3
Crackley Warks 51 B7
Crackleybank Shrops 61 C7
Crackpot N Yorks 100 E4
Cracoe N Yorks 94 C2
Craddock Devon 11 C5
Cradhlastadh W Isles 172 E3
Cradley Hereford 50 E2
Cradley Heath W Mid 62 F3
Crafthole Corn 5 D8
Cragg Vale W Yorks 87 B8
Craggan Highld 149 B6
Craggie Highld 165 C5
Craggie Highld 157 F8
Craghead Durham 110 D5
Crai Powys 34 B2
Craibstone Moray 159 D8
Craichie Angus 143 E5
Craig Dumfries 106 B3
Craig Dumfries 106 C3
Craig Highld 155 F6
Craig Castle Aberds 150 B3
Craig-cefn-parc Swansea 33 D7
Craig Penllyn V Glam 21 B8
Craig-y-don Conwy 83 C7
Craig-y-nos Powys 34 C2
Craiganor Lodge Perth 140 D3
Craigdam Aberds 160 E5
Craigdarroch Dumfries 113 E7
Craigdarroch Highld 156 D5
Craigdhu Highld 156 E5
Craigearn Aberds 151 C6
Craigellachie Moray 159 E6
Craigencross Dumfries 104 C4
Craigend Perth 134 B3
Craigend Stirl 133 F6
Craigendive Argyll 129 B5
Craigendoran Argyll 129 B8
Craigends Renfs 120 C4
Craigens Argyll 126 C2
Craigens E Ayrs 113 C5
Craighat Stirl 132 F3
Craighead Fife 135 D8
Craighlaw Mains Dumfries 105 C7
Craighouse Argyll 127 F3
Craigie Aberds 151 C8
Craigie Dundee 142 F4
Craigie Perth 134 B3
Craigie Perth 141 E8
Craigie S Ayrs 120 F4
Craigiefield Orkney 176 E3
Craigielaw E Loth 123 B7
Craiglockhart Edin 122 B5
Craigmalloch E Ayrs 112 E4
Craigmaud Aberds 161 C5
Craigmillar Edin 123 B5
Craigmore Argyll 129 D6
Craignant Shrops 73 F6
Craigneuk N Lnrk 121 D7
Craigneuk N Lnrk 121 C7
Craignure Argyll 130 B3
Craigo Angus 143 C6
Craigow Perth 134 D2
Craigrothie Fife 135 C5
Craigroy Moray 158 D5
Craigruie Stirl 132 B3
Craigston Castle Aberds 160 C4
Craigton Aberdeen 151 D7
Craigton Angus 142 D3
Craigton Angus 143 F5
Craigton Highld 164 E3
Craigtown Highld 168 D3
Craik Borders 115 D6
Crail Fife 135 D8
Crailing Borders 116 B2
Crailinghall Borders 116 B2
Craiselound N Lincs 89 E8
Crakehill N Yorks 95 B7
Crakemarsh Staffs 75 F7
Crambe N Yorks 96 C3
Cramlington Northumb 111 B5
Cramond Edin 122 B4
Cramond Bridge Edin 122 B4
Cranage Ches 74 C4
Cranberry Staffs 74 F5
Cranborne Dorset 13 C8
Cranbourne Brack 27 B7
Cranbrook Kent 18 B4
Cranbrook Common Kent 18 B4
Crane Moor S Yorks 88 D4
Crane's Corner Norf 68 C2
Cranfield Beds 53 E7
Cranford London 28 B2
Cranford St Andrew Northants 53 B7
Cranford St John Northants 53 B7
Cranham Glos 37 C5
Cranham London 42 F1
Crank Mers 86 E3
Crank Wood Gtr Man 86 D4
Cranleigh Sur 27 F8
Cranley Suff 57 B5
Cranmer Green Suff 56 B4
Cranmore I o W 14 E4
Cranna Aberds 160 C3
Crannich Argyll 137 D6
Crannoch Moray 159 D8
Cranoe Leics 64 E4
Cransford Suff 57 C7
Cranshaws Borders 124 C2
Cranstal I o M 84 B4
Crantock Corn 4 C2
Cranwell Lincs 78 E3
Cranwich Norf 67 E7
Cranworth Norf 68 D2
Craobh Haven Argyll 130 E3
Crapstone Devon 6 C3
Crarae Argyll 131 F5
Crask Inn Highld 164 B2
Crask of Aigas Highld 157 E5
Craskins Aberds 150 D4
Craster Northumb 117 C8
Craswall Hereford 48 F4
Cratfield Suff 57 B7
Crathes Aberds 151 E6
Crathes Castle and Gardens Aberds 151 E6
Crathie Aberds 149 E8
Crathie Highld 147 E8
Crathorne N Yorks 102 D2
Craven Arms Shrops 60 F4
Crawcrook T & W 110 C4
Crawford Lancs 86 D2
Crawford S Lnrk 114 B2
Crawfordjohn S Lnrk 113 B8
Crawick Dumfries 113 C7
Crawley Hants 26 F2
Crawley Oxon 38 C3
Crawley W Sus 28 F3
Crawley Down W Sus 28 F4
Crawleyside Durham 110 E2
Crawshawbooth Lancs 87 B6
Crawton Aberds 143 B8
Cray N Yorks 94 B2
Cray Perth 141 C8
Crayford London 29 B6
Crayke N Yorks 95 B8
Crays Hill Essex 42 E3
Cray's Pond Oxon 39 F6
Creacombe Devon 10 C3
Creag Ghoraidh W Isles 170 F3
Creagan Argyll 138 E3
Creaguaineach Lodge Highld 139 C7
Creaksea Essex 43 E5
Creaton Northants 52 B5
Creca Dumfries 108 B2
Credenhill Hereford 49 E6
Crediton Devon 10 D3
Creebridge Dumfries 105 C8
Creech Heathfield Som 11 B7
Creech St Michael Som 11 B7
Creed Corn 3 B8
Creekmouth London 41 F7
Creeting Bottoms Suff 56 D5
Creeting St Mary Suff 56 D4
Creeton Lincs 65 B7
Creetown Dumfries 105 D8
Creg-ny-Baa I o M 84 D3
Creggans Argyll 131 E6
Cregneash I o M 84 F1
Cregrina Powys 48 D3
Creich Fife 134 B5
Creigiau Cardiff 34 F4
Cremyll Corn 6 D2
Creslow Bucks 39 B8
Cressage Shrops 61 D5
Cressbrook Derbys 75 B8
Cresselly Pembs 32 D1
Cressing Essex 42 B3
Cresswell Northumb 117 E8
Cresswell Staffs 75 F6
Cresswell Quay Pembs 32 D1
Creswell Derbys 76 B5
Cretingham Suff 57 C6
Cretshengan Argyll 128 D2
Crewe Ches 73 D8
Crewe Ches 74 D4
Crewgreen Powys 60 C3
Crewkerne Som 12 D2
Crianlarich Stirl 132 B2
Cribyn Ceredig 46 D4
Criccieth Gwyn 71 D5
Crich Derbys 76 D3
Crichie Aberds 161 D6
Crichton Midloth 123 C6
Crick Mon 36 E1
Crick Northants 52 B3
Crickadarn Powys 48 E2
Cricket Malherbie Som 11 C8
Cricket St Thomas Som 11 D8
Crickheath Shrops 60 B2
Crickhowell Powys 35 C6
Cricklade Wilts 37 E8
Cricklewood London 41 F5
Cridling Stubbs N Yorks 89 B6
Crieff Perth 133 B7
Crieff Visitors' Centre Perth 133 B7
Criggion Powys 60 C2
Crigglestone W Yorks 88 C4
Crimond Aberds 161 C7
Crimonmogate Aberds 161 C7
Crimplesham Norf 67 D6
Crinan Argyll 128 A2
Cringleford Norf 68 D4
Cringles W Yorks 94 E3
Crinow Pembs 32 C2
Cripplesease Corn 2 C4
Cripplestyle Dorset 13 C8
Cripp's Corner E Sus 18 C4
Croasdale Cumb 98 C2
Crock Street Som 11 C8
Crockenhill Kent 29 C6
Crockernwell Devon 10 E2
Crockerton Wilts 24 E3
Crocketford or Ninemile Bar Dumfries 106 B5
Crockey Hill York 96 E2
Crockham Hill Kent 28 D5
Crockleford Heath Essex 43 B6
Crockness Orkney 176 G2
Croes-goch Pembs 44 B3
Croes-lan Ceredig 46 E2
Croes-y-mwyalch Torf 35 E7
Croeserw Neath 34 E2
Croesor Gwyn 71 C7
Croesyceiliog Carms 33 C5
Croesyceiliog Torf 35 E7
Croesywaun Gwyn 82 F5
Croft Leics 64 E2
Croft Lincs 79 C8
Croft Pembs 45 E3
Croft Warr 86 E4
Croft Motor Racing Circuit N Yorks 101 D7
Croft-on-Tees N Yorks 101 D7
Croftamie Stirl 132 F3
Croftmalloch W Loth 122 C2
Crofton Wilts 25 C7
Crofton W Yorks 88 C4
Crofts of Benachielt Highld 169 F6
Crofts of Haddo Aberds 160 E5
Crofts of Inverthernie Aberds 160 D4
Crofts of Meikle Ardo Aberds 161 D5
Crofty Swansea 33 E6
Croggan Argyll 130 C3
Croglin Cumb 109 E5
Croich Highld 164 E1
Crois Dughaill W Isles 171 H3
Cromarty Highld 157 C8
Cromblet Aberds 160 E4
Cromdale Highld 149 B6
Cromer Herts 41 B5
Cromer Norf 81 C8
Cromford Derbys 76 D2
Cromhall S Glos 36 E3
Cromhall Common S Glos 36 F3
Cromor W Isles 172 F7
Cromra Highld 147 E8
Cromwell Notts 77 C7
Cronberry E Ayrs 113 B6
Crondall Hants 27 E5
Cronk-y-Voddy I o M 84 D3
Cronton Mers 86 F2
Crook Cumb 99 E6
Crook Durham 110 F4
Crook of Devon Perth 134 D2
Crookedholm E Ayrs 120 F4
Crookes S Yorks 88 F4
Crookham Northumb 124 F5
Crookham W Berks 26 C3
Crookham Village Hants 27 D5
Crookhaugh Borders 114 B4
Crookhouse Borders 116 B3
Crooklands Cumb 99 F7
Croome Park, Pershore Worcs 50 E3
Cropredy Oxon 52 E2
Cropston Leics 64 C2
Cropthorne Worcs 50 E4
Cropton N Yorks 103 F5
Cropwell Bishop Notts 77 F6
Cropwell Butler Notts 77 F6
Cros W Isles 172 B8
Crosbost W Isles 172 F6
Crosby Cumb 107 F7
Crosby I o M 84 E3
Crosby N Lincs 90 C2
Crosby Garrett Cumb 100 D2
Crosby Ravensworth Cumb 99 C8
Crosby Villa Cumb 107 F7
Croscombe Som 23 E7
Cross Som 23 D6
Cross Ash Mon 35 C8
Cross-at-Hand Kent 29 E8
Cross Green Devon 9 F5
Cross Green Suff 56 D3
Cross Green Suff 56 D2
Cross Green Warks 51 D8
Cross Hands Carms 33 C6
Cross-hands Carms 32 B2
Cross Hands Pembs 32 C1
Cross Hill Derbys 76 E4
Cross Houses Shrops 60 D5
Cross in Hand E Sus 18 C2
Cross in Hand Leics 64 F2
Cross Inn Ceredig 46 D2
Cross Inn Ceredig 46 C4
Cross Inn Rhondda 34 F4
Cross Keys Kent 29 D6
Cross Lane Head Shrops 61 E7
Cross Lanes Corn 3 D5
Cross Lanes N Yorks 95 C8
Cross Lanes Wrex 73 E7
Cross Oak Powys 35 B5
Cross of Jackston Aberds 160 E4
Cross o'th'hands Derbys 76 E2
Cross Street Suff 57 B5
Crossaig Argyll 118 A5
Crossal Highld 153 F5
Crossapol Argyll 136 F1
Crossburn Falk 121 B8
Crossbush W Sus 16 D4
Crosscanonby Cumb 107 F7
Crossdale Street Norf 81 D8
Crossens Mers 85 C4
Crossflatts W Yorks 94 E4
Crossford Fife 134 F2
Crossford S Lnrk 121 E8
Crossgate Lincs 66 B2
Crossgatehall E Loth 123 C6
Crossgates Fife 134 F3
Crossgates Powys 48 C2
Crossgill Lancs 93 C5
Crosshill E Ayrs 112 B4
Crosshill Fife 134 E3
Crosshill S Ayrs 112 D3
Crosshouse E Ayrs 120 F3
Crossings Cumb 108 B5
Crosskeys Caerph 35 E6
Crosskirk Highld 168 B5
Crosslanes Shrops 60 C3
Crosslee Borders 115 C6
Crosslee Renfs 120 C4
Crossmichael Dumfries 106 C4
Crossmoor Lancs 92 F4
Crossroads Aberds 151 E6
Crossroads E Ayrs 120 F4
Crossway Hereford 49 F8
Crossway Mon 35 C8
Crossway Powys 48 D2
Crossway Green Worcs 50 C3
Crossways Dorset 13 F5
Crosswell Pembs 45 F3
Crosswood Ceredig 47 B5
Crosthwaite Cumb 99 E6
Croston Lancs 86 C2
Crostwick Norf 69 C5
Crostwight Norf 69 B6
Crothair W Isles 172 E4
Crouch Kent 29 D7
Crouch Hill Dorset 12 C5
Crouch House Green Kent 28 E5
Croucheston Wilts 13 B8
Croughton Northants 52 F3
Crovie Aberds 160 B5
Crow Edge S Yorks 88 D2
Crow Hill Hereford 36 B3
Crowan Corn 2 C5
Crowborough E Sus 18 B2
Crowcombe Som 22 F3
Crowdecote Derbys 75 C8
Crowden Derbys 87 E8
Crowell Oxon 39 E7
Crowfield Northants 52 E4
Crowfield Suff 56 D5
Crowhurst E Sus 18 D4
Crowhurst Sur 28 E4
Crowhurst Lane End Sur 28 E4
Crowland Lincs 66 C2
Crowlas Corn 2 C4
Crowle N Lincs 89 C8
Crowle Worcs 50 D4
Crowmarsh Gifford Oxon 39 F6
Crown Corner Suff 57 B6
Crownhill Plym 6 D2
Crownland Suff 56 C4
Crownthorpe Norf 68 D3
Crowntown Corn 2 C5
Crows-an-wra Corn 2 D2
Crowshill Norf 68 D2
Crowsnest Shrops 60 D3
Crowthorne Brack 27 C6
Crowton Ches 74 B2
Croxall Staffs 63 C5
Croxby Lincs 91 E5
Croxdale Durham 111 F5
Croxden Staffs 75 F7
Croxley Green Herts 40 E3
Croxton Cambs 54 C3
Croxton N Lincs 90 C4
Croxton Norf 67 F8
Croxton Staffs 74 F4
Croxton Kerrial Leics 64 B5
Croxtonbank Staffs 74 F4
Croy Highld 157 E8
Croy N Lnrk 121 B7
Croyde Devon 20 F3
Croydon Cambs 54 E4
Croydon London 28 C4
Crubenmore Lodge Highld 148 E2
Cruckmeole Shrops 60 D4
Cruckton Shrops 60 C4
Cruden Bay Aberds 161 E7
Crudgington Telford 61 C6
Crudwell Wilts 37 E6
Crug Powys 48 B3
Crugmeer Corn 4 B4

Crugybar Carms 47 F5
Crulabhig W Isles 172 E4
Crumlin = Crymlyn Caerph 35 E6
Crumpsall Gtr Man 87 D6
Crundale Kent 30 E4
Crundale Pembs 44 D4
Cruwys Morchard Devon 10 C3
Crux Easton Hants 26 D2
Crwbin Carms 33 C5
Crya Orkney 176 F2
Cryers Hill Bucks 40 E1
Crymlyn Gwyn 83 D6
Crymlyn = Crumlin Caerph 35 E6
Crymych Pembs 45 F3
Crynant Neath 34 D1
Crynfryn Ceredig 46 C4
Crystal Palace National Sports Centre London 28 B4
Cuaig Highld 154 E3
Cuan Argyll 130 D3
Cubbington Warks 51 C8
Cubeck N Yorks 100 F4
Cubert Corn 4 D2
Cubley S Yorks 88 D3
Cubley Common Derbys 75 F8
Cublington Bucks 39 B8
Cublington Hereford 49 F6
Cuckfield W Sus 17 B7
Cucklington Som 13 B5
Cuckney Notts 77 B5
Cuckoo Hill Notts 89 E8
Cuddesdon Oxon 39 D6
Cuddington Bucks 39 C7
Cuddington Ches 74 B3
Cuddington Heath Ches 73 E8
Cuddy Hill Lancs 92 F4
Cudham London 28 D5
Cudliptown Devon 6 B3
Cudworth Som 11 C8
Cudworth S Yorks 88 D4
Cuffley Herts 41 D6
Cuiashader W Isles 172 C8
Cuidhir W Isles 171 K2
Cuidhtinis W Isles 173 K3
Culbo Highld 157 C7
Culbokie Highld 157 D7
Culburnie Highld 157 E5
Culcabock Highld 157 E7
Culcairn Highld 157 C7
Culcharry Highld 158 D2
Culcheth Warr 86 E4
Culdrain Aberds 160 E2
Culduie Highld 155 F3
Culford Suff 56 B2
Culgaith Cumb 99 B8
Culham Oxon 39 E5
Culkein Highld 166 F2
Culkein Drumbeg Highld 166 F3
Culkerton Glos 37 E6
Cullachie Highld 149 B5
Cullen Moray 160 B2
Cullercoats T & W 111 B6
Cullicudden Highld 157 C7
Cullingworth W Yorks 94 F3
Cullipool Argyll 130 D3
Cullivoe Shetland 174 C7
Culloch Perth 133 C6
Culloden Highld 157 E8
Culloden Battlefield, Inverness Highld 157 E8
Cullompton Devon 10 D5
Culmaily Highld 165 E5
Culmazie Dumfries 105 D7
Culmington Shrops 60 F4
Culmstock Devon 11 C6
Culnacraig Highld 162 D4
Culnaknock Highld 152 C6
Culpho Suff 57 E6
Culrain Highld 164 E2
Culross Fife 133 F8
Culroy S Ayrs 112 C3
Culsh Aberds 161 D5
Culsh Aberds 150 E2
Culshabbin Dumfries 105 D7
Culswick Shetland 175 J4
Cultercullen Aberds 151 B8
Cults Aberdeen 151 D7
Cults Aberds 160 E2
Cults Dumfries 105 E8
Culverstone Green Kent 29 C7
Culverthorpe Lincs 78 E3
Culworth Northants 52 E3
Culzean Castle, Maybole S Ayrs 112 D2
Culzie Lodge Highld 157 B6
Cumbernauld N Lnrk 121 B7
Cumbernauld Village N Lnrk 121 B7
Cumberworth Lincs 79 B8
Cuminestown Aberds 160 C5
Cumlewick Shetland 175 L6
Cummersdale Cumb 108 D3
Cummertrees Dumfries 107 C8
Cummingston Moray 158 C5
Cumnock E Ayrs 113 B5
Cumnor Oxon 38 D4
Cumrew Cumb 108 D5
Cumwhinton Cumb 108 D4
Cumwhitton Cumb 108 D5
Cundall N Yorks 95 B7
Cunninghamhead N Ayrs 120 E3
Cunnister Shetland 174 D7
Cupar Fife 135 C5
Cupar Muir Fife 135 C5
Cupernham Hants 14 B4
Curbar Derbys 76 B2
Curbridge Hants 15 C6
Curbridge Oxon 38 D3
Curdridge Hants 15 C6
Curdworth Warks 63 E5
Curland Som 11 C7
Curlew Green Suff 57 C7
Currarie S Ayrs 112 E1
Curridge W Berks 26 B2
Currie Edin 122 C4
Curry Mallet Som 11 B8
Curry Rivel Som 11 B8
Curtisden Green Kent 29 E8
Curtisknowle Devon 6 D5
Cury Corn 3 D5
Cushnie Aberds 160 B4
Cushuish Som 22 F3
Cusop Hereford 48 E4
Cutcloy Dumfries 105 F8
Cutcombe Som 21 F8
Cutgate Gtr Man 87 C6
Cutiau Gwyn 58 C3
Cutlers Green Essex 55 F6
Cutnall Green Worcs 50 C3
Cutsdean Glos 51 F5
Cutthorpe Derbys 76 B3
Cutts Shetland 175 K6
Cutty Sark, Greenwich London 28 B4
Cuxham Oxon 39 E6
Cuxton Medway 29 C8
Cuxwold Lincs 91 D5
Cwm Bl Gwent 35 D5
Cwm Denb 72 B4
Cwm Swansea 33 E7
Cwm-byr Carms 46 F5
Cwm-Cewydd Gwyn 59 C5
Cwm-cou Ceredig 45 E4
Cwm-Dulais Swansea 33 D7
Cwm-felin-fach Caerph 35 E5
Cwm Ffrwd-oer Torf 35 D6
Cwm-hesgen Gwyn 71 E8
Cwm-hwnt Rhondda 34 D3
Cwm Irfon Powys 47 E7
Cwm-Llinau Powys 58 D5
Cwm-mawr Carms 33 C6
Cwm-parc Rhondda 34 E3
Cwm Penmachno Conwy 71 C8
Cwm-y-glo Carms 33 C6
Cwm-y-glo Gwyn 82 E5
Cwmafan Neath 34 E1
Cwmaman Rhondda 34 E4
Cwmann Carms 46 E4
Cwmavon Torf 35 D6
Cwmbach Carms 32 B3
Cwmbach Carms 33 D5
Cwmbach Powys 48 D2
Cwmbach Powys 48 F3
Cwmbâch Rhondda 34 D4
Cwmbelan Powys 59 F6
Cwmbran = Cwmbrân Torf 35 E6
Cwmbrân = Cwmbran Torf 35 E6
Cwmbrwyno Ceredig 58 F4
Cwmcarn Caerph 35 E6
Cwmcarvan Mon 36 D1
Cwmcych Pembs 45 F4
Cwmdare Rhondda 34 D3
Cwmderwen Powys 59 D6
Cwmdu Carms 46 F5
Cwmdu Powys 35 B5
Cwmdu Swansea 33 E7
Cwmduad Carms 46 F2
Cwmdwr Carms 47 F6
Cwmfelin Bridgend 34 F2
Cwmfelin M Tydf 34 D4
Cwmfelin Boeth Carms 32 C2
Cwmfelin Mynach Carms 32 B3
Cwmffrwd Carms 33 C5
Cwmgiedd Powys 34 C1
Cwmgors Neath 33 C8
Cwmgwili Carms 33 C6
Cwmgwrach Neath 34 D2
Cwmhiraeth Carms 46 F2
Cwmifor Carms 33 B7
Cwmisfael Carms 33 C5
Cwmllynfell Neath 33 C8
Cwmorgan Carms 45 F4
Cwmpengraig Carms 46 F2
Cwmrhos Powys 35 B5
Cwmsychpant Ceredig 46 E3
Cwmtillery Bl Gwent 35 D6
Cwmwysg Powys 34 B2
Cwmyoy Mon 35 B6
Cwmystwyth Ceredig 47 B6
Cwrt Gwyn 58 D3
Cwrt-newydd Ceredig 46 E3
Cwrt-y-cadno Carms 47 E5
Cwrt-y-gollen Powys 35 C6
Cydweli = Kidwelly Carms 33 D5
Cyffordd Llandudno = Llandudno Junction Conwy 83 D7
Cyffylliog Denb 72 D4
Cyfronydd Powys 59 D8
Cymer Neath 34 E2
Cyncoed Cardiff 35 F5
Cynghordy Carms 47 E7
Cynheidre Carms 33 D5
Cynwyd Denb 72 E4
Cynwyl Elfed Carms 32 B4
Cywarch Gwyn 59 C5

D

Dacre Cumb 99 B6
Dacre N Yorks 94 C4
Dacre Banks N Yorks 94 C4
Daddry Shield Durham 109 F8
Dadford Bucks 52 F4
Dadlington Leics 63 E8
Dafarn Faig Gwyn 71 C5
Dafen Carms 33 D6
Daffy Green Norf 68 D2
Dagenham London 41 F7
Daglingworth Glos 37 D6
Dagnall Bucks 40 C2
Dail Beag W Isles 172 D5
Dail bho Dheas W Isles 172 B7
Dail bho Thuath W Isles 172 B7
Dail Mor W Isles 172 D5
Daill Argyll 126 C3
Dailly S Ayrs 112 D2
Dairsie or Osnaburgh Fife 135 C6
Daisy Hill Gtr Man 86 D4
Dalabrog W Isles 171 H3
Dalavich Argyll 131 D5
Dalbeattie Dumfries 106 C5
Dalblair E Ayrs 113 C6
Dalbog Angus 143 B5
Dalbury Derbys 76 F2
Dalby I o M 84 E2
Dalby N Yorks 96 B2
Dalchalloch Perth 140 C4
Dalchalm Highld 165 D6
Dalchenna Argyll 131 E6
Dalchirach Moray 159 F5
Dalchork Highld 164 C2
Dalchreichart Highld 147 C5
Dalchruin Perth 133 C6
Dalderby Lincs 78 C5
Dale Pembs 44 E3
Dale Abbey Derbys 76 F4
Dale Head Cumb 99 C6
Dale of Walls Shetland 175 H3
Dalelia Highld 137 B8
Daless Highld 158 F2
Dalfaber Highld 148 C5
Dalgarven N Ayrs 120 E2
Dalgety Bay Fife 134 F3
Dalginross Perth 133 B6
Dalguise Perth 141 E6
Dalhalvaig Highld 168 D3
Dalham Suff 55 C8
Dalinlongart Argyll 129 B6
Dalkeith Midloth 123 C6
Dallam Warr 86 E3
Dallas Moray 158 D5
Dalleagles E Ayrs 113 C5
Dallinghoo Suff 57 D6
Dallington E Sus 18 D3
Dallington Northants 52 C5
Dallow N Yorks 94 B4
Dalmadilly Aberds 151 C6
Dalmally Argyll 131 C7
Dalmarnock Glasgow 121 C6
Dalmary Stirl 132 E4
Dalmellington E Ayrs 112 D4
Dalmeny Edin 122 B4
Dalmigavie Highld 148 C3
Dalmigavie Lodge Highld 148 B3
Dalmore Highld 157 C7
Dalmuir W Dunb 120 B4
Dalnabreck Highld 137 B7
Dalnacardoch Lodge Perth 140 B4
Dalnacroich Highld 156 D4
Dalnaglar Castle Perth 141 C8
Dalnahaitnach Highld 148 B4
Dalnaspidal Lodge Perth 140 B3
Dalnavaid Perth 141 C7
Dalnavie Highld 157 B7
Dalnawillan Lodge Highld 168 E5
Dalness Highld 139 D5
Dalnessie Highld 164 C3
Dalqueich Perth 134 D2
Dalreavoch Highld 164 D4
Dalry N Ayrs 120 E2
Dalrymple E Ayrs 112 C3
Dalserf S Lnrk 121 D8
Dalston Cumb 108 D3
Dalswinton Dumfries 114 F2
Dalton Dumfries 107 B8
Dalton Lancs 86 D2
Dalton Northumb 110 D2
Dalton Northumb 110 B4
Dalton N Yorks 95 B7
Dalton N Yorks 101 D6
Dalton S Yorks 89 E5
Dalton-in-Furness Cumb 92 B2
Dalton-le-Dale Durham 111 E7
Dalton-on-Tees N Yorks 101 D7
Dalton Piercy Hrtlpl 111 F7
Dalveich Stirl 132 B5
Dalvina Lodge Highld 167 E8
Dalwhinnie Highld 148 F2
Dalwood Devon 11 D7
Dalwyne S Ayrs 112 E3
Dam Green Norf 68 F3
Dam Side Lancs 92 E4
Damerham Hants 14 C2
Damgate Norf 69 D7
Damnaglaur Dumfries 104 F5
Damside Borders 122 E4
Danbury Essex 42 D3
Danby N Yorks 103 D5
Danby Wiske N Yorks 101 E8
Dandaleith Moray 159 E6
Danderhall Midloth 123 C6
Dane End Herts 41 B6
Danebridge Ches 75 C6
Danehill E Sus 17 B8
Danemoor Green Norf 68 D3
Danesford Shrops 61 E7
Daneshill Hants 26 D4
Dangerous Corner Lancs 86 C3
Danskine E Loth 123 C8
Darcy Lever Gtr Man 86 D5
Darenth Kent 29 B6
Daresbury Halton 86 F3
Darfield S Yorks 88 D5
Darfoulds Notts 77 B5
Dargate Kent 30 C4
Darite Corn 5 C7
Darlaston W Mid 62 E3
Darley N Yorks 94 D5
Darley Bridge Derbys 76 C2
Darley Head N Yorks 94 D4
Darley Moor Motor Racing Circuit Derbys 75 E8
Darlingscott Warks 51 E7
Darlington Darl 101 C7
Darliston Shrops 74 F2
Darlton Notts 77 B7
Darnall S Yorks 88 F4
Darnick Borders 123 F8
Darowen Powys 58 D5
Darra Aberds 160 D4
Darracott Devon 20 F3
Darras Hall Northumb 110 B4
Darrington W Yorks 89 B5
Darsham Suff 57 C8
Dartford Kent 29 B6
Dartford Crossing Kent 29 B6
Dartington Devon 7 C5
Dartington Cider Press Centre Devon 7 C5
Dartington Crystal Devon 9 C6
Dartmeet Devon 6 B4
Dartmouth Devon 7 D6
Darton S Yorks 88 D4
Darvel E Ayrs 121 F5
Darwell Hole E Sus 18 D3
Darwen Blkburn 86 B4
Datchet Windsor 27 B7
Datchworth Herts 41 C5
Datchworth Green Herts 41 C5
Daubhill Gtr Man 86 D5
Daugh of Kinermony Moray 159 E6
Dauntsey Wilts 37 F6
Dava Moray 158 F4
Davenham Ches 74 B3
Davenport Green Ches 74 B5
Daventry Northants 52 C3
David's Well Powys 48 B2
Davidson's Mains Edin 122 B5
Davidstow Corn 8 F3
Davington Dumfries 115 D5
Daviot Aberds 151 B6
Daviot Highld 157 F8
Davoch of Grange Moray 159 D8
Davyhulme Gtr Man 87 E5
Dawley Telford 61 D6
Dawlish Devon 7 B7
Dawlish Warren Devon 7 B7
Dawn Conwy 83 D8
Daws Heath Essex 42 F4
Daw's House Corn 8 F5
Dawsmere Lincs 79 F7
Dayhills Staffs 75 F6
Daylesford Glos 38 B2
Ddôl-Cownwy Powys 59 C7
Ddrydwy Anglesey 82 D3
Deadwater Northumb 116 E2
Deaf Hill Durham 111 F6
Deal Kent 31 D7
Deal Hall Essex 43 E6
Dean Cumb 98 B2
Dean Devon 6 C5
Dean Devon 20 E4
Dean Dorset 13 C7
Dean Hants 15 C6
Dean Som 23 E8
Dean Prior Devon 6 C5
Dean Row Ches 87 F6
Deanburnhaugh Borders 115 C6
Deane Gtr Man 86 D4
Deane Hants 26 D3
Deanich Lodge Highld 163 F7
Deanland Dorset 13 C7
Deans W Loth 122 C3
Deanscales Cumb 98 B2
Deanshanger Northants 53 F5
Deanston Stirl 133 D6
Dearham Cumb 107 F7
Debach Suff 57 D6
Debden Essex 55 F6
Debden Essex 41 E7
Debden Cross Essex 55 F6
Debenham Suff 57 C5
Dechmont W Loth 122 B3
Deddington Oxon 52 F2
Dedham Essex 56 F4
Dedham Heath Essex 56 F4
Deebank Aberds 151 E5
Deene Northants 65 E6
Deenethorpe Northants 65 E6
Deep Sea World, North Queensferry Fife 134 F3
Deepcar S Yorks 88 E3
Deepcut Sur 27 D7
Deepdale Cumb 100 F2
Deeping Gate Lincs 65 D8
Deeping St James Lincs 65 D8
Deeping St Nicholas Lincs 66 C2
Deerhill Moray 159 D8
Deerhurst Glos 37 B5
Deerness Orkney 176 F4
Defford Worcs 50 E4
Defynnog Powys 34 B3
Deganwy Conwy 83 D7
Deighton N Yorks 102 D1
Deighton W Yorks 88 C2
Deighton York 96 E2
Deiniolen Gwyn 83 E5
Delabole Corn 8 F2
Delamere Ches 74 C2
Delfrigs Aberds 151 B8
Dell Lodge Highld 149 C6
Delliefure Highld 158 F4
Delnabo Moray 149 C7
Delnadamph Aberds 149 D8
Delph Gtr Man 87 D7
Delves Durham 110 E4
Delvine Perth 141 E8
Dembleby Lincs 78 F3
Denaby Main S Yorks 89 E5
Denbigh = Dinbych Denb 72 C4
Denbury Devon 7 C6
Denby Derbys 76 E3
Denby Dale W Yorks 88 D3
Denchworth Oxon 38 E3
Dendron Cumb 92 B2
Denel End Beds 53 F8
Denend Aberds 160 E3
Denford Northants 53 B7
Dengie Essex 43 D5
Denham Bucks 40 F3
Denham Suff 55 C8
Denham Suff 57 B5
Denham Green Bucks 40 F3
Denham Street Suff 57 B5
Denhead Aberds 161 C6
Denhead Fife 135 C6
Denhead of Arbilot Angus 143 E5
Denhead of Gray Dundee 142 F3
Denholm Borders 115 C8
Denholme W Yorks 94 F3
Denholme Clough W Yorks 94 F3
Denio Gwyn 70 D4
Denmead Hants 15 C7
Denmore Aberdeen 151 C8
Denmoss Aberds 160 D3
Dennington Suff 57 C6
Denny Falk 133 F7
Denny Lodge Hants 14 D4
Dennyloanhead Falk 133 F7
Denshaw Gtr Man 87 C7
Denside Aberds 151 E7
Densole Kent 31 E6
Denston Suff 55 D8
Denstone Staffs 75 E8
Dent Cumb 100 F2
Denton Cambs 65 F8
Denton Darl 101 C7
Denton E Sus 17 D8
Denton Gtr Man 87 E7
Denton Kent 31 E6
Denton Lincs 77 F8
Denton Norf 69 F5
Denton Northants 53 D6
Denton N Yorks 94 E4
Denton Oxon 39 D5
Denton's Green Mers 86 E2
Denver Norf 67 D6
Denwick Northumb 117 C8
Deopham Norf 68 D3
Deopham Green Norf 68 E3
Depden Suff 55 D8
Depden Green Suff 55 D8
Deptford London 28 B4
Deptford Wilts 24 F5
Derby Derby 76 F3
Derbyhaven I o M 84 F2
Dereham Norf 68 C2
Deri Caerph 35 D5
Derril Devon 8 D5
Derringstone Kent 31 E6
Derrington Staffs 62 B2
Derriton Devon 8 D5
Derry Hill Wilts 24 B4
Derryguaig Argyll 137 E5
Derrythorpe N Lincs 90 D2
Dersingham Norf 80 D2
Dervaig Argyll 137 C5
Derwen Denb 72 D4
Derwenlas Powys 58 E4
Desborough Northants 64 F5
Desford Leics 63 D8
Detchant Northumb 125 F6
Detling Kent 29 D8
Deuddwr Powys 60 C2
Devauden Mon 36 E1
Devil's Bridge Ceredig 47 B6
Devizes Wilts 24 C5
Devol Invclyd 120 B3
Devon & Exeter Racecourse Devon 10 F4
Devonport Plym 6 D2
Devonside Clack 133 E8
Devoran Corn 3 C6
Dewar Borders 123 E6
Dewlish Dorset 13 E5
Dewsbury W Yorks 88 B3
Dewsbury Moor W Yorks 88 B3
Dewshall Court Hereford 49 F6
Dhoon I o M 84 D4
Dhoor I o M 84 C4
Dhowin I o M 84 B4
Dial Post W Sus 17 C5
Dibden Hants 14 D5
Dibden Purlieu Hants 14 D5
Dickleburgh Norf 68 F4
Didbrook Glos 51 F5
Didcot Oxon 39 F5
Diddington Cambs 54 C2
Diddlebury Shrops 60 F5
Didley Hereford 49 F6
Didling W Sus 16 C2
Didmarton Glos 37 F5
Didsbury Gtr Man 87 E6
Didworthy Devon 6 C4
Digby Lincs 78 D3
Digg Highld 152 C5
Diggerland, Cullompton Devon 10 D5
Diggerland, Langley Park Durham 110 E5
Diggle Gtr Man 87 D8
Digmoor Lancs 86 D2
Digswell Park Herts 41 C5
Dihewyd Ceredig 46 D3
Dilham Norf 69 B6
Dilhorne Staffs 75 E6
Dillarburn S Lnrk 121 E8
Dillington Cambs 54 C2
Dilston Northumb 110 C2
Dilton Marsh Wilts 24 E3
Dilwyn Hereford 49 D6
Dinas Carms 45 F4
Dinas Gwyn 70 D3
Dinas Cross Pembs 45 F2
Dinas Dinlle Gwyn 82 F4
Dinas-Mawddwy Gwyn 59 C5
Dinas Powys V Glam 22 B3
Dinbych = Denbigh Denb 72 C4
Dinbych-y-Pysgod = Tenby Pembs 32 D2
Dinder Som 23 E7
Dinedor Hereford 49 F7
Dingestow Mon 36 C1
Dingle Mers 85 F4
Dingleden Kent 18 B5
Dingley Northants 64 F4
Dingwall Highld 157 D6
Dinlabyre Borders 115 E8
Dinmael Conwy 72 E4
Dinnet Aberds 150 E3
Dinnington Som 12 C2
Dinnington S Yorks 89 F6
Dinnington T & W 110 B5
Dinorwic Gwyn 83 E5
Dinton Bucks 39 C7
Dinton Wilts 24 F5
Dinwoodie Mains Dumfries 114 E4
Dinworthy Devon 8 C5
Dippen N Ayrs 119 D7
Dippenhall Sur 27 E6
Dipple Moray 159 D7
Dipple S Ayrs 112 D2
Diptford Devon 6 D5
Dipton Durham 110 D4
Dirdhu Highld 149 B6
Dirleton E Loth 135 F7
Dirt Pot Northumb 109 E8
Discoed Powys 48 C4
Discovery Point Dundee 135 B6
Diseworth Leics 63 B8
Dishes Orkney 176 D5
Dishforth N Yorks 95 B6
Disley Ches 87 F7
Diss Norf 56 B5
Disserth Powys 48 D2
Distington Cumb 98 B2
Ditchampton Wilts 25 F5
Ditcheat Som 23 F8
Ditchingham Norf 69 E6
Ditchling E Sus 17 C7
Ditherington Shrops 60 C5
Dittisham Devon 7 D6
Ditton Halton 86 F2
Ditton Kent 29 D8
Ditton Green Cambs 55 D7
Ditton Priors Shrops 61 F6
Divach Highld 147 B7
Divlyn Carms 47 F6
Dixton Glos 50 F4
Dixton Mon 36 C2
Dobcross Gtr Man 87 D7
Dobwalls Corn 5 C7
Doc Penfro = Pembroke Dock Pembs 44 E4
Doccombe Devon 10 F2
Dochfour Ho. Highld 157 F7
Dochgarroch Highld 157 E7
Docking Norf 80 D3
Docklow Hereford 49 D7
Dockray Cumb 99 B5
Dockroyd W Yorks 94 F3
Dodburn Borders 115 D7
Doddinghurst Essex 42 E1
Doddington Cambs 66 E3
Doddington Kent 30 D3
Doddington Lincs 78 B2
Doddington Northumb 125 F5
Doddington Shrops 49 B8
Doddiscombsleigh Devon 10 F3
Dodford Northants 52 C4
Dodford Worcs 50 B4
Dodington S Glos 24 A2
Dodleston Ches 73 C7
Dods Leigh Staffs 75 F7
Dodworth S Yorks 88 D4
Doe Green Warr 86 F3
Doe Lea Derbys 76 C4
Dog Village Devon 10 E4
Dogdyke Lincs 78 D5
Dogmersfield Hants 27 D5
Dogridge Wilts 37 F7
Dogsthorpe P'boro 65 D8
Dol-fôr Powys 58 D5
Dôl-y-Bont Ceredig 58 F3
Dol-y-cannau Powys 48 E4
Dolanog Powys 59 C7
Dolau Powys 48 C3
Dolau Rhondda 34 F3
Dolbenmaen Gwyn 71 C6
Dolfach Powys 59 D6
Dolfor Powys 59 F8
Dolgarrog Conwy 83 E7
Dolgellau Gwyn 58 C4
Dolgran Carms 46 F3
Dolhendre Gwyn 72 F2
Doll Highld 165 D5
Dollar Clack 133 E8
Dolley Green Powys 48 C4
Dollwen Ceredig 58 F3
Dolphin Flint 73 B5
Dolphinholme Lancs 92 D5
Dolphinton S Lnrk 122 E4
Dolton Devon 9 C7
Dolwen Conwy 83 D8
Dolwen Powys 59 D6
Dolwyd Conwy 83 D8
Dolwyddelan Conwy 83 F7
Dolyhir Powys 48 D4
Doncaster S Yorks 89 D6
Doncaster Racecourse S Yorks 89 D7
Dones Green Ches 74 B3
Donhead St Andrew Wilts 13 B7
Donhead St Mary Wilts 13 B7
Donibristle Fife 134 F3
Donington Lincs 78 F5
Donington on Bain Lincs 91 F6
Donington Park Motor Racing Circuit Leics 63 B8
Donington South Ing Lincs 78 F5
Donisthorpe Leics 63 C7
Donkey Town Sur 27 C7
Donnington Glos 38 B1
Donnington Hereford 50 F2
Donnington Shrops 61 D5
Donnington Telford 61 C7
Donnington W Berks 26 C2
Donnington W Sus 16 D2
Donnington Wood Telford 61 C7
Donyatt Som 11 C8
Doonfoot S Ayrs 112 C3
Dorback Lodge Highld 149 C6
Dorchester Dorset 12 E4
Dorchester Oxon 39 E5
Dorchester Abbey, Wallingford Oxon 39 E5
Dordon Warks 63 D6
Dore S Yorks 88 F4
Dores Highld 157 F6
Dorking Sur 28 E2
Dormansland Sur 28 E5
Dormanstown Redcar 102 B3
Dormington Hereford 49 E7
Dormston Worcs 50 D4
Dornal S Ayrs 105 B6
Dorney Bucks 27 B7
Dornie Highld 155 H4
Dornoch Highld 164 F4
Dornock Dumfries 108 C2
Dorrery Highld 169 D5
Dorridge W Mid 51 B6
Dorrington Lincs 78 D3
Dorrington Shrops 60 D4
Dorsington Warks 51 E6
Dorstone Hereford 48 E5
Dorton Bucks 39 C6
Dorusduain Highld 146 B2
Dosthill Staffs 63 E6
Dottery Dorset 12 E2
Doublebois Corn 5 C6
Dougarie N Ayrs 119 C5
Doughton Glos 37 E5
Douglas I o M 84 E3
Douglas S Lnrk 121 F8
Douglas & Angus Dundee 142 F4
Douglas Water S Lnrk 121 F8
Douglas West S Lnrk 121 F8
Douglastown Angus 142 E4
Doulting Som 23 E8
Dounby Orkney 176 D1
Doune Highld 163 D8
Doune Stirl 133 D6
Doune Park Aberds 160 B4
Douneside Aberds 150 D3
Dounie Highld 164 E2
Dounreay Highld 168 C4
Dousland Devon 6 C3
Dovaston Shrops 60 B3
Dove Cottage and Wordsworth Museum Cumb 99 D5
Dove Holes Derbys 75 B7
Dovenby Cumb 107 F7
Dover Kent 31 E7
Dover Castle Kent 31 E7
Dovercourt Essex 57 F6
Doverdale Worcs 50 C3
Doveridge Derbys 75 F8
Doversgreen Sur 28 E3
Dowally Perth 141 E7
Dowbridge Lancs 92 F4
Dowdeswell Glos 37 C6
Dowlais M Tydf 34 D4
Dowland Devon 9 C7
Dowlish Wake Som 11 C8
Down Ampney Glos 37 E8
Down Hatherley Glos 37 B5
Down St Mary Devon 10 D2
Down Thomas Devon 6 D3
Downcraig Ferry N Ayrs 129 E6
Downderry Corn 5 D8
Downe London 28 C5
Downend I o W 15 F6
Downend S Glos 23 B8
Downend W Berks 26 B2
Downfield Dundee 142 F3
Downgate Corn 5 B8
Downham Essex 42 E3
Downham Lancs 93 E7
Downham Northumb 124 F4
Downham Market Norf 67 D6
Downhead Som 23 E8
Downhill Perth 141 F7
Downhill T & W 111 D6
Downholland Cross Lancs 85 D4
Downholme N Yorks 101 E6
Downies Aberds 151 E8
Downley Bucks 39 E8
Downside Som 23 E8
Downside Sur 28 D2
Downton Hants 14 E3
Downton Wilts 14 B2
Downton on the Rock Hereford 49 B6
Dowsby Lincs 65 B8
Dowsdale Lincs 66 C2
Dowthwaitehead Cumb 99 B5
Doxey Staffs 62 B3
Doxford Northumb 117 B7
Doxford Park T & W 111 D6
Doynton S Glos 24 B2
Draffan S Lnrk 121 E7
Dragonby N Lincs 90 C3
Drakeland Corner Devon 6 D3
Drakemyre N Ayrs 120 D2
Drake's Broughton Worcs 50 E4
Drakes Cross Worcs 51 B5
Drakewalls Corn 6 B2
Draughton Northants 53 B5
Draughton N Yorks 94 D3
Drax N Yorks 89 B7
Draycote Warks 52 B2
Draycott Derbys 76 F4
Draycott Glos 51 F6
Draycott Som 23 D6
Draycott in the Clay Staffs 63 B5
Draycott in the Moors Staffs 75 E6
Drayford Devon 10 C2
Drayton Leics 64 E5
Drayton Lincs 78 F5
Drayton Norf 68 C4
Drayton Oxon 52 E2
Drayton Oxon 38 E4
Drayton Ptsmth 15 D7
Drayton Som 12 B2
Drayton Worcs 50 B4
Drayton Bassett Staffs 63 D5
Drayton Beauchamp Bucks 40 C2
Drayton Manor Park, Tamworth Staffs 63 D5
Drayton Parslow Bucks 39 B8
Drayton St Leonard Oxon 39 E5
Dre-fach Ceredig 46 E4
Dre-fach Carms 33 C7
Dreamland Theme Park, Margate Kent 31 B7
Drebley N Yorks 94 D3
Dreemskerry I o M 84 C4
Dreenhill Pembs 44 D4
Drefach Carms 46 F2
Drefach Carms 33 C6
Drefelin Carms 46 F2
Dreghorn N Ayrs 120 F3
Drellingore Kent 31 E6
Drem E Loth 123 B8
Dresden Stoke 75 E6
Dreumasdal W Isles 170 G3
Drewsteignton Devon 10 E2
Driby Lincs 79 B6
Driffield E Yorks 97 D6
Driffield Glos 37 E7
Drigg Cumb 98 E2
Drighlington W Yorks 88 B3
Drimnin Highld 137 C6
Drimpton Dorset 12 D2
Drimsynie Argyll 131 E7
Drinisiadar W Isles 173 J4
Drinkstone Suff 56 C3
Drinkstone Green Suff 56 C3
Drishaig Argyll 131 D7
Drissaig Argyll 130 D5
Drochil Borders 122 E4
Drointon Staffs 62 B4
Droitwich Spa Worcs 50 C3
Droman Highld 166 D3
Dron Perth 134 C3
Dronfield Derbys 76 B3
Dronfield Woodhouse Derbys 76 B3
Drongan E Ayrs 112 C4
Dronley Angus 142 F3
Droxford Hants 15 C7
Droylsden Gtr Man 87 E7
Druid Denb 72 E4
Druidston Pembs 44 D3
Druimarbin Highld 138 B4
Druimavuic Argyll 138 E4
Druimdrishaig Argyll 128 C2
Druimindarroch Highld 145 E6
Druimyeon More Argyll 118 A3
Drum Argyll 128 C4
Drum Perth 134 D2
Drumbeg Highld 166 F3
Drumblade Aberds 160 D2
Drumblair Aberds 160 D3
Drumbuie Dumfries 113 F5
Drumbuie Highld 155 G3
Drumburgh Cumb 108 D2
Drumburn Dumfries 107 C6
Drumchapel Glasgow 120 B5
Drumchardine Highld 157 E6
Drumchork Highld 162 F2
Drumclog S Lnrk 121 F6
Drumderfit Highld 157 D7
Drumeldrie Fife 135 D6
Drumelzier Borders 122 F4
Drumfearn Highld 145 B6
Drumgask Highld 148 E2
Drumgley Angus 142 D4
Drumguish Highld 148 E3
Drumin Moray 159 F5
Drumlasie Aberds 150 D5
Drumlemble Argyll 118 E3
Drumligair Aberds 151 C8
Drumlithie Aberds 151 F6

Fowley Common Warr 86 E4
Fowlis Angus 142 F3
Fowlis Wester Perth 133 B8
Fowlmere Cambs 54 E5
Fownhope Hereford 49 F7
Fox Corner Sur 27 D7
Fox Lane Hants 27 D6
Fox Street Essex 43 B6
Foxbar Renfs 120 C4
Foxcombe Hill Oxon 38 D4
Foxdale I o M 84 E2
Foxearth Essex 56 E2
Foxfield Cumb 98 F4
Foxham Wilts 24 B4
Foxhole Corn 4 D4
Foxhole Swansea 33 E7
Foxholes N Yorks 97 B6
Foxhunt Green E Sus 18 D2
Foxley Norf 81 E6
Foxley Wilts 37 F5
Foxt Staffs 75 E7
Foxton Cambs 54 E5
Foxton Durham 102 B1
Foxton Leics 64 E4
Foxton Canal Locks Leics 64 F3
Foxup N Yorks 93 B8
Foxwist Green Ches 74 C3
Foxwood Shrops 49 B8
Foy Hereford 36 B2
Foyers Highld 147 B7
Fraddam Corn 2 C4
Fraddon Corn 4 D4
Fradley Staffs 63 C5
Fradswell Staffs 75 F6
Fraisthorpe E Yorks 97 C7
Framfield E Sus 17 B8
Framingham Earl Norf 69 D5
Framingham Pigot Norf 69 D5
Framlingham Suff 57 C6
Framlingham Castle Suff 57 C6
Frampton Dorset 12 E4
Frampton Lincs 79 F6
Frampton Cotterell S Glos 36 F3
Frampton Mansell Glos 37 D6
Frampton on Severn Glos 36 D4
Frampton West End Lincs 79 E5
Framsden Suff 57 D5
Framwellgate Moor Durham 111 E5
Franche Worcs 50 B3
Frankby Mers 85 F3
Frankley Worcs 62 F3
Frank's Bridge Powys 48 D3
Frankton Warks 52 B2
Frant E Sus 18 B2
Fraserburgh Aberds 161 B6
Frating Green Essex 43 B6
Fratton Ptsmth 15 E7
Freathy Corn 5 D8
Freckenham Suff 55 B7
Freckleton Lancs 86 B2
Freeby Leics 64 B5
Freehay Staffs 75 E7
Freeland Oxon 38 C4
Freeport Hornsea Outlet Village E Yorks 97 E7
Freester Shetland 175 H6
Freethorpe Norf 69 D7
Freiston Lincs 79 E6
Fremington Devon 20 F4
Fremington N Yorks 101 E5
Frenchay S Glos 23 B8
Frenchbeer Devon 9 F8
Frenich Stirl 132 D3
Frensham Sur 27 E6
Fresgoe Highld 168 C4
Freshfield Mers 85 D3
Freshford Bath 24 C2
Freshwater I o W 14 F4
Freshwater Bay I o W 14 F4
Freshwater East Pembs 32 E1
Fressingfield Suff 57 B6
Freston Suff 57 F5
Freswick Highld 169 C8
Fretherne Glos 36 D4
Frettenham Norf 68 C5
Freuchie Fife 134 D4
Freuchies Angus 142 C2
Freystrop Pembs 44 D4
Friar's Gate E Sus 29 F5
Friarton Perth 134 B3
Friday Bridge Cambs 66 D4
Friday Street E Sus 18 E3
Fridaythorpe E Yorks 96 D4
Friern Barnet London 41 E5
Friesland Argyll 136 C2
Friesthorpe Lincs 90 F4
Frieston Lincs 78 E2
Frieth Bucks 39 E7
Frilford Oxon 38 E4
Frilsham W Berks 26 B3
Frimley Sur 27 D6
Frimley Green Sur 27 D6
Frindsbury Medway 29 B8
Fring Norf 80 D3
Fringford Oxon 39 B6
Frinsted Kent 30 D2
Frinton-on-Sea Essex 43 B8
Friockheim Angus 143 E5
Friog Gwyn 58 C3
Frisby on the Wreake Leics 64 C3
Friskney Lincs 79 D7
Friskney Eaudike Lincs 79 D7
Friskney Tofts Lincs 79 D7
Friston E Sus 18 F2
Friston Suff 57 C8
Fritchley Derbys 76 D3
Frith Bank Lincs 79 E6
Frith Common Worcs 49 C8
Fritham Hants 14 C3
Frithelstock Devon 9 C6
Frithelstock Stone Devon 9 C6
Frithville Lincs 79 D6
Frittenden Kent 30 E2
Frittiscombe Devon 7 E6
Fritton Norf 68 E5
Fritton Norf 69 D7
Fritwell Oxon 39 B5
Frizinghall W Yorks 94 F4
Frizington Cumb 98 C2
Frocester Glos 36 D4
Frodesley Shrops 60 D5
Frodingham N Lincs 90 C2
Frodsham Ches 74 B2
Frogden Borders 116 B3
Froggatt Derbys 76 B2
Froghall Staffs 75 E7
Frogmore Devon 7 E5
Frogmore Hants 27 D6
Frognall Lincs 65 C8
Frogshail Norf 81 D8
Frolesworth Leics 64 E2
Frome Som 24 E2
Frome St Quintin Dorset 12 D3
Fromes Hill Hereford 49 E8
Fron Denb 72 C4
Fron Gwyn 82 F5
Fron Gwyn 70 D4
Fron Powys 48 C2
Fron Powys 60 D2
Fron Powys 59 E8
Froncysyllte Wrex 73 E6
Frongoch Gwyn 72 F3
Frostenden Suff 69 F7
Frosterley Durham 110 F3
Frotoft Orkney 176 D3
Froxfield Wilts 25 C7
Froxfield Green Hants 15 B8
Froyle Hants 27 E5
Fryerning Essex 42 D2
Fryton N Yorks 96 B2
Fulbeck Lincs 78 D2
Fulbourn Cambs 55 D6
Fulbrook Oxon 38 C2
Fulford Som 11 B7
Fulford Staffs 75 F6
Fulford York 96 E2
Fulham London 28 B3
Fulking W Sus 17 C6
Full Sutton E Yorks 96 D3
Fullarton Glasgow 121 C6
Fullarton N Ayrs 120 F3
Fuller Street Essex 42 C3
Fuller's Moor Ches 73 D8
Fullerton Hants 25 F8
Fulletby Lincs 79 B5
Fullwood E Ayrs 120 D4
Fulmer Bucks 40 F2
Fulmodestone Norf 81 D5
Fulnetby Lincs 78 B3
Fulstow Lincs 91 E7
Fulwell T & W 111 D6
Fulwood Lancs 92 F5
Fulwood S Yorks 88 F4
Fundenhall Norf 68 E4
Fundenhall Street Norf 68 E4
Funtington W Sus 15 D8
Funtley Hants 15 D6
Funtullich Perth 133 B6
Funzie Shetland 174 D8
Furley Devon 11 D7
Furnace Argyll 131 E6
Furnace Carms 33 D6
Furnace End Warks 63 E6
Furneaux Pelham Herts 41 B7
Furness Vale Derbys 87 F8
Furze Platt Windsor 40 F1
Furzehill Devon 21 E6
Fyfett Som 11 C7
Fyfield Essex 42 D1
Fyfield Glos 38 D2
Fyfield Hants 25 E7
Fyfield Oxon 38 E4
Fyfield Wilts 25 C6
Fylingthorpe N Yorks 103 D7
Fyvie Aberds 160 E4

G

Gabhsann bho Dheas W Isles 172 C7
Gabhsann bho Thuath W Isles 172 C7
Gablon Highld 164 E4
Gabroc Hill E Ayrs 120 D4
Gaddesby Leics 64 C3
Gadebridge Herts 40 D3
Gaer Powys 35 B5
Gaerllwyd Mon 35 E8
Gaerwen Anglesey 82 D4
Gagingwell Oxon 38 B4
Gaick Lodge Highld 148 F3
Gailey Staffs 62 C3
Gainford Durham 101 C6
Gainsborough Lincs 90 E2
Gainsborough Suff 57 E5
Gainsford End Essex 55 F8
Gairloch Highld 154 C4
Gairlochy Highld 146 F4
Gairney Bank Perth 134 E3
Gairnshiel Lodge Aberds 149 D8
Gaisgill Cumb 99 D8
Gaitsgill Cumb 108 E3
Galashiels Borders 123 F7
Galgate Lancs 92 D4
Galhampton Som 12 B4
Gallaberry Dumfries 114 F2
Gallachoille Argyll 128 B2
Gallanach Argyll 130 C4
Gallanach Argyll 136 B3
Gallantry Bank Ches 74 D2
Gallatown Fife 134 E4
Galley Common Warks 63 E7
Galley Hill Cambs 54 C4
Galleyend Essex 42 D3
Galleywood Essex 42 D3
Gallin Perth 140 E2
Gallowfauld Angus 142 E4
Gallows Green Staffs 75 E7
Galltair Highld 155 H4
Galmisdale Highld 144 E4
Galmpton Devon 6 E4
Galmpton Torbay 7 D6
Galphay N Yorks 95 B5
Galston E Ayrs 120 F5
Galtrigill Highld 152 D2
Gamblesby Cumb 109 F6
Gamesley Derbys 87 E8
Gamlingay Cambs 54 D3
Gammersgill N Yorks 101 F5
Gamston Notts 77 B7
Ganarew Hereford 36 C2
Ganavan Argyll 130 B4
Gang Corn 5 C8
Ganllwyd Gwyn 71 E8
Gannochy Angus 143 B5
Gannochy Perth 134 B3
Gansclet Highld 169 E8
Ganstead E Yorks 97 F7
Ganthorpe N Yorks 96 B2
Ganton N Yorks 97 B5
Garbat Highld 156 C5
Garbhallt Argyll 131 F6
Garboldisham Norf 68 F3
Garden City Flint 73 C7
Garden Village Wrex 73 D7
Garden Village W Yorks 95 F7
Gardenstown Aberds 160 B4
Garderhouse Shetland 175 J5
Gardham E Yorks 97 E5
Gardin Shetland 174 G6
Gare Hill Som 24 E2
Garelochhead Argyll 129 A7
Garford Oxon 38 E4
Garforth W Yorks 95 F7
Gargrave N Yorks 94 D2
Gargunnock Stirl 133 E6
Garlic Street Norf 68 F5
Garlieston Dumfries 105 E8
Garlinge Green Kent 30 D5
Garlogie Aberds 151 D6
Garmond Aberds 160 C5
Garmony Argyll 137 D7
Garmouth Moray 159 C7
Garn-yr-erw Torf 35 C6
Garnant Carms 33 C7
Garndiffaith Torf 35 D6
Garndolbenmaen Gwyn 71 C5
Garnedd Conwy 83 F7
Garnett Bridge Cumb 99 E7
Garnfadryn Gwyn 70 D3
Garnkirk N Lnrk 121 C6
Garnlydan Bl Gwent 35 C5
Garnswllt Swansea 33 D7
Garrabost W Isles 172 E8
Garraron Argyll 130 E4
Garras Corn 3 D6
Garreg Gwyn 71 C7
Garrick Perth 133 C7
Garrigill Cumb 109 E7
Garriston N Yorks 101 E6
Garroch Dumfries 113 F5
Garrogie Lodge Highld 147 C8
Garros Highld 152 C5
Garrow Perth 141 E5
Garryhorn Dumfries 113 E5
Garsdale Cumb 100 F2
Garsdale Head Cumb 100 E2
Garsdon Wilts 37 F6
Garshall Green Staffs 75 F6
Garsington Oxon 39 D5
Garstang Lancs 92 E4
Garston Mers 86 F2
Garswood Mers 86 E3
Gartcosh N Lnrk 121 C6
Garth Bridgend 34 E2
Garth Gwyn 83 D5
Garth Powys 47 E8
Garth Shetland 175 H4
Garth Wrex 73 E6
Garth Row Cumb 99 E7
Garthamlock Glasgow 121 C6
Garthbrengy Powys 48 F2
Garthdee Aberdeen 151 D8
Gartheli Ceredig 46 D4
Garthmyl Powys 59 E8
Garthorpe Leics 64 B5
Garthorpe N Lincs 90 C2
Gartly Aberds 160 E2
Gartmore Stirl 132 E4
Gartnagrenach Argyll 128 E2
Gartness N Lnrk 121 C7
Gartness Stirl 132 F4
Gartocharn W Dunb 132 F3
Garton E Yorks 97 F8
Garton-on-the-Wolds E Yorks 97 D5
Gartsherrie N Lnrk 121 C7
Gartymore Highld 165 C7
Garvald E Loth 123 B8
Garvamore Highld 147 E8
Garvard Argyll 127 C1
Garvault Hotel Highld 168 F2
Garve Highld 156 C4
Garvestone Norf 68 D3
Garvock Aberds 143 B7
Garvock Invclyd 129 C7
Garway Hereford 36 B1
Garway Hill Hereford 35 B8
Gaskan Highld 138 B1
Gastard Wilts 24 C3
Gasthorpe Norf 68 F2
Gatcombe I o W 15 F5
Gate Burton Lincs 90 F2
Gate Helmsley N Yorks 96 D2
Gateacre Mers 86 F2
Gatebeck Cumb 99 F7
Gateford Notts 89 F6
Gateforth N Yorks 89 B6
Gatehead E Ayrs 120 F3
Gatehouse Northumb 116 F3
Gatehouse of Fleet Dumfries 106 D3
Gatelawbridge Dumfries 114 E2
Gateley Norf 81 E5
Gatenby N Yorks 101 F8
Gateshead T & W 111 C5
Gateshead International Stadium T & W 111 C5
Gatesheath Ches 73 C8
Gateside Aberds 150 C5
Gateside Angus 142 E4
Gateside E Renf 120 D4
Gateside Fife 134 D3
Gateside N Ayrs 120 D3
Gathurst Gtr Man 86 D3
Gatley Gtr Man 87 F6
Gattonside Borders 123 F8
Gaufron Powys 47 C8
Gaulby Leics 64 D3
Gauldry Fife 135 B5
Gaunt's Common Dorset 13 D8
Gautby Lincs 78 B4
Gavinton Borders 124 D3
Gawber S Yorks 88 D4
Gawcott Bucks 52 F4
Gawsworth Ches 75 C5
Gawthorpe W Yorks 88 B3
Gawthrop Cumb 100 F1
Gawthwaite Cumb 98 F4
Gay Street W Sus 16 B4
Gaydon Warks 51 D8
Gayfield Orkney 176 A3
Gayhurst M Keynes 53 E6
Gayle N Yorks 100 F3
Gayles N Yorks 101 D6
Gayton Mers 85 F3
Gayton Norf 67 C7
Gayton Northants 52 D5
Gayton Staffs 62 B3
Gayton le Marsh Lincs 91 F8
Gayton le Wold Lincs 91 F6
Gayton Thorpe Norf 67 C7
Gaywood Norf 67 B6
Gazeley Suff 55 C8
Geanies House Highld 158 B2
Gearraidh Bhailteas W Isles 171 H3
Gearraidh Bhaird W Isles 172 F6
Gearraidh na h-Aibhne W Isles 172 E5
Gearraidh na Monadh W Isles 171 J3
Geary Highld 152 C3
Geddes House Highld 158 D2
Gedding Suff 56 D3
Geddington Northants 65 F5
Gedintailor Highld 153 F6
Gedling Notts 77 E6
Gedney Lincs 66 B4
Gedney Broadgate Lincs 66 B4
Gedney Drove End Lincs 66 B4
Gedney Dyke Lincs 66 B4
Gedney Hill Lincs 66 C3
Gee Cross Gtr Man 87 E7
Geilston Argyll 120 B3
Geirinis W Isles 170 F3
Geise Highld 169 C6
Geisiadar W Isles 172 E4
Geldeston Norf 69 E6
Gell Conwy 83 E8
Gelli Pembs 32 C1
Gelli Rhondda 34 E3
Gellideg M Tydf 34 D4
Gellifor Denb 72 C5
Gelligaer Caerph 35 E5
Gellilydan Gwyn 71 D7
Gellinudd Neath 33 D8
Gellyburn Perth 141 F7
Gellywen Carms 32 B3
Gelston Dumfries 106 D4
Gelston Lincs 78 E2
Gembling E Yorks 97 D7
Gentleshaw Staffs 62 C4
Geocrab W Isles 173 J4
George Green Bucks 40 F3
George Nympton Devon 10 B2
George Town Bl Gwent 35 D5
Georgefield Dumfries 115 E5
Georgeham Devon 20 F3
Gerlan Gwyn 83 E6
Germansweek Devon 9 E6
Germoe Corn 2 D4
Gerrans Corn 3 C7
Gerrards Cross Bucks 40 F3
Gestingthorpe Essex 56 F2
Geuffordd Powys 60 C2
Gib Hill Ches 74 B3
Gibbet Hill Warks 64 F2
Gibbshill Dumfries 106 B4
Gidea Park London 41 F8
Gidleigh Devon 9 F8
Giffnock E Renf 121 D5
Gifford E Loth 123 C8
Giffordland N Ayrs 120 E2
Giffordtown Fife 134 C4
Giggleswick N Yorks 93 C8
Gilberdyke E Yorks 90 B2
Gilchriston E Loth 123 C7
Gilcrux Cumb 107 F8
Gildersome W Yorks 88 B3
Gildingwells S Yorks 89 F6
Gileston V Glam 22 C2
Gilfach Caerph 35 E5
Gilfach Goch Rhondda 34 F3
Gilfachrheda Ceredig 46 D3
Gillamoor N Yorks 102 F4
Gillar's Green Mers 86 E2
Gillen Highld 152 D3
Gilling East N Yorks 96 B2
Gilling West N Yorks 101 D6
Gillingham Dorset 13 B6
Gillingham Medway 29 C8
Gillingham Norf 69 E7
Gillock Highld 169 D7
Gillow Heath Staffs 75 D5
Gills Highld 169 B8
Gill's Green Kent 18 B4
Gilmanscleuch Borders 115 B6
Gilmerton Edin 123 C5
Gilmerton Perth 133 B7
Gilmonby Durham 100 C4
Gilmorton Leics 64 F2
Gilmourton S Lnrk 121 E6
Gilsland Cumb 109 C6
Gilsland Spa Cumb 109 C6
Gilston Borders 123 D7
Gilston Herts 41 C7
Gilwern Mon 35 C6
Gimingham Norf 81 D8
Giosla W Isles 172 F4
Gipping Suff 56 C4
Gipsey Bridge Lincs 79 E5
Girdle Toll N Ayrs 120 E3
Girlsta Shetland 175 H6
Girsby N Yorks 102 D1
Girtford Beds 54 D2
Girthon Dumfries 106 D3
Girton Cambs 54 C5
Girton Notts 77 C8
Girvan S Ayrs 112 E1
Gisburn Lancs 93 E8
Gisleham Suff 69 F8
Gislingham Suff 56 B4
Gissing Norf 68 F4
Gittisham Devon 11 E6
Gladestry Powys 48 D4
Gladsmuir E Loth 123 B7
Glais Swansea 33 D8
Glaisdale N Yorks 103 D5
Glame Highld 153 E6
Glamis Angus 142 E3
Glamis Castle Angus 142 E3
Glan Adda Gwyn 83 D5
Glan Conwy Conwy 83 E8
Glan Conwy Conwy 83 D8
Glan-Duar Carms 46 E4
Glan-Dwyfach Gwyn 71 C5
Glan Gors Anglesey 82 D4
Glan-rhyd Gwyn 82 F4
Glan-traeth Anglesey 82 D2
Glan-y-don Flint 73 B5
Glan-y-nant Powys 59 F6
Glan-y-wern Gwyn 71 D7
Glan-yr-afon Anglesey 83 C6
Glan-yr-afon Gwyn 72 E3
Glan-yr-afon Gwyn 72 E4
Glanaman Carms 33 C7
Glandford Norf 81 C6
Glandwr Pembs 32 B2
Glandy Cross Carms 32 B2
Glandyfi Ceredig 58 E3
Glangrwyney Powys 35 C6
Glanmule Powys 59 E8
Glanrafon Ceredig 58 F3
Glanrhyd Gwyn 70 D3
Glanrhyd Pembs 45 E3
Glanton Northumb 117 C6
Glanton Pike Northumb 117 C6
Glanvilles Wootton Dorset 12 D4
Glapthorn Northants 65 E7
Glapwell Derbys 76 C4
Glas-allt Shiel Aberds 149 F8
Glasbury Powys 48 F3
Glaschoil Highld 158 F4
Glascoed Denb 72 B3
Glascoed Mon 35 D7
Glascoed Powys 59 C8
Glascorrie Aberds 150 E2
Glascote Staffs 63 D6
Glascwm Powys 48 D3
Glasdrum Argyll 138 E4
Glasfryn Conwy 72 D3
Glasgow Glasgow 121 C5
Glasgow Airport Renfs 120 C4
Glasgow Art Gallery & Museum Glasgow 121 C5
Glasgow Botanic Gardens Glasgow 121 C5
Glasgow Cathedral Glasgow 121 C6
Glasgow Prestwick International Airport S Ayrs 112 B3
Glashvin Highld 152 C5
Glasinfryn Gwyn 83 E5
Glasnacardoch Highld 145 D6
Glasnakille Highld 153 H6
Glasphein Highld 152 E2
Glaspwll Powys 58 E4
Glassburn Highld 156 F4
Glasserton Dumfries 105 F8
Glassford S Lnrk 121 E7
Glasshouse Hill Glos 36 B4
Glasshouses N Yorks 94 C4
Glasslie Fife 134 D4
Glasson Cumb 108 C2
Glasson Lancs 92 D4
Glassonby Cumb 109 F5
Glasterlaw Angus 143 D5
Glaston Rutland 65 D5
Glastonbury Som 23 F7
Glastonbury Abbey Som 23 F6
Glatton Cambs 65 F8
Glazebrook Warr 86 E4
Glazebury Warr 86 E4
Glazeley Shrops 61 F7
Gleadless S Yorks 88 F4
Gleadsmoss Ches 74 C5
Gleann Tholàstaidh W Isles 172 D8
Gleaston Cumb 92 B2
Gleiniant Powys 59 E6
Glemsford Suff 56 E2
Glen Dumfries 106 D2
Glen Dumfries 106 B5
Glen Auldyn I o M 84 C4
Glen Bernisdale Highld 152 E5
Glen Ho. Borders 123 F5
Glen Mona I o M 84 D4
Glen Nevis House Highld 139 B5
Glen Parva Leics 64 E2
Glen Sluain Argyll 131 F6
Glen Tanar House Aberds 150 E3
Glen Trool Lodge Dumfries 112 F4
Glen Village Falk 121 B8
Glen Vine I o M 84 E3
Glenamachrie Argyll 130 C5
Glenbarr Argyll 118 C3
Glenbeg Highld 137 B6
Glenbeg Highld 149 B6
Glenbervie Aberds 151 F6
Glenboig N Lnrk 121 C7
Glenborrodale Highld 137 B7
Glenbranter Argyll 131 F7
Glenbreck Borders 114 B3
Glenbrein Lodge Highld 147 C7
Glenbrittle House Highld 153 G5
Glenbuchat Lodge Aberds 150 C2
Glenbuck E Ayrs 113 B7
Glenburn Renfs 120 C4
Glencalvie Lodge Highld 164 F1
Glencanisp Lodge Highld 163 B5
Glencaple Dumfries 107 C6
Glencarron Lodge Highld 155 E6
Glencarse Perth 134 B3
Glencassley Castle Highld 163 D8
Glenceitlein Highld 139 E5
Glencoe Highld 138 D4
Glencraig Fife 134 E3
Glencripesdale Highld 137 C7
Glencrosh Dumfries 113 F7
Glendavan Ho. Aberds 150 D3
Glendevon Perth 133 D8
Glendoe Lodge Highld 147 D7
Glendoebeg Highld 147 D7
Glendoick Perth 134 B4
Glendoll Lodge Angus 142 B2
Glendoune S Ayrs 112 E1
Glenduckie Fife 134 C4
Glendye Lodge Aberds 150 F5
Gleneagles Hotel Perth 133 C8
Gleneagles House Perth 133 D8
Glenegedale Argyll 126 D3
Glenelg Highld 145 B8
Glenernie Moray 158 E4
Glenfarg Perth 134 C3
Glenfarquhar Lodge Aberds 151 F6
Glenferness House Highld 158 E3
Glenfeshie Lodge Highld 148 E4
Glenfiddich Distillery, Dufftown Moray 159 E7
Glenfield Leics 64 D2
Glenfinnan Highld 145 E8
Glenfoot Perth 134 C3
Glenfyne Lodge Argyll 131 D8
Glengap Dumfries 106 D3
Glengarnock N Ayrs 120 D3
Glengorm Castle Argyll 137 C5
Glengrasco Highld 153 E5
Glenhead Farm Angus 142 C2
Glenhoul Dumfries 113 F6
Glenhurich Highld 138 C2
Glenkerry Borders 115 C5
Glenkiln Dumfries 106 B5
Glenkindie Aberds 150 C3
Glenlatterach Moray 159 D5
Glenlee Dumfries 113 F6
Glenlichorn Perth 133 C6
Glenlivet Moray 149 B7
Glenlochsie Perth 141 B7
Glenloig N Ayrs 119 C6
Glenluce Dumfries 105 D6
Glenmallan Argyll 131 F8
Glenmarksie Highld 156 D4
Glenmassan Argyll 129 B6
Glenmavis N Lnrk 121 C7
Glenmaye I o M 84 E2
Glenmidge Dumfries 113 F8
Glenmore Argyll 130 D4
Glenmore Highld 153 E5
Glenmore Lodge Highld 149 D5
Glenmoy Angus 142 C4
Glenogil Angus 142 C4
Glenprosen Lodge Angus 142 C2
Glenprosen Village Angus 142 C3
Glenquiech Angus 142 C4
Glenreasdell Mains Argyll 128 E3
Glenree N Ayrs 119 D6
Glenridding Cumb 99 C5
Glenrossal Highld 164 D1
Glenrothes Fife 134 D4
Glensanda Highld 138 E2
Glensaugh Aberds 143 B6
Glenshero Lodge Highld 147 E8
Glenstockadale Dumfries 104 C4
Glenstriven Argyll 129 C5
Glentaggart S Lnrk 113 B8
Glentham Lincs 90 E4
Glentirranmuir Stirl 133 E5
Glenton Aberds 150 B5
Glentress Borders 123 F5
Glentromie Lodge Highld 148 E3
Glentrool Village Dumfries 105 B7
Glentruan I o M 84 B4
Glentruim House Highld 148 E2
Glenturret Distillery, Crieff Perth 133 B7
Glentworth Lincs 90 F3
Glenuig Highld 145 F6
Glenurquhart Highld 157 C8
Glespin S Lnrk 113 B8
Gletness Shetland 175 H6
Glewstone Hereford 36 B2
Glinton P'boro 65 D8
Glooston Leics 64 E4
Glororum Northumb 125 F7
Glossop Derbys 87 E8
Gloster Hill Northumb 117 D8
Gloucester Glos 37 C5
Gloucester Cathedral Glos 37 C5
Gloucestershire Airport Glos 37 B5
Gloup Shetland 174 C7
Glusburn N Yorks 94 E3
Glutt Lodge Highld 168 F4
Glutton Bridge Derbys 75 C7
Glympton Oxon 38 B4
Glyn-Ceiriog Wrex 73 F6
Glyn-cywarch Gwyn 71 D7
Glyn Ebwy = Ebbw Vale Bl Gwent 35 D5
Glyn-Neath = Glynedd Neath 34 D2
Glynarthen Ceredig 46 E2
Glynbrochan Powys 59 F6
Glyncoch Rhondda 34 E4
Glyncorrwg Neath 34 E2
Glynde E Sus 17 D8
Glyndebourne E Sus 17 C8
Glyndyfrdwy Denb 72 E5
Glynedd = Glyn-Neath Neath 34 D2
Glynogwr Bridgend 34 F3
Glyntaff Rhondda 34 F4
Glyntawe Powys 34 C2
Gnosall Staffs 62 B2
Gnosall Heath Staffs 62 B2
Goadby Leics 64 E4
Goadby Marwood Leics 64 B4
Goat Lees Kent 30 E4
Goatacre Wilts 24 B5
Goathill Dorset 12 C4
Goathland N Yorks 103 D6
Goathurst Som 22 F4
Gobernuisgach Lodge Highld 167 E6
Gobhaig W Isles 173 H3
Gobowen Shrops 73 F7
Godalming Sur 27 E7
Godley Gtr Man 87 E7
Godmanchester Cambs 54 B3
Godmanstone Dorset 12 E4
Godmersham Kent 30 D4
Godney Som 23 E6
Godolphin Cross Corn 2 C5
Godre'r-graig Neath 34 D1
Godshill Hants 14 C2
Godshill I o W 15 F6
Godstone Sur 28 D4
Godstone Farm Sur 28 D4
Godwinscroft Hants 14 E2
Goetre Mon 35 D7
Goferydd Anglesey 82 C2
Goff's Oak Herts 41 D6
Gogar Edin 122 B4
Goginan Ceredig 58 F3
Golan Gwyn 71 C6
Golant Corn 5 D6
Golberdon Corn 5 B8
Golborne Gtr Man 86 E4
Golcar W Yorks 88 C2
Gold Hill Norf 66 E5
Goldcliff Newport 35 F7
Golden Cross E Sus 18 D2
Golden Green Kent 29 E7
Golden Grove Carms 33 C6
Golden Hill Hants 14 E3
Golden Pot Hants 26 E5
Golden Valley Glos 37 B6
Goldenhill Stoke 75 D5
Golders Green London 41 F5
Goldhanger Essex 43 D5
Golding Shrops 60 D5
Goldington Beds 53 D8
Goldsborough N Yorks 95 D6
Goldsborough N Yorks 103 C6
Goldsithney Corn 2 C4
Goldsworthy Devon 9 B5
Goldthorpe S Yorks 89 D5
Gollanfield Highld 158 D2
Golspie Highld 165 D5
Golval Highld 168 C3
Gomeldon Wilts 25 F6
Gomersal W Yorks 88 B3
Gomshall Sur 27 E8
Gonalston Notts 77 E6
Gonfirth Shetland 175 G5
Good Easter Essex 42 C2
Gooderstone Norf 67 D7
Goodleigh Devon 20 F5
Goodmanham E Yorks 96 E4
Goodnestone Kent 30 C4
Goodnestone Kent 31 D6
Goodrich Hereford 36 C2
Goodrington Torbay 7 D6
Goodshaw Lancs 87 B6
Goodwick = Wdig Pembs 44 B4
Goodwood Racecourse W Sus 16 C2
Goodworth Clatford Hants 25 E8
Goole E Yorks 89 B8
Goonbell Corn 3 B6
Goonhavern Corn 4 D2
Goose Eye W Yorks 94 E3
Goose Green Gtr Man 86 D3
Goose Green Norf 68 F4
Goose Green W Sus 16 C5
Gooseham Corn 8 C4
Goosey Oxon 38 E3
Goosnargh Lancs 93 F5
Goostrey Ches 74 B4
Gorcott Hill Warks 51 C5
Gord Shetland 175 L6
Gordon Borders 124 E2
Gordonbush Highld 165 D5
Gordonsburgh Moray 159 C8
Gordonstoun Moray 159 C5
Gordonstown Aberds 160 C2
Gordonstown Aberds 160 E4
Gore Kent 31 D7
Gore Cross Wilts 24 D5
Gore Pit Essex 42 C4
Gorebridge Midloth 123 C6
Gorefield Cambs 66 C4
Gorey Jersey 17
Gorgie Edin 122 B5
Goring Oxon 39 F6
Goring-by-Sea W Sus 16 D5
Goring Heath Oxon 26 B4
Gorleston-on-Sea Norf 69 D8
Gornalwood W Mid 62 E3
Gorrachie Aberds 160 C4
Gorran Churchtown Corn 3 B8
Gorran Haven Corn 3 B9
Gorrenberry Borders 115 E7
Gors Ceredig 46 B5
Gorse Hill Thamesdown 38 F1
Gorsedd Flint 73 B5
Gorseinon Swansea 33 E6
Gorseness Orkney 176 E3
Gorsgoch Ceredig 46 D3
Gorslas Carms 33 C6
Gorsley Glos 36 B3
Gorstan Highld 156 C4
Gorstanvorran Highld 138 B2
Gorsteyhill Staffs 74 D4
Gorsty Hill Staffs 62 B5
Gortantaoid Argyll 126 B3
Gorton Gtr Man 87 E6
Gosbeck Suff 57 D5
Gosberton Lincs 78 F5
Gosberton Clough Lincs 65 B8
Gosfield Essex 42 B3
Gosford Hereford 49 C7
Gosforth Cumb 98 D2
Gosforth T & W 110 C5
Gosmore Herts 40 B4
Gosport Hants 15 E7
Gossabrough Shetland 174 E7
Gossington Glos 36 D4
Goswick Northumb 125 E6
Gotham Notts 76 F5
Gotherington Glos 37 B6
Gott Shetland 175 J6
Goudhurst Kent 18 B4
Goulceby Lincs 79 B5
Gourdas Aberds 160 D4
Gourdon Aberds 143 B8
Gourock Invclyd 129 C7
Govan Glasgow 121 C5
Govanhill Glasgow 121 C5
Goveton Devon 7 E5
Govilon Mon 35 C6
Gowanhill Aberds 161 B7
Gowdall E Yorks 89 B7
Gowerton Swansea 33 E6
Gowkhall Fife 134 F2
Gowthorpe E Yorks 96 D3
Goxhill E Yorks 97 E7
Goxhill N Lincs 90 B5
Goxhill Haven N Lincs 90 B5
Goybre Neath 34 F1
Grabhair W Isles 172 G6
Graby Lincs 65 B7
Grade Corn 3 E6
Graffham W Sus 16 C3
Grafham Cambs 54 C2
Grafham Sur 27 E8
Grafton Hereford 49 F6
Grafton N Yorks 95 C7
Grafton Oxon 38 D2
Grafton Shrops 60 C4
Grafton Worcs 49 C7
Grafton Flyford Worcs 50 D4
Grafton Regis Northants 53 E5
Grafton Underwood Northants 65 F6
Grafty Green Kent 30 E2
Graianrhyd Denb 73 D6
Graig Conwy 83 D8
Graig Denb 72 B4
Graig-fechan Denb 72 D5
Grain Medway 30 B2
Grainsby Lincs 91 E6

Grainthorpe Lincs 91 E7
Grampound Corn 3 B8
Grampound Road Corn 4 D4
Gramsdal W Isles 170 E4
Granborough Bucks 39 B7
Granby Notts 77 F7
Grandborough Warks 52 C2
Grandtully Perth 141 D6
Grange Cumb 98 C4
Grange E Ayrs 120 F4
Grange Medway 29 C8
Grange Mers 85 F3
Grange Perth 134 B4
Grange Crossroads Moray 159 D8
Grange Hall Moray 158 C4
Grange Hill Essex 41 E7
Grange Moor W Yorks 88 C3
Grange of Lindores Fife 134 C4
Grange-over-Sands Cumb 92 B4
Grange Villa Durham 110 D5
Grangemill Derbys 76 D2
Grangemouth Falk 133 F8
Grangepans Falk 134 F2
Grangetown Cardiff 22 B3
Grangetown Redcar 102 B3
Granish Highld 148 C5
Gransmoor E Yorks 97 D7
Granston Pembs 44 B3
Grantchester Cambs 54 D5
Grantham Lincs 78 F2
Grantley N Yorks 94 C5
Grantlodge Aberds 151 C6
Granton Dumfries 114 D3
Granton Edin 122 B5
Grantown-on-Spey Highld 149 B6
Grantshouse Borders 124 C4
Grappenhall Warr 86 F4
Grasby Lincs 90 D4
Grasmere Cumb 99 D5
Grasscroft Gtr Man 87 D7
Grassendale Mers 85 F4
Grassholme Durham 100 B4
Grassington N Yorks 94 C3
Grassmoor Derbys 76 C4
Grassthorpe Notts 77 C7
Grateley Hants 25 E7
Gratwich Staffs 75 F7
Graveley Cambs 54 C3
Graveley Herts 41 B5
Gravelly Hill W Mid 62 E5
Gravels Shrops 60 D3
Graven Shetland 174 F6
Graveney Kent 30 C4
Gravesend Kent 29 B7
Grayingham Lincs 90 E3
Grayrigg Cumb 99 E7
Grays Thurrock 29 B7
Grayshott Hants 27 F6
Grayswood Sur 27 F7
Graythorp Hrtlpl 102 B3
Grazeley Wokingham 26 C4
Greasbrough S Yorks 88 E5
Greasby Mers 85 F3
Great Abington Cambs 55 E6
Great Addington Northants 53 B7
Great Alne Warks 51 D6
Great Altcar Lancs 85 D4
Great Amwell Herts 41 C6
Great Asby Cumb 100 C1
Great Ashfield Suff 56 C3
Great Ayton N Yorks 102 C3
Great Baddow Essex 42 D3
Great Bardfield Essex 55 F7
Great Barford Beds 54 D2
Great Barr W Mid 62 E4
Great Barrington Glos 38 C2
Great Barrow Ches 73 C8
Great Barton Suff 56 C2
Great Barugh N Yorks 96 B3
Great Bavington Northumb 117 F5
Great Bealings Suff 57 E6
Great Bedwyn Wilts 25 C7
Great Bentley Essex 43 B7
Great Billing Northants 53 C6
Great Bircham Norf 80 D3
Great Blakenham Suff 56 D5
Great Blencow Cumb 108 F4
Great Bolas Telford 61 B6
Great Bookham Sur 28 D2
Great Bourton Oxon 52 E2
Great Bowden Leics 64 F4
Great Bradley Suff 55 D7
Great Braxted Essex 42 C4
Great Bricett Suff 56 D4
Great Brickhill Bucks 53 F7
Great Bridge W Mid 62 E3
Great Bridgeford Staffs 62 B2
Great Brington Northants 52 C4
Great Bromley Essex 43 B6
Great Broughton Cumb 107 F7
Great Broughton N Yorks 102 D3
Great Budworth Ches 74 B3
Great Burdon Darl 101 C8
Great Burgh Sur 28 D3
Great Burstead Essex 42 E2
Great Busby N Yorks 102 D3
Great Canfield Essex 42 C1
Great Carlton Lincs 91 F8
Great Casterton Rutland 65 D7
Great Chart Kent 30 E3
Great Chatwell Staffs 61 C7
Great Chesterford Essex 55 E6
Great Cheverell Wilts 24 D4
Great Chishill Cambs 54 F5
Great Clacton Essex 43 C7
Great Cliff W Yorks 88 C4
Great Clifton Cumb 98 B2
Great Coates NE Lincs 91 D6
Great Comberton Worcs 50 E4
Great Corby Cumb 108 D4
Great Cornard Suff 56 E2
Great Cowden E Yorks 97 E8
Great Coxwell Oxon 38 E2
Great Crakehall N Yorks 101 E7
Great Cransley Northants 53 B6
Great Cressingham Norf 67 D8
Great Crosby Mers 85 E4
Great Cubley Derbys 75 F8
Great Dalby Leics 64 C4
Great Denham Beds 53 E8
Great Doddington Northants 53 C6
Great Dunham Norf 67 C8
Great Dunmow Essex 42 B2
Great Durnford Wilts 25 F6
Great Easton Essex 42 B2
Great Easton Leics 64 E5
Great Eccleston Lancs 92 E4
Great Edstone N Yorks 103 F5
Great Ellingham Norf 68 E3
Great Elm Som 24 E2
Great Eversden Cambs 54 D4
Great Fencote N Yorks 101 E7
Great Finborough Suff 56 D4
Great Fransham Norf 67 C8
Great Gaddesden Herts 40 C3
Great Gidding Cambs 65 F8
Great Givendale E Yorks 96 D4
Great Glemham Suff 57 C7
Great Glen Leics 64 E3
Great Gonerby Lincs 77 F8
Great Gransden Cambs 54 D3
Great Green Norf 69 F5
Great Green Suff 56 D3
Great Habton N Yorks 96 B3
Great Hale Lincs 78 E4
Great Hallingbury Essex 41 C8
Great Hampden Bucks 39 D8
Great Harrowden Northants 53 B6
Great Harwood Lancs 93 F7
Great Haseley Oxon 39 D6
Great Hatfield E Yorks 97 E7
Great Haywood Staffs 62 B4
Great Heath W Mid 63 F7
Great Heck N Yorks 89 B6
Great Henny Essex 56 F2
Great Hinton Wilts 24 D4
Great Hockham Norf 68 E2
Great Holland Essex 43 C8
Great Horkesley Essex 56 F3
Great Hormead Herts 41 B6
Great Horton W Yorks 94 F4
Great Horwood Bucks 53 F5
Great Houghton Northants 53 D5
Great Houghton S Yorks 88 D5
Great Hucklow Derbys 75 B8
Great Kelk E Yorks 97 D7
Great Kimble Bucks 39 D8
Great Kingshill Bucks 40 E1
Great Langton N Yorks 101 E7
Great Leighs Essex 42 C3
Great Lever Gtr Man 86 D5
Great Limber Lincs 90 D5
Great Linford M Keynes 53 E6
Great Livermere Suff 56 B2
Great Longstone Derbys 76 B2
Great Lumley Durham 111 E5
Great Lyth Shrops 60 D4
Great Malvern Worcs 50 E2
Great Maplestead Essex 56 F2
Great Marton Blkpool 92 F3
Great Massingham Norf 80 E3
Great Melton Norf 68 D4
Great Milton Oxon 39 D6
Great Missenden Bucks 40 D1
Great Mitton Lancs 93 F7
Great Mongeham Kent 31 D7
Great Moulton Norf 68 E4
Great Munden Herts 41 B6
Great Musgrave Cumb 100 C2
Great Ness Shrops 60 C3
Great Notley Essex 42 B3
Great Oakley Essex 43 B7
Great Oakley Northants 65 F5
Great Offley Herts 40 B4
Great Orme Tramway, Llandudno Conwy 83 C7
Great Ormside Cumb 100 C2
Great Orton Cumb 108 D3
Great Ouseburn N Yorks 95 C7
Great Oxendon Northants 64 F4
Great Oxney Green Essex 42 D2
Great Palgrave Norf 67 C8
Great Parndon Essex 41 D7
Great Paxton Cambs 54 C3
Great Plumpton Lancs 92 F3
Great Plumstead Norf 69 C6
Great Ponton Lincs 78 F2
Great Preston W Yorks 88 B5
Great Raveley Cambs 66 F2
Great Rissington Glos 38 C1
Great Rollright Oxon 51 F8
Great Ryburgh Norf 81 E5
Great Ryle Northumb 117 C6
Great Ryton Shrops 60 D4
Great Saling Essex 42 B3
Great Salkeld Cumb 109 F5
Great Sampford Essex 55 F7
Great Sankey Warr 86 F3
Great Saxham Suff 55 C8
Great Shefford W Berks 25 B8
Great Shelford Cambs 55 D5
Great Smeaton N Yorks 101 D8
Great Snoring Norf 80 D5
Great Somerford Wilts 37 F6
Great Stainton Darl 101 B8
Great Stambridge Essex 42 E4
Great Staughton Cambs 54 C2
Great Steeping Lincs 79 C7
Great Stonar Kent 31 D7
Great Strickland Cumb 99 B7
Great Stukeley Cambs 54 B3
Great Sturton Lincs 78 B5
Great Sutton Ches 73 B7
Great Sutton Shrops 60 F5
Great Swinburne Northumb 110 B2
Great Tew Oxon 38 B3
Great Tey Essex 42 B4
Great Thurlkleby N Yorks 95 B7
Great Thurlow Suff 55 D7
Great Torrington Devon 9 C6
Great Tosson Northumb 117 D6
Great Totham Essex 42 C4
Great Totham Essex 42 C4
Great Tows Lincs 91 E6
Great Urswick Cumb 92 B2
Great Wakering Essex 43 F5
Great Waldingfield Suff 56 E3
Great Walsingham Norf 80 D5
Great Waltham Essex 42 C2
Great Warley Essex 42 E1
Great Washbourne Glos 50 F4
Great Weldon Northants 65 F6
Great Welnetham Suff 56 D2
Great Wenham Suff 56 F4
Great Whittington Northumb 110 B3
Great Wigborough Essex 43 C5
Great Wilbraham Cambs 55 D6
Great Wishford Wilts 25 F5
Great Witcombe Glos 37 C6
Great Witley Worcs 50 C2
Great Wolford Warks 51 F7
Great Wratting Suff 55 E7
Great Wymondley Herts 41 B5
Great Wyrley Staffs 62 D3
Great Wytheford Shrops 61 C5
Great Yarmouth Norf 69 D8
Great Yarmouth Sea Life Centre Norf 69 D8
Great Yeldham Essex 55 F8
Greater Doward Hereford 36 C2
Greatford Lincs 65 C7
Greatgate Staffs 75 E7
Greatham Hants 27 F5
Greatham Hrtlpl 102 B2
Greatham W Sus 16 C4
Greatstone on Sea Kent 19 C7
Greatworth Northants 52 E3
Greave Lancs 87 B6
Greeba I o M 84 D3
Green Denb 72 C4
Green End Beds 54 D2
Green Hammerton N Yorks 95 D7
Green Lane Powys 59 E8
Green Ore Som 23 D7
Green St Green London 29 C5
Green Street Herts 40 E4
Greenbank Shetland 174 C7
Greenburn W Loth 122 C2
Greendikes Northumb 117 B6
Greenfield Beds 53 F8
Greenfield Flint 73 B5
Greenfield Gtr Man 87 D7
Greenfield Highld 146 D5
Greenfield Oxon 39 E7
Greenford London 40 F4
Greengairs N Lnrk 121 B7
Greenham W Berks 26 C2
Greenhaugh Northumb 116 F3
Greenhead Northumb 109 C6
Greenhill Falk 121 B8
Greenhill London 40 F4
Greenhill Kent 31 C5
Greenhill Leics 63 C8
Greenhills N Ayrs 120 D3
Greenhithe Kent 29 B6
Greenholm E Ayrs 120 F5
Greenholme Cumb 99 D7
Greenhouse Borders 115 B8
Greenhow Hill N Yorks 94 C4
Greenigoe Orkney 176 F3
Greenland Highld 169 C7
Greenlands Bucks 39 F7
Greenlaw Aberds 160 C3
Greenlaw Borders 124 E3
Greenlea Dumfries 107 B7
Greenloaning Perth 133 D7
Greenmeadow Community Farm, Pontnewydd Torf 35 E6
Greenmount Gtr Man 87 C5
Greenmow Shetland 175 L6
Greenock Invclyd 129 C7
Greenock West Invclyd 129 C7
Greenodd Cumb 99 F5
Greenrow Cumb 107 D8
Greens Norton Northants 52 E4
Greenside T & W 110 C4
Greensidehill Northumb 117 C5
Greenstead Green Essex 42 B4
Greensted Essex 41 D8
Greensted Church, Chipping Ongar Essex 41 D8
Greenwich London 28 B4
Greet Glos 50 F5
Greete Shrops 49 B7
Greetham Lincs 79 B6
Greetham Rutland 65 C6
Greetland W Yorks 87 B8
Gregg Hall Cumb 99 E6
Gregson Lane Lancs 86 B3
Greinetobht W Isles 170 C4
Greinton Som 23 F6
Gremista Shetland 175 J6
Grenaby I o M 84 E2
Grendon Northants 53 C6
Grendon Warks 63 D6
Grendon Common Warks 63 E6
Grendon Green Hereford 49 D7
Grendon Underwood Bucks 39 B6
Grenofen Devon 6 B2
Grenoside S Yorks 88 E4
Greosabhagh W Isles 173 J4
Gresford Wrex 73 D7
Gresham Norf 81 D7
Greshornish Highld 152 D4
Gressenhall Norf 68 C2
Gressingham Lancs 93 C5
Gresty Green Ches 74 D4
Greta Bridge Durham 101 C5
Gretna Dumfries 108 C3
Gretna Green Dumfries 108 C3
Gretton Glos 50 F5
Gretton Northants 65 E5
Gretton Shrops 60 E5
Grewelthorpe N Yorks 94 B5
Grey Green N Lincs 89 D8
Greygarth N Yorks 94 B4
Greynor Carms 33 D6
Greysouthen Cumb 98 B2
Greystoke Cumb 108 F4
Greystone Angus 143 E5
Greystone Dumfries 107 B6
Greywell Hants 26 D5
Griais W Isles 172 D7
Grianan W Isles 172 E7
Gribthorpe E Yorks 96 F3
Gridley Corner Devon 9 E5
Griff Warks 63 F7
Griffithstown Torf 35 E6
Grimbister Orkney 176 E2
Grimblethorpe Lincs 91 F6
Grimeford Village Lancs 86 C4
Grimethorpe S Yorks 88 D5
Griminis W Isles 170 E3
Grimister Shetland 174 D6
Grimley Worcs 50 C3
Grimness Orkney 176 G3
Grimoldby Lincs 91 F7
Grimpo Shrops 60 B3
Grimsargh Lancs 93 F5
Grimsbury Oxon 52 E2
Grimsby NE Lincs 91 C6
Grimscote Northants 52 D4
Grimscott Corn 8 D4
Grimsthorpe Lincs 65 B7
Grimston E Yorks 97 F8
Grimston Leics 64 B3
Grimston Norf 80 E3
Grimston York 96 D2
Grimstone Dorset 12 E4
Grinacombe Moor Devon 9 E6
Grindale E Yorks 97 B7
Grindigar Orkney 176 F4
Grindiscol Shetland 175 K6
Grindle Shrops 61 D7
Grindleford Derbys 76 B2
Grindleton Lancs 93 E7
Grindley Staffs 62 B4
Grindley Brook Shrops 74 E2
Grindlow Derbys 75 B8
Grindon Northumb 124 E5
Grindon Staffs 75 D7
Grindonmoor Gate Staffs 75 D7
Gringley on the Hill Notts 89 E8
Grinsdale Cumb 108 D3
Grinshill Shrops 60 B5
Grinton N Yorks 101 E5
Griomsidar W Isles 172 F6
Grishipoll Argyll 136 C2
Grisling Common E Sus 17 B8
Gristhorpe N Yorks 103 F8
Griston Norf 68 E2
Gritley Orkney 176 F4
Grittenham Wilts 37 F7
Grittleton Wilts 37 F5
Grizebeck Cumb 98 F4
Grizedale Cumb 99 E5
Grobister Orkney 176 D5
Groby Leics 64 D2
Groes Conwy 72 C4
Groes Neath 34 F1
Groes-faen Rhondda 34 F4
Groes-lwyd Powys 60 C2
Groesffordd Marli Denb 72 B4
Groeslon Gwyn 82 E5
Groeslon Gwyn 82 F4
Grogport Argyll 118 B5
Gromford Suff 57 D7
Gronant Flint 72 A4
Groombridge E Sus 18 B2
Grosmont Mon 35 B8
Grosmont N Yorks 103 D6
Grosvenor Museum, Chester Ches 73 C8
Groton Suff 56 E3
Groudle Glen Railway I o M 84 E4
Grougfoot Falk 122 B3
Grouville Jersey 17
Grove Dorset 12 G5
Grove Kent 31 C6
Grove Notts 77 B7
Grove Oxon 38 E4
Grove Park London 28 B5
Grove Vale W Mid 62 E4
Grovesend Swansea 33 D6
Grudie Highld 156 C4
Gruids Highld 164 D2
Gruinard House Highld 162 E3
Grula Highld 153 G4
Gruline Argyll 137 D6
Grunasound Shetland 175 K5
Grundisburgh Suff 57 D6
Grunsagill Lancs 93 D7
Gruting Shetland 175 J4
Grutness Shetland 175 N6
Gualachulain Highld 139 E5
Gualin Ho. Highld 166 D5
Guardbridge Fife 135 C6
Guarlford Worcs 50 E3
Guay Perth 141 E7
Guernsey Airport Guern 16
Guestling Green E Sus 19 D5
Guestling Thorn E Sus 18 D5
Guestwick Norf 81 E6
Guestwick Green Norf 81 E6
Guide Blkburn 86 B5
Guide Post Northumb 117 F8
Guilden Morden Cambs 54 E3
Guilden Sutton Ches 73 C8
Guildford Sur 27 E7
Guildtown Perth 141 F8
Guilsborough Northants 52 B4
Guilsfield Powys 60 C2
Guilton Kent 31 D6
Guineaford Devon 20 F4
Guisborough Redcar 102 C4
Guiseley W Yorks 94 E4
Guist Norf 81 E5
Guith Orkney 176 C4
Guiting Power Glos 37 B7
Gulberwick Shetland 175 K6
Gullane E Loth 135 F6
Gulval Corn 2 C3
Gulworthy Devon 6 B2
Gumfreston Pembs 32 D2
Gumley Leics 64 E3
Gummow's Shop Corn 4 D3
Gun Hill E Sus 18 D2
Gunby E Yorks 96 F3
Gunby Lincs 65 B6
Gundleton Hants 26 F4
Gunn Devon 20 F5
Gunnerside N Yorks 100 E4
Gunnerton Northumb 110 B2
Gunness N Lincs 90 C2
Gunnislake Corn 6 B2
Gunnista Shetland 175 J7
Gunthorpe Norf 81 D6
Gunthorpe Notts 77 E6
Gunthorpe P'boro 65 D8
Gunville I o W 15 F5
Gunwalloe Corn 3 D5
Gurnard I o W 15 E5
Gurnett Ches 75 B6
Gurney Slade Som 23 E8
Gurnos Powys 34 D1
Gussage All Saints Dorset 13 C8
Gussage St Michael Dorset 13 C7
Guston Kent 31 E7
Gutcher Shetland 174 D7
Guthrie Angus 143 D5
Guyhirn Cambs 66 D3
Guyhirn Gull Cambs 66 D3
Guy's Head Lincs 66 B4
Guy's Marsh Dorset 13 B6
Guyzance Northumb 117 D8
Gwaenysgor Flint 72 A4
Gwalchmai Anglesey 82 D3
Gwaun-Cae-Gurwen Neath 33 C8
Gwaun-Leision Neath 33 C8
Gwbert Ceredig 45 E3
Gweek Corn 3 D6
Gwehelog Mon 35 D7
Gwenddwr Powys 48 E2
Gwennap Corn 3 C6
Gwenter Corn 3 E6
Gwernaffield Flint 73 C6
Gwernesney Mon 35 D8
Gwernogle Carms 46 F4
Gwernymynydd Flint 73 C6
Gwersyllt Wrex 73 D7
Gwespyr Flint 85 F2
Gwithian Corn 2 B4
Gwredog Anglesey 82 C4
Gwyddelwern Denb 72 E4
Gwyddgrug Carms 46 F3
Gwydyr Uchaf Conwy 83 E7
Gwynfryn Wrex 73 D6
Gwystre Powys 48 C2
Gwytherin Conwy 83 E8
Gyfelia Wrex 73 E7
Gyffin Conwy 83 D7
Gyre Orkney 176 F2
Gyrn-goch Gwyn 70 C5

H

Habberley Shrops 60 D3
Habergham Lancs 93 F8
Habrough NE Lincs 90 C5
Haceby Lincs 78 F3
Hacheston Suff 57 D7
Hackbridge London 28 C3
Hackenthorpe S Yorks 88 F5
Hackford Norf 68 D3
Hackforth N Yorks 101 E7
Hackland Orkney 176 D2
Hackleton Northants 53 D6
Hackness N Yorks 103 E7
Hackness Orkney 176 G2
Hackney London 41 F6
Hackthorn Lincs 90 F3
Hackthorpe Cumb 99 B7
Haconby Lincs 65 B8
Hacton London 41 F8
Hadden Borders 124 F3
Haddenham Bucks 39 D7
Haddenham Cambs 55 B5
Haddington E Loth 123 B8
Haddington Lincs 78 C2
Haddiscoe Norf 69 E7
Haddon Cambs 65 E8
Haddon Ches 75 C6
Haddon Hall Derbys 76 C2
Hade Edge W Yorks 88 D2
Hademore Staffs 63 D5
Hadfield Derbys 87 E8
Hadham Cross Herts 41 C7
Hadham Ford Herts 41 B7
Hadleigh Essex 42 F4
Hadleigh Suff 56 E4
Hadley Telford 61 C6
Hadley End Staffs 62 B5
Hadlow Kent 29 E7
Hadlow Down E Sus 18 C2
Hadnall Shrops 60 C5
Hadstock Essex 55 E6
Hady Derbys 76 B3
Hadzor Worcs 50 C4
Haffenden Quarter Kent 30 E2
Hafod-Dinbych Conwy 83 F8
Hafod-Iom Conwy 83 D8
Haggate Lancs 93 F8
Haggbeck Cumb 108 B4
Haggerston Northumb 125 E6
Haggrister Shetland 174 F5
Hagley Hereford 49 E7
Hagley Worcs 62 F3
Hagworthingham Lincs 79 C6
Haigh Gtr Man 86 D4
Haigh S Yorks 88 C3
Haigh Moor W Yorks 88 B3
Haighton Green Lancs 93 F5
Hail Weston Cambs 54 C2
Haile Cumb 98 D2
Hailes Glos 50 F5
Hailey Herts 41 C6
Hailey Oxon 38 C3
Hailsham E Sus 18 E2
Haimer Highld 169 C6
Hainault London 41 E7
Hainford Norf 68 C5
Hainton Lincs 91 F5
Hairmyres S Lnrk 121 D6
Haisthorpe E Yorks 97 C7
Hakin Pembs 44 E3
Halam Notts 77 D6
Halbeath Fife 134 F3
Halberton Devon 10 C5
Halcro Highld 169 C7
Hale Gtr Man 87 F5
Hale Halton 86 F2
Hale Hants 14 C2
Hale Bank Halton 86 F2
Hale Street Kent 29 E7
Halebarns Gtr Man 87 F5
Hales Norf 69 E6
Hales Staffs 74 F4
Hales Place Kent 30 D5
Halesfield Telford 61 D7
Halesgate Lincs 66 B3
Halesowen W Mid 62 F3
Halesworth Suff 57 B7
Halewood Mers 86 F2
Halford Shrops 60 F4
Halford Warks 51 E7
Halfpenny Furze Carms 32 C3
Halfpenny Green Staffs 62 E2
Halfway Carms 46 F5
Halfway Carms 47 F7
Halfway W Berks 26 C2
Halfway Bridge W Sus 16 B3
Halfway House Shrops 60 C3
Halfway Houses Kent 30 B3
Halifax W Yorks 87 B8
Halket E Ayrs 120 D4
Halkirk Highld 169 D6
Halkyn Flint 73 B6
Hall Dunnerdale Cumb 98 E4
Hall Green W Mid 62 F5
Hall Green W Yorks 88 C4
Hall Grove Herts 41 C5
Hall of Tankerness Orkney 176 F4
Hall of the Forest Shrops 60 F2
Halland E Sus 18 D2
Hallaton Leics 64 E4
Hallatrow Bath 23 D8
Hallbankgate Cumb 109 D5
Hallen S Glos 36 F2
Halliburton Borders 124 E2
Hallin Highld 152 D3
Halling Medway 29 C8
Hallington Lincs 91 F7
Hallington Northumb 110 B2
Halliwell Gtr Man 86 C5
Halloughton Notts 77 D6
Hallow Worcs 50 D3
Hallrule Borders 115 C8
Halls E Loth 124 B2
Hall's Green Herts 41 B5
Hallsands Devon 7 F6
Hallthwaites Cumb 98 F3
Hallworthy Corn 8 F3
Hallyburton House Perth 142 F2
Hallyne Borders 122 E4
Halmer End Staffs 74 E4
Halmore Glos 36 D3
Halmyre Mains Borders 122 E4
Halnaker W Sus 16 D3
Halsall Lancs 85 C4
Halse Northants 52 E3
Halse Som 11 B6
Halsetown Corn 2 C4
Halsham E Yorks 91 B6
Halsinger Devon 20 F4
Halstead Essex 56 F2
Halstead Kent 29 C5
Halstead Leics 64 D4
Halstock Dorset 12 D3
Haltham Lincs 78 C5
Haltoft End Lincs 79 E6
Halton Bucks 40 C1
Halton Halton 86 F3
Halton Lancs 92 C5
Halton Northumb 110 C2
Halton Wrex 73 F7
Halton W Yorks 95 F6
Halton East N Yorks 94 D3
Halton Gill N Yorks 93 B8
Halton Holegate Lincs 79 C7
Halton Lea Gate Northumb 109 D6
Halton West N Yorks 93 D8
Haltwhistle Northumb 109 C7
Halvergate Norf 69 D7
Halwell Devon 7 D5
Halwill Devon 9 E6
Halwill Junction Devon 9 D6
Ham Devon 11 D7
Ham Glos 36 E3
Ham London 28 B2
Ham Highld 169 B7
Ham Kent 31 D7
Ham Shetland 175 K1
Ham Wilts 25 C8
Ham Common Dorset 13 B6
Ham Green Hereford 50 E2
Ham Green Kent 19 C5
Ham Green Kent 30 C2
Ham Green N Som 23 B7
Ham Green Worcs 50 C5
Ham Street Som 23 F7
Hamble-le-Rice Hants 15 D5
Hambleden Bucks 39 F7
Hambledon Hants 15 C7
Hambledon Sur 27 F7
Hambleton Lancs 92 E3
Hambleton N Yorks 95 F8
Hambridge Som 11 B8
Hambrook S Glos 23 B8
Hambrook W Sus 15 D8
Hameringham Lincs 79 C6
Hamerton Cambs 54 B2
Hametoun Shetland 175 K1
Hamilton S Lnrk 121 D7
Hamilton Park Racecourse S Lnrk 121 D7
Hammer W Sus 27 F6
Hammerpot W Sus 16 D4
Hammersmith London 28 B3
Hammerwich Staffs 62 D4
Hammerwood E Sus 28 F5
Hammond Street Herts 41 D6
Hammoon Dorset 13 C6
Hamnavoe Shetland 174 E4
Hamnavoe Shetland 175 K5
Hamnavoe Shetland 174 E6
Hamnavoe Shetland 174 F6
Hampden National Stadium Glasgow 121 C5
Hampden Park E Sus 18 E3
Hamperden End Essex 55 F6
Hampnett Glos 37 C7
Hampole S Yorks 89 C6
Hampreston Dorset 13 E8
Hampstead London 41 F5
Hampstead Norreys W Berks 26 B3
Hampsthwaite N Yorks 95 D5
Hampton London 28 C2
Hampton Shrops 61 F7
Hampton Worcs 50 E5
Hampton Bishop Hereford 49 F7
Hampton Court Palace, Teddington London 28 C2
Hampton Heath Ches 73 E8
Hampton in Arden W Mid 63 F6
Hampton Loade Shrops 61 F7
Hampton Lovett Worcs 50 C3
Hampton Lucy Warks 51 D7
Hampton on the Hill Warks 51 C7
Hampton Poyle Oxon 39 C5
Hamrow Norf 80 E5
Hamsey E Sus 17 C8
Hamsey Green Sur 28 D4
Hamstall Ridware Staffs 62 C5
Hamstead I o W 14 E5
Hamstead W Mid 62 E4
Hamstead Marshall W Berks 26 C2
Hamsterley Durham 110 F4
Hamsterley Durham 110 D4
Hamstreet Kent 19 B7
Hamworthy Poole 13 E7
Hanbury Staffs 63 B5
Hanbury Worcs 50 C4
Hanbury Woodend Staffs 63 B5
Hanby Lincs 78 F3
Hanchurch Staffs 74 E5
Handbridge Ches 73 C8
Handcross W Sus 17 B6
Handforth Ches 87 F6
Handley Ches 73 D8
Handsacre Staffs 62 C4
Handsworth S Yorks 88 F5
Handsworth W Mid 62 E4
Handy Cross Devon 9 B6
Hanford Stoke 75 E5
Hanging Langford Wilts 24 F5
Hangleton W Sus 16 D4
Hanham S Glos 23 B8
Hankelow Ches 74 E3
Hankerton Wilts 37 E6
Hankham E Sus 18 E3
Hanley Stoke 75 E5
Hanley Castle Worcs 50 E3
Hanley Child Worcs 49 C8
Hanley Swan Worcs 50 E3
Hanley William Worcs 49 C8
Hanlith N Yorks 94 C2
Hanmer Wrex 73 F8
Hannah Lincs 79 B8
Hannington Hants 26 D3
Hannington Northants 53 B6
Hannington Thamesdown 38 E1
Hannington Wick Thamesdown 38 E1
Hansel Village S Ayrs 120 F3
Hanslope M Keynes 53 E6
Hanthorpe Lincs 65 B7
Hanwell London 40 F4
Hanwell Oxon 52 E2
Hanwood Shrops 60 D4
Hanworth London 28 B2
Hanworth Norf 81 D7
Happendon S Lnrk 121 F8
Happisburgh Norf 69 A6
Happisburgh Common Norf 69 B6
Hapsford Ches 73 B8
Hapton Lancs 93 F7
Hapton Norf 68 E4
Harberton Devon 7 D5
Harbertonford Devon 7 D5
Harbledown Kent 30 D5
Harborne W Mid 62 F4
Harborough Magna Warks 52 B2
Harbottle Northumb 117 D5
Harbour Park, Littlehampton W Sus 16 D4
Harbury Warks 51 D8
Harby Leics 77 F7
Harby Notts 77 B8
Harcombe Devon 11 E6
Harden W Mid 62 D4
Harden W Yorks 94 F3
Hardenhuish Wilts 24 B4
Hardgate Aberds 151 D6
Hardham W Sus 16 C4
Hardingham Norf 68 D3
Hardingstone Northants 53 D5
Hardington Som 24 D2
Hardington Mandeville Som 12 C3
Hardington Marsh Som 12 D3
Hardley Hants 14 D5
Hardley Street Norf 69 D6
Hardmead M Keynes 53 E7
Hardrow N Yorks 100 E3
Hardstoft Derbys 76 C4
Hardway Hants 15 D7
Hardway Som 24 F2
Hardwick Bucks 39 C8
Hardwick Cambs 54 D4
Hardwick Norf 67 C6
Hardwick Norf 68 F5
Hardwick Notts 77 B6
Hardwick Northants 53 C6
Hardwick Oxon 38 D3
Hardwick Oxon 39 B5
Hardwick W Mid 62 E4
Hardwick Hall Derbys 76 C4
Hardwicke Glos 36 C4
Hardwicke Glos 37 B6
Hardwicke Hereford 48 E4
Hardy's Green Essex 43 B5
Hare Green Essex 43 B6
Hare Hatch Wokingham 27 B6
Hare Street Herts 41 B6
Hareby Lincs 79 C6
Hareden Lancs 93 D6
Harefield London 40 E3
Harehills W Yorks 95 F6
Harehope Northumb 117 B6
Haresceugh Cumb 109 E6
Harescombe Glos 37 C5
Haresfield Glos 37 C5
Hareshaw N Lnrk 121 C8
Hareshaw Head Northumb 116 F4
Harewood W Yorks 95 E6
Harewood End Hereford 36 B2
Harewood House, Wetherby W Yorks 95 E6
Harford Carms 46 E5
Harford Devon 6 D4
Hargate Norf 68 E4
Hargatewall Derbys 75 B8
Hargrave Ches 73 C8
Hargrave Northants 53 B8
Hargrave Suff 55 D8
Harker Cumb 108 C3

South Cerney Glos 37 E7
South Chard Som 11 D8
South Charlton Northumb 117 B7
South Cheriton Som 12 B4
South Cliffe E Yorks 96 F4
South Clifton Notts 77 B8
South Cockerington Lincs 91 F7
South Cornelly Bridgend 34 F2
South Cove Suff 69 F7
South Creagan Argyll 138 E3
South Creake Norf 80 D4
South Croxton Leics 64 C3
South Croydon London 28 C4
South Dalton E Yorks 97 E5
South Darenth Kent 29 C6
South Duffield N Yorks 96 F2
South Elkington Lincs 91 F6
South Elmsall W Yorks 89 C5
South End Bucks 40 B1
South End Cumb 92 C2
South End N Lincs 90 B5
South Erradale Highld 154 C3
South Fambridge Essex 42 E4
South Fawley W Berks 38 F3
South Ferriby N Lincs 90 B3
South Garth Shetland 174 D7
South Garvan Highld 138 B3
South Glendale W Isles 171 J3
South Godstone Sur 28 E4
South Gorley Hants 14 C2
South Green Essex 42 E2
South Green Kent 30 C2
South-haa Shetland 174 E5
South Ham Hants 26 D4
South Hanningfield Essex 42 E3
South Harting W Sus 15 C8
South Hatfield Herts 41 D5
South Hayling Hants 15 E8
South Hazelrigg Northumb 125 F6
South Heath Bucks 40 D2
South Heighton E Sus 17 D8
South Hetton Durham 111 E6
South Hiendley W Yorks 88 C4
South Hill Corn 5 B8
South Hinksey Oxon 39 D5
South Hole Devon 8 B4
South Holme N Yorks 96 B2
South Holmwood Sur 28 E2
South Hornchurch London 41 F8
South Hykeham Lincs 78 C2
South Hylton T & W 111 D6
South Kelsey Lincs 90 E4
South Kessock Highld 157 E7
South Killingholme N Lincs 91 C5
South Kilvington N Yorks 102 F2
South Kilworth Leics 64 F3
South Kirkby W Yorks 88 C5
South Kirkton Aberds 151 D6
South Kiscadale N Ayrs 119 D7
South Kyme Lincs 78 E4
South Lancing W Sus 17 D5
South Leigh Oxon 38 D3
South Leverton Notts 89 F8
South Littleton Worcs 51 E5
South Lopham Norf 68 F3
South Luffenham Rutland 65 D6
South Malling E Sus 17 C8
South Marston Thamesdown 38 F1
South Middleton Northumb 117 B5
South Milford N Yorks 95 F7
South Millbrex Aberds 160 D5
South Milton Devon 6 E5
South Mimms Herts 41 D5
South Molton Devon 10 B2
South Moreton Oxon 39 F5
South Mundham W Sus 16 D2
South Muskham Notts 77 D7
South Newbald E Yorks 96 F5
South Newington Oxon 52 F2
South Newton Wilts 25 F5
South Normanton Derbys 76 D4
South Norwood London 28 C4
South Nutfield Sur 28 E4
South Ockendon Thurrock 42 F1
South Ormsby Lincs 79 B6
South Otterington N Yorks 102 F1
South Owersby Lincs 90 E4
South Oxhey Herts 40 E4
South Perrott Dorset 12 D2
South Petherton Som 12 C2
South Petherwin Corn 8 F5
South Pickenham Norf 67 D8
South Pool Devon 7 E5
South Port Argyll 131 C6
South Radworthy Devon 21 F6
South Rauceby Lincs 78 E3
South Raynham Norf 80 E4
South Reston Lincs 91 F8
South Runcton Norf 67 D6
South Scarle Notts 77 C8
South Shian Argyll 138 E3
South Shields T & W 111 C6
South Shields Museum T & W 111 C6
South Shore Blkpool 92 F3
South Somercotes Lincs 91 E8
South Stainley N Yorks 95 C6
South Stainmore Cumb 100 C3
South Stifford Thurrock 29 B7
South Stoke Oxon 39 F5
South Stoke W Sus 16 D4
South Street E Sus 17 C7
South Street London 28 D5
South Street Kent 30 C5
South Street Kent 30 D4
South Tawton Devon 9 E8
South Thoresby Lincs 79 B7
South Tidworth Wilts 25 E7
South Town Hants 26 F4
South View Hants 26 D4
South Walsham Norf 69 C6
South Warnborough Hants 26 E5
South Weald Essex 42 E1
South Weston Oxon 39 E7
South Wheatley Corn 8 E4
South Wheatley Notts 89 F8
South Whiteness Shetland 175 J5
South Widcombe Bath 23 D7
South Wigston Leics 64 E2
South Willingham Lincs 91 F5
South Wingfield Derbys 76 D3
South Witham Lincs 65 C6
South Wonston Hants 26 F2
South Woodham Ferrers Essex 42 E4
South Wootton Norf 67 B6
South Wraxall Wilts 24 C3
South Zeal Devon 9 E8
Southall London 40 F4
Southam Glos 37 B6
Southam Warks 52 C2
Southampton Soton 14 C5
Southampton International Airport Hants 15 C5
Southborough Kent 29 E6
Southbourne Bmouth 14 E2
Southbourne W Sus 15 D8
Southburgh Norf 68 D2
Southburn E Yorks 97 D5
Southchurch Sthend 43 F5
Southcott Wilts 25 D6
Southcourt Bucks 39 C8
Southdean Borders 116 D2
Southdene Mers 86 E2
Southease E Sus 17 D8
Southend Argyll 118 F3
Southend W Berks 26 B3
Southend Wilts 25 B6
Southend Airport Essex 42 F4
Southend-on-Sea Sthend 42 F4
Southend Sea Life Centre Essex 42 E4
Southernden Kent 30 E2
Southerndown V Glam 21 B7
Southerness Dumfries 107 D6
Southery Norf 67 E6
Southfield Northumb 111 B5
Southfleet Kent 29 B7
Southgate Ceredig 46 B4
Southgate London 41 E5
Southgate Norf 81 E7
Southgate Swansea 33 F6
Southill Beds 54 E2
Southleigh Devon 11 E7
Southminster Essex 43 E5
Southmoor Oxon 38 E3
Southoe Cambs 54 C2
Southolt Suff 57 C5
Southorpe P'boro 65 D7
Southowram W Yorks 88 B2
Southport Mers 85 C4
Southpunds Shetland 175 L6
Southrepps Norf 81 D8
Southrey Lincs 78 C4
Southrop Glos 38 D1
Southrope Hants 26 E4
Southsea Ptsmth 15 E7
Southstoke Bath 24 C2
Southtown Norf 69 D8
Southtown Orkney 176 G3
Southwaite Cumb 108 E4
Southwark London 28 B4
Southwater W Sus 17 B5
Southwater Street W Sus 17 B5
Southway Som 23 E7
Southwell Dorset 12 G4
Southwell Notts 77 D6
Southwell Minster Notts 77 D7
Southwell Racecourse Notts 77 D7
Southwick Hants 15 D7
Southwick Northants 65 E7
Southwick T & W 111 D6
Southwick Wilts 24 D3
Southwick W Sus 17 D6
Southwold Suff 57 B9
Southwood Norf 69 D6
Southwood Som 23 F7
Soval Lodge W Isles 172 F6
Sowber Gate N Yorks 102 F1
Sowerby N Yorks 102 F2
Sowerby W Yorks 87 B8
Sowerby Bridge W Yorks 87 B8
Sowerby Row Cumb 108 F3
Sowood W Yorks 87 C8
Sowton Devon 10 E4
Soyal Highld 164 E2
Spa Common Norf 81 D8
Spacey Houses N Yorks 95 D6
Spadeadam Farm Cumb 109 B5
Spalding Lincs 66 B2
Spaldington E Yorks 96 F3
Spaldwick Cambs 54 B2
Spalford Notts 77 C8
Spanby Lincs 78 F3
Sparham Norf 68 C3
Spark Bridge Cumb 99 F5
Sparkford Som 12 B4
Sparkhill W Mid 62 F4
Sparkwell Devon 6 D3
Sparrow Green Norf 68 C2
Sparrowpit Derbys 87 F8
Sparsholt Hants 26 F2
Sparsholt Oxon 38 F3
Spartylea Northumb 109 E8
Spaunton N Yorks 103 F5
Spaxton Som 22 F4
Spean Bridge Highld 146 F5
Spear Hill W Sus 16 C5
Speen Bucks 39 E8
Speen W Berks 26 C2
Speeton N Yorks 97 B7
Speke Mers 86 F2
Speke Hall Mers 86 F2
Speldhurst Kent 29 E6
Spellbrook Herts 41 C7
Spelsbury Oxon 38 B3
Spelter Bridgend 34 E2
Spencers Wood Wokingham 26 C5
Spennithorne N Yorks 101 F6
Spennymoor Durham 111 F5
Spetchley Worcs 50 D3
Spetisbury Dorset 13 D7
Spexhall Suff 69 F6
Spey Bay Moray 159 C7
Speybridge Highld 149 B6
Speyview Moray 159 E6
Spilsby Lincs 79 C7
Spindlestone Northumb 125 F7
Spinkhill Derbys 76 B4
Spinningdale Highld 164 F3
Spirit of the West, St Columb Major Corn 4 C4
Spirthill Wilts 24 B4
Spital Hill S Yorks 89 E7
Spital in the Street Lincs 90 F3
Spitfire and Hurricane Memorial, Manston Kent 31 C7
Spithurst E Sus 17 C8
Spittal Dumfries 105 D7
Spittal E Loth 123 B7
Spittal Highld 169 D6
Spittal Northumb 125 D6
Spittal Pembs 44 C4
Spittal Stirl 132 F4
Spittal of Glenmuick Aberds 150 F2
Spittal of Glenshee Perth 141 B8
Spittalfield Perth 141 E8
Spixworth Norf 68 C5
Splayne's Green E Sus 17 B8
Spofforth N Yorks 95 D6
Spon End W Mid 51 B8
Spon Green Flint 73 C6
Spondon Derby 76 F4
Spooner Row Norf 68 E3
Sporle Norf 67 C8
Spott E Loth 124 B2
Spratton Northants 52 B5
Spreakley Sur 27 E6
Spreyton Devon 9 E8
Spridlington Lincs 90 F4
Spring Vale S Yorks 88 D3
Spring Valley I o M 84 E3
Springburn Glasgow 121 C6
Springfield Dumfries 108 C3
Springfield Essex 42 D3
Springfield Fife 134 C5
Springfield Moray 158 D4
Springfield W Mid 62 F4
Springhill Staffs 62 D3
Springholm Dumfries 106 C5
Springkell Dumfries 108 B2
Springside N Ayrs 120 F3
Springthorpe Lincs 90 F2
Springwell T & W 111 D5
Sproatley E Yorks 97 F7
Sproston Green Ches 74 C4
Sprotbrough S Yorks 89 D6
Sproughton Suff 56 E5
Sprouston Borders 124 F3
Sprowston Norf 68 C5
Sproxton Leics 65 B5
Sproxton N Yorks 102 F4
Spurstow Ches 74 D2
Spynie Moray 159 C6
Squires Gate Blkpool 92 F3
Srannda W Isles 173 K3
Sronphadruig Lodge Perth 140 B4
SS Great Britain Bristol 23 B7
Stableford Shrops 61 E7
Stableford Staffs 74 F5
Stacey Bank S Yorks 88 E3
Stackhouse N Yorks 93 C8
Stackpole Pembs 44 F4
Staddiscombe Devon 6 D3
Staddlethorpe E Yorks 90 B2
Stadhampton Oxon 39 E6
Stadhlaigearraidh W Isles 170 G3
Staffield Cumb 108 E5
Staffin Highld 152 C5
Stafford Staffs 62 B3
Stagsden Beds 53 E7
Stainburn Cumb 98 B2
Stainburn N Yorks 94 E5
Stainby Lincs 65 B6
Staincross S Yorks 88 C4
Staindrop Durham 101 B6
Staines Sur 27 B8
Stainfield Lincs 65 B7
Stainfield Lincs 78 B4
Stainforth N Yorks 93 C8
Stainforth S Yorks 89 C7
Staining Lancs 92 F3
Stainland W Yorks 87 C8
Stainsacre N Yorks 103 D7
Stainsby Derbys 76 C4
Stainton Cumb 99 F7
Stainton Cumb 99 B6
Stainton Durham 101 C5
Stainton M'bro 102 C2
Stainton N Yorks 101 E6
Stainton S Yorks 89 E6
Stainton by Langworth Lincs 78 B3
Stainton le Vale Lincs 91 E5
Stainton with Adgarley Cumb 92 B2
Staintondale N Yorks 103 E7
Stair Cumb 98 B4
Stair E Ayrs 112 B4
Stairhaven Dumfries 105 D6
Staithes N Yorks 103 C5
Stake Pool Lancs 92 E4
Stakeford Northumb 117 F8
Stalbridge Dorset 12 C5
Stalbridge Weston Dorset 12 C5
Stalham Norf 69 B6
Stalham Green Norf 69 B6
Stalisfield Green Kent 30 D3
Stalling Busk N Yorks 100 F4
Stallingborough NE Lincs 91 C5
Stalmine Lancs 92 E3
Stalybridge Gtr Man 87 E7
Stambourne Essex 55 F8
Stambourne Green Essex 55 F8
Stamford Lincs 65 D7
Stamford Bridge Ches 73 C8
Stamford Bridge E Yorks 96 D3
Stamfordham Northumb 110 B3
Stanah Cumb 99 C5
Stanborough Herts 41 C5
Stanbridge Beds 40 B2
Stanbridge Dorset 13 D8
Stanbrook Worcs 50 E3
Stanbury W Yorks 94 F3
Stand Gtr Man 87 D5
Stand N Lnrk 121 C7
Standburn Falk 122 B2
Standeford Staffs 62 D3
Standen Kent 30 E2
Standen, East Grinstead W Sus 28 F4
Standford Hants 27 F6
Standingstone Cumb 107 F7
Standish Gtr Man 86 C3
Standlake Oxon 38 D3
Standon Hants 14 B5
Standon Herts 41 B6
Standon Staffs 74 F5
Stane N Lnrk 121 D8
Stanfield Norf 80 E5
Stanford Beds 54 E2
Stanford Kent 19 B8
Stanford Bishop Hereford 49 D8
Stanford Bridge Worcs 50 C2
Stanford Dingley W Berks 26 B3
Stanford in the Vale Oxon 38 E3
Stanford-le-Hope Thurrock 42 F2
Stanford on Avon Northants 52 B3
Stanford on Soar Notts 64 B2
Stanford on Teme Worcs 50 C2
Stanford Rivers Essex 41 D8
Stanfree Derbys 76 B4
Stanghow Redcar 102 C4
Stanground P'boro 66 E2
Stanhoe Norf 80 D4
Stanhope Borders 114 B4
Stanhope Durham 110 F2
Stanion Northants 65 F6
Stanley Derbys 76 E4
Stanley Durham 110 D4
Stanley Lancs 86 D2
Stanley Perth 141 F8
Stanley Staffs 75 D6
Stanley W Yorks 88 B4
Stanley Common Derbys 76 E4
Stanley Gate Lancs 86 D2
Stanley Hill Hereford 49 E8
Stanlow Ches 73 B8
Stanmer Brighton 17 D7
Stanmore London 40 E4
Stanmore Hants 15 B5
Stanmore W Berks 26 B2
Stannergate Dundee 142 F4
Stanningley W Yorks 94 F5
Stannington Northumb 110 B5
Stannington S Yorks 88 F4
Stansbatch Hereford 48 C5
Stansfield Suff 55 D8
Stanstead Suff 56 E2
Stanstead Abbotts Herts 41 C6
Stansted Kent 29 C7
Stansted Mountfitchet Essex 41 B8
Stanton Glos 51 F5
Stanton Mon 35 B7
Stanton Northumb 117 F7
Stanton Staffs 75 E8
Stanton Suff 56 B3
Stanton by Bridge Derbys 63 B7
Stanton-by-Dale Derbys 76 F4
Stanton Drew Bath 23 C7
Stanton Fitzwarren Thamesdown 38 E1
Stanton Harcourt Oxon 38 D4
Stanton Hill Notts 76 C4
Stanton in Peak Derbys 76 C2
Stanton Lacy Shrops 49 B6
Stanton Long Shrops 61 E5
Stanton-on-the-Wolds Notts 77 F6
Stanton Prior Bath 23 C8
Stanton St Bernard Wilts 25 C5
Stanton St John Oxon 39 D5
Stanton St Quintin Wilts 24 B4
Stanton Street Suff 56 C3
Stanton under Bardon Leics 63 C8
Stanton upon Hine Heath Shrops 61 B5
Stanton Wick Bath 23 C8
Stanwardine in the Fields Shrops 60 B4
Stanwardine in the Wood Shrops 60 B4
Stanway Essex 43 B5
Stanway Glos 51 F5
Stanway Green Suff 57 B6
Stanwell Sur 27 B8
Stanwell Moor Sur 27 B8
Stanwick Northants 53 B7
Stanwick-St-John N Yorks 101 C6
Stanwix Cumb 108 D4
Stanydale Shetland 175 H4
Staoinebrig W Isles 171 G3
Stape N Yorks 103 E5
Stapehill Dorset 13 D8
Stapeley Ches 74 E3
Stapeley Water Gardens, Nantwich Ches 74 D3
Stapenhill Staffs 63 B6
Staple Kent 31 D6
Staple Som 22 E3
Staple Cross E Sus 18 C4
Staple Fitzpaine Som 11 C7
Staplefield W Sus 17 B6
Stapleford Cambs 55 D5
Stapleford Herts 41 C6
Stapleford Leics 64 C5
Stapleford Lincs 77 D8
Stapleford Notts 76 F4
Stapleford Wilts 25 F5
Stapleford Abbotts Essex 41 E8
Stapleford Tawney Essex 41 E8
Staplegrove Som 11 B7
Staplehay Som 11 B7
Staplehurst Kent 29 E8
Staplers I o W 15 F6
Stapleton Bristol 23 B8
Stapleton Cumb 108 B5
Stapleton Hereford 48 C5
Stapleton Leics 63 E8
Stapleton N Yorks 101 C7
Stapleton Shrops 60 D4
Stapleton Som 12 B2
Stapley Som 11 C6
Staploe Beds 54 C2
Staplow Hereford 49 E8
Star Fife 134 D5
Star Pembs 45 F4
Star Som 23 D6
Stara Orkney 176 D1
Starbeck N Yorks 95 D6
Starbotton N Yorks 94 B2
Starcross Devon 10 F4
Stareton Warks 51 B8
Starkholmes Derbys 76 D3
Starlings Green Essex 55 F5
Starston Norf 68 F5
Startforth Durham 101 C5
Startley Wilts 37 F6
Stathe Som 11 B8
Stathern Leics 77 F7
Station Town Durham 111 F7
Staughton Green Cambs 54 C2
Staughton Highway Cambs 54 C2
Staunton Glos 36 C2
Staunton Glos 36 B4
Staunton in the Vale Notts 77 E8
Staunton on Arrow Hereford 49 C5
Staunton on Wye Hereford 49 E5
Staveley Cumb 99 F5
Staveley Cumb 99 E6
Staveley Derbys 76 B4
Staveley N Yorks 95 C6
Staverton Devon 7 C5
Staverton Glos 37 B5
Staverton Northants 52 C3
Staverton Wilts 24 C3
Staverton Bridge Glos 37 B5
Stawell Som 23 F5
Staxigoe Highld 169 D8
Staxton N Yorks 97 B6
Staylittle Powys 59 E5
Staynall Lancs 92 E3
Staythorpe Notts 77 D7
Stean N Yorks 94 B3
Stearsby N Yorks 96 B2
Steart Som 22 E4
Stebbing Essex 42 B2
Stebbing Green Essex 42 B2
Stedham W Sus 16 B2
Steele Road Borders 115 E8
Steen's Bridge Hereford 49 D7
Steep Hants 15 B8
Steep Marsh Hants 15 B8
Steeple Dorset 13 F7
Steeple Essex 43 D5
Steeple Ashton Wilts 24 D4
Steeple Aston Oxon 38 B4
Steeple Barton Oxon 38 B4
Steeple Bumpstead Essex 55 E7
Steeple Claydon Bucks 39 B6
Steeple Gidding Cambs 65 F8
Steeple Langford Wilts 24 F5
Steeple Morden Cambs 54 E3
Steeton W Yorks 94 E3
Stein Highld 152 D3
Steinmanhill Aberds 160 D4
Stelling Minnis Kent 30 E5
Stemster Highld 169 C6
Stemster Ho. Highld 169 C6
Stenalees Corn 4 D5
Stenhousemuir Falk 133 F7
Stenigot Lincs 91 F6
Stenness Shetland 174 F4
Stenscholl Highld 152 C5
Stenso Orkney 176 D2
Stenson Derbys 63 B7
Stenton E Loth 124 B2
Stenton Fife 134 E4
Stenwith Lincs 77 F8
Stepaside Pembs 32 D2
Stepping Hill Gtr Man 87 F7
Steppingley Beds 53 F8
Stepps N Lnrk 121 C6
Sterndale Moor Derbys 75 C8
Sternfield Suff 57 C7
Sterridge Devon 20 E4
Stert Wilts 24 D5
Stetchworth Cambs 55 D7
Stevenage Herts 41 B5
Stevenston N Ayrs 120 E2
Steventon Hants 26 E3
Steventon Oxon 38 E4
Stevington Beds 53 D7
Stewartby Beds 53 E8
Stewarton Argyll 118 E3
Stewarton E Ayrs 120 E4
Stewkley Bucks 40 B1
Stewton Lincs 91 F7
Steyne Cross I o W 15 F7
Steyning W Sus 17 C5
Steynton Pembs 44 E4
Stibb Corn 8 C4
Stibb Cross Devon 9 C6
Stibb Green Wilts 25 C7
Stibbard Norf 81 E5
Stibbington Cambs 65 E7
Stichill Borders 124 F3
Sticker Corn 4 D4
Stickford Lincs 79 D6
Sticklepath Devon 9 E8
Stickney Lincs 79 D6
Stiffkey Norf 81 C5
Stifford's Bridge Hereford 50 E2
Stillingfleet N Yorks 95 E8
Stillington N Yorks 95 C8
Stillington Stockton 102 B1
Stilton Cambs 65 F8
Stinchcombe Glos 36 E4
Stinsford Dorset 12 E5
Stirchley Telford 61 D7
Stirkoke Ho. Highld 169 D8
Stirling Aberds 161 D8
Stirling Stirl 133 E6
Stirling Castle Stirl 133 E6
Stisted Essex 42 B3
Stithians Corn 3 C6
Stittenham Highld 157 B7
Stivichall W Mid 51 B8
Stixwould Lincs 78 C4
Stoak Ches 73 B8
Stobieside S Lnrk 121 F6
Stobo Borders 122 F4
Stoborough Dorset 13 F7
Stoborough Green Dorset 13 F7
Stobshiel E Loth 123 C7
Stobswood Northumb 117 E8
Stock Essex 42 E2
Stock Green Worcs 50 D4
Stock Wood Worcs 50 D5
Stockbridge Hants 25 F8
Stockbury Kent 30 C2
Stockcross W Berks 26 C2
Stockdalewath Cumb 108 E3
Stockerston Leics 64 E5
Stockheath Hants 15 D8
Stockiemuir Stirl 132 F4
Stocking Pelham Herts 41 B7
Stockingford Warks 63 E7
Stockland Devon 11 D7
Stockland Bristol Som 22 E4
Stockleigh English Devon 10 D3
Stockleigh Pomeroy Devon 10 D3
Stockley Wilts 24 C5
Stocklinch Som 11 C8
Stockport Gtr Man 87 E6
Stocksbridge S Yorks 88 E3
Stocksfield Northumb 110 C3
Stockton Hereford 49 C7
Stockton Norf 69 E6
Stockton Shrops 60 D2
Stockton Shrops 61 E7
Stockton Warks 52 C2
Stockton Wilts 24 F4
Stockton Heath Warr 86 F4
Stockton-on-Tees Stockton 102 C2
Stockton on Teme Worcs 50 C2
Stockton on the Forest York 96 D2
Stockwood Park Museum, Luton Luton 40 C3
Stodmarsh Kent 31 C6
Stody Norf 81 D6
Stoer Highld 162 B4
Stoford Som 12 C3
Stoford Wilts 25 F5
Stogumber Som 22 F2
Stogursey Som 22 E4
Stoke Devon 8 B4
Stoke Hants 26 D2
Stoke Hants 15 D8
Stoke Medway 30 B2
Stoke Suff 57 E5
Stoke Abbott Dorset 12 D2
Stoke Albany Northants 64 F5
Stoke Ash Suff 56 B5
Stoke Bardolph Notts 77 E6
Stoke Bliss Worcs 49 C8
Stoke Bruerne Northants 52 E5
Stoke by Clare Suff 55 E8
Stoke-by-Nayland Suff 56 F3
Stoke Canon Devon 10 E4
Stoke Charity Hants 26 F2
Stoke Climsland Corn 5 B8
Stoke D'Abernon Sur 28 D2
Stoke Doyle Northants 65 F7
Stoke Dry Rutland 65 E5
Stoke Farthing Wilts 13 B8
Stoke Ferry Norf 67 E7
Stoke Fleming Devon 7 E6
Stoke Gabriel Devon 7 D6
Stoke Gifford S Glos 23 B8
Stoke Golding Leics 63 E7
Stoke Goldington M Keynes 53 E6
Stoke Green Bucks 40 F2
Stoke Hammond Bucks 40 B1
Stoke Heath Shrops 61 B6
Stoke Holy Cross Norf 68 D5
Stoke Lacy Hereford 49 E8
Stoke Lyne Oxon 39 B5
Stoke Mandeville Bucks 39 C8
Stoke Newington London 41 F6
Stoke on Tern Shrops 61 B6
Stoke-on-Trent Stoke 75 E5
Stoke Orchard Glos 37 B6
Stoke Poges Bucks 40 F2
Stoke Prior Hereford 49 D7
Stoke Prior Worcs 50 C4
Stoke Rivers Devon 20 F5
Stoke Rochford Lincs 65 B6
Stoke Row Oxon 39 F6
Stoke St Gregory Som 11 B8
Stoke St Mary Som 11 B7
Stoke St Michael Som 23 E8
Stoke St Milborough Shrops 61 F5
Stoke sub Hamdon Som 12 C2
Stoke Talmage Oxon 39 E6
Stoke Trister Som 12 B5
Stoke Wake Dorset 13 D5
Stokeford Dorset 13 F6
Stokeham Notts 77 B7
Stokeinteignhead Devon 7 B7
Stokenchurch Bucks 39 E7
Stokenham Devon 7 E6
Stokesay Shrops 60 F4
Stokesby Norf 69 C7
Stokesley N Yorks 102 D3
Stolford Som 22 E4
Ston Easton Som 23 D8
Stondon Massey Essex 42 D1
Stone Bucks 39 C7
Stone Glos 36 E3
Stone Kent 19 C6
Stone Kent 29 B6
Stone Staffs 75 F6
Stone S Yorks 89 F6
Stone Worcs 50 B3
Stone Allerton Som 23 D6
Stone Bridge Corner P'boro 66 D2
Stone Chair W Yorks 88 B2
Stone Cross E Sus 18 E3
Stone Cross Kent 31 D7
Stone-edge Batch N Som 23 B6
Stone House Cumb 100 F2
Stone Street Kent 29 D6
Stone Street Suff 56 F3
Stone Street Suff 69 F6
Stonebroom Derbys 76 D4
Stoneferry Hull 97 F7
Stonefield S Lnrk 121 D6
Stonegate E Sus 18 C3
Stonegate N Yorks 103 D5
Stonegrave N Yorks 96 B2
Stonehaugh Northumb 109 B7
Stonehaven Aberds 151 F7
Stonehenge, Amesbury Wilts 25 E6
Stonehouse Glos 37 D5
Stonehouse Northumb 109 D6
Stonehouse S Lnrk 121 E7
Stoneleigh Warks 51 B8
Stonely Cambs 54 C2
Stoner Hill Hants 15 B8
Stone's Green Essex 43 B7
Stonesby Leics 64 B5
Stonesfield Oxon 38 C3
Stonethwaite Cumb 98 C4
Stoney Cross Hants 14 C3
Stoney Middleton Derbys 76 B2
Stoney Stanton Leics 63 E8
Stoney Stoke Som 24 F2
Stoney Stratton Som 23 F8
Stoney Stretton Shrops 60 D3
Stoneybreck Shetland 175 L3
Stoneyburn W Loth 122 C2
Stoneygate Aberds 161 E7
Stoneygate Leicester 64 D3
Stoneyhills Essex 43 E5
Stoneykirk Dumfries 104 D4
Stoneywood Aberdeen 151 C7
Stoneywood Falk 133 F6
Stonganess Shetland 174 C7
Stonham Aspal Suff 56 D5
Stonnall Staffs 62 D4
Stonor Oxon 39 F7
Stonton Wyville Leics 64 E4
Stony Cross Hereford 50 E2
Stony Stratford M Keynes 53 E5
Stonyfield Highld 157 B7
Stoodleigh Devon 10 C4
Stopes S Yorks 88 F3
Stopham W Sus 16 C4
Stopsley Luton 40 B4
Stores Corner Suff 57 E7
Storeton Mers 85 F4
Stornoway W Isles 172 E7
Stornoway Airport W Isles 172 E7
Storridge Hereford 50 E2
Storrington W Sus 16 C4
Storrs Cumb 99 E5
Storth Cumb 99 F6
Storwood E Yorks 96 E3
Stotfield Moray 159 B6
Stotfold Beds 54 F3
Stottesdon Shrops 61 F6
Stoughton Leics 64 D3
Stoughton Sur 27 D7
Stoughton W Sus 16 C2
Stoul Highld 145 D7
Stoulton Worcs 50 E4
Stour Provost Dorset 13 B5
Stour Row Dorset 13 B6
Stourbridge W Mid 62 F3
Stourhead Garden Wilts 24 F2
Stourpaine Dorset 13 D6
Stourport on Severn Worcs 50 B3
Stourton Staffs 62 F2
Stourton Warks 51 F7
Stourton Wilts 24 F2
Stourton Caundle Dorset 12 C5
Stove Orkney 176 C5
Stove Shetland 175 L6
Stoven Suff 69 F7
Stow Borders 123 E7
Stow Lincs 90 F2
Stow Lincs 78 F3
Stow Bardolph Norf 67 D6
Stow Bedon Norf 68 E2
Stow cum Quy Cambs 55 C6
Stow Longa Cambs 54 B2
Stow Maries Essex 42 E4
Stow-on-the-Wold Glos 38 B1
Stowbridge Norf 67 D6
Stowe Shrops 48 B5
Stowe-by-Chartley Staffs 62 B4
Stowe Green Glos 36 D2
Stowe House and Gardens, Buckingham Bucks 52 F4
Stowell Som 12 B4
Stowford Devon 9 F6
Stowlangtoft Suff 56 C3
Stowmarket Suff 56 D4
Stowting Kent 30 E5
Stowupland Suff 56 D4
Straad Argyll 129 D5
Strachan Aberds 151 E5
Stradbroke Suff 57 B6
Stradishall Suff 55 D8
Stradsett Norf 67 D6
Stragglethorpe Lincs 78 D2
Straid S Ayrs 112 E1
Straith Dumfries 113 F8
Straiton Edin 123 C5
Straiton S Ayrs 112 D3
Straloch Aberds 151 B7
Straloch Perth 141 C7
Stramshall Staffs 75 F7
Strang I o M 84 E3
Stranraer Dumfries 104 C4
Stratfield Mortimer W Berks 26 C4
Stratfield Saye Hants 26 C4
Stratfield Turgis Hants 26 D4
Stratford London 41 F6
Stratford Racecourse Warks 51 D6
Stratford St Andrew Suff 57 C7
Stratford St Mary Suff 56 F4
Stratford Sub Castle Wilts 25 F6
Stratford Tony Wilts 13 B8
Stratford-upon-Avon Warks 51 D6
Strath Highld 169 D7
Strath Highld 154 C3
Strathan Highld 146 E2
Strathan Highld 167 C7
Strathan Highld 162 B4
Strathaven S Lnrk 121 E7
Strathblane Stirl 121 B5
Strathcanaird Highld 163 D5
Strathcarron Highld 155 F5
Strathcoil Argyll 130 B2
Strathdon Aberds 150 C2
Strathellie Aberds 161 B7
Strathkinness Fife 135 C6
Strathmashie House Highld 147 E8
Strathmiglo Fife 134 C4
Strathmore Lodge Highld 169 E6
Strathpeffer Highld 157 D5
Strathrannoch Highld 156 B4
Strathtay Perth 141 D6

Strathvaich Lodge Highld 156 B4
Strathwhillan N Ayrs 119 C7
Strathy Highld 168 C3
Strathyre Stirl 132 C4
Stratton Corn 8 D4
Stratton Dorset 12 E4
Stratton Glos 37 D7
Stratton Audley Oxon 39 B6
Stratton on the Fosse Som 23 D8
Stratton St Margaret Thamesdown 38 F1
Stratton St Michael Norf 68 E5
Stratton Strawless Norf 81 E8
Stravithie Fife 135 C7
Streat E Sus 17 C7
Streatham London 28 B4
Streatley Beds 40 B3
Streatley W Berks 39 F5
Street Lancs 92 D5
Street N Yorks 103 D5
Street Som 23 F6
Street Dinas Shrops 73 F7
Street End Kent 30 D5
Street End W Sus 16 E2
Street Gate T & W 110 D5
Street Lydan Wrex 73 F8
Streethay Staffs 62 C5
Streetlam N Yorks 101 E8
Streetly W Mid 62 E4
Streetly End Cambs 55 E7
Strefford Shrops 60 F4
Strelley Notts 76 E5
Strensall York 96 C2
Stretcholt Som 22 E4
Strete Devon 7 E6
Stretford Gtr Man 87 E6
Strethall Essex 55 F5
Stretham Cambs 55 B6
Strettington W Sus 16 D2
Stretton Ches 73 D8
Stretton Derbys 76 C3
Stretton Rutland 65 C6
Stretton Staffs 62 C2
Stretton Staffs 63 B6
Stretton Warr 86 F4
Stretton Grandison Hereford 49 E8
Stretton-on-Dunsmore Warks 52 B2
Stretton-on-Fosse Warks 51 F7
Stretton Sugwas Hereford 49 E6
Stretton under Fosse Warks 63 F8
Stretton Westwood Shrops 61 E5
Strichen Aberds 161 C6
Strines Gtr Man 87 F7
Stringston Som 22 E3
Strixton Northants 53 C7
Stroat Glos 36 E2
Stromeferry Highld 155 G4
Stromemore Highld 155 G4
Stromness Orkney 176 F1
Stronaba Highld 146 F5
Stronachlachar Stirl 132 C3
Stronchreggan Highld 138 B4
Stronchrubie Highld 163 C6
Strone Argyll 129 B6
Strone Highld 147 B8
Strone Highld 146 F4
Strone Invclyd 129 C7
Stronmilchan Argyll 131 C7
Stronsay Airport Orkney 176 D5
Strontian Highld 138 C2
Strood Medway 29 C8
Strood Green Sur 28 E3
Strood Green W Sus 16 B4
Strood Green W Sus 28 F2
Stroud Glos 37 D5
Stroud Hants 15 B8
Stroud Green Essex 42 E4
Stroxton Lincs 78 F2
Struan Highld 153 F4
Struan Perth 141 C5
Strubby Lincs 91 F8
Strumpshaw Norf 69 D6
Strutherhill S Lnrk 121 E7
Struy Highld 156 F4
Stryt-issa Wrex 73 E6
Stuartfield Aberds 161 D6
Stub Place Cumb 98 E2
Stubbington Hants 15 D6
Stubbins Lancs 87 C5
Stubbs Cross Kent 19 B6
Stubb's Green Norf 69 E5
Stubbs Green Norf 69 E6
Stubhampton Dorset 13 C7
Stubton Lincs 77 E8
Stuckgowan Argyll 132 D2
Stuckton Hants 14 C2
Stud Green Windsor 27 B6
Studham Beds 40 C3
Studland Dorset 13 F8
Studley Warks 51 C5
Studley Wilts 24 B4
Studley Roger N Yorks 95 B5
Stump Cross Essex 55 E6
Stuntney Cambs 55 B6
Sturbridge Staffs 74 F5
Sturmer Essex 55 E7
Sturminster Marshall Dorset 13 D7
Sturminster Newton Dorset 13 C5
Sturry Kent 31 C5
Sturton N Lincs 90 D3
Sturton by Stow Lincs 90 F2
Sturton le Steeple Notts 89 F8
Stuston Suff 56 B5
Stutton N Yorks 95 E7
Stutton Suff 57 F5
Styal Ches 87 F6
Styrrup Notts 89 E7
Suainebost W Isles 172 B8
Suardail W Isles 172 E7
Succoth Aberds 159 F8
Succoth Argyll 131 E8
Suckley Worcs 50 D2
Suckquoy Orkney 176 H3
Sudborough Northants 65 F6
Sudbourne Suff 57 D8
Sudbrook Lincs 78 E2
Sudbrook Mon 36 F2
Sudbrooke Lincs 78 B3
Sudbury Derbys 75 F8
Sudbury London 40 F4
Sudbury Suff 56 E2
Suddie Highld 157 D7
Sudeley Castle and Gardens Glos 37 B7
Sudgrove Glos 37 D6
Suffield Norf 81 D8
Suffield N Yorks 103 E7
Sugnall Staffs 74 F4
Suladale Highld 152 D4
Sulaisiadar W Isles 172 E8
Sulby I o M 84 C3
Sulgrave Northants 52 E3
Sulham W Berks 26 B4
Sulhamstead W Berks 26 C4
Sulland Orkney 176 B4
Sullington W Sus 16 C4
Sullom Shetland 174 F5
Sullom Voe Oil Terminal Shetland 174 F5
Sully V Glam 22 C3
Sumburgh Shetland 175 N6
Sumburgh Airport Shetland 175 M5
Summer Bridge N Yorks 94 C5
Summer-house Darl 101 C7
Summercourt Corn 4 D3
Summerfield Norf 80 D3
Summergangs Hull 97 F7
Summerleaze Mon 35 F8
Summerlee Heritage Centre, Coatbridge N Lnrk 121 C7
Summersdale W Sus 16 D2
Summerseat Gtr Man 87 C5
Summertown Oxon 39 D5
Summit Gtr Man 87 D7
Sunbury-on-Thames Sur 28 C2
Sundaywell Dumfries 113 F8
Sunderland Argyll 126 C2
Sunderland Cumb 107 F8
Sunderland T & W 111 D6
Sunderland Bridge Durham 111 F5
Sundhope Borders 115 B6
Sundon Park Luton 40 B3
Sundown Kiddies Adventureland, Rampton Notts 77 B7
Sundridge Kent 29 D5
Sunipol Argyll 136 C4
Sunk Island E Yorks 91 C6
Sunningdale Windsor 27 C7
Sunninghill Windsor 27 C7
Sunningwell Oxon 38 D4
Sunniside Durham 110 F4
Sunniside T & W 110 D5
Sunnyhurst Blkburn 86 B4
Sunnylaw Stirl 133 E6
Sunnyside W Sus 28 F4
Sunton Wilts 25 D7
Surbiton London 28 C2
Surby I o M 84 E2
Surfleet Lincs 66 B2
Surfleet Seas End Lincs 66 B2
Surlingham Norf 69 D6
Sustead Norf 81 D7
Susworth Lincs 90 D2
Sutcombe Devon 8 C5
Suton Norf 68 E3
Sutors of Cromarty Highld 158 C2
Sutterby Lincs 79 B6
Sutterton Lincs 79 F5
Sutton Beds 54 E3
Sutton Cambs 54 B5
Sutton London 28 C3
Sutton Kent 31 E7
Sutton Mers 86 E3
Sutton Norf 69 B6
Sutton Notts 77 F7
Sutton Notts 89 F7
Sutton N Yorks 89 B5
Sutton Oxon 38 D4
Sutton P'boro 65 E7
Sutton Shrops 61 F7
Sutton Shrops 74 F3
Sutton Som 23 F8
Sutton Staffs 61 B7
Sutton Suff 57 E7
Sutton Sur 27 E8
Sutton S Yorks 89 C6
Sutton W Sus 16 C3
Sutton at Hone Kent 29 B6
Sutton Bassett Northants 64 E4
Sutton Benger Wilts 24 B4
Sutton Bonington Notts 64 B2
Sutton Bridge Lincs 66 B4
Sutton Cheney Leics 63 D8
Sutton Coldfield W Mid 62 E5
Sutton Courtenay Oxon 39 E5
Sutton Crosses Lincs 66 B4
Sutton Grange N Yorks 95 B5
Sutton Green Sur 27 D8
Sutton Howgrave N Yorks 95 B6
Sutton In Ashfield Notts 76 D4
Sutton-in-Craven N Yorks 94 E3
Sutton in the Elms Leics 64 E2
Sutton Ings Hull 97 F7
Sutton Lane Ends Ches 75 B6
Sutton Leach Mers 86 E3
Sutton Maddock Shrops 61 D7
Sutton Mallet Som 23 F5
Sutton Mandeville Wilts 13 B7
Sutton Manor Mers 86 E3
Sutton Montis Som 12 B4
Sutton on Hull Hull 97 F7
Sutton on Sea Lincs 91 F9
Sutton-on-the-Forest N Yorks 95 C8
Sutton on the Hill Derbys 76 F2
Sutton on Trent Notts 77 C7
Sutton St Edmund Lincs 66 C3
Sutton St James Lincs 66 C3
Sutton St Nicholas Hereford 49 E7
Sutton Scarsdale Derbys 76 C4
Sutton Scotney Hants 26 F2
Sutton under Brailes Warks 51 F8
Sutton-under-Whitestonecliffe N Yorks 102 F2
Sutton upon Derwent E Yorks 96 E3
Sutton Valence Kent 30 E2
Sutton Veny Wilts 24 E3
Sutton Waldron Dorset 13 C6
Sutton Weaver Ches 74 B2
Sutton Wick Bath 23 D7
Swaby Lincs 79 B6
Swadlincote Derbys 63 C7
Swaffham Norf 67 D8
Swaffham Bulbeck Cambs 55 C6
Swaffham Prior Cambs 55 C6
Swafield Norf 81 D8
Swainby N Yorks 102 D2
Swainshill Hereford 49 E6
Swainsthorpe Norf 68 D5
Swainswick Bath 24 C2
Swalcliffe Oxon 51 F8
Swalecliffe Kent 30 C5
Swallow Lincs 91 D5
Swallowcliffe Wilts 13 B7
Swallowfield Wokingham 26 C5
Swallownest S Yorks 89 F5
Swallows Cross Essex 42 E2
Swan Green Ches 74 B4
Swan Green Suff 57 B6
Swanage Dorset 13 G8
Swanage Railway Dorset 13 G8
Swanbister Orkney 176 F2
Swanbourne Bucks 39 B8
Swanland E Yorks 90 B3
Swanley Kent 29 C6
Swanley Village Kent 29 C6
Swanmore Hants 15 C6
Swannery, Abbotsbury Dorset 12 F3
Swannington Leics 63 C8
Swannington Norf 68 C4
Swanscombe Kent 29 B7
Swansea = Abertawe Swansea 33 E7
Swanton Abbot Norf 81 E8
Swanton Morley Norf 68 C3
Swanton Novers Norf 81 D6
Swanton Street Kent 30 D2
Swanwick Derbys 76 D4
Swanwick Hants 15 D6
Swarby Lincs 78 E3
Swardeston Norf 68 D5
Swarister Shetland 174 E7
Swarkestone Derbys 63 B7
Swarland Northumb 117 D7
Swarland Estate Northumb 117 D7
Swarthmoor Cumb 92 B2
Swathwick Derbys 76 C3
Swaton Lincs 78 F4
Swavesey Cambs 54 C4
Sway Hants 14 E3
Swayfield Lincs 65 B6
Swaythling Soton 14 C5
Sweet Green Worcs 49 C8
Sweetham Devon 10 E3
Sweethouse Corn 5 C5
Sweffling Suff 57 C7
Swepstone Leics 63 C7
Swerford Oxon 51 F8
Swettenham Ches 74 C5
Swetton N Yorks 94 B4
Swffryd Bl Gwent 35 E6
Swiftsden E Sus 18 C4
Swilland Suff 57 D5
Swillington W Yorks 95 F6
Swimbridge Devon 9 B8
Swimbridge Newland Devon 20 F5
Swinbrook Oxon 38 C2
Swinderby Lincs 77 C8
Swindon Glos 37 B6
Swindon Staffs 62 E2
Swindon Thamesdown 38 F1
Swine E Yorks 97 F7
Swinefleet E Yorks 89 B8
Swineshead Beds 53 C8
Swineshead Lincs 78 E5
Swineshead Bridge Lincs 78 E5
Swiney Highld 169 F7
Swinford Leics 52 B3
Swinford Oxon 38 D4
Swingate Notts 76 E5
Swingfield Minnis Kent 31 E6
Swingfield St Kent 31 E6
Swinhoe Northumb 117 B8
Swinhope Lincs 91 E6
Swining Shetland 174 G6
Swinithwaite N Yorks 101 F5
Swinnow Moor W Yorks 94 F5
Swinscoe Staffs 75 E8
Swinside Hall Borders 116 C3
Swinstead Lincs 65 B7
Swinton Borders 124 E4
Swinton Gtr Man 87 D5
Swinton N Yorks 94 B5
Swinton N Yorks 96 B3
Swinton S Yorks 88 E5
Swintonmill Borders 124 E4
Swithland Leics 64 C2
Swordale Highld 157 C6
Swordland Highld 145 D7
Swordly Highld 168 C2
Sworton Heath Ches 86 F4
Swydd-ffynnon Ceredig 47 C5
Swynnerton Staffs 75 F5
Swyre Dorset 12 F3
Sychtyn Powys 59 D6
Syde Glos 37 C6
Sydenham London 28 B4
Sydenham Oxon 39 D7
Sydenham Damerel Devon 6 B2
Syderstone Norf 80 D4
Sydling St Nicholas Dorset 12 E4
Sydmonton Hants 26 D2
Syerston Notts 77 E7
Syke Gtr Man 87 C6
Sykehouse S Yorks 89 C7
Sykes Lancs 93 D6
Syleham Suff 57 B6
Sylen Carms 33 D6
Symbister Shetland 175 G7
Symington S Ayrs 120 F3
Symington S Lnrk 122 F2
Symonds Yat Hereford 36 C2
Symondsbury Dorset 12 E2
Synod Inn Ceredig 46 D3
Syon Park & House London 28 B2
Syre Highld 167 E8
Syreford Glos 37 B7
Syresham Northants 52 E4
Syston Leics 64 C3
Syston Lincs 78 E2
Sytchampton Worcs 50 C3
Sywell Northants 53 C6

T

Taagan Highld 154 D6
Tàbost W Isles 172 B8
Tabost W Isles 172 G6
Tackley Oxon 38 B4
Tacleit W Isles 172 E4
Tacolneston Norf 68 E4
Tadcaster N Yorks 95 E7
Taddington Derbys 75 B8
Taddiport Devon 9 C6
Tadley Hants 26 C4
Tadlow Beds 54 E3
Tadmarton Oxon 51 F8
Tadworth Sur 28 D3
Tafarn-y-gelyn Denb 73 C5
Tafarnau-bach Bl Gwent 35 C5
Taff's Well Rhondda 35 F5
Tafolwern Powys 59 D5
Tai Conwy 83 E7
Tai-bach Powys 59 B8
Tai-mawr Conwy 72 E3
Tai-Ucha Denb 72 D4
Taibach Neath 34 F1
Taigh a Ghearraidh W Isles 170 C3
Tain Highld 164 F4
Tain Highld 169 C7
Tainant Wrex 73 E6
Tainlon Gwyn 82 F4
Tai'r-Bull Powys 34 B3
Tairbeart = Tarbert W Isles 173 H4
Tairgwaith Neath 33 C8
Takeley Essex 42 B1
Takeley Street Essex 41 B8
Tal-sarn Ceredig 46 D4
Tal-y-bont Ceredig 58 F3
Tal-y-Bont Conwy 83 E7
Tal-y-bont Gwyn 83 D6
Tal-y-bont Gwyn 71 E6
Tal-y-cafn Conwy 83 D7
Tal-y-llyn Gwyn 58 D4
Tal-y-wern Powys 58 D5
Talachddu Powys 48 F2
Talacre Flint 85 F2
Talardd Gwyn 59 B5
Talaton Devon 11 E5
Talbenny Pembs 44 D3
Talbot Green Rhondda 34 F4
Talbot Village Poole 13 E8
Tale Devon 11 D5
Talerddig Powys 59 D6
Talgarreg Ceredig 46 D3
Talgarth Powys 48 F3
Talisker Highld 153 F4
Talke Staffs 74 D5
Talkin Cumb 109 D5
Talla Linnfoots Borders 114 B4
Talladale Highld 154 C5
Tallarn Green Wrex 73 E8
Tallentire Cumb 107 F8
Talley Carms 46 F5
Tallington Lincs 65 D7
Talmine Highld 167 C7
Talog Carms 32 B4
Talsarn Carms 34 B1
Talsarnau Gwyn 71 D7
Talskiddy Corn 4 C4
Talwrn Anglesey 82 D4
Talwrn Wrex 73 E6
Talybont-on-Usk Powys 35 B5
Talygarn Rhondda 34 F4
Talyllyn Powys 35 B5
Talysarn Gwyn 82 F4
Talywain Torf 35 D6
Tame Bridge N Yorks 102 D3
Tamerton Foliot Plym 6 C2
Tamworth Staffs 63 D6
Tan Hinon Powys 59 F5
Tan-lan Conwy 83 E7
Tan-lan Gwyn 71 C7
Tan-y-bwlch Gwyn 71 C7
Tan-y-fron Conwy 72 C3
Tan-y-graig Anglesey 82 D5
Tan-y-graig Gwyn 70 D4
Tan-y-groes Ceredig 45 E4
Tan-y-pistyll Powys 59 B7
Tan-yr-allt Gwyn 82 F4
Tandem W Yorks 88 C2
Tanden Kent 19 B6
Tandridge Sur 28 D4
Tanerdy Carms 33 B5
Tanfield Durham 110 D4
Tanfield Lea Durham 110 D4
Tangasdal W Isles 171 L2
Tangiers Pembs 44 D4
Tangley Hants 25 D8
Tanglwst Carms 46 F2
Tangmere W Sus 16 D3
Tangwick Shetland 174 F4
Tank Museum, Bovington Dorset 13 F6
Tankersley S Yorks 88 D4
Tankerton Kent 30 C5
Tannach Highld 169 E8
Tannachie Aberds 151 F6
Tannadice Angus 142 D4
Tannington Suff 57 C6
Tansley Derbys 76 D3
Tansley Knoll Derbys 76 C3
Tansor Northants 65 E7
Tantobie Durham 110 D4
Tanton N Yorks 102 C3
Tanworth-in-Arden Warks 51 B6
Tanygrisiau Gwyn 71 C7
Tanyrhydiau Ceredig 47 C6
Taobh a Chaolais W Isles 171 J3
Taobh a Thuath Loch Aineort W Isles 171 H3
Taobh a Tuath Loch Baghasdail W Isles 171 H3
Taobh a'Ghlinne W Isles 172 G6
Taobh Tuath W Isles 173 K2
Taplow Bucks 40 F2
Tapton Derbys 76 B3
Tarbat Ho. Highld 157 B8
Tarbert Argyll 127 D4
Tarbert Argyll 128 D3
Tarbert Argyll 118 A3
Tarbert = Tairbeart W Isles 173 H4
Tarbet Argyll 132 D2
Tarbet Highld 166 E3
Tarbet Highld 145 D7
Tarbock Green Mers 86 F2
Tarbolton S Ayrs 112 B4
Tarbrax S Lnrk 122 D3
Tardebigge Worcs 50 C5
Tarfside Angus 142 B4
Tarland Aberds 150 D3
Tarleton Lancs 86 B2
Tarlogie Highld 164 F4
Tarlscough Lancs 86 C2
Tarlton Glos 37 E6
Tarnbrook Lancs 93 D5
Tarporley Ches 74 C2
Tarr Som 22 F3
Tarrant Crawford Dorset 13 D7
Tarrant Gunville Dorset 13 C7
Tarrant Hinton Dorset 13 C7
Tarrant Keyneston Dorset 13 D7
Tarrant Launceston Dorset 13 D7
Tarrant Monkton Dorset 13 D7
Tarrant Rawston Dorset 13 D7
Tarrant Rushton Dorset 13 D7
Tarrel Highld 165 F5
Tarring Neville E Sus 17 D8
Tarrington Hereford 49 E8
Tarsappie Perth 134 B3
Tarskavaig Highld 145 C5
Tarves Aberds 161 E5
Tarvie Highld 156 D5
Tarvie Perth 141 C7
Tarvin Ches 73 C8
Tasburgh Norf 68 E5
Tasley Shrops 61 E6
Taston Oxon 38 B3
Tate Gallery London 28 B3
Tate Gallery, Albert Dock Mers 85 F8
Tate Modern London 28 B4
Tate St Ives Corn 2 B4
Tatenhill Staffs 63 B6
Tathall End M Keynes 53 E6
Tatham Lancs 93 C6
Tathwell Lincs 91 F7
Tatling End Bucks 40 F3
Tatsfield Sur 28 D5
Tattenhall Ches 73 D8
Tattenhoe M Keynes 53 F6
Tatterford Norf 80 E4
Tattersett Norf 80 D4
Tattershall Lincs 78 D5
Tattershall Bridge Lincs 78 D4
Tattershall Thorpe Lincs 78 D5
Tattingstone Suff 56 F5
Tatton House, Knutsford Ches 86 F5
Tatworth Som 11 D8
Taunton Som 11 B7
Taunton Racecourse Som 11 B7
Taverham Norf 68 C4
Tavernspite Pembs 32 C2
Tavistock Devon 6 B2
Taw Green Devon 9 E8
Tawstock Devon 9 B7
Taxal Derbys 75 B7
Tay Bridge Dundee 135 B6
Tayinloan Argyll 118 B3
Taymouth Castle Perth 140 E4
Taynish Argyll 128 B2
Taynton Glos 36 B4
Taynton Oxon 38 C2
Taynuilt Argyll 131 B6
Tayport Fife 135 B6
Tayvallich Argyll 128 B2
Tealby Lincs 91 E5
Tealing Angus 142 F4
Teangue Highld 145 C6
Teanna Mhachair W Isles 170 D3
Tebay Cumb 99 D8
Tebworth Beds 40 B2
Tedburn St Mary Devon 10 E3
Teddington Glos 50 F4
Teddington London 28 B2
Tedstone Delamere Hereford 49 D8
Tedstone Wafre Hereford 49 D8
Teeton Northants 52 B4
Teffont Evias Wilts 24 F4
Teffont Magna Wilts 24 F4
Tegryn Pembs 45 F4
Teigh Rutland 65 C5
Teigncombe Devon 9 F8
Teigngrace Devon 7 B6
Teignmouth Devon 7 B7
Telford Telford 61 D6
Telham E Sus 18 D4
Tellisford Som 24 D3
Telscombe E Sus 17 D8
Telscombe Cliffs E Sus 17 D7
Templand Dumfries 114 F3
Temple Corn 5 B6
Temple Glasgow 120 C5
Temple Midloth 123 D6
Temple Balsall W Mid 51 B7
Temple Bar Ceredig 46 D4
Temple Bar Carms 33 C6
Temple Cloud Bath 23 D8
Temple Combe Som 12 B5
Temple Ewell Kent 31 E6
Temple Grafton Warks 51 D6
Temple Guiting Glos 37 B7
Temple Herdewyke Warks 51 D8
Temple Hirst N Yorks 89 B7
Temple Normanton Derbys 76 C4
Temple Sowerby Cumb 99 B8
Templehall Fife 134 E4
Templeton Devon 10 C3
Templeton Pembs 32 C2
Templeton Bridge Devon 10 C3
Templetown Durham 110 D4
Tempsford Beds 54 D2
Ten Mile Bank Norf 67 E6
Tenbury Wells Worcs 49 C7
Tenby = Dinbych-y-Pysgod Pembs 32 D2
Tendring Essex 43 B7
Tendring Green Essex 43 B7
Tenston Orkney 176 E1
Tenterden Kent 19 B5
Terling Essex 42 C3
Ternhill Shrops 74 F3
Terregles Banks Dumfries 107 B6
Terrick Bucks 39 D8
Terrington N Yorks 96 B2
Terrington St Clement Norf 66 C5
Terrington St John Norf 66 C5
Teston Kent 29 D8
Testwood Hants 14 C4
Tetbury Glos 37 E5
Tetbury Upton Glos 37 E5
Tetchill Shrops 73 F7
Tetcott Devon 8 E5
Tetford Lincs 79 B6
Tetney Lincs 91 D7
Tetney Lock Lincs 91 D7
Tetsworth Oxon 39 D6
Tettenhall W Mid 62 E2
Teuchan Aberds 161 E7
Teversal Notts 76 C4
Teversham Cambs 55 D5
Teviothead Borders 115 D7
Tewel Aberds 151 F7
Tewin Herts 41 C5
Tewkesbury Glos 50 F3
Tewkesbury Abbey Glos 50 F3
Teynham Kent 30 C3
Thackthwaite Cumb 98 B3
Thainston Aberds 143 B6
Thakeham W Sus 16 C5
Thame Oxon 39 D7
Thames Ditton Sur 28 C2
Thames Haven Thurrock 42 F3
Thamesmead London 41 F7
Thanington Kent 30 D5
Thankerton S Lnrk 122 F2
Tharston Norf 68 E4
Thatcham W Berks 26 C3
Thatto Heath Mers 86 E3
Thaxted Essex 55 F7
The Aird Highld 152 D5
The All England Jumping Course, Hickstead W Sus 17 C6
The Arms Norf 67 E8
The Bage Hereford 48 E4
The Balloch Perth 133 C7
The Barony Orkney 176 D1
The Bluebell Railway, Sheffield Park E Sus 17 B8
The Bog Shrops 60 E3
The Bourne Sur 27 E6
The Braes Highld 153 F6
The Broad Hereford 49 C6
The Burrell Collection Glasgow 121 C5
The Butts Som 24 E2
The Camp Glos 37 D6
The Camp Herts 40 D4
The Chequer Wrex 73 E8
The City Bucks 39 E7
The Common Wilts 25 F7
The Craigs Highld 164 E1
The Cronk I o M 84 C3
The Dell Suff 69 E7
The Den N Ayrs 120 D3
The Dinosaur Museum, Dorchester Dorset 12 E4
The Eals Northumb 116 F3
The Eaves Glos 36 D3
The Flatt Cumb 109 B5
The Four Alls Shrops 74 F3
The Friars, Aylesford Kent 29 D8
The Garths Shetland 174 B8
The Green Cumb 98 F3
The Green Wilts 24 F3
The Grove Dumfries 107 B6
The Hall Shetland 174 D8
The Haven W Sus 27 F8
The Heath Norf 81 E7
The Heath Suff 56 F5
The Hill Cumb 98 F3
The Howe Cumb 99 F6
The Howe I o M 84 F1
The Hundred Hereford 49 C7
The Lee Bucks 40 D2
The Lhen I o M 84 B3
The Living RainForest W Berks 26 B3
The Long Man of Wilmington E Sus 18 E2
The Lost Gardens of Heligan, Mevagissey Corn 4 E4
The Lowry, Salford Gtr Man 87 E6
The Marsh Powys 60 E3
The Marsh Wilts 37 F7
The Middles Durham 110 D5
The Moor Kent 18 C4
The Moors Centre, Danby N Yorks 103 D5
The Mumbles = Y Mwmbwls Swansea 33 F7
The Murray S Lnrk 121 D6
The National Archives, Kew London 28 B3
The National Tramway Museum, Crich Derbys 76 D3
The Needles Old Battery I o W 14 F3
The Neuk Aberds 151 E6
The Oval Bath 24 C2
The Oval Cricket Ground London 28 B4
The Oxford Story, Oxford Oxon 39 D5
The Pole of Itlaw Aberds 160 C3
The Quarry Glos 36 E4
The Rhos Pembs 32 C1
The Rock Telford 61 D6
The Ryde Herts 41 D5
The Sands Sur 27 E6
The Stocks Kent 19 C6
The Tales of Robin Hood Nottingham 77 E5
The Throat Wokingham 27 C6
The Tutankhamun Exhibition, Dorchester Dorset 12 E4
The Vauld Hereford 49 E7
The Vyne Hants 26 D4
The World of Beatrix Potter, Bowness-on-Windermere Cumb 99 E6
The Wyke Shrops 61 D7
Theakston N Yorks 101 F8
Thealby N Lincs 90 C2
Theale Som 23 E6
Theale W Berks 26 B4
Thearne E Yorks 97 F6
Theberton Suff 57 C8
Theddingworth Leics 64 F3
Theddlethorpe All Saints Lincs 91 F8
Theddlethorpe St Helen Lincs 91 F8
Thelbridge Barton Devon 10 C2
Thelnetham Suff 56 B4
Thelveton Norf 68 F4
Thelwall Warr 86 F4
Themelthorpe Norf 81 E6
Thenford Northants 52 E3
Therfield Herts 54 F4
Thetford Lincs 65 C8
Thetford Norf 67 F8
Theydon Bois Essex 41 E7
Thickwood Wilts 24 B3
Thimbleby Lincs 78 C5
Thimbleby N Yorks 102 E2
Thingwall Mers 85 F3
Thirdpart N Ayrs 119 B8
Thirlby N Yorks 102 F2
Thirlestane Borders 123 E8
Thirn N Yorks 101 F7
Thirsk N Yorks 102 F2
Thirsk Racecourse N Yorks 102 F2
Thirtleby E Yorks 97 F7
Thistleton Lancs 92 F4
Thistleton Rutland 65 C6
Thistley Green Suff 55 B7
Thixendale N Yorks 96 C4
Thockrington Northumb 110 B2
Tholomas Drove Cambs 66 D3
Tholthorpe N Yorks 95 C7
Thomas Chapel Pembs 32 D2
Thomas Close Cumb 108 E4
Thomastown Aberds 160 E2
Thompson Norf 68 E2
Thomshill Moray 159 D6
Thong Kent 29 B7
Thongsbridge W Yorks 88 D2
Thoralby N Yorks 101 F5
Thoresway Lincs 91 E5
Thorganby Lincs 91 E6
Thorganby N Yorks 96 E2
Thorgill N Yorks 103 E5
Thorington Suff 57 B8
Thorington Street Suff 56 F4
Thorlby N Yorks 94 D2
Thorley Herts 41 C7
Thorley Street Herts 41 C7
Thorley Street I o W 14 F4
Thormanby N Yorks 95 B7
Thornaby on Tees Stockton 102 C2
Thornage Norf 81 D6
Thornborough Bucks 52 F5
Thornborough N Yorks 95 B5
Thornbury Devon 9 D6
Thornbury Hereford 49 D8
Thornbury S Glos 36 E3
Thornbury W Yorks 94 F4
Thornby Northants 52 B4
Thorncliffe Staffs 75 D7
Thorncombe Dorset 11 D8
Thorncombe Dorset 13 D6
Thorncombe Street Sur 27 E8
Thorncote Green Beds 54 E2
Thorncross I o W 14 F5
Thorndon Suff 56 C5
Thorndon Cross Devon 9 E7
Thorne S Yorks 89 C7
Thorne St Margaret Som 11 B5
Thorner W Yorks 95 E6
Thorney Notts 77 B8
Thorney P'boro 66 D2
Thorney Crofts E Yorks 91 B6
Thorney Green Suff 56 C4
Thorney Hill Hants 14 E2
Thorney Toll Cambs 66 D3
Thornfalcon Som 11 B7
Thornford Dorset 12 C4
Thorngumbald E Yorks 91 B6
Thornham Norf 80 C3
Thornham Magna Suff 56 B5
Thornham Parva Suff 56 B5
Thornhaugh P'boro 65 D7
Thornhill Caerph 35 F5
Thornhill Cumb 98 D2
Thornhill Derbys 88 F2
Thornhill Dumfries 113 E8
Thornhill Soton 15 C5
Thornhill Stirl 133 E5
Thornhill W Yorks 88 C3
Thornhill Edge W Yorks 88 C3
Thornhill Lees W Yorks 88 C3
Thornholme E Yorks 97 C7
Thornley Durham 110 F4
Thornley Durham 111 F6
Thornliebank E Renf 120 D5
Thorns Suff 55 D8
Thorns Green Ches 87 F5
Thornsett Derbys 87 F8
Thornthwaite Cumb 98 B4
Thornthwaite N Yorks 94 D4
Thornton Angus 142 E3
Thornton Bucks 53 F5
Thornton E Yorks 96 E3
Thornton Fife 134 E4
Thornton Lancs 92 E3
Thornton Leics 63 D8
Thornton Lincs 78 C5
Thornton Mers 85 D4
Thornton M'bro 102 C2
Thornton Northumb 125 E5
Thornton Pembs 44 E4
Thornton W Yorks 94 F4
Thornton Curtis N Lincs 90 C4
Thornton Heath London 28 C4
Thornton Hough Mers 85 F4
Thornton in Craven N Yorks 94 E2
Thornton-le-Beans N Yorks 102 E1

Thornton-le-Clay N Yorks 96 C2
Thornton-le-Dale N Yorks 103 F6
Thornton le Moor Lincs 90 E4
Thornton-le-Moor N Yorks 102 F1
Thornton-le-Moors Ches 73 B8
Thornton-le-Street N Yorks 102 F2
Thornton Rust N Yorks 100 F4
Thornton Steward N Yorks 101 F6
Thornton Watlass N Yorks 101 F7
Thorntonhall S Lnrk 121 D5
Thorntonloch E Loth 124 B3
Thorntonpark Northumb 124 E5
Thornwood Common Essex 41 D7
Thornydykes Borders 124 E2
Thoroton Notts 77 E7
Thorp Arch W Yorks 95 E7
Thorpe Derbys 75 D8
Thorpe E Yorks 97 E5
Thorpe Lincs 91 F8
Thorpe Norf 69 E7
Thorpe Notts 77 E7
Thorpe N Yorks 94 C3
Thorpe Sur 27 C8
Thorpe Abbotts Norf 57 B5
Thorpe Acre Leics 64 B2
Thorpe Arnold Leics 64 B4
Thorpe Audlin W Yorks 89 C5
Thorpe Bassett N Yorks 96 B4
Thorpe Bay Sthend 43 F5
Thorpe by Water Rutland 65 E5
Thorpe Common Suff 57 F6
Thorpe Constantine Staffs 63 D6
Thorpe Culvert Lincs 79 C7
Thorpe End Norf 69 C5
Thorpe Fendykes Lincs 79 C7
Thorpe Green Essex 43 B7
Thorpe Green Suff 56 D3
Thorpe Hesley S Yorks 88 E4
Thorpe in Balne S Yorks 89 C6
Thorpe in the Fallows Lincs 90 F3
Thorpe Langton Leics 64 E4
Thorpe Larches Durham 102 B1
Thorpe-le-Soken Essex 43 B7
Thorpe le Street E Yorks 96 E4
Thorpe Malsor Northants 53 B6
Thorpe Mandeville Northants 52 E3
Thorpe Market Norf 81 D8
Thorpe Marriot Norf 68 C4
Thorpe Morieux Suff 56 D3
Thorpe on the Hill Lincs 78 C2
Thorpe Park, Chertsey Sur 27 C8
Thorpe St Andrew Norf 69 D5
Thorpe St Peter Lincs 79 C7
Thorpe Salvin S Yorks 89 F6
Thorpe Satchville Leics 64 C4
Thorpe Thewles Stockton 102 B2
Thorpe Tilney Lincs 78 D4
Thorpe Underwood N Yorks 95 D7
Thorpe Waterville Northants 65 F7
Thorpe Willoughby N Yorks 95 F8
Thorpeness Suff 57 D8
Thorrington Essex 43 C6
Thorverton Devon 10 D4
Thrandeston Suff 56 B5
Thrapston Northants 53 B7
Thrashbush N Lnrk 121 C7
Threapland Cumb 107 F8
Threapland N Yorks 94 C2
Threapwood Ches 73 E8
Threapwood Staffs 75 E7
Threave Gardens Dumfries 106 C4
Three Ashes Hereford 36 B2
Three Bridges W Sus 28 F3
Three Burrows Corn 3 B6
Three Chimneys Kent 18 B5
Three Cocks Powys 48 F3
Three Counties Showground, Malvern Worcs 50 E2
Three Crosses Swansea 33 E6
Three Cups Corner E Sus 18 C3
Three Holes Norf 66 D5
Three Leg Cross E Sus 18 B3
Three Legged Cross Dorset 13 D8
Three Oaks E Sus 18 D5
Threehammer Common Norf 69 C6
Threekingham Lincs 78 F3
Threemile Cross Wokingham 26 C5
Threemilestone Corn 3 B6
Threemiletown W Loth 122 B3
Threlkeld Cumb 99 B5
Threshfield N Yorks 94 C2
Thrigby Norf 69 C7
Thringarth Durham 100 B4
Thringstone Leics 63 C8
Thrintoft N Yorks 101 E8
Thriplow Cambs 54 E5
Throckenholt Lincs 66 D3
Throcking Herts 54 F4
Throckley T & W 110 C4
Throckmorton Worcs 50 E4
Throphill Northumb 117 F7
Thropton Northumb 117 D6
Throsk Stirl 133 E7
Throwleigh Devon 9 E8
Throwley Kent 30 D3
Thrumpton Notts 76 F5
Thrumster Highld 169 E8
Thrunton Northumb 117 C6
Thrupp Glos 37 D5
Thrupp Oxon 38 C4
Thrushelton Devon 9 F6
Thrussington Leics 64 C3
Thruxton Hants 25 E7
Thruxton Hereford 49 F6
Thruxton Motor Racing Circuit Hants 25 E7
Thrybergh S Yorks 89 E5
Thulston Derbys 76 F4
Thundergay N Ayrs 119 B5
Thundersley Essex 42 F3
Thundridge Herts 41 C6
Thurcaston Leics 64 C2
Thurcroft S Yorks 89 F5
Thurgarton Norf 81 D7
Thurgarton Notts 77 E6
Thurgoland S Yorks 88 D3
Thurlaston Leics 64 E2
Thurlaston Warks 52 B2
Thurlbear Som 11 B7
Thurlby Lincs 65 C8
Thurlby Lincs 78 C2
Thurleigh Beds 53 D8
Thurlestone Devon 6 E4
Thurloxton Som 22 F4
Thurlstone S Yorks 88 D3
Thurlton Norf 69 E7
Thurlwood Ches 74 D5
Thurmaston Leics 64 D3
Thurnby Leics 64 D3
Thurne Norf 69 C7
Thurnham Kent 30 D2
Thurnham Lancs 92 D4
Thurning Norf 81 E6
Thurning Northants 65 F7
Thurnscoe S Yorks 89 D5
Thurnscoe East S Yorks 89 D5
Thursby Cumb 108 D3
Thursford Norf 81 D5
Thursford Collection, Fakenham Norf 81 D5
Thursley Sur 27 F7
Thurso Highld 169 C6
Thurso East Highld 169 C6
Thurstaston Mers 85 F3
Thurston Suff 56 C3
Thurstonfield Cumb 108 D3
Thurstonland W Yorks 88 C2
Thurton Norf 69 D6
Thurvaston Derbys 76 F2
Thuxton Norf 68 D3
Thwaite N Yorks 100 E3
Thwaite Suff 56 C5
Thwaite St Mary Norf 69 E6
Thwaites W Yorks 94 E3
Thwaites Brow W Yorks 94 E3
Thwing E Yorks 97 B6
Tibbermore Perth 134 B2
Tibberton Glos 36 B4
Tibberton Telford 61 B6
Tibberton Worcs 50 D4
Tibenham Norf 68 F4
Tibshelf Derbys 76 C4
Tibthorpe E Yorks 97 D5
Ticehurst E Sus 18 B3
Tichborne Hants 26 F3
Tickencote Rutland 65 D6
Tickenham N Som 23 B6
Tickhill S Yorks 89 E6
Ticklerton Shrops 60 E4
Ticknall Derbys 63 B7
Tickton E Yorks 97 E6
Tidcombe Wilts 25 D7
Tiddington Oxon 39 D6
Tiddington Warks 51 D7
Tidebrook E Sus 18 C3
Tideford Corn 5 D8
Tideford Cross Corn 5 C8
Tidenham Glos 36 E2
Tideswell Derbys 75 B8
Tidmarsh W Berks 26 B4
Tidmington Warks 51 F7
Tidpit Hants 13 C8
Tidworth Wilts 25 E7
Tiers Cross Pembs 44 D4
Tiffield Northants 52 D4
Tifty Aberds 160 D4
Tigerton Angus 143 C5
Tigh-na-Blair Perth 133 C6
Tighnabruaich Argyll 128 C4
Tighnafiline Highld 162 F2
Tigley Devon 7 C5
Tilbrook Cambs 53 C8
Tilbury Thurrock 29 B7
Tilbury Juxta Clare Essex 55 E8
Tile Cross W Mid 63 F5
Tile Hill W Mid 51 B7
Tilehurst Reading 26 B4
Tilford Sur 27 E6
Tilgate W Sus 28 F3
Tilgate Forest Row W Sus 28 F3
Tillathrowie Aberds 159 F8
Tilley Shrops 60 B5
Tillicoultry Clack 133 E8
Tillingham Essex 43 D5
Tillington Hereford 49 E6
Tillington W Sus 16 B3
Tillington Common Hereford 49 E6
Tillyarblet Angus 143 C5
Tillybirloch Aberds 151 D5
Tillycorthie Aberds 151 B8
Tillydrine Aberds 150 E5
Tillyfour Aberds 150 C4
Tillyfourie Aberds 150 C5
Tillygarmond Aberds 150 E5
Tillygreig Aberds 151 B7
Tillykerrie Aberds 151 B7
Tilmanstone Kent 31 D7
Tilney All Saints Norf 67 C5
Tilney High End Norf 67 C5
Tilney St Lawrence Norf 66 C5
Tilshead Wilts 24 E5
Tilstock Shrops 74 F2
Tilston Ches 73 D8
Tilstone Fearnall Ches 74 C2
Tilsworth Beds 40 B2
Tilton on the Hill Leics 64 D4
Timberland Lincs 78 D4
Timbersbrook Ches 75 C5
Timberscombe Som 21 E8
Timble N Yorks 94 D4
Timperley Gtr Man 87 F5
Timsbury Bath 23 D8
Timsbury Hants 14 B4
Timsgearraidh W Isles 172 E3
Timworth Green Suff 56 C2
Tincleton Dorset 13 E5
Tindale Cumb 109 D6
Tingewick Bucks 52 F4
Tingley W Yorks 88 B3
Tingrith Beds 53 F8
Tingwall Orkney 176 D2
Tinhay Devon 9 F5
Tinshill W Yorks 95 F5
Tinsley S Yorks 88 E5
Tintagel Corn 8 F2
Tintagel Castle Corn 8 F2
Tintern Abbey Mon 36 D2
Tintern Parva Mon 36 D2
Tintinhull Som 12 C3
Tintwistle Derbys 87 E8
Tinwald Dumfries 114 F3
Tinwell Rutland 65 D7
Tipperty Aberds 151 B8
Tipsend Norf 66 E5
Tipton W Mid 62 E3
Tipton St John Devon 11 E5
Tiptree Essex 42 C4
Tir-y-dail Carms 33 C7
Tirabad Powys 47 E7
Tiraghoil Argyll 136 F4
Tiree Airport Argyll 136 F1
Tirley Glos 37 B5
Tirphil Caerph 35 D5
Tirril Cumb 99 B7
Tisbury Wilts 13 B7
Tisman's Common W Sus 27 F8
Tissington Derbys 75 D8
Titchberry Devon 8 B4
Titchfield Hants 15 D6
Titchmarsh Northants 53 B8
Titchwell Norf 80 C3
Tithby Notts 77 F6
Titley Hereford 48 C5
Titlington Northumb 117 C7
Titsey Sur 28 D5
Tittensor Staffs 75 F5
Tittleshall Norf 80 E4
Tiverton Ches 74 C2
Tiverton Devon 10 C4
Tivetshall St Margaret Norf 68 F4
Tivetshall St Mary Norf 68 F4
Tividale W Mid 62 E3
Tivy Dale S Yorks 88 D3
Tixall Staffs 62 B3
Tixover Rutland 65 D6
Toab Orkney 176 F4
Toab Shetland 175 M5
Toadmoor Derbys 76 D3
Tobermory Argyll 137 C6
Toberonochy Argyll 130 E3
Tobha Mor W Isles 170 G3
Tobhtarol W Isles 172 E4
Tobson W Isles 172 E4
Tocher Aberds 160 E3
Tockenham Wilts 24 B5
Tockenham Wick Wilts 37 F7
Tockholes Blkburn 86 B4
Tockington S Glos 36 F3
Tockwith N Yorks 95 D7
Todber Dorset 13 B6
Todding Hereford 49 B6
Toddington Beds 40 B3
Toddington Glos 50 F5
Todenham Glos 51 F7
Todhills Cumb 108 C3
Todlachie Aberds 151 C5
Todmorden W Yorks 87 B7
Todrig Borders 115 C7
Todwick S Yorks 89 F5
Toft Cambs 54 D4
Toft Lincs 65 C7
Toft Hill Durham 101 B6
Toft Hill Lincs 78 C5
Toft Monks Norf 69 E7
Toft next Newton Lincs 90 F4
Toftrees Norf 80 E4
Tofts Highld 169 C8
Toftwood Norf 68 C2
Togston Northumb 117 D8
Tokavaig Highld 145 B6
Tokers Green Oxon 26 B5
Tolastadh a Chaolais W Isles 172 E4
Tolastadh bho Thuath W Isles 172 D8
Toll Bar S Yorks 89 D6
Toll End W Mid 62 E3
Toll of Birness Aberds 161 E7
Tolland Som 22 F3
Tollard Royal Wilts 13 C7
Tollbar End W Mid 51 B8
Toller Fratrum Dorset 12 E3
Toller Porcorum Dorset 12 E3
Tollerton Notts 77 F6
Tollerton N Yorks 95 C8
Tollesbury Essex 43 C5
Tolleshunt D'Arcy Essex 43 C5
Tolleshunt Major Essex 43 C5
Tolm W Isles 172 E7
Tolpuddle Dorset 13 E5
Tolvah Highld 148 E4
Tolworth London 28 C2
Tomatin Highld 148 B4
Tombreck Highld 157 F7
Tomchrasky Highld 147 C5
Tomdoun Highld 146 D4
Tomich Highld 147 B6
Tomich Highld 157 B7
Tomich House Highld 157 E6
Tomintoul Aberds 149 E7
Tomintoul Moray 149 C7
Tomnaven Moray 159 F8
Tomnavoulin Moray 149 B8
Ton-Pentre Rhondda 34 E3
Tonbridge Kent 29 E6
Tondu Bridgend 34 F2
Tonfanau Gwyn 58 D2
Tong Shrops 61 D7
Tong W Yorks 94 F5
Tong Norton Shrops 61 D7
Tonge Leics 63 B8
Tongham Sur 27 E6
Tongland Dumfries 106 D3
Tongue Highld 167 D7
Tongue End Lincs 65 C8
Tongwynlais Cardiff 35 F5
Tonna Neath 34 E1
Tonwell Herts 41 C6
Tonypandy Rhondda 34 E3
Tonyrefail Rhondda 34 F4
Toot Baldon Oxon 39 D5
Toot Hill Essex 41 D8
Toothill Hants 14 C4
Top of Hebers Gtr Man 87 D6
Topcliffe N Yorks 95 B7
Topcroft Norf 69 E5
Topcroft Street Norf 69 E5
Toppesfield Essex 55 F8
Toppings Gtr Man 86 C5
Topsham Devon 10 F4
Torbay Torbay 7 D7
Torbeg N Ayrs 119 D6
Torboll Farm Highld 164 E4
Torbrex Stirl 133 E6
Torbryan Devon 7 C6
Torcross Devon 7 E6
Tore Highld 157 D7
Torinturk Argyll 128 D3
Torksey Lincs 77 B8
Torlum W Isles 170 E3
Torlundy Highld 139 B5
Tormarton S Glos 24 B2
Tormisdale Argyll 126 D1
Tormitchell S Ayrs 112 E2
Tormore N Ayrs 119 C5
Tornagrain Highld 157 E8
Tornahaish Aberds 149 D8
Tornaveen Aberds 150 D5
Torness Highld 147 B8
Toronto Durham 110 F4
Torpenhow Cumb 108 F2
Torphichen W Loth 122 B2
Torphins Aberds 150 D5
Torpoint Corn 6 D2
Torquay Torbay 7 C7
Torquhan Borders 123 E7
Torran Argyll 130 E4
Torran Highld 152 E6
Torran Highld 157 B8
Torrance E Dunb 121 B6
Torrans Argyll 137 F5
Torranyard N Ayrs 120 E3
Torre Torbay 7 C7
Torridon Highld 154 E5
Torridon Ho. Highld 154 E4
Torrin Highld 153 G6
Torrisdale Highld 167 C8
Torrisdale-Square Argyll 118 C4
Torrish Highld 165 C6
Torrisholme Lancs 92 C4
Torroble Highld 164 D2
Torry Aberdeen 151 D8
Torry Aberds 159 F8
Torryburn Fife 134 F2
Torterston Aberds 161 D7
Torthorwald Dumfries 107 B7
Tortington W Sus 16 D4
Tortworth S Glos 36 E4
Torvaig Highld 153 E5
Torver Cumb 98 E4
Torwood Falk 133 F7
Torworth Notts 89 F7
Tosberry Devon 8 B4
Toscaig Highld 155 G3
Toseland Cambs 54 C3
Tosside N Yorks 93 D7
Tostock Suff 56 C3
Totaig Highld 152 D3
Totaig Highld 155 H4
Tote Highld 152 E5
Totegan Highld 168 C3
Tothill Lincs 91 F8
Totland I o W 14 F4
Totnes Devon 7 C6
Toton Notts 76 F5
Totronald Argyll 136 C2
Totscore Highld 152 C4
Tottenham London 41 E6
Tottenhill Norf 67 C6
Tottenhill Row Norf 67 C6
Totteridge London 41 E5
Totternhoe Beds 40 B2
Tottington Gtr Man 87 C5
Totton Hants 14 C4
Touchen End Windsor 27 B6
Tournaig Highld 154 B4
Toux Aberds 161 C6
Tovil Kent 29 D8
Tow Law Durham 110 F4
Toward Argyll 129 D6
Towcester Northants 52 E4
Towcester Racecourse Northants 52 E5
Towednack Corn 2 C3
Tower End Norf 67 C6
Tower Knowe Visitor Centre, Kielder Water Northumb 116 F2
Tower of London London 41 F6
Towersey Oxon 39 D7
Towie Aberds 150 C3
Towie Aberds 161 B5
Towiemore Moray 159 E7
Town End Cambs 66 E4
Town End Cumb 99 F6
Town Row E Sus 18 B2
Town Yetholm Borders 116 B4
Townend W Dunb 120 B4
Towngate Lincs 65 C8
Townhead Cumb 108 F5
Townhead Dumfries 106 E3
Townhead S Ayrs 112 D2
Townhead S Yorks 88 D2
Townhead of Greenlaw Dumfries 106 C4
Townhill Fife 134 F3
Townsend Bucks 39 D7
Townsend Herts 40 D4
Townshend Corn 2 C4
Towthorpe York 96 D2
Towton N Yorks 95 F7
Towyn Conwy 72 B3
Toxteth Mers 85 F4
Toynton All Saints Lincs 79 C6
Toynton Fen Side Lincs 79 C6
Toynton St Peter Lincs 79 C7
Toy's Hill Kent 29 D5
Trabboch E Ayrs 112 B4
Traboe Corn 3 D6
Tradespark Highld 158 D2
Tradespark Orkney 176 F3
Trafford Park Gtr Man 87 E5
Trago Mills, Newton Abbot Devon 7 B6
Trallong Powys 34 B3
Tranent E Loth 123 B7
Tranmere Mers 85 F4
Trantlebeg Highld 168 D3
Trantlemore Highld 168 D3
Tranwell Northumb 117 F7
Trapp Carms 33 C7
Traprain E Loth 123 B8
Traquair Borders 123 F6
Trawden Lancs 94 F2
Trawsfynydd Gwyn 71 D8
Tre-Gibbon Rhondda 34 D3
Tre-Taliesin Ceredig 58 E3
Tre-vaughan Carms 32 B4
Tre-wyn Mon 35 B7
Trealaw Rhondda 34 E4
Treales Lancs 92 F4
Trearddur Anglesey 82 D2
Treaslane Highld 152 D4
Trebah Garden, Mawnan Smith Corn 3 D6
Trebanog Rhondda 34 E4
Trebanos Neath 33 D8
Trebartha Corn 5 B7
Trebarwith Corn 8 F2
Trebetherick Corn 4 B4
Treborough Som 22 F2
Trebudannon Corn 4 C3
Trebullett Corn 5 B8
Treburley Corn 5 B8
Trebyan Corn 5 C5
Trecastle Powys 34 B2
Trecenydd Caerph 35 F5
Trecwn Pembs 44 B4
Trecynon Rhondda 34 D3
Tredavoe Corn 2 D3
Treddiog Pembs 44 C3
Tredegar Bl Gwent 35 D5
Tredegar Newydd = New Tredegar Caerph 35 D5
Tredington Glos 37 B6
Tredington Warks 51 E7
Tredinnick Corn 4 B4
Tredomen Powys 48 F3
Tredunnock Mon 35 E7
Tredustan Powys 48 F3
Treen Corn 2 D2
Treeton S Yorks 88 F5
Tref-y-Clawdd = Knighton Powys 48 B4
Trefaldwyn = Montgomery Powys 60 E2
Trefasser Pembs 44 B3
Trefdraeth Anglesey 82 D4
Trefdraeth = Newport Pembs 45 F2
Trefecca Powys 48 F3
Trefechan Ceredig 58 F2
Trefeglwys Powys 59 E6
Trefenter Ceredig 46 C5
Treffgarne Pembs 44 C4
Treffynnon Pembs 44 C3
Treffynnon = Holywell Flint 73 B5
Trefgarn Owen Pembs 44 C3
Trefil Bl Gwent 35 C5
Trefilan Ceredig 46 D4
Trefin Pembs 44 B3
Treflach Shrops 60 B2
Trefnanney Powys 60 C2
Trefnant Denb 72 B4
Trefonen Shrops 60 B2
Trefor Anglesey 82 C3
Trefor Gwyn 70 C4
Treforest Rhondda 34 F4
Trefriw Conwy 83 E7
Trefynwy = Monmouth Mon 36 C2
Tregadillett Corn 8 F4
Tregaian Anglesey 82 D4
Tregare Mon 35 C8
Tregaron Ceredig 47 D5
Tregarth Gwyn 83 E6
Tregeare Corn 8 F4
Tregeiriog Wrex 73 F5
Tregele Anglesey 82 B3
Tregidden Corn 3 D6
Treglemais Pembs 44 C3
Tregole Corn 8 E3
Tregonetha Corn 4 C4
Tregony Corn 3 B8
Tregoss Corn 4 C4
Tregoyd Powys 48 F4
Tregroes Ceredig 46 E3
Tregurrian Corn 4 C3
Tregynon Powys 59 E7
Trehafod Rhondda 34 E4
Treharris M Tydf 34 E4
Treherbert Rhondda 34 E3
Trekenner Corn 5 B8
Treknow Corn 8 F2
Trelan Corn 3 E6
Trelash Corn 8 E3
Trelassick Corn 4 D3
Trelawnyd Flint 72 B4
Trelech Carms 45 F4
Treleddyd-fawr Pembs 44 C2
Trelewis M Tydf 35 E5
Treligga Corn 8 F2
Trelights Corn 4 B4
Trelill Corn 4 B5
Trelissick Corn 3 C7
Trelissick Garden, Feock Corn 4 F3
Trellech Mon 36 D2
Trelleck Grange Mon 36 D1
Trelogan Flint 85 F2
Trelystan Powys 60 D2
Tremadog Gwyn 71 C6
Tremail Corn 8 F3
Tremain Ceredig 45 E4
Tremaine Corn 8 F4
Tremar Corn 5 C7
Trematon Corn 5 D8
Tremeirchion Denb 72 B4
Trenance Corn 4 C3
Trenarren Corn 3 B9
Trench Telford 61 C6
Treneglos Corn 8 F4
Trenewan Corn 5 D6
Trent Dorset 12 C3
Trent Vale Stoke 75 E5
Trentham Stoke 75 E5
Trentham Gardens, Newcastle-under-Lyme Staffs 75 F5
Trentishoe Devon 20 E5
Treoes V Glam 21 B8
Treorchy = Treorci Rhondda 34 E3
Treorci = Treorchy Rhondda 34 E3
Tre'r-ddôl Ceredig 58 E3
Trerule Foot Corn 5 D8
Tresaith Ceredig 45 D4
Tresawle Corn 3 B7
Trescott Staffs 62 E2
Trescowe Corn 2 C4
Tresham Glos 36 E4
Tresillian Corn 3 B7
Tresinwen Pembs 44 A4
Treskinnick Cross Corn 8 E4
Tresmeer Corn 8 F4
Tresparrett Corn 8 E3
Tresparrett Posts Corn 8 E3
Tressait Perth 141 C5
Tresta Shetland 175 H5
Tresta Shetland 174 D8
Treswell Notts 77 B7
Trethosa Corn 4 D4
Trethurgy Corn 4 D5
Tretio Pembs 44 C2
Tretire Hereford 36 B2
Tretower Powys 35 B5
Treuddyn Flint 73 D6
Trevalga Corn 8 F2
Trevalyn Wrex 73 D7
Trevanson Corn 4 B4
Trevarren Corn 4 C4
Trevarrian Corn 4 C3
Trevarrick Corn 3 B8
Trevaughan Carms 32 C2
Treveighan Corn 5 B5
Trevellas Corn 4 D2
Treverva Corn 3 C6
Trevethin Torf 35 D6
Trevigro Corn 5 C8
Treviscoe Corn 4 D4
Trevone Corn 4 B3
Trewarmett Corn 8 F2
Trewassa Corn 8 F3
Trewellard Corn 2 C2
Trewen Corn 8 F4
Trewennack Corn 3 D5
Trewern Powys 60 C2
Trewethern Corn 4 B5
Trewidland Corn 5 D7
Trewint Corn 8 E3
Trewint Corn 8 F4
Trewithian Corn 3 C7
Trewoofe Corn 2 D3
Trewoon Corn 4 D4
Treworga Corn 3 B7
Treworlas Corn 3 C7
Treyarnon Corn 4 B3
Treyford W Sus 16 C2
Trezaise Corn 4 D4
Triangle W Yorks 87 B8
Trickett's Cross Dorset 13 D8
Triffleton Pembs 44 C4
Trimdon Durham 111 F6
Trimdon Colliery Durham 111 F6
Trimdon Grange Durham 111 F6
Trimingham Norf 81 D8
Trimley Lower Street Suff 57 F6
Trimley St Martin Suff 57 F6
Trimley St Mary Suff 57 F6
Trimpley Worcs 50 B2
Trimsaran Carms 33 D5
Trimstone Devon 20 E3
Trinafour Perth 140 C4
Trinant Caerph 35 D6
Tring Herts 40 C2
Tring Wharf Herts 40 C2
Trinity Angus 143 C6
Trinity Jersey 17
Trisant Ceredig 47 B6
Trislaig Highld 138 B4
Trispen Corn 4 D3
Tritlington Northumb 117 E8
Trochry Perth 141 E6
Trodigal Argyll 118 D3
Troed rhiwdalar Powys 47 D8
Troedyraur Ceredig 46 E2
Troedyrhiw M Tydf 34 D4
Tromode I o M 84 E3
Trondavoe Shetland 174 F5
Troon Corn 3 C5
Troon S Ayrs 120 F3
Trosaraidh W Isles 171 J3
Trossachs Hotel Stirl 132 D4
Troston Suff 56 B2
Trottiscliffe Kent 29 C7
Trotton W Sus 16 B2
Troutbeck Cumb 99 D6
Troutbeck Cumb 99 B5
Troutbeck Bridge Cumb 99 D6
Trow Green Glos 36 D2
Trowbridge Wilts 24 D3
Trowell Notts 76 F4
Trowle Common Wilts 24 D3
Trowley Bottom Herts 40 C3
Trows Borders 124 F2
Trowse Newton Norf 68 D5
Trudoxhill Som 24 E2
Trull Som 11 B7
Trumaisgearraidh W Isles 170 C4
Trumpan Highld 152 C3
Trumpet Hereford 49 F8
Trumpington Cambs 54 D5
Trunch Norf 81 D8
Trunnah Lancs 92 E3
Truro Corn 3 B7
Truro Cathedral Corn 4 E3
Trusham Devon 10 F3
Trusley Derbys 76 F2
Trusthorpe Lincs 91 F9
Trysull Staffs 62 E2
Tubney Oxon 38 E4
Tuckenhay Devon 7 D6
Tuckhill Shrops 61 F7
Tuckingmill Corn 3 B5
Tuddenham Suff 55 B8
Tuddenham St Martin Suff 57 E5
Tudeley Kent 29 E7
Tudhoe Durham 111 F5
Tudorville Hereford 36 B2
Tudweiliog Gwyn 70 D3
Tuesley Sur 27 E7
Tuffley Glos 37 C5
Tufton Hants 26 E2
Tufton Pembs 32 B1
Tugby Leics 64 D4
Tugford Shrops 61 F5
Tullibardine Perth 133 C8
Tullibody Clack 133 E7
Tullich Argyll 131 D6
Tullich Highld 148 B2
Tullich Muir Highld 157 B8
Tullie House, Carlisle Cumb 108 D3
Tulliemet Perth 141 D6
Tulloch Aberds 143 B7
Tulloch Aberds 160 E5
Tulloch Perth 134 B2
Tulloch Castle Highld 157 C6
Tullochgorm Argyll 131 F5
Tulloes Angus 143 E5
Tullybannocher Perth 133 B6
Tullybelton Perth 141 F7
Tullyfergus Perth 142 E2
Tullymurdoch Perth 142 D1
Tullynessle Aberds 150 C4
Tumble Carms 33 C6
Tumby Woodside Lincs 79 D5
Tummel Bridge Perth 140 D4
Tunga W Isles 172 E7
Tunstall E Yorks 97 F9
Tunstall Kent 30 C2
Tunstall Lancs 93 B6
Tunstall Norf 69 D7
Tunstall N Yorks 101 E7
Tunstall Stoke 75 D5
Tunstall Suff 57 D7
Tunstall T & W 111 D6
Tunstead Derbys 75 B8
Tunstead Gtr Man 87 D8
Tunstead Norf 81 E8
Tunworth Hants 26 E4
Tupsley Hereford 49 E7
Tupton Derbys 76 C3
Tur Langton Leics 64 E4
Turgis Green Hants 26 D4
Turin Angus 143 D5
Turkdean Glos 37 C8
Turleigh Wilts 24 C3
Turn Lancs 87 C6
Turnastone Hereford 49 F5
Turnberry S Ayrs 112 D2
Turnditch Derbys 76 E2
Turners Hill W Sus 28 F4
Turners Puddle Dorset 13 E6
Turnford Herts 41 D6
Turnhouse Edin 122 B4
Turnworth Dorset 13 D6
Turriff Aberds 160 C4
Turton Bottoms Blkburn 86 C5
Turves Cambs 66 E3
Turvey Beds 53 D7
Turville Bucks 39 E7
Turville Heath Bucks 39 E7
Turweston Bucks 52 F4
Tushielaw Borders 115 C6
Tutbury Staffs 63 B6
Tutnall Worcs 50 B4
Tutshill Glos 36 E2
Tuttington Norf 81 E8
Tutts Clump W Berks 26 B3
Tuxford Notts 77 B7
Twatt Orkney 176 D1
Twatt Shetland 175 H5
Twechar E Dunb 121 B7
Tweedmouth Northumb 125 D5
Tweedsmuir Borders 114 B3
Twelve Heads Corn 3 B6
Twemlow Green Ches 74 C4
Twenty Lincs 65 B8
Twerton Bath 24 C2
Twickenham London 28 B2
Twickenham Stadium London 28 B2
Twigworth Glos 37 B5
Twineham W Sus 17 C6
Twinhoe Bath 24 D2
Twinstead Essex 56 F2
Twinstead Green Essex 56 F2
Twiss Green Warr 86 E4
Twiston Lancs 93 E8
Twitchen Devon 21 F6
Twitchen Shrops 49 B5
Two Bridges Devon 6 B4
Two Dales Derbys 76 C2
Two Mills Ches 73 B7
Twycross Leics 63 D7
Twycross Zoo, Ashby-de-la-Zouch Leics 63 D7
Twyford Bucks 39 B6
Twyford Derbys 63 B7
Twyford Hants 15 B5
Twyford Leics 64 C4
Twyford Lincs 65 B6
Twyford Norf 81 E6
Twyford Wokingham 27 B5
Twyford Common Hereford 49 F7
Twyn-y-Sheriff Mon 35 D8
Twynholm Dumfries 106 D3
Twyning Glos 50 F3
Twyning Green Glos 50 F4
Twynllanan Carms 34 B1
Twynmynydd Carms 33 C7
Twywell Northants 53 B7
Ty-draw Conwy 83 F8
Ty-hen Carms 32 B4
Ty-hen Gwyn 70 D2
Ty-mawr Anglesey 82 C4
Ty Mawr Carms 46 E4
Ty Mawr Cwm Conwy 72 E3
Ty-nant Conwy 72 E3
Ty-nant Gwyn 59 B6
Ty-uchaf Powys 59 B7
Tyberton Hereford 49 F5
Tyburn W Mid 62 E5
Tycroes Carms 33 C7
Tycrwyn Powys 59 C8
Tydd Gote Lincs 66 C4
Tydd St Giles Cambs 66 C4
Tydd St Mary Lincs 66 C4
Tyddewi = St David's Pembs 44 C2
Tyddyn-mawr Gwyn 71 C6
Tye Green Essex 55 F6
Tye Green Essex 42 B3
Tye Green Essex 41 D7
Tyldesley Gtr Man 86 D4
Tyler Hill Kent 30 C5
Tylers Green Bucks 40 E2
Tylorstown Rhondda 34 E4
Tylwch Powys 59 F6
Tyn-y-celyn Wrex 73 F5
Tyn-y-coed Shrops 60 B2
Tyn-y-fedwen Powys 72 F5
Tyn-y-ffridd Powys 72 F5
Tyn-y-graig Powys 48 D2
Ty'n-y-groes Conwy 83 D7
Ty'n-y-maes Gwyn 83 E6
Tyn-y-pwll Anglesey 82 C4
Ty'n-yr-eithin Ceredig 47 C5
Tyncelyn Ceredig 46 C5
Tyndrum Stirl 139 F7
Tyne Tunnel T & W 111 C6
Tyneham Dorset 13 F6
Tynehead Midloth 123 D6
Tynemouth T & W 111 C6
Tynemouth Sea Life Centre T & W 111 B6
Tynewydd Rhondda 34 E3
Tyninghame E Loth 124 B2
Tynron Dumfries 113 E8
Tynygongl Anglesey 82 C5
Tynygraig Ceredig 47 C5

Wel – Wil 255

Welsh End Shrops 74 F2
Welsh Frankton Shrops 73 F7
Welsh Highland Railway, Caernarfon Gwyn 82 E4
Welsh Highland Railway, Porthmadog Gwyn 71 D6
Welsh Hook Pembs 44 C4
Welsh National Velodrome Newport 35 F7
Welsh Newton Hereford 36 C1
Welsh St Donats V Glam 22 B2
Welshampton Shrops 73 F8
Welshpool = Y Trallwng Powys 60 D2
Welton Cumb 108 E3
Welton E Yorks 90 B3
Welton Lincs 78 B3
Welton Northants 52 C3
Welton Hill Lincs 90 F4
Welton le Marsh Lincs 79 C7
Welton le Wold Lincs 91 F6
Welwick E Yorks 91 B7
Welwyn Herts 41 C5
Welwyn Garden City Herts 41 C5
Wem Shrops 60 B5
Wembdon Som 22 F4
Wembley London 40 F4
Wembley Stadium London 40 F4
Wembury Devon 6 E3
Wembworthy Devon 9 D8
Wemyss Bay Invclyd 129 D6
Wenallt Ceredig 47 B5
Wenallt Gwyn 72 E3
Wendens Ambo Essex 55 F6
Wendlebury Oxon 39 C5
Wendling Norf 68 C2
Wendover Bucks 40 D1
Wendron Corn 3 C5
Wendy Cambs 54 E4
Wenfordbridge Corn 5 B5
Wenhaston Suff 57 B8
Wennington Cambs 54 B3
Wennington London 41 F8
Wennington Lancs 93 B6
Wensley Derbys 76 C2
Wensley N Yorks 101 F5
Wentbridge W Yorks 89 C5
Wentnor Shrops 60 E3
Wentworth Cambs 55 B5
Wentworth S Yorks 88 E4
Wenvoe V Glam 22 B3
Weobley Hereford 49 D6
Weobley Marsh Hereford 49 D6
Wereham Norf 67 D6
Wergs W Mid 62 D2
Wern Powys 59 C6
Wern Powys 60 C2
Wernffrwd Swansea 33 E6
Wernyrheolydd Mon 35 C7
Werrington Corn 8 F5
Werrington P'boro 65 D8
Werrington Staffs 75 E6
Wervin Ches 73 B8
Wesham Lancs 92 F4
Wessington Derbys 76 D3
West Acre Norf 67 C7
West Adderbury Oxon 52 F2
West Allerdean Northumb 125 E5
West Alvington Devon 6 E5
West Amesbury Wilts 25 E6
West Anstey Devon 10 B3
West Ashby Lincs 79 B5
West Ashling W Sus 16 D2
West Ashton Wilts 24 D3
West Auckland Durham 101 B6
West Ayton N Yorks 103 F7
West Bagborough Som 22 F3
West Barkwith Lincs 91 F5
West Barnby N Yorks 103 C6
West Barns E Loth 124 B2
West Barsham Norf 80 D5
West Bay Dorset 12 E2
West Beckham Norf 81 D7
West Bedfont Sur 27 B8
West Benhar N Lnrk 121 C8
West Bergholt Essex 43 B5
West Bexington Dorset 12 F3
West Bilney Norf 67 C7
West Blatchington Brighton 17 D6
West Bowling W Yorks 94 F4
West Bradford Lancs 93 E7
West Bradley Som 23 F7
West Bretton W Yorks 88 C3
West Bridgford Notts 77 F5
West Bromwich W Mid 62 E4
West Buckland Devon 21 F5
West Buckland Som 11 B6
West Burrafirth Shetland 175 H4
West Burton N Yorks 101 F5
West Burton W Sus 16 C3
West Butterwick N Lincs 90 D2
West Byfleet Sur 27 C8
West Caister Norf 69 C8
West Calder W Loth 122 C3
West Camel Som 12 B3
West Challow Oxon 38 F3
West Chelborough Dorset 12 D3
West Chevington Northumb 117 E8
West Chiltington W Sus 16 C4
West Chinnock Som 12 C2
West Chisenbury Wilts 25 D6
West Clandon Sur 27 D8
West Cliffe Kent 31 E7
West Clyne Highld 165 D5
West Clyth Highld 169 F7
West Coker Som 12 C3
West Compton Dorset 12 E3
West Compton Som 23 E7
West Cowick E Yorks 89 B7
West Cranmore Som 23 E8
West Cross Swansea 33 F7
West Cullery Aberds 151 D6
West Curry Corn 8 E4
West Curthwaite Cumb 108 E3
West Darlochan Argyll 118 D3
West Dean Wilts 14 B3
West Dean W Sus 16 C2
West Deeping Lincs 65 D8
West Derby Mers 85 E4
West Dereham Norf 67 D6
West Didsbury Gtr Man 87 E6
West Ditchburn Northumb 117 B7
West Down Devon 20 E4
West Drayton London 27 B8
West Drayton Notts 77 B7
West Ella E Yorks 90 B4
West End Beds 53 D7
West End E Yorks 96 F5
West End E Yorks 97 F7
West End Hants 15 C5
West End Lancs 86 B5
West End Norf 68 D2
West End Norf 69 C8
West End N Som 23 C6
West End N Yorks 94 D4
West End Oxon 38 D4
West End S Lnrk 122 E2
West End Suff 69 F7
West End Sur 27 C7
West End S Yorks 89 D7
West End Wilts 13 B7
West End Wilts 24 B4
West End W Sus 17 C6
West End Green Hants 26 C4
West Farleigh Kent 29 D8
West Felton Shrops 60 B3
West Fenton E Loth 135 F6
West Ferry Dundee 142 F4
West Firle E Sus 17 D8
West Ginge Oxon 38 F4
West Grafton Wilts 25 C7
West Green Hants 26 D5
West Greenskares Aberds 160 B4
West Grimstead Wilts 14 B3
West Grinstead W Sus 17 B5
West Haddlesey N Yorks 89 B6
West Haddon Northants 52 B4
West Hagbourne Oxon 39 F5
West Hagley Worcs 62 F3
West Hall Cumb 109 C5
West Hallam Derbys 76 E4
West Halton N Lincs 90 B3
West Ham London 41 F7
West Handley Derbys 76 B3
West Hanney Oxon 38 E4
West Hanningfield Essex 42 E3
West Hardwick W Yorks 88 C5
West Harnham Wilts 14 B2
West Harptree Bath 23 D7
West Hatch Som 11 B7
West Head Norf 67 D5
West Heath Ches 74 C5
West Heath Hants 27 D6
West Heath Hants 26 D3
West Helmsdale Highld 165 C7
West Hendred Oxon 38 F4
West Heslerton N Yorks 96 B5
West Hill Devon 11 E5
West Hill E Yorks 97 C7
West Hill N Som 23 B6
West Hoathly W Sus 28 F4
West Holme Dorset 13 F6
West Horndon Essex 42 F2
West Horrington Som 23 E7
West Horsley Sur 27 D8
West Horton Northumb 125 F6
West Hougham Kent 31 E6
West Houlland Shetland 175 H4
West-houses Derbys 76 D4
West Huntington York 96 D2
West Hythe Kent 19 B8
West Ilsley W Berks 38 F4
West Itchenor W Sus 15 D8
West Keal Lincs 79 C6
West Kennett Wilts 25 C6
West Kilbride N Ayrs 120 E2
West Kingsdown Kent 29 C6
West Kington Wilts 24 B3
West Kinharrachie Aberds 161 E6
West Kirby Mers 85 F3
West Knapton N Yorks 96 B4
West Knighton Dorset 12 F5
West Knoyle Wilts 24 F3
West Kyloe Northumb 125 E6
West Lambrook Som 12 C2
West Langdon Kent 31 E7
West Langwell Highld 164 D3
West Lavington Wilts 24 D5
West Lavington W Sus 16 B2
West Layton N Yorks 101 D6
West Lea Durham 111 E7
West Leake Notts 64 B2
West Learmouth Northumb 124 F4
West Leigh Devon 9 D8
West Lexham Norf 67 C8
West Lilling N Yorks 96 C2
West Linton Borders 122 D4
West Liss Hants 15 B8
West Littleton S Glos 24 B2
West Looe Corn 5 D7
West Luccombe Som 21 E7
West Lulworth Dorset 13 F6
West Lutton N Yorks 96 C5
West Lydford Som 23 F7
West Lyng Som 11 B8
West Lynn Norf 67 B6
West Malling Kent 29 D7
West Malvern Worcs 50 E2
West Marden W Sus 15 C8
West Marina E Sus 18 E4
West Markham Notts 77 B7
West Marsh NE Lincs 91 C6
West Marton N Yorks 93 D8
West Meon Hants 15 B7
West Mersea Essex 43 C6
West Midlands Safari Park, Kidderminster Worcs 50 B3
West Milton Dorset 12 E3
West Minster Kent 30 B3
West Molesey Sur 28 C2
West Monkton Som 11 B7
West Moors Dorset 13 D8
West Morriston Borders 124 E2
West Muir Angus 143 C5
West Ness N Yorks 96 B2
West Newham Northumb 110 B3
West Newton E Yorks 97 F7
West Newton Norf 67 B6
West Norwood London 28 B4
West Ogwell Devon 7 B6
West Orchard Dorset 13 C6
West Overton Wilts 25 C6
West Park Hrtlpl 111 F7
West Parley Dorset 13 E8
West Peckham Kent 29 D7
West Pelton Durham 110 D5
West Pennard Som 23 F7
West Pentire Corn 4 C2
West Perry Cambs 54 C2
West Putford Devon 9 C5
West Quantoxhead Som 22 E3
West Rainton Durham 111 E6
West Rasen Lincs 90 F4
West Raynham Norf 80 E4
West Retford Notts 89 F7
West Rounton N Yorks 102 D2
West Row Suff 55 B7
West Rudham Norf 80 E4
West Runton Norf 81 C7
West Saltoun E Loth 123 C7
West Sandwick Shetland 174 E6
West Scrafton N Yorks 101 F5
West Sleekburn Northumb 117 F8
West Somerset Railway, Minehead Som 21 E8
West Somerton Norf 69 C7
West Stafford Dorset 12 F5
West Stockwith Notts 89 E8
West Stoke W Sus 16 D2
West Stonesdale N Yorks 100 D3
West Stoughton Som 23 E6
West Stour Dorset 13 B5
West Stourmouth Kent 31 C6
West Stow Suff 56 B2
West Stowell Wilts 25 C6
West Strathan Highld 167 C7
West Stratton Hants 26 E3
West Street Kent 30 D3
West Tanfield N Yorks 95 B5
West Taphouse Corn 5 C6
West Tarbert Argyll 128 D3
West Thirston Northumb 117 E7
West Thorney W Sus 15 D8
West Thurrock Thurrock 29 B6
West Tilbury Thurrock 29 B7
West Tisted Hants 15 B7
West Tofts Norf 67 E8
West Tofts Perth 141 F8
West Torrington Lincs 90 F5
West Town Hants 15 E8
West Town N Som 23 C6
West Tytherley Hants 14 B3
West Tytherton Wilts 24 B4
West Walton Norf 66 C4
West Walton Highway Norf 66 C4
West Wellow Hants 14 C3
West Wemyss Fife 134 E5
West Wick N Som 23 C5
West Wickham Cambs 55 E7
West Wickham London 28 C4
West Williamston Pembs 32 D1
West Willoughby Lincs 78 E2
West Winch Norf 67 C6
West Winterslow Wilts 25 F7
West Wittering W Sus 15 E8
West Witton N Yorks 101 F5
West Woodburn Northumb 116 F4
West Woodhay W Berks 25 C8
West Woodlands Som 24 E2
West Worldham Hants 26 F5
West Worlington Devon 10 C2
West Worthing W Sus 16 D5
West Wratting Cambs 55 D7
West Wycombe Bucks 39 E8
West Wylam Northumb 110 C4
West Yell Shetland 174 E6
Westacott Devon 20 F4
Westbere Kent 31 C5
Westborough Lincs 77 E8
Westbourne Bmouth 13 E8
Westbourne Suff 56 E5
Westbourne W Sus 15 D8
Westbrook W Berks 26 B2
Westbury Bucks 52 F4
Westbury Shrops 60 D3
Westbury Wilts 24 D3
Westbury Leigh Wilts 24 D3
Westbury-on-Severn Glos 36 C4
Westbury on Trym Bristol 23 B7
Westbury-sub-Mendip Som 23 E7
Westby Lancs 92 F3
Westcliff-on-Sea Sthend 42 F4
Westcombe Som 23 F8
Westcote Glos 38 B2
Westcott Bucks 39 C7
Westcott Devon 10 D5
Westcott Sur 28 E2
Westcott Barton Oxon 38 B4
Westdean E Sus 18 F2
Westdene Brighton 17 D6
Wester Aberchalder Highld 147 B8
Wester Balgedie Perth 134 D3
Wester Culbeuchly Aberds 160 B3
Wester Dechmont W Loth 122 C3
Wester Denoon Angus 142 E3
Wester Fintray Aberds 151 C7
Wester Gruinards Highld 164 E2
Wester Lealty Highld 157 B7
Wester Milton Highld 158 D3
Wester Newburn Fife 135 D6
Wester Quarff Shetland 175 K6
Wester Skeld Shetland 175 J4
Westerdale Highld 169 D6
Westerdale N Yorks 102 D4
Westerfield Shetland 175 H5
Westerfield Suff 57 E5
Westergate W Sus 16 D3
Westerham Kent 28 D5
Westerhope T & W 110 C4
Westerleigh S Glos 23 B9
Westerton Angus 143 D6
Westerton Durham 110 F5
Westerton W Sus 16 D2
Westerwick Shetland 175 J4
Westfield Cumb 98 B1
Westfield E Sus 18 D5
Westfield Hereford 50 E2
Westfield Highld 169 C5
Westfield N Lnrk 121 B7
Westfield Norf 68 D2
Westfield W Loth 122 B2
Westfields Dorset 12 D5
Westfields of Rattray Perth 142 E1
Westgate Durham 110 F2
Westgate N Lincs 89 D8
Westgate Norf 81 C5
Westgate on Sea Kent 31 B7
Westhall Aberds 151 B5
Westhall Suff 69 F7
Westham Dorset 12 G4
Westham E Sus 18 E3
Westham Som 23 E6
Westhampnett W Sus 16 D2
Westhay Som 23 E6
Westhead Lancs 86 D2
Westhide Hereford 49 E7
Westhill Aberds 151 D7
Westhill Highld 157 E8
Westhope Hereford 49 D6
Westhope Shrops 60 F4
Westhorpe Lincs 78 F5
Westhorpe Suff 56 C4
Westhoughton Gtr Man 86 D4
Westhouse N Yorks 93 B6
Westhumble Sur 28 D2
Westing Shetland 174 C7
Westlake Devon 6 D4
Westleigh Devon 9 B6
Westleigh Devon 11 C5
Westleigh Gtr Man 86 D4
Westleton Suff 57 C8
Westley Shrops 60 D3
Westley Suff 56 C2
Westley Waterless Cambs 55 D7
Westlington Bucks 39 C7
Westlinton Cumb 108 C3
Westmarsh Kent 31 C6
Westmeston E Sus 17 C7
Westmill Herts 41 B6
Westminster London 28 B4
Westminster Cathedral London 28 B3
Westmuir Angus 142 D3
Westness Orkney 176 D2
Westnewton Cumb 107 E8
Westnewton Northumb 124 F5
Westoe T & W 111 C6
Weston Bath 24 C2
Weston Ches 74 D4
Weston Devon 11 F6
Weston Dorset 12 G4
Weston Halton 86 F3
Weston Hants 15 B8
Weston Herts 54 F3
Weston Lincs 66 B2
Weston Notts 77 C7
Weston Northants 52 E3
Weston N Yorks 94 E4
Weston Shrops 61 E5
Weston Shrops 61 B5
Weston Staffs 62 B3
Weston W Berks 25 B8
Weston Beggard Hereford 49 E7
Weston by Welland Northants 64 E4
Weston Colville Cambs 55 D7
Weston Coyney Stoke 75 E6
Weston Favell Northants 53 C5
Weston Green Cambs 55 D7
Weston Green Norf 68 C4
Weston Heath Shrops 61 C7
Weston Hills Lincs 66 B2
Weston-in-Gordano N Som 23 B6
Weston Jones Staffs 61 B7
Weston Longville Norf 68 C4
Weston Lullingfields Shrops 60 B4
Weston-on-the-Green Oxon 39 C5
Weston-on-Trent Derbys 63 B8
Weston Park Staffs 62 C2
Weston Patrick Hants 26 E4
Weston Rhyn Shrops 73 F6
Weston-Sub-Edge Glos 51 E6
Weston-super-Mare N Som 22 C5
Weston Turville Bucks 40 C1
Weston under Lizard Staffs 62 C2
Weston under Penyard Hereford 36 B3
Weston under Wetherley Warks 51 C8
Weston Underwood Derbys 76 E2
Weston Underwood M Keynes 53 D6
Westonbirt Glos 37 F5
Westonbirt Arboretum, Tetbury Glos 37 F5
Westoncommon Shrops 60 B4
Westoning Beds 53 F8
Westonzoyland Som 23 F5
Westow N Yorks 96 C3
Westport Argyll 118 D3
Westport Som 11 C8
Westray Airport Orkney 176 A3
Westrigg W Loth 122 C2
Westruther Borders 124 E2
Westry Cambs 66 E3
Westville Notts 76 E5
Westward Cumb 108 E2
Westward Ho! Devon 9 B6
Westwell Kent 30 E3
Westwell Oxon 38 D2
Westwell Leacon Kent 30 E3
Westwick Cambs 54 C5
Westwick Durham 101 C5
Westwick Norf 81 E8
Westwood Devon 10 E5
Westwood Wilts 24 D3
Westwoodside N Lincs 89 E8
Wetheral Cumb 108 D4
Wetherby W Yorks 95 E7
Wetherby Racecourse W Yorks 95 E7
Wetherden Suff 56 C4
Wetheringsett Suff 56 C5
Wethersfield Essex 55 F8
Wethersta Shetland 174 G5
Wetherup Street Suff 56 C5
Wetley Rocks Staffs 75 E6
Wettenhall Ches 74 C3
Wetton Staffs 75 D8
Wetwang E Yorks 96 D5
Wetwood Staffs 74 F4
Wexcombe Wilts 25 D7
Wexham Street Bucks 40 F2
Weybourne Norf 81 C7
Weybread Suff 68 F5
Weybridge Sur 27 C8
Weycroft Devon 11 E8
Weydale Highld 169 C6
Weyhill Hants 25 E8
Weymouth Dorset 12 G4
Weymouth Sea Life Park Dorset 12 F4
Whaddon Bucks 53 F6
Whaddon Cambs 54 E4
Whaddon Glos 37 C5
Whaddon Wilts 14 B2
Whale Cumb 99 B7
Whaley Derbys 76 B5
Whaley Bridge Derbys 87 F8
Whaley Thorns Derbys 76 B5
Whaligoe Highld 169 E8
Whalley Lancs 93 F7
Whalsay Airport Shetland 174 G7
Whalton Northumb 117 F7
Wham N Yorks 93 C7
Whaplode Lincs 66 B3
Whaplode Drove Lincs 66 C3
Whaplode St Catherine Lincs 66 B3
Wharfe N Yorks 93 C7
Wharles Lancs 92 F4
Wharncliffe Side S Yorks 88 E3
Wharram le Street N Yorks 96 C4
Wharton Ches 74 C3
Wharton Green Ches 74 C3
Whashton N Yorks 101 D6
Whatcombe Dorset 13 D6
Whatcote Warks 51 E8
Whatfield Suff 56 E4
Whatley Som 11 D8
Whatley Som 24 E2
Whatlington E Sus 18 D4
Whatstandwell Derbys 76 D3
Whatton Notts 77 F7
Whauphill Dumfries 105 E8
Whaw N Yorks 100 D4
Wheatacre Norf 69 E7
Wheatcroft Derbys 76 D3
Wheathampstead Herts 40 C4
Wheathill Shrops 61 F6
Wheatley Devon 10 E4
Wheatley Hants 27 E5
Wheatley Oxon 39 D5
Wheatley S Yorks 89 D6
Wheatley W Yorks 87 B8
Wheatley Hill Durham 111 F6
Wheaton Aston Staffs 62 C2
Wheddon Cross Som 21 F8
Wheedlemont Aberds 150 B3
Wheelerstreet Sur 27 E7
Wheelock Ches 74 D4
Wheelock Heath Ches 74 D4
Wheelton Lancs 86 B4
Wheen Angus 142 B3
Wheldrake York 96 E2
Whelford Glos 38 E1
Whelpley Hill Bucks 40 D2
Whempstead Herts 41 B6
Whenby N Yorks 96 C2
Whepstead Suff 56 D2
Wherstead Suff 57 E5
Wherwell Hants 25 E8
Wheston Derbys 75 B8
Whetsted Kent 29 E7
Whetstone Leics 64 E2
Whicham Cumb 98 F3
Whichford Warks 51 F8
Whickham T & W 110 C5
Whiddon Down Devon 9 E8
Whigstreet Angus 142 E4
Whilton Northants 52 C4
Whim Farm Borders 122 D5
Whimble Devon 9 D5
Whimple Devon 10 E5
Whimpwell Green Norf 69 B6
Whinburgh Norf 68 D3
Whinnieliggate Dumfries 106 D4
Whinnyfold Aberds 161 E7
Whippingham I o W 15 E6
Whipsnade Beds 40 C3
Whipsnade Wild Animal Park, Dunstable Beds 40 C3
Whipton Devon 10 E4
Whirlow S Yorks 88 F4
Whisby Lincs 78 C2
Whissendine Rutland 64 C5
Whissonsett Norf 80 E5
Whistlefield Argyll 129 A6
Whistlefield Argyll 129 A7
Whistley Green Wokingham 27 B5
Whiston Mers 86 E2
Whiston Northants 53 C6
Whiston Staffs 62 C2
Whiston Staffs 75 E7
Whiston S Yorks 88 F5
Whitbeck Cumb 98 F3
Whitbourne Hereford 50 D2
Whitbread Hop Farm, Beltring Kent 29 E7
Whitburn T & W 111 C7
Whitburn W Loth 122 C2
Whitburn Colliery T & W 111 C7
Whitby Ches 73 B7
Whitby N Yorks 103 C6
Whitby Abbey N Yorks 103 C7
Whitbyheath Ches 73 B7
Whitchurch Bath 23 C8
Whitchurch Bucks 39 B7
Whitchurch Cardiff 35 F5
Whitchurch Devon 6 B2
Whitchurch Hants 26 E2
Whitchurch Hereford 36 C2
Whitchurch Oxon 26 B4
Whitchurch Pembs 44 C2
Whitchurch Shrops 74 E2
Whitchurch Canonicorum Dorset 11 E8
Whitchurch Hill Oxon 26 B4
Whitcombe Dorset 12 F5
Whitcott Keysett Shrops 60 F2
White Coppice Lancs 86 C4
White Lackington Dorset 12 E5
White Ladies Aston Worcs 50 D4
White Lund Lancs 92 C4
White Mill Carms 33 B5
White Ness Shetland 175 J5
White Notley Essex 42 C3
White Pit Lincs 79 B6
White Post Notts 77 D6
White Post Farm Centre, Farnsfield Notts 77 D6
White Rocks Hereford 35 B8
White Roding Essex 42 C1
White Waltham Windsor 27 B6
Whiteacen Moray 159 E6
Whiteacre Heath Warks 63 E6
Whitebridge Highld 147 C7
Whitebrook Mon 36 D2
Whiteburn Borders 123 E8
Whitecairn Dumfries 105 D6
Whitecairns Aberds 151 C8
Whitecastle S Lnrk 122 E3
Whitechapel Lancs 93 E5
Whitecleat Orkney 176 F4
Whitecraig E Loth 123 B6
Whitecroft Glos 36 D3
Whitecross Corn 4 B4
Whitecross Falk 122 B2
Whitecross Staffs 62 B2
Whiteface Highld 164 F4
Whitefarland N Ayrs 119 B5
Whitefaulds S Ayrs 112 D2
Whitefield Gtr Man 87 D6
Whitefield Perth 142 F1
Whiteford Aberds 151 B6
Whitegate Ches 74 C3
Whitehall Blkburn 86 B4
Whitehall W Sus 16 B5
Whitehall Village Orkney 176 D5
Whitehaven Cumb 98 C1
Whitehill Hants 27 F5
Whitehills Aberds 160 B3
Whitehills S Lnrk 121 D6
Whitehough Derbys 87 F8
Whitehouse Aberds 150 C5
Whitehouse Argyll 128 D3
Whiteinch Glasgow 120 C5
Whitekirk E Loth 135 F7
Whitelaw S Lnrk 121 E6
Whiteleas T & W 111 C6
Whiteley Bank I o W 15 F6
Whiteley Green Ches 75 B6
Whiteley Village Sur 27 C8
Whitemans Green W Sus 17 B7
Whitemire Moray 158 D3
Whitemoor Corn 4 D4
Whitemore Staffs 75 C5
Whitenap Hants 14 B4
Whiteoak Green Oxon 38 C3
Whiteparish Wilts 14 B3
Whiterashes Aberds 151 B7
Whiterow Highld 169 E8
Whiteshill Glos 37 D5
Whiteside Northumb 109 C7
Whiteside W Loth 122 C2
Whitesmith E Sus 18 D2
Whitestaunton Som 11 C7
Whitestone Devon 10 E3
Whitestone Devon 20 E3
Whitestone Warks 63 F7
Whitestones Aberds 160 C5
Whitestreet Green Suff 56 F3
Whitewall Corner N Yorks 96 B3
Whiteway Glos 37 E5
Whiteway Glos 37 C6
Whitewell Aberds 161 B6
Whitewell Lancs 93 E6
Whitewell Bottom Lancs 87 B6
Whiteworks Devon 6 B4
Whitfield Kent 31 E7
Whitfield Northants 52 F4
Whitfield Northumb 109 D7
Whitfield S Glos 36 E3
Whitford Devon 11 E7
Whitford Flint 72 B5
Whitgift E Yorks 90 B2
Whitgreave Staffs 62 B2
Whithorn Dumfries 105 E8
Whiting Bay N Ayrs 119 D7
Whitington Norf 67 E7
Whitkirk W Yorks 95 F6
Whitland Carms 32 C2
Whitletts S Ayrs 112 B3
Whitley N Yorks 89 B6
Whitley Reading 26 B5
Whitley Wilts 24 C3
Whitley Bay T & W 111 B6
Whitley Chapel Northumb 110 D2
Whitley Lower W Yorks 88 C3
Whitley Row Kent 29 D5
Whitlock's End W Mid 51 B6
Whitminster Glos 36 D4
Whitmore Staffs 74 E5
Whitnage Devon 10 C5
Whitnash Warks 51 C8
Whitney Hereford 48 E4
Whitrigg Cumb 108 F2
Whitrigg Cumb 108 D2
Whitsbury Hants 14 C2
Whitsome Borders 124 D4
Whitson Newport 35 F7
Whitstable Kent 30 C5
Whitstone Corn 8 E4
Whittingham Northumb 117 C6
Whittingslow Shrops 60 F4
Whittington Glos 37 B7
Whittington Lancs 93 B6
Whittington Shrops 73 F7
Whittington Staffs 62 F2
Whittington Staffs 63 D5
Whittington Worcs 50 D3
Whittle-le-Woods Lancs 86 B3
Whittlebury Northants 52 E4
Whittlesey Cambs 66 E2
Whittlesford Cambs 55 E5
Whittlestone Head Blkburn 86 C5
Whitton Borders 116 B3
Whitton N Lincs 90 B3
Whitton Northumb 117 D6
Whitton Powys 48 C4
Whitton Shrops 49 B7
Whitton Stockton 102 B1
Whitton Suff 56 E5
Whittonditch Wilts 25 B7
Whittonstall Northumb 110 D3
Whitway Hants 26 D2
Whitwell Derbys 76 B5
Whitwell Herts 40 B4
Whitwell I o W 15 G6
Whitwell N Yorks 101 E7
Whitwell Rutland 65 D6
Whitwell-on-the-Hill N Yorks 96 C3
Whitwell Street Norf 81 E7
Whitwick Leics 63 C8
Whitwood W Yorks 88 B5
Whitworth Lancs 87 C6
Whixall Shrops 74 F2
Whixley N Yorks 95 D7
Whoberley W Mid 51 B8
Whorlton Durham 101 C6
Whorlton N Yorks 102 D2
Whygate Northumb 109 B7
Whyle Hereford 49 C7
Whyteleafe Sur 28 D4
Wibdon Glos 36 E2
Wibsey W Yorks 88 A2
Wibtoft Leics 63 F8
Wichenford Worcs 50 C2
Wichling Kent 30 D3
Wick Bmouth 14 E2
Wick Devon 11 D6
Wick Highld 169 D8
Wick S Glos 24 B2
Wick Shetland 175 K6
Wick V Glam 21 B8
Wick Wilts 14 B2
Wick Worcs 50 E4
Wick W Sus 16 D4
Wick Airport Highld 169 D8
Wick Hill Wokingham 27 C5
Wick St Lawrence N Som 23 C5
Wicken Cambs 55 B6
Wicken Northants 52 F5
Wicken Bonhunt Essex 55 F5
Wicken Green Village Norf 80 D4
Wickenby Lincs 90 F4
Wickersley S Yorks 89 E5
Wickford Essex 42 E3
Wickham Hants 15 C6
Wickham W Berks 25 B8
Wickham Bishops Essex 42 C4
Wickham Market Suff 57 D7
Wickham St Paul Essex 56 F2
Wickham Skeith Suff 56 C4
Wickham Street Suff 55 D8
Wickham Street Suff 56 C4
Wickhambreux Kent 31 D6
Wickhambrook Suff 55 D8
Wickhamford Worcs 51 E5
Wickhampton Norf 69 D7
Wicklewood Norf 68 D3
Wickmere Norf 81 D7
Wicksteed Park, Kettering Northants 53 B6
Wickwar S Glos 36 F4
Widdington Essex 55 F6
Widdrington Northumb 117 E8
Widdrington Station Northumb 117 E8
Wide Open T & W 110 B5
Widecombe in the Moor Devon 6 B5
Widegates Corn 5 D7
Widemouth Bay Corn 8 D4
Widewall Orkney 176 G3
Widford Essex 42 D2
Widford Herts 41 C7
Widham Wilts 37 F7
Widmer End Bucks 40 E1
Widmerpool Notts 64 B3
Widnes Halton 86 F3
Wigan Gtr Man 86 D3
Wigan Pier Gtr Man 86 D3
Wiggaton Devon 11 E6
Wiggenhall St Germans Norf 67 C5
Wiggenhall St Mary Magdalen Norf 67 C5
Wiggenhall St Mary the Virgin Norf 67 C5
Wigginton Herts 40 C2
Wigginton Oxon 51 F8
Wigginton Staffs 63 D6
Wigginton York 95 D8
Wigglesworth N Yorks 93 D8
Wiggonby Cumb 108 D2
Wiggonholt W Sus 16 C4
Wighill N Yorks 95 E7
Wighton Norf 80 D5
Wigley Hants 14 C4
Wigmore Hereford 49 C6
Wigmore Medway 30 C2
Wigsley Notts 77 B8
Wigsthorpe Northants 65 F7
Wigston Leics 64 E3
Wigthorpe Notts 89 F6
Wigtoft Lincs 79 F5
Wigton Cumb 108 E2
Wigtown Dumfries 105 D8
Wigtwizzle S Yorks 88 E3
Wike W Yorks 95 E6
Wike Well End S Yorks 89 C7
Wilbarston Northants 64 F5
Wilberfoss E Yorks 96 D3
Wilberlee W Yorks 87 C8
Wilburton Cambs 55 B5
Wilby Norf 68 F3
Wilby Northants 53 C6
Wilby Suff 57 B6
Wilcot Wilts 25 C6
Wilcott Shrops 60 C3
Wilcrick Newport 35 F8